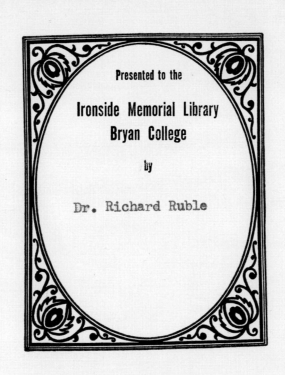
THE EDITOR

Robert E. L. Faris is presently Professor of Sociology and Chairman, Department of Sociology, University of Washington. He received his Ph.B., M.A., and Ph.D. from the University of Chicago. His former teaching affiliations were with Brown University, McGill University, Bryn Mawr College, and Syracuse University.

Professor Faris is the author of *Social Disorganization*, *Social Psychology*, and co-author (with H. W. Durham) of *Mental Disorders in Urban Areas*. His articles have appeared in *American Sociological Review*, *American Journal of Sociology*, and *Social Forces*.

HANDBOOK OF MODERN SOCIOLOGY

CONTRIBUTORS

Robert E. L. Faris • Otis Dudley Duncan • Irene B. Taeuber • Gideon Sjoberg • Philip M. Hauser • David Matza • A. Paul Hare • Leonard D Cain, Jr. • Saxon Graham • Otto N. Larsen • Ralph H. Turner • Lewis M. Killian • Judith Blake • Kingsley Davis • W. Richard Scott • Kaare Svalastoga • Frank R. Westie • Edward Gross • Morris Zelditch, Jr. • Burton R. Clark • Louis Schneider • Scott Greer • Peter Orleans • Norman Kaplan • Wilbert E. Moore • William R. Catton, Jr. • George Casper Homans • Matilda White Riley • James S. Coleman

HANDBOOK
OF MODERN
SOCIOLOGY

Edited by Robert E. L. Faris

RAND McNALLY & COMPANY
Chicago

RAND McNALLY SOCIOLOGY SERIES

Edgar F. Borgatta, Advisory Editor

ALFORD, *Party and Society*

BAKAN, *The Quality of Human Existence*

BORGATTA AND CROWTHER, *A Workbook for the Study of Social Interaction Processes*

CHRISTENSEN, ED., *Handbook of Marriage and the Family*

DEMERATH, *Social Class in American Protestantism*

FARIS, ED., *Handbook of Modern Sociology*

GLOCK AND STARK, *Religion and Society in Tension*

HADDEN AND BORGATTA, *American Cities: Their Social Characteristics*

KAPLAN, ED., *Science and Society*

MARCH, ED., *Handbook of Organizations*

NYE AND HOFFMAN, *The Employed Mother in America*

SCOTT, *Values and Organizations*

WARREN, *The Community in America*

WARREN, ED., *Perspectives on the American Community*

WEBB, CAMPBELL, SCHWARTZ, AND SECHREST, *Unobtrusive Measures*

Preface

Mercator's task was easier. All he had to do was to represent on a plane the surface features of a sphere. The builder of a general work on sociology, however, encounters the problem of projecting the multidimensional unity onto the single dimension of a line of type. The reader who remains alert to indications of order and unity in the complexity that characterizes modern sociology may be rewarded by many glimpses of pattern in the materials presented here.

A full coverage of the content of contemporary sociology would fill a massive encyclopedia. A handbook therefore must have omissions, and among the matter best left to other literature is the content that is standard enough to be available in general textbooks on sociology. In general the aim here is to summarize all of the major growing research areas of modern sociology and to indicate some of their interrelations by unifying chapters. Some arbitrary decisions have been necessary. Chapters on social change, and social disorganization, for example, were initially planned, but it soon became apparent that some of the subject matter on these topics would logically be distributed among several other chapters. It was therefore decided to treat these topics separately only in brief sections of Chapter 1.

At an early stage of planning over 80 topics for chapters were considered. In the necessary process of contraction a number of emerging sociological interests, including many with "Sociology of . . ." titles, were omitted. Some of these may never develop; the more successful will find their way into later handbooks of sociology.

The choice of topics and the general organization of the present work is the result of collaboration. The editor early sought the help of Kingsley Davis, Sanford M. Dornbusch, and Matilda W. Riley. After some interchanges by mail, this group, along with Mr. John Applegath of Rand McNally & Company, met in San Francisco for a long day of finishing the general outline of chapters and selection of authors. The editor found it necessary to make some minor modifications afterward, but the strength of the Handbook owes much to the above colleagues, and the editor hereby expresses thanks to them.

Gratitude is also due several other persons. Edgar F. Borgatta initiated the project and by long distance telephone persuasion induced the editor to undertake it. Along the way encouragement, advice, and technical help were extended by F. Edward Peacock, Lucia Boyden, Maralyn Robinson, and Jane Mitchell Lazars, all of Rand McNally & Company. Indispensable help in manuscript handling was also provided by Gwen A. Williams and Beulah E. Reddaway of the Department of Sociology Office of the University of Washington. Special appreciation is, of course, owed to the 28 authors who toiled so carefully to provide the rich contents of the book.

The pages that follow are vines that will grow and spread and in time should surely yield fruit for the good of mankind.

Robert E. L. Faris
University of Washington

Table of Contents

The Discipline
of Sociology

ROBERT E. L. FARIS

When the wise men of ancient Babylonia gazed at the night sky, they were not merely partaking of recreation, but were searching for meanings relevant to human affairs. The Greeks of old, also believing that planet-gods interfered with the destinies of mortals, directly sought divine favor. Elsewhere about the world, and throughout the millennia of prehistory, men have looked to deities, spirits of the dead, ghosts of totem animals, and other supernatural agents to give some understanding and control in the course of their hazardous lives.

Magic appears to have arisen in response to a desperate urgency to know, in situations where knowledge is out of reach. Magic is therefore most prevalent in extremely primitive cultures. But no peoples live in a purely magical cosmos. All possess some effective technology, and thus at least some elementary concept of causation. Every tool necessarily implies a causal viewpoint toward the materials on which it is used. Techniques of hunting and fishing depend on at least some regularity of behavior on the part of the animals and fish, and so rest on a principle of orderliness in nature. While such slight

degree of understanding of nature is not conventionally granted the title of science, it may reasonably be considered remotely ancestral to the sophisticated structure of modern tested knowledge.

A claim could also be made that in making use of techniques for influencing one another, preliterate peoples have a unformulated but on the whole effective grasp of an applied sociology. This is visible in the use of rewards, emblems of rank, rites, etiquette systems, child training methods, and other aspects of collective human life. Furthermore, explicit generalizations on human behavior are abundant in proverbs, legends, and ceremonial speeches. There is valid folk-sociology in such African proverbs as: "Distant firewood is good firewood," "Ashes fly back in the face of him who throws them," "When you go to the village of the tortoise and it eats earth, you eat some too," "Quick loving a woman means quick not loving a woman."

It is safe to say that all preliterate cultures must therefore possess an adequate system of implicit proto-sociology or they would never have survived. Thus all living peoples today necessarily have an unbroken cultural continuity with organized folk-sociological concepts which link present generations with prehistoric cultures. The technology of living together, of mutually regulating behavior, has always been as necessary to the human species as that of obtaining food, shelter, and protection from the varied perils of nature. Societies which failed sociologically, if there ever were any, must have quickly become extinct, leaving the earth to be inhabited only by those peoples with adequate concepts of human relations.

Thus it is that modern sociology rests on a foundation of organized cultural wisdom which evolved at an imperceptible rate in a remote and utterly unknown antiquity. The human animal has in fact lived in organized society long enough to have undergone an important amount of physiological adaptation to the conditions of social living, and thus even his biological human nature has become social nature through the workings of evolutionary development. Man is now biologically unable to be other than a social animal.

In view of this prehistoric origin of fundamental concepts of an essentially sociological character our twentieth-century sociology cannot be expected to produce with frequency any spectacular new discoveries of totally unsuspected laws. There is little in the content of modern sociology which has not been to some degree familiar in the folk-wisdom of earlier peoples. Our task today thus is not that of primal ground-breaking, but rather of systematically organizing what we already know, or think we partly know, so that the subject will achieve internal consistency as well as harmony with other sciences. And, perhaps even more important, the modern sociologists must apply systematic tests of all of its store of principles, so that the false generalizations so abundant in folk-sociology and in practical life will be discarded, allowing the principles which survive the methodological trials to form the content of an intellectually satisfying and practically applicable science.

SCIENCE AND HUMAN CONCERNS

Methodical investigation of general issues of knowledge is motivated not only by the pressure of human needs, but also by the kind of pure curiosity which emerges from man's highest mental powers. Scholars have long debated which of the two types of motivation has been more responsible for the creation of organized science, but it would appear reasonable to suppose that in the millennia before the emergence of writing it must have been mainly the practical concerns which dominated in the pursuit of both technology and whatever abstract generalizations were made from primitive knowledge. Pure curiosity could scarcely have been importantly productive before the emergence of the civilizations of the Mediterranean region, although from that time to the present it has motivated an increasing proportion of search for knowledge.

The most urgent need of prehistoric man must have been, as it is with most preliterate peoples today, that of getting food. Famine, one of nature's most established endemic cruelties, has always been a major source of fear. Along with their fight against hunger, prehistoric peoples had to sustain a variety of struggles against a hostile nature. They faced perils from extreme temperatures, violent weather, dangerous animals, and a variety of pestilences. The most urgent requirements were always for some kind of knowledge of how to assure survival of the community. Members of a small and simple food-gathering society ordinarily have little time left over for any activities other than providing for staying alive.

The funded technological wisdom made possible by civilization has of course altered this immediately dependent relationship of man to nature. In modern cities, at least, climate and weather have been virtually conquered, diseases are rapidly coming under control, the supply of food is a concern only by its over-abundance, and, except to the reckless tourists in national parks who expose themselves to laceration by mendicant bears, wild animals are no longer a threat.

But, as the perils of nature have been steadily reduced, we find new types continually emerging. With advancement of civilization we seem to be increasingly threatened by war, race conflict, population explosions, economic disruptions, crime, family disintegration, along with a variety of lesser manifestations of disorganization. Here the menaces are not consequences of natural forces, but of troubles of human relations—of interpersonal communication, interaction of masses, conflicts among organizations. The physical and biological sciences which have produced magnificent triumphs over the natural perils have solved no problems in this field of human interaction, rather they have, unintentionally to be sure, been among the major forces in creating them.

There is no reason to expect that mathematics, physics, chemistry, genetics, impressive as are their achievements, will ever contribute substantially to the solution of this class of difficulties. Nor will that category of knowledge known as the humanities, however much it contributes to the enjoyment of civilized living. Nations of peoples who love ballet, poetry, Mozart, and Shakespeare can fight to the death against others with identical tastes. For that matter, the gap of communication between science and humanities, viewed with lament by popular writers, is devoid of relevance to the question of surviving our modern perils.

Whatever hope there may be of using intelligence effectively must be in the application of adequate research methods to the creation of some organized and validated understanding of the principles of human behavior, social interaction, and the nature of organizations. This means that sociology in the broad sense, or social science, is the best, and probably the only, basis of hope for control over the modern threats to human survival.

Sociology, as will be pointed out more fully in later pages of this chapter, is a young field and was developed only after the major physical and biological sciences were relatively mature. Thus sociology, in its academic form, was able to proceed less from direct concern with immediate problems, than from broad philosophical interests. There has nevertheless been, for the better part of a century, a running factional debate of low intensity between the scholars who seek to build a relatively objective science of sociology and a minority which advocates that all effort be spent directly on pressing problems of the day.

The long range of experience fully justifies a policy of setting aside from practical assignments the all-too-rare scholars and scientists of highest ability, relieving them from urgent *ad hoc* engineering research so that they may pursue fundamental knowledge wherever it leads and without reference to the possibility of early application. In the long run much of this pure knowledge tends to be not only applicable, but capable of yielding vastly greater return for the manpower involved, than does the same amount of time given to *ad hoc* research. The history of science contains more than ample support for this policy; the point may be represented by the single example of the Fermi laboratory observations of the moderating influence of water on free neutrons. If Fermi had instead been given the assignment of producing a submarine that could circle the globe without refueling, the result would have been failure to produce the submarine and also absence of the basic discovery necessary to the development of the nuclear power which was soon to make such a submarine possible.

Sociology profits from the experience of all science and does not have to recapitulate the evolution of chemistry from an *ad hoc* alchemy. The policy presently dominant among most contemporary sociologists, in the United States at least and in some other nations, favors such a pursuit of general objective knowledge, relatively detached from the pressing problems of contemporary life. The sociologist who follows this course is protected from reproaches implying lack of responsibility by his realization that in his present state of knowledge he would probably handle the urgent practical problems of civilization little if any better than do the many men of affairs who at present have direct responsibility. He also knows that Rome is not really burning and that his ship is not sinking and that a nation which can comfortably spare billions for cosmetics can set aside a few millions for basic research into the causes of human and social behavior.

THE ENVIRONMENT OF MAN

All living things experience adaptation to environment. Prehistoric man spread over nearly all the land masses of the earth and found ways to survive in deserts, highlands, coral atolls, and arctic shores. Few forms of animal life have approached the versatility of the human in facing such a variety of environmental problems.

There is an understandable tendency naively to conceive of man primarily as a capable reasoning individual, who, when faced with an environmental problem, goes about solving it with a combination of trial-and-error manipulation and rational calculation. Such a process undoubtedly does occur with some frequency, and among all peoples. But this is far from an adequate representation of the principle way in which adaptation to environment is achieved.

The human response is never to a whole environment, if the latter is conceived in terms of the totality of surrounding topography and objects. It would be impossible to attend to every detail of the world about us; we obviously must select and interpret. The environment which we encounter is thus in part a man-made abstraction from the whole of our surroundings.

Furthermore, in common with many other living forms, but to a far greater extent, man modifies his environment, and in the modern metropolis he has in fact arranged the environment so that it is altered to suit his preferences far more than he adapts himself to it. Even so, the city dweller faces problems of living in this highly artificial environment.

Humans are inhabitants of cultures, and culture is as much or more a part of the environment as is the surrounding world of physical objects. Cultures are man-made, but are not made by man acting individually. Cultures evolve in a collective process, in which rational foresight is an extremely minor factor. The growth of cultures follows laws that do not correspond with any principles observable in individual psychology. The social level is, as Durkheim (1894) insisted, *sui generis*. A society and a culture has a life of its own, follows causal principles on a superorganic level, which cannot be reduced to any kind of sum of individual dispositions, qualities, or actions.

The confrontation of the physical world by a human being is done directly only in minor part. Man's world is encountered principally through the culture and society to which he belongs. His eyes see what his society permits or directs him to see. As Lévy-Bruhl (1910) contended at length, and modern psychological experiments prove, the power of the society over its members' individual mentalities, when unopposed by other social forces, is such as to make the individual almost impermeable to contradicting individual experience. Though processes of formal education in advanced societies attempt with partial success to liberate some of its members from this dependence on social influence, the phenomenon is not limited to prehistoric or preliterate peoples—it is still the overwhelming determiner of the relation of most of us to our universe.

It is this dominance of the person by organized social relations that makes it impractical to expect investigators to disclose the causes of behavior solely or even mainly by means of individual psychology. Human behavior cannot be completely explained by knowledge of individuals, however thorough.

The search for causation must also be directed toward the understanding of processes of interaction, the behavior of collectivities of various types, the nature of culture, the characteristics of organizations and their effects on their members. While this necessity has been clear to a few scholars for more than a century, the full realization of it in research activity has come only slowly. Our cultural habit, which influences the scholar along with other members of his society, is to perceive action as based on individual responsibility. To the sociologically unlearned person, for example, it appears intuitively obvious that wars are caused by a summation of hostilities within individuals and that peace is achieved through somehow implanting good will into person after person. The concept of organizations interacting as units, as wholes, on a superorganic level involving processes not existing in interpersonal interaction, and of this organizational interaction affecting the behavior of the members, is too sharply different from folk concepts to be widely grasped by the general public at the present time.

A major problem of contemporary sociology thus is the development of new conceptions and the perception of new processes not suspected in the folk-sociology of our ancestors. In the route to such new knowledge there lies an abundance of pitfalls and problems without precedent in other sciences. These of course do not discourage the sociologist, they merely set the conditions in which his activity of discovery must operate.

INDIVIDUALITY AND SOCIAL LIFE

The subsurface fish, if it were to have the capacity to think, would nevertheless not be able to develop a concept of ocean, although the medium in which he lives determines much of his shape and behavior. The human likewise has to get to a certain extent outside of himself in order to conceive of society. Influence of society is more easy to perceive in the behavior of other persons, but even the perception of systematically different ways of behavior on the part of strange peoples has not always led to the formulation of the concept of society. It is more characteristic of man, in his premodern condition, to view systematic differences of behavior as indications of general inferiority or derangement on the part of the persons who follow strange customs.

Many a concept seems intuitively clear and obvious after it is completely familiar. Any contemporary person would suppose that it stands to reason that wind is simply air in motion, and yet it has not been long since the prevalence of a general belief that air and wind are two different things.

The concepts of culture and society are now well established in the folk-understanding of civilized peoples, even though most of the necessary implications for behavior seem not to be. Most persons also sense the control of social influences on individual behavior, without seeming to realize fully their extent and power. Many persons alternately entertain the assumptions of free will and individual responsibility along with awareness of social influences. It appears, however, to be most difficult for a person to perceive social influences on himself. The typical citizen recognizes that his neighbor votes in response to pressures of tradition from his social group, all the while remaining confident that he assesses the candidates and issues logically and independently of any interfering influences.

The various means by which organized social groups control persons differ in visibility. Some aspects of the material culture are inescapable—the walls of a city, for example, are not too subtle for anyone to perceive. Official pressure from uniformed officials, police and soldiers, is almost equally conspicuous. That part of the law which is familiar to a population is also readily perceived as social control. Informal control, however, through spontaneous and sporadic expressions of disapproval and through the perception of the possibility of such expressions if breaches of custom were to be committed are more subtle.

The type of social control most difficult to sense, however, is that which operates by virtue of the fact that each person is a product of his society. To a considerable extent the society guides his behavior by virtue of having formed his nature. No one senses intuitively that in using his native tongue he is formed and controlled by his society. Similarly each person experiences the basic mores and attitudes of his people as his own preferences, rather than as the resultant of controlling forces. Cooley's aphorism, "Custom appears in the guise of nature," symbolizes the type of phenomenon in which the American views insects as in the nature of things inedible, even though he may readily perceive that the Hindu avoids the eating of beef by virtue of a completely arbitrary control by his society.

The concept of the human as a person with a responsible and free mentality, characterized previously as a theological viewpoint because of the support it has had in Christian doctrine, thus appears to be sociologically inadequate because it fails to recognize the amount of control which the person cannot resist because he is utterly unable to perceive it. The sociologist, however, need not relieve the individual from all responsibility on the ground that the latter is a helpless victim of forces beyond his control. Neither freedom nor control is absolute. There is an ample amount of freedom, and therefore a corresponding degree of responsibility, in the fact that every person, in civilization at least, experiences a unique combination of social memberships, influences, pressures, roles, and tasks. A considerable amount of individual freedom thus lies in this fact that each one of us experiences balanced pressures without specific and detailed direction from social control for every particular dilemma. The books of rules cannot cover every contingency, and in actual life the various sets of rules have much inconsistency. Thus no one can escape the frequent necessity of deciding. To say this, however, is not yet to settle the issue of how persons go about deciding. This is a problem to be solved by investigation, not to be given over by default to any particular theological doctrine. But this freedom, or even necessity, to make decisions is properly to be considered a basis of personal responsibility for much of our behavior. Even the most understanding sociologist is not likely to permit an embezzling bank employee to escape public sanctions on the convict's standard plea that "society is to blame." Society may, however, be the cause (though not blame) of the fact that he speaks English, drinks cow's milk, and opposes polyandry.

Thus, without denying a range of freedom for individual choices, and therefore a function for individual responsibility, the accumulated body of sociological knowledge points to a large and powerful force through which any society guides the behavior of its members. This force is least or absent in situations where social influences are undefined, inconsistent, in conflict, and it is strongest on matters concerning which the society is consistent and unanimous. The power of the society, at maximum strength, is in general greater than most of the familiar biological motives—"instincts," "drives," "needs." That is to say, men may starve to death in the presence of nutritious but arbitrarily tabooed edibles, observe incest restrictions, adopt celibate lives, sacrifice infants in response to social demands, and in other ways violate the "law of self-preservation" when a socially-instilled sense of honor demands it.

The causal relation, from society to person, is directional partly because of the inequality of the size of forces. In a sense the mass of a society or culture is not merely that of the living generation, but of its entire past. The infant is forced to speak his mother language not merely because he is outnumbered in his family or community, but because the organized language evolved over many centuries and has the solidity coming from the funded contributions made by all the generations before his own. Individuals do invent, and a small proportion of their inventions may be adopted into the culture, but in any generation, and for any one individual, the far greater determination is in the direction of society influencing the person rather than the converse. The point may be illustrated by the growth of a language; few persons succeed in introducing a new word. The difficulty is not in inventing a new phenomenon or concept, but in placing it in the language so that it actually comes into general use. In many cases, moreover, in which a term has been intentionally and successfully introduced into the language, a process of semantic drift, not controlled by any individual, quickly assimilates the term so that its eventual meaning may be importantly different from that intended by its original inventor.

Sociological theorists have sometimes been troubled by the contention that a society, which it would seem could only be a sum of individuals, and is therefore only an abstract concept, could operate as a force on real individuals. In some cases an accusation of mysticism is implied, but, from Durkheim (1894) on, modern sociologists have denied intending anything beyond the reality that a particular society or culture has an existence far beyond any member, and that it is always much older than a member can be. By virtue of being born into a system that is well-established a person is necessarily bound to be influenced by it. Individuals are real enough, to be sure, but the manifold linkages of relationship of various kinds produce functioning unities—families, corporations, governments, associations, and the like— which keep their special characteristics through the passage of generations of members, and constantly assimilate new members, altering their personal characters in the process. The persistence of a systematic pattern among persons, over a succession of generations, is reality enough. It is a reality we can and do count on in everyday life, as we commit our savings to life insurance companies, confidently assuming that some future officials, perhaps not now even members of the companies, will pay to our children, perhaps not yet born, the specified sums of money.

THE NATURE OF ORGANIZATION

Individual psychology would potentially account for all of human behavior were it not for the fact that in living together the human achieves organization. Human groups are not mere sums or aggregates, but are differentiated in systematic ways, and, as indicated above, the patterns of relationship have emergent qualities not present in the separate persons, and which are capable of contributing to causation on the organizational level itself.

Not all generalizations about people directly involve organization. Pluralistic behavior results from a number of persons being subjected to the same or similar influences. Tens of thousands of toilets are sometimes flushed simultaneously without direct intercommunication among the persons performing the action, as a consequence of the fact that they had been watching the same television program and therefore were freed from their chairs by the same commercial break. A considerable amount of vacation travel, attendance at sports attractions, purchases of faddish items, and other types of mass behavior are pluralistic in this sense, rather than organized. It is of course possible for pluralistic behavior to be mixed with organized behavior, and for parallel activity beginning in pluralistic fashion to turn into organization. For example, a spontaneous gathering of farmers to protest low prices of their produce may evolve into a permanent league for action.

Interaction processes constitute the basic fiber of organizations, but not all interaction culminates in permanent systems. Sociological research finds subject matter of interest in the entire range of such processes. Two-person, or dyadic, interaction is naturally a most elementary process, but turns out to be rich enough in its consequences to justify extensive research. Present-day investigators are also finding it rewarding to conduct research on three-person groups and on other small groups of every size. As the materials of Chapter 8 indicate, processes vary meaningfully in groups of varying size, and not all of the generalizations valid for small group interaction processes apply to large organizations.

Apart from person-to-person interaction in the direct contact of small groups there is a far more important amount of indirect role-interaction in formal organizations of various sizes and characteristics, and of an even more remote type of one-way interaction such as that involved in a person's response to his imagination of some possible individual or group reaction to himself, and also in the response a person may make as a consequence of his reading of literature, such as a response to some inspiring person who lived in a previous time.

Beyond the investigation of interaction processes themselves, the study of organization constitutes the heart of the discipline of sociology. In order to preserve clarity of meanings, it is useful to examine a sequence of concepts relevant and marginal to organization.

Aggregation refers to a mass of persons who are gathered in a compact space but lack systematic relations to one another, or any visible pattern of symbolic interaction. Pedestrians in a crowded shopping district, each going his own way, would constitute an aggregation.

Sum refers only to a number obtained by counting units and is necessarily an abstraction from such a reality as an aggregation or group. A naive assertion is sometimes made to the effect that a group or association "is nothing more than the sum of the members." In such a statement the concept of sum is undefined and useless.

Pattern designates relationships other than contiguity and summation. A heap of bricks is an aggregation and if counted can yield a sum. The same bricks, however, may be arranged to form such a pattern as an arch, which has an emergent quality not present in the separate bricks, or in a sum. Persons also may form patterns in lining up

at ticket windows, or sitting in rows at a theater.

Machine refers to a pattern in which moving interaction of parts yields further emergent characteristics. The parts of a clock may be arranged into a variety of static decorative patterns, but they form a machine only if they are formed into the particular dynamic interrelations that result in reporting of the time of day.

Organism designates a machine-like assembly of parts or elements but which have in addition the basic qualities of living things—the ability to assimilate material, the ability to adapt to varying conditions, the ability to reproduce themselves, and the like. Lichens, oysters, rabbits, and people are organisms.

The concept of *organization,* in some usage, may overlap with that of organism, and borderline examples may sometime blur precise distinctions. A rabbit may be referred to as an organization of cells, and a jellyfish may be regarded either as an organism or as a colony (used in zoology essentially synonymously with organization). The distinction which appears to serve well in sociology, however, is that an organization (of human beings) differs from an organism in that the former is composed of organisms as elements, and the elements (persons) have some separate existence from the organization and are capable of coming and going apart from their membership in the organization. Furthermore, in human organizations persons may belong simultaneously and successively to various organizations.

Although the above statement implies that a social organization is based on elements which are human individuals, one important qualification can be made. Because of multiple memberships, a person may more accurately be said to belong to a particular organization not with his whole self, but with a part, or aspect, of himself. That is, a man may be a husband and father at home, a judge in his occupational activity, a member of a school board, vice-president of a social club, and chairman of a fund drive committee. In each organization he participates with only the relevant aspect of himself; while conducting his duties in the courtroom his father-aspect does not participate.

This phenomenon of an organization composed of aspects of persons rather than whole organisms is unique to the human species. Many other animal species have organization, and some of the systems are impressively intricate. But the beehive is composed of whole bees, each of which has only the one membership and role, which it maintains throughout its short life.

The above distinctions serve to make unnecessary types of dispute once popular, on whether man is a machine, or society is an organism. Both answers would be clearly in the negative.

A pattern of bricks may involve differentiation of parts only with respect to location and contacts among bricks, but machine, organism, and organization derive their cohesion from the fact of complementary differentiation of elements. In human organization, the principle of unity does not derive from the fact that like attracts like (although this does occur and produces friendships and unorganized social groups) but from an emergent utility resulting from a particular differentiation of elements which can act in a concerted manner.

The familiar example of a football team serves well as an illustration of the functioning of complementary differences in an organization. Each of the 11 members has a unique and specified task to perform on each play, but the cohesion and effectiveness of the team does not come from either the congeniality of similarities or from the attraction of opposites. Differences for the sake of differences are not useful or welcome; there is no approval of noncomformity as such. Only the differences which fit into the patterns of the designed play are sought, and these are indispensable. An extreme form of disorganization of a football team would be an inevitable consequence of each member doing the same thing at the same time.

Athletic teams, military units, factory assembly lines, all furnish examples of tight and coherent forms of organization. A university is a looser and far more complex type, and there are all degrees of further extension and tenuousness in human organizations. Moreover, organizations themselves may constitute the elementary units in higher levels of complexity—organizations of organizations. Thus there are leagues of athletic teams, associations of colleges and universities, councils of learned societies, and a variety of organizations of national governments. Ultimately world-wide organized governmental and economic activity is interlocked into a grand but loose unity, which has been called by Wallas (1915) "The Great Society."

Organization is present, and important, among all humans and is obviously essential to sustain life itself. The most primitive human societies conduct their important functions for survival by efficient organization. Nowhere is spontaneous human nature trusted to ensure that food is obtained and shared, protection is achieved, harmony prevails, and the community reproduces itself. All men live by organization, and the human species would quickly die without it.

Dependence upon organization is great in direct proportion to the complexity of civilization. Each metropolitan dweller relies on the interrelated functioning of many systematically cooperating persons for fulfillment of his most simple needs. The milk delivered at his door comes to him by virtue of an immense coordination of farmers, truck drivers, processors, wholesalers, retailers, along with uncountable accessory functionaries who build the needed machinery, supply fuel for the transportation, and control the traffic through which vehicles must pass.

A partial attempt to assess the general place organization has in the life of civilized man would include at least the following three propositions.

Organization creates power. This generalization applies on all levels of complexity. Five good players of basketball without organization will be defeated in a game by five equally good men who are appropriately organized. Larger teams build ships, control great rivers, wage world wars, and shoot rockets to other planets. No mere *aggregation* of persons, however large, could handle tasks of this order of magnitude—organization is required.

Organization creates certainty. When we cannot find a Lieutenant Rowan to carry a message to Garcia, and such men are not ordinarily available to serve most of our desires, we find we can rely on an established organization. Certainty can never be absolute, but in general we find ourselves willing to put valuables in the mail with reasonable assurance that they will reach the intended destination. We send checks in advance to pay for goods, trusting that the items will be safely delivered. We allow banks and life insurance companies to hold money for us and in countless other ways put large amounts of faith in stable organizations.

Organization creates continuity. A perpetual charitable trust is enduring only because organizations succeed in their work. Again, continuity cannot be absolute, but endowments often achieve their intended purposes over a series of centuries. Our matter-of-fact confidence in extended contracts is illustrated by the 99-year lease from Columbia University of the land on which the Rockefeller Center buildings stand. The signers of the agreement felt confident that their action could bind persons not yet born to convey ownership of the land and buildings to other persons not yet born.

A naive view of human behavior, based on a popular understanding of behavioristic psychology, involves a conception of the human as only capable of acting in response to stimuli presented to sense organs and thus by implication responsive only to an immediate environment. In contrast the sociologist sees the human as mainly guided, regardless of environment, by formal institutional roles, which in turn are defined and enforced by mechanisms essentially timeless in their duration. In this sense all humans are organiza-

tion men and can be fully understood only to the extent that organizations are understood.

The foregoing statements showing the ways in which organizations differ in kind from sums or aggregations of individuals are not sufficiently obvious to be perceived by all writers who have been interested in the subject of human collective action. There have been, for example, political scientists who view a nation as essentially similar to a single human individual and to which treatment appropriate to an individual is likely to be successful. Others have viewed the characteristics of an organization as a sum of the characteristics of its members. Thus a simple polling of members of a labor union should presumably reveal the policies of the organization, though it is now well known that this does not necessarily or even usually work, for unions, business corporations, or nations. Thoreau (1949), in his *Civil Disobedience,* expressed a parallel thought in writing: "It is truly enough said that a corporation has no conscience, but a corporation of conscientious men *is* a corporation with a conscience." Had Thoreau been able to foresee the formulations of modern sociology he would have recognized that a corporation often acts on policies which are not products of, or always in harmony with, the consciences of the individual members.

Because of the differentiation of men within an organization, the influence of the various members on policy is never equal. The inner circle of management has more per capita influence than do members on the fringe. But, as indicated above, these officials do not take part in the organization with their whole personalities or their whole consciences, but with aspects of themselves, with their formal roles, which do not embrace their totality as persons. In the interaction of these role-aspects of persons with one another, and with the problems and environment of the organization, there emerges a unique product of policy and action on the collective level which cannot be explained by separate knowledge of members, however thorough the investigation of each individual, because the answer is not there. For this reason industrial sociology cannot succeed if it bases its research solely on attitudes and experiences of individual workers in the shops and individual employers in the offices. The interactions which dominate in this field are mainly interactions of organized collectivities—unions and manufacturing firms—and the processes are on a level which has characteristics of its own, not predictable even from complete knowledge of personal characteristics and interpersonal relations.

For the same reason, relations among nations will never be understood from a knowledge of characteristics of persons who are citizens of the various nations, however complete that knowledge. Public opinion polls, which compile separate statements of individuals, notoriously fail to account for national policies and international interaction. Political science can become mature only when understanding of the nature of organization is well developed.

Organizations are shaped by characteristics of membership, by environment and experience, and by their functions. For many organizations the function is the most important of the determiners and has some dominance over the other two. The function of a chemical manufacturing corporation, for example, is to produce and market chemical products at a profit, and the function of a major political party is to win elections and hold offices. Function need not be fully explicit in the minds of members, and often it is vaguely and incompletely perceived.

The fact of interrelation of function and structure is no obstruction to change in the organization, nor is sociological analysis of structure and function inconsistent with perception or study of change. Some organizations appear to grow in a sort of sympodial relation to environment, discovering in a gradual trial-and-error process the detailed elaboration of a function while at the same time building structure to fit the evolving concept. Here equilibrium and change go together with no necessary opposition.

SOCIAL CHANGE

As change is ubiquitous in modern times, scholars acquire a natural inclination to think of it as the natural condition of man and society. All history appears to be a record of uninterrupted and accelerating change. The sociologist therefore encounters a temptation to explain it by offering some sort of a general principle of instability in human nature and social organization. But this would explain nothing, and, to the extent that such a proposition were to be taken seriously, it could even tend to discourage research into causes of change.

In the broadest cosmic view of things the fact of continuous change cannot be denied. From the primordial explosion of matter on through the billions of years of universe expansion, there have been evolutions of galaxies, stars, planets, and on one or more planets evolution of life and a diversity of species, in a never-ending unidirectional process.

Over shorter periods, however, there seems to occur a reasonable amount of stability. The sun emits a fairly constant amount of energy, and its planets steadily hold to their courses in predictable orbits. On the earth, through all the flow of evolution of living things, there are plants, insects, and even vertebrates, which display records of structural stability over periods of millions of years.

Archeological examination of stone-age implements reveals a sequence of steady improvements from eoliths to finely polished stone tools, but this progress occurred over a great period of time. The Chellean hand-axe was manufactured and used in Europe for hundreds of thousands of years without visible improvement. This fact, along with other archeological evidence of long periods of stability in material cultures would seem to suggest that the cause of change might well be sought in some other principle than mere restlessness of human nature. At least it is worth while to compare observations showing change with others indicating periods of stability and to examine variations in rates of change from society to society and era to era. The Toda people of India, for example, were visited and described at two periods separated by most of the nineteenth century and were found to have changed very little in contrast to the revolutionary transformation of Western civilization in the same period (Rivers, 1906). Even transplanted Europeans, placed by accidents of history in remote environments, have been known to lose their taste for change. The English and Italian settlers of the south Atlantic island Tristan da Cunha furnish an impressive example of stability deliberately preserved. For example, cast-off clothing, donated to them from time to time by compassionate ship crews, was usually altered to minimize style change (Munch, 1945).

Other examples of deliberate attempts to avoid change are to be found in such religious sects as the Hutterites, who hold carefully to their separate customs and costumes in the midst of a North American environment of the mid-twentieth century (Eaton, 1953).

Even in completely modern civilization, where change is most rapid, we can observe that not every aspect of culture takes part in the process. There are familiar and commonplace ways that remain stable for centuries, untouched by any feverish impatience of human nature, or *elan vital* of society. Traffic customs, for example, such as keeping to the right (or to the left, as is done in Britain and some other lands) can be changed, but may remain long untouched by the seemingly omnipresent winds of change. And, to mention a material example, the violin has undergone negligible change in 250 years, in the same civilization which makes automobiles and airplanes obsolete in a decade.

If we should assume that both human nature and the nature of social organization tend to prefer stability, as long as satisfactory solutions of problems of living and working together reach an equilibrium, we would still have no trouble finding conditions, entirely external to sociology and psychology, which force disturbances and therefore initiate change. A number of such external conditions or events can present new problems, force migrations, render existing culture obsolete, bring contacts with alien peoples, and in other ways disturb the equilibrium. Lightning, for example, can cause forest fires and burn inhabitants out of their homeland. Floods and plagues may have similar effects. Population growth may also bring exhaustion of food supply and force migrations, which in turn may initiate contacts with other cultures with additional instigation of change for both peoples. Presumably these and similar physical events have influenced human societies all through the prehistoric millennia, never allowing any condition of equilibrium to become permanent. Fundamentally, therefore, some amount of change is perpetually forced, apart from any sociological principles bearing on the question, by occurrences external to man and society, which force him to seek new adaptations and cause him to come into contact with other cultures, inevitably to learn different ways from that experience.

Invention and Social Change

Consideration of the variety of material possessions of modern man provides the impression that mankind is perpetually disposed to invent, and by doing so to transform every aspect of his life. The proposition is true enough of contemporary man, viewed collectively. But the inventor is, in proportion to a population, a rare individual. The great majority of persons invent nothing in their entire lifetimes, and, of the persons who do invent, only a small proportion succeed in having their inventions established as a part of the culture and as a force for social change.

Ogburn (1922; 1933; 1946), in his pioneering labors on the subject, argued that most inventions have only a small amount of true originality, and that in fact most of them consist of minor additions to, or recombinations of, existing elements in the culture. As Ogburn (1922) wrote, "In the telegraph, for instance, electricity, coils, batteries and circuit are all known. The sound contrivance and the code seem the newer features, but these indeed have cultural predecessors in the electric bell, the alphabet, and signalling" (p. 88).

Inventions thus would tend to occur at a rate closely related to the number of existing elements ready to enter into new combinations. This "cultural base" of previously existing inventions appeared to Ogburn to be the principal factor in determining the rate of invention itself and in accounting for the further fact that the growth of the body of inventions appears to have an exponential character. That is, the more elements present to be combined, the larger the number of other possible combinations.

Ogburn further claimed, providing strong evidence in support, that until a cultural base contains the element necessary to an invention it is virtually impossible for the invention to be made, but when all the elements are present the occurrence of the invention is inevitable. If one inventor does not create the new device, another will. Thus even if Morse had not survived his childhood we would still have the telegraph, and if Daguerre had never lived we would have photography. In these instances the matter is not speculative, since other men did make these inventions independently, at about the same time. The impressive frequency of independent simultaneous inventions constitutes almost conclusive support for Ogburn's generalization. In his early work Ogburn listed 148 of these, and other scholars have since extended his list (Ogburn, 1922, pp. 90–102).

Thus explanation of the factor of invention in social change begins with the principle that, in a way, invention causes invention, in an ever-accelerating process. To be sure, some mental ability is required, but there is no certainty that this must be of a rare degree. Necessity is also acknowledged by Ogburn to be a factor, though hardly a "mother" of invention; extreme necessity fails to generate a particularly needed invention if the cultural base is not ready. It can also be granted that we have an abundance of clever inventions which bear no relation to necessity, other than the possible financial requirements of the inventor.

Ogburn, especially in his monumental work on Social Trends (1933), examined at length and in detail the many ways in which inventions have effects on all aspects of culture and social life. This of course need not be viewed as a theory of cultural determination by inventions, or as one-way influence of technology on society; effects may also flow in the opposite direction, and ideas may also shape history. Scholars have long been aware that certain early inventions and discoveries transformed the nature of human life—among these are the use of fire, stone tools, agriculture, the bow and arrow, the wheel, alphabetic writing, iron and steel, gunpowder, paper, printing, steam engines, gasoline engines, and many others.

The process never ends, but rather accelerates, as does the making of inventions. Effects of a particular invention are never fully traceable, since chain effects and branching spread into hopeless complexity. Ogburn, however, indicated with specific examples the sort of effects that appear to be connected with certain inventions of recent times. Among the obvious effects of the typewriter, for example, is the creation of a new career for women and thus a general emancipation of women, with consequent important alterations in the character of family life as well as unmeasurable changes in political processes. The vacuum tube, and its miniature successor the transistor, have led to a chain of consequences from the creation of radio and television to modern computers and automation mechanisms, with fundamental effects on family life and industrial organization, in a process which may yet be only in its infancy.

One invention may have effects in a variety of directions, and one effect may follow from the combined influence of many inventions. The transformation in modern nations from agricultural society to urban-industrial civilization is a consequence of such varied innovations as machines which lighten farm work, chemicals which increase farm yield, and the vast body of technological developments in laboratories and factories which contributed to these.

Even though the specific causal relations can only be partially described there could hardly be doubt that the combined social effects of all technical developments creates a continuous revolution that touches and transforms all aspects of human life, at speeds which up to the present stage of history are always more swift. Recent spectacular advances, in their infancy of development—such as the laser, particle physics, and molecular biology—are leading contemporary thinkers to speculate, sometimes with awe, on fantastic transformations in human life only a few decades in the future.

It is appropriate to mention here that the human has so far shown such versatility that he has quickly adapted to new devices and the styles of life that followed from them, so that young persons who have never known anything but a television and jet plane age still seem to us basically like the children familiar to our grandparents. Through all the revolutionary changes we not only keep many old customs and practices, but retain some confidence that when we build a stone building it will be used for the intended purpose 40 or more years later, and that when we take out a retirement annuity policy at age 30 the agreement will be kept 35 and more years later. The whirl of technological change thus does not abolish all conditions of stability.

Ideas, or concepts, are widely supposed to be social forces. It is unlikely that many sociologists would doubt this, in the face of historical accounts of the wars and crusades that seem to have been inspired by religious ideas, and the numerous revolutions, reforms, and social movements that appear to have derived so much force from such concepts as "liberty," "justice," "equality," and

from broad notions of race pride, nationalism, and convictions of "manifest destiny." The spread of missionaries about the world could be mainly accounted for by ideology. Images of utopia also appear to have inspired population movements and the founding of new settlements, and a large number of social movements of various sizes have drawn their power from ideas as diverse as health notions, affection for animals, virtue of property-sharing, and so on.

The idea of change may itself be considered as a factor in social change. The thought is as old as history, since the oldest writings contain laments about the departure of living generations from the superior ways of the past. Some ancients even considered change beneficial and sought it. But until about the beginning of the twentieth century it would appear that most peoples, while knowing that change occurs, tended to think of stability as more normal and preferable. A considerable amount of opinion appeared in the late nineteenth century, viewing the recent perceived changes as spectacular but mostly temporary, as if all of the possible science and invention would soon be achieved, and social conditions would permanently stabilize. For example, it has been reported that G. K. Chesterton predicted, early in the twentieth century, that hansom cabs would be seen on London streets at the end of the century, and about the same time Simon Newcomb is said to have predicted that man would never succeed in flying.

If these representations of earlier viewpoints are correct, we can recognize that a new and important emergent conception, arising in the present century, may constitute an unprecedented factor in social change. The new factor is the general public conception that change is more normal than stability, and a conviction that it is more desirable. Change thus becomes something not to be resisted, but to be sought, encouraged, and welcomed from year to year. While the World's Fair of 1893 in Chicago exhibited the new beauty of electric lighting, its main theme was a celebration of the voyage of Columbus, and its buildings were all of classical design. In the same city in 1933 another World's Fair looked only to the future, as nearly all major expositions have since done.

Along with this adaptation to an expectation of perpetual change has come a slower development of institutional adjustment. Legal systems still permit founding for perpetuity, but men are learning that old arrangements designed to last forever can be altered by later generations when it is necessary. There is ever less tendency to endow funds to last forever, or even to construct buildings to live, as does the Roman Pantheon, for 1,500 years and more. The transition of culture and society to a situation of continuous and accelerating change is still under way.

It may be in part a reflection of this concept of naturalness of change that an increasing proportion of organizations of various sorts conceive that they must grow continuously. Most business firms now seem to have this disposition, although it was not always so; some European business enterprises are said to have maintained a constant size out of preference. Perhaps the spreading of the modern spirit accounts for the decision of some colleges, long holding to a constant size, to begin to allow a certain amount of growth.

The above factors intermingle in complex ways. Machines alter ideas, and ideas create machines. Technology controls the death rate, causing populations to expand, forcing a collision of necessity with ideals and of one set of ideals with another. The interrelationship of forces is impossible to trace, but in summation they lead to what would appear to be irreversible trends in history—trends toward richness of material culture and complexity of society, intercommunication and interdependence among peoples, increasing flow of populations, and various others, along with a constant emergence of difficulties not previously known to man.

The broad historical process appears to be universal, but of course engages some regions before others. Historians and sociologists have given full attention to the possibility that separate civilizations tend to have natural life-cycles (Sorokin, 1937–1941; Spengler, 1926; Toynbee, 1947–1957). A few conceive that Western civilization at the present time is in the late stages of its cycle, and therefore probably facing early extinction as an organizational entity. Among sociologists, however, this is a minority point of view, and most would perceive a single process in the development of western civilization from its Mediterranean beginning to its present world-wide dominance. In this view there is but one civilization, with an origin that depended on the development of alphabetic writing—a process which was successful only once in the history of the world.

SOCIAL DISORGANIZATION

The term disorganization, when used with care, refers simply to some degree of separation of the linked patterns of interrelations which constitutes organization. Disorganization is organizational bonds coming apart and does not necessarily imply any sort of damage to the persons who compose the organization. It is possible to have an unhealthy organization even though all of its members are individually normal. Social disorganization, thus, is conceptually distinct from individual pathology, even though there may be some types of social disorganization that may impair the normality of member persons.

Social disorganization can be total, or partial to any degree. Total disorganization means that the organization ceases to exist, as in the case of dissolution of a partnership, disbanding of a social club, or abolition of a military unit. It is not per se good or bad and can be either welcomed as beneficial or dreaded as harmful, according to the utility of the organization. Used in this way, the concept is value-neutral, and thus disorganization is not properly employed as a synonym for "social problems" or other undesired human conditions.

Partial disorganization exists where the organizational pattern has defects or incompleteness which interfere with the performance of its functions. The consequences may range from trivial inefficiency to severe interference with functions and hence a variety of types of dissatisfaction in members and also in persons whose interests are served by the organization. Few organizations approach perfection in any case; the work of the world is done by organizations with defects of many kinds. Contending armies, like opposing football teams, carry on their contests even when their organizational patterns are severely disrupted. Again, the distinction between individual fitness and organizational health must be kept in mind; athletes and soldiers may be individually adequate and yet be defeated by better organized opponents.

A few of the most generally perceived causes of disorganization may be noted here, recognizing that future research is likely to elaborate and test these suggestions. Perhaps the foremost basis of failure lies in defectiveness of the design of the organizational pattern itself. Construction of teamwork bonds is an old art in military and political affairs, but has been only recently begun to be examined by science. It is widely believed, however, that the patterns do make important differences in the capacity of organizations to survive and to carry out their tasks. Some of the folk knowledge of principles of organization are recorded in treatises on administration in military, governmental, and business organizations. It is widely held, for example, that unnecessary complexity has disorganizing effects, and thus some corporations attempt to minimize the number of levels in the management structure. The pattern of lines of communication is also generally to be of significance, and some writers put special importance on the desirability of providing for communication upward as well as down through the levels of management. Also among the supposed factors in partial disorganization are shortcomings in clarity of role and task definition, and in responsibility and authority, as well as extreme rigidity of regulations which obstruct necessary flexibility.

Disruptive opposition can disorganize, and tactics of both military and athletic engagements involve intentional efforts to cause disorganization of the opposing forces. Natural obstacles may have similar effects—conditions on a high mountain can break into the integrative pattern of a climbing team, and severe conditions at sea can disorganize a ship's crew. Opposition from within, from secret subversion, can also be destructive in various degrees.

Internal conflict weakens organization in a variety of ways. Factions can damage cooperation, antagonisms can obstruct communications, distrust can confuse and slow down teamwork operations, and extreme hostilities can lead to sabotage and other deliberate interference with functions. A nation divided by antagonistic subdivisions may survive when not under severe pressure, but topple easily to enemy invasion under the strain of war, as is said to have been the case with France in 1940 (Gurvitch, 1943). Internal conflict in the Congo in the early 1960's brought about such a disruption of economic organization as to lead to widespread starvation.

Since the structure of any organization evolves to perform a function, organization defects may result from inadequacies, vagueness, and inconsistencies of function. Functions may also become obsolete, as in the case of organizations to support enforcement of obsolete laws. If an organization is formed to achieve a specific task, the fulfilling of its goal constitutes a crisis of function which may be fatal to an organization unless it can find a new and viable function. The Anti-Saloon League may be said to have died of success, and organizations formed to control a specific disease encounter the same kind of difficulty, which is sometimes solved by turning to some comparable disease. The Townsend Movement, organized in the early years of the depression of the 1930's, was built about the function of extracting old age pensions from Congress through strong political pressure. The enactment of social security legislation, however, along with the disappearance of the depression in the prewar and wartime prosperity, so weakened the function that the membership experienced a 97 per cent decline in the 15 years from 1936 to 1951 (Messinger, 1955). The remnant of an organization that survived seems to have been held together by a combined social and merchandising function, and it becomes a question of semantics whether the latter entity should be designated by the same name as the original Townsend Movement, even though there was continuity between the two.

Organizations for occasional action sometimes encounter difficulties during the periods when no action is required. There is apathy in the fire departments of fireproof cities and restlessness in military organizations during long periods without visible threats from potential enemies. Other protective organizations, such as community associations, associations of employed professionals, and labor unions, experience confusion of function in times when their welfare is secure. In some cases the leadership, in the interest of vitality of the organization, may even seek to provoke some oppression, to avoid extinction through inactivity.

As indicated above, quality of members and soundness of organizational design are conceptually independent, so that a team of able individuals may nevertheless suffer severe disorganization just as a good organization may sometimes be formed of low-quality members. There are some types of organization which can only be formed of members of specified high quality. Some, such as military and athletic organizations, may require individuals of strength, quickness, and endurance, while others may require a high level of intelligence. Inability to recruit and hold these necessary types of membership can thus become a cause of disorganization. Intricate economic systems, in fact, have quality requirements for the working populations such that nations with low levels of average education cannot fulfil.

Morale is generally conceived, by administrators as well as sociologists, as a factor in the soundness of an organization. Some confusion on the definition of the concept prevails in the literature, but there appears to be a fabric of mutual confidence, pride, and motivation that binds the members of an acting team in such a way that the whole health of the organization is supported. Although some writers refer to "individual morale," it is more common among sociologists to use the term to refer to a collective condition, which of course may have its effects on the motivation and spirits of individual members. High morale may be found in such groups as elite military teams, Rangers, Commandos, and the like, in which a unifying bond appears to create a collective will, pride, and confidence almost entirely submerging individual interests which have possible conflict with the purposes of the group. The extreme of low morale can apparently develop when the unity of a military group is totally shattered, as is said by some writers to have been the case among American soldiers imprisoned by the enemy in the Korean War of the mid-1950's.

Examination of concrete examples of malfunctioning in groups of many kinds suggests that disorganization may cause further disorganization in a circular process which can spread widely throughout the whole structure, just as failure in one part of a physiological organism may cause a sequence of troubles in a chain effect. This is not to say, however, that once started a process stops only with complete destruction. As indicated earlier, construction and reorganization processes are also omnipresent in human life, and in the long course of history the processes of organization have outstripped those of disruption. Thus, in spite of the variety of disorganization processes civilization becomes based on ever larger, more intricate, and powerful organization, and each person's survival and welfare depends ever less on his individual capacities and always more on the soundness of social organization.

THE PROBLEMS OF KNOWING IN THE SOCIOLOGICAL FIELD

The aspirant to sociological inquiry encounters the special difficulty of penetrating a subject of which he is an intimate part. The problem is more than that of understanding a part of one's own body or self; man has no trouble in examining objectively his own feet. The human mind, however, must make a special effort to get outside of itself in order to perceive the social matrix in which it is constantly being formed. The very idea of attempting this is an artificial one, for, as previously stated, natural intuition leads each person to conceive of himself as autonomous and in realistic and logical contact with all of his surroundings. The sociological problem here is to construct entities of a new order of emergence in which the thinking person is only a minor aspect and to find means of determining the nature and the ways in which these entities behave as cause and effect of personal behavior.

This difficulty is not, of course, a fatal obstruction to a science of sociology, although there is no lack of holders of such a pessimistic proposition. As stated earlier, even the unsophisticated person has little difficulty in perceiving the influences of society and culture in distant and strange peoples. An American needs no sociological instruction to recognize that a traditional Japanese society has much to do with guiding the behavior and mentality of its members, although he may be surprised and fascinated (and sometimes annoyed) to hear a foreign scholar generalize about the typical American person as a product of a distinctive society.

An important phase of the process of development of a science of society was of course the grand movement of ethnographic study by both amateurs and academic professionals in the pre-sociological period of inquiry. With the availability of enough world-wide observations on a variety of cultures it became not too difficult for such generalizers as Morgan, Spencer, Frazier, and Sumner to arrive at articulate observations of the phenomena of the superorganic level without employing mystical elements in their thinking.

The concepts of society and culture, once clearly pointed out, are readily comprehensible to the citizen who lacks sociological training. Thus some hard-won generalizations of the early sociologists are now becoming assimilated into the organized mass of folk-knowledge, and in so doing come to appear to the unsophisticated person to have intuitive reality. All this is to say that the idea of society as a part of the causal process was difficult until it was conceived and explained by pioneering scholars who possessed the ability and energy to generate it, after which it became easy enough for a school child to grasp.

When new knowledge, achieved by hard labor, eventually becomes clear to the nonspecialized population it loses glamor by reason of its familiarity. The small child, for example, now takes the marvel of television for granted, and many a bright high-school student understands it well enough to feel that he could easily have invented it if this had not already been done. The very obviousness of new and difficult concepts, once these have been made clear, constitutes another insidious barrier to further discovery, as it tends to trap persons into supposing that intuitive comprehension is a reliable instrument for investigation of new knowledge. There is always great folk-confidence in "common-sense" however many disastrous mistakes have been made in its name; it ever seems that it is the other person whose common-sense is defective. The scholarly equivalent of this faith in methodless intuition lies in an occasional fondness for the concept of *Verstehen,* which appears to play the function, for some knowledge-seekers at least, of liberating the investigator from the burdensome necessity of using various technical devices others have found useful in reducing sources of error and making knowledge reliable.

The gales of doctrine and passion can blow in any field of inquiry and have done so in most of them. The Inquisition interfered with cosmology, controversial storms have followed destructive courses in human physiology and medicine, and even in the coldly abstract fields of mathematics and logic factional disputes are not unknown. But, since no other field makes such rich contact with values, both sacred and secular, as does the study of human behavior and social relations, sociology has exceptional need for insulation from the obstructive influence of arbitrary doctrine. Much of Christian theology purports to offer explanations and solutions of questions under investigation by sociologists, and, to the extent that the threat of sociological competition is perceived by the fundamentalist believer, the scientific viewpoint is feared and fought as an enemy of sacred truth. Also, where Marxism, Freudianism, or any other secular formulation of an organized faith contain principles bearing on issues of sociology, there is similar interference with the goal of a scientific discipline.

Wherever political movements become joined with comprehensive theories of human and social behavior such impediments to the development of sociology have been formidable. In spite of the large contributions to the development of the field coming out of Europe, there has always been on that continent a considerable amount of obstruction of this sort. Some European sociologists, in fact, have pronounced the hope for an objective sociology to be entirely futile and have offered only the compensating device of the practice of requiring each author of a sociological treatise to provide an autobiographical confession of all his personal doctrines that determine his conclusions. The justification for such a practice is that a reader should thereby be able, on reading of the author's biases, to make the proper allowances for them. The weakness of the device, of course, is that it can only subtract from the confidence a reader may have in the work and gives no basis for finding any amount whatsoever of positive value in it.

Latin America has, of course, been an equally fertile ground for intense political doctrines which interfere with the development of sociology. In the report of a 1961 conference on the sociology of that continent it was stated that, "There are many people in Latin America who regard the work of empirical sociological research as a threat to values and social structures they consider vital to the cohesion of Latin American Society" (Wood & Wagley, 1961, p. 3). Undoubtedly the difficulty is even more extreme in some of the countries of Asia and Africa, and the flourishing of a scientific sociology in such regions is not soon to be expected.

Reduction of doctrinal interference is, however, far from impossible, and much freedom and objectivity has been achieved in the United States and in some parts of Europe and elsewhere during the past few decades. As universities have become stronger, and have gained the appreciation and confidence of the populations that support them, they are increasingly allowed to develop effective defenses against interference from outside. Nowhere is this protection absolute, but in many universities today the principal remaining doctrinal obstruction to objective investigation is the relatively minor one of the school-of-thought habit which constricts vision in an ever-decreasing proportion of academic sociologists.

The observation is frequently made that no scholar can ever be utterly without values and therefore completely objective and that consequently sociology cannot ever be free of value commitments. Freedom may be obtained, however, through the choice of particular research issues on which the scholar himself has no emotional preference for a particular outcome. A sociologist who happens to be either a fervent Zionist or an enthusiastic Nasser disciple may be inappropriate for research on comparative social mobility in Cairo and Tel Aviv, but need not be disqualified from undertaking research on juvenile delinquency in Toronto. For the mobility study it might be preferable to find a Swiss or a Scandinavian who, whatever emotional prejudices lurk in his character, may be sufficiently indifferent on the controversies which would interfere with the study in the Near East. Thus the fact that all men have values does not mean that prejudice bears on every possible issue, and it does not have to render impossible a value-free science of sociology.

By understandable selection, the field of sociology increasingly becomes occupied by scholars who are not discouraged by any of the variety of special obstacles discussed above. For each difficulty, fatal as it may seem to the person who lists it, the sociologists have persistently worked to devise means of surmounting it. The whole armament of research techniques, mentioned briefly below and treated more extensively in various chapters of this book, represents the dominant professional posture in relation to the critical pessimists (Lundberg, 1961).

The aim of science is always to explain, which is to say that causation is to be identified. The utility of science lies in prediction, control, and also in the choice of man's own courses of adaptation in situations in which control cannot be achieved, as in the case of behavior with respect to volcanic eruptions and climatic disasters. In plain terms, knowing the causes of things helps us to get what we want, and to avoid what we do not want.

The concept of causation would appear to present special difficulties for the study of human and social behavior. Apart from the fact of complexity, which seems formidable enough, there is the free-will issue, mentioned previously. If there is an uncaused proportion of human activity, and if this pervades the tangle of organized social relations, pursuit of causal explanations would appear to be hopeless. And if the only justification for research were the certainty that eventually complete causal explanation of all activity in every detail could be achieved, abandonment of the whole game would be the only course of action. But absolute con-

quest of problems is not possible in any field of knowledge; there are inherently unpredictable and unknowable things in physics and therefore necessarily in all other sciences. Physics, however, achieves much prediction and control of the behavior of gases, without embarrassment at failure to predict the exact behavior of each gaseous particle. If complete explanation were required for science, then science never was and never will be. Causation is inevitably a pragmatic achievement, useful though incomplete and imperfect. If there is any causation at all in human and social behavior, the discovery of it constitutes science.

Billiard balls may influence one another through physical collision. Persons may and do jostle in a crowd, but the larger part and more important forms of human interaction operate through communication in which symbols, meanings, imagination operate. There is, of course, a problem of accessibility of information regarding phenomena which lie within the imagination of a person, but if the material is never totally accessible, neither is it totally inaccessible. We can and do, much of the time, communicate with some success by means of language. There are also possibilities of inferring inarticulate meanings through experimental use of projective methods and other devices. In ordinary manipulation of persons we can alter behavior by means of changing the meanings of objects—adolescent pranksters sometimes cause their schoolmates to stop eating by pointing out the resemblance of a particular food to disgusting objects, thereby exemplifying both prediction and control in a simple sequence of behavior.

The statement that human behavior is not predictable, offered with tiresome frequency, can only mean that we will not be able to achieve complete predictability. If it is ever meant to imply that there is no predictability whatever, the statement is absurd. A large proportion of social life assumes predictability of behavior in a most obvious way. If you say "good morning" your acquaintance will respond in the same way, not every time of course, but with enough regularity to make life somewhat predictable. If you spank a small child he will cry. If you put down your coin, the news salesman will hand you the paper.

There is also a predictability and control in masses, apart from particular actions of individuals. A glamorous film actress may cause a change in hair fashions, an advertising campaign may cause massive change in cigarette preferences, a television debate may swing an election. All this is familiar and obvious, but perhaps by virtue of its familiarity tends to be overlooked when social causation is under discussion.

Probably the greatest and most reliable predictability in human affairs is the product of organization. The students and the professor appear in a classroom at nine o'clock in the morning because of formal arrangements in the institution of the university. Mail reaches its destination, department store purchases are delivered, electricity lights our homes—all because of predictable and controllable processes so commonplace that sociologists seldom mention them and virtually never conduct research on them; research properly is directed toward the less obvious matters, on which the answers are not yet a matter of common knowledge.

The pragmatic question that is inescapable in the pursuit of explanation of human behavior comes out of the fact that there is a wide and arbitrary choice of type and number of causal aspects of any general issue. When the coroner must report on the cause of death of a person whose body is found by a highway bridge abutment, he may report the cause as injury to the brain. The traffic statistician may find the relevant cause to be a failure of a steering mechanism. A court may find the event to be caused by a plot to murder by tampering with the car. A psychiatrist may look into the mind of the murderer for the sources of the causal delusion which instigated the train of events. Any and all of these causes may be real and the particular one each official finds of interest is related to the particular way in which his responsibility applies to the case. There is little point in debating which of the above is *the* cause.

While a historian may investigate the cause or causes of a particular event, the sociologist, by virtue of interest in general principles, seeks regularities of causation. He is less interested professionally in the cause of a particular incident of burglary than in the general causal factors in this class of criminal actions. The general causes never tell the whole story about a particular criminal event, but have the possibility of being far more useful in the long run.

It is assumed that a diligent search for general causation of organized human behavior will in time be usefully applicable, even though absolute certainty is forever out of the question. Nor do we need be discouraged by a degree of historical specificity in sociological principles. Statements of causal relations true today may not necessarily be as true 50 years hence, when the emergent processes of civilization alter both human nature and social organization. Urban ecology of the 1920's may have been partly specific to those times, and it may in fact be necessary to revise urban ecology as long as cities grow and change. This means that sociology may have to be an ever-moving science, and that if it is ever to be useful it must also move more rapidly than its subject matter evolves. Discouragement need not be the response to this outlook; the sociologist can at least feel confident that he need never sink into boredom from lack of questions to investigate.

The search in sociology thus is for practically useful rather than eternal and perfect causes, and pursuit of confidence takes the form of trying for relative rather than absolute certainty. We must accept reasonable progress in these directions because nothing more is possible. All people come to accept less than perfection as long as there is a sense of progress in the directions that matter.

Relevant questions may properly be asked on various levels, and the appropriate form of causation varies according to the levels. In the search for causes of crime it is rewarding to look for the reasons for high prevalence of crime in particular neighborhoods as well as for the processes of interpersonal influences by means of which each offender acquires his criminal techniques. It is equally legitimate to speak of the cause of the high neighborhood rate as of the causes of the sequence of experiences of the individual.

Overconcern with formulation of a broad and universally applicable meaning of "cause" can all too easily lead the theorist into a sterile image of colliding billiard balls, for which there is rarely a useful analogy in sociology. It is commonplace in the science of physiology to seek causes of deficiency conditions, such as scurvy, in which the cause is not impact of a colliding particle, but the *absence* of a usually present substance. While it may offend the formal theorist to speak of the absence of something as a cause, the understanding of the consequence of the deficiency is all that is needed to provide control.

INSTRUMENTS FOR
SOCIOLOGICAL RESEARCH

Each science has its own ways of gathering observations which are the basic materials from which causal statements are eventually extracted. The geologist looks at strata with unaided eye, the astronomer uses telescopes and spectroscopes, the biologist needs microscopes. The brass instruments of the sociologists, however, are largely conceptual. Most sociological data are gathered by visual observation or through communication, and instrumentation consists in the use of devices which reduce known sources of error and distortion in the data-gathering process.

For example, to observe (for the purpose of measurement, comparison, and extraction of causal generalizations) a condition of public opinion on an issue of popular concern it may be necessary to employ such devices as the following:

1. Draw the sample to be observed by random methods, to avoid biases that are inherent in the choices of subjects by the observer.

2. Phrase the questions and statements offered to the subjects in such a way that they are clearly understood and have identical meanings to respondents of all regions and socioeconomic levels.

3. Arrange the statements in such a sequence that responses to an early statement cannot influence in an undesired way any responses to later statements.

4. Employ interviewers who are trained in the skills known to be related to effective data-gathering, so that refusals are held to a minimum, candid responses are obtained, and interviewers' attitudes are effectively concealed.

5. Hold to a minimum emotional resistance to answering certain types of questions, by indirection, concealment of purpose of inquiry, and other devices.

6. Obtain responses in such a form that they may be arranged into a useful scale of attitude.

7. Observe and measure intensity as well as content of opinion.

Such devices, of which the above list is only an illustrative sample, are a part of the technical heritage of academic sociology and various research institutes and polling organizations, and to a considerable extent these and related devices are recorded in field manuals of such organizations and in textbooks on research methods in sociology.

Another sociological equivalent of the brass instrument is the observation laboratory, in which the observers of specimens of behavior are concealed behind a one-way mirror. Actual recording instruments, such as films and sound recorders, are generally used here.

Precision and objectivity sometimes have to be sacrificed in order to observe behavior which cannot be collected in formal interviews or generated in a laboratory. Thus studies of boy gangs, religious movements, neighborhood organizations, and various other natural developments must often be made by a participant observer, who may in some cases be required to conceal the fact that he is engaged in research.

Some of the data analyzed in the quest for sociological knowledge are gathered by other than research sociologists, or furnished by other agencies. Information from governmental censuses is among the important sources of sociological basic data. Other social sciences also furnish raw material for the sociologist, especially anthropology with its rich output of useful ethnographic information.

In addition to the technology of sociological data-gathering, the research equipment of sociology contains a rich and rapidly growing body of techniques for the extraction of causal generalizations from the data. The most important part of this instrumentation, of course, is the fund of statistical methods, which can uncover regularities in masses of data too bewildering in their complexity to give up their secrets to any kind of personal skill or intuition. Statistical methods can also furnish a bridge between qualities and quantities, by measuring frequencies of different qualities, and by extracting further quantitative generalizations from these frequencies. Relative importance of various factors in producing effects of combinations, or interactions, of the factors can be measured. Out of bewildering complexities of relationships of many variables, statistical techniques can sometimes discover a few pervading factors which provide the basis for a relatively simple explanation of much of the behavior reflected in the variables. These statistical, and related formal logical methods, employed in connection with modern high-speed computers, promise exponential progress in scientific knowledge of human and social behavior, providing that the data-gathering process itself, now becoming something of a bottle-neck, can be made sufficiently swift and accurate.

It should be mentioned, of course, that sociological methods will for some time and perhaps indefinitely permit the employment of informal methods in situations where elaborate techniques are difficult to apply or perhaps even inappropriate. Useful conclusions may still be made from information plotted on maps and diagrams and from other relatively simple observations and comparisons.

THE EMERGENCE OF MODERN SOCIOLOGY IN THE UNITED STATES

Sociology as we know it today took a long time to develop. As pointed out at the beginning of this chapter, it can be seen as a development covering thousands of years, most of that time progressing at a pace imperceptibly slow. Not until the past 50 years or so did the rate of progress become sufficiently rapid to justify a sense of confidence that the field is really viable. It appears from our present perspective that the two requirements for coming to this stage were the conceptualizing of a distinctive field and the development of some sense of research method. The first of these requirements was achieved mainly in the nineteenth and early twentieth centuries, and, as shown below, can be understood as much in terms of general conditions of civilization in those times, especially in the United States, as in terms of the exceptional mental efforts of able pioneer scholars.

In the middle of the nineteenth century, academic treatment of matters relating to society and human behavior was not at all differentiated into separate fields of social science. The fields of history and moral philosophy embraced all of this subject matter and what there was of human psychology as well. Philosophers and historians of the period were far more disposed to seek truth from famous writings of great thinkers than to attempt to convert their subject matter into a science.

Awareness of pathologies of human behavior and social institutions was not lacking, but this did not at once supply impetus toward discovery of new knowledge. For many persons, human betterment was to be found only in religion, and this hope was reflected in the considerable amount of revivalism and in the waves of organization of new religious movements in the nineteenth century. Some scholars—historians and moral philosophers—held to a faith that government and law could eventually be perfected to yield solutions to the major human problems. Political processes were thus seen as the central focus of the field of history: "History is past politics, and politics is present history." Politics, though, by its nature, was likely to remain more an art than a science for much time to come, since the political and legislative processes were in the hands of practical men in the legislatures and courts of every township and county. Conflict and skill, rather than objectivity and analysis, were and are dominant in this central topic of history.

Albion Small (1916) conceived that the Civil War was a significant factor in the unsettling of this complacent trust in the governmental process. As he saw it, scholars were made more sophisticated by the destruction of a popular illusion that "a constitution and laws enacted in pursuance thereof would automatically produce human welfare. . . . Some of these men reacted to the situation by trying to understand it as theorists and philosophers" (Small, 1916, p. 179). In 1865 scholars founded the American Social Science Association, which, without ever approaching the creation of a social science, may have been among the strategic initial threats to the complacent monopoly by philosophers and conventional historians of the relevant subject matter.

It is the nature of doctrines to succeed one another in the manner of fad and fashion, and not to accumulate as do technology and science. It took more than a half-century from the founding of the American Social Science Association to the time when dominance of doctrine weakened so that a cumulative process in sociology could begin to develop. This long delay cannot be attributed to deficiencies in the ability or energy of nineteenth-century scholars. Accomplishments characteristically tend to seem easy after they have been made, but the story of

the long struggle to define fields and develop methods gives a valuable impression of the magnitude of the problems faced by the early creators of the field of sociology. Their effort was of course intentional—English, French, German scholars played prominent parts in the discourse, and most of the mistakes made and false pathways followed in one country were duplicated in others.

If motivation for social science inquiry is supplied in part by concern with human troubles, it is not suprising that some scholars would start with a direct *ad hoc* humanitarianism. Small described the social science interest in the first two post-war decades as follows:

In brief, the period 1865–85 in the United States was a time of benevolent amateurishness with reference to questions which have since been distributed among the historical, political, economic, sociological, and philanthropic divisions of positive social science. There were a great many Americans of the type represented by most of the members of the Social Science Association, who had more or less of the spirit which William G. Sumner held up to ridicule in variations of the dictum: "The type and formula of most schemes of philanthropy or humanitarianism is this: A and B put their heads together to decide what C shall be made to do for D" (Small, 1916, p. 180).[1]

At the suggestion of the president of Cornell University, a "social science" course was instituted in 1884 to consist of "practical instruction calculated to fit young men to discuss intelligently such important social questions as the best methods of dealing practically with pauperism, intemperance, crime of various degrees and among persons of different ages, insanity, idiocy, and the like" (Small, 1916, p. 184). It was a long

---

[1] This passage, and the quotations from the same essay in the following pages are quoted by permission from the article by Albion W. Small, "Fifty Years of Sociology in the United States (1865–1915)," *American Journal of Sociology* Index to Volumes I–LII, 1895–1947. Published by The University of Chicago Press.

time before such "practical instruction" consisted of anything other than prevailing doctrine and well-meant but ineffectual proposals. For some time, of course, scholastic humanitarianism encountered strenuous opposition from Spencer, Sumner, and others, who saw futility or damage in any departure from strict laissez faire policies.

Humanitarian concerns of the type listed above in time became a part of the sociology empire, although as scientific research penetrated the subject matter, some of the topics came to be more appropriately studied in the disciplines of chemistry, physiology, psychology, and others. The tradition of directly applied humanitarianism lives on, however, in the academic field of social work and also in a variety of civic organized activities, from Junior League to Salvation Army.

An approach sharply contrasting to that of the humanitarian is made by the scholar who, in seeking systematic knowledge, concentrates on some single embracing central principle, which promises to relate all knowledge in his field into some kind of unity which provides control. We can sympathize with men who were tempted in this direction if we imagine the appearance of hopeless complexity and confusion in human and social behavior which must have bewildered the scholarly minds of the nineteenth century even more than it still discourages some contemporary scholars.

Lester Ward (1893), of course, was among the most conspicuous of the system-creators in America. He was a man of exceptional ability and energy and already a well-established scientist in the biological field when he decided to transfer his interests and methods into the new subject of sociology. Out of his experience as a museum investigator, classifier, unifier, and from his tireless workmanship, he produced a *Dynamic Sociology* which gave the subject, in his view, systematic organization and a coherent place in the grand unity of all science. Small noted that in later life Ward "grew more and more unable to abide anyone who showed signs of thinking that he might not have said the final word on the subject of sociology" (1916, p. 196).

Yet Ward's "final word" not only lacked immortality but perished with astonishing rapidity and is now all but forgotten except by scholars of the history of sociology. Nor has any other systematizer had better success in finding the one principle, or a few unifying principles, for sociology. Small (1916) came to perceive in 1915:

I think we have arrived at something better. The human lot is not reducible to as simple formulas as Ward supposed. Discovery and acceptance of this fact are long steps beyond satisfaction with a version of the human lot which makes it simpler than it is. We have discovered that human reactions have a baffling way of showing thoughtless independence of antecedent logic. We have discovered that we must pry into actual human facts to find out how they work; and that preconceptions which we carry into the facts, no matter how much presumption goes with them from knowledge of better analyzed relations, are quite likely to be discredited by the actual findings (Small, 1916, p. 197).

Small's remarks are instructive to present-day sociologists in showing the pioneer theorist's difficulty of conceiving of a subject matter and a method. For all of the good sense he reveals in his candid review of the troubles he and his colleagues experienced, he did not himself succeed in establishing a foundation of a cumulative science. He learned, as stated above, that a satisfying logical system would not serve and that it would be necessary to "pry into actual human facts." But Spencer, Ward, and many lesser creators gathered facts which were both human and actual, and their work did not lead into a science. Even some of the humanitarians became great surveyors of facts, and Charles Booth, in *Life and Labour of the People of London* produced enough facts to fill 17 volumes without either establishing the beginnings of a science or abolishing the human misery that shocked him into undertaking his immense task.

In a sense, sociology became organized before it began to exist. There had been a word for the subject since 1837, but its meanings were so vague and variable that sociology could claim fairly to be no more than an intention. But beginning in 1893, with the establishment of a Department of Sociology at the University of Chicago and soon after at other universities, and with the creation of the *American Journal of Sociology* only two years later, and the organization of the American Sociological Society in 1895, there existed a commitment which created a strenuous necessity to bring into existence some reality which the term could designate. If such a way of origin of an academic and scientific field of knowledge seems somehow eccentric, it should be recalled once more that interest in the ways of human behavior is as old as recorded history, and that for nearly a century there had been a conviction among philosophers of high standing that some such field should have an existence in the academic curriculum. There was confidence enough in the broad direction of motion, but confusion about the way of initially penetrating the confronting jungle of conceptions and proposals.

There were, to be sure, confident individuals urging particular courses. Small (1916) characterized the activity at the end of the nineteenth century in the following terms:

Our talk was of methodology for finding out something, but we did not find out much of anything by the use of the methodology. We were all the time more or less consciously tempering drills for our particular kind of boring, but we did comparatively little boring after we produced the drills. Many people get so interested in the tools that they forget all about the work which the tools are expected to do. The common problem of the social sciences is to understand people, past, present, and if may be future; but we get so wrought up in championship of our favorite *method* of approaching people that we may omit to deal very intimately with people themselves. As we have seen, the last decade of the nineteenth century was a time of much empty-seeming wrangling in the United States about the "province" of history, the "scope" of political economy, the "field" of political science, the "problems" of sociology. It was a time of attack and counterattack upon methods of procedure that were insisted upon in the various divisions of social science (Small, 1916, p. 220).

Franklin H. Giddings serves as an illustration of the spirit of dogmatic prophecy with his following route plan:

Sociology must go right from this time forth, as Mr. Spencer says that humanity does in the long run, because it has tried all possible ways of going wrong. Since contact and alliance are phenomena obviously more special than association or society, and imitation and impression are phenomena obviously more general, we must look for the psychic datum, motive, or principle of society in the one phenomenon that is intermediate. Accordingly, the sociological postulate can be no other than this, namely: The original and elementary subjective fact in society is *consciousness of kind*. By this term I mean a state of consciousness in which any being, whether low or high in the scale of life, recognizes another conscious being as of like kind with itself (Small, 1916, p. 222).

To Giddings it doubtless seemed obvious that baby chicks in a barnyard clustered together and followed the mother hen because of this sense of being of like kind. It is now known that a baby chick, under certain conditions, will follow an *unlike* animal—a dog, a horse, a human, or even a moving inanimate object which has no resemblance to itself. The mechanism of this "imprinting" behavior may as yet be unexplained but it could hardly be "consciousness of kind." Giddings' formulation was also gravely deficient in leaving out of consideration the equally basic principle of society as an organization of complementary differences, although Maine, Durkheim, and Toennies had effectively stated it over the course of several decades.

As the twentieth century opened, according to Small's (1916) disarming confession, sociology had not justified itself as a body of doctrine, as a point of view, or as a method of research. It was "more of a yearning," shared by volunteer leaders no one of whom was totally convincing to a single other individual who called himself a sociologist. These strong and impatient men tried to create

a type of sociology which starts where it hopes to end. That is, it virtually does what the conventional preacher does when he announces his text. Literally, it is then "all over but the shouting." The text is supposed to be the truth, the whole truth, and nothing but the truth, except that it is supposed also to be in itself proof of the truth and guaranty of the truth (Small, 1916, p. 262).

The above spirit of course inevitably gave rise to schools of thought, factions and rivalries, and bitter doctrinal struggles in which the interest in destruction of a rival sociology threatened to become greater than interest in the creation of knowledge. Sociology in the United States really began to move away from this destructive atmosphere during the first third of the twentieth century, as its bearers learned the value of the more patient activities of inductive study and moved toward the cultivation of modesty and objectivity. *The Polish Peasant in Europe and America,* by William I. Thomas and Florian Znaniecki (1927), devoted more words to the relatively minor problems of assimilation of immigrants in America than did Lester Ward to the grand system of all sociology, and the Polish Peasant study had a far more lasting effect on both the content and the research ways of sociology than did the entire Ward system. Sociologists came to see that a thorough study of a small research problem at least gives the promise of yielding knowledge in which some confidence can be placed and thus started in motion a research movement having the desired cumulative character.

Impatience dies hard, however, and in time the troubles of world wars, depressions, fears of world destruction by nuclear weapons, stimulated a revival of the appeals to drop objective research in favor of emergency activities. Sociologists were accused in some quarters of "fiddling while Rome burned" and "lecturing on navigation while the ship is sinking." At a research-planning conference of 35 assorted scholars who met in 1950 to devise a 10-year controlled experiment to measure the effects of community mental health problems, an actionist objected to the entire proceedings, protesting that "We don't have ten years." The research was not undertaken, more than 10 years passed, the ship did not sink and Rome did not burn, and we still do not know whether community mental health programs are effective. This knowledge will ultimately be obtained, by researchers who trust civilization to survive while they pursue the research activities appropriate to their responsibilities.

Although neither Small (1916) nor Giddings were able to provide a clear statement of the content and boundaries of sociology, it is much to the credit of both that they perceived the value of patience and objectivity and were able to inspire among their successors an energetic determination to create good methods and to trust the findings based on such methods to lead them along the proper pathways to a mature science. It is said that Small had the habit of saying to his graduate students, at the end of their training, that it was now their duty to go forth and make everything he had taught them out of date as soon as possible. With such a spirit dominating at the University of Chicago as well as at Columbia University, the two largest and most influential departments of sociology in the first quarter of the century, the inductive attitude for which American sociology became known was firmly established.

The choice among the wide ranges of possible subject matter was virtually settled during the decade of the 1920's. The resolution was symbolized, and to a certain extent accomplished, by the publication of the *Introduction to the Science of Sociology* by Robert E. Park and E. W. Burgess (1920). No other book had done so much to standardize the content of sociology. Ward's "science of sciences" was omitted, philosophy of history was turned back to historians, humanitarian concerns with poverty and related afflictions were located out toward the boundaries of the field. Drawing on European traditions, particularly those of Germany and France, Park and Burgess sensed promise in investigations of social processes, in interaction (social psychology), and in the nature of organization. The main content growth of sociology to the present time has involved in a central way the development of these aspects of the subject. These subject matter fields—social process, interaction, organization—constitute a unique territory for sociology, involving no boundary disputes with neighboring academic fields, and they continue to show increasing promise of results tending toward the goals of understanding, prediction, and control that in the long run motivate the whole enterprise of science.

THE RELATIONS
OF SOCIOLOGY TO OTHER
SOCIAL SCIENCE FIELDS

As the previous section has shown, the emergence of a new field is a consequence of a variety of historical factors as well as of abstract logical thinking, and it is hardly to be expected that the contemporary division of fields of knowledge be other than arbitrary and conventional, and subject to constant evolution and revision.

A recurring popular accusation holds that academic knowledge is separated into "watertight" compartments. If this were true the condition would constitute a costly obstruction to scientific advance, but the actual situation is that fields of knowledge are loosely defined and that many borderlines are so vaguely conceived that no definition of a separating line is taken seriously by investigators following the natural courses of research interest. There is free movement along the contiguous boundaries between astronomy, physics, chemistry, biology, psy-

chology, and sociology, and possibly even richer interactions along the frontiers of the various social science fields. While there have been times and places at which scholars have jealously sought to exclude rivals of neighboring sciences from their side of the boundary, the prevailing contemporary attitude is one of welcoming aid and collaboration from any qualified person, whether he carries credentials in the same discipline or a neighboring one.

It may be instructive to view briefly some ·of the characteristic relations of present-day sociology to other sciences and to speculate on the types of benefit accruing to sociology from these relationships.

The Relation
to Biology and Physiology

In previous pages it has been indicated that human behavior is not highly predictable from knowledge of human physiology, however complete. While man is an assuredly physiological organism, his behavior is organized by experience in collectivities whose natures are *sui generis* and not predictable from physiological knowledge alone. This does not mean, however, that causal relations between biology and sociology are totally lacking. The scientific problem is to assess the partial contribution of biology to human behavior.

In the most obvious way, biology imposes requirements and limitations on the range of human activities. Nature's regularities dictate that the human must obtain enough of the right kinds of food and must obtain protection against severe conditions and dangers. Within the immense variety of ways in which such requirements may be satisfied there seems to be virtually no physiological guidance that creates an effective preference for any particular foods or techniques. As far as physiology is concerned, the individual, or his culture, is free to work out any means at all to satisfy these requirements, and the present fund of sociological knowledge convincingly shows that for the most part it is culture that specifies the means of fulfilling physiological requirements.

After the demise of the instinct concept in the 1920's there remained only a trace of controversy relating to the above generalization. A few theorists clung to the conception that some physiological needs could provide at least a vague impulse in the direction of the activity which could satisfy the need, and at least one contemporary writer prefers to retain the term instinct for such motivating elements (Fletcher, 1957). Recent exhaustive examination of evidence on this point, however, justifies an almost decisive verdict against these vestigial doctrines. Apparently all of the specific direction of behavior required to satisfy demands of the physiological mechanisms is supplied by habits acquired in experience, and mainly in organized social experience. Custom does the work formerly thought to be performed by instinct, and adequacy of the culture supplants "wisdom of the body." This adequacy is not based on any hidden principle that guarantees correctness; cultures can be imperfect regarding such important matters as diet, but those cultures that allow too great an error necessarily must disappear.

Physiology also affects behavior by settling limits. Custom obviously cannot require men to run faster, jump further, lift more, than their mechanism can bear. This fact produces some differentiation in human populations, since individuals vary in size, strength, and agility. Far more differentiation in achieved strength and speed, however, is in fact produced by style of life. The maximum speed of running for most men is far below their potential maximum, since few men regularly train to do their best.

The contribution made by physiological limits to mental abilities is a more controversial matter. Here again it seems almost certain that few persons develop their potential mental performances to anything near the limit of physiological capacities. It seems reasonable to suppose that only those few persons who do train a certain ability to the limit may be differentiated among themselves by varying physiological limits—chess masters, for example, may conceivably achieve some ranking among themselves on this basis. But since the vast majority of all populations appear to use only a portion of their mental potentiality, it may be that nearly all actual differentiation of the population in respect to mental achievement is a product of variations in life experiences.

It would appear reasonable that sex differences in behavior are influenced by the universal contrast in average size and strength between males and females. Even this differentiation of physical tasks, however, may be mediated mainly through cultural adaptation to the recognized physiological differences. While women certainly are capable of hunting and fishing, it would be a principle of efficiency, in societies obtaining food supply by such activities, to organize such teamwork activity around men, since their skills would not have to be put aside during periods of child-bearing and infant care. It is probable that the necessity of periodic interruptions in the availability of women for important heavy tasks is the major influence that has dominated the manner in which world-wide cultural distinctions of roles have emerged. In many instances the liberation of women from muscular tasks has gone much further than physiology requires; the protected southern belle in the prewar aristocratic tradition of the Deep South was not expected to carry a bucket of water, though women porters in distant lands have been reported to be able to carry loads as heavy as a piano. If in contemporary suburban life in the United States it is the husband who mows the lawn and the wife who mends the clothes, this division of labor between the sexes could hardly be said to be dictated by their undoubted physiological differences in strength.

Physiological variations may of course have important causal relations to behavior in indirect ways, through the assignment of arbitrary meanings by the culture. If there is a standard belief that a red-headed boy is hot-tempered, this cultural fact may make

him so, regardless of the lack of a physiological relation of hair color and temperament. It is conceivable that blonde women
may give indications of stronger sexual inclinations for a similar reason. Social roles
may be similarly affected by extremes of
stature and by various visible features conspicuously varying from the normal. The
fictional Cyrano's behavior was overwhelmingly dominated by such a physiological
variation though there is never presumed to
be a direct physiological connection between
nasal dimensions and pugnacity.

It is a matter of sound practice for sociologists to be reasonably well-informed on such
firmly proved principles of biology as may be
directly relevant to human behavior; it
would be unwise to entertain principles of
sociology which are irreconcilable with firm
biological laws. This does not mean, however, that a proposed biological generalization in conflict with a sociological one must
always be right—each must be required to
face the same severity of methodological
criticism and neither should have an arbitrary advantage in the contest.

The soundness of physiological research
dealing with issues of human behavior may
depend not merely on application of experimental techniques which are found adequate
in laboratory sciences. Sophistication regarding the ordinary sources of error which regularly confront the sociologist can be just as
important to the achievement of reliable
findings. The point may be illustrated by the
following account of an investigation made
in the biochemical laboratory of the National Institutes of Mental Health (Hollingshead, 1961). Urine samples taken from
schizophrenic patients were found to differ
from those taken from control subjects in
containing a significantly higher amount of
four compounds and a significantly lower
amount of one other compound. The finding could be interpreted as a promising lead
toward the discovery of biochemical causation of mental abnormality. Further inquiry,
however, revealed that the biochemical differences were the *results* of unlike behavior

of the two groups of subjects. The four
compounds that were more abundant among
the schizophrenics turned out to be metabolites of substances in coffee, which the hos-
pitalized patients drank in greater amounts
than did the controls. The other compound,
more frequent among the controls, was a
derivative of oil of wintergreen, a common
ingredient of commercial toothpastes, but
lacking in the dentrifices isued to the
schizophrenics.

The Relation to Psychology

To the extent that psychology is a study
of the behavior of the individual human, its
relation to sociology is somewhat similar to
that of biology. The two fields make interlocking contact, but sociology is principally
concerned with interactions on a higher
emergent level. Sociology must be cautious
also here not to embrace attractive generalizations which are in clear opposition to
solidly proved findings of psychology.

Psychology in a sense looks in two directions—toward the relatively unvarying basic
mechanisms which might also be considered
a part of the field of human physiology, and
toward patterns of individual behavior
which derive their organization from experience, including social experience. There
is a perceptible differentiation of psychological investigators of these two directions, according to their preference for certainty
versus relevance.

Where relevance to the problem of explaining the activities of human beings is
dominant, the psychologist tends to be led
toward an interest in social psychology, in
which his observations are directed toward
whole persons (rather than such physiological details as the mechanism of the inner
ear) and their patterns of interaction. This
of course brings him into a field in which
there is virtually total overlap with the concerns of social psychology as handled by the
sociologist. Here then is a field of science
and an academic area shared by two conventional branches of science from the time

of the origin of the term social psychology. The overlapping, far from undesirable, appears to be both harmonious and productive, and its existence is a significant refutation of the "water-tight" compartmentalization indictment referred to previously.

The borderlines between individual psychology and social psychology need not and cannot be drawn precisely, no more than the borderline between social psychology and sociology. In general, observations of patterns of interaction and their effects would be thought of as activities of social psychology, and description and analysis of formal organizational structures as concerns of sociology. There is interpenetration almost everywhere, however, of interaction and structures, and few investigators show serious concern about which of these territories they are occupying at any particular time.

The Relation to Anthropology

The historical sequence which led to the development of the field of anthropology was unique in the sense that its subject matter was originally defined by a concept imported from biology rather than by concern with problems of explanation of human behavior. The concept of course was that of evolution, which emerged abruptly on the scientific scene after the publication of Darwin's major works. Darwin boldly placed man in the same evolutionary process that he proposed to account for the origins of all other species, and it was a natural thought to follow up his suggestions by developing a scientific discipline which would fit man and his works—prehistoric material cultures, contemporary cultures, and languages—in sequences of evolutionary stages. "Man in evolution" was thus the assignment accepted by nineteenth-century anthropologists, and during the more than half-century during which the formulation seemed promising, it made the study of human bones, stone axes, linguistic forms, and contemporary customs appear to fit into a coherent scientific discipline.

Early in the present century, however, the determination to tie all of anthropology to the evolutionary concept began to seem forced, and research scholars tended increasingly to follow leads inherent in their data rather than the directions prescribed by doctrine. A most obvious fact was eventually taken into account—skeletal changes in the human race take place extremely slowly, while cultures can develop and change in relatively brief periods of time. The cultural changes do not occur parallel to, or fit into, the pattern of change characteristic of biological evolution. As emphasis on parallel evolution consequently diminished, the logic of the combination of the above four types of subject matter into a single academic field came to appear unconvincing. It now remains to be seen how long habit, tradition, and academic bureaucracy can delay the relinquishing of physical anthropology to paleontology, of linguistics to the humanities fields, and of archeology to history.

Social anthropology, however, is mainly sociology, and there is little distinction between the two fields other than that resulting from the accidental and scientifically irrelevant differences in the routes by which the two fields came to their present interests. There is of course some practical division of labor in the fact that anthropologists undertake most of the descriptive studies of preliterate societies, although for more than a quarter of a century they have also conducted sociological research on communities in modern civilization. Also, until recently anthropologists mainly employed their personal skills in recording and interpreting a community or a society as a whole, while sociologists placed somewhat more confidence in the use of technical research methods and their application to problems of considerably smaller scope. At the present time, however, even this distinction is diminishing, and if present trends continue it may soon become pointless to attempt to distinguish between sociology and social anthropology. This statement, however, does not imply a prediction that the two academic departments will necessarily merge into one. The forces of organization—the fact that each discipline has national and international associations, as well as separate departmental establishments in most universities—may prove to have more power than does a pure sense of logic. This is not necessarily an undesirable condition; there is an unlimited amount of research and teaching work to be done, and a moderate degree of amicable rivalry may possibly contribute to productivity in both fields.

The Relation to Economics

If sociology had been developed before economics, the latter field might have been conceived as a subfield of sociology. Here again, however, history does not feel constrained to follow our present sense of logical arrangement of subject matter. Economics arose out of practical concerns, which could not be avoided in view of the great and highly visible consequences of human activities in such fields as manufacturing, trade, financing, and taxation. These mysteries affected the wealth of nations, and attention to them was a matter of national urgency. Practical action required a sense of dependable policy and therefore called for some kind of theoretical justification of a particular set of recommended actions. These were in due time drawn up and eventually grew into a discipline of economics. In the early stages certain observations seemed so true that research appeared to be unnecessary. When a buyer sees identical objects for sale at different prices, it hardly seems worth questioning the fact that he usually chooses the one with the lower price; only when goods are scarce and in high demand can the seller charge higher prices. From such commonplace observations it was not difficult to elaborate systematic implications which could form the basis of a policy for a person, a business firm, or a national government.

An economist, in the youthful period of the discipline, needed to be a man of per-

ception, of consistency of thought, and of skilled foresight, but he was not necessarily a scientist. Objective methical research in economics is a matter of recent times and was perhaps late in developing precisely because prescientific theoretical formulations had enough value to give useful service. The attractive emergent bodies of principles, however, eventually appeared to fail with enough frequency to bring economists to the perception of the necessity of creating a real science of those aspects of behavior which have been of traditional interest in their field. This of course means that they are in part learning to be sociologists and social psychologists, with specialization in wealth-getting and wealth-distributing aspects of behavior. It would appear to be a matter of inevitability that sociologists and economists will increasingly find themselves, perhaps sometimes to their own surprise, working on identical questions. Even now urban studies, population and demography research, and various types of mass behavior engage the interest of investigators in both fields. At the present time it would also seem likely that some of the technical fields of applied economics will always continue to be remote from sociological concerns, but along some of the common borderlines interaction and cooperation should be expected to increase indefinitely.

The Fields of Political Science and Law

Patterns of government and law are products of imperceptibly slow growth of coordinating customs. All societies have sytematic means of regulation of behavior of members, much of them through customs so informal that the peoples who follow them have never made them explicit and think of their own customs not as arbitrary rules, but as the way of nature. Elaborate teamwork, however, is needed for some kinds of hunting, fishing, warfare, and heavy construction, and for these activities the principles of organization and methods of controlling the behavior of the participants may be matters of conscious concern. Attention of the same sort may also, even in simple societies, be required for problems of internal harmony, justice, and any major decisions affecting the society. Out of such circumstances institutional arrangements tend to evolve, and these constitute the primitive forms of government. Deliberate invention is an extremely minor part of the process which generates such primitive institutions. Government is as ancient as political science is new.

Reflections and speculations concerning the nature of law and government have been devised by ancient philosophers and their successors in an uninterrupted tradition reaching to present times. The concept of a political science, however, is a contribution of nineteenth-century scholars. The *realization* of a political science is a development expected to occur in the second half of the twentieth century.

As in the case of economics, political science could logically be considered a part of sociology and perhaps also would have been so if it had not become established somewhat earlier than sociology. Also, as in the case of economics, the decisions relating to governmental affairs were so pressing and practical that informed men of judgment and skill could practice usefully as political scientists, even in the absence of anything resembling scientific research.

The research stage in political science may also have been delayed by the fact that expanding governments and diplomatic services have long been willing to employ a considerable number of college-trained persons whose knowledge of government has been mainly descriptive and theoretical. Little or no pressure has customarily come from governments to academic departments to stimulate objective research or to make the study of government an actual science.

The recent beginnings of a movement to build a body of research knowledge in political behavior may have been the consequence of influences from related social science fields. Research stimulation in universities, with support from foundations and encouragement from such bodies as the Social Science Research Council, may also constitute an important part of the motivation of scholars to further such a transformation of the political science field.

With respect to all of the fields bordering the discipline of sociology it might be said that interrelations with the latter subject are likely to become more penetrating in future years. Whether or not the academic and professional organizations take the trends into account, it is to be expected that scholars in neighboring fields will learn and make use of more sociology in the course of the study of their own problems, and even that their research will tend to have an increase in sociological content. Regardless of administrative borderlines the diffusion of sociological content and methods promises to extend generally through all of the social sciences.

THE PROSPECT FOR SCIENTIFIC SOCIOLOGY

Until sometime about the end of the second decade of the present century there was little perceptible development of a truly cumulative stage in sociology. There was a growing literature of systems, undoubtedly satisfying to their creators, but the prevailing relation among leading sociologists was more often one of rivalry than of cooperation. A cumulative stage, however, became perceptible during the 1920's and from that time on has taken the form of a gradual but clearly exponential growth. The organization of sociological knowledge is now increasingly based on research results, and, as previously stated, there is a corresponding decline in the tendency for individuals to create embracing theoretical systems of sociology on the basis of speculative thought.

As the foregoing review has also shown, this entrance into the new cumulative phase of sociology has been the consequence of the development of technical research methods and has been aided by a long-run confidence in research-based findings which releases the investigator from any special responsibility for making immediate contributions to human welfare.

The exponential character of the growth of sociological knowledge is made possible by the use of ever more efficient methods and also by acceleration in the numbers of trained sociologists and financial support of their research activities. It is reasonable to suppose that these factors will continue to have the same influence for as many decades in the future as it is profitable to try to foresee. The contemporary trends toward occupational and educational upgrading of the population should also make available a progressively larger fraction of the labor force for basic research in sociology along with other sciences and technological fields. The ever-expanding productivity of the economy should further contribute by making possible financial support adequate to the research needs. Even if these needs should now appear to be great it seems highly probable that all modern nations will in time come to appreciate the benefits of sociological research, which, as in the case of research in other fields of knowledge, eventually returns the costs many times over.

Concern is sometimes expressed over the possible undesirable consequences of the growth of a fully developed science of human and social behavior. A super-tyranny is feared as one conceivable result of the scientific manipulation of a society caught in the power of technologists equipped with complete knowledge of behavior principles. A newspaper essay (Kirk, 1961, p. 11) represents the "serious sociologist" as claiming to be ". . . the engineer and the architect of a new rational social order." Furthermore, "His opinion pools, his analyses of out-groups, his indices of prejudice, his statistical computations of popular choice . . . all are intended to convert mankind into a predictable and controllable species" (p. 11). At present, however, the distance to such a level of accomplishment is too great to provide more than such enjoyable shudders as are to be derived from reading science fiction. The prospect toward which the present behavior sciences are moving is rather that of reducing some of the sources of human unhappiness about which no controversy exists. As for absolute control of the behavior of a population, there is no reason to be sure that it will ever occur, or even that a developed science of behavior would move civilization in such a direction. It is fully as reasonable to hope that such knowledge could be applied to yield ever more human freedom, and thus to banish forever all possibility of tyranny.

Such speculations, however, are of little relevance to the character of present and proximate research activity. There is no reason to debate the human desirability of a more ample fund of knowledge than we now possess. An abundance of human needs is on hand and history has a way of generating an unlimited supply of new difficulties. The most likely prospect of the benefit of a growing science to human well-being is that it will help the human species to continue to use its intelligence and good will at the ever-increasing rate required by the ceaseless emergence of difficulties.

REFERENCES

Durkheim, E. Les règles de la méthode sociologique. Paris: Alcan, 1894.

Eaton, J. W., & Weil, R. J. The mental health of the Hutterites. Sci. Amer., December, 1953, 189, 31–37.

Fletcher, R. Instinct in man. New York: Int. Univers. Press, 1957.

Gurvitch, G. Social structure of pre-war France. Amer. J. Sociol., 1943, 48, 535–554.

Hollingshead, A. B. The epidemiology of schizophrenia. Amer. sociol. Rev., 1961, 26, 12.

Kirk, R. Is social science scientific? N.Y. Times Mag., June 25, 1961, 11–18.

Levy-Bruhl, L. Les fonctions mentales dans les sociétés inférieures. Paris: 1910.

Lundberg, G. A. Can science save us? New York: Longmans, 1961.

Messinger, S. Organizational transformation: A case study of a declining social movement. Amer. sociol. Rev., 1955, 20, 3–10.

Munch, P. A. *Sociology of Tristan da Cunha.* Oslo: 1945.

Ogburn, W. F. *Social change.* New York: Viking, 1922.

Ogburn, W. F. *The social effects of aviation.* Boston: Houghton, 1946.

Ogburn, W. F., & Gilfillan, S. C. *Recent social trends.* New York: McGraw, 1933.

Park, R. E., & Burgess, E. W. *Introduction to the science of sociology.* Chicago: Univer. of Chicago Press, 1920.

Rivers, W. H. R. *The Todas.* London: 1906.

Small, A. Fifty years of sociology in the United States (1865–1915). *Amer. J. Sociol.,* Index to Vols. 1–52, 1916.

Sorokin, P. A. *Social and cultural dynamics.* New York: American, 1937–1941.

Spengler, O. *The decline of the west.* New York: Knopf, 1926.

Thomas, W. I., & Znaniecki, F. *The Polish peasant in Europe and America.* New York: Knopf, 1927.

Thoreau, H. *Civil disobedience.* Chicago: Regnery, 1949.

Toynbee, A. J. *A study of history.* New York: Oxford, 1947–1957.

Wallas, G. *The great society.* New York: Macmillan, 1915.

Ward, L. *Dynamic sociology.* New York: Appleton, 1893.

Wood, B., & Wagley, C. The social sciences: Parochial or cosmopolitan. *Items,* Soc. Sci. Res. Council, 1961, 3.

CHAPTER 2   Social Organization and the Ecosystem

OTIS DUDLEY DUNCAN

Ibn Khaldûn (1332–1406) may well have been right when he asserted that social organization is necessary to the human species. The individual human being, he argued, is weak, defenseless, and incapable of securing by himself a minimum supply of food. Given the ability to think and hands that can manipulate instruments, however, men may cooperatively obtain nourishment, provide for their defense, and settle the world with their numbers. The pattern of social life is not uniform in space nor invariable over time, but "differences of condition among people are the result of the different ways in which they make their living." A knowledge of the principles governing human social organization is required if one is to be able to distinguish between the credible and the unlikely in reports of the doings of men. There is need for a new, independent discipline, for "any topic that is understandable and real requires its own special science." It should concern itself, among other things, with "the origin of races and dynasties . . . the synchronism of the earliest nations . . . the reasons for change and variation in past periods . . . towns and hamlets . . . large numbers and small numbers, sciences and crafts . . . changing general conditions, nomadic and sedentary life . . . all things expected to occur in civilization" (Ibn Khaldûn [1958], I, 249, 79, 13; for an assessment of Ibn Khaldûn as sociologist and human ecologist, see the translator's introduction and Liebling [1959]).

Of the many "new" sciences announced since the time of the great Arab philosopher of history, one—sociology—has staked the broadest claim to the subject matter of social organization. Another—ecology—has exploited most systematically the assumption that ways of life are a function of conditions of life. The aim of this chapter is to indicate in general terms the bearing of ecological considerations on the study of social organization. Space permits only an outline of the ecological principles that impinge most evidently upon the sociologist's concern with social organization. As for the subject matter of social organization as such, most of the chapters in this Handbook, in effect, provide the necessary elaboration of topics which are treated sketchily here.

BASIC ECOSYSTEM PROCESSES

A recent treatise with the arresting title, *The Sociology of Nature* (Reid, 1962), develops the subject of ecology from the standpoint of "mutual dependence [as] a governing principle." The concept of dependence is indeed a rich one, for dependence may assume various guises, may vary in degree, and may be more or less direct. It will suffice for the moment to take note of (1) the dependence of organic forms on others of like kind, i.e., intraspecies relationships; (2) the dependence of several kinds of organisms each upon at least some of the others in the interspecies community, or biocoenosis; and (3) the dependence, indirect or immediate, of all organisms upon the inanimate environment, together with the reciprocal influence upon the environment of its occupancy by living things. The last type of dependence, of course, is the most inclusive.

Ecologists use the term ecosystem to refer to a community together with its habitat. An ecosystem, then, is an aggregation of associated species of plants and animals, together with the physical features of their habitat. Ecosystems . . . can be of any size or ecologic rank. . . . At the extreme, the whole earth and all its plant and animal inhabitants together constitute a world ecosystem (Dice, 1955, pp. 2–3).

More briefly, according to Allee and collaborators (1949, p. 695), "The ecosystem may be defined as the interacting environmental and biotic system."

Definitions aside, we may begin by characterizing the ecosystem as a "natural unit . . . in which the exchange of materials between the living and nonliving parts follows circular paths," which are called "biogeochemical cycles" (Odum, 1953, p. 9). This statement needs amplification, first, to call attention to the exchanges between diverse living units as well as between such units and the nonliving surroundings. Second, the dependence of life upon environment involves not only the materials that follow circular paths, but also the noncircular flows of two other "commodities," energy and information.

Organisms are made up of certain fundamental *materials*. Some 30 or 40 of the 92 natural elements are known to be required by organisms, although oxygen, carbon, hydrogen, nitrogen, calcium, and phosphorous together make up about 99 per cent of the human body, for example, while the compound H_2O alone accounts for as much as 60 per cent of its mass. These materials are used over and over again. They are extracted from the environment by some organisms, passed along to other organisms, and returned finally to the environment to become available for a repetition of the cycle.

The flow of materials involved in growth, maintenance, and reproduction of organisms is accomplished only if work, an expenditure of *energy,* is done. "The acquisition of energy is therefore the primary and inescapable business of every living organism" (Simpson, Pittendrigh, & Tiffany, 1957, p. 6). Some general features of the pattern by which this primary business gets done are illustrated in Figure 1. Special note should be taken of the following: (1) The ecosystem as a whole from a physical standpoint is not a closed system but an *open system* with a continual input of energy from an external source. (2) The "strands of dependence" (Reid, 1962, chs. 4–5) in food chains represent, in general, asymmetric relations. (3) The flow of energy through the system, though temporarily arrested at one point or another by devices which accumulate and store energy, is subject to the Second Law of Thermodynamics. No transformation of energy can be 100 per cent efficient, but must be accompanied by some degradation of energy into the dispersed form of heat, which is not available to do work. Transfers of energy progress in a one-way fashion. The total amount of energy available to each link of a food chain is less than that available to the preceding ones. (4) Consequently, there is a flow but *no cycle* (circular path) of energy. The ecosystem continually loses potential energy as work is done, with the supply being replenished from the outside. "Civilization is

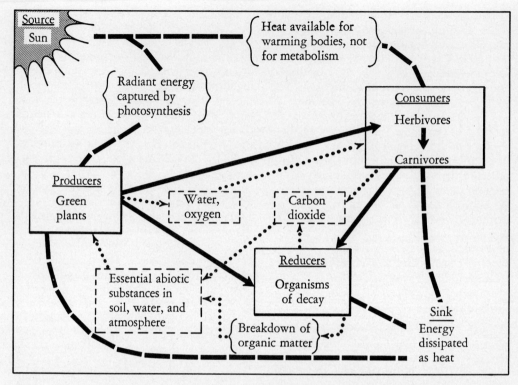

Fig. 1. Generalized pattern of energy flow via food chains in an ecosystem. Types of food chain are represented by solid lines, selected transfers of materials by dotted lines, the continuous entry of energy and the degradation of energy by dashed lines. Living components of the ecosystem are enclosed by solid lines, abiotic components by broken lines. This diagram is based on ideas of Alfred J. Lotka, who wrote: "The several organisms that make up the earth's living population, together with their environment, constitute one system, which receives a daily supply of available energy from the sun. . . . It is not so much the organism or the species that evolves, but the entire system, species and environment. The two are inseparable" (Lotka, 1925, p. 16).

just one of the remarkable natural proliferations that are dependent on the continuous inflow of the concentrated energy of light radiation" (Odum, 1953, p. 66).

Not all energy flows nor all work done in an ecosystem is via food chains. Other subsystems equally indispensable for life likewise require energy inputs. A prime example, the hydrologic cycle, is depicted schematically in Figure 2. The ultimate energy source for this subsystem is the same as that of food chains, namely, the heat and radiant energy of the sun. The transporting of water is accomplished in large part by processes external to living organisms, although these may play important roles in affecting the rate and pattern of flow. The kinetic energy of moving water serves certain organisms, moreover, not only by supplying this indispensable material for ingestion into the body, but also by moving other materials, including organisms themselves. It is also a supply that may be converted, given appropriate devices (water wheel, hydroelectric dynamo), into other forms of energy that may more readily be applied to accomplish useful work.

Flows of materials and energy occur in physical systems devoid of life. Life processes, though subject to the physical laws governing all such flows, are not adequately ex-

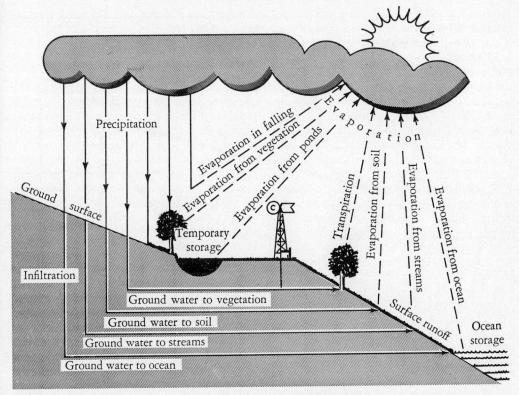

Fig. 2. The hydrologic cycle (Source: U.S. Department of the Interior)

plained by reference to these laws alone. Without attempting to dispose of the hoary question, "What is life?", we must add one principle that, however stated, is indispensable for even a minimal elucidation of the distinctive properties of life processes (including the social processes that comprise a subset thereof).

Living systems, at whatever level of integration—cell, individual, association or society, species population, interspecies aggregation—are complex structures of matter maintained by energy inputs. These inputs, however, must be not merely random but rather patterned or directed. The maintenance of structure calls for *information* or "instructions" on how the energy is to be expended. "Even the simplest living creature is an information-gathering and information-organizing structure" (Boulding, 1961, p. 35). How information enters a system, is transferred between unit parts of the system, is modified or elaborated within the system, is preserved, and is applied on behalf of system functions—all are questions to be resolved by investigation and not by definition or postulation. While we know at least some of the general laws governing transfers and transformations of materials and energy, as established by such disciplines as mechanics, thermodynamics, and chemistry, an analogous body of principles applying to information in a generic sense is not yet available. The subjects of "information theory" and "cybernetics" (Cherry, 1961), to which we owe the modern push to develop a generic concept of information, have as yet dealt only with some of the forms or types of information and have succeeded in quantifying only certain features of the transfer and application of information.

Admittedly, it may be quite premature to claim that a variety of phenomena diverse in form and level may usefully be subsumed under the concept "information." Yet one is impressed by the multiplicity of investigations in which some recognition is given to generic aspects of information. More than one observer has noted that " 'information' . . . is increasingly being recognized as a fundamental economic and technological 'stuff' comparable to matter and energy" (Siegel, 1960, p. 234). To give but one example, the general science periodicals bring almost monthly news of progress in cracking the "code" of the genetic "messages" which convey the "instructions" on which the whole organization of life in each new generation depends. Today's effort to generalize the information concept is perhaps no more radical for its time than were the hypotheses of energy conservation and interconvertibility of forms of energy a little more than a century ago.

The student of human society does not, of course, have to be persuaded of the importance of information in the social process, though the technical vocabulary of sociology tends rather to revolve about such terms as knowledge, culture, norms, and symbols. The general sociologist, however, is not yet accustomed to the idea that there is an intimate connection between human ecology and the "sociology of knowledge."

Given the currently fluid situation regarding the investigation of general properties of information as a component of ecosystems, the present statement must be cursory and no doubt inaccurate in some degree. The apparent importance of the idea is justification for the risk assumed. Perhaps it would be well to preface the succeeding paragraphs with an anticipation of the theme that motivates this discussion.

The salient feature of man's evolution is the expansion of his niche in the ecosystem. This expansion has involved (1) increase in numbers sustained by (2) increasing human resourcefulness in extracting the requisite supplies of energy and materials from the environment and (3) an elaboration of the patterns of organization of the human collective efforts involved in this activity. Both the tools and the organizational patterns enabling human expansion represent accumulations of information and the construction of numerous subsystems of information acquisition, processing, and application. Man has in effect created new forms of information as he has wrought matter into new combinations and devised new techniques of energy conversion not available to other species. Only a hopelessly anthropocentric view of the universe, however, can overlook the continuity of man's uses of materials, energy, and information with those of preceding and associated forms of life.

Our brief statement on the information concept is intended only to draw attention to some interrelations of materials, energy, and information, to some analogies among their respective patterns of flow, and to the crucial respects in which these analogies fail to hold.

As is implied by Figure 1, transfers of energy often take place via movements of materials. Thus, food consists of various materials in which is stored potential chemical energy that is released upon combustion, i.e., in exothermic reactions. The movement of water, as was pointed out, supplies kinetic mechanical energy to organisms appropriately situated with respect to the direction of flow, and the storage of water at some elevation represents potential energy that may be released by its subsequent fall. From the viewpoint of the organism, on the other hand, acquisition of the requisite supplies of materials and energy may well require an expenditure of energy in movement. The flows of materials and energy in an ecosystem, then, are closely linked in a variety of ways.

The same may be said of the relations of information flows to the other two. Messages, signals, and symbols often are carried by bits of material or pulsations of energy. Current research in molecular biology, for example, is leading to the identification of complex substances called "messenger RNA," which carry instructions from the genes to the protein-manufacturing apparatus. Signals and symbols always are physical events. The acquisition and transfer of information require expenditure of energy, though the amount of semantic "meaning" in a given item of information need not be proportional to the amount of energy expended in its receipt or processing.

To mention just one further aspect of the interrelations of the flows of materials, energy, and information, we note that information serves to control, that is, to modify, the rate and pattern of materials and energy flows as these are intersected by living units. This fact in no way exempts organisms from the operation of physical laws; it merely refers to the ability of organisms to influence favorably some of the conditions under which these laws operate.

From this mere sketch of some significant interrelations among the three classes of flows, we turn to a similarly abbreviated indication of salient analogies among their respective patterns. The following scheme, if not applied too mechanically, is helpful in summarizing certain parallelisms. For any ecosystem or subsystem thereof one may examine the flow of materials or energy or information from the standpoint of:

1. *Entry* into the system;
2. *Transformation* during the flow through the system;
3. *Transfer* from one unit or level of the system to another;
4. *Accumulation* and *storage* at some point within the system, followed by *retrieval* and resumption of the flow;
5. *Application* to the advantage of some (living) unit part of the system; and
6. *Dissipation,* i.e., temporary or ultimate loss to the system.

A description of flows, then, would run in terms of the spatiotemporal pattern and the quantities of flows manifesting each of these aspects. The description, however, would require more specialized terminology, according to (1) the focus on materials, on energy, or on information, and (2) the kind of subsystems under analysis. Some of the obvious subsystems are (a) the organism-environment system, wherein flows may be analyzed in terms of (individual) physiology and behavior; (b) the intraspecies population system, the analysis of flows which calls upon the apparatus of genetics, demography, and the disciplines that study social behavior; (c) the interspecies community, analysis whose flows (particularly of energy and materials) is a major preoccupation of traditional community ecology; and (d) "technological" systems, most conspicuously those devised by men, some features of which are under the control of living agents but which operate in good part as semiautonomous derivative or auxiliary (perhaps "artificial") systems and can be analyzed apart from their functions in more inclusive systems.

For illustration of the foregoing scheme, some of the processes of physiology and behavior that are analyzed in textbooks on animal biology are mentioned briefly.

1. Materials *enter* the organism from its environment, say, by respiration or ingestion. They are *transformed* metabolically and *transferred* from one part of the body to another in the alimentary canal or the blood stream. Some materials may be *accumulated* and *stored* for greater or lesser periods and *retrieved* subsequently. The *application* of materials in growth and repair of the organism's structure is more or less continuous, as is the *dissipation* or loss of materials (e.g., by excretions) to the environment. Ultimately, upon death, the organism's substance returns entirely to the environment.

2. Similarly, energy enters the system as food, the potential energy of which is released metabolically during transfers among cells and organs. Energy is accumulated at each "meal" and stored in the contents of the meal to be retrieved gradually as the organism does work, or some small part of

the surplus may be stored on a longer-run basis in fat tissues. Energy is applied in all the foregoing processes and in the work done by the organism on the external world. Since the body, like any heat engine, is much less than 100 per cent efficient, a considerable fraction of the energy intake is dissipated as heat to the organism's surroundings.

3. Finally, information flows are initiated by perception of either the state of the environment or the organism itself. More or less complex sets of elaborators process the information taken in by the receptors and transfer it to the relevant effectors, which may be said to "apply" the information in the exercise of choice, decision, or process control.

Information storage and accumulation are referred to as learning; the retrieval of learned information is the exercise of memory. Both capacities, in however rudimentary form, apparently are possessed by all animals. (The greatest versatility belongs to the species capable of symbolic learning, but symbols are intrinsically social mechanisms not adequately analyzed in the simple individual-environment framework.) The dissipation of information is implicit in the "noise" generated by competing perceptions, in forgetting, and in the changes of state that render information relevant at one instant obsolete at the next. The total amount of information "applied," therefore, is vastly less than that received by the organism. Death, again, is tantamount to the complete loss of information stored in learned symbol or response sets.

The flows just mentioned are, of course, basic to any others that may occur in intra- or interspecies aggregations. A comprehensive analysis of flows in an ecosystem would involve a number of complications of the individual-environment system. A few of these may be indicated.

As soon as the situation is one of a plurality of organisms, flows between individuals must be taken into account. The relevance of interspecies food chains to the flow of materials and energy already has been noted. Prominent among intraspecies flows is the feeding of the young, which is practiced by many diverse forms. A less evident example of a vital flow of materials can be demonstrated at various phylogenetic levels: ". . . many organisms, both plants and animals, change or 'condition' an unfavorable medium so that others following or associated with them can survive better and thrive when they could not do so in a raw, unconditioned medium" (Allee, 1958, p. 210). A variety of more or less rudimentary or complex social behaviors evidently depend on efficient means of information flow. Allelomimetic behavior is involved in the close coordination observed in flocks of geese or sheep or in schools of fish; two or more animals do the same thing at the same time, the behavior of each being responsive to the behavior of the others (Scott, 1958, pp. 18–22). More highly organized aggregations are based on one or another system of actual communication— that is, the conveying of information by vocal, visual, or chemical signs and signals (Scott, 1958, Ch. 9). In human groups, the more elementary communication systems are displaced, though not wholly, by the exchange of symbols. The capacity of symbol systems for conveying information is, of course, vastly greater than that of other communication systems.

Apart from language, the most distinctive feature of ecosystems that is due to the inclusion of man is the modification, or even the creation, of flows of materials, energy, and information occasioned by technology. Tools and techniques, in the first place, permit an intensification of the means of securing requisites. From this point of view, technology is an *extension* of the species capacities—often a very great extension indeed, as is exemplified by such aids to perception as the microscope or such auxiliary devices for moving materials as the bulldozer. Even more dramatic is the role of technology in setting up *artificial systems* that lack any clear counterpart on the intra-human level. Refinement of inorganic ores, generation of electricity, and printing of books are examples of incidents in the three types of flow which are intelligible only in the context of technological systems as such and not merely as adjuncts to organic behavior. The presence of man and his devices does, indeed, vastly complicate the operation of ecosystems, and this is the theme of much of the subsequent discussion.

The objective of the discussion to this point has been to indicate that a fundamental feature of any ecosystem and its component subsystems is the flows of requisite materials, energy, and information, and to indicate that there are both physical interrelations and formal similarities among these flows. One capital observation remains to be emphasized: The interesting analogies among the three flows break down in ways that are profoundly important for an understanding of ecosystems. The point can be summarized in a simple diagram (in which sociologists will recognize the form of a "Guttman scale"):

	Obeys conservation law?	Cyclical flow?
Materials	Yes ⎫	Yes
Energy	Yes ⎬	No
Information	No	No

The frame of reference here is the ecosystem as a whole and the time scale is one relevant thereto. The materials that make up the earth, including the substance of its living inhabitants, are indestructible (neglecting interconversion of matter and energy in nuclear processes), and their total quantity is essentially fixed. The law of conservation of matter guarantees that the substance on which life processes work constitutes a constant store or capital fund. This does not gainsay the fact that both organic and inorganic reactions constantly change the form of materials—complex molecules are built up and broken down, metals oxidize, and so on. In principle, then, the same matter is used by organisms over and over again and follows "circular paths" through the ecosystem —the paths of the hydrologic cycle, nitrogen cycle, carbon cycle, and phosphorous cycle, among others. The statement must be qualified in respect to elements required for some human technological systems. These may depend not so much on the mere existence of requisite materials in the earth's crust, but rather on *concentrations* of these materials sufficient to permit their *economical* extraction. While technological action does not destroy the material, it may well dissipate the concentration. Technology, therefore, is periodically running into shortages and contriving substitutes. To say that technology generates acyclic flows of materials may be only to say that technology—or a given technological regime—is an unstable subsystem. It is one, however, whose special dependence upon an accumulating stock of information may lead to the development of efficient compensating mechanisms. "The aim of conservation of natural resources in the broadest sense is to make acyclic processes more cyclic" (Odum, 1953, p. 19).

Energy, like matter, obeys a principle of conservation, the first law of thermodynamics: "The total sum of all kinds of energy in a closed system is constant. This means that energy which by natural and artificial processes is permanently converted from one form into another is never lost or generated from nothing." There is this qualification: In nuclear processes, "energy can be converted into matter and matter into energy. Hence the classical laws of the conservation of mass and the conservation of energy do not hold true each by itself; instead they fuse into the one universal law of the conservation of the sum of mass and energy" (Thirring, 1962, p. 19). But if energy can be neither created nor destroyed within the ecosystem (nuclear processes neglected), it is certainly not true that the ecosystem operates with a fixed quantity of energy available initially and perpetually to be used over and over again. On the contrary, the energy budget of the world ecosystem is approximately constant because of a continual inflow of energy into the system balanced by an equal loss of energy from the system resulting from radiation of the earth's heat into interplanetary space. The flow of energy is not cyclic, but one-way. It can be arrested by accumulators of one sort or another, but the energy output of any accumulator is less than the input. No transfer or conversion of energy is 100 per cent efficient. At the same time, not all ecosystems are equally inefficient. If the total amount of energy through-put is constant, or roughly so, there is room for much variation in the proportion of this through-put that actually sustains life. Indeed, it has been proposed as the most general law of biological evolution that the ecosystem as a whole evolves toward a state of maximum energy flux (Lotka, 1925; Lotka, 1945). If so, the explanation lies in what has been called the "antientropic trend" of information accumulation.

We have been treating information as a commodity that exists only in systems with living components, and rightly so. The students of cybernetics have, to be sure, exhibited mechanical contrivances—servomechanisms—that regulate their own action in accordance with instructions keyed to relevant states of the environment. As Lotka (1925, p. 340) noted in an interesting anticipation of cybernetics (wherein the term "information" appears in its modern sense), "It must not be supposed that the typical elements of the correlating apparatus, the receptors, adjustors and effectors, are wholly peculiar to living organisms. They can be very clearly recognized also in certain mechanisms of human construction." But these are precisely human technological systems, and we have as yet no examples of servomechanisms which are not of "human construction" and which regulate themselves other than by principles "built into" them by human contrivance. All this is to say that if life were to disappear, the quantity of information would reduce to zero, which it was, presumably, before life originated.

In this sense only is quantity of information subject to a conservation law. On the time scale of ecosystems and the evolution of

their living components, there is no definite limit on amount of information, save that imposed by the limitations on the supplies of energy and materials that may be available to convey and embody information. While the amount of material substance in the world ecosystem is virtually constant and the energy through-put of the ecosystem occurs at a nearly constant rate, the trend of evolution is toward an increase or continual accumulation of information in the ecosystem. The information extracted from the environment by one organism does not in equal measure reduce the amount of information available to any other organism, nor does what is learned by one diminish the amount that can be learned by another. A genetic population in expanding its numbers increases if anything its per capita information supply, even if per capita supplies of materials and energy be reduced. Evolution viewed as a "learning process" entails the incorporation of more information into population systems: "In the long view there has been an increase in the complexity of the genetical instructions" (Medawar, 1961, p. 38). Social organisms in sharing information increase the amount by increasing the distribution, rather than inversely. Information stored in symbolic systems, i.e., the form of information we term knowledge, may indeed be lost, but it is not intrinsic to the flow of information as it is intrinsic to the flow of energy that some portion of the supply must be dissipated into useless form at each transfer. As the species to which the use of symbols is unique, or virtually so, man enjoys the advantage of an "exosomatic heredity" (Lotka, 1945) independent of and superimposed upon genetic mechanisms. Cultural evolution, the elaboration of the content of the exosomatic inheritance, does indeed represent inheritance of acquired characteristics, a mechanism not known to operate at the genetic level.

Information, then, does not represent the flow of a fixed quantity over circular paths (materials) nor yet the through-put of an amount supplied at nearly constant rate (energy). It neither obeys a conservation law nor moves in cycles. In virtue of this freedom, information results in transformations of materials and energy virtually limitless in the variety of their manifestations, though it can, of course, accomplish nothing that is incompatible with the laws to which materials and energy are subject.

THE EVOLUTION OF MAN

The ecological point of view first became explicit in the context of an effort, by Darwin (1873), to understand the origins of diversity among organic forms and their ways of life. One premise of the present discussion is that the most fundamental postulates of human ecology still are best elucidated in an evolutionary framework. It is more natural than it may seem at first to develop the topic of this chapter from an initial consideration of the very evolution of man as a species. It will be possible to show, first, that our present understanding of the course of human evolution has been considerably influenced by attending to the ecological elements of the problem; and, second, that this understanding has significant implications for the conceptual framework of human ecology. The subject is an elusive one, however, and few if any investigators could be called expert in all its ramifications. What is offered here is mainly a reference to and commentary on some of the recent literature that is technically accessible to readers not versed in any of the lines of inquiry that are directly involved (see especially Dobzhansky, 1962; Spuhler, 1959; Tax, 1960; Tax & Callender, 1960; Washburn, 1961). While subsequent remarks derive largely from these and other sources cited, it is quite likely that the several authors' views are represented with considerable imprecision.

Homo sapiens is believed to be a descendant of tree-dwelling prehominid primates who lived during the Miocene epoch, about 12 million to 25 million years ago and earlier. These arboreal creatures had developed the ability to grasp with their hands, presumably as an adaptation to climbing, and the stereoscopic vision suited to operations in the three-dimensional environment of the forest canopy. While modern anthropoid apes, distant cousins of man rather than his ancestors, continue to live in a forest environment, the evolutionary transition from prehominid to protohominid involved the assumption of a terrestrial mode of life. This transition may well have been favored by a change of the environment toward drier conditions, with a resultant expansion of grasslands at the expense of forests. The circumstances must be rather conjectural, however, for there is a dearth of known primate fossils from the Pliocene epoch, which began some 12 million years ago.

A more reliable inference is that the australopithecines were well adapted for terrestrial life and presumably flourished in the more open habitat of parkland or savannah. These creatures, termed near-men by a well-informed investigator (Leakey, 1960a), were, if not direct ancestors of the genus *Homo,* a collateral branch of the human stock. Their appearance has been dated in the early part of the last geological epoch, the Pleistocene, the beginning of which has conventionally been taken as one million years ago. Very recent studies, however, based on potassium-argon dating of rock from the stratum where the fossil *Zinjanthropus* (assumed to be one of the australopithecines) was discovered in association with other Pleistocene forms, suggest a considerably earlier date. The significance of this result lies not only in the light that it may shed on the dating of the Pleistocene, but also in the fact that *Zinjanthropus,* regarded by its discoverer as a genus that "may well be directly ancestral to modern man" (Leakey, 1960b, p. 28), was apparently a maker as well as a user of tools.

Two anatomical characteristics of the australopithecines are critical: the assumption of fully upright posture with bipedal locomotion, and the beginning of a specialization of the hand in ways that facilitate precise and powerful manipulations (Napier,

1962). The two traits doubtlessly are related, for bipedalism completely freed the hands for manipulation, a matter of some considerable advantage to a form that, unlike the other primates, was to become increasingly dependent on the use of weapons in the taking of large animals for food. Here, as in other aspects of human evolution, it is easier to see how several modifications were adaptively interrelated than to discern a temporal or causal order of priority among them. While animals other than man may be said to use tools on occasion, the significant human development was that man became "the only mammal which is continuously dependent on tools for survival" (Bartholomew & Birdsell, 1953, p. 483).

Great things may have small beginnings, and it is not fanciful to derive some crucial features of human sociality from the ecology of the protohominids and early representatives of the genus *Homo*. The new habit of hunting in a more open habitat not only involved a shift of niche or ecological zone, but also involved the elaboration of cooperative behavior patterns. Hallowell (1961, p. 241) states: "A new ecological niche provided the opportunity for the exercise, at a new level of behavioral organization, of behavioral potentialities already present, as well as for the development of new behavioral patterns." Concerted collective action frequently is required for taking large game, and an advantage accrued to a species capable of transmitting precise information on the location of prospective food. Meat is a more concentrated food (more Calories per gram) than plant tissue, and a large number of Calories can be transported for consumption at some distance from the point of acquisition, with the kill being divided among individuals not participating in the chase. Females, who are often pregnant or tending infants, are not likely to specialize in hunting. Food sharing between the predatory male and his dependent mate and offspring was an early step toward an economic division of labor within the family, a crucial supplement to and, in some degree, replace-

ment for the strictly sexual bond between mates. Spuhler (1959, p. 7) suggested, moreover, "It is unlikely that the long dependency of human children—so important in the acquisition of culture by individuals—could develop in a society without food sharing."

Reference to what are usually considered the most distinctive human traits—possession of a large and versatile brain, and the ability to communicate symbolically—has been postponed intentionally. These capacities apparently were involved after the adaptations just mentioned (Washburn, 1960). Within the past decade, there has been a growing appreciation of the extent to which the selection pressures that issued in the evolution of *Homo sapiens* were determined by the prior ecological adaptations, social patterns, and cultural achievements of pre-*sapiens* forms. "It is probably more correct to think of much of our structure as the result of culture than it is to think of men anatomically like ourselves slowly discovering culture" (Washburn, 1959, p. 21).

The genetical theory of natural selection has shown that even a slight reproductive advantage can be decisive for the long-run course of evolution. Thus even the most rudimentary human skill or capacity would render biological success highly probable for its possessor, and populations experiencing genetic changes enhancing the advantage would leave disproportionate numbers of progeny and hence contribute disproportionately to the species gene pool. Tool-making ability, visual acuity, capacity for fine sensory-motor coordination, ability to communicate precisely, and the like were presumably subject to positive natural selection. This point may require a little clarification. In a genetic population system there occurs over time an entry of information from the environment into the population. Modern biology describes the "genetic system of a species as the whole of that which affects the flow of genetic information from one individual to another and from one generation to the next" (Medawar, 1961, p. 57). But heredity is non-Lamarckian; that is, "The environment does *not* imprint genetical instructions upon living things" (p. 87). Nevertheless, genetic systems undergo adaptive changes, explicable in part by the introduction of "new" information into the genes by mutations. Such of these mutations as are favorable are positively selected; the theory of evolution "declares that genetical instructions change in the course of time" (p. 36) in directions dictated at least in part by the state of the environment. In this sense, therefore, the genetic population system acquires and stores information ("learns") about the environment, although the time scale of the process is incomparably longer than that of the individual organism's perception, learning, and adaptive behavior. It is, therefore, not necessary to postulate a Lamarckian inheritance of acquired characteristics to predict that an organism which has become dependent on distinctively cultural modes of behavioral adaptation would experience selection on the basis of "capacity for culture."

The evolution from some predecessor species of the genus *Homo* to modern man is believed to have occurred entirely within the epoch of the Pleistocene. As the special relevance of Pleistocene conditions for human evolution has become more apparent, there has developed a preoccupation of physical anthropologists and archaeologists with problems of "Pleistocene ecology" (J. D. Clark, 1960; Howell, 1952). A number of students have commented on the rapidity of the evolution of modern man from the protohominid stage, and the point is well taken, even if we accept recent results suggesting an earlier date for the first "men" than had previously been contemplated. A relevant fact, in all likelihood, is that the Pleistocene was an era of profound environmental change. In the northerly latitudes of Europe, there were the four major periods of glacial advance and retreat that give the epoch its popular name, the Ice Ages. In Africa, which mounting evidence tends to assign more unequivocally to the position of the "cradle of mankind," environmental fluctuations occurred as a sequence of pluvial interspersed with dry periods (G. Clark, 1961). No doubt there were accompanying changes in vegetation patterns, water supply, and abundance of various types of game.

During the Pleistocene there was a far-flung distribution of hominid populations induced in part, no doubt, by migratory responses (Birdsell, 1957) to environmental changes and population pressure, for the cultural level and exploitative efficiency of these populations were not high enough to sustain high local population densities. As modern genetic theory has shown, the optimum condition for rapid evolution is a species population widely distributed over a diversity of environments and split up into small local groups (demes) that are partially but not wholly isolated genetically one from the other. Precisely this condition would be expected on the basis of the Pleistocene environment, given the Paleolithic technology of that period.

Some writers have suggested another, though not inconsistent, type of influence on the rate of human evolution. Leakey (1960b, p. 29) notes that evolutionary processes are accelerated in animals that undergo domestication: "When man became a toolmaker and began to exert control over his natural environment, he made himself in effect a 'domesticated animal.' It may well be that, upon becoming man, he initiated a major acceleration of his own rate of physical change in addition to his rapid cultural development." Dobzhansky (1962, p. 196) questions the applicability of the concept of domestication in this connection, but he does not deny "that the physical and genetic endowments of the human species now living have evolved as a result of and hand in hand with the development of culture . . . biological and cultural evolution are interdependent" (p. 193).

A related point has been made by Eiseley (1956), in a discussion that brings out the contrast between the well-known anatomical variability (polymorphism) of the human species and the apparent absence of appreciable racial variation in mental and emotional capacities. All living peoples are descendants of populations of culture-bearing animals. As dependence upon culture patterns, including linguistic communication, has been in effect for scores of thousands of years, it has constituted a continuous selective force favoring the perpetuation of the capacity to adjust to the exigencies of a human type of social life. Since these were much the same in essentials in all human groups, despite variation in culture content, the selection pressures were approximately equal.

In sum, man's morphological and intellectual capacity for culture evolved under the pressure of a complex social and technical life that was initiated by ecological adaptations of his prehuman ancestors. Modern man, the *Homo sapiens sapiens* of the systematist, arrived on the scene with his large brain perhaps no more than fifty thousand years ago, after a million years—maybe twice that long—of human evolution. His evolution was the product of an interplay of genetic, ecological, social, and cultural forces.

More to the point at hand, the genetic, social, and cultural changes accompanying the emergence of man represented ecological adaptations that, in total, produced a species with a distinctively human ecology. If we take the species characteristics of modern man as given, for purposes of post-Pleistocene ecological investigation, we must reckon with a creature having a number of attributes and capacities equipping it for a unique place in the ecosystem: (1) An anatomical structure that is generalized and versatile rather than specialized for particular kinds of defense or food-getting behavior; (2) a plasticity of behavior, with adaptation being based largely on learning and experience; (3) the ability to communicate symbolically and to socialize experience through interindividual transmission; hence (4) a social pattern based on conventional or normative definitions of differentiated

roles; (5) a cultural inheritance from pre-*sapiens* ancestors which, though meager in contrast to the cultural apparatus of contemporary man, was at the outset of *sapiens* existence so highly developed and powerful a means of coping with life conditions as to render human life apart from culture unimaginable; and as a concomitant of all these; (6) the potentiality for indefinitely elaborating technical procedures, social forms, and cultural preoccupations (Hallowell, 1956; Oakley, 1954; Spuhler, 1959). With the advent of modern man, the time scale of evolution was tremendously foreshortened, because cultural evolution was superimposed upon genetic evolution (Dobzhansky, 1962; Medawar, 1961) and had already attained sufficient momentum to guarantee that future changes in hominid ecology would occur largely on the basis of this new principle—though not entirely so, since racial differentiation, for example, appears to have occurred subsequently to the appearance of *Homo sapiens* (Howells, 1960). The ecology of man was, therefore, to be the ecology not merely of a peculiar organism, but the ecology of that animal's culture, social patterns, technology, and increasingly "artificial" environment.

THE EVOLUTION OF SOCIETY

Man, as the preceding remarks have indicated, always has been a social animal; he has, that is, maintained social organization of some kind throughout his tenure of the earth. Since man depends on his social organization for life itself, a concern with social organization must be one of the central preoccupations of human ecology. We know that human social organization has neither remained constant in time nor reproduced itself without alteration as peoples have occupied the several regions of the planet. The ecologist's interest in social organization must, therefore, encompass the variability of social organization in time and space. The interpretation of this variability in terms of the notion of social evolution is congenial to an ecological view of society, for, as will be shown, present conceptions of social evolution depend in considerable measure upon ecological concepts.

The discussion must not be allowed to founder on the controversies and misunderstandings that plague current treatments of social or cultural evolution. Actually, there can be no quarrel with the brute fact of social evolution. Some, at least, of the kinds of society now extant have not always existed. Their appearance in history, moreover, was not occasioned by a special act of creation out of nothing. If, therefore, we mean by evolution what Darwin meant, *descent with modification,* all known societies are a product of evolution. All descended from earlier societies and were modified in greater or lesser degree in the process. The establishment of this principle in respect to social and cultural phenomena, in fact, preceded and opened the way for its application to species of organisms. Like the acknowledged stimulus of Malthusian doctrine and the patent borrowing of a number of social-structural concepts, the transfer of the idea of evolution was a clear instance of influence running from social science to biology, rather than vice versa.

From a formal standpoint, four classes of interrelated problems arise in the investigation of social evolution:

1. What are the *units* of evolution? Evolution has been predicated of a considerable variety of levels and subsystems of sociocultural phenomena: linguistic, technological, kinship, stratification, political, and other systems, and such holistic units as patterns of social integration or premises of cultural orientation.

2. What are the *causes* of evolution? The search for causes or mechanisms usually is oriented to generic, repetitive types of instigators of evolution rather than to the unique or specific manifestations thereof in particular instances of evolutionary change.

3. What has been the concrete *course* of evolution? In principle, inquiry directed to this question seeks to identify, for the class of units in question, all instances of the class and to ascertain all the "genealogical" connections among them. In terms of explanation, as distinct from description, attention focuses on the particular combinations of causes or the particular values of causal variables present in the case of each recognizable modification. Thus the study of the course of evolution is literally a historical problem, as contrasted to a search for principles or causes, which seeks a generalized explanation of how evolution occurs. If the distinction seems insecure in its application to social evolution, it is plain enough in the theory of organic evolution, where there is a recognized division of labor between students of the principles of genetics on the one hand and the paleontologists and systematists (the currently preferred term for taxonomists) on the other (Goudge, 1961, Ch. 3).

4. Are there *trends* or patterns of evolution that recur from time to time or that can be predicated of the evolutionary process as a whole? Does evolution, for example, move generally, if not uniformly and inevitably, in the direction of increasing complexity, higher ecological efficiency, or augmented variety? Again, it is instructive to refer to the situation in the study of organic evolution, where certain trends can be identified and partially explained. These trends, however, appear neither to be invariant and irreversible nor to apply to the totality of evolution, save perhaps for "a tendency for life to expand, to fill in all the available spaces in the livable environments, including those created by the process of that expansion itself. . . . even this, although general, is not invariable" (Simpson, 1960, p. 243). More abstractly—and this would surely hold true of social as well as organic evolution—one can say that there is an overall "direction" of evolution, in the sense that evolution as a whole is not reversible in detail, nor can major sequences of evolution be shown to repeat themselves precisely. The overall course of evolution, therefore, can only be productive of novelty, despite parallels and

analogies between spatiotemporally distinct subsequences.

Given the alternate possibilities in the choice of unit and problem focus, it is not surprising that a variety of intellectual enterprises, some apparently incompatible with others, could develop, all of which purport to be inquiries into social or cultural evolution. Some progress has been made in reconciling apparent oppositions between them, on the basis of distinctions between "general" and "specific" evolution (Sahlins & Service, 1960) or among "universal," "unilinear," and "multilinear" evolution (Steward, 1955, Ch. 1). It is now apparent that students of "general" or "universal" evolution are focusing on the problem of trends in evolution with reference to the evolutionary process as a whole. The outcome of their studies typically is a scheme of "stages," representing a succession of ordered types or levels analyzed in terms of their general preconditions or causes, rather than in terms of particular genealogies. The enterprise termed multilinear evolution is addressed to the problem of parallels between comparable but distinct episodes of evolution, where genealogy is demonstrable within each episode. The search is for similarities both in sequence pattern and in specifiable causal factors. So-called specific evolution usually is concerned with a particular local sequence of evolution, in which genealogic relationships are to be worked out in some detail, while analysis is addressed to particular causal circumstances and adaptive responses. While this enumeration does not exhaust the possibilities of variation in conceptual orientations to social evolution, it should suggest that no necessary paradox inheres in the evident dissimilarity among kinds of evolutionary investigation. There is not yet a "synthetic theory" of social evolution to match the achievement of the biologists, during the last generation, in integrating the findings and conceptual schemes of paleontology, ecology, genetics, and systematics. One may be pessimistic about the possibility of such an achievement in the foreseeable future without denying the significance and legitimacy—if not urgency—of the problem of social evolution.

For purposes of the present discussion, the problem of units has already been partially resolved in the designation of the topic as "the evolution of society." No attention is given, therefore, to the evolution of language, philosophy, or the fine arts, even though these and other aspects of culture afford most instructive examples of methodological problems in evolutionary inquiry. (Language, indeed, represents the earliest and in some ways the most advanced field of evolutionary study, organic or cultural; see, e.g., Thieme [1958].) The implicit equation of "social evolution" to "the evolution of society," moreover, reflects a concern with the evolution of forms and features that apply to a society as a whole, rather than to component parts of society, such as the conjugal relationship or the role of the scientist, although, again, the limitation of scope is not meant to deny the importance of work with such units (Znaniecki, 1934, pp. 282–295; Znaniecki, 1940). These restrictions leave ample opportunity for selective attention to distinguishable properties of whole societies. The evolution of the subsistence patterns of societies, for example, may be compared with or related to that of their political patterns. Both are features of a society as a whole.

Although the presentation of substantive propositions deriving from evolutionary investigations is only illustrative, it will be possible to demonstrate the mutual relevance of ecological and evolutionary conceptual schemes in a variety of ways. Among the propositions advanced about the general *causes* of evolution, those referring to ecological considerations are prominent. Interpretations of the *course* of evolution, insofar as they go beyond the problem of historical reconstruction, almost invariably include specifications of ecological circumstance or response. Finally, most of the *trends* in social evolution that command general recognition are manifestly ecological in some direct sense

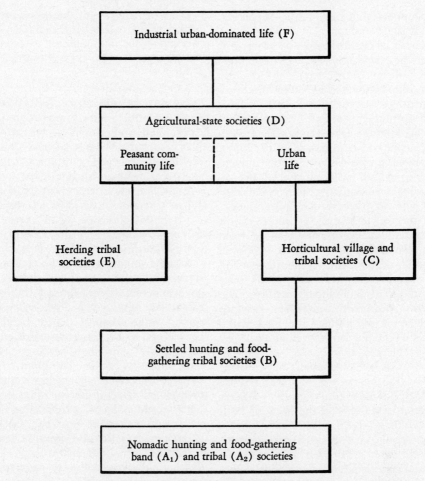

Fig. 3. A taxonomy of societies with respect to evolutionary stages, according to Goldschmidt (1959, p. 183). (Letter designations added for reference to figs. 4 and 5.)

or are immediately derivative from ecological trends.

A convenient set of material for discussion is Goldschmidt's (1959) thoughtful treatment of social evolution, the taxonomic outline of which is represented in Figure 3. Several pertinent observations can be made about this taxonomy without entering into the details of the content of each category or its spatiotemporal distribution. To begin, note that the categories represent a *sequence of stages*. The higher categories are those that appeared later, though the lower may

have persisted—indeed, contemporary or nearly contemporary representatives of each category or approximations to its type are known. The exception to a strict temporal ordering is the herding tribal society, which, on Goldschmidt's hypothesis, is a "devolution to a simpler mode of life," a late specialization occasioned by the achievement of animal domestication by certain horticultural and agricultural peoples.

Second, observe that the categories are a typology of *basic ecological forms*. Significantly, the ecological differentia are systems of exploitive technology, rather than, say, types of environment. An ecological approach to social evolution does not, therefore, require the assumption of environmental determinism, but rather that of a reciprocal relationship between technology and environment.

Goldschmidt's (1959) justification for basing an account of social evolution on ecological considerations is straightforward: Major differences between social systems are explained by social evolution. Social institutions, which serve to maintain social continuity and to preserve social integration, do not themselves evolve, but rather adjust to new conditions, originating either from environmental change or from technological development. Technology is cumulative and progressive, because useful inventions, once made and accepted, tend to be retained. Each advance in technology, moreover, expands the sphere of possibilities for further advances. Technological development frequently enlarges the interacting human aggregate and hence augments the effective numbers available to contribute and share new ideas. Technological change is subject to adaptive selection—on the basis of both utility within a group and its contribution to the survival of a given group in competition with others. The relevant ecological context, therefore, is not the strictly hypothetical isolated society, but the arena or field of interacting populations. The ramifications of Goldschmidt's argument need not be pursued further. The central thesis is that technological development has a variety of specifiable social effects—on group structure, values, status systems, role differentiation, authority systems, and ideology—by virtue of the fact that it alters the size and life conditions of a population, subject to the limitations imposed by the environment at any given stage of technological growth:

Whatever the nature of the society, the social imperatives continue. But the pattern in which they operate will vary, and this variation is dependent, in large measure, on the character of that technology and the size and circumstances of the population that it supports. For this reason, the institutions of society undergo evolutionary change (Goldschmidt, 1959, p. 180).

No dissent from these propositions is intended. Goldschmidt's (1959) argument is a careful one and cannot be shaken by any play on words. There is, however, a series of methodological and substantive considerations bearing upon his discussion which are suggestive from an ecological standpoint.

The taxonomy is *typological* in two senses. First, the categories are "pure" types more or less approximated in reality. There are evidently transitional or mixed instances of societies combining features of two types, significantly, these often occur "under special environmental circumstances." Second, the categories represent a "reduced property space," in the sense of Lazarsfeld and Rosenberg (1955, p. 16), in that several attributes conceptually capable of at least partially independent variation are involved. Each category represents an empirical clustering of specified values of two or more attributes. This second point is perhaps suggested by the rearrangement of Goldschmidt's (1959) taxonomy depicted in Figure 4, which incorporates some references to his textual description as well as a few extensions of his terminology. In this arrangement, no less than three attributes are involved: the subsistence technology, the form of local territorial units, and the pattern of political integration (this author's terms). The three attributes are highly correlated, in that a number of logically possible combinations of subcategories are empirically unobserved or are theoretically improbable. The correlation, nevertheless, is not perfect, for each attribute has certain subcategories that occur with two or three subcategories of another attribute.

Some additional characteristics of Goldschmidt's (1959) taxonomy are emphasized by this rearrangement. The number of subcategories of each attribute is minimal. As the author himself suggests, some of the

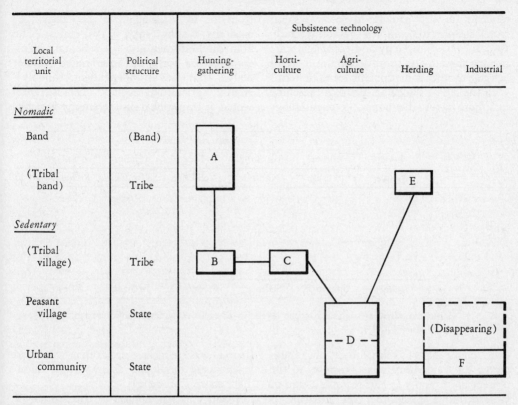

Local territorial unit	Political structure	Subsistence technology				
		Hunting-gathering	Horti-culture	Agri-culture	Herding	Industrial
Nomadic						
Band	(Band)	A				
(Tribal band)	Tribe				E	
Sedentary						
(Tribal village)	Tribe	B	C			
Peasant village	State			D		(Disappearing)
Urban community	State					F

Fig. 4. Alternative representation of taxonomy of societies according to Goldschmidt (1959, p. 183). (See Fig. 3 for meaning of letters.)

types might well be subdivided. In terms of sociopolitical integration, for example, Service (1962, Ch. 5) makes a good case for the "chiefdom" as a distinctive level beyond the tribe, while still confining his attention to "primitive" societies. Certainly the category of the state needs some elaboration. The city-state, conquest empire, feudal regime, national state, and (emerging) international leagues and organizations come to mind as types suggestive of an evolutionary sequence (though not necessarily a unilinear one). Indeed, the entire taxonomy is perhaps overly parsimonious at the higher levels. The top two categories, while they may have existed for only one-tenth of the time during which *Homo sapiens* has held tenure of the earth, or one one-hundredth of the time period of the hominid branch of evolution,

probably have accounted for 80 per cent of the human population of the earth and an even larger fraction of the impact of man on the ecosystem.

The taxonomy is not "genealogical" with respect to specific societies, although it embodies the hypothesis that a specified lower level was a requisite precondition for the emergence of the next higher one. (Goldschmidt [1959] specifies "continuity" as one of the general "mechanisms" of evolution.) The taxonomy does not purport, therefore, to represent the "course" of evolution in terms of the documented or inferred history of all known societies. It is, in fact, more nearly a taxonomy of levels of "general evolution" than of specific societies.

The primary hypothesis underlying this account of evolution is "the assumption of a tendency toward growth in social systems from simple to complex" (Goldschmidt, 1959, p. 106). Simplicity and complexity are not specified in any great detail, but it seems possible to infer some content for these terms with the aid of a scheme like that presented in Figure 5. (At this point, the terminology from the "self-sufficient" to the "exchange" economy. Krader (1957, p. 136) states: "The nomadic herdsmen and the sedentary farmers together form an interrelated whole; neither composes an independent economy." Again, agricultural society (D) is represented as transitional on the energy variable,

Type of Society	Level	Structural Variable				
		Political	Territorial	Food	Economy	Energy
	Simple	Local	Nomadic	Collection	Self-sufficient	Preindustrial
A₁		—	—	—	—	—
A₂		o	—	—	—	—
B		+	o	o	—	—
C		+	o	+	—	—
E		+	—	+	o	—
D		+	+	+	+	o
F		+	+	+	+	+
	Complex	Inter-local	Sedentary	Production	Exchange	Industrial

Fig. 5. Structural variables suggested by the taxonomy of societies by Goldschmidt (1959, p. 183). (See Fig. 3 for meaning of letters.)

is no longer that of Goldschmidt, but is suggested solely for illustrative purposes in the present discussion.) In this reconstruction of Goldschmidt's taxonomy, an attempt is made to specify a minimum number of structural variables, such that a unique combination of simple discriminations on each variable will suffice to define each of the taxonomic categories. At the same time, an attempt is made, without complete success, to designate variables whose interrelations over the relevant universe of observation would assume the pattern of a scale.

Although Goldschmidt's conceptualization lends itself most easily to presentation if the variables are treated as dichotomies, his own remarks and the plain facts of the case suggest that variation is a matter of degree. Hence, in the diagram, those types of society most clearly manifesting "transitional" features are identified with the symbol "O." The herding tribal society (E), for example, is one that exists in a "symbiosis" with sedentary peoples (Toynbee, 1961, p. 277), relying for some of its requisites on trading or raiding; in this regard, it is transitional

since it was in such societies that wind and water were developed as important inanimate sources of energy.

When it is represented in the fashion of Figure 5, the Goldschmidt (1959) taxonomy is seen as susceptible of considerable development (and this is, perhaps, all that one should ask of such a formulation at the present time). The component variables are capable of conceptual and observational refinement with respect to ranges of variation and patterns of covariation. Dissatisfaction with a dichotomous or trichotomous discrimination for each of the five variables may be translated back into an uneasiness about the fairly gross character of the original categories, since these elementary discriminations define those categories without ambiguity.

Subjecting the taxonomy to even a slight amount of conceptual manipulation discloses some lacunae and ambiguities. Can the matter of "scale" of social organization be treated as conceptually independent of the variables in Figure 5, and, if so, need it be explicitly introduced as a taxonomic criterion? To what extent is social evolution predicated on technological developments other than those suggested by the shift from food collecting to food production, and from animate to inanimate energy sources? Granted the paradoxical case of the Andean culture, in which the Inca ruled an empire using only the most rudimentary system of physical mnemonics (Toynbee, 1961, p. 275), how far can social evolution really proceed without literacy? As Steward and Shimkin (1961, p. 487) note, "the evolution of communications has been a critical factor in the changes in many major aspects of culture." Can one accept without qualification Goldschmidt's implicit hypothesis that evolution can be adequately characterized and its mechanism isolated while the internal structural differentiation of society remains a dependent variable?

The component of culture that Goldschmidt calls "ideology" may likewise invite an investigation that enlarges upon his characterization of it as a device which justifies the social order and provides the motivation for people to do what they must do in a society at a given level of social evolution. Toynbee's treatment of "universal churches" as a medium through which "civilizations of the third generation" were affiliated to "civilizations of the second generation" is suggestive of a positive and distinctive role of religion in social evolution (Toynbee, 1957, pp. 81–87). Coulborn, on the other hand, has suggested a key role for religion in the formation of the *primary* civilizations. His account runs strongly in ecological terms:

Each religion arose as a means of enabling the people of its society to survive. . . . for most of the societies at their origin . . . religion was vitally concerned with the need for water. Water was . . . the essential means of the societies' survival, and . . . it was the main aim of religion in the Egyptian, Mesopotamian, Middle American, and Andean societies, probably in the Indian and Chinese societies, and very possibly in the Cretan Society to secure water and to establish in men's minds the appropriate and necessary devotion to it (Coulborn, 1959, pp. 129–130).

Yet another formulation of the role of religion in social evolution is suggestive:

The nature and social functions of religion have . . . evolved. To the personalized relation between primitive man and supernatural forces . . . there was added ceremonialism, for such group purposes as procuring food. Religion at higher levels of sociocultural integration served to sanction national social and political purposes. A still different kind of religious emergence seems to have been the personalized or messianic religions that began about 600 B.C. (Steward & Shimkin, 1961, pp. 489–490).

With the emergence of "agricultural-state societies," we are on the threshold of "history," the period covered by increasing amounts of written documentation. While the aims of prehistory must be sharply circumscribed in view of the paucity and selectivity of available evidence, the profusion of the data of the historic period invites a plurality of objectives. To the prehistorian, an ecological approach comes naturally (G. Clark, 1957, Ch. 1). Students of the historic period must discipline themselves to a calculated abstraction if they wish to keep a firm grasp on ecological variables while not overlooking any sort of aid that the entire corpus of historic material may offer. Yet the same questions about the causes, the course, and the possible trends and patterns of social evolution apply to the historic as to the prehistoric period. The proposition to be maintained here is that the theme of ecological expansion is a serviceable orientation to these problems, whether the concern is with the appearance of new levels of social integration or with the genealogies and careers of the several major sociohistorical units whose definition and characterization have been achieved in recent macrohistorical scholarship.

The appearance of "agricultural-state societies" is virtually coterminous with what various writers have called the "agricultural revolution" (L. A. White, 1959), the "urban revolution" (Childe, 1950), and the "dawn of civilization" (Piggott, 1961). There is a considerable measure of agreement among students of this transformation that it occurred not only once, but in a half-dozen or so historical instances. These were, perhaps, not all strictly independent occurrences, but were nonetheless clearly distinct developments each having unique features, but all exhibiting some remarkable parallels and similarities. The locales in question were Mesopotamia (Sumer), Egypt, the Indus Valley, China, and, in the New World, the central Andes and Meso-America. (There is less agreement that the island of Crete in the Aegean Sea belongs in the list.)

Complex societies arose in each of these regions in the course of a series of interrelated developments, including intensification of subsistence activity, increase of population density, and heightened population concentration. The details of the initial changes—falling largely within the prehistoric period—are imperfectly known. There is enough information, however, to suggest that a number of contingent factors were at work. With a focus on Near East materials, Braidwood and Reed (1957) have reconsidered the whole question of delineating "developmental levels" of "subsistence patterns," and have shown cause for recognizing no less than eight levels: early Pleistocene food-gathering; late glacial and post-glacial specialized food-gathering; "vegeculture," a mixed food-getting combined with a specialized food-collecting level; incipient agriculture; primary village farming; the primary urban community, which, as far as subsistence level is concerned, represented an intensification of the village-farming pattern; various vegecultural-farming blends; and pastoral nomadism, a specialization from the village-farming level.

As an archaeologist, Braidwood (1952) is extremely sensitive to the difficulties posed by the identification of these levels in the archaeological record, and to the ambiguities presented by "blendings" of the various patterns and by chronological variations from this sequence. Certainly, in a comparative framework, one must recognize that each of the early complex societies gained this level of organization on the basis of distinctive ecological adjustments to unique environmental conditions (Adams, 1960). In the Near East, there was early established a symbiosis between plant cultivation and the management of domesticated animals; whereas, in the New World, where domesticable animals were largely absent, food production was somewhat differently organized. In the Western hemisphere, there was a distinctive roster of domesticated plants. Diversified farming, with a dependence on maize and a variety of vegetables, roots, and tubers, was perhaps more characteristic here than in the Near East, where cultivation of the small grains was perfected.

Much uncertainty surrounds the question of the role of "cities," in some strictly defined sense of the term, in the rise of complex societies. Mesopotamia, the Indus Valley, and northern Peru are known archaeologically to have produced sizeable settlements on a distinctively urban plan. Knowledge of early Egypt, however, derives from excavations of tombs rather than settlements, which fact has contributed a possibly spurious conception of the origin of a "civilization without cities." Similarly, the Mayan era of the Meso-American development has been interpreted largely through remains of monumental architecture whose pattern suggests the notion of "ceremonial centers" rather than cities as economic and residential units (Kraeling & Adams, 1960, pp. 124–164). Again, there is the distinct possibility of bias in the archaeological record. There is no doubt, however, that in all instances new patterns of population concentration followed upon gains in agricultural productivity, and urban communities of some type emerged somewhere along the line.

In this connection, attention may be directed to the argument presented by certain writers, notably Childe (1950; 1951a), who lay plausible stress on the creation of an economic surplus which becomes large enough to support activities other than primary food production. In theory, such a surplus might be accumulated even without increasing productivity per man or per acre, if only more producers, each with his relatively small surplus, were brought into sufficient proximity to allow the use of efficient methods of accumulation. This hypothesis is meant only to suggest how a demographic phase of ecological expansion could be a precondition for realizing the potential of a prior technological achievement. One could equally well argue that the repatterning of energy flows occasioned by demographic change might have significant implications for materials flows. It is supposed that in most, if not all, the early civilizations, water control—irrigation and drainage—became vital at some stage. Since water control on any worthwhile scale requires considerable numbers to effect it and to profit by it, some demographic expansion or redistribution may have been a critical intervening factor between an initial moderate rise in efficiency of food production and the emergence of complex organizational forms on the basis of that rise. The same could be argued concerning information flows, but the point is not to press for some kind of "demographic interpretation." Rather, it is suggested that changes great enough to be described as a transition from one "level" to another were almost certainly the outcome of expansion in several intercorrelated components of the human niche in the ecosystem.

The suggestion, then, is that ecological expansion, rather than the appearance of specific features of culture content or institutional form, be accepted as the key to the transition from one major "level" of social evolution to the next. In this light, the failure to discover exact parallels between the several distinct instances of the appearance of civilization becomes understandable. Each of the acknowledged "cradles of civilization" presented a distinctive set of environmental

problems, despite a certain similarity of their general situations. Obstacles to expansion cannot, therefore, have been identical in all these areas, and the factor that resulted in the overcoming of the immediately operative barrier to expansion at any given time need not have been the same. In each case, however, we do see at the basis of the formative complex society apparent population increase and redistribution along with technical-organizational innovations altering the flows of materials, energy, and information. We must be prepared to recognize formally dissimilar inventions as functionally equivalent in some measure. Draft animals and wheeled vehicles, used to advantage in Old World societies, were absent in the early American civilizations; yet, "every New World center developed roads, boats, and canals to a degree of efficiency which enabled them to achieve states as large as those of the Old World" (Steward, 1955, p. 201). There was no writing in pre-Spanish Peru; but the Inca not only had a means of reckoning and recording quantities based on patterns of knotted strings, but they also developed a remarkable system of roads and messenger service.

In point of fact, what is here called ecological expansion is used as an interpretive variable, under one name or another, in most efforts to discern a general pattern in social evolution beyond the point of the initiation of the first civilized societies.

Steward (1955, Ch. 11) has shown that, given broad similarity of their arid or semiarid environments, the early complex societies developed in remarkably parallel ways: "In the irrigation areas, environment, production, and social patterns had similar functional and developmental interrelationships" (Steward, 1955, p. 199). Without going into Steward's chronological and typological delineation of "developmental eras" in five of the major areas (he does not consider the Indus Valley) where civilization arose, we may review some of the phases of expansion he treats. Population increased in each area as the construction of irrigation works raised the limits of agricultural production. With increased farming productivity, some labor was released from subsistence activity and diverted to craft, construction, and transportation pursuits, in each of which fields technological innovations then resulted. At the same time, the increasing scale of production called for coordination and management, and these functions were preempted by a theocratic class, which virtually monopolized the emerging techniques of writing, mensuration, and record keeping. As the societies reached the population limits set by agricultural productivity, population pressure heightened the competition between local areas and regions, some of which embarked upon conquest and the building of empires. Limits to military expansion were soon reached, however, and the first empires were short-lived. Their exploitative policies weakened the productive base of tributary areas and engendered revolutions against the over-extended imperial authority. The breakdown of the latter initiated a period of Dark Ages, in which there was deterioration of irrigation works and decline of food production with consequent political disorganization. In some cases, the process of empire-building was resumed, initiating an era of cyclical conquests, either by a local state of the former empire or a predatory nomadic group. The militaristic organization geared to conflict supported the codification and systematization of law and learning and engendered innovations in political organization. The increasing regimentation and sharper social stratification, however, apparently diverted effort from potentially creative lines into standardized and closely administered artistic and economic production. The early ages of imperialism were not noted for technological inventiveness, but rather represented expansion, along other lines, to the limits set by previous technological achievements.

Despite considerable uncertainties—not so surprising in view of the recency of the adoption of an ecological viewpoint in respect to the problem at hand—the available evidence permits a tentative general char-

acterization of the innovations in energy, information, and materials flows accompanying the formation of the early complex societies.

Braidwood (1952), for example, has dealt with the problem of specifying key elements in the emergence of "civilization" from the general background of the "food-producing" society, continuing a discussion opened by Childe (1950; 1951a) in his description of the "urban revolution." The criteria of civilization suggested by Braidwood are: fully efficient food production, cities and urbanization, formal political state, formal laws embodying a new sense of moral order, formal projects and works, social classes and hierarchies, writing, and monumentality in art. Braidwood does not list, as does Childe, extensive "foreign" trade and the development of craft specialization, both attributed in some measure to new techniques of working materials, especially metallurgy.

The pattern of social evolution beyond the stage at which the first civilizations were established invites description from two points of view, the pulsatory and the cumulative. Again, the issue between them turns more on how the problem is stated than on divergent understandings of the facts. When attention is focused on such units as peoples, nations, states, dynasties, classes, ideologies, regions, and localities, and when history is written as a narrative of their careers and fortunes, there is an overwhelming impression of endless fluctuations. The prospect of unmanageable complexity created by the accumulation of such histories has stimulated significant efforts toward a systematics of historical societies. The towering achievement is that of Arnold Toynbee, who stated more clearly than any of the predecessor "philosophers of history" the problem of identifying units—"intelligible fields of study," as he calls them. His initial taxonomic proposals, dating from 1934, were subjected to a number of criticisms, and he has recently provided "A Re-Survey of Civilizations" (Toynbee, 1961, Ch. 18), which incorporates several modifications.

Meanwhile, proposals along similar lines have been advanced by other scholars taking Toynbee's work as a point of departure (Bagby, 1959; Coulborn, 1959; Kroeber, 1962; Quigley, 1961).

We need not be concerned here with the controversial questions raised by this type of work, which, surely, must be regarded as still in its initial stages. Instead, let us note some of its fruitful consequences for the problem at hand. One conception of "civilization" is that of a spatiotemporally localized society undergoing a sequence of changes, from its formation through a stage of expansion which is ultimately arrested, whereupon the society may undergo such disruption that its identity is lost. It should be noted at once that a sequence of this sort, whatever the details of the formulation, is regarded by none of the responsible scholars in the field as a mechanical inevitability. The dangers of analogies with the life cycle of an organism are fully appreciated. Such a sequence pattern, moreover, is something more than an arbitrary simplification of historical data. It embodies the hypothesis that ecological expansion is carried forward in a succession of relatively restricted locales wherein initial conditions are favorable, where antecedent changes have created new opportunities, and where critical innovations are in process of gaining acceptance and application. At the same time, expansion based on any particular set of propitious circumstances cannot be continued indefinitely, but must encounter limiting conditions. Whether a given civilization can circumvent the immediate set of limiting conditions and resume expansion on a new basis or whether the next phase of expansion occurs elsewhere is a contingent matter. Interestingly enough, however, geographic displacement, or the rise of new civilizations on "new ground," has been a recurrent phenomenon.

Although a civilization as a macrohistoric unit is regarded as an "intelligible field of study," it is not *ipso facto* a closed or self-contained unit. A salient feature of Toynbee's (1957) work, for example, is the concern with the contact between civilizations. Some formalization of this problem is provided in the concepts of "affiliated" and "satellite" civilizations, with the recognition that these are but convenient demarcations on a continuum ranging from minimal to extremely close contact. Indeed, among the most prominent of the conditions favoring or inhibiting expansion is the position of each nascent civilization with respect to environing civilizations in various stages of their own careers. Quigley (1961), too, treats "mixture" as an initial stage of the evolution of a civilization.

It is this last feature of the process of civilization that affords a basis for resolving any real issue between the pulsatory and the cumulative conceptions of social evolution. Toynbee himself, though his own interest is in the "spiritual progress" of mankind, has provided an illuminating metaphor:

. . . the successive rises and falls of the primary and the secondary civilizations are examples of a rhythm . . . in which the successive revolutions of a wheel carry forward the vehicle which the wheel conveys (Toynbee, 1957, p. 88).

There is no need to take a stand here on the question of the reality of the kind of progress Toynbee discerns, for his metaphor will serve to describe any cumulative process that is moved along by the succession of rising and falling civilizations. Thus, despite his "spiritual" bias, Toynbee (1957, Ch. 25) includes a number of the significant cumulative achievements of civilizations in his list of "imperial institutions" that "afford services" to "unintended beneficiaries": communication systems, official languages and scripts, legal codes, calendars, weights and measures, and money.

Is it not quite apparent that a major theme of culture history must be the transit between civilizations of the arts and practices which gained for mankind increasing control of the patterns and rates of flow of materials, energy, and information? Ironworking, achieved in Armenia before 1400

B.C., much later became an instrument of expansion for European agriculturalists, who had need of sturdy axes to clear the thick deciduous forests and of iron-tipped ploughs to turn the heavy sod of trans-Alpine Europe. The foot-stirrup, a Chinese invention of the fifth century A.D., was diffused to the West through Central Asia and played a key role in the revolution in military techniques in early Medieval Europe, thereby contributing to a profound change in social structure, the consolidation of feudalism (L. White, Jr., 1962). The potato, domesticated in the highlands of western South America and an element in the agricultural base of civilization there, was to become a factor in population expansion in modern western Europe, an expansion that had its catastrophic phases (Salaman, 1949). Alphabetic writing spread widely from its Syriac origin and gave advantages to the successor civilizations adopting it that have probably never been fully assessed.

The foregoing examples, of course, concern the cultural anthropologist's category, diffusion. Now, it is precisely the prominence of diffusion in the origins of the cultural apparatus of any people or locality that has persuaded some critics that the idea of evolution is inapplicable to human society or culture. But this only shows that the analogy between cultural and organic evolution—or, actually, between the concepts of a species and a society—is inexact. The most careful exponents of the idea of social evolution as a cumulative process do not ignore diffusion. They treat it as one of the primary mechanisms of social evolution (Childe, 1951b, Ch. 12; Ogburn, 1950, supplementary chapter).

Ecological expansion, then, is carried forward by an accumulation of culture content —advances in control of the flows of materials, energy, and information—both within and between civilizations. Our conception of expansion, however, is incomplete until there is explicit recognition of certain consequences of culture growth and of some correlative processes.

A most fundamental aspect of social evolution has been the expansion of the orbit of civilization. Paleolithic man had achieved a widespread distribution over the face of the earth, including the whole of the New World, the Arctic region in both hemispheres, and the subcontinent of Australia, as well as the African-Eurasian land mass. In few cases indeed (the somewhat specious example of Antarctica excepted) have civilized peoples been in the position of colonizing where earlier societies did not already exist. Civilizations at their origin were quite localized geographically: a few thousands of square miles in the valleys of the Tigris and Euphrates, the Nile, the Indus, and the Yellow rivers, the insular and peninsular excrescences of the Aegean Sea, a strip along the western coast of South America, and a restricted portion of southern Mexico and Central America. All subsequent efflorescences of civilization are historically continuous with the societies that achieved the transition in these few localities, some of which were, therefore, centers for all subsequent expansion.

This expansion assumed various forms. Historical maps familiarize us with the territorial extensions of the classic empires but seldom reveal how thinly populated were vast reaches of the controlled territory and how tenuous was the control in regions off the beaten track. Yet the cyclical conquests did, in the course of time, serve to bring barbarian peoples as well as barbarian lands into the sphere of advanced culture, even if the barbarians were the conquerors nearly as often as they were the conquered.

The demographic aspects of the spread of civilization are not well understood. Even the names given to many of the population groups caught up in the process are known only from incidental literary references. Yet one fact seems probable: "An urban culture seems to make and unmake its carrying population" (Turner, 1941, II, 1325). Early cities, in all likelihood, were centers of extinction, wherein high mortality due to recurrent epidemics left a vacuum to be filled by migration or literal importation of a working population. Conquerors, colonists, and administrators of the imperial regimes mixed their genes as well as their habits with those of the indigenous (if there were such) populations. The overall course of population, if generally upward, was hardly a smoothly rising trend. Yet, if the whole Paleolithic era had brought the entire standing crop of humanity to perhaps five million hunters and gatherers, the beginnings of food production and the subsequent three millennia of civilization witnessed a growth of population to a crudely estimated two to three hundred million by the beginning of the Christian era.

The counterparts to culture growth and demographic expansion were the increasing intensity of environmental exploitation, though, again, the trend was beset by many local fluctuations, and a heightening of interdependence between centers and hinterlands or among regions and peoples. The flow of tribute and trade, though its economic magnitude would seem puny by modern standards, became the lifeblood of the centers of military and cultural dominance. Trade routes allowed movement not only of goods and people, but of information as well. Though we think of the ancients as tradition bound, no major tradition, save at the price of ultimate extinction, failed to be enriched and transmuted in the processes of expansion, contact, and assimilation.

Our contemporary social sciences stem from but one of these traditions, as elaborated in the Hellenic and Western spheres of civilization. They came into being in a late phase of one thrust of expansion, that of modern Europe. Their historic preoccupation, however heavily disguised, has been with the pattern of that expansion and the structures it produced. Even today, as a growing concern with internationalism and economic development lend urgency to an interest in all peoples and places, bias remains in the implicit statement of the problem—how are backward peoples to be incorporated within the European pattern of economic growth and cultural cosmopolitanism? The process of social evolution has finally brought us to a confrontation with a predicament of its own making. Human ecology must henceforth be the ecology of man on the planet earth. Plain it now is, though the fact is far older than its recognition, that the destinies of all peoples are intertwined.

ECOLOGICAL EXPANSION: MODERN TIMES

While the cycles of earlier civilizations were being completed, central and northern Europe were in process of consolidation to a pattern of Neolithic barbarian settlement. The Roman expansion brought into the area much of the apparatus of civilization, however thinly spread. As the Graeco-Roman world, following the pattern of previous Near Eastern civilizations, reached the limits of its expansion, became disorganized, and was forced out of the bulk of Europe, the trans-Alpine region was bequeathed the legacy of the whole accretion of technological development from the ancient civilizations. At the same time, the disruption of the Roman Empire in the West meant that there was a minimal carry-over of the institutional structures of Hellenism (Ayres, 1962, Ch. 7; Mumford, 1934, pp. 107–109). The West then had at its disposal the instruments on which expansion could be based but was freed of the organizational framework suited only to an earlier pattern of expansion. The foundations of modern Europe were laid, moreover, in a period of active culture contact. The rise of Islam, the Crusades, and the Mongol invasions each resulted in the introduction into Europe of critical inventions. In the meantime, the already ancient civilizations of the Far East were far along in their commitment to a way of life based on the labor-intensive agrarianism typified by wet-rice culture, which produced populations subsisting at high densities and governed on a despotic pattern. The New World civilizations, still

in the first phases of their remarkable indigenous expansion, were to prove unequal to
the coming contest with the Europeans. In
short, the expansion of Europe is a prime
illustration of the Law of Evolutionary Potential, which implies that there is "a perfectly normal leapfrog effect which makes
backward forms potentially more effective
than advanced forms in the course of moving into a new stage" of evolution (Sahlins
& Service, 1960, p. 115).

Modern expansion, like that producing
each of the earlier levels of social evolution,
was composite. The notion of a single "industrial revolution" based on steam power
generated from fossil fuels—important as
that one development was—is incomplete
and myopic. In the field of energy technology alone, important components of European expansion date well before 1750. Significant increments in horsepower, beginning
no later than the early medieval period,
were gained in a number of ways. The horse
itself was in effect transformed into an engine when the introduction of the iron horse-
shoe improved its traction and a new form
of harness allowed the animal's pull to be
met at the shoulder and transmitted to a
vehicle, tool, or machine, in place of the
neck, where its effect was to prevent the
beast from breathing. Devices for converting
the energy of moving wind and water,
known in principle to the ancients, became
the foundation of industrial expansion in
consequence of a host of improvements in
wind- and water-mills and inventions of
auxiliary machinery. And Europeans were
literally blown all over the face of the globe
by winds whose force was captured with
increasing efficiency by sails (Cottrell, 1955,
Ch. 4).

In the field of materials one example may
suffice. Glass was an ancient discovery, but
crucial improvements date from the Medieval period. Windows, spectacles, the tele-
scope and microscope, chemical retorts, and
mirrors were some of the fruits of advances
in glass-making. Who can calculate their
effects on experimental science? Did the
mirror indeed give rise to introspective explorations by presenting the subject with a
sharply objectified self (Mumford, 1934, pp.
128–131)?

As for information, the West made the
fourth quantum leap in a series comprising
language itself, writing, the alphabet, and
printing from movable type. But this brings
us back to an earlier theme. If no "other
innovation outranks printing in the importance of its effects," it is equally true that
"no other presents a clearer case of cultural
cross-fertilization" (Ayres, 1962, p. 138) or
"technical syncretism" (Mumford, 1934, p.
107).

All these technological innovations, and
more—for even an encyclopaedia can only
sketch the significant developments, imperfectly though they are known—had produced a civilization in full course of expansion before the advent of "Steam: Key to
the Industrial Revolution" (Cottrell, 1955,
Ch. 5) or the "Fuel Revolution" (L. A.
White, 1959, p. 370). It follows that there is
some difficulty in identifying the specific
contribution of fuel technology to European
expansion, apart from other elements in the
composite.

Some perspective is afforded, however, by
the data in Table 1. The United States in
1850 was not a low-energy economy, for its
per capita use of inanimate energy was already greater than that of dozens of countries today, and it made lavish use of animal
power. Yet the expansion from this relatively high base was rapid enough to justify
such extravagant language as "fuel revolution." During the century covered by these
data, population grew in a ratio of 6.5:1
(1950 compared to 1850), but work output
by 65:1; hence horsepower hours per capita
were 10 times as great in the later as in the
earlier year. The vast bulk of this gain was
due to the expanding use of the fossil fuels
and was predicated, of course, upon the invention of several kinds of engines and
motors, as well as machines that could be
driven by them. From 1850 to 1900 the per
capita output from inanimate energy sources

TABLE 1

ESTIMATED ANNUAL WORK OUTPUT PER CAPITA, BY SOURCE OF ENERGY,
FOR THE UNITED STATES: 1850–1950

Source	1850	1900	1950
	Horsepower Hours Per Capita[a]		
All sources	44.3	103.5	444.9
Renewable	41.3	33.8	41.0
Human workers	5.6	5.5	4.2
Work animals	23.2	22.2	2.5
Windmills and sailing vessels	6.0	1.3	0.1
Water wheels (direct drive)	3.9	2.8	0.4
Hydroelectric	—	1.6	33.7
Fuel wood	2.6	0.4	0.1
Exhaustible	3.0	69.7	403.9
Coal	3.0	68.7	147.3
Petroleum	—	0.9	166.0
Natural gas	—	0.1	90.6

[a] Computed from estimates by Dewhurst and Associates (1955, Appendix 25–3, Table L).

was merely added on to that of men and animals; after 1900, there was an absolute reduction in per capita use of muscle power, as both animals and people were displaced by machines.

One of the important implications of this revolution turns on the distinction between the renewable and nonrenewable energy sources. Hydroelectric energy, rapid as its expansion was in relative terms, just compensated for the declining rates of use of other renewable sources. Mid-twentieth-century industrial civilization, therefore, rested upon an exceedingly impermanent resource base, and the technologists of industrial society already were becoming preoccupied with the problem of effecting a transition to a new base, atomic energy, even though the prospect of fossil fuel exhaustion seemed remote in the time perspective of day-to-day economic activity (Brown, 1954).

There is evidence enough, then, that, with human ecological expansion occurring on an industrial basis, the previous stages have been left behind. It is much less certain that enough experience has yet accumulated to permit definitive characterization of industrialism itself as a "stage." An attempt to sketch some basic ecological relationships in industrial society must, therefore, be prefaced with the disclaimer of any hypothesis that these relationships are in a condition of stable equilibrium.

Industrial society is, most obviously, one in which technology assumes an increasingly dominant role. Flows of requisites increasingly are mediated by technological systems instead of being the outcome of a direct interchange between human activity and the environment. Contriving and operating technological systems become key functions, symbolized by a particular occupational role, the engineer. What is this role? One gesture toward a definition that is especially congenial to the present viewpoint reads as follows:

By and large engineers are paid by society to work on systems dealing with problems whose solutions are of interest to that society. These systems seem to group conveniently into (a) systems for material handling, including transformation of and conservation of raw and processed materials; (b) systems for energy handling, including its transformation, transmission, and control; and (c) systems for data or information handling, involving its collection, transmission, and processing (Harmon, Franzini, Ireson, & Kline, 1953, p. 258).

If the increase in the significance of this role can be roughly gauged by the numbers involved, the following series—number of "technical engineers" per one thousand of the economically active population in the United States—is informative:

1900	.... 1.3	1940	.... 5.7
1910	.... 2.1	1950	.... 9.2
1920	.... 3.2	1960	....12.8
1930	.... 4.5		

The expansion of the engineering profession, 1900 to 1960, was 10 times as great as that of the entire working force.

With regard to materials, technological expansion means using increasingly varied kinds of materials and processing them through more and more elaborate transformations to secure closely specified and highly specialized properties. Materials in use become more remotely related to the original input of raw materials. Flows of materials become so voluminous and so intricate in pattern as to defy statistical description. The most valiant effort to date has resulted in a table that shows for each of some two hundred industries, the amount of its output (dollar value) purchased by each other industry as well as the amount taken by various sectors of "final demand" (Cumberland, 1956). Since, in this classification, only a small fraction of the industries are "services," the bulk of the information in the table applies to the actual physical movement of goods. The movement is in an "inter-industry" space, as far as the statistical definitions are concerned, but movement in geographic space is implied in most instances.

Two things are especially impressive about such an input-output table. First, despite the formidable amount of detail in the two hundred by two hundred matrix, the "industries" in many cases are fairly heterogeneous aggregates. The variety of goods produced under such a rubric as "office supplies" or "industrial organic chemicals" is quite great. Second, the number of cells in the table with nonzero entries is substantial. This means that nearly every industry is dependent for both supplies and markets on a considerable number of other industries. Indeed, it was a recognition of the complexities occasioned by this interdependence that led to the efforts of economic statisticians to estimate input-output relationships. A change in the level of production in any one industry will react back on the industries supplying its inputs, then on the industries providing inputs to its suppliers, and so on. Even approximate calculation of the ramifying effects of changes in an interdependent system of this kind has called for new developments in matrix mathematics and computer techniques.

If to the complexities of inter-industry analysis is added a concern with geographic patterns of materials flows, the tasks of description and analysis become too formidable for present-day data-collection and processing procedures to handle, even though conceptual expositions of the problem exist and the problem is soluble in principle (Isard, 1960, Ch. 8; Isard & Kavesh, 1954). The scanty amount of direct information on geographical flows indicates that even a sizeable region—and, a fortiori, a local area—is far from self-contained with respect to such flows. An industrial ecosystem, indeed, is one in which a fairly definite spatial hierarchy emerges, even though it can be described in only very general terms. There is a "core" area, comparatively small in geographic extent but containing a concentration of population and economic activity; it carries out the bulk of the activity which transforms materials into economic goods. Throughout a much larger area some manufacturing is carried on; typically it has to do with the early stages of a production sequence—"processing," as contrasted with "fabricating," to suggest a very crude distinction. Processing activities often are located in terms of access to natural resources and raw materials production. Since these tend to reflect local or regional environmental features, the character of processing activity varies considerably over space. Figure 6 depicts some of the elements of this type of spatial structure.

Much of the foregoing discussion applies

to flows of energy as well as materials, for all transformations and movements of materials require energy inputs, whether these derive from human effort directly or, as is characteristic of industrialism by definition, mostly from nonhuman sources. So basic is the energy supply to the materials flows that it has been claimed that there is no such thing as a shortage of materials, if only sufficient energy be available to concentrate and process the materials in the earth's crust and atmosphere (Brown, 1954, Ch. 6). An indication has been given (see Table 1) of the amounts of energy involved in running an industrial society. Some recognition should also be given to the extent to which the system depends on interconversion of forms of energy. Large amounts of coal (potential chemical energy) are burned to produce heat energy, changing water to steam, which drives generators (kinetic mechanical energy) producing energy in electrical form; the latter is transmitted over considerable distances and applied to drive motors (mechanical energy), to which are attached the machines doing useful work. The accompanying diagram of energy flows in the United States (Figure 7) makes it clear that only a minor fraction of all energy produced is used in primary form; the bulk of it is processed through various stages before finding its way to users.

Industrialism represents a "technologizing" of information flows no less than materials and energy flows. The volume of information required is far greater than at any prior stage of evolution; flows are increasingly mediated by complex technology; whole sectors of the economy come to specialize in one or another phase of the production, distribution, and application of information; and this specialization fosters a high degree of functional and territorial interdependence among parts of the system.

Something of the magnitude and complexity of information flows in an industrial system is conveyed by a recent survey by Machlup (1962) in which an effort is made to catalog the varieties of information

(Machlup prefers the term knowledge), to analyze the division of labor in knowledge-production and dissemination, and to estimate the quantities of manpower and money allocated to these functions. The study (pp. 361–362) indentifies five sectors of the information industry in the United States and estimates that total expenditures for their products amounted to $136 billion in 1958, or no less than 29 per cent of the nation's (adjusted) Gross National Product. Expenditures by sector, in percentages of the total of $136 billion, were as follows:

Education 44.1
Research and development 8.1
Media of communication 28.1
Information machines 6.5
Information services (incomplete) . . 13.2

Total 100.0

Another estimate of considerable interest, despite the inadequacies of statistical time series, indicates that the growth rate of the aggregate of information industries was about 2.5 times as great as that of the remainder of the economy during the decade preceding 1958 (Machlup, 1962, p. 374).

Another kind of observation on the role of information flows in an industrial system is that a high proportion of all transactions and transfers of materials, energy, and information is registered in exchanges of money or claims to money. Of all devices to facilitate movement of information, money may be second only to writing itself in its significance for the operation of a system of interdependent differentiated parts. As it happens, in the United States, a goodly proportion of exchanges expressed in monetary terms are mediated by banks, and the volume of banking activity is, therefore, suggestive of the amount of one kind of information flowing in the system. A significant example is given in Table 2. The Federal Reserve System in the United States is divided into 36 zones, the territories of the 12 Federal Reserve Banks and the 24 branches. Most transactions across the boundaries of zones

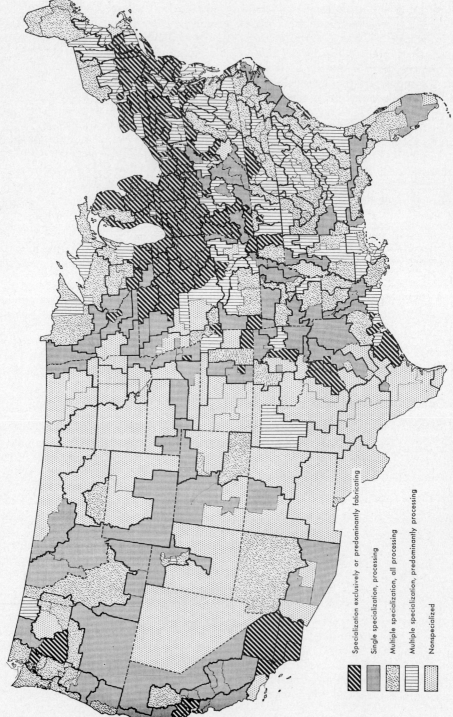

Specialization exclusively or predominantly fabricating

Single specialization, processing

Multiple specialization, all processing

Multiple specialization, predominantly processing

Nonspecialized

Fig. 6. Type of Manufacturing Specialization, 1950, by State Economic Areas (Source: Perloff, 1963, p. 45).

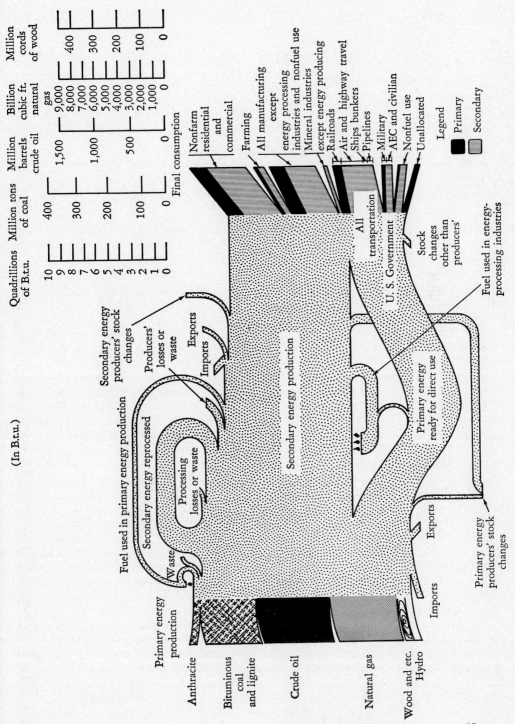

Fig. 7. Consolidated origin and distribution of all energy in the United States, 1954 (Source: Teitelbaum, 1961).

TABLE 2

INTERDISTRICT SETTLEMENT FUND CLEARINGS BETWEEN
SELECTED FEDERAL RESERVE SYSTEM ZONES
FOR A TOTAL OF FOUR WEEKS IN 1957[a]

To	Credits ($ million) Sent by					
	Boston	Atlanta	St. Louis	Kansas City	Minneapolis	San Francisco
Boston	—	15	30	13	29	47
Atlanta	19	—	12	9	5	41
St. Louis	26	18	—	149	32	48
Kansas City	11	6	136	—	56	81
Minneapolis	29	3	21	45	—	182
San Francisco	57	47	45	88	202	—

[a] Unpublished records of the Federal Reserve System; see Duncan, Scott, Lieberson, Duncan, & Winsborough (1960, Ch. 6).

are reflected in clearings of the Interdistrict Settlement Fund. Records of these clearings, therefore, reflect the volume of transactions *between* regions of the country. The full record comprises a 36 by 36 table compiled weekly; an illustrative excerpt from this table appears in Table 2. The reader may be impressed by the considerable magnitudes of the flows, even between widely separated regions. He may also perceive a tendency for the volume of flows to assume a definite spatial orientation (compare, e.g., flows to and from the St. Louis and Kansas City zones) as well as a tendency for volume to be related inversely to distance. These characteristics are confirmed upon closer analysis of the entire flow table (Duncan, Scott, Lieberson, Duncan, & Winsborough, 1960, Ch. 6). The money amounts themselves represent a staggering quantity of information processing—pen-pushing and paper-shuffling. The transactions lying behind them make up an intricate territorial division of labor which can function at a high level of output only if information moves rapidly and inexpensively.

Implied in the emergence of industrialism is an evolution of environment. Technological systems operate in many respects in an "artificial" environment of structures, artifacts, and installations. A journalist's report on *The World Beneath the City* (Daley,

1959) describes a fantastic environment of pipes, mains, wires, railroad tracks, tunnels, and conduits under the streets, sidewalks, and buildings. of New York. As Wagner (1960, p. 225) indicates, the environment of modern industrialism "represents the incorporation of more different natural substances into an artificial complex than are found under any other technical system." Besides creating a pervasive "artificial" environment, therefore, technology makes ever-increasing demands upon and alterations of the "natural" environment. Technology is, in effect, a redefinition of the environment. As Zimmermann (1951, Part 1) has argued, the positive and negative features of the environment—"resources" and "resistances"—are strictly relative to the technology available to exploit or cope with the external world. Deposits of each substance whose useful properties are learned become "resources" as the knowledge is put into effect. For this reason, the environment of industrial technology is vastly richer in resources than that of any prior regime.

It is sometimes claimed that technological advance has rendered man increasingly "independent" of his environment. This inherently ambiguous statement is likely to be misleading. Its measure of truth is made evident by considering a spatially delimited population and the region of the earth's surface it inhabits. It is then the case that industrial technology may "free" the population from sole dependence on the resources of the region, inasmuch as resources are made available from many other regions. It also is true that the hazards and resistances of the region can be confronted more confidently, since they can be overcome by means not indigenous to the region. Both aspects of freedom from the *local* environment, however, put the population in a position of greater dependence upon environmental resources of other regions. The industrial technology that fosters interregional interdependence, moreover, simultaneously intensifies the exploitation of, and hence dependence on, resources in all regions. Taking more from the environment and reacting back upon the environment in more varied and drastic ways, industrial man has carried the process of "living into" the environment beyond any precedent. How far the process has gone can be made evident only by pooling the information of a small army of specialists, as in the monumental symposium, *Man's Role in Changing the Face of the Earth* (Thomas, 1956).

To the biologist, who achieves a welcome simplification of his problem by regarding human factors as external to nature, man's role often seems to be that of a creature who tampers with, plunders, disrupts, damages, interferes with, and spoils the balance of the ecosystem. Despite the colorful terminology, the biologist's perception is sound: Industrialized peoples do effect pervasive and ramifying changes in the ecosystem. Not all of these changes, whatever their short-run advantage to some segment of an industrial society, are likely to be to the ultimate net benefit of mankind. Problems like the pollution of water and air, the local exhaustion of mineral deposits and stands of timber, and the disappearance of useful wildlife, become evident as they impinge upon the health, pleasure, and incomes of persons directly affected. Much of the aggregate effect of environmental deterioration may be masked, however, by a statistical illusion.

The efforts of air pollution control officers are recompensed by salaries. These salaries, since they are earned in the labor market, appear in the national accounts as part of the Gross National Product—rightly so, for the national welfare is undoubtedly greater because of these efforts than it would be in their absence. Yet, another system of bookkeeping would show expenditures for mitigating industrialism's untoward effects on the environment as loss rather than gain.

The point is not to make a romantic case against industrialism—evolution, as we have seen, is essentially irreversible—but to bring home the ecologist's basic point: A way of life and its setting comprise an interdependent unity. Either is regarded as extrinsic to the other only at the peril of overlooking the interrelations on which depends the viability of the system as a whole.

At least since the writings of Karl Marx, it has been recognized that industrialism ushered in a new era in human population growth. A vivid restatement of the idea of demographic eras has been provided by Deevey (1960). He posits three main surges in world population. The first, beginning, say, one million years ago with the emergence of tool-making, accomplished the dispersion of humanity over much of the face of the globe and brought the total numbers to a few million. The second, commencing roughly ten thousand years ago with the development of food production, brought an increase to a few hundreds of millions. The third, the industrial era, getting under way within the last thousand years, has brought the total to some three billion, with a current growth rate sufficient to double that total within forty years. What the equilibrium population might be in a world fully industrialized no one yet knows how to calculate.

Within each of these eras, of course, there occurred population fluctuations which were more or less localized and of varying amplitude and duration. As distinct from transitions between major eras, these may perhaps be regarded as variations around an equilibrium or as erratic movements toward equilibrium between numbers and the requisites for their support.

Demographers are prone to make a sharp distinction between the first two eras and the third on the basis of the mechanism of growth. Broadly speaking, the growth surge in all three eras must have been primarily the result of a lowering of mortality (increase in life expectancy). The approach toward equilibrium in the first two eras, however, presumably was accompanied by a rise in mortality. In the third era it is hoped, on the basis of the recent experience ("demographic transition") of European peoples, that equilibrium can be reached on the basis of lowered fertility, so that demographic balance might for once be maintained by "controlled" vital rates. It must be observed, however, that the termination of the growth surge of the industrial era through a rise in mortality is "unthinkable" only because we *hope* that it will not occur. Actually, such a rise is all too thinkable, if world politics should unloose a major war, if the world economy should be disrupted, or if public health measures and controls should be impaired. Industrial populations are like the acrobat on a tight rope—their position is unstable, even though they possess vast skill and resourcefulness in coping with incipient displacements.

There is another significant feature of the third era. The first two growth surges were directly supported by advances in techniques of securing food. The industrial era, however, is one whose characteristic advances are in the field of inanimate energy sources. How these worked indirectly to secure the requisite augmentation of food supply is a problem that is poorly understood. Several suggestions are plausible. The industrial revolution (recall that we are dating its origin much earlier than the conventional period of the steam engine and textile machinery) afforded energy supplies for bringing more land under cultivation. Improvements in the arts of navigation and ocean transport, like later developments in land transportation,

enhanced interregional accessibility and thereby mitigated, if they did not eliminate, localized famines. They assured a more regular and varied diet in nonfamine periods as well. Furthermore, the age of exploration brought about a "veritable revolution," as M. K. Bennett (1954) calls it, in which New World food crops spread to Africa and Eurasia, and Old World plants and domesticated animals were introduced into the Americas. "The productivity of agriculture was greatly enhanced as the number of crops available and able to grow in a given locality was enlarged" (p. 36). Finally, there was a slow "scientific revolution" in agriculture, of which the medieval introduction of the three-field rotation system was the harbinger (Lynn White, 1962, Ch. 2). In our own time, we have seen what applied genetics and soil chemistry have done for yields per acre, given a literate class of agricultural producers receiving the information output of the centers of scientific research.

The other aspect of lowered mortality, which is indeed unique to the industrial era, is the "control" of disease. One thinks first of the dramatic results of mass immunization, pest eradication, and antibiotic therapy in recent decades. The process of disease control, however, has a somewhat longer history. Guardians of the public health and urban sanitarians were able to achieve important reductions of death rates in the nineteenth century, proceeding on the basis of empiricism and common sense in the absence of sound general theories of etiology (Rogers, 1962). It is not often realized, moreover, that diseases have their own patterns of evolution, adapting to the life conditions of the host in sometimes obscure ways. An experienced public health officer was once heard to remark that, if a disease is on the increase, no measure of control can halt it; while if it is on the downgrade, control measures must be instituted quickly, else the disease will disappear of its own accord. McKeown and Record (1962) note that the trend in scarlet fever was responsible for about one-fifth of the decline in mortality in nineteenth-century England and Wales. The disease has fluctuated greatly in severity.

These changes . . . appear to have been largely independent of the environmental changes which we have been discussing in relation to the other infections, and there is no reason to differ from the general opinion that they have resulted from a change in the nature of the disease. This change was probably due mainly to variation in the virulence of the hæmolytic streptococcus rather than to modification of man's response to it (McKeown & Record, 1962, p. 117).

Elton (1927, pp. 52–53) observes that the Black Death (plague) disappeared after the plague-carrying black rat (*Rattus rattus*) was driven out of Europe by the brown rat (*R. norvegicus*), which was adapted to life in the urban sewers "being installed in some of the European towns as a result of the onrush of civilisation." The ecologist is led to wonder what might happen if rat-control programs in seacoast cities were really to succeed in eliminating *R. norvegicus*. Would a niche then be opened up again for *R. rattus,* which is still to be found on the ships plying between world ports?

Accompanying the major population surges were changes in population distribution that are almost equally diagnostic of the three eras. As we have seen, Paleolithic man spread all over the globe, reaching the New World as early as about thirty thousand years ago. As each principal region was opened up, we may assume on Birdsell's argument (1957) that it was quickly populated to an equilibrium density, a low one by subsequent standards. Population concentration—i.e., local variation in density—was comparatively slight, as population tended to be fairly uniformly spread. Variation in density was a rather direct reflection of climatic and topographic factors (Birdsell, 1953).

During the second era, when growth was based on the spread of food production, population concentration was heightened. Density rose especially in areas of high soil fertility as they were brought under cultivation and in areas where control of water supply was achieved. Preindustrial cities in some instances attained substantial size, but there were not many extremely large ones. It is doubtful that more than 10 or 15 per cent of the population in any of the ancient empires was urban.

The industrial era, as it brought advances in agricultural technique, afforded the basis for heightened population density in agricultural areas. Its major contribution to the increase of population concentration, however, was the stimulus of industrialism to the growth of towns and cities—not only those that were the sites of manufacturing establishments, but also those which collected and concentrated the raw materials and agricultural support of the industrial towns and served as distribution centers for rural hinterlands. The more recent phases of industrialism assumed a pattern that Gras (1922) has called the "metropolitan economy," typified by the emergence of centers of control, coordination, and mediation of the production-distribution processes of industrializing societies. An excellent description is to be found in a neglected paper by one of the founders of human ecology, McKenzie (1927):

The expansion of Western civilization is a result of the development of transportation and communication. The region of dominance expands as the agencies of communication improve. . . . as the impediments to movement are overcome, the world becomes organized on the pattern of a spider's web. The entire physical shell through which civilization functions is becoming a complexly interrelated entity in which the fundamental relation of parts is that of dominance and subordination. The axiate pattern of spatial distribution with the relation of dominance and subordination among the interdependent parts is becoming a world distribution pattern. . . . The extension of the market made possible by modern communication is producing regional specialization of production, and therefore territorial integration, to a degree unknown in the past. The modern world is integrated through information collected and distributed from fixed centers of dominance. . . . Modern dominance penetrates new parts of the world in catastrophic fashion; that is, large-scale industry or business breaks into undeveloped or differently developed parts of the world in a sudden and mature form. It is only the large organization that can afford to invade new parts of the world. Consequently the invasion comes, not as a slow growth, but as a sudden burst of power producing revolutionary effects upon the space and sustenance relations of the indigenous inhabitants. . . . The world's centers of gravity are always in process of change. Old centers lose their relative importance as new factors enter to disturb the equilibrium. Some of the factors are temporary and accidental; others are associated with permanent trends. The world is gradually becoming a closed area (McKenzie, 1927, pp. 32, 35, 37, 42, quotations rearranged).

McKenzie's observations assume, of course, a historical background of developments in social organization accompanying the ecological changes previously described. As we have seen, industrialism represents an accumulation of technological advances; it is predicated on a much more far-reaching division of labor than any previous stage of expansion. The early civilizations had already introduced a symbiosis (sometimes, perhaps, verging toward the parasitic form) between nonproducers and producers of food and were able to accumulate sufficient resources to sustain some specialization of functions within the former sector. The division of labor was nonetheless fairly rudimentary. As Childe (1951a) notes, there were some spectacular early examples of "foreign trade," and the Romans performed the feat of feeding an urban proletariat with the grain produced throughout a wide territory. Yet these instances are impressive because regional self-sufficiency or a near approximation thereto was the norm. Industrialism, however, generates a demand for such a varied list of raw materials that no region can contain them all. Correlatively, it achieves the technologically possible economies of scale on the basis of extreme

specialization of function, only if the market is large, which usually means territorially extended.

There is, no doubt, a reciprocal relationship among the division of labor, population growth, and technological expansion. Adam Smith laid it down as an axiom that the division of labor is limited by the extent of the market, and Durkheim (1947) concerned himself with the social mechanisms through which an extension of the market is translated into an increased differentiation of functions (Schnore, 1958). Ayres (1962, p. xvi) has provided a vigorous plea for due recognition of the technological factor: "As it is the state of the industrial arts that gives occasion to exchange, so the extent of the market must always be limited by the state of the industrial arts." Here, as in all cases of cumulative processes, or "circular causation," our appreciation of the reciprocal character of multiple influences outruns our skill in analyzing their interrelations.

The major point for the moment is that a process creating differences or divisions is likely to give rise to mechanisms which link the divisions or bridge the differences. Industrialism, beyond the point of its earliest manifestations, brings into being a pattern of centers, routes, and rims and a stratification of functions into those of the center, those of the field, and those relating center and field. No simple one- or two-dimensional representation of this structure can convey all the principles of differentiation or all the types of linkage between functions and places.

Systematic classifications of labor-force data, however, reveal some basic aspects of the structure. In Table 3 there is a demonstration of how the composition of the labor force by broad functional categories varies by size of community. Extractive industries (principally agriculture and mining) are, of course, "field" activities par excellence; they bulk larger in the total of gainful pursuits the smaller the community and especially in territory lying outside sizeable nucleated settlements. Processing industries, being ori-

TABLE 3

PERCENTAGE DISTRIBUTION OF THE EMPLOYED LABOR FORCE BY BROAD INDUSTRY CATEGORIES, BY SIZE OF PLACE, FOR THE UNITED STATES: 1950[a]

Size of Place	Percentage Distribution					
	All industries[b]	Extractive	Manufacturing		Services	
			Processing	Fabricating	Local	Non-local
Urbanized areas						
3,000,000 or more	100.0	0.7	10.3	23.3	29.3	36.4
1,000,000 to 3,000,000	100.0	0.6	11.9	22.7	29.0	35.8
250,000 to 1,000,000	100.0	1.5	12.1	17.8	31.9	36.7
50,000 to 250,000	100.0	1.7	14.6	18.4	31.7	33.6
Other urban						
25,000 or more	100.0	2.5	14.7	15.2	33.9	33.7
10,000 to 25,000	100.0	4.5	15.6	13.5	34.4	32.0
2,500 to 10,000	100.0	7.6	15.5	11.0	35.5	30.4
Rural						
Nonfarm	100.0	15.8	16.5	12.1	29.1	26.5
Farm	100.0	76.2	6.2	3.6	6.8	7.2

[a] Duncan, Scott, Lieberson, Duncan, & Winsborough (1960, p. 60).
[b] Base excludes "Construction" and "Industry not reported."

ented toward resource extractors as sources of inputs, reproduce this pattern, albeit in attenuated form. Fabricating, by contrast, gravitates toward "centers" located fairly high up in the hierarchy. Service activities can be roughly classified into those whose clientele is in the immediate vicinity of the service installation and those with a considerable volume of nonlocal contacts. Nonlocal service activities—particularly business and financial services, wholesale trade, and certain transportation services—are concentrated toward the larger centers, and the local services account for a higher proportion of activity in small places.

Intensive analysis along lines suggested by such relationships demonstrates that one salient principle of industrial social organization is an *urban hierarchy* (Duncan et al., 1960, Ch. 3). Viewed in terms of specific oc-

cupations rather than the broad industry categories just mentioned, the most striking feature of the hierarchy is the concentration of *clerical* jobs in large centers. No less than 18 per cent of the employment in the largest places was in this occupation group in 1950; the percentage was 14 per cent in places of 50,000 to 100,000 and only 9 per cent in places of 1,000 to 2,500 inhabitants (Duncan & Reiss, 1956, p. 96). The presumption is that variation in proportion of clerical jobs reflects a tendency for the information-handling, coordinating, and administrative tasks to be concentrated in large centers, irrespective of the functional class of the activity in which these tasks are performed. · It is not necessary to rely wholly on statistics of labor force distribution—although these are the most comprehensive available— to demonstrate a territorial hierarchy of function and control. Pappenfort (1959), for example, discovered a gradient of dominance by major centers in the management of manufacturing enterprises in his study of the respective location patterns of branch plants and their home offices.

Human ecologists doubtless have made the most progress in uncovering the territorial or settlement aspects of the division of labor in industrial societies. Their concern with general principles of organizational morphology has not carried over so much into investigations wherein the spatial axis of classification is absent. The division of labor needs to be analyzed in terms of the kinds of units that are formed, their scale of operations and patterns of control, and the extent of concentration evidenced by their distributions with respect to size of personnel complement, amount of resources, and volume of output. The theme of "big business" and "small business," for example, can be approached morphologically as well as from the strictly economic point of view.

According to a recent and novel compilation of census data on "enterprises" (U.S. Bureau of the Census, 1963), there were in 1958 some 270,000 companies engaged primarily in manufacturing. They operated some 380,000 geographically distinct establishments and employed more than 17,000,000 workers. Now, the vast bulk of these companies represented quite small operations. About 72 per cent of them were single-unit (one establishment per company) companies employing fewer than 20 persons each. In the aggregate, this 72 per cent accounted for only 6.5 per cent of all employees of manufacturing companies. At the opposite extremes of size, scale, and complexity of operations were some 363 companies, only 0.13 per cent of the total, in the category of multi-unit, multi-industry companies, each employing 5,000 or more workers and operating an average of 170 establishments each. This mere .13 per cent of all companies accounted, in total, for no less than 40 per cent of all employees of manufacturing companies. (A multi-industry company is one

with establishments—that is, plants or factories—in 2 or more of the 855 individual industries used in classifying establishments in the 1958 censuses of manufactures and business.)

Similar indications of wide variation in company size and concentration of employment in large concerns are observed in sectors other than manufacturing. The multi-unit pattern of organization, however, has become most widespread there. The percentages of total employment accounted for by multi-unit companies varied as follows over the six major sectors covered by the censuses: manufacturing, 67.4; mineral industries, 56.7; retail trade, 40.2; public warehousing, 34.6; wholesale trade, 29.8; selected service trades, 27.5.

The conception of industrial social organization that begins to form upon inspection of such statistics, partial as is their coverage and crude as their analytical categories may be, is that of multiple organizational pyramids. We have no comprehensive enumeration of organizational units, and few indeed of their functional linkages are adequately depicted in statistics. Yet it can be surmised that the complex social structure arising in the course of industrialization comprehends a spectrum of organizational types. At one end is the "political" sector, which provides us with the model of a nested or partially nested hierarchy of governmental jurisdictions—a hierarchy paralleled, incidentally, by one comprising the structure of the organizations (parties) which are oriented to the securing and the exercise of the powers of government. At the other end is the model of a plurality of autonomous, variable and stratified, but functionally equivalent units—the economist's model of a system of "pure competition," now evidently absent from most sectors of the economy, but typified by the aggregate of consumption units or households. Varying between these extremes are the several industries or sector-aggregates of related industries each of which, as we have seen, comprises a collection of units highly variable in size and scale and functionally linked to other units of the same or different category in a variety of patterns.

To this complex array of what Hawley (1950, Ch. 12) has called "corporate" units must be added an account of the various types of "categoric" units which intersect the former in various ways. Some analysis of their proliferation in modern industrial society has been given in Boulding's *The Organizational Revolution* (1953). This work emphasizes innovations in information technology as a basis for the large-scale combinations of individuals and units with like interests, as exemplified by labor unions, trade associations, farmers' organizations, pressure groups, professional associations, and the like.

Sociologists have approached the problem of social stratification primarily from the standpoint of persistent patterns of inequality among persons or families with respect to prestige status, levels of living, and the correlates thereof. The foregoing remarks should point to the desirability of enlarging the concept of stratification. Not only individuals or families, but also populations of any kind of organizational units may be stratified. Stratification may be manifested not only in simple inequality in respect to command of resources, but may also take the form of interunit, intersectoral, and interarea linkages with a hierarchical or partially hierarchical arrangement of control. Relations between corporate and categoric units, though inadequately depicted by the simple metaphor of "strata," represent the exercise of dominance, albeit diffused by the intricacy of the patterns of such relations.

In summary, ecological expansion in the phases of social evolution influenced by industrialism may be characterized by a formula, the four terms in which have been called the "ecological complex" (Duncan, 1959; Duncan, 1961): technological accumulation at an accelerated rate; intensified exploitation of environment; demographic transition (now popularly known as "population explosion"); and organizational revo-

lution. As the causal interconnections of these developments are further elucidated by research, a truly ecological understanding of social organization may emerge. Perhaps one day a human ecologist will write the treatise of which he can say, with Ibn Khaldûn:

In the work, I commented on civilization, on urbanization, and on the essential characteristics of human social organization, in a way that explains to the reader how and why things are as they are. . . .

HUMAN ECOLOGY

In the foregoing pages, little has been said of human ecology as a discipline. The concern has been not to outline the concepts of a specialized science, but to convey some implications of a point of view. There is, indeed, cause for uncertainty as to whether human ecology is, or should be recognized as, a field in its own right or a subfield of one of the established academic departments. A little intellectual history may make an interesting epilogue, since the problems with which our predecessors grappled have found no final solutions.

The word ecology (œcology), a derivative from the Greek *oikos* (household), although it was used by Henry David Thoreau and apparently was familiar to his correspondents (Oehser, 1959), appeared in scientific discourse as a proposal of Ernst Haeckel, a disciple of Charles Darwin (Stauffer, 1957). Darwin (1873) had a keen appreciation of the "infinitely complex relations" of a species "to other organic beings and to their physical conditions of life" (p. 49) as well as the extent of "our ignorance on the mutual relations of all organic beings; a conviction as necessary, as it is difficult to acquire" (p. 61). He had, of course, developed the hypothesis that all the grand and wondrous complexity in the interdependence of forms of life could be explained (in principle) as a consequence of natural selection working upon variable heredity, given the impulse of all manifestations of life to expand. The insight that expansion played a key role in evolutionary differentiation, Darwin tells us, came as he pondered the theses of Thomas R. Malthus on population growth and the means of subsistence.

Although Darwin expected his doctrine to clarify the history of man, neither he nor Haeckel was ready to extend the ecological viewpoint to the explicit concern with human populations. A period of preparation was needed. In the late decades of the nineteenth century, plant ecology was firmly established, and application of ecological principles in animal population and community studies came early in the twentieth century.

It is curious that the Ecological Society of America, whose official journal began publication in 1920, included, at the time of its founding, members eager to consider human ecology as part of the discipline. Efforts along this line soon died out after a few exploratory sessions and tentative gestures. Ecologists were not equipped for the task. Even more important, they were not prepared to grapple with the implications of the proposition that "the ecological system of the existing twentieth-century world must include the twentieth-century man as its dominant species—dominant, that is, in the sense of dynamic ecology as the most influential, the controlling member of his associate group," which was put to them by an able member of their own ranks in a paper, "The Humanizing of Ecology" (Forbes, 1922). As an eminent animal ecologist (Darling, 1955, p. 121) later noted somewhat ruefully, "When some bold spirit began talking of human ecology he was promptly excommunicated." It fell, therefore, to the social scientists to pick up the idea of human ecology. This was appropriate enough, since ecology had been from its outset largely preoccupied with interrelations of organisms dependent one upon the other, and not with the mere "external physiology" of the individual. It was, in other words, a sociological orientation to the world of life. (For a time, the term "phytosociology"

actually competed with "plant ecology.")

Within the social science arena, the period of preparation for human ecology had been equally long if not longer. Intellectual appreciation of environmental factors was at least as old as the Greeks. The thoughts of Ibn Khaldûn which clearly adumbrate our present concerns were paralleled by discussions of subsequent European thinkers, Montesquieu for one (Durkheim, 1960b). As social science, *strictu senso,* emerged from political and moral philosophy in the nineteenth century, empirical studies were made by a series of vigorous investigators now easily recognized as the forerunners of present-day human ecologists (Theodorson, 1961, pp. 8–21). In this, as in other areas, the availability of reliable statistical information was certainly one of the foundation stones of empirical social science, which inherited an important legacy from the earlier tradition of demography or "political arithmetic," a field, interestingly enough, in which both natural and social scientists had made important contributions (Cole, 1957). Thus, there was a substantial basis laid for the labors of such a prodigious worker as Charles Booth, who busied himself in late nineteenth-century London discovering the very regularities of urban morphology that were to become the mainstay of human ecology in America a generation or two later. Not to neglect the conceptual side, it can be observed that the turn of the century found Émile Durkheim in France expounding his notions of "social morphology" (Durkheim, 1960a) while C. H. Cooley in this country was proposing a new discipline of "territorial demography." Both, it seems, had been influenced by and were reacting to German developments in "Anthropogeographie." A brief account of these developments appears in the translators' preface to Halbwachs' (1960) little volume, which was the summation of the French tradition by a scholar who had had a fructifying contact with the American human ecologists.

As it happened, just at the time the Ecological Society of America was engaged in its abortive foray into human ecology, sociologists at the University of Chicago, guided by Robert E. Park, had seized upon the term to designate the study of the "forces at work within the limits of the urban community—within the limits of any natural area of human habitation, in fact—which tend to bring about an orderly and typical grouping of its population and institutions" (Park, 1925; reprinted in Park, 1952, p. 14). Upon the foundation of a community's ecology, it was assumed, was erected a structure of economic, political, and moral life. This view proved useful as a temporary scaffolding for an impressive body of field research which, indeed, constituted much of the demonstration that a systematic empirical science of society is a realistic possibility. In time, attention was to become focused more on defects in the scaffolding than on the qualities of the structure it had served to produce. There was spawned a literature of critiques and polemics. It is possible to arrange the history of human ecology, if attention is confined to the writings of sociologists, in terms of the positions taken by the adversaries in the controversies. A useful anthology of these writings has been organized on this principle (Theodorson, 1961).

It appears, nevertheless, that the "criticisms of the classical position" which Theodorson has brought together missed the most important point while identifying serious symptomatic weaknesses in the "classical" writings. It was perfectly true, as the critics asserted, that human ecology in the exposition of Park, for example, rested on an *analogy*. He likened the "natural area" of human habitation to the plant community in which an "economy" develops on the basis of unconscious, impersonal relations of competitive cooperation. The analogy conveyed an insight, for, as far as we can tell, such complex forms of human settlement as the metropolis may indeed come into existence without a preconceived design and perform functions that are not realizations of the desires of anyone in particular. In identifying the "biotic" aspect of the human

community with processes that are not explicit in the verbal tradition and linguistic communication of the group, however, Park left to human ecology a subject matter that could be defined only in residual terms. The insight that some social processes yield important but latent and unanticipated structural patterns was ultimately to be overburdened by the analogy initially used to convey the insight.

It must be acknowledged that there is no real harm in using the patterns disclosed by animal and plant ecology as models for initial characterizations of human communities. Boulding (1958, pp. 14-16), for example, conveys a vivid sense of the extent of interdependence in human affairs by indicating how human society is "something like" an ecosystem. At the same time, the analogy quickly plays out, as all analogies must. More important, it lays no firm basis for elaborating a genuinely ecological approach to human collective life. You cannot throw away what is most distinctively human—communication with symbols, custom, and the artificial or cultural transformations man makes in his environment—and treat the residue as the ecology of the species. There is no need, of course, to adopt such a strategy. The whole burden of this chapter has been to show how human culture and social organization develop ecologically. A partitioning of the world of human affairs into the ecological and the nonecological is not used. When examined from an ecological standpoint, social evolution and social organization are subject matter for human ecology. They can, of course, be examined from other viewpoints as well (Duncan & Schnore, 1959).

It is probably true, however, that arguments about conceptual issues of this sort become tiresome and are forgotten before all their nuances can be stated and evaluated. In point of fact, the progress of human ecology was resumed when interest waned in establishing or discrediting its claims as a school of thought and turned toward a more careful examination of its problems.

In retrospect, the turning point was a paper by Hawley (1944) in which, entirely contrary to the then prevailing tenor of criticism, he asserted: "Probably most of the difficulties which beset human ecology may be traced to the isolation of the subject from the mainstream of ecological thought." Identifying that mainstream as a concern with generic features of the problem of organization as experienced by populations constrained to cope with the exigencies of their environments, Hawley (1950) went on to provide the only systematic and comprehensive presentation of an empirically grounded conceptual framework for human ecology that has yet been published. (The useful textbook by Quinn [1950], which appeared at the same time, was primarily a summary of the Chicago-style urban research studies.) The present chapter, though explicit references are few, is to be regarded as primarily an extension of some of the elements in Hawley's work.

Since 1950—though relevant work had been accumulating for quite some time— two major factors have influenced the development of human ecology at the hands of sociologists. First, a considerable volume of empirical work has been reported in which some of the classic preoccupations of human ecologists were represented in studies having a wider empirical basis and controlled by increasing methodological sophistication. In this work there can be discerned, as well, a determination to investigate social organization from an ecological standpoint for the sake of the intrinsic interest of such inquiry, rather than as a mere baseline for inquiries governed by quite different conceptual schemes. No adequate summary of post-1950 research in human ecology exists, but portions of the work have been reviewed by Duncan (1957; 1959).

The second influence was the growing pressure of the interest in human ecology and the productivity in that area on the part of scientists in disciplines other than sociology. A review of ecological work in the field of *anthropology* (Helm, 1962) discloses not only that this discipline long has had an implicit concern with ecological problems, but also that recent formulations have secured a firm place for this concern in the anthropologist's general outlook on man and society. Some of the signal contributions from anthropology have been mentioned earlier in this chapter. *Geography,* recovering at last from its traumatic encounter with environmentalism, has been able to become more convincing on behalf of its early claim (Barrows, 1923) that many of the geographer's inquiries represent ecological interpretations of phenomena on the earth's surface (Wagner, 1960). The term medical or human ecology has been applied increasingly to the field traditionally called *epidemiology* (Gordon, 1958; Rogers, 1962). The new terminology signifies a recognition that health is indeed a man-society-environment relation, and not a scalar quantity that can be measured or manipulated apart from this relation. If the medical ecologists' interest in social organization as such is slight, their readiness to capitalize on the conceptual insights and methodological skills of sociologists, not to mention the recent availability of large quantities of federal funds for public health research, has re-awakened sociological interest in one of the topics where human ecologists first made an important impact (Faris & Dunham, 1939). Still other fields are exhibiting more or less serious interest in ecology as a source of concepts, hypotheses, and procedures. It may suffice only to mention that *psychology,* remote from ecology though its traditional concerns have been, has witnessed an interesting attempt to attack some of its basic conceptual problems from an ecological point of view (Barker, 1960). In sum, the sociologist who would remain receptive to progress in elucidating the basic principles of human ecology finds that he cannot suffer his interest to be confined to a narrow range of subject matter. On our earlier argument, a pluralistic environment should bode well for the expansion of human ecology.

REFERENCES

Adams, R. M. Early civilizations, subsistence and environment. In C. H. Kraeling & R. M. Adams (Eds.), *City invincible.* Chicago: Univer. of Chicago Press, 1960. Pp. 269–295.

Allee, W. C. *The social life of animals.* (rev. ed.) Boston: Beacon Press, 1958.

Allee, W. C., Emerson, A. E., Park, O., Park, T., & Schmidt, K. P. *Principles of animal ecology.* Philadelphia: W. B. Saunders, 1949.

Ayres, C. E. *The theory of economic progress.* (2nd ed.) New York: Schocken Books, 1962.

Bagby, P. *Culture and history.* Berkeley: Univer. of California Press, 1959.

Barker, R. G. Ecology and motivation. In M. R. Jones (Ed.), *Nebraska symposium on motivation.* Lincoln: Univer. of Nebraska Press, 1960. Pp. 1–49.

Barrows, H. H. Geography as human ecology. *Ann. Ass. Amer. Geographers,* 1923, **13**, 1–14.

Bartholomew, G. A., Jr., & Birdsell, J. B. Ecology and the protohominids. *Amer. Anthrogist,* 1953, **55**, 481–498.

Bennett, M. K. *The world's food.* New York: Harper, 1954.

Birdsell, J. B. Some environmental and cultural factors influencing the structuring of Australian aboriginal populations. *Amer. Naturalist,* 1953, **87** (suppl.), 171–207.

Birdsell, J. B. Some population problems involving Pleistocene man. *Cold Spring Harbor Sympos. quant. Biol.,* 1957, **22**, 47–68.

Boulding, K. E. *The organizational revolution.* New York: Harper, 1953.

Boulding, K. E. *Principles of economic policy.* Englewood Cliffs, N.J.: Prentice-Hall, Inc., 1958.

Boulding, K. E. *The image: Knowledge in life and society.* (paperback ed.) Ann Arbor: Univer. of Michigan Press, 1961.

Braidwood, R. J. *The Near East and the foundations for civilization.* Eugene: Oregon State System of Higher Education, 1952.

Braidwood, R. J., & Reed, C. A. The achievement and early consequences of food-production: A consideration of the archeological and natural-historical evidence. *Cold Spring Harbor Sympos. quant. Biol.,* 1957, **22**, 19–31.

Brown, H. *The challenge of man's future.* New York: Viking, 1954.

Cherry, C. *On human communication.* New York: Science Editions, 1961.

Childe, V. G. The urban revolution. *Town Planning Rev.,* 1950, **21**, 3–17.

Childe, V. G. *Man makes himself.* New York: Mentor Books, 1951. (a)

Childe, V. G. *Social evolution.* New York: Schuman, 1951. (b)

Clark, G. *Archaeology and society.* Cambridge, Mass.: Harvard Univer. Press, 1957.

Clark, G. *World prehistory: An outline.* Cambridge: Cambridge Univer. Press, 1961.

Clark, J. D. Human ecology during Pleistocene and later times in Africa south of the Sahara. *Curr. Anthro.,* 1960, **1**, 307–324.

Cole, L. C. Sketches of general and comparative demography. *Cold Spring Harbor Sympos. quant. Biol.,* 1957, **22**, 1–15.

Cottrell, F. *Energy and society.* New York: McGraw, 1955.

Coulborn, R. *The origin of civilized societies.* Princeton, N.J.: Princeton Univer. Press, 1959.

Cumberland, J. H. Interindustry analysis, new tool in economics. *Scientif. mon.,* 1956, **83**, 189–197.

Daley, R. *The world beneath the city.* Philadelphia: Lippincott, 1959.

Darling, F. F. Pastoralism in relation to populations of men and animals. In J. B. Cragg & N. W. Pirie (Eds.), *The numbers of man and animals.* Edinburgh: Oliver & Boyd, 1955. Pp. 121–127.

Darwin, C. *On the origin of species by means of natural selection.* (new ed. from the sixth Eng. ed., with additions and corrections) New York: D. Appleton, 1873.

Deevey, E. S., Jr. The human population. *Scientif. Amer.* 1960, **203** (3), 194–204.

Dewhurst, J. F., & Associates. *America's needs and resources: A new survey.* New York: Twentieth Century Fund, 1955.

Dice, L. R. *Man's nature and nature's man: The ecology of human communities.* Ann Arbor: Univer. of Michigan Press, 1955.

Dobzhansky, T. *Mankind evolving.* New Haven, Conn.: Yale Univer. Press, 1962.

Duncan, O. D. Population distribution and community structure. *Cold Spring Harbor Sympos. quant. Biol.,* 1957, **22**, 357–371.

Duncan, O. D. Human ecology and population studies. In P. M. Hauser & O. D. Duncan (Eds.), *The study of population*. Chicago: Univer. of Chicago Press, 1959. Pp. 678–716.

Duncan, O. D. From social system to ecosystem. *Sociol. Inquiry*, 1961, **31**, 140–149.

Duncan, O. D., & Reiss, A. J., Jr. *Social characteristics of urban and rural communities, 1950*. New York: Wiley, 1956.

Duncan, O. D., & Schnore, L. F. Cultural, behavioral, and ecological perspectives in the study of social organization. *Amer. J. Sociol.*, 1959, **65**, 132–146.

Duncan, O. D., Scott, W. R., Lieberson, S., Duncan, Beverly, & Winsborough, H. H. *Metropolis and region*. Baltimore: The Johns Hopkins Press, 1960.

Durkheim, E. *The division of labor in society*. (from the first and fifth Fr. eds., 1893 & 1926) G. Simpson (trans.). Glencoe, Ill.: Free Press, 1947.

Durkheim, E. *Montesquieu and Rousseau: Forerunners of sociology*. Ann Arbor: Univer. of Michigan Press, 1960. (a)

Durkheim, E. Sociology and its scientific field. In K. H. Wolff (Ed.), *Emile Durkheim, 1858–1917*. Columbus: Ohio State Univer. Press, 1960. Pp. 354–375. (b)

Eiseley, L. C. Fossil man and human evolution. In W. L. Thomas, Jr. (Ed.), *Current anthropology*. Chicago: Univer. of Chicago Press, 1956. Pp. 61–78.

Elton, C. *Animal ecology*. London: Sidgwick & Jackson, 1927.

Faris, R. E. L., & Dunham, H. W. *Mental disorders in urban areas*. Chicago: Univer. of Chicago Press, 1939.

Forbes, S. A. The humanizing of ecology. *Ecology*, 1922, **3**, 89–92.

Goldschmidt, W. *Man's way: A preface to the understanding of human society*. New York: Holt, Rinehart & Winston, 1959.

Gordon, J. E. Medical ecology and the public health. *Amer. J. med. Sci.*, 1958, **235**, 337–359.

Goudge, T. A. *The ascent of life*. Toronto: Univer. of Toronto Press, 1961.

Gras, N. S. B. *An introduction to economic history*. New York: Harper, 1922.

Halbwachs, M. *Population and society: Introduction to social morphology*. O. D. Duncan & H. W. Pfautz (trans.). New York: The Free Press of Glencoe, 1960.

Hallowell, A. I. The structural and functional dimensions of a human existence. *Quart. Rev. Biol.*, 1956, **31**, 88–101.

Hallowell, A. I. The protocultural foundations of human adaptation. In S. L. Washburn (Ed.), *Social life of early man*. Chicago: Aldine, 1961. Pp. 236–255.

Harmon, W. W., Franzini, J. B., Ireson, W. C., & Kline, S. J. Abstract report of the Stanford University Committee on Evaluation of Engineering Education. *J. engin. Educ.*, 1953, **44**, 258–260.

Hawley, A. H. Ecology and human ecology. *Soc. Forces*, 1944, **22**, 398–405.

Hawley, A. H. *Human ecology: A theory of community structure*. New York: Ronald Press, 1950.

Helm, J. The ecological approach in anthropology. *Amer. J. Sociol.*, 1962, **67**, 630–639.

Howell, F. C. Pleistocene glacial ecology and the evolution of "classic Neanderthal" man. *Southwest. J. Anthro.*, 1952, **8**, 377–410.

Howells, W. W. The distribution of man. *Sci. Amer.* 1960, **203** (3), 112–127.

Ibn Khaldûn. *The Muqaddimah: An introduction to history*. F. Rosenthal (trans.). New York: Pantheon, 1958. 3 vols.

Isard, W. *Methods of regional science*. New York: Wiley, 1960.

Isard, W., & Kavesh, R. Economic structural interrelation of metropolitan regions. *Amer. J. Sociol.*, 1954, **60**, 152–162.

Krader, L. Culture and environment in interior Asia. In *Studies in human ecology, Social Science Monographs*, III. Washington: Pan American Union, 1957. Pp. 115–138.

Kraeling, C. H., & Adams, R. M. (Eds.) *City invincible: A symposium on urbanization and cultural development in the ancient Near East*. Chicago: Univer. of Chicago Press, 1960.

Kroeber, A. L. *A roster of civilizations and cultures*. Chicago: Aldine, 1962.

Lazarsfeld, P. F., & Rosenberg, M. *The language of social research*. Glencoe, Ill.: Free Press, 1955.

Leakey, L. S. B. *Adam's ancestors: The evolution of man and his culture*. (4th ed.) New York: Harper, 1960. (a)

Leakey, L. S. B. The origin of the genus *Homo*. In S. Tax (Ed.), *Evolution after Darwin*. Vol. 2. *The evolution of man*. Chicago: Univer. of Chicago Press, 1960. Pp. 17–32. (b)

Liebling, A. J. The round of history. *The New Yorker*, 1959, 35 (38), 206–233.

Lotka, A. J. *Elements of physical biology.* Baltimore: Williams & Wilkins, 1925.

Lotka, A. J. The law of evolution as a maximal principle. *Human Biol.*, 1945, 17, 167–194.

Machlup, F. *The production and distribution of knowledge in the United States.* Princeton, N.J.: Princeton Univer. Press, 1962.

McKenzie, R. D. The concept of dominance and world-organization. *Amer. J. Sociol.*, 1927, 33, 28–42.

McKeown, T., & Record, R. G. Reasons for the decline of mortality in England and Wales during the nineteenth century. *Pop. Stud.*, 1962, 16, 94–122.

Medawar, P. B. *The future of man.* New York: Mentor, 1961.

Mumford, L. *Technics and civilization.* New York: Harcourt, 1934.

Napier, J. The evolution of the human hand. *Sci. Amer.*, 1962, 207 (6), 56–62.

Oakley, K. P. Skill as a human possession. In C. Singer, E. J. Holmyard, & A. R. Hall (Eds.), *A history of technology.* Vol. 1. New York & London: Oxford Univer. Press, 1954.

Odum, E. P. *Fundamentals of ecology.* Philadelphia: W. B. Saunders, 1953.

Oehser, P. H. The word "ecology." *Science*, 1959, 129, 992.

Ogburn, W. F. *Social change.* (new ed. with suppl. ch.) New York: Viking, 1950.

Pappenfort, D. M. The ecological field and the metropolitan community: Manufacturing and management. *Amer. J. Sociol.*, 1959, 64, 380–385.

Park, R. E. *Human communities: The city and human ecology.* Glencoe, Ill.: Free Press, 1952.

Perloff, H. S., with Dodds, Vera W. *How a region grows.* Suppl. Paper No. 17. New York: Committee for Economic Development, March, 1963.

Piggott, S. (Ed.) *The dawn of civilization.* New York: McGraw, 1961.

Quigley, C. *The evolution of civilizations.* New York: Macmillan, 1961.

Quinn, J. A. *Human ecology.* New York: Prentice-Hall, Inc., 1950.

Reid, L. *The sociology of nature.* (rev. ed.) Baltimore: Penguin, 1962.

Rogers, E. S. Man, ecology, and the control of disease. *Publ. Hlth Repts,* 1962, 77, 755–762.

Sahlins, M. D., & Service, E. R. (Eds.) *Evolution and culture.* Ann Arbor: Univer. of Michigan Press, 1960.

Salaman, R. N. *The history and social influence of the potato.* Cambridge: Cambridge University Press, 1949.

Schnore, L. F. Social morphology and human ecology. *Amer. J. Sociol.*, 1958, 63, 620–634.

Scott, J. P. *Animal behavior.* Chicago: Univer. of Chicago Press, 1958.

Service, E. R. *Primitive social organization: An evolutionary perspective.* New York: Random House, Inc., 1962.

Siegel, I. H. Scientific discovery, invention, and the cultural environment. *The Patent, Trademark, and Copyright J. Res. Educ.*, 1960, 4, 233–248.

Simpson, G. G. *The meaning of evolution.* (paperbound ed.) New Haven, Conn.: Yale University Press, 1960.

Simpson, G. G., Pittendrigh, C. S., & Tiffany, L. H. *Life: An introduction to biology.* New York: Harcourt, 1957.

Spuhler, J. N. (Ed.) *The evolution of man's capacity for culture.* Detroit: Wayne State Univer. Press, 1959.

Stauffer, R. C. Haeckel, Darwin, and ecology. *Quart. Rev. Biol.*, 1957, 32, 138–144.

Steward, J. H. *Theory of culture change: The methodology of multilinear evolution.* Urbana: Univer. of Illinois Press, 1955.

Steward, J. H., & Shimkin, D. B. Some mechanisms of social evolution. *Daedalus, Proc. Amer. Acad. Arts Sci.*, 1961, 90, 477–497.

Tax, S. (Ed.) *Evolution after Darwin.* Vol. 2. *The evolution of man.* Chicago: Univer. of Chicago Press, 1960.

Tax, S., & Callender, C. *Evolution after Darwin.* Vol. 3. *Issues in evolution.* Chicago: Univer. of Chicago Press, 1960.

Teitelbaum, P. D. *Energy production and consumption in the United States: An analytical study based on 1954 data.* Report of Investigations, No. 5821. Washington: U.S. Bureau of Mines, 1961.

Theodorson, G. A. (Ed.) *Studies in human ecology.* Evanston, Ill.: Row, 1961.

Thieme, P. The Indo-European language. *Sci. Amer.*, 1958, 199 (4), 63–74.

Thirring, H. *Energy for man.* (Harper Torchbook ed.) New York: Harper & Row, 1962.

Thomas, W. L., Jr. *Man's role in changing the face of the earth*. Chicago: Univer. of Chicago Press, 1956.

Toynbee, A. J. *A Study of history*. Abridgement of Vols. VII–X by D. C. Somervell. New York: Oxford Univer. Press, 1957.

Toynbee, A. J. *A study of history*. Vol. 12. *Reconsiderations*. London: Oxford Univer. Press, 1961.

Turner, R. *The great cultural traditions*. New York: McGraw, 1941. 2 vols.

U.S. Bureau of the Census. *Enterprise statistics: 1958*. Part 1. *General Report*. Washington: Government Printing Office, 1963.

Wagner, P. L. *The human use of the earth*. Glencoe, Ill.: Free Press, 1960.

Washburn, S. L. Speculations on the interrelations of the history of tools and biological evolution. In J. N. Spuhler (Ed.), *The evolution of man's capacity for culture*. Detroit: Wayne State Univer. Press, 1959. Pp. 21–31.

Washburn, S. L. Tools and human evolution. *Sci. Amer.*, 1960, 203 (3), 62–75.

Washburn, S. L. (Ed.) *Social life of early man*. Chicago: Aldine, 1961.

White, L. A. *The evolution of culture*. New York: McGraw, 1959.

White, L., Jr. *Medieval technology and social change*. Oxford: Clarendon, 1962.

Zimmermann, E. W. *World resources and industries*. (rev. ed.) New York: Harper, 1951.

Znaniecki, F. *The method of sociology*. New York: Farrar & Rinehart, 1934.

Znaniecki, F. *The social role of the man of knowledge*. New York: Columbia Univer. Press, 1940.

CHAPTER 3 Population and Society[1]

IRENE B. TAEUBER

The field of population studies extends from inherent growth and structure to widely ramified interdisciplinary and multidisciplinary subjects. Population is a focus of approach in many fields and an organizing principle for many associations. Distribution and migration may be studied as geographic, economic, or social facts. Birth and death are proper subjects for biologists and chemists as well as for demographers and behavioral scientists. Moreover, demographic processes are influenced by the society in which they occur and the characteristics, aspirations, and activities of the people who are both units for demographic analysis and members of society. Social structures and processes are influenced by demographic structures and processes.

In the long run, the numbers, the distribution, and the growth of population may be viewed as dependent variables. In the short run, population status and changes may be facts to which adjustments must be made. The distinction between relative variability over time and relative fixity at specific times is an essential focus in the formulation of research, policy, and operational plans. It is an analytical convention with major elements of artificiality, however, since interactions of demographic and other factors are continuing processes. Population changes are propulsions to social change. The increase of youth in a peasant village or the increase of aged in a mature society necessarily alter the balance if not the forms of social functioning. Social changes are also propulsions to population changes. The hopes and frustrations that send peasants cityward alter the balances of births and deaths and the rural-urban distribution of the population. Family values and individual orientations to self or ancestors condition marriage and childbearing.

The analysis of the interrelations of population, society, and the person is complex in conceptualization and implementation. Associations are multiple and diverse; cultures and chronological sequences thwart universalistic theory and limit the generalization of empirical findings. If the statement is

---

[1] Since the topic of this chapter encompasses such a broad field, it is impossible to cite specifically to the primary sources, the analytical studies, and the general literature. References to publications most directly relevant to the subjects considered here are located at the end of the chapter.

doubted, consider the question of the relation of lineage organization to the survival of the individual and the persistence of the group, in relation to a theory or generalization that is valid across cultures, modernization levels, and time periods.

Since population status and dynamics are so widely and so intimately associated with social structure, function, and dynamics, broad discussion can contribute little beyond platitudes and unverified if not unverifiable generalizations. Limitation of topic is indicated in brief discussion, but overly severe limitation would bar documentation of the major significance of demographic analysis in sociological research. Hence the subject selected here is population growth. This topic is at once the widest in scope and impact and the most incisively developed in formal demography.

GROWTH IN SPACE
AND TIME

The increase of man's numbers on earth has been an evolutionary process, with primacy passing gradually from the biological to the cultural aspects. The physical remains of man, his artifacts, and his imprint on land are the sole sources of information for most of the long period of species, subcultural, and early cultural evolution. The transition from development that was basically biological to change that was increasingly cultural was extremely slow. Abstraction, speech, and social transmission through verbal communication evolved long before the pictographs and the writing that yielded a physical and relatively permanent record of the mental activities and the social interactions that were basically human and cultural rather than simply biological. Writing itself permitted wider and more cumulative transmission and thus swifter and more efficiently guided change. In the period after pictographs and writing, sources of knowledge of man and society increased in type and depth. Tomb inscriptions, mythologies, legends, and quasi-historical records

are late supplements to the deductions from bones and habitation spots.

Admittedly, sources for the study of early man and early society are limited and faulty. Social analysis remains largely speculative, but the extent and type of population growth can be deduced with considerable plausibility and some major certainties. The prime fact is that numbers were few and increase was slight. Perhaps evolutions occurred in several places; perhaps there was dispersion from a single site. Studies in primate biology suggest the pattern when ecological factors were little influenced by culture. Studies of isolated primitive peoples suggest the variations and the vicissitudes when technology was simple and response more adaptive than manipulative.

Diversities in population change were perhaps more prevalent than uniformities. Some peoples may have achieved stable ecological balance. Other peoples and cultures failed, in the final sense that insufficient births, excessive deaths, or some faulty relationship of the two led to physical extinction. A few peoples increased in numbers and moved outward over wider areas. Increase, dispersion, and assimilative capacities operated on increasingly massive scales, and some few peoples reached fairly large numbers in the classical periods. The population of the Roman Empire was perhaps 50 million at the death of Augustus in 14 A.D.; the population of China was perhaps 60 million under the Han Dynasty.

Sustained and fairly uniform movements are relatively new, even for European populations. Hazards multiplied with the weakening and disappearance of the power of Imperial Rome. In the dark ages of the late ancient and early medieval periods, famines, epidemics, and civil strife contributed to and were further reinforced by economic and political disintegration. Ecclesiastical order and agricultural expansion were basic in new integrations. Curiously enough, the stirrings that foretold the modern world became more active, creative, and cumulative in the period of recovery after the devastation and depopulation of the Black Death. Advances in productivity, the growth of urban areas, commercial and financial expansion within and outside Europe, intellectual awakenings, and scientific advances operated in some proportions to stimulate population growth. Conversely, the increasing populations in the period after the Black Death stimulated economic and social advance, urban life, commercial and geographic expansion, and intellectual progress.

In 1650, a millenium and a half after the great days of Romans and Hans, the total population of the earth is estimated to have been only 500 million (see Table 1). Most

impact of the commercial and industrial expansion of the barbarians from the West on the great cultures of the East was not even envisioned.

World population, perhaps 500 million in 1650, increased to 2.5 billion in 1950. Increase was slow and erratic at first, but gradually it became more regular and rapid. The average annual growth per one thousand total population was three from 1650 to 1750, four from 1750 to 1800, five from 1800 to 1850, six from 1850 to 1900, and eight from 1900 to 1950. Even these slow rates of growth generated large absolute increases. Growth amounted to 200 million in the cen-

TABLE 1

The Growth of World Population, 1650 to 1950[a]
(population in millions)

Area	1650	1750	1800	1850	1900	1950
World	545	728	906	1,171	1,608	2,406
Africa	100	95	90	95	120	199
Northern America	1	1	6	26	81	166
Latin America	12	11	19	33	63	162
Asia[b]	327	475	597	741	915	1,272
Europe[c]	103	144	192	274	423	594
Oceania	2	2	2	2	6	13

[a] Source: United Nations. Department of Social Affairs, Population Division. *The determinants and consequences of population trends.* New York, 1953. Table 2, p. 11.
[b] Excluding the Asian portion of the U.S.S.R.
[c] Including the Asian portion of the U.S.S.R.

figures for the seventeenth century are estimates; many are only conjectures. The broad picture of the earth's population and its increase is etched sharply, though, whatever the error in detail. In 1650, as today, the central core of the earth's population was Asian. The 40 per cent of the population that was not Asian was largely European or African. The Americas had received few immigrant increments to their indigenous "Indian" populations, while Oceania was still the habitat of its indigenous people. The expansion of Europeans that peopled North America, Latin America, and Oceania was commencing. The slave trade that later depopulated Africa was beginning. The

tury from 1650 to 1750, 400 million in the century from 1750 to 1850, and 1.4 billion in the century from 1850 to 1950.

Thus in the long formative eras, the stone and metal ages, and the further period to the beginnings of modern history, human population increased to 500 million. Then numbers multiplied fivefold in three hundred years. This multiplication occurred with an average annual increase of five per one thousand.

Today the accepted figure for average annual growth is 18 per 1,000, but this figure is regarded generally as too low. Given at least 3 billion people increasing at rates of growth four or more times those of recent centuries, simple forward projections for a few more centuries yield numbers that are not possible on a finite earth. Given present logistics, transfer of appreciable proportions of the increasing numbers to outer space is not possible.

It has always been obvious that growth must slow down sometime. It is now evident that the timing of such slowing may be a critical factor in determining man's future on earth. The projection of the trends of the past into the future has been the usual demographic technique for illustrating the possible or the probable for the future. The trends of the past, projected far into the future, are today the improbable or the impossible. But, if the future cannot be an ordered projection of the past, what can that future be?

Neither the analysis of the changing populations of the past nor the estimation of the probable populations of the future is a simple task. Analysis must go beyond the simple numbers of growth curves to the consideration of fertility, mortality, migration, and the factors that condition their levels and their changes. It is appropriate, therefore, to glance at the balances of births and deaths in the past before plunging into the maelstrom of statistics, figures, and estimates that at once simplify and compound the problems of population projection today.

PROCESSES OF GROWTH

Population growth is a biological process in man as in other species. Man's reproductive potential is limited, for the child-bearing years of women are a brief period in the central span of life, the usual birth is a single one, and average birth intervals are considerably more than a year. The period of gestation, childhood, adolescence, maturity, and senescence is long. The slow maturity and the long productive period are functional, for the years of youth permit the endowment of the person with culture and the years of maturity permit the enrichment and transmission of the heritage. This bio-logical span of life means, however, that man's numbers are not immediately responsive to changing conditions nor can they be responsive. Death is the only quick regulator of numbers. But if death is too frequent, the problem becomes the survival of the species, not the superabundance. If changing frequencies of births are the prime regulators, adjustment proceeds with lags that are measured in quarter centuries. The infant born this year in the United States has more than an even chance of surviving beyond the end of the first quarter of the twenty-first century.

Given today's levels of science and technology, survival itself does not seem a major population problem. The question commonly debated, rather, is the level of the birth rate and the superabundant production of babies. This is a relatively new state in man's evolution. In the prescientific relationship, numbers of births and deaths had to be balanced delicately in relation to each other if biological heritages and cultural transmissions were to be continuing processes. Births had to be numerous enough to replace deaths if the people were to survive. Decimations could not be so frequent or so severe that people declined in numbers and finally disappeared. This would suggest maximum fertility and minimum mortality as an optimal relationship. If growth should be overrapid, however, culture, economy, and society might deteriorate and growth itself vanish in rising death rates.

Thus one is tempted to formulate a theory of demographic equilibrium in which births, deaths, and, therefore, population growth are balanced delicately in relation to resources, skills, economic organization, and social institutions. There are difficulties, though, for there are few instances in which resources, contact, communication, and the rewards and hazards of nature are unchanging. If there were such instances, there might be optimal balances of births and deaths. If external conditions should then change or vital balances shift, however, adjustments would be difficult, if indeed they could occur at all. There is no simple adjustment of current population to current conditions except in a dynamic setting that is in no way a stable equilibrium model. Biological and social factors alike make it unlikely that births of a specific year are adjusted delicately to manpower needs of later decades. Moreover, mobility is a basic aspect in the lives of most peoples, if not an inherent characteristic of man himself. So migration, expansion, contact or conflict, and changing rates of growth are more characteristic of man than is acquiescent equilibrium in an unchanging natural environment.

A few island peoples in remote seas may have achieved an interrelated structure of birth and death rates that have evenly replaced the numbers then living in ideal relationship to the environment of nature, culture, and other men. It is apparent, however, that none of the great cultures or the numerous peoples trace lineage to such equilibrium relationships. Here the question of growth processes is the complex one of the varying structures of fertility, mortality, and migration that place peoples and societies in continuing forward movements.

If there are principles of continuity in replacement and regularity in mobility, demography may become a predictive science. What are the variations and associations among fertility, mortality, and migration in differing temporal and developmental periods? What are the relations between and within cultures, ethnic groups, specific areas, and broad regions? Are there demographic principles without temporal, cultural, or technical specificities?

These queries are invitations to social as well as demographic research. Since man became man, vital rates and migrations have mirrored both social and biological processes. In all periods and in all areas, vital rates vary in relation to values, mores, and the conditioning factors of sustenance, hazards, and milieu. Migrations occur whether in response to opportunity or as consequence of deprivation, and they too are structured in origin, course, and consequence. Man's reactions to his increasing numbers are likewise diverse. Sometimes there are fatalistic adjustments to or acquiescent acceptance of increasing pressures on subsistence. Sometimes there are acquisitive expansions. Sometimes there are propulsions to greater and more productive efforts. Variability and alternate responses have been characteristic of most populations at most periods in the past. They are likely to be characteristic of most populations in the future.

PREMODERN

Fluctuating levels and episodic variations in mortality have largely determined man's changing numbers throughout most of his existence as a biological species with a culture. The intensity of the values associated with family, community, and lineal succession suggest that sufficiency of offspring may have been a paramount need for most peoples throughout most of history. It cannot be assumed, however, that people adjusted to hazardous life and prevalent death merely through producing many children. Regulations of marriage and family, compulsions and taboos in sex relations, concepts of proper rearing of children, mores of selective care, and practices if not ethics of selective survival are almost universal.

The possibilities for and the implications of varying relations between fertility and mortality may be noted for a hypothetical country that is densely settled and premodern. The people live in villages, and they cultivate the soil by hand techniques. Ways of living, habits of work, and health practices are ancient folkways. There is no native scientific technology, and there is little impact from outside. The expectation of life at birth fluctuates at around 25 years; the death rate averages 40 per 1,000 total population. The birth rate is higher than the death rate in good years, lower than the death rate in bad years and also averages 40 per 1,000 total population. The population changes upward and downward, but with no continuing trend in either direction.

Perhaps the hypothetical country has values and institutions so conducive to frequent childbearing that the birth rate averages 55 rather than 40. If the society remains premodern, a birth rate of 55 cannot exist alongside a death rate of 40 for any long period of time, for such rates yield a natural increase of 1.5 per cent a year. What adjustments can provide sustenance and amenities for a population with an increase of this magnitude?

Among the possibilities, there may be some increase in the density of settlement on land that is already cultivated; there may be expansion of cultivated areas; or there may be some emigration. Unfortunately, neither alone nor in combination can such adjustments relieve the problems caused by an increase of 1.5 per cent a year for many years. Hence the solution becomes a shift from the relationship of birth and death rates that produces rapid growth to a relationship that produces lesser growth. Birth rates may decline, or death rates may rise. These changes may occur separately or concurrently. Changes in birth rates can only occur slowly, for these involve altered reproductive mores and institutional frames. Changes in death rates, however, may occur swiftly, for some specific causes of death are independent of local values and individual volitions. Perhaps increasing population pressures, increasing instabilities, and weakened resistances initiate a cycle of cataclysms and decimations.

The specific forces and forms of changes in birth rates are many. Economic difficulties may result in later or less frequent marriages. Search for work and sustenance may remove men from families. Folkways of birth prevention may spread, or those already widespread may be practiced more assiduously. The realities of family pressures may manifest themselves in abortion and infanticide. Although any combination of these changes or actions may produce some decline in the number of live births, decline is not likely to be sufficient to relieve major pressures of population on available subsistence. If there is severe malnutrition and reduced vitality, there may also be declining productivity, increasing susceptibility to disease, and lessened reproduction. Famine, epidemic, flight, and prevalent death have been the penalties of undue increase in numbers throughout much of man's history.

The debate over the priorities between changes in fertility and changes in mortality in the demographic balances of premodern peoples is generally oversimplified. Given an initial level of fertility and slight temporal changes in that level over time, mortality determines growth. However, levels of fertility are related to levels of mortality in stable and in dynamic situations. The peoples whose descendants became the world's massive populations and the carriers of its great cultures had to have birth rates high enough to yield growth over decades and millennia. Death rates also had to be sufficiently limited to permit growth at existing levels of fertility. Many peoples and cultures never even achieved a relation of birth and death rates that permitted permanent survival. Some of these vanished in cataclysms, and others moved slowly to extinction as deaths exceeded births and numbers became continually smaller.

The declining population of the island of Yap in Micronesia was studied by German, Japanese, and American investigators. Until recently, numbers of births were too few to replace the existing population. Each cohort of children was smaller than the one preceding it, and each group of women in the childbearing ages less than the previous one. Depopulation was in process. In recent years, however, there has been a reversal. The low birth rates are now high and death rates low. The problem has become that of increase rather than decline, but this has been a response to the impact of external forces of a modern type, not a reversal of indigenous balances of births and deaths.

The hypothetical country of high but precariously balanced birth and death rates is a generalized model of most of the countries of the world prior to the development of science, technology, and industrial society. Its greatest and most enduring manifestation was China. Slow and often interrupted growth and expansion occurred over the millennia, with underlying continuities in social organization, family institutions, and economic folkways. Tenacious viability in difficult conditions, peripheral expansions, and assimilative propensities were factors in the generation and preservation of the world's largest cohesive ethnic group. Under Manchu rule from the middle of the seventeenth century to the early twentieth century, population responded in classic form to efficient administration, economic development in a historic context, expanded areas, and new food crops. The *paochia* household records suggest an increase from 278 million in 1780 to 430 million in 1850. Increasing pressures on available resources, however, were but one manifestation of a culminating disintegration that reached its climax in the Tai-p'ing Rebellion of the mid-nineteenth century. The Ching (Manchu) kept the semblance of power until 1911; the Republic of China struggled for effective power from 1911 to 1949; the Peoples Republic of China achieved it in 1949. Their census registration of 1953–1954 indicated a mainland population of 582 million.

Whatever the comparative errors in figures, it is obvious that there had been massive growth over the centuries from the Ching conquest of the middle of the seventeenth century to the Communist conquest of the middle of the twentieth century. There had been no comprehensive transformation from a premodern to a scientific and technological base. The balance of births and deaths remained premodern. Increase and decline alternated in various areas in certain years in response to the abundance or the sparsity of food, the absence or the presence of epidemics, and the state of civil order.

The initial impact of modernization in China under a Communist form of organization was similar to that which occurred elsewhere: a reduction in mortality with no correlated decline in fertility. The response to the resultant growth that threatens subsistence and advance alike has been a move toward governmental policy to stimulate birth control. China has joined, not the modern nations, but the demographically underdeveloped ones struggling for the modernization of economy and the control of population.

While China remained largely premodern, two great transformations were occurring elsewhere. The first, discussed below, was indigenous in Europe; the second (pp. 103–120) was an indirect and partial impact of European transformations on colonial and related areas.

TRANSITION TO THE MODERN

The distinctive demographic pattern of the modern world has been a mortality reduced to low levels by economic and scientific achievements, and a fertility reduced to low levels by planned regulation in accord with family decisions concerning desired numbers of children. Once mortality was reduced to such low levels that further declines were necessarily small, fertility became the major variable. Population growth remained a biological process. Death was pushed back, but man remained mortal. Children were born as of old, but conscious decisions became the predominant forces in the level and variability of fertility. In this greatest advance of science, man assumed control of his own numbers.

The demographic transition from high to low birth and death rates came initially and proceeded furthest in Europe. The agricultural and commercial advances, the applications of science and technology in industry and in health and welfare, and the democratization of opportunity were associated factors in the generation of continuing declines in mortality. There were social and psychological aspects of economic transformations, however, and there were social forces compelling economic and political modernization. There were the Renaissance and the

Reformation, the wider integrations of political democracies, and the advances of education. There were altered functions for families and altered roles for women. Children changed from economic assets to family responsibilities as education became available or required. Birth rates declined, often initially in urbanizing areas and among rising middle classes, but sooner or later in total populations.

These generalizing arguments on birth and death rates and the relations between them have been phrased primarily in a context of demographic change and variability in differing types of societies. Either demographic or social change may be viewed as the independent variable. If there is a demographic aspect to the viability of a society, there is also a social aspect to the viability of a population. There are two great sagas of demographic viability or, alternately, cultural viability—those of the Europeans and those of the Chinese. There are no more striking contrasts in the diversities and interdependencies in population change over the millennia than those of the Europeans, with substantial modernization, and the Chinese, with modernization still largely to be achieved. It cannot be assumed, however, that modernization with its low birth and death rates is an ethnic or a cultural characteristic. Some predominantly European peoples in parts of Latin America that are not modernized maintain the high birth rates of the historic societies. Birth and death rates among the modernized Japanese are among the lowest in the world, and intrinsic population change is negative.

Demographic modernization was largely an unplanned byproduct of social and economic modernization. What happened to balances of births and deaths in countries that did not modernize? Some few, relatively small and isolated, long remained in the condition of the hypothetical country of pp. 87–88. Most were influenced to some degree by the great currents of change initially generated in European societies and economies. The result was neither undisturbed balance nor transition to new balance in demographic process. It was, rather, the generation of deep instabilities. In the eighteenth and nineteenth centuries, there were migrations of developing peoples and expansions of imperial states. In this era, the impact of technically advanced on technically retarded societies was partial and biased. In the twentieth century there are awakened peoples, ardent nationalisms, and conflicting ideologies. There is international cooperation in development, but there are also the insecurities of social revolution, internal subversion, and military hegemony. Along with these shifting social and political forces, there is the most widespread, persistent, and rapid growth in population that has occurred anywhere at any time in world history.

The following section will assume the complexities in origin and the multiplicities in association among all peoples in this swiftly changing era. The discussion will concern the changing numbers and the varying birth and death rates whose differences are altering the rates of population growth in the world, its major regions, and some of the larger countries. Southeast Asia will then be considered as illustrative of the continuities and alterations in growth patterns in a region where peoples and colonial powers were diverse. The case of Japan will be noted throughout as one of demographic modernization without the Graeco-Roman tradition, the Christian religion, the Protestant ethic, the Caucasian biological heritage, or an alphabetic language, but will not be summarized separately. The population and society of the United States will be presented as indicative of the emerging dimensions of demographic dynamics and structures in the setting of an affluent metropolitan country.

WORLD POPULATION: GROWTH AND PROJECTIONS

The basic processes and interrelations of population growth are universal. Specificities and variations are related to pre-existing population status, which in turn conditions further growth. No country without an industrializing economy, an economically based urbanization, widespread education, and a modernizing status and role of women has achieved the low birth and death rates characteristic of the modern era, and no country with such comprehensive modernization has failed to achieve low birth and death rates.

Within any definitions of high and low birth rates there is substantial variation. The premodern people may have a birth rate as low as 37 per 1,000 total population or a rate as high or even higher than 50. The modern people may have a birth rate of 25 or somewhat higher, but apart from exceptional circumstances it will be less than 30. Many mature modernized countries have birth rates considerably below 20, some in the 12 to 15 range. Here, of course, reproduction is inadequate for replacement, and the population must eventually decline if low fertility persists and there is no major and continuing immigration.

In the past, given the necessarily high levels of mortality, peoples without birth rates that would now be classified as high could not survive biologically. These high birth rates were fairly stable, for they were associated with the institutions and values of slowly changing societies. Levels of death rates over periods of years and changes in such levels were the major factors influencing growth. The differential increase of the populations in the various regions of earth and the changing patterns of such differentials reflected varying and changing mortality more than varying and changing fertility. Growth in the eastern Mediterranean in the period of Greek hegemony, growth in Japan during the first century of Seclusion under the Tokugawa, growth in China in the early period of Ching rule, and growth in Europe from the fourteenth century to the eighteenth or even the nineteenth were associated with developments that permitted long-continued reductions in death rates.

As peoples modernized birth rates began to decline, whether in association with advanced age at marriage, lesser prevalence of marriage, or limited childbearing among the married. Fertility became a variable in change. In the period of transition among European peoples, roughly from the mid-eighteenth to the mid-twentieth centuries, mortality declined slowly to low levels and eventually ceased to be a major variable except in years of war or instability. The changing levels of a declining fertility gradually became the major variable within and among countries. Eventually there was low mortality and low fertility with a consequent low rate of population growth. Fluctuations continued, but they occurred within narrow limits if the basis for evaluation is that of man's demographic evolution. Among European peoples overseas in the United States, Canada, Australia, and New Zealand, there were increases in fertility and higher rates of population growth that were associated with rising levels of fertility rather than declining levels of mortality. (This phenomenon will be considered later specifically for the United States.) But here, also, fertility was the major factor of variability. Furthermore, these increases in fertility were contained below the upper limits of fertility defined as low.

The people who have not yet become modern include the major portion of those in Asia, Africa, and Latin America. Here, with the exception of some of the tribal societies and the more modernized countries of Israel, Japan, and Argentina, levels of indigenous fertility are far higher than those once prevalent in Europe. In the completely premodern and nondevelopmental situation, therefore, death rates must have also been substantially higher than those that once prevailed in Europe. Potential growth was greater should there be changes that failed to touch fertility but reduced mortality. The realization of this potential for rapid growth has been in process as modern political, economic, and social developments impinged on societies still basically traditional in social structure and tradi-

TABLE 2

THE POPULATION OF THE WORLD AND ITS INCREASE, 1920 TO 1960[a]

Area	Population in Millions					Annual Rate of Increase 1950–1960	Rates per 1,000 Population 1956–1960	
	1920	1930	1940	1950	1960		Births	Deaths
World[b]	1,811	2,015	2,249	2,510	2,995	1.8	36	18
Africa	141	157	176	206	254	2.2	47	25
Northern	47	53	61	71	88	2.2	45	23
Other	94	104	115	135	166	2.1	48	27
America	208	244	277	329	405	2.1	34	13
Northern[c]	117	135	146	167	199	1.8	25	9
Middle	30	34	41	51	66	2.7	42	15
South	61	75	90	111	140	2.3	42	19
Asia[d]	966	1,072	1,212	1,386	1,679	1.9	41	22
South West	43	47	53	60	77	2.6	48	22
South Central	326	362	410	472	559	1.7	41	24
South East	110	128	155	175	214	2.0	41	21
East	487	535	594	679	829	2.0	40	20
Europe[e]	329	356	381	395	427	0.8	19	11
Northern and Western	115	122	128	133	142	0.7	18	11
Central	112	120	127	128	139	0.8	19	11
Southern	102	114	126	134	146	0.9	21	10
Oceania[f]	9	10	11	13	16	2.4	24	9
U.S.S.R.	158	176	192	181	214	1.7	25	8

[a] Source: United Nations. Statistical Office. *Demographic yearbook 1961*. New York, 1962. Table 2.
[b] All data are adjusted estimates.
[c] Excluding Hawaii.
[d] Excluding the Asian portion of the U.S.S.R.
[e] Excluding the European part of the U.S.S.R.
[f] Including Hawaii.

tionally village-oriented and with an agricultural economy.

The concurrent results of these varying levels and changes in birth and death rates are the major factors in the world picture of population change and vital rates given in Table 2. Migration is a lesser factor in the growth that is now occurring, but remains apparent as immigration into Australia, Canada, the United States, and some other countries and as emigration primarily from Europe. In general, though, even in the countries just listed, it is a minor factor in comparison with natural change.

Birth rates are estimated at 40 or more per 1,000 population in Africa, Asia, and Latin America. They are less than 20 in Europe. In Northern America, Oceania, and the U.S.S.R. they are about 25 per 1,000. In the high fertility regions, death rates are far lower than birth rates and growth is appreciable. In the years from 1956 to 1960, it was estimated to be close to or even higher than 2 per cent a year.

Death rates in the underdeveloped countries, although reduced, are higher than those in the developed countries. In Northern America, Oceania, and the U.S.S.R., birth rates around 25 and death rates of 8 or 9 yield rates of natural increase of 1.7 or 1.8 per cent a year. These rates are somewhat similar in levels to those in the underdeveloped countries, but they are far different in the matrix of forces that produce them and in their implications for future growth.

In the developed countries of fairly rapid increase in population, crude death rates are already so low that further reductions in age-specific rates are unlikely to compensate for the impact of age structures more heavily weighted with the aging and the aged. Birth rates are largely subject to voluntary control. Many couples have the number of children they desire, and they then limit further childbearing. In the underdeveloped areas, there are major possibilities for further declines in death rates. In fact, many countries now have death rates much lower than those attributed to them in Table 2. Birth rates remain traditional in levels and in the factors associated with their reduction. In so far as modernization has influenced fertility, it has tended toward the increases of heightened vitality, improved health, and altered institutions and taboos. Reductions in child marriage, lessened revulsion toward widow remarriage, improved care for girl babies and children, and spreading avoidance of infanticide are among the reasons leading to some increases in fertility. However, the predominant factor in present and future growth is reduced and still declining mortality.

Slowing growth can come through reduced fertility only as the people themselves transfer marital relations and childbearing from the customary and therefore natural sector of values and behavior to the rational sector wherein decisions are made and effective actions taken to implement them. Perhaps a qualifying note should be introduced, for scientific and technological advances might yield means and procedures extraneous to family and village living whereby births, as well as deaths, could be reduced by central actions that are neither determined by economic activities nor influenced by institutions and values in agrarian village society. Such means and procedures are not yet available, nor do they seem imminent. Nor is it feasible to speculate on whether governments would or would not make the collective decisions to manipulate the birth rates of their peoples.

Population replacement is continuing. So, therefore, is the differential growth of the regional populations. If fertility remains unchanged at high levels while mortality continues to decline, population will grow at increasing rates on bases that become continually larger. Projections made several years ago in the Secretariat of the United Nations are presented in Table 3. As a preface to commenting on these results, three points should be emphasized. First, present populations are generally underestimated: In many countries, base populations and birth rates were too low, while death rates declined more rapidly than assumed. Second, the estimates presented here are illustrative of the population growth that would occur if birth rates did not change throughout the century. These estimates are not predictions that birth rates will be so resistant to change as to be practically identical in 1900, 1950, and 2000. Third, the assumption of continuing declines in mortality is not a prediction. Given unchanging fertility and further declines in mortality, economic expansion would have to be rapid to maintain the increasing population at current subsistence levels. If economic expansion did not occur, death rates would have to rise. But sufficient economic expansion could hardly occur unless it were linked with general economic development. That development, in turn, is inhibited if not barred by the high fertility, the load of dependent youth, the consumption and developmental expenditures, and the limited savings that are products of existing population structures and their continuing dynamics.

The logical inference from present interrelations and trends concerning the future is instability. The projection of unchanging fertility and continually declining mortality

TABLE 3

ESTIMATED AND PROJECTED POPULATIONS FOR DEVELOPED AND DEVELOPING AREAS
IN THE TWENTIETH CENTURY[a]
(Projected populations: declining mortality, high fertility)

Year	Developed[b]	Developing			
		Total	Africa	Asia[c]	Latin America
Population in Millions					
1900	554	996	120	813	63
1925	700	1,207	147	961	99
1950	838	1,659	199	1,297	163
1975	1,115	2,741	331	2,107	303
2000	1,448	5,459	663	4,145	651
Per Cent Increase					
1900–1925	26.4	21.2	22.5	18.2	57.1
1925–1950	19.7	37.4	35.4	35.0	64.6
1950–1975	33.0	65.2	66.3	62.5	85.9
1975–2000	29.9	99.2	100.3	96.7	114.8
Per Cent of World Total					
1900	35.7	64.3	7.7	52.4	4.1
1925	36.7	63.3	7.7	50.4	5.2
1950	33.6	66.4	8.0	51.9	6.5
1975	28.9	71.1	8.6	54.6	7.9
2000	21.0	79.0	9.6	60.0	9.4

[a]Source of data: United Nations. Department of Economic and Social Affairs. *The future growth of world population*. New York, 1958. Table 5.
[b] Europe, the U.S.S.R., Australia, New Zealand, Japan, and Northern America.
[c] Excluding the Asian portion of the U.S.S.R. and Japan.

yields a condition that sooner or later becomes incompatible with reality. The actuality of the populations that are projected requires the economic and social developments whose associated changes include the demographic modernization of declining fertility.

The population growth of the twentieth century is presented in Table 3 for world regions and subregions in quarter centuries. The first two quarters are matters of record. Population in the period from 1900 to 1950 is subject to error of estimation, for data are limited and inaccurate. The populations of the years from 1950 to 2000 are necessarily only estimated. These are the populations that would exist if stabilities in fertility and declines in mortality continued to the end of the century. The multiplication of numbers in the century is astounding: 1.8 billion in 1900, 2.5 billion in 1950, and 6.9 billion in 2000.

The distinction in the population dynamics of developed and underdeveloped countries is etched sharply in the historic and projected course of growth in the twentieth century. The percentage increase changed relatively little in the developed countries. Growth amounted to less than one-third in each succeeding quarter century. Rates of growth moved sharply upward in the underdeveloped countries—from less than one-fifth in the first quarter century to almost double in the last quarter century.

The redistribution of world population is a continuing process. The developing areas had about one-third the population of the earth in 1900. If projected trends are realized, they will have less than one-fifth in 2000. The underdeveloped areas had less than two-thirds of the population of the earth in 1900. If trends continue, they will have almost four-fifths at the end of the century.

Further comments will concern the period from 1950 to 1975, for the extent of the conjecture is reduced thereby. Birth rates have not declined in any large underdeveloped countries between 1950 and 1963, the time of this writing. Research on demographic and social changes supports the inference that rapid declines in fertility are not likely in the 12 years between 1963 and 1975. Hence, the discussion of 1975 is a consideration of what will be, subject to the major and even critical question of the death rate.

If the world is viewed as a unit, its total population and the various age groups consist increasingly of persons who lack the opportunities in education and experience essential to full and creative participation. In 1950, 74 per cent of those below age 15 and 44 per cent of those aged 60 and over lived in underdeveloped areas. In 1975, underdeveloped areas will include 79 per cent of all people on earth below age 15, but only 45 per cent of those aged 60 and over. Given the continuation of economically backward areas, the economically advanced areas include ever declining proportions of earth's people.

Some Projected Populations

Geographic regions of the surface of the earth need be neither cultural, economic, nor political units. Combined populations become doubtfully significant if the major similarity is mere contiguity. Given disparate economic and social units and nationalism as emotion, motivation, and developmental force, the facts and projections of growth can be assessed more firmly in terms of national units. Hence, summary data on population changes projected for the years 1960 and 1975 are given in Table 4 for Mexico and Brazil in Latin America and for Indonesia, Pakistan, India, and Mainland China in Asia. The years 1960 and 1975 were selected to minimize conjectural elements. All persons who will be age 12 and over in 1975 are already born, and birth rates in the next decade or so are not likely

to decline appreciably if there is reasonable continuity between future and past experience and reasonable consistency between the actual behavior of people and that which social knowledge would lead one to anticipate.

In the 15 years from 1960 to 1975, given the validity and accuracy of the assumptions and the projections, Mexico's population will increase almost 60 per cent and India's a little over 40 per cent. The populations of the other four countries will increase about 50 per cent. The increase will be more rapid for the younger than the older age groups, for recent declines in mortality have had their major impact in infancy and childhood.

It is rates of increase such as those given in Table 4 that have made greater numbers of governments and larger proportions of demographers conclude that population growth is the most critical and the most nearly insoluble problem of our era. It is critical because it retards if it does not bar economic and social development. In many areas, it also contributes to political instability. It is so nearly insoluble because solutions cannot be forced by governments, no matter how dictatorial. Resolution comes through the determinations of couples who decide to limit the number of children they will have and take effective action to do so.

The lethargies and pressures of the present and the complicated requirements for movement are alike demonstrated in the increasing numbers of youth aged 5 to 14. These are the ages of elementary school attendance, if there are schools to attend. If children in the ages from 6 to 12 or 14 are not going to school, the next generation will be as widely illiterate, as inadequately educated, and as pervasively unskilled as the present one. One of the major drives in underdeveloped countries is universal education. Moreover, education and the improvement of the quality of human resources are increasingly emphasized as strategic approaches to development. Yet these countries must provide schools, teachers, and supplies for children now aged 5 or 6 to 14, at the same time

IRENE B. TAEUBER

TABLE 4

POPULATION PROJECTIONS FOR SIX COUNTRIES, 1960 TO 1975, ON ASSUMPTIONS
OF DECLINING MORTALITY AND HIGH AND UNCHANGING FERTILITY[a]

Country and Age Group	Population in Thousands		Increase	
	1960	1975[c]	Amount in Thousands	Per Cent
Total population				
Mexico	34,119	54,462	20,343	59.6
Brazil	66,085	98,297	32,212	48.7
Indonesia	93,344	137,376	44,032	47.2
Pakistan[b]	95,387	145,630	50,243	52.7
India[b]	423,600	600,600	177,000	41.8
Mainland China[b]	732,900	1,112,700	379,800	51.8
School ages (5–14)				
Mexico	9,181	14,635	5,454	59.4
Brazil	16,701	25,809	9,108	54.5
Indonesia	21,363	34,666	13,303	62.3
Pakistan	24,323	38,752	14,429	59.3
India	100,100	150,300	50,200	50.1
Mainland China	182,800	292,700	109,900	60.1
Productive ages (15–59)				
Mexico	17,210	27,091	9,881	57.4
Brazil	35,125	50,963	15,838	45.1
Indonesia	51,521	72,289	20,768	40.3
Pakistan	50,137	74,036	23,899	47.7
India	233,300	316,600	83,300	35.7
Mainland China	376,800	551,300	174,500	46.3

[a] Source for projections in quinquennial ages: Mexico: United Nations. Department of Social Affairs. Population Division. *Future population estimates by sex and age.* Report 1. *The population of Central America (including Mexico), 1950–1980.* New York, 1954. Table 2. Brazil: Report 2. *The population of South America, 1950–1980.* New York, 1955. Table 4. Indonesia: United Nations. Department of Economic and Social Affairs . . . Report 3. *The population of South-east Asia (including Ceylon and China: Taiwan) 1950–1980.* New York, 1958. Table 6. Pakistan, India, and Mainland China: Report 4. *The population of Asia and the Far East, 1950–1980;* Pakistan, Table xvii, p. 109; India, Table viii, p. 100; Mainland China, Table iv, p. 96 (low mortality, 1953 birth rate of 41.6). New York, 1959.

[b] Pakistan and India, 1961 to 1976; Mainland China, population as reported from the investigation and registration of 1953 extended to 1963 and then projected to 1978.

[c] High projections.

that they develop further schools, teachers, and supplies for 40 to 60 per cent more children only 15 years from now. While this drive for elementary education is proceeding, higher schools, colleges, technical schools, and universities must be provided if the country is to have the intermediate and advanced technical, scientific, managerial, and administrative personnel so essential for the further development of economy, society, and government. If the breakthrough is not achieved, if today's children are not educated, then the workers and the parents of the decades after 1975 will not be educated and the attempt to move forward will either end in frustration or proceed against the manifold and numerically larger problems of ill-trained manpower.

The self-perpetuating mechanisms of the traditional societies are nowhere more apparent than in education. The large families, the severe burdens of children on families and communities, and the deterrents to individual opportunity and national economic growth are all part of a complex of forces that preserve the traditionalism and the lack of education. These in their turn perpetuate the early marriages, the abundant childbearing, and the high rates of population growth.

Are considerations of rates of population growth such as these realistic? Is the projected growth actually occurring today? Are there alternatives to its continuation to 1975? These and other queries are basically the question of the validity of the estimated present and future levels of death rates. The major enigma here, as elsewhere in demography, is China. A registration and investigation of the population in late 1953 and early 1954 indicated a mainland population of 582 million. Published data are too limited to permit evaluation, and data from further counts or national registration systems are lacking. If the birth rate was 41.6 and the death rate 20.4 in 1953, and if the birth rate did not change while the death rate declined in the general Asian pattern to 1963, then the population was 733 million in 1963. It should be noted that this is a population already projected for a decade on the basis of plausible assumptions rather than statistical data. If population was 733 million in 1963 and the death rate continued to decline regularly and rapidly while the birth rate remained stable, the population would exceed one billion by 1975. But the major evidence is that the course of economic development and the path of the death rate have not been smooth in recent years, particularly since the difficulties of the Great Leap of 1958 and the series of years when agricultural production was deficient. In the case of China, then, the population projected for 1960 differs from the actual population of that year by an unknowable amount. The projection from 1960 to 1975 is the forward movement of a population known to be too large through the use of estimated vital rates whose relations to reality are not known.

For the other countries, and particularly for India and Pakistan, the census counts of 1961 indicated that populations had been underestimated. Fertility may have been higher than it was assumed to be or, more probably, death rates had declined more rapidly than had been assumed. There may also have been problems with the comparative completeness and accuracy of the enumerations of 1951 and 1961. Whatever the explanations, true populations were higher than estimated. Thus the projected populations for 1975 are less than the ones likely to exist, if death rates continue to move downward on the projected curves and birth rates do not decline.

No queries of data, no skepticism concerning specific assumptions, no more refined demographic analysis can do other than alter the outer forms of the populations projected for 1975. It is no longer possible to question the existence of a major dilemma posed by the declines in death rates without commensurate declines in birth rates.

Southeast Asia: Demographic and Other Diversities[2]

Asia is the center of the world's population and of its population problems. Almost 1.75 billion people live in the deep arc below the Soviet border. In the frame of this vast and populous area, Southeast Asia seems almost insignificant. It includes 17 per cent of Asia's land area, 13 per cent of its population. Density is less than half that in South Central Asia, two-thirds that in East Asia. Cursory readings and listenings today suggest the strategic significance of this region so diverse and divided within itself. But still, why worry about population? There is a rich resource potential. There are great rivers still to be harnessed and rice lands still to be developed. Yet increasing numbers of the countries within the region view population growth itself as a major if not insuperable hazard to advance. Diversities within a broad context of similarities challenge comparative demographic analysis of the inter-

---

[2] This section is a modification of a lecture given in October, 1963, and published, pp. 51–61 in: *Asia; A Selection of Papers Delivered before the Asia Society*. 1, Spring, 1964. 92 pp. Included with the permission of the Asia society as the introduction to the Indonesia Council's 1963–1964 series.

relations among development potential, low productivity, and high population growth.

The focus of time. There have been few smoothly moving developments in Southeast Asia in the past, and few scholars envision either stability or development as the sole pattern of the future. Cultures have advanced and populations have grown until economies could produce and sustain the irrigation works of a Ceylon or the monumental structures of an Angkor Vat. Then cultures declined, decimated survivors dispersed, and the jungles returned. Former major peoples came to be only marginal minorities, while new peoples filtered down from the Chinese border regions—Burmese, Thai, and Annamites. Buddhism and Hinduism diffused eastward. The faith of the prophet spread through Malaya, Indonesia, and upward into Mindanao and beyond. Political and social structures became compounds, almost layers, of indigenous and imposed forms. Here would have been a paradise for demographers had there been records, surveys, or chronicles to report the almost infinite diversities in space and time within a region that lacked only Western man.

Western man came to Southeast Asia as colonialism became Asia's prevalent form of political and economic organization. But colonialism contributed further to the diversities within the region. Ruling powers differed in the various areas and at the various time periods as Spain, Portugal, and Imperial Germany yielded to the Netherlands, Britain, France, Japan, and the United States of America. Colonial contacts were channeled to colonial powers, not to countries within the region. Intercountry diffusions were blocked, modernization of an elite directed toward different models. Hanoi communicated with Paris, Singapore with London, Jakarta with The Hague, Taipeh with Tokyo.

In Southeast Asia, as elsewhere, enlightened colonialism preserved folkways, social institutions, and kin-oriented values that would be maladjustments in developing societies and economies. Colonialism largely created the populations, the pressure areas, and the rates of growth that are the present problems and the future hazards of the independent countries of the region. This unanticipated consequence merits further comment on process and result.

The population growth of Southeast Asia in the period of Western expansion is one of the astounding phenomena in world demographic history. Early figures are conjectural. Java may have had more than the 5 million people that Lord Raffles attributed to it in 1815; Mainland Southeast Asia may have had more than the 10 million people that Professor Dobby attributed to it for 1800. Whatever the precise figures, numbers were small, not only in the seventeenth century but throughout the eighteenth century.

In the nineteenth and early twentieth centuries, colonialism involved a tripartite approach of sector production for export, local production for subsistence, and cultural continuity for stability. The demographic consequence was the maximization of population growth along with the minimization of changes that might have slowed growth. All factors favored the maintenance of high birth rates. Catholicism and Islam are faiths peculiarly appropriate to generating or maintaining high birth rates. Folk practices of birth limitations that had once existed came to be defined as immoral or barbarian. This occurred in all areas, whatever the former religion and whoever the governing power. If birth rates had been high, no new forces operated to lower them. If birth rates had been low, many forces operated to increase them. Only a few remote peoples labelled as pagans retained habits of adaptive fertility that presumably had once been widespread.

The death rates of normal times and the hazards of catastrophe were alike reduced. Regularized production and improved distribution lessened the frequency and impact of famine. Sanitary cordons, isolations, and eventually innoculations operated similarly to reduce deaths from epidemics. There were extensions of health and sanitation, and there were new food crops. Increasing peoples cultivated more land areas with improved practices, improved seeds, and the controlled waters of irrigation works. As populations multiplied many-fold, per capita food production kept pace, sometimes increased. The situation could have been labelled Malthusian were it not for the fact that the Malthusian controls of death were pushed aside.

There were extensions of education, but schooling was limited to a few years, and most of it was in the vernacular. There were cities, but few natives were other than quiescent performers at lower echelons of achievement and status.

This picture of evolving growth is a generalized one. It is derived from the rich and varied historical records of status, trends, and relationships in the Philippines under Spain and the United States, Indonesia under the Dutch, the Tonkin Delta under the French, Taiwan under the Japanese, and Thailand under the Thai. Growth occurred at increasing rates in the subareas and in the total area. A region that had been sparsely settled in 1820 reached a population of 110 million in 1920. Numbers increased almost one-half between 1920 and 1940. The total population in 1940 was 155 million. The Pacific War devastated economies and broke the evolutionary continuities of colonialism. What populations might have been and what adjustments might have been made had colonialism continued are hardly relevant to the present or the future of Southeast Asia. Revolution replaced slow change. Sovereign nations replaced colonies. Instability and war replaced imposed order. Ideological confrontations alien to the region replaced imposed imperial indoctrinations. And all this occurred within a single decade.

The postwar years. Questions of population growth in Southeast Asia were generally dismissed in cavalier fashion in the early years after the victory over Japan, if indeed they were considered at all. Initially the struggles for independence and viable governments were paramount. Population remained a remote question in areas where the struggles for social integration and political survival continued.

The population problems of Southeast Asia were generally ignored outside as well as within the region. Outsiders with global views saw India, Pakistan, and China as problem areas. The growth of Japan's population was viewed with alarm, but not that of Southeast Asia. Here were the fabled Outer Islands of the Indies, the empty spaces of Mindanao, the mighty rivers whose valleys had a rice potential sufficient for another India or a second China. Ironically, the same demographers who made the quiescent assessments of Southeast Asia cited Taiwan and Java as the classic instances of Malthusian growth. Neglect, optimism, and acceptance alike ended in the first decade or so of independence. The omen of the Southeast Asian problem, as well as the world problem, was Ceylon. The year was 1947.

In late 1946 and early 1947 the houses of Ceylon were sprayed with DDT. The death rate dropped 40 per cent within a single year. Nothing happened at family or village level to provide land or jobs for those surviving who otherwise would have died. Nothing happened to family values that was conducive to immediate and comparable reductions of birth rates. The death rate was largely disassociated from the complex of subsistence agriculture, low vitality, and illiteracy. It remained disassociated. The birth rate had been associated with agrarian occupations, village life, poverty, malnutrition, and ignorance. It remained so associated. Modern science, technology, and technical assistance were spectacularly successful in one field—the reduction of death rates. Success was qualified, if it came at all, in the fields of economic development and social advance. Birth rates tended to remain largely in the domain of nature, increasingly measured in census and survey data and in vital statistics. Some nations now move experimentally toward policies to reduce births, but this will be reserved for later consideration.

For Southeast Asia as a whole, the population that had been 171 million in 1950 reached 214 million in 1960—an increase of 25 per cent within a decade. The rate of increase was also increasing within the decade, as death rates declined to ever lower levels.

If there are to be no major alterations in stabilities and trends, the population of Southeast Asia will reach 300 to 400 million by 1980 and will exceed 600 million by the end of the century. Continuity in development for another 40 years implies the addition of 400 million people to the population of the region. There are only two assumptions involved in the projection of almost astronomic future populations for Southeast Asia: (1) Death rates continue to move downward; (2) birth rates do not decline.

The first uncertainty in the estimated future population is that numbers may be reduced by increased death rates, whether from the slow dying of economic deterioration or the decimation of famine, epidemic, or war. This would be a solution to problems of numbers, but hardly one that would be desired by those in Southeast Asia who survived, or by thoughtful people outside the region.

The second uncertainty in the projected populations is the future of birth rates. If birth rates should decline along with and eventually more rapidly than death rates, growth would slow and finally vanish. If this should occur, the political, social, and economic problems of growth might be transitional difficulties, as they were in earlier periods in Europe, Northern America, Oceania, and Japan.

The idea of demographic solution through family planning in Southeast Asia may seem naive to serious students of the population problems of underdeveloped areas. It may appear as sheer hallucination to those who know the cultures or the subcultures of the villages. But before one surveys present status, one must examine the facts of population growth and lay to rest that ancient and recurring mirage of the governments

and peoples of Southeast Asia—that resettlement from Luzon or Cebu to Mindanao and transmigration from Java to Sumatra are solutions to the population problems of the areas of origin or of destination. Hence, the dimensions of the population growth and the population difficulties of the Philippines and Indonesia must be briefly noted.

The Phillippines. The Phillippines are intriguing areas for cultural demographers. Almost all relationships are found within the island, but in a pattern that is distinctively Filipino. It is neither Southeast Asian nor Spanish nor American, but a selective synthesis of all. It is not Catholic or Muslim or primitive, but some interpenetrated layering of the original and the later religions. Economic and social diversities are also extensive. Here are major resources for an industrial economy; here are large areas for agricultural expansion. But here also is apalling poverty, and an under cultivation of resources that parallels an underutilization of manpower. Here is the sprawling Manila metropolitan area, so American in many ways, so Filipino in others, and here also are the barrios. Here are the most educated people in developing Asia with a drive for education that awes the observer. These educated people with their aspirations for education, high income, upward mobility, and upper-class status have, nevertheless, one of the world's highest birth rates. The presumed cause might be the influence of Catholicism, but birth rates are low or falling in all the Catholic countries of Europe, whether Roman, Greek, or Eastern, whether capitalist or Communist. The Philippines, along with Latin America, may seem to be exempt from this one facet of modernization. However, major statistical activities are being carried on by the government. There are training centers and institutes to provide personnel and locus for research. Interest in population and research and plans for research are already widespread, including not alone the Ateneo of Manila but the Ateneo of Mindanao.

Growth of population has been phenomenal in the Philippines. When Ferdinand Magellan came in 1521 there were perhaps half a million people in the islands. In 1903, the first census taken under United States auspices indicated a population of less than eight million. Population had increased fifteen-fold in the four centuries of Spanish theocracy. The crown and the church of Spain had avoided spectacular depopulation such as that which followed conquistadores and cross in Mexico and had then established a basis for living and a value structure that were conducive to high birth rates.

Death rates declined gradually and erratically over the period of United States rule. Birth rates remained unchanged. The Philippine population was less than eight million in 1903. It was 16 million in 1939. Numbers had more than doubled in little more than a third of a century. And after 400 years of Spanish rule and 40 years of American trusteeship, the potential for growth was high. There was postponement of marriage, but almost all women eventually married. There were regional and subcultural differences in the fertility of the married, but almost all women who married had children. Fertility was lowest among the peoples called pagan (or perhaps relevant data were most deficient). Fertility was relatively low among the Iloconos, very high among the Muslims and in the completely Catholic provinces. In 1939, the average number of children ever born, for each 1,000 women aged 45 to 54 who were or had been married, was 6,711 for the Christian provinces. Fifty-three per cent of all ever-married women in this age group had had seven or more children.

The human losses of the Pacific War were limited. Given the already developed state of the people and the assistance of the United States, health services were expanded rapidly and death rates reduced sharply. The results of the 1960 census corroborated what had long been suspected. The birth rate of the Philippine population was well over 50 per 1,000. The death rate was about 20. The rate of natural increase was somewhere between 3 and 3.5 per cent a year. With death rates declining, the rate of growth may approach or even exceed 4 per cent a year.

A growth rate of 3.5 or 4 per cent a year is a demonstration of the human potential for reproduction, but it is much more. It is a problem of major import for families, communities, and the nation. Family expenditures for consumption rise, but individual shares become less adequate. Land is limited, and now there are several sons to inherit family-owned land, or to seek for land if the parental role is tenancy. Schools are limited, and those that do exist are crowded. Facilities and teachers must increase 3.5 per cent a year if the educational system is not to deteriorate. Maturing youth leave the land for work in cities. There is urbanization without economic development sufficient to provide jobs and incomes for all those who seek them.

Savings are negligible, while capital formation is limited and inefficient. Neither the economists of the Philippine government nor those of the International Bank can develop a feasible plan for economic growth with the high rate of population increase. Another nation is forced to begin a gingerly indirect approach to the problems of reducing the rates of childbearing among its people.

There is the relatively empty island of Mindanao, but its development will be a contribution to economic advance rather than a demographic solution. Given an efficient administration with a firm mandate and adequate finances, almost one million people would have to be resettled in Mindanao each year to care for the population increase of the other islands. This would involve land development, transportation and communication, and towns and facilities in Mindanao, plus the movement of the people, and their care until returns from activities were adequate for maintenance. The Filipino, moreover, with his drives and Western-oriented mobility, is not a candidate for peasant settlement in Mindanao. He wants Manila, and to Manila he goes. And so the pursuit of solution through migration to Mindanao is another vain search for Eldorado.

What of the future population of the Philippines? It is expected to reach 33 million in 1965. If birth rates remain at present levels and death rates continue to decline, population will increase further from 33 million in 1965 to 48 million in 1975. This will be an increase of almost one-half within a decade. The increase of the Philippines in the decade from 1965 to 1975 will be equal to the entire population of the Philippine Islands in 1939. Here, quiet and virtually unnoticed, is an extraordinary crisis in population growth and economic development coming upon a people whose culture, religion, and *élan* are little prepared either to recognize it or to solve it.

Indonesia. The classic population problem of the world is that of Indonesia. People are concentrated in agrarian Java. Resources for an industrial economy are concentrated in the outer islands. The problem is not inherently insoluble, but postponements may make it so. Again, the historic focus and the numerical aspects are essential bases for analysis of the present and assessment of the future.

In the early nineteenth century, the colonial administration of the Dutch began to penetrate all phases of life, maintaining peace, introducing minimum public health, teaching basic hygiene, and fostering better agricultural techniques. The native peoples of Java and Madurs increased from about 5 million in 1816 to 13 million in 1861, 30 million in 1905, 41 million in 1930. By 1930 Java was one of the most densely settled agricultural areas in the world. Population per square mile of total land area had reached 818 in all Java, 1,274 in Jogjakarta.

There was a long hiatus of statistics in the Indies from the census of 1930 to the census of 1960. The total population, 60 million in 1930, had reached almost 95 million in 1960. Not even war, civil war, starvation, disease, or malnutrition had eliminated growth. If the birth rate remains at its esti-

mated level and the death rate declines, population will increase from 93 million in 1960 to 137 million in 1975—an increase of 44 million within a period of 15 years. In this brief span, men in the productive ages needing land or jobs will increase 40 per cent. If there is to be advance, schools and teachers must be provided for that major portion of the 21 million youth aged 5 to 14 who are not now in school, plus 13 million additional children who will be in the same age group in 1975.

The outlook for smooth transition to demographic modernization is somber indeed, given continuities in the values, attitudes, and activities that have shaped the past. The population problem has long existed in the Indies, and it has long been ignored. Malthusians viewed Javanese growth with awe, but failed to descend from the verbal level to the painstaking research and the intricate planning involved in advancing the social changes and providing the contraceptive services that would lead to declining birth rates. Marxism-Leninism denied the economic determinism of the past and affirmed the freedom of human reproduction from mundane limits of food and fiber in the future. No one pointed out that in Indonesia the children brought mouths for eating and hands for working, but found too little food and too little work.

The great mirage of Indonesia is transmigration from Java to Sumatra. Planned transfers, if achieved, would remove only 12 per cent of the population increase from Java. Given a natural increase of some three million people a year, agrarian settlement is a hopelessly antiquated idea for solution to the problem of numbers.

But Indonesia does have the wealth of the outer islands. It has a population that, given the breakthrough to development, could participate in modernization of an advanced scientific and technical type. For Indonesia certainly, for other areas perhaps, there is no middle ground. Continuity in population growth leads sooner or later to increased death rates. The continuing quest for agrarian solutions through transmigration intensifies the difficulties of that thrust into modernization which offers the only solution.

Indonesia's people and their increasing numbers are products, rather than causes, of that long, quiescent, and generally myopic period that was the Indonesian past. The questions are the Indonesian future, not the Indonesian past. If there is any place in the contemporary world where population growth should be generating compulsive pressures for swift modernization, that place is Indonesia.

Other countries. The exploration of cultural, demographic, and political interrelations could continue. There are the countries once called Indochina, where the extraordinary density of population in the Tonkin delta existed alongside almost empty areas, and where divided countries, divided ideologies, and war follow along lines of the demographic diversities. There is Malaya, where population problems have been fundamentally those of ethnic diversity, where today such problems are those of the Chinese and the Malays. There is Thailand, long acclaimed as a country that could easily support a hundred million people. A recent census and several surveys indicate that the birth rate, once believed low, is actually above 50 per 1,000. The population, 24 million in 1960, may increase to 48 million in 1980. Given constant birth rates and declining death rates, a population of one hundred million would be reached by the end of this century.

Past, present, and future. The evolution and status of the Southeast Asian countries has been traced in terms of population. Here there has come to be major unity rather than diversity. That unity lies in the coexistence of very high birth rates and declining death rates, and hence in rates of population increase that, continued, jeopardize not alone economic development and social advance, but human survival itself. An overlay of the great Asian cultures followed by the selective penetrations of colonial powers was apparently conducive to relaxing the fertility controls in the indigenous populations but not adequate to stimulate new controls. Neither country nor religion can be awarded the badge of achievement for the growth that is now occurring. Fertility is almost equally high in the Catholic Philippines, Muslim Indonesia, and Buddhist Thailand. Nor can the colonial powers be blamed, for Spain and the United States governed in the Philippines; the Dutch ruled Indonesia; the French, Indochina; the British, Malaya; and, as noted earlier, Thailand was never a colony.

The future is now forming. Neither statisticians nor seers can discern more than vague shadows of the outlines. The great forces determining tomorrow's populations lie within the region. There have been major declines in birth rates among an Asian people, the Japanese. Birth rates are now declining in the Ryukyus, Taiwan, Hong Kong, and Singapore. Thailand debates national policy at the highest levels—to develop public health services that will contribute to declining birth rates and so to swifter economic and social advance. The Indonesian problem is known to the Indonesians, the Philippine problem to the Filipinos. But needs are great, science and technology are limited, and time is brief.

Transition and Transformation: The United States

Northern America was sparsely settled in the early seventeenth century. The indigenous people were few and widely dispersed. Some Spanish had moved northward into areas that are now the United States, but there was no continuing push from colonizing people. The French were moving into Canada, but numbers were few and the period of continuing immigration was brief. The first permanent English settlements were made on the East Coast early in the eighteenth century.

One hundred and seventy years after the Pilgrims landed in Massachusetts, the newly established United States of America ordered the first count of its people. The year was 1790. The total population was 3.9 million, excluding Indians and others beyond the settled frontiers. The land area was 865,000 square miles; density was less than five per square mile. One hundred and seventy years after this first census, the eighteenth decennial census was taken. The year was 1960. A total population of 179 million occupied a land area of 3.5 million square miles. Density was 50 per square mile.

Many of the transitions that made the United States feasible as a populous, unified, and relatively integrated nation occurred in the first half of the country's history when population was increasing and diffusing without benefit of statisticians or census takers. If there is a period at which the population potential and the population problems of the United States are comparable with those of today's underdeveloped and newly sovereign nations, it is the late eighteenth and early nineteenth centuries, roughly the period measured in the data of the censuses of 1790, 1800, and 1810. The more appropriate comparison for the United States of America is Europe, though, for the native peoples of the land were not the ones who achieved independence. The free population was mainly European in origin. The growth and the westward movement was a component in European growth and expansion, a variant of the modernization that has occurred in all European nations and among all European peoples. There was an African population in the colonial period and in 1790, but in the late eighteenth and the first half of the nineteenth centuries, acculturation proceeded under chattel slavery. The contrasts of African demography in Africa and among Africans overseas becomes a fruitful approach to processes of social change and the persistence or emergence of subcultural differentiations.

This multiple comparative focus is one of the major justifications for consideration of the demography of a specific country. The other is the unique value of the United States as a case study in the demography of the affluent society.

Increase and expansion. European society had ancient institutions that limited marriage and retarded childbearing, ancient folkways whereby births remained within the appropriate limits. America was settled by common people from Europe, probably downwardly biased in class selection but deficient also in the physically weak, the mentally limited, and the socially derelict. The mores of family limitation must have been pervasive in the European homeland. In the new situation, however, institutional deterrents and economic barriers were reduced and birth rates increased to high levels. The forces of the increase and the validity of various functional interpretations may be debated. The demographic facts are firmly based and subject to question only within narrow limits. In the eighteenth and early nineteenth centuries, birth rates in the United States of America were above 50 per 1,000 total population. Population increase amounted to more than 30 per cent each decade (see Figure 1). Since immigration was slight in this period, the major factor in the growth must have been natural increase. A high rate of natural increase in turn indicates that death rates must have been fairly low for a people without modern medicines in a land where doctors were few and health services limited. The conditions of living in the New World should have been favorable to death rates lower than those in the Europe of the period. Towns were few, villages were small, and farmers lived on scattered homesteads. Epidemics decimated the populations of limited areas, but not those of great regions. Climate was temperate, and food was adequate. Neither famine nor severe malnutrition were widespread after the early difficult years when agricultural cultivation was being established in an unknown and often hostile environment. There were Indian and other conflicts, but few of the European immigrants and their descendants were involved outside the frontier areas. Moreover, losses were slight

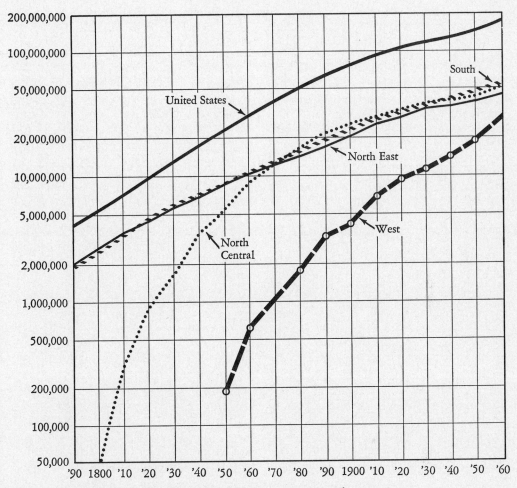

Fig. 1. Population of the United States and regions: 1790 to 1960.

among those who had guns and other superior technologies.

The demographic impact of the ways and conditions of living in the new land differed for the white population that soon became the majority, the indigenous population whom the Europeans labelled as "Indians," and the Africans who came as chattel slaves. Here, as in other countries throughout the world, the fate of the simpler people involved disorganization, displacement, and decimation. The Indians met pressures on their living space, deterioration of their hunting grounds, and conflict, while also

subjected to the germs, the alcohol, and the guns of the newcomers. Some became extinct; many declined until few remained. There was some assimilation. Eventually, for the ones that remained distinct, there was recuperation and rapid increase with the lowered death rates and the high birth rates that are characteristic, here and elsewhere, for retarded, isolated, and subsidized minorities.

The development of the African population was distinctive whether viewed with reference to other groups in the United States or Africans in Africa and elsewhere.

The slave trade presumably depopulated much of Central Africa. Mortality was high in the movement across the Atlantic and in the islands of conditioning in the Caribbean. It must also have been high in many areas of the mainland, as new hazards were met at the same time that patterns of submission were being established. By the early nineteenth century, though, fertility was high and mortality was lowered. The African as property was capital investment and saleable product. Maximum numbers of surviving children and minimum hazards to health and life were economically advantageous. Whether these or the social and cultural factors were paramount, natural increase was rapid.

Ethnic differentiations associated with color have always been present in the United States. Death rates long remained higher for the Negroes than for the whites. Birth rates long remained high, aside from the factors of disorganization and disease that resulted in lowered birth rates in the central cities of the North. Eventually, the balance of health, institutional, and other factors was altered and the birth rates of Negroes in central cities rose to relatively high levels. Overall, though, the growth of the Negro population was distinctive primarily in the economic, social, and motivational complex influencing fertility and the nutritional and health complex influencing mortality. The high birth rates in the rural setting, the current high birth rates in the great cities, and the correlates of upward social mobility are the anticipated aspects of change in a developing society. The differential fertility within the Negro population is similar to that in the white population. Perhaps here, as in the case of the European immigrant groups of the late nineteenth and early twentieth centuries, there is convergence toward, and merging in, a total population that is itself in process of change. With the African, as with the Indian, the model for acculturation was European in origin and modified European in outline. The Negro became American in language, religion, and culture. Pre-sumably, therefore, further merging into the larger society will be accompanied by the elimination of the demographic differentiations that still exist.

In the early period, only the Indian population was declining, and it was but a small portion of the total. The white majority and the Negro minority were increasing rapidly. Estimates of the population of the United States at varying future periods, based on the projection of the rates of growth of the late eighteenth and early nineteenth centuries, indicated very large populations and presumably serious population difficulties ahead. There were fears that the pressures of the Old World would appear in the new. Elsewhere in the world at different time periods, nations feared their high rates of growth and estimated future populations in numbers so large that realization of the projected numbers was not possible. Today, the projected growth of the underdeveloped areas and the world that is rousing such widespread alarm pertains to the final decades of the century. Controversy is in the realm of the conjectural, for there cannot be objective analysis of the history of the decades from 1960 to 2000 prior to the passing of that history. In the case of the United States, the test of history is available. There is a numerical record of a century and a half. Fears and predictions of demographic doom have had little relationship to future realities. The United States does not have rural densities comparable to those in the river valleys of monsoon Asia. The people do not suffer from the poverty of the lands where man is plentiful, knowledge limited, and resources few. In this instance, the course of development thwarted the fears of human inundations.

In the focus of comparative demography, the role of empty lands and unused resources is distinctive to the United States, along with those few other countries that are truly continental in the scope of their lands and resources: U.S.S.R., Canada, and Brazil. The United States has again and again increased its lands and its resources.

The Louisiana Purchase of 1803 and the Oregon Cession of 1846 gave the increasing nucleus of the east the world's most fruitful agricultural lands—lands that were almost empty from the Mississippi River to the Pacific Ocean, from New Orleans to the Canadian border. Spain ceded Florida in 1819. The mid-century additions of Texas, the Southwest, and California provided the expansion frontier for the industrial mid-twentieth century. Hawaii and Alaska contributed farther to area and diversity. Expansion that involved colonial relationships, however, was repudiated, ideologically and in the fact of Philippine independence.

If the economy and the society had remained agrarian, rural, and isolated, it is probable that population would have increased until the new lands were occupied as the old had been. Deaths would have functioned again as regulators of growth, such as has been the pattern for many populations in many countries. New lands on the frontiers, new crops, irrigation, and efficient administration permitted the increase of numbers for limited periods. But then there was the ancient poverty and the ancient balance of birth and death rates at high levels. In the United States, the advance of science and technology and the education of the people altered economic activity, social structure, population distribution, and growth processes. Rapid economic development made rapid population increase an asset rather than a liability.

Declining fertility came largely as a correlate of economic and social change. It seemed to provide a fundamental solution to problems of population growth and the economic and social interrelations of such growth. Fears concerned the severity of the decline and the imminence of depopulation, for this was the problem of the future if the long trends of the past should continue. Recently, however, increases in fertility have focused current controversies on the question of whether or not the United States is moving toward major pressures of population on natural resources, rates of economic

growth, social flexibilities, and individual opportunities.

Perhaps the most difficult questions of American demography and society are the ones that are seldom asked: Why did the path of development tend toward social and demographic convergence among ethnic, linguistic, and other groups? Why did rates of population growth slow as a result of declining birth rates rather than increasing death rates?

The answers to these and many other fundamental questions concerning population growth are more than demographic. Urbanization, industrialization, and the demographic transition are interrelated processes today; they were interrelated in the past; presumably they will remain so in the future. Hence the following sections note the growth of cities, the occupational transformations of a once agricultural population, and the educational advance of a once largely illiterate people.

Growth and urbanization. The demographic epic of the United States involves growth, migration, and transformation. The story is customarily envisioned as the movement of pioneers in covered wagons, as the impact of a frontier that was filled in 1890, as the continuity of an agrarian structure wherein family farms produced abundantly, nurtured youth in proper settings, and contributed manpower to cities and industrial regions. This, along with the Statue of Liberty and the land of opportunity for the oppressed, is part of the vision of the new world. It is also part of the mythology of a people whose origins involve private space, simple economies, firm social structures, and known codes of propriety and ethics. As demography, it is simplification.

The United States has always had less densely settled areas and less developed regions, and most people in most periods have been free to move if they so desired. Migration became and remained part of a way of life. The feasible and profitable frontier areas were also the areas of most rapid growth, wherever the frontier and whatever

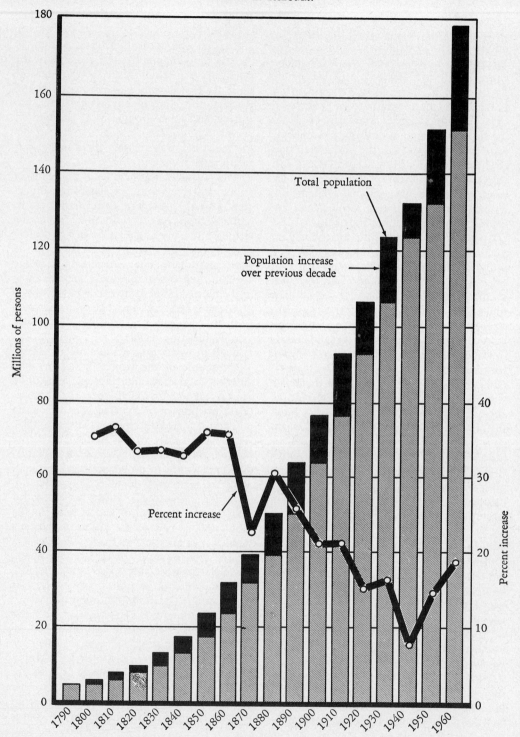

Fig. 2. Total population, decennial, population increase, and per cent of increase: 1790 to 1960.

the time. This onward and outward movement is apparent in the growth of the populations of regions and subregions over time (see Figure 2). There was westward expansion within the northern regions, but the populations of the combined regions have had, and still have, a major part of the population of the nation. The cities received immigrants from Europe, Canada, and other parts of the United States, while cities and rural areas alike contributed migrants to the more westerly regions. The South grew primarily by virtue of that portion of its natural increase which it retained.

The major areas of growth have been peripheral to the developed areas. In most of the nation's history, this growth involved westward migrations. In the years from the Revolutionary to the Civil wars, the most rapidly increasing population was that of the Northwest Territory. People numbered 51,000 in 1800, 6.9 million in 1860. Forward bases and technological advances in agriculture and transportation were preconditions for massive migrations and effective utilization of the lands beyond the Mississippi. Thus major parts of the Louisiana Purchase and the Pacific Northwest became great settlement areas only in the last half of the nineteenth century. The population was 1.6 million in 1850. It increased to 5.3 million in 1870, 12.8 million in 1890, and 20.0 million in 1910. By 1910, though, the region was already contributing migrants to other areas. In the half century from 1910 to 1960, the exodus became so great that there was widespread decline in the rural population.

The increase of the population in Florida and the areas acquired in mid-century eventually surpassed that in the northwest push from the Mississippi to the Pacific Northwest. In 1860, there were 1.3 million people in these southerly areas. By 1900 the population was over 4.3 million, little more than one-fourth that of the northern areas west of the Mississippi. By 1920, the southern expansion areas had a population almost half that of the states formed from the Louisiana Purchase and the Northwest Cession. By 1960, the rapidly increasing southern populations had surpassed the slowly increasing or even declining populations of the great heartland that had provided the unique epic of rural America. Change continues, with the most rapid increases of the last decade occurring in Florida, the Southwest states, and California. There was also rapid growth in the farthest and newest of the states, particularly Alaska. Here immigration from the other states occurred along with the rapid natural increase of an indigenous population whose intact birth rate existed alongside a low death rate and a white population heavily weighted with young and newly married members of the armed forces.

This growth and expansion of the American population across an empty and rich continent was never merely the outward filtration of simple agrarian peoples. The earliest occupants here moved beyond the institutions of church and school and the amenities of the middle classes, but churches and schools were priorities in new areas. Migration was a channel of upward mobility in the agricultural class itself, and the driving motivations for children involved education, especially for daughters. Then, too, trade, transportation, and industry were aspects of expansion, for agriculture itself was oriented to the market. Towns and cities grew as economic centers, nucleii of contacts, and meccas for the youth of the farms and villages. Professional, managerial, and technical workers migrated along with farmers and laborers. The only simple measure of this complex process of growth, expansion, concentration, and differentiation is the proportion of the population that is urban. For the United States and the expansion areas, as for the conventional regions and divisions, urban population increased more rapidly than rural from the first census in 1790 to the most recent one in 1960 (see Figure 3). In 1790, 5.1 per cent of the total population was urban. Not until 1910 did the figure pass 50 per cent. In 1960, by current definitions, almost 70 per cent of the

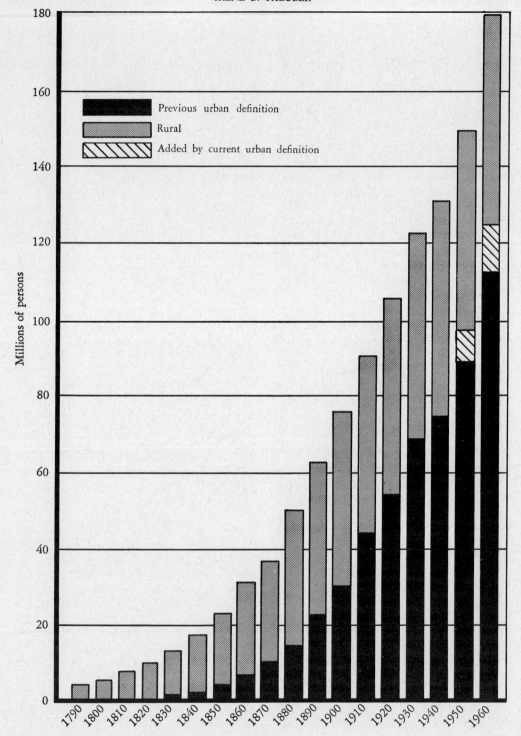

Fig. 3. Urban and rural population: 1790 to 1960.

total population of the United States was urban.

Urbanization has been essential to the formation of the industrial economy. It has also been essential to the preservation and advance of the agricultural economy. Cities grew in labor force and in population through their own natural increase, migration from the rural areas, and immigration from abroad. Rural areas preserved some balance between opportunities and people through the exodus of their youth. Agriculture itself was industrialized; agricultural productivity was based on science and technology. Rural children attended school, and rural families adopted urban ways of living along with the attitudes and values of the larger culture. Some rural people were poor and retarded, but some urban people were likewise disadvantaged.

From 1790 to 1900 and even later, urban residence and nonagricultural employment were highly correlated. "Rural" was so closely identified with "agriculture" that the one could be estimated from the other. With the acceleration of urbanization, the industrial revolution in agricultural production, the advance of transportation and communication, and rising real incomes, the rural population became primarily a sector of the nonagricultural population defined in terms of place of residence. Urban people moved outward, and great outer areas of interpenetrated urban and rural living became the characteristic mark of affluent America. Technology was obliterating not simply the population dependent on agriculture, but the age-old distinction of the city people and the rural folk.

Something of the forces in occupation and education that are continuing aspects and products of the urban ways of life and value structures must be noted, for these are basic to the formation and differentiation of the urbanized population of an increasingly metropolitan society.

Occupational transformations. The United States developed, or was developed by, the most productive agricultural population that has existed anywhere at any time. Then, in the last half of the eighteenth century, that population declined continually and with increasing speed in response to further advances in the technology, productivity, and opportunity that created it.

The agricultural and nonagricultural sectors of the labor force long increased together, but the rate of increase was higher in the nonagricultural sector. Proportions working in agriculture therefore declined, even while numbers continued to increase. In the early nineteenth century, three-fourths or more of the total gainfully occupied population was in agriculture. In 1870, slightly more than half was in agriculture. It was 37.5 per cent in 1900, 21.2 per cent in 1930. Relative decline continued to 17.4 per cent in 1940, 11.8 per cent in 1950, and 6.3 per cent in 1960.

The persistence of long time developments and the immensity of the changes of the twentieth century are alike apparent in the trends in the numbers of men occupied in agriculture. In 1910, there were 10.4 million men gainfully occupied in agriculture. Increase had been continuous throughout the national history, probably even from the time the colonists landed in Jamestown and Plymouth in the early seventeenth century. Then, as agricultural productivity soared, manpower in agriculture started to decline in numbers, slowly at first, then more speedily. In the years from 1910 to 1940, decline amounted to 10 per cent each decade. From 1940 to 1950 and again from 1950 to 1960, decade decline was 35 per cent. In 1960, there were 3.9 million men in agriculture as contrasted with the 10.4 million men of 1910.

The implications of a change of this order of magnitude are major and pervasive. In each of the last two decades, about half of all the counties of the United States have declined in total population. Depopulation is in process in the great agricultural center of the Mississippi-Missouri Valley and the high plains, as in many areas of the South. The sons and daughters of the farmers turned away from agriculture; farmers themselves left as lands were consolidated. The towns, the cities, and the industrial regions were formed in substantial part by youth from the farms and their descendants in later generations. Rural traditions and mores vied with immigrant diversities in the intermixture and amalgam through and from which metropolitan America was formed. The tenant farmers of the South in the cities of the North and the West are lineal successors to the youth of the Corn Belt in an earlier period and the youth of New England in a still earlier period.

Thus one of the great transformations is nearing completion. Families now remaining on farms are too few to contribute any major numbers of maturing youth to urban residence and nonagricultural occupations. But a new and different transformation results from the slowing and virtual completion of the rural farm and agricultural transformation. The oncoming generations will be in major part urban born and urban reared. Increasingly, movement and mobility involve metropolitan populations in interrelations with each other. Conjecture permits only hypothetical outlines of the structure and dynamics of a metropolitan society whose people are indigenous urbanites. It would be desirable to approach the analysis of demographic and social processes in the past, with the focus on indigenous urbanites rather than indigenous agriculturalists. But space and time alike preclude this approach here.

The character of the growing occupations in recent decades is a clue if not the key to the economy and society that is emerging. Manual workers, including craftsmen and foremen, operatives, and laborers, have changed little as a proportion of the total occupied population. They constituted 36 per cent of the gainfully occupied in 1900, 40 per cent in 1920, 1940, and 1960. Within the group, though, operatives were increasing while laborers were declining. Service workers increased slowly, but this was the net result of a major and continuing decline

in private household workers along with major and continuing increases in other service workers, including waiters, counter and fountain workers, bartenders, beauticians, and others. In general, white collar workers increased, manual workers changed fairly slowly, and service workers increased somewhat.

The phenomenal trends in occupational activities are blunted in the customary social and economic classification. These trends involve the decline of farm workers and other laborers along with the rise of professional, technical, and kindred workers among men and women and the rise of occupations for women. The decline in farm workers has been noted previously. Men who worked as laborers in 1960 were numerically about the same in 1900 and in 1960; relative to the total occupied, there was a decline from 15 per cent in 1900 to 8 per cent in 1960. Men in the professional, technical, and related fields increased from 4.2 million in 1900 to 16.2 million in 1960; as a percentage of the occupied, numbers rose from 3 per cent in 1900 to 10 per cent in 1960. Rates of increase are still growing. Numbers in 1960 were 55 per cent larger than those in 1950.

Trends in employment and the occupational structure for women are as striking as those for men. The percentage of women aged 14 and over in the labor force increased from 26 per cent in 1940 to 29 per cent in 1950 and 34 per cent in 1960. In the latter year, 45 or more per cent of the women from ages 18 to 24 were in the labor force, 35 per cent at ages 25 to 34, 45 or more per cent at ages 40 to 54, 30 per cent at ages 55 to 59, and 17 per cent at ages 60 to 64. With prevalent early marriages and a period of domestic responsibility that involves three or more children on the average, women work outside the home in increasing numbers. This is particularly true, though, for the years when children are in high school and college and in the years when the family is again simply a husband-wife one.

The entrance of the industrial revolution

into the home and related fields, the types of opportunities available, and the definitions of roles and responsibilities for women are all involved in the increasing coexistence of the reproductive and the economic roles of women. In 1900, one-fifth of all employed women were in agriculture; in 1960, the proportion was one-fiftieth. In 1900, almost 30 per cent of all employed women were private household workers; in 1960, 8 per cent. The percentage of employed women who were operatives was also declining. The great increases occurred in clerical and related occupations, in service occupations outside the household, and in professional, technical, and related occupations.

The occupational transformation mirrors the process of industrialization and, in recent years, automation. In 1900, 56 per cent of all workers were either farmers or laborers; in 1960, 16 per cent. In 1900, 3 per cent of all workers were professional or technical; in 1960, 10 per cent. Perhaps the most startling fact concerning the society of contemporary United States is the simple one that there are now more professional and technical workers than laborers, other than

farm and mine, and more professional and technical workers than farm operators, managers, and laborers combined. Together professional, technical, managerial and related workers, and officials outnumber laborers and farmers. Hands, brawn, and folk skills have limited utility in the contemporary labor market. Ability, education, and discipline are the essential requirements. Workers with lesser innate abilities, low education, and little discipline are increasingly marginal in the moving economy and society. The process is cumulative, for the definitions of the levels of ability and education that signify competence are themselves advancing.

Education. The early colonial population was largely unschooled and illiterate. Schools were built soon, mainly on the initiative of local communities. By 1850, more than 90 per cent of the native white people were literate. Illiteracy remained prevalent in frontier areas and was almost universal in the slave population. By 1900, however, illiteracy had declined to 5 per cent for native whites, 13 per cent for foreign-born whites, and 44 per cent for Negroes. Illiteracy was already ceasing to be a significant measure

TABLE 5

UNITED STATES. MEDIAN YEARS OF SCHOOL COMPLETED BY MEN, BY AGE,
FOR URBAN AND RURAL AREAS, 1960[a]

Age in 1960	Year when Aged 25–29	Total	Residence in 1960		
			Urban	Rural Nonfarm	Rural Farm
25 and over		10.3	10.9	9.0	8.6
25–29	1960	12.3	12.4	12.0	11.5
30–34	1955	12.1	12.3	11.1	10.6
35–39	1950	12.1	12.2	11.0	10.0
40–44	1945	11.6	12.0	10.2	8.9
45–49	1940	10.3	10.9	9.0	8.7
50–54	1935	9.4	10.1	8.7	8.5
55–59	1930	8.7	8.9	8.4	8.3
60–64	1925	8.5	8.7	8.3	8.2
65–69	1920	8.3	8.4	8.1	8.1
70–74	1915	8.1	8.2	7.7	7.9
75 and over	1910	8.0	8.1	7.3	7.5

[a] Source of data: U. S. Bureau of the Census. *1960 Census of population.* Vol. 1. *Characteristics of the population.* Part D. Detailed characteristics. United States Summary. Washington, 1961. Table 173.

of educational differences for the modal areas and groups in the population.

Participation in the moving economy and the urbanizing society required increasingly higher levels of educational attainment. The extent to which these higher levels were achieved is suggested in Table 5, where median years of school completed are given for the male population as of 1960 by age in the different areas of residence.

Since final educational level is achieved approximately by ages 25 to 29, persons of specific ages in 1960 may be taken as crudely representative of the educational levels of the population at the time they were aged 25 to 29. Educational levels for successive age groups differed widely, whether comparisons are made among color groups, residential areas, or regions. In 1910, the major differentiation was that between whites and nonwhites, rather than between residential groups within a color dichotomy. In the half century from 1910 to 1960, education advanced substantially for all groups, with growth coming first in the urban areas, later in the rural nonfarm areas, and last in the rural farm areas. Even in 1960 the advance for nonwhites remained limited in the rural sectors.

The trends of educational levels for the age groups suggest the dimensions of the future. The interrelations and the social and demographic correlates of educational levels in recent decades are suggested in Table 6, where the relative prevalence of functional illiteracy (four years school attendance or less) and college graduation are given for all persons aged 25 and over for the years 1940, 1950, and 1960. The superiority of the urban over the rural is major, as is that of the white over the nonwhite. These are relationships known to perceptive observers of the contemporary scene. Four aspects of the relationships are not so obvious. First, overall, and in each type of residence, the numbers of the functionally illiterate are substantially larger for whites than for nonwhites. Second, the differentials are less, the increases over time greater, in the urban than in the rural areas. Third, migration takes portions of all groups, and particularly the Negro, from disadvantaged rural areas to advanced urban areas. Fourth, the convergences of opportunities and achievements, in younger ages in all groups and all residential areas, will transform the educational levels of the adult population as these younger groups mature to become in turn the prime productive workers, the aging, and the aged.

Processes. The increase, expansion, redistribution, and changing characteristics of the population of the United States have already been noted. The processes involved include international migration, natural increase, and internal migration.

In the years from 1820 to 1961, more than 42 million immigrants entered the United States, most of them from Europe. The strength of the exodus from Europe became apparent in the 1840's, when 1.7 million immigrants from the continent entered the United States. Migration from western and northern Europe was the major component in a great swell that carried the number of immigrants to 5.2 million in the 1880's. As these regions of Europe industrialized and reduced their rates of natural increase, the number of emigrants dwindled. The new streams of immigrants to the United States came mainly from the eastern and southern portions of the continent.

In six of the eleven years from 1905 through 1915 more than a million migrants entered the United States. There was a hiatus during the late years of World War I, but as the tides resumed, migration became a major question of public policy. The maturing of the population and the economy of the United States, fears of ethnic and cultural diversity, and ethnocentrism were factors in a political decision for limitation. The resulting law was based on quotas according to ethnic origin, defined as the presumed contribution of the group to the population of 1920. The quota for total immigration was about 150,000 a year, but no quotas were applied to the countries of the Americas.

TABLE 6

UNITED STATES. FUNCTIONAL ILLITERACY AND COLLEGE EDUCATION AMONG PERSONS
AGED 25 AND OVER, BY COLOR, FOR URBAN AND RURAL AREAS, 1940 TO 1960[a]

Year, Color and Residence	Population in Thousands			Per cent completing	
	Total Aged 25 and Over	Educational level			
		4 Years or Less	College 4 Years or More	4 Years or Less	College 4 Years or More
Total					
1940	74,776	10,105	3,407	13.7	4.6
1950	87,885	9,522	5,304	11.1	6.2
Urban	59,050	5,406	4,273	9.4	7.4
Rural	28,834	4,116	1,032	14.7	3.7
1960	99,438	8,303	7,625	8.4	7.7
Urban	71,052	5,178	6,290	7.3	8.9
Rural	28,386	3,124	1,336	11.0	4.7
Nonfarm	21,163	2,308	1,130	10.9	5.3
Farm	7,223	816	205	11.3	2.8
White					
1940	68,000	7,322	3,320	10.9	4.9
1950	79,515	6,893	5,123	8.9	6.6
Urban	53,395	4,048	4,117	7.8	7.9
Rural	26,119	2,845	1,005	10.1	3.9
1960	89,581	5,989	7,278	6.7	8.1
Urban	63,574	3,785	5,986	6.0	9.4
Rural	26,007	2,204	1,292	8.5	5.0
Nonfarm	19,399	1,649	1,093	8.5	5.6
Farm	6,609	555	199	8.4	3.0
Nonwhite					
1940	6,776	2,782	88	41.8	1.3
1950	8,370	2,629	182	32.6	2.3
Urban	5,655	1,358	155	24.9	2.8
Rural	2.715	1,271	26	48.7	1.0
1960	9,857	2,314	347	23.4	3.5
Urban	7,478	1,394	304	18.6	4.1
Rural	2,378	920	44	38.7	1.8
Nonfarm	1,764	660	37	37.4	2.1
Farm	614	261	7	42.4	1.1

[a] Source of data: U.S. Bureau of the Census. *1960 Census of population.* Vol. 1. *Characteristics of the population.* Part C. General social and economic characteristics. United States Summary. Washington, 1961. Table 76.

When quotas were adopted, it was assumed that immigrants would no longer contribute significantly to the population of the United States. In the years from the great depression to the end of World War II, net international movements were indeed slight. But again, as in so many aspects of demography, conclusions proved to be specific as to time and circumstances. Refugees, nonquota migrants, and special groups have contributed to the numbers and the qualitative transformation of international migration in recent years. Two and one-half million immigrants were admitted in the decade from 1951 to 1961. These new immigrants were mainly selected from professional, scientific, technical, and scholarly groups.

Immigrants who remained in the United States were reported in the data of the successive censuses as the foreign-born. Immigrants were mainly young adults, so native-born children were soon added to the population amalgam. Many of these first generation natives were recognizable as such, in the communities in which they lived, and in their affiliations, identifications, and roles. In census data, they were labelled as native-born of foreign or mixed parentage. As the children of immigrants became young adults, married, and had children, they became native-born of native parentage, no longer distinguished from the descendants of the earliest migrants to Massachusetts or Virginia.

The transformation in the nativity composition of Whites is far advanced. The foreign-born are aging or aged, as are the native-born of foreign or mixed parentage. Children, youth, and increasing proportions of those in the productive and reproductive ages are now native-born of native parentage. Since the Negroes are predominantly descendants of seventeenth- and eighteenth-century immigrants, the population of the United States as a whole is becoming native in the third or further generations.

Natural increase has always predominated in population growth, but a dichotomy of immigration and natural increase is somewhat artificial. Immigrants and their descendants (the native-born), contribute to births and deaths within the United States. Since the earlier immigrants were a selection of lower socioeconomic levels, their presence retarded declines in birth and in death rates.

The levels of death rates in the United States remained conjectural through the first half of the nineteenth century, for there were neither national nor regional registration systems. From 1850 onward, mortality declined slowly but with considerable regularity. In Massachusetts, the expectation of life at birth for males was 38.3 years in 1850, and 46.1 years in 1901–1902. In the death registration states, the expectation of life at birth for males was 53.6 years in 1920, 60.8 years in 1940, and 66.5 years in 1959. The expectation of life at birth for females first exceeded the proverbial 3 score years

and 10 in 1950; in 1959, it was 73 years. Death rates per 1,000 total population were 17.2 in 1900, 10.8 in 1940, and 9.5 in 1960. Rates standardized to the age distribution of the population of 1940 were 17.8 in 1900, 10.8 in 1940, and 7.7 in 1960.

The trend of birth rates was downward from the early nineteenth century to the thirties of this century. The birth rate that had been 55 per 1,000 total population for 1815–1825 had declined below 40 by 1880. It was 30 in 1910, 21 in 1930, and below 19 in 1935. Further decline was believed probable, but instead the birth rate increased to 19.4 in 1940 and 25.0 in 1950. The maximum crude rate for the recent period was 25.3 in 1957. Annual declines then carried the rate down to 23.4 in 1961. Current and potential increase is substantial for a population believed to be facing decline only a quarter century ago.

In the earlier part of the twentieth century, there were major convergences in vital rates for whites and nonwhites. Convergence has continued in mortality, but it seems to have been slowed in fertility. In 1961, birth rates were 22.3 for whites, 31.6 for non-whites. More refined measures corroborate the validity of the differentials in levels. From 1957 to the present, however, both crude rates and gross reproduction rates have declined for nonwhites as for whites. Moreover, social, economic, and educational differentials in fertility have been and remain similar for whites and nonwhites. Numbers of children ever born to women aged 25 to 34 are shown for white and nonwhite women by marital status in Table 7.

The associations involved in the long decline in fertility have been documented fully and incisively. Fertility was lower in upper social and economic groups, among the educated, and in urban areas. Theories of the interrelations of industrialization, urbanization, secularization, altered roles for women, altered values of children, and declining fertility have been formulated. There were some interesting deviations, particularly a somewhat higher fertility among members of

TABLE 7

UNITED STATES. CUMULATIVE FERTILITY OF WOMEN AGED 25 TO 34, BY COLOR.
MARITAL STATUS, AND RESIDENCE, 1910 AND 1940 TO 1960[a]
(children ever born per 1,000 women)

Year and Residence	All Women			Ever-Married Women		
	Total	White	Nonwhite	Total	White	Nonwhite
1910	1,982	1,913	2,543	2,550	2,485	3,040
1940	1,391	1,353	1,715	1,758	1,717	2,093
1950	1,646	1,621	1,853	1,854	1,825	2,096
Urban	1,432	1,423	1,509	1,644	1,635	1,716
Rural	2,123	2,056	2,743	2,294	2,214	3,065
1960	2,236	2,187	2,590	2,447	2,379	2,963
Urban	2,104	2,059	2,392	2,330	2,269	2,731
Rural	2,585	2,507	3,374	2,746	2,642	3,889
Nonfarm	2,534	2,466	3,252	2,681	2,590	3,732
Farm	2,798	2,680	3,781	3,021	2,867	4,423

[a] Source: U.S. Bureau of the Census. *1960 Census of population. General social and economic characteristics*. United States: Summary. Final Report PC(1)-1C. Washington, 1961. Table 81.

the highest income groups in the most developed areas. It was assumed, however, that the generally inverse relationships would be maintained and that downward movements would continue.

By the middle thirties, as already noted, the childbearing of women was insufficient for the replacement of the women. Given the continuation of the trends and relationships, numbers of births would be fewer than numbers of deaths, and the national population would decline. In the process, ever declining proportions in the younger ages would exist alongside ever increasing proportions in the older ages. There would follow profound, and generally undesirable, effects on economic growth, social institutions, political rationality, and innovation.

The rise in fertility was viewed initially as an adjustment, i.e., a cumulation of births postponed in the depression years and an advance of births associated with early war marriages. As it became apparent that there was a higher level of fertility, research was directed toward the inherent dynamics of the process of replacement, the values of children in terms of the numbers that couples wished or expected to have, and the social and psychological factors associated with family ideals and reproductive per-

formance. Continuing and ever more intensive research on the processes, levels, and interrelations of fertility with economic, social, religious, and political factors is essential to the formulation of theory that accords with the developing realities.

Estimates of future populations, based on the declining fertility of the past, indicated precipitant decline in total numbers in the latter part of this century, but the decline is not occurring. Projections of future populations on the assumption of continuity in current levels or current dynamics in fact suggest major increases in total numbers in future years. The population that was 181 million on July 1, 1960, will reach approximately 210 million by July 1, 1970, if the fertility levels of the fifties continue.

The change from inherent decline to substantial growth has involved sharp transitions in age structure and major shifts in rates of increase for functional age groups from one time period to another. These aspects are not mentioned further here, for they are discussed, with special reference to population in the productive ages and the labor force, in Chapter 5.

Given high rates of natural increase, the mechanization of agriculture with the corre-lated release of the agricultural labor supply,

the concentration of population in metropolitan areas, and the growth of the southern coastal areas from Florida to California,
it is apparent that migrations of major mag-

nitude must have occurred and must still
be occurring. This is indeed true (see Table
8). The out-migrations from the South constitute a near exodus. The population aged

TABLE 8

UNITED STATES. REGIONS. NET CHANGES BY MIGRATION OR AREA CHANGES, 1950 TO
1960, PERSONS 15 TO 44 YEARS OF AGE IN 1960, BY NATIVITY AND RACE,
BY RESIDENCE[a]

(net change per 100 expected without migration or area change)

Region, Residence Nativity, and Race	Age groups						
	Age 10 and Over	15 to 19	20 to 24	25 to 29	30 to 34	35 to 39	40 to 44
All areas							
Northeast	− 0.4	− 0.2	0.0	4.0	3.7	1.7	− 0.3
North Central	− 0.8	− 1.2	− 3.0	2.8	2.8	− 0.3	− 0.7
South	− 2.3	− 2.7	− 8.5	−10.3	−5.7	− 2.6	− 1.1
West	17.9	18.4	31.3	35.1	26.9	20.9	14.9
Urban							
Northeast	1.3	4.0	9.1	8.7	2.7	1.1	0.2
North Central	6.5	12.0	24.9	22.8	6.0	2.4	2.9
South	18.0	25.7	45.6	33.0	10.8	9.3	10.8
West	32.7	38.2	65.2	68.7	43.0	31.7	26.1
Rural							
Northeast	− 6.9	−13.4	−27.0	−11.7	8.1	4.5	− 2.5
North Central	−13.9	−19.7	−39.0	−27.4	− 4.3	− 6.2	− 8.4
South	−21.5	−22.7	−41.9	−41.9	−24.6	−17.5	−15.3
West	−15.6	−16.6	−22.7	−22.8	−11.4	− 8.5	−14.2
Native White							
All areas							
Northeast	− 3.1	− 3.7	− 7.2	− 4.0	− 2.0	− 2.1	− 2.8
North Central	− 2.8	− 3.5	− 7.1	− 2.6	− 1.1	− 2.8	− 2.4
South	− 0.6	− 1.0	− 5.4	− 6.9	− 3.0	−0.6	0.3
West	15.6	15.7	24.5	27.7	22.2	17.9	13.2
Urban							
Northeast	− 2.0	0.0	0.3	− 1.1	− 4.3	− 3.6	− 2.8
North Central	4.2	9.2	20.0	15.3	0.5	− 1.2	0.8
South	19.0	26.9	49.4	34.8	10.7	10.2	12.0
West	30.0	34.6	56.5	58.4	36.5	28.0	24.1
Rural							
Northeast	− 7.0	−14.5	−28.4	−13.0	7.4	3.8	− 2.9
North Central	−14.0	−20.1	−39.7	−27.9	− 4.3	− 6.2	− 8.3
South	−19.0	−21.2	−39.5	−37.8	−19.1	−14.0	−13.3
West	−16.0	−17.8	−26.5	−25.6	−12.0	− 9.0	−14.2
Negro							
All areas							
Northeast	25.3	28.8	65.8	74.3	39.8	20.6	12.1
North Central	24.8	27.7	50.2	70.8	39.1	19.3	14.7
South	−11.7	− 9.5	−22.5	−26.8	−19.1	−13.3	− 7.9
West	52.2	63.0	157.2	155.9	68.3	35.9	23.8
South							
Urban	9.7	18.5	24.2	17.0	4.7	1.1	3.6
Rural	−31.2	−27.4	−50.8	−56.8	−43.8	−31.7	−23.0

[a] Source of data: U.S. Bureau of the Census. *1960 Census of population. Detailed characteristics.*
United States: Summary. Final Report PC(1)-1D. Washington, 1961. Table 233. Census survival
ratios used in aging.

25 to 29 in the rural areas of the South in 1960 was only three-fifths that expected in the absence of migration or urban expansion during the decade from 1950 to 1960. Losses through net migration or area changes amounted to 38 per cent for native whites and 57 per cent for Negroes.

The areas of destination were cities, particularly those of the West. As a result of the balance of rural and urban, white and nonwhite changes, the Northeast and the North Central regions had only slight net changes in persons in the productive ages, through migration, while the South lost such persons. The remainder of the nation contributed to the rapid gain of the West.

The almost phenomenal migrations of the decade are abundantly documented in data (the census of 1960) on place of birth and place of residence and on place of residence in 1960 and 1955, both tabulated in detail by age and sex. The major redistributions were those of youth. The movements for the rural areas were major, whatever the region of residence or the nativity or color group. Native whites moved in cross currents in all regions, with major destinations being California and the Southwest, the Inner Gulf Coast, and Florida. Negroes moved in patterns comparable to those of native whites with a single great exception. For them, movement away from the South was unidirectional.

Given the high rates of natural increase, internal migration was a lesser factor than natural increase in the changes of the decade for all regions other than the West. Even with the exodus of Negroes, as shown in Table 8, more Negroes were enumerated in the South in 1960 than in 1950. Natural increase of Negroes was also more important than net migration in the decade in many of the cities of the North. However, migrants brought the practices and values of their areas of origin with them and so contributed to the relatively high birth rates of their areas of destination. In the northern and western regions in 1960, more than one-third of the Negro women aged 15 to 34

were net in-migrants of the decade from 1950 to 1960. The rural South lost almost half the expected number of Negro women in the ages from 15 to 34 in 1960. The net increase of the urban South amounted to only one-fourth of the rural loss. The net loss of Negro women to the South was equivalent to three-fourths of the rural loss.

Mobility within metropolitan areas compounds the patterns of distribution and the measurement of the interrelations of social, economic, and demographic factors. As already noted, the in-migrant Negro women bring the high fertility patterns of the rural South to the North and West. The outward-moving whites in urbanized areas concentrate the childbearing of the native whites, and particularly the native whites of native parentage, in the areas outside central cities. The movements are massive, influencing all aspects of life and all institutions in central cities and outer areas alike. Thirty-seven per cent of the white population living in the central cities of the standard metropolitan statistical areas (SMSA) of the North in 1955 and remaining in the same SMSA in 1960 lived outside the central city in that year. Again, in the central cities of the North, whites who reported residence outside the SMSA in 1955 and were therefore in-migrants of the five-year period were only one-third as numerous as the whites who had been in the central city in 1955, remained in the SMSA in 1960, but moved outside the central city by 1960. For Negroes, in-migrants to the central cities of SMSA from outside the SMSA were more than twice as numerous as the internal migrants from the central city to the outer areas.

The question of the future. Questions of the future of the population of the United States are basic ones for research, as well as for projection or planning in many fields other than the demographic. The formulation of hypotheses is difficult, for the affluent metropolitan population and society are new. The American future cannot be a direct continuation of the American past. The farm-to-city migrants of the future will necessarily be few and will be declining percentages of all migrants. Rural backgrounds yield to multigenerational urban and metropolitan backgrounds. The aged foreign-born and the aging native-born of foreign or mixed parentage are replaced by natives of native parentage. The indigenous metropolitan population whose major movements are within or between metropolitan areas is now becoming numerically dominant in most subregions of the country.

Projections to the present based on established trends and relationships of a century and a half and the theory associated therewith once suggested very low birth rates for today's urbanized and metropolitan population. Projections of the trends and relationships of the present period into the future yield continuing and substantial rates of population growth. Is this projection then invalid? Neither empirical evidence nor theoretical formulations permit an answer in the affirmative—or in the negative.

Today's rates of growth, long sustained, would threaten the standard of living and hence the conditions that yield the abundant reproduction in the metropolitan context. Arguments of functional disutility are not necessarily consonant with behavior, however. The answers to questions of the interrelations of growth with opportunities and motivations in the indigenous metropolitan population must receive intensive analysis if evaluations of future populations are to be other than computational exercises.

REALITIES, IDEOLOGIES, AND POLICIES

Throughout most of man's history, death has been the regulator of growth. Levels of nutrition, shelter, and sanitation may be adequate for some people at some periods but inadequate for most people at most periods. Premature death by famine, epidemic, and disorder were episodic in the past, if not recurrent. Why, then, should population problems become a major preoccupation in a period when famine and epidemic are curbed and reduced mortality permits rapid growth? It is obvious that people create their own definitions of problems. Today's definition of the population problem is in terms of the over sufficiency of births on regional and global bases. Current definitions are not related to the historic or contemporary changes in levels of well being or to the prevalence of the excess deaths. Rather, they concern primarily that which is inherent in the future if the rates of growth continue. Since the rates cannot continue indefinitely in a finite world, the critical question is when, where, and even whether, growth will be terminated by declining fertility rather than by increasing mortality.

Definitions of problems in terms of the super abundance of fertility are relatively new among technical demographers. A few decades ago, the major problems were defined as those of incipient population decline in advanced industrial nations. France, for example, has long been concerned with her slow rate of population growth. Population policies are so pervasive that they amount to an appreciable redistribution of national income in favor of families with children. In the decades between World War I and World War II, birth rates reached such low levels in many countries that fear of decline became acute. Population policy was pronatalist policy. Germany, Italy, and Japan had policies to increase numbers as aspects of their expansionist and militaristic ideologies. None were particularly successful in increasing birth rates, however.

In the period when Europeans and Japanese were turning to consideration of policy if not policy itself, it was argued widely that developments had disproved Malthus, that the problem was no longer man's propensity to reproduce more rapidly than his sustenance, but his unwillingness to reproduce adequately in an industrial and urban setting. Publicists in the advanced countries tended to ignore the increasing populations of the agrarian areas, particularly those under colonial guidance. Publicists in the colonial countries blamed imperialism for their economic woes and denied a demographic basis in the multiplication of their numbers.

In the early postwar years, population was recognized in the emphasis on population statistics and population research in the structure of the Secretariat of the United Nations. However, population growth receded as a primary variable for specific policy. In Western Europe, initial postwar spurts were followed by birth rates sufficient for replacement. The Communist ideology defined problems as economic rather than demographic. Apparent overpopulation, in their view, was a product of capitalism and imperialism.

The solutions to the problems of population growth in underdeveloped areas were seen widely as matters for economic rather than demographic policy. Birth and death rates were associated closely with economic and social conditions. If conditions were changed, it was supposed, birth and death rates would change. Since industrialization, urbanization, and advancing education would result in declining birth rates along with declining death rates, rates of population growth would remain fairly low. It was a persuasive hypothesis, derived from the distillation of Western experience in modernization. Whether it would have been valid in the developing world that was envisioned is not determinable, for two major factors altered the projected pattern of demographic and social-economic interrelations.

First, the economic development and the social modernization that were plotted so hopefully proved to be halting in implementation. That which was theoretically possible and that which was feasible in social context diverged sharply.

Second, great and unanticipated advances in science and technology came in medical chemistry and biology, producing insecticides, antibiotics, and inoculations. The new techniques were applied externally, in the sense that no economic and social changes were necessary preconditions, associations, or immediate consequences. Death rates were disassociated from the subsistence–low-productivity–illiteracy–village complex, while birth rates remained associated. Rates of natural increase moved upward to 2, 3, or more per cent a year, with little reference to the extent of economic development, or even the fact of any development.

The Secretariat of the United Nations made a series of projections, first in the period of association between birth and death rates and relevant transition theory as to future movements and second in the period of disassociation. Each series of projections implied more rapid growth and larger populations than the preceding one. Actual populations have even gone above the high estimate of the series of projections. As billions mount on billions in the populations projected for future dates, there is a striking and incontrovertible picture of what lies ahead, given that continuing decline in mortality which all peoples desire and that persistence in fertility which is the heritage of the past and the overt indicator of the limited changes of the present.

Given high rates of population growth and limited economic development, persistent high population increase has become a villain blamed for difficulties in economic development. Indeed it is a major deterrent. India has pioneered in government policies to reduce birth rates through stimulating contraceptive practice or sterilization. Pakistan has developed central government policy. Egypt, Turkey, Korea, and other countries have policies or consider establishing them. Communist China has vacillated in propaganda and action to reduce births, while maintaining a legal basis that permits contraception, induced abortion, and sterilization for health reasons.

Propaganda and ideological forces are inextricably intertangled in the movements toward national, bilateral, and general international action in the population field. Viewpoints so prevalent in the United States—expressions of concern over the "explosion" of population—have been labelled by the Communists as Malthusian, Neo-Malthusian, imperialistic, or even cannibalistic. The Marxist-Leninist argument notes that people are producers as well as consumers and affirms that each form of social organization has its own law of population growth. In so far as there are population problems, therefore, they are only the products of a capitalism that generates an oversupply of the proletariat. Thus, they can be solved quite simply through transfer to socialist forms of organization. Or so runs the argument.

The Roman Catholic church affirms the moral obligations of responsible parenthood, but accepts only celibacy or periodic abstinence as means of limitation. The Protestant churches increasingly define planned parenthood as a moral obligation. Islam, Buddhism, and Confucianism have no explicit commands or taboos in this field.

If social actions and the consequences of actions were straightforward, it might be assumed that Catholicism among the religions and communism among the political forms would be most conducive to high fertility. Institutionalized religion and operational government are only aspects of society, however, and are interpenetrated with traditional values and responsive to secular institutions. The industrialized and urbanized Catholic peoples of Europe have long had low fertility. In recent years birth rates have declined rapidly in Catholic Southern Europe. Latin America with its high birth rates is often cited as indicative of the impact of Catholicism, but Argentina and Uruguay with their low birth rates and Chile with its rate at an intermediate level are alike Latin and Catholic. Fertility is very high in the Catholic Philippines, but it is also very high in Buddhist Thailand and Islamic East Pakistan.

Perhaps the most glaring error in the direct movement from ideology to assumed consequence involves the Communist-capitalist comparison. Marxism today rejects antinatalist policy based on arguments from macroeconomics. But health and opportunities for women and children are high values. So in the U.S.S.R., most of the Communist countries of Eastern Europe, and the Peoples' Republic of China, contraception, induced abortion, and sterilization are included in health services.

The move to government policy that is overtly or covertly demographic is widespread and increasing in the underdeveloped areas. This in itself merits social analysis. There are new and increasingly intensive forms of social action in fields where guidelines in research and experience are limited. Sociologists, social psychologists, and social statisticians are already involved, along with demographers, in the planning, analysis, and evaluation of experiments and operating programs.

RESEARCH, COMMITMENT, AND ACTION

The advance of the birth rate in the United States to levels that sustain rapid population increase has generated or intensified many social and economic problems. Relatively high fertility and disproportionately rapid increase compound and complicate the problems of the social integration and the economic advance of the Negro population. In the United States, there is no major central consideration of specifically antinatalist policy at the level of the national government. There is, however, major concern with the consistency of our national and international postures and with the responsibilities of public health and welfare agencies.

The major research questions in the United States concern motivations and behavior of the modal population that has a prevalent ideal of a three to four child family and that on the average approaches the realization of the ideal. These questions extend beyond demographic measurement. In so far as there is consideration of policy, it involves the problem of influencing volitions, and hence childbearing, by people living at material levels where decisions are more complex than the simple economic ones of whether an additional child can or cannot be supported.

International developments likewise intensify the needs for research. A December, 1962, resolution of the United Nations general Assembly concerned population growth and economic development. An original provision for technical assistance in population policy to nations desiring it was defeated. What remained, however, included the collection of census and vital statistics data, the analysis of such data, and the analysis of population growth with emphasis on social and economic interrelations.

Technical assistance to underdeveloped countries wishing it is likely to increase, probably at both governmental and private levels, a theory supported by analysis of past and present and evaluation of the future for many countries. It is stated here in relationship to two major areas of intensive research. One is biomedical research on the physiology of reproduction, and the other is research in motivation and communication. Both have immediate importance, for today there is neither the science, the technology, nor the operational knowledge of how to reduce birth rates speedily and sharply in the underdeveloped setting. Thus, again the recognition of a problem leads to research whose contributions to scientific knowledge may be major, and whose consequences may ramify far beyond the anticipated demographic ones.

Today there is dispute concerning the relative roles of means and motivations in the persistent high fertility in the underdeveloped areas. There are also questions of social change, of readiness for change, of the slowly rational and the irrationally quick in the adoption of the new. Given scientific advances in fertility control equivalent to those in mortality control, what would be the response of governments in their policies and programs and of people in their personal lives? Given the rapidly increasing numbers of children in peasant families and communities with consequent pressures on family

living, schools, opportunities for advance, and the availability of land, what will be the attitudes to family planning in future years? Questions, whose answers can be only speculative in advance of the development, are abundant.

The present populations, the present rates of growth, and the present precarious balances of population and productivity are facts of the present, and heritages to the future. Given the rapidity of the growth and the acuteness of the problems associated therewith, population will long remain a component in the differentiation of nations and in the difficulties of the underdeveloped ones. This much is apparent. Given advancing science and technology relevant to production, nutrition, fertility control, organization, motivation, and the induction of social change, it would be as naive to predict the population of the year 2000 from that of the year 1960 as it was to predict the population of the year 1960 from that of the year 1920.

Concepts of natural economic balances had limited relevance to the analysis of the demographic transitions of the early modernizing peoples. Concepts of natural demographic transitions that accompany industrialization and urbanization may have limited relevance to the transformations of the future. Doubtless there are general relationships that hold through time, space, and cultural diversity. In this sense there may be continuity, but the specificity of the relationships differ according to the form of the economy and the state of the arts. The speed of change and the interrelations in change are related to the fields in which, and the speed at which, science and technology develop. Given the widening chasms between the affluent and the traditional peoples, along with the imbalance in technologies relevant to mortality and those relevant to fertility control, the continuities may be so altered that present relationships disappear and future prospects are indeterminate.

The critical difference of the present from the past is in magnitude of growth. The critical difference with reference to the future is the speed of adaptive transition that is required. The realities are both demographic and social. Population research is an open and rewarding field for sociologists. It is also one where research promises to contribute to the alleviation or reduction of one of the most nearly insoluble problems of our era—the rapid increase of population in the underdeveloped areas.

REFERENCES

United Nations

United Nations. Department of Social Affairs. Population Division. *The determinants and consequences of population trends. A summary of the findings of studies on the relationships between population changes and economic and social conditions.* Population Studies No. 17. New York, 1953.

United Nations. Department of Economic and Social Affairs. *The future growth of world population.* Population Studies No. 28. New York, 1958.

United Nations. Department of Social Affairs. Population Division. *Future population estimates by sex and age.* Rept 1. *The population of Central America (including Mexico), 1950–1980.* New York, 1954.

United Nations. Department of Social Affairs. Population Division. *Future population estimates by sex and age.* Rept II. *The population of South America, 1950–1980.* New York, 1955.

United Nations. Department of Economic Affairs. *Future population estimates by sex and age.* Rept III. *The population of South-east Asia (including Ceylon and China: Taiwan), 1950–1980.* New York, 1958.

United Nations. Department of Economic Affairs. *Future population estimates by sex and age.* Rept IV. *The population of Asia and the Far East, 1950–1980.* New York, 1959.

United Nations. Economic Commission for Asia and the Far East. *Population trends and related problems of economic development in the ECAFE region.* Published as: *Economic bulletin for Asia and the Far East.* X (1). New York, June, 1959.

United Nations and UNESCO in cooperation with the International Labour Office. *Urbanization in Asia and the Far East.* Proceedings of the Joint UN/UNESCO Seminar (in cooperation with the International Labour Office) on urbanization in the ECAFE region, Bangkok, 8–18 August, 1956. Calcutta, India: UNESCO Research Centre on the Social Implications of Industrialization in Southern Asia, 1957.

United Nations. Statistical Office. *Demographic yearbook, Annuaire demographique.* 1948–—— New York, 1949——.

International Conferences

United Nations in cooperation with the International Union for the Scientific Study of Population. *Proceedings of the World Population Conference, Rome* (1954). New York, 1955.

Union internationale pour l'étude scientifique de la population. *International Population Conference, Wien, 1959.* Wien, im Selbstverlag, 1959. *International Population Conference, Discussions.* Paris, 1962.

Periodicals

France. Institut national d'études démographiques. *Population. Revue trimestrielle de l'institut . . .* 18ièm, annee, 1963.

Milbank Memorial Fund. *Milbank Memorial Fund Quart.,* 1963, 41.

Population Investigation Committee. *Population Studies. Quart. J. Demography.* 1963, 16.

Princeton University. Office of Population Research and Population Association of America. *Population Index.* 1963, 29.

United Nations. Department of Economic and Social Affairs. *Population Bulletin.* No. 1, December, 1951, 2. Irregular.

Collections of Studies

Cold Spring Harbor Symposium on Quantitative Biology. *Population studies: Animal ecology and demography.* Vol. XXII. Cold Spring Harbor, Long Island, New York: The Biological Laboratory, 1957.

Hauser, P. M. (Ed.) *Population and world politics.* Glencoe, Ill.: Free Press, 1958.

Hauser, P. M., & Duncan, O. D. (Eds.) *The study of population: An inventory and appraisal.* Chicago: Univer. of Chicago Press, 1959.

Milbank Memorial Fund. *Demographic studies of selected areas of rapid growth.* Proceedings of the 1944 Annual Conference. . . . New York, 1944.

Milbank Memorial Fund. *Approaches to problems of high fertility in agrarian societies.* Proceedings of the 1951 Annual Conference. . . . New York. 1952.

Milbank Memorial Fund. *The interrelations of demographic, economic, and social problems in selected underdeveloped areas.* Proceedings of the 1953 Annual Conference. . . . New York, 1954.

Milbank Memorial Fund. *Current research in human fertility.* Proceedings of the 1954 Annual Conference. . . . New York. 1955.

Milbank Memorial Fund. *Trends and differentials in mortality.* Proceedings of the 1955 Annual Conference. . . . New York, 1956.

Milbank Memorial Fund. *Selected studies of migration since World War II.* Proceedings of the 1957 Annual Conference. . . . New York, 1958.

Milbank Memorial Fund. *Thirty years of research in human fertility: Retrospect and prospect.* Proceedings of the 1958 Annual Conference. . . . New York, 1959.

Milbank Memorial Fund. *Population trends in Eastern Europe, the USSR, and Mainland China.* Proceedings of the 1959 Annual Conference. . . . New York, 1960.

Milbank Memorial Fund. *Emerging techniques in population research.* Proceedings of the 1962 Annual Conference. . . . New York, 1963.

National Bureau of Economic Research. *Demographic and economic change in developed countries.* A conference of the Universities—National Bureau Committee for Economic Research. Princeton, N.J.: Princeton Univer. Press, 1960.

Spengler, J. J., & Duncan, O. D. (Eds.) *Demographic analysis, selected readings.* Glencoe, Ill.: Free Press, 1956. (a)

Spengler, J. J., & Duncan, O. D. (Eds.) *Population theory and policy, selected readings.* Glencoe, Ill.: Free Press, 1956. (b)

United States: Official

U.S. Bureau of the Census. *U.S. Census of population: 1960. United States summary.* Washington: Government Printing Office, 1961–1963.

U.S. Bureau of the Census. *General population characteristics.* Final Report PC(1)—1B. Washington: Government Printing Office, 1961.

U.S. Bureau of the Census. *Number of inhabitants.* Final Report PC(1)—1A. S1–S36. Washington: Government Printing Office, 1961.

U.S. Bureau of the Census. *General social and economic characteristics.* Final Report PC(1)—1C. Washington: Government Printing Office, 1962.

U.S. Bureau of the Census. *Statistical abstract of the United States, 1962.* (83rd ed.) Washington: Government Printing Office, 1962.

U.S. Bureau of the Census. *Detailed characteristics.* Final Report PC(1)—1D. Washington: Government Printing Office, 1963.

United States: Other

Freedman, R., Whelpton, P. K., & Campbell, A. A. *Family planning, sterility, and population growth.* New York: McGraw, 1959.

Hill, R., Stycos, J. M., & Back, K. W. *The family and population control: A Puerto Rican experiment in social change.* Chapel Hill: Univer. of North Carolina Press, 1959.

Lee, E. S., Miller, Ann R., Brainerd, Carol P., & Easterlin, R. A. *Methodological considerations and reference tables.* Vol. 1. *University of Pennsylvania population redistribution and economic growth, United States, 1870–1950.* Philadelphia: American Philosophical Society, 1957.

Kuznets, S., Miller, Ann R., & Easterlin, R. A. *Analysis of economic change.* Vol. 2. *University of Pennsylvania population redistribution and economic growth, United States, 1870–1950.* Philadelphia: American Philosophical Society, 1960.

Taeuber, C., & Taeuber, Irene B. *The changing population of the United States.* New York: Wiley, 1958.

Westoff, C. F., Potter, R. G., Jr., Sage, P. C., & Mishler, E. G. *Family growth in metropolitan America.* Princeton, N.J.: Princeton Univer. Press, 1961.

Whelpton, P. K., & Kiser, C. V., et al. *Social and psychological factors affecting fertility.* New York: Milbank Memorial Fund, 1946–1958.

Other Areas

Coale, A. J., & Hoover, E. M. *Population growth and economic development in low-income countries: A case study of India's prospects.* Princeton, N.J.: Princeton Univer. Press, 1958.

Japanese National Commission for UNESCO. *An outlook of studies on population problems in Japan.* Vol. 5. *Retrospect and prospect.* Tokyo: UNESCO, 1962.

Smith, T. E. *Population growth in Malaya. A survey of recent trends.* London and New York: Royal Institute of International Affairs, 1952.

Taeuber, Irene B. *Asian populations: The critical decades.* House of Representatives, Committee on the Judiciary, Subcommittee No. 1, Study of Population and Immigration Problems. Special Series No. 4. Washington: Government Printing Office, 1962.

Taeuber, Irene B. *The population of Japan.* Princeton, N.J.: Princeton Univer. Press, 1958.

Thompson, W. S. *Population and progress in the Far East.* Chicago: Univer. of Chicago Press, 1959.

Policy

Agarwala, S. N. *Attitude towards family planning in India.* Institute of Economic Growth, Occasional Papers, No. 5. New Delhi, India: Asia Publishing Co., 1962.

Rock, J. D. *The time has come. A Catholic doctor's proposals to end the battle over birth control.* New York: Knopf, 1963.

Kiser, C. V. (Ed.) *Research in family planning.* Papers presented at a conference sponsored jointly by The Milbank Memorial Fund and the Population Council, Inc. Princeton, N.J.: Princeton Univer. Press, 1962.

Koya, Y. *Pioneering in family planning. A collection of papers on the family planning programs and research conducted in Japan.* Tokyo: Japan Medical Publishers, Inc., 1963.

Gardner, R. N. *Population growth: A world problem.* Bull. Dept. of State, Publ. No. 7485. Washington: Government Printing Office, 1962.

Fagley, R. M. *The population explosion and Christian responsibility.* New York: Oxford Univer. Press, 1960.

Hauser, P. M. (Ed.) *The population dilemma.* The American Assembly, Columbia University. Englewood Cliffs, N.J.: Prentice-Hall, Inc., 1963.

CHAPTER 4   The Rural-Urban Dimension
in Preindustrial, Transitional,
and Industrial Societies

GIDEON SJOBERG

An examination of rural-urban patterns in different types of society is our goal. This, in turn, requires major modifications of, and amendments to, the earlier efforts of Sorokin and Zimmerman (1929; Sorokin, Zimmerman & Galpin, 1930——) and Redfield (1941), among others. For these writers, and followers in their tradition, have overlooked some crucial facets of the rural-urban dimension made discernible by recent social research on societies throughout the world. Moreover, the social revolution currently under way in societies that are shifting from a preindustrial to an industrial technology has brought to light patterns that a few decades ago were at most only dimly perceived.

The chapter begins with an extended evaluation of the existing theoretical perspectives and a proposed reformulation. It then briefly treats the demographic structure of rural and urban communities over time and space. All this serves as a foundation for the ensuing discussion of rural-urban patterns in preindustrial civilized societies, in developing (or modernizing) ones, and in industrial orders. That the rural-urban dimension differs significantly in these socie-

ties, dependent as they are upon distinctive kinds of technology, is the chief hypothesis.

EXISTING THEORETICAL ORIENTATIONS

Traditional Theories

Sociologists are properly interested in theorizing about the differences, readily visible, between city and country. Even within an advanced industrial order one need only travel from a large metropolis to a small rural community to perceive, intuitively at least, a variety of differences in the inhabitants' way of life. In the ancient world, philosophers recognized that the city stood apart from the rural hinterland in its basic economic activities. But only since the time of Ibn Khaldûn (1958), in the fourteenth century, and Giovanni Botero (1956), some centuries later, have serious efforts been made to describe and explain some of the divergencies between city and country.

In the post-Comtean era, numerous sociologists have interested themselves in rural-urban contrasts, so much so that during the 1920's rural and urban specialists emerged within the sociological discipline. Actually, however, differences between rural and urban communities have in one way or another preoccupied most well-known sociologists. Maine's (1930) status and contract, Durkheim's (1947) organic and mechanical solidarity, Tönnies' (1940) *Gemeinschaft* and *Gesellschaft,* Becker's (1950) sacred and secular, all these and others reflect a common concern with an issue that has long plagued sociologists—namely, what happens (and why) when a social order is transformed from one wherein most people reside in small villages and are committed to working the land from dawn to dusk, to one where the vast majority of inhabitants are urban-based and committed to the furtherance of a scientific-industrial way of life? Unfortunately, rural-urban sociologists have in recent years become so involved with minor details that they have tended to neglect the broader implications of their investigations.

The study of rural-urban patterns was in the past considered to be a far more significant topic. After World War II many American sociologists came to disregard rural-urban differentials. American society had by then attained a high degree of industrial-urbanization, and the rural sector that persisted was steadily being drawn into the urban orbit. As a result, the fundamental problems to which sociologists addressed themselves also shifted. With the advent of a mature industrial-urban order, sociologists were no longer interested in the processes of transformation, but rather were concerned with whether people had realized their hopes and expectations within the new order. The fundamental research focus became the difference between the ideal and the actual normative orders.

By the late 1950's, however, perhaps earlier, some sociologists began to take a second look at their research topics. The great world revolution within what are variously termed underdeveloped, modernizing, or transitional societies could no longer be ignored. This transition involves a shift from a pre-industrial, largely rural, order to an industrial, largely urban, society. As the world's people awaken and the revolution generates ever greater strains, one notices a revival of interest by American sociologists in the preoccupations of Durkheim, Weber, and members of the Chicago School. Then, too, those social scientists who live and work in transitional societies are little challenged by the study of ideal versus actual patterns; rather they are, understandably, concerned with the major issue facing their own society: the transmutation from a preindustrial to an industrial-urban order.

Use of Multiple Criteria in Rural-Urban Differentiation

Sorokin and Zimmerman, Redfield, and Wirth rank among those who have employed multiple criteria in distinguishing between rural and urban communities. Sorokin and Zimmerman, the mentors of many leading American rural sociologists, including T. Lynn Smith (1947) and Loomis (1957), delineated the rural and urban worlds on the basis of the following criteria: (1) occupational differences, (2) environmental differences, (3) differences in community size, (4) differences in density of population, (5) differences in population homogeneity and heterogeneity (i.e., in terms of acquired "socio-psychical" characteristics—language, beliefs, patterns of behavior, etc.), (6) differences in social mobility, (7) differences in the direction of migration, (8) differences in social differentiation, and (9) differences in the systems of interaction (Sorokin & Zimmerman, 1929, Ch. 2).

Thus, Sorokin and Zimmerman (1929) took as the basis for their schema such factors as community size and environment, as well as the more strictly social ones of homogeneity, differentiation, and interaction. This formulation is largely classificatory, for no variables are explicitly set forth which might be used to explain the existence of differences between the rural and the urban sectors.

Wirth and Redfield, drawing upon the theoretical and empirical studies of Park (1952) and other Chicago sociologists—who in turn were influenced by such European sociologists as Simmel—saw the city as the main variable for explaining certain social phenomena. Wirth's (1938) chief contribution, "Urbanism as a Way of Life," was essentially a theoretical effort, whereas Redfield (1941) developed his folk-urban orientation in the process of research on four communities in Yucatan, Mexico: a folk or preliterate village, a small peasant community, a town, and the city of Merida. Moreover, Wirth concentrated upon the city and had relatively little to say about the rural or folk order, whereas Redfield (1947) dealt extensively with the folk society.

The city, according to Wirth (1938), is distinguished from the rural community by greater size, heterogeneity, and density. Its development is accompanied by the emergence of a secular order, a breakdown in the normative and moral fabric of everyday existence, and the rise of secondary group relations and controls. For Wirth, urbanism as a way of life involves a fluid and mobile sort of existence.

Redfield summarized his own theoretical position as follows:

For the purposes of this investigation the isolation and homogeneity of the community are taken together as an independent variable. Organization or disorganization of culture, secularization, and individualization are regarded as dependent variables. The choice of isolation and homogeneity as independent variables implies the hypothesis that loss of isolation and increasing heterogeneity are causes of disorganization, secularization, and individualization. Even if this should be established, it would not follow that these are the only causes of these effects or that these are the only covariant or causal relationships to be discovered in the same data (Redfield, 1941, p. 344).

In a later article Redfield (1947) elaborated a typology of the folk society which has had a strong impact on the thinking of numerous sociologists and anthropologists. He argued that ". . . we may characterize the folk society as small, isolated, nonliterate, and homogeneous, with a strong sense of group solidarity" (Redfield, 1947, p. 297).

Use of a Single Criterion in Rural-Urban Differentiation

One approach is to differentiate between rural and urban communities by size—the number of inhabitants (e.g., Browning, 1962; Duncan & Reiss, 1956; Schnore, 1961). According to Hope Tisdale (Eldridge):

Urbanization is a process of population concentration. It proceeds in two ways: the multiplication of points of concentration and the increase in size of individual concentrations. . . . Consistent with the definition of urbanization, cities may be defined as points of concentration (Tisdale, 1942, p. 311).

Although Geertz (1962) indicated that Julian Steward employed the single criterion of occupation and Wittfogel differential access to power to distinguish between rural and urban communities, Geertz's interpretation is a debatable one. Certainly, no other single criterion apart from size is widely employed for separating rural from urban centers.

A Critical Evaluation

The Sorokin-Zimmerman formulation has invited less criticism than has the Wirth-Redfield framework. In part this is because the former is more descriptive than analytical. The latter, by attempting to move beyond description, with the city as the explanatory variable, raises a host of larger issues.

A salient weakness in Redfield's (1941) formulation (and to a degree in Wirth's [1938]) is the fact that, although the folk order is a closed, self-contained system and the city (or urban community) only a partial system, the two are nonetheless contrasted. But they are not really comparable entities: One is a whole while the other is merely a part of a broader system. One can, of course, legitimately compare an urban community with its rural counterpart, as Sorokin and Zimmerman (1929) did, for both are subsystems within a broader society. In fairness to Redfield, it must be remarked that he rectified his error in later writings (Redfield, 1956). Despite this many sociologists and anthropologists continue to employ Redfield's earlier perspectives.

A second drawback to the Redfield-Wirth formulation, and to a degree that of Sorokin and Zimmerman, is the assumption that rural people exhibit a high degree of homogeneity and stability, whereas urbanites evince marked heterogeneity and instability. While such is generally the case, at least in relative terms, it is easy to overemphasize the differences. Actually, peasant communities have often displayed serious tensions and instabilities (Foster, 1960–1961; O. Lewis, 1960–1961).

Conversely Redfield and Wirth, along with many of their latter-day followers, have exaggerated the amount of divisiveness and fluidity in the urban normative order. Indeed it can be argued that Wirth and to a degree Redfield were captives of their particular era. Life in the urban communities of the United States during the 1920's and 1930's was, from the perspective of newcomers to the city, quite disorganized and unstable. Yet Wirth and many other students of the city have failed to give due attention to the myriad of informal structures within this setting. Thus, slums are indeed organized, though in their own fashion. For one thing, visiting patterns among the urban poor, though not as intensive as those in most rural communities, nevertheless exist and cannot be ignored. Then, too, Lenski (1963), on the basis of his study of the religious factor in Detroit, wrote:

. . . what is startling about our present study is the finding that communalism survives, and even thrives, in heart of the modern metropolis, though admittedly in a guise which makes its recognition difficult for those accustomed to associating communalism with geographically isolated and numerically small populations (Lenski, 1963, p. 328).

Third, those who employ the Wirth-Redfield framework, as well as the followers of Sorokin and Zimmerman, have by and large failed to analyze rural and urban communities—both of them partial systems—within the context of the broader social order in which they are imbedded. As a result there are surprisingly few solid sociological studies documenting the impact upon the local setting of large-scale extracommunity structures—government bureaucracies, corporations, religious structures, etc.—and the interaction between the local and the national systems.

Finally, many of the rural-urban differences posited by sociologists are not as universal as was once supposed. Most specialists (e.g., Smith, 1947) on rural and urban communities have considered large families more a rural than an urban phenomenon. But in preindustrial civilized societies this has certainly not been the case. So, too, the notion that the city is much more secular than the rural community is open to serious qualifications. These points will be discussed in greater detail below.

Up to now this discussion has concentrated upon those orientations that have utilized multiple criteria for differentiating between rural and urban communities. What about the unidimensional perspective employed by Eldridge and many modern demographers? The use of community size as the sole criterion for distinguishing among communities facilitates measurement, a fact demonstrated by a variety of significant studies in recent years (e.g., Duncan & Reiss, 1956; Schnore, 1961). But this approach embodies serious weaknesses as well. In order to analyze their data from a cross-cultural perspective, researchers who employ community size often introduce other criteria into their definitions of rural or urban, though without making this explicit. After all, communities in, say, the five thousand to ten thousand population category may differ widely in their social characteristics, according to whether they form part of pre-industrial civilized societies, transitional orders, or industrial ones. Hope Tisdale (Eldridge) (1942) implicitly recognized this and observed that as technology advances ever greater population concentration (i.e., urbanization) becomes possible. In keeping with this reasoning, we hold technology constant in the analysis of rural-urban patterns in different types of society.

More generally, the severest criticism launched against rural-urban studies, whether these embody the multiple-criteria or the single-criterion approach, is that any particular set of rural-urban differentials is the product of a given cultural system. Thus rural-urban differentials can (and do) vary widely from one culture to the next. Oscar Lewis (1951) in his criticism of Redfield (1941) in part espoused this position, and Pocock, challenging the entire field of rural-urban studies, wrote:

The city is an *Indian* city and the village an *Indian* village and in this article I have tried to suggest a manner in which these differences of habitation can be transcended. . . . The sociology of India's urban and rural population may not be divided between urban and rural sociologies (Pocock, 1960, p. 81).

Dewey (1960), in his more temperate critique of rural-urban study, a critique which defines rural and urban in demographic terms, maintained that, although differences exist between rural and urban communities, they are not particularly important. He contended that one should not confuse *Gemeinschaft* and *Gesellschaft* with rural and urban, respectively; the former are often more descriptive of types of society than of rural-urban differences.

A PROPOSED FORMULATION

Given the above criticisms, why study rural-urban differences (and interrelation-

ships)? Although one should not exaggerate the importance of rural-urban contrasts, they are real enough to contemporary ideologists and policy-makers in societies all over the world. But defense of rural-urban research need not rest solely on pragmatic grounds. Only by examining rural-urban differences and interrelationships can social scientists hope to formulate theories that will satisfactorily account for some of the revolutionary changes that are occurring in transitional societies today. Any adequate theory in this realm must make due allowance for the shift from a basically rural to an urban or metropolitan mode of existence.

Yet, in order to analyze rural-urban patterns effectively, one must recognize that rural and urban communities are subsystems within larger wholes such as nation-state systems. Neither the local urban community nor its rural counterpart are microscopic representations of the broader society. Anthropologists and sociologists are discarding the notion, carried over from earlier research in preliterate communities, that intensive investigation of the local community necessarily explains the functioning of the total society.

It also bears repeating that the concepts "rural" and "urban" are analytical constructs that the sociologist employs when he studies aspects of social systems. Is there a rural-urban continuum or a rural-urban dichotomy? Sociologists may for analytical reasons treat the rural-urban divergency as a dichotomy. But we must not confuse an analytical distinction with empirical reality, for obviously a gradation exists from the relatively small, isolated village, through the larger village, to the market town, the small city, the larger city, and finally to the dominant community (or communities).

One source of confusion is the failure to recognize that often the communities anthropologists label as "rural" or as "villages" are actually small market towns that provide the much smaller, truly rural communities with economic, political, and other services. Thus the community of Tepoztlan, the focus of so much debate, is frequently observed in improper perspective. Lewis' data demonstrate that Tepoztlan, a community of over four thousand persons at the time he last studied it, has long been the seat of governmental control and an economic nexus for a group of smaller communities, a number of them containing fewer than five hundred residents (O. Lewis, 1951, pp. 26–29). The inhabitants of these much smaller places—rural villages—have undoubtedly looked upon Tepoztlan as an avenue to the outside world.

Similar misinterpretations are involved in some of the so-called village studies in India (e.g., Carstairs, 1960; Opler & Singh, 1948). Some of the significant ground-breaking investigations such as that by Opler and Singh (1948) were of communities with several thousand persons. Although many of the inhabitants therein gain their livelihood from agriculture, these communities have also been market centers and seats of governmental power for a broad region. It is of some moment that as late as 1951 the number of communities in India with fewer than five hundred inhabitants—the true villages —was greater than the number of all larger communities combined (Bose, 1954).

Against this background a more satisfactory definition of rural and urban, based on multiple criteria, can now be set forth. An urban center, in contrast to a rural one, is characterized by larger size, higher density, and a preponderance of persons engaged in nonagricultural economic activity. These nonagriculturists must include a group of literate persons. The existence of a literate element is an especially meaningful cutting-point in distinguishing between the folk society (or the protocity) and the truly urban community which forms part of the preindustrial civilized society (Sjoberg, 1960, pp. 32ff.; cf. Goody & Watt, 1963).

From this vantage point, the peoples of Africa south of the Sahara, prior to the European invasion, were not part of any "civilized society": i.e., a society with a literate element and city life (Fallers, 1961).

Here modern cities were imposed upon relatively advanced folk societies. This region, and others like it, deserves special treatment, for some of the generalizations made herein do not apply to it.

We now examine rural-urban patterns in three "constructed types" of society: the preindustrial civilized (or feudal), the transitional (or modernizing or developing), and the industrial. The prime variable for distinguishing among these societies is the level of technology involved. Technology here means the kinds of tools, energy, and know-how employed. In the preindustrial civilized order, the tools and technological knowledge are relatively simple (though more complex than in the folk society), and the populace must rely primarily upon animate sources of energy. In the industrial system, on the other hand, the tools are exceedingly complex, energy stems from inanimate sources, and much of the applicable knowledge derives from the scientific method.

For each of the above societal types it is possible to describe certain interrelationships, and similarities and differences, between rural and urban communities that recur in numerous societies and across many cultural boundaries. The framework is admittedly neo-evolutionary, though it is not the nineteenth-century evolutionary approach that assumed that all societies advance through certain fixed stages.

Although technology is here the chief explanatory variable, others will be utilized as well. Certainly the nature of the city itself accounts for some differences between city and country. Furthermore, rural-urban patterns are often shaped by the power structure (e.g., Keyfitz, forthcoming). Thus we differentiate between the patterns in Communist and in non-Communist nations, patterns that derive from divergent power structures as well as from distinctive value systems. The variable of cultural values in fact accounts for many of the differences among societies belonging to any given type. However, excessive attention to values as a determinant of rural and urban forms can lead to undue emphasis upon the unique and a disregard of the general. Social scientists can discern and analyze the unique patterns only in terms of some broader standard.

RURAL-URBAN PATTERNS IN HISTORICAL-DEMOGRAPHIC PERSPECTIVE

Long before men created cities they lived in villages. Cities are recent, having emerged first in the Mesopotamian riverine area sometime about 3500 B.C. The precise dating of these earliest cities is impossible, and the estimates vary considerably, largely because different scholars employ different criteria in defining the concept "urban." Those who tend to emphasize permanent structures, as do some archeologists, label as cities certain communities that sociologists would classify as preurban or protourban (Sjoberg, 1960, pp. 32ff.).

The earliest cities were by modern standards mere towns; they sheltered perhaps five thousand to ten thousand persons. Even so, these communities were the end product of centuries, even millennia, of technological and organizational development (Braidwood & Willey, 1962). Only after a sizeable economic surplus was assured could some members of the community be permanently freed from the incessant struggle for food, clothing, and shelter to devote themselves to the governmental and intellectual pursuits that paved the way to literacy and urban living.

One factor that made a sizeable surplus possible was a significant advance in technology. With improved means of transportation, food and other supplies could be drawn from a broader territorial base. First and foremost, however, were technological gains in agriculture. In most of the regions that first spawned city life—the Mesopotamian riverine area, the Nile River Delta, the Hwang-ho Valley in China, the Indus Valley—large-scale irrigation was developed and grain crops domesticated. Grains are of spe-

cial importance because they are highly nourishing and can be stored for a relatively long period of time. The Maya developed maize—a superior food crop so easily cultivated that a considerable surplus could be gained without recourse to irrigation and to the more highly-developed implements of the Asiastic–North African urban complex— and so were able to create cities in spite of possessing only stone-age tools.

But technology alone could not make city life possible. Just as significant was the development of a body of complex organizational knowledge. Marx, and more recently Wittfogel (1957), postulated a hydraulic determinism whereby the system of social power and the techniques of social organization essential for the support of complex societies supposedly rest upon man's ability to build and control irrigation systems. Durkheim's (1947) more sophisticated formulation recognized that as the division of labor (not just in the sphere of irrigation) becomes more complex, an organizational hierarchy is required to integrate and harmonize the activities of specialists. Of course, some kind of specialization apparently was required to provide the surplus necessary to support the administrative hierarchy.

Although advances in technology and organizational knowledge were imperative for the rise of cities, it is also significant that cities, both in the Old World and the New, developed first at natural points of contact for peoples of diverse cultures (i.e., in certain natural corridors). In Mesopotamia, Egypt, and China these were riverine valleys. In Middle America the corridor was the isthmus that connects North and South America. The consequent mingling of persons with a variety of skills and concepts evidently stimulated innovations of the sort that enhanced man's control over his environment and eventually permitted the development of cities and civilization.

A detailed treatment of the spread of cities out of their centers of origin need not detain us here (see Sjoberg, 1960). Certainly, well before the Christian era cities had spread over much of Eurasia. But it was not until the Roman Empire reached its zenith that cities were diffused into much of Europe, and many more centuries elapsed before vast areas of Soviet Asia and North and South America came to be urbanized.

Before the Industrial Revolution in Europe only a small proportion of the world's people lived in cities: in most societies less than 10 per cent, perhaps only 5 per cent. It appears that few cities reached the one hundred thousand mark until after the Industrial Revolution. A few modern scholars contend that some cities in China, for instance, attained populations of a million (Durand, 1960), but this is doubtful. Studies by Russell (1958) and Mols (1955) on cities in traditional Europe and the Near East have done much to reduce the estimates of the size of preindustrial cities. The decrease

sources of energy—made possible the support of large urban populations. Davis documented this urbanization as seen in Table 1 (Davis, 1955).

TABLE 1

PERCENTAGE OF WORLD'S POPULATION LIVING IN CITIES[a]

	Cities of 20,000 or More	Cities of 100,000 or More
1800	2.4	1.7
1850	4.3	2.3
1900	9.2	5.5
1950	20.9	13.1

[a] Source: Davis, 1955, p. 433.

Despite the trend, different parts of the world display considerable variation in the proportion of urban and rural populations. The data in Table 2 highlight this fact.

TABLE 2

URBAN AND RURAL POPULATIONS, BY CONTINENTS, ca. 1960[a]

Continent	Population	Per Cent in Communities of Different Size			
		100,000 and Over	20,000– 99,999	1,000–5,000 to 19,999	1,000–5,000 or Less
North America	265,257,000	49.70	8.85	14.65	26.8
South America	139,231,000	27.32	8.19	11.00	53.5
Europe[b]	638,561,000	29.60	12.51	11.24	46.7
Asia[c]	1,650,258,000	12.33	5.37	3.79	78.5
Africa	252,192,000	8.09	3.66	3.62	84.6
Oceania[d]	16,249,000	43.33	3.69	14.44	38.5
Total	2,961,748,000	19.92	7.20	6.75	66.1

[a] Source: Hoyt, 1962, p. 31.
[b] Includes U.S.S.R.
[c] Excludes U.S.S.R.
[d] Includes Hawaii.

in the estimates can be attributed in part to the realization that preindustrial city families (except within the small upper class) were not as large as earlier writers presumed.

The dramatic increase in the proportion of urban dwellers began with the Industrial Revolution. Only a vast expansion in technological knowledge—specifically the ability to create new tools and tap greatly improved

Obviously, North America and Oceania are the most highly-urbanized continents and Asia and Africa the least. Yet statistics on such a gross scale can conceal variations within these broad blocs that are at times as great as the variations between or among them. In Europe there is much unevenness (between, for example, northwestern and southern Europe) in the distribution of urban inhabitants, and still more striking variations appear among nations in South America.

Hoyt (1962) collated data for nations throughout the world. To do so he relied upon the *Worldmark Encyclopedia of Nations,* the *Britannica Book of the Year for 1961,* International Urban Research's *The World's Metropolitan Areas,* and U.N.'s *Demographic Yearbook, 1960.* There are a number of limitations to Hoyt's study. Some inconsistencies and errors appear in the

tables, table headings, and the like. Also, judged by the estimates Hoyt used for India's population, some of his data are very crude. Finally, the category of one thousand to five thousand is, as Hoyt fully recognized, most inadequate, for the demographic dividing line between rural and urban communities is not standard across national boundaries (cf. United Nations, 1961). Yet the data are useful. The materials for selected countries appear in Table 3.

TABLE 3

Population Distribution by Community Size for Selected Countries, *ca.* 1960

Nation	Population	Per Cent in Communities of Different Size			
		100,000 and Over	20,000–99,999	1,000–5,000 to 19,999	1,000–5,000 or Less
North America					
U.S.A.	179,593,000	61.9	9.8	14.0	14.3
Canada	18,049,000	44.6	9.4	21.0	25.0
Puerto Rico	2,427,000	30.3	9.9	2.1	57.7
Cuba	6,743,000	25.4	12.5	19.1	43.0
Mexico	34,626,000	23.8	6.6	13.6	55.9
Guatemala	3,759,000	10.1	0.7	14.2	75.0
South America					
Argentina	20,956,000	52.1	8.1	4.8	35.0
Colombia	14,132,000	33.3	16.3	10.4	40.0
Chile	7,627,000	32.2	15.9	15.0	36.9
Uruguay	2,800,000	30.7	9.6	9.7	50.0
Brazil	65,743,000	20.7	5.5	11.6	62.3
Ecuador	4,298,000	18.1	2.3	...	79.6
Peru	10,857,000	14.3	9.2	20.8	55.7
Europe					
United Kingdom[b]	52,157,000	59.1	10.9	10.2	19.8
West Germany[c]	55,584,000	47.6	13.8	13.6	25.0
Netherlands	11,480,000	42.5	14.3	13.2	30.0
Denmark	4,547,000	38.9	8.8	21.3	31.0
Spain	30,128,000	29.2	14.6	6.2	50.0
Ireland (Rep.)	2,834,000	26.9	10.6	4.0	58.5
France	45,540,000	26.4	15.5	14.1	44.1
U.S.S.R.	214,400,000	23.9	12.0	12.0	52.1
Italy	49,368,000	23.8	20.2	4.0	52.0
Norway	3,587,000	21.8	11.8	10.6	55.8
Greece	8,300,000	21.6	14.5	5.9	58.0
Finland	4,456,000	18.7	15.4	2.9	63.0
Romania	18,256,000	14.5	8.8	8.7	68.0
Czechoslovakia	13,649,000	14.3	7.3	29.6	48.8
Yugoslavia	18,655,000	7.4	3.2	3.2	86.0
Africa					
Union of South Africa	15,841,000	25.4	7.6	19.0	48.0
Egypt	25,365,000	23.7	11.8	7.9	56.6
Algeria	10,930,000	12.7	4.6	0.7	82.0

TABLE 3 (Cont'd.)

POPULATION DISTRIBUTION BY COMMUNITY SIZE FOR SELECTED COUNTRIES, *ca.* 1960

Nation	Population	Per Cent in Communities of Different Size			
		100,000 and Over	20,000–99,999	1,000–5,000 to 19,999	1,000–5,000 or Less
Congo					
(Leopoldville)	13,821,000	6.0	3.2	1.4	89.4
Nigeria	34,296,000	4.5	. . .	1.3	94.2
Sudan	11,615,000	2.9	1.9	0.9	94.3
Tanganyika	9,238,000	1.4	1.7	1.1	95.8
		Asia			
Israel	2,114,000	47.6	18.9	3.5	30.0
Japan	93,419,000	47.3	29.5	3.3	20.0
Syria	4,539,000	27.3	1.3	. . .	71.3
China (Taiwan)	10,611,000	24.2	4.7	6.1	65.0
Korea, South	24,502,000	18.8	8.2	5.4	67.6
Turkey	27,829,000	16.2	7.2	5.4	71.2
Philippines	27,456,000	12.5	32.8	10.9	43.8
China (Mainland)	690,000,000	10.0	3.0	3.0	84.0
Indonesia	92,600,000	9.9	2.2	6.9	81.0
India	408,050,000	9.7	4.7	2.8	82.7
Ceylon	9,612,000	9.0	. . .	8.6	82.4
Pakistan	86,823,000	5.6	2.5	2.9	89.0
Burma	20,662,000	5.2	2.4	2.8	89.6
		Oceania			
Australia	10,281,000	56.2	4.9	19.5	19.4
New Zealand	2,372,000	32.2	4.2	9.3	54.3

[a] The data presented by Hoyt for Hawaii (which he places in Oceania) are here combined with those for the United States.
[b] Hoyt's data for England and Wales, Scotland, and Northern Ireland are here combined.
[c] The data from Hoyt for West Germany and West Berlin are combined.

Tables 2 and 3 indicate that the greatest proportion of the world's people still live in small communities. Nevertheless, there is a great deal of variability among societies in their proportions of rural and urban. In turn, the amount of urbanization is closely associated with industrialization. Unfortunately, measuring this association, using nations as units, poses special problems. Controversies arise in the selection of the appropriate index or indexes of industrialization. Also, nations are not fully self-sufficient or independent units. As a result not all cities are formed by processes within nations. Calcutta and Madras, for example, were creations of a colonial power (Great Britain), and cities such as Athens and Cairo have drawn upon the scientific knowl-edge and resources of advanced industrial nations in Europe for their development.

If, however, one compares countries at the extremes of the scale—the United States, Canada, the United Kingdom, West Germany, Belgium, or Australia—with India, Burma, Pakistan, Ceylon, or Indonesia—then no matter how one measures industrial development (gross energy consumption per capita, per cent of persons employed in industry, or amount of money invested in scientific knowledge) there is a negative association between industrialization and the proportion of people living in small rural communities (cf. Gibbs & Schnore, 1960; Ginsburg, 1961; Schnore, 1961).

I. Z. Husain (1962), in line with research carried out by the United Nations, utilized

TABLE 4

CLASSIFICATION OF COUNTRIES BY THE DEGREE OF INDUSTRIALIZATION
ACCORDING TO PER CAPITA INDUSTRIAL OUTPUT IN 1959[a]

Industrial Class I: $200 and Over

(1) United States, (2) Canada, (3) Germany (Fed. Rep.), (4) United Kingdom, (5) Belgium, (6) Netherlands, (7) Denmark, (8) New Zealand, (9) Norway, (10) Australia, and (11) Finland

Industrial Class II: $100 to $199

(1) Israel, (2) Yugoslavia, (3) Italy, (4) Union of South Africa, (5) Ireland, (6) Puerto Rico, and (7) Chile

Industrial Class III: $50 to $99

(1) Japan, (2) Portugal, (3) Greece, (4) Spain, (5) Argentina, and (6) Lebanon

Industrial Class IV: Under $50

(1) Rhodesia, (2) Colombia, (3) Philippines, (4) Peru, (5) Ecuador, (6) Brazil, (7) Turkey, (8) Syria, (9) China (Taiwan), (10) China (Mainland), (11) Congo (Leopoldville), (12) Korea,[b] (13) UAR (Egypt), (14) India, (15) Burma, (16) Pakistan, (17) Ceylon, and (18) Indonesia

---

[a] Source: Husain, 1962, p. 23.
[b] South Korea apparently.

an index of industrial development that reflects the extent to which a society's population is employed in manufacturing, together with the productivity of labor so employed.

Examination of the materials in Table 4 in light of the rural-urban patterns in these countries reveals an apparently close associa-

more. In fact, some relatively nonurbanized societies may contain large metropolitan centers. As a result, Wilkinson (1960, p. 360) found it useful to distinguish between the degree of urbanization and metropolitanization, a pattern he described for the world scene via the following typology:

	Western Europe and Anglo-America	Latin America	The East and Africa
Industrialization	High	Moderate/Low	Medium/Low
Urbanization	High	High	Low
Metropolitanization	High	Low	High

tion (at the extremes) between industrialization and urbanization. Such nations as Finland and Yugoslavia, however, deviate from the expected pattern. In line with the reasoning above, it can be surmised that these countries' close ties with highly industrialized societies partially compensate for their definite agrarian orientation.

Although there is a close association between urbanization and industrialization, some so-called agrarian societies embrace millions of urbanites. Thus, on Mainland China about 70 million people reside in communities of one hundred thousand or

Overall, the association between industrialization and metropolitanization is not as high as that between industrialization and urbanization.

As for the future, the urbanization process, barring an atomic war, will continue. Even for the United States much larger urban agglomerations can be foreseen. Although today the New York Metropolitan Area contains about 15 million people, Hauser (1960) has envisioned the emergence of "strip cities" in America, one of which would run from Boston to Washington, D.C. In part the growth of such cities will result from a relatively rapid expansion of the total societal population.

Underdeveloped countries, as they consciously strive to industrialize, are likely to intensify their rates of urbanization. This, combined with large societal populations, may lead to cities whose size staggers the imagination. Davis (1962) speculated about the future size of cities in India. Basing his predictions on a number of assumptions, including the nature of future population growth in India, Davis has foreseen cities of

although the transition between city and village in the civilized societies of antiquity was not as sharp as that in later preindustrial orders in, for example, China, India, the Middle East, and Europe, the city has always stood apart.

Everywhere and at all times the city has dominated the countryside: politically, economically, and culturally. To be sure, the sphere of influence of preindustrial cities has been much less than that of modern urban centers. Thus, for the small city in medieval

TABLE 5

ESTIMATED SIZE OF MAJOR CITIES IN INDIA IN 1970 AND 2000
(in millions of inhabitants)[a]

Metropolis[b]	Type of Estimate of Proportion in Cities[c]			
	Low		High	
	1970	2000	1970	2000
Calcutta	12.0	35.6	16.0	66.0
Delhi	6.0	17.8	8.0	33.0
Bombay	4.0	11.9	5.3	22.0
Madras	3.0	8.9	4.0	16.5
Bangalore	2.4	7.1	3.2	13.2

[a] This is an abbreviated version of Davis' table (1962, p. 25).
[b] Rank according to relative position in the year 2000.
[c] Each type of estimate yields two series of figures for the specific cities, according to whether the 20,000+ or the 100,000+ class is utilized. On the whole the differences are not great; we have accordingly taken the mean of the two.

enormous size, with perhaps as many as 66 million in Calcutta by the year 2000 (Davis, 1962, pp. 22–26).

RURAL-URBAN PATTERNS IN PREINDUSTRIAL CIVILIZED SOCIETIES

Frankfort (1956, pp. 61–62) argued that in Mesopotamia and "as recently as the European Middle Ages our contrast 'urban-rural' was unknown." If he meant by this that agriculturists were settled on the outskirts of the cities (just as occurs today in transitional societies), then we would agree with this proposition. But if he intended to say that the city was not differentiated from the rural community, then we must demur. For

England, a day's journey seems to have been the ordinary limit for bringing in food and various other necessities (Russell, 1960, p. 67). Political capitals such as Rome, however, have dominated, and drawn upon the resources of, the entire society and have cast their shadows even beyond the political frontiers.

The city's dominance over the village, including greater urban prestige and status, has been associated with the ruling group's residence therein. The largest landlords, who have owned property directly or indirectly through the governmental, educational, or religious structures they have controlled, have resided chiefly in cities, the centers of power and authority. In some societies, as in England, it was the custom for large landlords to spend part of the year at their country estates, and some eventually retired thereto, but they also maintained houses in the city, and especially important personages resided in the capital. The term landed gentry as applied to such persons, especially in European historical literature, has led many social scientists to assume, falsely, that "landed" necessarily means "domiciled in the countryside."

Why have the elite clustered in cities? First of all, urban life maximizes personal contact among the political, religious, and educational leaders. Today in industrial-urban centers certain managerial functions are most effectively carried out through face-to-face contacts. This has been even more the case in preindustrial settings, where mass communication media that facilitate the interchange of ideas and information have been lacking. The pressures for personal communication among societal leaders must have had a great deal to do with the first emergence of cities; moreover, this functional requirement partially accounts for the elite's residence in the central district rather than on the fringes.

Not only has urban residence maximized personal communication among members of the elite, but the city's (and especially the capital city's) position astride the major communication routes has enhanced the ruling group's ties with the lesser bureaucrats in the provincial capitals and with other communities in the outlying regions.

Not least among the city's attractions for the upper class have been the presence of the military and (usually) the protection of city walls. Typically, armies have been quartered in and about cities; the absence of efficient communication media has made rural regions difficult to control. Also urban living has offered social and intellectual advantages —libraries, universities, religious institutions, theaters, and the like, not available in the rural community.

All these factors have added prestige to urban living. The notion that rural peoples are unsophisticated is not unique to indus-

trial societies. They have always looked to, and wherever possible have tried to emulate, urban life-ways. Foster (1960, p. 96) observed that some types of dress worn by peasants in mid-twentieth-century Spain reflect the styles of the urban populace of many decades (or even some centuries) ago, styles long since abandoned in the cities.

The preindustrial city's prestige has been further reinforced by its political and economic dominance over the countryside. To a large extent the peasants have worked for and functioned under the control of urban leaders. Urban dwellers have provided organizational skills, especially those pertaining to the maintenance of a stable economic and political structure, and the fortunes of the peasantry have usually shifted with the waxing and waning of the urban communities they have supplied. Thus peasants seem to have prospered more when empires (and cities) have flourished than during periods when the political structure has been highly fragmented.

Yet it is significant that whereas the countryside has supported the city, mainly via its agricultural produce, the preindustrial city has produced few goods for ruralites, providing instead the necessary political and economic organization. Urban manufactures in preindustrial civilized societies have been destined primarily for city-dwellers.

Whether the urban elite has owned land directly, or has controlled it indirectly through its dominance of the church and governmental hierarchies that have owned the land, the result has been the same: The lot of the peasants has usually been worse than that of the city dwellers, even those in the lower class. Through rent, taxation, sharecropping, or like methods, all reinforced by the religious ideology, peasants in traditional China, Tibet, Egypt, and elsewhere have been induced to send to the urban markets, especially for the benefit of the urban elite, many items they could easily have consumed themselves (e.g., Carrasco, 1959; Hsiao, 1960; Shaw, 1962). In all this the peasants have rather passively accepted their lot, for until recently they have had little notion of alternative modes of existence.

City and village usually have been linked by a complex social network. Itinerant merchants, tax collectors, or other governmental officials have passed to and fro between these subsystems. Kinship ties have formed another bridge between urban and rural centers. For instance, according to Eberhard (1952, pp. 15–16), during one period of Chinese history the gentry family typically had an urban and a rural branch, and, if in a struggle for power the urban branch were exterminated, the country cousins usually managed to survive and thereby perpetuate the family. (It seems likely that the country branches of the gentry lived in small towns, not in little rural villages.)

The prime locus of city-country ties has been the market town. At regular intervals peasants have flocked thereto from the farms, with merchants and others arriving from the larger cities. Through these market towns produce from the farms has flowed in the direction of the city and information from the cities has diffused to the countryside (e.g., Cohn & Marriott, 1958; Yang, 1944).

Returning to the matter of rural-urban differences in preindustrial civilized societies, divergencies can be found in the political, economic, educational, family, and class structures. But for an understanding of these patterns, it is necessary to elaborate upon the class structure in this type of society.

The city has harbored not only the elite but also members of the lower class and outcaste groups (outcastes have typically been more urban than rural). Yet the city's lower class and outcaste elements have had more in common with the villagers, except perhaps in the economic sphere, than with the urban upper stratum, a fact of considerable import for the analysis of rural-urban patterns in transitional orders today.

Consider, for example, the family system. The ideal patterns as realized by the urban elite in preindustrial societies such as China, India, and those in the Middle East have found no real counterpart in the rural communities. The upper-class family is the extended type with several generations (typically the father, mother, unmarried children, married sons and their wives and children) living in one household, i.e., under a single roof. Through this extended family system (an economic unit), as well as through links with other families in its class, the elite has been able to sustain its political and economic leadership. Members of the same family or broader kinship group assist one another in achieving positions of authority in the principal bureaucracies: educational, political, and religious. Conversely, the large extended family generally can be sustained only by persons who command positions of power and authority in the system.

On the other hand, for the lower class in the city and in the village, life is a constant struggle for bread. Some members of the family must move about in search of a livelihood. This mobility, along with the higher mortality rates, tends to fragment the family and keep it small. As a result, the conjugal type (or more usually the *famille souche*) is typical of the lower class and most outcastes, rural or urban. The popular notion that the largest families in single households tend to be found in rural areas is not a valid generalization for preindustrial civilized societies.

Rural and urban family patterns differ also with respect to the role of women. In the countryside women have usually enjoyed greater "freedom" than those living in the city. A dramatic instance of this has occurred in the cultural context of the Middle East, where urban women in preindustrial cities have gone veiled while rural women have typically appeared in public with the face uncovered. Moreover, in preindustrial-urban centers, irrespective of the cultural setting, lower-class women have been less cloistered than those in the elite. Women both in the urban lower class and among the peasantry have had to work outside the home to help support the family.

Another dimension to rural-urban differentiation appears in the area of religious values and practices. Urban peoples generally have been considered more secular than the inhabitants of rural communities. However, in preindustrial societies the city has been the chief source of both change and tradition. Sociologists have stressed the city's function in generating change almost to the exclusion of the latter.

Despite the city's role in social change and despite the frequently expressed view that cities are inherently "evil," some cities have been regarded as highly sacred places. After all, the great religions of history—Buddhism, Hinduism, Islam, and Christianity—were primarily products of the urban environment. For example, it was to the cities of the Mediterranean littoral, not to the villages and hamlets, that Christianity was first transmitted and established. Preindustrial cities, in fact, have been the sites of the highest forms of religious worship. Lhasa has been considered holy by Buddhists in Tibet. For the Hindus, Benares, with its immediate ancestor Kasi, has been the fountainhead of religion and of traditional learning for over two thousand years. Jerusalem has served as a sacred symbol for a number of different religious groups. But in some respects Mecca is the most striking instance. One of the basic tenets of Islam is that a Muslim must, if at all possible, make a pilgrimage to Mecca at least once. Thus, through its portals have passed an endless stream of pilgrims from all parts of the world. Such evidence indicates that cities are not always foci of secularization, nor are they necessarily prejudicial to religious values (cf., Vidyarthi, 1961).

Most significant, the ideals have been urban rather than rural in character. For it is the urban elite, not the villagers or lower-class urban people, who perpetuate the ideal religious norms as set forth in the religious writings. This pattern continues to the present day in, for example, the Indonesian city studied by Geertz (1960, pp. 228ff.). After all, indoctrination into the complexities of religion in preindustrial civilized societies has demanded considerable time and funds. Intensive knowledge of the scriptures is available only to those who command the necessary formal education. Moreover, the ideal religious rites have usually been so costly that only the upper class has performed them regularly. For these reasons, the religious practices and beliefs of rural, as well as lower-class urban, peoples form part of the "little" rather than the "great" tradition of the society (Redfield & Singer, 1954).

Other significant rural-urban differences have appeared in the realm of education and language. Formal education in the preindustrial civilized order has been heavily concentrated in the cities, and literacy has tended to be a monopoly of the elite. So also, products and ideas from abroad usually reach the city first and only much later spread to the small towns and villages. In keeping with the city's dominance in the educational sphere, the urban populace, notably the elite, speak that form of the language considered to be the standard.

RURAL-URBAN PATTERNS IN TRANSITIONAL SOCIETIES

Nowadays most preindustrial societies are striving for an industrial tomorrow, recognizing that the social orders with power, prestige, and status in the contemporary world are industrial, not preindustrial, in nature.

Transitional societies, of course, differ in many respects. They include former folk orders (as in Africa south of the Sahara), as well as societies that are emerging from a preindustrial civilized past (the latter are stressed herein). Both categories of modernizing, or transitional, societies include peoples that have only recently shaken off a colonial status. The different social systems in the transitional category, moreover, vary greatly in their human and natural resources.

As a result of this diversity, the initial propositions made in this section are of necessity on a high level of generalization. Afterwards some refinements will be introduced, at least by taking into account the political context within which industrialization is occurring. For a distinction is made here between industrial urbanization within totalitarian orders and industrialization within systems that claim to adhere to a more democratic model. This distinction forces us to compare rural-urban patterns in Communist countries with those in the non-Communist world.

In attempting to delineate rural-urban differences and interrelationships in transitional societies, one frequently encounters conflicting evidence and interpretations. In part the confusion stems from certain initial assumptions (e.g., those concerning the nature of social reality) that social scientists make before they proceed with their analysis. Moreover, sociologists still think of the rural-urban differences in transitional societies in terms of American or West European patterns.

As for specific rural-urban relationships and differences in these societies, cognizance must be taken of the large-scale movement of persons from the rural to the urban sector, one consequence of the industrialization process. Much of city growth is a result of this in-migration. But it must also be recognized that in most of these societies the urbanization process is taking place within the context of a population explosion.

The proportion of urban growth attributable to internal migration, in contrast to natural increase within cities, varies considerably among nations. In Latin America, for example, in-migration accounted for about 71 per cent of the urban growth in Venezuela (1941–1950), but only for about 42 per cent of the urban growth in Mexico (1940–1950) (Hauser, 1961, p. 110).

With rapid population increase, rural communities experience severe social and economic pressures. Even with large-scale out-migration the total population of rural communities may actually increase (e.g., Seklani, 1960). In many societies, as in India, landholdings have become highly fragmented as children of each successive generation inherit smaller and smaller parcels of land. A large landless laboring group has arisen in

many underdeveloped countries; there is both much unemployment and much underemployment of the labor force (Unemployment and underemployment in India . . . , 1962). Consequently, the factors leading to rural-to-urban migration in transitional societies differ from those in advanced industrial systems:

As between the advanced and the less developed countries, there is a fundamental difference in the underlying causes of the transfer of manpower. Lower levels of income are a universal reason for movement. But different causes operate to reduce the level of incomes in agriculture in relation to other incomes. In the advanced countries labour leaves the land because agriculture is growing in efficiency. Income per head in agriculture tends to fall in relation to incomes in other occupations because food production increases more rapidly than the demand for food. In the less developed countries, however, incomes from agriculture tend to fall relative to other incomes because (a) population on the land increases more rapidly than food output; (b) new investment is concentrated in industrial production and urban development generally; and (c) the prices of primary products in world markets are falling. These income-depressing factors may operate singly or together. Agriculture is an underprivileged sector of the economy, suffering from a chronic excess of labour and shortage of capital (International Labour Office, 1960, pp. 209–210).

Furthermore, urban residence commands increased social prestige and offers greater access to special political, economic, and educational facilities (e.g., Tumin, 1961; Whetten, 1961). If one is to improve his lot he must move to the city.

These migration patterns produce various strains and tensions, about which little is known. Migrants and nonmigrants often differ in age, sex, and amount of education. The resulting shift in age and sex distributions within both villages and cities generates new kinds of social arrangements. For example, because young adults abandon the rural areas for the city more frequently than do other age groups, the villages lose and the cities gain many persons who are in the most productive years of life.

Further, one needs to distinguish between the temporary and the permanent urban in-migrant. In many developing societies a size-able group of migrants enter the cities with no thought of staying (e.g., Meinkoth, 1962, p. 25). But many do remain and some who return to the village eventually find their way back to the urban community. This movement to and fro helps to reduce the social distance between city and country.

It is now time to examine the question: Are the differences between rural and urban communities in underdeveloped countries increasing or decreasing? Hoselitz (1962), for one, has contended that these communi-ties are moving further apart, socially and culturally. Certainly, many cities in transi-tional societies are undergoing marked trans-formation, not only in size but in their social organization as well. The traditional stratification, familial, economic, political, and religious systems are breaking down and newer industrial forms are emerging. Yet these changes do not necessarily mean that the differences between the rural and the urban sectors are greater than ever before. Rather, the evidence suggests that contra-dictory forces are at work (e.g., Lambert, 1962).

When evaluating rural-urban contrasts in transitional societies, one must bear in mind the carry-overs from the preindustrial past. In societies such as India, many of the large cities, and particularly their suburbs, include a sizeable number of agriculturists (Davis, 1951, p. 138). This leads to a certain overlap in the occupational structure of city and village. Rural and urban sectors also merge because their lower-status inhabitants share what Lewis (O. Lewis, 1961, pp. xxiv–xxvii) has termed "the culture of poverty." The unfavorable economic situation of lower-class urbanites and peasants prevents them from sustaining the patterns of either the traditional elite or the emerging industrial-urban middle class. As in preindustrial civil-ized orders, poverty imposes serious strains upon the family structure, and religious be-liefs are frequently but "corrupted" versions of the high-status forms. Although indus-trialization is slowly improving the eco-nomic position of the lower strata, many persons are still held in the grip of this widespread culture of poverty.

Various forces, however, are changing the nature of the rural-urban distinctions. As cities expand in size and over space, some villages in the immediate environs are liter-ally being absorbed into the urban complex (e.g., Singh & Harit, 1960). More impressive in its impact is the increase in scale of the economic and political spheres. Improved transportation now enables the city to range much more widely for its raw materials and to distribute its products more broadly as well. Pred, on the basis of his research on the industrialization of Göteborg, Sweden, and his review of the pertinent literature, concludes:

. . . the technological innovations in manufac-turing processes associated with industrial revo-lution lead to lower unit production costs and attendant scale shifts, which in turn necessitate a spatial extension of market and supply areas. Similarly, the cheapening of transport inputs, the expansion and intensification of the rail-road network . . . encourage . . . a greater feasibility for industrial agglomeration, and an increased tendency toward geographic speciali-zation of manufacturing activities—all of which imply expanded scales of production and longer and larger flows of raw materials and finished products (Pred, 1962, p. 107).

As industrialization proceeds, city and village become increasingly interdependent. Not only does the city rely upon the agricul-tural produce of the countryside, but it be-gins to send finished goods (such as farm machinery or chemical fertilizers) to the villages. As the rural communities are drawn into this new economic order geared to industrial-urbanization, changes in the age-old rural-urban marketing patterns, though painfully slow in some countries, are occurring. Thus there is movement toward greater standardization, such as the sorting of produce by size and quality.

With the expansion of the villager's economic horizons, the traditional social structure, especially the status hierarchy, undergoes considerable revision (Epstein, 1962), as does also the peasant's world view (Sanders, 1962, pp. 308ff.). Although, as Banfield (1958) demonstrated in his study of an Italian village, the peasant social structure may be highly resistant to change, the forces at work in many modernizing societies are such as to transform peasants into farmers (Sanders, 1962, pp. 308ff.; cf. Franklin, 1962).

In greater or lesser degree, the state has been intervening in the lives of the peasants. Land reform programs, for instance, have been carried out in numerous societies; such plans are not unique to the Communist sphere. Furthermore, the proliferation of mass communication media may expose the villager to much the same kind of news and ideas that the urbanite receives. Although there is considerable variation within and among societies in the impact of mass media on village life (cf. deYoung & Hunt, 1962, with Hirabayashi & El Khatib, 1958), radio, movies, television, and to a lesser degree popular writings do hurdle the barriers surrounding the traditional village (deYoung, 1955, p. 173; Geddes, 1963; Lerner, 1958). This contact with the outside world is accentuated by modern means of transportation—buses, automobiles, and highways. One result is greater identification of the villagers with the broader nation-state system, its political leaders, and the ideology of nationalism.

Because of the monumental changes in mass communication and transportation, it is difficult to compare patterns in present-day transitional societies with those for Europe in the eighteenth century. Clearly one must not assume (without substantial data) that the differences today are greater than those in the past.

But neutralizing these tendencies toward the blending of the rural and urban sectors are certain divisive forces. First of all, in transitional societies, it is the upper socio-economic elements, overwhelmingly urban in residence, who are the first to acquire the complicated technical knowledge associated with industrialization. They do this through participation in the formal educational structure, especially the universities, of advanced industrial-urban orders. In recent decades a familiar sight in universities of the United States and Europe (including nations in the Soviet bloc) has been the many students and exchange professors from modernizing societies. Nations seeking to industrialize and urbanize are thus in a position to draw upon the industrial world's accumulated knowledge of more than a century and a half. Urban residents, more than ruralites, are in the forefront of this process.

The most highly-educated persons, moreover, tend to cluster in the largest cities. In some transitional societies, like Mexico and Greece, the pre-eminence of the capital city in every sphere is striking (e.g., Browning, 1962; McNeill, 1957). This extreme centralization in part results from the dearth of skilled human resources, such as managers, scientists, or engineers, who, to function effectively, require sustained personal contacts with others of their kind. The high concentration of specialists in just a few cities does seem to have functional advantages for economic development. For one thing, decentralization of industrial activities and their distribution over a number of medium-sized cities—a proposal advanced by the economist John P. Lewis (1962, Ch. 7)—might prevent efficient use of some kinds of technical skills.

The identification of the educated sector with the city accentuates the gap between rural and urban communities in other ways. Whether in Cuba (Nelson, 1950), Guatemala (Whetten, 1961), India, southern Italy, or elsewhere, the number (and quality) of village teachers is far below that in the urban sector. Carlyle (1962, p. 134) stated that in 1954 Italy had 120,000 unemployed primary school teachers; yet the southern part of

Italy, the most heavily agrarian and impoverished region, displayed a serious lack of qualified teaching personnel. As a consequence of this pattern, rural birth definitely becomes a limiting factor in educational achievement (e.g., Tumin, 1961, p. 57).

The tendency of many educated persons to reject the traditional forms for the industrial-urban model generates other kinds of patterns. Here again the data are limited. However, Cohn's (1958) research in India and especially Friedl's research and analysis of the situation in Greece (Friedl, forthcoming), suggest that as the educated come to embrace the industrial-urban forms, the peasantry and lower-class urbanites, groups that continue to have many social characteristics in common, look increasingly to the values of the older preindustrial-urban elite. As a result the city, or more specifically the upper socioeconomic element within it, tends to become more liberal (or, as many term it, "Westernized") at the same time that other sectors of the society are becoming more conservative. The economic gains that industrialization offers eventually filter down to the urban lower class and the rural people, greatly increasing their ability to emulate the traditional ideals. An increase in the standard of living, combined with a lowered mortality rate, leads to larger families. Also, as some formal education becomes available to persons in the lower strata, they gain a greater understanding of the traditional religious norms (cf. Barclay, 1963). Also, their improved economic situation makes it possible for them to carry out more of the traditional religious rites (at the very time that many in the upper strata are abandoning these ceremonies). Although the mass media may, as indicated above, orient rural dwellers in the direction of industrial-urban forms, the findings of Friedl and Cohn help to describe and explain, at least to a degree, the differential rates and kinds of change within transitional cities and societies.

The research findings of Stycos (1963) in Peru support this interpretation of social change in modernizing societies. Stycos has indicated that, in the short run, modernization in Peru may increase the fertility of the Indian element by bringing their mating patterns more in line with those of Mestizo culture. The Mestizos, the privileged stratum, have been the carriers of the traditional ideal norms which the Indian lower socioeconomic groups are now attempting to emulate. Also, in Europe today some of the distinctions between rural and urban communities apparently have resulted from the peasants' adoption, during the last century or more, of feudal values, for they had at last acquired the means to attain some of the traditional ideals.

Another facet to the problem of rural-urban relationships in transitional societies that deserves special attention concerns the adjustment to the urban milieu of in-migrants from rural areas. As stated above, urban in-migrants may create special links between city and village. One reason for the perpetuation of the new urbanite's bonds with his village or region of origin is that he tends to settle in communities within the city containing others like him. He may in fact have moved to the city because of personal ties with earlier migrants. Misra's (1959, p. 78) social survey of the city of Jamshedpur, India, revealed that 74.96 per cent of the in-migrants before 1940 and 76.53 per cent between 1940 and 1955 were attracted toward Jamshedpur because they already had friends and relatives living there. Over 80 per cent of these in-migrants came from rural, rather than urban, areas. Although this is perhaps an extreme case, it nevertheless dramatizes the importance of interpersonal relations in rural-to-urban movement.

Also, through these subsystems, similar in function to the immigrant communities in American cities, in-migrants come to acquire basic knowledge about the urban social order. In urban centers in modernizing societies, a person is often employed through the intervention of friends or relatives. A.F.A. Husain, on the basis of his study of Dacca, Pakistan, concluded:

Probably in most cases a close relative or at any rate a fellow villager is responsible for introducing a person to a factory or to rickshaw employment. Most factories having more applicants than vacancies, people already in employment keep a watch on possible vacancies and inform their relatives beforehand. It is not unusual also for a young man to come from the village and live with a relative until a vacancy occurs (A.F.A. Husain, 1956, p. 130).

The in-migrant also learns through his friends how to avoid police dragnets and in general how to survive and even to enjoy himself.

At the same time, these subsystems in the city permit and encourage links between the members and their regions of origin (Bruner, 1961; Friedl, 1959; Hauser, 1961, pp. 184ff.; Siguan, 1959). This may take the form of visits to the home village, especially on festive occasions. More significant, these social groupings serve as vehicles for sustaining in the urban milieu certain ceremonies and traditions of the rural areas in question. These cultural survivals operate particularly in the noneconomic sphere (Mayer, 1961). Thus, Wagley (1961), when discussing urban in-migrants, stated: "The vast majority of them are, in a sense, peasants living in the city" (Wagley, 1961, p. 211). Nevertheless, urban residence does induce significant changes in the lifeways of in-migrants, and city dwellers, with their greater prestige, influence the villagers far more than the villagers influence them (e.g., Miner & De Vos, 1960).

In the course of research on the transitional city the inevitable question arises: Are these enclaves functional or dysfunctional to industrial-urban development? By linking the urban in-migrant to his past they ease his adjustment to the new environment; but, looked at from the viewpoint of the broader society, they may retard industrial-urbanization (Sjoberg, forthcoming). The issue is whether one is concerned with individuals or subgroups in the immediate present, or with the long-run development of the society

as a whole. This leads now to an examination of the political context within which industrialization is proceeding.

Political Structure, Ideology, and Rural-Urban Patterns

The nature of the power structure strongly affects the course of industrial-urbanization, and political ideologies can either support or inhibit this process. Rural-urban differentials in transitional societies appear to differ according to whether the society is committed to a totalitarian form of government or to a democratic one. But still further refinements in this typology can be made. The totalitarian model in particular can be divided into two subtypes: one which strongly encourages industrial-urban development and one which firmly resists it (cf. Coser, 1963). The second type—the anti-industrial-urban authoritarian model—is only mentioned here. Spain and Portugal, as well as some countries in Latin America and Asia, display this form of government. Spain under Franco has for several decades sought to maintain its peasant-based order dominated by a traditional feudal elite, which includes the large landlords and the church hierarchy. Although during the past few years the situation has been changing, resistance to the emergence of a full-fledged industrial-urban order continues strong (Crow, 1963).

Totalitarian industrial-urban development. More significant here are those totalitarian orders that are striving to further industrial-urban development. The prime examples are nations within the Communist orbit. Although there are certain significant differences within this bloc, particularly between China and the Soviet Union (Zauberman, 1962), one can perceive a number of common policies regarding rural-urban patterns. The writings of Galbraith (1962) and Nove (1961), among others, are helpful in the analysis of the Communist model.

Following Marx, the leaders in Communist countries have usually taken a strong antirural stand (Mitrany, 1951). For a number of decades in Russia, and today in China, the formation of an industrial-urban order has been considered the main goal, and the political leaders have instituted policies intended to destroy the traditional peasant way of life.

Yet the role of Marxism in all this is complex. Most writers commenting on the Chinese revolution, and more recently on that in Viet Nam, seldom, if ever, discuss these upheavals in terms of a rural-urban conflict. But unlike the Russians, the Chinese Communists (Gillin, 1960; Johnson, 1962) have used, and now the Viet Cong is attempting to use, the peasantry as a means of acquiring political control of the society. Mao Tse-tung and his followers departed from the teachings of Marx and Lenin by organizing a revolution of the peasants rather than of the urban proletariat (attempts to achieve the latter were unsuccessful). It appears that in part the peasants have united because of their resentment of the traditional urban elite, which has included large landowners.

The Communist leaders in China have utilized the peasants as a means to an end. Once in power they have apparently reverted to more traditional Marxist doctrine, which disparages the worth of the peasantry and seeks to bring them into the industrial-urban sphere as quickly as possible. For the leaders know that today only an industrial power can maintain a position of dominance on the world scene.

Barrington Moore (1954) and Jasny (1962), among others, probed some of the reasons why the Soviet Union undertook to collectivize agriculture; many of the same reasons apply to China, especially during its "great leap forward" (Hughes & Luard, 1961; Yang, 1959).

First, collectivization has served to uproot the traditional rural structure—including the long-standing emotional bond between the peasant and his little plot of land. And, just as significant, land reform (in terms of collectivization) has destroyed the power base of the traditional landlord group (Maynard, 1962).

Second, collectivization—government ownership of agricultural lands—has resulted in larger farms, which the Soviets have assumed to be essential for mechanization. (Recent experience in Japan, as indicated below, seems to cast doubt on this premise.)

Third, destruction of the peasant's identification with the land, plus the mechanization of agriculture, has pushed many persons into the urban labor market. Such movement is essential to development of an industrial-urban complex.

Fourth, collectivization has permitted much more immediate control over any agricultural "surplus," including direct expropriation of this surplus for the benefit of urban residents. If small, independent farmers were permitted to handle the production and marketing of their crops, they would consume more and deliver less to the markets. The direct political control has also made it possible for the state to pay low prices for agricultural produce; in effect the peasant is called upon to assume a sizeable share of the social cost of industrial-urbanization (Jasny, 1962).

Fifth, the centralization of small, private holdings, and in many cases the merging of villages, have permitted closer surveillance of the peasantry by the authorities, and easier indoctrination into the officially approved norms and values. The peasant owner of a small plot of land has generally been viewed as a potential source of capitalistic revival.

In essence, the Communists, first the Soviets and now the Chinese, have been mainly intent upon building (and glorifying) industrial cities. The policy is to industrialize and urbanize as rapidly as possible through whatever means. The stress is on heavy rather than light industry. Yet the Soviets have viewed with some concern the growth of very large cities. They are pro-urban only up to a point; indeed, on more than one occasion, the leaders have talked about limiting the size of cities, but without much effect (Laqueur & Labedz, 1962, pp. 170–185).

Not only have the Communists aspired mainly to an industrial-urban order, but, as noted above, they have used maximum political coercion to push the populace along the road to this ideal. It is assumed, for instance, that through a high degree of state organization, more efficient use can be made of persons who might otherwise remain unemployed or underemployed in the rural communities.

Democratic industrial-urban development. Quite in contrast to this totalitarian model is the so-called democratic one. The democratic model in transitional societies is generally much more proagrarian than is the totalitarian one. Considerable attention is directed to agrarian reform, however, and, indirectly at least, to modification or destruction of the feudal elite, including the traditional landlord group. But more than this, there is interest in preserving the villages and small towns. The fundamental principle here is that solid social improvements in the agrarian sector, through land reform and extensive capital investment, can substantially increase the production of an agrarian surplus. This, along with some assistance from advanced industrial-urban orders, would not only better the standard of living of the societal population, but if such a plan were fully realized, the common man (especially the peasant) would not have to pay such a heavy share of the social and economic cost of building an industrial-urban order.

By way of illustration, the Alliance for Progress in Latin America reflects just this kind of ideology, for this program is heavily directed to the rural sector; the terms industrialization and urbanization appear only infrequently in most statements of policy (Kennedy, 1961; cf. Haar, 1963). Also, the programs of the governments of South Viet Nam (Fishel, 1961, Ch. 4) and India, with the support of policy-makers in the West, have had much the same kind of orientation. The first five-year plan in India

was committed to building up agriculture rather than urban industry, after which more attention was to be paid (and to a degree has been paid) to the industrial sector.

Specifically, the democratic model's perspective on industrialization and urbanization in the transitional society emphasizes short-range goals. Priority is given to light industry and to programs calling for decentralization of production, often in the form of handicrafts in the villages and small towns. Conversely, there is a general fear of the large city with its slums, its poverty, and the potential instability it breeds.

The democratic model, as developed in the United States and transmitted to many developing societies, seems to embody a number of antiurban values that prevail among intellectuals in this country (White & White, 1962). These values in turn may be reinforced by the intellectual climate of the recipient societies. One need only examine the *Economic Weekly,* or the writings of Indians in *India's Urban Future* (Davis, 1962), to sense that many intellectuals in India view large-scale industrial-urbanization with genuine alarm. Some even remain sympathetic to the Gandhian conception of India, with its symbol of the spinning wheel standing for the village handicrafts as the economic orientation for India in the future.

Evaluation of the Contrasting Models

Although there is little in the way of solid sociological analysis of the ideological models concerning the relative stress that should be accorded the rural and urban sectors during the period of modernization, it seems clear that these models have manifold implications for developing nations. Ideas have consequences.

A fundamental issue is whether nations should press for rapid industrialization, with the expectation that the population today will bear the heaviest cost, or whether they should seek an easier transition through policies calculated to improve the rural sector of the economy. Both the democratic and the totalitarian models embody built-in contradictions as well as serious moral and political dilemmas.

The Communist model, which stresses industrial-urbanization, has encountered some major obstacles. One is the failure of the leadership to inspire confidence in the very group upon whom the society depends for its food (Bauer, Inkeles, & Kluckhohn, 1956, Ch. 19). Negation of the peasant way of life and the paucity of investment in the agricultural sector do little to stimulate food production. First the Soviets, and apparently now the Chinese Communists, have accommodated to this problem through frequent policy alterations. The pattern seems to be to squeeze the peasant for all he's worth, to extract as much from him as possible, then to relax the pressures, increase his freedom, and tighten the wrench again. Thus the strictures upon small, private plots have been tightened or relaxed according to the state of the peasant's morale or the needs of the society for agricultural produce.

The Chinese seem to face special difficulties in the agricultural sphere, for they must feed a huge and rapidly expanding population. The range of expert opinion regarding the future of the Chinese agricultural system is wide, to judge by the contradictory reactions of specialists like Eckstein, Hudson, Lindsay, MacLeish, K. Walker, and R. Walker (Comment "on China's descending spiral," 1962) toward the pessimistic theorizing of Joseph Alsop (1962).

Apart from any personal political preference, it appears necessary to recognize that if a preindustrial civilized society is to industrialize *rapidly* it can do so only in the context of a one-party state exercising a high degree of totalitarian or authoritarian rule (Sjoberg, 1963). Only charismatic totalitarian leaders can give direction to the uneducated mass populace, and their ideological fervor is apparently required to break the "cake of custom" that survives from the preindustrial past. Of course, the low level of literacy and the perennial poverty of the common man are not, if one accepts Lipset's analysis (Lipset, 1963), conducive to the establishment of a democratic order. Then, too, if these societies are to reach industrialization before the predictable population explosion becomes a crushing reality, they must move rapidly, for greatly expanding population would more than consume any food surplus that moderate agricultural reforms could produce.

RURAL-URBAN PATTERNS IN INDUSTRIAL SOCIETIES

The industrial-urban order is composed of several subtypes. One includes societies, like the United States, that have urbanized and industrialized without having to discard a feudal social structure. Another includes societies, such as Western Europe and Japan, that have emerged from a preindustrial civilized past. The differences in the rural-urban patterns within these two subtypes cannot be explored in this chapter.

These subtypes notwithstanding, rural and urban interrelationships in advanced systems differ markedly from those in preindustrial and modernizing societies. First and foremost, industrial societies are dominated by metropolitan agglomerations. Most people live in or near the large cities which dominate the political, economic, and cultural landscape of the society. But these metropolitan centers arrange themselves into a hierarchy: Some dominate a limited region, whereas others like New York, Washington, D.C., London, or Moscow affect the total society of which they are a part and exert influence on the international scene as well.

With metropolitanization of society and advancing industrialization (including the proliferation of mass media and rapid means of transportation), the regional structure undergoes marked change. One can no longer speak of rural-oriented regions, only of urban ones. In the United States, Western Europe, and the Soviet bloc, the older regional distinctions, based largely upon agrarian and cultural traits, have become homogenized: The "mass society" is now a reality. But along with this homogenization of regional traits has emerged a special kind of heterogeneity, based upon occupational specialization of a highly technical sort. This differentiation in turn has fostered functional specialization among urban centers, though not necessarily among the largest ones (Duncan, Scott, Lieberson, Duncan & Winsborough, 1960).

With the rise of the industrial city, new familial, stratification, economic, religious, educational, and entertainment structures have emerged (e.g., Parsons, 1960). These differ markedly from those in the preindustrial city. For example, the ideal family form in the industrial-urban center is no longer the extended family living under one roof but the conjugal type, and the religious norms tend to be permissive rather than prescriptive. Furthermore, the industrialization process has greatly reduced the rural-urban differentials in each of the organizational spheres (e.g., Fuggitt, 1963; Nelson, 1957). Although certain differences persist in the United States (e.g., Duncan & Reiss,

The decrease in rural-urban differentials, especially in the economic realm, has been truly dramatic. The farmer has been released from his age-old position behind the hoe and the plow. Industrial machinery—tractors, cotton pickers, hay balers—as well as scientific farming practices such as the use of chemical fertilizers have been exported to the rural areas. Mass production is no longer confined to the urban factory system.

Mass industrialization in the agricultural sphere is a recent development. Loosely speaking, it became established in the United States in the 1920's, but it was only after World War II that industrialization of agriculture, with its stress upon technology and upon the rationalization of labor and marketing facilities, really came to dominate in Europe. The whole pattern of European agriculture, which in a country like France was, prior to World War II, quite traditional in its economic and social organization, has been greatly transformed (cf. Higbee, 1963; Rambaud, 1961; Sternberg-Sarel, 1961). Some statistics for the United States (Table 6) and Western Europe (Table 7)

TABLE 6

NUMBER OF TRACTORS, MOTOR-TRUCKS, AND HORSES AND MULES
IN THE UNITED STATES[a]

(in thousands)

Year	Tractors	Motor-Trucks	Horses and Mules[b]
1900	..	..	20,004
1910	1	..	23,321
1920	246	139	25,199
1930	920	900	18,738
1940	1,545	1,047	13,932
1950	3,394	2,207	7,604
1957 (prel.)	4,600	2,900	3,574

[a] Source: U.S. Bureau of the Census, *Historical statistics*, 1960, pp. 284–285, 289–290.
[b] See source for manner in which horses and mules were counted in the various years.

1956) and in countries of Western Europe (e. g., Beijer, 1963; Robertson, 1961; Swedner, 1960), the dominant trend has clearly been toward a breakdown in the traditional distinctions (e.g., Williams, 1956; Wurzbacher, 1961).

show the amount and spread of farm mechanization.

Certain types of mechanized equipment have also become widespread in Eastern Europe and the Soviet Union (Michal, 1960, p. 79). The Soviets have been especially at-

TABLE 7

NUMBER OF TRACTORS, SELECTED COUNTRIES IN WESTERN EUROPE[a]

Country	Thousands			Per 1,000 ha. of Agricultural Land	
	Prewar	1950	1957	Prewar	1957
Western Europe	206.9	862.8	2,377.8	2	18
Germany	30.3	139.0	600.0	2	42
Norway	2.8	10.9	38.0	3	38
United Kingdom	50.0	325.0	450.0	4	36
Sweden	22.6	63.8	133.9	6	34
Denmark	3.5	17.2	76.8	1	25
Netherlands	4.0	21.0	51.8	2	22
France	36.0	144.0	535.0	1	16
Italy	35.8	56.9	188.0	2	11
Greece	1.1	4.1	13.0	0.3	4
Spain	5.0	14.8[b]	29.4	..	1
Portugal	0.6	2.3	5.7	0.1	1

[a] Source: Dewhurst, Coppock, Yates, and Associates, 1961, p. 496.
[b] 1949–1952 average.

tracted to use of heavy machinery on farms, as well as to the merging of collective farms into ever larger units. Japan, too, has mechanized much of its agriculture, but in a different fashion. Whereas the U.S.S.R. has, in a manner of speaking, created large farms in order to accommodate large tractors, Japan has built small tractors for small farms:

The most recent and spectacular development has been the remarkable popularity and expansion in the use of hand tractors, or power cultivators—3- to 7-horsepower machines much like rototillers. In 1947 there were 7,000 in use, 35,000 in 1953, 85,000 in 1955, and estimates for 1961 run as high as 1,000,000. These machines are used to cultivate the land and take the place of the work animal and plow. They can be used in both wet and dry fields and constitute a major technological breakthrough in paddy cultivation (Hall, 1963, pp. 30–31).

But the industrialization of agriculture involves not merely tools but a whole set of ideas associated with them. Thus in the United States and Western Europe, great strides have been made toward efficiency in agricultural production, marketing proced-

ures, and the processing of produce. It is significant that, with some exceptions such as Denmark and the Netherlands, the 1960's will mark the first time in history that a significant number of European farm operators have received formal training in pertinent scientific management practices (Coppock, 1963, p. 164).

The move from transitional to advanced industrial orders also involves a shift in the kind of food produced and consumed. As urban dwellers become more prosperous, they import somewhat more food from the countryside, but far more significant is a change in the kinds of food purchased Where Europeans were formerly willing mainly to consume grains, they now demand more livestock and poultry products (Coppock, 1963, Ch. 6). A somewhat similar process is under way in Japan:

. . . marked enlargement of livestocks and fruits markets . . . the strong demand for processed foodstuffs accompanying the high level consumption structure has brought about the rapid increase of agricultural products for foodstuff processing, such as beer, barley, livestocks, fruits, high class vegetables (Agricultural economy in Japan, 1962, pp. 585–586)

On the other hand, the demand for rice and wheat became stagnant. Some Japanese farmers, however, especially the more tradition-bound ones, have experienced considerable difficulty in adapting to the modern market conditions.

Industrialization affects not only farmers and farm laborers but also the nonagriculturists in the small towns. As the farmer becomes urban-oriented in his sale of produce, he purchases more urban products, including fertilizers and mechanized equipment as well as some of the luxury goods associated with urban living. The consequences of this for traditional towns in such countries as England and France have been serious. One has been the obliteration of many traditional handicrafts of these towns (Mendras, 1960).

The decline of population in the small towns and villages has itself generated economic, political, and other social tensions (although these vary considerably among societies). An illustration is provided by certain strains in the political structure of contemporary American society. Even during the present century, rural voters have been able to exert an influence greater than their actual numbers would warrant (Baker, 1955), because the system of representation in state legislatures and in the United States House of Representatives was determined in an agrarian age. Adjustments in the institutional arrangements have lagged behind the often drastic shifts in population. Until a United States Supreme Court decision opened up the possibility of using the courts to achieve equity for urban voters, movement toward fair representation was indeed slow. Rural representatives understandably have been reluctant to yield greater representation to urban politicians and in the process vote themselves out of office.

Industrial-urbanization and the relative decline of the rural sector have generated other problems. One of these concerns inequities between rural and urban populations in the standard of living. In most societies rural peoples have profited less than urban inhabitants during the period of industrialization and urbanization (Agriculture in Japan, 1963; Bellerby, 1956). This has led the farmer, as during the Populist era in the United States, to demand greater economic equality with the urban dweller. During recent decades a number of nations, including the United States, Great Britain, and Germany and others in Western Europe, have sought to provide farmers with special economic advantages, notably through various forms of subsidy such as price supports. Not only have these been designed to provide the rural sector with a larger share of the rewards of industrialization, but nations have used them to sustain a degree of self-sufficiency in agricultural production for nationalistic and military reasons. Such agricultural policies are impeding the economic and political integration of Western Europe (Coppock, 1963).

Two somewhat contradictory problems have emerged in the rural sector of industrial orders: agricultural overproduction and rural poverty. The process of subsidization, plus the growth of scientific agriculture, has generated vast surpluses in the United States. Coppock (1963) argued that, if present policies continue, Western Europe will also be plagued with such surpluses in the future.

As a result of the differential impact of industrial urbanization upon regions and communities within nations (e.g., Ford, 1962; Nordström, 1962), some rural areas have prospered whereas others have fallen behind economically and socially and now stand out as islands of poverty. In the recent past these latter have been one source of support for extremist movements that have threatened the fabric of industrial-urban democracies. In Germany certain rural areas apparently lent much support to Hitler during his rise to power (Heberle, 1951), and in Sweden certain outlying rural communities have nourished the small Communist movement (Davison, 1954–1955). More recently, highly rural Quebec has been prominent as a politically disturbed area in Canada. While the Quebec issue involves ethnic tensions, some of the chief localities of discontent have been the small towns and rural communities that remain outside the industrial-urban sphere.

Numerous difficulties plague industrial-urban systems as they strive to integrate the more isolated, poverty-stricken rural communities into modern society. Beijer (1963), in a very extensive survey of the literature on rural-to-urban migration in 12 European countries, points up the persistence of strains as societies attempt to incorporate ruralities into the urban social setting. These tensions are likely to be heightened as automation destroys many of the semi-skilled and unskilled urban occupations to which inmigrants from the depressed farming regions have historically aspired. The inhabitants of outlying rural communities who lack technical skills are perhaps more difficult to assimilate than are lower-class urban peoples. Although little comparative data are available on this issue, it is clear that the latter group at least has been exposed to the urban environment—an experience the poorer rural dweller lacks.

The inhabitants of depressed rural communities are perhaps now in the position of falling further and further behind in their knowledge of urban technical and social skills. To be sure, the mass media and the formal educational structure, in particular, are strategic in assimilating these outlying rural dwellers into the industrial-urban way of life (Schwarweller & Brown, 1962). However, many rural communities in, for example, Mississippi and West Virginia in the United States or those in the more impoverished regions of Western European nations, experience serious difficulties in staffing their schools, for the most qualified personnel continually drift toward the cities.

Finally, the decline of the rural sector awakens efforts on the part of some elements of the population to cling to the rural past, or at least to an idealized image of that past. After all, rural communities in industrial-urban orders are frequently the repositories of traditional values and norms in the family, religious, and political realms. The "moral fiber" of the rural dweller is often viewed as superior to that of the urbanite. Thus, during the past century and a half in the United States and Western Europe, many intellectuals, as well as substantial segments of the broader populace, have voiced strong antiurban and anti-industrial sentiments. Numerous city planners in Europe and the United States implicitly assume that the rural community embodies the ideal form of social organization—one based upon primary group relations—and, that insofar as possible, such should be transplanted to and nurtured in the cities as well. Therefore the urban community should consist of various small communities or well-defined neighborhoods. Then, too, in the political arena, where the strains have been intense, the conservatives have typically objected to the scientifically based industrial-urban order and have sought to glorify the agrarian past with its supposedly simple life. Indeed, few social theorists outside the Marxian tradition have championed the cause of industrial cities over that kind of society wherein most people inhabit small towns and villages and are committed to cultivating the soil.

The above generalizations apply principally to industrial democracies in the West. Although some of the propositions also hold for industrial systems under Communist control, certain qualifications concerning rural-urban patterns in the Soviet Union and similar areas must be inserted.

First of all, the Soviets have adopted as a purposive policy the elimination of all contrasts between the rural and urban sectors of society (Vucinich, 1960); they are carrying to the logical extreme their ideological negation of the peasant way of life. At one time in the early 1950's there was even talk of constructing *agrogorods* (loosely, agricultural cities) as one means of bringing the city into the countryside (Armstrong, 1961, pp. 207–209). Although this idea has been abandoned, collective farms during the 1950's were regrouped into larger units, and industrialization has moved forward, with the continuing intention of bringing the farming operation in line with the urban factory system (Armstrong, 1961, p. 323).

Yet, side by side with the highly advanced industrial-urban subsystem in the U.S.S.R. is a depressed and rather backward rural sector. Although some rural regions or communities have been more fully incorporated into the industrial-urban orbit than have certain more isolated ones (Dunn & Dunn, 1962; Kalb, 1962; Vucinich, 1960) and, although economic gains have been made in the post-Stalin era, the inhabitants of rural areas in general suffer many more economic, educational, political, and other social liabilities than does the urban populace.

Specifically, agriculture remains the Achilles heel of the Soviet system (Grossman, 1962; Nove, 1961). Agricultural production has lagged so much that, according to Harris (1963), the diet of the Russian people is poorer than that in nonindustrial nations in eastern and southern Europe. The problem is today compounded by rising expectations for a quality diet on the part of the urban managerial and professional class.

There are a number of reasons for this disparity between the industrial-urban and the rural-agricultural sectors (Nove, 1961; Prybyla, 1962). One is the insufficiency of capital investment in the latter. Second, although mechanization has advanced considerably, its application is uneven, being limited to a few basic operations—plowing, sowing, and harvesting of grain crops; many operations are still performed manually. Moreover, the machinery that exists is often inefficiently employed. Third, some writers believe that Soviet agriculture is overbureaucratized, thereby hampering the adaptation of agricultural practices to local conditions; the planners in Moscow attempt to determine too many features of the program for agriculture. Fourth, negative values toward farm labor may have siphoned off many of the aggressive and skilled workers into urban areas. Fifth, the collective farmers lack social and economic incentives. Whereas collectivization may have encouraged mechanization and political control of the rural communities, it has undermined the farmer's historic sense of independence; he no longer has a vested interest in increasing production.

The one country within the Communist orbit that has made considerable progress in increasing agricultural productivity is Poland. Here, after Gomulka's rise to power and in line with the de-Stalinization campaign, de-collectivization was permitted. Today the farmer works his own plot of land for his own profit (Crossman, 1963). As a "control case," Poland's agricultural gains lend support to the propositions that collectivization gives the peasant little motivation to produce and that governments have as yet been unable to organize collective farms in a rational and efficient manner.

SUMMARY AND CONCLUSIONS

This chapter has sought to delineate three types of rural-urban relationships, each corresponding to a stage in the technological development of society: the preindustrial civilized, the transitional or modernizing, and the industrial. This perspective involves a major reformulation of existing theoretical perspectives.

Although certain features are shared by all three societies, significant variations exist in the kinds of economic, political, educational, familial, religious, and recreational differentials between city and countryside in the three societal types. Herein the emphasis has been on the form of rural-urban differences and interrelationships, rather than on specific cultural patterns.

Looking to the future, it can, first of all, be predicted that conflicts between the rural and urban sectors in transitional societies will intensify. At the very least, the arguments over how best to achieve some reasonable balance between rural and urban development will continue. One can also expect a continued narrowing of the rural-urban hiatus in industrial societies, though undoubtedly some differences will long persist.

One can foresee an expansion in the role of rural areas as leisure-time regions for urban dwellers. With the now-possible production of special kinds of foods, say, from algae, by urban industries, a fundamental economic difference between city and country could even disappear.

To end on a note of caution, the present state of knowledge concerning rural-urban patterning across cultures is incomplete, especially with respect to rural-urban patterns in transitional societies, and the available data permit only plausible hypotheses. Undoubtedly some key problems still await definition, as sociologists and other social scientists seek to describe and explain the modern world revolution.

REFERENCES

Agricultural economy in Japan. *Oriental economist*, 1962, 30, 585–587.

Agriculture in Japan. *Oriental economist*, 1963, 31, 141–143.

Alsop, J. On China's descending spiral. *China Quart.*, 1962 (11), 21–37.

Armstrong, J. A. *The politics of totalitarianism*. New York: Random House, Inc., 1961.

Baker, G. E. *Rural versus urban political power*. New York: Doubleday, 1955.

Banfield, E. C. *The moral basis of a backward society*. Glencoe, Ill.: Free Press, 1958.

Barclay, H. B. Muslim religious practice in a village suburb of Khartoum. *Muslim World*, 1963, 53, 205–211.

Bauer, R. A., Inkeles, A., & Kluckhohn, C. *How the Soviet system works*. Cambridge, Mass.: Harvard Univer. Press, 1956.

Becker, H. *Through social values to social interpretation*. Durham, N.C.: Duke Univer. Press, 1950.

Beijer, G. *Rural migrants in urban setting*. The Hague, Netherlands: Martinus Nijhoff, 1963.

Bellerby, J. R. *Agriculture and industry: Relative income*. London: Macmillan, 1956.

Bose, A. The first census of free India. *Mod. Rev.*, 1954, 95, 114–117.

Botero, G. The greatness of cities. R. Peterson (Trans.). In G. Botero (Ed.), *The reason of state and the greatness of cities*. London: Routledge & Kegan Paul, 1956.

Braidwood, R. J., & Willey, G. R. (Eds.) *Courses toward urban life*. Chicago: Aldine, 1962.

Browning, H. Urbanization in Mexico. Unpublished doctoral dissertation, Univer. of California (Berkeley), 1962.

Bruner, E. M. Urbanization and ethnic identity in north Sumatra. *Amer. Anthrogist, 1961, 63, 508–521.

Carlyle, M. *The awakening of southern Italy*. New York: Oxford Univer. Press, 1962.

Carrasco, P. *Land and polity in Tibet*. Seattle: Univer. of Washington Press, 1959.

Carstairs, G. M. A village in Rajasthan: A study in rapid social change. In M. N. Srinivas (Ed.), *India's villages*. (2nd ed.) London: Asia Publishing House, 1960. Pp. 36–41.

Cohn, B. S. Changing traditions of a low caste. *J. Amer. Folklore*, 1958, 71, 413–421.

Cohn, B. S., & Marriott, M. Networks and centers in the integration of Indian civilization. *J. soc. Res.* (Ranchi, India), 1958, 1(1), 1–9.

Comment "on China's descending spiral." *China Quart.*, 1962 (12), 19–56.

Coppock, J. O. *North Atlantic policy—The agricultural gap*. New York: Twentieth Century Fund, 1963.

Coser, L. Prospects for the new nations. *Dissent*, 1963, 10, 43–58.

Crossman, R. H. S. The Polish miracle. *Commentary*, 1963, 35, 210–219.

Crow, J. *Spain*. New York: Harper & Row, 1963.

Davis, K. *The population of India and Pakistan*. Princeton, N.J.: Princeton Univer. Press, 1951.

Davis, K. The origin and growth of urbanization in the world. *Amer. J. Sociol.*, 1955, 60, 429–437.

Davis, K. Urbanization in India: Past and future. In R. Turner (Ed.), *India's urban future*. Berkeley: Univer. of California Press, 1962. Pp. 3–26.

Davison, W. P. A review of Sven Rydenfelt's *Communism in Sweden*. *Publ. Opin. Quart.*, 1954–1955, 18, 375–388.

Dewey, R. The rural-urban continuum: Real but relatively unimportant. *Amer. J. Sociol.*, 1960, 66, 60–66.

Dewhurst, J. F., Coppock, J. O., Yates, P. L., & Associates. *Europe's needs and resources*. New York: Twentieth Century Fund, 1961.

deYoung, J. E. *Village life in modern Thailand*. Berkeley: Univer. of California Press, 1955.

deYoung, J. E., & Hunt, C. L. Communication channels and functional literacy in the Philippine barrio. *J. Asian Stud.*, 1962, 22, 67–78.

Duncan, O. D., & Reiss, A. J., Jr. *Social characteristics of urban and rural communities, 1950*. New York: Wiley, 1956.

Duncan, O. D., Scott, W. R., Lieberson, S., Duncan, B., & Winsborough, H. H. *Metropolis and region*. Baltimore: The Johns Hopkins Press, 1960.

Dunn, S. P., & Dunn, E. Directed culture change in the Soviet Union: Some Soviet studies. *Amer. Anthrogist*, 1962, 64, 328–339.

Durand, J. The population statistics of China, A.D. 2-1953. *Pop. Stud.*, 1960, 13, 209–256.

Durkheim, E. *The division of labor in society*. G. Simpson (Trans. & Ed.). Glencoe, Ill.: Free Press, 1947.

Eberhard, W. *Conquerors and rulers: Social forces in medieval China*. Leiden, Holland: Brill, 1952.

Epstein, T. S. *Economic development and social change in south India*. Manchester, Eng.: Manchester Univer. Press, 1962.

Fallers, L. Are African cultivators to be called "peasants"? *Curr. Anthro.*, 1961, 2, 108–110.

Fishel, W. R. (Ed.) *Problems of freedom: South Vietnam since independence*. New York: The Free Press of Glencoe, 1961.

Ford, T. R. (Ed.) *The southern Appalachian region: A survey*. Lexington: Univer. of Kentucky Press, 1962.

Foster, G. M. *Culture and conquest: America's Spanish heritage*. New York: Viking Fund Publications in Anthropology, No. 27, 1960.

Foster, G. M. Interpersonal relations in peasant society. *Hum. Organ.*, 1960–1961, 19, 174–178.

Frankfort, H. *The birth of civilization in the Near East*. New York: Doubleday, 1956.

Franklin, S. H. Reflections on the peasantry. *Pacific Viewpoint*, 1962, 3, 1–26.

Friedl, E. The role of kinship in the transmission of national culture to rural villages in mainland Greece. *Amer. Anthrogist*, 1959, 61, 30–38.

Friedl, E. Lagging emulation in post-peasant society: A Greek case. *Amer. Anthrogist*, forthcoming.

Fuggitt, G. The city and countryside. *Rural Sociol.*, 1963, 28, 246–261.

Galbraith, J. K. The poverty of nations. *Atlantic Mon.*, 1962, 210 (4), 47–53.

Geddes, W. R. *Peasant life in Communist China*. Ithaca, N.Y.: Society for Applied Anthropology, Monograph No. 6, 1963.

Geertz, C. *The religion of Java*. Glencoe, Ill.: Free Press, 1960.

Geertz, C. Studies in peasant life: Community and society. In B. J. Siegel (Ed.), *Biennial review of anthropology, 1961*. Stanford: Stanford Univer. Press, 1962. Pp. 1–41.

Gibbs, J. P., & Schnore, L. Metropolitan growth: An international study. *Amer. J. Sociol.*, 1960, 66, 160–170.

Gillin, D. Peasant and Communist in modern China: Reflections on the origins of the Communist-led peasant movement. *South Atlantic Quart.*, 1961, 60, 434–446.

Ginsburg, N. *Atlas of economic development*. Chicago: Univer. of Chicago Press, 1961.

Goody, J., & Watt, I. The consequences of literacy. *Comp. Stud. Soc. Hist.*, 1963, 5, 304–345.

Grossman, G. Structure and organization of the Soviet economy. *Slavic Rev.*, 1962, 21, 203–222.

Haar, C. M. Latin America's troubled cities. *For. Affairs*, 1963, 41, 536–549.

Hall, R. B., Jr., *Japan: Industrial power of Asia*. Princeton, N.J.: Van Nostrand, 1963.

Harris, C. D. U.S.S.R. resources: Agriculture. *Focus*, 1963, 13(5), 1–6.

Hauser, P. *Population perspectives*. New Brunswick, N.J.: Rutgers Univer. Press, 1960.

Hauser, P. (Ed.) *Urbanization in Latin America*. Paris: UNESCO, 1961.

Heberle, R. *Social movements*. New York: Appleton-Century-Crofts, Inc., 1951.

Higbee, E. *Farms and farmers in an urban age*. New York: Twentieth Century Fund, 1963.

Higbee, E. The French paysan is angry. *N.Y. Times Mag.*, October 27, 1963, 20–21 +.

Hirabayashi, G. K., & El Khatib, M. F. Communication and political awareness in the villages of Egypt. *Publ. Opin. Quart.*, 1958, 22, 357–363.

Hoselitz, B. F. The role of urbanization in economic development: Some international comparisons. In R. Turner (Ed.), *India's urban future*. Berkeley: Univer. of California Press, 1962. Pp. 157–181.

Hoyt, H. *World urbanization*. Washington: Urban Land Institute, Tech. Bull. 43, 1962.

Hsiao, K. *Rural China: Imperial control in the nineteenth century*. Seattle: Univer. of Washington Press, 1960.

Hughes, T. J., & Luard, D. E. T. *The economic development of Communist China, 1949–1960*. New York: Oxford Univer. Press, 1961.

Husain, A. F. A. *Human and social impact of technological change in Pakistan*. I. Dacca, Pakistan: Oxford Univer. Press, 1956.

Husain, I. Z. A measure of underdevelopment. *AICC econ. Rev.*, 1962, **14**, 19–26.

Ibn Khaldûn, *The Muqaddimah, an introduction to history*. F. Rosenthal (Trans.). New York: Pantheon, 1958. 3 vols.

International Labour Office. *Why labour leaves the land: A comparative study of the movement of labour out of agriculture*. Geneva, Switzerland: Author, 1960.

Jasny, N. *Essays on the Soviet economy*. New York: Praeger, 1962.

Johnson, C. A. *Peasant nationalism and Communist power*. Stanford: Stanford Univer. Press, 1962.

Kalb, M. G. Khrushchev's economic problems. *Reporter*, 1962, **27**(11), 21–23.

Kennedy, J. Alianza para progreso: Address by President. . . . and text of message to Congress. *Bull. Dept. State*, 1961, **44**, 471–478.

Keyfitz, N. The political economy of urbanization in developing countries: The Southeast Asia case. In P. Hauser & L. Schnore (Eds.), *The study of urbanization*. New York: Social Science Research Council, forthcoming.

Lambert, R. D. The impact of urban society upon village life. In R. Turner (Ed.), *India's urban future*. Berkeley: Univer. of California Press, 1962. Pp. 117–140.

Laqueur, W., & Labedz, L. (Eds.) *The future of Communist society*. New York: Praeger, 1962.

Lenski, G. *The religious factor*. (rev. ed.) New York: Doubleday, 1963.

Lerner, D. *The passing of traditional society*. Glencoe, Ill.: Free Press, 1958.

Lewis, J. P. *Quiet crisis in India*. Washington: Brookings Institution, 1962.

Lewis, O. *Life in a Mexican village: Tepoztlán restudied*. Urbana: Univer. of Illinois Press, 1951.

Lewis, O. Some of my best friends are peasants. *Hum. Organ.*, 1960–1961, **19**, 179–180.

Lewis, O. *The children of Sánchez*. New York: Random House, Inc., 1961.

Lipset, S. M. *Political man*. New York: Doubleday, 1963.

Loomis, C. P., & Beegle, J. A. *Rural sociology: The strategy of change*. Englewood Cliffs, N.J.: Prentice-Hall, Inc., 1957.

McNeill, W. H. *Greece*. New York: Twentieth Century Fund, 1957.

Maine, H. *Ancient law*. (new ed.) London: J. Murray, 1930.

Mayer, P. *Townsmen or tribesmen*. Cape Town, South Africa: Oxford Univer. Press, 1961.

Maynard, J. *The Russian peasant and other studies*. New York: Collier Books, 1962.

Meinkoth, M. R. Migration in Thailand with particular reference to the northeast. *Econ. Bus. Bull.* (Temple Univer.), 1962, **14**(4), 3–45.

Mendras, H. The rural exodus and industrialization. *Diogenes*, 1960 (30), 104–119.

Michal, J. M. *Central planning in Czechoslovakia*. Stanford: Stanford Univer. Press, 1960.

Mighell, R. L. *American agriculture*. New York: Wiley, 1955.

Miner, H., & De Vos, G. *Oasis and casbah: Algerian culture and personality in change*. Ann Arbor: Anthropological Papers, Museum of Anthropology, Univer. of Michigan, No. 15, 1960.

Misra, B. R. *Report on socio-economic survey of Jamshedpur city*. Patna, India: Patna Univer. Press, 1959.

Mitrany, D. *Marx against the peasant*. London: Weidenfeld & Nicholson, 1951.

Mols. R. *Introduction à la démographie historique des villes d'Europe du XIVe au XVIIIe siècle*. II. Louvain, Belgium: Univer. de Louvain, 1955.

Moore, B., Jr. *Terror and progress: USSR*. Cambridge, Mass.: Harvard Univer. Press, 1954.

Nelson, L. *Rural Cuba.* Minneapolis: Univer. of Minnesota Press, 1950.

Nelson, L. Rural life in a mass-industrial society. *Rural Sociol.,* 1957, **22,** 20–30.

Nordström, O. Population and labour problems in Sweden's depopulated districts. *Econ. & Hist.,* 1962, **5,** 30–45.

Nove, A. *The Soviet economy.* New York: Praeger, 1961.

Nove, A. The Soviet model and under-developed countries. *Int. Affairs,* 1961, **37,** 29–38.

Opler, M. E., & Singh, R. D. The division of labor in an Indian village. In C. S. Coon (Ed.), *A reader in general anthropology.* New York: Holt, 1948. Pp. 464–496.

Park, R. E. *Human communities.* Glencoe, Ill.: Free Press, 1952.

Parsons, T. *Structure and process in modern societies.* Glencoe, Ill.: Free Press, 1960.

Pocock, D. F. Sociologies—urban and rural. *Contributions Indian Sociol.,* 1960 (4), 63–81.

Pred, A. *The external relations of cities during "industrial revolution": With a case study of Göteborg, Sweden: 1868–1890.* Department of Geography, Univer. of Chicago, Research Paper No. 76, 1962.

Prybyla, J. S. Problems of Soviet agriculture. *J. Farm Econ.,* 1962, **44,** 820–836.

Rambaud, P. Eléments pour une sociologie de la montagne. *Rev. française sociol.,* 1961, **2,** 272–281.

Redfield, R. *The folk culture of Yucatan.* Chicago: Univer. of Chicago Press, 1941.

Redfield, R. The folk society. *Amer. J. Sociol.,* 1947, **52,** 293–308.

Redfield, R. *Peasant society and culture.* Chicago: Univer. of Chicago Press, 1956.

Redfield, R., & Singer, M. The cultural role of cities. *Econ. Develpm. cult. Change,* 1954, **3,** 53–73.

Robertson, I. M. L. The occupational structure and distribution of rural population in England and Wales. *Scot. geograph. Mag.,* 1961, **77,** 165–179.

Russell, J. *Late ancient and medieval population.* Philadelphia: Transactions of the Amer. Philosophical Society, 48, 1958.

Russell, J. The metropolitan city region of the Middle Ages. *J. region Sci.,* 1960, **2,** 55–70.

Sanders, I. T. *Rainbow in the rock.* Cambridge, Mass.: Harvard Univer. Press, 1962.

Schnore, L. The statistical measurement of urbanization and economic development. *Land Econ.,* 1961, **37,** 229–245.

Schwarweller, H. K., & Brown, J. S. Education as a cultural bridge between eastern Kentucky and the great society. *Rural Sociol.,* 1962, **27,** 357–373.

Seklani, M. Villes et campagnes en Tunisie: Évaluations et prévisions. *Population,* 1960, **15,** 485–512.

Shaw, S. J. *The financial and administrative organization and development of Ottoman Egypt 1517–1798.* Princeton, N.J.: Princeton Univer. Press, 1962.

Siguan, M. *Del campo al suburbio.* Madrid, Spain: Consejo Superior de Investigaciones Científicas, 1959.

Singh, I. P., & Harit, H. L. Effects of urbanization in a Delhi suburban village. *J. soc. Res.* (Ranchi, India), 1960, **3**(1), 38–43.

Sjoberg, G. *The preindustrial city: Past and present.* Glencoe, Ill.: Free Press, 1960.

Sjoberg, G. *Political structure, ideology, and economic development.* Bloomington, Ind.: Carnegie Faculty Seminar, Department of Government, 1963.

Sjoberg, G. Cities in developing and in industrial societies. In P. Hauser & L. Schnore (Eds.), *The study of urbanization.* New York: Social Science Research Council, forthcoming.

Smith, T. L. *The sociology of rural life.* (rev. ed.) New York: Harper, 1947.

Sorokin, P., & Zimmerman, C. *Principles of rural-urban sociology.* New York: Holt, 1929.

Sorokin, P., Zimmerman, C., & Galpin, C. J. (Eds.) *A systematic source book in rural sociology.* Minneapolis: Univer. of Minnesota Press, 1930———. 3 vols.

Sternberg-Sarel, B. Grands et moyens proprietaires dans deux villages de l'Hérault. *Rev. française sociol.,* 1961, **2,** 259–271.

Stycos, J. M. Culture and differential fertility in Peru. *Pop. Stud.,* 1963, **16,** 257–270.

Swedner, H. *Ecological differentiation of habits and attitudes.* Lund, Sweden: CWK Gleerup, 1960.

Tisdale, Hope. The process of urbanization. *Soc. Forces,* 1942, **20,** 311–316.

Tönnies, F. *Fundamental concepts of sociology.* C. P. Loomis (Trans. & suppl.). New York: American Book Co., 1940.

Tumin, M. *Social class and social change in Puerto Rico.* Princeton, N.J.: Princeton Univer. Press, 1961.

Unemployment and underemployment in India, Indonesia, Pakistan, and the Philippines. *Inter. Labour Rev.,* 1962, 86, 369–387.

United Nations, *Demographic yearbook, 1960.* New York: United Nations, 1961.

U.S. Bureau of the Census. *Historical statistics of the United States: Colonial times to 1957.* Washington: Government Printing Office, 1960.

Vidyarthi, L. P. *The sacred complex in Hindu Gaya.* London: Asia Publishing House, 1961.

Vucinich, A. Soviet ethnographic studies of cultural change. *Amer. Anthrogist,* 1960, 62, 867–877.

Wagley, C. The Brazilian revolution: Social changes since 1930. In R. Adams et al. (Eds.), *Social change in Latin America today.* New York: Vintage Books, 1961. Pp. 177–230.

Whetten, N. *Guatemala: The land and the people.* New Haven, Conn.: Yale Univer. Press, 1961.

White, M., & White, L. *The intellectual versus the city.* Cambridge, Mass.: Harvard Univer. Press & Massachusetts Institute of Technology Press, 1962.

Wilkinson, T. O. Urban structure and industrialization. *Amer. sociol. Rev.,* 1960, 25, 356–363.

Williams, W. M. *Gosforth: The sociology of an English village.* Glencoe, Ill.: Free Press, 1956.

Wirth, L. Urbanism as a way of life. *Amer. J. Sociol.,* 1938, 44, 1–24.

Wittfogel, K. *Oriental despotism.* New Haven, Conn.: Yale Univer. Press, 1957.

Wurzbacher, G. *Das Dorf in Spannungsfeld industrieller Entwicklung.* Stuttgart: Ferdinand Enke, 1961.

Yang, C. K. *A north China rural market economy.* New York: Institute of Pacific Relations, 1944.

Yang, C. K. *A Chinese village in early Communist transition.* Cambridge, Mass.: Technology Press, 1959.

Zauberman, A. Soviet and Chinese strategy for economic growth. *Inter. Affairs,* 1962, 38, 339–352.

CHAPTER 5 Labor Force

PHILIP M. HAUSER

The labor force is a field of interest to the sociologist, primarily, but not solely, as a subfield of demography. Demographers are interested in the labor force as a large and significant component of the total population. It is that part of the population which is contributing to the production of goods and services, which is in the work force, as distinguished from the "dependent" population. The demographer, as demographer, studies the size, territorial distribution, and composition of the labor force, the changes therein, and the components of such changes. These components may be identified as entrance to the labor force, withdrawal from the labor force as through territorial movement (migration), and labor force mobility (change of status). This statement parallels the definition of demography by Hauser and Duncan (1959, p. 23).

The sociologist, including the sociologist-demographer, however, has a broader interest in the labor force. The demographer, qua demographer, primarily focuses on the labor force as a dependent variable and on the explanation of variance in labor force phenomena in terms of demographic and other labor force data considered as independent variables. The sociologist, however, is more likely to be concerned with the labor force as an independent as well as a dependent variable and with relating changes in the size and composition of the labor force to cultural, social organizational, and social psychological variables. The sociologist also has developed specialized interests with respect to the labor force evident in studies in the sociology of work, in investigations of specific occupations and professions, and in the wide spectrum of activities relating to industrial sociology. Finally, the sociologist often draws on labor force data, especially occupational data, for studies in social stratification, social mobility, and human ecology (see chapters 2, 15, 17).

Focus on work and on the labor force is of relatively recent origin. The consideration of a population of workers, as distinguished from the population in general, implies a society in which work is differentiated from other activities which fill the life space, such as recreation, play, education, worship, and politics. Work is not necessarily sharply differentiated from other life activities in pre-industrial, folk societies. Behavior in a Balinese village incident to the erection of a temple may involve a series of activities, all of which are considered essential to the achievement of the objective without the sharp differentiation which our culture would impose upon the behavior. More specifically, the Balinese do not separate the behavior which we would identify as "recreation" (the dance) from "religion," from "community action," from "work."

In the evolution of our society, activities incident to the production of goods and services have been increasingly detached from the other activities of life. Such activity, identified as work, takes place, usually, in a specific place, during specified intervals of time, and under explicit contractual conditions. It is usually easy to determine when a person is or is not at work. This general rule, however, is beset with exceptions, so that what constitutes work or labor force participation is even in our society an arbitrary matter dependent upon where dividing lines are placed. For example, the housewife who conducts her own household duties in the United States, and in most industrialized countries, is not regarded as in the labor force, that is, she is not considered as among the persons in the working population. But the maid or housekeeper who performs the same type of activity for remuneration in money or kind is generally defined as doing work and as in the labor force. To define and measure the labor force thus becomes a highly technical matter.

The development of interest in the labor force, in general as well as in sociology, and the evolution of the relevant concepts and methods of measurement are well illustrated in the history of the census and other statistical activities in the United States. It was not an accident that it was not until the Fourth Decennial Census of the United States, in 1820, that an inquiry was included in the Census that had any relation to work. The Congress of the United States saw no reason for getting information on workers in the nation prior to 1820, despite the fact that the Senate had been memorialized by at least two learned societies to obtain such information prior to the Second Decennial Census in 1800. The American Philosophical Society, through its president, Thomas Jefferson, in addition to obtaining other types of information, asked the Congress to "furnish a curious and useful document of the distribution of society in the States and of the conditions and vocations of our fellow citizens." Jefferson called for a table showing

the number of free male inhabitants, of all ages, engaged in business, under the following or such other descriptions as the greater wisdom of the legislature shall approve, to wit: (1) Men of the learned professions, including clergymen, lawyers, physicians, those employed in the fine arts, teachers, and scribes in general. (2) Merchants and trades, including bankers, insurers, brokers, and dealers of every kind. (3) Marines. (4) Handicraftsmen. (5) Laborers in agriculture. (6) Laborers of other descriptions. (7) Domestic servants. (8) Paupers. (9) Persons of no particular calling, living on their income . . . (Wright, 1900, p. 19).

Jefferson with obvious statistical insight also cautioned that "care be taken that every person be noted but once in the table, and that under the description to which he principally belongs." A similar memorial was also forwarded to the Senate by the Connecticut Academy of Arts and Sciences through its president, Timothy White. The Senate in its "greater wisdom" ignored the memorials.

Even in the Census of 1820, the schedule called for information only on the number of persons engaged in three classes of occupations: agriculture, commerce, and manufacturing. This Census showed that there were some 2.5 million persons with specified occupations in the above three categories, of whom 2.1 million, or 83 per cent, were in agriculture; 349,000, or 14 per cent, were in manufacturing; and 72,000, or less than 3 per cent, were in commerce.

Interest in the working population was slight enough so that all questions about occupation were omitted in the Census of 1830 (Wright, 1900). Inquiries relating to work, however, did reappear in the Census of 1840. The evolution of the census questions about work from 1840 through 1870 may be interpreted as an indication of our changing society—one becoming transformed from a primarily rural, agricultural order to an industrialized and urbanized one. That is, it may be concluded that the little interest shown in the working population manifest in the United States prior to 1870 was an indication of the preindustrial, preurban status of the nation. In a society in which the predominant proportion of the population was engaged in agriculture and in which the entire family continued to operate as a productive as well as a consuming unit, there was not much reason to be curious about what was obvious. Almost all persons, including children, did something to contribute to the production of the limited schedule of goods and services that characterized living at the time.

It is only since 1870 that reasonably comparable statistics relating to the working population of the United States have been collected (Edwards, 1943). Moreover, significant changes occurred both in the concept and measurement of the working population and components thereof as our society continued to become more highly industrialized and urbanized and as increasingly large proportions of our population worked as employees for employers, that is under "contractual" relationships.

CONCEPTUAL FRAMEWORK

The labor force affords the sociologist an opportunity for methodological as well as substantive study. The development of the present conceptual framework for investigation of the labor force, as well as the specific methods of measurement utilized, constitute one of the best-documented case histories that may be found on the evolution of a census inquiry or sample social survey. Over the past 25 years, the use of the sample survey to measure the labor force of the United States and changes in its composition has

especially added to the methodology of the sample survey as well as to knowledge about the working population.

The conceptual approach employed in the United States Census of 1870, itself a product of earlier census experience, set the pattern for measuring the workers in the United States in subsequent censuses until 1940. According to the Census returns from 1870 to 1930, the working population of the United States was composed of persons who reported an occupation. A "gainful worker" was a person above a specified age (prior to 1940 usually taken as 10 years of age) who reported a "gainful occupation" to the census enumerator. A "gainful occupation" was "an occupation by which the person who assumes it earns money, or money equivalent, or in which he assists in the production of marketable goods" (U.S. Bureau of the Census, 1933, p. 29).

The gainful worker approach employed in the decennial censuses of the United States seemed satisfactory enough until after the 1930 Census. It is to be recalled that the stock market break occurred in the fall of 1929, so that the 1930 Census, conducted as of April 1, was taken in a climate of rapidly deteriorating economic conditions highlighted by a mounting volume of unemployment. The 1930 Census, in consequence, included provisions to obtain a count of the unemployed. The publication of the census unemployment statistics, however, produced more critical reaction than enlightenment. The census reported seven classes of unemployed according to the nature of the unemployment (U.S. Bureau of the Census, 1931). These data confused both technicians and the general public, and the statistics, instead of resolving the question about the number of unemployed, stimulated a great public debate about census concepts and procedures (Arner, 1933; Myers & Webb, 1937; Persons, 1931; Van Kleeck, 1931). Moreover, the situation was not alleviated by the continued rise in unemployment during the depression thirties. Unemployment and relief of the distress of the unemployed became the nation's foremost problem. But the actual volume of unemployment remained unknown until subsequent statistical developments in the later thirties and in the forties indicated that about a fourth of the nation's labor force had been idled during the trough of the depression (U.S. Bureau of the Census, 1960, p. 63).

Rising concern with the volume of unemployment in the 1930's and interest in the characteristics of the unemployed focused attention on the deficiencies of the then current estimates of the unemployed as well as on the inadequacies of the census data. It led to a series of important experiments with both concept and methods of measurement (Dedrick & Hansen, 1938; Webb, 1939). The glare of the public spotlight made it clear that the facts about the most important problem facing the nation simply were not available. The seriousness of the unemployment problem and its political importance gave great impetus to many state and local efforts to count the unemployed. Out of these censuses and surveys a new concept and method of measuring the work force emerged. Interestingly enough, these state and local surveys were in large part financed with federal funds designed to help to alleviate the distress of white collar workers.

The critical analyses which resulted from the confusion and debates of the thirties, together with the experimental surveys and censuses, pointed up the deficiencies of the gainful worker approach for measuring the working population in our highly industrialized and urbanized society. Three major deficiencies in the conceptual framework became apparent. One was the absence of a clear-cut time referent in respect to work force activity. The respondent in reporting his gainful occupation did so without being asked to indicate whether he was still working at the occupation, or whether he had retired from the work. Second, the respondent, if a young person or a housewife who had never previously worked, often had no occupation to report, especially if he had

never been trained for any specific type of work. In consequence, the response obtained was often a "status" response rather than a "behavioristic" one. Since there was no clear-cut time reference or activity involved in the inquiry or the response, the number of gainful workers enumerated in this manner did not actually refer to the labor supply at work or seeking work at any particular time. As a result, a third serious deficiency became evident: It was not possible to measure changes in the labor supply from time to time, or changes in either employment or unemployment, by means of the gainful worker approach.

The experimental surveys during the thirties culminated in the "Census of Partial Employment, Unemployment and Occupations" in 1937, conducted at the express direction of the Congress and in the development of a monthly sample survey designed by the Works Progress Administration to measure the volume of employment and unemployment. The new conceptual framework which emerged came to be known as "the labor force" approach as distinguished from "the gainful worker" approach (Ducoff & Hagood, 1947; Long, 1942; Hauser, 1949; U.S. Bureau of the Census, 1958).

Two essential elements were contained in the new approach that were missing in the older one. First, the labor force concept, so far as possible, was made behavioristic, that is response was based on activity, specifically the activity of working or seeking work. Second, it required a specific time reference—activity during a specified week, the week preceding the interview. Under the new labor force approach, the working population became the population working or seeking work during a specified week.

In addition, the labor force concept changed the lower age limit for the definition of "workers," raising it from 10 to 14 years of age, and it excluded inmates of certain institutions who were not regarded as in the labor market—institutions such as penal and mental institutions and homes for the aged, infirm, and needy. Such institutions might have people actually contributing to the production of goods and services but not for the market.

Under the labor force approach, the working force of the nation was regarded as made up of two major groups: the employed and the unemployed. A great majority of each of these groups under most conditions were determined on a behavioristic basis. That is, the employed, in the main, were taken as those who actually worked at any time for pay or profit or at unpaid family work during the specified week. The unemployed, in the main, were regarded as those who actually sought work during the specified week.

Unfortunately, the complexity of working patterns in our society did not permit a rigidly behavioristic definition of either employment or unemployment. It was necessary, for example, to include as employed not only those who actually worked but, also, those with a job who for good reasons did not actually work during the period under observation. This included persons on vacation during the week, those temporarily ill, those in outdoor work such as construction who were unable to work because of inclement weather, those who were on strike, and others. While it may be true that such persons should be omitted from the employed group when a measure of labor input is desired, as for example in productivity studies, it is also clear that they should not be omitted from a current measurement of the labor supply and not regarded as part of the labor supply seeking work.

Similarly, the unemployed necessarily had to include not only those actively seeking work but also persons actually in the labor market who for specified reasons were not actively seeking employment during the week of observation. An obvious example is the worker in a one-plant town who was not actively seeking work because there was no place to seek it, but who would report to work whenever the factory reopened. Other examples include persons not seeking work because of temporary illness or on a short lay-off with specific instructions to return to work.

Because of necessary compromises of this type, the labor force concept, while based on a behavioristic approach, nevertheless encompasses status relations in including both "inactive" employed and unemployed workers. Under most conditions these inactive groups are relatively small, but under some situations they may loom relatively large and raise questions of interpretation and policy.

Despite shortcomings and difficulties of the type indicated, the labor force concept has great advantages over the gainful worker concept in our economy. In having a definite time reference, the labor force approach provides a clear basis for anchoring current series, and it thus makes possible the measurement of changes in the labor force over short periods of time. It becomes possible, for example, to measure monthly, seasonal, and annual changes in the labor supply, as is not possible with the gainful worker approach. In comparison with the gainful worker approach, the labor force concept comes much closer to providing a picture of the labor supply in a given labor market at a specified period of time.

The shift from agricultural and entrepreneurial enterprise to industrial activity and employee-employer relationships outmoded the gainful worker approach or, in any case, pointed up its deficiencies. The advent of mass unemployment with its attendant interruption of income flow during the thirties created duress and hardship for about a fourth of the nation's workers, and focused unprecedented national attention on the work force and on unemployment. The development of interest in the labor force and its components may be taken, then, as a product of the new problems arising in the transition from a rural, agricultural society to an urbanized, industrial one.

PROBLEMS OF MEASUREMENT

The conceptual framework, the gainful worker or the labor force, indicates the objectives of work force measurement—the desiderata. To attain these objectives, specific methods of measurement must be employed. These methods include sample design, the development of a schedule and specific inquiries for interviewing respondents, an interview situation, processing of the data, analysis of the data, and a program for evaluating the validity, reliability, and precision of response. Information obtained about the size and composition of the labor force is, then, in a fundamental sense, a function not only of the conceptual framework used but, also, of specific forms of measurement employed. Thus, the comparability of information about the work force from canvas to canvas, whether census or sample survey, depends both on the conceptual framework and the methods of measurement.

The materials available on the development of gainful worker and labor force statistics constitute perhaps the fullest documentation of the effect of differences in conceptual framework and methods of measurement on the information obtained. These materials, therefore, provide not only essential information for analyzing and understanding work force statistics but, also, generic insights into the problems and limitations of census and sample survey methods in general. Intensive study of the methodological development of the labor force materials, in fact, raises fundamental questions about the validity and reliability of much of the data obtained through census and survey methods upon which the social scientist, including the sociologist, is dependent (U.S. Bureau of the Census, 1963a; U.S. Bureau of the Census, 1963b; U.S. Bureau of the Census, 1963c).

By reason of differences in concept, it is readily apparent that the work force data obtained historically by means of the gainful worker and labor force approaches, respectively, could not be expected to be comparable without adjustment. It is perhaps not as readily apparent that census and survey results utilizing the same conceptual framework, either the gainful worker or the labor force approach, also pose difficult problems of comparability because of differences in methods of measurement. Hence, although the concept "gainful worker" remained essentially the same from 1870 to 1930 in the decennial census of the United States, the data from census to census are not strictly comparable. Unanticipated and unintended variations in operating procedures, including changes in wording of instructions to enumerators, introduced important discontinuities in the census series. For example, analysis of the returns of children as gainful workers indicates that they were relatively underenumerated in the censuses of 1890 and 1920 and overenumerated in 1910 and 1900. Likewise, gainfully occupied women 20 years of age and over were apparently overcounted in 1910 and undercounted in 1920. To achieve comparability of census data on gainful workers from 1870 to 1930, a number of adjustments in the data are necessary, even though the same concept was employed in both periods (Edwards, 1943, pp. 87-156).

Similarly, there are many problems of measurement in the labor force statistics which adversely affect comparability between the monthly sample and the decennial census and, also, the comparability of the data from census to census and from month to month in the sample survey. Fourteen major improvements were made in current population surveys affecting the labor force statistics between 1942 and 1958 (U.S. Bureau of the Census, 1958, pp. 11-13), and additional changes have been made since (President's Committee to Appraise Employment and Unemployment Statistics, 1962; U.S. Bureau of the Census, 1963b). In respect to the comparability of the monthly sample survey and decennial census data, the differences in type and experience of the enumerator and in the complexity of the interview situation are among the factors which affect the returns. That is, as a result of the better controlled situation in the monthly survey, there can be little doubt that the small sample monthly results are more accurate than the results of the complete decennial census enumeration (U.S. Bureau of the Census, 1953, p. 52).

As various methodological improvements were introduced into the Monthly Report on the Labor Force, the data were from time to time adjusted to provide a comparable time series (U.S. Bureau of the Census, 1960; U.S. Bureau of the Census, 1962). With continued improvements, it may be anticipated that further adjustments will continue to be made.

Let us turn next to the consideration of some of the things that have been learned about the labor force—the substantive results of the conceptual and methodological developments which have been described.

LABOR FORCE PARTICIPATION

Movement into and out of the labor force, that is, mobility in labor force participation, frames all other forms of labor mobility. All other types of labor force change—changes in occupation, industry, class of worker, job, employer, place of work, or combinations of these—necessarily occur within the framework of change in labor force participation itself. Likewise, changes in labor force status, that is, changes in employment or unemployment also occur within the framework of changes in labor force participation.

Explanation of changes in the size and composition of the labor force in terms of components of change represent in a formal

TABLE 1

PARADIGM FOR STUDY OF CHANGE
IN LABOR FORCE PARTICIPATION

Types of Change	Factors Associated with Change													
	Demo-graphic		Economic		Cultural		Social-Organi-zational		Social-Psycho-logical		Political		All Others	
	Net	Gross	Net	Gross	Net	Gross	Net	Gross	Net	Gross	Net	Gross	Net	Gross
Annual Entrances With-drawals														
Secular Entrances With-drawals														
Cyclical Entrances With-drawals														
War Entrances With-drawals														
Seasonal Entrances With-drawals														
All other Entrances With-drawals														

sense the major interest of the demographer in labor force analysis. The broader sociological interest in the labor force, as has been indicated above, includes interest in relating changes in the size and composition of the labor force not only to changes in labor force participation rates but, also, to the factors associated with these changes.

Since it is the broader sociological interest which is of concern here, let us consider a paradigm for the study of changes in labor force participation. Such a paradigm may be constructed in at least three dimensions (Hauser, 1954b, pp. 8-46). First, changes in labor force participation may be considered in terms of the usual time series categories, that is, as secular, cyclical, seasonal, and other. Second, each of these types of changes may be analyzed as gross as well as net, that is, as involving continuous in-and-out movements which produce measurements of net change as measurements are taken at given points in time. Third, each of the changes, gross and net, may be further analyzed in terms of the factors producing or associated with the change, and these may be categorized in various ways, such as cultural, social-organizational, social-psychological, economic, demographic, political, and others. This paradigm is presented in tabular form as a three dimensional table (see Table 1). The cross-classification of the first two dimensions of change would produce labor force analysis paralleling demographic analysis. Introduction of the third dimension, the nonlabor force factors producing change, results in labor force studies, that is, broader studies involving sociological analysis, economic analysis, and the like (Hauser & Duncan, 1959, pp. 2-3).

The paradigm may, of course, be greatly expanded. Among the desirable expansions would be the introduction of geographic space as a factor, including individual labor markets, and the consideration of the family, rather than the individual worker, as the labor force unit. Moreover, the analysis could be conducted not only in terms of the labor force in the aggregate, but, also, in terms of its various components by sex, age, color, nativity, and other characteristics.

Each of the time categories of the paradigm will now be considered, with special attention to the types of knowledge acquired and gaps in such knowledge pointing to opportunities for sociological research.

Secular Changes—Trends in Size and Composition of the Labor Force

Changes in work activity must be seen against the broad perspective of basic changes over time in the economy and in the social order. Table 2 presents some indexes of the fundamental changes which have occurred in the United States between 1870 and 1950. Over these eight decades, the population of the United States increased almost fourfold, from 40 million to 151 million. During the same period, the work force increased fivefold, from 13 million to 65 million. Although the number of workers increased almost fivefold, labor input increased only threefold. That is, total labor input, as measured by millions of man-years of work activity, increased from 17 million to 48 million between 1870 and 1949 (assuming a man-year equals 52 weeks of work per year at 50 hours per week). Labor input in agriculture, by the same measurement, actually declined from 9.4 million man-years to 7.6 million man-years, while nonagricultural labor input increased sixfold, from 7 million to 40 million man-years. The fact that labor input did not increase as rapidly as workers is explained by the decline in the length of the workweek. Over these eight decades, the length of the workweek declined by about one-third, from an average of 61 hours in nonagricultural activities to 40 hours.

A major factor contributing to an understanding not only of the changing work pattern but, also, the changing character of work itself is given by the transformation which occurred during these 80 years in the form of energy utilized in the production of goods and services. Over the period, as a

TABLE 2

SELECTED INDICATORS OF CHANGE
IN THE UNITED STATES CIRCA 1870 TO CIRCA 1950

Item	Circa 1870	Circa 1950
Total population (millions)[a]	39.8	150.7
Total labor force (millions)[a]	12.9	64.7
Labor input[b]		
Total (millions man years)	16.5	48.0
Agricultural	9.4	7.6
Nonagricultural	7.1	40.4
Hours work per week (nonagricultural)[b]	61	40
Horsepower hours of energy[b]		
Total (billions)	27.8	410.4
Mineral fuels and water supply	3.2	386.2
Work animals	20.3	12.1
Human workers	4.3	12.1
Distribution of labor force (per cent)[a]	100	100
Production of physical goods	75	46
Services	25	54
Per capita Gross National Product[a]		
Current prices	$165	$1,876
Constant prices (1929)	$223	$1,233

[a] Source: U.S. Bureau of the Census. *Historical statistics of the United States, colonial times to 1957.* Washington: Government Printing Office, 1960.
[b] I. Frederick Dewhurst & Associates. *America's needs and resources.* New York: Twentieth Century Fund, 1947 (Revised, 1955).

whole, equivalent horse power hours of energy increased almost fifteen-fold, from 28 billion to 410 billion. Energy of human workers, however, increased but threefold, rising from 4.3 billion equivalent horse power hours of energy to 12 billion. The contribution of work animals actually decreased, falling from 20 to 12 billion equivalent horse power hours of energy.

The most spectacular change was, of course, represented by the great increase in energy supplied by mineral fuels and water supply. These sources of energy for production of goods and services increased from 3.2 billion equivalent horse power hours of energy in 1870 to 386 billion by 1950, more than a 120-fold increase. The tremendous increase in nonhuman energy was the major factor in greatly increased per capita gross national product. For the period 1869–1873, per capita gross national product in current prices was $165. By 1950, per capita gross

national product in current prices had increased to $1,876. The same figures in constant 1929 prices were $223 for the period 1869–1873 and $1,233 in 1950, a five-and-a-half-fold increase.

The eight decades from 1870 to 1950 were characterized, then, by an increase in productivity, providing a huge increase in the flow of goods and services to the American people even while hours of work per week declined. These were the concomitants of the transformation of the American economy from predominantly agricultural to predominantly industrial during this period. For the time being, however, one should ignore the changed character of work and focus on patterns of work activity. That is, consider the trends in respect to labor force participation for the total population and on an age and sex specific basis.

Data for the United States and for a number of foreign countries, despite their imperfections, permit at least a broad analysis of trends in labor force participation. Taking into consideration the basic social and economic changes which have occurred over the years, labor force participation rates in the United States as presented in Table 3 as well

crease in that of women (Bancroft, 1958, p. 31). In contrast, the work participation of males in the intermediate ages has changed very little. Males 25 to 64 years of age may, indeed, be regarded as the central core of the labor force in our society. This element

TABLE 3

WORK FORCE PARTICIPATION RATES
FOR THE UNITED STATES: 1890 TO 1960

Year	Gainful workers 10 years & over[a]	Labor force 14 years & over based on decennial census[b]	Labor Force 14 years & over based on Current Population Reports[c]
1960	—	—	58.3
1950	—	53.5	57.7
1940	—	52.7	55.3
1930	49.5	53.2	55.9
1920	51.3	54.3[d]	—
1910	52.3		—
1900	50.2	53.7	—
1890	49.2	52.2	—
1880	47.3	—	—
1870	44.4	—	—

[a] Source: Alba M. Edwards. *Comparative occupation statistics for the United States, 1870 to 1940.* Bureau of the Census. Washington: Government Printing Office, 1943, p. 90. Data are adjusted for comparability.
[b] U.S. Bureau of the Census. *Historical statistics of the United States, colonial times to 1957.* Washington: Government Printing Office, 1960, p. 71.
[c] *Ibid.,* p. 71, and U.S. Bureau of the Census. *Statistical abstract of the United States, 1962.* Washington: Government Printing Office, 1963, p. 215.
[d] Adjudged unreliable.

as the data for other countries (Long, 1958, Ch. 12) show remarkable stability. This conclusion is warranted no matter which of the series of data is utilized. Long is much impressed with this phenomenon. He states: "the propensity to be 'in the labor force' seems one of the most stable elements in the labor market, varying hardly at all except in long, slow trends, requiring years to consummate. . ." (Long, 1958, p. 243).

The relative stability of the total labor force participation rate, however, is the net effect of conflicting trends in specific age and sex labor force rates. Whichever of the series of data is utilized, it is clear that over the years there has been a great secular decline in the work participation of young persons and of older males and a considerable in-

of the population has little alternative but to work and, consequently, shows little mobility over time in respect to labor force participation. Over the past 80 years in the United States, then, young persons under 20 and males 65 and over have withdrawn from the work force, while adult women have almost exactly replaced them.

Despite imperfections of the data, the facts, with respect to total, age, and sex, of labor force participation rates can be set forth rather clearly. The same cannot be said with respect to the factors associated with the changes which have occurred. A number of studies are available, however, which have come to grips with various aspects of this problem.

Edwards (1943, pp. 183-190) has pointed

to important effects of the changing economy on the composition of the labor force and especially on the decreased demand for workers in agriculture and increased demand for workers in white collar and service pursuits. Durand, and Jaffe and Stewart (Durand, 1948, pp. 47–160; Jaffe & Stewart, 1951, pp. 235–414) have studied changes in the labor force as a function of various economic and cultural changes, including the changing role of women, increased educational requirements and exposure, changes in family composition, changes in the role of older persons, and shifts from rural non-farm to urban residence. Palmer and Ratner (1949) have shown how the changes in industrial and occupational structure have influenced labor force participation, particularly of women. Wolfbein and Jaffe (1946) traced in some detail the effects of demographic changes in labor force participation and composition. Dewhurst and his associates (1955, pp. 721–753) have dealt with changes in labor force composition and the nature of work in relation to the changing economy, including changes in technology and productivity. Bancroft (1958, pp. 1–30) has analyzed changing patterns of labor force participation, emphasized the changing role of women, focused on the part-time labor force, and considered family employment patterns. The National Manpower Council has issued a number of policy-oriented reports, which contain research materials. Especially useful is the volume *Womanpower* (National Manpower Council, 1957, pp. 43–318) which comprehensively treats women in the labor force.

Various studies have focused on the general problem of explaining changes in labor force participation in terms of income level or wage structure (Dornbusch, 1952; Douglas, 1934; Douglas & Schoenberg, 1937; Durand, 1948). The most comprehensive of these, including a summary of the previous literature, is by Long (1958).

Such research as has been completed points to gaps in knowledge about the labor force which the sociologist can help to fill.

Durand, for example, in tracing in some detail the effects of demographic changes on the labor force, concludes that: "taken together, demographic factors are a fairly important part of the explanation of the past rise in the ratio of the labor force in the total population, the reduction in the labor force participation of males, and increase in the female labor force. In the future these same demographic factors can be expected to continue their influence on long range labor force trends, acting on the whole much the same way that they have acted in the past" (Durand, 1948, p. 83). But Wolfbein and Jaffe in their analysis of the labor force participation rate changes, after standardizing the population for various demographic changes between 1890 and 1930, conclude that: "social and economic forces are much more important than measurable demographic factors in accounting for changes in the proportion of the population in the labor force" (Wolfbein & Jaffe, 1946, p. 396).

Long, in his analysis of changes in the labor force in terms of changing levels of income and employment, recognizes that economic factors alone cannot explain labor supply behavior. After an examination of previous literature and the introduction of new analytical materials, Long acknowledges that the answer to the simple postulates of the classical economists remains inconclusive. He explicitly points to the noneconomic factors involved, such as changing attitudes, social class, social life, changing conditions of work, intensity in the effort of the worker, unionization, and changing leisure time activity, as factors which are operative in determining labor force participation (Long, 1958, pp. 26–33). Thus, although he demonstrates that changes in income do influence the labor force, if other things do not change too much, the "other things" are of major explanatory value and remain to be studied. By the reference to other things Long is, in effect, pointing to opportunities for sociologists. His own analysis, incidentally, provides perhaps the best explanation of why the increase in labor force participation of females has almost exactly balanced the decreased labor force participation of younger persons and older males. The explanation lies in the fact that intermediate aged females, by reason of higher education than older males, pushed them out of the labor force. With the increased family income resulting from female employment, it became increasingly possible for younger persons to prolong their schooling and thus to decrease their work activity.

The available literature discloses that, on the whole, much remains to be done to fill in the information called for by the paradigm to explain changes in labor force participation. Some study has been made of economic and demographic factors as they affect the labor force, but the surface has barely been scratched in the consideration of cultural, social-organizational, social-psychological, and other factors that operate to change the total, and age and sex specifically, labor force participation. The gaps in knowledge are, of course, greatly increased if one adds the additional dimensions to the paradigm, such as geographic areas, including specific labor markets; the analysis of the labor force in terms of family rather than individual worker units; and consideration of various groupings of the population classified by race, nativity, and other characteristics.

Little beyond speculation yet appears in the literature on the interrelationship between labor force changes and the transition from the extended to the nuclear family, the changing role of women, the increasing regulation of family size, and changes in social stratification and social mobility. Similarly, little study has yet been made of the effect of the changing political scene on labor force participation, although increasing government interventionism has undoubtedly exerted important influences on work activity. The "bloodless revolutions" of the New Deal and the Fair Deal have undoubtedly greatly affected workers and patterns of work activity. The social security system especially, including unemployment compensation and old age and survivors insurance, has undoubtedly exerted powerful influences.

Within the broad framework of demographic, economic, cultural, social organizational, and political forces influencing the labor supply in our society, social psychological factors, including personal decision-making, undoubtedly play a major role. Personal choice to some extent is involved with respect to such matters as education and training and entrance into, and withdrawal from, the labor force. There is much need for basic research into the factors affecting personal motivation and incentive with respect to labor force activity within the broad context of the influences exerted by the changing social, economic, and political orders.

On the whole, the types of data available are still too fragmentary and unsatisfactory to permit investigations of the type implied in the paradigm. The Bureau of the Census and the Bureau of Labor Statistics, in expanding the information available about the labor force, have taken steps in the right direction. The official data thus far collected by government agencies, however, need supplementation in the form of more intensive field investigations.

Although the basic forces accounting for the secular trends in labor force participation are far from fully understood, it is possible to make projections of observed trends to obtain some notions of future labor force size and composition. That is, within the framework of demographic projections, it is possible to project age and sex specific labor force participation rates. It would be a mistake to regard such projections as predictions of what the future will bring, but they do provide some feel for the potential size and composition of the nation's work force. Important in interpreting short-term projections of the labor force (those extended for not more than 14 years) is the fact that they do not involve estimates of changes in fertility. Such short-range projections, since they deal entirely with population already born, avoid the major hazard in interpreting projections as "predictions," that is, the uncertainties introduced in estimating future fertility. The actual labor force by sex and age for 1955 and projections for 1965 and 1975 together with labor force participation rates are shown in Table 4.

the increasing work activity of women 25 to 64 years of age. In contrast with pre-World War II patterns, the highest rates of female labor force activity are to be found in the middle years instead of the earlier premarital years of life. By 1975, with the

TABLE 4

TOTAL LABOR FORCE AND LABOR FORCE PARTICIPATION RATES, BY AGE AND SEX: 1955 AND PROJECTIONS, 1965 TO 1975[a]

Age and Sex	Total Labor Force (1,000)				Labor Force Participation Rates			
	1955 (actual)	1965	1970	1975	1955 (actual)	1965	1970	1975
Total	68,899	79,872	87,092	94,775	58.0	57.8	57.8	57.9
Male, 14 years and over	48,040	53,206	57,443	62,353	82.3	79.1	78.4	78.4
14 to 19 years	3,378	5,034	5,534	5,896	49.0	47.2	46.6	46.9
14 to 17 years	1,696	2,549	2,783	2,861	36.1	34.9	34.4	34.2
18 and 19 years	1,682	2,485	2,751	3,035	76.5	73.7	72.6	72.1
20 to 24 years	4,832	5,923	7,587	8,423	89.5	87.0	86.3	86.0
25 to 34 years	11,462	10,836	12,173	15,123	96.5	96.5	96.5	96.5
35 to 44 years	10,835	11,544	10,999	10,940	96.9	96.9	96.9	96.9
45 to 54 years	8,879	10,200	10,725	10,917	95.1	95.1	95.1	95.1
55 to 64 years	6,129	7,036	7,721	8,183	86.4	86.4	86.4	86.4
65 years and over	2,525	2,633	2,704	2,871	38.5	34.0	32.2	31.0
Female, 14 years and over	20,859	26,666	29,649	32,422	34.5	37.6	38.3	38.5
14 to 19 years	1,987	2,896	3,180	3,374	29.7	28.2	27.8	27.9
14 to 17 years	899	1,448	1,588	1,642	19.8	20.6	20.4	20.4
18 and 19 years	1,088	1,448	1,592	1,732	50.9	44.7	43.6	42.7
20 to 24 years	2,458	3,032	3,866	4,311	45.8	45.3	45.2	45.2
25 to 34 years	4,266	4,372	4,905	6,077	34.8	38.7	38.9	39.1
35 to 44 years	4,814	5,631	5,470	5,478	41.4	45.5	47.0	47.9
45 to 54 years	4,160	5,941	6,555	6,814	43.5	52.1	54.5	56.0
55 to 64 years	2,394	3,636	4,313	4,779	32.2	40.6	43.0	44.4
65 years and over	780	1,158	1,360	1,589	10.3	11.7	12.2	12.6

[a] Source: U.S. Bureau of the Census. *Statistical abstract of the United States, 1962.* Washington: Government Printing Office, 1963, p. 216.

These projections indicate an increase of almost 26 million workers in the labor force of the United States between 1955 and 1975. Of this increase, 11.6 million will be women; 14.3 million men. Over this 20-year period, the labor force participation of all males 14 years and over will decline from 82.3 to 78.0 per cent, while labor force participation rates of women will increase from 34.5 to 38.5 per cent. The most notable changes in patterns of labor force activity which are revealed by the projections can be seen in

persistence of present trends, labor force participation of women 45 to 54 years of age would increase from 43.5 per cent in 1955 to 56.0 per cent. The most significant change shown in the projection for males is the continued decline in work activity of men 65 years of age and over.

Cyclical Change

With the advent of industrialization, the American economy has been subject to fluctuations in levels of economic activity—the swings in the business cycle. The most violent of these swings was heralded by the crash of the stock market in 1929 and the onset of the depression in the 1930's. The severity of that depression generated some basic changes in the relation between government and business and introduced new policies and agencies designed to mitigate the extreme swings in the cycle. Certainly it is true that since the 1930's, although the economy has continued its cyclical expansions and contractions, the swings, except for those induced by World War II, of course, have been relatively moderate. The term depression has virtually disappeared from use in favor of such terms as "recession," or "adjustment."

It might reasonably be expected that swings in the business cycle would influence patterns of labor force activity. Efforts to study the relationship between the business cycle and work activity have produced at least four theories and, on the whole, conflicting evidence and indefinite conclusions. In large measure, the unsatisfactory state of knowledge about the effects of the business cycle on work activity are the result of inadequate data. Decennial census statistics are too widely spaced to permit the measurement of labor force changes resulting from swings in the business cycle. Moreover, because of limitations in concept and defects in measurement, they have not been adequate to do so in any case. The monthly series of labor force statistics, available only since 1940, is of too recent origin to permit intensive historical investigation. Furthermore, the combination of changes in various forms of measurement, together with the relatively low amplitude of business cycle surveys during the lifetime of the current monthly series, does not permit the analysis that is necessary. Similarly, data are not available to permit definitive conclusions about the relations between the business cycle and work activity in other countries.

The four theories attempting to explain the relationship between the trade cycle and

work activity include the mercantilist theory, neoclassicial theory, the additional worker theory, and a type of merger of the neoclassical and additional worker theories. Mercantilist theory contends that increased wages would tend to reduce the amount of labor offered (Douglas, 1934, p. 270). Neoclassical economic theory holds that the labor force expands under conditions of prosperity and contracts under conditions of depression (Marshall, 1898, Book IV, Ch. 4, Book VI, Ch. 2). In direct conflict with this theory is the additional worker theory set forth by Woytinsky (1940). According to this theory the loss of employment by the primary worker results not only in his seeking employment but leads, also, to other members of the family joining in the search for work. In this manner, the loss of one job may result in more than the addition of one person to the ranks of the unemployed. Long and Humphrey have challenged this theory, and empirical studies give conflicting results. A type of merger of the neoclassical and additional worker theories contends that additions to the labor force occur with high and low economic activity, whereas withdrawals from the labor force are associated with balanced prosperity (Humphrey, 1940; Long, 1942). A number of contemporary economists believe, with the mercantilists, that "at least a part of the nation's supply curve of labor has a pronounced negative slope, which means that the higher the price paid for labor the less labor will be supplied" (Lester, 1947, p. 104).

In view of the unsatisfactory character of the data, definitive conclusions about the effect of the business cycle on labor force participation are not possible. Better data and additional research to test the theories remain to be achieved.

The sociologist's interest in the labor force coincides with the interest of the economist in seeking explanations of variations in labor force patterns associated with swings in the business cycle. The interest of the sociologist, however, is usually broader and includes interest in the impact of cyclical changes in work activity on behavior and social organization. The available studies are necessarily far from definitive, but they point to important vistas of research opportunity in the future (Angell, 1936; Bakke, 1940; Cavan & Ranck, 1938; Komarovsky, 1940; Stouffer & Lazarsfeld, 1937). The sociologist's interest in variations in labor force activity with swings in the business cycle is broader than the economist's, also, in including concern with the entire spectrum of independent variables as set forth in the paradigm. The sociologist's interest in the play of economic factors is also much more general than the economist's because the former is neither as interested nor as equipped to pursue such study.

A major aspect of cyclical changes in the labor force is that relating to fluctuations in the level of unemployment. This, however, will be dealt with separately below. Let us next turn to the consideration of the impact of World War II on labor force activity—an impact paralleling cyclical activity which helps to throw light on other forms of labor force changes.

War Time Changes

One type of short-run change in labor force activity that has been measured in an unprecedented way by reason of the availability of the monthly series of data is the impact of the war. By reason of the fact that the "Monthly Report on the Labor Force" was initiated prior to 1940 and has been conducted ever since, it was possible to follow the expansion and contraction of the labor

TABLE 5

DEVIATION OF LABOR FORCE FROM "NORMAL," BY AGE AND SEX,
UNITED STATES, 1945 AND 1946[a]
(numbers of persons in thousands)

	April 1946				April 1945			
	Actual Labor Force[b]	"Normal" Labor Force	Deviation from "Normal" (— denotes less than "normal")		Actual Labor Force[b]	"Normal" Labor Force	Deviation from "Normal" (— denotes less than "normal")	
			Number	Per Cent of "Normal"			Number	Per Cent of "Normal"
Both sexes	60,304	58,843	1450	2.5	66,246	58,163	8083	13.9
Male, total	43,626	42,788	838	2.0	46,407	42,496	3911	9.2
14–19 years	3,431	2,552	879	34.4	4,737	2,615	2122	81.1
20–24 years	4,832	5,386	−554	−10.3	5,829	5,401	428	7.9
25–34 years	10,504	10,948	−444	− 4.1	10,575	10,462	113	1.1
35–44 years	9,045	9,070	− 25	− 0.3	9,453	9,334	119	1.3
45–54 years	8,084	7,863	221	2.8	8,017	7,749	268	3.5
55–64 years	5,349	5,019	330	6.6	5,385	4,998	387	7.7
65 years and over	2,381	1,950	431	22.1	2,411	1,937	474	24.5
Female, total	16,678	16,066	612	3.8	19,839	15,667	4172	26.6
14–19 years	1,930	1,227	703	57.3	2,720	1,268	1452	114.5
20–24 years	2,876	3,037	−161	− 5.3	3,405	3,034	371	12.2
25–34 years	3,784	4,508	−724	−16.1	4,551	4,365	186	4.3
35–44 years	3,677	3,543	134	3.8	4,089	3,404	685	20.1
45–54 years	2,651	2,305	346	15.0	2,964	2,149	815	37.9
55–64 years	1,350	1,112	238	21.4	1,620	1,118	502	44.9
65 years and over	410	334	76	22.8	490	329	161	48.9

[a] Derived from U.S. Bureau of the Census data. Not adjusted to more recent changes in monthly survey.
[b] Includes Armed Forces.

force during and after World War II. The effect on the labor force of mobilization and demobilization is shown in Table 5. The "actual" labor force is shown both for April, 1945, taken as a measurement of the labor force at the height of mobilization, and for April, 1946, taken as a measurement after demobilization. The "actual" labor force is compared with the "normal" labor force, i.e., the labor force size and composition that would have obtained had the prewar trends continued.

The major conclusion to be drawn from the World War II experience is that the labor force in the United States, at least under conditions of duress, can be extremely flexible. It increased by almost 11 million workers between 1940 and 1945, the peak of the war effort. From a work force of almost 55 million persons in April, 1940, there were about 66 million workers, including the armed forces, in April, 1945. Of the increase of 11 million workers during this five-year period, only 3 million can be regarded as normal increase. The additional 8 million may be regarded as an "abnormal" increment in the labor force, that is, the increment resulting from the pressures of war. The great wartime increase in the total labor force made it possible to maintain the civilian labor force at about its prewar size, while permitting the expansion of the armed forces from about three hundred thousand to 12 million persons.

Comparison of differences between the actual and the normal labor force both at the peak of mobilization and after demobilization discloses the sources of labor reserves drawn upon by the war effort. In April, 1945, the actual labor force of some 66.2 million persons was 8 million, or 13.9 per cent above the normal labor force of 58.2 million persons. Actual male labor force was 9.2 per cent above normal, female labor force 26.6 per cent above normal. Of the abnormal increment to the labor force, almost 4.2 million were females as contrasted with only 3.9 million males. Females, of course, constituted a larger reserve for meeting the

exigencies of the war labor market than did males who were, in the main, already in the labor force before the onset of the war.

Investigation of changes by age discloses that by far the largest single group contributing to the abnormal increment in the labor force was young persons 14 to 19 years of age. About 2.1 million young men and 1.5 million young women of this age were in the labor force who would not have been workers (including the armed forces) except for the impact of the war. Young males were in the labor force at a level about 81 per cent above normal and young women at a level about 115 per cent above normal.

Older persons 65 years of age and over contributed the next largest share to the abnormal increment in workers. About half a million older males, about 25 per cent in excess over normal, and 161,000 older females, about 49 per cent over normal, swelled the ranks of the labor force. The third largest contribution to the abnormal labor force increment was made by women 35 to 65 years of age, who contributed about 2 million workers. Males 20 to 64 years of age contributed an additional 1.3 million workers, a relatively small contribution because they were already largely in the labor force.

As a result of these changes, the civilian labor force remained approximately the same size between 1940 and 1945, i.e., between 54 and 55 million persons. Male civilian workers, however, decreased by over 6 million, whereas female civilian workers increased by over 5.5 million.

After demobilization, the labor force displayed great flexibility in contracting as it had done in expanding. Between April, 1945, and April, 1946, the total number of workers decreased by almost 6 million, dropping to a level of 60.3 million. By April, 1946, the total labor force was only 2.5 per cent in excess of normal—males 2 per cent and females 3.8 per cent in excess.

The excess of some 800,000 males, however, was the net effect of a deficit of over 1 million males, mainly 20 to 34 years of age, and an excess of about 1.8 million males 14 to 19 years of age or over 45 years of age. The deficit in males 20 to 34 years of age was of course largely explained by the veterans who, under the G.I. Bill, were in school. Their places were more than filled by young males still in the military establishment and by older workers who were able to remain in the labor force under conditions of relatively full employment.

Similarly, the excess of approximately 600,000 females in the labor force was the net effect of a deficit of about 900,000 women, mainly in the ages 20 to 34 years and an excess of other age groups, especially young women 14 to 19 years of age. The relatively large deficits represented women of reproductive age who were not available for the labor force by reason of the dramatic upsurge in marriage and birth rates after demobilization. Their places were easily filled by the other age groups of women.

These changes in labor force participation, clearly traceable to the impact of the war, have undoubtedly had a major effect. For example, the war increased the propensity for females to work and produced a major change in the working life pattern of women in our society (see pp. 180–181). Similarly, though perhaps in lesser degree, the wartime work experience has profoundly affected the attitudes and behavior of each of the age and sex groups which constituted the abnormal increment to the work force. But relatively little has as yet been done by sociologists to trace the consequences of these changes.

Seasonal Changes

Many social and economic activities are influenced by the changing seasons. The swing in the number of employed persons from peaks in mid-summer to lows in mid-winter has been regularly reported by the "Monthly Report on the Labor Force" (U.S. Department of Labor, monthly). Unemployment actually fluctuates from a low of about 20 per cent below average in October, to a high of 15 per cent above the annual average in February and June (President's Com-

mittee to Appraise Employment and Unemployment Statistics, 1962, p. 351).

The problem of seasonal variation in the labor force and its components is undoubtedly of greater concern to the economist than to the sociologist. The economist's concern arises largely from his desire to interpret month-to-month changes as indicative of secular trend. Such an interpretation is not possible without adjustment for seasonality—a problem which is quite complex. However, the sociologist who would work with time series that may similarly be influenced by seasonality, such as crime or delinquency, must deal, also, with seasonality in labor force activities if a relationship is to be established. It is sufficient for the present purpose to call attention to the complex nature of the problem and to point to the new avenues of research opportunities that lie therein.

Gross Changes

A census or a sample survey provides a cross-section measurement of the characteristics of a population at a given interval of time stipulated in the operational design. Such data may be used to measure change from census to census or survey to survey. The measurements thus obtained, however, are measurements of "net" change from date to date. Completely obscured in such measurements are the "gross" changes—the many changes that occur between the dates on which the cross-section measurements were made.

When net change measurements are made there is apparently little change in labor force participation rates in the short-run and great stability, as has been noted, even in the longer run. The illusory nature of the apparent stability in labor force participation rates becomes apparent when gross changes are examined. Such gross change tabulations have been published from time to time since 1945. The data for 1951 are summarized in Table 6 by sex and age.

In 1951, there was an average of 62.9 million persons in the labor force for the year.

TABLE 6

GROSS CHANGES IN THE CIVILIAN LABOR FORCE BY SEX AND AGE, UNITED STATES, 1951[a]

Gross Change	Total (in thousands)	Age				
		14-19 yrs.	20-24 yrs.	25-44 yrs.	45-64 yrs.	65 yrs. and over
Total						
Average number in labor force	62,871	4984	6668	28,712	19,486	3024
Average monthly gross change	6,627	1797	816	1,939	1,516	560
Number additions	3,320	952	383	968	758	259
Number reductions	3,307	845	433	971	758	301
Average gross change as percentage of average labor force	10.5	36.1	12.2	6.8	7.8	18.5
Male						
Average number in labor force	43,647	2967	3999	20,156	14,062	2465
Average monthly gross change	2,419	1009	273	352	431	356
Number additions	1,192	537	114	163	209	170
Number reductions	1,227	472	159	189	222	186
Average gross change as percentage of average labor force	5.5	34.0	6.8	1.7	3.1	14.4
Female						
Average number in labor force	19,224	2018	2670	8,556	5,424	558
Average monthly gross change	4,208	789	543	1,586	1,086	205
Number additions	2,128	416	269	804	550	89
Number reductions	2,080	373	274	782	536	116
Average gross change as percentage of average labor force	21.9	39.1	20.3	18.5	20.0	36.7

[a] Compiled from Bureau of the Census. Annual report on the labor force for 1950 and 1951. *Cur. Pop. Repts.*, Series P-50, Nos. 31 and 40, March, 1951 and May, 1952, Tables 3, 16, and 17. Data are rounded independently in thousands and may not add to totals.

This was the average of the 12 monthly reports for the year. There was also, however, an average of 6.6 million gross monthly changes in the labor force during that year. That is, there was an average of 3.3 million additions to the labor force each month and an average of 3.3 million withdrawals. Hence, to maintain the average of 62.9 million persons in the labor force for the year, there were a total of 79.5 million entrances to and exits from the labor force during the year: some 39.8 million entrances and 39.7 million exits.

To maintain an average labor force of 43.6 million males for the year, there were a total of 29 million gross changes made up of 14.3 million entrances to the labor force and 14.7 million exits. To maintain an average of 19.2 million females in the labor force during the year, there were 50.5 million gross changes: 25.5 million entrances and 25.0 million exits from month to month.

For the labor force as a whole, in 1951, the average gross changes constituted 10 per cent of the average number of persons in the labor force. Male gross changes were less than 6 per cent of the average number of male workers, whereas female gross changes made up 22 per cent of the average female total. Male mobility in respect to labor force participation was thus much smaller than female. Particularly was this the case for males 25 to 64 years of age who, in our culture, have virtually no alternative to labor force participation. Gross labor force changes for males 25 to 44 years of age made up less than 2 per cent of the average number of male workers in this age group; and gross changes of males 45 to 64 years of age made up only 3 per cent of the average number of such male workers.

The highest mobility in labor force participation is found at the younger and older ages for workers of each sex. For young male workers 14 to 19 years of age, gross changes made up about one-third of the average number; and for young female workers gross changes made up almost two-fifths of the average number. Among workers 65 years of age and over, gross changes were 14 per cent of the average number for males and about 38 per cent for females.

The pattern of gross changes in the labor force participation of females suggests the complex role of women in our society—the interchange of their roles as homemakers, on the one hand, and as members of the labor force, on the other. Among young women 20 to 24 years of age, gross changes made up about 20 per cent of the average number in the labor force, whereas for males of this age, gross changes were only about 7 per cent. In contrast with the relative stability of males between 25 and 64 years of age, female gross changes in these age groups make up about one-fifth of their average number.

This type of gross change analysis cannot be interpreted to apply to individuals, that is, they refer to entrances and exits in the labor force. It is probably true for gross changes, as for other forms of labor mobility, that a relatively small proportion of workers contributes a disproportionately large share of the mobility (Palmer, 1954, p. 36).

An explanation of gross changes in terms of the paradigm would undoubtedly be illuminating for work activity and also for participation in other activities. It would shed light on the roles of females and of other members of the family. It would undoubtedly have important explanatory value for phenomena such as family disorganization and juvenile delinquency on the one hand and savings, consumer expenditures, and instalment buying on the other. Gross change data make it clear that the labor force is a much more dynamic entity than is ever indicated by net change measurements and has significance for every aspect of labor force research. Gross change data have special implications for interpretation of unemployment data as will be indicated in the discussion of unemployment.

WORKING LIFE

By reason of the complex character of work activity and problems of data collection, most of the information available about the labor force is cross-section information—measurements taken as of a given point or interval in time. In the absence of longitudinal data on the labor force, a limited form of longitudinal analysis is made possible by the application of life-table technique to labor force activity (U.S. Department of Labor, 1950; U. S. Department of Labor, 1956). The utilization of life-table methods has made possible the measurement of the average length of working life in relation to total life expectation and has illuminated, also, for males, the pattern of entrance into, and exit from, labor force activity. Such data, however, it must be stressed, are based on cross-section measurements as of a given interval of time and indicate longitudinal patterns only on the assumption that the cross-section patterns of work activity and mortality were to continue to operate. True longitudinal analysis must necessarily await the availability of data permitting a cohort analysis of both labor force activity and mortality. Data on the working life of males, based on statistics for 1950, are presented in Table 7.

For the age group 15 to 19 years, an average of 53.6 years of life remained in 1950, of which 47.9 years would be spent in the work force and 5.7 years in retirement. For the age group 50 to 54 years, an average of 22.6 years of life remained, of which 16.6 years would be spent in the work force and 6.0 years in retirement. In view of the great attention paid to retirement, it is significant to observe that for the age group 65 to 69,

TABLE 7

ABRIDGED TABLE OF WORKING LIFE FOR MALES IN THE UNITED STATES, 1950[a]

Age	Number Living of 100,000 Born Alive			Accessions to the Labor Force per 1,000 in Population	Separations from the Labor Force (per 1,000 in Labor Force)			Average Number of Remaining Years of—		
	In population	In Labor Force			Due to All Causes	Due to Death	Due to Retirement	Life	Labor Force Participation	Retirement
		Number	Percent of Population							
	(within age interval)				(between successive age intervals)			(at beginning of age interval)		
10 to 14 years	477,806	21,000	(b)	...	5.3	5.3	...	...	...	...
15 to 19 years	475,282	251,899	53.0	483.5	8.5	8.5	...	53.6	47.9	5.7
20 to 24 years	471,255	418,003	88.7	354.0	9.8	9.8	...	48.9	43.2	5.7
25 to 29 years	466,652	448,453	96.1	73.3	10.7	10.7	...	44.4	38.6	5.8
30 to 34 years	461,671	446,436	96.7	6.0	15.1	14.1	1.0	39.8	34.0	5.8
35 to 39 years	455,169	439,693	96.6	...	23.3	21.3	2.0	35.2	29.3	5.9
40 to 44 years	445,488	429,450	96.4	...	42.6	33.4	9.2	30.8	24.9	5.9
45 to 49 years	430,539	411,165	95.5	...	70.9	51.5	19.4	26.6	20.6	6.0
50 to 54 years	408,140	382,019	93.6	...	116.3	77.4	38.9	22.6	16.6	6.0
55 to 59 years	375,956	337,608	89.8	...	195.5	109.7	85.8	19.0	13.0	6.0
60 to 64 years	332,858	271,612	81.6	...	337.2	142.3	194.9	15.7	9.7	6.0
65 to 69 years	217,261	180,022	64.4	...	485.9	180.1	305.8	12.7	7.2	5.5
70 to 74 years	279,537	92,553	42.6	...	558.6	247.5	311.1	10.1	5.9	4.2
75 years-over	287,742	61,289	21.3	...	...	...	...	...	...	...

[a] Source: Stuart Garfinkle. Changes in working life of men, 1900–2000. *Mon. Labor Rev.*, March, 1955, p. 300.
[b] Only persons 14 years old and over are enumerated in the labor force.

an average of 12.7 years of life remained in 1950 of which 7.2 years would be spent working and 5.5 years in retirement.

Similar analyses have been done for different time periods, making possible the type of information presented in Table 8. In 1900, the average male in the United States could look forward at birth to a life of 48.2 years

TABLE 8

AVERAGE LENGTH OF LIFE AND WORKING LIFE FOR MALES IN THE UNITED STATES, 1900 TO 2000[a]

Year	At Birth			At Age 20		
	Average Number of Remaining Years of—			Average Number of Remaining Years of—		
	Life	Working Life	Outside Labor Force	Life	Working Life	Retirement
1900	48.2	32.1	16.1	42.2	39.4	2.8
1940	61.2	38.3	22.9	46.8	41.3	5.5
1950	65.5	41.9	23.6	48.9	43.2	5.7
1955	66.5	42.0	24.5	49.5	43.0	6.5
2000	73.2	45.1	28.1	53.8	45.1	8.7

[a] Source: Stuart Garfinkle. Changes in working life of men, 1900–2000. *Mon. Labor Rev.*, March, 1955, Table 1, p. 299.

He would spend on the average 32.1 years in the work force and 16.1 years outside the work force, including the time spent both before beginning his work career and after retirement. At age 20, the male in the United States, in 1900, had an average of 42 years of life remaining, of which 39.4 years would be working life and 2.8 years life spent in retirement. By 1955, this situation had materially changed. At birth, the male could look forward to a life expectation 18.3 years greater than that of his counterpart in 1900. Of the gain of 18.3 years, 9.9 years would be added to his working life and 8.4 years to his life outside the labor force. The male in 1955, at age 20, had gained some 7.3 years of life expectation over his counterpart in 1900. Of the gain of 7.3 years of life at age 20, 3.6 years would be added to his working life and 3.7 years to his life in retirement. Thus, between 1900 and 1955, the average male at age 20 had increased his working life by 11 per cent and more than doubled his life in retirement.

Projection of these trends to the year 2000 makes possible an interesting comparison of changes in average life and working life in the first half of this century with changes anticipated during the second half. At birth the male gained some 17.3 years of life during the first half of the century and would gain an additional 7.7 years during the second half. In consequence, he added 9.8 years to his working life during the first half of the century and may add an additional 3.2 years during the second half. He also gained 7.5 years of life outside the labor force during the first half of the century and may gain an additional 4.5 years during the second half. Thus, during the first half of the century, the male at birth gained some 36 per cent in average life expectation, adding 31 per cent to his working life and 47 per cent to years spent outside the labor force. During the second half of the century, should the trend continue, he can anticipate an additional gain of 12 per cent in total life, a gain of 8 per cent in working life, and a gain of

19 per cent spent outside the labor force.

At age 20, the male in the United States gained some 6.7 years during the first half of the century in total years of life, 3.8 years in work life, and 2.9 years in retirement. During the second half of the century he may, at age 20, gain an additional 4.9 years of life, 1.9 years of work life, and 3.0 years of life in retirement. Thus, during the first half of the century, the male at age 20 gained some 16 per cent in total life, 10 per cent in working life, and more than 100 per cent in life in retirement. During the second half of the century he can anticipate an additional 10 per cent gain in life remaining at age 20, a 4 per cent gain in work life, and a more than 50 per cent gain in retirement.

Tables for women completely comparable with those for men cannot be calculated because women do not tend to remain in the labor force continuously. But a different and useful type of measurement is possible (U.S. Department of Labor, 1956). The average remaining lifetime for women together with average numbers of years of work remaining by marital status is shown in Table 9.

In 1950, the female at age 15 had an average remaining life time of 58.5 years. She had 15.8 years of work remaining— 16.0 years for single women, 13.2 years for married women with their husbands present, and 25.6 years for women widowed, separated, or divorced. At age 30, the woman in 1950 had 44.3 years of life time remaining, of which 10.9 years would be in the work force. For single women of this age 21.6 years of work remained; for married women with husband present 9.7 years; for widowed, separated, divorced women, 18.9 years. Throughout the life span, single women and widowed, separated, or divorced women spend considerably longer periods in work activity than do married women with their husbands present.

Examination of labor force participation rates for women points to significant changes in patterns of work activity dur-

TABLE 9

AVERAGE LENGTH OF LIFE AND WORKING LIFE AT SELECTED YEARS FOR FEMALES
IN THE UNITED STATES, 1950[a]

Age	Average Life Remaining	Average Number of Years of Work Remaining			
		All Women	Single Women	Married, Husband Present	Widowed, Separated, Divorced
15	58.5	15.8	16.0	13.2	25.6
20	53.7	14.5	15.1	12.2	24.1
30	44.3	10.9	21.6	9.7	18.9
40	35.1	7.8	17.6	7.0	12.8
50	26.4	4.5	10.8	4.0	7.0
60	18.5	2.0	5.1	1.8	2.6

[a] Source: Stuart Garfinkle. Tables of working life for women, 1950. *Mon. Labor Rev.,* October, 1956, Table 12.

ing and since World War II. Prior to the war, the labor force participation reached a peak for women 20 to 24 years of age and, as marriage and household responsibility superseded work activity, diminished from that period to the end of the work span. During the war this pattern changed significantly. The premarital peak in labor force participation was matched by the reentry of women into the labor force at about age 35, after which they worked for at least 10 years before tapering off their work activities. This pattern has persisted. In consequence, at the present time young women enter the labor force after leaving school and continue to work, even after marriage, until their childbearing and childrearing activities begin. With the birth of

their first child they tend to leave the labor force, beginning at about age 23, and they become homemakers until their last child enters school. When this occurs, at about age 35, they tend to re-enter the labor market and remain in it, until about age 45, at which time they begin to taper off their work activities.

According to the 1950 census, the proportion of married women with husbands present who were in the labor force showed a peak of 28 per cent at age 22. Labor force participation declined to 20 per cent at age 29, rose again to almost 28 per cent at age 40, and then declined to 10 per cent by age 60. The working life of the unmarried woman was quite different. In 1950, about four-fifths of the single women between 25

TABLE 10

AVERAGE LENGTH OF LIFE AND WORKING LIFE FOR FEMALES AT BIRTH
IN THE UNITED STATES, 1900 TO 1955[a]

Year	Life Remaining	Working Life Remaining	Years Outside Labor Force
1900	50.7	6.3	44.4
1940	65.9	12.1	53.8
1950	71.0	15.2	55.8
1955	72.9	18.2	54.7

[a] Source: Seymour L. Wolfbein. The length of working life. Paper presented at Fourth International Gerontological Congress, Merano, Italy, July, 1957. (Mimeographed)

and 35 were in the labor force, three-fourths were still working at age 45, and more than half at age 60.

Changes in life expectancy and years in work activity for women are also available, as shown in Table 10. At birth, the average female in the United States in 1900 had a life expectancy of 50.7 years. She could, during her life, expect to work some 6.3 years and spend 44.4 years outside the labor force. By 1955, her expectation of life had increased by 22.2 years to 72.9 years. She could expect to work 18.2 years during her life time and spend 54.7 years outside the labor force. Thus, between 1900 and 1955, female expectation of life increased by some 44 per cent. Work expectancy, however, almost tripled, while years spent outside the labor force increased by 23 per cent. It is apparent that working life tables provide a significant measurement of the changed role of women.

The paradigm presented above provides a scheme for examining factors associated with the changes in expectation of life and working life. To the general sociologist, the changes in expectation of life and working life and their interrelationships can be regarded as independent variables, as well as dependent ones, with important explanatory power for many of the changes in behavior and social organization which have occurred over the years. The use of these data as independent variables in sociological research has scarcely begun.

OCCUPATION

The changes which have been discussed in the size and composition of the labor force reflect, of course, the profound changes which have occurred in the United States by reason of industrialization and urbanization. These changes have affected not only patterns of labor force participation but, also, the nature of work itself.

Without question the most significant change over the years has been the shift from agricultural to nonagricultural work activities. Although the data have many limitations, it is clear that the predominant proportion of the work force of the United States, about 72 per cent, were farm workers in 1820. By 1900, the proportion of workers engaged in farm occupations had shrunk by almost 50 per cent and was at a level of approximately 37 per cent. By 1960 only 6.3 per cent of the labor force was in agriculture.

At the beginning of the century nearly three-fourths of all the workers in the United States were engaged in the production of physical goods and a little less than a fourth in service occupations. In 1960, 54 per cent of the work force was engaged in providing services—42 per cent in white collar occupations, 12 per cent in household service and other service occupations. Only 46 per cent of the workers were engaged in the actual production of physical goods. This shift, signifying the great transformation which has occurred in the nature of work, was the product, on the one hand, of technological advance and, on the other, of the rise in income and the level of living that has generated increasing demand for services as well as for goods. Data showing occupational changes since 1900 for each sex are shown in Table 11.

The decline in production workers is entirely attributable to the decline in farm workers and in nonfarm laborers. In 1900, well over a third of the work force, 37.5 per cent, were either farmers or farm laborers, as contrasted with only 6.3 per cent in 1960; and 12.5 per cent of the work force was made up of nonfarm laborers in 1900 as compared with only 5.5 per cent in 1960. By 1960, farm workers were only one-sixth as great a proportion of the total work force as in 1900, and nonfarm laborers constituted less than half of the 1900 proportion. The decline in farm and nonfarm labor occupations more than offset the increases which occurred in the proportions of craftsmen and operatives (largely machine tenders).

The increase in workers providing services, including white collar services, was

TABLE 11

Major Occupation Group of Experienced Labor Force for the United States, 1900 to 1960
(per cent distribution)[a]

Major Occupation Group	Both Sexes							Males			Females		
	1900	1910	1920	1930	1940	1950	1960	1900	1950	1960	1900	1950	1960
Total	100.0	100.0	100.0	100.0	100.0	100.0	100.0	100.0	100.0	100.0	100.0	100.0	100.0
White Collar	17.6	21.4	25.0	29.4	31.1	36.6	42.2	17.6	30.5	35.4	17.8	52.5	56.3
Professional, technical, and kindred workers	4.3	4.7	5.4	6.8	7.5	8.6	11.4	3.4	7.2	10.4	8.2	12.2	13.3
Managers, officials, proprietors, except farm	5.9	6.6	6.6	7.4	7.3	8.7	8.5	6.8	10.5	10.8	1.4	4.3	3.8
Clerical and kindred workers	3.0	5.3	8.0	8.9	9.6	12.3	14.9	2.8	6.4	7.2	4.0	27.4	30.9
Sales workers	4.5	4.7	4.9	6.3	6.7	7.0	7.4	4.6	6.4	7.0	4.3	8.6	8.3
Service	9.1	9.6	7.9	9.8	11.7	10.5	11.8	3.1	6.2	6.5	35.5	21.5	22.8
Private household workers	5.4	5.0	3.3	4.1	4.7	2.6	2.8	0.2	0.2	0.2	28.7	8.9	8.4
Other service workers	3.6	4.6	4.5	5.7	7.1	7.9	8.9	2.9	6.0	6.3	6.8	12.6	14.4
Manual	35.8	38.2	40.2	39.6	39.8	41.1	39.7	37.6	48.4	49.7	27.8	22.4	19.1
Craftsmen, foremen, and kindred workers	10.6	11.6	13.0	12.8	12.0	14.2	14.3	12.6	19.0	20.6	1.4	1.5	1.3
Operatives and kindred workers	12.8	14.6	15.6	15.8	18.4	20.4	19.9	10.4	20.6	21.2	23.8	20.0	17.2
Laborers, except farm and mine	12.5	12.0	11.6	11.0	9.4	6.6	5.5	14.7	8.8	7.8	2.6	0.9	0.6
Farm	37.5	30.9	27.0	21.2	17.4	11.8	6.3	41.7	14.9	8.5	19.0	3.7	1.9
Farmers and farm managers	19.9	16.5	15.3	12.4	10.4	7.4	3.9	23.0	10.0	5.5	5.9	0.7	0.6
Farm laborers and foremen	17.7	14.4	11.7	8.8	7.0	4.4	2.4	18.7	4.9	3.0	13.1	2.9	1.3

[a] Source: 1900–1950, U.S. Bureau of the Census. *Historical statistics of the United States, colonial times to 1957.* Washington: Government Printing Office, 1960, Table D 72-122, p. 74; 1960, U.S. Bureau of the Census. *U.S. census of population: 1960, general social and economic characteristics, U.S. summary.* Washington: Government Printing Office, Final Report PC(1)-1C.

183

led by the almost fivefold expansion in the proportion of clerical and related occupations. Clerical workers made up 14.9 per cent of the 1960 work force, as compared with only 3.0 per cent of that in 1900. The other white collar occupational groups, however, also increased rapidly. The proportion of professional, technical, and kindred workers increased almost threefold, that of sales workers by about two-thirds, and that of managers, officials, and proprietors (except farm) increased by almost half.

Although there was a great increase in the relative size of the labor force providing services rather than goods, workers specifically classified as service workers in the census did not increase as rapidly as did white collar workers. Service workers as a whole increased by about one-third between 1900 and 1960, rising from 9.1 to 11.8 per cent. But this increase was the net effect of an almost 50 per cent decline in the proportion of private household workers and of more than a doubling in the proportion of other service workers (barbers, beauticians, cooks, policemen, firemen, janitors, waitresses, and others).

The changing occupational composition of the labor force (changes in specific ways of making a living) was the result of advancing technology making the economy much less dependent than it previously was on human muscle power and much more dependent on professional, technical, and clerical skills and of modifications in the way of life which have changed consumption patterns. These changes have altered the sex division of labor and contributed materially to the changed role of women. The gateway to the work force has been increasingly opened to women as work shifted from emphasis on brawn to emphasis on brain and dexterity—on education and skill. The changes over time in the occupational composition of the American labor force are dramatically evident, not only in the increased work activity of women but, also, in the character of work that women do.

In 1960, over half of all women workers, 56.3 per cent, had white collar pursuits, and well over a fifth, 22.8 per cent, were directly classified as "service workers." Almost four-fifths of all female workers were providing services and only a fifth were engaged in the production of physical goods. "Clerical and kindred" tasks accounted for almost one-third of all the occupations pursued by women.

Between 1900 and 1960, the proportion of clerical workers in the female work force increased almost eightfold. The proportion of female managers, officials, and proprietors (except farm) more than doubled; female sales workers doubled; and the female professional, technical, and kindred workers (including school teachers) increased by almost two-thirds.

The proportion of service workers among women in the labor force (not including the white collar occupations) declined by about one-third. This decrease is the net effect of an almost three-fourths decline in the proportion of private household workers and a doubling of that of workers in the other services.

Despite the increased importance of operatives in the economy (12.8 per cent of all workers in 1900 compared with 19.9 per cent in 1960), female operatives declined, as a proportion of all women workers, by about a fourth. The proportion of female craftsmen and laborers also decreased, even though it was small in 1900. Although the statistics for women in agriculture are subject to relatively great error because of problems of definition and response, there can be no doubt that the decrease in the proportion of females in agriculture between 1900 and 1960 was substantial.

The pattern of male work activity is quite different from that of females. In 1960, almost three-fifths of the male work force, 58.2 per cent, was still engaged in producing goods rather than services, as contrasted with only one-fifth of female workers. The proportion of male workers producing goods, however, had shrunk from four-fifths in 1900, at which time more than half were in agriculture.

In 1960, the largest group of male workers, over a fifth, were operatives, followed closely by craftsmen, also about a fifth of the total. The proportion of operatives among male workers doubled between 1900 and 1960 and that of craftsmen increased by two-thirds. In contrast, the remaining category of manual workers, laborers—except farm—declined by almost 50 per cent during this period. In 1960, only 8.5 per cent of the male workers were in agricultural pursuits, in contrast with 41.7 in 1900. The proportion of farmers declined about three-fourths and that of farm laborers by more than four-fifths.

Among male white collar workers the proportion of professional, technical, and kindred occupations showed a threefold increase between 1900 and 1960, that of clerical workers more than doubled, and more than 50 per cent increases were recorded in the proportion of managers, officials, proprietors, and sales workers.

The great changes in the character of work and in the occupations of men and women have undoubtedly exerted major influences on personal attitudes, behavior, and roles. When regarded as independent variables, these changes afford the sociologist the opportunity to account for many types of changes in the person and in the social order. Little has as yet been done to trace their impact on ways of making a living and redefinitions in the sex division of labor. Sociologists, however, have utilized occupational data extensively in studies of social stratification and social mobility (see Chapter 15). Interest has heightened also in studies of the sociology of work and in the study of industrial occupations and professions (see Chapter 17). There can be little doubt that extensive and intensive use of the occupational data in relation to phenomena of central interest to sociologists would open new avenues of interesting and fruitful research.

UNEMPLOYMENT

Among the most significant changes which have occurred in the transition from an agrarian to an urban society is the great increase in the proportion of the work force who are employees, that is who depend on a "job" to make their livelihood. This fundamental shift from "status" to "contract" has made a large proportion of workers dependent upon a relationship with an employer. Any termination of this relationship resulting in the worker's unemployment interrupts the flow of income and therefore access to means of subsistence.

Unemployment has been a catastrophic experience for the worker and his family throughout the history of our industrial civilization. During the depression 1930's, however, unemployment reached such magnitude (one in every four workers) that the government was forced to step in in an unprecedented manner to alleviate the distress of the unemployed. Among the more significant of the "New Deal" reforms was the provision for unemployment compensation introduced as an element in the Social Security system. By means of this program the government assumed responsibility for maintaining some flow of income when the worker lost his job, both to ameliorate the hardships of unemployment and to provide a stimulus to economic recovery.

Although the floors and ceilings established to mitigate the swings of the business cycle have greatly dampened the fluctuations in employment, unemployment levels still rise and fall. Unemployment rates by sex from 1940 to 1962 are shown in Table 12. The data clearly reveal the four recessions, or economic adjustments, our economy has experienced since the end of World War II, as evidenced by unemployment peaks in 1949, 1954, 1958, and 1961. These peaks, however, were well below the unemployment rate in 1940 (14.6 per cent), which in turn was well below the peak rate of unemployment of 24.9 per cent experienced in 1933 at the bottom of the depression.

TABLE 12

UNEMPLOYMENT RATES BY SEX, 1940–1962[a]
(annual average)

Year	Both Sexes	Male	Female
1962	5.6	5.3	6.2
1961	6.7	6.5	7.2
1960	5.6	5.4	5.9
1959	5.5	5.3	5.9
1958	6.8	6.8	6.8
1957	4.3	4.1	4.7
1956	4.2	3.8	4.9
1955	4.4	4.2	4.9
1954	5.6	5.3	6.1
1953	2.9	2.8	3.3
1952	3.1	2.8	3.7
1951	3.3	2.9	4.4
1950	5.3	5.1	5.8
1949	5.9	5.9	6.0
1948	3.8	3.6	4.1
1947	3.9	3.7	3.2
1946	3.9	4.4	2.8
1945	1.9	1.8	2.2
1944	1.2	1.0	1.7
1943	1.9	1.5	2.7
1942	4.7	4.3	5.8
1941	9.9	9.5	11.2
1940	14.6	14.3	15.5

[a] Source: U. S. Bureau of the Census. *Historical statistics of the United States, colonial times to 1957.* Washington: Government Printing Office, 1960, and Bureau of Labor Statistics.

The incidence of unemployment varies greatly by industrial and occupational sector of the economy and within occupational and industrial groupings, by sex, age, color, and other characteristics of the population. Analysis of the data reveals, however, that although the volume and rate of unemployment fluctuates over a wide range, the differential pattern of unemployment remains the same. That is, it is the same groups which show the highest incidence of unemployment (Hauser, 1957, pp. 243–278).

Female unemployment is almost always appreciably higher than male. Unemployment among the young workers of each sex is considerably above that of workers of intermediate age. Unemployment of older workers also tends to be high, but the data are not clear on this point, partly because the older worker tends to leave the labor force when he cannot find a job. Nonwhite unemployment is always above that of the white population and frequently twice as high. Married persons with a spouse present, both male and female, have lower unemployment rates than do the single, divorced, or separated people. Unemployment rates of wage and salary workers tend to be well above the average in agriculture, forestry, fishery, construction, retail trade, domestic service, personal service other than domestic, amusement and recreation, and nondurable goods manufacturing. On the other hand, unemployment rates for workers in finance, insurance, real estate, and the professional and related services tend to be uniformly low. Considered by occupation, unemployment rates are relatively low for white collar workers and high for nonfarm laborers, operatives, craftsmen, and foremen.

Unemployment rates, as currently defined, do not necessarily measure the differential vulnerability of workers to loss of a job. That is, the conventional unemployment rate includes among the unemployed not only those who have been disemployed, that is, who have lost their jobs, but, also, those who are seeking work from a previous status of not in the labor force. In consequence, the unemployment rates tend to be inflated for those elements of the population whose mobility in respect to labor force participation is high. Thus, the high mobility in labor force participation of women, young workers, and old workers reported above is a factor in the relatively high unemployment rates of these groups. In all likelihood the in-and-out movements of the nonwhite population also tend to inflate their unemployment rates.

Data are available on unemployment by sex, showing gross changes. A "disemployment" rate may be calculated from these data—a rate showing loss of jobs by persons actually employed (Hauser, 1957, p. 248). Female disemployment rates are lower than male. Thus, once a job is obtained, the vulnerability of the female to loss of employment is below that of the male, even though the conventional unemployment rates show the reverse relationship. It would be highly desirable to have data for similar analyses for the other population groupings. Gross data that make this possible are not yet available. It should be stated, however, that the magnitude of the differences by age and by color, and by occupation and by industry, are such that they are not likely to be reversed by gross change analysis. On the other hand, there can be little doubt that high mobility in labor force participation tends to inflate unemployment rates.

In the study of unemployment, further differentiation of the unemployed is possible and desirable. For example, long-term and short-term unemployment can be differentiated by reason for unemployment.

Sociologists have evidenced some interest in unemployment as an area of study, but the surface of the problem has scarcely been scratched. This despite the fact that unemployment is probably among the more catastrophic and critical experiences both of the person and the family. Unemployment considered as an independent variable undoubtedly has great explanatory power for many types of personal and social phenomena, ranging from delinquency and crime to marital discord and suicide. The increasing availability and richness of data about unemployment and the unemployed is opening up new areas of research opportunities for the sociologist.

CONCLUDING OBSERVATIONS

Data are available with respect to many characteristics of the labor force, in addition to those discussed above, which could more effectively be utilized by the sociologist. These include: wage or salary income; the class of worker composition of the labor force, that is, whether workers are employees in government, employees in private industry, own account workers or unpaid family workers; part time and full time employment; multiple job holders; industrial com-

position; and employment status, that is, whether employed or unemployed. Each of these subjects, in turn, may be considered in cross-classification with one another and with general demographic characteristics such as age, sex, color, urban-rural residence, region, and the like. There is a largely unexplored area in the investigation of labor force phenomena in terms of family units rather than individual workers (Kitagawa, 1956). Finally, there is a great need for comparative labor force studies, international and cross-cultural. Needless to say, comparative international studies of the labor force greatly compound the problem of data comparability.

Of increasing importance, also, is interest in the labor force as an element in economic growth in the developing areas of the world. A major barrier to economic development is to be found in the illiteracy, lack of skills, and other qualitative deficiencies in the work force. Economists have recently shown a great interest in investment in human resources as an important factor in achieving economic development, and sociologists, also, have been focusing attention on this problem (Galenson, 1962; *Journal of Political Economy,* 1962; Moore & Feldman, 1960).

Concern with the work force as an object of research within the social sciences has been primarily the province of economists. In recent years, however, sociologists have shown increasing interest in various aspects of the labor force. In focusing research activity on work and the work force, contemporary sociologists are following with some considerable delay the lead of some of the pioneers of sociology, for example, Spencer and Durkheim (Durkheim, 1947; Spencer, 1897, Vol. II, Part III).

The sociologist, by showing greater interest in the labor force as a field of investigation can undoubtedly both gain and contribute much. On the one hand, labor force data can shed light on a wide range of personal and social phenomena, and, on the other, in bringing his frame of reference and methods of analysis to bear, the sociologist can undoubtedly make significant contributions to a better understanding of labor force phenomena.

REFERENCES

Angell, R. C. *The family encounters the depression.* New York: Scribner, 1936.

Arner, G. B. L. The census of unemployment. *J. Amer. statist. Ass.,* March, 1933, 28, Proceedings Suppl., 48–53.

Bakke, E. W. *The unemployed worker.* New Haven, Conn.: Yale Univer. Press, 1940.

Bancroft, Gertrude. *The American labor force, its growth and changing composition.* Social Science Research Council in cooperation with the U.S. Bureau of the Census. New York: Wiley, 1958.

Cavan, R. A., & Ranck, K. H. *The family and the depression.* Chicago: Univer. of Chicago Press, 1938.

Dedrick, C. L., & Hansen, M. H. *Census of unemployment 1937, final report.* Vol. IV. *The enumerative check census, census of partial employment, unemployment and occupations: 1937.* Washington: Government Printing Office, 1938.

Dewhurst, J. F., & Associates. *America's needs and resources, a new survey.* New York: Twentieth Century Fund, 1955.

Dornbusch, S. The family in the labor force. Unpublished doctoral dissertation, Univer. of Chicago, 1952.

Douglas, P. H. *The theory of wages.* New York: Macmillan, 1934.

Douglas, P. H., & Schoenberg, Enka. Studies of the supply curve of workers. *J. polit. Econ.,* February, 1937, 45, 45–79.

Ducoff, L. J., & Hagood, Margaret Jarman. *Labor force definition and measurement.* New York: Social Science Research Council, 1947. Bull. No. 56.

Durand, J. *The labor force in the United States, 1890 to 1960.* New York: Social Science Research Council, 1948.

Durkheim, E. *The division of labor in society.* George Simpson (Trans.). Glencoe, Ill.: Free Press, 1947.

Edwards, Alba M. *Comparative occupation statistics for the United States, 1870 to 1940.* Washington: Government Printing Office, 1943.

Galenson, W. *Labor in developing economics.* Berkeley and Los Angeles: Univer. of California Press, 1962.

Garfinkle, S. Changes in working life of man, 1900–2000. *Mon. Labor Rev.,* March, 1955, 18, 297–300.

Hauser, P. M. The labor force and gainful workers—concept, measurement and comparability. *Amer. J. Sociol.,* January, 1949, 54(4), 338–355.

Hauser, P. M. The labor force as a field of interest for the sociologist. *Amer. sociol. Rev.,* August, 1951, 16, 530–538.

Hauser, P. M. Changes in the labor force participation of the older worker. *Amer. J. Sociol.,* January, 1954, 59(4), 312–323.(a)

Hauser, P. M. Mobility in labor force participation. In E. W. Bakke et al. (Eds.), *Essays in labor mobility.* New York: Wiley, 1954.(b)

Hauser, P. M. Differential unemployment and characteristics of the unemployed in the United States, 1940–1954. In National Bureau of Economic Research, *The measurement and behavior of unemployment.* Princeton, N.J.: Princeton Univer. Press, 1957. Pp. 243–278.

Hauser, P. M., & Duncan, O. D. *The study of population: An inventory and appraisal.* Chicago: Univer. of Chicago Press, 1959.

Humphrey, D. D. Alleged additional workers in the measurement of unemployment. *J. polit. Econ.,* June, 1940, 48, 412–419.

Jaffe, A. J. & Stewart, C. D. *Manpower resources and utilization.* New York: Wiley, 1951.

Jaffe, A. J. *People, jobs and economic development.* Glencoe, Ill.: Free Press, 1959.

Journal of Political Economy. October, 1962, 70(5), Part 2. (Suppl.)

Kitagawa, Evelyn M. *The family as a unit in the work force—a review of the literature.* Chicago: Univer. of Chicago, Population Research and Training Center, October, 1956. (Hectographed)

Kleeck, Mary Van. The federal unemployment census of 1930. *J. Amer. statist. Ass.,* March, 1931, 26, 189–200. (Suppl.)

Komarovsky, Mirra. *The unemployed man and his family.* New York: Dryden, 1940.

Lester, R. A. *Economics of labor.* New York: Macmillan, 1947.

Long, C. D. The concept of unemployment. *Quart. J. Econ.*, November, 1942, 57, 1–30.

Long, C. D. *The labor force under changing income and employment.* National Bureau of Economic Research. Princeton, N.J.: Princeton Univer. Press, 1958.

Marshall, A. *Principles of economics.* London: Macmillan, 1898.

Moore, W. E., & Feldman, A. S. *Labor commitment and social change in developing areas.* New York: Social Science Research Council, 1960.

Myers, H. B., & Webb, J. N. Another census of unemployment? *Amer. J. Sociol.*, January, 1937, 62, 521–533.

National Manpower Council. *Womanpower.* New York: Social Science Research Council, 1954.

Palmer, Gladys L. *Labor mobility in six cities.* New York: Columbia Univer. Press, 1957.

Palmer, Gladys L., & Ratner, Ann. *Industrial and occupational trends in national employment.* Philadelphia: Univer. of Pennsylvania, Industrial Research Dept., Research Rept. No. 11, 1949.

Persons, C. E. Census reports on unemployment in April 1930. *Ann. Amer. Acad. polit. soc. Sci.*, March, 1931, 154, 12–16.

President's Committee to Appraise Employment and Unemployment Statistics. *Measuring employment and unemployment.* Washington: Government Printing Office, 1962.

Spencer, H. *Principles of sociology.* New York: Appleton, 1897.

Stouffer, S. A., & Lazarsfeld, P. *Research memorandum on the family in the depression.* New York: Social Science Research Council, 1937.

U.S. Bureau of the Census. *Fifteenth census of the United States: 1930; unemployment.* Vol. 1. Washington: Government Printing Office, 1931.

U.S. Bureau of the Census. *Fifteenth census of the United States, population.* Vol. 5. *General report on occupations.* Washington: Government Printing Office, 1933.

U.S. Bureau of the Census. Annual report on the labor force. *Current Pop. Repts.* Series P-50, No. 31. Washington: Bureau of the Census, March, 1951.

U.S. Bureau of the Census. Annual report on the labor force. *Current Pop. Repts.* Series P-50, No. 40. Washington: Bureau of the Census, May, 1952.

U.S. Bureau of the Census. *U.S. census of population: 1950.* Vol. II. *Characteristics of the population.* Part 1. *United States Summary.* Washington: Government Printing Office, 1953.

U.S. Bureau of the Census. Concepts and methods used in the current employment and unemployment statistics prepared by the Bureau of the Census. *Current Pop. Repts.* Series P-23, No. 5. Washington: Bureau of the Census, May 9, 1958.

U.S. Bureau of the Census. *Historical statistics of the United States, colonial times to 1957.* Washington: Government Printing Office, 1960. (a)

U.S. Bureau of the Census. *The post enumerative survey, 1950.* Washington: Government Printing Office, Technical Paper No. 4, 1960. (b)

U.S. Bureau of the Census. *U.S. census of population: 1960. General social and economic characteristics, U.S. summary.* Final Rept. PC(1)-1C, 1962.

U.S. Bureau of the Census. *Accuracy of census statistics with and without sampling.* Washington: Government Printing Office, Technical Paper No. 2, 1963. (a)

U.S. Bureau of the Census. *The current population survey, a report on methodology.* Washington: Government Printing Office, Technical Paper No. 7, 1963. (b)

U.S. Bureau of the Census. *The current population survey reinterview program, some notes and discussion.* Washington: Government Printing Office, Technical Paper No. 6, 1963. (c)

U.S. Bureau of the Census. *Statistical abstract of the United States, 1962.* Washington: Government Printing Office, 1963. (d)

U.S. Department of Labor. *Monthly report on the labor force* (monthly).

U.S. Department of Labor, Bureau of Labor Statistics. *Tables of working life, length of working life for men.* Washington: Government Printing Office, Bull. No. 1001, 1950.

U.S. Department of Labor, Bureau of Labor Statistics. *Tables of working life for women, 1950.* Washington: Government Printing Office, Bull. No. 1204, 1956.

Webb, J. N. Concepts used in employment surveys. *J. Amer. Statist. Ass.,* March, 1939, 34, 49–61.

Wolfbein, S. L. The length of working life. Paper read at Fourth International Gerontological Congress, Merano, Italy, July, 1957. (Mimeographed)

Wolfbein, S. L., & Jaffe, A. J. Demographic factors in labor force growth. *Amer. sociol. Rev.,* August, 1946, 11(4), 392–396.

Woytinsky, W. S. *Additional workers and the volume of unemployment in the depression.* Washington: Social Science Research Council, 1940.

Wright, C. D. *The history and growth of the United States census.* Washington: Government Printing Office, 1900.

CHAPTER 6 Position and Behavior Patterns of Youth

DAVID MATZA

The surprising thing about youth is how little is known about it despite the considerable number of studies and essays on one or another of its aspects. One may learn a great deal about the correlates of different phases of adolescence or youth (Clausen & Williams, 1963), but he may still know very little directly about these self-same aspects. One knows something about the socialization processes by which children assume one or another youthful style, but considerably less about the variety, shape, and texture of the styles themselves. From the less empirical literature on youth, one may learn much about what is wrong with alleged characteristics of modern youth, but is not enlightened regarding the details of these characteristics and the particular youth to whom they presumably pertain. The present chapter will focus on the shape and texture of these youthful patterns and the position of youth on which the diversity of styles is presumably founded.

"Youth" is here used in a meaning broader than the usual connotation of "adolescence." It includes adolescence, but needs not culminate with the end of adolescence. Rightly or wrongly, adolescence has come to be associated with the teen-age years. Youth, however, may, under certain conditions, last well into the thirties or middle-age. Youth ends with the attaining of potentially self-sufficient adulthood. Adolescence has been similarly defined (Muuss, 1962, p. 4), but the word is usually less acceptable when used in such a broad scope. There is less reservation about conceiving of a 13-year-old youth. Such usage is not uncommon. Thus, the present conception of "youth" will be similar to that commonly used with reference to "adolescence"—the period between childhood and adulthood.

Youth is a period in the temporal ordering of society (Moore, 1963). It is a period whose beginning and end are more or less explicitly punctuated. As Ruth Benedict (1938), and other anthropologists after her, reminded readers, some societies make a great effort to celebrate and ritualize passage into youth and, subsequently, into adulthood. Other societies, however, are notorious for their lack of activity in these respects. Despite the great variability in the patency of the beginning and end of youth, all societies apparently conceive of the category (Eisenstadt, 1962, pp. 28–29) and manage to supply commonly understood *social indica-tions* of onset and conclusion. These indi-cations may themselves lack consistency and coherence, in which case they are *diffuse,* or they may coincide on a particular point in time, in which case they are *specific.*

Contemporary America tends to the lazy end of the spectrum, allowing the definitions of the beginning and end of youth to lie latent in common understandings and fail-ing to supply a specific occasion on which diverse indications coalesce. But this should not be taken to mean that common under-standings of the beginning and end of youth are lacking. The social indications of the start of youth in our society, and many oth-ers, have included publicly or privately visi-ble aspects of biological pubescence (Ausubel, 1954; Lander, 1942; Muuss, 1962, pp. 19–23; Sarnoff, 1962, pp. 384–385). Moreover, the beginnings of youth are indicated in the partial subsiding of parental dominance and a concurrent license to utilize guardedly one's new sexual equipment in some pale or playful imitation of adult heterosexuality. Finally, in many modern societies the be-ginning of youth is indicated by a license—not a right—to engage in some imitation of adult work. Thus indicated, youth is a step, albeit a halting one, toward socially defined adulthood.

The conclusion of youth is obviously the assumption of adult status and, within the limits set by other prevalent systems of stratification, the ascription of first-class citizenship. With adulthood, one is at least a first-class subject within one's estate or caste and, at best, a first-class citizen in one's community. Excellent and persistent social indicators of the time at which the assumption of adulthood is warranted in-clude the formation of new kinship ties by marriage, the begetting of children, the en-trance into the labor force by taking or searching for full-time and permanent em-ployment, and the establishment of a new and separate place of residence.

The conclusion of youth, like its begin-ning, may be obvious or latent, diffuse or specific, early or late. There is no avoiding this ambiguity and variability—both among and within societies (Muuss, 1962, pp. 8–10). If there are common understandings regarding when entry into and exit from youth take place, it is perhaps risky to rely too heavily on the variable propensities of societies explicitly to ritualize passage in accounting for stressful or tranquil youth. Common understandings of the general conditions of entry and exit may easily substitute for ritualized celebration in as-suaging the anxiety presumably felt by youth who lack a concise date of gradua-tion into one or another age grade. To suppose otherwise is to assume that rigid and meticulous social organization is some-how less productive of tension than are flexible and imprecise arrangements.

THE POSITION
OF MODERN YOUTH

Most analyses of youth have proceeded from a picture of their emergent position in modern society. The problems and po-tentialities of youth, both as seen from with-in and by ex-youth, derive from their position in society and their relations with adults. The consequences of the position of youth may be mediated through the special families encountered by them, and mollified or aggravated but not negated. The position of youth is the general circumstance within which adult agencies of variable character perform their work. Thus, any analysis of youth seems incomplete without a consid-eration of this position.

A common error in most portrayals of youth is an exaggeration of those aspects making for stress, turmoil, and, subsequent-ly, for deviance and a variety of other psy-chic misfortunes. Literary essayists and posi-tivist sociologists alike have shared in a common mood which stresses the sense in which growing up in the way preferred by adults is harder and more fraught with obstacles today than at some usually un-specified previous time (Coleman, 1961a;

Goodman, 1960). Such a mood should immediately arouse suspicion since it partakes of the general, and for the most part unwarranted, intellectual gloom connected with the negative assessment of modernity (Grana, in press). Moreover, a negative and pessimistic assessment of youth based on a purported degeneration of their position should be subjected to special scrutiny because of the common tendency of ex-youth to romanticize their own experiences and disparage those of succeeding cohorts.

Ameliorated Dependency

Youth is a dependent status (Parsons, 1962, pp. 110–111), which means that it suffers from special liabilities or penalties and enjoys special protections, indulgences, and privileges. The special status is most explicit in law, where youth receive special treatment and are subject to special provisions up to ages ranging from about 16 to the mid-twenties, depending on the particular jurisdiction and matter at hand. The dependent status of youth is also apparent in the special treatment and support accorded in other major institutions, ranging from the family to industry. Special provisions are often enacted in law (Abbott, 1938), but some are merely customary in character. The mere fact that someone is young grants him special treatment. This special treatment is a mixture of the sort of liability and indulgence that is generally characteristic of dependent status.

Sometimes youth are accorded special indulgence, sometimes special stringency. In either case dependency is a peculiar status. This status is best summarized in political rather than economic or social terms: It is a deficiency in citizenship (Marshall, 1950). Dependents are only limited citizens.

In what sense has the dependent status of youth been ameliorated? One important answer seems obvious and is implicit, though strangely only rarely explicit, in the many studies of child-rearing in America. The major secular drift described in these studies is a transformation of parental domination from reliance on physical coercion to one or another form of manipulation or persuasion. This drift has produced the profound amelioration inherent in the substitution of persuasion for brutality. Children today are protected from the coarsest physical forms of adult domination by both custom and law and, though not always effectively, from flagrant abuse by parents, teachers, and other officials. The secular trend and the increasing correspondence between the social classes were summarized by Bronfenbrenner:

It is now a matter of scientific record that patterns of child rearing in the United States have changed appreciably over the past twenty-five years. . . . Middle class parents especially have moved away from the more rigid and strict styles of care and discipline advocated in the early 1920's and '30's toward modes of response involving greater tolerance of the child's impulses and desires, free expression of affection, and increased reliance on "psychological" methods of discipline, such as reasoning and appeals to conscience, as distinguished from more direct techniques like physical punishment. . . . At the same time, the gap between the social classes in their goals and methods of child rearing appears to be narrowing, with working class parents beginning to adopt both the values and techniques of the middle class (Bronfenbrenner, 1961, p. 7).

Moreover, Bronfenbrenner (1961) indicated that the trend may be extended back to the early part of the twentieth century, suggesting that, at least during the present century, not merely cyclical variation is being witnessed. Bronfenbrenner based this judgment on a study of Californians reared in the early 1900's, and in the late 1920's and 1930's (Bronson, Katten, & Livson, 1959). Thus, according to Bronfenbrenner, the trend to greater reliance on persuasion and less on coercion has continued in the same direction from the early 1900's to the present.

The narrowing gap between the social classes continues to attract the attention of students of child-rearing. In one recent study, the results showed that the differences in the child-rearing patterns between working- and middle-class seem to have almost vanished (Kohn, 1959). The methods used in showing both the trend toward persuasion and the increasing similarity between the classes in the use of this technique may be challenged, but the challenge lacks credibility. The findings of these studies confirm the common sense and literary impression that persuasion has been replacing coercion.

The above trend is related to a tendency toward permissiveness, which has appeared within educational as well as family systems. Whatever the precise meaning attached to the term permissiveness, it indicates a rise in the indulgence granted young persons and a decrease in their liabilities and duties. There have, of course, been countertrends in permissiveness and the freedom of movement, choice, and action inherent in it, for instance, the instituting of curfew restrictions for youth in many large cities. These, however, have remained largely unenforced. Despite such countertrends, the secular trend toward permissiveness has hardly been reversed. Youth today enjoy greater indulgence of their freedom of choice and movement than formerly, and, in that measure, their status of dependency has been ameliorated.

The lessening of youthful dependency has been accomplished in a variety of other ways, each balancing the previously overwhelming liabilities and duties with newly granted protection and indulgence. Best seen in this light are such innovations as protective legislation and persistent restrictions on the conditions of child labor, the creation of special courts for juveniles, the emergence of the probation system which originally was mainly a special dispensation for minors, the progressive movement in education which was inspired and animated by a dedicated child-centeredness, and the considerable gains in financial allowance dispensed to youth by increasingly generous parents.

What have been the consequences of amelioration? A satisfactory answer is suggested by a reiteration of the fact that while dependency has been ameliorated, it still exists. Moreover, another answer is suggested by stressing the sense in which youth are a minority group (Friedenberg, 1959, p. 7; Friedenberg, 1963a, pp. 149–158). Minority can mean both a small fraction of a population and not having attained the age of maturity, blended in "minority group" as it pertains to ethnic fractions of the population. It is not that minors are treated as a fractional ethnic group; rather, ethnic fractions have been treated like minors.

Youth are not only *a* minority group. Symbolically, they are *the* minority group in that they have provided a paradigm for imputations and policy regarding disliked ethnic fractions. A conception of youth as a minority group suggests the probable consequences of the shift in position implicit in the amelioration of dependent status. Minorities whose dependence is lessened but not abolished manifest some standard features. The reaction of youth to improvement of their position has been partially similar to that of ethnic fractions. It has been different, too, since youth are a special kind of minority.

Young persons display considerable uncertainty and vacillation regarding their proper place in society. Amelioration, with the persistence of second-class citizenship, hardly leads to contentment and satisfaction; instead, it whets the previously undeveloped appetite for freedom and equality and makes some persons restless. This has been noted many times in the study of ethnic minorities and more generally disadvantaged sections of the population. Moreover, individuals whose dependency has been ameliorated come to forget their place in society, often because they no longer know what it is and neither do their majority benefactors. Thus, youth come to occupy a marginal status in society, and so it has been described by many writers. The incumbents of marginal position typically experience some measure of status anxiety. Irving Sarnoff described the marginality of youth:

In our society . . . the adolescent is generally obliged to live for many years as a "marginal man." . . . That is, his social status is rather ambiguous, for he is considered neither an adult, nor yet a child; neither permitted to share the prerogatives of adults nor enjoy the irresponsibility of prepubescent childhood; neither taken completely seriously by adults nor ignored by them as they might ignore the antics of a young child . . . (Sarnoff, 1962, p. 392).

Kurt Lewin, too, in an earlier statement, attributed much of the tension of youth to their marginal position in society. Lewin, like Sarnoff and other recent writers, focused on the sense in which youth is currently marginal without sufficiently stressing the historical shifts which produced that legacy (Muuss, 1962, p. 90). Consequently, one often overlooks the fact that the ambiguity of youthful status emanates from an improvement, or amelioration, of position, rather than increased deprivation or degeneration.

A consequence of status ambiguity is a persistent uncertainty regarding the proper stance with which members of the minority are to interact with those of the majority, and the pathetic misunderstandings which normally attend uncertainty. For instance, the question of whether or not a youth knows his proper place is more important, and in some sense of greater social import to many adult law-enforcement officials than whether or not the youth has actually engaged in any violation of the law (Werthman & Piliavin, 1963). After this is established, interaction proceeds in one direction or another depending in some measure on the minority member's response to the query.

Place uncertainty may result in a higher predisposition to deviant modes of conduct in that it may generate hostility to the social order and its official agents or engender alienation from the norms and sentiments which regulate social behavior. While this is likely, one cannot be certain that place uncertainty will culminate in high rates of deviation, since many things obviously intervene between an affinity and an accomplished and registered act. Less conjectural is the idea that place uncertainty will result in greater *imputation of deviance* to minority members than to those of majority status.

Normally, place uncertainty means that official agents of the majority have a certain touchiness regarding the activities of those in minority position. They are touchy both because they suspect the minority of falling short of the standards of maturity and because they are uncertain regarding where they stand with their inferiors. The touchiness of adults is countered by a pushy show of youthful defiance, since many minority members mistake favors for rights and are resentful when reminded of their actual position. As a result of the mutual touchiness and the strained interaction which ensues, the chances of discovering and registering deviant acts are maximized. Moreover, given the wide latitude of youthful violations implicit in modern juvenile codes, police apprehension and subsequent citation for mere disrespect or other behavior unbecoming a person of minority status can and does occur. Given the circumstance of place uncertainty, police, like other adults, are apt to be highly sensitive to the respect accorded them by youth, and youth are apt to act in a way which is taken to be disrespectful. Thus, the initial imputation of deviant tendencies, coupled with the intensely touchy relations between the official registrars of deviance and youth, may serve to produce something of a self-confirming prophecy, especially if, as alleged by some sociologists, such reinforced imputations serve to structure self-conception and to shape the opportunities for association or affiliation (Becker, 1963; Lemert, 1951).

Place uncertainty and attendant difficulties are aggravated by the spiraling tendency by which expectations outrun realities. In another context, this has been termed the "revolution of rising expectations." Two forms of rising expectations may be distinguished, one rather unreasonable, the other quite reasonable and perhaps more common. The first, "runaway expectations," refers to a situation in which aspirant equals forget to surrender the indulgence and protection that befit them as ameliorated dependents but appear unseemly among first-class citizens. Women and youth are among the best examples of minorities which include persons who seem to aspire to more than full equality. Thus, for instance, some women desire deference and chivalry as well as freedom and equality. Some youth desire pampering and coddling as well as being treated as adults. Runaway expectations manifest themselves in an apparent ambivalence regarding equality and are a rather normal affliction among these special minorities that have been perpetually integrated in social circles which include majority members. An excellent instance of such a social circle is, of course, the family.

But however reasonable, the expectations of many women and youth surpass what is normally allowed. Their expectations are not runaway, merely galloping. An important aspect of "galloping youthful expectations" is implicit in Kingsley Davis' (1944) observation that the contemporary domination of the principle of merit results in tension and subsequent conflict. Davis felt that such a principle, when widely extended, provides a basis for intergenerational dispute regarding rightful incumbency in scarce positions and relative claims over scarce goods and services. Furthermore, the failure of such lofty principles to attain realization provides a setting for youthful resentment and a sense of injustice.

It is easy to exaggerate the proportion of youth who seriously experience such resentment. Though youth, like any minority, have their disgruntled and malcontented members, a large proportion of them accept the indulgence of adults and exhibit satisfaction instead of resentment. Thus, a third section, perhaps the largest, seems hardly touched by the rising expectations experienced by more obstreperous and thus visible youth. These are the staid and contented youth who have only recently begun to be noticed (Bealer & Willits, 1961; Danserau, 1961; Reiss, 1961). Such a contented type is most likely to appear and gain influence among minorities, like women and youth, who enjoy easy access to majority members. Moreover, the prominence of contented youth is especially enhanced by the unique feature of youthful minorities—the realistic expectation that with the passage of time majority status will be ascribed.

Youth are thus a minority who realistically look ahead to maturity and therefore majority. The conventionality of modern youth is mainly based on this aspiration to adulthood. The deviance is based on temporary minority status and the difficulties arising from touchy relations with adults. Moreover, youthful adherence to a variety of deviant forms is increased in the measure that adulthood must be achieved through adequate performance and conduct, rather than simply being gained with mere passage of time. Thus, youth who perform very badly in elementary or secondary schools are likely to have the realistic aspiration to adulthood interfered with and to that extent are less bound to convention. Such youth often engage in delinquent behavior. On the other hand, since youthful deviance is partially based on the prolonged period during which some are requested to exhibit patience and to continue as mere aspirants to majority status, it may not appear until the end of the long educational regimen—most notably in the American graduate school—and typically takes a bohemian or radical turn.

Prolonged Aspiration and Diversion

Statistics on years spent in school all show a consistent and sharp rise in the past century (Trow, 1961). One cannot, however, jump to the conclusion that increase in schooling produces a concomitant rise in the stressful condition of youth, at least until one knows what duration is subjectively considered "prolonged" by youth themselves. One may suggest that the duration of youth is subjectively prolonged when some youth believe that certain occupations warrant little preparation, or when they imply through sustained truancy, for instance, that whatever the theoretical value of educational preparation, it has failed to help them. Each of these states characterizes some sizable, though not necessarily major, segment of youth. However, overall satisfaction with the long period of youth may prevail despite the reluctance by some young persons to grant legitimacy to educational preparation. Youth is a period of remarkable contemporaneous engagements which serve to obscure the future. If these engagements of "youth culture" may divert youth from study, they may also divert them from their dissatisfaction with study taken as preparation for adulthood.

The long period and the tempo of American schooling provide the occasion for leisure and diversion as well as a period for aspiration and preparation. The long duration of education does not rest solely on the higher skill requirements of an advanced technology (Muuss, 1962). There is little doubt that education could proceed faster and consequently youths could be more quickly brought to adulthood. However, other values are involved. As Naegele suggested:

We have increasingly come to expect childhood to be in some sense happy, light, carefree. Yet as childhood moves more and more into the province of the schools, we come to have various second thoughts as to this apparent light-heartedness. The debate about education is directly a debate about priorities and realities in adult life (Naegele, 1962, pp. 53–54).

Despite the second thoughts alluded to by Naegele, the persistence of the slow tempo of schooling, best symbolized by the summer vacation, indicates that the earlier ideas continue to dominate.

Second, our school system includes in its curriculum liberal, or impractical, subjects. Not all courses, or even most, are directed toward the technical proficiencies necessary for one or another career. Liberal education is an "inefficiency," but one that is more or less treasured by the professionals most immediately concerned with the school system. Thus, many courses taken in secondary school or college are valued by educational authorities on their own merits, rather than as a means to a job. A great assortment of interesting and otherwise worthwhile courses in the educational curriculum, with little or no relevance to any subsequent career, are offered because they contain the minimal aspects of the cultural heritage Americans wish to give to future citizens.

A third source of prolonged schooling may be found in occupational or professional rivalries. Occupations, especially those which are in close interaction with technical or staff professions, come to require higher and higher degrees of education partially to expedite the wielding of authority over those who are initially more educated or to achieve a greater measure of colleagueship with superior professions than currently exists. Thus, for instance, business executives "need" more education partially because they must legitimately supervise Ph.D. chemists, and social workers "need" more education partially because they wish to work on a collegial basis with psychiatrists. Each occupation desires to control its own entrance requirements. The time spent in school thus is only partially related to concern for the interests of youth.

Ameliorated dependence and prolonged aspiration and diversion combine to give youthful behavior its complex and markedly inconsistent character. The indulgences and freedom granted during youth produce a discontent and anxiety arising from a confused and often unrealized aspiration to equality, but they also permit a sort of frivolous euphoria. Similarly, the prolonging of education provides an opportunity for leisure or an occasion for boredom, frustration, and resentment. The peculiar com-

bination of precocious resentment and leisured euphoria facilitates the third feature of
the position of modern youth. The period
of youth is only loosely integrated into the
wider society. It is, in relative terms, a free
sector in the social order.

Loose Integration
and Partial Autonomy

The term alienation has served to obscure
the obvious fact that integration in social
systems is a matter of degree. Full alienation connotes, among other things, a feeling
of sustained opposition to the system, but
this feeling is not necessarily a feature of
loosened integration.

Relative freedom from conventional controls initially follows from the normal subsiding of parental domination before the
responsibility of self-support has appeared.
Relative freedom is further facilitated by
the social changes implicit in ameliorated
dependence, the potentialities of prolonged
and undemanding education, and the combination of resentment and euphoria elicited
by these changes.

Eisenstadt (1951; 1962) suggested the general conditions under which youth groups
are likely to emerge in society. He felt that
they appear in societies in which the family
is not directly linked to the productive sectors of the economy. Implicit in his theory
is the idea that age periods during which
the family subsides in importance and occupation has yet to appear are prone to the
development of semiautonomous and relatively unregulated youth groupings.

Youth culture, more properly youth subculture, is neither clearly separated from
adult conventions nor unified within itself.
Youth subculture is not so separated from
adult culture because it is manned by persons who in the past have been dominated
by conventional families and look forward,
or aspire, to subsequent entry into conventional life. Thus, the leisured diversions
which make up much of the substance,
temporary for each member, of youth

subculture are themselves highly colored by
activities and precepts which appear in adult
life. Youth subculture is at least in part an
adaptation of adult sentiments and practices
to the special conditions of youthful existence (Elkin & Westley, 1955).

The integration of youth subculture and
its separation from conventional adult life
are both recognized in Coleman's *Adolescent
Society* (1961), despite the fact that Coleman's main purpose was to document the
fundamental separation. He related the separation to the "setting-apart" of children in
the school system, to the tendency of schools
to take on more and more in the form of
extracurricular activities, and to the increased duration of education and training.
Consequently, suggested Coleman, the adolescent is "cut off from the rest of society,
forced inward toward his own age group,
made to carry out his whole social life with
others his own age" (Coleman, 1961a,
p. 3). Most of the important interactions,
according to Coleman, take place within the
adolescent society. There are "only a few
threads of connection with outside adult
society" (Coleman, 1961). Coleman suggested that the basic cause of this separation
may be found in the emergence and character of the school system. Thus, youth subculture, according to Coleman, is an unintended consequence of the organization of
the school system. Youth have been placed
in a collective context in which segregation
from adult life has been imposed, and they
have responded accordingly.

Whether separation is nominal or real,
however, depends on the content of youth
subculture. If a content different from that
of the adult culture appears, one may speak
of a separate youth subculture. If the substance of youth subculture is similar to that
of adults, then despite the predominance of
peer interaction one must exercise considerable caution in conceiving of a separate
world of youth. Coleman's (1961a) findings
—his data more than his interpretation—indicate a state of affairs somewhere between
separation and integration. Coleman was,

of course, aware of this, despite the main thrust of his argument which is toward the thesis of separation.

Youth subculture is intertwined with adult culture (Berger, 1963) and is highly pluralistic. Despite its connection with adult sentiments and its internally heterogeneous character, one may nevertheless note the existence of youth subculture and describe some of its manifestations. Youth subculture is by now a world-wide phenomenon, first occurring in advanced countries but increasingly apparent in emerging nations. Many perceptive observers have correctly stressed the central and initiating role played by American youth (Denney, 1962). Teenage culture has been among the most important exports of the United States. To many Europeans, it has been a disturbing matter.

Youth relations, suggested Smith, "are largely informal and are composed of intimacy and sentiment" (E. Smith, 1962, p. 2). The subculture of youth is largely an informal system of highly localized and ephemeral units. It is for the most part not anchored in conventional formal organization, though portions of it may base their operation in one or another adult-sponsored house or area. There is some tendency to avoid adult supervision. Smith, relying heavily on Simmel's (1906, pp. 462–463) assertion regarding the universality of secrecy among youth, suggested the prevalence of youthful inclination to evade regular supervision.

Solidarity and concealment . . . may be viewed as universal characteristics of youth culture. . . . The universality of secrecy suggests that youth will manifest varying degrees of withdrawal from adult socializing institutions. . . . The activities and interactions of youth will be hidden behind a veil of secrecy erected to escape the supervision and control of adults (E. Smith, 1962, p. 2).

Part of what youth are hiding must surely confirm the worst suspicions of their excluded elders; behind the veil they sometimes do disapproved of things. But there are at least two other sorts of activities that are concealed from adults.

First, youth, in a variety of ways, play at being adults. These games take many forms, some of which pay tribute to a public figure, some to members of private and intimate circles. One example of such activity consists of the playful conversion of informal and intimate ball-playing to out-and-out fantasies in which youthful players openly pretend before one another to be grown-up major league baseball stars. Only peculiar and specially defined adults are privy to public fantasies of this sort. Another example consists of the pretenses by which boys and girls act considerably more "grown up" than they and almost everyone else knows they are. Such aping of adults may be exhibited before peers, but to allow the conventional adult to observe would be embarrassing and in some circles an unpardonable admission of the respect accorded adulthood despite the frequent disclaimers. The staging of disdain of adulthood requires the obscuring of imitation and respect. Many adult observers, their vision being obstructed, have been deceived by the front.

Second, secrecy helps maintain the uncommitted character of youthful identity. Young persons toy with a variety of styles which they later discard. Even during engagement with a particular style, there frequently is little commitment to the precepts and practices underlying it. Publicity regarding identity, especially publicity which reaches conventional adults, minimizes the chances of playful engagement and maximizes the chances that character will be typed and lead to commitment.

Thus, seclusion upholds an inner secret of youth: fickle playing rather than commitment to identities. Conventional adults are likely to view the behavior implicit in one or another style completely out of context. They see it as harboring commitment, duration, and, thus, danger or a precocious closing of adolescence. Secrecy is therefore valuable to the youthful players since it minimizes the possibility that a temporary impression will endure as a stereotype.

THE PURSUIT OF IDENTITY

Adult identity is relatively focused and narrow. Presumably, men find identity in work, or, if work is too stultifying, perhaps in some seriously pursued avocation. Women invest their identity in kinship units, in the perceived occupational status of husbands, in their own roles as housewives, and in the character of their progeny. Increasingly, of course, women seek identity in an occupation or career. Youth, on the other hand, is the period of pursuit of *general* identity, a search which is simultaneously less intellectually demanding and more psychically tiring than that encountered during adulthood. Youth is engaged in self-discovery, except that it is not a self that is typically discovered but rather an already available style with which one's self can be comfortably associated. Identity here consists of generalized *preoccupations* instead of specific occupations (Eisenstadt, 1962; Erikson, 1950; Erikson, 1962; Muuss, 1962).

Because of the emerging position of youth, more or less stable identities have appeared within American life. These identities have grown into traditional styles which have been assumed and put aside by one cohort of youth after another. No style claims a majority of youthful adherence. Many youth vacillate among different identities, some of which will be discussed on the following pages, and most include in their wanderings shorter or longer stays in conventional amalgams which combine the features of analytically distinctive styles.

Scrupulosity

Scrupulosity is the most conformist of youthful styles. Among such persons, one finds little trace of the hedonism, expressiveness, and rebellion which presumably characterize youth culture. An expert on the incidence and forms of scrupulosity de-

scribed it in the following way: "The term scrupulosity is well known to those devoted to pastoral work. . . . It may be taken to mean an unhealthy and morbid kind of meticulousness which hampers a person's religious adjustment" (Riffel, 1963, p. 39).

For the sociologist, however, the defining element of scrupulosity is the meticulous adherence to religious and moral precepts. Scrupulosity may take the form of meticulous avoidance of temptation, a studied devoutness unbecoming to frivolous youth, a seriousness regarding church and parochial study, or a deeply introspective mentality. Whether such a style masks a deep emotional disorder, as is frequently alleged, is of little concern here, for almost all of the styles of youth to be described have been held by one writer or another to be the manifestation or symptom of a deep or transient disturbance. It remains to be shown, however, that abnormality is more representative of scrupulous youth than, say, the occasional athlete who turns out to be a pervert.

Scrupulosity, like most youthful styles, has a putative social base among students in the widespread system of Catholic parochial education. There is undoubtedly scrupulosity among youth who are devoted to other religious or secular faiths, but it is difficult to obtain information on these young people. Thus the present discussion must focus on Catholic scrupulosity.

The proportion of Catholic youth attending parochial school in America is high. Moreover, the proportion of those engaging in scrupulosity for longer or shorter interludes is sufficiently large to make it an important youthful phenomenon. Numerically, scrupulosity seems of roughly the same order of magnitude as that youthful style at the other end of the spectrum which nowadays attracts so much public attention—juvenile delinquency.

Though it is obviously difficult to know with certainty the frequency with which youth take on the style of scrupulosity, there are a few studies which give a rough idea.

The data reported in these studies seem unusually plausible since the conditions of true response are more or less built into the attributes of the style and the generally negative assessment it receives. Scrupulous persons, like delinquents, might have a motive to deny their condition, but, unlike delinquents, they cannot because of their scrupulosity.

Riffel summarized the few available reports on the frequency of scrupulosity:

Though accurate figures on the extent of scrupulosity among Catholic adolescent students are hard to obtain, the data of several reports are available. Mullen (1927) reported in a study of 400 Catholic school girls that 26% of them admitted to habitual scrupulosity. A Fordham study (Riffel, 1958) corroborated this earlier report of Mullen. This study was based on 490 students divided between sophomore high school and sophomore college years. . . . Of the high school students, 26% admitted to current scrupulosity, but in college the number had declined to 14%. . . . Boys and girls were included in the sample and the percentage of boys admitting to scrupulosity was almost precisely the same as that for girls (Riffel, 1963, p. 42).

Even if one assumes no scrupulosity whatsoever among parochial students in other denominations, which hardly seems reasonable, and no scrupulosity whatsoever among nonparochial school youth, which is considerably more reasonable, he is still left with a national rate of scrupulosity of at least 2 or 3 per cent, which is of the same order of magnitude as that of juvenile delinquency.

Scrupulosity, like delinquency and most other styles of youth, varies in frequency by specific age within the time period of youth. Considerably higher proportions of high school than college youth assume this style. Riffel (1963) stressed the transitory quality of scrupulosity, though he was careful to avoid the common view that it is very short-lived. According to his findings, scrupulosity is a stylistic phase that is assumed and acted on for a year or two, then apparently dispensed for yet another. Some

smaller proportion of young persons maintain scrupulosity for somewhat longer periods of time. Scrupulosity, like delinquency, seems to be a passing phase for certain kinds of youth and more or less impervious to correctional intervention. A few persons may develop commitment to the style or for other reasons maintain the identity into adulthood and perhaps even for a lifetime.

Studious Youth

Scholars and achievers, along with the scrupulous, are among the conforming youth. Studious youth conform because they are preoccupied by the official purpose of youth, aspiration and preparation, and for the same reason reduce their participation in diversion and leisure.

Preoccupation with officially-approved study accompanied by the reasonable anticipation of moral success during adulthood would seem calculated to achieve prestige. One might, therefore, expect studious youth to occupy the position of highest prestige among their peers. That they do not seems to be the general conclusion of most research. The findings of research are, in this case as in so many others, similar to those reached by less systematic commentators.

The position of studious youth is tenable, nevertheless, because the rewards and acclaim of scholastic achievement are large and established, though not perhaps as high and exclusive as we intellectuals might like. It is also tenable because studious youth are not so rare and isolated as to be unable to form cliques which function to insulate and protect members against the hostility or seduction emanating from nonstudious youth.

Implicit in the view that studious youth are vulnerable is the belief that they are so dispersed as to lack a demographic base for clique structure. This belief gives rise to the oft-expressed fear that initially studious youth run the danger of being discouraged by peers and anti-intellectual adults and thus deterred from serious enterprise. But if a delinquent subculture may flourish, why suppose that a studious subculture, nurtured as it is by official authority, cannot also survive. Surely, the demographic base is ample. For youth, both academically-oriented scholars and vocationally-oriented careerists (Clark & Trow, 1960), compose a demographic base for insulated and protective studious cliques. This does not mean they study together, though occasionally they may; rather, it means that they may support one another's studious propensities. Nor does this imply a separate studious sector within youth subculture. There is shifting from this style to others and vice versa though there is perhaps greater stable commitment to this studious style of youth than to other styles, because it is more adult-like in character, because its preoccupation is more securely linked to the realm of occupation, and because persistent performance —the amassing of a good and steady scholastic record—is a main criterion of success in this style.

Studious youth may hold to a tenable style despite the threats and seductions emanating from other styles and despite the ambivalence and uncertainty which studious youth themselves exhibit. Introspective ambivalence may be an essential and frequently misleading feature of the studious style. Thus, studious youth themselves are among the many critics of their style. They are often in the curious position of verbally wishing for the diversions which abound among the youth who surround them. But denunciation may have little effect on the tenacity with which they pursue study. They know that substantial rewards await scholastic performance. It is that realization that probably accounts for the hostility of nonstudious youth in the first place.

An impression of the proportion of youth who are in some measure oriented to studies may be found in Coleman's *Adolescent Society* (1961). He found that in large high schools about 6 per cent of the boys are identified by peers as scholars. Another 1 per cent are considered to be both scholars and athletes. In small high schools, a little less than 9 per cent are identified as scholars, and another 2 per cent are thought of as athlete-scholars. Moreover, the scholars are surrounded by many students whose attitudes seem generally sympathetic to studious enterprise (Coleman, 1961a, p. 147).

Coleman (1961a) suggested that occupational aspirations may be taken as indications of values, some of which provide supportive attitudes to the scholars. Thus, a favorable orientation toward an attractive representative of an occupation which requires conscientious study may indicate a supporting attitude toward scholarship.

The high school students in Coleman's (1961a) study were asked: "If you could be any of these things you wanted, which would you most want to be?" The available responses—jet pilot, nationally famous athlete, missionary, and atomic scientist— may be taken respectively as orientations to adventure, sports, morality, and scholarship. About 25 per cent chose atomic scientist. Even if one assumes that all who were identified as scholars chose atomic scientist, and surely many did not, he is left with more than 15 per cent of high school youth who, while not scholars, seem sympathetic to scholarship.

The secure status of studious youth and the tenability of the enterprise inherent in that status is indicated in many studies of youthful opinion. Though the interpretations convey a tone of complaint and an expressed wish that the status of studious youth were even higher, the findings themselves leave little doubt regarding their established position (Tannenbaum, 1962, Ch. 2). Coleman's (1961a) is one of many studies that legitimately stresses the preponderance of frivolous pursuits among youth, but in so doing minimizes the established and substantial minority given to studious concerns. The secure establishment of a studious style within the subculture is obscured by its minority position, its failure to advertise its advantaged place, and the uncertainty and ambivalence with which the studious themselves hold to such a style. Partly, their ambivalence is a response to blandishments and taunts emanating from more diverted youth. Partly, however, the ambivalence is intrinsic to the studious style itself which, being less distracted by external diversion and more given to solitary study, is perhaps more prone to introspection and self-scrutiny. Some of the anti-studious sentiment which abounds in opinion surveys of youth may actually emanate from studious youth themselves. The ambivalence may function to reduce the level of hostility directed toward the studious. Self-doubt is a mark of the intellectual which also appears among studious youth. It would be a mistake to suppose that the self-scrutiny and self-doubt of intellectuals, or studious youth, are tantamount to style- or self-rejection.

Tannenbaum's (1962) findings regarding the unfavorable attitudes of high school youth toward the studious are best seen in the light of the ambivalence maintained by youth who are themselves oriented in a studious direction. The students in Tannenbaum's sample were asked to respond in stereotypical fashion to eight adolescent types constructed by dichotomizing three attributes. The attributes were brilliance, conscientiousness or studious effort, and sports-mindedness. The highest-regarded type was the brilliant, nonstudious, and sports-minded, while the lowest was brilliant, studious, and nonathletic. Between the two extremes, athletic orientation consistently attracted esteem while studious effort consistently repelled it. Thus far, there is nothing surprising in Tannenbaum's findings. Beyond this, however, he found virtually no relationship

between character ratings and the respondent's own academic abilities . . . [or] the educational accomplishments of their parents. . . . Correlations hovered around zero . . . indicating that for the population studied, the value of information on intelligence and levels of parental education in predicting character rat-

ings was negligible (Tannenbaum, 1962, p. 58).

This absence of any relation between the rating of the constructed character types and the background and performance of the raters was

one of the most significant outcomes of the study. Even in the case of the brilliant-studious-non-athlete, rated significantly lower than any of the others, there was no evidence of higher regard shown by those who might identify more closely with this character on the basis of ability and dedication to school work (Tannenbaum, 1962, p. 58).

Tannenbaum (1962) felt that this may indicate a conformity on the part of studious youth to the atmosphere of anti-intellectualism current in high school. Whatever this finding *may* indicate, it surely demonstrates the persistence of a segment, in this case a large one, of studious youth, whatever their expressed attitude. Tannenbaum's study, as it happens, was of a middle-class high school in Brooklyn in which the student body was 75 per cent Jewish. Jews exemplify, perhaps better than any other American group, a culture which provides support for studious youth. The antistudious rhetoric of Jewish and other youth seems to be an element of the style of this group. It should not be confused with actual vulnerability to frivolous diversion or rejection of the studious effort implicit in the style.

Sports and Athletes

Sports are perhaps the most important of the conventional styles which divert attention from the officially defined purposes of youth. In the Coleman (1961a) study, the proportion of male youth identified by peers as athletes was slightly under 6 per cent in large schools. Another 1 per cent combined scholarly with athletic virtuosity. In small schools a little over 9 per cent were identified as athletes by peers. An additional 2 per cent were seen by their peers as coupling scholarly with athletic skill (Coleman, 1961a, p. 147).

The dominance of sports among American youth has drawn the attention of many observers. Typically, though not always, a disapproval of athletic dominance has accompanied the assertion of its central role in youth (Coleman, 1961a; Gorer, 1958; Laski, 1948). The major basis for this has been the claim that its seductive potency is so high that it diverts energy and attention from studies.

One of Coleman's (1961a) purposes in *Adolescent Society* was to document the prevalence of athletic orientation among high school youth and to designate the limited though large section of youth in which sports predominate.

High school boys were asked: "If you could be remembered here at school for one of the three things below, which one would you want to be?" Of the responses, 31.5 per cent of the boys chose brilliant student; 45.1 per cent, athletic star; and 23.4 per cent, most popular (Coleman, 1961a, pp. 28-29). The responses differ substantially from parental responses to the same question regarding their sons. Of the parents, 77 per cent would prefer boys to be remembered as brilliant students; 9 per cent as athletic stars; and 14 per cent, as the most popular student (Coleman, 1961a, pp. 32-33). Girls were asked: "Suppose you had the chance to go out with . . . [any of the following]. Which one would you rather go out with?" Of their answers 35 per cent said star athlete; 17 per cent, best student; and 48 per cent, best looking boy (Coleman, 1961a, pp. 30-31). Thus, if one grants the utility of such indicators, common sense impressions are supported. A strong case can be made for the predominance of sports among boys, the fact that this predominance is not especially reflected in parental sentiments and that athletic prowess has some limited appeal to girls.

Coleman, among others, tended to view this predominance as a problem or failing and suggested a remedy, or palliative, by intellectual contests to provide prestige for studious youth (Coleman, 1960, pp. 337-347; Coleman, 1961b, pp. 33-43). His desire to ameliorate the position of scholars led him to consider the meaning and appeal of sports among youth. He was forced to consider this question because he wished to provide a structural alternative to sports— something which performs the same variety of functions. The discussion of the basis of athletic appeal is interesting but incomplete. Thus, his suggested alternative, intellectual contests, remains unconvincing even if one shares the antiathletic bias implicit in Coleman's corrective approach, because intellectual contests do not fulfill the variety of functions performed by sports. Coleman was able to maintain the possibility of substituting intellectual for athletic contests because he ignored many other important functions performed by sports—functions which could not be served by intellectual contests.

Coleman's (1960; 1961b) discussion of the functions of sports and the basis of their appeal is essentially an elaboration of one of the points made by Waller (1932) in *Sociology of Teaching*. Waller's analysis of the appeal of sports is still the fullest and most perceptive attempt by a sociologist to answer the difficult question of the meaning of sports. Waller began, like Coleman, by noting the central role of athletics among youth. He said of the activities of youth within the educational system:

Of all activities athletics is the chief and most satisfying. It is the most flourishing and most revered culture pattern. It has been elaborated in more detail than any other culture pattern. Competitive athletics has many forms. At the head of the list stands football, still regarded as the most diagnostic test of the athletic prowess of any school. Then comes basketball, baseball, track, etc. (Waller, 1932, pp. 112-113).

Waller went on to consider the basis of athletic pre-eminence:

[We may also] account for the favorable influence of athletics upon school life in terms of changes effected in group alignments and the individual attitudes that go with them. It is perhaps as a means of unifying the entire school group that athletics seems most useful from the sociological point of view. There is a tendency for the school population to split up into its hostile segments of teachers and students and to be fragmented by cliques among both groups. . . . This condition [of potential conflict] athletics alleviates. Athletic games furnish a dramatic spectacle of the struggle of picked men against the common enemy, and thus is a powerful factor in building up a group spirit which includes students of all kinds and degrees and unifies the teachers and the taught (Waller, 1932, p. 115).

This notion of athletics as a device for enhancing the unity or solidarity of schools was stressed by Coleman (1960; 1961a; 1961b). For Coleman, however, it was the sole basis of athletic appeal, whereas for Waller it was only one of a variety of bases.

Coleman concluded by contrasting the predicament of studious youth with the fortunate position of athletes. It is this contrast which stimulates Coleman's recommendation to promote intellectual contests by which studious youth, too, could serve as collective embodiments of scholastic unity.

The outstanding student, by contrast, has few ways—if any—to bring glory to his school. His victories are purely personal ones, often at the expense of his classmates, who are forced to work harder to keep up with him. Small wonder that his accomplishments gain little reward, and are often met by such ridicule as "curve raiser" or "grind," terms of disapprobation having no analogues in athletics (Coleman, 1961a, p. 309).

By limiting his explanation of the appeals of sports to this single contribution, Coleman (1961a) was not driven to ask why athletics has emerged as *the* agency of school cohesion and therefore had little reason for exercising caution in commending intellectual contests as structural substitutes for football games. As soon as one considers other functions of sports and thus other bases of appeal, the case for intellectual contests is weakened and the case for the continued predominance of sports among youth is strengthened. These other functions are no more speculative, and no less, than the thesis which bases the appeal of sports on its service as a collective representation.

Many of the other possible social functions of sports are discussed by Waller (1932). Waller was able to capture some of the sense in which sports, but not intellectual contests, may exemplify masculinity, heroism, goodness, and danger and thus represent a tenable subject for drama and pageantry.

Waller stressed the contribution made by athletics in supporting an *adult-dominated* scholastic order. Athletic contests in many cases have emerged as increasingly routinized and institutionalized ways of channeling violent rivalries between towns, neighborhoods, and schools (Kittermaster, 1958, pp. 84-85; Rudolph, 1962, p. 378). Early athletic contests were frequently symbolic contests between fierce and violent rivals in which the conflict was increasingly limited by rules of the game and chosen representatives of each side. The routinization of violence in sports has never been quite complete in that there is a persistent tendency for uncontrolled violence to break through the limitations set by the rules, in the form of rough or dirty playing, and for the spectators to join the field of battle. Thus, the athletic contest may occasionally erupt into more total conflict, despite its long institutionalization. Normally, however, the official goal of civil order is well served by the routinized violence embodied in many athletic contests. The contest is still a fight in the crucial sense that physical force and prowess constitute essential elements of sports. The fight is controlled by the rules of the game—the instituted sanctions that attend flagrant violation—and, most important, by the limitation on participation to a few chosen representatives. Thus, as has been argued by some of its defenders, sports have played an important civilizing function. The peculiar and distinctive feature of sports is that it has maintained and encouraged physical force and strength while effectively controlling it.

Waller (1932) suggested the sense in which athletics have been a traditional means of social control. He also sensed the precariousness with which that purpose is served.

Competition between schools in athletics comes to a focus on games. The game is in fact disguised war. There is a continual tendency for the game to revert to actual war. . . . Everyone treats the game as a fight, and thinks of it as a fight, except perhaps the referee. It is small wonder that the political order consisting of the rules and the referee to back them, is maintained with such difficulty and only by penalities which impose the direst disabilities upon the offenders. There is, it is true, a whole code of sportsmanship which arises from the conflict situation, a code which internalizes the rules and makes for the principle of fair play (Waller, 1932, pp. 113–114).

Thus, the appeal of sports among youth is enhanced by the fact that it is a forceful contest approved and even applauded by adults and the authorities among them. Sports have been traditionally viewed by adults as a means of stylizing and thus controlling violence. Moreover, athletics, and the associated codes of sportsmanship, have frequently been taken as the playground on which subsequently useful moral precepts are learned. This function can be exaggerated and idealized, but there is some correspondence between the moral demands of adult life and the particular code of sportsmanship prevalent in youthful games. A statement of correspondence or approximation need not be a mindless celebration of sports as character-building.

Waller (1932) suggested that athletics may expedite social control in yet another important sense. Athletes are, by the social definition of their endeavor, discouraged from engaging in many excesses which are commonly associated with youthful deviance. During the athletic seasons, athletes are enjoined to be "in training"; they are to refrain from smoking, drinking, staying out late, and other forms of dissipation which violate the expectations of adult authority and are seen by many as precursors to more serious delinquency. Whether such undesired precocious activity is always controlled by the Spartan requirements of training or whether such regimen is in fact necessary is of little consequence. What is important is that the athlete guided by its stern demands symbolizes the expectations of adults regarding clean-living among youth. Simultaneously, the high position awarded athletes serves to dramatize and glamorize the rewards of avoiding disssipation and other forms of early presumption of adulthood. In this way, as in others, the athlete is doing adult's work.

Athletes may simplify the problem of police work in school. The group of athletes may . . . furnish a very useful extension of faculty-controlled social order. . . . [There is] a close correspondence between athletic prowess and clean-living (Waller, 1932, pp. 116–117).

One final service of athletics warrants mention. There has never been any discernible *substantive similarity* between scholastic preparation and occupational goals. Substantive similarity is reserved for apprenticeship systems of preparation and for the small part of our scholastic system, usually in the performing arts or in graduate education, that has maintained important elements of apprenticeship. In almost all of a modern educational system there is little visible substantive connection between studying to be something and actually being that thing. There is formal connection, both direct and indirect, but the tasks of study and preparation bear little resemblance to concrete tasks in any particular occupation. Consequently, though adults expect youth to aspire, the very meaning of aspiration, and thus its impact, is obscure to youth. An important function of athletics is to make real the conception of aspiration.

Thus, sports links aspiration to diversion. Moreover, it joins youth to the adult social order in its functions as an agency of official social control. Athletics are the handmaiden of convention despite their harboring within them the spirit of exuberance, violence, prowess, freedom, and other attributes commonly imputed to youth. Thus, they are among the best examples of the social duplicity by which control is instituted through the illusion of autonomy. The substance of athletics contains within itself—in its rules, procedures, training, and sentiments—a paradigm of adult expectations regarding youth.

Like most actors who do important work for social systems and are paid in tenuous currency which is not always forthcoming, athletes are not as impressed with their lot as outsiders are. Thus, the high standing attributed to athletic youth does not necessarily result in a subjective feeling of satisfaction and contentment. The imagery of Saturday's hero is quite common among athletic youth, and in a variety of ways they display the same minority mentality as intellectuals or any other group which exists within a pluralistic system and feels its efforts insufficiently rewarded. Like others in their position, athletes are frequently more impressed with the liabilities of their enterprise than its more celebrated perquisites. These liabilities may include the humiliations of persistent defeat, grueling and dull periods devoted to practice and drill, the limitations on free and enjoyable leisure inherent in training regulations, the anti-athletic biases of an influential and vocal minority of teachers and students—especially female—which often result in the dehumanizing stereotype of the "jock," the special fears concerning one's fortune after the typically very brief period of celebrity, and the very obvious dangers of incapacitating injury. Thus, the mood of those who main-tain the athletic style may as much approximate that emanating from the demeaning ordeal of Sisyphus as that of Olympus.

Rebellious Youth

The final style of youth is a familiar one. Youth are generally known for rebelliousness, and, if one is careful to specify the small proportion who are rebellious, it is useful and informative to describe this contingent. Youth do seem more vulnerable to rebellious posture than either children or adults (Matza, 1961; Matza & Sykes, 1961). During the life cycle, maximum rebelliousness is generally reached during youth (Almond, 1954, pp. 218–220; Bernard, 1957, pp. 421, 444; Dunham & Knauer, 1954; Ernst & Loth, 1952; Lane, 1959, pp. 216–217; McCord, McCord, & Zola, 1959, p. 21; Parkinson, 1961, pp. 277–278; Parry, 1933, p. 2). This apparently holds for three forms of rebelliousness—delinquency, radicalism, and bohemianism.

Delinquency, radicalism, and bohemianism are forms of rebelliousness which apparently have a special appeal to youth. Each is a tradition that has distinct anticivil implications. Each is in some sense a threat to the stability and order of an on-going social system, though each threatens different aspects of that system. Delinquency does not denounce bourgeois property arrangements, but it clearly violates them. Moreover, the delinquent rejects bourgeois sentiments of methodism and routine, especially as they appear within the school system, which appears to be his major target of hostility. The bohemian's attitude toward property is typically one of condescending indifference, though he is appalled by the commercialization of art that he associates with property arrangements. His ire is reserved for the puritanical and methodical elements of the bourgeois ethos, especially as they pertain to personal and social relations. Moreover, the bohemian is typically antagonistic to recent trends in bourgeois society. He is opposed to the mechanized, organized, centralized, and increasingly collectivized nature of modern society, Capitalist, Socialist, or Communist. Radicalism, by contrast, envisages a less general denunciation. Particularly in the varieties of revolutionary Marxism, which represent the most important examples of modern radicalism, the primary focus of attack has been on the Capitalist system of economic domination, on the imperialist role allegedly played by such systems, and, most recently, on the threats to world peace presumably initiated or aggravated by Capitalist nations. The methodical, the puritanical, and, especially, the industrial aspects of the bourgeois order have been more or less embraced by most radicals.

Delinquency, radicalism, and bohemianism are most pronounced during youth, but they differ with respect to the specific age of vulnerability within youth. Since the duration of youth turns on the completion of schooling and preparation rather than chronology, it is not surprising that stage of education seems a more decisive point of division than chronological age. Youth who leave school earliest seem most vulnerable to delinquency. Delinquency is primarily a high-school-age phenomenon. Radicalism and bohemianism, especially in America, can be found in institutions of higher education. Its adherents are typically drawn from those whose education terminates during college, with the attainment of a bachelor's degree, or with some graduate work of indeterminable duration. Especially susceptible are persons whose studies are concentrated in areas without a clear-cut career route and without a demanding or exact curriculum. Bohemians seem so regularly concentrated in departments of English, art, and music that one is tempted to suggest that their real rebellion is not against society-at-large, but against the faculties in the respective departments and the standards of art they profess.

The modes of rebelliousness, furthermore, differ with respect to their ambitions. Delinquents have no designs on society; there is no desire on the part of delinquents to reconstruct society. Thus they are aberrant (Merton, 1961, pp. 725-727). Radicals, on the other hand, do wish to reshape society in the form of their own ideological predilections. Thus, they are the archetype of the nonconformist (Merton, 1961, pp. 725-727). Bohemians fall somewhere between, typically wishing to develop a private and insulated way of life, but rarely having any aspiration to convert the rest of society.

Finally, the modes of youthful rebelliousness differ with respect to assessments regarding their moral worth. In the case of delinquents, the judgments seem more or less to coincide with those belonging to conventional society (Sykes & Matza, 1957). There is no serious belief in either camp in the moral worth of the delinquent enterprise. There has been, however, considerable dispute regarding the moral value of radicalism and bohemianism. Many intellectuals attribute worth to each of these enterprises, and radicals and bohemians themselves, unlike delinquents, are convinced of the moral value of their doctrines and actions.

Beyond these general similarities and differences, each mode of youthful rebellion may be described separately, remembering that it is extremely unlikely that radicals, bohemians, and delinquents taken together and defined generously constitute even 5 per cent of the youthful population.

Juvenile delinquency. There are many perceptive accounts describing the behavior of juvenile delinquents and their underlying sentiments. Perhaps no style of youth has been better covered and described (Bloch & Niederhoffer, 1958; Bordua, 1961; Cloward & Ohlin, 1960; Cohen, 1955; Cohen & Short, 1958; Finestone, 1957; Griffith, 1948; Kobrin, 1951; Miller, 1958; Shaw & Moore, 1931; Thrasher, 1936; Yablonski, 1962). Although there have been important differences of opinion in the interpretation of this material and in the relative stress placed on various components, there has been some consensus on the content of delinquent values and sentiments.

The distinctive feature of the spirit of delinquency is the celebration of prowess. Each of the themes stressed in the delinquent tradition develops an aspect of the meaning of "prowess." First, delinquents are deeply immersed in a search for excitement, thrills, or "kicks." The approved style of life is an adventurous one. Activities pervaded by displays of daring and charged with danger are highly valued. The fact that an activity involves breaking the law and, thus, an eliciting of the game of "cops and robbers" is often the element that provides the air of excitement. "Kicks" or "action" may come to be defined as "any act tabooed by 'squares' that heightens and intensifies the present moment of experience and differentiates it as much as possible from the humdrum routines of daily life" (Finestone, 1957, p. 5). In courting danger and provoking authorities, the delinquent does not simply endure hazards; he creates them in an attempt to manufacture excitement. For many delinquents, "the rhythm of life fluctuates between periods of relatively routine and repetitive activities and sought situations of greater emotional stimulation" (Miller, 1958, pp. 10–11).

Second, to attain prowess is to seek and receive the material rewards of society while avoiding, in the manner of a leisure class, the canons of school and work with their implicit commitments to methodism, routine, and security. Delinquents commonly exhibit a disdain for "getting on" in the realms of school and work. Instead, there is a sort of aimless drifting or perhaps grandiose dreams of quick success.

The delinquent must be financed if he is to attain the luxury of the sporting life. Although some writers have coupled the delinquent's disdain of work with a disdain of money, it seems unlikely that money is renounced in the delinquent code; more likely, it is treated in a special but not unprecedented way. Money is valued, but not for purposes of a careful series of expenditures or long-range objectives. Money for the delinquent is a luxury. It is something to be attained in windfall amounts

and subsequently squandered in gestures of largesse and other exhibitions of conspicuous consumption.

An age-old method of attaining such luxury income is gambling. Most of the other techniques involve victimizing others. Simple expropriation—theft and its variants—must be included, of course, but it is only one of a variety of ways of "scoring" and does not always carry great prestige in the eyes of delinquents (Finestone, 1957). Other forms of prowess include chicanery or manipulation, which may take the form of borrowing from gullible and sympathetic "squares" or more elaborate forms of hustling like exhorbitant initiation fees into otherwise defunct clubs; an emphasis on "pull," frequently with reference to obtaining a "soft" job assumed available only to persons with influential contacts; and the exploitation of females for gain.

A third theme running through the accounts of juvenile delinquency centers on aggressive masculinity. The code of the warrior, which in some ways the delinquent code reflects, calls for aggressive manliness, including reluctance to accept slights on one's honor (Margolis, 1960). The delinquent's readiness for aggression is particularly stressed in the analysis of juvenile gangs in slum areas of large cities. It is in such gangs that one finds the struggles for "turf," and, thus, it is in these cases that the applicability of the warrior code is most apparent. Cloward and Ohlin (1960) pointed out that one can be led into error by viewing conflict-oriented delinquents as typical of all delinquents. Yet the gang delinquent's use of honor, or "rep," and the proof of courage, or "heart," seems to express in extreme form the idea that aggression is a demonstration of toughness and, thus, masculinity. It is this idea which pervades delinquent thought.

Student radicalism. Relative to the many accounts of delinquency, there are few systematic descriptions of student radicalism in the United States (Iversen, 1959; Wechsler, 1953). Enough exists, however, to proceed with a tentative description of this tradition.

Radicalism among students did not begin in the decade of the thirties, although there is little question that it reached its height during that period. The Intercollegiate Socialist Society was organized in 1905, and in 1921 Calvin Coolidge decried student radicalism (Iversen, 1959, p. 13). Despite the internecine struggles within the revolutionary socialist movement since 1905, some aspects of the radical tradition have remained relatively stable.

First among the stable components is the vision of the apocalypse. This refers to "the belief that the evil world as we know it, so full of temptation and corruption, will come to an end one day and will be replaced by a purer and better world" (Shils, 1960, p. 59). This tradition has its origins in the apocalyptic outlook of the prophets of the Old Testament and has been passed down through the early Christians and adherents of heretical sects. Its modern recipients are "the modern revolutionary movements and above all the Marxian movements." The tradition is best reflected in "doctrinaire politics, or the politics of the ideal" (Shils, 1960, p. 60).

Whatever its general importance in revolutionary socialism, the politics of the ideal seems peculiarly well suited to the predispositions of youthful rebelliousness. This sort of politics seems consistent with Davis' description of youth's mixture of idealism and cynicism (Davis, 1940; Davis, 1944). In the politics of the ideal, perception and assessment become bifurcated with respect to idealism and cynicism. On this side of the apocalypse, one views and interprets events critically and cynically; on the other side, or in some contemporary foreshadowing of the future, one views and interprets events idealistically and generously.

The second component of the spirit of student radicalism is populism. "Populism is the belief in the creativity and in the superior worth of the ordinary people, of the uneducated and the unintellectual"

(Shils, 1960, p. 60). Because of the central role of populism in modern radicalism, revolutionary movements have tended to equate the apocalypse with the liberation of the folk. The particular folk has varied: In the Russian social revolutionary movement, it was the peasant; in traditional Marxism, it was the industrial proletariat; in the anarchism of Bakunin, it tended to be the *Lumpenproletariat*. American student radicalism, largely unaware of these esoteric distinctions, has tended to lump these populist ideals together in a compote consisting of migrant farm workers, unskilled and semiskilled industrial workers, and Negroes.

Among students, the appeal of populism is not simply an outgrowth of traditional radical propensities. Just as the apocalyptic mentality has a special appeal to youth, so, too, does populism. Students have a special liking for populism because it is a vehicle for an effective attack on the professional authority and a way of defending against unflattering assessment of themselves. For the radical, and bohemian, too, a belief in populism allows students who perceive themselves as avant-garde to deflect the contrary judgments of academic elders.

A third component of the student radical spirit is evangelism, which is well suited to the exuberance and impetuosity characteristic of rebellious youth. Without it, radicalism would be too serious an enterprise to compete effectively for rebellious youth. Thus, evangelism seems as important in the bolstering of internal enthusiasm as in its alleged purpose of gaining new adherents. By encouraging excursion, it allows student radicals to stray from the dull routine of the radical enterprise (Wechsler, 1953) and challenges their capacities for argumentation, intimidation, persuasion, and seduction.

The substance of student radicalism is unconventional political action. Its round-of-life consists of taking stands on concrete issues, circulation of petitions, distribution of leaflets, sale of literature, raising funds, demonstrations and rallies, frequent meetings, discussions, debates, and the like. The mundane character of most of these activities is more or less obscured by the context within which they are viewed. This context is provided by the general characteristics of unconventional politics.

Radical politics is less attentive than conventional politics to the administrative by-laws which govern collegiate activity. Thus, elements of excitement and risk are introduced. Moreover, radical politics is revolutionary rather than simply reformist. This adds meaning and drama to concrete activities and provides a basis for vicarious excitement by requiring identification with actual revolutions taking place elsewhere. Furthermore, radical politics is ideological rather than "market" (Bell, 1960) politics, and, thus, a sense of moral superiority attaches to the activities of the enterprise. Finally, radical politics is year-round rather than seasonal, and so imparts a sense of urgency rarely apparent in conventional politics. In summary, each of the characteristics of unconventional politics conspires to transform the mundane to the extraordinary.

Bohemianism. Bohemianism is a socio-artistic enterprise which appeared as a widespread phenomenon in the first part of the nineteenth century in France (Parry, 1933, p. ix). Since then it has spread to many parts of the world, but particularly to Europe and the United States. Despite indigenous sources in the United States and internal influences, the periods of rise and fall of American bohemianism have coincided fairly well with its cycles in France (Parry, 1933). "Beat," the most recent form of American bohemianism, is best viewed as a response to recurrent internal conditions, most notably postwar prosperity, as well as a reflection of developments on the French scene, especially the emergence of café existentialism.

The failure to understand the traditional character of bohemianism in selected American locales and to see its ebb and flow as a reflection of recurrent social process, internal and external, has been largely responsible for alarmist interpretations of beat. Beat has been viewed, alternatively, as a sign of incipient nihilist rebellion and a symbol of hedonistic withdrawal from public life. It has been interpreted as a symptom of some deeper malady and a dark foreboding of what is to come. Interpretations of this sort occur whenever deviant patterns are not viewed in their historical context (Sisk, 1961).

The first and major component of bohemianism is romanticism. Romanticism "starts with the appreciation of the spontaneous manifestations of the essence of concrete individuality. Hence it values originality . . . that which is produced from the 'genius' of the individual (or the folk), in contrast with the stereotyped and traditional actions of the philistine" (Shils, 1960, p. 57). The commitment to spontaneity and originality has had many manifestations among traditional bohemians, particularly in the graphic arts (Barrett, 1958; Rosenberg, 1959). Among beats, however, greater stress has been placed on development of originality and spontaneity in other art forms. Most notable among these have been the celebration of improvisation in modern jazz, poetry, and the novel. For this reason, among others, jazz and jazz musicians have occupied an exalted role in the beat realm. Kerouac, the most notable literary exponent of improvisation, has occupied a similarly exalted position (Kerouac, 1957; Kerouac, 1958a; Kerouac, 1958b).

The exaltation of spontaneity in artistic endeavor is reflected in the bohemian view of the folk. Bohemianism, like radicalism, has a distinctive form of populism, which is best termed "primitivism." Its authentic folk hero was, of course, the gypsy. Because of the gypsy's chronic unavailability, however, it was not long before the notion of primitive folk had expanded to include more available peoples. The closest approximation that could be found in urban society was the *Lumpenproletariat,* and it is this group that has occupied a central place in the bohemian's primitivist mystique (Malaquais, 1958). In the modern form of bohemianism, the idealized folk is the lower-class Negro (Mailer, 1957). The Negro, however, is not the first American ethnic group to be granted this dubious honor. East European Jews, too, have been perceived by previous bohemians as the incarnation of primitive folk (Parry, 1933, p. 35).

Closely connected to the celebration of the primitive is the tradition of dedicated poverty. "A neighborhood where the poor live, the poor who are resigned to their poverty, is the best environment in which to live 'the life.' This is a cardinal principle which the beat share with the bohemians of the past" (Lipton, 1959, p. 59). Although the dedication to poverty is, in part, a natural outgrowth of a commitment to primitivism, it is simultaneously a conscious way of avoiding the corrupting influence of the commercial world.

A final aspect of romanticism, consistent with primitivism, consists of a more or less complete rejection of bureaucratic-industrial society. This may be referred to as medievalism and is best described as an apocalyptic view without the apocalypse. Medievalism accepts the first part of the apocalyptic formula, man's fall from grace, but makes no provision, as in radicalism, for man's redemption.

The second component of the bohemian tradition is insistence on the expression of authentic inner feelings. Thus, bohemianism has been marked by an intense moodiness. Mood is not to be suppressed or obscured; rather, it is to be indulged, pursued, and exhibited. Mood is a crucial part of inner, or authentic, experience and, thus, deserves unhampered expression. Because of this dedication to the full expression of mood, bohemianism has always been somewhat perplexing to the outsider who expects some consistency of temperament to accompany a reasonably coherent viewpoint.

Bohemianism has long had two faces which, although often combined in the career of the same person, have been manifested in two roughly differentiated streams. There is frivolous bohemianism, reminiscent in many respects of aristocratic "dandyism," and there is morose bohemianism, initiated by Poe and popularized by Baudelaire (Parry, 1933, pp. 11–12). After Baudelaire, the two moods persist and are reflected in beat in the modern distinction between "hot" and "cool":

By 1948 the hipsters, or beatsters, were divided into cool and hot. . . . The cool today is your bearded laconic sage . . . before a hardly touched beer in a beatnik dive, whose speech is low and unfriendly, whose girls say nothing and wear black. "The "hot" today is the crazy talkative shining-eyed (often innocent and open-hearted) nut who runs from bar to bar, pad to pad, looking for everybody, shouting, restless, lushy, trying to "make it" with subterranean beatniks who ignore him (Kerouac, 1961, p. 73).

Thus, in the insistence on the authentic display of mood and in the development of frivolous and morose subtraditions, bohemianism has pushed to the limits of human expression. It has had a manic and a depressive character.

Even for the morose, however, the solitary life receives little authorization in the bohemian view. The unfriendly, laconic sage in Kerouac's description had, after all, "made the scene." Bohemians must have "scenes," since bohemianism has always referred to a collecting of like-minded eccentrics (Lipton, 1959; Parry, 1933; Rigney & Smith, 1961).

Monasticism, which is the formation of insulated communities of adherents, is an explicit attempt on the part of bohemians to regain the sense of community which, according to their ideology, no longer exists in the broader society. The clubs, cafés, dives, or pads, which are their monasteries, are places where the bonds of familiarity can be assumed and, except for the danger of the police interloper, one hardly need "check out" a scene before feeling secure in it. Not all persons are welcome in the places of congregation. Bohemians are not evangelists; on the contrary, the newcomer must prove in a variety of ways that he belongs (Rigney & Smith, 1961).

Bohemians have long realized that both the unauthentic (pretenders or "phonies") and the outright conventional (tourists or "squares") are greatly fascinated by the bohemian life (Rigney & Smith, 1961, p. 181). But because of their stress on authenticity, bohemians have been guarded in their relations with phonies and squares. They are also dimly aware of the fate that, sooner or later, befalls all bohemias: The persistence with which the squares and phonies discover their haunts has meant that virtually no bohemian "monastery" can long survive.

The substance of bohemianism has two important and interrelated elements. First, there is the creation of unconventional art, which may be distinguished from the conventional variety in three major ways. It is disaffiliated from the major institutions which provide the machinery for the production and distribution of art. Among these institutions are the modern university, with its direct and indirect subsidization of the arts, and the modern industries of mass communication which deal commercially in art (publishing firms) and in commercialized art (advertising). Second, stylistic innovation is characteristic of bohemian art. In each of the arts, the bohemian has been an experimenter in new styles of expression.

The third feature of unconventional art applies to its subject matter. Bohemian art has frequently dealt with the forbidden, the censorable. In his attempt to plumb the depths of human existence, the bohemian has often been guilty of confusing or equating the two meanings of "depths." This equivocation was an outgrowth of the bohemian's peculiar style of populism in which authentic life coincides with primitive life, with life as it is lived in the lowest orders of society and the underworld. His own descent into the lowest orders, resulting from his dedicated poverty, allows him to extend the province of his subject matter in an important manner. If the bohemian feared the *Lumpenproletariat* or if he discovered that their behavior was not always censorable, he could always turn to what is,

after all, the most frequent subject matter of bohemian art—bohemians.

This brings us to the second and interrelated element of the bohemian enterprise, the pursuit of unconventional personal experience. It is interrelated, because, whatever its motive among bohemians, it has persistently performed a crucial function for young, aspiring painters, poets, sculptors, and novelists. It has provided them with a subject matter to which to apply their variable talents.

In the pursuit of unconventional personal experience, there is no assurance of success. Some sorts of experience involve higher risks of failure than others—the pursuit of sexual conquest, for instance, is less likely to culminate successfully than is the use of alcohol to lessen inhibitions. Thus, a cataloguing of the forms of experience traditionally pursued by bohemians should not be mistaken for an accurate rendition of what bohemians typically do. More time seems spent in pursuit than in actual experience.

Two sorts of unconventional experience are pursued. First, there is the search for hedonistic experiences which overlap considerably with activities that are currently deemed illegal in the United States. These are generally nonvictimizing offenses and include such misdeeds as sexual excess, homosexuality, intemperate use of alcohol, disturbing the peace, use of narcotics, and speeding in automobiles. Since many of these activities held popularity among bohemians during the nineteenth century (Parry, 1933, p. 11), it should not be assumed that beats have attained new levels of hedonistic experience.

Second, there is a quest for transcendence which is closely related to the problem of creativity and represents an experimenting with the limits to which human perception may be pushed. It is as an attempt to transcend the mundane restrictions on human perception that can best be understood in three highly esoteric activities of the beats: religious mysticism as manifested in Buddhist meditation, or the "Zen kick" (Kerouac, 1958a); the flirtation with and acceptance of psychosis, or the "insanity bit" (Krim, 1960); and the hallucinogenic use of drugs (Lipton, 1959, p. 178).

CONCLUSION

The aim of this chapter has been to summarize and organize some of the accumulated sociological knowledge regarding youth by means of a description of a variety of styles of youth behavior. Many youth, of course, do not, during most of their younger years, maintain these styles in a pure form. Most youth probably engage in conventional composites, which in varying mixes blend the styles of scrupulosity, scholarship, sports, and one or another mode of rebelliousness. These blends are so varied as to defy enumeration. Moreover, there are other styles about which very little is known.

REFERENCES

Abbott, Grace. *The child and the state*. Chicago: Univer. of Chicago Press, 1938. 2 vols.

Almond, G. A. *The appeals of communism*. Princeton, N.J.: Princeton Univer. Press, 1954.

Ausubel, D. P. *Theory and problems of adolescent development*. New York: Grune & Stratton, 1954.

Barrett, W. *Irrational man*. New York: Doubleday, 1958.

Bealer, R. C., & Willits, Fern K. Rural youth: A case study in the rebelliousness of adolescents. *Ann. Amer. Acad. polit. soc. Sci.*, November, 1961, **338**, 63–69.

Becker, H. S. *Man in reciprocity*. New York: Frederick A. Praeger, 1956.

Becker, H. S. *The outsiders: Studies in the sociology of deviance*. New York: The Free Press of Glencoe, 1963.

Bell, D. *End of ideology*. Glencoe, Ill.: Free Press, 1960.

Benedict, Ruth. Continuities and discontinuities in cultural conditioning. *Psychiatry*, May, 1938, **1**, 161–167.

Berger, B. M. On the youthfulness of youth cultures. *Soc. Res.*, Autumn, 1963, **30** (3), 319–342.

Berger, B. M. Adolescence and beyond: An essay review of three books on the problems of growing up. *Soc. Probs*, Spring, 1963.

Bernard, Jessie. *Social problems at midcentury*. New York: Dryden, 1957.

Bettelheim, B. The problem of generations. *Daedalus*, Winter, 1962, 68–96.

Bloch, H., & Niederhoffer, A. *The gang*. New York: Philosophical Library, 1958.

Bordua, D. Delinquent subcultures: Sociological interpretations of gang delinquency. *Ann. Amer. Acad. polit. soc. Sci.*, November, 1961, **338**, 119–136.

Boys' Club of America. *Needs and interest study of 11, 12, and 13 year-old boys club members*, 1963.

Bronfenbrenner, U. The changing American child. In E. Ginzberg (Ed.), *Values and ideals of American youth*. New York: Columbia Univer. Press, 1961. Pp. 71–84.

Bronson, W. C., Katten, E. S., & Livson, N. Patterns of authority and affection in two generations. *J. abnor. soc. Psychol.*, 1959, **58**, 143–152.

Brossard, C. *Who walk in darkness*. New York: New Directions, 1952.

Clark, B. R., & Trow, M. Determinants of college student subculture. Unpublished manuscript, Berkeley, Center for the Study of Higher Education, 1960.

Clausen, J. A., & Williams, Judith R. Sociological correlates of child behavior. *Child Psych.*, 62nd Yearb. nat. Societ. Stud. Educ., 1963, Part I.

Cloward, R. A., & Ohlin, E. E. *Delinquency and opportunity*. Glencoe, Ill.: Free Press, 1960.

Cohen, A. K. *Delinquent boys*. Glencoe, Ill.: Free Press, 1955.

Cohen, A. K., & Short, J. F. Research in delinquent subcultures. *J. Soc. Iss.*, 1958, **14**, (3), 20–37.

Cohen, A. K., & Short, J. F. Juvenile delinquency. In R. K. Merton & R. A. Nisbet (Eds.), *Contemporary and social problems*. New York: Harcourt, 1961. Pp. 77–126.

Coleman, J. The adolescent subculture and academic achievement. *Amer. J. Sociol.*, January, 1960, **65**, 337–347.

Coleman, J. *The adolescent society*. Glencoe, Ill.: Free Press, 1961.(a)

Coleman, J. Athletics in high school. *Ann. Amer. Acad. polit. soc. Sci.*, November, 1961, **338**, 33–43.(b)

Danserau, H. K. Work and the teen-ager. *Ann. Amer. Acad. polit. soc. Sci.,* November, 1961, 338, 44–52.

Davis, A. Socialization and adolescent personality. In N. B. Henry (Ed.), *Adolescence, 43rd Yearb. nat. Societ. Stud. Educ.,* 1944. Part I.

Davis, K. Sociology of parent-youth conflict. *Amer. sociol. Rev.,* August, 1940, 5, 523–535.

Davis, K. Adolescence and the social structure. *Ann. Amer. Acad. polit. soc. Sci.,* November, 1944, 236, 8–16.

Denny, R. American youth today. *Daedalus,* Winter, 1962, 124–144.

Dunham, W. H., & Knauer, M. E. The juvenile court and its relationship to adult criminality. *Soc. Forces,* March, 1954, 32, 290–296.

Eisenstadt, S. N. *From generation to generation.* Glencoe, Ill.: Free Press, 1956.

Eisenstadt, S. N. Archetypal patterns of youth. *Daedalus,* Winter, 1962, 28–46.

Elkin, F., & Westley, W. A. The myth of adolescent culture. *Amer. sociol. Rev.,* December, 1955, 20, 680–684.

Erikson, E. *Childhood and society.* New York: Norton, 1950.

Erikson, E. Fidelity and diversity. *Daedalus,* Winter, 1962, 5–27.

Ernst, M. L., & Loth, D. *Report on the American Communist.* New York: Holt, 1952.

Feldman, G., & Gartenberg, M. *The beat generation and the angry young men.* New York: Dell, 1958.

Finestone, H. Cats, kicks, and color. *Soc. Probs,* 1957, 5, 3–13.

Friedenberg, E. *The vanishing adolescent.* Boston: Beacon, 1959.

Friedenberg, E. The image of the adolescent minority. *Dissent,* Spring, 1963, 10, 149–158.(a)

Friedenberg, E. The isolation of the adolescent. In W. C. Bier, S. J. (Ed.), *The adolescent: His search for understanding.* New York: Fordham Univer. Press, 1963. Pp. 11–20.(b)

Goodman, P. *Growing up absurd.* New York: Random, 1960.

Gorer, G. The all-American child. In B. Meltzer, H. Doby, & P. Smith (Eds.), *Education in society.* New York: Crowell, 1958. Pp. 53–58.

Grana, C. *Bourgeois and bohemia.* New York: Basic Books, in press.

Griffith, Beatrice. *American me.* Boston: Houghton, 1948.

Hess, R. D., & Goldblatt, Irene. The status of adolescents in American society. *Child Develpm.,* 1957, 28, 459–468.

Hollingshead, A. B. *Elmstown's youth.* New York: Wiley, 1949.

Iversen, R. W. *The Communists and the schools.* New York: Harcourt, 1959.

Keniston, K. Social change and youth in America. *Daedalus,* Winter, 1962, 145–171.

Kerouac, J. *On the road.* New York: Viking, 1957.

Kerouac, J. *Dharma bums.* New York: Viking, 1958. (a)

Kerouac, J. *The subterraneans.* New York: Grove, 1958. (b)

Kerouac, J. The origins of the beat generation. In T. Parkinson (Ed.), *A casebook on the beat.* New York: Crowell, 1961. Pp. 68–76.

Kittermaster, R. Sport and education. In A. Natan (Ed.), *Sport and society.* London: Bowes and Bowes, 1958. Pp. 82–88.

Knowles, J. *A separate peace.* New York: Macmillan, 1960.

Kobrin, S. The conflict of values in delinquent areas. *Amer. sociol. Rev.,* 1951, 16, 653–661.

Kohn, M. Social class and the exercise of parental authority. *Amer. sociol. Rev.,* June, 1959, 24, 352–366.

Krim, S. The insanity bit. In Krim, S. (Ed.), *The beats.* Greenwich: Fawcett, 1960. Pp. 60–77.

Lander, J. The pubertal struggle against the instincts. *Amer. J. Orthopsychiatry,* July, 1942, 12, 456–461.

Lane, R. E. *Political life.* Glencoe, Ill.: Free Press,1959.

Laqueur, W. Z. *Young Germany: A history of the German youth movement.* New York: Basic Books, 1962.

Laski, H. *American democracy.* New York: Viking, 1948.

Lemert, E. M. *Social pathology: A systematic approach to the theory of sociopathic behavior.* New York: McGraw, 1951.

Lipset, S. M. *Political man.* Garden City: Anchor, 1963.

Lipton, L. *The holy barbarians.* New York: Messner, 1959.

McClelland, D., Atkinson, J., Clark, R., & Lowell, E. *The achievement motive.* New York: Appleton-Century-Crofts, 1953.

McCord, W., McCord, Joan, & Zola, I. *Origins of crime*. New York: Columbia Univer. Press, 1959.

McIntosh, P. C. The British attitude to sport. In A. Natan (Ed.), *Sport and society*. London: Bowes and Bowes, 1958. Pp. 13–24.

Mailer, N. The white Negro. *Dissent*, Summer, 1957, 4, 276–293.

Malaquais, Jean. Critique of "White Negro." *Dissent*, Winter, 1958 5, 73–75.

Margolis, J. Juvenile delinquents: Latter-day knights. *Amer. Schol.*, Spring, 1960, 29, 211–218.

Marshall, T. H. *Citizenship and social class, and other essays*. Cambridge: Cambridge Univer. Press, 1950.

Matza, D. Subterranean traditions of youth. *Ann. Amer. Acad. polit. soc. Sci.*, November, 1961, 338, 102–118.

Matza, D., & Sykes, G. Juvenile delinquency and subterranean values. *Amer. sociol. Rev.*, October, 1961, 26, 712–719.

Merton, R. K. Social problems and sociological theory. In R. K. Merton & R. A. Nisbet (Eds.), *Contemporary social problems*. New York: Harcourt, 1961. Pp. 697–737.

Miller, W. Lower class culture as a generating milieu of gang delinquents. *J. soc. Iss.*, 1958, 14 (3), 5–19.

Moore, W. *Man, time and society*. New York: Wiley, 1963.

Muuss, R. E. *Theories of adolescence*. New York: Random House, Inc., 1962.

Naegele, K. Youth and society. *Daedalus*, Winter, 1962, 47–67.

Parkinson, T. Phenomenon or generation. In T. Parkinson (Ed.), *A casebook on the beat*. New York: Crowell, 1961. Pp. 276–290.

Parry, A. *Garrets and pretenders: A history of bohemianism in America*. New York: Covici-Friede, 1933.

Parsons, T. Age and sex in the social structure of the United States. *Amer. sociol. Rev.*, October, 1942, 7, 604–616.

Parsons, T. Youth in the context of American society. *Daedalus*, Winter, 1962, 97–123.

Powers, E., & Witmer, Helen. *An experiment in the prevention of delinquency: The Cambridge-Somerville youth study*. New York: Columbia Univer. Press, 1951.

Reiss, I. L. Sexual codes in teen-age culture. *Ann. Amer. Acad. polit. soc. Sci.*, November, 1961, 338, 53–62.

Remmers, H. H., & Radler, D. H. *The American teenager*. Indianapolis: Bobbs, 1957.

Riffel, P. A. Sex and scrupulosity. In W. C. Bier, S. J. (Ed.), *The adolescent: His search for understanding*. New York: Fordham Univer. Press, 1963. Pp. 39–51.

Rigney, F., & Smith, L. D. *The real bohemia*. New York: Basic Books, 1961.

Rosenberg, H. *The tradition of the new*. New York: Horizon, 1959.

Rudolph, R. *The American college and university*. New York: Knopf, 1962.

Sarnoff, I. *Personality dynamics and development*. New York: Wiley, 1962.

Shaw, C. R., & Moore, M. E. *The natural history of a delinquent career*. Chicago: Univer. of Chicago Press, 1931.

Shils, E. A. *The traditions of intellectuals*. In G. de Huszar (Ed.), *The intellectuals*. Glencoe, Ill.: Free Press, 1960. Pp. 55–61.

Simmel, G., The sociology of secrecy and of secret societies. *Amer. J. Sociol.*, January, 1906, 11, 441–497.

Sisk, J. P. Beatniks and tradition. In T. Parkinson (Ed.), *A casebook on the beat*. New York: Crowell, 1961. Pp. 194–200.

Smith, E. A. *American youth culture*. Glencoe, Ill.: Free Press, 1962.

Sykes, G. M., & Matza, D. Techniques of neutralization. *Amer. sociol. Rev.*, December, 1957, 22, 664–670.

Tannenbaum, A. J. *Adolescent attitudes toward academic brilliance*. New York: Teachers' College, 1962.

Thrasher, F. M. *The gang*. Chicago: Univer. of Chicago Press, 1936.

Trow, M. The second transformation of American secondary education. *Int. J. comp. Sociol.*, September, 1961, 2, 144–166.

Waller, W. *The sociology of teaching*. New York: Wiley, 1932.

Wechsler, J. A. *The age of suspicion*. New York: Random House, Inc, 1953.

Werthman, C., & Piliavin, I. Preadolescent delinquency as a relationship to authority. Unpublished manuscript, Berkeley, Center for the Study of Law and Society, 1963.

Yablonski, L. *The violent gang*. New York: Macmillan, 1962.

CHAPTER 7 Interpersonal Relations
in the
Small Group

A. PAUL HARE

Small groups have from 2 to about 20
members. Even larger groups can be considered "small" if face-to-face interaction is
possible, and collections of fewer than 20
individuals may actually contain several
smaller groups. The *social interaction* in a
small group can be seen as a function of
man's *biological nature* and *personality*, on
the one hand, and *role, culture,* and *environment,* on the other. "Environment" refers to the natural and man-made nonhuman elements which form the situation in
which the interaction occurs. Man's *biological nature* and his *environment* represent a
different order of data from the other elements of the system, since they can be measured independently of the behavior one
wishes to predict. However, the social nature of the individual and that of the group
are both abstractions from the same behavior. The individual's tendencies to behave which are consistent as he moves from
group to group are his *personality*. The set
of expectations shared by group members
associated with a position in a group, no
matter what individual fills the position,
are called *role*. The sum of the expectations
for the roles of all members of a group plus

the expectations for behavior for members
in general is the *culture* of a group This
includes patterns of behavior which are
transmitted from one generation to the next
—ways of thinking, acting, and feeling.

With this general outline of the usual
elements in an interactional system and
some notion of the definition of a small
group, we will examine the *behavior* of individuals in interaction. Some observers
focus on *inter*personal behavior, such as cooperative problem-solving. Some focus on
*intra*personal behavior, as evidenced in tension or anxiety. Still others focus on aspects
of *individual performance* which may characterize an individual whether he is alone
or in a group. In this chapter, we will be
concerned primarily with *inter*personal behavior, although other material will be included when it is relevant.

The review of the literature undertaken
in this chapter is based on the *Handbook
of Small Group Research* (Hare, 1962) and
includes additional references covering the
period 1959–1962. Since an extensive bibliography of small group research would require more pages than have been allotted
for this chapter, only a sample of the refer-

ences to research has been included, and
more attention is given to recent work and
to summaries of earlier research. Recent reviews covering much of the same material
have been written by Borgatta (1960), Homans (1961), Klein (1961), and Golembiewski (1962). A bibliography which includes
unpublished material, especially military research, has been edited by Terauds, Altman,
and McGrath (1960).

For readers who wish to sample original
material, three sets of readings contain most
of the major articles: *Readings in Social
Psychology* (Maccoby, Newcomb, & Hartley, 1958); *Group Dynamics* (Cartwright &
Zander, 1960); and *Small Groups* (Hare,
Borgatta, & Bales, 1955). The journals
which carry the more relevant articles are
the *Journal of Abnormal and Social Psychology, Sociometry,* and *Human Relations.*

For a review of methods of research, the
chapters in the *Handbook of Social Psychology,* edited by Lindzey (1954), cover
the laboratory and field methods most frequently used. Two methodological approaches which have come into prominence
since 1954 are the use of formal mathematical models, represented by Berger, Cohen, Snell, and Zelditch (1962), *Types of
Formalization in Small-Group Research,*
and the use of computers, represented by
recent journal articles especially in *Behavioral Science.*

Among the pioneering works in the small
groups field that have stimulated much of
present-day research are the following (in
alphabetical order): Asch (1955), Bales
(1955), Festinger, Schachter, and Back
(1950), Leavitt (1951), Moreno (1953),
Roethlisberger and Dickson (1939), Sherif
(1956), White and Lippitt (1960), and
Whyte (1943).

In the remainder of this chapter, the
literature on interpersonal relations in the
small group is presented in two ways: first,
by considering the central tendencies of the
interaction process and group structure and,
second, by emphasizing the deviations from
typical patterns which may result from var-

iations in such factors as leadership, communication network, and group size.

NORMS AND SOCIAL CONTROL

Support for many of the generalizations
in this section is found in the collection of
articles edited by Berg and Bass (1961),
Conformity and Deviation, which includes
reviews of research as well as new articles
by several authors active in this area. Another collection of articles covering conformity produced by mass media as well
as small group interaction is *Personality and
Persuasibility,* edited by Hovland and Janis
(1959). Other recent reviews and critiques
are De Montmollin (1958), Yarrow, Campbell, and Yarrow (1958), Hollander (1959;
1960b), Hovland (1959), Jahoda (1959),
and Willis (1961). Over the past 10 years,
there has been more research on the issue of
conformity than any other aspect of interaction in small groups.

Formation of Norms

Group members tend to form and conform to norms. Norms are rules of behavior, proper ways of acting, which have
been accepted as legitimate by members of
a group. Norms specify the kinds of behavior that are expected of group members.
These rules or standards of behavior to
which members are expected to conform
are for the most part derived from the
goals which a group has set for itself.

When the individual's norms and goals
are in accord with those of the group, his
behavior will meet approval. However, if
the individual finds that his behavior deviates from the group norms, he has four
choices: to conform, to change the norms,
to remain a deviant, or to leave the group.
Of course, he may also be removed from
the group without his consent. The literature on the formation of norms and social
control in the small group deals with the
first three types of behavior, *conformity,
change,* and *pressures on the deviant.* Cur-

rent research with leaderless groups has little to say about the choice to leave the group, since most of these experimental groups are disbanded after only a few meetings.

The Autokinetic Effect and Group Norms

Sherif (1935) uses the autokinetic effect to demonstrate the relation between individual and group norms. Each subject is placed in a dark room and asked to judge how far a dot of light which is actually stationary appears to move. Under these conditions, each subject develops a range in which he makes his estimates. When these same individuals are placed together in groups of two and three members, their judgments converge in a group standard or norm. If the subjects make their first judgments in a group, their judgments tend to converge even more rapidly. The group norm persists for the individual member when he faces the same stimulus alone at a later time.

The same experimental results have been obtained by others using slightly different experimental designs (e.g., in groups in which all responses other than that of the subject are tape-recorded) (von Cranach, 1960; Downing, 1958; Endler, 1960) and are predictable enough to be used as a classroom demonstration (Ray, 1951).

Effects of Group Opinion on Judging Line Lengths

Solomon Asch (1955) designed a study to yield objective measures of conformity of an individual's psychophysical judgments when confronted by an incorrect majority opinion.

In this experiment, several persons are instructed by the experimenter to give incorrect judgments in what is ostensibly an experiment in visual perception. The stimulus materials are two sets of white cards. In one set, each card displays a single black line (the standard). Each card of the other set bears three lines, one being the same length as the standard, the other two being perceptibly longer or shorter. The task is to match the correct line of the three with the standard.

When a subject is faced with an incorrect majority opinion, there is a significant increase in his errors, always in the direction of the majority. In this case, nearly 37 per cent of the subjects' responses are in error, as compared with almost no error in the control groups.

The subjects who yield on more than half of the critical trials are categorized by Asch into those who distort their perception, those who distort their judgment (decide they are inaccurate and the group is accurate), and those who distort their action, yielding overtly only because of a great need not to appear deviant in the group.

General Conditions Affecting Conformity

The experiments by Sherif (1935) and Asch (1955) give evidence of the general tendency to conform to norms; other types of experiments suggest the conditions which affect the extent to which a person may conform. Although all of the physical and social factors which affect any type of behavior also bear on conformity, a few factors have received most of the attention in the literature. An individual is more likely to conform to group opinion in the following cases: if the object to be judged is ambiguous; if he must make his opinion public; if the majority holding a contrary opinion is large; and if the group is especially friendly or close knit. The influence of each of these factors is subject to the individual's awareness that his opinions are deviant. If individuals make judgments and remain unaware of the judgments of others, no tendency toward conformity can be expected.

Homans (1961) has suggested that conformity can be seen as a case of the economic principle: that the individual tries to maximize his reward and minimize his cost in any transaction. Thus, the individual will conform to group opinion if the cost of deviation is high and the rewards (e.g., liking) for conformity are high or if he perceives any other combination of reward and cost which yields some profit. The individual is least likely to conform when the cost exceeds the reward.

Generalizations derived from research on conformity are organized in this section under three headings: the object about which a judgment is to be made, the subject who is making the judgment, and the situation in which the group has the primary influence.

Conformity and the object. Individuals are called upon to make judgments about two general classes of objects: those which are unambiguous, such as the length of a line or the number of dots on a card; and those which are ambiguous, such as the merit of a painting. In addition to objects that have real ambiguity, there are also objects for which there is actually an objective standard of judgment, although they are perceived as ambiguous by the subjects. Generally, the greater the ambiguity of the object, the greater the influence of other group members in determining the judgment of the subject.

The relative influence of perceived ambiguity is illustrated by a series of studies in which pairs of individuals are asked to identify the objects in drawings which become progressively more or less ambiguous as the experiment progresses. When the drawing is complete in all its details, the partner's opinion has no influence (Luchins, 1945). The same effect has been noted with other kinds of ambiguous objects. Even though the object is ambiguous or difficult to judge, subjects who are correct when there is an objective standard are less likely to be influenced by others in the group (Luchins, 1955).

When the phenomenon is actually ambiguous, the subject cannot be objectively "correct" in his judgment, but the subjects who are more certain of their judgments are, again, less likely to be influenced by other group members (Sherif & Harvey, 1952).

When the object is unambiguous, group opinion has little impact on individual judgment (Luchins & Luchins, 1956). If the subject is particularly suggestible, however, or if the situation is more coercive, as in the Asch experiment (1955), he will conform to some extent even when there is an objective standard.

Since the social value of any object is always ambiguous in the sense that it varies from group to group and is a product of group interaction, the individual is forced to compare himself with a group on many issues (Festinger, 1962; Radloff, 1961). As a result, value judgments are more subject to group pressure than factual judgments (Blau, 1960). Value judgments about behavior are of special concern for the individual where the nature of the response is relative to the deviation of the behavior from the norm, since he attempts to learn which response will follow from any given behavior so that he can predict the consequence of his act (Gerard & Rabbie, 1961; Kelley, 1955, p. 49).

Conformity and the subject. The individual brings with him into the judgment situation certain tendencies to conform or not conform which may be related to his personality, his skill or previous success with the task, and prejudgments about the phenomena which are "anchored" in some other group. An example of personality as a variable is an experiment in which 64 subjects with various combinations of two personality traits, anxiety and neuroticism, were given social approval or disapproval of their opinions in a five-to-seven-minute discussion with two role-players. All of the subjects participated more when approved. The high-neurotic subjects were more rigid in holding their opinions when under disapproval, especially when they were also high-anxious (Cervin, 1955a; Cervin, 1956).

No differences in behavior between emotionally stable and unstable subjects were observed, however, in a similar situation when the subjects were praised rather than subjected to disapproval (Cervin, 1955b).

A similar relationship between nonconformity and high neuroticism was found in a hospital study in which neurotic patients from a psychiatric ward conformed less in an experiment using autokinetic effect than did patients from the medical wards (Levine, Laffal, Berkowitz, Lindemann, & Drevdahl, 1954).

Some studies report that subjects who receive high scores on the F Scale of "authoritarianism" conform more than low "F" subjects (Katz & Benjamin, 1960; Nadler, 1959). (Since the publication of the F Scale, a number of authors have questioned whether the Scale actually measures authoritarianism, conformity, or some type of response set. Recent articles in this series are by Gage and Chatterjee [1960], Small and Campbell [1960], Couch and Kenniston [1961], Edwards and Walker [1961a; 1961b], and Taylor [1961a; 1961b]. Some of the same criticisms have been made about other personality scales of the same type.) Whatever the device for measuring conformity, however, whether it be a paper-and-pencil test as in the case of the F Scale, a measure of conventionality derived by comparison of a subject with the mean response of his group, or a test of the Asch type, subjects who conform in one situation are likely to conform in another.

Other related characteristics of conforming individuals appear to be a high need to be approved by others, a low need to be outstanding as an individual, and a feeling that parental figures are harsh, punitive, restrictive, and rejecting. Sex also appears to be a factor, since women are found to yield more to a bogus group norm than men (Tuddenham, 1961). Younger subjects also tend to yield more (Di Vesta & Cox, 1960) unless they are very young children who are hardly aware of the social pressure to conform (Hunt & Synnerdahl, 1959).

The fact that self-confident subjects will resist pressures to conform (Di Vesta, 1959) has already been indicated in the discussion of the effects of the ambiguity of the stimulus. Self-confidence can result from skills which the subject brings with him, or it can be built up experimentally by allowing the subject to experience success in a series of individual trials before he is placed in a group (Gerard, 1961a).

An individual may also be a nonconformist in one group if his opinions are well "anchored" in another group. The family, for example, is one of the principal reference groups for many subjects (Rosen, 1955b). The general tendency for individuals to have particular reference groups in mind is usually discussed in relation to large aggregates such as religious groups, political parties, or nations (Hovland, Janis, & Kelley, 1953). In small group studies in which individuals' opinions have first been anchored in a reference group, however, a similar effect is observed (Blake & Mouton, 1961a).

A reference for opinion need not be a whole group, it may be a single person whose opinion is highly valued. The presence of a highly valued person within a group makes group members appear to agree with each other, when in fact the members are similar only in that they agree with the central person. When that person's opinion shifts, all other opinions also shift.

Conformity and the situation. The aspects of the situation relevant to conformity are those which have to do with the subject's "commitment" to the group. The subject is more apt to conform if his alternative is to go on record as a deviant in a group to which he is highly attracted and whose influential members disagree with him (Festinger & Aronson, 1960).

Opinions given in public are often different from those expressed in private. Generally, the views that are expressed in public or that may possibly be made public are more conforming (Gerard, 1961b; Raven, 1959; Smith, 1959), although this is not always the case, since the first persons to vote publicly are often the ones who are the most confident of their opinions (Carment, 1961). Some of the early responders will influence later responses. In such a case, the opinions of the first to answer will turn out to represent majority opinion because they had a part in the formation of the majority (Shaw, 1961). Other individuals who are equally confident of their opinions will turn out to be deviants.

Whether he conforms or is deviant, if a person expresses his opinion (or intended course of action) publicly, he is more likely to follow up the opinion with appropriate behavior than if the opinion is given privately, especially if the group restraints against giving an opinion are high (Schachter & Hall, 1952).

Festinger and others have developed a "theory of cognitive dissonance" which applies to the small group as well as to instances of mass persuasion (Brehm & Cohen, 1962; Cohen, Brehm, & Latane, 1959; Festinger, 1962; Festinger & Carlsmith, 1959; Zajonc, 1962; Zimbardo, 1960). They found that, although the subject does change his private opinion to conform to his public opinion, the more he is forced to change his opinion in public, the less likely he is to change privately. For example, if a subject is paid $20 for saying that an unenjoyable task is enjoyable, he will have less reason subsequently to like the task than does a subject paid only $1. The first subject can afford to maintain his private opinion, since the amount of pay he receives is not "dissonant" with the idea that the task is really quite unenjoyable. The second subject, however, is moved to feel that the task cannot have been too bad in the first place since he accepts such a relatively small amount of money to make a contrary public statement.

In work groups or living groups, members who are highly attracted to the group either for its prestige, its productivity, or the friendship of its members conform more to the standards of the group than do members who place a low value on these criteria (Festinger, Schachter, & Back, 1950).

The attraction to the group may be increased if members first have to undergo a severe initiation.

In a panel study of 2,500 ninth and tenth grade students from 15 high school groups, the students who were chosen as "liked" were more often conforming in their behavior than those who were disliked. The authors suggest that the high-status members may be surrounded by conformity-approving relationships (with those who like them) and deviance-disapproving relationships (with those who dislike them). These networks may be more effective for social control than the networks of low-status members which tend to be made up exclusively of deviance-disapproving relationships (Riley & Cohn, 1958). In some ad hoc experimental groups, however, the amount of convergence on a norm (such as the number of dots in a square) may not be correlated with the amount of liking of the members for the group (Bovard, 1953) or of the group for a particular member (Dittes & Kelley, 1956).

The relation between friendship and conformity is evident in the Relay Assembly Test Room study which was part of the Western Electric Researches (Roethlisberger & Dickson, 1939). Over a five-year period, high correlations between the fluctuations of the output rates of several of the girls began to appear in the data, especially between girls who were friends and sat next to each other. Although this group had only five members, it does illustrate the point that behavior, in this case the output of relay assemblies, may be highly correlated with the norms of some subgroup, here the pair, whatever may be its relation to the norms of the group as a whole. This effect is also evident in gangs of boys, which would be rated as highly cohesive subgroups of a larger society from whose norms they consciously deviate (Sherif & Cantril, 1947).

The size of the majority whose opinions oppose those of the individual member is directly related to the amount of influence on his opinion (Asch, 1955). In some experiments, subjects are found to be more anxious, as measured by their galvanic skin response, when disagreeing with the majority (Smith, 1936).

Having even one person support the subject increases the number of times he will hold out against a majority (Asch, 1955). The support will be especially effective if it comes from the leader or a high-prestige person. As group size increases, there is an increase in the number of opportunities to form subgroup coalitions representing minority opinions.

Most of the studies on the influence of group norms on individual judgment deal only with the results of the subject's internal struggle to reconcile his own opinion with the weight of the contrary opinion. If one wishes to maximize conformity, he must add direct appeals to change opinion and coercion to the types of "pressures toward uniformity" discussed up to this point. The influence of the direct appeal will be discussed in a section on changing the norms, but the effects of coercion are not treated in detail, since everyday examples of police and military action give evidence of its effectiveness.

The influence of "majority" opinion, of course, extends beyond the small face-to-face group. In a number of early studies (e.g., Dashiell, 1935), individuals were given information about the majority opinions of such large groups as the student body of a high school or a college, or all adults in general. In all of these studies, his information led to shifts in the direction of greater conformity with indicated majority opinion.

The size of the majority is related to the amount of influence on a subject only if the members of the majority have equal or higher status than the subject. If a minority or a subgroup of equal size has high status through power, popularity, or expert knowledge, the minority view will prevail. Subjects who are aware of the opinions of a person with high power, such as a teacher in a classroom of students, will limit the range of their opinions and conform more to the opinions of the high-status person.

A member who is an expert, either because he has demonstrated his skill in the past or because he appears at the moment to have the ability to make correct decisions, will have more influence than one who is not as successful. The expert tends to have more influence in the absence of any apparent homogeneity of opinion in the group and under conditions which allow him to defend his position with rational arguments.

Leaders Also Conform

Group leaders, who would be expected to have the greatest power to bring about a change in the group norms, also find it difficult to resist the influence of the norms once they are established (Harvey, 1960). Sherif (1935) noted that, in cases where one person took the initiative in an initially leaderless group, the group norm which was then established would reflect his judgment. But if the same member changed his individual norm after the group norm was established, he was no longer followed. Further evidence for this hypothesis is found in a study of nursery school children (Merei, 1949).

We see, then, that group leaders conform to the norms, but for reasons different from those of the followers. Where the follower may conform because he is coerced by majority opinion, the leader's opinion may be close to that of the group because he played a major part in the formation of group opinion. Since the leader's influence on the group is usually measured by the number of members who agree with his opinion, it is often difficult to tell whether he is the most "conforming" or the most "influential." On the other hand, the leader may be accorded more freedom to deviate from the norms than are other members who are less secure of their status in the group. Leaders, as well as others who appear to conform, are often the most popular members of the group.

Norms of the Primary Group

Some indication of the relative influence of the norms of a small primary group, such as a family or peer group, and of a large secondary group, such as a religious or occupational group, has already been given in the discussion of the anchorage of opinions in reference groups. In general, the norms of the primary group are more important for the individual than those of the secondary group (Baur, 1960).

Disasters which affect a whole community, such as floods and tornadoes, bring out ordinarily latent conflicts between loyalties to primary and secondary groups. Under disaster conditions, the loyalty to the primary group is usually the most demanding, but, if a person is trained as a disaster worker or is responsible for the work of a large organization, he may stay by his post (Killian, 1952).

In another example, the food preferences of a sample of urban children were found to be closer to those of their small peer groups than to the larger religious organization which specified certain food taboos (Rosen, 1955a).

Conflicts in group norms have been most apparent over the years in industry, where the systematic attempts on the part of management to overcome "soldiering" or "goldbricking" among the workers go back at least to Taylor's first efforts at "Scientific Management," when he persuaded men in a steel mill to shovel coal from coal cars individually rather than in groups. Once freed from the influence of a group norm, his workers were able to earn 60 per cent more wages and were no more fatigued than when working under the old pace (Taylor, 1903). This same tendency for the informal group to depress the output rate has been noted in the Western Electric Researches (Roethlisberger & Dickson, 1939) and in other industrial studies. Similar findings have been duplicated in the laboratory, where highly cohesive groups produce substantially less than those with lower co-hesiveness, when the group standard is for lower production (Schachter, Ellerton, McBride, & Gregory, 1951; Seashore, 1954).

The norms of the primary group are not always in conflict with those of the secondary group. They may provide informal social control which is more effective than the formal control of the larger organization in fulfilling the goal of the organization (Gross, 1953). Several examples of this come from experiences in armies during World War II where soldiers in both the American army and the German *Wehrmacht* derived their motivation to fight from their loyalty to their military primary group rather than from their acceptance of strategic or political goals (Shils, 1950; Shils & Janowitz, 1948). The success in ending segregation in the American armed services during the same war has also been attributed to the fact that Negroes became comembers of primary groups with white soldiers and thus shared common loyalties (Mandelbaum, 1952).

To follow-up the war experience, the hypothesis that primary group affiliation is related to institutional group morale was tested with a sample of students from a large university. In this instance, the number and strength of the ties in a friendship group did not appear to be related to "institutional morale," as measured by the extent of the desire to remain in college if the subject was not doing well academically (Zentner, 1955).

Pressures on the Deviant

Since individuals generally perceive their opinions as being closer to group norms than they actually are, the deviant, who tends to be marginal to the group and less informed about group decisions, may not be aware of the norms or of the extent of his deviation. Under these conditions, his own attempts at self-control may not bring him close enough to the group standard to satisfy the other group members. Whether or not the deviant is aware of his behavior, the group members cannot tolerate deviation without being forced to re-examine their concept of reality (Festinger, 1954). As a result they make overt attempts to secure the conformity of the deviant.

Interaction with the deviant increases when the group first recognizes his deviancy, but falls off if he begins to conform or if other members think that he is a lost cause (Berkowitz & Howard, 1959; Schachter, 1951). In one study of high school students in clubs, the amount of pressure on the deviant was also related to the attractiveness of the club for the other members. The higher the club was rated by its members, the greater was the pressure exerted toward the deviant (Emerson, 1954). Rejection of the deviant appears to be an almost universal phenomenon, as indicated by experimental evidence from a number of different cultures (Israel, 1956; Schachter et al., 1954). However, an exception is found in a study which was made in England; there the presence of the deviate, persisting quietly and unaggressively with his own choice, seems to have reinforced the strength of other individual opinions. Other group members appeared to reason, "If he won't give up his choice, why should I?" (De Monchaux & Shimmin, 1955). In addition to punitive control of the deviant, the group exerts positive control by giving more support to the opinions of well-liked members (Horowitz, Lyons, & Perlmutter, 1951). (Hollander [1958; 1960a] suggested that each group member has a certain amount of "idiosyncracy credit" and that a member will deviate from the group norm to the extent that he is allowed to do so.)

Changing the Norms

Since norms are formed through group interaction, they can also be changed through group interaction. Although some patterns of behavior, such as fads of dress, speech, and mannerisms, change through contagion, a group discussion is generally found to result in more change than other forms of persuasion, such as lectures or directives.

Examples of behavior change are found in the "action research" of Lewin (1947) and his colleagues during World War II. They were seeking the best way to convince housewives to buy low priority foods which they were not accustomed to eating. Lewin brought together key persons or "gate-keepers" who exert the major influence on some small group to which they belong. In the case of food habits, the housewife is the "gate-keeper" who exerts the major influence on the family diet. More housewives changed their behavior and attitudes about various types of foods after participating in a group discussion than after hearing a lecture on the value of eating these same new foods. Once the new group standard had been formed through group discussion, it was easier for the housewives to change their behavior to conform to the new standard.

Additional studies report similar changes in pattern over a wide range of behavior (Cartwright, 1951): Community problems are solved, alcoholics cured, productivity raised, group skills improved, student attitudes changed, and personality patterns changed.

When discussion groups are compared for effectiveness in bringing about change in opinion, the groups in which the opportunities for discussion are maximized are found to be the most effective. The amount of participation is usually controlled through some "democratic" leader who urges all members to take part in the discussion (Hare, 1953; Preston & Heintz, 1949). The discussion leader tends to have more success in changing opinions if he is the "natural" group leader rather than a leader, such as an instructor, who has joined the group only for this purpose.

The evidence indicates that the important element in changing norms is less the provision of an opportunity to discuss the problem than it is the action of the discussion in the breaking down of the old value system before the adoption of a new one, an emotional as well as an intellectual process. In the process of change, group members tend to show the greatest resistance to change just before they yield to the new set of values. An intensified version of this technique of breaking down old values was developed in China after the Korean War as part of the Chinese political re-education program (Biderman, 1959; Lifton, 1961; Schein, 1960; Schein, Schneier, & Barker, 1961).

If, however, the change of "opinion" involves only learning new information without changing commitment from an old to a new norm, then information from an expert, teacher, or book may be as effective as group discussion.

INTERACTION AND DECISION PROCESS

In the research on the interaction and decision process in small groups, the major emphasis has been on the problem the group faces in establishing an equilibrium between the time spent on the task and the time spent on the social-emotional problems of maintaining the group structure. In connection with this research, a number of investigators have developed category systems or methods of content analysis which make it possible to break the interaction process into small units and to assign each unit to one of the categories. A category system may have as few as two categories, such as action and silence (Chapple, 1942) or it may have over one hundred categories (Ruesch & Prestwood, 1950). Some systems record only one type of verbal content, such as personal pronouns (Conrad & Conrad, 1956), while others are used to score words, gestures, and any form of body activity which indicates the individual's mental state (Leary, 1957).

The category system developed by Bales (1950) is one of the most commonly used methods of coding interaction. Bales takes as his unit act a bit of behavior (usually verbal) which can provide enough of a stimulus to elicit a meaningful response from another person. In practice this is usually a sentence. Each sentence or comparable act is given a score to indicate the type of task behavior or social-emotional behavior which appears to the observer to dominate the act. There are 12 categories in all. The first three categories, "shows solidarity," "shows tension release," and "shows agreement," are classified as positive reactions. These coupled with the three negative reactions, "shows disagreement," "shows tension," and "shows antagonism," constitute social-emotional behavior. The six categories describing task behavior are also grouped in sets of three. "Gives suggestion," "gives opinion," and "gives information" are problem-solving attempts and "asks for information," "asks for opinion," and "asks for suggestion" are questions.

An analysis of the typical actions and reactions in a small discussion group (Bales, 1955; Psathas, 1960) shows that about half (56 per cent) of the acts during a group session are problem-solving attempts, and the remaining 44 per cent are positive reactions, negative reactions, and questions. In this two-sided process, the reactions act as a constant feedback on the acceptability of the problem-solving attempts.

A speaker's first remark is likely to be a reaction, and, if he continues speaking, the probability is very high that his second act will be a problem-solving attempt.

Positive reactions outnumber negative reactions two to one. This indicates that the members share a common definition of the situation and can make problem-solving attempts which will be in line with the group's goals most of the time.

Although an action is usually followed immediately by the "appropriate" reaction, the reaction may be stored (remembered) and appear at a later time either in its original form or perhaps in a disguised form (Thibaut & Coules, 1952).

Group Differences in Task and Social-Emotional Activity

In groups of long standing, the style of the leaders, the social class of the members, the personalities of the members, or other factors may produce characteristic differences between groups in their patterns of task and social-emotional activity. For instance, "democratic" leaders, who act positively toward their group members and set a standard for cooperative activity between members, tend to receive positive reactions, and "authoritarian" leaders provoke negative reactions and intermember hostility (White & Lippitt, 1960).

Social class influence is shown in a study of 10 adolescent clubs, 5 with members from the lower class and 5 with members from the middle class. The lower-class members were more aggressive with each other and collaborated more with the adult leader; the middle-class members directed more collaborative and aggressive acts to the club president, a peer (Maas, 1954).

Group differences which result from the personalities of members are best illustrated by studies which contrast groups of mental patients where extremes of activity in the task area (compulsiveness) and the social-emotional area (hysteria) as well as extremes of inactivity (withdrawal) have been observed (Roberts & Strodtbeck, 1953). Similarly, subjects whose emotional balance has been changed through the use of drugs or alcohol will have a different pattern of social-emotional activity (Bruun, 1959; Lanzetta, Wendt, Langham, & Haefner, 1956; Lennard, Jarvik, & Abramson, 1956; Takala, Phikanen, & Markkanen, 1957).

It is also possible to alter the characteristic pattern of task or social-emotional activity by stimulating one category of act. For this purpose, less extensive methods than changing the leadership style of the group composition can be used. For example, paired subjects increase their rate of giving opinion when the experimenter reinforces their opinions by repetition or agreement (Verplanck, 1955).

Norms are established within groups which tend to regulate the frequency and duration of member interaction and the channels through which communications are allowed to travel. The principal content category associated with a high interaction rate varies from group to group and over time within the same group, depending upon the problem the group faces at the moment.

Individual Interaction Characteristics

Perhaps the most consistent finding in all of the research on social interaction is that individuals differ in their rates of interaction. The person who initiates the most action tends to receive more than anyone else and to address more of his remarks to the group as a whole than to specific individuals (Bales, Strodtbeck, Mills, & Roseborough, 1951; Stephan & Mishler, 1952). In a series of studies, Matarazzo and Saslow (1961) and others have shown that different personality types have typical patterns of action and silence.

Since relative rate and direction of interaction are such basic dimensions of individual and group activity, they are perhaps the first things to be affected by any changes in the group. As the size of the group is increased from 3 to 12 members, the differences between the relative interaction rates of members tend to disappear, while the difference between the leader and the average member becomes more apparent (Bales et al., 1951; Stephan & Mishler, 1952). The rate of interaction for any one member is inversely related to the rates of the other members composing the group and directly related to the freedom to participate allowed by the communication net. An individual's communication rate can be increased by removing the high interactors from the group (Knutson, 1960; Stephan & Mishler, 1952), by having the leader encourage participation (Bovard, 1951), or by placing him in a favorable position in the communication net, which may mean simply having him sit at the head of the table (Strodtbeck & Hook, 1961).

Previous experience and training can also affect the participation rate of the group member. In a therapeutic setting, therapists who had been psychoanalyzed were found to be more active with their patients than therapists who had not been psychoanalyzed (Strupp, 1955c).

Both the form and content of an individual's interaction pattern are predetermined in part by his role and his personality. Therapists who had been trained to be "nondirective" were found to "reflect" more of the patient's statements and to show less inclination to set therapeutic goals than were analytically oriented therapists (Strupp, 1955a; Strupp, 1958). In a similar comparison of social workers with psychiatrists, the social workers were found to reassure the patients more; whereas inexperienced psychiatrists explored more of the patient's problems but did not interpret as much. In both professions, however, differences in content which were related to level of training were greater than differences between professions (Strupp, 1955b). The inexperienced therapists who were less certain of their role tended to be more limited in their range of behavior.

Some indication of the effect of personality type on interaction content is evident in a study of the content of a problem-solving discussion held by six pairs of men. The subjects judged to be "emotionally mature" made more statements which had mutual satisfaction as their aim, while the immature subjects made more statements for self-gratification (Lichtenberg, 1955).

Phase Movement in Discussion

The balance between task and social-emotional activity maintains itself during the entire meeting. When problem-solving discussion meetings are divided into three time-periods, however, the predominant type of activity shifts from one phase to another in a manner which reflects the stages in the group's progress toward a decision (Bales & Strodtbeck, 1951). The rate of acts of information decreases steadily from initial to final phase, and the rate of acts of suggestion rises. Acts of opinion increase in the middle phase and then fall off again. Both positive and negative reactions increase in rate from the initial to the final phase, the positive reactions increasing more rapidly in the final phase. In phase one, the group members are collecting information; in phase two, evaluating the information; and in phase three, pressing for a decision with a concomitant increase in support of some members and rejection of others.

The increase in positive and negative reactions may be connected mainly with the social-emotional problems of the group process. Since the ratio of negative to positive reactions tends to be higher in response to suggestions than to factual statements, the decision point is the critical event of the process. Once the decision point has been passed, the rates of negative reaction usually fall off and the rates of positive reaction rise sharply. Joking and laughter, indicating solidarity and tension release, become more frequent. Having settled the problems of the task for the time being by the decision, the group apparently turns its attention to the emotional states of the individuals and their social relationships.

The nature and duration of the phases of discussion are directly related to the task of the group; an example is provided by a study of therapy groups in which the Bales categories for interaction process analysis were used (Talland, 1955). In these groups, the phases described above did not appear nor was there any tendency to establish equilibrium, since the group did not have to reach a decision and the therapist's job was to keep the level of emotional involvement sufficiently high so that the patients would talk about their problems.

As the phases change in an initially leaderless group, the persons who play the roles of leaders and followers may change, if some persons have greater skill in one type of activity or find the emotional climate which accompanies a particular phase more compatible with their personalities.

Meeting-to-meeting trends. In addition to shifts or phase movements in activity within a single meeting, patterns of activity in groups also change from meeting to meeting.[1] In a series of four meetings, members of one set of initially leaderless groups gradually spent less time in task behavior and more time in positive social-emotional behavior as the series progressed from the first to last meeting. Negative social-emotional behavior rose briefly in the second meeting during the "status struggle" in which the hierarchy was established (Heinicke & Bales, 1953). Phase movements similar to these have also been noted in discussion groups over a longer series of meetings (Philp & Dunphy, 1959; Theodorson, 1953).

If the members of the group take part in a series of meetings, each of which has a different set of group members, the effect is the same as if the group is meeting for the first time. Although the task and other aspects of the situation remain the same, the individuals must take time to get to know the other group members at the beginning of each meeting. Group structure is not given an opportunity to develop, and the status struggle usually reflected in the interaction pattern of the second meeting does not take place (Borgatta & Bales, 1953).

Phase movement and trends in psychotherapy. A modification of the Bales categories was used in an analysis of communication between psychotherapists and their patients (Lennard, Bernstein, Hendin, & Palmore, 1960). A major theme throughout the study was the analysis of the process through which the patient learns his patient role with the possibility of later transferring what he has learned about role patterns in

therapy to other significant role relationships. The "socialization" of the patient in his role appeared to be more of a conscious effort at the beginning of the therapy. As therapy progressed the amount of discussion about therapy itself and about the reciprocal therapist-patient roles tended to decrease. There was a similar decrease within each session. At the same time, there was an increase in the amount of communication about affect as the patient learned to put his thoughts and feelings into words. The therapist and patient established rather stable "norms" for their interaction rate, with the patient talking most of the time. In a given hour, however, if the patient talked less, the therapist talked more. When patient and therapist differed initially in their expectations about the activity of the therapist, the therapist spent more time in the socialization process.

The Equilibrium Problem

The status struggle that takes place in the second session of the laboratory groups leaves less time and energy available to group members for performance of the task (Shaw, 1959). In industry, for example, the most productive teams were found to spend less time on "within"-team interaction (Horsfall & Arensberg, 1949). When carpenters and bricklayers who were accustomed to being assigned to work teams each day by their foremen were given a chance to choose the men they would prefer to work with, they showed marked differences in performance when compared with teams composed in the usual way (Van Zelst, 1952). In the groups of "buddies," job satisfaction increased, labor and material costs dropped, and labor turnover decreased practically to zero. These effects presumably occurred because the "buddies" did not have to spend as much time in the solution of status problems.

This tendency of the group to swing back and forth between attempts to complete the task and attempts to maintain the group

---

[1] A theory of group development is given by Bennis and Shepard (1956) and Shepard and Bennis (1956).

and to satisfy the needs of its members has been identified by Bales as the equilibrium problem (Bales, 1953). Pendulum-like swings in activity occur as members become more absorbed in the task, neglecting individual member needs, and then lose sight of the task, turning their attention to group solidarity.

As noted in the industrial studies, the time spent on the task can be increased by selecting members who have similar feelings about the criteria for establishing group structure and therefore spend less time on the "status struggle." Since persons choose as friends others with a similar personality type or basic orientation, the sociometric test in which individuals are asked to choose others whom they would like as teammates is in a sense an indirect way of selecting compatible personality types. If one knew enough about the types of personalities which would get along together, one could eliminate the question of liking and simply put persons of appropriate types in the same group with the expectation that productivity would increase. This has been done successfully with naval recruits and college students, at least on the personality dimension of affection or "personalness" (Schutz, 1958). When subjects who preferred close intimate relations with others (as a personality characteristic) were placed in a group and given a series of tasks, they were more productive than mixed groups composed of some subjects who liked close intimate relations and some who wanted to keep others at a distance.

The Initial Phase of the Act

The remaining pages of this section give a more detailed analysis of research on the initial phase of the social act. This includes a description of the individual's perceptions of himself and others, and the part these perceptions play in the imagined interaction between self and others through which the individual pretests his behavior.

Before the individual acts, he first imagines himself carrying out the act and then imagines the response of another person to his action. If the imagined response is not favorable, he will modify his intended action before actually carrying it out. In either event, the actual behavior of the other person serves as a check on his perceptions. The perceptions of the "self" and "other person" are then modified to correspond to the new evidence presented by actual behavior.

Group members are generally aware of their behavior and of the effect that it is having on other group members (Crowell, Katcher, & Miyamoto, 1955). Behavior is apt to be least self-conscious in a small group in which the individual is highly involved (Goffman, 1957) and most self-conscious in larger groups which provide some time for reflection between acts.

First impressions. Although the perception of another person usually changes as new information is gathered about him, one's first impression of a person may color all subsequent information. An example of the influence of first impressions is found in the research on group "cohesiveness" (Schacter et al., 1951) in which subjects were told that they were either (1) similar to each other in interests and personality, and would get along well together, or (2) mismatched, and would probably not do very well together. After a short period of interaction during which the subjects solved some problems together, the subjects who had been told that they would like each other reported that they did like each other better than those who had been told that they would not be attracted to each other.

The group basis of perception. Individuals are continually making observations. The perceptions which remain the same over a long period of time are here called attitudes. The concept of attitude has been used historically in a number of different ways, and the present definition is only one among several current meanings (Allport, 1954). The attitudes which are transmitted from one generation to the next play a major role in defining the categories in which persons will be socially perceived. The individual's perception, at any given time, is a function of the attitudes of the society transmitted in culture, the more transient perceptions of other members of the small group involved in the action of the moment, and an idiosyncratic component which results from the personality of the perceiver and the perceived and other unique situational factors. The fundamental part of the individual's perceptual base is, however, in his assessment of the perceptions of his group (Cartwright, 1952; Zander, 1958). Although the influence of the group on individual judgment has already been discussed, some further indication of the influence of the group on judgments of the self and others will be given here.

The self-concepts of men living in a dormitory in four-man living units have been found to be influenced by others' perceptions of them over a period of months of living together (Manis, 1955). In another study, the ways in which individuals rated themselves on 4 personality traits in 10 college classroom and fraternity groups of 8 to 48 persons were analyzed. The subjects' self-perceptions were compared with the actual feelings of others in the group about these traits, with their perceptions of others' attitudes, and with their perception of the attitudes of the members of most groups or a generalized other. The self-perceptions were found to be related to the actual attitudes of others in the group. The self-perceptions were even more related to the subjects' perceptions of others' attitudes, however, and most closely related to the subjects' estimates of the generalized attitude (Miyamoto & Dornbush, 1956).

The group's perception of an individual has more influence on his self-perception when he is highly attracted to the group and when the other group members place a high value on his participation (Festinger, Torrey, & Willerman, 1954; Stotland, Thorley, Thomas, Cohen, & Zander, 1957). Under these conditions, the individual pays more attention to the opinions of the group, and the group members in turn are more explicit in their valuation of the individual.

The group basis of the perception of others is also evident in the research on attitudes toward different classifications of people. The concept of stereotype refers to the group prejudgment of a class of persons which so colors the "first impression" that the individual characteristics which do not fit the stereotype are suppressed (Cronbach, 1955).

Perceptual accuracy. Individuals differ in ability to perceive accurately the characteristics of others. Some of the factors relevant to this differential perception are found in the age, sex, and personality of the perceiver, in the characteristics of the perceived, and in the content area in which the predictions are to be made (Steiner, 1959).

To measure the ability to perceive accurately, one must first rule out the accuracy which could be expected if only chance factors were operating and then, since the subject may project his own values on the other person, one must rule out the apparent accuracy which results only from the fact that the subject and the object are similar (Gage & Cronbach, 1955). Other difficulties in dealing with data on social perception are a variety of technical problems which can occur in the collection and analysis of data which make this type of analysis "a breeding ground for artifacts" (Cronbach, 1958).

Perceptual accuracy apparently increases with age, at least among children, since eleven-year-olds show greater perceptive ability than seven-year-olds (Dymond, Hughes, & Raabe, 1952). Sex is also a factor, since the general notion in the folklore that women are more intuitive (perceptive) than men is borne out by some experimental results (Exline, 1960a).

When the relationship between empathic ability and personality is explored through direct and projective tests, high-empathy persons appear to be outgoing, optimistic, warm, emotionally secure, and interested in others. Low empathy is associated with rigidity, introversion, emotionality, self-centeredness, and interpersonal incompetence (Chance, 1958; Dymond, 1949; Dymond, 1950).

Further evidence of the relationship between personality and perception comes from a series of experiments with college-age subjects who were classified on the single personality dimension of authoritarianism. In one experiment, those rated high authoritarians on a personality test were paired with low authoritarians for a twenty-minute general discussion. In a second experiment, high authoritarians were paired with high, and low with low. After the discussion, the high authoritarians rated their partners as high on authoritarianism whether they were high or low; whereas the low authoritarians thought all their partners were either middle or high. Apparently, the highs thought that everyone was just as high as they were; whereas the lows thought that no one could be as low as they (Crockett & Meidinger, 1956). High authoritarians were even found to rate a "stimulus person" as high without any intervening interaction (Kates, 1959). This finding suggests that twenty minutes of interaction did little to alter the highs' original perception that most people are authoritarian.

Some other distortions of perception related to personality factors result from being overanxious to see others' behavior as related to a particular goal the individuals may have or from being unwilling to accept indications of hostility from another person who may be thwarting the goal (Pepitone, 1950). There are also general tendencies in individuals either to overestimate or underestimate the position of themselves or others in the hierarchies based on interpersonal choice (Schiff, 1954).

If individuals have similar feelings for each other their perceptions will tend to be more accurate because otherwise they may mask their feelings to avoid conflict (Tagiuri, Bruner, & Blake, 1958). An individual may also attempt to mask his feelings if he does not trust another group member (Mellinger, 1956).

Perception of friends. In general, if one subject likes another, he tends to think that his liking is returned; and if he likes two other subjects, he will perceive them as liking each other (Kogan & Tagiuri, 1958). (Also, if a person dislikes something about himself, he will tend to dislike others who appear to like what he dislikes [Deutsch & Solomon, 1959]. These generalizations are consistent with Heider's theory of "structural balance" [Davol, 1959].)

Group members who have many friends in the group are generally more accurate in their perception of the informal group structure and of the characteristics of others in the group than are individuals who are relatively isolated. Accuracy of perception of the informal hierarchies on the part of well-liked members of the group may result from the fact that, when friendship choices are openly reciprocated, the place of the self in a hierarchy is more evident. The isolated person who may like others but is less sure of the extent to which his liking is returned may not be as accurate in his judgment.

Pairs of friends tend to be more accurate in the perception of each other's personalities than pairs of nonfriends, partly as a result of increased knowledge of the other person from continued social interaction and partly as a result of a tendency to project one's own values on a friend.

This tendency of subjects to describe others whom they like best as more similar to themselves than are those they like least presumably reflects some of the common interests which brought the pair together as friends in the first place. Marital happiness for 20 university student couples, for example, was found to be positively associated with similarity of self-perception of mates (Corsini, 1956). Further evidence of the relation between similarity of values and perception of friends is found in a study in which each of 90 college women classified 100 self-referent statements in a Q sort for her self-concept, ideal self-concept, and her perception of her first- and second-best friend. The perception of each friend's personality was more similar to the ideal self-concept ($r = .42$) than to the self-concept ($r = .33$) of the subject. Here, the ideal self appeared to be a composite of traits valued both in the self and others (McKenna, Hoffstaetter, & O'Connor, 1956).

Changing perception through interaction. Evidence for both the consistency and change of perception as a result of interaction between two individuals has been presented in the literature (Cronbach, 1955). On the one hand, research on the importance of "first impressions" indicates that judgments of persons once formed are slow to change; and, on the other hand, research on friendship suggests that the longer two individuals know each other and the more intimate their interaction, the greater will be the accuracy of the interpersonal perceptions (Bieri, 1953). Since individuals may or may not increase their perceptual accuracy as a result of interaction, further evidence must be presented to permit the prediction of the conditions under which increased accuracy of perception occurs. It might be expected, for example, that persons with high test scores on insight or empathy would increase their accuracy more than those with low scores. However, in one study, after 30 minutes of interaction in 12-man, leaderless discussion groups, subjects with high empathy scores were not able to estimate the way in which one member's personality traits would be viewed by the other members any more effectively than were low scorers (Bell & Stolper, 1955).

Whether or not the subject focuses attention on himself or the other person does seem to make a difference, since, in one experiment, paired interaction increased the accuracy of a member's prediction of another's values, if he focused attention on the other person; but it changed the prediction toward the member's own values and away from those of his partner when he focused attention on himself (Lundy, 1956).

Apparently, close contact on a work basis does not increase the accuracy of perception to the same extent as interaction on a basis of friendship (Block & Bennett, 1955). When changes in accuracy of perception do occur as a result of increased communication or intimacy between the members of a pair, the changes can be expected to be more pronounced if the members initially have the same underlying attitudes (Runkel, 1956).

Perception and adjustment. Although it might be supposed that the person with the greatest insight should be able to make the best adjustment to the group, the evidence to support this generalization is not clear. Some studies suggest a positive relationship between adjustment and the ability to estimate one's own position as seen by the group (Green, 1948), as well as the tendency to be more accurate in the perception of others (Baker & Sarbin, 1956; Gage, 1953). Other studies report no correlation between insight and effectiveness in interpersonal relations (Gage & Exline, 1953; Lemann & Solomon, 1952).

These conflicting findings may indicate that insight or accuracy of perception is a necessary but not sufficient condition for effectiveness, since some deviant members may be well aware of their position in the group and yet be unable to get along well with the other group members. Steiner (1955) suggested that accurate social perception should promote "interpersonal competence" and group efficiency if (1) the group members are motivated to cooperate, (2) the accurately perceived qualities are relevant to the activities of the group, (3) members are free to alter their own behavior in response to their perceptions of other members, (4) the behavioral changes that are a consequence of accurate social perception are the kinds which produce a more thoroughly integrated system. Whenever any one or more of these conditions is not met, accurate social perception will not affect adjustment to the group.

In cases in which perceptual accuracy and level of adjustment are related, changes in the individual's level of adjustment brought about by therapy can be expected to change his perceptions, and vice versa (Butler, 1952). For example, 21 patients who received counseling were given projective tests before and after therapy. In these tests, the patients' own self-descriptions were less loaded with feeling after therapy (Dymond, Seeman, & Grummon, 1956).

Leader's perception. The same factors which affect the perceptions of the average group member also operate on the perceptions of the leader. Moreover, since the leader is in the center of the communication net and is usually selected or arises because of his ability to put himself in the place of others, his perceptions of others tend to be more accurate than those of the average member, although it has been suggested that some of this apparent superiority may be a statistical artifact (Campbell, 1955). As evidence of the superior perceptual accuracy of leaders, school teachers were found to perceive accurately the choice structure of their classes (Gronlund, 1956a), and teachers who were the most accurate in perceiving the structure of the classroom also perceived accurately the structure of their own peer group of teachers (Gronlund, 1956b). The leader, on the other hand, may perceive himself more favorably than he is perceived by other members of the group (Gebel, 1954).

As a result of his favored position, the leader is usually superior to nonleaders and isolates in his ability to judge group opinion on issues which are relevant to the group's activity (Chowdhry & Newcomb, 1952; Exline, 1960b). However, if all members of the group actually share the same opinion on an issue and there is a high rate of interaction among group members, the difference in perception between leaders and nonleaders may not appear (Hites & Campbell, 1950).

The importance of being in the center of the communication net for accurate perception is further demonstrated by evidence from studies in which communication between all members is maximized either because the groups are small or because the members have known each other longer. In these cases, all members may be able to predict group opinion or group structure more accurately than members of groups with less effective communication, although one study of high school students in discussion groups of 14 to 16 members revealed that estimates of group opinion on certain issues were no more accurate after discussion than they were without discussion (Stone & Kamiya, 1957).

In the previous discussion of perceptual accuracy and adjustment, the average individual's social adjustment was not found to be clearly related to his perceptual ability. Nevertheless, leaders who are more discriminating in their social perception are apparently better able to organize group activity. The most preferred co-worker chosen by members of winning high school basketball teams and highly rated college surveying teams was found to be the one who in turn perceived his preferred and rejected co-workers as differing and perceived little similarity between himself and his co-workers (Fiedler, 1954). Since subjects tend to perceive those they like as similar to themselves, Fiedler concludes that the member who differentiates in his perceptions of other group members is also the one who maintains enough emotional distance from others and has enough task orientation to make him an effective team leader (Fiedler, 1958). Similar findings have been reported with small military units (Hutchins & Fiedler, 1960). (Steiner and McDiarmid [1957] suggest that Fiedler's Assumed Similarity Score can be broken into two components: (1) the perceived discrepancy between the overall "goodness" of the traits possessed by the two co-workers, and (2) the perceived dissimilarity between the patterns of traits possessed by the two co-workers. Foa [1958] noted that variables such as assumed similarity, empathy, and conformity will be correlated if they are composed of similar "facets," e.g., actor, observer, level, and alias.)

This positive association between ability to influence and perceptual accuracy was also evident in a study of a 17-man training group. Members whose perceptions were accurate in that their judgments of the power of others agreed with the average group judgment were considered effective by observers and valuable and powerful by the other group members (Smith, Jaffe, & Livingston, 1955).

The results of any attempt to change the perceptions of leaders can be expected to vary with the personality of the leader and the situation in which he finds himself (Maas, 1950).

GROUP STRUCTURE

As groups grow in size and complexity, individuals tend to specialize in some aspect of the interaction process. The expectations for behavior in these specialties are represented by the roles of the group members (Bates, 1956; Bates & Cloyd, 1956; Gross, McEachern, & Mason, 1958; Levinson, 1959; Southall, 1959).

Some evidence that behavior in a role does not always agree with the expectations for that role is reported in two studies of the relationship between the ideologies of aircraft commanders and educational administrators and their actual behavior (Halpin, 1955). In both cases, the "ideologies" of the leaders in the categories of "initiating group structure" and "consideration" were considerably higher than the ratings of actual behavior made by their subordinates.

Individuals vary in their ability to play a given role (Sarbin & Jones, 1955). The expectations for a role are met most easily by the individual whose personality fits the role (Borgatta, 1961; Rapoport & Rosow, 1957; Smelser, 1961). General conformity to role expectations is also greater when the role is well defined (Videbeck & Bates, 1959).

Some of the consequences for a group if a member does not fulfill his role expectations are illustrated in a study of the effects of clear and unclear role expectations on group productivity and defensiveness. College students played the game of "Twenty Questions" in groups of five members. Each group contained two confederates who remained silent throughout the game. When the silence on the part of these two members was unanticipated, the productivity and satisfaction of the other participants decreased and their defensiveness increased. The groups did better if the silent subjects announced that they would remain silent before the experiment began, thus altering the expectations for their roles in the group (Smith, 1957).

The concept of role as it is used in the literature does not generally involve all aspects of behavior. Rather, each author tends to limit his description of role to some aspects which are particularly relevant to his experiment. In some cases, the subject's position in a communication network (e.g., central person, member, or isolate) is seen as the most important aspect of the role; in others, his typical interaction rate or pattern (e.g., the person who talks most) is considered; and in others, his primary content area (e.g., task leader versus social-emotional leader) is selected.

Development of the Informal Structure

The studies which deal with the development of the informal structure in the group tend to focus on the network of positions rather than on the roles or expectations for behavior which go with the positions. In many of these studies, the researcher is concerned with development of the simplest type of network, the straight-line hierarchy, in which a subject's position is operationally defined by the sum of the ratings he receives on some criterion.

In laboratory experiments, when the experimenter leaves the members to their own devices in developing a structure, the group is referred to as an "initially leaderless group." In other cases, the roles are assigned by the experimenter before the group begins its task or are developed in response to some style of leadership which has been planted in the group.

In most large organizations and in many types of small groups, there is a formal structure, a set of "official" positions which incorporate the accepted division of labor for the group's task. Other positions are "unofficial" and make up the informal structure.

All aspects of the work situation including the formal structure influence the development of the informal structure. In some groups, the formal structure and informal structure may be the same. This would be especially true in clubs which developed first on an informal basis and were later formalized. In either case, the structure tends to develop around the leader or some other type of central person, such as the tyrant, idol, or scapegoat (Redl, 1942).

The attempts of children to establish a hierarchy (Hanfmann, 1935) are perhaps more apparent than those of college-age students, who characteristically wait until the second meeting of a laboratory discussion group before launching their struggle for status.[2] The greater the agreement among members concerning the potential status of individuals in an initially leaderless group, the less time it will take to solve the status problem.

Shifts of position are most evident in experimental groups or in groups in which the informal structure is not reinforced by a formal structure. If the power differences between members are obvious and firmly fixed from the start, the positions of the top men are less likely to be challenged by those down the line. However, there is a tendency

in a three-man group for the two-man coalition to attack the high-power person or, in the opposite case, to withstand attack from below from a low-power person. This coalition is seen as a basic structural type in the three-person group (Mills, 1953; Simmel, 1902).

In most discussion groups in which members have approximately equal amounts of information and no one holds more cards or points at the outset, the leadership rank is established by the relative amount of talking of each member. The person who talks the most generally wins most of the decisions and becomes the leader.

Whyte's (1943) study of gangs of corner boys in an Italian urban area provides many examples of the development and maintenance of an informal structure in a group. Other similar examples are described by Bloch and Neiderhoffer (1958).

Differentiation in Hierarchies

Although the hierarchies of task and social-emotional positions may at first appear to be undifferentiated, they tend, particularly in large groups, to separate as the group grows older. In the initially leaderless group, the most apparent differentiation of informal roles is the gradual development of a task leader and a best-liked person or social-emotional leader. In a series of four meetings of groups which met to discuss human relations problems (Bales, 1953), the member most chosen as "liked" was usually also chosen for "best ideas" and "guidance" in the first meeting, but this coincidence of choice became less likely in later meetings. In fact, when observations for all four meetings were summarized, the member who ranked highest on "guidance" and "best ideas" and who initiated most of the activity in the group was found to be the member who was disliked most (i.e., received the most negative votes) and ranked only third on liked choices. The second or third man on "guidance" and "best ideas" was usually best liked.

---

[2] Some authors use the term status to refer to the rank of a group member on some criterion. Although "status" has also been used as synonymous with "position" in everyday usage, the term seems to be associated with a less well-defined set of expectations than the term position. When an original author has used the term status in this way, his usage has been adopted in many instances in reporting the results of his research.

When the same person is capable of playing both the task and social-emotional leader roles, he usually favors being best liked and gives up the task leader role. In ten cases where the same person played both roles in the first meeting of an initially leaderless group, the "best ideas" role was dropped nine times in favor of the "liked" role. In the remaining case, the person dropped both roles (Bales, 1953).

Investigation of an established group will usually uncover similar differences between choices on a task and social-emotional basis, where the top man in either category may be regarded as a leader if he initiates most of the activity in his specialty. However, high rank in these two categories is not always correlated with all criteria for leadership (Gibb, 1950).

The tendency for role differentiation which involves sharing the leadership activity may be resisted by members of groups who expect to have a strong central leader. In high-level conferences in business, industry, and government, for example, leadership sharing was found to be negatively related to group cohesion and member satisfaction unless the group had an urgent problem to solve (Berkowitz, 1953).

In mixed sex groups, men tend to play the task leader role and initiate more activity; whereas women tend to specialize in the social-emotional area, providing more reactions (Strodtbeck & Mann, 1956). Men also more often play the role of "joker," engaging in tension release (Davis, 1961). Two types of "joker" role have been observed: An individual who uses sarcastic wit is perceived by other group members as powerful but unpopular; and one who uses clowning wit is seen as popular but powerless (Goodchilds, 1959).

Since roles develop in a group in response to the requirements of the task and the particular constellation of individuals who compose the group, the specific content of any role may be expected to vary primarily with the group's task and secondarily with the characteristics of the members. In groups which have a life which is longer than any of the individual members, the task requirements would be less variable than the social-emotional requirements.

Culture and Role Differentiation

In the typical middle-class family in the United States and Great Britain, the father is the task leader and the mother the social-emotional leader (Bott, 1955; Bott, 1956; Kenkel, 1957; Parsons et al., 1955), but this is not always the case in other cultures or even within all subcultures to be found in the United States. Strodtbeck (1951) observed husband-wife interaction in three subcultures in the southwestern United States and found differences in the amount of activity and power of the husband and wife in each of the cultures.

Role Collision, Incompatibility, and Confusion

Group members usually agree about some specific attributes of a member's role (especially in highly cohesive groups) (Hall, 1955), but in some areas, their expectations for role behavior are contradictory or ill-defined. The clash of expectations concerning some aspects of a role have usually been called "role conflict." Role conflicts can arise in a number of different ways. In role collision, two different individuals have roles which are in conflict in some respect; in role incompatibility, the same individual plays roles which have contradictory expectations; and in role confusion, there is a lack of agreement among group members about the expectations for a given role. Although examples of these types of role problems can be found in research on small groups (Exline & Ziller, 1959), most of the examples occur in larger segments of society.

INTERPERSONAL CHOICE

Individuals indicate their interpersonal choices in a variety of ways; through frequency of association, formal elections, and ratings of other group members elicited by observers and experimenters. Ratings of the last type, popularized by Moreno (Moreno, 1953; Moreno et al., 1960), have been called "sociometric" ratings.

An analysis of "sociograms," which depict the patterns of interpersonal choice, is useful in identifying the position of an individual in the informal structure of a group, but does not reveal the behavior which is associated with the position. The ratings on several criteria are often combined; thus, individuals are identified as "overchosen" or "underchosen" in the informal structure without reference to the particular position which they hold. Although the "overchosen" members tend to be those who prefer close relationships with others, they are not necessarily the informal leaders.

The sociometric test has been used widely in studies of children in school populations. Here the principal problem for research has often been to determine the basis of friendship between pairs of children. The friendship bonds between individuals tend to be influenced by proximity and by similarities in individual social characteristics, interests or values, and personality.

Sociometric ratings are often used to derive measures of morale or cohesiveness, since individuals who are highly attracted to a group tend to be the most productive if the norms of the group specify high productivity. A measure of cohesiveness may then be used to predict productivity.

Reciprocal Choice

When an investigator asks the subjects to rate all other members of the group using some criterion of choice, the data include not only those choices which the individuals have consciously made before the experimenter arrives on the scene, but also those choices that have been made only for the purpose of the questionnaire, which played no major part in the development of the social structure. An individual who is ranked low by another individual may, therefore, be someone who is disliked or someone who is relatively unknown to the first person. When group members are relative strangers, mutual choices might occur simply by chance. In general, however, choices are not random, since in every group some persons are chosen more and some chosen less than would be expected if only chance factors were operating. Reciprocation of choice will not appear, however, unless a sociometric question is asked which makes reciprocation of choice possible. For example, mutual choices would not be expected if subjects were asked to nominate the best potential leaders in the group. Mutual choice would be expected with a criterion of "sit next to" or "room with."

Subjects who are told that others like them will reciprocate the presumed choice unless the actual behavior of the other person gives no evidence of liking (Backman & Secord, 1959).

Subgroups

The tendency for the group to split into subgroups becomes marked as the group size increases. The typical sociometric chart of interpersonal choices shows a series of interlocking subgroups as the informal group structure. So characteristic is the tendency for members of groups to form subgroups on some choice basis, that, even when the subgroups are imposed by some outside condition, the amount of friendly interaction within the subgroups increases and the number of social isolates in the group decreases.

The relative nature of positions in an informal structure is evidenced by the fact that if "overchosen" or central members and "underchosen" or fringe members are separated from each other into new groups, a new informal structure will form in each group in which some members will again be "overchosen" and others "underchosen" (Powell et al., 1956).

In a series of studies in a summer camp

for boys, Sherif and his colleagues (Sherif, Harvey, White, Hood, & Sherif, 1961) experimentally demonstrated that an increase in hostility toward some outgroup is usually associated with an increase in affection for members of the ingroup.

Consistency of the Informal Structure

Since the institution or alteration of the formal structure of a group is usually obvious to everyone, including the investigator, little attention has been given to the consistency of the formal structure. On the informal side, the persistence of the structure based on interpersonal choice is usually studied by administering sociometric tests at several points in a group's life. A number of investigators find high correlations between successive tests, indicating that the informal structure persists or becomes more apparent over a period of time.

The reliabilities of sociometric tests used in 53 studies have been analyzed in detail by Mouton, Blake, and Fruchter (1955a). The authors concluded that there is enough evidence to justify the hypotheses that the consistency of sociometric choices between test and retest will be greater under the following conditions:

1. The time interval between test and retest is short.

2. The subjects are adults or near-adults.

3. The subjects have known each other for a long time before the first test.

4. The criterion of choice by which judgments are made is relevant to the activity of the group.

5. A large number of discriminations is required by the technique of choosing.

6. The group from which the choices are made is large.

Bases of Friendship

Most people choose each other for a variety of reasons. The generalization that "birds of a feather flock together" is supported by most of the studies of friendship, although

there is also evidence that "opposites attract."

The process by which persons are initially attracted to each other and finally become "reciprocal choices" or friends can be represented by four types of relationship: (1) proximity, (2) similar individual characteristics, (3) common interests or values, (4) similar personality traits (Newcomb, 1960). Presumably the relationship involving similar personality traits is more intense than that involving proximity, although most research does not compare different types of relationship.

Proximity is the first factor to operate, since persons who live near each other, or are near to each other, on the job or in school (Byrne, 1961b) become friends more often than persons who live or work farther apart. Once acquainted, persons who are attracted to each other seek each other out at lunch or other places of possible contact and so increase the "chance" of being together. Friendship groups continue longest if the members have a work relationship with each other.

Persons who choose each other tend to have similar individual characteristics, such as age, intelligence, sex, and athletic ability, although an occasional study reports no association between these variables and friendship formation (Bonney, 1946).

Although individuals may be drawn together at first because of common attributes, their friendship is more likely to continue if they have common interests or values (Byrne, 1961a). For instance, in a study of the Supreme Court as a small group, three cliques were identified. The membership in these cliques appeared to be related to the ideology of the judges (Snyder, 1958). Being an "old-timer" at camp or in the factory provides the type of common experience upon which friendship is based, and religion, ethnic group, and social class may provide a common value orientation. Social class, in addition to providing a common value orientation, often serves to restrict the contacts of members of a given class to others within the same class. The gross effects of class differences on behavior are seldom apparent in small group research, since the school populations which provide the subjects for most of the experiments present a sample of a very limited range of the total society.

Finally, friendship is related to personality in that individuals with the same personality type tend to choose each other (Maisonneuve, 1954), and marriage partners with similar personality traits are found to be more satisfied with their spouses (Burchinal, Hawkes, & Gardner, 1957).

Subjects are also found to choose others whose personalities they describe as being similar to their own positive traits and to reject others whom they describe as being similar to their own negative traits. However, as with the evidence on social characteristics and friendship, not all studies agree on the similarities in the personalities of friends, and some studies report no significant correlations (Reilly, Commins, & Stefic, 1960). In one study of married couples, assertive persons were found to marry receptive persons. Other personality needs such as abasement, achievement, approach, and autonomy appeared to be generally complementary (Winch, 1955). In another study with a school population, friends were not found to be similar in neuroticism (Thorpe, 1955). This somewhat conflicting evidence may only mean that friends are similar on some but not all of their personality characteristics (Bowerman & Day, 1956; Rosow, 1957).

Overchosen Members

Certain types of personalities appear to be more "popular," since persons with these characteristics are chosen more often on sociometric tests. Specifically, girls in one college who were rated as generous, enthusiastic, and affectionate were chosen more often than those who were rated as stingy, apathetic, and cold (Lemann & Solomon, 1952); girls with scores near the median on dominance, security, and femininity were the most chosen in another college (Lindzey & Urdan, 1954). These same personality characteristics (with the exception of femininity) have been found to be associated with popularity in a summer camp for boys (Hunt & Solomon, 1942). Popularity appears to be related to the extent to which a person exemplifies the group ideal (Turk, 1961). If a person is popular, he may be receiving votes from some who are not like him in personality as well as from some who are, since popularity involves only one-way choices.

In many cases, the "popular" person may represent the "ideal" or "norm" of the group simply because the indications of what is "ideal" and who is "popular" are derived from the same source. That is, the observer asks group members on one occasion to indicate their preferred personality traits. The average rating on a trait then becomes a "norm." At another time, the observer asks who is preferred for work or play. Since the majority of the group, who represent the norm, will tend to choose others like themselves, the individuals receiving the most choices will also represent the norm. The use of the same population to derive measures of "normal" and "popular" may also account for the "accuracy" of perception of popular members. When college subjects in a class of 48 were divided into 5 work-groups, the popular members were found to be more "accurate" than the task leaders in their "perception" of the popularity of others and of certain group dimensions (those suggested by Hemphill, 1956). Here "accuracy" was measured by agreement with the group as a whole (Bugental & Lehner, 1958).

The individuals in the group who receive the most choices from all the group members also choose each other. They make more positive choices, have patterns of choice and rejection which differ from "isolates," and are highly chosen by members of other subgroups within the same social system. Part of the correlation between choices inside and outside of a given small group may be accounted for by the finding that status differences from large organizations carry over into ad hoc training groups so that individuals who have high "outside" status are chosen in the ad hoc group over those with low "outside" status (Horwitz, Exline, & Lee, 1953). In small discussion groups, these overchosen members also reveal a pattern of interaction which one would associate with leadership (Borgatta & Bales, 1956).

Apparently, being well liked does not make a person especially friendly to those less popular, even though they may be friendly to him. However, the popular person will be more concerned about his status if it is subject to change (Berkowitz & Macaulay, 1961).

Popularity and Skill

High-choice status has also been found to be positively related to skill in recreational groups, such as bowling teams (Whyte, 1943) and also to combat effectiveness, individual productivity in work groups (Jackson, 1959), and influence and apparent skill in laboratory groups (Kleiner, 1960; Whitmyre, Diggery, & Cohen, 1961; Zander & Havelin, 1960). (The individual's perception of his skill, of course, may not be accurate. In one study of informal groups which were competing at dart-throwing, the high-status members tended to overestimate their own performance [Harvey, 1953]. Other group members also tended to overestimate the skill of well-liked members [Sherif, White, & Harvey, 1955].) Popularity shows a negative correlation with accident-proneness, sickness, and disciplinary offenses (Mouton, Blake, & Fruchter, 1955b). The positive relation between skill and popularity in industry, however, may not be evident in cases in which choice status in the group depends more upon the extent to which a person conforms to the production standards set by the informal group than to the overall production level of the whole industry (French & Zander, 1949).

Morale and Cohesiveness

Interpersonal choices, in addition to indicating the informal structure of a group, can also be used to form an index of morale or cohesiveness. Groups are said to have high morale or to be cohesive if members are highly attracted to the group. The terms "morale" and "cohesiveness" have generally been used interchangeably. Some authors form an index of the ratio of ingroup to outgroup sociometric choices which they call an "index of morale" (Zeleny, 1939); others call a similar index an "index of cohesiveness" (Martin, Darley, & Gross, 1952); and still others call it an "index of cohesiveness-morale" (Fessenden, 1953).

The term cohesiveness is generally favored by investigators whose work follows the pattern set by Lewin. They use an index of attractiveness to the group which is based on any one or a combination of choices in the task or social-emotional areas. One should be cautious, however, about combining the results of studies which use different sociometric criteria for their indices. Attraction based on "likeability" and attraction based on "task ability," for example, may lead to different forms of interaction (Blau, 1962). If the group members come together with work as the primary goal, they will probably spend little time on the social activity which would be characteristic of a group formed on an affectional basis. Some studies have reported no relationship between different operational measures of cohesiveness (Eisman, 1959; Ramus-Nienhuis & Van Bergen, 1960).

Where a distinction is made between cohesiveness and morale, cohesiveness is most frequently used to represent the "desire to belong to a group," and morale is used to emphasize a "disposition to act toward a goal" (Albert, 1953). In one methodological study of the concept of morale, for example, the concept is defined as "an average feeling of contentment or satisfaction about the major aspects of the work situation" (Campbell & Tyler, 1957).

An index of the attractiveness of the group for its members is often desired since the extent of the attractiveness is also found to be related to significance of the group as a reference group for judgments about the self and others. Once an individual has dropped out of a group which has lost its attraction for him (Sagi, Olmsted, & Atelsek, 1955), the group will no longer be important as a positive reference group.

A group will tend to become cohesive if it is formally well organized, the members are individually motivated to do the task, and the group is successful. In addition, a group will appear more attractive to its members if they have to undergo a severe initiation to join (Aronson & Mills, 1959). At the other end of the continuum, in a school for delinquent girls, it was observed that cottages with a low percentage of choices made within the cottage were marked by a high degree of deviant behavior and low interest in controlling this behavior (Moreno, 1953). The relative number of within-group choices as an index of cohesiveness is less appropriate for children, since the number and strength of interpersonal relationships is correlated with age. Very young children make few choices either in or out of a group.

In industrial plants where the personal bonds are well established and newly recruited members are easily incorporated, labor turnover is lower than in plants which are similar in geographic location, technology, and labor force, but where the bonds between members are weak and no informal group standards are enforced (Fox & Scott, 1943; Mayo & Lombard, 1944), absenteeism and turnover are especially high among the new workers in such plants. High ingroup choice is also related to effective performance on field problems by infantry rifle squads (Goodacre, 1951).

In an extensive study of group cohesiveness in industrial work-groups, data were drawn from 228 machine factory work-groups ranging in size from 5 to 50 members. Members of high-cohesive work-groups exhibited less anxiety than did members of low-cohesive work-groups. Productivity varied less among the members of the high-cohesive groups, although those groups differed more frequently and in greater amounts from the plant norm of productivity than did the low-cohesive groups. The amount of cohesiveness in a group was positively related to the degree of prestige which the members of the group attributed to their own jobs, the opportunities for interaction as measured by the size of the group (i.e., the larger the group, the fewer opportunities for interaction), and the length of time members had been together on the job (Seashore, 1954).

LEADERSHIP

The most frequently studied role in the small group is that of the leader. Leadership can be varied by selecting an individual with a given set of personality characteristics or by training an individual to perform a given set of behaviors. Variations in leadership style produce the greatest effect on interaction when selection and training are combined. In this section, the general traits of leaders and the functions of leadership for which an individual might be trained are summarized. Since leader selection is of particular importance to the armed forces, many of the studies of small group leadership have used military personnel. A leaderless group discussion has been used to predict leader potential for a variety of tasks, and the differences in the skills required for leadership in manual and intellectual tasks have led to the development of a number of situational tests and assessment techniques.

Although in most groups a single individual has the most power and authority and is recognized as the formal leader, the leadership functions may be divided formally or informally among several group members. A common division of leadership separates the roles of task leader, primarily concerned with task performance, and social-emotional leader, or best-liked man, primarily concerned with affectional relationships and member satisfaction. A collection of articles that illustrate many of the generalizations in this section is edited by Petrullo and Bass (1961) and extensive summaries of the literature are given by Bass (1960) and Verba (1961).

Leadership Traits

The variety of traits which a leader may have is the same as that of any other group member, except that the leader is usually found to have a higher rating on each "good" trait. While correlations between "good" personality traits and leadership are generally positive, they are rarely large. Thus, only a little of the variance in leader behavior can be accounted for by his traits (Gibb, 1954). There are indications that certain traits such as intelligence, enthusiasm, dominance, self-confidence, social participation, and equalitarianism frequently characterize leaders (Blake & Mouton, 1961b; Borg, 1960; Kirscht, Lodahl, & Haire, 1959; Mussen & Porter, 1959; Rosen, Levinger, & Lippitt, 1961). Usually, however, the relation of the trait to the leadership role is more meaningful if the detailed nature of the role and the characteristics of the followers are considered.

Leaders who emerge in leaderless group discussions tend to be more authoritarian in their behavior than leaders who are appointed (Carter, Haythorn, Shriver, & Lanzetta, 1951). Presumably this occurs because more dominating behavior is required to establish a position of leadership in a group than to maintain one (Hare, 1957). In laboratory groups, leaders who are "elected" gain more acceptance from their followers than those who appear to "take over" (French & Raven, 1960).

Leadership Functions

An indication of the functions which are common to the leader role regardless of the group situation is obtained from Hemphill's (1949) extensive questionnaire study of leadership qualities. In this study, each respondent to the questionnaire gave a description of the different groups to which he belonged and also reported his observations of the leaders' behavior. Five functions were identified which were common to leaders of all groups: (1) advance the purpose of the group, (2) administer, (3) inspire greater activity or set the pace for the group, (4) make the individual member feel secure of his place in the group, (5) act without regard to his own self-interest. Leader functions which are similar to some or all of those on Hemphill's list also appear in a number of other studies (Bartlett, 1959; Stogdill & Coons, 1957; Warriner, 1955; Wilson, High, & Comrey, 1955).

In terms of the interpersonal categories of task and social-emotional behavior, the leader's function can be seen as that of facilitating behavior in each area which will maximize productivity on the group's task. Whether or not he fulfills these functions, the leader, through his activity in the group, is a major determiner in establishing the point at which the group will reach equilibrium along each dimension of interaction (Back, 1948).

Since the problem of role confusion is present for the leader as well as for the others in the group, the determination of leader functions will depend upon who is asked. In the armed forces, where status differences are clear cut, the military rank of the individual determines both his own conception of leadership and the types of leadership others expect of him.

The customs of many military organizations require social distance between leaders and followers and place a low value on the "consideration" of commanders for their troops. These customs may increase group effectiveness, not so much because the men will not follow a leader with whom they are too familiar, but rather because a leader who is too close to his men may find it more difficult to reach efficient decisions when he is influenced by his feelings about his men (Fiedler, 1957).

Individuals with different personality dimensions have divergent expectations for the leader. When subjects are ranked on an Authoritarian-Equalitarian Scale, two distinct sets of expectations for leadership are found. Authoritarians accept status-laden, strongly directive leadership, demand that others adhere to ingroup values, and interact with the leader as a person rather than as a role (Medalia, 1955; Sanford, 1950). A similar dependent state may characterize the emotional atmosphere of a group during the early phases of group formation (cf. Bion, 1961), indicating that the functions expected of the leader will vary with the stages in group development.

The Central Person

The "leader," in the usual sense, is only one type of central person who may have the power to control the activity of a group. In a family, for example, a sick child may have more influence on family activity than the father or mother who usually takes the leader role. Other types of central persons may appear as objects of identification, as objects of drives, and as ego supports. Redl (1942) described 10 of these types: patriarchal sovereign, leader, tyrant, idol, scapegoat, organizer, seducer, hero, bad influence, and good example. All of the types of central persons have in common the fact that they have influence over other group members (Cartwright 1959; Janda, 1960).

The influence of a member in the informal structure will be enhanced if he is placed in a formal position of leadership (Maier & Solem, 1952). An individual will also try to exert more influence if he is placed in the leader role (Gerard, 1957).

Selection of Leaders

In addition to personality and performance tests (Carter & Nixon, 1949), a fre-

quently used technique for the selection of formal leaders is the observation of the leaderless group discussion. First developed by the German army during World War I (Ansbacher, 1951), this technique was taken over by the British and American armies and is now used by other organizations. In a series of researches on this subject, Bass and his associates observed college students, officer candidates, and business executives in four-to-ten-man groups (Bass, 1960; Bass, 1961). As the candidates discussed a series of problems in a group in which no leader had been appointed, observers recorded the amount of time each member talked and rated each member's behavior on a series of scales which had been found to be valid for identifying leadership potential. A high rating on leadership in an initially leaderless group of this type was found to have a positive correlation with leadership in training performance of army personnel, status of supervisors in an oil company, and other criterion measures of leadership (Ames, 1955; Bass, 1960; Borgatta, 1954; Kiessling & Kalish, 1961).

The possibility that one observer may be able to select the leader in an initially leaderless group simply by judging his appearance has been investigated without success (Mason, 1957).

Consistency of Leadership Behavior

The assumption of individual consistency in leadership behavior lies behind all leader assessment techniques. Individuals who receive a high rating on leadership behavior in one situation are generally expected to take the leader role in other situations. The consistency is especially high if the social characteristics of the members, group size, and task remain the same even though specific group members may be changed. Conversely, consistency will be low if these or other factors are varied (Hemphill, Pepinsky, Shevitz, Jaynes, & Christner, 1956). A change in the personalities of the followers from high authoritarian to low authoritarian results in less authoritarian behavior on the part of the leader regardless of his authoritarian rating (Haythorn, Couch, Haefner, Langham, & Carter, 1956a; Haythorn et al., 1956b), and a change in the communication network may result in an entirely different person's assuming leadership (Bavelas, 1950).

Once an individual has established himself as the leader in an initially leaderless group situation, he may continue in the role even if another leader is appointed (Borg, 1957).

Leadership Training

The effectiveness of the leader can generally be improved by giving him training for the type of group he has to lead. In experimental training programs, youth leaders have become more democratic, foremen have gained more acceptance from employees in introducing work changes, and college students have improved their discussion leadership techniques (Maier & Hoffman, 1960).

Not all training programs are successful, however. In one study in which foremen were trained in "consideration," a comparison of tests taken before and after the school session seemed to show more consideration; but in actual practice, the same foremen were less considerate (Fleishman, 1952). A second program of the same type produced no differences in the foremen's test scores (Harris & Fleishman, 1955).

A number of books have been written during the past 30 years to help the individual improve his leadership technique. Only a sample of these appear in the bibliography (Andrews, 1955; Bellows, 1959; Laird & Laird, 1956; W. M. Lifton, 1961; Whyte, 1953).

Authoritarian versus Democratic Leadership

Authoritarian versus democratic leadership styles are the two most common types of leadership which have been imposed upon experimental groups. As in any situation, the group will be more effective when the members' expectations about the behavior appropriate for that situation are met. Where group members anticipate a democratic organization, as they do in educational settings such as children's clubs, discussion groups, or classrooms, the democratic style produces the most effective group. In industry or the army, however, where members anticipate forceful leadership from their superiors, a more authoritarian form of leadership results in a more effective group.

The classic experiments in this area by Lewin, Lippitt, and White in 1939–1940 resulted in an increased interest in the scientific study of group dynamics. The first experiment compared the group atmospheres created by authoritarian and democratic leaders, and the second experiment added a laissez faire leader (White & Lippitt, 1960). The second experiment, which corroborated the findings of the first, studied clubs of 11-year-old boys who were equal with respect to certain of the personal and sociometric characteristics and degree of interest in the task. All clubs met in the same clubroom setting, two at a time in adjacent meeting spaces with a common equipment box. Four adults played the roles of "authoritarian," "democratic," and "laissez faire" leaders in rotation so that, with minor exceptions, each adult played each leader role in each of the groups. The same activities were used in each club; the democratic clubs were allowed to select an activity, and then that activity was imposed on the authoritarian clubs. In the laissez faire situation, there were a number of potential activities of the same types as those selected by the democratic clubs.

The members of the authoritarian groups showed more dependency on the leader and more hostile and apathetic behavior among members. The members of the laissez faire groups showed little dependency on the leader but greater irritability and aggressiveness among members and dissatisfaction with the task. The democratic group showed less dependency on the leader, more friendliness, and more satisfaction with the activities of the club. The autocratic groups surpassed the others in quantity of output, but the products of the democratic groups were judged to be of the best quality.

Variations of studies on the authoritarian-democratic theme use somewhat similar leader roles with discussion groups rather than activity groups (Bevan, Albert, Loiseaux, Mayfield, & Wright, 1958; Fox, 1957; Ziller, 1957a; Ziller, 1958). In general, when leaders who have an active and positive relationship with their discussion groups are contrasted with those who hold negative attitudes, a greater incidence of supportive acts among members is reported for the positively led groups, and a greater incidence of opposing acts is found in the negatively led groups. In addition, the members accept opposing behavior more readily in the negatively led groups, so that opposers receive high popularity ratings and are more highly satisfied with the group decision.

Some of these same effects were observed in a study of the relationship between the behavior of B-29 commanders in the air corps and the attitudes of their crew members. When the leader was considerate, the friendship, willingness, and confidence of the members increased (Christner & Hemphill, 1955). In another study of military groups, men were more likely to engage in tension releasing activities in their leisure hours if their commanding officer was arbitrary in his leadership style (Selvin, 1960). Experiments with discussion groups have compared "participatory" leaders, who take part in the discussion and try to ensure an equal chance for participation to all group members, and "supervisory" leaders, who do not take part but whose job it is to make sure the group finishes the discussion on time. The data indicate that participatory leadership is more effective as a technique for changing opinion. The participatory leader has more influence on the group

decision, and the followers are better satisfied with the result of the group decision, apparently because each has had an opportunity to express his opinion even though it may not have been accepted by the group (Hare, 1953; Preston & Heintz, 1949).

It can be assumed that the leader who facilitates free discussion among the members will be more effective when the group task requires free discussion among peers. Many tasks, however, require for their successful completion more frequent participation by the more skillful members and a hierarchy of power and influence (Horowitz & Perlmutter, 1955). Because other variables can influence the outcome of "authoritarian" or "democratic" leadership attempts, the relation between leader style and productivity does not appear consistently (Anderson, 1959).

Teacher-Centered versus Learner-Centered Classes

In learning situations, two contrasting styles have been called "teacher-centered" and "learner-centered." Task-centered, demanding teachers are found to elicit from students hostility, apathy, and other signs of withdrawal; whereas accepting, student-supportive teachers decrease anxiety and produce greater interaction and positive feeling among members both in class and outside the classroom. Women appear to be more affected by these changes in the classroom situation than men (McKeachie, 1958).

Some observers report more learning in the "learner-centered" classes, although some students prefer the more directive classes for examination preparation. Little difference has been found when students from both types of classes are given the same examination. In addition, permissive instruction may increase the ambiguity of the teaching situation unless group members have the skills to set and achieve goals (McKeachie, 1954). Dull children may do better under "teacher-centered" instruction (Calvin, Hoffmann, & Harden, 1957).

Differences similar to those between "teacher-centered" and "learner-centered" classes have been found between large lecture groups and small discussion groups.

Democratic Leaders in Autocracies

In industrial organizations and the armed services, where members expect the leader to play an autocratic role, attempts to introduce more democratic procedures usually result in member dissatisfaction and low productivity similar to that usually associated with autocratic leadership in a democratic culture (cf. Berkowitz, 1953). In other industrial studies, high productivity in a shop has been found to be associated with a well-differentiated and authoritative style of leadership (Gekoski, 1952; Kahn & Katz, 1953).

In an air corps study, bomber-crew critiques of training problems were held under the direction of different types of leaders (Torrance, 1953). Crews with critiques which were structured by having a well-defined leader and procedure more frequently showed improvement in a subsequent problem-solving situation than did crews with less structured critiques. In addition, crews with an unstructured, nonauthoritarian leader and those who had no leader assigned but held a "self-critique" did no better than crews receiving no critique.

Similar findings are reported in studies of the smallest autocracies, the doctor and patient in a therapeutic interview. Here, progress is found to be associated with high frequencies of directive, interpretive remarks on the part of the therapist (Dittman, 1952; Keet, 1948; Wiener, 1955).

Distributed Leadership

Studies of initially leaderless groups often report that the leadership functions are distributed between a task leader and a social-emotional leader (Bales, 1958; Bales & Slater, 1955; Parker, 1958) or that the individual who receives the most nominations for leadership is not necessarily the one who is best liked (Hollander & Webb, 1955). Similar differences appear in organized groups. In the air corps, for example, both in behavior and ideology, the educational administrators showed greater consideration for the enlisted men and less organizing activity than did aircraft commanders (Halpin, 1955).

An exception to this tendency to distribute leader functions has been observed in labor mediations which involve only three persons: the mediator, a representative of management, and a representative of labor. It is the function of the labor mediator to guide the parties toward a settlement by his suggestions and powers of persuasion and thus to provide task leadership. Yet, because of the dispute separating and often alienating the parties, none of the three is in a position to serve as the social-emotional leader. As a result, the mediator must also perform this second type of leadership (Landsberger, 1955).

COMMUNICATION NETWORK

In large military and industrial organizations, a subsegment of the organization often serves as an information-processing center. There, the information is collated, displayed, evaluated, and decisions are made which affect the entire operating organization. Frequently some of the members involved are separated physically from one another and communicate by telephone and other devices in restricted networks. The frequency of concern with problems of communication in restricted networks has led to experimentive exploration of the properties of different sorts of networks.

The communication network is a factor in the situation which can be varied independently of the task or of the style of leadership in the group, although it is usually closely associated with it. When a task requires a particular type of communication network for optimum performance, the leader's style tends to place limits on the frequency, duration, and direction of member communications. However, all three variables—task, communication network, and leadership—are similar in that they are ways of manipulating the situation for the group by setting norms for the form or content of interaction.

A number of the studies using formal communication networks discussed in this section are also reviewed by Glanzer and Glasner (1961).

Relative Rates of Communication

Mechanical constrictions on communication, of course, constitute an extreme and obvious case of conditions that prevent the full and free interaction of each member with every other member. At one end of the continuum, subjects who are not allowed to communicate cannot be expected to have much effect on each other (Vinacke, 1957). But even in discussion groups where physical conditions of intercommunication are optimized, spatial location plays some part. For example, members tend to address more communication to persons seated opposite them at a table than to those next to them, presumably because of easier eye contact (Hearn, 1957; Sommer, 1959; Steinzor, 1950), and persons seated at the ends of the table in more "central" positions tend to dominate the discussion (Hare & Bales, 1963; Sommer, 1961; Strodtbeck & Hook, 1961). However, when the leaderless group is used as a technique for leader selection, seating position has little effect on final leadership ratings received by members (Bass & Klubeck, 1952). Presumably the difficulties of spatial location and interactive contact decrease as the size of the group decreases in a discussion situation. In a situation of this kind, the communication network is probably derived more from the expectations of the members than from other more mechanical considerations.

In free communication situations a gradient of activity-rates, rather than of equal participation, among members is the usual thing (Bales et al., 1951; Stephan & Mishler, 1952). Members who talk the most generally also receive the most interaction. This is probably a result, in part, of the tendency for a remark made by one person to be answered by some other, who may then continue to address the former speaker. In ad hoc problem-solving groups, about half of the remarks are addressed to the group as a whole and about half to particular other members—that is, in pair relationships (Bales et al., 1951). About half of the total content is devoted to substantive contributions while the other half is devoted to positive reactions, negative reactions, and questions. Both of these balances suggest that freely communicating groups devote about as much of their time to feedback (i.e., indications to the sender that the message has been received) as to specific problem-solving attempts. Low participators do not talk to each other as much as high participators talk among themselves. The network of communication is thus in effect restricted more or less spontaneously by the members, so that links between low participators tend to drop out as size increases, especially above size seven. It appears to be generally true that status distinctions show a high positive correlation with amount of participation, although status based on popularity is not as highly related as status based on task criteria in task-oriented groups (Bales, 1953; Bales & Slater, 1955; Hurwitz, Zander, & Hymovitch, 1953). In free discussion groups, the communication network and the network of interpersonal choice are interdependent, but also each is in some degree independently variable, so that the congruence is seldom perfect.

Centrality and Control

In a series of reports which systematically examine some features of the communication network, Shaw (1954a) found that subjects who have the greatest freedom of communication are generally more satisfied with the group, send more messages, and are more often recognized as leaders. (Mulder [1960b] suggested that member satisfaction with a position in the communication network is less related to centrality or amount of activity than it is to the amount of power the individual has over others in the group.)

In another experiment involving four-man groups in three controlled communication conditions, the wheel, the slash, and the circle (Gilchrist, Shaw, & Walker, 1954; Shaw, 1954c), centrality was found to vary inversely with the time required to complete an activity and directly with individual morale, the number of items transmitted, and the probability that a person would be chosen as the leader. These experiments used essentially individual problems, such as mathematical problems. The group was said to have completed the problem when each person in the network knew the answer.

Using four-man groups in star, slash, and "comcon" (all channels open) nets, it was also found that the groups which met once a day for 10 days solved problems faster, sent fewer messages, and were better satisfied as time passed (Shaw & Rothschild, 1956).

Increasing the amounts of information given to a person has an effect similar to increasing his centrality index. Using a systematic rather than random distribution of information in a net has the effect of allowing the members to reach faster solutions, with fewer errors and greater satisfaction, since they can group the data in their messages (Shaw, 1956). However, in group tasks which require each man to perform a separate function, the most efficient distribution of information is one which permits each individual the most autonomy in reaching his own decision and putting it into effect (Lanzetta & Roby, 1956).

It is also necessary for the central person

in the network to reach a decision when the task calls for group participation. If the central person simply collects or transmits information and leaves the decision to some other member, his group will not be as effective (Mulder, 1960a).

The relationship between leader style and communication network is evident in a controlled communication experiment using the wheel, kite, and comcon nets, in which authoritarian (appointed) leadership resulted in better group performance than nonauthoritarian leadership (Shaw, 1955). In the authoritarian situation, morale was lower but errors were lower. Morale was found to be related to the independence of action permitted; and saturation, or the input and output requirements placed upon a position, was shown to be related to performance.

Personality versus Position in the Communication Network

Although behavior has been conceptualized as involving a compromise between the tendencies of personality and the expectations of role, relatively few pieces of evidence have been presented to indicate the results which may be expected from the interaction of personality and role. Some evidence is provided by two studies of communication networks which deal primarily with the area of control.

In the first study, 10 4-man groups of college subjects solved 3 problems in a star communication network. Each group contained one subject who had been previously rated high on ascendance, one rated low, and two rated moderate. A high scoring person was expected to dominate the interaction. In some groups, the highly ascendant person occupied the central position, and in other groups, the lowest person was given central position. In the latter case, position in the network appeared to be the dominant factor since, after the first trial, the low ascendants in the center behaved like the highs, and the highs in peripheral positions became more passive. In each case, the subject in the center was more satisfied (Berkowitz, 1956).

In the second experiment, 44 previously unacquainted college subjects in 3-man groups each received notes which created variations in his centrality and autonomy. Autonomy in the network was measured by the subject's access to task-relevant information. Each of the subjects had high or low autonomy needs as measured by a paper-and-pencil test. After the experiment, the subjects who had been given positions of high autonomy were the most satisfied, especially when they had high autonomy needs. No differences in satisfaction appeared to accompany differences in centrality. However, a subject perceived another's performance as more valuable if the other person held a position more central than his own. Differences in the relative autonomy of positions seemed to have no effect on the perception of value (Trow, 1957).

An inconsistency between the amount of communication required by a position in a network and the popularity of the person in the position can affect group performance in a manner similar to inconsistencies between personality and role. Wheel networks with unpopular central members were found to be less efficient than those with popular central members (Mohanna & Argyle. 1960).

Feedback in Restricted Networks

In a situation where there is one-way communication and the receiver of the information is given no opportunity to "feed back" acknowledgments, questions, of negative reactions to the sender, accuracy, and confidence are reduced for both sender and receiver (Leavitt & Mueller, 1951). An initial reaction of hostility on the part of the receiver toward the sender tends to appear. Accuracy can improve with time, but not as rapidly as with feedback, and depends more on the sender than the receiver. An initial period with free feedback appreci-

ably improves subsequent communication without feedback. The feedback condition requires more time, but with experience the amount of time decreases. Receivers who are permitted to communicate back to a person who has sent them an act of hostility show more postexperimental friendliness to the instigator than those not permitted to communicate (Thibaut & Coules, 1952). Apparently, one-way communication prevents not only expressive catharsis, but also the opportunity for building new understanding and norms by which the members manage their social relationships and their process of communication. From this basic impairment other problems may develop.

Certain Communication Networks and Group Performance

An experiment by Leavitt (1951) provides an example of some of the effects that certain communication networks can have on group performance. One hundred male undergraduates were divided into 20 groups of 5 men each. Each group member was seated in a booth in a laboratory in either a circle, a chain, a "Y," or a wheel network, making a total of five groups for each network. The task of each group was to discover by passing notes which symbol was held in common from a set of symbols given to each man.

The results indicated that the circle network, at one extreme, was active, leaderless, unorganized, erratic, and yet enjoyed by its members. The wheel, at the other extreme, was less active, had a distinct leader, was organized, less erratic, and yet unsatisfying to most of its members. These findings have been replicated in groups with a much longer series of trials (Cohen, Bennis, & Wolkon, 1961). In one repetition with three-man groups, the members in the wheel network used less time to solve the problem of the common symbol than did members in a circle network, although the difference was not statistically significant.

Members in the wheel, however, took longer to solve more complex problems which required simple arithmetical computations (Shaw, 1954b). For an even more complex task, that of the discussion of a human relations problem, a star network required more time than a slash network, and a slash used more than a comcon network (all channels open). No differences in satisfaction or number of messages were found (Shaw, Rothschild, & Strickland, 1957). It is possible that in solving problems requiring some skill, the wheel network is more efficient only when the person in the center of the net is the most skillful member of the group.

In a similar experiment (Smith, 1951), the circle network permitted members to adapt more readily to a change requiring the breaking and relearning of a previously established set. The greater amount of interaction and feedback which characterizes the decentralized network seems to decrease the probability of gross unanimous errors, to increase adaptability in the face of new demands for relearning, and to increase average member satisfaction; however, it results in some cost in quantity of messages, duplication of effort, and general confusion.

Another experiment demonstrates the results of extreme conditions of lack of communication and feedback. Members of 30 6-man groups were required to close their eyes and then to raise a number of fingers so that the total would equal a number (e.g., six, five, or some smaller number) which the experimenter had previously announced. Under these conditions, only a few subjects were able to solve the problem (Berg, 1955).

Developing a Task Hierarchy

The Leavitt experiment was repeated (Guetzkow, 1960; Guetzkow & Dill, 1957; Guetzkow & Simon, 1955) and modified so as to study the development of the task hierarchy within each type of communication network. Using the same problem of discovering the common symbol on a set of cards, five-man groups were tested in wheel, circle, and all-channel networks. Between each trial, the group members were allowed a two-minute period in which to organize the group. In the wheel, the activity during this two-minute period was centered on discovering the organization which was already present; in the all-channel and circle networks, the members sought to develop an efficient hierarchy. In the circle, the members tended to select a three-level hierarchy, and in the all-channel group, the members formed either a two- or three-level hierarchy. As soon as the members of a group had worked out a hierarchy, they improved in the task. Fewer task messages and more social-emotional messages were sent after the hierarchy was established. On the first few trials, more messages were sent to those subjects who gave good information or who provided the right answer. As these channels began to be used more than others, they were gradually incorporated into the developing communication network. The all-channel networks were the slowest to establish hierarchies because the members had to make a selection from so many channels. In a related experiment, members of groups with experience in a wheel network organized themselves in a chain when placed in a circle network (Cohen & Bennis, 1961).

Noise

The differences between networks become more pronounced as "noise" is introduced into the communication channels. Here "noise" refers to anything which interrupts the messages sent (Heise & Miller, 1951) or makes it difficult to understand and solve the problem, such as the introduction of irrelevant information (Shaw, 1958).

To counteract the effects of "noise" in the information theory sense, groups repeat the same information several times as a means of reducing error (Christie, Luce, & Macy, 1952; Macy, Christie, & Luce, 1953).

GROUP SIZE

Some of the effects of increasing size will be considered as they relate to the form and content of interaction. Since the number of potential relationships between group members increases rapidly as a group grows larger, the larger group tends to break into subgroups with a more rigid hierarchy of positions. When the time for discussion is limited, the average member has fewer chances to speak and intermember communication becomes difficult. Morale declines since the former intimate contact between members is no longer possible. Although the larger group has in its membership a greater variety of resources for problem-solving, the average contribution of each member diminishes, and it becomes more difficult to reach consensus on a group solution. The pair and the three-person group have special characteristics of intimacy and of power structure which give each group some unique aspects. Although the optimum size for a group varies with the task, a five-man group is found to have some advantages for problems which can be solved by group discussion.

Natural Size

In terms of effective participation in group activity, it may be that certain group sizes are more "natural" and occur more frequently than others under particular conditions. Age seems to be a variable which is related to size in this way. The increasing maturity associated with age appears to permit effective participation in larger groups. Preschool children tend to play first individually, although in parallel, then in pairs, and later in larger groups (Parten, 1933).

Another variable which appears to be associated with "natural" sizes is the rural-urban continuum. Rural high school youth form cliques of about three persons; whereas town youth are more likely to form cliques of four to five persons (Hollingshead, 1949). The smaller size of the rural cliques seems to result primarily from the fact that the rural youth live farther apart.

Frequency and duration of contact between members is to some extent conditioned by size, as well as the reverse. Among college students, as the size of the group increases, the frequency, duration, and intimacy of contact decreases (Fischer, 1953). Studies of the frequency of occurrence of small groups of different sizes, collected data by observation and from records of the sizes of groups formed by pedestrians, shoppers, play groups, work groups, and congressional committees. The frequency of occurrence of groups of different sizes was found to be a negative function of size. The function described appears smooth, and the mean size was close to 2.4 (Coleman & James, 1961; James, 1953). Face-to-face groups seem to tend to gravitate to the smallest size—two.

Size and Satisfaction

The importance of the individual's relationship with a small group as a factor contributing to his satisfaction with the task is further indicated by evidence that infantry men in the American army, coal miners in Great Britain, and college students are more satisfied with smaller work groups (Chesler, Van Steenberg, & Bruchel, 1955; Schellenberg, 1959; Trist & Bamforth, 1951).

In general, as the size of the group decreases, the strength of the affectional ties between members increases, with the dyad allowing the possibilities for the greatest degree of intimacy.

Size and the Emergence of Leadership

As size increases, it presumably becomes more difficult for each member to keep each other group member in mind as a separate, differentiated person. Observers reach maximum agreement on leadership assessment at size 6, as compared with sizes 2, 4, 8, and 18 (Bass & Norton, 1951). It may be that leadership tends not to emerge so clearly in the even sizes below 6, and that above that size, the observer may begin to run into cognitive difficulties. The coincidence of these findings suggests that the ability of the observing individual to perceive, keep track of, and judge each member separately in a social interaction situation may not extend much beyond the size of 6 or 7. If this is true, one would expect members of groups larger than that size to tend to think of other members in terms of subgroups, or "classes" of some kind, and to deal with members of subgroups other than their own by more stereotyped methods of response.

Size and Number of Relationships

Possibly a more relevant way of viewing size as a variable is to consider the number of possible relationships in the group by pairs and larger subgroups rather than by the number of persons. As the number of individuals increases, the number of possible relationships increases much more rapidly than size (Bavelas, 1959).

It may be expected, then, that when there is a desire for intimate and highly developed relationships or a need for fine coordination, there will also be a tendency toward the restriction of size. It is worth noting that the appearance of a leader can permit a reduction of the psychological complication of the group to a series of pair relationships of each member with the leader for certain purposes of coordination. The development of leadership is possibly in part an alternative to an actual reduction in the size of the group.

Several investigators associate the emergence of leadership with increasing size of the group. In the restaurant industry, increasing size of the organization is related to increasing difficulty in coordinating activities (Whyte, 1949). A large questionnaire study found that leader behavior in many different types of groups differs as size increases (especially above size 31). The demands upon the leader role, moreover, become more numerous and exacting, and member tolerance for leader-centered direction of group activities becomes greater (Hemphill, 1950). In initially leaderless groups, correlations between observer ratings of members on "initiative," "insight," "leadership behavior," and "authoritarianism" are greater in groups of eight than those of four (Carter, Haythorn, Meirowitz, & Lanzetta, 1951). A similar increase in correlation between prediction of leadership skill made from TAT analysis and the amount of change toward consensus in group discussion appears when groups of 5 are compared with groups of 12 (Hare, 1952), since the larger groups "demand more skill from the leader." In a study of adjustment over time in a group of machine shop workers, the underlying emotional tone fluctuates as size increases—from an initial period of aggression and withdrawal to a period of dependency on the leader and then back to aggression and withdrawal (Rice, 1951). Members of larger groups tend to form subgroups with spokesmen for their opinions (Hare, 1952; Homans, 1950).

Size and Time for Communication

The time available per member for overt communication during a meeting of any given length decreases as the group size increases (Hare, 1952). In addition, an increased proportion of the members report feelings of threat and inhibition of impulses to participate as size is increased (J. R. Gibb, 1951).

Not only does the average amount of participation per member diminish as group size is increased, but the distribution of participation also varies (Bales et al., 1951). Generally, in discussion groups of three to eight, all members address some remarks to the group as a whole, but typically only one member, the top participator, addresses more to the group as a whole than to specific other members. As group size increases, an ever larger proportion of the participators have total amounts of participation under their "equal" share, that is, under the mean for the group. At the same time, at least where a participating leader is appointed, the gap between the top participator and the others tends to grow proportionately greater as size increases. When the designated leader of a group is excluded, the gradient of total acts initiated by the remainder of the members tends to follow a simple curve that flattens as the size of the group increases (Stephan & Mishler, 1952). In one experiment involving a group of four males, each individual had sufficient latitude or space for interaction, so the basic abilities of each individual could be expressed; in a group of eight, however, only the more forceful individuals were able to express their abilities and ideas, since the amount of freedom in the situation was not sufficient to accommodate all the group members (Carter et al., 1951).

Increased Resources versus Diminishing Returns

While increasing size may be viewed as a limiting condition in certain respects, it is obviously not a constricting factor in every way. Many abilities or resources needed in task performance tend to have an additive character; these may include such things as the number of items of information which can be absorbed and recalled; the number of critical judgments available to correct errors of information and inference; the number of ideas or suggestions available for solution of problems; the range of values likely to be brought to bear; as well as the range of technical skills, abilities, and amount of muscular power available to implement decisions. For example, in a word-building task, the number of words built in a given time increases as the group size is increased from 3 to 10 (Watson, 1928).

The familiar phenomenon of "diminishing returns," however, tends to set in at some point. The addition of a person to a group of a given size may not represent a unit addition to task ability. The tendency for difficulty of coordination to increase with size is one factor that may lead to diminishing net returns, but there are other factors also. In audience-like groups of 8 different sizes, from 1 to 96 persons (J. R. Gibb, 1951), the absolute number of volunteered ideas for the solution of a problem produced within a set time followed a negatively accelerated increasing function. The negative acceleration may be due to some limit to the number of solutions available and reluctance to repeat, or it may have resulted from the increasing difficulty faced by the experimenter in recording all suggestions as they occurred. However, the proportion of subjects who reported feelings of threat or inhibition of their impulses to participate increased with size. The same experiment included a situation which increased feelings of threat by creating a more formal procedure. This situation also leads to a reduction in the number of ideas proposed. One infers then that increased feeling of threat may reduce participation as size increases and thus may create an obstacle to the completion of the task.

On a task requiring physical pulling power, a four-man group was found to be the most efficient (Moede, 1927). Above that size, the pulling power per member decreased by 10 per cent with each additional member. One would suppose that difficulty of coordination may be an interfering factor in this case.

On a concept formation task (Twenty Questions), groups of two persons obtained the answer in shorter time, used fewer questions, and failed less often at the task than did individuals (Taylor & Faust, 1952). Groups of four failed least often but were not otherwise superior to groups of two. Here we see, apparently, gains from having available a larger pool of questions to ask, and from the exercise of critical judgment in eliminating poor ideas or testing closure on the solution, but both sources of gain are subject to diminishing returns. The number of man-minutes required per problem increases with size. This, of course, is typically the case. However, for many practical purposes, where the task requires some absolute level of effectiveness within a set time to avoid complete failure, the lowered efficiency per unit of time per man may be a secondary consideration.

A number of early experiments include the finding that groups have a lower probability of failure or a greater probability of accuracy in problem-solving than do individuals, since the groups have greater resources for ideas, error-checking, and memory (Barnlund, 1959; Dashiell, 1935; Perlmutter, 1953; Perlmutter & de Montmollin, 1952; Ziller, 1957b). However, the only clearly demonstrated gain so far is essentially of a statistical sort: Four judgments are better than one for the same nonsocial reason that four thermometers are better than one. The group effect is essentially a trend toward homogeneity or reduction of variance. In a secondary way this usually increases the accuracy of individual judgments, or the size of the majority vote, but it does not by itself increase the accuracy of group judgment (Johnson, 1955, p. 471). Thus "pooled" judgments of individuals who do not meet as a group may be as accurate as group opinion (Anderson, 1961; Faust, 1959). If the true value of the variable being judged is bracketed by the range of individual judgments, and if the errors are only of a random kind, the tendency to converge toward a group norm of judgments will increase the accuracy of the average individual judgment. If the true value is outside the range of judgments, the average error of the judgments will not be changed by the convergence effect.

The greater variety of opinion available as size increases may give some advantage of critical power but has as its price the greater difficulty of reaching consensus. The difficulty is apparently most marked when the task is primarily one of modifying opinion in the absence of any clear objective criteria for judgment. For example, groups of 6 took longer on tasks of this sort than groups of 3 (South, 1927), and groups of 12 took longer on a group decision than groups of 5 (Hare, 1952). On the other hand, if the task is a technical one with clear criteria of correct performance and requires some absolute level of intelligence, speed, or the like, the larger group may have a higher probability of containing some member who can obtain an answer easily acceptable to the others once it is presented (Lorge & Solomon, 1960).

Changes in the Content of Interaction

The frequency with which certain categories of acts appear tends to vary with group size (Hamblin & Miller, 1961). In groups of two to seven engaged in a group decision problem, where the criteria of the goodness of the solution depends upon the values of the members (Bales & Borgatta, 1955), as size increases, the rate of giving information and suggestion increases and the rate of asking for opinion, giving opinion, and showing agreement decreases. These changes are consistent with the hypothesis that as size increases there is a tendency toward a more mechanical method of introducing information (by round-robin procedure, for example), a less sensitive exploration of the point of view of the other, and a more direct attempt to control others and reach solution whether or not all group members indicate agreement. All these effects are reasonably associated with the increasing constriction of time available per person.

Rates of showing tension tend to decrease with size; but joking and laughter increase, which may indicate a tendency for less direct involvement of members in task success and for tension to be displaced into humor rather than be reduced directly through serious attempts to resolve opinion differences. In this sense, it is suggested that unresolved differences appear to be more tolerable in larger groups and may be handled by devices such as compartmentalization rather than by resolution.

The Dyad

In addition to the effects of size which show an increasing or decreasing trend are certain unique characteristics of groups of two (Becker & Useem, 1942). Dyads tend to have high rates of showing tension and consistently avoid disagreement and antagonism. Members have high rates of asking for opinion but avoid giving opinion, and concentrate rather on exchange of information and agreement (or acknowledgment) (Bales & Borgatta, 1955; Borgatta & Guerrin, 1960). This pattern is consistent with an interpretation that in groups of two a delicate balance of power exists when, as in ad hoc experimental groups, there are few group norms regarded as binding except those to which both members currently assent. In such a case, there is no "public opinion," no majority to which either can appeal. Either member can prevent task completion by disagreement or withdrawal. Both members have to proceed within certain limits to avoid this reaction on the part of the other. Two asymmetric roles tend to develop; that is, the members tend to specialize in different types of overt behavior. The differences appear in practically all categories of behavior. Apparently there is a tendency for one member to gravitate toward a more active role and exercise the power of initiative while the other tends toward a more passive role and holds the power of veto.

Even and Odd Sizes

Above size two there are significant differences between groups with an even or odd number of members (Bales & Borgatta, 1955). Groups of even size (four and six) have higher rates of showing disagreement and antagonism and lower rates of asking for suggestion and possibly of showing agreement than groups of odd size (three, five, and seven). These effects are attributed to the fact that in even sizes a division of the group into two subparts of equal size is possible. Thus, in cases of disagreement in even-size groups, the probability of a majority and a minority is lower than in odd sizes, and this in turn may increase the probability that disagreements will remain deadlocked between two subgroups.

The Triad

The power of majority over minority is especially marked in groups of size three, since any minority must be a single person, who is thus left isolated without the support of any other group member, at least with respect to the immediate discussion.

If the power distribution in the group is unequal, these observations may not hold, since the most powerful member may prevail (Caplow, 1956), or the weakest person may initiate a coalition with the strongest (Kelley & Arrowood, 1960; Stryker & Psathas, 1960; Vinacke & Arkoff, 1957). In mixed sex groups, both sexes when in the majority tend to ally against the minority of the opposite sex (Bond & Vinacke, 1961).

In laboratory discussion groups of three persons (Mills, 1953; Mills, 1956), a relationship in which the two top participators disagree with each other and seek the support of the third low member is unstable during meeting and tends to change toward the end of the meeting to a supporting coalition between the two higher participators with the low man excluded. In laboratory groups such as these, any pattern, once clearly formed, tends to be preserved with minimal alteration when a fourth member (a newcomer) is added to the group (Mills et al., 1957). In more permanent groups of three (father, mother, and son), no one person is singled out for exclusion in a series of decisions (Strodtbeck, 1954).

In another study on coalitions, a third member was forced to change his behavior pattern completely by two role players who first allowed him to form a coalition with one of them, and then combined against him. He changed his opinion less often than his behavior, and he tended to retain his liking for the original partner in spite of the overt desertion (Mills, 1954).

The Optimum Size

A final comment may be made on the relation of size to member satisfaction. In one study, members of 5-man groups were more satisfied with the discussion than members of 12-man groups (Hare, 1952), and in another study of discussion groups, the optimal size appeared to be 5 (Bales, 1954; Slater, 1958). Below size five, members complain that the group is too small, although amount of talking time available to each increases. This may be a reflection of the strains associated with the face-to-face relationship which have been noted above in the description of the two-, three-, and four-man groups, and of the odd and even effects. Above size five, members complain that the group is too large, and this may be due to the restriction on the amount of participation. Size five combines the characteristics that: (1) a strict deadlock is not possible with an odd number of members; (2) the group tends to split into a majority of three and a minority of two, so that being in a minority does not isolate the individual but allows him sources of gratification; and (3) the group appears to be large enough for the members to shift roles easily and for any individual to withdraw from an awkward position without necessarily having the issue resolved.

REFERENCES

Albert, R. S. Comments on the scientific function of the concept of cohesiveness. *Amer. J. Sociol.*, 1953, 59, 231–234.

Allport, G. W. The historical background of modern social psychology. In G. Lindzey (Ed.), *Handbook of social psychology.* Reading, Mass.: Addison-Wesley, 1954. Pp. 3–56.

Ames, R. Leaderless group discussion and experience in group leadership. *Calif. J. educ. Res.*, 1955, 6, 166–169.

Anderson, N. H. Group performance in an anagram task. *J. soc. Psychol.*, 1961, 55, 67–75.

Anderson, R. C. Learning in discussions: A resume of the authoritarian-democratic studies. *Harv. educ. Rev.*, 1959, 29, 201–215.

Andrews, R. E. *Leadership and supervision.* U.S. Civil Service Comm., Personnel Mgmt Ser. No. 9. Washington: Government Printing Office, 1955.

Ansbacher, H. L. The history of the leaderless group discussion technique. *Psychol. Bull.*, 1951, 48, 383–391.

Aronson, E., & Mills, J. The effect of severity of initiation on liking for a group. *J. abnorm. soc. Psychol.*, 1959, 59, 177–181.

Asch, S. E. Opinions and social pressure. *Sci. Amer.*, 1955, 193(5), 31–35.

Back, K. W. Interpersonal relations in a discussion group. *J. soc. Iss.*, 1948, 4, 61–65.

Backman, C. W., & Secord, P. F. The effect of perceived liking on interpersonal attraction. *Hum. Relat.* 1959, 12, 379–384.

Baker, Bela O., & Sarbin, T. R. Differential mediation of social perception as a correlate of social adjustment. *Sociometry*, 1956, 19, 69–83.

Bales, R. F. *Interaction process analysis: A method for the study of small groups.* Reading, Mass.: Addison-Wesley, 1950.

Bales, R. F. The equilibrium problem in small groups. In T. Parsons, R. F. Bales, & E. A. Shils (Eds.), *Working papers in the theory of action.* New York: The Free Press of Glencoe, 1953. Pp. 111–161.

Bales, R. F. In conference. *Harv. bus. Rev.*, 1954, 32, 44–50.

Bales, R. F. How people interact in conferences. *Sci. Amer.*, 1955, 192(3), 31–35.

Bales, R. F. Task roles and social roles in problem solving groups. In Eleanor E. Maccoby, T. M. Newcomb, & E. L. Hartley (Eds.), *Readings in social psychology.* (3rd ed.) New York: Holt, 1958. Pp. 437–447.

Bales, R. F., & Borgatta, E. F. Size of group as a factor in the interaction profile. In A. P. Hare, E. F. Borgatta, & R. F. Bales (Eds.), *Small groups: Studies in social interaction.* New York: Knopf, 1955. Pp. 396–413.

Bales, R. F., & Slater, P. E. Role differentiation in small decision-making groups. In T. Parson, R. F. Bales, J. Olds, M. Zelditch, & P. E. Slater (Eds.), *The family, socialization, and interaction process.* New York: The Free Press of Glencoe, 1955. Pp. 259–306.

Bales, R. F., & Strodtbeck, F. L. Phases in group problem solving. *J. abnorm. soc. Psychol.,* 1951, 46, 485–495.

Bales, R. F., Strodtbeck, F. L., Mills, T. M., & Roseborough, Mary E. Channels of communication in small groups. *Amer. sociol. Rev.* 1951, 16, 461–468.

Barnlund, D. C. A comparative study of individual, majority, and group judgment. *J. abnorm. soc. Psychol.,* 1959, 58, 55–60.

Bartlett, C. J. Dimensions of leadership behavior in classroom discussion groups. *J. educ. Psychol.,* 1959, 50, 280–284.

Bass, B. M. *Leadership, psychology, and organizational behavior.* New York: Harper, 1960.

Bass, B. M. Some aspects of attempted, successful, and effective leadership. *J. appl. Psychol.,* 1961, 45, 120–122.

Bass, B. M., & Klubeck, S. Effects of seating arrangement on leaderless group discussions. *J. abnorm. soc. Psychol.,* 1952, 47, 724–727.

Bass, B. M., & Norton, Fay-Tyler M. Group size and leaderless discussions. *J. appl. Psychol.,* 1951, 35, 397–400.

Bates, A. P., & Cloyd, J. S. Toward the development of operations for defining group norms and members' roles. *Sociometry,* 1956, 19, 26–39.

Bates, F. L. Position, role, and status: A reformulation of concepts. *Soc. Forces,* 1956, 34, 313–321.

Baur, E. J. Public opinion and the primary group. *Amer. sociol. Rev.,* 1960, 25, 208–219.

Bavelas, A. Communication patterns in task oriented groups. *J. accoustical soc. Amer.,* 1950, 22, 725–730.

Bavelas, A. Group size, interaction, and structural environment. In B. Schaffner (Ed.), *Group processes: Transactions of the fourth conference.* New York: Josiah Macy, Jr. Foundation, 1959. Pp. 133–179.

Becker, H., & Useem, Ruth H. Sociological analysis of the dyad. *Amer. sociol. Rev.,* 1942, 7, 13–26.

Bell, G. B., & Stopler, Rhoda. An attempt at validation of the Empathy Test. *J. appl. Psychol.,* 1955, 39, 442–443.

Bellows, R. *Creative leadership.* Englewood Cliffs, N.J.: Prentice-Hall, Inc., 1959.

Bennis, W. G., & Shepard, H. A. A theory of group development. *Hum. Relat.,* 1956, 9, 415–437.

Berg, I., & Bass, B. M. (Eds.) *Conformity and deviation.* New York: Harper, 1961.

Berg, J. Cooperation without communication and observation. *J. soc. Psychol.,* 1955, 41, 287–296.

Berger, J., Cohen, B. P., Snell, J. L., & Zelditch, M., Jr. *Types of formalization in small-group research.* Boston: Houghton, 1962.

Berkowitz, L. Sharing leadership in small, decision-making groups. *J. abnorm. soc. Psychol.,* 1953, 48, 231–238.

Berkowitz, L. Personality and group position. *Sociometry,* 1956, 19, 210–222.

Berkowitz, L., & Howard, R. C. Reactions to opinion deviates as affected by affiliation need (n) and group member interdependence. *Sociometry,* 1959, 22, 81–91.

Berkowitz, L., & Macaulay, Jacqueline R. Some effects of differences in status level and status stability. *Hum. Relat.,* 1961, 14, 135–148.

Bevan, W., Albert, R. S., Loiseaux, P. R., Mayfield, P. N., & Wright, G. Jury behavior as a function of the prestige of the foreman and the nature of his leadership. *J. publ. Law,* 1958, 7, 419–449.

Biderman, A. D. Effects of Communist indoctrination attempts: Some comments based on an Air Force prisoner-of-war study. *Soc. Probs,* 1959, 6, 304–313.

Bieri, J. Changes in interpersonal perceptions following social interaction. *J. abnorm. soc. Psychol.,* 1953, 48, 61–66.

Bion, W. R. *Experiences in groups: And other papers.* New York: Basic Books, 1961.

Blake, R. R., & Mouton, Jane S. Loyalty of representatives to ingroup positions during intergroup competition. *Sociometry,* 1961, 24, 177–183.(a)

Blake, R. R., & Mouton, Jane S. Perceived characteristics of elected representatives. *J. abnorm. soc. Psychol.,* 1961, 62, 693–695.(b)

Blau, P. M. Patterns of deviation in work groups. *Sociometry,* 1960, 23, 245–261.

Blau, P. M. Patterns of choice in interpersonal relations. *Amer. sociol. Rev.,* 1962, 27, 41–55.

Bloch, H. A., & Neiderhoffer, A. *The gang: A study in adolescent behavior*. New York: Philosophical Library, 1958.

Block, J., & Bennett, Lillian F. The assessment of communication. *Hum. Relat.*, 1955, 8, 317–325.

Bond, J. R., & Vinacke, W. E. Coalitions in mixed-sex triads. *Sociometry*, 1961, 24, 61–75.

Bonney, M. E. A sociometric study of the relationship of some factors to mutual friendships on the elementary, secondary, and college levels. *Sociometry*, 1946, 9, 21–47.

Borg, W. R. The behavior of emergent and designated leaders in situational tests. *Sociometry*, 1957, 20, 95–104.

Borg, W. R. Prediction of small group role behavior from personality variables. *J. abnorm. soc. Psychol.*, 1960, 60, 112–116.

Borgatta, E. F. Analysis of social interaction and sociometric perception. *Sociometry*, 1954, 17, 7–31.

Borgatta, E. F. Small group research: A trend report and bibliography. *Curr. Sociol.*, 1960, 9 (3), 173–272.

Borgatta, E. F. Role-playing specification, personality, and performance. *Sociometry*, 1961, 24, 218–233.

Borgatta, E. F., & Bales, R. F. Task and accumulation of experience as factors in the interaction of small groups. *Sociometry*, 1953, 16, 239–252.

Borgatta, E. F., & Bales, R. F. Sociometric status patterns and characteristics of interaction. *J. soc. Psychol.*, 1956, 43, 289–297.

Borgatta, E. F., & Guerrin, R. F. The two-person group: Some notes on theory and research. *Sociol. soc. Res.*, 1960, 45, 3–13.

Bott, Elizabeth. Urban families: Conjugal roles and social networks. *Hum. Relat.*, 1955, 8, 345–384.

Bott, Elizabeth. Urban families: The norms of conjugal roles. *Hum. Relat.*, 1956, 9, 325–341.

Bovard, E. W., Jr. Group structure and perception. *J. abnorm. soc. Psychol.*, 1951, 46, 398–405.

Bovard, E. W., Jr. Conformity to social norms and attraction to the group. *Science*, 1953, 118, 598–599.

Bowerman, C. E., & Day, Barbara R. A test of the theory of complementary needs as applied to couples during courtship. *Amer. sociol. Rev.*, 1956, 21, 602–605.

Brehm, J. W., & Cohen, A. R. *Explorations in cognitive dissonance*. New York: Wiley, 1962.

Bruun, K. Significance of role and norms in the small group for individual behavior changes while drinking. *Quart. J. Stud. Alcohol*, 1959, 20, 53–64.

Bugental, Daphne E., & Lehner, G. F. J. Accuracy of self-perception and group-perception as related to two leadership roles. *J. abnorm. soc. Psychol.*, 1958, 56, 396–398.

Burchinal, L. G., Hawkes, G. R., & Gardner, B. Personality characteristics and marital satisfaction. *Soc. Forces*, 1957, 35, 218–222.

Butler, J. M. The interaction of client and therapist. *J. abnorm. soc. Psychol.*, 1952, 47, 366–378.

Byrne, D. Interpersonal attraction and attitude similarity. *J. abnorm. soc. Psychol.*, 1961, 62, 713–715.(a)

Byrne, D. The influence of propinquity and opportunities for interaction on classroom relationships. *Hum. Relat.*, 1961, 14, 63–69.(b)

Calvin, A. D., Hoffman, F. K., & Harden, E. L. The effect of intelligence and social atmosphere on group problem solving behavior. *J. soc. Psychol.*, 1957, 45, 61–74.

Campbell, D. T. An error in some demonstrations of the superior social perceptiveness of leaders. *J. abnorm. soc. Psychol.*, 1955, 51, 694–695.

Campbell, D. T., & Tyler, Bonnie B. The construct validity of work-group morale measures. *J. appl. Psychol.*, 1957, 41, 91–92.

Caplow, T. A theory of coalitions in the triad. *Amer. sociol. Rev.*, 1956, 21, 489–493.

Carment, D. W. Ascendant-submissive behavior in pairs of human subjects as a function of their emotional responsiveness and opinion strength. *Canad. J. Psychol.*, 1961, 15, 45–51.

Carter, L. F., Haythorn, W., Meirowitz, Beatrice, & Lanzetta, J. The relation of categorizations and ratings in the observation of group behavior. *Hum. Relat.*, 1951, 4, 239–254.

Carter, L. F., Haythorn, W., Shriver, E., & Lanzetta, J. The behavior of leaders and other group members. *J. abnorm. soc. Psychol.*, 1951, 46, 589–595.

Carter, L. F., & Nixon, Mary. Ability, perceptual, personality, and interest factors associated with different criteria of leadership. *J. Psychol.*, 1949, 27, 377–388.

Cartwright, D. Achieving change in people: Some applications of group dynamics theory. *Hum. Relat.*, 1951, 4, 381–392.

Cartwright, D. Emotional dimensions of group life. In M. L. Reymert (Ed.), *Feelings and emotions.* New York: McGraw, 1952. Pp. 439–447.

Cartwright, D. (Ed.) *Studies in social power.* Ann Arbor: Univer. of Michigan Press, 1959.

Cartwright, D., & Zander, A. (Eds.) *Group dynamics: Research and theory.* Evanston, Ill.: Row, 1953. (2nd ed.: 1960)

Cervin, V. Experimental investigation of behavior in social situations: I. Behavior under opposition. *Canad. J. Psychol.*, 1955, 9, 107–116.(a)

Cervin, V. Experimental investigation of behavior in social situations: II. Individual behavioral effects of change in group attitude from opposition to cooperation. *Canad. J. Psychol.*, 1955, 9, 155–160.(b)

Cervin, V. Individual behavior in social situations: Its relation to anxiety, neuroticism, and group solidarity. *J. exp. Psychol.*, 1956, 51, 161–168.

Chance, June E. Adjustment and prediction of others' behavior. *J. consult. Psychol.*, 1958, 22, 191–194.

Chapple, E. D. The measurement of interpersonal behavior. *Trans. N.Y. Acad. Sci.*, 1942, 4, 222–233.

Chesler, D. J., Van Steenberg, N. J., & Brueckel, Joyce E. Effect on morale of infantry team replacement and individual replacement systems. *Sociometry*, 1955, 18, 587–597.

Chowdhry, Kamla, & Newcomb, T. M. The relative abilities of leaders and non-leaders to estimate opinions of their own groups. *J. abnorm. soc. Psychol.*, 1952, 47, 51–57.

Christie, L. S., Luce, R. D., & Macy, J., Jr. *Communications and learning in task oriented groups.* Cambridge, Mass.: Research Laboratory Electronics, 1952.

Christner, Charlotte A., & Hemphill, J. K. Leader behavior of B-29 commanders and changes in crew members' attitudes toward the crew. *Sociometry*, 1955, 18, 82–87.

Cohen, A. M., & Bennis, W. G. Continuity of leadership in communication networks. *Hum. Relat.*, 1961, 14, 351–367.

Cohen, A. M., Bennis, W. G., & Wolkon, G. H. The effects of continued practice on the behaviors of problem-solving groups. *Sociometry*, 1961, 24, 416–431.

Cohen, A. R., Brehm, J. W., & Latane, B. Choice of strategy and voluntary exposure to information under public and private conditions. *J. Pers.*, 1959, 27, 63–73.

Coleman, J. S., & James, J. The equilibrium size distribution of freely-forming groups. *Sociometry*, 1961, 24, 36–45.

Conrad, Dorothy C., & Conrad, R. The use of personal pronouns as categories for studying small group interaction. *J. abnorm. soc. Psychol.*, 1956, 52, 277–279.

Corsini, R. J. Understanding and similarity in marriage. *J. abnorm. soc. Psychol.*, 1956, 52, 327–332.

Couch, A., & Kenniston, K. Agreeing response set and social desirability. *J. abnorm. soc. Psychol.*, 1961, 62, 175–179.

Cranach, M. L. von. Experimente zur urteilsbildung in strukturierten gruppen (Experiments towards formation of judgment in structured groups). *Z. exp. angew. Psychol.*, 1960, 7, 427–450.

Crockett, W. H., & Meidinger, T. Authoritarianism and interpersonal perception. *J. abnorm. soc. Psychol.*, 1956, 53, 378–382.

Cronbach, L. J. Processes affecting scores on "understanding of others" and "assumed similarity." *Psychol. Bull.*, 1955, 52, 177–193.

Cronbach, L. J. Proposals leading to analytic treatment of social perception scores. In R. Tagiuri & L. Petrullo (Eds.), *Person perception and interpersonal behavior.* Stanford, Calif.: Stanford Univer. Press, 1958. Pp. 353–379.

Crowell, Laura, Katcher, A., & Miyamoto, S. F. Self-concepts of communication skill and performance in small group discussions. *Speech Monogr.*, 1955, 22, 20–27.

Dashiell, J. F. Experimental studies of the influence of social situations on the behavior of individual human adults. In C. Murchison (Ed.), *A handbook of social psychology.* Worcester, Mass.: Clark Univer. Press, 1935. Pp. 1097–1158.

Davis, J. A., Gebhard, Ruth U., Huson, Carolyn, & Spaeth, J. L. *Great books and small groups.* New York: The Free Press, 1961.

Davol, S. H. An empirical test of structural balance in sociometric triads. *J. abnorm. soc. Psychol.*, 1959, 59, 393–398.

De Monchaux, Cecily, & Schimmin, Sylvia. Some problems in experimental group psychology: Considerations arising from cross-cultural experiments on threat and rejection. *Hum. Relat.*, 1955, **8**, 53–60.

Deutsch, M., & Solomon, L. Reactions to evaluations by others as influenced by self-evaluations. *Sociometry*, 1959, **22**, 93–112.

Dittes, J. E., & Kelley, H. H. Effects of different conditions of acceptance upon conformity to group norms. *J. abnorm. soc. Psychol.*, 1956, **53**, 100–107.

Dittman, A. T. The interpersonal process in psychotherapy: Development of a research method. *J. abnorm. soc. Psychol.*, 1952, **47**, 236–244.

Di Vesta, F. J. Effects of confidence and motivation on susceptibility to informational social influence. *J. abnorm. soc. Psychol.*, 1959, **59**, 204–209.

Di Vesta, F. J., & Cox, L. Some dispositional correlates of conformity behavior. *J. soc. Psychol.*, 1960, **22**, 259–268.

Downing, J. Cohesiveness, perception, and values. *Hum. Relat.*, 1958, **11**, 157–166.

Dymond, Rosalind F. A scale for the measurement of empathic ability. *J. consult. Psychol.*, 1949, **13**, 127–133.

Dymond, Rosalind F. Personality and empathy. *J. consult. Psychol.*, 1950, **14**, 343–350.

Dymond, Rosalind F., Hughes, Anne S., & Raabe, Virginia L. Measurable changes in empathy with age. *J. consult. Psychol.*, 1952, **16**, 202–206.

Dymond, Rosalind F., Seeman, J., & Grummon, D. L. Patterns of perceived interpersonal relations. *Sociometry*, 1956, **19**, 166–177.

Edwards, A. L., & Walker, J. N. A note on the Couch and Kenniston measure of agreement response set. *J. abnorm. soc. Psychol.*, 1961, **62**, 173–174.(a)

Edwards, A. L., & Walker, J. N. Social desirability and agreement response set. *J. abnorm. soc. Psychol.*, 1961, **62**, 180–183.(b)

Eisman, Bernice. Some operational measures of cohesiveness and their interrelations. *Hum. Relat.*, 1959, **12**, 183–189.

Endler, N. S. Social conformity in perception of the autokinetic effect. *J. abnorm. soc. Psychol.*, 1960, **61**, 489–490.

Exline, R. V. Effects of sex, norms, and affiliation motivation upon accuracy of perception of interpersonal preferences. *J. Pers.*, 1960, **28**, 397–412.(a)

Exline, R. V. Interrelations among two dimensions of sociometric status, group congeniality and accuracy of social perception. *Sociometry*, 1960, **23**, 85–101.(b)

Exline, R. V., & Ziller, R. C. Status congruency and interpersonal conflict in decision-making groups. *Hum. Relat.*, 1959, **12**, 147–161.

Faust, W. L. Group versus individual problem-solving. *J. abnorm. soc. Psychol.* 1959, **59**, 68–72.

Fessenden, S. A. An index of cohesiveness-morale based on the analysis of sociometric choice distribution. *Sociometry*, 1953, **16**, 321–326.

Festinger, L. Theory of social comparison processes. *Hum. Relat.*, 1954, **7**, 117–140.

Festinger, L. *A theory of cognitive dissonance.* Stanford, Calif.: Stanford Univer. Press, 1962.

Festinger, L., & Aronson, E. The arousal and reduction of dissonance in social contexts. In D. Cartwright & A. Zander (Eds.), *Group dynamics: Research and theory.* Evanston, Ill.: Row, Peterson, 1960. Pp. 214–231.

Festinger, L., & Carlsmith, J. M. Cognitive consequences of forced compliance. *J. abnorm. soc. Psychol.*, 1959, **58**, 203–210.

Festinger, L., Schachter, S., & Back, K. *Social pressures in informal groups: A study of human factors in housing.* New York: Harper, 1950.

Festinger, L., Torrey, Jane, & Willerman, B. Self-evaluation as a function of attraction to the group. *Hum. Relat.*, 1954, **7**, 161–174.

Fiedler, F. E. Assumed similarity measures as predictors of team effectiveness. *J. abnorm. soc. Psychol.*, 1954, **49**, 381–388.

Fiedler, F. E. A note on leadership theory: The effect of social barriers between leaders and followers. *Sociometry*, 1957, **20**, 87–94.

Fiedler, F. E. *Leader attitudes and group effectiveness.* Urbana: Univer. of Illinois Press, 1958.

Fischer, P. H. An analysis of the primary group. *Sociometry*, 1953, **16**, 272–276.

Fleishman, E. A. The leadership role of the foreman in industry. *Enging Expt Sta. News*, Ohio State Univer., 1952, **24**, 27–35.

Foa, U. G. The contiguity principle in the structure of interpersonal relations. *Hum. Relat.*, 1958, **11**, 229–238.

Fox, J. B., & Scott, J. F. *Absenteeism: Management's problem.* Boston: Graduate School of Business Administration, Harvard University, 1943.

Fox, W. F. Group reaction to two types of conference leadership. *Hum. Relat.,* 1957, 10, 279–289.

French, J. R. P., Jr., & Raven, B. The bases of social power. In D. Cartwright & A. Zander (Eds.), *Group dynamics: Research and theory.* Evanston, Ill.: Row, 1960. Pp. 607–623.

French, J. R. P., Jr., & Zander, A. The group dynamics approach. In A. Kornhauser (Ed.), *Psychology of labor management relations.* New York: American Book, 1949. Pp. 71–80.

Gage, N. L. Accuracy of social perception and effectiveness in interpersonal relationships. *J. Pers.,* 1953, 22, 128–141.

Gage, N. L., & Chatterjee, B. B. The psychological meaning of acquiescence: Further evidence. *J. abnorm. soc. Psychol.,* 1960, 60, 280–283.

Gage, N. L., & Cronbach, L. Conceptual and methodological problems in interpersonal perception. *Psychol. Rev.,* 1955, 62, 411–422.

Gage, N. L., & Exline, R. V. Social perception and effectiveness in discussion groups. *Hum. Relat.,* 1953, 6, 381–396.

Gebel, A. S. Self-perception and leaderless group discussion status. *J. soc. Psychol.,* 1954, 40, 309–318.

Gekoski, N. Predicting group productivity. *Personnel Psychol.,* 1952, 5, 281–292.

Gerard, H. B. Some effects of status, role clarity, and group goal clarity upon the individual's relations to group process. *J. Pers.,* 1957, 25, 475–488.

Gerard, H. B. Disagreement with others, their credibility, and experienced stress. *J. abnorm. soc. Psychol.,* 1961, 62, 559–564.(a)

Gerard, H. B. Some determinants of self-evaluation. *J. abnorm. soc. Psychol.,* 1961, 62, 288–293.(b)

Gerard, H. B., & Rabbie, J. M. Fear and social comparison. *J. abnorm. soc. Psychol.,* 1961, 62, 586–592.

Gibb, C. A. The sociometry of leadership in temporary groups. *Sociometry,* 1950, 13, 226–243.

Gibb, C. A. Leadership. In G. Lindzey (Ed.), *Handbook of social psychology.* Reading, Mass.: Addison-Wesley, 1954. Pp. 877–920.

Gibb, J. R. The effects of group size and of threat reduction upon creativity in a problem-solving situation. *Amer. Psychogist,* 1951, 6, 324.

Gilchrist, J. C., Shaw, M.E., & Walker, L. C. Some effects of unequal distribution of information in a wheel group structure. *J. abnorm. soc. Psychol.,* 1954, 49, 554–556.

Glanzer, M., & Glasner, R. Techniques for the study of group structure and behavior: II. Empirical studies of the effects of structure in small groups. *Psychol. Bull.,* 1961, 58, 1–27.

Goffman, I. Alienation from interaction. *Hum. Relat.,* 1957, 10, 47–60.

Golembiewski, R. M. *The small group.* Chicago: Univer. of Chicago Press, 1962.

Goodacre, D. M. The use of a sociometric test as a predictor of combat unit effectiveness. *Sociometry,* 1951, 14, 148–152.

Goodchilds, Jacqueline D. Effects of being witty on position in the social structure of a small group. *Sociometry,* 1959, 22, 261–272.

Green, G. H. Insight and group adjustment. *J. abnorm. soc. Psychol.,* 1948, 43, 49–61.

Gronlund, N. E. Generality of teachers' sociometric perceptions: Relative judgment accuracy on several sociometric criteria. *J. educ. Psychol.,* 1956, 47, 25–31.(a)

Gronlund, N. E. The general ability to judge sociometric status: Elementary student teachers' sociometric perceptions of classmates and pupils. *J. educ. Psychol.,* 1956, 47, 147–157.(b)

Gross, E. Some functional consequences of primary controls in formal work organizations. *Amer. sociol. Rev.,* 1953, 18, 368–373.

Gross, N., McEachern, A. W., & Mason, W. S. Role conflict and its resolution. In Eleanor E. Maccoby, T. M. Newcomb, & E. L. Hartley (Eds.), *Readings in social psychology.* (3rd ed.) New York: Holt, 1958. Pp. 447–459.

Guetzkow, H. Differentiation of roles in task-oriented groups. In D. Cartwright & A. Zander (Eds.), *Group dynamics: Research and theory.* Evanston, Ill.: Row, 1960. Pp. 683–704.

Guetzkow, H., & Dill, W. R. Factors in the organizational development of task-oriented groups. *Sociometry,* 1957, 20, 175–204.

Guetzkow, H., & Simon, H. A. The impact of certain communication nets upon organization and performance in task-oriented groups. *Mgmt Sci.,* 1955, 1, 233–250.

Hall, R. L. Social influence on the aircraft commander's role. *Amer. sociol. Rev.*, 1955, 20, 292–299.

Halpin, A. W. The leader behavior and leadership ideology of educational administrators and aircraft commanders. *Harv. educ. Rev.*, 1955, 25, 18–22.

Hamblin, R. L., & Miller, L. K. Variation interaction profiles and group size. *Sociol. Quart.*, 1961, 2, 105–117.

Hanfmann, Eugenia P. Social structure of a group of kindergarten children. *Amer. J. Orthopsychiat.*, 1935, 5, 407–410.

Hare, A. P. A study of interaction and consensus in different sized groups. *Amer. sociol. Rev.*, 1952, 17, 261–267.

Hare, A. P. Small group discussions with participatory and supervisory leadership. *J. abnorm. soc. Psychol.*, 1953, 48, 273–275.

Hare, A. P. Situational differences in leader behavior. *J. abnorm. soc. Psychol.*, 1957, 55, 132–135.

Hare, A. P. *Handbook of small group research.* New York: The Free Press of Glencoe, 1962.

Hare, A. P., & Bales, R. F. Seating position and small group interaction. *Sociometry*, 1963, 26, 480–486.

Hare, A. P., Borgatta, E. F., & Bales, R. F. (Eds.) *Small groups: Studies in social interaction.* New York: Knopf, 1955.

Harris, E. F., & Fleishman, E. A. Human relations training and the stability of leadership patterns. *J. appl. Psychol.*, 1955, 39, 20–25.

Harvey, O. J. An experimental approach to the study of status reactions in informal groups. *Amer. sociol. Rev.*, 1953, 18, 357–367.

Harvey, O. J. Reciprocal influence of the group and three types of leaders in an unstructured situation. *Sociometry*, 1960, 23, 57–68.

Haythorn, W., Couch, A. [S.], Haefner, D., Langham, P., & Carter, L. F. The behavior of authoritarian and equalitarian personalities in groups. *Hum. Relat.*, 1956, 9, 57–74. (a)

Haythorn, W., Couch, A. [S.], Haefner, D., Langham, P., & Carter, L. F. The effects of varying combinations of authoritarian and equalitarian leaders and followers. *J. abnorm. soc. Psychol.*, 1956, 53, 210–219.(b)

Hearn, G. Leadership and the spatial factor in small groups. *J. abnorm. soc. Psychol.*, 1957, 54, 269–272.

Heinicke, C., & Bales, R. F. Developmental trends in the structure of small groups. *Sociometry*, 1953, 16, 7-38.

Heise, G. A., & Miller, G. A. Problem solving by small groups using various communication nets. *J. abnorm. soc. Psychol.*, 1951, 46, 327–336.

Hemphill, J. K. Situational factors in leadership. *Ohio State Univer., Educ. Res. Monogr.*, 1949, No. 32.

Hemphill, J. K. Relations between the size of the group and the behavior of "superior" leaders. *J. soc. Psychol.*, 1950, 32, 11–22.

Hemphill, J. K. Group dimensions: A manual for their measurement. *Ohio State Univer. Bur. Bus. Res. Monogr.*, 1956, No. 87.

Hemphill, J. K., Pepinsky, Pauline N., Shevitz, R. N., Jaynes, W. E., & Christner, Charlotte A. The relation between possession of task-relevant information and attempts to lead. *Psychol. Monogr.*, 1956, 70(7), No. 414.

Hites, R. W., & Campbell, D. T. A test of the ability of fraternity leaders to estimate group opinion. *J. soc. Psychol.*, 1950, 32, 95–100.

Hollander, E. P. Conformity, status, and idiosyncrasy credit. *Psychol. Rev.*, 1958, 65, 117–127.

Hollander, E. P. Some points of reinterpretation regarding social conformity. *Sociol. Rev.*, 1959, 7, 159–168.

Hollander, E. P. Competence and conformity in the acceptance of influence. *J. abnorm. soc. Psychol.*, 1960, 61, 365–370.(a)

Hollander, E. P. Reconsidering the issue of conformity in personality. In H. P. David & J. C. Brengelmann (Eds.), *Perspectives in personality research.* New York: Springer, 1960.(b)

Hollander, E. P., & Webb, W. B. Leadership, followership and friendship: An analysis of peer nominations. *J. abnorm. soc. Psychol.*, 1955, 50, 163–167.

Hollingshead, A. B. *Elmtown's youth.* New York: Wiley, 1949.

Homans, G. C. *The human group.* New York: Harcourt, 1950.

Homans, G. C. *Social behavior: Its elementary forms.* New York: Harcourt, 1961.

Horowitz, M. W., Lyons, J., & Perlmutter, H. V. Induction of forces in discussion groups. *Hum. Relat.*, 1951, 4, 57–76.

Horowitz, M. W., & Perlmutter, H. V. The discussion group and democratic behavior. *J. soc. Psychol.,* 1955, 41, 231–246.

Horsfall, A. B., & Arensberg, C. M. Teamwork and productivity in a shoe factory. *Hum. Organization,* 1949, 8(1), 13–25.

Horwitz, M., Exline, R. V., & Lee, F. J. *Motivational effects of alternative decision-making processes in groups.* Urbana: Bureau of Educational Research, Univer. of Ill., 1953.

Hovland, C. I. Reconciling conflicting results derived from experimental and survey studies of attitude change. *Amer. Psychogist,* 1959, 14, 8–17.

Hovland, C. I., & Janis, I. L. (Eds.) *Personality and persuasibility.* New Haven, Conn.: Yale Univer. Press, 1959.

Hovland, C. I., Janis, I. L., & Kelley, H. H. *Communication and persuasion: Psychological studies of opinion change.* New Haven, Conn.: Yale Univer. Press, 1953.

Hunt, J. McV., & Solomon, R. L. The stability and some correlates of group-status in a summer camp group of young boys. *Amer. J. Psychol.,* 1942, 55, 33–45.

Hunt, R. G., & Synnerdahl, Vonda. Social influence among kindergarten children. *Sociol. soc. Res.,* 1959, 43, 171–174.

Hurwitz, J. I., Zander, A., & Hymovitch, B. Some effects of power on the relations among group members. In D. Cartwright & A. Zander (Eds.), *Group dynamics: Research and theory.* Evanston, Ill.: Row, 1953. Pp. 483–492.

Hutchins, E. B., & Fiedler, F. E. Task-oriented and quasi-therapeutic role functions of the leader in small military groups. *Sociometry,* 1960, 23, 393–406.

Israel, J. *Self-evaluation and rejection in groups.* Stockholm: Almqvist & Wiksell, 1956.

Jackson, J. M. Reference group processes in a formal organization. *Sociometry,* 1959, 22, 307–327.

Jahoda, Marie. Conformity and independence. *Hum. Relat.,* 1959, 12, 99–120.

James, J. The distribution of free-forming small group size. *Amer. sociol. Rev.,* 1953, 18, 569–570.

Janda, K. F. Towards the explication of the concept of leadership in terms of the concept of power. *Hum. Relat.,* 1960, 13, 345–363.

Johnson, D. M. *The psychology of thought and judgment.* New York: Harper, 1955.

Kahn, R. L., & Katz, D. Leadership practices in relation to productivity and morale. In D. Cartwright & A. Zander (Eds.), *Group dynamics: Research and theory.* Evanston, Ill.: Row, 1953. Pp. 612–628.

Kates, S. L. First-impression formation and authoritarianism. *Hum. Relat.,* 1959, 12, 277–286.

Katz, I., & Benjamin, L. Effects of white authoritarianism in biracial work groups. *J. abnorm. soc. Psychol.,* 1960, 61, 448–456.

Keet, C. D. Two verbal techniques in a miniature counseling situation. *Psychol. Monogr.,* 1948, 62, No. 294.

Kelley, G. A. *The psychology of personal constructs.* New York: Norton, 1955.

Kelley, H. H. Salience of membership and resistance to change of group-anchored attitudes. *Hum. Relat.,* 1955, 8, 275–290.

Kelley, H. H., & Arrowood, A. J. Coalitions in the triad: Critique and experiment. *Sociometry,* 1960, 23, 231–244.

Kenkel, W. F. Influence differentiation in family decision making. *Sociol. soc. Res.,* 1957, 42, 18–25.

Kiessling, R. J., & Kalish, R. A. Correlates of success in leaderless group discussion. *J. soc. Psychol.,* 1961, 54, 359–365.

Killian, L. M. The significance of multiple-group membership in disaster. *Amer. J. Sociol.,* 1952, 57, 309–314.

Kirscht, J. P., Lodahl, T. M., & Haire, M. Some factors in the selection of leaders by members of small groups. *J. abnorm. soc. Psychol.,* 1959, 58, 406–408.

Klein, Josephine. *Working with groups.* London: Hutchinson & Co., Ltd., 1961.

Kleiner, R. J. The effects of threat reduction upon interpersonal attractiveness. *J. Pers.,* 1960, 28, 145–155.

Knutson, A. L. Quiet and vocal groups. *Sociometry,* 1960, 23, 36–49.

Kogan, N., & Tagiuri, R. Interpersonal preference and cognitive organization. *J. abnorm. soc. Psychol.,* 1958, 56, 113–116.

Laird, D. A., & Laird, Eleanor C. *The new psychology of leadership.* New York: McGraw, 1956.

Landsberger, H. A. Interaction process analysis of professional behavior: A study of labor mediators in twelve labor-management disputes. *Amer. sociol. Rev.*, 1955, 20, 566–575.

Lanzetta, J. T., & Roby, T. B. Effects of work-group structure and certain task variables on group performance. *J. abnorm. soc. Psychol.*, 1956, 53, 307–314.

Lanzetta, J. T., Wendt, G. R., Langham, P., & Haefner, D. The effects of an "anxiety-reducing" medication on group behavior under threat. *J. abnorm. soc. Psychol.*, 1956, 52, 103–108.

Leary, T. *Interpersonal diagnosis of personality.* New York: Ronald Press, 1957.

Leavitt, H. J. Some effects of certain communication patterns on group performance. *J. abnorm. soc. Psychol.*, 1951, 46, 38–50.

Leavitt, H. J., & Mueller, R. A. H. Some effects of feedback on communication. *Hum. Relat.*, 1951, 4, 401–410.

Lemann, T. B., & Solomon, R. L. Group characteristics as revealed in sociometric patterns and personality ratings. *Sociometry,* 1952, 15, 7–90.

Lennard, H., & Bernstein, A. (with Helen C. Hendin & E. B. Palmore). *The anatomy of psychotherapy: Systems of communication and expectation.* New York: Columbia Univer. Press, 1960.

Lennard, H., Jarvik, M. E., & Abramson, H. A. Lysergic acid diethylamide (LSD-25): XII. A preliminary statement of its effects upon interpersonal communication. *J. Psychol.*, 1956, 41, 185–198.

Levine, J., Laffal, J., Berkowitz, M., Lindemann, J., & Drevdahl J. Conforming behavior of psychiatric and medical patients. *J. abnorm. soc. Psychol.*, 1954, 49, 251–255.

Levinson, D. J. Role, personality, and social structure in the organizational setting. *J. abnorm. soc. Psychol.*, 1959, 58, 170–180.

Lewin, K. Frontiers in group dynamics: II. Channels of group life: Social planning and action research. *Hum. Relat.*, 1947, 1, 143–153.

Lichtenberg, P. Emotional maturity as manifested in ideational interaction. *J. abnorm. soc. Psychol.*, 1955, 51, 298–301.

Lifton, R. J. *Thought reform and the psychology of totalism: A study of "brain-washing" in China.* New York: Norton, 1961.

Lifton, W. M. *Working with groups: Group process and individual growth.* New York: Wiley, 1961.

Lindzey, G. (Ed.) *Handbook of social psychology.* Reading, Mass.: Addison-Wesley, 1954.

Lindzey, G., & Urdan, J. A. Personality and social choice. *Sociometry,* 1954, 17, 47–63.

Lorge, I., & Solomon, H. Group and individual performance in problem solving related to previous exposure to problem, level of aspiration, and group size. *Behav. Sci.,* 1960, 5, 28–38.

Luchins, A. S. Social influences in perception of complex drawings. *J. soc. Psychol.*, 1945, 21, 257–273.

Luchins, A. S. A variational approach to social influences on perception. *J. soc. Psychol.*, 1955, 42, 113–119.

Luchins, A. S., & Luchins, Edith H. Discovering the source of contradictory communications. *J. soc. Psychol.*, 1956, 44, 49–63.

Lundy, R. M. Assimilative projection and accuracy of prediction in interpersonal relations. *J. abnorm. soc. Psychol.*, 1956, 52, 33–38.

Mass, H. S. The role of members in clubs of lower-class and middle-class adolescents. *Child Develpm.*, 1954, 25, 241–251.

Maas, H. S. Evaluating the individual member in the group. In National Conference of Social Work, *Group work and community organization, 1953–1954.* New York: Columbia Univer. Press, 1954. Pp. 36–44.

Maccoby, Eleanor, E., Newcomb, T. M., & Hartley, E. L. (Eds.) *Readings in social psychology.* (3rd ed.) New York: Holt, 1958.

McKeachie, W. J. Student centered *versus* instructor centered instruction. *J. educ. Psychol.*, 1954, 45, 143–150.

McKeachie, W. J. Students, groups, and teaching methods. *Amer. Psychogist,* 1958, 13, 580–584.

McKenna, Sister Helen V., S.S.J., Hofstaetter, P. R., & O'Connor, J. P. The concepts of the ideal self and of the friend. *J. Pers.,* 1956, 24, 262–271.

Macy, J., Jr., Christie, L. S., & Luce, R. D. Coding noise in a task-oriented group. *J. abnorm. soc. Psychol.*, 1953, 48, 401–409.

Maier, N. R. F., & Hoffman, L. R. Using trained "developmental" discussion leaders to improve further the quality of group decisions. *J. appl. Psychol.*, 1960, 44, 247–251.

Maier, N. R. F., & Solem, A. R. The contribution of a discussion leader to the quality of group thinking: The effective use of minority opinions. *Hum. Relat.*, 1952, 5, 277–288.

Maisonneuve, J. A contribution to the sociometry of mutual choices. *Sociometry*, 1954, 17, 33–46.

Mandelbaum, D. G. *Soldier groups and Negro soldiers.* Berkeley: Univer. of California Press, 1952.

Manis, M. Social interaction and the self concept. *J. abnorm. soc. Psychol.*, 1955, 51, 362–370.

Martin, W. E., Darley, J. G., & Gross, N. Studies in group behavior: II. Methodological problems in the study of interrelationships of group members. *Educ. Psychol. Measmt,* 1952, 12, 533–553.

Mason, D. J. Judgments of leadership based upon physiognomic cues. *J. abnorm. soc. Psychol.*, 1957, 54, 273–274.

Matarazzo, J. D., & Saslow, G. Difference in interview interaction behavior among normal and deviant groups. In I. A. Berg & B. M. Bass (Eds.), *Conformity and deviation.* New York: Harper, 1961. Pp. 286–327.

Mayo, E., & Lombard, G. F. F. *Team work and labor turnover in the aircraft industry of Southern California.* Boston: Graduate School of Business Administration, Harvard Univer., 1944.

Medalia, N. Z. Authoritarianism, leader acceptance, and group cohesion. *J. abnorm. soc. Psychol.*, 1955, 51, 207–213.

Mellinger, G. D. Interpersonal trust as a factor in communication. *J. abnorm. soc. Psychol.*, 1956, 52, 304–309.

Merei, F. Group leadership and institutionalization. *Hum. Relat.*, 1949, 2, 23–39.

Mills, T. M. Power relations in three-person groups. *Amer. sociol. Rev.*, 1953, 18, 351–357.

Mills, T. M. The coalition pattern in three-person groups. *Amer. sociol. Rev.*, 1954, 19, 657–667.

Mills, T. M. Development process in three-person groups. *Hum. Relat.*, 1956, 9, 343–354.

Mills, T. M. in collaboration with Gauslaa, Løchen, Y., Mathiesen, T., Nørstebø, G., Ramsøy, O., Skirbekk, S., Skårdal, O., Torgersen, L., Tysnes, B., & Øyen, Ø. Group structure and the newcomer: An experimental study of group expansion. *Univer. Oslo Inst. Sociol., Stud. Soc.,* No. 1, 1957.

Miyamoto, S. F., & Dornbush, S. M. A test of interactionist hypotheses of self-conception. *Amer. J. Sociol.*, 1956, 61, 399–403.

Moede, W. Die richtlinien der leitungspsychologie. *Industr. Psychotechn.*, 1927, 4, 193–209.

Mohanna, A. I., & Argyle, M. A cross-cultural study of structured groups with unpopular central members. *J. abnorm. soc. Psychol.*, 1960, 60, 139–140.

Montmollin, Germaine de. Les processus d'influence sociale (Processes in social influence). *Ann. Psychol.*, 1958, 58, 427–477.

Moreno, J. L. *Who shall survive?* (rev. ed.) Beacon, N.Y.: Beacon House, 1953.

Moreno, J. L. with Jennings, Helen H., Criswell, Joan H., Katz, L., Blake, R. R., Mouton, Jane S., Bonney, M. E., Northway, Mary L., Loomis, C. P., Proctor, C., Tagiuri, R., & Nehnevajsa, J. *The sociometry reader.* New York: The Free Press of Glencoe, 1960.

Mouton, Jane S., Blake, R. R., & Fruchter, B. The reliability of sociometric measures. *Sociometry*, 1955, 18, 7–48.(a)

Mouton, Jane S., Blake, R. R., & Fruchter, B. The validity of sociometric responses. *Sociometry*, 1955, 18, 181–206.(b)

Mulder, M. Communication structure, decision structure and group performance. *Sociometry*, 1960, 23, 1–14.(a)

Mulder, M. The power variable in communication experiments. *Hum. Relat.*, 1960, 13, 241–257.(b)

Mussen, P. H., & Porter, L. W. Personal motivations and self-conceptions associated with effectiveness and ineffectiveness in emergent groups. *J. abnorm. soc. Psychol.*, 1959, 59, 23–27.

Nadler, E. B. Yielding, authoritarianism, and authoritarian ideology regarding groups. *J. abnorm. soc. Psychol.*, 1959, 58, 408–410.

Newcomb, T. M. Varieties of interpersonal attraction. In D. Cartwright and A. Zander (Eds.), *Group dynamics: Research and theory.* Evanston, Ill.: Row, 1960. Pp. 104–119.

Parker, S. Leadership patterns in a psychiatric ward. *Hum. Relat.*, 1958, 11, 287–301.

Parsons, T., Bales, R. F., Olds, J., Zelditch, M., & Slater, P. E. *Family socialization, and in-*

teraction process. Glencoe, Ill.: Free Press, 1955.

Parten, Mildred B. Social play among preschool children. *J. abnorm. soc. Psychol.,* 1933, **28**, 136–147.

Pepitone, A. Motivational effects in social perception. *Hum. Relat.,* 1950, **3**, 57–76.

Perlmutter, H. V. Group memory of meaningful material. *J. Psychol.,* 1953, **35**, 361–370.

Perlmutter, H. V., & Montmollin, Germaine de. Group learning of nonsense syllables. *J. abnorm. soc. Psychol.,* 1952, **47**, 762–769.

Petrullo, L., & Bass, B. M. (Eds.) *Leadership and interpersonal behavior.* New York: Holt, Rinehart & Winston, 1961.

Philp, H., & Dunphy, D. Developmental trends in small groups. *Sociometry,* 1959, **22**, 162–174.

Powell, R. M., et al. An experimental study of role taking, group status, and group formation. *Sociol. soc. Res.,* 1956, **40**, 159–165.

Preston, M. G., & Heintz, R. K. Effects of participatory *versus* supervisory leadership on group judgment. *J. abnorm. soc. Psychol.,* 1949, **44**, 345–355.

Psathas, G. Phase movement and equilibrium tendencies in interaction process in psychotherapy groups. *Sociometry,* 1960, **23**, 177–194.

Radloff, R. Opinion evaluation and affiliation. *J. abnorm. soc. Psychol.,* 1961, **62**, 578–585.

Ramuz-Nienhuis, Wilhelmina, & Van Bergen, Annie. Relations between some components of attraction-to-group. *Hum. Relat.,* 1960, **13**, 271–277.

Rapoport, Rhona, & Rosow, I. An approach to family relationships and role performance. *Hum. Relat.,* 1957, **10**, 209–221.

Raven, B. H. Social influence on opinions and the communication of related content. *J. abnorm. soc. Psychol.,* 1959, **58**, 119–128.

Ray, W. S. *A laboratory manual for social psychology.* New York: American Book, 1951.

Redl, F. Group emotion and leadership. *Psychiatry,* 1942, **5**, 573–596.

Reilly, Mary St. A., Commins, W. D., & Stefic, E. C. The complementarity of personality needs in friendship choice. *J. abnorm. soc. Psychol.,* 1960, **61**, 292–294.

Rice, A. K. The use of unrecognized cultural mechanisms in an expanding machine shop; with a contribution to the theory of leadership. *Hum. Relat.,* 1951, **4**, 143–160.

Riley, Matilda W., & Cohn, R. Control networks in informal groups. *Sociometry,* 1958, **21**, 30–49.

Roberts, B. H., & Strodtbeck, F. L. Interaction process differences between groups of paranoid schizophrenic and depressed patients. *Int. J. group Psychother.,* 1953, **3**, 29–41.

Roethlisberger, F. J., & Dickson, W. J. *Management and the worker.* Cambridge, Mass.: Harvard Univer. Press, 1939.

Rosen, B. C. Conflicting group membership: A study of parent-peer group cross pressures. *Amer. sociol. Rev.,* 1955, **20**, 155–161.(a)

Rosen, B. C. The reference group approach to the parental factor in attitude and behavior formation. *Soc. Forces,* 1955, **34**, 137–144.(b)

Rosen, S., Levinger, G., & Lippitt, R. Perceived sources of social power. *J. abnorm. soc. Psychol.,* 1961, **62**, 439–441.

Rosow, I. Issues in the concept of need-complementarity. *Sociometry,* 1957, **20**, 216–233.

Ruesch, J., & Prestwood, A. R. Interaction processes and personal codification. *J. Pers.,* 1950, **18**, 391–430.

Runkel, P. J. Cognitive similarity in facilitating communication. *Sociometry,* 1956, **19**, 178–191.

Sagi, P. C., Olmsted, D. W., & Atelsek, F. Predicting maintenance of membership in small groups. *J. abnorm. soc. Psychol.,* 1955, **51**, 308–311.

Sanford, F. H. *Authoritarianism and leadership.* Philadelphia: Institute for Research in Human Relations, 1950.

Sarbin, T. R., & Jones, D. S. An experimental analysis of role behavior. *J. abnorm. soc. Psychol.,* 1955, **51**, 236–241.

Schachter, S. Deviation, rejection, and communication. *J. abnorm. soc. Psychol.,* 1951, **46**, 190–207.

Schachter, S., Ellertson, N., McBride, Dorothy, & Gregory, Doris. An experimental study of cohesiveness and productivity. *Hum. Relat.,* 1951, **4**, 229–238.

Schachter, S., & Hall, R. Group-derived restraints and audience persuasion. *Hum. Relat.,* 1952, **5**, 397–406.

Schachter, S., Nuttin, J., De Monchaux, Cecily, Maucorps, P. H., Osmer, D., Duijker, H.,

Rommetveit, R., & Israel, J. Cross-cultural experiments on threat and rejection. *Hum. Relat.*, 1954, 7, 403–439.

Schein, E. H. Interpersonal communication, group solidarity, and social influence. *Sociometry*, 1960, 23, 148–161.

Schein, E. H., Schneier, I., & Barker, C. H. *Coercive persuasion.* New York: Norton, 1961.

Schellenberg, J. A. Group size as a factor in success of academic discussion groups. *J. educ. Sociol.*, 1959, 33, 73–79.

Schiff, H. Judgmental response sets in the perception of sociometric status. *Sociometry*, 1954, 17, 207–227.

Schutz, W. C. *FIRO: A three-dimensoinal theory of interpersonal behavior.* New York: Holt, 1958.

Seashore, S. E. Group cohesiveness in the industrial work group. Ann Arbor: Univer. of Michigan Press, 1954.

Selvin, H. C. *The effects of leadership.* New York: The Free Press of Glencoe, 1960.

Shaw, M. E. Group structure and the behavior of individuals in small groups. *J. Psychol.*, 1954, 38, 139–149.(a)

Shaw, M. E. Some effects of problem conplexity upon problem solution efficiency in different communication nets. *J. exp. Psychol.*, 1954, 48, 211–217.(b)

Shaw, M. E. Some effects of unequal distribution of information upon group performance in various communication nets. *J. abnorm. soc. Psychol.*, 1954, 49, 547–553. (c)

Shaw, M. E. A comparison of two types of leadership in various communication nets. *J. abnorm. soc. Psychol.*, 1955, 50, 127–134.

Shaw, M. E. Random versus systematic distribution of information in communication nets. *J. Pers.*, 1956, 25, 59–69.

Shaw, M. E. Some effects of irrelevant information upon problem-solving by small groups. *J. soc. Psychol.*, 1958, 47, 33–37.

Shaw, M. E. Some effects of individually prominent behavior upon group effectiveness and member satisfaction. *J. abnorm. soc. Psychol.*, 1959, 59, 382–386.

Shaw, M. E. A serial position effect in social influence on group decisions. *J. soc. Psychol.*, 1961, 54, 83–91.

Shaw, M. E., & Rothschild, G. H. Some effects of prolonged experience in communication nets. *J. appl. Psychol.*, 1956, 40, 281–286.

Shaw, M. E., Rothschild, G. H., & Strickland, J. F. Decision process in communication nets. *J. abnorm. soc. Psychol.*, 1957, 54, 323–330.

Shepard, H. A., & Bennis, W. G. A theory of training by group methods. *Hum. Relat.*, 1956, 9, 403–413.

Sherif, M. A study of some social factors in perception. *Arch. Psychol.*, 1935, 27, No. 187.

Sherif, M. Experiments in group conflict. *Sci. Amer.*, 1956, 195(5), 54–58.

Sherif, M., & Cantril, H. *The psychology of ego-involvements.* New York: Wiley, 1947.

Sherif, M., & Harvey, O. J. A study of ego functioning: Elimination of stable anchorages in individual and group situations. *Sociometry*, 1952, 15, 272–305.

Sherif, M., Harvey, O. J., White, B. J., Hood, W. R., & Sherif, Carolyn W. *Intergroup conflict and cooperation: The robbers cave experiment.* Norman, Okla.: Univer. Book Exchange, 1961.

Sherif, M., White, B. J., & Harvey, O. J. Status in experimentally produced groups. *Amer. J. Sociol.*, 1955, 60, 370–379.

Shils, E. A. Primary groups in the American army. In R. K. Merton & P. F. Lazarsfeld (Eds.), *Continuities in social research: Studies in the scope and method of "The American Soldier."* Glencoe, Ill.: Free Press, 1950. Pp. 16–39.

Shils, E. A., & Janowitz, M. Cohesion and disintegration of the Wehrmacht in World War II. *Publ. Opin. Quart.*, 1948, 12, 280–315.

Simmel, G. The number of members as determining the sociological form of the group. *Amer. J. Sociol.*, 1902–1903, 8, 1–46, 158–196.

Slater, P. E. Contrasting correlates of group size. *Sociometry*, 1958, 21, 129–139.

Small, D. O., & Campbell, D. T. The effect of acquiescence response-set upon the relationship of the F scale and conformity. *Sociometry*, 1960, 23, 69–71.

Smelser, W. T. Dominance as a factor in achievement and perception in cooperative problem solving interactions. *J. abnorm. soc. Psychol.*, 1961, 62, 535–542.

Smith, A. J., Jaffe, J., & Livingston, D. G. Consonance of interpersonal perception and individual effectiveness. *Hum. Relat.*, 1955, 8, 385–397.

Smith, C. E. A study of automatic excitation resulting from the interaction of individual and group opinion. *J. abnorm. soc. Psychol.*, 1936, 31, 138–164.

Smith, E. E. The effects of clear and unclear role expectations on group productivity and defensiveness. *J. abnorm. soc. Psychol.*, 1957, 55, 213–217.

Smith, E. E. Individual versus group goal conflict. *J. abnorm. soc. Psychol.*, 1959, 58, 134–137.

Smith, S. L. Communication pattern and the adaptability of task-oriented groups: An experimental study. Cited in A. Bavelas, Communication patterns in task-oriented groups. In D. Lerner & H. Lasswell (Eds.), *The policy sciences: Recent developments in scope and method.* Stanford, Calif.: Stanford Univer. Press, 1951. Pp. 193–203.

Snyder, Eloise C. The Supreme Court as a small group. *Soc. Forces,* 1958, 36, 232–238.

Sommer, R. Studies in personal space. *Sociometry,* 1959, 22, 247–260.

Sommer, R. Leadership and group geography. *Sociometry,* 1961, 24, 99–110.

South, E. B. Some psychological aspects of committee work. *J. appl. Psychol.,* 1927, 11, 348–368.

Southall, A. An operational theory of role. *Hum. Relat.,* 1959, 12, 17–34.

Steiner, I. D. Interpersonal behavior as influenced by accuracy of social perception. *Psychol. Rev.,* 1955, 62, 268–274.

Steiner, I. D. Human interaction and interpersonal perception. *Sociometry,* 1959, 22, 230–235.

Steiner, I. D., & McDiarmid, C. G. Two kinds of assumed similarity between opposites. *J. abnorm. soc. Psychol.,* 1957, 55, 140–142.

Steinzor, B. The spatial factor in face to face discussion groups. *J. abnorm. soc. Psychol.,* 1950, 45, 552–555.

Stephan, F. F., & Mishler, E. G. The distribution of participation in small groups: An exponential approximation. *Amer. sociol. Rev.,* 1952, 17, 598–608.

Stogdill, R. M., & Coons, A. E. (Eds.) Leader behavior: Its description and measurement. *Res. Monogr., Bureau Bus. Res., Ohio State Univer.,* 1957, No. 88.

Stone, P., & Kamiya, J. Judgment of consensus during group discussion. *J. abnorm. soc. Psychol.,* 1957, 55, 171–175.

Stotland, E., Thorley, S., Thomas, E., Cohen, A. R., & Zander, A. The effects of group expectations and self-esteem upon self-evaluation. *J. abnorm. soc. Psychol.,* 1957, 54, 55–63.

Strodtbeck, F. L. Husband-wife interaction over revealed differences. *Amer. sociol. Rev.,* 1951, 16, 468–473.

Strodtbeck, F. L. The family as a three-person group. *Amer. sociol. Rev.,* 1954, 19, 23–29.

Strodtbeck, F. L., & Hook, L. H. The social dimensions of a twelve-man jury table. *Sociometry,* 1961, 24, 397–415.

Strodtbeck, F. L., & Mann, R. D. Sex role differentiation in jury deliberations. *Sociometry,* 1956, 19, 3–11.

Strupp, H. H. An objective comparison of Rogerian and psychoanalytic techniques. *J. consult. Psychol.,* 1955, 19, 1–7.(a)

Strupp, H. H. Psychotherapeutic technique, professional affiliation, and experience level. *J. consult. Psychol.,* 1955, 19, 97–102.(b)

Strupp, H. H. The effect of the psychotherapist's personal analysis upon his own techniques. *J. consult. Psychol.,* 1955, 19, 197–204.(c)

Strupp, H. H. The performance of psychoanalytic and client-centered therapists in an initial interview, *J. consult. Psychol.,* 1958, 22, 265–274.

Stryker, S., & Psathas, G. Research on coalitions in the triad: Findings, problems and strategy. *Sociometry,* 1960, 23, 217–230.

Tagiuri, R., Bruner, J. S., & Blake, R. R. On the relations between feelings and perception of feelings among members of small groups. In Eleanor E. Maccoby, T. M. Newcomb, & E. L. Hartley (Eds.), *Readings in social psychology.* (3rd ed.) New York: Holt, 1958. Pp. 110–116.

Takala, M., Pihkanen, T. A., & Markkanen, T. The effects of distilled and brewed beverages: A physiological, neurological, and psychological study. *Finnish Found. Alcohol Stud.,* 1957, 4.

Talland, G. A. Task and interaction process: Some characteristics of therapeutic group discussion. *J. abnorm. soc. Psychol.,* 1955, 50, 105–109.

Taylor, D. W., & Faust, W. L. Twenty questions: Efficiency in problem solving as a function of size of group. *J. exp. Psychol.,* 1952, 44, 360–368.

Taylor, F. W. Group management. *Trans. Amer. soc. mech. Enging*, 1903, 24, 1337–1480.

Taylor, J. B. The "yeasayer" and social desirability: A comment on the Couch and Kenniston paper. *J. abnorm. soc. Psychol.*, 1961, 62, 172. (a)

Taylor, J. B. What do attitude scales measure: The problem of social desirability. *J. abnorm. soc. Psychol.*, 1961, 26, 386–390.(b)

Terauds, Anita, Altman, I., & McGrath, J. E. *A bibliography of small group research.* Arlington, Va.: Human Sciences Research, Inc., April, 1960.

Theodorson, G. A. Elements in the progressive development of small groups. *Soc. Forces*, 1953, 31, 311–320.

Thibaut, J. W., & Coules, J. The role of communication in the reduction of interpersonal hostility. *J. abnorm. soc. Psychol.*, 1952, 47, 770–777.

Thorpe, J. G. A study of some factors in friendship formation. *Sociometry*, 1955, 18, 207–214.

Torrance, E. P. Methods of conducting critiques of group problem-solving performance. *J. appl. Psychol.*, 1953, 37, 394–398.

Trist, E. L., & Bamforth, K. W. Some social and psychological consequences of the longwall method of coal-getting. *Hum. Relat.*, 1951, 4, 3–38.

Trow, D. B. Autonomy and job satisfaction in task-oriented groups. *J. abnorm. soc. Psychol.*, 1957, 54, 204–209.

Tuddenham, R. D. The influence of a distorted group norm upon judgments of adults and children. *J. Psychol.*, 1961, 52, 231–239.

Turk, H. Instrumental values and the popularity of instrumental leaders. *Soc. Forces*, 1961, 39, 252–260.

Van Zelst, R. H. An interpersonal relations technique for industry. *Personnel*, 1952, 29, 68–76.

Verba, S. *Small groups and political behavior: A study of leadership.* Princeton, N.J.: Princeton Univer. Press, 1961.

Verplanck, W. S. The control of the content of conversation: Reinforcement of statements of opinion. *J. abnorm. soc. Psychol.*, 1955, 51, 668–676.

Videbeck, R., & Bates, A. P. An experimental study of conformity to role expectations. *Sociometry*, 1959, 22, 1–11.

Vinacke, W. E. Some variables in buzz sessions. *J. soc. Psychol.*, 1957, 45, 25–33.

Vinacke, W. E., & Arkoff, A. An experimental study of coalitions in the triad. *Amer. sociol. Rev.*, 1957, 22, 406–414.

Warriner, C. K. Leadership in the small group. *Amer. J. Sociol.*, 1955, 60, 361–369.

Watson, G. B. Do groups think more efficiently than individuals? *J. abnorm. soc. Psychol.*, 1928, 23, 328–336.

White, R. K., & Lippitt, R. O. *Autocracy and democracy.* New York: Harper, 1960.

Whitmyre, J. W., Diggery, J. C., & Cohen, D. The effects of personal liking, perceived ability, and value of prize on choice of partners for a competition. *J. abnorm. soc. Psychol.*, 1961, 63, 198–200.

Whyte, W. F. *Street corner society: The social structure of an Italian slum.* Chicago: Univer. of Chicago Press, 1943.

Whyte, W. F. The social structure of the restaurant. *Amer. J. Sociol.*, 1949, 54, 302–310.

Whyte, W. F. Leadership and group participation. *Bull. 24, New York State Sch. Industr. Labor Relat.*, Cornell Univer., 1953.

Wiener, M. The effects of two experimental counseling techniques on performances impaired by induced stress. *J. abnorm. soc. Psychol.*, 1955, 51, 565–572.

Willis, R. H. Social influence and conformity —some research perspectives. *Acta Sociol.*, 1961, 5, 100–114.

Wilson, R. C., High, W. S., & Comrey, A. L. An iterative analysis of supervisory and group dimensions. *J. appl. Psychol.*, 1955, 39, 85–91.

Winch, R. F. The theory of complementary needs in mate-selection: Final results on the test of the general hypothesis. *Amer. sociol. Rev.*, 1955, 20, 552–554.

Yarrow, Marian R., Campbell, J. D., & Yarrow, L. J. Interpersonal change: Process and theory. *J. soc. Issues*, 1958, 14(1), 60–63.

Zajonc, R. B. The concepts of balance, congruity, and dissonance. *Publ. Opin. Quart.*, 1962, 24(2), 280–296.

Zander, A. Group membership and individual security. *Hum. Relat.*, 1958, 11, 99–111.

Zander, A., & Havelin, A. Social comparison and interpersonal attraction. *Hum. Relat.*, 1960, 13, 21–32.

Zeleny, L. D. Sociometry of morale. *Amer. sociol. Rev.,* 1939, 4, 799–808.

Zentner, H. Primary group affiliation and institutional group morale. *Sociol. soc. Res.,* 1955, 40, 31–34.

Ziller, R. C. Four techniques of group decision making under uncertainty. *J. appl. Psychol.,* 1957, 41, 384–388.(a)

Ziller, R. C. Group size: A determinant of the quality and stability of group decisions. *Sociometry,* 1957, 20, 165–173.(b)

Ziller, R. C. Communication restraints, group flexibility, and group confidence. *J. appl. Psychol.,* 1958, 42, 346–352.

Zimbardo, P. G. Involvement and communication discrepancy as determinants of opinion conformity. *J. abnorm. soc. Psychol.,* 1960, 60, 86–94.

CHAPTER 8 Life Course and Social Structure

LEONARD D CAIN, JR.

A social structure may be viewed as a system of statuses, and among the universal criteria in the articulation of a status system is the age of its members. In spite of the observed ubiquity of age status and of the abundance of descriptive data on the subject, supplied by historians, anthropologists, demographers, researchers in social welfare, and others, sociologists have yet to devote more than passing attention to these data and to their implications for the total social structure.

Although Linton (1940), among others, has observed that age-sex patterns are more pervasive and significant than the family in most social structures, few texts in the principles of sociology, or curriculum offerings in colleges and universities, evidence endorsement of this observation. *Sociological Abstracts,* for example, has as yet no category on aging or the life course. Information on the life course is more likely to be introduced into sociological writings through the problems approach, especially the problems of the adolescent or the aged, than in any other way.

Data on the life course are overwhelming in their abundance and their diversity (Cain,

1959). Biological researches on aging continue apace; studies of the aging organism, of particular organs, even particular types of cells, have been reported in large numbers. Demographic data on age composition and trends among populations around the world are becoming increasingly accurate and refined. Anthropological field reports abound in data on the relevance of age to the determination of status (Simmons, 1945; Wilson, 1951). Historians on occasion have reported and interpreted the significance of age status patterns to the understanding of an epoch (Fleming, 1933; Pinchbeck, 1956; Richardson, 1933). The bureaucratization of organizations and the rationalization of personnel records and policies provide social scientists with rich opportunities to gain insight into life course phenomena. Interest of social psychologists and educators in human development has led to numerous studies of motor skills and learning abilities at various stages of the life course (Pressey & Kuhlen, 1957). Public-opinion polling and survey research have typically designed their inquiries to incorporate age as a major variable. Thus, data on the life course accumulate. It is the present task to sort out and

272

to order some of these diverse and often scattered data and to try to achieve some significant theoretical progress from these endeavors.

This chapter has three major purposes: (1) to identify, isolate, and systematize a life course, or age status, frame of reference; (2) to review pertinent research, including studies of age status in marital, religious, political, economic, educational, legal, welfare, and other institutions, and of interaction patterns among age peers and between generations; and (3) to propose needed research and theoretical exploration which may contribute to the advancement of a sociology of age status.

AN AGE STATUS FRAME OF REFERENCE

Biological Conditions

The evolution and involution of the human organism have been studied by metaphysicians, philosophers, and scientists, but many factors contributing to the growth and decay of organs and cells remain unknown. Cultural man has made significant intrusions into the senescent tendencies of biological man, through dietary variations, studies of psychological and physiological strains, surgery and other organic repair, and, more recently, actual replacement of worn-out or damaged organs. Although the purpose of this chapter does not include extensive review of biological theories concerning age and aging, it is essential that biological characteristics of man at various stages of the life course be recognized as limiting factors in the construction of age status patterns.

Freeman (1960) emphasized the unfolding of a built-in, genic inheritance through the life course. "The mechanism for aging could be thought of as under regulation of a complex biologic mechanism which regulates the rate of the body's total progression in the general pattern of senescence" (p. 29). Aging is regulated by abiotrophy, the "in-

herent nature of tissues to manifest the accepted characteristics of aging according to species type, regulated by genetic endowment, and paced by ecologic forces" (p. 30).

Shock (1962), in reviewing large numbers of research contributions, reported that different organs in the human body reduce their functional efficiency with age at widely varying rates, and that the organisms as a whole also have varying rates of maturation and deterioration.

Comfort (1956) presented one of the more comprehensive summaries of research on the biology of aging, including a classification and critique of the major theories of human aging. "To a great extent human history and psychology," Comfort wrote, "must always have been determined and moulded by the awareness that the life-span of any individual is determinate, and that the expectation of life tends to decrease with increasing age" (p. 5).

Comfort quotes Warthin's "uplifting generalization" that *involution* is a biologic entity equally important with *evolution* in the broad scheme of the immortal process of life. . . . age, the major involution, is due primarily to the gradually weakening *energy-charge* set in action by the moment of fertilization, and is dependent upon the potential fulfillment of function by the organism" (Comfort, 1956, p. 5).

Biological theories of aging have fallen into three categories, none of which has clear-cut historical development, according to Comfort. The first, fundamentalist theories, seek to encompass the entire senescent process, or treat aging as an inherent process of living matter; the second, epiphenomenalist theories, attribute senescence to particular physiological conditions; the third, general development theories, associate senescence with the cessation of somatic growth. Under the fundamentalist category may be placed theories concerned with "wear and tear" of cells, deterioration of cell colloids, or inherent deterioration of nervous, endocrine, vascular, or connective tissues. Under the epiphenomenalist classification may be placed theories which associate aging with production of intestinal bacteria, accumulation of metabolites, or even the action of gravity, heavy water, or radiation on the human organism.

Among the general development theories, Comfort identified Bidder's contribution as the most recent and among the most important. "Senescence is a correlate of the evolution of determinate growth and of a final absolute size" (p. 12). Bidder argued that the acquisition of a regulator capable of terminating organismic growth when a specific, efficient size was reached, was vital in the evolution of certain land animals, including man. This regulator has produced in man a maximally effective physique between approximately the ages of 20 and 40, the span of years in which men are called upon to contribute most to the nurture and protection of the young. According to Bidder, "the dwindling of cartilage, muscle and nerve cell, which we call senescence, did not affect the survival of the species." In a reference to the emergence of advanced cultural patterns, Bidder observed: "Probably no man ever reached 60 years old until language attained such importance in the equipment of the species that long experience became valuable in a man who could neither fight nor hunt" (Comfort, 1956, p. 12).

Many biological characteristics, especially those few which provide visible bench marks for change of status, have relevance to age status analysis. The long period of infant dependence on adults has bearing on the length and quality of childhood status. The changes in bodily form and function identified by the concept of puberty have provided cues for many societies to alter status. The span of fecundity typically has relevance both for marriage and morals. Changes in endurance, strength, dexterity, and coordination have bearing both on learning and on performance, and thereby are clues for age status determination.

The link between advancing biological knowledge and age status remains only dimly perceived. In fact, contradictory trends appear on occasion. For example, although biological and psychological research repeatedly confirms that chronological age is a poor predictor, in individual cases, of strength and skill retention and learning potential, bureaucratically oriented societies are continuing, even extending, the use of chronological age in assigning status; among illustrations are compulsory retirement policies and age-peer promotions in schools.

Likewise, the prospective use of biological discoveries in modifying age status remains unclear. Bleyer (1958), in a study of rates of abnormality of children born to mothers of different ages, discovered that children born to mothers over 35 years of age were more likely to have physical and mental defects than children born to younger mothers. Legal restraints and moral controls are often employed to reduce the birth rate among very young mothers. Are there prospects that data of the type reported by Bleyer may lead to restraints on child bearing by older mothers?

Cross-currents of biological and social developments have produced some strange paradoxes. The age of puberty has dropped precipitously in technologically progressive countries, apparently as a result of improved diet and medical care, but even as sexual and physiological maturity comes earlier, greater intellectual and emotional demands in these same countries call for a postponement of social maturity. Not only longevity, but the years of vigor are being extended among those peoples whose economies and political pressures are calling for ever earlier removal from the work force.

Finally, attention needs to be called to an ideological component in the application of biological theories of aging, especially the extension into social definitions of the description of senescence as a period of deterioration or decline. Kutner (1962) has charged that most current interpretations of growing old are couched in the language of despair. He found that aging has been described variously as "a decremental process," "progressive impairment of function," a "flight of irregular stairs, down which some journey more quickly than others," or "as the period in life in which losses exceed gains" (p. 6). Kutner also has taken exception to Tibbitts' characterization of the early years as exhibiting "enlargement, differentiation, and refinement of capacities," and the later years as displaying "decline, decrement, and loss of function" (p. 5). Rather, Kutner argued, "Sociological research suggests that the decrements of aging are produced at least as much by circumstances (such as compulsory retirement, age-segregation, youth-oriented community facilities, death of family and friends) as by any intrinsic aging phenomenon" (p. 5).

These biological references are partial and fragmentary. The purposes in presenting them have been, first, to acknowledge that biological characteristics act as limiting factors as well as clues in the determination of age status, and, second, to suggest that societies may take considerable liberties with biological conditions in status demands related to age.

Demographic Conditions

Societies are typically composed of members with chronological ages which form a continuum; ordinarily, the older the age category, the smaller the percentage of the total population. For short periods, of course, a society may have a concentration in one or more limited age categories—witness the establishment of the *kibbutzim* in Palestine in the wake of a youth movement, or the settlement of frontier America. Other factors than selective migration also may produce aberrations of population composition. War, depression, epidemics, infanticide, and birth-control policies may affect birth and death rates as well as migration. The shift from a combined high birth rate and death rate, which is the pattern typical of so-called underdeveloped countries, to a low birth and death rate, the pattern typical of industrially advanced countries, shrinks the percentage of the population in the younger age categories and expands the percentage in the older categories. Although it is conceivable that a society may disrupt the tendency toward formation of an age continuum by, for example, drastic forms of infanticide or birth control, or by gerontocide, it may be concluded that, for most societies, in the long run the population is likely to conform, when plotted by age and sex, to a pyramidal pattern.

Demographic projections of changing age composition have led to a wide variety of interpretations of consequences for the social structure. Spengler (1941), in the midst of the Great Depression and its low birth rate, predicted that the aging of the population would lead to a gerontocracy in business and government, unless means were developed which would assure that younger men would be assigned key decision-making roles. Dickinson (1958), in the context of the post-World War II baby boom in Western Europe, the United States, and Australia and New Zealand, projected not only a reversal of the trend toward the aging of the populations of these countries, but what he called a "younging" of the electorate, which would rebuff socialistic trends and return to individualism and free private enterprise. Bouthol (1953) suggested a correlation between a nation's willingness to engage in war at a particular period and the presence in that nation's population of a "surplus" of young men who might otherwise indulge in internal agitation or revolt.

Nations exhibit considerable variations in the age composition of their populations (Hauser & Vargas, 1960). In 1950, France, Belgium, Great Britain, Ireland, Sweden, and Austria reported more than 10 per cent of their populations to be 65 years or older. In sharp contrast, Togoland, Gold Coast (now Ghana), Greenland, Mozambique, Brazil, and Formosa had only 2.5 per cent or less in the older age category (Hauser & Vargas, 1960).

Nations with the largest percentages of older persons are typically those with the largest percentages in the "productive" age span, 15–64 years. The six countries with the highest percentage of aged, listed above, have a productive population ranging from 60.4 per cent to 68.0 per cent, whereas the six lowest-ranking countries contain a productive population ranging from 54.3 per cent to 63.1 per cent. Furthermore, most of the European nations report between 20 and 30 per cent to be children under 15 years of age, whereas many underdeveloped countries report that children comprise 40 to 45 per cent of the total.

National populations have been arbitrarily divided into three groups on the basis of percentage of older population. "Young" populations are those with less than 4 per cent 65 years and over; "mature" populations contain 4–7 per cent older population; and "aged" populations have at least 7 per cent 65 years and older. The young nations, characterized by high birth and death rates and short life expectancy, are typically agricultural and economically underdeveloped. The old nations are, for the most part, industrially developed representatives of Western European civilization.

The increasing refinement of demographic data on a comparative, world-wide basis provides important background data for the sociologist of the life cycle. Hauser has posed some significant issues which can be better understood through analysis of demographic data on age composition and trends. He wrote: "If youth means vigor and age debility, the Western and free nations may be handicapped in the intense competition—economic, social, political, and perhaps military—which seems to lie ahead. But youth has not always triumphed over age, and age has many virtues and strengths not possessed by youth" (Hauser & Vargas, 1960, p. 52).

Not only does the age composition vary among nations, but among segments within nations as well (Cowgill, 1957; Cowgill, 1958; Misra, 1959; Vance, 1954). Higher rural birth rates and the rural-to-urban migration of youth have often resulted in urban areas containing disproportionately large percentages in the productive years, and the rural areas having disproportionately large percentages of the young and the old. Within cities, some new, low-cost, suburban housing developments have produced census tracts with a median age under 20 years, whereas older sections of the cities may contain census tracts with median ages of 45 or 50 years. Extensive interstate migration has resulted in high percentages of the aged in New England and the midwestern states in the United States. The emergence of communities with atypical age compositions —e.g., college towns, old folks' villages— have resulted in development of distinctive institutional responses. Long-range consequences of imbalanced ecological distribution of age categories upon political behavior and welfare demands, for example, are only partially understood.

Demographers have made effective use of their data to contribute to a general sociology of age status. An outstanding contribution is Daric's *Vieillissement de la population et prolongation de la vie active* (1948). This study included an analysis of the impact of an aging population on the economic, political, military, and other social organizations in France. Information on the French public's responses to prospective prolongation of the work span was included. Finally, Daric combined data on general demographic trends with data on skills and learning potentials of older workers to propose programs to overcome biases and fears regarding extension of the work period. The French demographers Sauvy (1948; 1953) and Paillat (1962), among others, have also made significant contributions. The papers presented at a 1948 conference convened by the Alliance Nationale contre la Dépopulation (1948) deserve thorough study by all students interested both in the demography and general sociology of aging.

The United Nations report, *The Aging of Populations and Its Economic and Social Implications* (1956), made ingenious use of demographic data on age composition to project trends in several countries and to assess the social and economic implications thereof. In the United States, the Taeubers' (1958) study of the changing population is an effective reference. Davis (Davis & Combs, 1950) has made significant contributions to age status analysis by building from demographic data.

As with the discussion of the biology of aging, this review of data on demography is partial. The purpose is to emphasize that biological and demographic factors act as restraints in the erection of age status systems, but not as determinants.

Sociological Determinants of the Life Course

Solon, the Athenian poet and lawmaker born in the seventh century, B.C., suggested a 10-stage life course of seven years each:

A boy at first is the man; unripe; then he casts his teeth;
Milk-teeth befitting the child he sheds in his seventh year.
Then to his seven years God adding another seven,
Signs of approaching manhood show in the bud.
Still, in the third of the sevens his limbs are growing; his chin
Touched with a fleecy down, the bloom of the cheek is gone.
Now, in the fourth of the sevens ripen to greatest completeness
The powers of the man, and his worth becomes plain to see.
In the fifth he bethinks him that this is the season for courting,
Bethinks him that sons will preserve and continue his line.
Now in the sixth his mind, ever open to virtue,
Broadens, and never inspires him to profitless deeds;
Seven times seven, and eight; the tongue and the mind.
For fourteen years together are now at their best.

Still in the ninth is he able, but never so nimble
In speech and in wit as he was in the days of his prime.
Who to the tenth has attained, and has lived to complete it,
Has come to the time to depart on the ebb-tide of Death (Vischer, 1947, p. 121).

Poets and playwrights have long been recorders and interpreters of the patterns as well as the vagaries of the life course. Some, such as Solon, have emphasized biological maturation, others have eulogized youth or old age. But many creative artists have portrayed life as transition, or preparation for transition, have described a succession of age statuses, have unfolded the life course, and have sought to identify purpose therein.

There are several approximate synonyms for the concept "life course." With little question, "life cycle" is the concept found most often in social scientific literature. The concept "aging," although often used to refer to the aged only, has also been used to refer to the entire life course. The "stages of life" and "life span" convey similar meaning. The process of "maturation" and the pattern of a "career" are often applied to most of the span of life.

In addition to the above social-psychological, human-development-oriented concepts, other terms, including Mead's (1939) "life plot" and Benedict's (1946) "arc of life," have been advanced to approach the life course culturalogically. Mead, for example, has traced the "plot" of the culturally directed shifts in status throughout the life course of the Balinese. The infant, according to the Balinese, comes from the purity of a heavenly world, decreasing in purity upon birth. The child increases in purity until adolescence, only to decrease in purity again upon marriage. The trend toward purity again resumes, until, upon attainment of great-grandparenthood, the state of purity is again reached, and the old person, "like a new-born infant, is but an uneasy occupant of this profane world."

Similarly, Benedict has adopted the concept "arc of life" to contrast the statuses assigned to Japanese and Americans at successive stages of the life course. She identified the Japanese arc of life as "a great shallow U-curve with maximum freedom and indulgence allowed to babies and to the old." Increasing restrictions are placed upon the growing child, and "having one's own way" reaches a nadir immediately before and after marriage. Culturally imposed restrictions continue, according to Benedict, through the adult years until, at age 60, both men and women again become almost as unhampered by shame and cultural restrictions as small children. The arc of life in the United States is precisely the reverse; the U-curve is turned upside down. The young child is firmly disciplined. Restrictions are relaxed as the child becomes a man. The adult years become the "high point of freedom and initiative." Restrictions appear again with senescence, "as men lose their grip or their energy or become dependent."

For purposes of this paper, "life course" is used to refer primarily to those successive statuses individuals are called upon to occupy in various cultures and walks of life as a result of aging, and "age status" refers to the system developed by a culture to give order and predictability to the course followed by individuals.

Life course theory had an auspicious advance in the first decade of this century, notably through the publication of *Altersklassen und Männerbünde,* by Hans Schurtz (1902); *Primitive Secret Societies,* by Hutton Webster (1908); and the classic *Les Rites de Passage,* by Arnold van Gennep (1960). By the end of the nineteenth century, anthropologists had already amassed copious field notes and published numerous descriptive studies of the rapidly disappearing preliterate societies. Although Linton (1942, p. 591) has complained that the early ethnographers often failed to record terms used to distinguish among age-sex categories, Schurtz, Webster, and Van Gennep were able to use these early studies to good ad-

vantage. Whereas the works of Schurtz and Webster were concerned primarily with the processes by which groups of young males were initiated into adult statuses, Van Gennep dealt systematically with status patterns throughout the life course.

That Van Gennep anticipated or, rather, constructed an age status frame of reference is clearly indicated by his observation that life is composed of "a series of passages from one age to another and from one occupation to another. . . ." These successive stages include "birth, social puberty, marriage, fatherhood, advancement to a higher class, occupational specialization, and death" (1960, pp. 2–3). The shift from membership in one group to another or from one social situation to another is, according to Van Gennep, accompanied by ritual. Three types of rites of passage—separation, transition, and incorporation—may be distinguished. Periodically during the life course, an individual participates in special rites as he divests himself of one age status (separation), makes a change of age status (transition), and becomes incorporated into the next status in a structured succession of statuses (incorporation). Movement through the life course is not steady, but pulsating. Van Gennep has again written, with simple eloquence, that life "is to act and to cease, to wait and rest, and then to begin acting again, but in a different way. And there are always new thresholds to cross" (p. 189). He lists as major thresholds birth, adolescence, maturity, old age, death, and, for believers, afterlife.

From the promising theoretical developments at the turn of the century, as exemplified by Van Gennep, the subsequent utilization of an age status frame of reference, especially the concept "rite of passage," has been disappointing. Miles (1935), in an essay, "Age and Human Society," collected and ordered considerable data on aging, including materials on demography, on biological and psychological theories of aging, on age-related changes in skills and intelligence, and on welfare needs of older people.

But it was Linton who, along with Parsons (1942), sought most directly to revive interest in age status as a significant component of social structure. A thorough examination of his article "Age and Sex Categories" (Linton, 1942) is appropriate.

The work of Linton. Linton suggested that traditional institutional approaches do not provide an adequate basis for understanding personality formation and social structure. In addition, analysis of various ways societies classify and organize their members is needed. One means utilized to classify and organize is the age-sex characteristics of the members. Linton emphasized that ordinarily societies use age and sex as classificatory devices only; members in a given category are not likely to constitute a formal social group, although at least a modicum of age-category solidarity is in evidence in most societies. Furthermore, certain culture patterns are frequently transmitted and nurtured by a particular age category; a distinctive language among adolescents, or secrets not divulged by adults until the youth is accepted as an adult, are examples.

Physiologically, maturation is slow, and changes in the organism are almost imperceptible in the short run. About the only exceptions are birth, arrival of puberty, the loss of reproductive powers (for the female), and death. Societies have exploited the considerable range of choices in developing age status systems, both in the age of entry and the age span of each status and in the prestige attached to a particular stage.

Linton suggested that age-sex classificatory systems "are sufficiently divorced from physiological considerations to make possible almost any amplification of formal categories and almost any choice of transition points" (1942, p. 592). Only birth and death, Linton observed, are universally recognized transition points, and these are not necessarily the termini of the life course, since some societies attribute a status from conception rather than from birth or "christening," and some societies grant status to the deceased.

Linton identified seven age-sex statuses as universal: infant, usually sexually undifferentiated; boy; girl; adult man; adult woman; old man; old woman. In most societies more male than female age statuses are discernible, and the female frequently is assigned adult status at a younger chronological age than the male. Although purely physiological considerations would suggest that the absence of sexual differentiation of infants would continue into childhood, Linton observed that status distinction between boy and girl takes place as a means of preparing the child for the subsequent and highly differentiated adult statuses. Many of the sex status differentiations of adults may be removed with the attainment of old age.

Linton gave considerable attention to the transition from childhood to adulthood. Although, physiologically, there are distinctive changes in puberty, and although sexual maturity precedes reproductive maturity by possibly three years, not all societies have recognized a distinctive adolescent status. Some societies do recognize an interim status, some prolong childhood and launch the individual directly into adulthood, some start adult status early.

Ceremonial observance ordinarily accompanies some, but not all, of the transitions from one age status to another. All, or almost all, societies perform rites of passage for entry into adulthood; these are more likely to be associated with marital than with pubertal rites. A rather small percentage of societies conducts rituals for transition from infancy into childhood, but the transition calling forth least ritual recognition is that from adult to old age status. Linton noted a progressive degeneration of rites of passage in the American society. Puberty rites have deteriorated more than marital rites, although the former remain strong among Roman Catholics in the lower socioeconomic class, through emphasis on religious confirmation, and among the highest socioeconomic class, through the ostentatious debuts of daughters.

Linton also observed that the behavior expected of an individual at one phase of his life course may be sharply different from the expectations at a subsequent stage. "Nevertheless," he stated, "we know that the average individual in all societies is able to make the transition from one age category role to another without serious personality disturbances and to function successfully in roles which often appear quite incompatible" (1942, p. 601). However, an individual is less likely to encounter difficulty in accommodating to new age status demands if the transition has been gradual.

Linton concluded with observations on the transition from adulthood to old age. The incentive to step from the adult status into old age may result from the prospect of enhanced prestige (although adult accomplishment, rather than growing old per se, seems to be a prerequisite for prestige in old age) or from the prospect of being relieved from many adult obligations.

Although most of Linton's seminal hypotheses have been tested and elaborated, efforts to maintain focus on the general age-sex relationship to the social structure have been few. It is to one of the notable exceptions, Eisenstadt's *From Generation to Generation* (1956), that we now turn.

The work of Eisenstadt. Eisenstadt's is one of the boldest efforts so far to theorize about social structure using age as the significant variable. Although his hypotheses relate primarily to the varying means by which societies prepare youths for, and introduce them into, the adult status, his work represents a great stride toward the development of a sociology of age status. Age status expectations, he suggested, "constitute one of the strongest, most essential links between the personality system of individuals and the social system in which they participate" (1956, p. 32). These expectations provide means by which individuals define their rights and obligations in interaction with others; they also provide a basis for defining and distinguishing the types of units within a social structure.

Eisenstadt built his study around the concept "age grade," especially the youth grade in its interaction with the adult age grade. An age grade incorporates a "broad definition of human obligations and potentials at a given stage of life" (p. 22). Through a system of statuses assigned to the age grades, individuals plot "The broad contours of human life, of their own expectations and possibilities, and place themselves and their fellow-men in various positions . . ." (p. 23).

Much of the importance of age differentials is linked with responsibilities of transmitting the social heritage to newcomers, namely, the newborn. This necessitates status distinction between the transmitter of the heritage and the recipient, between the adult and the child. The transmitting process, or socialization, includes normative elements; restraints and responsibilities placed upon the child are legitimized in the context of the superior social experience of the adult in contrast to that of the child.

In addition, according to Eisenstadt, the child associates with age peers, with whom the child recognizes a mutuality of interests, a recognition which is reinforced by adults. A function of establishing status distinctions on the basis of age is to enable the younger to learn from the older and thereby acquire ability to perform responsible roles so that social continuity may be maintained. The difference between adult and child statuses is emphasized so that the child can become an adult. The problem Eisenstadt defined for himself was to determine the relationship between social structure and age-homogeneous groups. That is, under what structural conditions do youth groups and youth movements emerge and function?

Essentially, Eisenstadt hypothesized that, in social structures in which the family or kinship system is the basic unit of the division of labor, values develop which emphasize particularistic interaction patterns, provide multiple responsibilities, and promote status ascription. In these societies, age-heterogeneous relationships thrive, and distinctive youth groups play only minor roles. In contrast, in social structures in which the kinship unit does not provide the context for the division of labor, or may even impede the attainment of adult status by children, age-homogeneous groups are likely to emerge to challenge the authority of the adults. An extensive array of data, mainly from anthropological sources, confirms the hypotheses.

The work of Prins. Repeatedly, the concepts "age set," "age class," and "age grade" are to be found in anthropological publications. As early as 1929, Radcliffe-Brown sought to provide consistency in the use of age organization terms. More recently, Prins (1953) has further refined this terminology and has added significant illustrative material as well.

Prins defined "age class" as "an institutionalized group with a definite task during a given period in the social life of the community, with a proper name and with a historical permanence, even when all members have died." An "age set" is "the sumtotal of the persons, the man-power thus, of the institutionalized group called 'class,' or . . . the number of people initiated together, but without reference to any specific task." And an "age grade," according to Prins, indicates "a recognized position in the tribal structure, attributing a well-defined number of rights and duties to the set of a certain class which occupies that position during a given period. . . . In short, an age-grade indicates the prerogatives of those who belong to a certain class" (p. 10). Put in other words, an "age set" is composed of the persons who ritually move into adulthood together, and who maintain a distinctive group identity over a period of time, possibly throughout life; "age class" is used to identify the group attributes and responsibilities of the members of an age set, when those responsibilities are formalized; and "age grade" refers to one of a series of statuses which, combined, encompass the life course. Typically, the age grade system is a multi-purpose institution, embodying legal, political, religious, educational, military, and other functions.

To illustrate the distinction among the above classifications and to detail the role of age (classes, sets, or grades), Prins turned to the social structure of three East African tribes, the Galla, the Kipsigis, and the Kikuyu.

The Galla have established a system of five age classes of eight years' length each. Every eighth year, the surviving members of the oldest recognized class move "outside" the system, and those recruited into the new age set appropriate the name of the oldest class for reuse and perpetuation of the class cycle. Also, of course, every eight years each of the other four classes moves up one age grade.

Peculiarly, membership in each newly created set is not dependent on chronological age but on kinship, that is, on being the son of a member of the class being moved outside the system. Therefore, it is questionable whether the term age set ought to be used to identify the new recruits, although ordinarily societies which emphasize age classes recruit members for newly forming sets from the young only. The Galla system calls for recruitment to an age class on the basis of patrilineal descent, not on age. The awarding of priority to lineal descent over approximate chronological age has led, concluded Prins, to "a complete perversion even of the widest concept of social age" (p. 64).

The age class system of the Kipsigis appears to be much less complicated, at least in implementation, than that of the Galla. The Kipsigis have established seven age classes, with recruitment into each class lasting about 15 years. Therefore, a cycle begins anew every 105 years. Only three age grades are distinguishable—boyhood, warriorhood, and elderhood. There is no rite of passage into the first grade, except birth itself, and no rite upon leaving the third, except the fact of death.

Since a cycle lasts longer than a century, not all classes are actually staffed with members at a given time. Prins identified four periods for each class as it proceeds full circle: (1) a period of "rest," during which members have died and the next phase of the cycle has not yet arrived; (2) a period in which future class members are being born, but are not yet initiated as warriors; (3) a period in which the class occupies the grade of warrior and strengthens itself by recruitment of new members during this 15-year period; and (4) a period of decline, in which members become elders and eventually die, only to have, for the age class, a new period of rest.

The most complicated use of age in the assignment of status reported by Prins is that of the Kikuyu. Age sets, formed annually, flow steadily rather than intermittently into the age grade system. Six age grades are delineated: junior warrior status, or the youth age set, occupied by an individual for about six-and-a-half years during the age span of 14–23 years; senior warrior status, occupied for about 10 years during the age span from 20–32 years; learning elder status, occupied ordinarily for about 14 years, or until the oldest child is to be circumcised; junior elder status; senior elder status; and priestly status. Since contingencies other than age enter increasingly into acquisition of the next successive age status, Prins reported no clear chronological age spans for the later grades. In fact, it is marriage rather than age per se which transfers an individual from warrior to elder status; the final, priestly status is achieved only by those who have had all their children circumcised and who no longer have wives of childbearing age.

The life course is complicated for the Kikuyu by the fact that, periodically, a shift of the political power structure takes place. The society is divided into tribal halves, with membership determined by a system of alternating patrilineal generations. If the father is a Maina (the name of one of the two political categories, or "parties"), the son is a Mwangi (the name of the other); the grandson is, like his grandfather, a Maina. Although about half of the total population is in each category, only those elders belonging to one category exercise formal leadership during a 30- or 40-year time span, then turn over leadership roles to the elders of the other category. Therefore, if, during a given period, Maina elders are in control, Mwangi elders serve only as consultants, in what Prins called the "shadow" grade of elder.

The three case studies confirm, Prins suggested, that an age class system provides for an individual a secure position which spreads far beyond the widest compass of kin. The system also makes it possible for an individual to rise steadily from the lowest to the highest rung of the social ladder merely by aging and by conforming to the generally recognized norms. Prins concluded his study with the observation that effective age class systems give coherence to a society and balance to personal lives, through the maintenance of an efficient military force, an educational system, welfare protections, a regulated family life, and an effective judicial procedure and political system.

Prins's contribution to age status analysis has been reviewed in some detail, not as an introduction to a survey of mankind's great variety of usages of age in determination of status and the pace and direction of the life course, but rather to give examples of man's versatility in the use of age and to draw sharp contrast to age status systems developed in industrial societies.

Before attempting to delineate an age status frame of reference, one additional perspective on aging ought to be introduced. For lack of a more concise term, this will be called the human development approach. The psychologist-philosopher Jung (1960), the psychoanalysts Erikson (1959), Linden and Courtney (1953), and Bühler (1935; 1961), and the social psychologist Strauss (1959) provide diverse examples of this approach to the life course.

The work of Jung. In sharp contrast to Freud and the many psychoanalysts and others who have emphasized personality formation during the first years of life, Jung gave emphasis to individuation during the middle periods of life. In "The Stages of Life" (*Die Lebenswende*), published in 1931, Jung focused on young adulthood and middle age as the significant periods of the life course. He divided the life course into four stages, employing the concept "arc of life" in a manner which apparently transcends cultural variations. The first segment of the arc, childhood, provides problems for adults, although children are not conscious of problems of their own. During the second and third stages, individuals are conscious of the problems confronting them. To complete the arc of life, one again becomes a problem for others. During the first period, the childish stage of consciousness, the individual is dependent on his parents, not himself, and therefore has no major problems. Jung identified childhood as the "anarchic or chaotic state," which lasts until the age of puberty. Youth, the second stage, extends from puberty until middle life, or to about 35 or 40 years of age. Jung did not see fit to label the age period after 40, nor did he suggest the chronological age at which one becomes old. But it is apparent in context that Jung's third stage is comparable to what is usually called middle age and possibly later maturity, whereas his fourth stage is closely related to the onset of senility.

Although Jung identified four stages, he also divided life into "morning" and "afternoon." That which is effective and proper for the first half of life is improper for the second half. "For a young person it is almost a sin . . . to be preoccupied with himself; but for the aging person it is a duty and a necessity to devote serious attention to himself" (1960, p. 399). The first half of life is properly devoted to individual development, entrenchment in the outer world, reproduction, and care of children. But, Jung added, "Money-making, social achievement, family and posterity are nothing but plain nature, not culture. Culture lies outside the purpose of nature. Could by

any chance culture be the meaning and purpose of the second half of life?" (p. 400). In addition, Jung noted that masculine and feminine characteristics often begin to reverse themselves at about age 40; males develop feminine traits, females, masculine traits.

Although transformations from one stage to the next are, apparently, inherent in the aging process itself, Jung insisted that many individuals traverse the life course without conscious awareness of the inherent transformations. Especially, many embark upon the second half of life wholly unprepared.

To recapitulate, Jung has intertwined a biological-psychological view of maturation with cultural factors which tend either to transcend, through culture, or to deny, through ignorance, the changing needs resulting from maturation.

The work of Erikson. Erikson (1959) has suggested an eight-phase pattern for the life course and the positive and negative alternatives available to the individual as he seeks ego identity during psychological crises of each stage. Table 1 reveals his

TABLE 1

EGO IDENTITY "ALTERNATIVES"
AT SUCCESSIVE STAGES
OF THE LIFE CYCLE[a]

Stage		Psychological Crisis (positive and negative alternatives)
I	Infancy	Trust vs. Mistrust
II	Early Childhood	Autonomy vs. Shame, Doubt
III	Play Age	Initiative vs. Guilt
IV	School Age	Industry vs. Inferiority
V	Adolescence	Identity vs. Identity Diffusion
VI	Young Adult	Intimacy vs. Isolation
VII	Adulthood	Generativity vs. Self-Absorption
VIII	Mature Age	Integrity vs. Disgust, Despair

[a] Source: Erikson, 1959, p. 121.

schema in compact form. He associated the life course with the interplay of the human organism's sequential development of loco-motor, sensory, and social capacities with culturally provided opportunities and limi-tations. Thus, personality unfolds through the "organism's readiness to be driven to-ward, to be aware of, and to interact with, a widening social radius" (p. 52), from the personality's origin in the image of the mother to its termination with an image of mankind.

The work of Linden and Courtney. Lin-den and Courtney, in emphasizing the po-tential contributions of persons in later maturity, offered poignant criticism of bio-logical and some psychological frames of reference for the life course. Biologists, they suggested, have long associated adulthood with procreation and parenthood. Linden and Courtney charged that biologists often identify reproduction as the primary func-tion of organisms; therefore, after a parent has reared his young, he is no longer needed for the survival of society. "The psychologic investigators with an apparent biologic ori-entation seem to have been bent on finding means for sustaining juvenescence, keeping alive sexual-reproductive interest, and thus postponing individual terminus as they view it" (1953, p. 906). Linden and Courtney made a frontal attack on these interpreta-tions and strategies of old age. Since human societies, they argued, require an extended period for socialization of the young as well as complex means of preserving and com-municating the heritage of the society, the older person has responsibilities not found among other animals. Therefore, "the aging human individual is just beginning some of his most important functions when parent-hood ceases" (p. 908).

Both evolescence and senescence are dy-namic. The major difference between evo-lescence and senescence is found in the direction of resolution of conflict. The evo-lescent period of the life course begins with almost complete dependence and develops, along with a progressive rebellion against this dependency on older members of soci-ety, in the form of egocentric strivings for gratification and pleasure. The evolescent period tends to produce group fragmenta-tion. Persons in the senescent period, with orientation toward the public rather than themselves, contain and restrain private pleasure-seeking and thereby prevent cul-tural disintegration.

The restraint exercised by mature mem-bers functions both to protect the young against social perils and to preserve the cul-ture. Likewise, Linden and Courtney hy-pothesize, the senescent develop a general outlook on life which is actually broader and less selfish than that of younger persons. Whereas the young view themselves as the dauntless masters of mankind, the old view themselves as participants in the improve-ment of society.

Although the aged have incipient contri-butions to make to a society, Linden and Courtney charged that cultural bias has un-necessarily relegated the older person to a status of rejection in some so-called ad-vanced countries.

The concepts "climacterium" and "invo-lution" restricted appreciation of the poten-tial contributions to society of the aging person. Inadequate information, the absence of an adequate conceptual scheme, and lack of interest have hampered the development of an understanding of old age.

Finally, Linden and Courtney have sought to compress their hypotheses about the stages of the life course into a diagram (Figure 1). With the exception of interrup-tive regressions at puberty and at an involu-tionary period in the mid-forties, the life course proceeds rather steadily from the instinct supremacy of infancy to the su-premacy of evaluative retrospection in old age. This process was called "the develop-ment of social vision."

The work of Bühler. Bühler (1935), mainly through biographical studies of the activities and productivity of large numbers of persons as they mature, also has devel-oped a general theory of maturation. She has accepted biological maturation as one of the "determining parameters" upon which

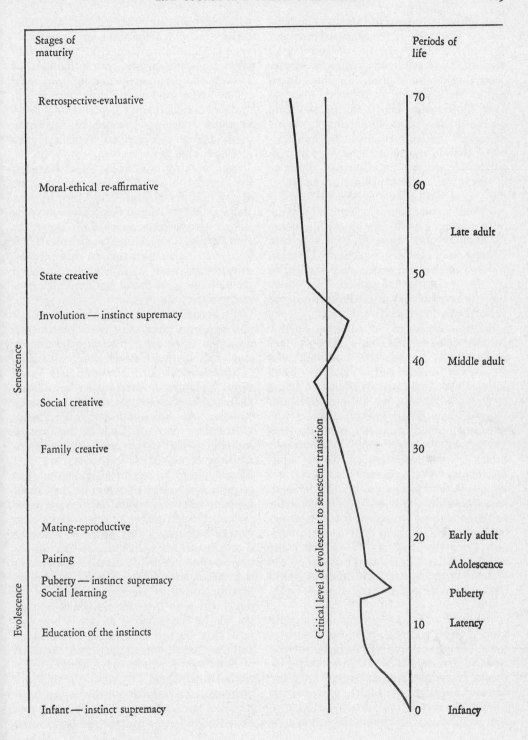

lives unfold. Maturation influences psychosomatic development, the general dimensions of human activity, and the ebb and flow of productivity. Review of studies of sensory perception, motor control, learning and retention abilities, and intelligence indicate a peak functional potential during the third decade of life, with decline setting in shortly thereafter. The dimensions of human activity, that is, the range of involvement in responsible assignments, appear to culminate at about age 30 and ordinarily remain at peak level until about age 50. Bühler has proposed a life course schema involving three successive periods: (1) expansiveness, (2) stability, and (3) reductiveness. In considering peak ages of productivity, however, Bühler's review suggested four distinctive patterns: (1) early culmination, (2) middle-age culmination, (3) late culmination, and (4) irregular, extended culmination.

Bühler contributed, in addition, the hypothesis that four basic tendencies of life—need-satisfaction, adaptive self-limitation, creative expansion, and upholding of the internal order—are closely related to stages of maturation. Although all four tendencies may be in operation at every stage of life, the young child primarily exhibits need-satisfaction, the older child adaptive self-limitation, the adolescent and young adult the tendency of creative expansion, and persons in their forties and beyond the tendency of establishing internal order. "It seems to be an unconscious tendency to establish internal equilibrium as well as integratedness before the end of life and after the individual has gone through most of the cycle of life of maintaining himself, adapting, and producing and reproducing" (1961, p. 368).

The work of Strauss. Strauss has properly warned about treating age status systems as static. He criticized social psychologists who view human development "either as attainment, or as sets of variations on basic themes" (1959, p. 91). He charged that the scientific observer too often presumes to have omniscience, to "know the end against which persons are matched" or "the basic themes on which variations are composed" (p. 91). Strauss maintained, however, that only a portion of the transformations of identity and perspective emanate from institutions. Also important is "the open-ended, tentative, exploratory, hypothetical, problematical, devious, changeable, and only partly-unified character of human courses of action" (p. 91).

Still in a critical vein, Strauss argued that efforts to isolate a well-regulated set of age statuses yield a static, nonhistorical view of the life course. Generation succeeds generation without appreciable alteration. But, Strauss insisted, this "model of a regulated, and rather unchanging, series of age-graded passages of status is far too simple a model to be very useful for studying modern societies" (p. 134).

Strauss accepted the significant role of age and aging in personality development, but he added emphasis to the historical dimension. The age status system itself is flexible. "Definitions of who is approximately of the same age, who is much older or a little older, who is almost as old or somewhat younger, are all social categories, hence, changeable" (p. 139). Both in the lives of individuals and of age sets, distinctive intrusions occur. These intrusions are first identifiable in the historical dimension, but acquire sociological relevance as they mold generational patterns and modify age status systems. The sequence of age statuses may change little over a long period of time, but the demands and privileges of the statuses may change rapidly. It becomes the task of the sociologist of age status, suggested Strauss, to seek to incorporate in the emerging theory both those factors which contribute to the perpetuation of age status patterns through time (institutional demands) and those which contribute to new demands of those who accede to adult statuses (generational demands).

Strauss, in advancing a revised sociological model of human development, proposed two major alterations in current theory. He first suggested that socialization continues beyond adolescence and that changes in later life are not necessarily mere variants of attributes acquired in earlier years. Essentially, Strauss has advocated that the socialization process be looked upon as a lifelong process.

Ordering the statuses. The assortment of interpretations of aging and the variety of approaches to the life course highlight both the rich heritage upon which a sociology of age status may be built and the difficulty in winnowing a consistent theoretical kernel from the chaff of ideology and speculation. To impose an order on these diverse contributions now is before us. Societies confront not only the existential factors of having members who, because of age differentials, have varying potentials and strengths, and of having a particular demographic composition, but also the factor of aging of individuals. Every member of a society is called upon to move through a succession of age statuses. Every society, therefore, has the tasks of preparing individual members for subsequent age statuses, of absorbing them into the successive statuses along with removing them from the formerly occupied status, and of proclaiming to, or providing other means of communicating to, the society that the transfers have been accomplished. Societies typically employ rites of passage to herald the shift to the next age status.

Since the chronological ages of members form a continuum, and since a society would find it unmanageable to establish a status system based on the uniqueness of the age of each member, every society has also established means of grouping persons of approximately the same age into what have been called age sets and of designating a relatively few age-sex categories to provide distinctiveness among the categories.

Still another task of every society is to provide for a system of relationships among members of different age categories. Institutional patterns of deference have been devised in some cultures; patterns under the broad label of generational phenomena have been identified by historians, political scientists, and sociologists.

The age continuum of populations and the aging of members of societies place demands upon societies which result in at least five distinguishable status accommodations: (1) differentiation of statuses on the basis of age—an *age status system;* (2) formalized means by which individual members are prepared for subsequent age statuses—*socialization;* (3) formalized means by which individual members are transferred from one age status to another—*rites of passage;* (4) identification of persons of comparable ages as distinctive categories—*age grading;* and (5) establishment of interaction patterns among those of different age sets—*generational phenomena.*

The coherence and persistence of social structure and institutions undergo continuous strain from demands generated by age and aging phenomena. Persons occupying particular statuses are ever changing. Even as some are being prepared to occupy key statuses, others are being removed from those statuses. When the phenomenon of generations, resulting from the prospectively unique and distinctive experiences of age sets which grow up in variable historical climates is also considered, the "threat" of life course to stable social structure becomes clear.

The emergence of complex, industrialized societies has produced at least two major innovations in the use of age in forming and articulating social structure. First, generational criteria have become ambiguous. The combination of giving credence simultaneously to familial and to sociopolitical criteria in providing generational identity, and of requiring older members of society to continue to learn—new job skills, new political loyalties, new neighborhood accommodations, new orientations—has complicated the task of maintaining identity through generational attachment. Nonetheless, data to follow indicate that the concept of generation has a significant role, if not *the* significant role, in the development of a sociology of age status.

Second, separate institutions have been assigned responsibility for establishing age status sequences, frequently with the result that individuals experience asynchronization in moving through the life course. The use of age for defining legal status, for example, may not result in a status pattern synchronous with career patterns, and family responsibilities do not synchronize with earning capacity; a married adult may simultaneously be a student preadult. Although age status asynchronization is present at most stages of the life course in complex societies, it is probably most pronounced in the transition from youth to adulthood. The significance of asynchronous movement through the life course will become more evident with the presentation of data on the life course in the several major institutions—marital, educational, religious, political, legal, and economic.

LIFE COURSE PATTERNS IN THE MAJOR INSTITUTIONS

Life Course and the Family

The family structure provides one of the more convenient ways to trace the life course. It is the family which typically provides infants and children with their most significant statuses. From courtship to marriage, through parental statuses to grandparenthood, and possibly to the status of family ancestor, most individuals' life courses may readily be followed.

The family itself also exhibits a life course, or cycle. From an arbitrarily chosen beginning for the family cycle, say, with marriage, the family expands in size, then retracts with the departure of children from the family household for the purpose of marriage, and the cycle begins anew. The counterpart of the successive statuses of child, parent, and grandparent is, for the family cycle, the successive functions as the family of orientation, the family of procrea-

tion, and the family of gerontation (Belknap & Friedsam, 1949). Fortes (1958) also has identified three stages of the developmental cycle of the family: the expansion phase; the dispersion, or fission, phase; and the replacement phase. The first spans the period from marriage through the time in which children remain dependent on their parents; the second spans the period from the departure of the first child to the departure of the last child from the family household, usually through marriage; and the third includes the postparental years, during which the inheritor of the father's family status assumes the key status in the kinship system.

The life cycle of the family has great significance to the sociologist, but the concern here is primarily with the life course of individuals in the family. Waller and Hill (1951) have identified a sequence of statuses related to family roles. Beginning with the post-childhood period, they identify a general "mate finding period," which in turn has three stages, "rating and dating," "courtship," and "engagement." With marriage, another sequence of stages normally unfolds. These include: "married-pair living (including the honeymoon)"; parenthood, subdivided into "child-bearing," "child-rearing," and "child-launching" periods; and, finally, the combination of grandparent and mother- or father-in-law status.

Glick (1955) has combined data on age of marriage, age of parents at the birth of their children, age of parents when their children marry, and on longevity to develop a schema for the life course in the family and to identity changes in the age of shift from status to status. Between 1890 and 1950 the age at first marriage for both husband and wife dropped, from a median of 26.1 years to 22.8 years for the husband, from 22.0 to 20.1 years for the wife. The lowering of the age of termination of the child-bearing period during this 60-year span was even more pronounced. In 1890, the median age of the father at the birth of his last child was 36.0 years; in 1950 it was 28.8; the median age of the mother dropped from 31.9 to 26.1 years. The trend toward earlier marriage, combined with earlier termination of the childbearing period, has produced a considerable lowering of the median age of the launching of the last child through marriage. In 1890 the median age of the father when the last child married was 59.4 years; in 1950 the age was 50.3. For the mother, the shift was from 55.3 to 47.6 years. Whereas in 1890 at least one spouse had died, on the average, two years before the launching of the last child, and therefore the majority of marriages did not include a postparental status for husband and wife, by 1950 a husband and wife could expect to have nearly 14 years together after their children had married and before one of them died. The emergence and elongation of the "empty nest," or postparental period, together with the prospect that great-grandparents will be commonplace, have as yet unmeasured consequences for the entire social structure.

Lansing and Kish (1957) have somewhat reversed the Glick approach by emphasizing not the chronological age but the role of the individual in the family at a given period. They hypothesized: "To understand an individual's social behavior it may be more relevant to consider which stage in the family life cycle he has reached than how old he is" (p. 513). Thus, it may be more significant to know how old the children in a family are than how old the parents are. To be the father of a teenage daughter elicits certain behavior patterns, whether the father be 30 or 70 years of age. Further studies along the lines suggested by Lansing and Kish are vitally needed to advance a sociology of age status.

Most interpretations of the dynamics of American family structure have concluded that a shift from an extended, three-generation kinship structure to a compact, two-generation conjugal structure has taken place as urbanization and industrialization have proceeded. The typical contemporary American family, according to Parsons

(1959), emphasizes the parental status and de-emphasizes the grandparental status. Thus, the aged are supposed to become "ex-family" (Beard, 1949). Linton (1959), like Parsons, accepted the interpretation that the kinship family had deteriorated under the impact of industrialization in Western Europe and America. However, Linton observed that certain new trends, external to the family structure, may contribute to the re-establishment of the kinship structure. For example, unions may increasingly restrict apprenticeship to offspring of members, and bureaucratization may promote nepotism; in both instances, younger members of the family would become dependent on older members.

It is profitable, in seeking to understand age status and family structure, to extend the Linton argument. Under what conditions have conjugal families arisen? Do those conditions exist today? Theories of the changing structure of the American family have been developed from data of a period in which mobility, both horizontal and vertical, was extensive. Immigration and rural-to-urban migration contributed to alienation between familial generations. As America becomes urban and middle class, and as immigration becomes less and less a factor in the population, cultural and class differences between parent and offspring are likely to become less apparent.

A series of superficially unrelated trends, it may be tentatively advanced, combine to give plausibility to the emergence of new forms of the three-generation family. Bureaucratization, which, in contrast to the period of entrepreneurial emphasis in careers, postpones peak earning power to the later years of the work span, places highest income in the hands of workers when their conjugal family responsibilities may have already ended. Likewise, the trend to increased employment of middle-aged women provides capital which may be used to subsidize married children and grandchildren. Furthermore, the institutionalization of seniority patterns, although occasionally corroded by automation, helps protect the security and earning power of older workers. Additional fringe benefits, such as nontransferable sick leave and pension schemes, and longer vacations based on years of employment, may encourage workers to forego temptations to migrate; permanence of residence increases the prospects of strong kinship ties (Litwak, 1960). Finally, the postponement of entry into the labor force for educational reasons, combined with trends in earlier marriages, provides an open invitation for older parents, with peak incomes, to subsidize their married children.

A number of studies indicate that kinship "self-help" patterns are emerging. Sussman (1953) has found a widespread pattern of subsidy of married children by their parents. Brady (1955) also found an increasing expenditure by the older person on his children and grandchildren. Studies in Great Britain, especially in East London (Kerr, 1958; Shaw, 1954; Townsend, 1957; Young & Willmott, 1957) have shown strong kinship ties to be in evidence. A study by Young and Geertz (1961) of the relationship of the aged to their adult children in suburbs of London and San Francisco led to the conclusion that their data "support the notions that old people generally maintain close links with their children and that the mother-daughter tie is the central nexus of the kinship network of industrial societies" (p. 140).

The trends cited above have monumental implications for the entire social structure, and especially for age status within the family. Current programs which presume the necessity of providing family substitutes for the welfare and related needs of the elderly may properly be re-examined. It will be ironic indeed if sociologists, by clinging to the theory that industrialization "naturally" produces the conjugal family, become unwitting contributors to a self-fulfilling prophecy by justifying programs which artificially alienate the old from the adult generation.

The life course within the family has been studied extensively. This short review has touched only a few of the issues treated by family sociologists. What is apparent, however, is that the changing length of the stages in the life course, and the increasing resources available to the older parent, necessitate a continuing alertness by the sociologist lest his models of the family structure become outmoded.

Life Course and Socialization

Although the concept "socialization" has typically been employed to describe those processes by which an infant obtains a cultural perspective or a child is groomed for adult statuses, recent studies have extended the concept to include those processes by which adults are prepared to assume new statuses. Goldfrank (1945), in an interpretation of socialization among the Pueblo Indians, has observed that "a study of the period of infancy alone would give few clues to the personality structure exhibited by the Pueblo adult" (p. 537). Whitehead (1962), commenting on the dynamics of industrialized societies, suggested that an individual, as he traverses the life course, "will be called upon to face novel situations which find no parallel in his past. The fixed person for the fixed duties, who, in older societies was such a godsend, in the future will be a public danger" (p. 3). Adult resocialization thus becomes as important as the socialization of the infant and child. From one perspective, then, socialization may be defined simply as the preparation for a subsequent (age) status. All socialization is, therefore, anticipatory.

Socialization is more than the transmission of a heritage. A society must also develop means of "absorbing each new generation into its structure" (Davis, 1940, p. 217). And, especially in complex, dynamic societies, socializing agents are called upon either to anticipate changes in status so that the younger, upon moving into the status of the older, can play a role that the older has not experienced, or to develop educational strategies which will prepare individuals to socialize themselves. Inkeles (1955) has noted that Soviet refugee parents have frequently been able to adopt socialization practices for their children which are quite different from Soviet practices. Iga (1957), in a study of Japanese American Issei child-rearing practices, observed that the immigrant parents have cast aside efforts to socialize their children to Japanese values and, instead, have endeavored "to adapt themselves to the new order of things which their children have accepted" (p. 278). Riesman and Roseborough (1955) commented that a striking aspect of American socialization patterns is that "people are prepared for roles their parents have not played, indeed, that no one has yet played: they are prepared . . . for jobs not yet invented and for consumption of goods not yet on the market" (p. 3). Mueller (1959), for example, has admonished, "To plan the education of the sixteen- to twenty-year-old [female] for the future needs of the forty-year-old and sixty-year-old is all but impossible, but it is the responsibility which cannot be circumvented" (p. 46). Mueller further suggested that this will require prophetic skills in estimating the problems and imperatives of a dynamic world 25 years hence. These challenges place awesome burdens on educators and other socialization agents. The implications for age status systems are hardly known at all.

That the concept "socialization" has become a vital tool to sociologists of age status is illustrated in studies of preparation for professional roles, preparation for the "empty nest" period in the family, preretirement education, and accommodation to old age. Becker and Carper (1956), in a study of graduate students, suggested, "One of the most compelling instances of personal change and development in adult life in our society is to be found in the typical growth of an 'occupational personality' in the young adult male . . ." (p. 289). A study of the socialization of student nurses, by Williams and Williams (1959), reviewed the demands upon students to modify their attitudes toward death, body odors, and the exposed human body. Lortie's study of preparation for the legal profession (1959), Dornbusch's study of Coast Guard Academy training (1955), and observations by Hughes (1956) and Merton (Merton, Reader, & Kendall, 1957) on medical school socialization are other examples of the application of socialization to adult learning.

Since the "empty nest" period is rather new for the American family, few postparental couples have had role models to accommodate to this change in family structure. Deutscher (1962), however, found that most older couples from a middle-class, urban group he studied moved from parental to postparental status without great difficulty.

Preretirement education is increasingly being adopted by large employers as a means of easing their older workers into retirement status. The proper roles of unions, governmental agencies, and the employers in providing the planning for and implementation of these programs are still being debated (Mack, 1958). Questions concerning choice of pension schemes, retirement residence, changing dietary and health needs, use of leisure time, among others, indicate that preretirement programs assume the educability of the older adult.

Differential responses of the young and the old to questions concerning which age category they would turn to for advice and help led Payne (1960) to conclude: "Youngsters accept as agents of socialization those persons who are older than themselves. . . . On the other hand, the oldsters were accepting as agents of their own socialization, either their own children or their children's surrogates. To do so represents a direct and complete role reversal" (p. 362).

Indeed, the younger learn from the older. Thereby societies perpetuate themselves. However, the process of socialization is more than learning to become an adult. The adult in the complex world of today must continue to learn, to revise his image of himself and the world. The mature not only have to learn old age statuses while growing old, but they may have to redefine what old age statuses are. The young, especially in industrial employment, are called upon to socialize the old. Processes of socialization alter the life course in new ways. The social structure is constantly altered to provide new agents of socialization.

Life Course and Religion

Although "folk" knowledge has occasionally related age to religious behavior and belief—"Kids and old folks go to church," or "The older you get, the more religion you get"—sociologists, including sociologists of religion, have infrequently studied age as a variable in religious behavior and beliefs. Recent studies have dealt with religious performance by age, but the theological roots of age status remain relatively unexplored.

A notable exception is the study of the child in the Puritan society of early New England by Fleming (1933). The Puritans hardly recognized a separate childhood status, especially within the religious domain. The theological doctrine of total depravity encouraged the practice of forced precocity among the young. The need for confession of sins and redemption by the unregenerate and unsaved, including the young, led Fleming to conclude: "The logical outcome of the theology [of total depravity] was contrary to an appreciation of child nature. . . . Children were regarded as children of wrath. . . . Hence the urgency of the situation, the obligation to press the conversion experience as far back as possible . . ." (p. 67). It was not until the mid-nineteenth century, through the endeavors of Horace Bushnell and others who promoted a Sunday School movement for children, that a separate and distinct child status was recognized in Puritan America, according to Fleming.

In sharp contrast to the age status consequences of a theology of total depravity are those of Hinduism and Buddhism. Hinduism, according to Huston Smith (1959), has isolated four wants of man: to experience pleasure, to achieve worldly success, to perform duties, and to accomplish liberation. These four wants, in the sequence listed, dominate, or may dominate, successive stages in the life course. The doctrine of reincarnation removes urgency from the progression through all four stages during one lifetime.

The first two wants, pleasure and success, represent the Path of Desire, and the latter two, the performance of duties and the quest for liberation, represent the Path of Renunciation. Smith's tracing of the four successive statuses of student, householder, retiree, and that of the *sannysin* ("one who neither hates nor loves anything" [p. 58]) is not fully correspondent with successive satisfaction of the four wants of man, but there is close relationship. With marriage and becoming a householder, the first three wants may be successively fulfilled. The family itself provides opportunity for pleasure, the vocation provides opportunity for success, and eventually the responsibilities of citizenship may lead to the exercise of duties for the community. Finally, with retirement providing opportunity for isolation from the world's burdens and taunts, man may seek to discover himself, by discovering that "complete release from every limitation is synonymous with absolute anonymity" (1958, p. 58). Thus, one completes the journey upon the Path of Renunciation.

T'ien (1949), in a study of the age status system of the Tai tribes, which inhabit the Yunnan-Burma frontier, has suggested the influence of Buddhism on social structure. Four distinct stages in the life course are discernible. The first and third stages, corresponding roughly to childhood and adulthood, are essentially devoid of religious responsibilities. The second and fourth stages, corresponding to youth and later maturity, are, in sharp contrast, thoroughly religious. During childhood, nurture and support are supplied by the family, and religious demands are minimal. During youth, religious instruction from the elders is stressed, and religious responsibilities are assumed. During adulthood, reponsibilities for producing and supporting children release members from religious obligations once more. Upon retirement, the member again may assume religious responsibilities, especially as instructor of the young adult and as ritual leader. Full achievement of the fourth stage, however, comes through relinquishing economic pursuits and family roles and giving material possessions to the temple.

T'ien has emphasized that movement through the successive stages is not based on chronological aging per se, but on achievement. The child must be willing to assume religious roles and instruction before moving to the second stage. Marriage, which is not determined precisely by chronological age, returns the individual to secular status. And only those willing to renounce material gain and to serve in religious capacities are granted the title of Paga, signifying movement into the fourth and final stage of the life course. T'ien coins the phrase "social age" to define this nonadherence to chronological age in shifts in status. "The essence of this new concept is the sequence of social life-history, as distinct from the growth, aging, and decline of the physical body" (1949, p. 50).

From these brief reviews of Hinduism's approach to aging and of a case study of a Buddhist society's development of a social structure built predominantly on age criteria, it becomes apparent that a society's theological system may have profound implications for age status. Although some of the materials to follow indicate the interpreters' grasp of the theology of the West, most of the data on age and religion presented by sociologists fail to incorporate the perspectives of Smith or T'ien.

Starbuck (1899) drew the conclusion from interviews with 237 persons on questions of religious belief and aspirations that "the belief in God . . . grows in importance as the years advance." Subsequent research does not confirm Starbuck's thesis. Rather, "religious life-profiles," to borrow Fichter's term, reveal varying intensities of belief in God and of participation in religious activities, with a frequent decline in concern over religious matters in old age.

Fichter's (1954) study of religious participation in Easter services, mass, and communion, by age categories of a sample of members of a southern Roman Catholic parish, indicated fluctuation through the life course, although the data are not longitudinal, and a generational phenomenon instead of aging per se may be a contributing factor. Youths under 20 reported a firm devotion to religious observances; participation tended to decline for those in their twenties; and a nadir of participation was reported by those in their thirties. From this decline in performance of religious duties, participation improves in the forties and fifties, although the intensity is not so great as for those in their teens.

Fukuyama (1961) has isolated four major dimensions of religious behavior and has included age as a variable in studying the emphasis individuals give to each of the dimensions. The first, the cognitive dimension, relates to what people *know* about religion; the second, the cultic dimension, seeks to determine what people actually *practice* in religion; the third, the creedal dimension, deals with what individuals *believe* about religion; and the final, or devotional dimension, seeks to measure what people *feel* and *experience* about religion.

In a study of over four thousand members of urban Protestant churches and of all ages, the index of the cognitive dimension revealed little variation among the several age categories. The cultic dimension index, however, showed a decline in religious practice from the teens to the twenties, with a high increase in the thirties, a continuing increase through the fifties, and a tapering off in the decades past 60. In both the creedal and devotional dimensions the indices reflect a steady increase in religious orientation from decade to decade. Fukuyama was cautious in his interpretation of the significance of his study, as he pointed out that, not being longitudinal, the trends it revealed did not indicate a life course phenomenon or a generational phenomenon.

Orbach (1961) has sought both to review some of the major studies on religious status by age and to add new understandings through reporting his own empirical study. The inconsistencies in previous studies and his own data challenge the frequently held notion that old age heralds an intensification of interest in religion. First, Orbach observed, "religion has variously been a dominant and a subsidiary force in society." Thus, during a period of dominance, both the young and old could be expected to have an intensified interest in religion, and for the young in such a period, some of this interest may continue into old age because of generational factors rather than aging per se. Orbach concluded his interpretation by reporting that his data do not corroborate either the hypothesis that the aged turn toward religion or that religiosity increases with age.

Barron (1958) has concluded that religiosity plays a surprisingly modest role in the overt behavior of most older people, but that religious concerns have a chronologically accelerative role in the inner, subjective aspects of the lives of older people. Rather than a turning to religion with aging, Barron suggested that "most people simply persist in the religious patterns of their earlier age-statuses" (p. 33).

Argyle (1959) has sought to amass and criticize psychologically oriented studies of age and religious behavior. These several studies suggest two peak periods of religious activity, adolescence and old age, with the years 30–35 representing the period of least activity. Argyle associated religiosity in adolescence with turmoil and perplexity, which lead eventually to a decision to cast aside the religion of childhood completely or to seek conversion and continuation in the faith. In contrast, religiosity in old age is associated with fear of death.

The "process of disengagement" with aging, a theory advanced by Cumming and Henry (1961), has special relevance for the religious status of the aged. Dean and Newell (1961), working within the disengagement context, developed a Religious Piety index for a sample of respondents 50 years of age and older. Piety tends to increase in the years 60–64, as does church attendance, but a steady decline in piety and in attendance after the crisis of retirement led Dean and Newell to conclude that concern for transcendental matters, including death, decreases in old age.

These brief accounts of some of the studies of religion and age reveal inconsistencies and incompleteness. Studies of the significance of religious rites of passage are meager. The data on religious participation by age categories are growing. Descriptive reports on religious programs for youth and the aged and on strategies of adult religious education may aid sociologists considerably. Social psychological studies of identity and changing self-images with aging occasionally isolate the religious factor. But the combined efforts of a substantial sociology of religion and a fledgling sociology of age status are needed to resolve the inconsistencies in the studies reported above and to clarify the functions of religious institutions and values in assigning age statuses and in assisting individuals through the life course.

Life Course and Political Behavior

Studies of the age composition of both leaders and members of political organizations are available to sociologists. Party platforms and legislative strategies reflect an increasing interest by politicians in the voting strength of various age groupings, especially the elderly. Also available are a number of interpretations of the influence of aging upon an individual's political behavior and of the aging of a whole population upon a nation's political values and fortunes.

In preliterate and agrarian societies, in which wisdom is often a corollary of age, political power is typically vested in the elders. Frazer (1905), for example, elaborated a theory of the origin of political leadership which identified gerontocracy as the earliest form of political control. Contemporary complex political systems, however, provide a setting in sharp contrast to that of a preliterate society. Establishment and extension of suffrage rights, the development of education instead of aging as the source of wisdom, and the general dynamics of societies with their changing age status patterns contribute new contingencies in understanding political behavior.

Michels observed in 1915 that, "owing to the technical type of modern civilization, age has lost much of its value, and therefore has lost, in addition, the respect which it inspired and the influence which it exercised" (1959, p. 76). Yet, many of the nations of the world entered the 1960's under the leadership of men born in the nineteenth century. Adenauer of Germany was born in 1876; Nehru of India, Mao Tsetung of Communist China, and Chiang Kai-shek of Nationalist China were born in the 1880's; and Macmillan of Great Britain, Eisenhower of the United States, DeGaulle of France, Khrushchev of the Soviet Union, Franco of Spain, Tito of Yugoslavia, and Ikeda of Japan were born in the 1890's. Generalizations about ages of top leaders may be premature.

However, studies of the age composition of party members and legislative officials have provided a more substantial basis for analysis. Gerth (1940) discovered that the age composition of the Nazi party in Germany shifted with the changing fortunes of the party. Youths in large numbers joined the party shortly before its ascension to power in 1933; however, members in the middle-age span increased their numerical strength considerably in the ensuing three years. All the while, the percentage of the Nazis in the older age categories remained considerably lower than in the Social Democratic party.

Studies by Ross (1948) and Duverger (1955) on the age composition of legislative bodies have contributed new knowledge to the role of aging in politics. Ross found that the members of the British House of Commons who represented the more democratic and decentralized parties typically achieved elective office at a later age than their more autocratic colleagues. Therefore, conservative parties are represented by younger men than the liberal parties. Duverger, in a study of the French National Assembly, found, as did Ross, that deputies from the democratic, decentralized parties had a higher average age than those from the more centralized parties. The explanation Duverger provided for this rather unexpected discovery was that, first, sons from the upper classes substitute formal education for the more elongated task of working up through the ranks of party organization in preparing for office, and, second, elected officials from the more democratic parties are less likely to have independent income to rely upon in case of political defeat, and therefore are more likely to manipulate party structure so as to entrench themselves in office.

Although some political offices have formal restrictions on tenure, a cardinal rule of politics is that the incumbent has the advantage in an election contest. The application of the rule of seniority in legislative organization gives the incumbent added power to aid his constituents. The placing of the incumbent's name at the top of the ballot is an aid in getting elected. In so far as incumbency breeds incumbency, officeholders are likely to stay in office into their old age.

Whether retention of incumbents in office leads to an emphasis on conservatism has not been effectively answered by social scientists. Gusfield's study (1957) of the leadership of the WCTU casts some light on the issue. A "conviction-oriented old guard" has been able to withhold power from the "public-oriented newcomers," not so much through incumbency directly, since tenure in office is limited, but through rules which permit an incumbent to appoint her likely successor. In another study, MacRae (1954) found that those who remained in a state legislature through several terms have a better chance of re-election than freshman legislators. In addition, the more senior members in the legislature tend to have been more "loyal" to their party than the newcomers. Thus, legislators who are successful in getting re-elected have learned to resist being mavericks.

Both age composition of the electorate and voting behavior by age groups have provided clues to the political process. In the United States, the percentage of persons of voting age (21 and over) who were also 65 and over was, in 1880, 6.8. By 1960, the potential electorate who were over 65 had more than doubled, to 15.1 per cent. With the increase in the birth rate since World War II, the increase in the percentage of the electorate in the old age category has been temporarily halted. Efforts to lower the voting age, to give counterbalance to the aging tendency, have been successful only in a few states (Georgia, Kentucky, Alaska, and Hawaii).

Probably of greater significance than age composition is the voting behavior of various age categories in the electorate. Survey research directed by Lazarsfeld (Lazarsfeld, Berelson, & Gaudet, 1952) and Campbell (Campbell & Kahn, 1952) reveals that the young voters do not exercise their right to vote as frequently as the middle aged, but that voting among the aged drops off once again. Lipset (1960) has sought to explain these variations by suggesting a relative absence of group pressures on the young and the old. The young adult has not yet settled into the full life of the community, and the aged have lost many social contacts. Another conclusion of these studies has been that voters tend to strengthen their identification with a given party the longer they have been committed to the party. The twofold task of a party, then, is to recruit the young into the party and to prod the old to go to the polls.

One of the persistent questions related to politics and age is to what extent aging, of individuals and of the electorate in general, is correlated with political conservatism. The emergence of the Townsend Movement and similar protests of the *status quo* suggests that the aged may not be necessarily conservative. Pollak (1943), in a study of consumer habits and stands on political issues by the aged, rejected the proposition that aging leads to conservatism. Fisher's questioning of a positive correlation between aging and conservatism (1952) has led to a scattered number of investigations. But, for the most part, Schmidhauser's questions (1958), "How do older persons exercise their influence? Are older people as a group in American society any more self-seeking than other social groupings? Do they constitute a cohesive group in any sense? Do they vote as a bloc?" (p. 124), remain unanswered.

Life Course and Legal Age

Legal age may be defined as the designation, in statutes or other legal expressions, of some chronological age or age span as the basis for proscriptive, prescriptive, or permissive behavior.

As suggested earlier, legal age may be replacing rites of passage in industrial societies as the primary means of effecting a clearly recognized transition from one age status to another. Public rites may no longer proclaim a shift in status, but for the insurance agent, the bartender, the county clerk, the social security official, the employer, the policeman, and the school administrator, particular birthdays of their "clients" and the ensuing alteration of legal status have great significance. Somewhat ironically, the functions of legal age, rooted almost exclusively in chronological age, are expanding at the same time that students of learning ability and of changes in stamina, strength, and coordination with age are confirming that individuals mature and age at greatly varying paces.

Ordinarily, legal age distinctions are sharply defined, that is, an individual is either old enough or not old enough to perform certain acts and assume certain privileges. One is or is not old enough to sign contracts, to vote, to be eligible for social security benefits. There are, of course, variations from the bimodal pattern. One is eligible for military draft during a certain span of years. Often, state-level fair employment practice legislation extends from the middle years to age 65. And there are occasional reports of efforts to remove suffrage rights from the aged or to reduce privileges of the aged to make contractual arrangements.

The defined nature of legal age provides major importance to "coming of age." The granting of suffrage is a case in point. The age of 21 has become a widespread standard in determining eligibility to vote, although in recent decades in the United States there have been periodic demands to lower the voting age to 18 years, usually with the slogan, "old enough to fight, old enough to vote." In a 1953–1954 survey of age of eligibility to vote in 59 countries (Anonymous, 1954), results indicated that 30 of the 59, including most of the West European and North American nations, had established 21 years as the minimum; that 17 nations, including 8 Soviet bloc nations, 8 Latin American nations, and Israel, had adopted a minimum of 18 years. Only 4 countries, Turkey, the Netherlands, Denmark, and Italy, required a minimum age over 21.

The age of responsibility for illegal acts also illustrates the same categoric nature of legal age. Although "degree of understanding" has been established in British common law since the time of Edward III, chronological age has been used as the convenient and fair means of distinguishing the delinquent from the criminal. The type of crime is also often significant; a 15-year-old thief who murders a storekeeper may immediately become an adult for purposes of prosecution, whereas he would have remained within the jurisdiction of the juvenile court if the storekeeper had merely been wounded. Surveys of terminal ages for classification as a juvenile delinquent instead of a criminal by Bogatto and Jewell (1958), Callahan (1958), and Ludwig (1955), indicate the diversity of practices in coming of age for purposes of standing trial.

Other fertile fields for analysis of coming of age are to be found in compulsory school attendance laws, in marriage laws, in eligibility to enter contractual agreements, and in legal protections and constraints in child labor (Callahan, 1958).

Since 1950 several states have added regulations to fair employment practices legislation forbidding discrimination in employment because of age (Anonymous, 1952). Many of the legislative acts are patterned after the pioneering Massachusetts bill of 1950, which read in part:

It shall be an unlawful practice: (1) For an employer by himself or his agent, because of the race, color, religious creed, national origin, age or ancestry of any individual, to refuse to hire or employ or to bar or to discharge for employment such individual . . . (Anonymous, 1962).

The enforceability of these laws, now on the statutes in at least 14 states, remains in doubt. Their effectiveness is only dimly perceived, and their consequences for the employment status of older workers is hardly known.

A survey by Gerig (1955) of minimum pensionable ages in 50 nations revealed that an eligibility range of from 50 years (Uruguay) to 70 years (Canada, Ireland, and Norway) existed. Gerig also reported that alterations in pensionable age have been used to promote high economic productivity or high employment.

Finally, the economic status of the aged has been enhanced by favorable tax legislation. Strecker (1962) has reviewed these tax benefits for older Americans and has raised questions concerning their equity. At age 65, an individual may double his personal income tax exemption from $600 to $1,200;

thus, an older married couple may have a tax-free income of $2,400. In addition, social security benefits are tax free, although only a portion of the contribution was taxable. Other special provisions for the aged include deduction of all medical expenses, rather than those over 3 per cent of adjusted gross income.

Legal age provisions are evident in many and diverse laws. However, neither the legal profession nor sociology has focused attention on the functions of legal age or the impact on the entire social structure. Two somewhat distinct types of legal age regulations may be isolated. One deals with the age of responsibility and the achievement of majority, that is, the shift from the status of "infant" to "adult." The other type is more diffuse and of more recent origin and deals primarily with effecting status changes in the older years. The former stems from British common law, the latter seems to have more easily traceable political roots.

Legal age has produced its own asynchronous life course patterns. The "old enough to fight, old enough to vote" argument is only one illustration among many. An individual may acquire adult economic responsibilities through marriage before he is old enough to work. He may be old enough to sign a contract to enlist in the armed forces years before he is old enough to sign a contract to purchase an automobile. However, there are few, if any, trends which might suggest that legal age "weapons" will be used to coordinate and synchronize stages in the life course. Rather, legal age is likely to continue to be used in particularistic ways; law enforcement agencies, welfare agencies, insurance companies, and political pressure groups of many sorts, will continue to make their specialized demands upon legislators.

Life Course, Career Patterns, and Economic Status

The concept "career" denotes the addition of the temporal dimension to the division of labor. In a sense, during the life course an individual experiences his personal division of labor, including minimally a "preparation for work" stage, a "breadwinner" stage, and a "retirement" stage. The breadwinner stage frequently involves a periodic modification or reassignment of work; this, strictly speaking, encompasses a career. Hughes (1937) has distinguished between the objective and subjective perspectives on career. Objectively, career, in a rigidly structured system, is a "series of statuses and clearly defined offices." Even if the division of labor is not highly structured, jobs typically include "sequences of position, achievement, responsibility, and even of adventure." Subjectively, in contrast, career is the "moving perspective in which the person sees his life as a whole and interprets the meaning of his various attributes, actions, and the things which happen to him" (1937, pp. 409–410).

Mannheim (1952) proposed that career be used in a more restrictive sense than Hughes's. A career "is the rationing or gradual distribution of success through a number of stages" (p. 248). To Mannheim a career is possible only "in societies where the future is predictable, where the distribution of power is no longer a matter of dispute, and where some sort of plan can be made and executed on the basis of pre-existent decisions" (p. 250). Bureaucratically organized societies, therefore, are, for Mannheim, prerequisite to the conversion of jobs to careers. Use of the concept "career" in this chapter more closely approximates the definition of Hughes than that suggested by Mannheim.

A number of efforts to identify career patterns have been made. Bühler (1935), who interrelated the "objective" and "subjective" aspects of career, has distinguished five stages: the "exploratory" stage, which typically spans the years from 17 to 28; the "selective" stage, which lasts from approximately 28 to 43; the "testing" stage, which represents a five-year period in the mid-forties in which the individual looks "both ways," that is, he reassesses his career to date and re-evaluates his prospects for future success; the "indulgence" stage, lasting from possibly 48 to 64, during which the individual maximizes self-gratification; and, finally, the "completion" stage, during which the retiree lives upon memories of past accomplishments.

Miller and Form (1951) have also identified five stages in a work career, but include the entire life course. The stages are: preparatory period (0–15 years); initial work period (15–18 years); trial work period (18–34 years); stable work period (34–64 years); and retirement. Household chores typically provide the child with his first work experience. Part-time jobs or summer work may introduce the high school youngster to the work force. Then, according to Miller and Form, the young worker may spend 15 or more years in "shopping around," in experimenting with a variety of jobs. Before his mid-thirties, the typical worker can be expected to have settled into a job that will constitute his life work.

Of course, there are many variations on the Bühler and the Miller and Form typologies. Men and women experience vastly different career patterns. Bureaucrats and entrepreneurs experience dissimilar patterns. Bendix (1956), for example, observed that entrepreneurs "need not spend their time in moving up an administrative hierarchy" (p. 233) and therefore are likely to achieve success at a rather early age. Careers of industrial bureaucrats, in contrast, involve "gradual advancement from job to job within an administrative hierarchy" (p. 233) and therefore bring success rather late. Prolonged educational requirements for entry into the professions lead to some careers being launched rather late; athletes, entertainers, soldiers, and others may be old at the same chronological age that physicians, diplomats, and attorneys are young. Careers, it may be suggested, are not only associated with age but, probably more significantly, with aging. Typically, promotion of an employee to a more rewarding office is associated with experience, formal preparation, or display of skill rather than with the age of the employee.

Sociological literature contains a growing list of studies of particular facets of careers. Cressey's study of the taxi-dancer (1932) revealed a career of short duration, including "a series of cycles of a regressive character." Floro's examination of city managers (1955) led to the distinguishing of two career patterns, one which involved the city manager's moving frequently from city to city in upward escalation, the other which involved achievement of prominence in one place. Floro emphasized that job security for city managers resulted not from entrenchment in one city's administration but from the prospect of moving to another city.

Hall (1948) identified four stages in a medical career. First, the "generating of an ambition" sustains the medical student. Next, the medical student must gain admittance to one or more of the medical institutions; the contacts he makes as an intern are crucial in determining the pattern of successive stages. The third stage, according to Hall, involves acquiring, retaining, and improving a clientele, and eventually transferring the clientele to a selected young successor. Hall also identified a fourth stage, the development of a "set of informal relationships with colleagues," which apparently overlaps the period of the prior two stages.

Chinoy's study of automobile workers (1955) emphasized the discrepancy between the career dream and the career accomplishments of many industrial workers. The young worker often considers his first job in the automobile industry temporary; yet, the longer the worker stays on the job, the less likely is he to be able to break away from it, although the dream of becoming an entrepreneur or farmer may prolong the period of his professing that he will break away soon. Eventually, the worker faces the day of reckoning, when he is called upon to admit that he is "trapped," that his American dream of being his own boss is not to be fulfilled.

A theoretical article by Becker and Strauss

(1956) has incorporated the themes of most previous career studies and has pointed to needed further research. Careers are "patterned sequences of passage," or "movement through structures." Career paths are called escalators, and they lead an individual upward or downward. Career patterns are expected to provide satisfaction and reward to individuals, but at the same time are called upon to withhold and delay satisfaction, at least for some, so that incentive to advance to successive stages in the career can be retained (p. 253).

Career patterns in complex societies are sure to remain multiple and diverse, regardless of standardization flowing from bureaucratization and unionization. The challenges before the sociologist are many. Von Mises (1946) stated, "It is evident that youth is the first victim of the trend toward bureaucratization. . . . The rising generation is at the mercy of the aged" (p. 97). Yet, the many studies which decry the loneliness and absence of authority of the aged suggest that gerontocracy is not the inevitable outcome of bureaucratization.

The function of seniority in patterning the life course for workers is only vaguely comprehended. Harbison (1940) concluded that "widespread application of seniority results in automatic discrimination against long-service workers who have the misfortune to be displaced from their regular jobs" (p. 858). The consequences of total plant shutdowns, or the abandonment of a set of job classifications through automation, for the workers with seniority, have been studied only in rare instances (Sheppard, Ferman, & Faber, 1960).

During this century the extension of longevity and the maintenance of health have contributed to an increase in the work-life span of the average worker. However, the extension of schooling and the lowering of retirement ages are likely to result in a shortening of the work-life span. Early entry into a career, and the shortening of the hours in the work week and work year, suggest the possibility of new multiple career patterns for individuals, either through tandem careers or moonlighting. For example, military personnel may complete one career, with substantial retirement benefits, well before the age of 40. The Secretary of Defense (U.S. Department of Defense, 1961), in noting this, has recommended that retired military personnel prepare for further public service roles, especially in teaching. Reissman (1956) has examined postmilitary career positions of high-ranking officers. Insofar as retirement programs provide for eligibility for pensions and other benefits for employees with as little as 30, or even 20 years' service, and insofar as fair employment practices legislation or other factors provide protection for older applicants to secure jobs, the pattern of tandem careers is likely to increase. Similarly, the holding of two jobs simultaneously becomes more manageable with the decline in the demands of a job and more tempting with an increase in the demands for consumer goods. The implications for these, and other emerging career patterns, on pension plans and retirement programs, on training programs of many sorts, on self-identity and meaning in life, await discovery by the social scientific researcher.

Age Status Asynchronization

Since most research on the life course has not been "cross-institutional," summary comments on the asynchronous pattern, especially in American culture, must remain tentative. Although a majority of men and women marry during their early twenties and complete their reproductive period within a decade or so thereafter, many do not follow this pattern. Divorce and remarriage may produce a second family. Some persons marry late, or start a family late.

Often independent of the family structure are the economic role and career pattern. Some parents are able to afford a home with a bedroom for each child only after the children have become adult and departed. Income tax exemptions for children, aid from grandparents, and long-term home financing loans have contributed to the lessening of asynchronization of family needs and family earning power, but only partially. At the other extreme, increasing numbers of workers approaching retirement have living relatives of the previous generation who are in various ways dependent on the worker. Compulsory retirement at a time when family responsibilities remain high may increase.

Not many decades ago, colleges were for young people 17 to 21. Now, the Secretary of Defense encourages even retired military personnel to return to college to obtain teaching credentials; housewives whose children are in school are flooding many campuses; refresher courses for the already employed are common. Higher education no longer functions mainly as a preparation for adulthood.

The greatest evidence of age status asynchronization is in evidence at the coming of age period. A person of 15 may be treated as an adult for certain criminal offenses, but may be viewed as a preadult for several years beyond that age in other circumstances. The "old enough to fight, old enough to vote" argument is one of very few efforts to counteract age status inconsistencies.

Added to life course discontinuities, as outlined by Benedict (1938), therefore, are age status discontinuities at one point in time. Institutional exclusiveness in the formation of age status patterns undoubtedly provides a culture with many advantages, such as efficiency and fluidity. However, the accompanying strains on the persons caught in status ambiguities may be a high price to pay. In the introduction to *The Rites of Passage,* Kimball insisted, "There is no evidence that a secularized urban world has lessened the need for ritualized expression of an individual's transition from one status to another." Rituals of passage have become so individualistic, Kimball asserted, that they are "now found for many only in the privacy of the psychoanalyst's couch. . . . Individuals are forced to accomplish their transitions alone and with private

symbols" (Van Gennep, 1960, xvii–xviii). The substitution of legal age for ritual appears to reinforce the personal rather than the social dimension of status transitions.

AGE STATUS AND SOCIAL CHANGE
Generational Phenomena

Social structures persist through the institutionalization of behavior patterns. The process of socialization ordinarily prepares younger members of society to occupy statuses vacated by older members. In this manner cultures display a continuity, a persistence over long periods of time. Possible disruptions in behavior patterns through the steady replacement of personnel are thereby held to a minimum. Generations seem to follow upon generations in a smooth flow.

Historical circumstances, however, appear to provide varying contexts in which people born at different periods achieve maturity. Some young men achieve maturity only to go to war. Some grow up under depression conditions, others in times of prosperity. Children once were taught in uncongested classrooms. A baby boom brought congestion and double sessions to a sizeable portion of America's school children. Do these different environments for growing up produce individuals who, because of generational distinctiveness, accommodate to institutions in distinctive ways? If so, does this add a dimension to age status beyond that of the institutionalized status patterns?

Although historians have used the generations concept in ex post facto analyses of epochs or periods of history, and although social scientists regularly distinguish between an older and a younger generation, sociologists as yet have given relatively little attention to generational phenomena. Survey researchers have become increasingly wary, in the absence of longitudinal studies, of accepting age as the variable in interpreting differences in behavior or attitude between the young and the old (Fichter, 1954; Fukuyama, 1961). The current group of old people, for example, may display certain characteristics, not because of their age, but because of general affiliations.

The concept of generation is much used and abused. The family structure provides one meaningful application of the concept, to distinguish between parents and children, but this use has limited applicability. Generation is also used frequently as a concept somewhat comparable to age set, to identify those individuals who are approximately the same age and who therefore were supposedly similarly influenced by certain types of events—wars, depressions, new literary and art forms, and the like.

Mannheim (1952) has contributed a provocative interpretation of generations, distinguishing between the positivist position and the romantic-historical position. To a positivist, a generation is seen as an identifiable span of time, say, 25 or 30 years, and as a link in a chain of progress. The romanticist, on the other hand, internalizes time; a generation cannot be measured as a span of time, but rather is based on a common sharing of experiences of a purely qualitative sort. From this perspective, peoples of all ages experience the dominating intellectual and social themes in basically the same way. A generation, then, lasts as long as a single art form or mode of expression prevails (Mannheim, 1952, pp. 276–277, 281–282).

Rintala (1958) has associated membership in a generation with all persons who have undergone basically similar experiences during their crucial, formative years, 17 to 25. Subsequent expressions can be expected to reflect the impact of the commonly shared experiences.

But, the question remains, How are generational termini established? Only in retrospect, by historians? Or can sociologists establish theoretical statements about generation formation?

Foote has noted that, "the turning points between generations are more sociological than chronological. . . . What distinguishes one generation from another is not a se-

quence of small gradations but rather marked qualitative divergencies, occurring rather suddenly" (1960, pp. 6–7). These divergencies, produced by dramatic historical events, act as "watersheds," Foote suggested, which route persons who mature during the dramatic events of a period in a different historical direction from their predecessors.

Berger (1960) has not only confronted the question of the length of a generation, but also that of whether chronological age is a sufficient criterion to place a particular individual within a generational category. Berger cited arguments which would suggest a telescoping of the span of a generation from several decades to hardly more than one decade. He also reviewed evidence indicating an extension of adolescence, at least youth, to the age of 30 or possibly 40. "Americans are members of the 'younger generation' from the time they begin to stay out at night to the time they begin to grow bald and arthritic . . ." (1960, p. 13). This extension of the span of youth suggests an elongation of the generational span. Paradoxically, the prolongation of the period of irresponsibility may explain the proliferation of quasi-generational phenomena. The young have increased opportunity to go about proclaiming they represent a new *Zeitgeist,* but to proclaim generational newness is not necessarily to represent it, Berger hinted.

But Berger's main contribution to generational analysis is to point out the inadequacy of age per se in determining to what generation an individual may belong. He observed that "members of the same age-groups may experience their most productive or representative period in different decades, [and] what they produce may be affected by different series of events" (p. 15). He then advanced the research and theoretical challenge. Although chronologically determined age groups are important in cultural analysis, their fuller significance is to be achieved only by considering "the structural variables which not only give a cultural meaning to age but which locate one in a 'school of thought,' give one a distinct 'perspective,' and a place within an intellectual tradition . . ." (p. 18).

A characteristic of our times, however, is that intellectual traditions are concocted rather than exhibited. Berger observed that intellectuals seek to "collapse the historical process" in locating their place in history. They try to write history before it has been made; thus, "intellectuals create the myth of their time." Berger failed to answer, however, the question, "Myth for whom?" Mainly other intellectuals? Not all are valiantly seeking to create, or even identify, the *Zeitgeist*. Still, the transmitted age status patterns, the encumbrances of legal age, of parental responsibilities, of career prospects and seniority systems, confront the bulk of the members of the complex societies. The social scientists, along with the philosophers and the writers, are participants both in viewing the status system objectively and in revamping it.

With only limited evidence of the incorporation of generational phenomena into life course and age status analysis, it may be premature to suggest that progress in generational theory holds the key to the development of a meaningful sociology of age status. Nonetheless, it is likely that the descriptive tracing of the life course through successive stages, even with added effort to fathom the consequences for the social structure of the status asymmetry in evidence among institutions, will prove inadequate to build a sound theory. Patterns of interaction between generations, partially surveyed in the following section on age movements, and factors contributing to the formation of ad hoc age sets, or peer groups, which may in time be identified as generational phenomena, clearly need thorough examination by sociologists.

Youth and Old Age Movements

The young have from time to time balked at accepting the values of their parents. Organized efforts by the young to establish alternative patterns of living have been called youth movements. On other occasions adults have organized youths themselves and have molded the young in the patterns of the adults. Likewise, the aged have on infrequent occasions become dissatisfied with their status and have formed organizations to protest and to seek to alter that status. At other times, adults have avoided the prospect of old age protest by establishing organizations for the aged which are under the supervision and direction of the adults. Thus, four distinct types of "age movements" may be isolated: (1) youth movements, which are indigenous to the youth themselves; (2) youth "movements," or organizations, which are supervised by adults; (3) old age movements, which are indigenous to the aged themselves; and (4) old age "movements," or organizations, which are supervised by adults.

Ebeling (1945) has distinguished between a "genuine 'movement' *of* youth," emerging from the youths themselves, and the " 'organization' *for* youth," directed from above by adults. Youth movements are spawned in conditions of frustration and disillusionment, political chaos and economic crisis, which lead to revolt against the elders. In contrast, youth organizations thrive under conditions of "stability, comparative prosperity and gradual rate of change." The young accept service rendered by adults rather than adopt the strategy of revolt (pp. 3–4).

The aged, after relinquishing the reins of authority, have, at least in the United States, ordinarily accepted the plans of the adults in the organization of recreational, welfare, and other programs. However, the Townsend Movement, which reached its pinnacle in the mid-1930's, demonstrated clearly that the aged were capable of revolting against the status accepted by the adults as appropriate for the old.

Kohn (1935) has also distinguished between "youth movements" and "youth organizations," but has suggested a third adult-youth relationship, in which youth movements have been captured by adults and rechanneled into political activity dominated by the state, political party, or church. This third category has been labeled by Windham Lewis (1932) "youth politics." Prime examples are the Hitler Jugend, the Komsomol, and the Italian Balilla.

Many youth movements have been short-lived and only partly successful at best. Germany, the place of birth of a number of youth movements during this century, experienced the absorption of the surge of youthful protest into the Nazi system. Student movements, with special emphasis on political reform and on the promotion of international peace, have frequently functioned as thorns in the sides of adult politicians, but their goals have not often been immediately realized. Youths have been in the forefront in the Negro demonstrations in the United States. In fact, there is evidence that the young, including children, are sometimes the major activists in these protest demonstrations, and that the leadership among Negroes may be found among those youth who have demonstrated and have been beaten and jailed.

The establishment of *kibbutzim* in Palestine represented the culmination of a successful movement of Jewish youths dissatisfied with the vulnerable, segregated lives of their parents in Germany and East European cities. Spiro (1956), in a comprehensive study of the kibbutz Kiryat Yedidim (a fictional name), has traced not only the youth movement in process but the social structural consequences of the aging of the founders of a community which was established essentially without an age status system. The youth movement produced an egalitarian community founded on the principle that differential power and prestige were to be associated with ability to work in agricultural pursuits, not with age. Within one generation, the founders, as middle-aged parents, found themselves incapable of competing with their own sons and daughters, and the ideology of equalitarianism became ambiguous, even dysfunctional.

Old age movements seem insignificant and inconsequential when compared with youth movements. Only in the United States, mainly through the Townsend Movement of the 1930's and the more recent California Institute of Social Welfare, have old age movements sustained themselves. Yet, the continuing increase in the percentage of the aged, coupled with a continued process of isolation and diminution of prestige, provide conditions favorable to old age movements. Furthermore, the development of gerontology heralds a social movement whose dimensions and direction are not yet understood. Although gerontology regularly associates itself with scientific endeavors, the gerontological literature, gerontological organizations and conferences, and the proclaimed commitments of many gerontologists display the characteristics typically associated with a social movement. Membership in the movement is recruited primarily from public welfare and research agencies, as well as charitable and religious organizations with a commitment to improve the living conditions of the aged, rather than from the aged themselves. A major task confronting sociology is the study of gerontology as a social movement.

Holtzman (1954) has provided one of the most significant assessments of old age movements. He attributed their rise in America to the country's accent on youth and the isolation of the aged from any means of effective political expression. The depression provided a catalyst for a protest movement by the aged. The redirection of old age movements into old age politics, as witnessed by the increased interest shown by the political parties in the welfare of the aged, led Holtzman to conclude that old age movements would wane in significance.

Without doubt the Townsend Movement, with its scheme of "old age revolving pensions," is the classic example of an organized protest by the aged against their deteriorating economic condition and loss of prestige. Although the Townsend Plan was not legislated into existence, the political offensive mounted by the physician from Southern

California and his army of the aged contributed to the hasty adoption of the Social Security Act of 1935 and has probably been indirectly responsible for the expanded attention both Republicans and Democrats have given to the older voter and his expressed needs. The Townsend motto, "Youth for Work, Age for Leisure," has not been officially adopted by any governmental agency, but efforts to lower the age of retirement and to maintain a high retirement income persist.

The pension movement associated with the California Institute of Social Welfare, often identified as the McLain Movement, has been analyzed by Pinner, Jacobs, and Selznick (1959). Their study focused upon the characteristics, resources, aspirations, and anxieties of the supporters of George McLain and the institute which he heads. The program is most attractive to "slightly privileged" older citizens who maintain some income from property, investments, or similar sources, but who have felt a reduction of prestige with old age. Paradoxically, many "conservative" property owners flocked to a movement which advocates "socialistic" reforms.

Although there is a paucity of data on both youth and old age movements, it is clear that during this century both the young and the old have joined with their age peers to seek to alter their status. Students continue to play roles in organized movements to modify political systems and policies. Other dissatisfactions of youths, as expressed by acts of delinquency, produce potential recruits for youth movements. And the aged, often forced into isolation from job, family, and previous organizational ties, retain the potential of formal organization at almost any time.

REFERENCES

Alliance Nationale contre la Dépopulation. *Trois journées pour l'étude scientifique du vieillissement de la population, 22–23–24 Avril, 1948.* Fascicule 1–6. Paris: Author, 1948.

Anonymous. Age discrimination in employment: An FEPC misfit. *Yale Law J.,* 1952, 61, 574–584.

Anonymous. The question of lowering the voting age to eighteen. *Cong. Digest,* 1954, 33, 67–96.

Anonymous. *Basic materials on the administration of the age provisions of the New York law against discrimination.* New York: New York State Commission for Human Rights, 1962.

Argyle, M. *Religious behavior.* Glencoe, Ill.: Free Press, 1959.

Barron, M. L. The role of religion and religious institutions in creating the milieu of older people. In D. L. Scudder (Ed.), *Organized religion and the older person.* Gainesville: Univer. of Florida Press, 1958. Pp. 12–33.

Beard, B. B. Are the aged ex-family? *Soc. Forces,* 1949, 27, 274–279.

Becker, H. S., & Carper, J. W. The development of identification with an occupation. *Amer. J. Sociol.,* 1956, 61, 289–298.

Becker, H. S., & Strauss, A. Careers, personality, and adult socialization. *Amer. J. Sociol.,* 1956, 62, 253–263.

Belknap, I., & Friedsam, H. Age and sex categories as sociological variables in the mental disorders of later maturity. *Amer. sociol. Rev.,* 1949, 14, 367–376.

Bendix, R. *Work and authority in industry.* New York: Wiley, 1956.

Benedict, Ruth. Continuities and discontinuities in cultural conditioning. *Psychiatry,* 1938, 1, 161–167.

Benedict, Ruth. *The chrysanthemum and the sword.* Boston: Houghton, 1946.

Berger, B. How long is a generation? *Brit. J. Sociol.,* 1960, 11, 10–23.

Bleyer, A. *Childbearing before and after thirty-five: Biologic and social implications.* New York: Vantage Press, 1958.

Bogatto, R., & Jewell, T. M., Jr. Age and related jurisdictional problems of the juvenile courts. *Texas Law Rev.,* 1958, 36, 323–346.

Bouthoul, G. *La guerre.* Paris: Letinier Presses Universitaires de France, 1953.

Brady, D. S. Influence of age on savings and spending patterns. *Mon. Labor Rev.,* 1955, 78, 1240–1244.

Bühler, Charlotte. The curve of life as studied in biographies. *J. appl. Psychol.*, 1935, 19, 405–409.

Bühler, Charlotte. Meaningful living in the mature years. In R. Kleemeier (Ed.), *Aging and leisure.* New York: Oxford Univer. Press, 1961. Pp. 345–387.

Cain, L. D., Jr. The sociology of aging: A trend report and bibliography. *Curr. Sociol.*, 1959, 8, 57–133.

Callahan, P. Legal status of young adults (under 21: Your rights and duties). *Legal Almanac Series*, No. 46. New York: Oceana Publications, 1958.

Campbell, A., & Kahn, R. L. *The people elect a president.* Ann Arbor: Institute for Social Research, Univer. of Michigan, 1952.

Chinoy, E. *Automobile workers and the American dream.* New York: Doubleday, 1955.

Comfort, A. *The biology of senescence.* New York: Rinehart, 1956.

Cowgill, D. O. Trends in the ecology of the aged in American cities, 1940–1950. *J. Geront.*, 1957, 12, 75–80.

Cowgill, D. O. Ecological patterns of the aged in American cities. *Midwest Sociogist*, 1958, 20, 78–83.

Cressey, P. *The taxi-dance hall: A sociological study in commercialized recreation and city life.* Chicago: Univer. of Chicago Press, 1932.

Cumming, Elaine, & Henry, W. E. *Growing old: The process of disengagement.* New York: Basic Books, 1961.

Daric, J. *Vieillissement de la population et prolongation de la vie active.* Paris: Presses Universitaires de France, 1948.

Davis, K. The child and the social structure. *J. educ. Sociol.*, 1940, 14, 217–229.

Davis, K., & Combs, J. W. The sociology of an aging population. In D. B. Armstrong (Ed.), *The social and biological challenge of our aging population.* New York: Columbia Univer. Press, 1950.

Dean, Lois R., & Newell, D. S. The evidence for disengagement in attitude and orientation changes. In Elaine Cumming & W. E. Henry (Eds.), *Growing old: The process of disengagement.* New York: Basic Books, 1961. Pp. 75–105.

Deutscher, I. Socialization for postparental life. In A. M. Rose (Ed.), *Human behavior and social processes.* Boston: Houghton, 1962. Pp. 506–525.

Dickinson, F. G. The younging of the electorates. *J. Amer. med. Ass.*, 1958, 166, 1051–1057.

Dornbusch, S. M. The military academy as an assimilating institution. *Soc. Forces*, 1955, 33, 316–321.

Duverger, M. *Political parties: Their organization and activity in the modern state.* Barbara North & R. North (Trans.). New York: Wiley, 1955.

Ebeling, H. *The German youth movement: Its past and future.* London: New Europe, 1945.

Eisenstadt, S. N. *From generation to generation: Age groups and social structure.* Glencoe, Ill.: Free Press, 1956.

Erikson, E. H. Identity and the life cycle. *Psychol. Iss.*, 1959, 1(1).

Fichter, J. H. *Social relations in an urban parish.* Chicago: Univer. of Chicago Press, 1954.

Fisher, L. H. The politics of age. In M. Derber (Ed.), *The aged and society: A symposium on the problems of an aging population.* Champaign, Ill.: Industrial Relations Research Association, 1952. Pp. 157–167.

Fleming, S. *Children and Puritanism: The place of children in the life and thought of the New England churches, 1620–1847.* New Haven, Conn.: Yale Univer. Press, 1933.

Floro, G. K. Continuity in city-manager careers. *Amer. J. Sociol.*, 1955, 61, 240–246.

Foote, N. The old generation and the new. In E. Ginzberg (Ed.), *The nation's children.* Vol. 3. *Problems and prospects.* New York: Columbia Univer. Press, 1960. Pp. 1–24.

Fortes, M. Introduction. In J. Goody (Ed.), *The developmental cycle in domestic groups. Cambridge papers in social anthropology,* No. 1. Cambridge: Cambridge Univer. Press, 1958.

Frazer, G. *Lectures on the early history of the kingship.* London: Macmillan, 1905.

Freeman, J. T. The geriatric limb on the gerontology tree. In N. W. Shock (Ed.), *Aging: Some social and biological aspects.* Publication 65. Washington, D.C.: American Association for the Advancement of Science, 1960.

Fukuyama, Y. The major dimensions of church membership. *Rev. relig. Res.*, 1961, 2, 154–161.

Gerig, D. S. Pensionable age under old-age

pension schemes. *Int. labour Rev.*, 1955, 72, 262–282.

Gerth, H. The Nazi party: Its leadership and composition. *Soc. Forces*, 1940, 18, 517–541.

Glick, P. C. The life cycle of the family. *Marr. fam. Living*, 1955, 17, 3–9.

Goldfrank, Esther S. Socialization, personality and the structure of Pueblo society. *Amer. Anthropol.*, 1945, 47, 516–539.

Gusfield, J. R. The problem of generations in an organizational structure. *Soc. Forces*, 1957, 35, 323–330.

Hall, O. The stages in a medical career. *Amer. J. Sociol.*, 1948, 53, 327–336.

Harbison, F. H. Seniority in mass-production industries. *J. polit. Econ.*, 1940, 48, 851–864.

Hauser, P. M., & Vargas, R. Population structure and trends. In E. W. Burgess (Ed.), *Aging in western societies*. Chicago: Univer. of Chicago Press, 1960. Pp. 29–52.

Holtzman, A. Analysis of old age politics in the United States. *J. Geront.*, 1954, 9, 56–66.

Hughes, E. C. Institutional office and the person. *Amer. J. Sociol.*, 1937, 43, 404–413.

Hughes, E. C. The making of a physician. *Hum. Organ.*, 1956, 14, 21–25.

Iga, M. The Japanese social structure and the source of mental strains of Japanese immigrants in the United States. *Soc. Forces*, 1957, 35, 271–278.

Inkeles, A. Social change and social character: The role of parental mediation. *J. soc. Iss.*, 1955, 11, 12–23.

Jung, C. G. The stages of life. *The collected works of C. G. Jung*. Vol. 8. *The structure and dynamics of the psyche*. New York: Pantheon Books, 1960. Pp. 387–403.

Kerr, M. *The people of Ship Street*. London: Routledge & Kegan Paul, 1958.

Kleemeier, R. (Ed.) *Aging and leisure*. New York: Oxford Univer. Press, 1961.

Kohn, H. Youth movements. In E. R. A. Seligman (Ed.), *Encyclopedia of the social sciences*. Vol. 15. New York: Macmillan, 1935. Pp. 517–520.

Kutner, B. The social nature of aging. *Gerontologist*, 1962, 2, 5–8.

Lansing, J. B., & Kish, L. Family life cycle as an independent variable. *Amer. sociol. Rev.*, 1957, 22, 512–519.

Lazarsfeld, P. F., Berelson, B., & Gaudet, Hazel. *The people's choice*. New York: Harcourt, 1952.

Lewis, W. *Doom of youth*. London: Chatto & Windus, 1932.

Linden, M. E., & Courtney, D. The human life cycle and its interruptions. *Amer. J. Psychiat.*, 1953, 109, 906–915.

Linton, R. A neglected aspect of social organization. *Amer. J. Sociol.*, 1940, 45, 870–886.

Linton, R. Age and sex categories. *Amer. sociol. Rev.*, 1942, 7, 589–603.

Linton, R. The natural history of the family. In Ruth N. Anshen (Ed.), *The family: Its function and destiny*. (rev. ed.) New York: Harper, 1959. Pp. 30–52.

Lipset, S. M. *Political man: The social basis of politics*. New York: Doubleday, 1960.

Litwak, E. Occupational mobility and extended family cohesion. *Amer. sociol. Rev.*, 1960, 25, 9–21.

Lortie, D. C. Laymen to lawmen: Law school, careers, and professional socialization. *Harvard educ. Rev.*, 1959, 29, 353–369.

Ludwig, F. J. *Youth and the law: Handbook on laws affecting youth*. Brooklyn: Foundation Press, 1955.

Lydall, H. The life cycle in income, saving, and asset ownership. *Econometrica*, 1955, 23, 131–150.

Mack, Margery J. An evaluation of a retirement-planning program. *J. Geront.*, 1958, 13, 198–202.

MacRae, D., Jr. The role of the state legislator in Massachusetts. *Amer. sociol. Rev.*, 1954, 19, 185–194.

Mannheim, K. *Essays on the sociology of knowledge*. New York: Oxford Univer. Press, 1952.

Mead, Margaret. On the concept of plot in culture. *Trans. New York Acad. Sci.*, 1939, II, 2(1), 24–28.

Merton, R. K., Reader, G. C., & Kendall, Patricia L. *The student physician: Introductory studies in the sociology of medical education*. Glencoe, Ill.: Free Press, 1957.

Michels, R. *Political parties*. E. Paul & Cedar Paul (Trans.). New York: Dover Publications, 1959.

Miles, W. R. Age and human society. In C. A. Murchison (Ed.), *A handbook of social psychology*. Worcester, Mass.: Clark Univer. Press, 1935. Pp. 596–682.

Miller, D. C., & Form, W. *Industrial sociology: An introduction to the sociology of work relations*. New York: Harper, 1951.

Misra, B. R. *Report on socio-economic survey of Jamshedpur city.* Patna, India: Patna Univer., Department of Applied Economics and Commerce, 1959.

Mueller, Kate H. *Educating women for a changing world.* Minneapolis: Univer. of Minnesota Press, 1954.

Orbach, H. L. Aging and religion: A study of church attendance in the Detroit metropolitan area. *Geriatrics,* 1961, 16, 530–540.

Paillat, P. Some features of aging in the French active population. In C. Tibbitts & Wilma Donahue (Eds.), *Social and psychological aspects of aging: Aging around the world.* New York: Columbia Univer. Press, 1962. Pp. 3–17.

Parsons, T. Age and sex in the social structure of the United States. *Amer. sociol. Rev.,* 1942, 7, 604–616.

Parsons, T. The social structure of the family. In Ruth N. Anshen (Ed.), *The family: Its foundation and destiny.* (rev. ed.) New York: Harper, 1959. Pp. 241–274.

Payne, R. Some theoretical approaches to the sociology of aging. *Soc. Forces,* 1960, 38, 359–362.

Pinchbeck, I. The state and the child in sixteenth century England. *Brit. J. Soc.,* 1956, 7, 273–285; 1957, 8, 59–74.

Pinner, F. A., Jacobs, P., & Selznick, P. *Old age and political behavior: A case study.* Berkeley: Univer. of California Press, 1959.

Pollak, O. Conservatism in later maturity and old age. *Amer. sociol. Rev.,* 1943, 8, 175–179.

Pressey, S. L., & Kuhlen, R. G. *Psychological development through the life span.* New York: Harper, 1957.

Prins, A. H. J. *East African age-class systems: An inquiry into the social order of Galla, Kipsigis, and Kikuyu.* Groningen, The Netherlands: Wolters, 1953.

Radcliffe-Brown, A. R. Age organisation terminology. *Man,* 1929(13).

Reder, M. W. Age and income. *Amer. econ. Rev.,* 1954, 44, 661–670.

Reissman, L. Life careers, power and the professions: The retired army general. *Amer. sociol. Rev.,* 1956, 18, 215–221.

Richardson, B. E. *Old age among the ancient Greeks.* London: Oxford Univer. Press, 1933.

Riesman, D., & Roseborough, H. Careers and consumer behavior. In L. H. Clark (Ed.), *Consumer behavior.* Vol. 2. *The life cycle and consumer behavior.* New York: New York Univer. Press, 1955. Pp. 1–18.

Rintala, M. The problem of generations in Finnish communism. *Amer. Slav. e. European Rev.,* 1958, 17, 190–202.

Ross, J. F. S. *Parliamentary representation.* (2nd ed.) London: Eyre & Spottiswoode, 1948.

Sauvy, A. Social and economic consequences of the aging of western Europe populations. *Pop. Stud.,* 1948, 2, 115–124.

Sauvy, A. Vieillissement de la population. décadence, renaissance. *Econ. & Humanisme,* 1953, 12, 23–34.

Schmidhauser, J. R. The political behavior of older persons: A discussion of some frontiers of research. *West. pol. Quart.,* 1958, 11, 113–124.

Schurtz, H. *Altersklassen und männerbünde.* Berlin: Reimer, 1902.

Shaw, L. A. Impressions of family life in a London suburb. *Sociol. Rev.,* 1954, 2, 179–194.

Sheppard, H. L., Ferman, L. A., & Faber, S. *Too old to work—too young to retire: A case study of a permanent plant shutdown.* U.S. Senate, Special Committee on Unemployment Problems. Washington, D.C.: Government Printing Office, 1960.

Shock, N. The physiology of aging. *Scient. Amer.,* 1962, 206, 100–110.

Simmons, L. W. *The role of the aged in primitive society.* New Haven, Conn.: Yale Univer. Press, 1945.

Smith, H. *The religions of man.* New York: Harper & Row, 1958.

Spengler, J. J. Some effects of changes in the age composition of the labor force. *S. econ. J.,* 1941, 8, 157–175.

Spiro, M. E. *Kibbutz: Venture in utopia.* Cambridge, Mass.: Harvard Univer. Press, 1956.

Starbuck, E. D. *The psychology of religion.* New York: Scribner, 1899.

Strauss, A. *Mirrors and masks.* Glencoe, Ill.: Free Press, 1959.

Strecker, R. L. Taxation of retirement provision. *Law contemp. Probs,* 1962, 27 (issue on *Problems of the Aging*), 67–88.

Sussman, M. B. The help pattern in the American middle class family. *Amer. sociol. Rev.,* 1953, 18, 22–28.

Taeuber, C., & Taeuber, Irene. *The changing population of the United States.* New York: Wiley, 1958.

T'ien, J. K. Pai cults and social age in the Tai tribes of the Yunnan-Burma frontier. *Amer. Anthrogist,* 1949, 51, 46–57.

Townsend, P. *The family life of old people: An inquiry in London.* London: Routledge & Kegan Paul, 1957.

United Nations, Department of Economic and Social Affairs. The aging of populations and its economic and social implications. *Population Studies,* No. 26. New York: Author, 1956.

U.S. Department of Defense, Office of Armed Forces Information and Education. *Teaching: A second career.* Pamphlet 7–10. Washington, D.C.: Author, 1961.

Vance, R. P. The ecology of our aging population. *Soc. Forces,* 1954, 32, 330–335.

Van Gennep, A. *The rites of passage.* M. B. Vizedom & G. L. Caffee (Trans.). Chicago: Univer. of Chicago Press, 1960.

Vedder, C. B. *Gerontology: A book of readings.* Springfield, Ill.: Thomas, 1963.

Vischer, A. L. *Old age: Its compensations and rewards.* New York: Macmillan, 1947.

Von Mises, L. *Bureaucracy.* New Haven, Conn.: Yale Univer. Press, 1946.

Waller, W., & Hill, R. *The family: A dynamic interpretation.* (rev. ed.) New York: Dryden, 1951.

Webster, H. *Primitive secret societies.* New York: Macmillan, 1908.

Whitehead, A. N. Cited in L. H. Evans, & G. E. Arnstein, *Automation and education: Hypothesis for a partial answer.* Washington, D.C.: National Education Association, January, 1962.

Williams, T. R., & Williams, Margaret M. The socialization of the student nurse. *Nursing Res.,* 1959, 8, 18–25.

Wilson, Monica. *Good company: A study of Nyakyusa age-villages.* London: Oxford Univer. Press, 1951.

Young, M., & Geertz, Hildred. Old age in London and San Francisco: Some families compared. *Brit. J. Sociol.,* 1961, 12, 124–141.

Young, M., & Willmott, P. Family and kinship in East London. *Institute of Community Studies,* No. 1. London: Routledge & Kegan Paul, 1957.

CHAPTER 9　Sociological Aspects of Health and Illness

SAXON GRAHAM[1]

The discussion of the life cycle in the preceding chapter noted that there are various changes in the biological equipment with which each individual is furnished at various times in his life. These take the form of variations in strength, physical coordination, endurance, disease immunity, and reproductive capacity. As age increases, these capacities increase to a maximum; later there may be a degeneration in various of them at various intervals. The recognition given changes in these capacities, particularly the relatively abrupt changes, such as puberty and menopause, differs from society to society. Similarly, the roles attaching to each variation alter. Thus, there is a continual interaction between biological change and sociological response. So intimately are these two aspects of man related that in some cultures, the sociological "response" to a given biological change may actually predate the change.

The intimate relationship between biological and sociological responses observed in

the normal process of the life cycle is equally apparent in those instances of deviation from the normal known as illness or disease. Sociological factors are intimately related to every aspect of the biological condition of nonhealth. This obtains even in the definition of disease. Schizophrenia in one culture or time may be an illness, and, in another, a qualification for certain types of shaman. Again, among the stimuli resulting in clinical illness, sociological factors are almost always present, putting the individual in contact with the toxic or infectious agent or protecting him from it. The responses of the individual's milieu to his illness and the different roles he assumes in response to given illnesses are strictly sociologically determined, although they are influenced by and have an influence upon the nature and course of his illness. Relevant sociological structures include the organization of the hospital and physician-patient relationships.

Sociological factors are also vital in preventive medicine. Both the existence and form of preventive medicine are determined largely by the value system of the society in a particular period of its existence. Granted that a preventive medicine does

[1] The author wishes to thank Drs. Edward Marra and Warren Winkelstein of the State University of New York at Buffalo for their critical reading of this chapter.

exist, relationships between both the individual physician and his patient and between the lay and medical publics determine whether a given preventive measure will be utilized. Once a biological preventive to a given medical problem has been developed, there always remains the sociological problem of securing its acceptance by the patient and the lay and professional community.

Human biology and sociology deal with two aspects of the same organism; certainly human biology is the natural science most closely related to sociology. Sociologists and human geneticists use similar methods in studies of familial aggregation of disease, and it is always difficult to separate the sociological from the genetic factors in deducing from their results. It is hardly surprising that in those particular aspects of human biology dealing with the etiology, treatment, and prevention of illnesses, sociological factors such as individual roles and cultural patterns should play such an important part. The sociobiological relationships relating to the etiology, prevention, and treatment of illness will be the subject of this chapter.

DEFINITIONS OF HEALTH AND ILLNESS

As in other facets of science, definitions of pathological phenomena have been much circumscribed by the development of biological knowledge, the intellectual orientation of the culture, and the society's value system. Thus, in some underdeveloped societies, the malaise and apathetic approach to life associated with infestation by certain parasites is a normal condition of life and is not considered a state of disease as it would be in the urban middle and upper classes (but not necessarily in the rural lower classes) of the United States. Similarly, a "touch of the liver," a bacterial enteritis, is a common complaint, but not necessarily an illness, in France. In the middle-class urban United States, where emphasis has been placed less upon the gastronomic de-

lights of cuisine than upon its hygiene, the gastric and intestinal symptoms so loosely defined in France are unusual and avoided wherever possible. The mere question of the presence or absence of a diseased state is answered in terms of the expectations in the culture.

Once a condition of nonhealth has been recognized, the problem of the definition of the kind of illness, disease, or other abnormality involved arises. Here again, the medical orientation of the society plays a part. The host of diseases classified as "fevers" by nineteenth-century physicians have today resolved themselves into a number of separate disease entities which are not only identified but are amenable to preventive measures as well as therapy. Most recently, something similar has taken place with regard to cancer. Cancers may possess some common elements; they generally involve the growth of abnormal cells. They differ, however, with respect to the site of the body involved, the histology of the tumor cells, their relation to metabolic processes, the therapies which are effectual, and many facets of their etiology. Thus, the large group of diseases which the layman often conceives of simply as cancer has been found to comprise a number of entities as distinct as those which formerly comprised the "fevers."

Fortunately for students of cancer epidemiology considerable progress has been made in distinguishing the various neoplastic diseases. Equally reliable diagnostic procedures are available for many communicable diseases, but not for all diseases. In many pathological states, for example in some cases of coronary artery disease, the condition may not be discernable until its lethal effects have been shown. In these instances, the investigator is reduced to studying persons who have died of the disease, who constitute a significant proportion of those having single attacks. The material the student can gather on deceased persons is so limited and biased by the fact of death that he is hard put to generalize to the living.

Even in diseases where definition comes in time for adequate investigation, the details of diagnosis may be confused—as in the case of arthritis (Cobb, Merchant, & Thompson, 1957). Again, in the definition of hypertension in an individual, confusion is generated by potentially great changes in blood pressure from time to time and from one set of examining circumstances to another (Diehl & Lees, 1929). In many of the various mental illnesses, definition is extremely difficult and even the most experienced clinicians differ greatly in diagnosis. Few areas of medical diagnosis find definition as hazy.

To this point, we have been discussing the definition of disease states from the point of view of the medical scientist. We have seen that his definition is at odds with the absolute biological reality in various degrees, and that the divergence is determined by the extent of medical knowledge and interest at any given time in any given culture. Definition is also relative to who does the defining within the culture. The layman's recognition or nonrecognition of what his physician conceives as illness determines the roles he will play, his relationships with others, his demands for medical care, and the medical facilities which must be made available to him. Consider the case of two men killed by a speeding ambulance. On autopsy, both are found to have had a mild coronary infarct earlier in life. One had felt chest pain and had experienced shortness of breath, sought medical advice, curtailed certain activities, and followed a prescribed regimen. He had taken six weeks off from work, followed the role of a cardiac patient, and his family and friends reacted in kind. The other had passed his seige of pain off as a gastric disturbance of greater than usual intensity and continued business as usual, although he had wondered occasionally at his loss of breath. Both men had the same symptoms; neither died of the condition. But the demands for medical care and their relationships with family members and others were quite different

because of their different conceptions of disease. Thus, the layman's conception of disease definition must also be considered.

In short, in the sociological study of epidemiology or medical care, the definitions made of case groups are always influenced to some extent by the varying recognition by the patient that something is wrong and by whether or not he seeks medical advice in answer to his symptoms. Research in a given disease of mild symptoms may show, for example, that the upper classes have a higher incidence than the lower. The question must then be considered as to whether this was because the upper classes have a higher standard of physical performance than the lower, and easier access to medical care for diagnosing even mild symptoms.

To this point, we have discussed the definition of illness. The other side of the coin, health, has often been thought of as simply the absence of illness. However, with the conquering of many of the traditional scourges of mankind, scientists thinking of the medical concerns of the future have conceived of health as implying optimum functioning of the individual and group, physically, mentally, and socially. Indeed, the definition of health given by the World Health Organization is that "state of complete physical, mental, and social well-being." The burden of this definition is that even comparatively minor physical and mental abnormalities will be of concern to the medical scientist and epidemiologist. Furthermore, social maladjustments also would be within their purview. It may be argued that this is carrying medicine into areas traditionally staked out by sociology for research and social work for action. It may also be argued that in view of the current social problems these disciplines need all the help they can get.

EPIDEMIOLOGY

Almost every branch of biology takes some part in developing knowledge of the etiology of pathological processes; these include sciences whose major source of research data is the controlled experiment and observation conducted in the laboratory on either animals, man, or tissue derived from them. Epidemiology, however, is the major science dealing with large masses of human population, their biosocial characteristics, and the way these relate to the distribution of disease in that population. Although epidemiology originated in the studies of etiology of epidemics in human populations, it has developed interest in the etiology of all human diseases. Like medicine itself, epidemiology has, in quest of its answers, made a marriage of a variety of biological sciences. Thus, in the study of conditions ranging from measles to mongolism to atherosclerosis, contributions from virology, chromosome study, and the biochemistry of nutrition, among other disciplines, are used as they apply to masses of people.

The key phrase here, for sociologists, is "masses of people." Many of the genetic, virological, nutritional, and other biological characteristics of individuals in these populations are closely related to such demographic characteristics as race, socioeconomic status, ethnic background, and fertility. Confronted with these observations, the sociological intuition envisions the possibility that still other aspects of social behavior may be related to states of health, aspects such as occupational behavior, religious prescriptions, recreational patterns, dietary habits, and factors of family relationships.

The common observation of both the clinician and layman that various aspects of human behavior may predispose to or protect against illness is congruent with the sociological view. The result has been that sociologists recently have increased their work in the area of epidemiology. At the same time, imaginative physician-epidemiologists have been more frequently concerned with details of human behavior and relationships. Studies of sociological variables have been pursued in research on the etiology of such varied conditions as coronary disease (Kannel, Dawber, Kagen, Revotskie,

& Stokes, 1961), hypertension (Boe, Hummerfelt, & Wedevang, 1956), ulcerative colitis (Lilienfeld, 1960), alcoholism (Strauss & Bacon, 1953), lung cancer (Dorn, 1959; Hammond & Horn, 1958), congenital abnormalities (Pasamanick & Lilienfeld, 1955), neuroses (Hollingshead & Redlich, 1953; Pasamanick, Rogers & Lilienfeld, 1956; Srole, Langner, Michael, Opler & Rennie, 1962), and injuries from skiing (Haddon, Ellison & Carroll, 1962) and automobile accidents (McCarroll & Haddon, 1962). Scientific method dictates that the investigated phenomenon be observed in detail and that relationships among the details be investigated to furnish explanations for the phenomenon. Application of this method has led epidemiologists from both medicine and sociology minutely to examine the characteristics of dietary, smoking, and driving behavior and of interpersonal relationships as they relate to various pathological states. Knowledge of the causes of a given condition provides suggestions as to various methods of prevention and therapy.

The Etiological Chain of Events

For the purposes of this discussion, we will define disease as a tissue change to a morbid state brought about by some endogenous or exogenous biochemical or biophysical agent. Most often, the tissue change is the last in a series of events or factors, many of which are social, that put the host in contact with the pathogenic agent (Graham, 1960). The first might be membership in a particular social group—for example, watch dial painters; next, this group may exhibit a particular behavior pattern—e.g., its members may form a point on the brush with the lips; next, the host might be exposed to a vector or carrier of the agent—in this case, a paint for illuminated dials; and finally, an agent, a radioactive ingredient of the paint that in some still undiscovered way brings about sarcoma, a fatal malignant bone tumor (Martland, 1931). The categories of factors leading to disease usually are membership in a social group engaging in a pathogenic behavior pattern, consequent exposure to a vector or carrier of the agent, and the agent itself which brings about the tissue change. Whether or not a disease is clinically evident may depend greatly upon host characteristics, inherited or acquired. Thus, some individuals appear to have a genetic predisposition to diabetes, which, together with certain dietary behavior, may result in this particular illness. The same diet in another individual will not produce the disease because these host characteristics are absent. Similarly, the tubercle bacillus may or may not bring about a clinically recognizable condition, depending on the state of the host, possibly including his genetic endowment, nutrition, and other factors relating to socioeconomic status.

All of the above steps in pathogenesis do not necessarily appear in the history of a given disease. Indeed, in a very few conditions, genetic predisposition plus time for the illness to manifest itself are the only factors which can be chronicled: mongolism and other congenital anomalies and probably sickle-cell anemia are examples. Sometimes a behavior pattern may be pervasive in a society, and not peculiar to any one social group. Thus, in the United States a majority of adult males smoke cigarettes; although the habit is less manifest in some occupational, ethnic, or other social groups (such as clergymen, Italian-Americans, or jet pilots), it is generally pervasive. The first in the chain of factors, membership in a group, is less important in distinguishing those exposed to this vector. Among adolescents, however, the chain of factors has a high probability of starting with group membership, such as belonging to a family in which most members smoke (Horn, Courts, Taylor & Solomon, 1959); the host is then introduced to the pattern which puts him in contact with the vector, cigarette smoke, and the agent in the smoke which produces lung cancer.

Occasionally, the social situation seems to be in itself the precipitating factor. This may occur in instances where, in susceptible hosts, a trying social situation brings about an endocrine disturbance in the body which might cause disease. Similar situations, in susceptible hosts, might contribute to development of neuroses through unknown mechanisms, perhaps biochemical. It is possible, too, that traumatic social situations operating together with other exogenous agents on susceptible hosts may help to produce certain cases of hypertension, peptic and duodenal ulcer, ulcerative colitis, asthma, or alcoholism.

From the point of view of prevention, the chain of factors leading to disease may be interrupted at any stage, and the disease thereby controlled. Thus, Percival Pott prescribed bathing to eighteenth-century English chimney sweeps as a preventive measure against scrotal cancer. His prophylaxis worked even though he had not identified the agent in soot causing the disease. A century earlier, James Lind suggested the eating of limes by English sailors to prevent scurvy long before the properties of ascorbic acid were understood. Similarly, today, a large proportion of lung cancer deaths could be prevented through abandonment of the cigarette-smoking habit. This could be done even though it is not known which of the specific chemical fractions of cigarette smoke which produce tumors in animals are also carcinogenic to humans. It is not necessary, obviously, to recognize the agent that causes the tissue change in order to effect prevention.

Rather, if health is to be preserved, once a link in the pathogenic chain has been found, this knowledge must be applied. This problem, a social one, is very difficult. Lind's prophylaxis against scurvy is a case in point. Scurvy was a disease serious enough to kill 100 of 160 men accompanying Vasco da Gama on his voyage of 1498. Nevertheless, not until a century after Lind gave his recommendation did the British Admiralty institute use of citrus fruit among its sailors. In our own time, even though there is more evidence regarding the relationship between dental caries and fluoridation of public water than between most other diseases and their preventive measures, the prophylaxis, for obscure sociological reasons, is not being universally applied.

The strategy of epidemiological investigation devolves from the etiological chain of factors and events described above. In instances where there are hints as to the relationship between a behavior pattern and a disease, as in the case of cigarette smoking and lung cancer, the investigation may begin with the suggested behavior trait. In such instances, hunches are derived from knowledge of a close relation between the possibly pathogenic substance and the given organ, in this case, the inhaled smoke and the lung.

Where no correlational hypotheses suggest themselves, the strategy must be revised. The fact that, as we pointed out earlier, membership in particular social groups may be the first step in an etiological chain suggests that investigation of the presence of disease in occupational, ethnic, religious, regional, social class, recreational, racial, or other social groups may be profitable. If a given disease is found to occur with more or less frequency in a given social class, further investigation can look into the specific behavioral trait characterizing the group which might be responsible for fomenting or protecting against the disease. The first stage of epidemiologic investigation, therefore, may be that of isolating unusual incidence of disease in given subcultures in the society. Research into many of the chronic diseases has reached only to this stage today. Investigation of some other diseases has turned up other kinds of evidence, in addition to the demographic. In these instances, it is important for the development of a coherent and complete theory of the etiology of the given disease that the sociological findings be consistent with those of the other disciplines. Indeed, one function of sociological epidemiology is to investigate the extent to which relationships of behavior patterns to disease are consistent with what is known regarding biophysical and biochemical relationships (S. Graham, 1960).

Inherent in this description of the etiological chain is the point made earlier that epidemiology must be a marriage of a variety of disciplines. Indeed, it must use whatever may shed light on the development of disease. The variety of scientific data utilized in this research is great. Geological studies of outcroppings of radioactive rock in the vicinity of homes where congenital anomalies occurred have proved useful (Gentry, Parkhurst, & Gulin, 1959). Soil science has been referred to in studies of gastric cancer (Tromp & Diehl, 1955). These data are used to supplement the more conventional epidemiological resources of biology, sociology, chemistry, and physics. An example of the variety of sources of data utilized in the epidemiology of some diseases is shown in the case of lung cancer.

Over a score of studies comparing smoking habits of lung cancer and control patients in hospitals have been undertaken (Levin, Goldstein & Gerhardt, 1950). These have consistently shown a relationship between lung cancer and smoking cigarettes. These have been retrospective studies based on hospital series, with the biases these populations entail. In addition, however, prospective studies have been conducted in which large samples of healthy people were asked about their smoking habits and were then followed through several years to determine the incidence of lung cancer in the various smoking categories. Three of the four prospective studies used a minimum of 180,000 individuals chosen from various populations in the United States, and the other used the physician population of Great Britain; for all, a result similar to those of the retrospective studies was obtained (Doll & Hill, 1956; Dorn, 1958; Hammond, 1962; Hammond & Horn, 1955). It is noteworthy that, in these studies, a dose-response relationship was established; thus, the incidence of lung cancer increased with each increase in amount of cigarettes smoked per day. Similarly, the longer the period for which individuals had stopped smoking, the lower was their lung cancer risk.

Further investigations have been undertaken to determine whether the relationships exist in particular subpopulations which in themselves are more subject to lung cancer, such as urban groups. The smoking relationship persists even here. Multivariate analysis of a variety of other factors also associated with lung cancer indicates that, while a few others are etiologically related, the smoking factor is extremely large in comparison (Hammond, 1955; Levin, 1962).

In addition to these many population studies, much laboratory research has been undertaken on histological and biochemical facets of the relationship between smoking and lung cancer. For example, pathologic studies have been done of the cells in the tracheobronchial trees of smokers of various amounts of cigarettes and of nonsmokers. In the autopsy studies of Auerbach, the bronchial epithelium of nonsmokers was usually normal, but only .2 per cent of heavy smokers and .1 per cent of lung cancer cases showed normal epithelium. Carcinoma *in situ* (a tumor of malignant characteristics which has not yet invaded surrounding tissues) was found in 75 per cent of heavy smokers as compared to none of nonsmokers (Auerbach, Stout, Hammond & Garfinkel, 1961).

Studies of the effect of tobacco smoke on the epithelia of freshly slaughtered cattle showed an inhibition of action of the cilia, the waving grasslike processes that waft foreign matter out of the respiratory passages. In many studies, the application of tobacco tars to the skin of mice resulted in the growth of many malignant and nonmalignant neoplasms. It is interesting that applications of tar from filter cigarettes resulted in less cancer to the mice than those from nonfilters (Bock, Moore, Dowd & Clark, 1953). Also indicating a dose-response relationship is the fact that smoke condensate from cigarettes yielding large amounts of tar resulted in more tumors than that from cigarettes lower in tar. Applications of chemically isolated fractions of cigarette smoke to the skin of mice have indicated a large number of fractions which are carcinogenic. In short, many studies using the methodologies and knowledge of several disciplines—including sociology, biochemistry, and pathology—have been completed. It it interesting that the findings of each are consistent with those of the others. Equally important is the point that everything is grist for the epidemiological mill.

Methodological Problems

The chief methodological problems of epidemiology and, indeed, many of those of medicine in general, are not unfamiliar to sociologists. All of these disciplines have the human animal as focus for study. The problems of obtaining physical and biological measurements and accurate verbal histories of past experiences on samples large and unbiased enough for meaningful study are as pressing for the human biologist as for the sociologist. This is particularly true for epidemiology, which, in its study of social groups and behavior related to disease, relies most heavily on sociological research techniques and knowledge.

A typical sociological problem of methodology which is also encountered in epidemiology concerns the source of groups for study. The most studied sociological group (but not the most preferred) is college sophomores, and the most studied epidemiological group is patients. Traditionally, physicians, being case oriented, have studied patients. As they have become more sophisticated, larger and larger numbers have been studied, both in trials of therapeutic measures and in epidemiological studies. Typically, the epidemiological study of this kind has gathered together information on a series of cases with the disease being investigated in a given hospital population and on a series of patients with other diseases in the same hospital. These have been compared as to their past medical, social, or other characteristics. Various measurements have been easy to make on such accessible groups.

Although studies utilizing this design are still frequently employed as first screening devices for the testing of hypotheses (for certain hypotheses and measurements, such as medical ones, they are most effective), some drawbacks inhere in them. First, people who do not go to the hospital for the disease under consideration are omitted from study. Where the variable studied is sociological, and it often is, the probable bias in hospital studies generally is apparent. All hospitals cater to certain categories of patients more than to others, on the basis of social class, ethnic background, religion, race, and even occupation (in the case of union hospitals), the bias depending a great deal on the characteristics of the groups which originally sponsored the hospitals. Thus, studies limited to individual hospitals can involve considerable bias.

Most hospital studies, but by no means all, are retrospective, and this suggests another facet of the problem of choice of study groups. In retrospective study, the investigator is confronted with those individuals possessing various traits who are left for study after a period of time has passed. The sociologist encounters this problem in studies of social mobility, in which he interviews in the community to determine differences in the occupational histories of the fathers of male subjects and of the subjects themselves. He may not find all of the individuals who have fathers with certain occupations because in these cases the occupation of the father is associated with an increased probability that the son will leave the community under study. Thus, the upward mobility of a laborer's sons may be greater than is shown from investigation of a given community because a large proportion of the upwardly mobile sons moved to other communities to increase their status. Exactly the same problem is encountered by epidemiologists when they are reduced to studying a population decimated by death or mobility.

An alternative and less biased procedure would be to study individuals prospectively in experimental designs. Thus, as in research on retrolental fibroplasia, the stimulus under investigation (large amounts of oxygen in the incubators, the conventional mode of treatment at the time) was applied randomly on premature infants to assess the damage to eyes associated therewith. In this procedure, there was no loss of patients. The stimulus was applied randomly, and those receiving it were compared to controls who received less oxygen, also randomly selected from the same population (Kinsey & Hemphill, 1955). This procedure, of course, although prospective and incorporating the positive values of the true experiment, involves some of the bias resulting from analysis of a restricted population group.

Experimental studies carried out on larger populations increase the capacity to generalize from results. A classical experimental epidemiological study is that comparing two similar Hudson River communities, one randomly chosen to have its water fluoridated and the other, not to have such treatment. The children in these communities were followed for 10 years to discover whether there were differences in the incidence of dental caries among them (Ast, Smith, Wachs & Cantwell, 1956). Even here, however, bias inheres in the choice of communities for study.

Because of the difficulty and expense of manipulating human beings in experimental studies, most prospective research carried out in epidemiology is not experimental. The prospective studies of lung cancer, for example, utilize the traditional "experiment provided by nature" which the sociologist sometimes uses. This, of course, is not an experiment at all. The independent variable has not been applied randomly to the subjects. In the studies of lung cancer, subjects were asked about their smoking habits and then followed for a number of years to determine the occurrence of disease in the smokers and nonsmokers. The bias inherent in the self-selection of smoking by the subjects rather than through random procedures could cast doubt on the findings if they were not supported by other data offering epidemiological, pathological, and biochemical evidence. Even with this qualification, however, prospective studies are to be preferred to retrospective ones for most purposes because they allow the investigator to control time effects. He can examine all individuals exposed to the dependent variable, not just those left to him as in retrospective designs. Nonetheless, prospective designs are used less often than retrospective simply because of the expense and time involved. However, if the sciences are to progress, investment of the necessary time and other resources must be made in research where the effects of time on the independent and dependent variables can be measured. This is as true for general sociological investigation as it is for epidemiological studies.

One problem which has been of some concern among epidemiologists concerns the incidence as opposed to the prevalence of disease. This problem also involves the occurrence of phenomena in time. Incidence is the number of new cases developing in a given point of time. Prevalence is the number of cases, new and old, current at a given point of time. For epidemiological study, where the investigator wishes to examine the *occurrence* of disease after the application of a given stimulus, either naturally or through his own manipulation, incidence is the logical choice for study. As Hollingshead pointed out, the lower classes may bulk large in a population of current cases of psychosis partly because they are less likely to receive treatment, and therefore remain cases for a longer time. The study of prevalence here would reveal the lower classes to have a larger amount of psychosis than might be the case if only new cases were studied. This discovery might furnish a false lead regarding factors related to cause

of the disease (Hollingshead, 1961; Hollingshead & Redlich, 1954).

Although the study of incidence is most useful to the epidemiologist, the study of prevalence is most useful to the investigator interested in the number of facilities which must be made available for the rehabilitation or treatment of persons with a certain condition. All cases needing the facilities are interesting to him, not merely new cases (MacMahon et al, 1960).

In a few respects, the problems of epidemiology differ somewhat from those of sociology. Almost inevitably, epidemiologists study disease, which, thankfully, is usually a rare entity. Sociologists are often concerned with less rare types of phenomena. Everyone has social class, but relatively few have the disease under question in a given study. For this reason, socio-epidemiological research often uses samples which seem unnecessarily large to the sociologist studying more widely distributed variables. This is not to say that many sociologists are not concerned with rare phenomena; criminologists are a case in point. Again, this is not to say that epidemiologists concern themselves only with rare entities; the younger generation among them are taking a more pure-science approach and are becoming concerned with the etiology of variations in universally distributed phenomena. Winkelstein's interest in the complete range of blood pressure, rather than simply in high blood pressure, is a case in point (Winkelstein, Warren, personal communication).

Age, on the other hand, is almost a universal preoccupation for epidemiologists but is less investigated by sociologists. Because age is so intimately related to most biological states in the human being, and because the usual changes associated with maturation and degeneration of the body are so pervasive, the effects of age in itself must be dissociated from whatever phenomena are under investigation in socio-epidemiology. The same principle can be followed with profit in general sociology. To return to the example of social mobility as measured by the occupations of fathers of upper- and lower-class sons, one would expect possibly spurious findings if the age of the subjects is not accounted for. The lower classes contain more young people than the upper, if class is measured by income, median rental, house type, and participation in voluntary associations. The association is maintained regardless of the class position of the fathers. Thus, the traditional finding that samples of upper-class sons have larger proportions of upper-class fathers than do samples of lower-class sons, where age is ignored, probably yields an underestimation of the difference. This is because the group of lower-class sons may contain more young individuals. Many of these come from upper-class families and are in low rental, low income, and other groups because they are young. After growing older and completing education these persons may have a higher than average probability of attaining the status of their fathers. For this reason such investigations should be conducted using age-specific or age-adjusted analyses. Where age is linked to social change as far as the individual is concerned, it becomes an important concern for general sociological research. Even here, then, epidemiology and sociology have very similar methodological problems.

Sociological Factors Related to Disease

The discussion of the chain of factors leading to the clinical recognition of disease noted that membership in a social group often entails a behavior pattern which puts the host into contact with a pathogen. Thus, membership in given social class, ethnic, religious, occupational, or other group is often related to unusual risk of a given disease. Examinations of incidence in such gross demographic categories put the investigator further away from etiological knowledge of the agent causing the tissue change than he would be if he searched for the individual items of behavior which in themselves might set the stage for dis-

ease. Frequently, however, there is no suggestion as to what those items of behavior might be, so the demographic approach must be utilized. From the sociological point of view, the demographic relationships discovered stimulate speculations about behavioral characteristics of the social groups involved which might predispose to or protect against the disease. Several studies have shown, for example, that the highest incidence of tuberculosis (Terris, 1948) is in the lower classes. For some reason, although a very large proportion of the population of the United States is exposed to the tubercle bacillus, a very small percentage develops clinical symptoms and active disease. The fact that the lower classes have more than their share of the disease suggests that factors relating to the lower-class environment, possibly crowding, poor diet, bad ventilation, or air pollution may determine whether or not an individual exposed to the bacillus develops clinically recognizable symptoms.

Trachoma, a disease of the eyes, is apparently concentrated in members of the lower classes in certain non-Western societies, perhaps because hygienic precautions against infection are less easily applied in them (May, 1958). Schistosomiasis is a similar case (Affifi, 1948). Poliomyelitis, on the other hand, has been found in a few studies to be more frequent in the upper classes than the lower. One theory (Corriell, Schaeffer, Felton, Fernandez-Moran & Bierly, 1956; Hammon, 1947) to account for this is based on the assumption that infection in infancy allows the individual to develop protective antibodies to the disease without the dramatic symptoms exhibited by individuals exposed later in life. Infants in large families are likely to be exposed to the disease by reason of crowding and to develop antibodies at an early age. These, of course, are more likely to be lower-class individuals, and the disease, therefore, manifests itself (as paralytic poliomyelitis) at a greater rate in the upper classes.

Much is known about the etiology of the

above-mentioned diseases. Nevertheless, to complete the understanding of their pathogenesis, the sociological relationships must be reconciled with the microbiological, and the theories available to account for the relationships between social environment and such diseases as tuberculosis and poliomyelitis, for example, must be further tested. In a large class of diseases, even less is known about potential agents. Frequently these are termed chronic or noninfectious to distinguish them from the infectious diseases discussed above. This is a slippery designation, however, because some of the infectious diseases can be chronic, and some of the illnesses discussed below may be infectious.

One theory of cancer etiology, for example, is that it may be caused by a virus, perhaps acting with a cocarcinogen which triggers the development of disease. This theory may apply even though the etiology of cancers at different sites is likely to be different: The virus and/or the cocarcinogen may vary from site to site. That the cocarcinogen for many sites of cancer may be associated with socioeconomic status is suggested by a number of studies in many parts of the world. These show, for example, that the decrease in socioeconomic status is associated with an increase in the incidence of cancers of the following sites: cervix uterus, stomach, esophagus, and lung. An increase in class status concides with an increase in cancer of the breast, corpus uterus, and probably the testis (Clemmesen & Nielsen, 1951; Cohart, 1955; Graham, Levin & Lilienfeld, 1960).

With reference to diseases of the circulatory system, there is some evidence that hypertension increases with decreases in socioeconomic status (Boe et al., 1956). On the other hand, deaths from coronary artery disease have been found in a number of studies to be more characteristic of the upper classes than the lower (Breslow & Bnell, 1960). Hospitalization for mental depression may be less associated with socioeconomic status than for neurosis and psychosis, which are

found more frequently in the lower classes (Faris & Dunham, 1939). Alcoholism is another disease which may have higher rates in the lower classes.

Ethnic background has also been related to a variety of diseases. Thus, one study suggested that the prevalence of hyperthyroidism among Winnipeg school children was higher among those deriving from countries of Eastern Europe than from Western Europe (Abbott, 1932). It is interesting that the rates decreased from east to west, declining in regular fashion from a high among children deriving from Poland, to a somewhat lower rate among German-Americans, to increasingly lower rates in the French, English, Irish, and Icelandic children. It was hypothesized that this may have been related to dietary differences in the cultures of the peoples involved. A study of mortality among ethnic groups shortly after many of them arrived in this country suggested that Italian-Americans had especially high rates of death from pneumonia. German-Americans evidenced unusually low rates of pneumonia and of tuberculosis. These relationships with pneumonia and tuberculosis, of course, may reflect differences in the socioeconomic characteristics of the ethnic groups.

Interesting correlations between ethnic background and coronary artery disease have been found in Israel. There, the Oriental Jews (Yemenites) were found to have appreciably lower rates of mortality from this disease than were the European Jews (Ashkenazim) (Toor, Katchalsky, Agmon, & Allaloub, 1960). The Yemenites were of lower socioeconomic status and ate less animal protein and fats. The intake of dietary animal fats is probably related to blood cholesterol levels. If it should be established that such levels are related to the development of the fatty plaques which contribute to the narrowing of coronary arteries and to myocardial infarction (Doyle, Heslin, Hilleboe, Formel & Korns, 1957; Kannel, Dawber, Kagen, Revotskie, & Stokes, 1961), the low rates among the Yemenites may be explained. On the other hand, there are further behavior patterns which distinguish Yemenites from other Jews in Israel.

Still other relationships between ethnic background and coronary artery disease have been shown in work in the United States. Thus, the Irish may have lower rates of the disease than other Western European groups (Graham, 1956). If this relationship is real, it may obtain because of some trait of the Irish, such as their high alcohol intake. Preliminary findings of Baedenkopf and associates (1963) suggest that persons with low alcohol intakes have more thickening of the coronary artery wall and therefore perhaps higher risks of infarction than those with higher alcohol ingestion. If it should be found that the lower classes ingest more alcohol than the upper, their lower mortality from heart disease might thereby be explained. This is a hypothesis only, but the possibility must be considered that characteristics of ethnic and class groups other than or in addition to ingestion of animal fats may be related to coronary disease.

Whether or not alcohol ingestion is related to class, alcohol addiction appears to be correlated with ethnic variations. Thus, various researches suggest that there is less alcoholism among Italians in the United States than among other ethnic groups. Irish- and Scandinavian-Americans, on the other hand, appear to have unusually high rates (Haggard & Jellinek, 1952). The very permissive attitude of the Irish toward drinking as a recreation may be associated with this finding (Bales, 1962). So might the Italian conception of alcohol as a food to be ingested mainly with meals. Such explanations, of course, are after the fact; nevertheless, the discovered ethnic relationships may point to variables which should be examined further as characteristics of drinkers with and without alcoholism.

Cancer at various sites has also been related to ethnic background. Cross-cultural studies, for example, have shown that the Japanese have unusually high rates of mortality from gastric cancer and unusually low rates of breast cancer (Segi, Fujisaku & Kurihara, 1957). The English and Americans have outstanding mortality rates from lung cancer (World Health Organization, 1959). Within the United States, evidence from two studies shows that cancers of the lung and esophagus have an unusually high rate among Polish-Americans; whereas cancers of the pharynx and colon occupy similar positions among Italian-Americans (Graham, Levin, Lilienfeld & Sheehe, 1963; Haenszel, 1961a). The foreign-born population in the United States considered as a whole have been found to have higher risks of cancer of the lung, stomach, esophagus, and cervix than do the native born.

Potentially useful relationships have also been found between religion and some diseases. Although incidence of the disease is difficult to measure, Jews have been reported to have low rates of alcoholism as compared with Catholics and Protestants in the United States. The rate of alcoholism among Jews reportedly increases with generation after immigration and with decline in orthodoxy. Sociologists investigating this phenomenon suggest that the low rate among Jews may be related to the fact that Jews utilize wine in their religious services, giving it some sanctity. They have also proposed that the permissive attitude toward male drinking to the point of befuddlement, present, for example, in the immigrant Irish culture, is not only absent but frowned upon in Jewish culture (Snyder, 1962).

Jews also have much lower rates of mortality from cancer of the cervix than Protestants or Catholics. This has been found both in cross-cultural comparisons between Israel and the United States and within the United States (Dorn, 1954). Some facet of Jewish culture may provide protection against the disease. In view of the superior hygiene associated with the practice of circumcision, investigators hypothesized that the Jewish practice of circumcising might furnish this protection (Wynder & Mantel). Whether this is the case or not is problematical; the results of the few studies done on the subject are equivocal (Lilienfeld & Graham, 1958).

Still other relationships exist among diseases and religion. Thus, Jews may have higher risks of leukemia (MacMahon & Koller, 1957). This provocative finding suggests that some trait of the Jewish subculture in American society may be promoting the disease. A possible factor here is the greater exposure of Jews to diagnostic radiation which in some research has been shown to be related to the disease (Lilienfeld, 1959). Again, some findings indicate that Protestants may be particularly prone to testicular cancer: One series adjusted for differences in social class, rural-urban residence, and native or foreign birth, showed Protestant patients to have higher risks than Catholic ones (Graham, n.d.). Further research on this point it highly desirable.

Throughout this discussion of ethnic background and religion as related to diseases of various kinds, it has been assumed that some sociological characteristic of the groups under investigation is responsible for the relationship discovered. The hypothesis must be entertained, however, that the crucial trait is not wholly sociologic but, in part at least, genetic. There is some evidence, for example, to indicate a common gene pool among Jews, present among Jews of all nationalities (Sachs & Bat-Miriam, 1957), and which may protect against or promote the diseases we have discussed. Similarly, genetic differences between Italians and Poles may account for their different risks for the various cancers; the same may be said for differences in alcoholism risks.

The Human Ecology of Disease in Vietnam

The discussion of individual sociological variables related to a variety of diseases cannot provide a completely coherent picture of the relationship between man-made, physical, and biological environments and disease. Hence, a description of the ecology of major diseases in Vietnam will be under-

taken. Ecological description of disease includes consideration of the physical, biological, and cultural environments. In this case, stress is placed on the topography of the area, its arthropod and rodent populations, its agriculture and plant life, and various aspects of culture.

The interior of Vietnam is mountainous. The mountains give way to hills and hills to plains to the east and south as the land meets ocean. The culture is primarily Chinese. The Indian influence found most strongly in Burma and Thailand tapers off in the more easterly parts of the Indo-Chiese peninsula; its frontier is in Cochin-China. One also finds some admixtures of the island cultures of the south, which show themselves particularly in the pile-housing of the rural Vietnamese. For the most part, the language, old modes of dress, diet, manners, and philosophy are influenced mainly by Chinese culture in the coastal and hill areas. Even the name which the area had until recently, Annam, meaning "Peaceful South" in Vietnamese and some Chinese dialects, suggests the relationship of the area to China. The relationship remains close despite the past century of domination by the French and the French colonial policy of assimilation.

A malaria-bearing mosquito thrives in the hilly region between the shoreline and mountains (May, 1958). Pile housing similar to that used in Indonesia is utilized in this area, however, so that humans are usually above the line of flight of mosquitos. The fowl, pigs, and other animals, kept underneath the houses in the shelter they provide, are the major loci for malaria. However, the hill people are prey to other diseases, mostly of an infectious nature. In common with other peoples in the Chinese culture area, they use human feces for fertilizer. This practice results in the spread of many diseases. The people, for example, wear shoes only rarely, walking directly on the hook-worm infested soil. The cultivation of land is so intensive here that food storage space is available only in or near the house. As a result, food is polluted by rats carrying plague. In the lowland areas, the use of night soil as fertilizer, plus inadequate water control in river delta regions, provides effective transmission of cholera. This is particularly a problem in time of floods. One important disease of a noninfectious nature also affects these people. This is beriberi, a thiamine deficiency disease common in rice-producing areas, which results from a diet which is limited in the main to polished rice.

Thus, many factors affect the ecology of disease in this society. The crowded population, the necessary intensive use of land and all materials, including possible fertilizers, the limited diet, the housing type, the characteristics of arthropod and rodent vectors of disease, the topography, and the agricultural techniques, together with an absence of modern medicine and public health organizations, produce a characteristic disease picture.

The Epidemiology of Gastric Cancer

An examination of the manner in which a variety of sociological variables are related to a number of different diseases provides an intimation of the potential of these relationships for suggesting hypotheses about the etiology of disease. It is also instructive to examine the epidemiology of a particular disease exhaustively. This kind of study indicates the way the discovery of one relationship suggests the possible existence of others, and it demonstrates the efforts to develop theories which can account for and make mutually consistent all of the relationships discovered. The epidemiology of gastric cancer is an especially useful example, particularly because sociological variables figure so prominently in its epidemiology.

Gastric cancer, like few other cancers, is declining in incidence almost yearly. Formerly, it was the cancer of highest incidence (and mortality) among males; its average annual incidence in New York State in 1942 was 26.8 per 100,000 among males, and 16.1 among females. By 1961, however, its incidence had fallen to 15.4 among males and 8.8 in females (N.Y. State Department of Health, 1961).

A number of biological conditions, which are perhaps associated with its early phases or which perhaps set the stage for its later development, may be related to this disease. Thus, one biological factor, gastric achlorhydria, has been found among approximately 70 per cent of cases but among only 10 per cent of controls (Berkson & Comfort, 1953; Comfort, Butsch & Eusterman, 1937–1938).

Another medical condition which, it has been hypothesized, may be related to the disease, is pernicious anemia (Rigler, Kaplan & Fink, 1945). Here again, it is difficult to obtain numbers of such patients large enough to contain sufficient individuals who develop gastric cancers. The hypothesis is reasonable, however, in view of the fact that the prolonged deficiency of vitamin B_{12} associated with pernicious anemia could result in damage to the gastric mucosa.

Gastric ulcers have also been hypothesized to serve as loci in which gastric cancers can develop. This suggestion is difficult to examine because the presence of an ulcer in the stomach may be obscured by the subsequent development of cancer at the same site. From the epidemiological point of view, diseases such as gastric ulcers, if they are precursors, must be examined to discover the mechanism by which they could develop the cancer. In addition, the problems remain of discovering the epidemiology of these promoting conditions and of that large proportion of gastric cancers which is not related to them.

Another important hypothesis relating medical conditions to etiology of stomach cancer has to do with dentition; fortunately, the easy access to teeth makes large-scale surveys of this factor possible, if not inexpensive. The small studies of dentition to date are equivocal, but current large-scale investigations may shed more light on the problem.

In addition, some evidence suggests a modest familial aggregation in this disease. A fair number of studies of this factor have been completed (Graham & Lilienfeld, 1958). Usually these compare the incidence of gastric cancer among the kin of cases as compared with the kin of controls. These studies show approximately twice as much gastric cancer in the relatives of cases as among those of controls. Thus, some genetic predisposition to the disease may run in families. Also, some behavior pattern may run in these families, which accounts for the disease. One way of examining these possibilities is to look into the incidence among nonblood kin living in the households, as compared to that among the blood kin. Woolf tried this and found that spouses of the cases had rates like those of the kin of controls; the blood kin of the cases had higher rates (Woolf, 1956). Woolf's is the only such study of the problem, although a number are currently under way; nevertheless, it suggests that at least a small amount of gastric cancer may be related to a genetic predisposition.

A number of sociological characteristics may be associated with the disease. It was noted earlier that gastric cancer is inversely related to socioeconomic status. This relationship has been found in Denmark, England and Wales, New Haven, and Buffalo. In addition, occupational relationships have been reported—workers exposed to iron dust experience greater risks (Kraus, Levin, & Gerhardt, 1957). Controlling on age, rural-urban residence, smoking, color, and marital status, it has been found that 12.5 per cent of cases, as compared to 1.0 per cent of controls, worked at jobs involving exposure to iron dust. Other research shows higher risks with increasing age, urban as opposed to rural residence (Levin, Haenszel, Carroll, Gerhardt, Handy & Ingraham, 1960), smoking (Dorn, 1958), and Negro as compared to white racial background (Haenszel, 1961). Further studies controlling on residence, carcinogenic occupation, socioeconomic status, and smoking show

that foreign-born have about two-and-one-half times the risk of native-born individuals among the Roswell Park Memorial Institute patient population. Polish-American females have unusually high risks (Graham, Levin, Lilienfeld & Sheehe, 1963).

Intercultural data also show differences. Thus, the Japanese, Finns, Chileans, and Icelandic populations appear to have elevated risks of the disease. The Japanese relationship is reinforced by the finding that the Japanese in the United States have higher risks than other American ethnic groups. However, their risk in the United States is lower than that in Japan, suggesting (because they are probably genetically little different from Japanese in Japan) that their new culture must have introduced something to protect them against the disease. It is particularly interesting that the Japanese in Hawaii have rates intermediate between those in the United States and Japan (Smith, 1956). The Japanese character of the Hawaiian-Japanese culture may be similarly intermediate. Another interesting ethnic relationship is the unusually high rates of gastric cancer among some of the Polynesian peoples. High rates have been suggested for the Samoans (Thieme, 1963). Investigation has also revealed higher than usual rates among the native Hawaiians, part-Hawaiians (Quisenberry, 1960), and, particularly, the Maori of New Zealand (Rose, 1963). Investigation is currently going on among other Polynesian groups to determine whether the relationship exists for them all. Research is needed to discover possible reasons for these relationships.

Because there apparently is a sociological as well as a genetic relationship with this disease, diet has suggested itself as a possibly relevant factor. Some item of diet, or perhaps the frequency or manner of eating, the temperature at which food and drink is taken, the use of alcohol, the type of cooking, or the use of condiments may be related to protection against or predisposition to this disease. Research could profitably begin by examining the diets of the groups of varying incidence noted above. Preliminary examination of dietary data already gathered at Roswell Park Institute suggests that higher risks of the disease may be related to frequent ingestion of potatoes, beer, animal fats and to irregular eating habits (Graham & Levin, n.d.). Sociological investigations suggest that the first, second, and last of the above mentioned variables are perhaps more characteristic of the lower than the upper classes; thus, this relationship is consistent with the marked socio-economic gradient of gastric cancer incidence. It is obvious that much research must be done on the epidemiology of this disease. Nevertheless, it is quite possible that the leads furnished by the sociological aspects of this epidemiology will be among the most valuable in directing attention to factors bringing about the tissue change known as gastric cancer.

PREVENTION OF DISEASE

The purpose of sociologic epidemiology is multifaceted. Most obviously it satisfies the curiosity of the scientist about relationships among phenomena which interest him. From the point of view of applied science and social value, in addition, it provides information useful in devising preventive measures for various diseases. These preventive measures may be applied at any point in the etiological chain of events.

Some of the most effective preventive devices depend upon changing the host so that he can withstand the onslaught of disease. Thus, the vaccines developed for use against poliomyelitis, diphtheria, typhoid, typhus, small pox, and measles operate through exposing the host to a small amount of micro-organisms which stimulate production of antibodies capable of protecting him in event of exposure to the disease in question. This procedure alone has been among the most successful in reducing deaths from disease, certainly more effective than the therapeutic measures

which would have had to be applied had the host been unprepared.

Another successful tactic involving attack on some phase of the etiological chain has been that directed against insect vectors which carry pathogenic microorganisms to man. One example is the insect which carries the infection known as the Aleppo button in North Africa. This arthropod resides through part of its life-cycle in the mud walls of human residences traditionally used in that part of the world. Changing the housing type in many communities has removed the menace by eliminating one environment necessary to the insect for life. Draining and treating pools of stagnant water to reduce areas of residence for anopheles mosquitos has likewise reduced malaria, particularly in South and Central America. Control of rodent and insect life has similarly meant control of vectors which carry plague and typhus to human hosts. Where the human animal figures importantly in bringing susceptible hosts into contact with the microorganism, as in syphilis and tuberculosis, control measures are based on keeping individuals already ill with these diseases out of contact with the uninfected.

Still other links in the etiological chain have been utilized for disease prevention. In the case of some noninfectious diseases, Potts's prescription of frequent baths for chimney sweeps reduced scrotal cancer; Lind's, of the use of lemons and limes reduced scurvy among British sailors; Goldberger's, of the use of animal protein as a source of niacin reduced pellagra in American southern mill towns. In the last-named cases, the adding to or removal of some element from the environment of the host has protected him very effectively from the disease in question. Similar preventive results could doubtless be obtained against dental caries were more communities to fluoridate their drinking water and against lung cancer were more individuals to stop smoking cigarettes.

All of these successes have been achieved

through prevention. For many of the diseases in question, if preventive measures are not applied and the individual develops a clinical case of disease, no therapeutic measures are very successful. Thus, dental treatment, which depends upon cutting out the affected area, is hardly a cure for caries.

ing, expensive, painful, or ineffective in varying degrees. The major hope of an individual's not succumbing is to avoid being affected in the first place. Although the major orientation of both the public and the medical community is toward therapy rather than prevention, treatment of many of the

TABLE 1

DEATH RATE, 1900–1959, AND DEATHS, 1959, FROM SELECTED CAUSES, UNITED STATES

	Death Rate per 100,000[a]							Number of Deaths
	1900	1910	1920	1930	1940	1950	1959	1959[b]
Cause of Death All Causes	1,719.1	1,468.0	1,298.9	1,132.1	1,076.4	963.8	941.7	1,659,000
Infectious Diseases								
Tuberculosis, all forms	194.4	153.8	113.1	71.1	45.9	22.5	6.7	11,730
Syphilis and its sequelae	12.0	13.5	16.5	15.7	14.4	5.0	1.8	3,190
Typhoid fever	31.3	22.5	7.6	4.7	1.0	0.1	...	.....
Dysentery, all forms	12.0	6.0	4.0	2.8	1.9	0.6	0.2	290
Diphtheria	40.3	21.1	15.3	4.9	1.1	0.3	0.0	60
Whooping cough	12.2	11.6	12.5	4.8	2.2	0.7	0.2	280
Acute poliomyelitis	...	2.9	0.9	1.2	0.8	1.3	0.3	540
Measles	13.3	12.4	8.8	3.2	0.5	0.3	0.2	380
Influenza and pneumonia, exclusive of pneumonia of newborn	202.2	155.9	207.3	102.5	70.3	31.3	32.5	57,320
Chronic Diseases								
Malignant Neoplasms	64.0	76.2	83.4	97.4	120.3	139.8	147.1	259,090
Diabetes Mellitus	11.0	15.3	16.1	19.1	26.6	16.2	16.0	28,160
Major cardiovascular renal diseases	345.2	371.9	364.9	414.4	485.7	510.8	519.7	⊁15,610
Ulcer of stomach and duodenum	2.7	4.0	3.6	6.2	6.8	5.5	5.9	10,460
Accidents								
Motor-vehicle accidents	...	1.8	10.3	26.7	26.2	23.1	20.0	35,320
All other accidents	72.3	82.4	59.7	53.1	47.0	37.5	30.7	54,030

[a] Based on population enumerated as of April 1 for 1940 and 1950 and estimated as of July 1 for other years.
[b] Estimated; based on a 10 per cent sample of death certificates.

The five-year survival rate for persons having lung cancer is from 2 to 4 per cent for males, with many survivors succumbing after the initial five-year period. The therapies for lung cancer, tuberculosis, small pox, malaria, and many of the other diseases mentioned above are variously time-consuming

conditions noted above is quite ineffective. Even if therapy does produce results, the individual suffering and social cost involved in caring for an affected individual is so great that prevention of the disease in the first place is much to be preferred. As can be seen in Table I, spectacular reductions in death from infectious diseases have been recorded in the last half-century. Most of these gains are the result of preventive rather than therapeutic measures.

Effective Organization of Prevention

Individual physicians acting on their own have used many preventive measures, particularly the immunizing ones, in dealing with their private patients. They have also cooperated with departments of public health or such agencies as the Rockefeller Foundation which have been interested in preventive medicine in areas where public health organizations needed aid. Even though individual physicians are generally less oriented toward prevention than therapy, in our time they have been quick to adopt preventive measures which have been shown to be effective. Because individual practices are not directed toward masses of people, however, the efforts of public health organizations, which are so oriented, have offered needed supplemental preventive medicine.

In the United States, the public health organization is the arm of preventive medicine par excellence, although it also provides some help for the therapy of certain illnesses for special classes of people, such as the aged or indigent. Such organizations on the national and state and often county or city level have several sections oriented toward prevention. These include statistical divisions to record the health status of the community and thereby to allow the early detection of epidemics. Epidemiological sections make inquiries of the sort described earlier in this chapter and apply etiological knowledge already available to investigations of the sources of infection of particular outbreaks of disease.

Sanitary engineering sections are also usually available to control water supplies and sewage disposal to make them unable to carry infection to the populace. Nursing sections act as therapeutic adjuncts to private medicine, participate in health education aimed at prevention, and carry out pre-ventive and control measures such as examining and keeping under observation contacts of individuals having such diseases as tuberculosis and syphilis. Public health physicians organize mass immunization efforts that often involve the cooperation of the private physicians in their communities. In addition to all of these activities, health education directed toward the prevention of disease is carried on by all of the public health functionaries mentioned above and by special divisions within the health department. Because public health departments work primarily with publics, sociologists and cultural anthropologists are employed in the more sophisticated departments to make studies of these publics in the fields of analytic epidemiology, the utilization and availability of medical care, organizational problems, and medical innovation.

Means for Prevention

Probably the most effective means of prevention of disease are those applied to masses of people. Preferably, they are effected without the individual decisions of the beneficiaries each time a measure is to be carried out. Thus, the treatment of public sewage for reduction of spread of disease has often required only the votes of elected representatives of people in a community to be effected and to provide protection for years afterward. Similarly, former Surgeon General Thomas Parran's persuasion of major baking corporations to add vitamin supplements to their bread dough, and earlier programs oriented toward the iodizing of table salt, have provided automatic protection to the consuming public. Extremely effective measures of the same kind were the draining and treating of swamps to reduce breeding places for malaria-carrying mosquitos. All of these measures required decisions only by the representatives of the affected individuals. Moreover, in most cases, decision was needed just once. All of this made such public health innovations comparatively easy to introduce.

A large class of measures, however, does involve the decisions of individuals, and with these the problems are much magnified. The problems are numerous, such as: persuading individuals to have preventive physical and dental examinations at regular intervals; persuading them to have their children immunized against the infectious childhood diseases, such as diphtheria, tetanus, poliomyelitis, and small pox; influencing potential smokers not to adopt the habit and current smokers to abandon it; motivating people to correct their dietary habits to reduce obesity. Each of these measures is an innovation to the individual who has not been confronted with it before. Each requires a decision on his part, and in some cases, such as dietary alterations and immunizations requiring boosters, call for repeated decisions. How to get people to make the right decisions for protection of their own health is one of the most substantial problems facing the medical community today. In the case of many diseases, medical knowledge and technology is advanced to the point that prevention may be easily effected. It is not nearly so often true that individuals can be persuaded to apply this knowledge to protect the health of themselves or their families.

As a result, there are outbreaks of diseases for which adequate medical preventives exist. An example of this was the serious epidemic of poliomyelitis in Chicago some years *after* Salk vaccine had been developed, tested, and made available for mass use. The medical knowledge was available for control of this disease, but the sociological knowledge for applying this control to masses of people had not yet been developed.

This sociological knowledge will not be available until considerably more is known about the process of innovation. Once sufficient knowledge is developed, techniques can be devised to apply it to the problems of public health innovation. In the meantime, public health innovation itself is a useful focus for study by sociologists interested not so much in problems of public

health as in this aspect of social change.

So far in this discussion attention has centered upon public health innovation in the densely populated, large societies, such as the United States and countries of Western Europe. Similar problems exist in other cultures as well, and these can serve equally well as testing grounds for hypotheses regarding innovation. Here the anthropologist as well as the sociologist is concerned, and the potential contributions to the public health are even larger in terms of numbers of lives saved because such societies are less advanced than those in the area of Western civilization. The gains possible from the introduction of simple innovations such as pit privies or the boiling of drinking water can provide spectacular reductions in mortality from such infectious diseases as dysentery. In addition, the development of various anthropological tests of hypotheses regarding innovation would buttress relevant sociological knowledge. If either of these disciplines is to develop to the extent of allowing prediction of change, such theoretical knowledge must be generated.

The Innovation Process

Innovation, of course, cuts across the whole medical activity, therapeutic and preventive, as well as all human affairs. One very interesting area of investigation is the subject of innovation of drugs among the medical fraternity. Bernhard Stern has described the resistances encountered by a variety of procedures when they were introduced in the nineteenth century (Stern, 1941). More recently, Katz and Menzel have investigated the practitioner's prestige, training, contacts with extracommunity physicians, knowledge regarding current trends in medicine, and membership and participation in professional organizations as related to whether or not he accepts innovation in medicaments (Menzel & Katz, 1958). Hence innovation can be studied at any juncture in the investigation of the social aspects of medicine. Innovation is, moreover, an especially vital process in the prevention of disease, and one which could bring about the saving of hundreds of thousands of lives with no increase in strictly medical knowledge. For this reason, we discuss it here primarily as it relates to prevention. The sociological study of innovation, aside from its advantages in developing predictive science, offers one of the current best hopes for advance in prevention of disease.

We may define innovation as the introduction of any idea, behavior pattern, or material item new to the individual or group. Thus, the process would include the introduction of new language patterns, ideologies, and tools; it would also include the cessation of use of material items, behavior, or ideas. Sociologists have been mainly concerned with additions to culture, but the changes involved in dropping old elements are also of interest and, in a real sense, are innovations. Probably factors operating in the acceptance and rejection of *accumulative* innovations are similar to those operating in relation to *displacement* innovations.

As Linton dramatically demonstrated, most of the innovations presented to any society for acceptance or rejection are transmitted by diffusion from other societies (Linton, 1936). Perhaps this is somewhat less true in the case of contemporary medical innovations in the United States and Western European cultures than for inventions not deriving from the scientific method. While some significant contributions to Western medicine have come from other cultures—such as the recent introduction of rauwolfia and related compounds—many have been invented within the society.

In some instances, medical inventions are the result of deliberate research planning, particularly as organized by the drug industry. In addition, it appears that they sometimes occur by accident. In either instance, they develop out of the current state of what Ogburn called the culture base (Ogburn, 1928). Inventions are new combinations of elements currently in the culture, or they are combinations of these with basic discoveries which have been developed out of the current equipment in the culture. Inventions, in short, must be developed out of something; very often the inventor-scientist is the individual with the imagination to visualize new relationships in currently existent data or new possibilities for the use of inventions. The scientist hardly needs to be shown the debt any invention owes to the work of individuals who have previously investigated the phenomena involved. Thus Salk's development of a killed virus poliomyelitis vaccine depended very much on the earlier work of Enders in culturing the virus. The motivation for Enders' work, in turn, goes back over one hundred years to the finding that infecting the individual with small amounts of a given agent stimulates formation of protective mechanisms against the disease. This discovery in turn was reinforced by the earlier suggestion that given microorganisms can cause disease (Shryock, 1947).

Even as inventions develop out of the current culture content and from orientations in the society toward investigation, so does the acceptance or rejection of innovations, whether created by invention or transmitted by diffusion. A new item always encounters an existing cultural configuration (Linton, 1936). If it can fit among the items already present without displacing some vital ones, if it can provide an improvement in terms of the pre-existing cultural configuration, if it is compatible with the culture, other things being equal, it may be accepted. Thus, it is a commonplace that societies confronted with Western medicine accept those parts which appear to fit into pre-existing culture and reject those which do not (Paul, 1955).

Frequently aspects of medicine which societies have accepted are treatments for diseases for which they have no remedies of their own. Contact with Westerners usually has meant contact also with new diseases for which the native medicine had no therapies. Western therapies for these diseases have been accepted, even as Western solutions to problems for which the culture already contained remedies were rejected. Kluckhohn has shown that while the Navaho have accepted some modern drugs, they have also rejected some treatments requiring long hospitalization (Kluckhohn & Leighton, 1948). They prefer the big "sing," with visits from friends and relatives and the generous administration of tender loving care, to the impersonal, aseptic, efficient, and often drab and downright depressing atmosphere of many hospitals.

In one South American society many aspects of Western medicine, including hospitalization, were rejected until some mothers received help from Western physicians during childbirth. The efficiency of the new medicine was so dramatically and quickly proven by the greatly reduced infant and maternal mortality rates that this part of Western medicine was accepted at the same time that others were rejected. Thus, where advantages are quickly demonstrable, acceptance is more likely to occur than where they are subtle, require a lengthy period for demonstration, and are abstract rather than concrete. Just as vocabulary is more easily introduced than grammar, and the names of Christian saints and the words of Christian hymns more readily accepted than the abstractions of Christian theology, so it is easier to influence modern Americans to accept chemotherapeutic psychiatry than psychoanalytic treatment.

In the process of actively introducing innovations, it has been suggested that it is easier to introduce a small item, unencumbered by theory, and with no potential for upsetting pre-existing configurations, than it is to introduce a large complex innovation (Kroeber, 1948). Thus, in a Mexican society, the germ theory may not quickly displace the theory of *el ojo* (the evil eye) as an explanation for disease causation (Saunders, 1955). It may, however, be comparatively easy to introduce the idea of using pit privies as an improvement in sewage disposal. Even in this instance of the attempt to introduce a concrete and apparently

simple item, however, difficulty has been encountered. Villagers supplied with cement slabs to use in constructing privies often have used them instead as doorsteps.

Innovation must somehow be made compatible with the pre-existing complexion of the culture. For example, if the society habitually boils water to make tea, and, if the aim of the innovator is to get the members to drink nothing but boiled water, he is more likely to meet success if he prescribes tea to them. The opposite result was obtained in attempts to introduce surgery to the Athabaskan Indians of Alaska (Parran, 1950). This culture holds that (1) if blood is allowed to flow, part of the soul flows away with it, and that (2) if a part of the body is removed, it will provide an enemy with a means of putting a curse on it and thereby on its former owner. In the face of such an ethos it would be safer to attempt to introduce modern medicine by starting with the introduction of drugs, injections for prevention, and the like. Once the Athabaskans begin to see the effectiveness of these means, they might become more hospitable to the idea of surgery.

In an African culture, an attempt was made at prevention by utilizing incomplete knowledge of this culture. The villagers were continually exposed to infestation with parasites through their habit of sitting on the earthen floors of their huts; this brought them into contact with the organisms left there in the feces of the cattle with which they shared their quarters. Attempts were made to persuade the villagers to keep their cattle outside the huts, but these were unsuccessful; the cattle provided needed company for the housewives and were, in a sense, part of the family. Noting that chairs were in use in this group, the innovator had enough chairs shipped to the area to provide for all members. These were distributed but were not used except by the chief's family. Closer investigation revealed that the use of chairs was a prerogative of the chief only; his underlings would not presume to use them.

This example suggests the importance of group pressures in acceptance and rejection. Redfield, Linton, and Herskovits, in their outline suggesting factors in culture change, note the importance of prestige in acceptance of innovations (Redfield, Linton, Herskovits, 1935). If the first accepters have high prestige in the group, the innovation stands a better chance of acceptance than otherwise. If the innovation is thought to be associated with those parts of the population having high prestige in open-class societies where emulation is not prohibited, it is more likely to be accepted. Emilio Willems has described the adoption of the horse-complex by German emigrants to Brazil, a group which in the main clung tenaciously to Germanic ways. Their acceptance of the horse-complex of the gauchos, he suggested, may have been related to the fact that, in the old country, the man on horseback was the landowner, the man of prestige, the man whom many of these immigrants had formerly looked up to as they tilled their fields. When they had an opportunity to adopt a similar role, with practical benefits, they did so (Willems, 1944).

The public health officer interested in introducing an innovation uses this principle when he undertakes to expose his idea to various of the strategically placed groups in the community's power structure (Willie & Notkin, 1958). If he receives a positive reaction from the county medical society, the county supervisors, hospital administrators, the local medical school, the newspapers, and school leaders, he feels justifiably that his innovation may be accepted by the rest of the population.

Complex societies are, by definition, composed of many groups with differing ideologies, including, of course, differing notions about which groups are prestigeful. Innovators concerned with introducing fluoridation have frequently tried to add support to their suggestions by reference to the authority of groups of high prestige, particularly those of physicians and scientists. Their efforts, however, have failed in many communities where there have been large majorities of individuals suspicious of physicians and anti-intellectual to the point of derogating science; these majorities have frequently been mobilized to react negatively to referenda on the question. Thus, at times the fluoridation controversy has stirred intense feelings and has split communities into bitterly opposed parties (Mausner & Mausner, 1955).

Often this kind of division has been along class lines, with persons trained to some degree to appreciate science and intellectual activity aligned for, and the less educated, against fluoridation. Those for fluoridation have used means which they employ commonly in persuading others, i.e., arguments based on logical deduction from carefully gathered facts. The opposition commonly has utilized the means most congenial and effective in their own subculture: appeals to emotion, for instance, that fluoridation is a Communist plot designed to poison the populace and is an infringement of democratic rights. In short, both proponents and opponents have turned to the means of persuasion most effective in their own subculture. Neither approach has had much effect in convincing members of the opposing group of the rightness of any stand.

Numerous communities not only have vetoed fluoridation but have been torn by conflict along pre-existing lines of division. Such has been the response to an issue on which scientific knowledge is as convincing as is generally the case in the field of public health.

The situation is parallel regarding Krebiozen. This is an alleged anticancer drug whose composition has changed constantly, thus making clinical trials difficult to conduct. Tests of its efficacy are unconvincing; they have been conducted without proper control groups under judgment conditions which are not blind and thus unprotected from personal bias. No reputable medical scientist would accept such findings; yet uninformed elements in various communities have been mobilized to inquire why the medical profession has not accepted use of this drug. In this case, persons having the same characteristics as those against fluoridation have attempted to force the introduction of an innovation which persons favoring fluoridation reject. The means of persuasion are as before: The rejecters use reason and rigorously obtained scientific data, and the accepters employ such emotional suggestions as that organized medicine is selfishly responsible for keeping the drug out of the hands of practitioners. The fact that patients would surely beat a path to the door of a physician with a "cure" for cancer, if such a unitary solution could be found, the fact that any physician would sacrifice much if he could have a drug which would save his patients from death, does not figure in the calculations of the accepter groups. On the other hand, the immunity to logical appeals of the pro-Krebiozen group is not easily apparent to those who oppose its use. Further research is obviously required to discover factors responsible for the implacable stands of persons opposing worthwhile health innovations and promoting less useful ones. Certainly, effective contact with information on the characteristics of the innovation has not been achieved in those cases. Their attitude may be a result of lack of familiarity with scientific approaches and a resentment of organized medicine. There is evidence that they conceive organized medicine to be a powerful and affluent monolith, unresponsive to the needs of the society. Those engaged in "selling" Krebiozen have frequently used appeals assuming this.

In some communities, effective contact with some innovations may promote quick acceptance among all subcultures. Thus, for example, acceptance of poliomyelitis vaccine in the 1956 field trials was common in all the subcultures in communities where it was introduced (Francis, Korns, Voigt, Boisen, Hemphill, Napler, & Tolchinsky, 1954). A large proportion of all the various social class, racial, and educational groups accepted the invitation to participate in the field trials. At the same time, there were differences in the extent of participation in the various groups, and it is instructive to compare groups with low as opposed to high participation. In Buffalo, in all but one census tract, participation was higher among Negroes than among whites (Winkelstein & Graham, 1959). Examination by tracts suggests that the racial factor is important even when economic and other tract-specific differences are held constant. This may be related to the greater acquaintance of Negroes with public health activities and routines, for Negroes have accepted other similar public health innovations as well (Anderson, 1952; Burke, Schenck & Thrash, 1949). Immunization was administered through the schools in these trials, but it may have been that the familiarity of Negroes with public health clinics and their routines (studies show that a larger percentage of Negroes than of whites receive their medical care from such clinics [National Health Survey, 1960]) made the shots, given under similar conditions, more acceptable to them.

In addition to racial variations, social class differences were found to be significant. Thus participation was greater among persons of high socioeconomic status, in both the Buffalo total population study and a sampling of 1,100 persons in 10 states (Francis et al., 1954). The finding in Buffalo was the same for students in both public and parochial schools. The educational advantage of the upper classes may have been partially responsible for the relationship, although increases in participation with increases in education occurred only in the upper half of the socioeconomic continuum (Winkelstein & Graham, 1959). It is possible that the greater contact with scientific procedures and knowledge associated with higher education may have had some effect in increasing participation by these classes, just as familiarity with clinic procedures may have influenced acceptance by the Negro population. Clausen's study of field trials in suburban Washington, and a recent Dade County, Florida, study of vaccine acceptance, showed similar relationships (Clausen, Seidenfeld, Deasy, 1958; Johnson, Jenkins, Patrick, Northcutt, n.d.). One of the most crucial relationships in the Buffalo investigation had to do with previous contacts of these populations with poliomyelitis. It was hypothesized that of the various townships in Erie County, New York, the ones accepting the vaccine in largest degree would be those which had recently experienced the greatest incidence of poliomyelitis. Investigation showed this to be the case. Thus, those townships in which contact with the disease had been greatest and those in whose culture the concept of a vaccine might be most compatible were those which most readily accepted the vaccine (Winkelstein & Graham, 1959).

Contact with the new factor is of importance in the innovation process at two levels. It provides the acquaintance necessary for the decision as to whether or not to accept, and degree of contact is related to opportunity for the innovation to be fitted into the pre-existing cultural configuration. Innovations vary with respect to contact accessibility, and the social structure has an important influence on facilitating or reducing contact. Research on television, for example, has shown that contact is easily obtained; the operation and advantages and disadvantages of television are readily apparent. The card game, canasta, though, introduced at about the same time that television became widely available, was almost never accepted without previous personal instruction in how to play the game. Contact with this innovation depended on acquaintance with someone knowing the game and thus acceptance was much more difficult to achieve than with television. A similar situation obtained for acceptance of health insurance. Although Blue Cross was available to individuals in New Haven, it received much less acceptance by separate individuals than by members of employed groups, educated with regard to the protective features of the insurance and urged as groups to obtain policies. The characteristics of the social structure thus operated to promote differential acceptance of Blue Cross along occupational lines. There are suggestions, in addition, that the reason canasta was more widely accepted in high social classes was that the innovation was introduced to the United States by upper-class travelers who had learned the game in South America. The need for personal instruction and the fact that recreational interaction takes place along social class lines may have produced this social class variation in acceptance (Graham, 1956).

Another example of the way in which social structure can affect such contact is in the differential acceptance of Western innovations by the sexes among the Navaho. Males accepted many more innovations than did females, and Kluckhohn speculates that this may have been because Navaho males had had more extensive contact with white culture than females (Kluckhohn & Leighton, 1948). Research in Pittsburgh has suggested that where contact with an innovation is available in the family, family members are more likely to accept it. Thus chest films for tuberculosis, lung cancer, and other chest diseases were more likely to be obtained by persons living in families where another member had previously obtained a chest film than in families where no such contact was available (Thompson & Pell, 1955).

Various elements of the social structure have been utilized purposefully by the tobacco industry to counteract the effect on the public of acquaintance with scientific findings on the health hazards of cigarette smoking. The result has been that a very large proportion of the population in the United States is confused about these findings, and only a small proportion has stopped smoking (stopping smoking is a displacement innovation in terms of our original definition). Part of this confusion has been wrought by the fact that the tobacco industry annually spends about $150 million to advertise cigarettes via the mass media. As it has become more concerned about sales reductions, the amount spent on advertising has increased (*Fortune,* 1963). When the first findings regarding the high risk of lung cancer associated with smoking in studies on large populations were published in the press in 1954, tobacco sales fell; the industry quickly formed a research committee to search into the question and especially to criticize the findings of reputable scientists. Evidence against cigarette smoking is based on so many well-designed studies, however, that no unbiased scientist can be unimpressed. Nevertheless, scientific research is like art in that the most admirable individual examples are subject to many questions. Newspaper articles carried by the various national press wire services reporting on scientific findings frequently concluded with paragraphs in which the tobacco industry research committee questioned the legitimate project in terms such that the laymen reading the article could only be confused. The fact that tobacco is the economic mainstay in eight southern states whose congressmen are among the most senior and influential in Washington and the fact that a large advertising industry and most units in the mass communications network in the United States benefit hugely from the sums spent by the tobacco industry make for further confusion of the public.

This has been less true in Great Britain where very positive educational efforts have been made; information campaigns have also been carried out in Italy and Sweden (Royal College of Physicians, 1962). This is not to say that a few governmental and other agencies in the United States have not carried out educational activities. The health commissioners of the states of New York and California, the United States Surgeon General, the surgeon general of the United States Air Force, the American College of Chest Surgeons, the American Cancer Society, the American Heart Association, and numerous other scientific and governmental bodies have attempted to make known the dangers of cigarettes, but the voices of these organizations are lost in the welter of advertising by the tobacco industry. Here is an instance where contact with knowledge regarding advantages and disadvantages of an innovation is purposefully obscured by organizations skillfully manipulating various parts of the social structure.

The skill of these organizations is, in the main, empiric, however, and is probably successful more because of the strength of the smoking habit and because of the huge sums of money expended than because of the intellectual application of any scientifically derived principles. The generation of such principles by sociologists could be of great benefit. Research of interest would concern the nature of innovation and, if it were also conducted on health innovations, might obtain measurable improvements in the public health. This could further provide scientific bases to the efforts of health education divisions of health departments.

Research to date on innovation suggests that, although similar processes probably operate in the acceptance or rejection of all innovations, the elements involved differ for innovations of different types. This conclusion grows out of the principle of compatibility outlined above. An innovation, to be accepted, must be compatible with the characteristics of the culture in the group receiving it. It would follow, then, that different innovations are acceptable in different degree by given groups in the population. For example, in the New Haven research described above, Blue Cross was accepted by similar proportions of all social classes, television acceptance varied inversely with class, and canasta varied directly with class (Graham, 1956).

This does not obviate the possibility that research on innovations which have characteristics in common, such as public health innovations, might not reveal common factors in the acceptance of each, knowledge of which could be useful in attempting to introduce new public health items as they develop. Research on compatibility and acceptance in various groups could identify the groups most likely to have high acceptance and rejection potentials for future health innovations. We might predict that upper-class individuals, persons educated to appreciate the scientific approach to problems, persons with past experience with diseases in question, persons oriented to preventive medicine (as shown by previously having regular dental and medical checkups, immunizations, chest films, taking steps to ensure hygiene in their environments, and the like) would be most likely to accept future health innovations. For example, accepters of poliomyelitis vaccine in the 10 state field trial sample had previously more frequently obtained immunizations (Francis et al., 1954). Again, contact with an innovation which is made through membership in and close identification with groups may be effectively used to secure acceptance of compatible innovations. Education through unions, religious organizations, and organizations employing workers could thus be effective, possibly, in introducing health innovations. Efforts directed at groups identified by research as being potential rejectors might be particularly effective in reducing rejection.

The above are only suggestions. It cannot be emphasized too strongly that, aside from the satisfaction of studying innovation for its own sake, research directed at health innovations can be among the most rewarding types of medical investigation. For, as noted earlier, effective medical technology has already been devised for many current problems. The development, by innovation research, of means of introducing this technology, both in Western and non-Western cultures, could result in the saving of much grief and pain and thousands of lives.

THE ORGANIZATION OF THERAPY

In instances where preventive medical knowledge is absent or where sociological knowledge of how to apply medical preventives is not available, the individual may succumb to a pathogen and become ill. Then various facets of the complex structure of organization for therapy may be called into play. As indicated in Table I, therapeutic problems have changed in the last century. Effective preventive measures have made such former scourges as smallpox so rare that the average American neophyte physician has difficulty in diagnosing them. These achievements have been made in part by effective application of bacteriological principles of immunization and hygiene. Applications of bacteriology to the therapeutic process have also been made in the creation of aseptic conditions in surgery, which increased its success astonishingly (Shryock, 1947). Other advances have been made in drug therapy; particularly effective have been the sulfonamides and various antibiotics. In short, in less than one hundred years, therapeutic as well as preventive processes have moved from a state where neither had much effectiveness to that shown in the reductions in death noted in Table I.

Most of the diseases against which these successes have been recorded are acute in nature; their duration is short and dramatic. The chronic diseases, cancer and some cardiovascular illness particularly, require long care, frequently involving hospitalization for lengthy periods, and therapy is much less successful than for the acute disorders.

Hospital Functions

The current organization of medical practice has been much affected by the foregoing developments in therapy. Most profound has been the effect on the hospital. Until recently the hospital was a place to go to die, and it continues to be viewed as such by many. Nevertheless, the recent success of the hospital is demonstrated on every hand, for example, with almost every birth experienced by women in the urban United States. As a result, the public attitude has turned from an extreme distrust of physicians and hospitals to a reliance on medicine that makes national drives for funds to combat a host of diseases, as a rule, successful. Hospitals are numerous, and the number of beds available to potential patients is increasing yearly. Hospitals are now used as the setting for many procedures formerly carried out in the home or not carried out at all. Besides therapeutic successes, other factors related to hospital functions and interactions between the hospital and its clients are responsible for these developments.

An important function of the hospital from the point of view of potential patients is the provision of emergency care. This service can be overlooked in the emphasis upon the growing role of hospitals in providing care for chronic illness. Emergency care depends upon speedy provision of facilities, and this is available only where there is fast transportation and some concentration of potential patients around the hospital. It is perhaps trite to cite the growth of urbanism and fast transportation in the United States as factors important in fostering the growth of hospitals; they have had profound influences on almost every aspect of the social structure. Nevertheless, their importance may have been lost upon planners who, in establishing hospitals under the Hill-Burton Act in rural areas, have done so merely on the basis of providing so many hospital beds per one thousand population. The lack of success and closing of some of these hospitals are probably related to the fact that in some rural areas there is neither concentration of population nor transportation speedy and cheap enough to make the hospital effective.

Also influential in the growth of hospitals are some aspects of relationships between hospitals and their important functionaries, the physicians. The hospital provides a ready aseptic setting. The obstetrician of the turn of the century would bring one or two vans of equipment to the patient's home for a delivery; he now needs only to bring the patient to the equipment. The hospital also centralizes needed equipment which is so large, complex, and expensive that no one physician could provide it for himself. Examples are huge X-ray machines, operating-room and after-care paraphernalia, and

numerous laboratory services. In addition, the hospital centralizes resources which are too rarely needed for the individual physician to have constantly available but which may be life-saving to one patient. Examples are little-used but sometimes very necessary drugs and rare blood types. The centralization factor is so important that, other things being equal, the patient in a large hospital which can afford to centralize more rare, expensive, and bulky items, has access to more therapeutic resources and presumably has a better chance of recovery than does the patient in a small hospital. Hospitals thus provide settings in which the physician can most easily provide the best care for his patient; this has been a big spur to the increase in their number.

Other conveniences provided by the hospital to the physician and parenthetically to his patient, arise from the centralization of patients in the hospital, which enables the practitioner to treat many more persons on a given day than he could by extensive home visits. The hospital also furnishes a centralization of physicians of various specialties, and physicians are often quick to take advantage of the resulting opportunities for consultation. Finally, the concentration of patients and of physicians of various specialties makes the hospital a valuable teaching ground. Traditionally, medical training was carried out through a master-apprentice relationship. The hospital now allows apprentices to group together and learn from each other; it allows them to observe the techniques of a variety of physicians; it allows them to see various kinds of patients in their training years, and to observe certain illnesses which they otherwise might not see during many years of practice (Becker, Geer, Hughes, & Strauss, 1961). This function of the hospital has been especially important in the last twenty years, a period of much increased formalized training for specialization. In a two- or three-year residency period, a young physician can make rich acquaintanceship with rare conditions, and these experiences can serve as a basis for later practice and continuing development throughout the rest of his career.

Organization and Statuses in the Hospital

In providing these various functions, the hospital has developed to the point where it is a community in itself. In addition to obvious departmentalization along medical specialty lines, such as medicine, surgery, gynecology, psychiatry, and pediatrics, there is a host of other sections providing important services to all of the aforementioned departments: nursing, housekeeping, laundry, nutrition, maintenance, and records. Although hospitals were formerly run primarily by physician-administrators, as they have grown ,and developed bureaucratic character, professional "lay" administrators have come into being, complete with graduate degrees to justify their new "professional" status. As many other occupational groups have done, hospital administrators often seek to professionalize their status by creating various ranks within it and by setting up educational and other qualifications (which to others may seem unnecessary) to ensure the quality of performance within the group.

The service departments are usually closely organized under the central administration of the hospital, but most of them feel the pressure of more than one line of authority—they must also respond to the demands of the medical specialty departments (H. L. Smith, 1958). The various medical specialty departments are operated by individuals who have traditionally been independent and who jealously guard against any infringement on this independence even though they are organized into the hospital structure (Wessen, 1958). Medical specialists are particularly defensive with respect to the lay administrator. Susser and Watson have suggested for this reason that the hospital is acephalous; certainly it is potentially so, for each department head is an authority almost unto himself as far as his department

is concerned (Susser & Watson, 1962). In the United States, his title often is Chief, and not without reason. Underlings in the department, especially full-time ones, are definitely subordinate, and lines of authority are strictly observed. Static battle lines separate the various departments in their competition for scarce resources. Nevertheless, since the average physician is dedicated to the welfare of patients, critics of the profession notwithstanding, cooperation is engendered. Furthermore, intradepartmental protocol and respect for lines of authority are reflected in deference often shown by department chiefs to the chief of medicine, chief of surgery, or M.D.-administrator. Authority is much more highly recognized in this profession than, say, in the academic milieu.

Similarly, lines of authority are clearly defined for nurses in the hospital. The hospital's acephaly, or more accurately, multicephaly, is, however, one source of potential friction. The nursing structure is headed by a chief, like other departments, but nurses are assigned to given floors or services where they are expected to take at least some of their orders from physicians attending the patients in these areas. A third source of demands on the nurse is the patient. Therefore, conflicts may ensue among the demands on nurses from these various sources. It is the administrators and physicians, however, with whom the nurse carries on a continuing relationship, and, within limits imposed by good medical care, it is they whom she is most anxious to please.

Perhaps for this reason as well as for many others, Koos (1955) suggests, patients often conceive of hospitals as lonely places. Activity around them is ceaseless from early morning until late at night, but most of it does not involve their own interaction. Attention is fixed on physical rather than social needs, and the focal individual to the patient, his physican, frequently spends only seconds even on these. A number of writers have noted that the patient often feels his environment to be an impersonal one which he cannot control, yet one which he must admit is very important to his well-being.

So little time is spent by hospital professionals in orienting the patient socially that in hospital situations where the patient spends more than a few days, and where he has contact with other patients because he is ambulatory or is in a ward with others, his orientation to hospital routines and expectations is accomplished more by other patients than by the professional staff. The extent to which this orientation differs from that which is conceived as functional by the professional staff can be a source of conflict within the hospital. Regardless of the frustration encountered by the patient in an environment which occasionally seems to be run for everyone's convenience but his own, if he stays long enough, Coser (1960) reports, he finds it a home-away-from-home. The long-term patient develops patterns of interaction which become familiar and functional to him and needs to do very little for himself. These circumstances can make termination of hospitalization as difficult for him as the original assimilation.

The Physician

The focus of activity in the hospital is the patient; yet because the organization is structured to serve him by means designated by the physician, the latter is as important to the continuation of the structure as the patient. Medical care, after all, can be administered on a patient-physician basis through clinic or office, though to be sure not as effectively as in the hospital. The physician is the key individual.

In the extrahospital culture, too, the physician has a unique status. He acts in a specialty function, but he is not otherwise important in the political or economic life of the community. Need for his services is ordinarily not urgent, but occasionally he is needed as individuals in no other status. He deals in life and death, and his prestige in the community devolves partly from this.

Other sources of the physician's high prestige in the United States include the fact that in the early life of the country, physicians were, with the clergy, one of the major educated groups. The economic power deriving from their work, the tradition of well-being associated with this status, their recruitment from the upper classes, all have combined to maintain high prestige for physicians. Organized efforts by the American Medical Association, which receives generous support from most but not all practicing physicians, have buttressed the physician's economic position in the national community and have sought to protect the professional image.

Even though the physician is a highly prestigeful member of the community (North & Hatt, 1949), he is still criticized occasionally as not justifiably occupying a status involving high prestige and economic rewards. It is probable, however, that, in the minds of most members of the society, the physician will continue to have high prestige. This may in part result from characteristics of the profession which are understood but often not expressed by laymen or even by its members. First are the obvious unattractive features of long, expensive, frustrating, and arduous training, and the burdensome hours of practice, in excess of the working day of many other statuses in the community. In addition, the physician does work which emotionally is very taxing: He is responsible for death as well as for life, and his personal mechanisms for dealing with this responsibility are never perfect. Many laymen hesitate even to visit hospitals because of the aura of fear and distaste attaching to them. The physician not only uses the hospital as his major locus of activity, but he is ultimately responsible for what goes on there. Furthermore, the physician must sublimate his aversion to the aesthetically unattractive features of dealing with the bodily functions of his normal patients and, even more, of his ill ones.

Physicians generally are recruited from the upper classes (Kendall & Merton, 1958).

Only a relatively small percentage have fathers who are blue-collar workers. Because of the long preparation required, upper-class derivation is to be expected. The physician ordinarily must secure a bachelor's degree and undergo four years of medical school, the first two consisting of basic science and its medical applications and the last two of experience in dealing with patients in various services of the teaching hospital (Becker et al., 1961). This is expensive training; medical school tuition is often higher than that in other schools in the university. Following medical school, at least one year of internship is required, during which the neophyte usually must depend upon some source of income other than present earnings. A large percentage of medical students continue training beyond internship and into residency in a specialty, which requires several more years of experience with relatively little income deriving from the activity. It is mainly in the upper classes that the parents' income is sufficient for such training and that motivation for postponement of economic and reproductive activity is strongly supplied.

Medical education is expensive not only to the student and his family. It involves a lavish use of professional personnel in the first two basic science years, and even more so in the clinical years when the medical student is in the metaphase of becoming a physician. Multiple instructors are often used in single courses in the first two years, and the student has intimate contact with his teachers in dealing with patients thereafter. His is a technical education, and his teachers are earnest in their desire to turn him into the best therapist possible.

The curriculum is crowded; students are pushed to the limits of their abilities, which because of selective recruitment are often considerable. The students are unusually bright individuals, and, contrary to the case in the average graduate school where a relatively small percentage of scholars finish their work to obtain the Ph.D. or Sc.D., M.D. students go through the training period in a group, taking classes together, and, for the most part, obtaining the M.D. together. The course is arduous, but the number failing to finish is much smaller than in the graduate school. In all but a few medical schools, the curriculum is dominated by subject matter required for application in therapy. Little information is imparted concerning the process of acquiring this knowledge; the procedures and spirit of scientific inquiry are, except in a few schools, missing from this training; students are trained to use scientifically derived facts, and the overloaded, application-oriented curriculum allows little opportunity for thinking along lines of scientific inquiry.

Among the better students who ultimately go on to specialize, there may be a reawakening of interest in scientific inquiry which they may have experienced in their undergraduate years. Specialization upon a broad general base of training makes it possible to encompass the huge amount of knowledge accumulated in most specialties and to leave perhaps some time for interest in how the knowledge is gathered, in hypotheses which require further testing, and in inconsistencies among scientifically derived findings.

Medical Specialization

The nonmedical individual may grasp an impression of the amount of growth of medical knowledge by referring to the list of journals subscribed to by the library of an average medical school. No individual could become intimately acquainted with all the developments reported in the scores of journals dealing with various aspects of medicine. Specialization is a way out of this dilemma. By specializing, the student-physician can begin to learn much about a single subject, can feel secure in his field. Specialization has been criticised for its failure to direct treatment to the "whole patient," and because some specialists have not recognized signs in patients that would mean something crucial to generalists. Specialization has also been said to result in impersonalization of treatment—a lack of understanding from first hand of the patient's and his family's history in the way that the "family doctor" once understood it. Although specialization has been criticised on all these grounds, it has continued to proliferate. The better students, and those who can afford the extra time and money required for the additional training, usually elect to specialize. Thus, in spite of criticism, the trend will probably continue and enlarge.

New specialties develop unceasingly. Within general surgery, specialties have developed in gastrointestinal surgery, chest surgery, neurosurgery, and others. Within internal medicine, the specialties of cardiology and endocrinology have developed. As knowledge has increased in the field, anaesthesiology has evolved from an activity carried on by nurses to one demanding specialization by a physician (Lortie, 1958). Specialization makes it possible for one individual to be a good physician in one field rather than a poor physician practicing general medicine.

It is axiomatic in sociology that a specialist cannot operate without other specialists. This poses additional problems for the organization of medical practice. Where the patient has an ill-defined complaint of unrecognized origin, he may find it necessary to make contact with specialist after specialist, often enduring the same tests and diagnostic procedures many times before a solution to his problem is found. This costs him much time and money, and the practitioner much time. In a few instances, solutions have been developed in the shape of clinics, such as the Mayo Clinic, where a number of specialists in various fields are grouped together; here the patient can easily seek the help of the individual he needs, for communication between him and the physicians and the physicians among themselves is maximized. Other structures having similar functions have also been developed, and it is probable that more will evolve in the future.

The Organization of Therapeutic Relationships

Medical practice in the United States and many Western countries has traditionally been organized on the basis of solo practice. Under this scheme, one physician deals with patients as individuals. He gradually develops his practice as he grows up professionally, he inherits a practice from a relative, or he buys a practice from a retiring physician. He is paid by the patient for each service rendered. Thus, he has the problems of the small business man—of securing enough income to support himself, charging for service differentially according to the patients' incomes, collecting payment, making payments on expensive equipment, maintaining an office, employing various paramedical personnel, making proper investments of surplus funds, and the like (Albright, 1958). At the same time, his dedication to the principles of practice leads him to furnish care to people unable to pay.

In a pattern of more recent development, an occasional physician already in practice offers a younger man a partnership with him. The two split costs and income, with the senior man taking the larger share. They also split the schedule of practice, allowing one individual to take certain days and evenings off while the other is on call. The result is more income per physician, usually, and certainly more leisure (Medical Economics, 1956). From the patient's point of view, it means the greater accessibility of a physician. With two practicing most of the time, the patient does not need to wait as long for attention. On the other hand, he often sees first one physician and then the other for a given complaint, making necessary some duplication in history-taking, examination, and other procedures. Where patient and partnership are associated over a period of time, these drawbacks to the organization are lessened.

Modern practice has seen a continuation of solo practice. This may still be the most frequent form. Nevertheless, more and more partnerships have been formed, and some physicians have gone beyond this to establish group practices. Frequently such groups consist of a number of general practitioners, plus specialists in the more popular fields such as obstetrics, pediatrics, and internal medicine, and the group maintains access to consultants in less used fields such as radiology, psychiatry, surgery, and proctology. This kind of organization has the same advantages and disadvantages as partnership practice. The physicians generally make more money, have more free time to count on, but they also provide less continuity of practice from the patient's point of view. The resulting potential for increased impersonality and fragmentation of the patient's care, however, may be offset by the additional advantages.

Typically, in group practice, the patient selects for himself the general practitioner in the group who seems to appeal to him. He consults him initially for all complaints, and, where necessary, the GP can refer the patient to the appropriate specialist in his group. Meanwhile, most of the testing done on the patient can be conducted in the group's headquarters, the results are accessible to all physicians concerned, and the patient is billed only once for them. Because several physicians are available to use and pay for diagnostic and therapeutic facilities, several kinds otherwise available only in hospitals or separate laboratories can be supported in the group. Because communication is easy, discussion of patients' problems among the physicians can take place with less delay and lost time. Freidson has reported that some patients feel that group practice presents an unwanted clinic atmosphere, impersonalization, and long waits for care (Freidson, 1961). It is quite possible, however, that as the patient becomes more acquainted with his group, the most serious charge, that of impersonalization, will disappear. It is also quite possible that this form of practice will increase: Its positive advantages in income, leisure, and convenience for the practitioner, and of effective referral and availability of facilities for the patient, are solutions to very pressing problems.

Payment for Care

As noted above, traditional methods of payment for medical care involved a fee-for-service to the physician or the hospital. This form has never been entirely satisfactory. The need for a solution became especially acute during the depression of the 1930's. At this time, a solution, which is traditional in Western free-enterprise, laissez faire thinking, was devised. It was based on spreading of risk of hospitalization through insurance on a community basis, through employee contributions, and was first put into practice by a group of teachers in Texas. Since then the idea has spread throughout the United States, and a very large proportion of the population is now covered for hospitalization costs (O. W. Anderson, 1954). The insurance mechanism was later applied to surgical costs, which were covered by similar plans. Both nonprofit organizations such as Blue Cross and Blue Shield and commercial companies have gone into the field. The extreme critic of such types of insurance argues as he may about any insurance: that it spreads the risk, that the individual does not pay for his own care when he needs it, and that he pays for the care of others even though he rarely uses the service himself. Research on the utilization of health insurance suggests that a very small percentage of the subscribers use a very large percentage of the service, and, to this extent, such critics are correct (Densen, Shapiro & Einhorn, 1959). Nevertheless, the constant reminder that the currently healthy individual may be next to face the devastating costs of today's medical care is incentive enough to make this insurance quite popular.

The drawbacks of health insurance, however, are, first, that a significant though small

proportion of the population is not covered
(O. W. Anderson, 1954). The fact that
most people subscribe through employees'
organizations means that lone workers or
those who do not work are not enrolled.
Farmers, the unskilled, the sporadically employed, and other unorganized groups are
not covered. Second, not all medical needs
are supplied by insurance. The costs of
drugs, office calls, dental services, and
opthalmological services are frequently not
included. In addition, utilization of the service often requires at least some payment to
physicians on a fee-for-service basis, which
some individuals cannot afford. The fact
that coverage is geared mainly to provide
for costs related to hospitalization leads to
lack of provision for preventive services and
for small complaints that if uncared for
may eventually lead to expensive ailments.
One solution to this problem was originated
by then Mayor Fiorello La Guardia for employees of the City of New York. Under
this plan, the employees had subscriptions
in what is called the Health Insurance Plan
of Greater New York (Baehr, 1953). (This
form of organization has been extended to
many other occupational groups in that city
and has been applied in California, as well.)
Under this scheme, the family is covered by
the conventional Blue Cross-Blue Shield
policies, and, in addition, has a subscription
to HIP. The HIP pays a fee to a physicians'
group practice organization, such as those
described above. The family can then visit
the group headquarters, select a general
practitioner, and receive all care in the subscription period without further payment.
Under such a plan, it is in the group's
interest to practice the best preventive medicine possible. This presumably reduces the
number of complaints that become major
and so require a large portion of the group's
services. From the patient's point of view,
the advantages are obvious: For a capita fee,
usually paid by his union or employer, he
has easy access to as much preventive and
therapeutic service as he needs or thinks
he needs.

Distribution of Medical Care

It hardly can be claimed, as do some
organized medical groups, that all of the
people—even in the prosperous United
States—now have adequate medical care.
National studies show that rural people,
Negroes, the less educated, the poorer, the
migrant workers, the aged, and the unemployed do not have access to as much medical care as do the rest of the population
(National Health Survey, 1960). Old age
is a time when illness is most likely to occur and when economic resources usually
are least able to provide for it. According
to the democratic ethic, in basic equipment,
such as minimum education, political advantage, and the like, the population should
be equal. It is repugnant to such an ethic
that in a matter of life and death—in medical care—even a small proportion of the
population should receive less than adequate
protection. Nevertheless, furnishing such
care often requires the purchase of expensive drugs, machinery, and the services of individuals who have sacrificed much to train
themselves and have economic needs similar
to those of other groups in the population.
Medical care cannot be provided free, even
under a socialistic organization. Some part
of the national resources must be devoted to
it, and while the costs may be met through
a variety of means, they must be met.

An adequate system of medical care
should: provide for all people; respect traditional patient-physician relationships including confidentiality and the right to select or
reject each other; provide for all aspects of
care, including house, office, and hospital
calls, drugs, prostheses, laboratory service,
and hospital care. It should also be organized
so as not to interfere with the practice of
medicine through increasing the physician's
paper work and administrative chores. It
should provide preventive care and be organized so as to encourage this. It must be
attractive enough in conditions of practice
and remuneration to draw the very intelligent and unusually energetic persons who

are needed for the practice of medicine. It should extend the use of controls organized by the professionals themselves, such as the tumor conferences current in hospitals today, to provide the best care it is possible to render. Training facilities to keep graduated physicians abreast of developments in their fields also should be developed in local medical schools and time to attend such seminars should be provided to the physicians. It is possible that perhaps through extension of the medical insurance concept these modes of medical practice could be carried out in a free enterprise milieu without disturbing traditional relationships. It is not possible to do this without organization, and in organization the individual gives up some of his freedom. Nevertheless, the advantages to be gained from organization in terms of better incomes to physicians and better diagnostic and therapeutic services have been demonstrated ever since the hospital began to proliferate. Physicians are aware of these and are enjoying many of them in the group practices of today.

The advantages of reorganization may outweigh the disadvantages. It is possible that in the United States, the distribution of the medical care of the future may build upon the mechanisms currently in the culture: group practice, the hospital, and the medical insurance concept.

REFERENCES

Abbott, A. C. Simple goitre. *Canad. Med. Ass. J.*, 1932, 27, 236–239.

Affifi, M. A. *Bilharzial cancer.* London: Lewis, 1948.

Albright, R. Economics of doctor-patient relations. In E. G. Jaco (Ed.), *Patients, physicians and illness.* Glencoe, Ill.: Free Press, 1958. Pp. 506–516.

Anderson, O. W. *National family survey of medical costs and voluntary health insurance.* New York: Health Information Foundation Preliminary Report, January, 1954.

Anderson, R. J. Rationale and results. Community-wide chest x-ray survey. *Publ. Hlth Serv. Pub.*, 1952, 222, 7.

Ast, D. B., Smith, D. J., Wachs, B., & Cantwell, K. T. Newburgh-Kingston caries—fluorine study. XIV. Combined clinical and roentgenographic dental findings after ten years of fluorine experience. *J. Amer. Dent. Ass.*, March, 1956, 52, 314–325.

Auerbach, O., Stout, A. P., Hammond, E. C., & Garfinkel, L. Changes in bronchial epithelium in relation to cigarette smoking and in relation to lung cancer. *New Eng. J. Med.*, August, 1961, 265, 253–267.

Baehr, G. H. I. P.—an alternative to national compulsory medical insurance. *Conn. State Med. J.*, 1953, 17(1), 29–35.

Bales, R. F. Attitudes towards drinking in the Irish culture. In D. J. Pittman and C. R. Snyder (Eds.), *Society, culture and drinking patterns.* New York: Wiley, 1962. Pp. 167–187.

Beadenkopf, W. Personal communication, 1963.

Becker, H. S., Geer, Blanche, Hughes, E. V., & Strauss, A. L. *Boys in white: Student culture in medical school.* Chicago: Univer. of Chicago Press, 1961.

Berkson, J., & Comfort, M. The incidence of development of cancer in persons with achlorhydria. *J. nat. Cancer Inst.*, 1953, 13, 1087.

Bock, F. G., Moore, G. E., Dowd, J. E., & Clark, P. C. Carcinogenic activity of cigarette smoke condensate. *J. Amer. Med. Ass.*, August, 1962, 181(8), 668–672.

Boe, J., Hummerfelt, S., & Wedevang, F. *The blood pressure in a population.* Bergen: A. S. John Griegs Boktrykkeri, 1956.

Breslow, L., & Buell, P. Mortality from coronary heart disease and physical activity of working. *J. chron. Dis.*, 1960, 11, 421–444.

Burke, M. H., Schenck, H. C., & Thrash, J. A. Tuberculosis studies in Muscogee County, Georgia. II. X-ray findings in a community-wide survey and its coverage as determined by a population census. *Publ. Hlth Rep.*, 1949, 64, 263ff.

Clausen, J., Seidenfeld, M., & Deasy, Leila. Parent attitudes toward participation of their children in polio vaccine trials. In E. G. Jaco (Ed.), *Patients, physicians and illness.* Glencoe, Ill.: Free Press, 1958. Pp. 119–129.

Clemmesen, J., & Nielsen, A. Social distribution of cancer in Copenhagen, 1943–1947. *Brit. J. Cancer*, 1951, 5, 159–171.

Cobb, S., Warren, J., Merchant, W. R., & Thompson, D. J. An estimate of the prevalence of rheumatoid arthritis. *J. chron. Dis.*, 1957, 5(6), 636–643.

Cohart, E. M. Socioeconomic distribution of cancer of female sex organs in New Haven. *Cancer*, 1955, 8, 34–41.

Comfort, M. W., Butsch, W. L., & Eusterman, G. B. Observations on gastric acidity before and after development of carcinoma of the stomach. *Amer. J. Dig. Dis. Nutrit.* 1937–1938, 4, 673–681.

Corriell, L. L., Schaeffer, K., Felton, H. M., Fernandez-Moran, H., & Bierly, M. Z. A serologic and clinical survey of poliomyelitis in Caracas, Venezuela, and Galveston, Texas. *Amer. J. publ. Hlth*, 1956, 46, 1431–1438.

Coser, Rose Laub. A home away from home. In Dorian Apple (Ed.), *Sociological studies of health and sickness.* New York: McGraw, 1960. Pp. 154–172.

Densen, P. M., Shapiro, S., & Einhorn, Marilyn. Concerning high and low utilizers of service in a medical care plan, and the persistence of utilization levels over a three year period. *Milbank mem. Fund Quart.*, 1959, 37 (3), 217–250.

Diehl, H. D., & Lees, M. D. Variability of blood pressure, II. *Arch. Int. Med.*, February, 1929, 44, 229–237.

Doll, R., & Hill, A. B. Lung cancer and other causes of death in relation to smoking: Second report on mortality of British doctors. *Brit. med. J.*, 1956, 2, 1071–1101.

Dorn, H. F. Cancer morbidity survey: A tool for testing theories of cancer etiology. Paper read at Amer. Publ. Hlth Ass., Buffalo, October 14, 1954.

Dorn, H. F. Smoking and cancer. Social Statistics Section Proceedings, Amer. Stat. Ass., 1958, Chicago.

Dorn, H. F. Tobacco consumption and mortality from cancer and other diseases. *Publ. Hlth Rep.*, 1959, 74(7), 581–593.

Doyle, J. T., Heslin, A. S., Hilleboe, H. E., Formel, P. F., & Korns, R. E. A progressive study of degenerative cardiovascular diseases in Albany. *Amer. J. Publ. Hlth*, 1957, 47 (4), suppl., 25–32.

Embattled tobacco's new strategy. *Fortune*, January, 1963, 67, 100–131.

Faris, R. E. L., & Dunham, H. W. *Mental disorders in urban areas.* Chicago: Univer. of Chicago Press, 1939.

Francis, T., Korns, R. F., Voigt, R. F., Boisen, M., Hemphill, F. M., Napler, J. A., & Tolchinsky, E. An evaluation of the 1954 poliomyelitis vaccine field trials. *Amer. J. publ. Hlth*, 1954, 44, 1526–1536.

Freidson, E. The organization of medical practice and patient behavior. *Amer. J. publ. Hlth*, 1961, 51 (1), 43–52.

Gentry, J. T., Parkhurst, Elizabeth, & Gulin, G. V., Jr. An epidemiological study of congenital malformations in New York State. *Amer. J. publ. Hlth*, 1959, 49 (4), 1–22.

Graham, S. Class and conservatism in the adoption of innovations. *Human Relat.*, 1956, 9 (1), 91–100.

Graham, S. Ethnic background and illness in a Pennsylvania county. *Soc. Probs*, 1956, 4 (1), 76–82.

Graham, S. Social factors in the epidemiology of cancer at various sites. *Ann. New York Acad. Sci.*, December, 1960, 84(17), 807–815.

Graham, S. unpublished data, Buffalo, 1962.

Graham, S., & Levin, M. L. unpublished data, Buffalo, 1962.

Graham, S., Levin, M. L., & Lilienfeld, A. M. The socioeconomic distribution of cancer of various sites in Buffalo, N.Y., 1948–1952. *Cancer*, 1960, 13(1), 180–191.

Graham, S., Levin, M. L., Lilienfeld, A. M., & Sheehe, P. Ethnic derivation as related to cancer at various sites. *Cancer*, 1963, 16 (1), 13–27.

Graham, S., & Lilienfeld, A. M. Genetic studies of gastric cancer in humans: An appraisal. *Cancer*, 1958, 11 (5), 945–958.

Haddon, W. Jr., Ellison, A. E., & Carroll, R. E. Skiing injuries: Epidemiological studies. *Publ. Hlth Rep.*, 1962, 77(11), 975–985.

Haenszel, W. Cancer mortality among the foreign-born in the United States. *J. nat. Cancer Inst.*, 1961, 26 (1), 37–132.(a)

Haenszel, W. Incidence of and mortality from stomach cancer in the United States. *Acta Unio Int. Contra Cancrum*, 1961, 17 (3), 347–364. (b)

Haggard, H. W., & Jellinek, E. M. *Alcohol explored.* New York: Doubleday, 1942.

Hammon, W. McD. Comparative epidemiology of poliomyelitis in certain California cities. *Amer. J. publ. Hlth*, 1947, 37, 1545–1558.

Hammond, E. C. Smoking and cancer: Consideration of some statistical aspects. Paper presented at the Annual Meeting of the American Statistical Association, New York City, December 27, 1955.

Hammond, E. C. The effects of smoking. *Scient. Amer.*, 1962, **207** (1), 39–51.

Hammond, E. C., & Horn, D. Smoking and death rates—report on forty-four months of follow-up of 187,783 men. *J. Amer. Med. Ass.*, 1958, **166**, 1159–1308.

Hollingshead, A. B. Some issues in the epidemiology of schizophrenia. *Amer. soc. Rev.*, 1961, **26** (1), 5–13.

Hollingshead, A. B., & Redlich, F. C. Social stratification and psychiatric disorders. *Amer. sociol. Rev.*, April, 1953, **18**, 163–169.

Hollingshead, A. B., & Redlich, F. C. Schizophrenia and the social structure. *Amer. J. Psychiat.*, 1954, **110** (9), 695–701.

Horn, D., Courts, F. A., Taylor, R. M., & Solomon, E. S. Cigarette smoking among high school students. *Amer. J. publ. Hlth*, 1959, 49(11), 1497–1511.

How much are physicians earning? *Med. Econ.*, October, 1956, 116–117.

Johnson, A. L., Jenkins, C. D., Patrick, R., & Northcutt, T. J., Jr. Epidemiology of polio vaccine acceptance. *Florida State Board of Hlth, Monogr.*, No. 3.

Kannel, W. B., Dawber, T. R., Kagen, A., Revotskie, N., & Stokes, J., III. Factors of risk in the development of coronary heart disease—6-year follow up experience: The Framingham study. *Ann. int. Med.*, 1961, **55**, 33–50.

Kendall, Patricia L., & Merton, R. K. Medical education as a social process. In E. G. Jaco (Ed.), *Patients, physicians and illness*. Glencoe, Ill.: Free Press, 1958. Pp. 321–350.

Kinsey, V. E., & Hemphill, F. M. Etiology of retrolental fibroplasia and preliminary report of cooperative study of retrolental fibroplasia. *Trans. Amer. Acad. Opthol. & Otolaryng.*, January–February, 1955, **59**, 15–24.

Kluckhohn, C., & Leighton, Dorothea. *The Navaho*. Cambridge, Mass.: Harvard Univer. Press, 1948.

Koos, E. L. Metropolis—what city people think of their medical services. *Amer. J. Publ. Hlth*, 1955, **45** (12), 1551–1557.

Kraus, A. S., Levin, M. L., & Gerhardt, P. R. A study of occupational associations with gastric cancer. *Amer. J. Publ. Hlth*, 1957, 47(8), 961–970.

Kroeber, A. L. *Anthropology*. New York: Harcourt, 1948.

Levin, M. L. Smoking and cancer: Retrospective studies and epidemiological evaluation. In G. James and T. Rosenthal (Eds.), *Tobacco and health*. Springfield, Ill.: Charles C. Thomas, 1962. Pp. 163–171.

Levin, M. L., Goldstein, H., & Gerhardt, P. Cancer and tobacco smoking. *J. Amer. Med. Ass.*, May 27, 1950, **143**, 336–338.

Levin, M. L., Haenszel, W., Carroll, B. E., Gerhardt, P. R., Handy, V. E., & Ingraham, S. C., II. Cancer incidence in urban and rural areas of New York State. *J. nat. Cancer Inst.*, 1960, **24** (6), 1243–1257.

Lilienfeld, A. M. Diagnostic and therapeutic x-radiation in an urban population. *Publ. Hlth Rep.*, 1959, 74 (1), 29–36.

Lilienfeld, A. M. Personal communication, 1960.

Lilienfeld, A. M., & Graham, S. Validity of determining circumcision status by questionnaire as related to epidemiological studies of cancer of the cervix. *J. nat. Cancer Inst.*, 1958, **21** (4), 713–720.

Linton, R. *The study of man*. New York: D. Appleton-Century Co., 1936.

Lortie, D. C. Anesthesia: From nurse's work to medical specialty. In E. G. Jaco (Ed.), *Patients, physicians and illness*. Glencoe, Ill.: Free Press, 1958. Pp. 405–412.

McCarroll, J. R., & Haddon, W., Jr. A controlled study of fatal automobile accidents in New York City. *J. chron. Dis.*, 1962, **15** (8), 811–826.

MacMahon, B., & Koller, E. K. Ethnic differences in the incidence of leukemia. *Blood*, 1957, **12** (1), 1–10.

MacMahon, B., Pugh, T. F., & Ipsen, J. *Epidemiologic methods*. Boston: Little, Brown, 1960.

Martland, H. S. The occurrence of malignancy in radioactive persons. *Amer. J. Cancer*, 1931, **15**, 2435–2516.

Mausner, B., & Mausner, Judith. A study of the anti-scientific attitude. *Scient. Amer.*, 1955, **192** (2), 35–39.

May, J. M. *The ecology of human disease*. New York: M. D. Publications, 1958.

Menzel, H., & Katz, E. Social relations and innovation in the medical profession: The epidemiology of a new drug. In E. G. Jaco (Ed.), *Patients, physicians and illness.* Glencoe, Ill.: Free Press, 1958. Pp. 517–528.

National Health Survey. Health statistics: Volume of physician visits, U.S., July 1957–June 1959. *Publ. Hlth Serv. Pub.,* 1960, 584 (B19), 4–5.

New York State Department of Health, Bureau of Cancer Control. *Ann. Rep.,* 1961.

North, C. C., & Hatt, P .K. Jobs and occupations: A popular evaluation. In L. Wilson & W. L. Kolb (Eds.), *Sociological analysis.* New York: Harcourt, 1949. Pp. 464–473.

Ogburn, W. F. *Social change.* New York: Viking, 1928.

Parran, T. Personal communication, 1950.

Pasamanick, B., & Lilienfeld, A. M. Association of maternal and fetal factors with development of mental deficiency. I. Abnormalities in the prenatal and paranatal periods. *J. Amer. Med. Ass.,* September 17, 1955, 159, 155–160.

Pasamanick, B., Rogers, Martha E., & Lilienfeld, A. M. Pregnancy experiences and the development of behavior disorders in children. *Amer. J. Psychiat.,* 1956, 112 (8), 613–618.

Paul, B. D. *Health, culture and community.* New York: Russell Sage, 1955.

Quisenberry, W. B. Sociocultural factors in cancer in Hawaii. *Ann. New York Acad. Sci.,* 1960, 84 (17), 795–806.

Redfield, R., Linton, R., & Herskovits, M. A memorandum for the study of acculturation. *Amer. Anthrop.,* 1935, 38, 149–152.

Rigler, L. G., Kaplan, H. S., & Fink, D. L. Pernicious anemia and the early diagnosis of tumors of the stomach. *J. Amer. med. Ass.,* 1945, 128, 426–432.

Rose, R. J., Personal communication, 1963.

Royal College of Physicians of London. A report of the Royal College of Physicians of London on smoking in relation to cancer of the lung and other diseases. *Smoking & Hlth,* New York: Pitman Publishing Co., 1962.

Sachs, L., & Bat-Miriam, Mariassa. The genetics of Jewish populations: I. Fingerprint patterns in Jewish populations in Israel. *Amer. J. Hum. Genet.,* 1957, 9(2), 117–126.

Saunders, L. *Cultural differences and medical care.* New York: Russell Sage, 1955.

Segi, M., Fujisaku, S., & Kurihara, M. Geographical observations on cancer mortality by selected sites on the basis of standardized death rate. *Gann,* June, 1957, 48, 219–225.

Shryock, R. H. *The development of modern medicine.* New York: Knopf, 1947.

Smith, H. L. Two lines of authority: The hospital's dilemma. In E. G. Jaco (Ed.), *Patients, physicians and illness.* Glencoe, Ill.: Free Press, 1958. Pp. 468–477.

Smith, R. L. Recorded and expected mortality among the Japanese of the United States and Hawaii with special reference to cancer. *J. nat. Cancer Inst.,* 1956, 17, 459–473.

Snyder, C. R. Culture and Jewish sobriety. In D. J. Pittman & C. R. Snyder (Eds.), *Society, culture and drinking patterns.* New York: Wiley, 1962. Pp. 188–225.

Srole, L., Langner, T., Michael, S., Opler, M. K., & Rennie, T. A. C. *Mental health in the metropolis: Midtown Manhattan study.* Vol. I. New York: McGraw, 1962.

Stern, B. J. *Society and medical progress.* Princeton, N.J.: Princeton Univer. Press, 1941.

Straus, R., & Bacon, S. D. *Drinking in college.* New Haven, Conn.: Yale Univer. Press, 1953.

Susser, M. W., & Watson, W. *Sociology in medicine.* London: Oxford Univer. Press, 1962.

Terris, M. Relation of economic status to tuberculosis mortality by age and sex. *Amer. J. publ. Hlth, August,* 1948, 38, 1061–1070.

Thieme, J. C. Western Samoa, unpublished data, 1963.

Thompson, D. J., & Pell, S. Participation in the Allegheny County mass chest x-ray campaign, 1953. *Publ. Hlth Rep.,* 1955, 70(7), 669–680.

Toor, M., Katchalsky, A., Agmon, J., & Allalouf, D. Anthrosclerosis and related factors in immigrants to Israel. *Circulation,* 1960, 12, 265–279.

Tromp, S. W., & Diehl, J. C. A statistical study of the possible relationship between cancer of the stomach and soil. *Brit. J. Cancer,* 1955, 9(3), 349–355.

Wessen, A. B. Hospital ideology and communication between ward personnel. In E. G. Jaco (Ed.), *Patients, physicians and illness*. Glencoe, Ill.: Free Press, 1958. Pp. 448–468.

Willems, E. Acculturation and the horse complex among German-Brazilians. *Amer. Anthrop.* 1944, 46, 153–161.

Willie, C. V., & Notkin, H. Community organization for health: A case study. In E. G. Jaco (Ed.), *Patients physicians and illness*. Glencoe, Ill.: Free Press, 1958. Pp. 148–159.

Winkelstein, W., Jr., & Graham, S. Factors in participation in the 1954 poliomyelitis vaccine field trials, Erie County, New York.

Amer. J. Publ. Hlth, 1959, 49 (11), 1454–1466.

Woolf, C. M. A further study on the familial aspects of carcinoma of the stomach. *Amer. J. hum. Genet.*, 1956, 8 (2), 102–109.

World Health Organization. Malignant neoplasms according to location in selected countries. *Epidemiological and vital statistics Rep.*, 1959, 12, 181–225.

Wynder, E. L., & Mantel, N. Statistical considerations on circumcision and cervical cancer. *Amer. J. Obst. Gynecol.*, 1960, 79 (5), 1026–1030.

CHAPTER 10 Social Effects of Mass Communication

OTTO N. LARSEN

The reader should begin with an awesome fact: All over the world more and more people are spending more and more time in exposure to the media of mass communication. The present task is to inquire into how sociologists have come to grips with the social consequences of this fact. The goal is to review what has been done and to suggest what might be done to enhance understanding of the social effects of mass communication. By mass communication is meant the relatively simultaneous exposure of large heterogeneous audiences to symbols transmitted by impersonal means from an organized source for whom audience members are anonymous. The study of how an individual or even an aggregate of individuals reacts to particular media messages does not necessarily constitute an assessment of social effects. Nor does impact flow automatically from the fact that a given set of symbols has been disseminated. Such propositions become apparent as the research terrain is approached. Efforts by sociologists to map this territory include the social systems analysis of Riley and Riley (1959), the functional reviews by Wright (1959; 1960), and the phenomenistic approach by Klapper

(1960). These works stem from compatible orientations, and they signal growing sociological interest in mass communication. Along with Hovland's (1954) earlier synthesis, they construct a base from which the present review is challenged to build.

FACETS OF COMMUNICATION

The case for sociological concern with communication has long been so compelling that a restatement of it cannot avoid the use of trite phrases. Communication is basic to any social system. Every form of collective action rests on meanings shared through some pattern of communication. Society can exist only because most people's definitions of most important situations coincide at least approximately most of the time. Communication is the means for establishing this consensus. It is the key to the question of how social order can be achieved amid continuing requirements for flexibility and change. Communication is necessary though not sufficient for this condition. This is suggested by an event that took place on the international scene in 1963. The United States and the Soviet Union signed an agreement to establish a "hot line" emergency communication link directly between Washington and Moscow to help reduce the risk of war by accident or miscalculation. The White House statement on the agreement concluded: "This age of fast-moving events requires quick, dependable communications for use in time of emergency. . . . This agreement is a limited but practical step forward in arms control and disarmament. We hope agreement on other more encompassing measures will follow" (New York *Times*, June 21, 1963).

In formulating and testing generalizations about the forms, processes, and consequences of interhuman behavior, sociologists study what happens when two or more persons or groups are in a position to influence one another. Communication is a pivotal concept that enters into this research both as a dependent and as an independent variable. In broad terms, the sociologist is interested in the conditions that give rise to various kinds and degrees of communication, and he is interested in how these kinds and degrees of communication affect the behavior of men and the founding and functioning of social structures. Furthermore, in sociological as well as in common usage, communication refers both to a process and to an end product. Everyone is engaged in acts of communication, but not all of these efforts result in communication. The communicative act involves a transfer of information from one place to another. To communicate is to attempt to establish a "commonness" between two points. For this to happen, messages must be formulated, transmitted over some channel, received, and evaluated. There are three main sources of stimulation for the performers of these acts: (1) They react to each other; (2) they react to past experience; and (3) they react to objects or events in the external common environment. The feedback that the participants get from their own messages and from each other becomes the corrective basis for achieving a greater degree of communication. Communication, thus, refers to the process through which a set of meanings embodied in a message is conveyed in such a way that the meanings received are equivalent to those which the initiator of the message intended.

This identification of elements and processes in communication systems specifies the essentials of communication for sociological purposes. Communication begins with contact between persons, but contact does not necessarily result in communication. There must be a transmission of meanings before communication has taken place. This is achieved through alternate and reciprocal stimulation and response among participants. Any act of communication is then, first of all, an *interact*. Even where media of mass communication are employed, there must be some form of interaction before a degree of communication is achieved or can be assessed.

At one end of a mass communication chain is the source of information, a complex organization, itself a product as well as a potential molder of social forces. At the other end are the receivers of information. Taken as a whole they constitute a "mass"—large numbers of persons coming from all walks of life. But seen in terms of the ways they sense, interpret, and act on information, the audience members, though anonymous to the mass communicator, are embedded in a network of primary and secondary groupings highly relevant for understanding the mass-communicative process (see, e.g., Johnstone, 1959). The source and the audience of mass media material are brought together by impersonal transmission mechanisms, but even the operation of these distribution systems is influenced by social contexts. Clearly, then, sociological elements are involved in all the links of a mass communication chain. Furthermore, since the chain is forged in the culture of a particular society, sociologists can contribute some understanding of its form as well as its function from this broad perspective.

Certain elements of the general definition of mass communication offered in the first paragraph of this chapter underscore some contrasts between the mass and the interpersonal communicative process (for an elaboration of differences see Westley & MacLean, 1955). In the interpersonal case, more sensory channels are usually involved in each communicative act (persons can see, hear, and even touch and smell each other). The result is that direct information and auxiliary cues move rapidly back and forth between persons each of whom is serving both as a sender and a receiver in the communicative act. A nod, a yawn, or a wink may sometimes constitute important feedback to assist or obstruct the emergence of mutual understanding.

In mass communication, the flow of information is largely in one direction. The ratio of output to audience to input from audience is very large. Technology has made it possible for the few to speak directly and almost incessantly to the many. There is also a technology to increase a reverse flow in the form of audience ratings, opinion polls, and marketing research (see, e.g., Lucas & Britt, 1963), but even if this were widely used there would still be an important time lag in the interaction between the mass communicator and the audience. As a result, it is often difficult to determine whether a message has reached a given audience. It is even more onerous to ascertain whether the message has had any effect, direct or indirect (see, e.g., Deutschmann, 1963). Despite these complications, the basic elements in mass and interpersonal communicative acts are closely parallel. In both instances participants encode and transmit messages, select and decode messages, and elicit responses (Schramm, 1963, p. 7). Furthermore, to elicit a particular response or effect through either interpersonal or mass communication requires that at least three conditions be met: (1) The message must gain someone's attention; (2) it must be understood as intended; and (3) the response must be within the capacity of the participants, sanctioned by them and by their relevant associates.

These conditions prescribe minimal essentials for effective communication. Other conceptual problems remain. A basic one may be seen in a distinction that can be made between *effective* and *successful* communication implied in the second condition above. When expression and impression correspond, communication has been effective. When the expression is received and evaluated favorably, the communicative encounter may also be described as having been successful. When instructors assert with positive intent that "sociology is a science," students may be able to reproduce the statement and thus get the message exactly as it was expressed. This is effective communication. If the expression is evaluated unfavorably, however, communication has not been successful.

Not all social situations nor all types of discourse place equal stress on effectiveness and success in communication. The advertiser and the preacher usually seek to meet both goals. The role of the professor, however, is such that he is often satisfied to be effective without striving to be successful. He wants the student to understand a point of view, not necessarily to react favorably or subscribe to it. Other combinations are also possible. A professor may find that while he is not effective he may be quite successful in communication. This is indicated when students fail a course but yet proclaim that they "got a lot out of it" or "enjoyed it very much" or "agreed with everything that was said." Comparable instances may be found in circumstances ranging from interpersonal to international relations. Teen-agers expressing love or some diplomats exchanging views at the United Nations are likely to be ineffective but successful acts of communication. After exposure to a dramatic film about science and the work of scientists, audiences at the Seattle World's Fair developed more positive attitudes and feelings about science, but their conceptions of science became more vague (Taylor, 1963). Apparently the film was more successful than effective. On the other hand, it is easy to imagine that some of the exchanges that might take place over the new emergency link of communication between Washington and Moscow might well be more effective than successful.

In the material that follows there is explicit and implicit concern with the social consequences of various combinations of effective-ineffective-successful-unsuccessful communicative acts. These distinctions are particularly pertinent when communication takes place through the mass media where it becomes useful to consider the intent of the communicator in evaluating the social consequences of the act. That such distinctions can be important in assessing the social impact of the media is clearly implied in the following observations:

If a campaign increases the proportion of people in possession of certain information, it is effective. Yet if this new information is not related to relevant attitudes or behavior, these remain much as they were before the campaign. Similarly, a blood bank drive that brings in the necessary donors, a political campaign that mobilizes the electorate, a bond campaign that steps up sales, or a crusade for souls that attracts new members to the churches is effective. Yet the real impact of such an "effective" mass media campaign, as judged by its ability to effect change in individuals, is often rather minimal. Studies have found, for example, that new bond-subscribers are primarily people who expected to buy bonds anyhow and were looking for an opportunity to do so; that most new church members, attracted by evangelists' appeals, are essentially religious but, for one reason or another, had not taken the step of formally affiliating with a church—and they might not stay long now. To effect basic changes requires social reinforcement. Hence, it is possible to achieve high effectiveness in communication, like high efficiency, without producing any great impact or lasting orientation (Lang & Lang, 1961, p. 143).

IMAGE OF THE FIELD AND THE PROCESS OF MASS COMMUNICATION

Curiosity is the only visa necessary for the initial entry into any research domain. Since the present chapter may in some sense be taken as an invitation to join ranks with those concerned with mass communication research, it is necessary to note what a student might observe should his curiosity propel him toward the study of mass communication.

At first glance, machines loom larger than men or social forms. Mass communication involves a complex technology, most of it recent in origin, much of it being transformed even before it is locked in place for full operation. The output is a torrent of symbols. Words and pictures cascade over each other so that an escape to silence requires effort. Professional training is not necessary to identify the presence of the media; their ubiquity is established in common experience. Television signals now bounce off satellites to bring metropolitan images to remote villages where men have barely dropped their spears to begin the struggle to achieve literacy.

The interrelationship of sociology and technology is of two kinds. One involves the study of the social situation that gives rise to invention and development. The other involves the study of the effects upon man and society of the uses of invention and discovery. Students of mass communication have principally been concerned with the latter, although if the role of the communicator is thought of as an extension of the technology he manipulates, then the former may also be said to be receiving attention. That is, mass media investigations, while mainly directed toward audience behavior, are increasingly interested in the social circumstances that influence the decisions of the mass communicators, including the interrelationship of communicator and audience (Riley & Riley, 1959, pp. 568–578). Indeed, it is now contended that the impact of mass communication can be understood only if the specific decisions of mass communicators, their relation to power holders, and the distribution and withholding of information from communication channels are included in the analysis

(Lang & Lang, 1961, p. 434). This approach has some similarity to the traditional task of the sociologist of knowledge who sought out the structural determinants of thought and ideas.

A student choosing to direct his attention to the mass media faces some minor risks as he sets out to study the major issues implied in the concern with social effects. For example, he may become suspect because he appears to enjoy his work. Leisure and labor are perceived as confused. Going to the movies, watching television, and reading comic books, even when cloaked with the vesture of participant-observation, can seem somewhat remote from basic research and respectable scholarly pursuit. But here, as elsewhere in sociology, it is not the subject matter but its treatment that provides the ultimate test of scientific worth.

If successful scholarship should allay the doubt of peers and self, yet other conditions can arise to redirect the research effort. The student of mass communication can develop a skill and a product with high utility. If he knows how to learn something about the effects of mass communication, there is always someone interested in having this turned to the problem of being more effective. The practicing arts of persuasion beckon. It is more than a matter of advertising and commerce; the urge to engineer consent and to practice public relations emanates today from all the major institutions. Even the profession of sociology is concerned about its image (Berger, 1963, pp. 1–24). The issue here is not that sociology should avoid being harnessed to practical demands, but that these demands, plentiful as they are in the field of communications, cannot by themselves constitute a basis for the sociology of mass communication.

Should our hypothetical student push beyond such preliminary cautions and plunge into the literature, what would he find? Implied in some of the early research, and in much of the early and even present-day discussion, is a model of the mass-communicative process that may be said to depict the media as a giant hypodermic needle: In the hands of a few skilled operators the needle persistently pecks and plunges away at the passively poised body of the masses and the response is direct and immediate. Two assumptions are implicit in this conception: (1) Modern urban society is an atomized mass of disconnected individuals, and (2) there is a direct stimulus-response relationship between the sending and receiving of mass media content in such a society. Historically, this conception was nourished by the uncritical use of dramatic materials presumably showing the power of the press in generating the Spanish-American War, the effectiveness of propaganda efforts in World War I, the operation of the Goebbel's propaganda machine in the 1930's, the inciting influence of a radio play like "The War of the Worlds," and the rise of Madison Avenue into a position of eminence in commerce and politics. Several generations of students from a variety of introductory social science courses are likely to remember these materials principally as illustrations of the powerful and directly operating impact of mass communication.

There is, of course, a more fundamental ground for such impressions of media operation. This is found in the early prominence and the lingering persistence of an individualistic frame of reference in mass communications research. Two recent appraisals (Brouwer, 1962; Ennis, 1961) converge in their estimates of what factors contributed to this orientation that conceives of media audiences as disparate, independent individuals. Both authors mention the psychological backgrounds and interests of the early pioneers in communications research as being influential. Brouwer mentioned (1962, p. 304) that the models guiding opinion studies and the availability of certain data-gathering techniques have been instrumental in centering media studies on the individual. He also stressed market research as a factor, whereas Ennis (1961, p. 121) posed this as a question and concluded as a "modest guess" that the habit of businessmen to think of audience-consumer problems in psychological or personal terms did nothing to stimulate alternative modes of thinking about the mass communicative process.

But alternative modes did develop. In the 1940's, studies began to appear (e.g., Lazarsfeld, Berelson, Gaudet, 1944) that made it clear that under most conditions the assumptions of the hypodermic needle conception were not tenable. People are not as easily manipulated by the mass media as had been feared or hoped. Individuals, even in urban society, are interconnected, and such social linkages were shown to play an important part in mediating and thus modifying, sometimes amplifying sometimes muting, the influence of mass communication. Group structure and interpersonal relations intervene between the mass communicator and the audience. Selectivity in exposure and reaction to mass media content thus began to be seen as arising out of the stimulation of organized social processes rather than as being merely a matter of personal interests of isolated individuals. In short, sociological variables began to appear in the analysis of the process and effects of mass communication.

Thus, empirical studies and critical conceptualization (e.g., Friedson, 1953) began to alter the image of the mass communicative process. The working model now maturing is one where the relationship between the mass communicator and the audience is seen as interdependent, indirect as well as direct, and one that is affected by an immediate as well as an extended social context.

CONCEPTUALIZING THE EFFECTS OF MASS COMMUNICATION

The proper form in which to conceptualize the problem of the impact of the mass media is to ask under what conditions specified effects will prevail. Berelson recognized this when he outlined an answer elegant in form but devoid of substance: "Some kinds of *communication* on some kinds of *issues,* brought to the attention of some kinds of *people* under some kinds of *conditions,* have some kinds of *effects*" (Berelson, 1948, p. 172). The present task is to critically examine how subsequent efforts have adhered to the magnet of this structure, particularly as it pertains to the formulation of kinds of effects.

There is high concern in many quarters about the effects of mass communication. This concern has produced a large number of studies bearing on particular mass media effects. But scientific achievement does not depend so much upon the verification of independent hypotheses as it does upon the systematic arrangement of concepts and findings under abstract theories that are rich in their logical implications as well as accurate in their empirical claims (Schrag, 1961, p. 51). Here the work has not begun in mass communication; in fact, a groundwork is barely visible. The primitive state of affairs is revealed in an examination of how effects have been thought about, how basic terms have been defined, and what attention has been directed toward the logical ordering of concepts.

General Characterization of Social Effects

The staggering statistics on the supply and consumption of mass media material are often taken as evidence that mass communication has influenced to some degree nearly every aspect of social life in modern society. An inventory of such effects, stated without qualifying conditions, would include propositions of the following order:

(1) The development of the mass media has created or stimulated vast new complexes of activities centering on the manipulation of symbols—e.g., advertising, public relations, entertainment, market research.

(2) By narrowing physical, temporal, and social distances, mass communication has widened the public that is taken into account. A leader in any area of activity can no longer say "the public be damned" without at least first acknowledging that the public should in some way be informed.

Mass communication has become the major means for expediting the flow of information, thus extending the horizon of every man's environment.

(3) Mass communication has not only introduced new content into the patterns of conversation and interpersonal interaction but has also become a force for the standardization of basic speech patterns and other language habits.

(4) The mass media have become a major arbiter of social status. The media manipulate prestige and authority simply by giving or withholding attention and recognition to persons, issues, organizations, and movements.

(5) Mass communication has given new emphasis to personality as a factor in social and political life. The media are a major source for identifying and evaluating heroes and villains and thus provide significant role models that serve as socializing agents in society.

(6) Mass communication has altered family patterns. The media challenge traditional lines of authority by influencing the basis for family formation through the portrayal of romantic values, by offering guidance on family problems, by redefining parental roles and reinforcing the prerogatives of children, and by creating new choice points in the budgeting of family recreational activities.

(7) Mass communication, coupled with mass production, has magnified material values, created "thing" consciousness, and generally elevated the perception of the importance of the economic sector of society.

(8) Mass communication has speeded the processes of cultural diffusion, has brought urban values and attitudes to rural settings, and has generally served as an agent fostering social change.

These statements illustrate the depth and form of concern with social effects of mass communication. Dramatic as they may appear, they are cautiously phrased compared with what might have been expressed had they been formulated around the presumed impact of the media on individuals (see,

e.g., Wertham, 1962). The eight statements are not a logically interrelated set of testable propositions. They are merely a number of descriptive assertions that suggest a classification of effects along political, economic, and other institutional lines. Some ordering or typology of general effects would be a useful step in building a structure of scientific explanation wherein claims go beyond the data already observed. But the limits of the kind of ordering implied above are soon reached. As indeed is the utility of a classification of effects by the various media (e.g., Steinberg, 1958, pp. 115–182), by social problem areas such as delinquency (e.g., Wright, 1959, pp. 92–100), or by even more general categories such as those employed by Schramm (1949) in organizing the research literature according to (1) effects of communication on the individual, (2) persuasive effects, (3) effects of different media, and (4) effects on public taste.

Directional Typology of Effects

Hovland (1954, p. 1090) observed that there was no adequate conceptual framework within which to classify the diverse types of mass media effects reported in the literature. While this situation still obtains, some relevant efforts have been made to approach the problem. Klapper (1960), faced with the need of finding an organizational scheme for his comprehensive survey of the literature, developed a classification of media effects. His system of concepts was not derived from a general theoretical base. Instead he employed the strategy of ascertaining whether the data from available studies suggested an underlying order in terms of a basic dimension. Accordingly, he formulated a typology around the direction of effects revealed in the research on the impact of persuasive communication on attitudes and opinions. The basis of his decision, expressed as follows, reveals the great difficulties encountered and the rationale employed:

A list of topical categories is obviously unfeasible, since it would necessarily involve all topics of human thought. A distinction in terms of immediate effects, short range effects, and long range effects involves difficult and perhaps arbitrary classifications, and would suffer, at least at present, from the virtual lack of objective studies of anything that might properly be called long term effect. Various other possibilities present similarly complex classification problems, all of which are intensified by the fact that the pertinent studies were never planned to fit into any such overall structure. Mass communication research has, in fact, been notoriously devoid of any organizing theoretical framework. But the data themselves do suggest an organization scheme. If the findings are viewed in reference to what might be called the *directions of effect,* marked consistencies are discernible; cross-topical findings can be brought into some sort of order; and many of the identified causative factors can be treated in relation to the directional typology. Such an organizational scheme, in short, appears to offer wide possibilities of integration with few organizational trappings.

Logic and common sense indicate that the possible "directions of effect" are limited. In reference to any given topic, a persuasive communication may:

a. create opinions or attitudes among persons who previously had none on the topic in question; *or*
b. reinforce (i.e., intensify or buttress) attitudes which already exist; *or*
c. diminish the intensity of existing attitudes without actually accomplishing conversion; *or*
d. convert persons to a point of view opposite to the one they held; *or*
e. (at least theoretically) have no effect at all (Klapper, 1960, p. 278).

In his text discussion, Klapper (1960) treated these definitions as *creative, reinforcement, minor change, conversion,* and *no effects.* To provide a simple hypothetical illustration of their application, Figure 1 presents a situation where it is assumed that an issue emerges on which the audience position is known before and after exposure to mass communication. It is further assumed that at either time point the audience will register only one of four reactions to the

issue: positive, negative, neutral, or no opinion. The before and after combinations of these 4 positions produce 16 states of audience response which may be typed employing the directional definitions supplied by Klapper. That an investigator would confront some thorny decisions in consistently applying the directional typology to research findings becomes apparent as the 16 decisions in Figure 1 are faced. That Klapper

Audience Position before Exposure	Audience Position after Exposure	Type of Effect
Positive	Positive	NO EFFECT
	Neutral	MINOR CHANGE
	Negative	CONVERSION
	No opinion	CONVERSION (?)
Neutral	Positive	REINFORCEMENT
	Neutral	NO EFFECT
	Negative	REINFORCEMENT
	No opinion	CONVERSION (?)
Negative	Positive	CONVERSION
	Neutral	MINOR CHANGE
	Negative	NO EFFECT
	No opinion	CONVERSION (?)
No opinion	Positive	CREATIVE
	Neutral	CREATIVE
	Negative	CREATIVE
	No opinion	NO EFFECT

Fig. 1 Typology of direction of effects by persuasive mass communications on opinions and attitudes.

did confront these and other difficulties, partly because of some looseness in the definitions and partly because of the nature of the available data, will be noted in the following discussion of each of these effects.

Creative effects. Mass communication is thought to be a force for creative effects when new issues arise or when issues are evoked that are unrelated to existing attitude clusters. A sociologist might characterize the setting for creative effects as follows: Under conditions of rapid social change many persons have no place to anchor an opinion, no vital culture through which to filter direct media impact. Where social norms are in flux, the media may reach the audience directly and carry heavy weight (e.g., Wilensky, 1961).

Strictly stated in terms of the definitional requirements of the various effects in the directional typology, the efficacy of mass communication in creating opinion can be gauged only in reference to issues on which, at the time of exposure, people are known to have no opinion at all. To ascertain the existence and validity of this blank slate is no simple matter. For example, the sensible use of a directional typology rests on research procedures adequately refined to distinguish accurately between "no opinion" and a "neutral" response. Without this, as Klapper noted (1960, p. 54), mass communication could be credited with creating opinions where it is in reality reinforcing predispositions. Thus, Klapper favored the view that neutrality represents a reasoned position rather than a lack of opinion. Following this formulation, Figure 1 thus shows that creative effects develop only when there is a shift in audience position from "no opinion" before exposure to "positive," "neutral," or "negative" positions after exposure.

Clear-cut demonstration of the creative effect is difficult. Even if something new does appear, it is perceived through established structures or soon fitted into them through an active definitional process. Recent experience in advertising makes this clear. With the advent of television, advertisers made strong efforts to appeal directly to the approximately 40 million children in the United States between the ages of 2 and 12 —a market presumably particularly susceptible to creative effects. New products emerged, and new messages about old products were forcefully directed to children. However, evidence has been mounting to suggest that even very young children today see so much advertising that they have developed a high degree of sophistication and have grown as hostile to hard-sell ads as their parents (Bart, 1963). At least the creative effect here may refer as much to an attitude set about advertising as it does to the creation of material wants or an inclination to buy.

Two general areas particularly appropriate for the study of creative effects are implied above. One is in the marketing and diffusion of new products. The other is in the study of the socialization of children's attitudes. Before discussing these, a third prospect may also be noted. In sociology, the study of collective behavior usually involves populations having no previous experience with the phenomena at hand. But since this often concerns unique and bizarre behavior, the possibilities for generalization may also be impaired. In studying media effects, this consideration must be balanced against the advantage of working in a context where the assumption of little likelihood of any structured opinion before exposure is most fully warranted.

One study from the literature on collective behavior may be cited to illustrate the mass media potential with respect to creative effects. This study (Medalia & Larsen, 1958) depicts the three moves from the pre-exposure position of no opinion to the positive position ("believers"), the neutral position ("undecided"), and the negative position ("skeptics"). Furthermore, this study suggests that the probabilities are not the same for the occurrence of each of these subtypes under the general condition that presumably prompts the creative effect—the appearance and treatment of a new and unstructured stimulus situation.

The new and unstructured event projected by the mass media concerned repeated reports that some unusual agent was causing widespread damage to automobile windshields in the form of pitting marks that grew into bubbles in the glass about the size of a thumbnail. Emergency appeals were made by local authorities to the state and federal government. Hundreds of persons "cried wolf" and telephoned the police (Medalia, 1959–1960). Many persons covered their windshields with floor mats or newspapers. Conjecture as to cause included vandalism, meteoric dust, and sand-flea eggs hatching in the glass, but centered ultimately on possible radioactive fallout from H-bomb tests. Research by physical scientists revealed that there was no evidence of pitting that could not be accounted for by ordinary road damage. But contrary beliefs emerged as people were looking *at* their windshields for the first time instead of *through* them. The event was created mainly by highly contradictory news stimuli. Interviews with a random sample of 964 telephone respondents in the city where this event occurred showed that shortly after it had taken place 92.6 per cent had heard about it. Three out of four of these persons got the news first from the mass media. Awareness had been created. In effect, the vast majority had moved from "no opinion" to a structuring of the situation, at least in this limited sense, and the mass media were directly instrumental at this level. But what kind of creative effect took place? What were the perceived definitions of the situation? Here the movement from no opinion to positive, neutral, or negative positions may be illustrated. Four days after the peak presentation of the windshield news in the press, 50 per cent of the respondents were believers. That is, they were positive in their contention that there had been unusual pitting activity and that this had been caused by some unusual physical agent. Another 26 per cent were undecided. They had heard many explanations but, even after probing, were unwilling to suggest one most likely cause. They may be said to have moved from no opinion to a neutral position. Another 21 per cent were skeptics; they were dubious of anything other than people noting ordinary road damage. The final 3 per cent of the respondents refused to express any opinion on the cause of the situation.

The findings of this study directly support the common contention that the media are effective in bringing events to the attention of audiences. In fact, this was a mass media generated event. The media definition of the situation was a key force in the creation of the emergent patterns of belief, or at least in the fact that beliefs had to emerge to cope with the event at all. Content analysis suggested that the media had employed a strategy of extracting every possible human interest lead in covering the event. Rather than turning immediately and forcefully to relevant institutional sources (including their own editorial mechanisms) whose definitions traditionally serve as social controls, mystery was maximized in the press as "ghostly little pellets" and "elusive B-B snipers" were highlighted. Out of such material came the incubation of a creative effect.

The creative effect occupies a basic position in a directional typology by virtue of the obvious fact that some attitude, opinion, value, or behavior structure must exist before the other effects have any meaning. That these evolve in complex social contexts variously subject to mass media influences is apparent from any review of socialization studies in sociology (e.g., Elkin, 1960). Students of mass communication and socialization can readily find common ground. To be concerned with socialization, the ongoing process by which the individual acquires the culture of his group and internalizes its social norms is to be concerned with a creative effect. Certain data suggest that the mass media may be playing an increasingly prominent role in the socialization processes of modern society. For example, the average North American child, from age 3 to 16, spends one-sixth of his waking hours watching television. This is as much time as he spends in school, and more time than he devotes to any other activity except sleep and play (Schramm, Lyle, & Parker, 1961). While this represents exposure to only one form of mass communication, careful analysis of the media habits of children suggests that television may be the key to any media socialization influences. In the words of Schramm, Lyle, and Parker, "It is television, more than any other channel, that builds the 'set' with which a child approaches the mass media. All other media choices are judged against what he has come to expect of television" (1961, p. 27).

The intense degree to which children are exposed to television is impressive. Coupled with the kind of content available for viewing, the potential for socialization would appear to be great. In dramatic movement, and sometimes in color, this medium scans a vast environment and offers a range of role-taking models not ordinarily found in family, neighborhood, and school settings. The content may teach the ways of society by portraying as Elkin phrased it, "the duties of the detective, waitress, or sheriff; the functions of the hospital, advertising agency, and police court; behavior in a night club or airplane; the language of the prison, army, or courtroom; the relationships between nurses and doctors or secretaries and their bosses" (1960, p. 71). The socialization potential of television content, however, does not derive alone from variety in settings, situations, and character types, but may emerge from unity in the portrayal of underlying values and ideals. This is suggested in a recent content analysis (Larsen, Gray & Fortis, 1963) that asked, "What do television programs such as animated cartoons, westerns, drama, situational comedy, and others, portray in common?" The study revealed that television deals in patterned ways with basic goals and the mechanisms for their achievement. On this level, all types of programs present similar models of behavior. Potentially, the finding bearing most significantly on the prospects for socialization was that television programs of all types consistently project content in which socially approved goals are most frequently achieved by methods that are not socially approved.

Clearly, a study of the media habits of children provides a good base for the assessment of the creative effects of mass communication. But, impressive as findings on audience exposure may be and pregnant as the patterns of content might appear, these features alone do not establish how much, if any, socializing influence the mass media have. The tasks that remain are first to establish how children perceive, identify with, and use mass media content and then to try to sort out this impact from the continuing influence of other agencies of socialization in which audience members function before, during, and after exposure to mass communication.

Some studies specifically designed to bear on these tasks are beginning to appear. The work of Schramm and his associates (1961, pp. 57–74) on the use of television by children in North America and the excellent English study of television by Himmelweit, Oppenheim, and Vince (1958) are major contributions. In addition, Zajonc's (1954–1955) study of children's identification with characters in radio space serials and Forer's (1955) study of the response of adolescents to a radio program called "Mind Your Manners" are relevant. More recently, Gerson (1963) conducted a sociological investigation of the general array of mass media as agencies of socialization in the cross-sex behavior of adolescents. Through interviews and by questionnaire he collected data from over six hundred Negro and white adolescents in the San Francisco area bearing on both creative and reinforcement effects of mass communication. In getting at the creative effect, Gerson asked his respondents if they ever received any ideas or advice about dating and related activities from the various forms of mass communication. To measure reinforcement, he asked his respondents if they ever tried out ideas they already had about dating and related matters. All segments of his population reported using the media more for the former purpose than for the latter. Furthermore, Gerson found that a family-school context in which an adolescent is not integrated is more likely to generate the use of the mass media as a socializing agency than is the social context in which the person is well integrated. Under all the conditions treated in the analysis, this relationship was stronger among Negro adolescents than among white. The findings of this study clearly suggest how the mass media may have important social effects when there is a discontinuity in the socializing function of traditional institutions such as the family and the school.

Much work remains to be done. In a brief but penetrating discussion, Wright (1959, pp. 92–100) outlined the problems and the prospects that confront investigators who would turn to this area of research. In particular, Wright pointed to three needs. Data are needed on the communications behavior of people of various age levels. More evidence is needed on the use of the media (advertently or inadvertently) as sources of social norms. And, finally, more information is needed on the extent to which people absorb social norms from the mass media, consciously and unconsciously, directly and indirectly. Work along these lines could produce knowledge of the capabilities as well as the limits of mass communication in the complex process of socialization and in the generation of creative effects.

Perhaps the most viable area in current communications research bearing directly on creative effects and tangentially on all other effect processes is the study of the diffusion of new ideas, products, and practices. Diffusion studies are extensions of traditional research on mass media "campaigns" that proceed from a more sophisticated frame of reference than does this earlier work. Rather than focusing narrowly on the effects of media per se, diffusion studies follow the itinerary of social and technical change through mass and interpersonal communication in both formal and informal networks of social relations (e.g., Katz, 1961).

The growing number of books reporting and appraising diffusion studies (e.g., De Fleur & Larsen, 1958; Karlsson, 1958; Katz & Lazarsfeld, 1955; Lionberger, 1960; Rogers, 1962) clearly marks this as an area of sociological significance and one of considerable promise for dealing with problems of process and effects of mass communication. A number of briefer references may also be cited for readers interested in the evolution and the future potential of this field. Katz (1960), a leader in vitalizing research in this area, reminded students of mass communication of the relevance of a long tradition of diffusion research in rural sociology. Katz, Levin, and Hamilton (1963) extended this review over a number of other disciplines to provide a groundwork and a set of critical problems for further study. The rigorous work of Rapoport (1953), Hagerstrand (1960), Coleman (1961b), and Dodd (1963) in developing mathematical models of diffusion represents a direction bound to be elaborated in this field in the future.

Viewed sociologically, a complete diffusion study would include the investigation of the following seven features (Katz, Levin, Hamilton, 1963, p. 240): the (1) *acceptance,* (2) over *time,* (3) of some specific *item*—an idea or a practice, (4) by individuals, groups or other *adopting units,* linked (5) to specific *channels* of communication, (6) to a *social structure,* and (7) to a given system of values, or *culture.* Diffusion studies are directed toward analyzing factors in the adoption of innovations, thus this line of research focuses on what in the present context would be called a creative effect. Not all studies included in the diffusion literature encompass the full set of seven factors in the definition above. A common research design is to test the power of a selected set of predictor variables to "explain" the variance in adoption rate in terms of multiple correlation techniques (e.g., Bose, 1962; Rogers & Havens, 1962). In some studies theoretical problems of general interest to sociologists, such as those centering on the impact of the legitimacy of norms and the effect of social integration, are salient features (Boyle, 1963; Menzel, 1960). In every case it is apparent that it takes a great deal of ingenuity and labor to make complete diffusion processes accessible for empirical research.

Throughout the diffusion process, from awareness through decision-making to adoption, there is, of course, a flow of information. A large number of studies dealing with a variety of items in a range of settings indicate that mass media and interpersonal communication are complementary forces in accomplishing change or a creative effect. The first persons to change, usually called innovators, are more likely to be influenced by mass or impersonal media, the later adopters by interpersonal channels (e.g., Deutschmann, 1962). It is in dealing with innovators, then, that the claim for the creative effect of the mass media is most direct, although since the innovator sets the stage for total change by injecting the new item into the social system, there is a larger sense in which this effect may also be conceptualized and analyzed in diffusion studies. There are problems, however, in suggesting that the identification of innovators and their characteristics might be a route to ferreting out this effect of mass communication.

The picture that one gets of the innovator from diffusion studies is not entirely consistent. For example, the work of rural sociologists (Lionberger, 1960, p. 54) and some anthropologists (Barnett, 1953, Ch. XIV) supports a conception of innovators as persons usually isolated from the local community. On the other hand, studies of the diffusion of new drugs among doctors (Coleman, Katz, & Menzel, 1957) indicated the opposite to be true—innovators were among the most integrated into the local medical community. Boyle (1963) attempted with some success to resolve this apparent conflict through a reformulation and test of a theory suggesting that the critical factors are the consonance of the innovation to the individual and its legitimacy in terms of the norms of the community. But questions still remain about the characteristics of the innovator and his influence on legitimizing the item by adopting it.

Rogers (1962, pp. 193–207) reviewed evidence from the literature and combined it with certain theoretical writings to cast a chapter entitled, "Innovators as Deviants: In Step with a Different Drummer." A critical reading of this chapter reveals some conceptual difficulties and leaves a number of unanswered questions. For example, Rogers did not use conformity and deviance as polar opposites, and his attempt to clarify

innovation in terms of Merton's paradigm is clouded because of an inconsistency in his conceptualization of norms. There may be considerable merit in viewing the innovator as a deviant, but in order to do so there needs to be a clear indication of what he is deviating from—the modal pattern of adoption behavior or shared conceptions specifying what is appropriate or inappropriate behavior in a situation. Further effort is needed to explain the deviation of the innovator. Does he deviate because means are not available for him legitimately to achieve socially accepted goals, or does he deviate because he gives up the goals and wants to formulate his own and develop means for achieving them? The reasons behind the deviation may be important in determining whether or not the individual will communicate with others concerning the innovation and how others in the system will respond to these communications and view the consequences of adoption. Furthermore, it will have to be determined whether the deviant is an innovator because he is a cosmopolitan, or cosmopolitan because he is a deviant.

In other words, the deviant's relation to the system norms, his position in the social structure, and his position in the communication system will have to be dealt with in any theory of the diffusion of innovation which contends that the innovator is a deviant.

Reinforcement. The formulation and application of the reinforcement concept is particularly critical. It bears a considerable burden as the central conclusion of Klapper (1960) and others (e.g., Davison, 1959) in evaluating the effects of mass communication. A prime theme in the current research literature is that reinforcement of attitudes and behavior patterns is the major impact of the mass media. In Klapper's estimate, reinforcement is the most likely outcome of media influence, followed in order by minor change and the creative effect, with conversion trailing along as the most rare result (Klapper, 1960, pp. 51, 58).

The definition of reinforcement used by Klapper (1960) in the explanatory notes of his technical appendix (see p. 278) parenthetically includes the terms "intensify or buttress" as synonymous with reinforcement. While this does not specify how much, it certainly implies that reinforcement involves strengthening attitudes that already exist to some degree. This definition is employed in Figure 1 and indicates that under the directional typology the reinforcement effect could only occur when an audience shifts from a neutral position to a positive or negative position after exposure to the media. Thus, in this simple framework of four possible reactions to an issue, the logic of Klapper's full definitional system would seem to rather markedly limit the opportunities for the fruition of this important effect.

Perhaps sensing this restraint when applying the term to a classification of research findings, Klapper relaxed the definition in his text discussion when he observed, "Within a given audience exposed to particular communications, reinforce-

directional classification of effects, even if refined measures of the direction and intensity of response were employed.

One such additional factor relevant to the present framework is the mass communicator's intent. In a general way, Klapper (1960) limited his consideration of effects to those occurring in a situation of "persuasive communications." Presumably this means that communicative intent is a variable that can be identified and dealt with. In a research setting, intent could be directly inquired into, or inferred from, systematic analysis of media content. For the present purposes, a trichotomy of communicative intent is assumed and represented as a "positive," "neutral," and "negative" stance of the media on a given issue. When the framework of Figure 1 is modified explicitly to include this factor only implicitly treated by Klapper (1960), then conditions emerge where it appears legitimate to infer that constancy of audience position represents reinforcement. The two additional instances where this inference appears justified may be represented as follows:

Audience Position before Exposure	*Mass Communicator's Intent*	*Audience Position after Exposure*	*Type of Effect*
Positive	Negative	Positive	REINFORCEMENT
Negative	Positive	Negative	REINFORCEMENT

ment, or at least constancy of opinion, is typically found to be the dominant effect" (Klapper, 1960, p. 9). He then proceeded to use as major evidence for the reinforcement effect the occurrence of constancy of opinion in a number of studies (Klapper, 1960, p. 17).

Given Klapper's (1960) definitional system, this ambiguity poses a serious question bearing on the continued use of the directional typology. If constancy of opinion, which is relatively easy to identify empirically, is taken as an indication of reinforcement, what, then, constitutes "no effect"? Apparently some additional factors must be considered in making decisions about the

Here the interpretation is that constancy of opinion represents reinforcement because the audience withstood media efforts to convert them to a position opposite to that held before exposure to mass communications. Had the media content (intent) been neutral rather than structured opposition, constancy of audience position would not merit being termed reinforcement but simply "no effect." The same judgment would appear obvious in the case where the audience maintained neutrality in the face of positive or negative intent through the mass communicative effort.

Going beyond the problem of conceptualizing reinforcement effects, two additional questions may be posed: (1) What mechanisms appear to operate in the service of reinforcement? and (2) If it is acknowledged that reinforcement is the major directional effect of mass communication, what are the social consequences of this fact?

In response to the first question, Klapper (1960, pp. 50–51) identified the following factors as instrumental in mediating impact and negotiating the reinforcement effect: predispositions and the derived processes of selective exposure, perception, and retention; the group, and the norms of groups, to which the audience member belongs; interpersonal dissemination of communication content; opinion leadership; and the nature of commercial mass media in a free enterprise society (the necessity to attract and hold the largest possible audience).

The second question calls for an interpretation of the reinforcement effect. The prominence of this effect means that attitudes and behavior cannot be altered at the mere whim of the mass communicator. It suggests that in the main audiences do not look for new experiences in exposure to the mass media but for a repetition and elaboration of old experiences. Thus a prominent interpretation of the social consequences of reinforcement (e.g., Lazarsfeld & Merton, 1948) is that the media serve mainly to sanctify the status quo.

This conclusion does not exhaust the possible social significance of reinforcement effects. Research has not been directed toward the long-range consequences of general audience reinforcement. Nor has it been concerned with the conditions under which reinforcement might lead to activation, apathy, or other effects. Reinforcement has been measured mainly in terms of individual perceptions. Sociologists might well ask, Is there a consequence on the social level to reinforcement on the individual level that would not necessarily support the interpretation of the conservative function of the media noted above? This is suggested in the following statement that serves as a forceful reminder of the need for further

analysis of reinforcement as a social effect:

Many mass media campaigns increase polarization, the counterpart on the aggregate level to individual reinforcement . . . a mass media campaign can contribute to polarization without directly converting any single individual. Political debate as well as major events lead to a "strain for consistency." They force the undecided to line up. If those who were previously neutral move predominantly to support one side, the aggregate balance may be upset. This happened in Truman's campaign of 1948. Assuming that mass communications do little more than keep old issues alive, the stress on bread-and-butter issues by Truman reactivated the eroding loyalties of enough Democrats to win the election. If reactivation reinforcement benefits one side more than the other, changes in the balance can occur (Lang & Lang, 1961, p. 431).

Minor change. In Klapper's (1960) directional typology this effect refers to a diminishing intensity of attitudes short of conversion—the converse of reinforcement. In others words, a minor change is a reduction in partisanship. This drift is depicted in Figure 1 as movement away from the structured positive or negative positions toward the neutral position.

The basis for terming such a shift a "minor" change is not clear, except that it represents less change than the more dramatic conversion possibility. But so, for that matter, does reinforcement, a shift in degree in the opposite direction. This being the case, a more apt description of minor change would be to call it something like neutralization. This is more than an exercise in semantics. The new label immediately signifies that a minor change of this sort may indeed have major social consequences. On the one hand, movement toward neutrality might make the audience more receptive to balancing various views providing a more reasoned structure in the event of reactivation to new commitments. On the other hand, the generalized change of a population from a structured to a neutral position through mass communication might be the first step in a "deactivation" effect that could lead to alienation, apathy induction, or narcotization. Klapper (1960) missed an opportunity here to expand his two-page discussion of "minor changes" with such important materials from his own research tradition as the penetrating analysis of political apathy in *Voting* (Berelson, Lazarsfeld, McPhee, 1954, pp. 305–323). This is perhaps accounted for by the fact that in his text discussion Klapper did not strictly adhere to the requirements of his own definition of minor change; he did not refer to "diminishing degrees" but only to "minor change, as in intensity of opinion" (1960, p. 15) or to slight changes or wavering (1960, p. 43). Such terms, of course, could also refer to reinforcement.

Klapper's discussion of the conditions attendant to minor change includes the following statement:

It is perhaps not remarkable that people should be more inclined to change slightly than they are to change a great deal, and attempts to

including the fact that it is widely taken as the definitive statement of the effects of mass communication), as there is in the statement above, an implication that change, particularly conversion, ought to be the major intent of the media. Since Klapper deliberately limited his concern to "persuasive communications," this orientation is perhaps understandable. In the statement above, however, he seems by virtue of the curious choice of words—e.g., "deterred," "imperfection"—to imply that minor change is in the "wrong" direction. He thus appears to be more concerned with the effectiveness of the media than with the social effects of mass communication. In either case, it is now appropriate to analyze the major contention which describes the general conditions that presumably foster minor change. This will be done by considering the intent of the communicator (which Klapper did) as a variable (which Klapper did not do) under conditions where minor change has taken place. The combined conditions may be depicted as follows:

Audience Position before Exposure	Mass Communicator's Intent	Audience Position after Exposure
Positive	Positive	Neutral
Positive	Neutral	Neutral
Positive	Negative	Neutral
Negative	Positive	Neutral
Negative	Neutral	Neutral
Negative	Negative	Neutral

explain this fact may seem unnecessary . . . such changes are apparently not as deterred by predispositions, group norms, and other extra-media factors as is conversion. The incidence of minor change might be looked upon as manifesting imperfections in the processes which ordinarily hinder change. The fluctuations of opinion, short of conversion, simply may not constitute a psychological threat sufficiently critical to bring all the defensive forces into full play (Klapper, 1960, p. 44).

There is throughout Klapper's (1960) book (a significant work in many respects,

In each instance above there is a minor change—a neutralization effect. But are the general extramedia conditions that Klapper (1960) described as generally attendant to minor change operative in the same way or degree in each case regardless of media intent? While research has not been directed toward this question, it may be fruitful to speculate that the variable of communicative intent does make a difference. On logical grounds, it is thus hypothesized that the more consonant the intent of the communicator is with the audience position before exposure (positive-positive or negative-negative), the more intense the extramedia influences would have to be to bring about a minor change. It follows that the more dissonant the intent of the communicator is with the audience position before exposure (positive-neutral, negative-neutral and then positive-negative, negative-positive), the less intense the extramedia influences would have to be to bring about a minor change. Whether these formulations are correct or not, they suggest that the general formula stating the importance of the intervention of extramedia social and psychological conditions in arresting conversion and resulting in minor change needs thorough checking and considerable refinement. Some important strides in the direction of sorting out and formalizing relationships between influence attempts and social dispositions can be found in the work of Ferguson and Smith (1963).

Conversion. Conversion effects of mass communication apparently occur relatively infrequently. This conclusion, drawn from empirical studies, has not deterred investment of resources in attempts to engineer conversion via mass communication. There are no signs to suggest an abatement of campaigns to change loyalties from one political party to another (see, e.g., Key, 1958, p. 521), to shift positions on such issues as fluoridation (e.g., Hirabayashi, 1963), or to switch preferences from "Brand X to Brand Y" (e.g., Coleman, 1961a). While intensive efforts to bring about this type of effect may only occasionally be successful, even rare occurrences can have major social impact. The most obvious example is when the conversion of a small proportion of the electorate brings a new political party into power. In certain decision structures, the movement of a minority can often markedly swing the outcome of a contest.

Another way in which a minor incidence of conversion can have major impact is suggested from diffusion studies. Conversion can "snowball" through interpersonal chan-nels and emerge as major social change. Change of this order starts somewhere with someone. In the complex diffusion and decision-making process that starts with the establishment of awareness of an innovation and sometimes leads to significant social change, there are leaders and laggards and there are people who hold out to the very end. In examining the characteristics of the leaders in the critical first stage of the adoption process, there are grounds for associating creative effects of mass communication with the innovators—the first to accept something new—and to associate conversion effects with early-adopters—those who follow in the footsteps of the innovators and subsequently are instrumental in influencing others to follow (see, e.g., Larsen, 1962).

Thus in assessing conversion as a social effect of mass communication, the frequency of occurrence criterion is not alone adequate to the task. This criterion is often stressed in discussions noting limitations of the mass media in directly producing either conversion or creative effects. As a result, there is a tendency to overlook what a minimal demonstration of such effects might do in given social structures. A study design limited to simple before-and-after measurement of response to media exposure cannot be expected to reveal these potentials. The full assessment of any effects requires their study over time. This may be particularly important for conversion and creative effects since they have a quality of dramatic visibility that may set them up as prototypes generating a chain reaction of social consequences.

Some caution must also be observed in accepting the conclusion that conversion effects are relatively infrequent occurrences. Klapper (1960, p. 63) called attention to two reporting techniques, commonly exercised in mass media studies, which have a tendency to mask the incidence of this effect. One is the practice from before-and-after tests to report conversion only in terms of change in the direction intended by the mass communicator. The other is to report "net change" unaccompanied by reports of integral changes which led to the net effect. Both practices may cloak instances where persons, after exposure to mass communication, shifted to a point of view opposite to that they originally held.

In his criticism of these practices, Klapper (1960) made his closest approach to applying the full implications of the definitional distinctions in his directional typology. He made explicit use of both mass communicative intent and original position of the audience to distinguish conversion from reinforcement and to underscore various overlooked possibilities for the emergence of conversion effects. He did not, however, follow through to clarify other conceptual problems, such as those that emerge in Figure 1 where systematic variation in the before-and-after position of the audience is portrayed.

In the instance where audience position at two points in time is considered, the shift from negative to positive or from positive to negative positions obviously constitutes conversion following Klapper's (1960) definition. His system of definitions, however, does not clearly imply how a shift from positive, neutral, or negative positions before exposure to "no opinion" after exposure should be termed. As noted earlier, there are difficulties in specifying empirical referents to "no opinion" and sharply distinguishing it from the neutral position, although this is done fairly routinely in survey research (see, e.g., Key, 1961, p. 398). Nonetheless, the "no opinion" position is an essential part of the directional typology since it provides the base for specifying creative effects. Movement from "no opinion" to some structured position as a result of exposure to mass communication is termed a creative effect.

Using Klapper's (1960) typology, what may shifts in the reverse direction be termed? Such shifts resemble "minor change," but since they appear as a change in quality beyond that of a matter of degree it would seem appropriate to distinguish

them from minor change or "neutralization." Being qualitative shifts, they could be classified as conversion effects. Here, however, the difficulty is that a move to "no opinion" from a structured position seems to be of a different order from a shift from one structured position to another. Allowing for considerable simplification, the contrast might be illustrated in the difference in moving from a theistic to an atheistic position in religion as compared to moving from either of these to an agnostic position. The first shift represents a move from one structured position to another, presumably its opposite. This is a conversion effect, using Klapper's definition. The second shift represents a move from structured positions (belief or disbelief) to an unstructured position (withholding belief). In Figure 1, both types of shift are labelled conversion, but a question mark has been inserted behind the latter to signify the difficulty in classification encountered in this area of the directional typology. Perhaps a more accurate description of shifts to unstructured from structured positions would be to call them "deactivation" effects. Something similar to this is implied in Klapper's discussion of media attendance and audience passivity toward the end of his book (pp. 234–248), but no effort is made to fit the concept of passivity into the directional typology.

Such classification problems are mainly of logical interest in the present context. In the absence of research, however, it is of interest to speculate about empirical possibilities. Under what conditions could this special direction of effect be achieved via persuasive communication? One way in which it might occur is for the media to avoid a frontal attack on established attitudes and attempt to bring about a change in the frame of reference in which an issue is evaluated by an audience. Questions highly relevant in one context can become meaningless when approached from another. Thus, for example, a person might have structured views when an issue is perceived in a humanistic or theological framework, and these views could truly dissolve to "no opinion" when the issue is shifted to a scientific framework where it might be ruled out as irrelevant. This phenomenon is sometimes experienced when a person shifts his professional commitment. William Graham Sumner, who moved from the ministry to academic sociology, is reported to have said, "I never consciously gave up a religious faith; it was as if I had put my beliefs into a drawer, and when I opened it up there was nothing there at all" (Keller, 1935, p. 543).

When attention is directed to conditions bearing on conversion from one structured position to another, conjecture can be supplemented by the findings of empirical scrutiny. Klapper (1960) carefully sifted and sorted an extensive literature, not limited to mass media studies, to try to construct some general propositions descriptive of the conditions under which such conversion occurs. Since his search rests on a postulate that the communicative process is basically the same regardless of which direction of effects emerge, his conclusion is that conversion comes about whenever there is a weakening of the protective nets of resistance which normally thwart change and produce reinforcement. Thus, anything that relaxes or atypically redirects the operation of the selective mechanisms of exposure, perception, and retention, or anything that reduces the restraining influence of group affiliation, tends to enhance the conversion capability of the media. This can occur, for example, when audience members experience cross-pressures, when issues are of low salience, or when group discussion of communications clarifies previously confused norms or reveals new and more basic counternorms.

Klapper (1960) supplemented his discussion of the conditions conducive to conversion with an extensive examination of features bearing on persuasive communications, such as the credibility of the communicator, one-sided versus two-sided presentations of content, the effect of threat appeals, and others (pp. 98–132). He asserted, however, that the data do not permit valid distinctions to be drawn between factors contributing to reinforcement versus those contributing to conversion. Had Klapper turned to available theoretical formulations, a number of which have been designed to account for attitude change as an effect of communication, he might have illuminated this and other issues involving the conversion effect. For example, he made no reference to Festinger's (1957) theory of cognitive dissonance, Heider's (1946) balance theory, Osgood and Tannenbaum's (1955) congruity theory, or Newcomb's (1953) ABX model of communication. More recent publications, for which Klapper cannot be held accountable, reveal the continuing promise of these formulations in unraveling knotty questions about attitude change. Particularly relevant illustrations include a concise review of general theories by Maccoby and Maccoby (1961), a major description and evaluation of dissonance theory by Brehm and Cohen (1962), a laboratory experiment on communicator credibility and communication discrepancy as determinants of opinion change by Aronson, Turner and Carlsmith (1963), and a field experiment on communication, perception, and behavior by Spitzer (1963). The strength of this work lies in the richness of the questions generated by the theoretical formulations and the rigor of the research controls afforded by laboratory-like conditions. The challenge that remains for students of mass communication is to capture the former, while relinquishing the latter in favor of undertaking research on conditions generating effects in a naturalistic setting or in a situation involving true mass media of communication as opposed to laboratory approximations.

The foregoing presentation has attempted to summarize Klapper's (1960) work in developing a directional typology of media effects. Any classification system may be defended on the grounds that it organizes data and reveals possible connections between classes of events. As Brown (1963, p. 170) indicated, to organize data so as to reveal testable connections between certain classes of events or processes is to organize data in the most scientifically useful manner possible. To be sure, there are shortcomings to Klapper's formulation in this regard, but his pioneering effort must be applauded as a step in the right direction. The critical commentary included in the present treatment was intended to suggest some cautions and a few lines of effort that may improve completeness and precision in future efforts to conceptualize mass media effects. In concluding this section of the present chapter, note is now taken of a few additional gropings to work out a vocabulary appropriate to this task.

The Expanding Vocabulary of Effects

The vocabulary of mass media effects has been expanding as research continues in a variety of disciplines. To the early trio of effects—*activation, reinforcement, conversion*—enunciated in a classic study of mass communications in a political context (Lazarsfeld, Berelson, & Gaudet, 1944), have come additions, variations, and some refinements beyond those noted in Klapper's (1960) directional typology. The vocabulary now includes apathy, boomerang, and sleeper effects. Reference to effects is also made in terms of narcotization, alienation, privatization, reactivation, polarization, and mobilization. Most of these terms have an ad hoc origin, some overlap in meaning, and occasionally they are joined together at different levels of abstraction; none of these circumstances particularly contributes to a systematic ordering of effects.

Such terms have come into use as investigators sought to make distinctions between media effects on attitudes and acts, between short and long range effects, between single exposure and campaign effects, between intended and unanticipated effects, and between effects on individuals versus those on a social systems level. Some of the terms

may be seen as variations on a theme of change emerging from a concern with common criteria. For example, the boomerang effect may be said to represent *negative conversion* while the sleeper effect represents *delayed conversion*. The former emerges in an analysis of change that begins with a consideration of the intent of the communicator; the latter includes this criterion plus an extension of the time dimension. Thus the boomerang effect is used in the literature to refer to media exposure that produces a result the opposite from that intended by the communicator (Klapper, 1960, p. 117). The sleeper effect, on the other hand, refers to an initial rejection of a communicator's point of view, followed, after a period of time, by a "coming around" to his position (see, e.g., Catton, 1960; Hovland, Janis, & Kelley, 1953, pp. 19–55).

While the time dimension must necessarily enter into any formulation of effects, not all conceptualizations emphasize the communicator's intent as a criterion. Some effect concepts focus more on audience response, while the communicator's intent is absent or only implicit in the definition. For example, *privatization* is used to describe the condition where the individual is overwhelmed by the flood of information brought to his attention through mass communication and reacts by turning to matters in his private life over which he presumably has greater control (see, e.g., Kris & Leites, 1947). The effect termed *apathy,* on the other hand, refers not to indifference to mass media material, or withdrawal from it, but is used to describe the condition where having information about the world gives the individual a false sense of mastery over his environment. The apathy effect occurs when a person spends so much time absorbing mass media material that he takes little direct action; he may believe that to be an informed citizen is equivalent to being an active citizen (see, e.g., Wright, 1959, p. 12). This is also referred to as the *narcotization* effect of mass communication

(Lazarsfeld & Merton, 1948). It could also be termed a *deactivation* effect.

When attention is directed toward *activation* effects, the emphasis is on a definitional criterion of audience response implicitly linked to communicator's intent, and the focus is usually on mass-media-induced changes in acts rather than attitudes. The activation effect initially described the instance where, following exposure to mass communications, subjects were moved to some overt act such as casting a vote, contributing money, writing a letter, or purchasing a product. When the shift is from an analysis of the responses of individuals to a consideration of changes in social patterns, activation has been termed *mobilization* (Lang & Lang, 1961, p. 435). Mendelsohn (1962) was critical of traditional research on the activation effect, terming it static in concept, and constructed a scale to measure the processes that induce action. This scale permits the analysis of the cumulative interconnection of three types of response to media messages: (1) rudimentary response (ability to recall message); (2) emotional response (recall plus affirmative answers to items concerning the message, the source, and so on; and (3) active response (1 and 2 plus learning relevant to positive decision, recommendation of message content to others, and indications that communications will be pursued further). The distinction between rudimentary and emotional responses is similar to that made early in this chapter between effective and successful communication.

There is also reference in the literature to a type of effect where the focus is on what happens to the message content as it is processed through the channels of communication. This effect may appear to be of lesser interest to sociologists than those mentioned above, but its occurrence has relevance for understanding the mass communicative process as a whole as well as bearing on the development of particular social effects. As has been seen, the fundamental problem in any communication system is that of reproducing at one point either exactly or approximately a message selected at another point. In information theory, where engineering purposes are paramount, all sources of error that distort the message in encoding, decoding, or while the message is in transit over the channel are lumped together under a single name, *noise* (Crowley et al., 1962, pp. 304–320). In most systems, therefore, some provisions are made to combat the effects of noise; the principal device is some form of redundancy. In mass communication networks, the term *refraction* has been employed to designate the reduction of fidelity in the transmission of content, whether such distortion comes from technological or nontechnological sources (Lang & Lang, 1961, pp. 438–443). When the message alteration occurs at the receiving end of the communication chain, however, the patterns of change have been described either in terms of an *embedding* process (the leveling, sharpening, and assimilation of Allport & Postman, 1947) or as a *compounding* pattern (DeFleur, 1962). The potential importance of these processes for the study of mass communication effects was demonstrated in a community diffusion experiment by DeFleur. He challenged the contention of many investigators that the embedding process is but a "questionable laboratory paradigm." DeFleur documented how individuals who receive a mass communicated message after it has passed through a number of removes from persons who received direct exposure are likely to receive a shorter version, selectively edited and distorted in accord with prevailing stereotypes, verbal habits, and cultural themes (pp. 68–70).

The above materials indicate the manner in which the vocabulary expressing the effects of mass communication has been growing. Of course, the invention of nomenclature must not be equated with the discovery of new principles or the extension of old ones. Many of the concepts making up the current dictionary of effects reflect the fact that much of the research in mass communication has tended to view persons as "targets" of communications impact rather than as a part of a total communication process. Stated otherwise, the majority of social science propositions about the impact of mass communication have been generated by research designed to meet the operational needs of communicators and propagandists (Lang & Lang, 1961, p. 425). Such needs are likely to result in research oriented to ask, "What will be the effects of mass communications?" rather than "Will mass communications have an effect?" or, more appropriately for social science purposes, "Under what conditions will mass communications have what effect?"

As the question of social effects is more adequately conceptualized, media impact over time and the reciprocal relationship between communicator and audience are being more thoroughly studied. In addition, research is being directed not only toward the question of what the media do to audiences, but also toward how audiences use the mass media. What is emerging is a reformulation of the question initially posed by Lasswell (1948), "Who says what in which channel to whom with what effect?" that has guided much of mass media analysis. This conceptualization stresses the communicator's view of the mass communicative process. The newer orientation, in essence, is asking, "In mass communication, who gets what from whom, by what means, and what do they do with it?" The merit of this approach is apparent, both from a reexamination of old studies and in the formulation of recent work such as in studies of audience reactions to radio serials (Herzog, 1944), daily newspapers (Berelson, 1949; Lyle, 1962), weekly newspapers (Janowitz, 1952; Larsen & Edelstein, 1960), and television (Steiner, 1963). These investigations produce evidence to demonstrate that the use of the media goes far beyond the manifest intent of the mass communicator. They thus reach into the zones of social effects of particular concern to sociologists (e.g., Wilensky, 1964).

DEFINING THE NORMS OF MEDIA OPERATION

On January 31, 1954, the Fourth Sunday after Epiphany, parishioners in a large metropolitan congregation found the following message in their church bulletin:

The motion picture "Julius Caesar," which has been widely advertised as an excellent film for general patronage, and which carries an A-1 Legion of Decency Rating, is appearing at the Music Box Theater. Although this picture in itself is unobjectionable, you are reminded that upon taking the Pledge of the Legion of Decency, you promised to avoid motion picture houses which show indecent or immoral pictures as a matter of policy. The Music Box Theater would seem by all standards to be such a house, and accordingly, you should wait to see the picture "Julius Caesar" until the film is shown elsewhere. The above applies also to the Lake City Theater, which is showing for the third time in recent months a condemned film ("The Moon is Blue" is playing currently at the Lake City Theater).

The response to this appeal is not known. The recurrent situation that such an effort symbolizes, however, can be of considerable significance in understanding the process of mass communication. This is just one of many efforts by organizations to mobilize a membership response to some form of mass communication. In addition to the use of boycotts, publications are often banned and sometimes burned, subscriptions are suspended, advertising is withdrawn, or box offices are picketed. Extreme reactions of this sort, as well as milder forms of audience response, such as letters to the editor or telephone calls to a radio or television station, when they take a collective form, can be influential feedback that may bring a redefinition in the mode of operating a medium of mass communication.

Audience feedback is of great interest in the sociology of mass communication. First, it reflects a conception of the social effects of mass communication; in its impact it matters little whether this is a generally valid conception or not. Second, to study this pattern of reaction, transmission, and accountability is to study how the norms of media operation are defined through the reciprocal relationship between the mass media and public opinion. Third, to study this phenomenon is to come to grips with public opinion in a distinctly sociological way. This way was aptly characterized by Blumer:

Insofar as public opinion is effective on societal action it becomes so only by entering into the purview of whoever, like legislators, executives, administrators, and policy makers have to act on public opinion . . . the individual takes into account different views only to the extent to which such views count. And views count pretty much on the basis of how the individual judges the "backing" of the views and the implication of the backing. It is in this sense, again, that the organization of the society with its differentiation of prestige and power enters into the character of public opinion (Blumer, 1948, p. 545).

The central task of a mass communication organization is to formulate the content that is transmitted to the audience. Since there are always alternative ways in which messages may be formulated and presented and since the mass communicator is usually under considerable pressure of time, the decision-making process is not a simple one. For example, a key role in the processing of information is that of the trained professional who makes the initial contact, direct or indirect, with an originating source. Reporters have four main techniques to gather information: direct observation of an event, search of secondary documents such as morgue clippings and reference works, the receipt of unsolicited information via tips or from government or press agent handouts, and direct interviewing of people who are involved in, concerned with, or informed about a news event (Webb, 1963, p. 1). Journalistic tradition in Western societies permits the reporter in this role to exercise considerable independent judgment in defining what is relevant.

What the professional perceives, however, and what he chooses to process depends on many factors. Research is mounting to clarify the functioning of the social frames of reference in which the communicator operates (Breed, 1955; Edelstein & Schulz, 1963; Gieber & Johnson, 1961; Pool & Shulman, 1959). It is clear that all communicators are enmeshed in critical social relations with sources, colleagues, employers, reference groups, and their "publics." Whatever the balance of these forces, it is highly unlikely that the role of professionals in the mass media can simply be that of observing the environment and passing unmodified and unselected information into the channels of mass communication.

In making content decisions, the few (the communicators) are influenced to some degree by a conception of the many (the audience). Sociological interest is focused therefore on the ways in which the communicator develops this image and on the social consequences of this process. In those systems based on direct economic support from the audience, the mass communicator is highly sensitive to the ups and downs in sales, whether they be of books, magazines, newspapers, or tickets at the box office. The market mechanism serves as a feedback route.

Apart from reacting to economic indexes, the mass communicator is also subject to the appraisal of fellow professionals, the response of intermedia critics (book, movie, and television reviewers), the scrutiny of government agencies, and the reactions voluntarily submitted from the audience. In some media, particularly in the early stages of their development, communicators are probably more sensitive and vulnerable to feedback from sources external to their medium than in others. Sensitivity to some of these influences in American television is suggested in an observation by Chairman Henry of the Federal Communications Commission, "I agree the broadcasters are afraid of economic and governmental sanctions. Certainly they'd be afraid to dissect a scandal in Congress. They *are* in a very delicate position. And I imagine potential sponsors don't want to get involved either. I'm told that really controversial programs are not, in general, conducive to sponsorship" (Efron, 1963, p. 20). That such a condition may have potent consequences is noted in a blunt statement by Henry Morgan, a television performer, who, when asked about his relationship to sponsors and network vice-presidents, commented, " 'They' are more frightened of opinions even than the audience is. The whole aim of broadcasting today is not to instruct, entertain nor edify. The machine is set up merely to be inoffensive. Completely, everlastingly, and soddenly, boringly inoffensive" (Wilner, 1963, p. 13).

Before further examining the general function of public opinion in mass media performance, it would be well to get a characterization of what the media should be doing in a broader sense than that suggested in the indictment of one particular performer. What follows, then, is not a culling of controlled experiments or field studies nor a series of quotations from authoritative sources, but, rather, a distillation of the main streams of argument about what norms should be governing mass communication today. These arguments feed small tributaries of reaction which sometimes have a way of merging into a flood of effective public opinion.

Contending Positions

A "great debate" revolves around the role of mass communication in modern society. Some sociologists and many social critics are asking if mass communication enhances social and political involvement and cultural creativity or if it induces apathy, indifference, and standardization and thus constitutes a mechanism for the manipulation of the masses and the concentration of power. The contest centering on such a question is only partly a function of the scarcity of reliable knowledge about the social effects

of mass communication. It also represents a deep division of values in society and, indeed, different conceptions of the nature of society itself. In part, too, it reflects different interpretations of where the mass media are perceived to be in their evolution from a technological invention to a social institution.

Berelson (1961) brought together three approaches to the appraisal of mass communication representing the viewpoints of intellectual critics ("Academicus"), mass communicators ("Practicus"), and social scientists ("Empiricus"). Noting that these three viewpoints are prominent in contemporary society, but that usually each camp talks only to itself, Berelson presented a perceptive conception of each ideal type in a simulated debate designed to reveal contrasting assumptions and to force transactions between positions. The labels for each position may call to mind such social critics as Dwight McDonald, such media managers as David Sarnoff, and such researchers as Paul Lazarsfeld. In reality it is unlikely that any spokesman, particularly one of eminence, would be found to represent only one position. These three major orientations nevertheless compete for the allegiance of both students and users of mass communication by projecting standards for the evaluation of media performance. Such efforts can set forces in motion to redefine the norms of media operation. What follows is a broad characterization of these three contending positions, a simplified personification of a range of actual viewpoints.

Academicus. This designation characterizes a person who first of all is concerned with values and who turns his critical attention toward the mass media. To Academicus, the overriding goal is to build a "better" society. The mass media, he believes, exert influence on what sort of society exists. When the many defects of society are taken into account, the mass media must be held to some degree responsible. There is, he insists, a duty on the part of media operators to look forward to long-run cultural goals instead of rationalizing approaches that bring private profits.

Academicus gathers his evidence from the literature of moral action and correctness, as well as from objective studies of Empiricus. It should be emphasized that almost all effective critics are persons of some background in the sciences or humanities, whose experience qualifies them to know something of how a society works and how the mass media might effect goals and values. Thus Academicus is not typically a stereotype of a nineteenth-century romanticist in a twentieth-century English department, but rather is an informed and articulate spokesman whose concern for values is shared by a wide enough public so that he can make himself a significant social force. Often this is true because the strength of his conviction is in his concern for values more than for his command of evidence.

Academicus is a worrier. He sees himself as the appointed guardian of cultural values. A central problem for him in evaluating mass communication is that of serious art versus mass or popular culture (for an analytic essay on the issues see Bell, 1962). A fit topic, says Academicus, must deal with a subject of importance and reality. A work must increase awareness of social problems and the general human condition. A basic assumption is that deviance from existing cultural values is not necessarily wrong and that a deviating person need not be either "reinstated to the fold" or destroyed in media portrayals. A related assumption is that endings need not always be shown as happy, but should follow logically from the action and forces in play. Academicus believes that media content is degrading modern man with an alluring diet of *kitsch* by presenting fantasy instead of reality. Media should be more realistic so that man can find workable solutions to real problems.

Academicus insists that the mass media be used as a tool to raise the general level of knowledge and intelligence. He is convinced that in the hands of responsible agents values, norms, and tastes can be elevated through mass communication. Thus the media may evoke responses to whatever message is disseminated. The media, to him, are chains, outlines, and forms in general structure. He "knows" that a message will somehow filter through, be received, and acted upon. He allows that the media have much more power than Empiricus could ever show.

For Academicus the operation of mass communications is divisible into the present function in society and the ideal function. The present is taken up with the transmission of diluted values and trivia leading to escape. The ideal and attainable function is that of purifier and uplifter of culture, not entertainment and escape, but instruction in the complexities and tragi-drama of life. Moreover, Academicus believes he holds the key: A society cannot really be free, or good, unless it is led by persons who have already had a glimpse of freedom or the good and undertakes to lead the greater number out into the light.

Empiricus. In some respects the stand of Empiricus is less readily characterized than is that of Academicus or Practicus. A debate tends to call for preferences, commitment, and recommendations and thus is a more alien context for Empiricus than for those who have substantively structured positions.

Empiricus is more comfortable as an investigator than as debater. In the former, he is a measurer: precise, objective, value free, or at least a value relativist. His attitude is, "I don't know, but I'll try to find out." He is optimistic that his findings will accrue to the benefit of all. As a debater, he tends to become a mediator. He feels under pressure to have to say more than his present findings truly permit. He does not mind whether his work is used to quench or to add fuel to the fires of the present debate, but he would rather start a new fire of his own. His counsel, however cautious, nevertheless can have real consequences, although in general it appears to be of a conservative sort.

Empiricus is the voice that warns Academicus and Practicus to re-examine their premises, to be sure of their evidence, and to revise their arguments as new knowledge dictates. He argues that it does not make sense to criticize or defend the media on the basis of intuition or vague impressions. He admonishes his debate colleagues to wait, to refrain from militant crusading (for either reform or defense of conditions) until more is known. He is the voice that tells the public that the "great debate" is premature or improperly cast and that to judge the cultural level of the media at a given point in time may be dubious and perhaps a dangerous practice. He appeals for further research.

When pressed for current research findings, his reply is to stress their limitations. He sees mass communication as a device used by society and by individuals for information, entertainment, education, social facilitation, and many other purposes, some intended and some not intended by the mass communicators. He suspects that the media can be either functional or dysfunctional, but notes that research is required to spell out the conditions for each.

He feels less guilty about watching television than do other people he knows. Sometimes he is asked to appear as an expert on a panel discussion. When this occurs, he states tentative conclusions and asks irritating questions. The invitations often are not repeated after the first performance. This, for Empiricus, is good. It leaves more time for research.

Practicus. Practicus is the media operator. Technical and management problems are part of his daily routine. Mass communication to him is not an abstraction. Since he has the responsibility of maintaining his medium in a competitive market place he is conscious of intricacies and subtleties not perceived by his debate colleagues. This shapes his thinking in ways which are often incompatible with the more abstract perspectives of his colleagues. Yet Practicus has criticized the media while nonpractitioners have defended them.

Practicus is a businessman. He manages capital and seeks a profit. Since his business is something of a public utility he is also moved by a sense of social responsibility. Struggling toward professionalization, he sees himself engaged in balancing such factors as freedom of the press, the public's right to know, truth, popular entertainment, and his own need to make a profit.

He develops a working philosophy to help achieve a balance. The keystone, simply expressed, is "give the audience what it wants." A person who would challenge public choice, freely expressed, challenges the very heart of the democratic process and free enterprise. The dollar ballot determines what the consumer wants. Empiricus and his knowledge can help, but the outcome must be the same: concentrate the effort on satisfying the largest possible number. Says Practicus, we are in a catering business where a few mistakes can be fatal.

Practicus agree that the contents of the mass media have consequences. Unlike Empiricus, he asserts and defends a value position, albeit a different one from that supported by Academicus. If his product reinforces the status quo and social stability, what is wrong with that? John Doe may not know what he wants to see on television, but he can tell you if he likes one program better than another. Give John Doe what he favors most of the time. If it strengthens his beliefs and supports society's norms and values, so much the better. Practicus further contends that it is one of his important functions to offer respite and relaxation. In the outside world, man is confronted by problems of every variety and intensity. The media can give him rest from worries and care. Practicus believes that Academicus is an alarmist; for his part, he sees little in the mass media menu of popular entertainment that has a harmful effect. What is more, he contends that Empiricus has not been able to come up with any real evidence to the contrary.

Epilogue: enter Publicus. Confrontation of contending positions either through hypo-

CHARACTERISTICS	ACADEMICUS	PRACTICUS	EMPIRICUS

Concept of Self, Typical Attitudes	EDUCATOR
	Intellectual
	Critic
	Academic Elite
	  —prescriptive
	  —theoretical
	  —abstract
	  —progressive
		BUSINESSMAN
		Economic being
		Expert
		Button-pusher
		  —realistic
		  —defensive
		  —practical
		  —concrete
		  —"democratic"
			SCIENTIST
			Observer
			Testor
			Analyst
			  —objective
			  —reserved
			  —dubious
			  —curious
			  —relativistic

Actual Responsibility for Media Content	LOW (Little involvement; much ignored by Practicus	HIGH (Full involvement, sets standards, responds in economic terms)	MODERATE (Increasing involvement, but considerable detachment)
Habitual Reaction to Media; Approach	PRESCRIPTIVE Critical and deprecatory	RATIONALIZES Defends and idealizes	HYPOTHESIZES Avoids value judgments

Functional Assessment of Media	MEDIA DYSFUNCTIONAL
	Limits choice
	Retards innovation
	Lowest made normal
	Escapist
	Materially oriented
		MEDIA FUNCTIONAL
		Extends culture
		Enhances democracy
		Performs service
		  —informs
		  —correlates
		  —entertains
		Stimulates economy
			MATTER OF CRITERIA
			Under what conditions?
			For what sector of the population?
			For what time period?
			Functions and dysfunctions may be simultaneously present

View of How Media Ought to be Used	TO EDUCATE, TO ACHIEVE VALUED ENDS To raise cultural level To inform more accurately	TO GIVE PUBLIC WHAT IT WANTS AND TO SHOW A PROFIT To do what it does even better	UNCERTAIN UNTIL MORE IS KNOWN Use now as a field of investigation

Fig. 2. Three approaches to the media of mass communication: An abstracting and extension of traits suggested by Berelson (1961).

thetical description as above or through an actual symposium (see, e.g., Jacobs, 1960) leaves gaps for interested persons who may find merit and fault in each position. Further features of the three orientations are outlined in Figure 2. Implicit in the whole comparison is the assumption that all three are potentially powerful forces. This power is ultimately derived from the linkages they have with each other and from the relationship that each has with the public, including the media audiences. The setting for this symbiotic drama may be likened to a large ocean-going vessel: Staggering Practicus is at the helm, petulant Academicus predicts shipwreck and sea dragons, Empiricus intently counts the barnacles, and Publicus rides more or less serenely in the cabin, trusting that there is a lifeboat on the deck.

While escape from the mass media would appear to be merely a matter of canceling subscriptions or flicking a switch to OFF, Publicus, intermittently and variously, draws concepts from the contending positions to engage in responses to the media other than mere withdrawal. Mixed reactions are necessarily the case, since the mass audience is a myth and indeed encompasses counterparts to the three positions. The audience for television, for example, includes protesters, embracers, and accommodaters (Glick & Levy, 1962). Accordingly, in the court of public opinion the authority of Academicus, Empiricus, or Practicus is subject to continuing scrutiny and contest as well as to confirmation and use.

Academicus projects ideals and visions of higher standards and thus nourishes protest about current conditions. His strength lies in his creative thinking, his power of expression, and the status of whatever his particular professional calling might be. His linkage with the general public is not always direct, but he can serve as an opinion leader when his ideas are taken from specialized forums and transmitted and amplified by other disseminators. To the skeptics, however, he seems to be saying, "Give the masses what I think they should have, for I know better than they what is good for them." He fears, perhaps, that the desire of the urban multitudes to participate in a culture of their own liking and choice will undermine "high" culture by corrupting the sources of talent that have cultivated it. Does a new tyranny lurk in the elite position that he represents? Would he institute formal means of regulation and control whose powers may ultimately extend beyond his present goals? Or would it be fairer to say that he merely wants evidence of growth rather than dictatorial prescriptive powers, or assurance that responsible, moral men will be in control? If this be the case, can he become interested in devoting his talent and influence to devising practical mechanisms so that bit by bit a move can be made from mediocrity?

Empiricus sees himself as a scientist, impartial and objective in his findings. His importance mounts as the need for information rises. But he has detractors, too. Since he appears to stand between Academicus and Practicus as a tool for any problem, the genuineness of his neutrality is called into question. Some suspect that he is merely Academicus with his emotions turned off. If

Academicus is thought of as a theorist of popular culture, a more realistic appraisal of the mutual interests of Empiricus and Academicus can be found in Katz and Foulkes (1962). Others find him a mere pawn of Practicus, busily engaged in devising rating systems that make popularity the test of performance with the result that the media content appeals to the lowest common denominator instead of aspiring to the highest common multiple. This charge is a continuing topic of congressional investigation and public discussion (see, e.g., Smith, 1963). Still others complain of his failure to formulate important questions, his misuse of language, his lack of imagination, his naive detachment from the audience, and his self-righteous "discovery" from time to time of "facts" that any fool knew intuitively all along (e.g., Kempton, 1961).

Despite these and other criticisms, it appears certain that the work and influence of Empiricus will loom even larger in the future of mass communications than it has in the past. A new role for the public, and a new responsibility for Empiricus, is evolving in the process. Even in planning investigations, researchers are beginning to speak not only to their fellow researchers and to sponsors, but also to relevant publics. Noting that research is being done on the public every day on behalf of all kinds of organizations and that the results of this research play a major part in shaping policies and in justifying them to the public, Lazarsfeld asserted that one cannot be a responsible citizen in an "age of social research" without some understanding of what research is all about, its uses, abuses, potentials, and limitations (Lazarsfeld, 1963, p. 410). Speaking directly to the concerns of the present context he also contended that "If research is to play a part in the 'great debate' of which Dr. Berelson has written, the researchers themselves have a public responsibility to indicate the limitations of their own efforts and the range of questions which remain to be answered" (Lazarsfeld, 1963, p. 410). For the realm of television, he then went on to outline (Lazarsfeld, 1963, pp. 411–422) the following five areas where research is needed: (1) the detailed study of the audience's experience; (2) experiments in changing public preferences; (3) studies of the long-range effects of television; (4) research on matters of taste; and (5) research on decision-making in the broadcasting industry.

The above could with little modification be a program for Empiricus in his future approach to any of the media. Inquiry into the last point, which Lazarsfeld described not only as a difficult area to study but one where probably the greatest gap in knowledge of the media exists, would reveal the nature of the actual relationship between Practicus and Publicus. Practicus argues, as previously stated, that the mass media "give the people what they want" and that the viewers, listeners, and readers ultimately determine the content of the media by their choices of what they will read, view, or hear. Whether or not this is a valid characterization of the role of the audience in relation to the media, it is only an arc of circular reasoning unless there is independent evidence of what the people do want. Empiricus can, and to some extent now does, provide this kind of evidence. If his studies are sophisticated enough to go beyond reactions to established patterns of content to probable response to untried alternatives, his efforts might even interest Academicus.

In making decisions about what content to offer Publicus, Practicus is not unmindful of the prescriptions of Academicus or the real or potential findings of Empiricus, but he is also subject to many other forces. Certainly the decisions that are made and the symbols that emerge are more than a product governed by artistic and professional considerations. They are also molded by social, economic, and political norms developed within the organization and penetrating from outside. The inputs into the mass communication system from the total society need to be studied. Clearly, the large-scale production of mass media messages entails a complex organization that operates in a broad social context of positive and negative pressures which push and pull the mass communicators in various directions with respect to performance.

Publicus enters into this picture not only as a consumer in a mass market, where he counts mainly in terms of his numbers, but also as a critic, where he counts in terms of some organization with a political as well as an economic potential. Practicus is sometimes subject to the militant voice of a sensitive and organized pressure group. Crusades by such groups have activated local, state, and national political bodies, leading to the threat or the actual imposition of censorship of mass communication (see, e.g., Winick, 1959). Historically, in the United States in particular, such action has more often led to adjustments by media organizations through the establishment of some form of "self-regulation." This means that the industry taxes itself to establish an organization to police itself. Codes of good practice are formulated, media content is reviewed before release, and other efforts are made to head off the kind of public criticism that gave rise to self-regulation in the first place.

The manner in which this came about for the motion picture industry has been thoroughly documented and analyzed (Inglis, 1947). The outline of a similar process for the medium of comic books has also been reported (Lundberg, Schrag, & Larsen, 1963, pp. 236–241). Both cases reveal the mechanics and the power of public opinion in influencing mass communication, after mass communication has, for some reason, incited public opinion. There is, in other words, a close reciprocal relationship between Practicus and Publicus.

For sociologists interested in general problems of social control, and specifically concerned with the emergence and application of organizational norms, studies of the development of self-regulation for all the mass media would clearly be instructive. There are also reasons why students of mass communication should maintain an interest in self-regulation. The interpretation of the codes governing media content reflect how media organizations diagnose current public opinion, manners, morals, and customs. Analysis of code changes and review decisions would continue to illuminate the relationship between public opinion and mass communication. While it is known that self-regulation has been successful in warding off public criticism and achieving new esteem for the media, very little is known about the internal consequences of the operation of the review mechanisms over time. For example, it would be important to explore what happens to professional creativity and the opportunities for innovation as the rough edge of controversy is constantly cut from materials. How do professionals internalize the norms specified in the code and in the practices established by the reviewers? That this does take place is suggested by the experience of the comic-code authority as revealed in an analysis of their work by the writer. During the first three months of 1957, the code authority brought about revisions in 38 per cent of the books reviewed before release. The percentages for the same three month period in succeeding years were as follows: 1958, 33 per cent; 1959, 28 per cent; and 1960, 8 per cent. For the whole year of 1962, the code administrator (*CMAA Newsletter,* August, 1963) reported that 1,047 books were reviewed, and of these 13 per cent were found to need some revisions in order to be able to carry the seal of approval.

In addition to studying the possible impact of code decisions on media professionals, it would also be of interest to study systematically how review practices standardize media content. Some possibilities are indicated in the following statements given to the writer in an interview with a comic-code reviewer:

In a number of cases we have used the Code directive "Criminals shall not be presented so as to be rendered glamorous, etc." Now "Billy the Kid" and other outlaws are depicted as having committed minor indiscretions but not real crimes, and, while they are wanted by law men, they are really not criminals.

Our present problems involve stories about teenagers, in which they are shown as becoming interested in "gang" boys or girls. Of course, they always take a moral course in the end, but we watch out for too detailed expositions of the behavior of gang members depicted as horrible examples. In these stories we play down quarrelsome parents and slum conditions used as explanations of anti-social behavior in the children (Moscow, 1960).

The impact on readers of such "safe" content is not known. Nor is the long-run social implication of these procedures and similar ones applied to more important media, such as television. For the present, however, such decisions by the comic-code authority, along with an active public relations program, has succeeded in converting former critics to tolerant, and indeed friendly, admirers of this medium. A vast array of church, civic, veteran, and business organizations now approve of comic magazines, and some have even made public awards to the industry. The United States Chamber of Commerce in 1960 awarded the Comics Magazine Association a silver plaque "for outstanding achievement in the business and public interest." For the eighth consecutive year since the Comics' Code became operative, the National Office for Decent Literature in 1962 did not list any comics' magazine titles as "Disapproved for Youth" (Darvin, 1963). On the level of silencing critical organizational reaction, then, self-regulation has been a success. From other perspectives, however, some students are critical of this form of internal censorship, asserting that it constitutes a serious challenge to the traditional conception of a free press (e.g., Twomey, 1957).

Self-regulation is a delicate mechanism created and sustained by the forces of public opinion. This being the case, it has within it the seeds of its own dissolution. When public opinion relaxes its vigilant stance toward a medium, as a result of the success of self-regulation, some elements within the mass communications industry may begin to withdraw their support of self-regulation. Once stability and some respectability have been achieved for their medium and the public pressure is off, they may feel that the problem is solved. If this process proceeds, "less reliable" entrepreneurs may re-enter the field to begin to produce content that once again calls forth public response, and a cycle of influence giving rise to regulation may again be repeated. This time the possibility of government censorship might be more seriously considered in order to maintain a continuing form of regulation.

Some of the elements in the above sketch have appeared and reappeared in the history of self-regulation in American mass communication. They currently are prominent in the field of comic magazines. The President of the CMAA, in his 1963 annual address, said:

We now represent a reduced percentage of the industry as a result of the addition of another large publisher to the ranks of non-members, and to that extent the effectiveness of our program has narrowed. Unfortunately a considerable number of titles, published by non-members, appear on newsstands without the Code Authority's seal of approval. We cannot, under the circumstances, provide the public and the wholesaler and retailer protection against the infiltration of objectionable material in comics magazines on an industry wide basis. Furthermore, the absence of the seal on these comics magazine covers is an open invitation to others who may come into the field in the future to avoid Code standards and the regulatory process (Goldwater, 1963).

This official then took cognizance of the elemental force in self-regulation. He called on the public, on voluntary organizations, and on the organs of opinion to "lend their voices and their influence to assure the program's effective continuance by clearly urging the non-member firms to participate in it" (Goldwater, 1963).

To study self-regulation, which many see as the only realistic alternative to formal censorship in modern society, is to study a system in dynamic equilibrium. From this line of inquiry it would appear that one of the major social effects of mass communication is to generate its own regulation and control.

REFERENCES

Allport, G. W., & Postman, L. The psychology of rumor. New York: Holt, 1947.

Aronson, E., Turner, Judith A., & Carlsmith, J. M. Communicator credibility and communication discrepancy as determinants of opinion change. J. abnorm. soc. Psychol., 1963, 67, 31–36.

Barnett, H. G. Innovation: The basis of cultural change. New York: McGraw, 1953.

Bart, P. Advertising: Children's role debated. N.Y. Times west. Ed., July 29, 1963, p. 14.

Bell, D. Modernity and mass society: On the varieties of cultural experience. Stud. publ. Communic., 1962, 4, 3–34.

Berelson, B. Communications and public opinion. In W. Schramm (Ed.), Communications in modern society. Urbana: Univer. of Illinois Press, 1948. Pp. 167–185.

Berelson, B. What missing the newspaper means. In P. F. Lazarsfeld & F. N. Stanton (Eds.), Communications research, 1948–1949. New York: Harper, 1949. Pp. 111–129.

Berelson, B. The great debate on cultural democracy. Stud. publ. Communic., 1961, 3, 3–14.

Berelson, B., Lazarsfeld, P. F., & McPhee, W. N. Voting. Chicago: Univer. of Chicago Press, 1954.

Berger, P. L. Invitation to sociology: A humanistic perspective. Garden City, N.Y.: Doubleday, 1963.

Blumer, H. Public opinion and public opinion polling. Amer. socio. Rev., 1948, 13, 542–554.

Bose, S. P. Peasant values and innovation in India. Amer. J. Sociol., 1962, 57, 552–560.

Boyle, R. P. The diffusion and adoption of innovations: A study of an Indian student community. Unpublished masters thesis, Univer. of Washington, 1963.

Breed, W. Social control in the news room. Soc. Forces, 1955, 33, 326–335.

Brehm, J. W., & Cohen, A. R. *Explorations in cognitive dissonance.* New York: Wiley, 1962.

Brouwer, M. Mass communication and the social sciences: Some neglected areas. *Int. soc. Sci. J.,* 1962, 14, 303–319.

Brown, R. *Explanation in social science.* Chicago: Aldine, 1963.

Catton, W. R., Jr. Changing cognitive structure as a basis for the sleeper effect. *Soc. Forces,* 1960, 38, 348–354.

Coleman, J. S. Consumer behavior and computer simulation. Paper read at Amer. Ass. Adv. Agen. Meetings, Chicago, October, 1961.(a)

Coleman, J. S. Diffusion in incomplete social structures. Paper read at West. Mgmt Sci. Conf., Cambria Pines, California, November, 1961.(b)

Coleman, J. S., Katz, E., & Menzel, H. The diffusion of an innovation among physicians. *Sociometry,* 1957, 20, 253–270.

Crowley, T. H., Harris, G. G., Miller, S. E., Pierce, J. R., & Runyon, J. P. *Modern communications.* New York: Columbia Univer. Press, 1962.

Darvin, L. (Ed.) No comics disapproved by NODL in 1962. *CMAA Newsletter,* April, 1963.

Davison, W. P. On the effects of communication. *Publ. Opin. Quart.,* 1959, 23, 343–360.

DeFleur, M. L. Mass communication and the study of rumor. *Sociol. Inquiry,* 1962, 32, 51–70.

DeFleur, M. F., & Larsen, O. N. *The flow of information.* New York: Harper, 1958.

Deutschmann, P. J. Communication in an Andean village. Paper read at Ass. Educ. Journ. Conv., Chapel Hill, North Carolina, August, 1962.

Deutschmann, P. J. Measurement in communication research. In R. O. Nafziger & D. M. White (Eds.), *Introduction to mass communications research.* (2nd ed.) Baton Rouge: Louisiana State Univer. Press, 1963. Pp. 207–237.

Dodd, S. C. *The probable acts of man.* Iowa City: State Univer. of Iowa, 1963. 2 vols.

Edelstein, A. S., & Schulz, J. B. The leadership role of the weekly newspapers as seen by community leaders: A sociological perspective. *Journ. Quart.,* in press.

Efron, Edith. Why the timid giant treads softly. *TV Guide,* 1963, 11, 15–21.

Elkin, F. *The child and society.* New York: Random House, Inc., 1960.

Ennis, P. H. The social structure of communication systems: A theoretical proposal. *Stud. publ. Communic.,* 1961, 3, 120–144.

Ferguson, J., & Smith, R. B. A theory of informal social influence. In W. N. McPhee, (Ed.), *Formal theories of mass behavior.* New York: The Free Press of Glencoe, 1963. Pp. 74–103.

Festinger, L. *A theory of cognitive dissonance.* Evanston, Ill.: Row, Peterson, 1957.

Forer, R. The impact of a radio program on adolescents. *Publ. Opin. Quart.,* 1955, 19, 184–194.

Freidson, E. Communications research and the concept of the mass. *Amer. soc. Rev.,* 1953, 18, 313–317.

Gerson, W. M. Social structure and mass media socialization. Unpublished doctoral dissertation, Univer. of Washington, 1963.

Gieber, W., & Johnson, W. The city hall beat: A study of reporter and source roles. *Journ. Quart.,* 1961, 38, 289–297.

Glick, I. O., & Levy, S. J. *Living with television.* Chicago: Aldine, 1962.

Goldwater, J. L. Annual report of president. *CMAA Newsletter,* August, 1963.

Hagerstrand, T. On monte carlo simulation of diffusion. Unpublished paper, Univer. of Lund, Sweden, 1960.

Heider, F. Attitudes and cognitive organizations. *J. Psychol.,* 1946, 21, 107–112.

Herzog, Herta. What do we really know about daytime serial listeners? In P. F. Lazarsfeld & F. N. Stanton (Eds.), *Radio research, 1942–3.* New York: Duell, Sloan & Pearce, 1944. Pp. 3–33.

Himmelweit, Hilde T., Oppenheim, A. N., & Vince, Pamela. *Television and the child.* New York: Oxford Univer. Press, 1958.

Hirabayashi, Esther. Mass media and fluoridation: A study of a fluoridation plebiscite. Unpublished masters thesis, Univer. of Washington, 1963.

Hovland, C. I. Effects of the mass media of communication. In G. Lindzey (Ed.), *Handbook of social psychology.* Cambridge, Mass.: Addison-Wesley, 1954. Pp. 1062–1103.

Hovland, C. I., Janis, I. L., & Kelley, H. H. *Communication and persuasion*. New Haven, Conn.: Yale Univer. Press, 1953.

Inglis, Ruth A. *Freedom of the movies*. Chicago: Univer. of Chicago Press, 1947.

Jacobs, N. (Ed.) Mass culture and mass media. *Daedalus*, 1960, 89, 271–418.

Janowitz, M. *The community press in an urban setting*. Glencoe, Ill.: Free Press, 1952.

Johnstone, J. W. C. Social context and mass media reception. *Stud. Publ. Communic.*, 1959, 2, 25–30.

Karlsson, G. *Social mechanisms*. Glencoe, Ill.: Free Press, 1958.

Katz, E. Communication research and the image of society: Convergence of two traditions. *Amer. J. Sociol.*, 1960, 65, 435–440.

Katz, E. The social itinerary of technical change: Two studies in the diffusion of innovation. *Hum. Organ.*, 1961, 20, 70–82.

Katz, E., & Foulkes, D. On the use of the mass media as escape. *Publ. Opin. Quart.*, 1962, 26, 377–388.

Katz, E., & Lazarsfeld, P. F. *Personal influence*. Glencoe, Ill.: Free Press, 1955.

Katz, E., Levin, M. L., & Hamilton, H. Traditions of research on the diffusion of innovation. *Amer. sociol. Rev.*, 1963, 28, 237–252.

Keller, A. G. *Reminiscences of William Graham Sumner*. New Haven, Conn.: Yale Univer. Press, 1935.

Kempton, M. Social notes on the A.S.A. meetings. *Sociol. Inquiry*, 1961, 31, 180–181.

Key, V. O., Jr. *Politics, parties, and pressure groups*. New York: Crowell, 1958.

Key, V. O., Jr. *Public opinion and American democracy*. New York: Knopf, 1961.

Klapper, J. T. *The effects of mass communication*. Glencoe, Ill.: Free Press, 1960.

Kris, E., & Leites, N. Trends in 20th century propaganda. In Géza Róheim (Ed.), *Psychoanalysis and the social sciences*. New York: International Univer. Press, 1947. Pp. 393–409.

Lang, K., & Lang, Gladys E. *Collective dynamics*. New York: Crowell, 1961.

Larsen, O. N. Innovators and early adopters of television. *Sociol. Inquiry*, 1962, 32, 16–33.

Larsen, O. N., & Edelstein, A. S. Communication, consensus and the community involvement of urban husbands and wives. *Acta Sociologica*, 1960, 5, 15–30.

Larsen, O. N., Gray, L. N., & Fortis, J. G. Goals and goal-achievement methods in television content: Models for anomie? *Sociol. Inquiry*, 1963, 33, 180–196.

Lasswell, H. D. The structure and function of communication in society. In L. Bryson (Ed.), *The communication of ideas*. New York: Harper, 1948. Pp. 37–51.

Lazarsfeld, P. F. Some reflections on past and future research on broadcasting. In G. A. Steiner, *The people look at television*. New York: Knopf, 1963. Pp. 410–422.

Lazarsfeld, P. F., Berelson, B., & Gaudet, Hazel. *The peoples' choice*. New York: Duell, Sloan & Pearce, 1944.

Lazarsfeld, P. F., & Merton, R. K. Mass communication, popular taste and organized social action. In L. Bryson (Ed.), *The communication of ideas*. New York: Harper, 1948. Pp. 95–118.

Lionberger, H. F. *Adoption of new ideas and practices*. Ames: Iowa State Univer. Press, 1960.

Lucas, D. B., & Britt, S. H. *Measuring advertising effectiveness*. New York: McGraw, 1963.

Lundberg, G. A., Schrag, C. C., & Larsen, O. N. *Sociology*. New York: Harper, 1963.

Lyle, J. Immediate vs. delayed reward use of newspapers by adolescents. *Journ. Quart.*, 1962, 39, 83–85.

Maccoby, N., & Maccoby, Eleanor E. Homeostatic theory in attitudes change. *Publ. Opin. Quart.*, 1961, 25, 538–545.

Medalia, N. Z. Who cries wolf? The reporters of damage to police in a pseudo-disaster. *Soc. Probs*, 1959–1960, 7, 233–240.

Medalia, N. Z., & Larsen, O. N. Diffusion and belief in a collective delusion: The Seattle windshield pitting epidemic. *Amer. soc. Rev.*, 1958, 23, 180–186.

Mendelsohn, H. Measuring the process of communications effect. *Publ. Opin. Quart.*, 1962, 26, 411–416.

Menzel, H. Innovation, integration, and marginality. *Amer. sociol. Rev.*, 1960, 25, 704–713.

Moscow, Mrs. Warren. General explanations of code revisions. Interview and memorandum, August 24, 1960.

Newcomb, T. H. An approach to the study of communicative acts. *Psychol. Rev.*, 1953, 60, 393–404.

Osgood, C. E., & Tannenbaum, P. H. The principle of congruity in the prediction of attitude change. *Psychol. Rev.*, 1955, **65**, 42–55.

Pool, I. S., & Shulman, I. Newsmen's fantasies, audiences, and newswriting. *Publ. Opin. Quart.*, 1959, **23**, 145–158.

Rapoport, A. Spread of information through a population with socio-structural bias. *Bull. Math. Biophysics*, 1953, **15**, 523–546.

Riley, J. W., Jr., & Riley, Mathilda W. Mass communication and the social system. In R. K. Merton, L. Broom, & L. S. Cottrell, Jr. (Eds.), *Sociology today*. New York: Basic Books, 1959. Pp. 537–578.

Rogers, E. M. *Diffusion of innovations*. New York: The Free Press of Glencoe, 1962.

Rogers, E. M., & Havens, A. E. Predicting innovativeness. *Sociol. Inquiry*, 1962, **32**, 34–42.

Schrag, C. Some demerits of contemporary sociology. *Pac. soc. Rev.*, 1961, 4, 43–51.

Schramm, W. The effects of mass communication: A review. *Journ. Quart.*, 1949, **26**, 397–409.

Schramm, W. (Ed.) *The science of human communication*. New York: Basic Books, 1963.

Schramm, W., Lyle, J., & Parker, E. B. *Television in the lives of our children*. Palo Alto: Stanford Univer. Press, 1961.

Smith, D. TV ratings: The debate grows. *N.Y. Times west. Ed.*, August 17, 1963, p. 7.

Spitzer, S. P. Perception and interpersonal behavior following focal communication. Unpublished doctoral dissertation, Univer. of Washington, 1963.

Steinberg, C. S. *The mass communicators*. New York: Harper, 1958.

Steiner, G. A. *The people look at television*. New York: Knopf, 1963.

Taylor, J. B. *Science on display: A study of the United States science exhibit Seattle world's fair, 1962*. Seattle: Univer. of Washington Institute for Social Research, 1963.

Twomey, J. New forms of social control over mass media content. *Stud. Publ. Communic.*, 1957, **1**, 38–44.

Webb, E. J. The interview or the only wheel in town. Unpublished paper, Northwestern Univer., 1963.

Wertham, F. The scientific study of mass media effects. *Amer. J. Psychiat.*, 1962, **119**, 306–311.

Westley, B. H., & Maclean, M. S., Jr. A conceptual model for communications research. *Audio-Visual Communic. Rev.*, 1955, **3**, 3–12.

Wilensky, H. L. Social structure, popular culture, and mass behavior: Some research implications. *Stud. Publ. Communic.*, 1961, **3**, 15–22.

Wilensky, H. L. Mass society and mass culture. *Amer. soc. Rev.*, 1964, **29**, 173–197.

Wilner, N. Everything is going down the drain. *TV Guide*, 1963, **11**, 12–14.

Winick, C. *Taste and the censor in television*. New York: Fund for the Republic, Inc., 1959.

Wright, C. R. *Mass communication*. New York: Random House, Inc., 1959.

Wright, C. R. Functional analysis and mass communication. *Publ. Opin. Quart.*, 1960, **24**, 605–620.

Zajonc, R. Some effects of space serials. *Publ. Opin. Quart.*, 1954, **55**, 367–374.

CHAPTER 11   Collective Behavior

RALPH H. TURNER

The assumption that there is a special field of study which can be called "collective behavior" rests primarily upon apparent contrasts with normal social and institutional behavior. It is the unusual character of mob behavior, of social movements in which otherwise meek individuals dare to threaten the established powers, of rumor process in which normally critical people seem to accept the improbable without a second thought, of dancing and revelrous behavior in which modest and sedate people make public spectacles of themselves, and of panic in which usually considerate people trample others to death, which leads investigators to single out a special field of study. Formal definitions are efforts to find theoretically sound and empirically objective grounds for the intuitive separation. But the formalization of the distinction is contingent upon some conception of normal behavior, whether explicit or implicit. Conceptions of normal behavior have undergone steady change as the understanding of normal social processes has progressed, and each such change has required a reassessment of the boundaries of collective behavior.

Three such changes have had profound effects on the conception of the field. Initially the subject matter of crowds and related phenomena was approached from the point of view that the individual had come under the sway of the group, yielding his independent judgment in the face of some overpowering collective force. Although this view still plays a large part in popular thinking, the sociological developments, from Bagehot (1869 [1948]) and Sumner (1906 [1940]) to the recent reference group theorists and the psychological research of Sherif (1935) and Asch (1951), have stressed the degree to which normal behavior is under group control and influence. If the entire framework of objects, alternatives, and criteria within which supposedly individual discretion is exercised is itself a group product, constantly reinforced and modified by group process, then the intensification of group control over the individual in collective behavior may be an illusion. The phenomena of collective behavior must then be marked by the *manner* in which social control operates rather than by its presence or degree of effectiveness, if the criterion of control is not to be abandoned entirely.

A second common-sense distinction emphasized the unpredictability of collective behavior. Observers were struck by the discontinuity between the normal behavior of an individual and the tendencies revealed in the crowd. They were also struck by the supposed propensity for a crowd to shift its object suddenly and unpredictably. But developments in psychology and especially the influence of psychoanalysis have convinced most students that much of the behavior of individuals in unusual situations would have been predictable from a sufficient knowledge of the hidden layers of his personality. The resentments that find expression in mobs or revolutionary movements and the selfishness expressed in panic can often be discovered in the individual by sophisticated procedures of psychological detection and used as a basis for prediction. Similarly, a better understanding of schisms in normal community life render many shifts in the course of crowd, public, and movement behavior understandable. The simplest and most prevalent basis for predictions in social sciences is the assumption that whatever people have been observed doing at time *one* they will continue to do at time *two*. As relational paradigms take the place of such simple continuity models in predicting behavior in conventional situations, the problem of predicting collective behavior becomes less distinctive.

A third and more sociologically sophisticated basis for distinguishing the field of collective behavior was aptly stated in Park and Burgess' commentary on the crowd: "The distinction between control in the crowd and in other forms of society is that the crowd has no tradition. It has no point of reference in its own past to which its members can refer for guidance. It has therefore neither symbols, ceremonies, rites, nor ritual: it imposes no obligations and creates no loyalties" (Park & Burgess, 1921, p. 790). But the stress on spontaneity and the discontinuity from conventional norms and social structure (Blumer, 1939 [1946]; Lang & Lang, 1961; Turner & Killian, 1957) seems less clear when the complexity of normal social structure and social norms is recognized. There is seldom only a single rule applicable to a particular situation, and the application of different rules indicates different courses of action. Careful examination of a wide range of collective behavior reveals few instances that are not specifically justified by their participants on the basis of some extant social norm and which cannot be shown to have some continuity with tradition. If there is a reasonable distinction to be made on this score, it must rest on the complex character of the relationship of collective behavior to established norms and social structure and not on a total discontinuity.

There is another type of difficulty in defining collective behavior which derives from the fact that such behavior is often thought to be coexistent with institutional or organized group behavior. While the extreme forms of panic and mob behavior can serve as relatively pure instances of collective behavior, it is necessary to recognize a collective behavior component in such otherwise institutional phenomena as fashion, financial cycles, organizational morale, and intraorganizational power plays. That the course of group life in any particular situation may have to be explained as a product of the simultaneous operation of an institutional causal system and a collective behavior causal system has been explicitly acknowledged (Blumer, 1939 [1946]; Lang & Lang, 1961; LaPiere, 1938; Turner & Killian, 1957). But defining collective behavior as a component of group behavior rather than simply as what happens in designated types of groups requires a refined understanding of its distinctive processes.

The conclusion toward which one is forced by this discussion is that a satisfactory definition depends on successive refinements of inadequate definitions based on the understanding acquired by working with these definitions. At present the most productive developments may stem from consideration of the peculiar character of the relationships between the behavior and organization of collective behavior and the conventional social norms and social organization. It is altogether possible that the search will ultimately undermine all of the traditional dynamic distinctions between collective behavior and organizational behavior and suggest that no special set of principles is required to deal with this subject matter. Past developments suggest that investigators should stress continuity rather than discontinuity with conventional behavior.

The following discussion of collective behavior begins by exploring certain alternative theoretical approaches to the field. Because of its prototypical character, the crowd will be used as the focus for the discussion, and the theories applied to other forms of collective behavior. Next will come an examination of the essential conditions for the emergence of collective behavior and consideration of the simple processes by which people arrive at collective definitions as a basis for collective action. Finally, the factors and processes associated with the transformation of collective behavior into its various developed forms will be reviewed. (Social movements, which are in large part instances of collective behavior, are treated in Chapter 12.)

THEORY OF COLLECTIVE BEHAVIOR

Treatments of the dynamics of collective behavior reflect three different kinds of theory which have been presented with varying degrees of explicitness. *Contagion* theories explain collective behavior on the basis of some process whereby moods, attitudes, and behavior are communicated rapidly and accepted uncritically. *Convergence* theories explain collective behavior on the basis of the simultaneous presence of people who share the same predispositions and preoccupations. *Emergent norm* theories see collective behavior as regulated by a social norm which arises in a special situation.

Contagion Theory

Some form of contagion, whereby unanimous, intense feeling and behavior at variance with usual predispositions are induced among the members of a collectivity, has been the focal point for most sociological study of collective behavior. From the early work of Bagehot (1869 [1948]), LeBon (1896), and Tarde (1901), through the American tradition of Ross (1921), Park and Burgess (1921), Young (1945), Blumer (1946), and the Langs (1961), this approach has played a major part. The foremost problem which this type of theory sets for the investigator is to explain how people in collectivities come to behave (a) uniformly, (b) intensely, and (c) at variance with their usual patterns. In differing degrees theorists of this bent accept LeBon's "law of the mental unity of crowds." "Under certain given circumstances, and only under those circumstances, an agglomeration of men presents new characteristics very different from those of the individuals composing it. The sentiments and ideas of all the persons in the gathering take one and the same direction, and their conscious personality vanishes" (LeBon, 1896, pp. 23–24). The solutions to this problem focus upon psychological mechanisms such as imitation, suggestion, and emotional contagion, through which dissemination takes place, and anonymity and restricted attention, which neutralize ordinary behavior anchorages.

In summarizing a common view of the process leading to this condition of unanimity and intensity, Blumer (1939 [1946]) contrasted the *circular reaction* of the crowd with the *interpretative interaction* of normal groups. The former "refers to a type of interstimulation wherein the response of one individual reproduces the stimulation that has come from another individual and in being reflected back to this individual reinforces the stimulation" (Blumer, 1946). Responses in the latter form of interaction follow upon interpretation, rather than directly upon the stimulus behavior, and are therefore likely to be different from the stimulus behavior. Since social structure ordinarily makes its impact through the interpretation phase, crowd behavior is thought to exhibit characteristics of herd behavior in animals (Blumer, 1939 [1946]; Trotter, 1919). It is similarly argued that the stripping away of "structured expectations of the participants" means that "psychological categories to supplement the categories of social structure" are required to explain collective behavior (Lang & Lang, 1961, p. 12).

Suggestion is the psychological mechanism upon which reliance has most often been placed. When writers such as Trotter (1919) asserted that suggestion is fundamental to all social behavior or Tarde (1901) that imitation is the basic process, suggestion in the crowd must be distinguished on the basis of the unusual limitation in the sources of suggestion. Tarde, accordingly, made the physical contiguity of crowd members a crucial criterion for the existence of the crowd. Trotter concluded that the degree to which the suggestion appears to emanate from the herd and embody the herd view determines its acceptance. Writers who distinguish the crowd according to the preponderance of suggestion and suggestibility are then led to search for the conditions which determine degrees of suggestibility. McDougall (1927) attributed suggestibility especially to the crowd's sense of power and to emotional excitement. Prestige, either of an individual or of the group, is the source characteristic most consistently viewed as conducive to acceptance of suggestion. Psychological research, beginning with Binet (1900), has accumulated a great deal of evidence on the conditions of suggestibility under laboratory conditions, whose extrapolation to crowd situations need not be of concern here.

Investigators have often asserted an inherent contagiousness of emotionally expressive behavior as the key mechanism in crowd behavior. McDougall enunciated a principle of primitive sympathy, that "each instinct . . . is capable of being excited in one individual by the expressions of the same emotion in another" (McDougall, 1927, p. 25). The fact that a situation is one that evokes emotional expression and that the emotion is a simple rather than complex one determines that contagion will take place. Control of a crowd by playing the national anthem, during which people must inhibit all emotional expression, is an effort to interrupt contagiousness of this sort.

The place of leaders in giving direction to crowds has generally been stressed, usually following the tradition of LeBon who asserted that the crowd seeks leaders and that "the leader has most often started as one of the led" (LeBon, 1896, p. 118). The opposite viewpoint, that there must be a leader before a crowd comes into being, was asserted by Gabriel Tarde (1901). Freud (1921) made a similar assumption the basis for a serious attempt to locate a more satisfactory mechanism than suggestion to account for the subservience of members to the group. Freud drew upon the similarity between crowd behavior and neurotic behavior and proposed that the explanation for suggestibility in groups be found in the harnessing of libidinal (or love) energy. An organized group is held together by two kinds of ties: to the leader and among the members. The suppression of the normal ambivalence among members of a group indicates that some new kind of libidinal tie must be at work since no other force would be strong enough to nullify negative reactions. The mechanism which accounts for the readiness of members to accept suggestions uncritically from others in the group is identification. Identification is the earliest form of emotional tie, but one which gives way to object-choice as the individual matures. When object-choice is blocked, however, there is a regression to identification. In groups the members form intense attachments to a common leader. Object-choice is blocked because the leader cannot reciprocate with an exclusive attachment to any of the group members. Consequently the members' attachments are transformed into identifications with the leader and with their fellows. Identification with their fellows is a protective device against special privilege: If I cannot possess the leader, neither must you, and complete uniformity and equality must be the rule among us. It is this two-way identification which makes for the rapid dissemination and uncritical acceptance of suggestion in the crowd.

Social contagion, imitation, suggestion, emotional contagiousness, and identification are the processes variously assumed to come into operation as vehicles for social contagion. In addition there are mechanisms which are believed to neutralize the normal inhibitions and social pressures against types of behavior which occur in the crowd. Normal social control is effective largely because the individual is known and identified and held responsible for his actions. In a large crowd people lose sight of individuals and mix with strangers before whom they can act without shame. Restriction of attention is another device which enables the present crowd to take the place of the normal range of reference groups in legitimating a course of action. If ability to carry out a course of action successfully is often a consideration in judging it legitimate, the apparent power of the crowd adds to its displacement of the usual behavioral anchorages.

While writers from the contagion point of view have in common their conception of crowd behavior as "not volitional but impulsive" (McDougall, 1920 [1927]), they differ in the manner in which they distinguish it from organized group behavior. Freud nowhere made any sharp distinction, while Tarde (1901) and Trotter (1919) differentiated in degree rather than kind. LeBon (1896), on the other hand, made the sharpest distinction on the basis of his law of mental unity. The preponderance of interpretative interaction (Blumer, 1939) and the control of interaction by shared expectations (Lang & Lang, 1961) have also been noted as characteristics of organized groups which distinguish them from crowds.

While not denying that there are differences, Park and Burgess cautioned that none of the writers had "succeeded in distinguishing clearly between the organized or 'psychological' crowd, as LeBon calls it, and other similar types of social groups" (Park & Burgess, 1921, p. 876).

There are certain common difficulties in the use of contagion theory as an approach to collective behavior. First, characterizations seem to rely excessively on the extreme and rare instances of behavior which the sociologist has no opportunity to observe for himself. The revivals, riots, demonstrations, and other events that sociologists visit appear to lack the contagiousness that purportedly whips disinterested bystanders into an emotional fury. Since the reports which support the contagion theories best are historical accounts by untrained and horrified observers, it is even conceivable that theorists have merely reconstructed the nightmare experienced by an observer in the face of something threatening and incomprehensible to him. But even if the reports are correct but apply only to rare events, it would be unwise to adopt the exceptional aberration as the model for collective behavior as a whole.

Second, the idea that crowds require a level of psychological explanation which organized groups do not require perpetuates a somewhat dubious conception of the human being as an animal with a removable veneer of socialization. Writers who employ the same level of explanation for crowd and organized groups escape this inconsistency, though they may do so as Freud (1922) did by extending the classical crowd model to include organized groups.

Third, the mechanisms cited to explain contagion appear to resist empirical verification. Least substantiated is the notion that the crowd develops out of love of a leader. There appear to be abundant instances in which shifting leadership is the rule and in which the leader only emerges after considerable crowd development has taken place. There may well be some contagiousness about a state of excitement, but it is doubtful that specific emotions are transmitted apart from some awareness of a situation to which they are appropriate responses. Suggestion is probably the best verified mechanism, but psychological research has led to narrower and narrower circumscription of the conditions under which suggestion takes place.

Fourth, contagion theory affords little basis for predicting the kinds of shifts which occur in crowd behavior. Contagiousness is perhaps the explanation for the existence of the shifting currents which have often been ascribed to crowds. But it affords no clues to the selective response that leads to a shift on one occasion and resistance on another.

Finally, contagion theory has nothing to offer in a study of the organization of collective behavior. Unless the simplistic model of the crowd as an undifferentiated mass of persons accepting suggestions uniformly is correct, a different sort of theory is essential to provide clues to differentiation of function within the crowd.

Convergence Theory

While the most popular interpretations of collective behavior (i.e., contagion) have stressed the temporary transformation of individuals under group influence, there has always been an undercurrent of suspicion that participants were merely revealing their "true selves" and that the crowd served merely as the excuse. When this suspicion is exalted into the key assumption about which the analysis of crowds is focused, the writer is guided by a theory which accounts for crowd behavior on the basis of the *convergence* of a number of persons who share the same predispositions. The predispositions are activated by the event or object toward which their common attention is directed. The course of action of the crowd would have been predictable had the observers known sufficiently the composition of the group and the latent predispositions of its members.

For investigators employing this kind of theory, the problem of identifying a mechanism and specifying conditions under which contagion will create a homogeneous crowd out of a heterogeneous aggregate evaporates, as the product of a faulty assumption. The problems instead become those of identifying relevant latent tendencies in masses of people, the circumstances that will bring people with similar latencies together, and the kinds of events which will trigger these tendencies. There are three major ways in which the assumption of convergence has been used, not all of which merit the designation "theory." These are the identification of a special class or category of persons as crowd-prone, equation of the crowd with psychopathy, and the application of attitude and learning theory.

Popular accounts of crowd behavior lean heavily on the "outsider" theme. The medieval dancing manias were attributed to groups of dancers who entered the villages from outside, the Russian pogroms were attributed to a "barefoot brigade" traveling from place to place, and outside "agitators" are currently blamed for industrial and racial strife. Newspaper reports of race riots in the United States have often stressed the role of uniformed military personnel who come from outside of the local community and who take advantage of the stereotype of the military person on a pass. Such popular accounts vary in the degree to which they acknowledge a supplementary role for contagion.

Serious studies have put less emphasis on outsiders, but have been concerned with categories of people within the community who are not fully committed to the dominant mores. Distinguishing between the active mob participants and others, Cantril (1941) cited the findings of private investigation to show that, in the Leeville, Texas, lynching of 1930, the active members were chiefly from the lowest economic bracket, and several had previous police records. The poorest whites were the class most likely to compete for employment with Negroes and were most likely to find their own status threatened by the presence of Negroes more successful than themselves. The lack of commitment to lawful procedure among criminal elements and the aggravated state of relations between poor whites and Negroes created a reservoir of people who were ready for a lynching upon a minimum of provocation.

The view that man has an evil nature which can show itself upon occasion is an old one which has been given an intellectually respectable imprint by introduction of the psychoanalytic concept of the unconscious. Jung, while invoking a contagion principle by speaking of "a sort of collective possession . . . which rapidly develops into a psychic epidemic," attributed a key role in such manifestations to latent psychotics. They are the dangerous "sources of infection" because, "their chimerical ideas, upborne by fanatical resentment, appeal to the collective irrationality and find fruitful soil there, for they express all those motives and resentments which lurk in more normal people under the cloak of reason and insight" (Jung, 1959, p. 14).

Extensive elaborations of the latent pathology explanation for crowd behavior were made by Martin (1920) and Meerloo (1950). Martin said that "a crowd is a device for indulging ourselves in a kind of temporary insanity by all going crazy together" (Martin, 1920, p. 37). Released in the crowd are the primitive impulses of hate and egotism which in normal circumstances are repressed. For a crowd to develop, it is merely necessary that a sufficient number of persons with the same unconscious wishes assemble and that one person strike the blow that all the others unconsciously want to deliver.

An effort to retain elements of the pathology approach while eliminating some of the extremities of Martin's (1920) and Meerloo's (1950) analyses is found in the frustration-aggression approach. Dollard, Doob, Miller, Mowrer, and Sears (1939) applied the general proposition that frustration universally creates instigations to aggression in proportion to the extent of frustration and that, where aggression against a perceived source of frustration is blocked, aggression will be redirected toward available and safe objects. In a review of lynchings of Negroes in the United States, Dollard et al. showed a connection between the amount of frustration that poor southern whites have experienced, as indicated by economic indices, and the incidence of lynchings directed against Negroes. The high incidence of race riots in the United States during the period of readjustment after World War I and the frequency of wild-cat labor strife and race riots during the second and third years of World War II have likewise been attributed to accumulating frustrations. In such explanations the object of crowd behavior need have nothing directly to do with the source of frustration.

The most careful development of a convergence type of theory is to be found among psychologists working in the learning theory tradition. The classic statement of this view was made by Allport (1924) and has been translated into the language of modern learning theory by Miller and Dollard (1941). Attacking LeBon's (1896) references to crowds in the French Revolution, Allport asserted,

It was the *individual citizen* who did this—the man who "in a state of isolation" had for many years felt the same hatred and cherished the same spark of vengeance or lust for freedom that was now bursting into flame in the crowd. Nothing new or different was added by the crowd situation except an intensification of the feeling already present, and the possibility of concerted action. The individual in the crowd behaves just as he would behave alone, *only more so* (Allport, 1924, p. 295).

Allport suggested that the term social facilitation is more appropriate than contagion. "By the similarity of human nature the individuals of the crowd are all set to react to their common object in the same manner, quite apart from any social influence. Stimulations from one another release and augment these responses; but they do not originate them" (Allport, 1924, p. 299).

Convergence theorists perform a valuable task in deflating the exaggerated claims of some contagion formulations. A compromise which stresses the importance of pre-existing attitudes while acknowledging that contagion may absorb persons without appropriate predispositions, in extreme circumstances, is logically tenable. The crucial empirical question of the power of contagion remains unanswered, however.

Apart from the unresolved empirical question there are some limitations to convergence theory. First, shifts in crowd behavior are difficult to explain under this approach. If the behavior in the crowd reflects the common predispositions of its members, then the development of the crowd should bring a clearer and more consistent, rather than a shifting, pattern to the fore. The one line of explanation available to convergence theory is that more intense impulses which are also more thoroughly repressed take longer to gain expression than surface impulses. Consequently, a crowd begins by expressing a fairly superficial but thinly repressed tendency, which then gives way to the deeper impulse whose repression is overcome by crowd facilitation. The test of this explanation would require examination of a large number of detailed accounts of actual crowds in which shifts occurred.

Second, like contagion theory, convergence theory offers no framework from which to approach organization in the crowd, unless it be the perpetuation of pre-existing relations within the crowd or the boosting of persons whose repressions are least intense to the positions of leaders.

A third limitation is more serious. It was a discovery of some importance that people have latent tendencies which they do not ordinarily express or recognize in themselves. That behavior in the crowd is an expression of these latencies is an observation that allows a more parsimonious explanation for phenomena that had mystified

and terrified observers. But as the understanding of these latencies has progressed, it has also become clear that people have not one but often several latent tendencies which are relevant to a given situation. So long as there was thought to be only a single applicable latency, prediction of crowd behavior on the basis of convergence in connection with an appropriate stimulus situation seemed easy. But with the recognition of multiple latencies the original problem re-emerges in new form: Which of the latencies will make its appearance? The door is reopened for contagion or some other process to select from among several potential courses of action.

Finally, part of the simplification achieved by convergence theory arises from ruling out of analysis a portion of the phenomenon which is crucial in other theories. The Miller-Dollard (1941) formulation, in keeping with other statements from this point of view, concerns itself solely with the intensity of response, taking for granted the kind or direction of response in the crowd. The direction is taken for granted because it is assumed to be an automatic response to the nature of the situation. It is necessary, then, to assume that the situation is self-evident and that it is defined individually. But the "collective" definition of the situation may be the crucial part of crowd development, during which a situation which is ambiguous to individual perceptions is defined as dangerous, as reprehensible, as defenseless, or whatever other characterization serves to indicate the appropriate behavior. If the crowd determines how the situation is defined, the fact that people respond to the situation according to their predispositions may be true but of slight predictive utility.

Emergent Norm Theory

Although convergence theories discount the sometimes exaggerated reports of contagion, they do not ordinarily dispute the unanimity, uniformity, and spontaneity attributed to the crowd by contagionists. A third type of theory makes its departure by challenging the empirical image of the crowd which both of these theories seek to explain. Turner and Killian (1957) suggested that the tendency for an observer to be overwhelmed by any dramatic happening and to see in wholes rather than in details leads to faulty observation and reporting of crowd behavior. The conspicuous actions of a few individuals are attributed to the entire group, and sentiments appropriate to the behavior and the situation are imputed to all of the members.

Observers trained to correct for these tendencies often report that many individuals in a crowd are merely amused or interested bystanders, some are even talking about other matters, and some may be quietly unfriendly to the dominant orientation of the crowd (Lee & Humphrey, 1943). The whole aggregation is characterized by *differential expression,* the behavior of a part of the crowd being taken by observers and crowd members as the sentiment of the crowd, and variant views and sentiments being sufficiently unrecognized to avoid destroying the illusion of unanimity. These observations raise an empirical question, but they also suggest a continuity between simpler and more commonplace phenomena and the dramatic episodes usually stressed. Observations of the former can be used as a basis for generalizations about the latter.

Emergent norm theory defines the key problem not as explaining why an unnatural unanimity develops, but as explaining the imposition of a pattern of differential expression which is perceived as unanimity by crowd members and observers. Taking the cue from the work of Sherif (1935) and Asch (1951), one can explain differential expression as the consequence of a social norm. The shared conviction of right, which constitutes a norm, sanctions behavior consistent with the norm, inhibits behavior contrary to it, justifies proselyting, and requires restraining action against those who

dissent. Because the behavior in the crowd is different either in degree or kind from that in noncrowd situations, the norm must be specific to the situation to some degree—hence *emergent* norm. Specific further problems that take pre-eminence when these assumptions are made include accounting for the neutralization or inapplicability of existing norms, specifying the process by which a collectivity comes to acknowledge a norm as the rule of that body, and accounting for the character of the norm.

There are several important differences between emergent norm theory and contagion theory in their characterizations of the crowd. The first concerns the view that complete uniformity is a collective illusion. The image of Nazi crowds attacking Jewish merchants often distorted the true situation in which a few storm-troopers acted while a crowd of persons afraid to voice dissent stood silently by. A "crowd of looters" taking advantage of an overturned ice cream truck in southern California turned out upon careful observation to include many groups of two or three persons who disapproved of the looting, but who by their overt passivity gave some collective support to the activities of the minority.

The second difference is between the spontaneous induction of emotion under contagion and the imposition of conformity under the impact of a norm. Under contagion people find themselves spontaneously infected with the emotions of others so that they want to behave as others do; under a norm people first experience the social pressure against nonconformity and do not necessarily share the emotion themselves, as Asch's (1951) experiments have shown. The crowd suppresses incongruous moods, and a prevalent fear of the crowd expressed both by observers and members of even recreational crowds facilitates the imposition of the norm. Far from being "infected" by the crowd mood, the newcomer observes it, suppresses any inappropriate mood, and then seeks actively to determine the nature of the situation which gives rise to it.

A third difference between normative and contagion theory is that the former is equally applicable to quiet and excited states, while the latter generally views contagion as a direct function of arousal. Moods of dread or of reverence may be as genuinely crowd phenomena as moods of violence and revelry. The observer who ran excitedly into the crowd at the site of a plane crash asking, "What happened?" was promptly silenced by disapproving gestures; students, present at a bonfire which exploded with injury to several persons, even though too far away to have observed the events directly, found it difficult to develop the proper mood for the subsequent homecoming dance.

Fourth, a conspicuous part of the symbolic exchange involved in the development of a crowd is the act of seeking and supplying justifications for the course of action of the crowd, or the recasting of conventional norms in a humorous or outgroup context so as to nullify their impact. Lynchings and riots never occur without extensive preparation, which consists of the development of collective assurance that the intended victims are outside of the ordinary moral order. Students cutting classes for a victory celebration were heard by observers to seek assurance that enough students would join to prevent professors from attempting to hold classes. Much of the content of the discussion and rumor which occurs in the crowd serves to define with group support the "facts" which are specifically necessary to determine the applicability of a particular norm. An empirical test of the two theories could be made by a content analysis of the exchanges that take place in observed crowds. The prime emphasis under contagion theory would be on communications which are expressive of the dominant emotion of the crowd and suggestions for action in accordance with the mood. While the latter would also be anticipated under norm theory, the former would be replaced by communications which have a normative character and which serve to indicate the applicability of a norm.

Fifth, limits to the development of crowd emotion and behavior are more readily explained as a function of a norm than as a product of contagion. The principle of contagion envisages a spiral of mutual reinforcement and neutralization of inhibitions typically leading the crowd to more extreme actions than were envisaged at its beginning. The evidence that southern lynchings were often followed by generalized devastation of Negro neighborhoods or that crowds soon get out of the hands of their original leaders appears to lend support to the spiral nature of contagion. Contradictory examples are available, however, and pose problems for contagion theory. In conventionalized crowds, the person whose expression of religious fervor (in a revival) or of abandonment of conventional mores (in an expressive jazz session) goes too far for the crowd serves to dampen the crowd mood rather than to facilitate its further development. Under contagion theory it might be argued that the crowd is not yet ready for the suggestion in question, but the fact that such crowds regularly reach limits beyond which they do not go calls this explanation into question. The further observation, drawn from careful historical research, that even so classical a crowd action as the storming of the Bastille during the French Revolution failed to follow up its action by attacks on the highly available director of the prison (Rudé, 1959), suggests that popular imagery of crowds has given insufficient attention to limits on crowd development. If an emergent norm defines behavior which is not usually acceptable as the rule in the crowd, it will usually also define the upper limits of acceptable behavior. Normative theory further gives rise to the hypothesis that many forms of crowd behavior are rendered possible as much by the conviction that behavior will not exceed certain upper limits as by the interstimulation of like-minded participants.

A final difference concerns the stress on anonymity which plays a part in many treatments of the crowd from a contagion viewpoint. Since social identity, by which the individual thinks of himself in certain stable social contexts and is recognizable to others, is a prime link in the chain of social control, its relevance is crucially different. If the crowd is a phenomenon of released impulse, then anonymity—the neutralization of identity—is important in eliminating the controls which ordinarily keep impulses in check. If the crowd represents behavior under an emergent norm, it is important that the individual in the crowd have an identity so that the control of the crowd can be effective over him. The latter assumption gives rise to the hypothesis that the control of the crowd is greatest among persons who are known to one another, rather than among anonymous persons.

Whereas convergence theory stresses the continuity between normal *individual* behavior and crowd behavior, emergent norm theory stresses the continuity between normal *group* behavior and crowd behavior. Just as behavior in normal groups gives rise to, and is governed by, norms, so the crowd generates and is governed by normative control. There is likewise a continuity between crowd norms and the norms which are usually in effect, the crowd supplying an atypical resolution of a long-standing normative conflict, defining a situation in which "emergency" norms can be invoked, or providing collective sanction for the conviction that the usual normative order has ceased to operate.

THE EMERGENCE OF COLLECTIVE BEHAVIOR

The question, "When does collective behavior take place?" must be divided into three more specific parts. First, by the nature of the definition of the field, collective behavior occurs only (but not always) when the established organization ceases to afford direction and supply channels for action. Hence one is led into the theory of social organization and disorganization to uncover the major circumstances which produce such failure affecting considerable numbers of people. Smelser spoke of *structural strain,* "an impairment of the relations among and consequently inadequate functioning of the components of action" (Smelser, 1963, p. 47). The impairment occurs when the problem at hand cannot be handled without reconsidering the more general foundations upon which a specific application of a means, motive, norm, or value is based. Thus the strain which produces collective behavior is distinguished from routine problems by its more far-reaching implications for the culture and organization of the society.

The second question is, "Why action rather than inaction?" In the absence of norms to specify action or organizational means to facilitate action, people may simply fail to act at all. The third problem is to discover the basis for the coordination of individual responses into collective behavior. Individual responses may be so disparate and uncoordinated that orderly procedures are disrupted but no collective response develops.

Although each consideration leads one to a different set of sources for collective behavior, the elements are not in practice fully independent. The social organization is only adequate or inadequate in relation to action tendencies. Similarly, the existence of relationships among people which facilitate coordination can enhance otherwise insufficient action tendencies, which in turn renders an otherwise adequate social organization insufficient.

Developmental Models

Conditions which give rise to collective behavior may be sought either according to a factorial or a developmental model. Factorial studies which relate the incidence of lynchings to decline in the price of cotton, attacks on constituted authority to runaway inflation, panic to low of confidence in leadership, or financial crazes to the opening of seemingly unlimited new opportunities for development supply the starting point for a more refined analysis of causation. But collective behavior is the product of a serial development, such that the conditions which facilitate the transition from stage I to stage II are not identical to the conditions which facilitate transition from stage II to stage III. It is the merit of the oft-used *life-cycle* or *natural history* approach "to permit us to discover the additional conditions that have to be present if a movement (or other collective behavior) is to proceed from any given stage to the next. . . . Through such analysis we can find explanations for movements that make impressive beginnings and then fail of further achievement . . ." (Turner & Killian, 1957, pp. 319–320). In a specific instance the failure of a social movement to develop after an impressive beginning could be attributed to such circumstances as the absence of an established communication network linking the populations whose interests were at stake and the failure to develop a program which did not threaten other values of the relevant population, both of which conditions were not essential to the initial stage of demonstration and enthusiasm (Jackson, Peterson, Bull, Monsen, & Richmond, 1960). While explicitly denying that order of occurrence is crucial, Smelser (1963) translates concepts from the development approach into the distinctive *value added* approach. He suggested a set of stages having general applicability to a wide range of collective behavior, each stage taking a specific form which is somewhat different for each type of collective behavior. The stages are structural *conduciveness* of the social order to collective behavior, social *strain, crystallization of beliefs* appropriate to the particular form of collective behavior, *precipitating factors, mobilization* for action, and efforts at *social control* of the collective behavior by outside persons and agencies. The specific implication of the developmental model is that the conditions leading to the development of collective behavior cannot be ascertained wholly apart from an examination of the actual process of development of the behavior.

Convergence Approaches

Under the parsimonious convergence approach, collective behavior culminates in the simultaneous development in many people of a sufficiently intense action tendency. Such development is achieved through learning or frustration of impulse, which is then activated by an appropriate incident. Social organization enters into the explanation as (1) the source of tension and (2) the basis for uniform tendencies in a collection of people. Frustrations leading to accumulating aggression and arising out of disadvantageous economic conditions or political subordination (Dollard et al., 1939; Hovland & Sears, 1949) and anxiety accumulating out of a succession of experiences which shake confidence in the future (Cantril, 1940) are among the conditions most frequently cited.

The incident which precipitates the crowd is often of minor apparent importance, or unrelated to the source of accumulated tension. An extended period of learning is required to connect incident with tension. Thus, although the southern poor white's troubles stemmed from economic, technological, and political conditions largely beyond his control and understanding, he had learned over the years to identify the unsubservient Negro as his primary threat (Cantril, 1941). The incident of Negro transgression of the color line was sometimes all that was then necessary to set in motion the community clamor for a lynching. The traditional religious teachings and the consequences of permitting only Jews to engage in money-lending during a period of growing demand for risk capital made it easy to see the pogrom in magicoreligious terms as expiatory and in instrumental terms as the redistribution of illgotten wealth.

Contagion Approach

Social unrest is often viewed as a preparatory stage for translating individual action tendencies into collective action and preparing people to accept new forms of behavior. For individual unrest to be incorporated into circular reaction and become social unrest (Blumer, 1946), individuals must be sensitized to one another. Aggregations, audiences, and casual crowds, awareness of undergoing derangement of living routines together, and prior interaction supply the initial sensitization. Possible evidence for the effect of prior sensitization, though subject to alternative interpretation, is supplied by French's (1944) experimental study in which groups, consisting of basketball teams, developed fear in response to a threat of fire more quickly than other groups of five students who had not previously known one another. Social unrest leads to milling, which in turn sets the stage for collective excitement and then social contagion. These stages involve increasing suggestibility and declining critical facility, and increasingly exclusive preoccupation with persons engaged in the common milling process. The focus of the milling process about an exciting event provides the basis for translation into crowd behavior.

The Langs, speaking of mass contagion, add that "the emergence of a leader who represents the 'typical' qualities of his following is the essential feature in the transformation of behavior in the elementary collectivity" (Lang & Lang, 1961, p. 228). Earlier, in the discussion of Freud, the contradictory evidence regarding leadership was noted; it should now be added that "typical" must be employed in a very limited and special sense if the statement is to be accepted. While the leader must reflect the same preoccupations and some of the same weaknesses as his followers, he must radiate a sense of competence, assuredness, and self-righteousness which the followers lack. But with the latter characteristics, acceptance of his leadership takes on less of the character of suggestibility and contagion and more of the quality of response to a definer of norms.

Emergent Norm Approach

A normative approach places equal weight on prior sensitization and shared derangement, less dependence on suggestibility and excitement or the psychological mechanism of identification, and greater stress on locating the conditions and sequences under which a new or special rule comes to be recognized and accepted as the basis for a coordinated response. From the normative viewpoint, situations of collective behavior are of varying complexity. In the simplest situation an event occurs for which the social organization offers insufficient directives or means for action. The normative implications are slightly complicated when the necessity to replace a temporarily inoperative social organization is added to the absence of directive. Successively greater complications enter when the operative social order must be set aside and when it must be actively opposed as a condition for carrying out the indicated action. It is useful to examine these situations in order of increasing complexity.

The occurrence of events which are inadequately defined in the group culture or for which there is no prior organization is endemic in all societies. Analysis of how collective behavior arises, if at all, in such situations as an automobile accident or failure of a teacher to arrive promptly at the beginning of a class period should reveal the elementary requirements for collective action.

Illustrative accounts of such episodes indicate that very little action is entirely individual, but that the coordination of behavior tends to remain limited to subgroups rather than to encompass the entire aggregation. Students typically leave the unstaffed class in groups after making decisions among themselves, and spectators at an automobile accident or fire form small groups, not necessarily limited to persons who have known each other previously. At the same time, in cases in which some action is required of people, a striking awareness of the larger group is common, and focus of attention on the actions of a few conspicuous individuals is general. In all cases some reduction of the usual barriers to interaction among strangers seems to occur. Collective action of the whole is largely a matter of registering approval or disapproval of actions and suggestions from individuals or small groups.

Participants in such episodes are primarily concerned with three types of cues. First, there is much concern with rules—what people are supposed and not supposed to do in such situations, except when the rule is universally understood. Second, there are attempts to define the situation, explain the teacher's absence, account for the accident, and the like, which often take the form of assigning fault or absolving from blame. When the rule is clear-cut, these considerations become the dominant ones, and a satisfactory definition appears to be as essential to action as the rule. Third, there is attention to, and search for, leadership, with appraisal of leader credentials, and with heavy dependence upon leaders to legitimate rules and assume the onus of starting action (Redl, 1945). The importance of finding a rule and formulating a conception of the situation with group sanction as a precondition to collective action is suggested by the instance of a university class in which members were still milling in the classroom and the hall without leaving, one-half hour after the professor walked out without explanation in the middle of his lecture. In more complex situations, the requirement of comprehensibility probably takes the form of demand for an ideology which will supply a basis for action.

There is greater complexity when the necessity to act in a situation of collective significance without adequate organizational direction and means is combined with a disruption of existing organization. Here is the typical disaster situation in which police, civilian defense officials, militia, fire depart-

ments, and other such groups should normally be directing action, but in which the organization of these groups has been impaired by the disaster. The emergence of such behavior cannot be explored apart from the relationships with the existing order. A similar situation exists when the social order is disrupted by rebellion, leaving elemental economic and social functions uncared for.

Beginning with the wartime studies of the effects of bombing on civilian morale and organization, there has been a concerted program of study of the effects of natural and man-made disasters (Disaster Research Group, 1961). A certain amount of effort has been devoted simply to dispelling popular misconceptions of mass panic, widespread looting, bitter conflict, and far-reaching mental illness in the wake of these episodes (Form & Loomis, 1956; Fritz & Williams, 1957). The greatest attention has been to strictly psychological effects, to effects on the normal social organization, and to the administrative and planning aspects of disaster, rather than to the emergence and nonemergence of collective behavior.

When disasters strike with a warning, there is a period characterized by reluctance on the part of officials to issue advance information for fear of creating panic and a tendency on the part of the populace to discount warnings. Evidence points toward a dominating tendency, both individual and collective, to cling to the established order and resist efforts to invoke innovative behavior until the threat is directly and dramatically apparent. Even in evacuation people stop to dress respectably and carry articles which provide symbolic linkage with the conventional order but lack survival utility.

When the disaster strikes, particularly if it is without warning, there is a brief stage of immobility in which people underreact to the event, failing to comprehend its magnitude, and either fail to act at all or act in grotesquely inappropriate fashion (Moore, 1956). A stage of vigorous activity then follows with emphasis on activity for its own sake. A spirit of generosity and compassion breaks down many conventional barriers, though help is often given to those who need it least and in an inefficient manner. Form and Nosow (1958) found an initial preoccupation with helping and searching for specific persons, such as family and close friends. After these had been located or assisted, attention shifted toward all others in need, irrespective of personal ties. Only after these two phases did people generally turn attention to their own injuries and losses. The initial concern about family and intimates, even to the extent of overlooking others in greater need and close at hand, has been well documented, and is the reason for much of the failure of local organizations to work effectively during this period (Killian, 1952). Barton noted, however, that it has never been adequately established that the majority of people actually participate in the rescue activities (Baker, 1962), and self-reports gathered by interviews may well be biased in a favorable direction.

Perhaps the most interesting observation about this stage of activity is the special character of the solidarity which develops. Professional rescue workers and other "outsiders" complain of noncooperation and often meet bitter hostility at the same time that residents of the disaster area are showing exceptional compassion toward one another. An outside group, however, such as the Salvation Army, whose workers participate in the sentiments of the victims, is readily accepted (Form & Nosow, 1958). The solidarity seems to be of the mechanical type (Durkheim, 1893 [1947]), based upon similarity of experience and sentiment rather than upon an interdependent division of labor. A sharp ingroup-outgroup dichotomy carries resentment against those who behave and feel as outsiders. When the complex social order is disrupted, the re-establishment of order may proceed best by instituting first the simpler, more "primitive" mechanical solidarity as a transitional step toward a new or reinstated organic solidarity.

Completion of the immediate tasks of rescue and decline of the heightened mechanical solidarity mark the transition to the reorientation stage during which time there is a general tendency to restore customary controls, and old hostilities reawaken within the community. The beginning of this stage sometimes incorporates such vigorous expressions of criticism and complaint that it has been called the brick-bat phase (Moore, 1956). With surprising rapidity the pre-disaster social order is reinstated with little immediate evidence of the more profound long-run changes which Sjoberg (Baker, 1962) believed may occur later.

The principal details of disaster response have been gleaned from the study of temporary crises in relatively smoothly functioning social orders where largely naturalistic definitions of events prevailed. Hence one can only guess at the answers to some of the most crucial questions for collective behavior research. Except for the well-known disorganization of behavior on occasions when the location and nature of danger cannot be identified, there seems to be only a brief period for comprehending and defining the situation before some kind of action gets underway. Where magical and teleological conceptions prevail, there may be a longer period of definition required as a prelude to even limited collective action. Observers have reported surprise at how little looting and deliberate selfishness occurs under these circumstances. But their reports deal with basically solidary communities in which the disaster is not likely to be experienced as an opportunity to unseat an oppressive system or seek revenge. Although propriety forestalled open expression of such sentiments, there were abundant rumblings in poorer sections of Los Angeles, at the time of the 1962 fire in the wealthy Bel Air and Brentwood neighborhoods, to the effect that "it couldn't have happened to a better group."

Still a further level of complexity is introduced when collective behavior takes place in the presence of a functioning social situation which does not supply avenues for the expression of certain strong action tendencies. Collective behavior then involves setting aside the established organization, usually temporarily. Reports of the frontier revivals in the United States during the early nineteenth century suggest the importance of these events in removing men and women from the daily routine and creating the occasion for abandonment of the usual restraints on behavior. Huizinga's (1924 [1954]) account of the late middle ages describes recurrent excesses of collective behavior. Because of the general sameness of life, people overreacted to small variations from the routine and made up for a general boredom by entering wholeheartedly into widely unrestrained collective behavior of many sorts. Vigilante actions often have this character, being viewed by the participants as temporary supplanting of constituted organization in response to an event (crime wave, or exceptionally heinous crime) which cannot be handled quickly or drastically enough by the accepted organization, or because incumbents are unwilling or unable to make the organization function effectively. Here, in addition to requirements noted already, symbolic legitimation from the established order seems to be essential. Expressions of tolerance from representatives of the established order, participation by people who provide a link to the established order, and adherence to ritual borrowed from the established order are nearly universal elements in such collective behavior.

The difference is only one of degree between collective behavior which develops because of strong impulses for which the social order provides no outlet and collective behavior which develops because the social order must be actively opposed. The bulk of riots, wildcat strikes, violent demonstrations, and the like fall in this group; though many incorporate much less real opposition to the social order than is supposed.

Common to all forms of collective behavior are (a) the discovery of a special but legitimate rule and (b) the development of a conception of the situation to which the rule is the appropriate guide. The nearer the situation is to the complex end of the continuum, the more complex is the fashion in which three general conditions must be met. First, there must be justification from the existing order, even in antiorganization behavior. The impact of an established order upon the normative conceptions of its members is such that value conflict or value change within the established culture, the opportunity to borrow legitimating rituals from the traditional order, and defection or support from some representatives of the order are generally necessary to give the collective behavior legitimacy. Second, there must be justification for repudiating the established order. The more extreme collective behavior seldom develops except as the culmination of long-standing divisions in society involving groups that are set apart from the main order by double lines of division, such as duplicating class and regional lines. Communication breakdown is crucial because lack of access to the legitimate order is a prime justification for use of exceptional means; but even then extreme collective behavior seldom occurs without incidents interpreted as repudiation of appeals and good faith by the established order. Third, there must be a conviction of ingroup rightness and effectiveness. This conviction is supplied through the opportunity to establish mechanical solidarity and through the prior development of an ideology which supplies the necessary definition of the situation and of the significance of the collectivity's action.

COMMUNICATION IN COLLECTIVE BEHAVIOR: RUMOR

Because collective behavior involves coordination of the behavior of many people, it necessarily rests upon a substratum of communication which may be studied in its own right. Communication through channels which are not institutionalized, concerning subject matter which cannot be entirely validated by reference to the established culture, may be a prelude or concomitant of more active forms of collective behavior, or it may take place apart from any more fully developed activity. The term which most closely corresponds to this aspect of collective behavior is *rumor*.

Definitions and approaches to the study of rumor correspond loosely to the three types of theories of collective behavior. Rumor may be viewed as the widespread transmission of certain "information," with stress on a common receptiveness to a particular kind of tale. This convergence approach points to the study of individual differences in willingness to believe. A contagion view of rumor stresses the dissemination itself, apart from the content, and points research toward isolating the circumstances conducive to rumor-proneness. A third point of view places less emphasis on the dissemination of a designated message, but treats rumor as the process of forming a normatively relevant collective definition of a situation. This emergent norm approach then directs research toward discovering how a given conception comes to be identified as "right," justifying its imposition on others.

Incidence

It has long been recognized that rumor abounds at times of disaster or excitement or intergroup competition and conflict. Efforts to identify conditions more precisely have generally concentrated on either individual states of readiness or social conditions facilitating transmission. A long tradition of the first type of explanation is neatly summarized in a formulation advanced by Allport and Postman (1947), in which rumor intensity (which includes incidence of rumor and rapidity and extensiveness of transmission) is asserted to be an unknown function of the product of *interest* in the matter being transmitted and *ambiguity* (i.e., incompleteness or unverified character of information).

That people will talk about matters which interest them, more than about items that do not, is an observation that few will dis-

pute. While ambiguity has likewise been stressed by nearly every writer on rumor, there may be a simple tautology here. Ambiguity is built into most definitions of rumor, so that the investigator either "plants" an intrinsically ambiguous story or in field observation reports as rumor only communication about unverified information. A more general principle, that the intensity of communication will be greater concerning incomplete or unverified information than about well-verified material, is probably incorrect, as illustrated by the rapid transmission and extensive discussion of important news events and the highly effective "grapevines" in large-scale organizations through which information leaks by way of known key members.

Ambiguity may still be a valid principle if interpreted broadly. At the close of World War II a variety of rumors were given widespread currency and credency among first generation Japanese in Hawaii (Lind, 1946). The rumors commonly held that Japan had actually won the war and that the American government was attempting to conceal the facts from her citizens for as long as possible. The actual information supplied Americans about the victory was certainly as well verified as could be without individual firsthand trips to Japan, and yet the rumors persisted for as long as a year. By supplying details of imagined conspiracy and by seizing on obscure items of news which were susceptible of reinterpretation, the Japanese were able to alleviate ambiguity brought on by their own inability to accept the true facts. In the same manner rumors associated with disasters often assimilate events to a teleological frame of reference when a perfectly complete and unambiguous naturalistic account is available. Thus in some fashion it can be shown that the afflicted people deserved their misfortune, or that the event related to some supernatural purpose.

A special case of ambiguity was cited by Rose (1951) in accounting for exceptionally high rumor rates in the stock market. Since making profit in the stock market depends on anticipating changes before others know and act on them, it is essential to get advance information before it gets into legitimate channels and to move without waiting for verification of information. The ambiguity is not inherent in the information, most of which can be verified fairly quickly, but in the competitive pressure to get and act on information before others have it.

Readiness to give and receive communication, reflecting prior interpersonal relationships, affects rumor incidence. While acknowledging that rumor may be a substitute for knowledge in a crisis situation, LaPiere (1938) attributed rumor generally to status seeking in congenial (or recreational) relations. In congenial relationships there is no institutional or task mechanism to identify and reinforce leadership, so that relating a dramatic and interesting account which is new to others in the group serves as a mechanism for establishing leadership. The more general principle that rumor is facilitated by a fluid social organization and minimized by a fully defined status structure finds support in Larsen and Hill's (1958) observation that status differentiations in two boys camps were obstacles to the communication of rumor. The high rate of rumor in such authoritarian systems as the army appears to constitute negative evidence, unless rumor spreads largely among persons of equal rank.

Differential Participation

In a neighborhood, an organization, or even a compact group, not all persons participate equally in the rumor process. Differential participation includes differences in hearing, attending, believing, and relaying rumors. Festinger (1948) found that persons with relatively more friends, rather than mere acquaintances, were more likely to have heard a rumor which circulated in a housing project.

Variation in belief is attributed to three types of variables: rationality, consistency with preconceptions, and utility. Rationality refers to the disposition of the individual to employ independent checks before accepting an unsubstantiated story as true, and the opportunities provided by the individual's situation for making such checks. In Cantril's (1940) classic study of the "Invasion from Mars" scare, resulting from a realistic radio program, educational level was a major variable distinguishing between persons who disbelieved or made independent checks on the truth of the account and those who accepted the program as a news report. On the other hand, Putney and Cadwallader (1954) found no tendency toward disbelief on the part of graduate students exposed to false radio news reports of an atom bomb attack on nearby Portland, Oregon. Danzig, Thayer, and Galanter (1958) found no relationship between education and attempts to confirm a rumor that a dam had burst above Port Jervis, New Jersey.

The tendency to believe what conforms to prior belief and supports existing feelings has been more consistently confirmed in a variety of settings. For example, Allport and Lepkin (1945) distributed questionnaires listing 12 rumors of waste and special privilege that were current in 1945. Among the 537 returnees, a high degree reported belief was associated with adverse attitudes toward rationing, lack of faith in fellow Americans' contributions to the war effort, feeling of being inconvenienced by shortages, and lack of close friends in the war zone.

A more complex relationship can be inferred from the study by Festinger, Cartwright, Barber, Fleischl, Gottsdanker, Keysen, and Leavitt (1948) dealing with a rumor, circulated in a housing project, which identified a research worker as a Communist agent. The effect of the rumor was to discredit the new leadership in the project and strengthen the old. People who stood to gain from the rumor were more likely to have heard the rumor than others. To the more obvious principle that people talk about what interests them has been added that people transmit what they believe will interest others. Transmission should thus be a function of the availability of potentially interested persons.

Position in the group is probably a determinant of transmission. Festinger (1948) found that people who were more highly involved in community activities in the housing project were also more likely to repeat the rumor if they heard it.

As stated in Chapter 10, in 1954 a widespread belief was diffused throughout Seattle, Washington, that some mysterious agent was causing automobile windshields to become pitted. Many persons attributed the pitting to some unknown consequence of atomic test explosions. Medalia (1959–1960) conducted telephone interviews with a sample of 70 persons who had reported windshield damage to the police. As a group these people were of higher than average education. Middle-class contacts were especially likely to report damage to cars other than their own. The author concluded that ". . . persons who are oriented by status to community responsibility and leadership will play a more significant role in alerting their fellow-citizens to the threat of disaster . . ." (Medalia, 1959–1960, p. 239). It is not, of course, possible to tell from such data whether the people also contributed disproportionately to the informal diffusion of interpretations, or whether reporting to official agencies merely took the place of other modes of transmission.

The obvious hypothesis that people transmit what they believe and not what they do not believe raises a footnote question about the importance of belief in the rumor process. G. Smith (1947) presented 13 pro-Russian and 13 anti-Russian statements to university students, applying the labels "fact" and "rumor" on the second administration. While the "fact" label increased acceptance, the "rumor" label had little effect, suggesting that rumors are not necessarily summarily rejected when so identified. Prasad (1935) reported two rumors, namely the forecast of total deluge and destruction and of a change of sex, which circulated widely,

following the Indian earthquake of 1934, although they were not believed.

In empirical study of rumor, subjects are often asked to indicate their belief or disbelief. For example, 61.5 per cent of a sample of respondents reported complete belief, after one exposure to the message, that the dam had broken above Port Jervis (Danzig, Thayer & Galanter, 1958). Such questions assume that the hearer first applies a test of belief or disbelief before he transmits or acts on the message. But in many circumstances of normal life people act on the basis of images which are not subjected to such a test. Thus, under questioning, people readily deny belief in the racial stereotypes upon which they have acted. Furthermore, action often occurs, as on the stock exchange, with full awareness that the facts cannot be ascertained beforehand. It may be more accurate to say that a rumor must meet a test of credibility if it is to be passed, but that degree of belief need not be a variable in determining transmittal. Prasad (1935) noted that the very circulation and repetition of a variety of rumors expressing the same emotion can give rise to the feeling that anything can happen, thus stretching the normal limits of credibility. Allport and Lepkin (1945) noted that belief was higher for rumors that had been heard before than for rumors heard for the first time. But here in the artificial and highly rationalistic situation of questionnaire completion a sharp distinction between belief and disbelief is imposed which has little counterpart in the real situation. Shibutani noted that "A rumor need not necessarily be believed to be effective. Some rumors simply give expression to sentiments that have been aroused and by their presence in the context of communication serve to disseminate those feelings" (Shibutani, 1944, p. 162).

Content and Distortion of Rumor

It is generally agreed that rumor is not a stable phenomenon, especially in its initial stages, but changes content. The commonest popular view is that a simple and true fact undergoes elaboration and exaggeration or distortion so that it gives way to a misleading rumor. There is evidence, however, suggesting that the rumor process may sometimes have built-in mechanisms which counteract tendencies toward distortion. Schachter and Burdick (1955), in their study of planted rumor in a girls' school, found no indication of distortion. They were not able to watch for the emergence and change of secondary themes, but the core content was faithfully reproduced. Caplow (1947) reported, on the basis of his experience in preparing monthly rumor reports for an army regiment, that "the veracity of rumors was high." Major events were usually reported accurately in rumor channels before official announcements were made. Caplow suggested that surprising accuracy, which others have remarked on, on the basis of military experience, arises when rumors travel through well-established channels. Because of *recirculation,* individual variations in interpretation can be checked against the common version, and communications from persons known to be unreliable are discounted. Furthermore, rumors were known to emanate from persons "in the know," or were checked with such people often during circulation.

Support for the hypothesis that rumor exchange and recirculation may enhance rather than lessen accuracy can be inferred from Diggory's (1956) study of response to a rabies outbreak among foxes in Montgomery County, Pennsylvania. On the basis of interviews with three hundred persons in three counties, Diggory concluded, "The *greater* the proximity of the threat, the greater the number of sources from which people derived information about it, the greater the importance of word-of-mouth communication as a first source and otherwise, *the less the tendency to overestimate the seriousness of the threat,* the greater the amount of anxiety, and the greater the number of changes in behavior" (italics supplied) (Diggory, 1956, p. 51).

The most carefully developed theory concerning the character of change and distortion in rumor content is that of Allport and Postman (1947). They proposed that, with successive telling, rumors undergo leveling— becoming "shorter, more concise, more easily grasped and told"—and sharpening—"selective perception, retention, and reporting of a limited number of details from a larger context." Just what becomes leveled and what sharpened is governed by the process of *assimilation*—"the powerful attractive force exerted upon rumor by the intellectual and emotional context existing in the listener's mind" (Allport & Postman, 1947, p. 100). The processes are illustrated and tested on the basis of laboratory experiments. The first subject describes a still picture, seen projected on a screen, to a second person who relays it to a third, the chain consisting of seven or more persons. Leveling is verified by the loss of about 70 per cent of the details during five or six transmissions, though little loss takes place after this time, as verified by Zaidi (1958) in replication research. What is not leveled is by definition sharpened. But sharpening also includes alterations of status, number, action, and other characteristics which serve to emphasize the main themes of the story. Assimilation is merely a name for the principle that the teller puts something of his own personality into the story and is illustrated by a wide range of alterations which make the story more consonant with his biases and expectations.

The Allport-Postman (1947) formulation has been widely debated, the principal issue being whether the laboratory situation replicates the essential features of rumor or whether the differences are in such essential matters that the principles cannot be applied to true rumor. Debate does not hinge on assimilation and sharpening, both of which have been generally recognized under other names but which Allport and Postman have been able to elaborate in substantial fashion. The controversy concerns whether leveling occurs in real situations.

Peterson and Gist (1951) used rumors which circulated in a midwestern city, following the reported rape-murder of a 15-year-old girl, to contradict the principle of leveling. Here a great variety of detail came and went, new themes being added to the accounts at certain times and some showing considerable imaginativeness. Individual rumors did not have independent careers but were part of the general speculation and discussion.

DeFleur (1962), on the other hand, reported verification in a field experiment of the Allport-Postman (1947) theory. Seventeen per cent of housewives in a small community were each given a pound of coffee and told a simple slogan, with the promise of another pound if they remembered the slogan three days later. In addition, thirty thousand leaflets were dropped, promising a pound of coffee to all who knew the slogan. DeFleur contrasted the "embedding" process (Allport & Postman, 1947) with the "compounding" pattern in which the basic message remains intact but acquires additional propositions or interpretive statements. The former was verified through the presence of leveling, as demonstrated by the tendency for the six-word slogan to become even shorter by three "removes" from the original contact. However, this experiment is as limited as the laboratory experiments in its lack of emotional arousal and occasion for invention and speculation. A systematic study of rumors relating to the real purpose of the leaflet drops would have been more to the point.

The respects in which the laboratory chain experiments differ from the normal rumor situation can be summarized as follows: (1) Interest and emotional arousal are not present in the laboratory. (2) The hearer's role in the laboratory is passive; in an actual rumor situation he questions, challenges, and agrees with the teller so that he is less likely to lose detail in which he is interested and is more likely to encourage the teller to elaborate. (3) Multiple

hearing and telling by each participant are not usually incorporated in laboratory experiments. (4) Only a single version of the rumor is usually circulated in laboratory experiments, while multiple versions are probably the rule in field rumor situations. (5) The rumor is planted, complete and sufficient for the purposes of the experiment, in the laboratory; but invention of the rumor is an integral part of the real process. Rumor can often be described as proceeding from an invention stage to a transmission stage, to a stage of saturation and decline. Snowballing, if it occurs at all, probably takes place in the first stage when an ambiguous situation is being explored or cues are being elaborated into a full-scale account. By planting a complete and adequate account, the experimenter in effect begins the experiment with the second stage, so that all he can observe is the declining phases.

The concept of assimilation is consistent with the many discussions of rumor in personal functional terms, in all of which the content given to the rumor is explained on the basis of its support of some purpose of the individuals involved. Firth (1956) divided rumors observed in Tikopia into the prosaic enlargements or explanations of ordinary experiences and the fantastic or extraordinary rumors which incorporate claims of special knowledge and power. The latter type of rumor serves as a social instrument in the hands of individuals or groups to improve their status positions. By facilitating adjustments to changing conditions in the social structure, such rumor can also contribute to stability of the social order.

Perhaps the function most generally attributed to rumor is that of bringing about what Festinger, Cartwright, Barber, Fleischl, Gottsdanker, Keysen, and Leavitt (1948) referred to as cognitive clarity, or Cantril (1941), "the pursuit of meaning." Prasad has argued that the content of rumor serves to justify the emotions people feel, whether of exhilaration or fear or suspicion, by presenting imagery consistent with the feelings.

Rumor as a Group Phenomenon

The rumor process itself creates an organization, with at least the beginnings of differentiation into roles. As is true of any organizational phenomenon, some dialectic must develop between pressures to stabilize and pressures to modify the organization. Rumor, then, should be subject simultaneously to reinforcement of elements which strengthen the initial structure and to the introduction of elements which would alter it if accepted. The simplest examples deal with the prestige structure. Prestige is established by laying claim to a rumor or rumor element which is accepted and which attracts interest or by claiming a special capacity to credit or discredit rumor elements. Larsen and Hill (1958, p. 505) reported that, on the basis of before-after sociometric tests in their boys camp study, "transmitters gained in popularity while decreasing in sociability; receivers lost in popularity while increasing in sociability." Eileen Irvin (Turner & Killian, 1957) noted that, in a specific rumor situation, those persons who happened on the scene first enjoyed considerable prestige because of their supposedly superior knowledge, a prestige which many of them cultivated by assuming an authoritative manner of communication. At the same time, dissenting interpretations were advanced, and the continued prestige of the first-comers was dependent upon discrediting the reinterpretation. As LaPiere (1938) observed, rumor creates a division into leader and audience, but the leader is in constant danger of losing his audience.

Probably the largest gap in rumor research lies in the absence of studies dealing with the rise and decline of prestige during the career of the rumor—the actual contest for prestige, the manner in which authenticity claims are related to prestige struggle, and the successive distortion and correction of rumor content which results. It is worth noting that the veracity characteristic of much rumor may itself be a product of the prestige to be gained by discrediting additions and inventions by persons not in a valid position to add to the rumor. In addition, other types of differentiation of roles besides that into tellers, hearers, and verifiers may exist.

RUMOR AS COLLECTIVE DECISION-MAKING

Many aspects of rumor are not adequately understood by assuming the convergence of like-minded people who engage in a chain-like transmission process or merely the uncritical diffusion of mood and imagery. Indications abound that rumor is often a collective process in which each individual's belief and participation are subordinated to a group process. Hence comes the view of Shibutani (1948), Turner and Killian (1957), and others that rumor should be treated as a collective decision-making process in which norms emerge to coordinate the action of individual members. The full rumor process occurs, they continued, (1) when a collective definition is necessary to permit the development of a group course of action or to provide collective support for the parallel actions of all of the members, (2) under circumstances in which traditional understandings fail to supply a basis for definition, and institutional arrangements do not adequately coordinate action.

The two crucial differences between this and other approaches are to regard rumor not as content but as process and not as individual but as collective. Instead of concentrating simply on the content of a particular message, the investigator studies a process in which the group concerns itself about a matter which demands or foretells collective action. The process begins by seizing upon cues, of which the principal one is sometimes but not always a rumored report, and moves toward agreement and the imposition of conformity upon all persons involved.

Collective Decision and Culture

Unlike subhuman animals, human beings do not act apart from conceptions of the situations in which they participate. But, as stressed by the pragmatist philosophers, the formation of conceptions is a part of the action process. Conceptions are developed, tested, selected, and rounded out as part of a preparation for action or as a support for action already under way. Those aspects of the situation on which definitional efforts are concentrated are the features most relevant for action, and the terms in which they are defined center in the alternative action possibilities. Shibutani (1944) pointed out that as the rapid succession of events leading up to relocation of American Japanese on the West Coast during World War II took place, rumors developed at each stage which offered guidance in decisions regarding whether to leave the area or stay, whether to send children east to school or not, whether to sell property or not, and so on. As each stage passed, the rumors relevant to the decisions which could only have been made at that stage also disappeared from the scene.

In Hawaii the rumor complex that Japan had actually won the war forestalled the major life readjustments which the defeat demanded of first generation Japanese (Lind, 1946). The primary loyalty to Japan, the commitment to the superiority of Japanese over occidental values, and the general failure to come to terms with the host culture had been kept alive by constantly looking to the motherland as the world leader. Defeat was strictly in America's own interest, for now she would acknowledge Japanese primacy, and her own culture would become enriched in consequence. But defeat of Japan meant the end of a way of life, the necessity to come to terms with American culture, and the acceptance of dominance by the younger generation. In the former example, rumor helped to permit new patterns of behavior; in the latter, rumor facilitated the continuance of old but threatened patterns. In both instances the focus for investigation is not primarily on the transmission of a particular story, but on the collective effort to develop a conception of the situation which will indicate clearly the appropriate course of action.

What is relevant for the action of only a single person cannot become the concern of collective definition because the individual will not be able to get others to participate with him in a rumor process. Furthermore, a situation whose action potentialities for different people are quite dissimilar will not readily generate rumor because there will be insufficient points of articulation among the diverse conceptions generated by the different people. Similarly, rumor does not spread among persons who witness the same event together unless the event has some common implication for them. On the scene of an automobile accident the rumor process may even be localized by age groupings when the age of a driver is a consideration in defining the situation. It is the action potential of the situation which must be shared, rather than simply the objective experience.

There is, however, a more fundamental basic for the collective character of the decision-making, arising out of the ultimate dependence of the individual upon group validation for the faith be places in his own perceptions. The process of collective definition (though not specifically in the context of rumor) has been well explained by Maurice Halbwachs (1925) and Charles Blondel (1952). Halbwachs pointed out that individual experience must be placed in the framework of shared group memories if it is to be remembered. Blondel noted the manner in which the individual identifies his own feelings by finding their place in the shared repertoire of motives which he verifies by communication with others. These processes assume the pre-existence of a group framework for experience: a culture. They assume, furthermore, that the meanings of experience are not self-evident but are derived from the categories in the culture. The very nature of the objects toward which people act derives from the organization supplied to experience by the cultural framework. But back of the dependence upon cultural validation of experience is the individual's organization of experience by reference to the *immediate* group. The culture is the framework employed by the group, and the individual is taught to master the culture so that he need not refer each experience back to the immediate group in order to assign meaning to it. In a sense culture is the group's proxy in validating experience.

In certain circumstances, however, the proxy is withdrawn and the individual must go back to the group itself to determine the meaning of his experience. This happens when the experience cannot be comfortably encompassed in the established cultural framework, or when individual use of the collective framework is negated by one's usual reference groups. *Rumor is a process of referring back to the group for a verified conception of a situation which will enable individuals to act with at least a modicum of confidence.*

Four kinds of situations are standing sources of rumor in this sense. First, whenever long-standing cleavages exist in society, some sort of stable accommodation is the condition upon which the pursuit of everyday matters must rest. Business activities proceed upon the assumption of a stable accommodation between labor and management; community behavior assumes an accommodation between majority and minority groups. Any events which threaten the stable accommodations also undermine the basis for the continuation of everyday affairs. Hence, as Firth (1956) observed among the Tikopia, recurring waves of rumor center in the major cleavages in the society.

Second, the formal structure of a society is a device to facilitate individual and collective action. Because of its rigidity, however, it frequently also serves as an obstacle to the circulation of information and the formation of appropriate definitions of sit-

uations. To the degree to which the formal structure does block the formation of such collective definitions, the *grapevine* emerges as a way of achieving the appropriate group definitions. As Bauer (1953) observed regarding Soviet Russia, the grapevine has come to be an essential feature of social life. Participation in the grapevine does not indicate unfriendliness to the regime, but merely that some matters cannot be adequately defined through the formal structure of communication.

Third, rumor arises when events occur which threaten the normal understandings underlying daily action. The report of a fatal automobile accident does not create rumor in California because the risk has long since been assimilated into the attitude of the typical driver. But invasion of a private dwelling and murder of a housewife by a prowler has not similarly been accepted as one of the risks which a husband takes every morning as he leaves for work. Anything which suggests that the woman encouraged the prowler, or that the family had disreputable associations, or that the prowler was a parolee who should have been kept in prison will help to assimilate the event into the normal assumptions which allow the husband to depart for work each morning without apprehension, and the wife to remain home.

Fourth, rumor arises in circumstances in which there is strong incentive to engage in a form of collective activity against which norms are ordinarily operative. Firth (1956) noted the strange circumstance that the Tikopia readily accept a false rumor that a ship has been sighted, even though they repeatedly express awareness of the unreliability of rumor. But the collective acceptance of the rumor supplies group sanction for dropping the daily routine, making a joyful trip, and engaging in spontaneous congeniality. The infrequency and importance of the ship's coming justifies the departure from normal obligations. Collective agreement in defining the situation sanctions each individual's abandonment of usual tasks, regardless of whether the ship eventually comes or not. Abandonment of routine or the resolution of situations of normative conflict is the function served by rumor in such circumstances.

Normative decision-making. The process of seeking a collective decision through rumor is normative in at least two respects. First, tests of the authority of the teller are a regular part of normal rumor process. Either the teller is able to represent himself as a person with authority—in a position to know—or he can attribute the rumor to a source which is authoritative. A hypothesis which deserves careful test is that the mere claim to first-hand knowledge by a person without authoritative social status in the community is insufficient to instigate rumor; rumor develops in such circumstances only when a person with authoritative social status can be cited as having credited the account. In the Port Jervis incident (Danzig et al., 1958) it is of special interest that the dam was widely and repeatedly rumored to have burst for a full day before the precipitate departure of a large fraction of the population. Had the latter action been merely a product of the culmination of accounts, a rising curve of departures rather than a sudden mass exodus would have occurred. The crucial fact seems to be that the effective rumor was spread by officials of the fire department.

Second, contrary to the impression that irresponsible people spread rumors, evidence has been adduced that the very involvement in community affairs and sense of responsibility supply motivation for discussion and dissemination. If more discriminating research verifies this observation and shows further that concern for the community leads people to round out rumor reports, a rather different process from the dissemination of falsehood by suggestible people would be indicated.

The sources for the normative character of the collective decision-making in rumor are twofold. First, it has been observed that the concluding phase of any group decision-making session is a period of heightened social control. Although the experimental evidence deals only with task-oriented small group interaction, the reasoning has a more general foundation. Once a general trend toward agreement has been sensed, there is an intensified tendency to bring disagreement to an end by imposing acquiescence upon the dissenters. If collective action, or inaction, is required, the necessity to coordinate the behavior of individuals is an obvious enough basis for applying pressure. But even when the adaptations parallel individual actions, such as fleeing from a threatened town, the action to be taken is a departure from normal behavior. The dissenters imply that the majority is silly or deviant, and, if the group decision is not borne out by events, the evacuees will be fools by contrast with the more level-headed citizenry. The view that, "We are all in this together; we must act as one," prevails.

The second basis relates to the earlier discussion of ultimate dependence for the veracity of experience upon group support. The ultimate faith in one's own perceptions is not based upon mere support of the majority; it is based upon the assurance of unanimity among all who are capable of valid perceptions. Once the faith is well-established, lack of consensus can be handled in noncritical situations by assuming that others did not see or interpret matters adequately. Decision in the normal cultural framework allows uncertainties about the application of cultural categories to serve as explanation for disagreements. But when the proxy is withdrawn and individuals must fall back directly upon the group in a critical situation, the only way in which the individual can have confidence in his judgment is by discovering consensus. Hence the social pressure toward consensus is magnified, and usual tolerances fall into abeyance.

Selective Definition

The process by which a group comes to accept one particular definition out of all those which might have been made and which might have been predicted from a knowledge of shared predispositions within the group is very little understood. It can be described as a matter of directed selective attention, whereby the group attends to some features of the situation and ignores others. Some of the mechanisms which guide selective attention follow:

Keynoting. Keynoting refers to the phenomenon in which a gesture or symbolic utterance made to an undecided and ambivalent audience crystallizes sentiment. If the keynote appropriately embodies one of the competing images, it encourages others who hold the same image to express it. To the ambivalent, the keynote and the rash of supporting expressions shift the balance in favor of the keynoted image. If the keynote is not followed by supporting expressions, its effect is lost, and those who favor a contrasting image may be emboldened to assert it. Effective keynoting presumes considerable latent support which has not been expressed because of ambivalence or uncertainty regarding the views of others in the group.

There is also a strong tendency for perception and attention to be guided by action-in-process. Once a group starts to take action in a particular direction the members tend to see events in a manner which facilitates and justifies completion of the action. As the orientation toward action becomes more intense, images are favored which indicate immediate and direct rather than delayed and indirect action.

Events have their own keynoting effect, as the most current happening (a reported rape, a sex killing) assumes disproportionate importance. The event strengthens one image at the expense of others and silences the dissenter, whose representation of his image is likely to sound weak even to himself. Thus the careless word of a public official or the panicky self-defense of a frightened person may so reinforce one image as to move the collectivity in the direction of some precipitate action.

Symbolization. The material and the product of the rumor process are symbols. The rumor process serves to bring symbols into selective salience and to reconstitute their meanings in relation to shared requirements for action. The process is a crucial component of all stages of collective behavior from milling through the translation of the symbols into action. The symbols are the currency which represents the collective *object* (Blumer, 1946; Lang & Lang, 1961), or the *belief system* (Smelser, 1963), which in turn shapes the ultimate form that collective behavior will take. In a broad sense the symbols function to indicate the *implementation* of the situation, to clarify its claim to *legitimacy,* and to supply a basis for *coordination*. The characteristics of symbols in collective behavior can be described under these headings.

In order to indicate the appropriate implementation, the symbol must have applicability to the situation and must formulate the situation in such a fashion as to simplify and clarify action. Aside from referring to the situation at hand in some crucial sense, the symbol must be nonspecific in character. Words like "liberty," "peace," and "states' rights" have sufficiently vague referents that they can be fitted to many different kinds of situations—sometimes even with contradictory implications—and people with rather different viewpoints can join in their use.

Levy-Bruhl (1910) suggested a distinction between *cognitive* and *mystical* types of symbols. The characteristics which distinguish the referent for a cognitive symbol are supposed to be sharply separable from the feelings which the object arouses in the observer or user. A mystical symbol, on the other hand, not only fails to make the distinction but the object tends to be identified primarily by the response it arouses rather than by its objective characteristics. In this sense the symbols with maximum applicability to situations of potential collective behavior are mystical rather than cognitive. A "traitor" can be any person who arouses fear regarding the traditional national image; "fraternité" can evoke a good feeling of brotherly acceptance without stirring up troublesome problems of who must associate with whom.

An important part of simplifying a situation so as to clarify action is the elimination of connotations which arouse ambivalence. Just prior to the 1943 disturbances in Los Angeles (Turner & Surace, 1956), the symbol "Mexican" was replaced in the major local newspaper by the symbol "zoot-suiter." The former symbol had connotations, related to the romanticized past of southern California, which were not likely to be totally forgotten. These favorable connotations may have inhibited many people from acting or tolerating action in accordance with the growing connotations of the same word of delinquency and dependency. The new symbol had no favorable connotations, so it aroused no ambivalence and the choice of action was simplified.

The presence of a villain figure in most collective behavior has often been attributed to the displacement of blocked hostile tendencies, but may be as adequately explained on the basis of its simplifying effect. The conception that events are the consequence of willed human action comes earlier in each individual's intellectual development than does the conception of naturalistic causation. To establish a foundation for social control, societies further train their members to assign greater salience to teleological than to naturalistic explanation of events in most social interaction. Thus, the "cause" of an automobile accident is laid to the carelessness of the driver in not seeing the bend in the road, rather than to centrifugal force. Drivers are taught to assume "responsibility." Defining a situation in terms of personal responsibility not only explains what happened in familiar and simple terms, it also indicates a few courses of action which promise high probabilities of success. The responsible person can then be persuaded, coerced, or replaced, any of which are much simpler than a naturalistic

diagnosis and prescription for changing the situation. According to the previously enunciated principle, action is simpler in relation to a villain than to a mistaken person, because the former arouses no ambivalence.

Following a study of responses to several disasters, Bucher (1957) asserted that blaming is much less common than is generally supposed. Before blaming can occur the following sequence is said to be necessary: (1) The disaster cannot be accounted for by conventional explanations; (2) power to alleviate the conditions is thought to reside in identifiable persons who are high in some relevant hierarchy; and (3) the responsible agents are believed to be unwilling to take remedial action and to stand in opposition to basic values. Of seven disasters studied, only the sequence of three airplane crashes in civilian neighborhoods within two months at Elizabeth, New Jersey, supplied all of the essential conditions for blaming.

The conclusion that blaming is infrequent seems divergent from common observation, and the conditions for blaming sound more like the steps necessary for *post hoc* logical justification of blaming than the workings of normal human reactions. Blaming is ordinarily a phenomenon of arousal and social interchange employing mystical symbols. Blaming is also normally one side of an ambivalent response which can be crystallized as appropriate symbols become salient. The quiet reasonable atmosphere of the interview may have been exactly what was necessary to render such symbols inappropriate.

If one assumes that all norms imply legitimation by reference to a larger group or superior authority, the legitimation function of the symbol is accomplished by linking the definition of the present situation to other situations and linking the developing course of action to already sanctioned courses of action. Two of the major ways in which this function is achieved are exemplified in the many tracts which appeared in connection with successive political disturbances in France during the nineteenth century (Belin-Milleron, 1951). Each succeeding disturbance borrowed symbols from the earlier movements, altering their meanings and contexts but linking the current effort to favorably valued efforts in the past. Symbols were also regularly employed in sets rather than singly, so that each symbol was strengthened in association (liberté, egalité, fraternité!). In another sense the symbol serves to translate the situation from one with particularistic significance into one with universalistic import.

Coordination. This function includes unifying and empowering aspects. The effective symbol can only unify potential participants in collective behavior if it avoids connotations which call attention to the separate interests of segments of the group and if it makes salient objects toward which responses by a wide range of people will be fairly uniform. In accounting for the culmination of long-standing discontent among the Japanese-American internees at Poston during World War II, Leighton (1945) named two unifying symbols. The primary obstacle to effective organization for protest and bargaining with the Center administration had been the cleavages between American- and Japanese-born internees and a variety of less pervasive factionalisms. The symbol of the "dog" (the informer) rooted in Japanese tradition and the symbol of the "martyr" supplied objects which could unify all groups of internees. When the first generation attempted to apply symbols of Japanese nationalism, however, the unity was destroyed, and the old factionalisms stifled further coordination.

It has already been noted that power and right are not sharply separated in practice, so that whatever affords an impression of legitimacy to the group thereby enhances its sense of power, and whatever conveys a sense of strength reinforces the sense of rightness. Symbolic references to invincibility shade imperceptibly into legitimating symbols of manifest destiny, the "wave of the future." Likewise, the self-congratulation of the collectivity with respect to its right-

eousness and with respect to its strength are generally merged. The emergence of a hero symbol provides both the assurance of success, because of the superhuman capabilities of the hero, and the guarantee of rightness. These kinds of self-assuring symbolization enable people to abandon disparate definitions of the situation and courses of action in one unifying orientation.

PANIC AND THE INDIVIDUALISTIC CROWD

Smelser (1963, p. 131) defined panic as "a collective flight based on a hysterical belief." The latter is "a belief empowering an ambiguous element in the environment with a generalized power to threaten or destroy." On the other hand, Meerloo did not make flight the specific criterion of panic. "One speaks of panic when a dangerous occurrence causes a spontaneous, disorganizing reaction in the individual or the community. . . . The socially important factor is the sudden reaction, the decomposing effect, the disintegration of the social formation or the individuality which results" (Meerloo, 1950, p. 11). In the second of these two typical definitions, the immobility and aggressiveness which may precede flight or serve as alternative responses are combined with flight in defining panic because of their assumed psychological equivalence. The restriction to flight has more commonly served sociologists' purposes.

A still more restricting definition is required to focus on what is distinctive about panic flight as contrasted with other forms of flight. MacCurdy (1943) remarked that it is crucial that "fear is not proportionate to the actual risk of injury." Similarly, interest in panic has often centered on the tendency of persons in flight to disregard the welfare and even the lives of others. Quarantelli brought in these two aspects by defining panic as "an acute fear reaction marked by a loss of self-control which is followed by non-social and non-rational flight behavior" (Quarantelli, 1953, p. 9).

Others have noted that in panic there is specifically no effort to correct the dangerous condition and that there is "behavior of a non-useful or self-destructive sort" (Wolfenstein, 1957, p. 85).

Convergence theory is probably more nearly adequate as an approach to panic than to any other form of collective behavior. A great deal has been learned about variations in individual tolerance for threat, the effects of physiological and situational variables on response to fear, and the fear-inducing characteristics of various kinds of stimuli (Biderman & Zimmer, 1961). Cantril (1940) was able to locate individuals who fled the supposed invasion by Martians when listening singly to the "War of the Worlds" radio broadcast. In light of well-documented cases of individual panic behavior, much of collective panic can be explained simply on the basis of possession by intense and disorienting terror.

Many writers distinguish between *solo panic* and *mass panic,* the latter depending upon some contagious process to account for the simultaneity and intensity of the flight behavior. But certain considerations make even this distinction merely a relative one. First, the definition of the situation as one of intense danger may be a product of the collective decision-making referred to earlier. Second, social pressures and definitions often determine whether people translate their fear into flight behavior or whether, like many aboard the sinking *Titanic,* they conceal their fear behind heroic behavior. Third, any behavior which alters the usual recognition of interpersonal obligations, so that one's fellows are abandoned in time of crisis or trampled in haste to escape, is unlikely without some evidence of deterioration of the normal reciprocities which constitute the moral order. Those who fled from the Martian invasion may have drawn inferences regarding all three of these aspects from the context in which the broadcast was presented, and many were able to interpret the normal movement of people on the streets as evidence of widespread flight behavior.

Definition of the Situation

From the definitions of panic it is clear that there must be something unusual about the way in which the danger is perceived if panic is to result. Meerloo (1950) likened human panic to the response of an animal which has first been conditioned to certain stimuli and then has these stimuli withdrawn or changed. Even the undue delay of anticipated dangerous and calamitous events can precipitate panic. "For many people this uncertain anticipation and continual mobilization of attention is more difficult to bear than the real danger itself. They surrender to fear in order to get rid of their uncertainty." Others have noted that panic is never a response simply to past or completed misfortune; it always stems from an orientation toward future calamity.

There appears to be a sensitive mixture of expectation and lack of preparation in panic. Familiarity with accounts of what might happen in a fire, a sea disaster, an earthquake, or a military rout supply the basis for a violent reaction. But such events are viewed as improbable or remote and no preparation is made to cope with them. When the event is actually recognized as being at hand, the combination of long-suppressed fantasies and the vital sense of unpreparedness provokes a response of desperation.

Smelser remarked that the precipitating event serves to "focus generalized anxiety on a specific event or situation." This leads to the formation of fears of immediate objects, and thus creates something definite from which to flee. ". . . it 'confirms' the generalized suspicions and uneasiness of anxious people" (Smelser, 1963, pp. 147, 150). The uneasiness may be merely the fear that unusual good fortune cannot continue indefinitely, as during business booms, or a cumulative reaction to conspicuously dangerous situations. The important consideration is that the event is suited to the character of the extant anxieties.

Even the intense terror which arises from

the foregoing circumstances does not ensure a response of flight. Indeed, resignation may be more common. Fritz and Williams (1957) attempted to specify just how a situation must be perceived if panic is to develop.

Panic is most likely to occur when (a) people perceive an immediate, severe danger, (b) they believe there is only one or at best a limited number of escape routes from the danger, (c) they believe these escape routes are closing (not closed) so that escape must be made quickly, and (d) there is a lack of communication to keep them informed of the situation (Fritz & Williams, 1957, p. 44).

The last condition lends ambiguity and lack of direction to the urgent situation. The possibility of escape is the basis for action, and the probability that only the first will escape translates panic into a reasonable effort of self-preservation in relation to the situation as it has come to be defined in the collectivity. Again attention is turned to the all-important process of collective definition and to the further conditions which distinguish between panic and non-panic in the presence of these necessary but insufficient conditions.

The development leading to collective panic may be a sudden crisis situation or the gradual crystallization of collective definition culminating from an initial stage of milling (Quarantelli, 1953). In the former instance people respond to the crisis situation by looking to others nearby for cues which re-inforce the definition of danger and indicate the response of flight. In this kind of situation the quick action of a perceptive individual may prevent panic. Emergent panic develops from verbal interaction. The changing conception of the situation may not be accompanied by an intensification of the realistic danger.

Impairment of Organization

If one assumes that people are socialized into membership in society, mass panic can-not be explained wholly on the basis of the way in which the danger itself is perceived. There must be a basis for repudiation or neutralization of the normal organizational framework within which problem situations are approached. LaPiere (1938) made the lack of regimental leadership in a crisis situation a specific condition for the development of panic. Since the urgency does not allow for decision-making by discussion, societies often prepare for such situations by training members to accept authoritative leadership unquestioningly and to follow routinized patterns (e.g., fire drill). The frustrated expectation of authoritative leadership signals the failure of the normal organization.

Freud's (1922) account of panic draws upon a theory of normal group organization which depends upon love of a leader. When the beloved leader dramatically fails his followers, they are not only left without direction and emotional support, but the basis for their identification with their fellows is destroyed. All the normally repressed interpersonal hostility comes to the fore, and violent aggressiveness is added to the disillusionment. The more intensely people have devoted themselves to the leader and identified with their peers, the more violent the panic. Thus, to Freud, panic is the antithesis of other forms of crowd behavior, occurring just because of the failure of the processes which account for the latter.

The Langs (1961) proceeded from Freud's (1922) formulation to interpret panic as a process of demoralization which, though it can be essentially an intra-individual development, is a progressive retreat from group goals. Its ultimate development is a state of *privatization*. Underlying demoralization is disruption of the socially sanctioned cognitive definitions by which nature and society are transformed into a meaningful world for action, and disruption of affective ties. The two elements are interdependent, so that continued internal dissension makes a group panic-prone. Privatization, or the undermining of primary group ties, follows impact and leads to disruption of group norms that anchor individual behavior in the larger secondary group. Once the group norms are neutralized, mutual facilitation intensifies the action tendencies which eventuate in panic.

Recognition that some form of disruption of group bonds is a necessary intervening step between crisis and panic points to a prime condition in accounting for instances in which panic does not follow the four conditions suggested by Fritz and Williams (1957). Morale in a group permits members to withstand crises and even to undergo severe deprivation or death together.

Individualistic Crowd

The tendency to treat panic as a special and distinctive phenomenon is warranted by its drama, but not by the character of relationships among the participants. Mintz (1951) designed a simple laboratory experiment which, without the accompaniment of emotional arousal and desperate aggressiveness, can serve as a paradigm for the social-relational aspects of panic. Several cones were placed in a bottle whose mouth was large enough for only one cone to be withdrawn at a time. Each subject held a string attached to one of the cones. Water admitted to the bottle from the bottom at a steady rate supplied a time limit for removing the cones. When the experiment was defined as a study in cooperation whose object was to remove all the cones as quickly as possible, subjects spontaneously took turns and removed the cones without jams. When rewards were offered to individuals for removing their cones before they became wet and fines assessed for delays, jams generally developed. The latter were likened to the crush of people attempting to escape a theater fire. Feelings would not, of course, run high enough in the laboratory experiment to cause personal injury, but the pattern might still be regarded as similar.

From this perspective, panic is merely a specific instance of a more general class of phenomena including situations in which competition for a scarce object leads to disregard for order and fairness, and rivalry is intensified to the extent of causing widespread cheating. Transportation was chronically in short supply during World War II, and, in one instance, a tightly packed crowd of people surged back and forth beside an interstate bus with such force that after 15 minutes only five people had been able to gain entry. The number of persons on hand dramatically exceeded the capacity of the bus. The bus driver's repeated assurances that there was another bus were met with skepticism. Much of the swarming may have reflected a determination that no one should get aboard until the driver assumed responsibility for a fair seating procedure. Not only panic-selling but the "panic-buying" in some economic crazes reflects the same displacement of usual norms for the sake of competitive individual goals.

It has been charged (Brown, 1954) that military panic does not follow Mintz's experimental pattern because the soldiers' selfish interests are not in competition. However, soldiers are always taught that the survival of each depends on the loyalty of all, so that the defection of a few may turn the tide of battle against the rest. A more serious criticism is that someone must still explain how the reward situation gets structured in this way. The value of a paradigm of this character is to redirect attention in the search for determinants of panic behavior.

Freud (1922) made suggestibility dependent upon identification, which is nullified in panic, but most observers agree with the Langs (1961) in assigning an important part to some form of group facilitation or incitement to panic. If panic is an instance of a broader phenomenon in which a uniform pattern of pursuit of individual goals in disregard of normal consideration for others is disseminated or imposed rather uniformly among members of a collectivity, it is appropriate to speak of an *individualistic* crowd (Turner & Killian, 1957). This phenomenon is in contrast to the usual *solidaristic* crowd in which the presence of others governed by the same impulse or norm is an aid to each person's pursuit of his own behavior.

From the normative standpoint, two aspects of the individualistic crowd are to be stressed. First is the moral neutralization of standard norms because of dramatic evidence that conventional reciprocities have broken down. Since norms often require that the individual forego some gratification, the sense of their rightness depends upon the faith that relevant others are also adhering to these or equivalent rules. Because of a general faith in social order, it is not necessary that such evidence be constantly forthcoming, and occasional evidence of violations by others can be discounted. The loss of position if one or two persons step out of order is minimal; if all orderly process is abandoned, the personal moral imperative is nullified.

Second is the collective support for the pursuit of individual survival or gain. Here is the typical collective behavior situation in which society, as the ultimate definer of norms, withdraws the proxy from the culture and in which the immediate group stands in place of the larger society in defining the permitted and the obligatory. Under the full impact of such an emergent norm the individual buyer will be more ashamed to have a friend see him edged away from the sales table than to be seen pushing and shoving for an advantageous position. It is in this connection that the example of one or a few people continuing to follow the conventional norms may sometimes interrupt the individualistic development.

FORMS OF COLLECTIVE BEHAVIOR

If collective behavior develops in a solidaristic direction, it may still take divergent forms. It may develop as a public or as a crowd. And if it takes the form of a crowd, it may be *acting* or *expressive*. An attempt will now be made to specify what is distinc-

tive about the processes in each type of behavior and what leads collective behavior to take one path or another.

PUBLIC AND CROWD

The distinction between the public and the crowd dates back to the earliest efforts to conceptualize the phenomena of collective behavior. There has always, however, been some confusion between two criteria for differentiating these forms. One type of criterion has referred to the character of the decision-making, action, or interaction; while the other has distinguished the public, as a collection of people physically separated, from the crowd, consisting of people in physical contiguity with each other. As early as Tarde (1901) and as recently as Lang and Lang (1961), writers have emphasized the importance of physical contiguity in promoting crowd process and physical separation in facilitating development of the public. Contiguity-separateness is not of interest intrinsically, but because of the contribution it makes as a determinant of the "form and effects of the interaction" (Park & Burgess, 1921). Hence, although the characteristics of public behavior are more common in diffuse collectivities and the characteristics of crowd behavior in compact collectivities, the phenomena are most fruitfully defined without reference to this variable.

Park and Burgess described the public as engaging in discussion with its members acting upon one another critically. Discussion implies (Blumer, 1939 [1946]) that the members of a public are *divided* in their opinion regarding an issue and are seeking to arrive at a collective opinion. Discussion means interpretative interaction rather than the circular reaction characteristic of the crowd. The crowd, according to Park and Burgess (1921), engages in no discussion, but simply mills; all its members are dominated by a collective impulse, and action is impulsive. The criterion of rationality has often been employed, as in Dawson and Gettys' (1948) contrast between the collective-emotional behavior of the crowd and the element of rational deliberation in publics. It has also been observed that the culmination of collective behavior in the public is the registration of opinion, while the crowd characteristically takes some more direct action.

Because the typical public depends upon the same kinds of rumor and symbolization processes as the crowd, the criterion of rationality may be illusory. Organization of collective behavior about the assumption that there is an issue and that there will continue to be some divergences of opinion serves more clearly to set public apart from crowd.

The habit of thinking of the public primarily in highly institutionalized settings has led investigators to question whether there is a public in the sense of a collectivity rather than the simple sum of individual opinions. The bulk of research dealing with public opinion is concerned with the determinants of the opinions which individuals hold or register, rather than with any collective processes. The use of contagion framework in approaching collective behavior tends to leave the public outside of the theoretical orbit of the field, since contagion has less applicability to public than crowd.

The public takes on the character of a collectivity insofar as (1) certain definitions of the issue and permissible alternative stances emerge out of the interaction and are accepted as the basis for discussion by the members and (2) there is orientation both within and without the public to the public as if it were an entity, with attempts constantly being made to assess the opinion of the public. The natural boundaries of the public mark off persons who are concerned about the issue and discuss it from those who do not.

The emergent norms in the public define the issues, the positions which can be taken, the criteria for admission to the public, and the legitimate criteria by which public opinion is identified. Although the public tolerates disagreement, the terms for toleration are discussion on the basis of one of the accepted definitions of the issue and from the standpoint of one of the legitimate alternative positions. Agreement on the issue is seldom complete, and much of the discussion consists of attempting to promote a particular definition of the issue. As events occur and as actions are taken in response to public opinion, preponderant definitions of issues change so that old arguments are then felt to be irrelevant. Cantril (1942) illustrated dramatically the shifts in issues from month to month during the period prior to full United States involvement in World War II.

The process whereby the public determines what positions relative to a given issue are to be regarded as making sense is the least researched aspect of the public. Best documented is the observation that the number of recognized positions is an inverse function of intensity of interest and sense of urgency. ". . . as a greater sense of urgency prevails there is a tendency toward the consolidation of positions ultimately into only two opposing views" (Turner & Killian, 1957, p. 236). On the basis of this observation the crowd becomes the limiting case of the public, with only one position acknowledged as legitimate.

Of perhaps equal importance with urgency in determining the tolerance of multiple alternatives is the correspondence between interest group divisions and other lines of division in society and with institutional communication barriers. The right to differ is granted to persons who in other respects share in an underlying value consensus and who can cite legitimate values to support their opinion. Where class and race or nationality correspond exactly, where religious and nationality barriers coincide, and where an elaborate etiquette formalizes relations between groups with opposed interests, differences are more likely to lead to crowd than public action and more to publics which recognize only two polarized alternatives than to publics which recognize a range of positions.

The opportunity for the registration of

public opinion and the expectations and character of the group which is to be influenced also help to determine whether public or crowd will develop and whether two or several alternative viewpoints will be recognized. The Langs observed that "A public opinion situation exists whenever in a large society, where action requires some implied consent, the decision-makers are guided by some assessment of public opinion before they act" (Lang & Lang, 1961, p. 385). The institutionalized practice of balloting on simple dichotomous choices undoubtedly constrains the public. Similarly the institutional arrangement whereby issues are settled indirectly, by selecting between persons, probably forges a linkage between the two kinds of judgment, further restricting the range of recognized alternatives in public discussion. It is hypothesized that the tendency toward polar positions is further facilitated by two other characteristics of the relationship between public and decision-makers. The more extensive and intimate the communication between public and decision-makers, the less the tendency to limit alternatives to polar positions. A complex public opinion requires greater intimacy and richness of communication if it is to be received and understood; ineffectual communication is met by simplification. The expectation that decision-makers will directly obey the mandates of public opinion fosters simple polar positions, while the expectation that they will listen and then make independent reasonable decisions fosters a wider range of alternatives. Only by simplifying the choice to two alternatives, between which a clear majority can be determined, can it be established that decision-makers are following the public's dictates.

Assessments of public opinion are continuously being made by persons inside and outside of the public. Since public opinion in an objective sense is myth, an important aspect of public decision-making consists of accepting or repudiating the various assessments of opinion. The presence of a democratic ideology, for example, means that opinion polls and votes will be accorded major legitimacy. Where other ideologies prevail such assessments are often treated as irrelevant and misleading. Frequently the formalized registration of public opinion is only fully possible on a related issue rather than on the matter centrally at hand. When this is the case, the public either accepts or rejects the registration as indicating opinion on the major issue.

Membership in a public is ordinarily differentiated into members of relevant interest groups and the "disinterested," and into instigators, receivers, and opinion leaders. Communications are accepted and interpreted according to these categories. Excessive personal interest often leads to complete denial of participation in the public, as does misrepresenting oneself as disinterested though actually a member of an interest group. The public also tends to define outer orbits, refusing communications from persons viewed as having no legitimate basis for concerning themselves with the issue. Ordinarily this means a decision regarding the group that is affected. There is probably a positive correlation between the flexibility with which the outer orbit is defined and the tolerance of multiple positions about the issue at hand.

Active and Expressive Crowds

At least from the Western instrumentalist point of view, the crowd which uses force or a show of force to register its demands or which deals physical vengeance on the object of its hatred seems to be perpetrating an understandable evil. But, from the same point of view, those types of crowd behavior in which people are swept up in a flurry of dancing, engage in a babbling which they call "speaking with tongues," see visions, or engage in public displays of behavior which flaunt customary reserve require a special form of explanation. This difference, with the associated implication that a somewhat different set of principles is required to generalize about each, has led to the established distinction between the acting crowd and the expressive or dancing crowd.

Blumer distinguished the expressive crowd as introverted: "its impulses and feelings are spent in mere expressive actions . . . which give release to tension without having any other purpose" (Blumer, 1939 [1946], p. 182). But increasing experience in empathizing with bizarre actors has made investigators reluctant to deny purpose in such behavior. Indeed, much contemporary analysis of expressive behavior consists of disclosing the supposed conscious or unconscious symbolism by which the behavior reveals the purposes of the participants. The emphasis is shifted in Swanson's (1953) distinction between the acting crowd members' effort to manipulate the environment external to themselves and the expressive crowd members' aim to manipulate self-images and norms of participation. The criterion that expressive crowd behavior is an end in itself is conveyed by Brown's (1954) reference to the behavior as consummatory.

Some dissatisfaction with the distinction has been frequent, however; even Brown noted that the "expressive mob is a wastebasket category including all those that show no other behavioral tendency" (Brown, 1954, p. 840). LaPiere (1938) disposed of expressive behavior by substituting *revelous* and *fanatical* behavior classified according to purpose. The Langs (1961) similarly substituted classification by objective with *mass conversion* and *crystallization* covering what might have been treated as expressive crowds. Expressive phenomena are incorporated in Smelser's concept of the *craze,* defined as "mobilization for action based on a positive wish-fulfillment belief" (Smelser, 1963, p. 171). The craze in this sense includes speculative economic booms and fads.

Expressive phenomena, however treated, are often viewed as incomplete developments toward becoming an acting crowd. The craze and panic, in Smelser's (1963) terminology, concern only the "facilities" component of action, while the hostile outburst extends to the mobilization component.

Blumer spoke of the expressive crowd as failing to develop any image of a goal or objective, such as does the acting crowd. Because of the aroused tension, "the crowd has to act, but it has nothing toward which it can act, so it merely engages in excited movements" (Blumer, 1946, p. 183). Similarly, Dawson and Gettys (1948) distinguished the three types of crowds, *expectant, expressive,* and *active,* as also stages in crowd development.

The behavior of a waiting audience illustrates this view. Clapping, stamping, chanting, in unison, are common manifestations. But it may be an error to identify these tensional behaviors, which are aimed at hastening events, with the attainment of mystical experience or with the moral holiday which characterized V-J Day in the western seaport cities of the United States. The underlying condition of tension is present, as in other forms of crowd behavior, but probably serves only in much the same way to establish a readiness to set aside the usual norms.

A classification which facilitates generalization at a sociological level must be one which relates to the organizational and interactional characteristics of phenomena, rather than their individual purpose characteristics. Just as individualistic and solidaristic crowds are distinguished by their internal relationships, acting and expressive crowds are distinguished by their external relationships. People in a crowd do not merely act; they act with an objective in mind, and the action unfolds according to the evidence they receive regarding the effects of their action. The acting crowd is a crowd whose members are watching for evidences of the effects of their actions on some social objects outside of the crowd, and who are encouraged, discouraged, satisfied, or shift to different objects according to the responses of the others. Thus a lynching turns into a riot when the lynchers meet with opposition; a focused attack spreads to include a wider range of objects when the responses of the initial victims either legitimate the action or make it excessively easy. The emergent norm which governs the behavior of the acting crowd incorporates the response of the social objects as a crucial condition in defining appropriate behavior. In contrast, the feedback to which members of an expressive crowd attend is the response of the fellow crowd members and their own subjective experience.

The normative support of the crowd members for one another is somewhat different in the two instances. In both instances crowd members support the emergent definition of the situation. But in the acting crowd the members support a definition of legitimate behavior toward designated outsiders; while in the expressive crowd the members support a definition which makes sensible behavior which would not normally be so regarded and gives significance to subjective sensations which would otherwise be meaningless or disturbing. Attention is specifically directed away from outsiders in the expressive crowd. The gratifications of engaging in the latest fad are entirely dependent upon participation in the fad by other persons and by constant recruitment of new faddists. The many party-behavior play-acting departures from the mores of marriage, of institutional authority, and of cultural routine are dependent upon participation by others who share in the mock rebellion and in the common understanding of the limited meaning of the actions. Vital expressions of enthusiasm for country, religion, or school require the participation of others to protect against the definition of such expressions as unsophisticated.

One justification for regarding the expressive crowd as an incomplete development of an acting crowd is found in the instances in which the former has developed into the latter. Student sports rallies opposed by the police have turned into violent crowds; European dancing crowds have become pogroms. Such transformation is partly a consequence of the establishment of an emergent moral universe in the crowd, which can then define the norms applicable to each

situation newly encountered. But partly it results from the fact that representatives of the institutional structure outside of the crowd are prone to fear the expressive crowd, to define it and treat it as an acting crowd, and to frustrate the crowd and force themselves into its sphere of attention, thus fostering translation into an acting crowd.

No serious study has been directed toward identifying the circumstances which cause crowd development to take the expressive or acting direction. A sacred, other-wordly emphasis leads to religious expressive behavior in circumstances which have led to crowds that actively demand reform or take matters into their own hands in a secularized setting. But as the religious expressive crowd declines concomitantly with increasing secularism, it is quite possible that orgies and fads, both secular expressive forms, increase. Similarly, there are institutionalized forms of acting crowd behavior, such as the criminal chase associated with the traditional hue-and-cry, which may decline with secularism. Hence there may be no simple relationship between expressive-active tendency and sacred-secular settings.

The expressiveness of crowds is sometimes attributed to the unavailability of the objects of hostile or favorable action. But from the same body of theory which supplies such interpretations comes the expectation that the acting crowd will find a scapegoat, thus changing its object while retaining its acting character.

An informative example is supplied by the different sorts of crowd behavior practiced by university students in different countries. In contrast to many other countries where students are regular participants in active political crowds, American student crowd behavior is almost entirely of the secular expressive sort. In Japan and some of the Latin and European countries the prestige and responsibility of the student status are high, while in the United States the association of gainful work with maturity makes studentship a relatively unarticulated status, viewed partly as perpetuating

the impotence and irresponsibility of childhood. The American student is accorded
little power or responsibility, and his panty
raids and athletic expressive crowds are
looked on with greater tolerance than would
be any incursion into attempts to alter by
action the situation he finds himself in. The
students who riot are more likely to come
from countries in which one expects to be
looked up to and listened to just because
he is a student.

These variables of sense of power and
socially defined responsibility may contribute to acting crowd development in general.
Working class violence has been associated
with some sense of class identity and some
experience with the power of the class. Negro crowd behavior in the United States has
shifted from almost exclusively expressive
forms to more active behavior as the conviction of power and the evidence of outside support have increased.

Two instances of crowd behavior which
fall somewhere between the extremes of
acting and expressive forms are instructive.
In 1943 there were extensive riots in the
Harlem district of New York City in which
Negroes destroyed white-owned property
and symbolic objects within Harlem, but
failed to move out into white districts, thus
averted a pitched racial battle such as developed in Detroit the same year. In the winter
of 1944–1945, at the Tule Lake relocation
center, interned Japanese-Americans engaged
in a mass renunciation of American citizenship, partly as protest against their treatment
and partly to forestall resettlement outside
of the center (Thomas & Nishimoto, 1946).
In both instances the behavior was limited
to at least partially symbolic actions because
of the fear of consequences of more active
efforts to alter the situation. The widespread
incidence of expressive crowds among suppressed populations, as in the preliminary
stages of nationalistic developments, reflects
this same unwillingness to face the repressive consequences of any direct action upon
persons or institutions outside.

The expressive form of crowd behavior
has a further advantage—the participants
can dramatize an act of protest without
actually making the choice to abandon their
present situation. In circumstances of strong
lingering ambivalence, expressive behavior
can serve the protest side without frustrating
the loyalty side. Thus the American teen-
ager can engage in forms of expressive crowd
behavior which allow him to play-act a
revolt against adult authority and the conventional mores, while still holding to both
apart from the crowd situation. The dancing
crowds of the declining middle ages probably contained a population not sufficiently
emancipated from the traditional order to
take direct action against it. But the protest
side of ambivalent attitudes could be satisfied by engaging in such collective unconventional behavior.

CONTROL OF
COLLECTIVE BEHAVIOR

There is a continuous two-way interaction
between any instance of collective behavior
and the larger society. In spite of exaggerated
claims, participants in collective behavior
are never fully divorced from their conventional anchorages; the emergent norms are
always in some sense exceptional applications of conventional norms; the institutional stratification, cleavages, and communication channels continually re-emerge in
collective behavior. Society responds to instances of collective behavior not only to
impose control, but to redefine its organization and values. The direct effects of collective behavior through killing individuals,
destroying buildings, pre-empting justice,
and obstructing institutional procedure are
minor; the indirect effects which arise out
of the societal reaction to instances of collective behavior are often vast.

Mediating Public

The principal mechanism through which
society is affected by any instance of collective behavior is a special public concerned

with the instance of behavior, whose issue is how the collective action should be defined. Every crowd, every panic, and many publics are "contained" within such larger publics, which mediate society's control of them and their impact on the society. Among the crucial questions which the public seeks to answer are the following: (1) What is it about? Are the students having a fling or are they part of a sinister plot to challenge the established order? Are the strikers demonstrating for bread and butter or are they acting petulantly or seeking to impede technological advance? (2) Where does justice lie? In this respect the mediating public always pre-empts an umpire's task, identifying the rules applicable to the situation and applying them to the collective behavior. (3) What is the probable course of the collective behavior? Will it lead to further episodes? If a cause is being advanced, what are its prospects for success? No large public will retain interest in, or give support to, a cause which is defined as foredoomed to failure.

The immediate effects of such definition are on the course of the collective behavior itself. Continued recruitment is facilitated or discouraged, and selectivity of recruitment is influenced by the definition. The frequent tendency for collective behavior in one location to touch off a rash of similar phenomena over a wide area is no doubt built upon the meaning which the public assigns to the actions. For example, the inconsequential act of daubing a swastika on a synagogue becomes a relatively easy and safe way of doing momentous harm to a minority group. The public definition constitutes a pressure on persons in authority, influencing their decision whether to act repressively or to give official blessing to the action.

Because of its intimate relationship to strains and hiatuses in the social order, collective behavior seldom fails to be interpreted by the mediating public as an expression of larger and more enduring trends and issues in the society. When lynchings were common in the southern United States, participants and local publics defined them as vigilante actions, concerned only with the enforcement of justice for particular crimes. The larger national public, however, refused to define lynchings as anything but an expression of long-standing racial repression. The long-range effects of lynching —a contribution to discrediting the traditional racial order—were determined by this latter definition. Small episodes of labor strife developing out of local irritants are often interpreted in relation to a supposed hidden larger issue and have their long range effect on this basis. One of the hazards of collective behavior as a means of presenting small grievances is that the collective action itself will become the object of attention by a mediating public, and the limited issue will be sidetracked through preoccupation with a larger issue as defined by that public.

The public, as it defines the collective action in relation to more enduring social strains and preoccupations, does so in at least four important respects. First, it sees the collective action as *precipitating* an issue. Discontent and tensions which have been covert are brought into the open. The episode forces discussion of matters which have been ignored. A great deal of official communication is often devoted to denying the long-range significance of the events, whether it be the Los Angeles community denying that the zoot suit episodes of 1943 were either riots or expressions of interethnic conflict, or a colonial power denying that nativistic demonstrations reflect discontent over foreign rule. The open discussion of a point of strain is likely to lead to new ways of viewing it.

Second, the definition of a collective incident by the mediating public becomes *committing* to many individuals and interest groups. Interested groups and officials are placed under pressure to take stands with the episode supplying a focus more concrete than mere definitions of abstract issues. People and groups known to have been involved in the incident find themselves committed. The process of translating a generalized concern into a dramatic alignment of pros and cons is thus begun.

Third, the collective incident is taken as *exemplifying* action which was otherwise merely contemplated. The collective action resembles "trying on" a suit of clothes to see how it looks off of the rack, and produces similar surprises. A group of boys who joined a race riot for the excitement withdrew in fear and horror after a brief participation. The reserved individual may discover a different side of himself after participating in the ecstasy of an expressive crowd. The enactment of protest, by destroying property or by defying governmental or industrial authority, gives the participants the opportunity to discover what it is like to confront authority with force, and the members of the public an opportunity to see and evaluate protest in action. In particular, the values which are in conflict in the situation come into sharper focus, so that it is possible to see how far property rights or individual determination must be infringed in the protest process.

Finally, the incident is defined as *identifying* the character of the persons and the interests represented on various sides of an issue. Incidents are often attributed to social movements, in which case the motives of participants in the movement are identified on the basis of the interpretation of the incident. Nonviolent actions, when observed by a public whose members are at least partly favorable to their purpose, probably contribute toward an image of righteousness and an assurance of good intention which strengthens the integration movement. It has long been recognized that worker violence in labor disputes generally swings sympathy away from the labor movement.

The mediating public normally outlasts the episodes of collective behavior, continuing its work of interpretation for a considerable period. The ordinary collective behavior episode may be viewed as an incomplete action, but one that must in time come to completion. The public persists as the vehicle for this completion tendency. If a satisfactory definition of the event is not reached currently, the public remains as the arena for continuing discussion. If further action is required to complete or correct the action of the crowd, the public makes this action its concern. In occasional instances of racial conflict the public has defined the riot as a disgrace and has dictated a program of reconstruction for the Negro area. After a disastrous panic a public usually arises which seeks to cope with the terrible fear that "it could have happened to anyone." The long-range effect of collective behavior may be either to further the aims of those who precipitate crowd behavior or to hasten resistance against them. Public definition and redefinition of the incident, during and afterwards, determines which the effect will be.

Conventionalization

Processes of conventionalization are at work from the start, in every instance of collective behavior, because of the continual reassertion of the institutional order. It has often been observed that demonstrations tend to get out of the control of organizers, and that unknown persons emerge as crowd leaders. But like other journalistic conceptions of collective behavior, these observations are both exaggerated and incomplete. Leadership of this character tends to be transitory because of the inexperience of the emergent leader and the waning enthusiasm of followers. The more dramatic incidents of attacks on institutional leaders appear, on fuller examination, to reflect long-standing contention between rival leadership. Thus the mayor of Omaha, who was himself the victim of attempted lynching when he sought to block a Negro lynching in 1919, had been a central figure in bitter partisan feuding for some time previously. Repudiation of NAACP leadership by a Chicago Negro crowd, in July, 1963, came in the context of recent successes of more activist Negro organizations. The effect of the lapse of institutional leadership is usually to provoke institutional leaders to adopt more radical positions in their efforts to regain leadership. But in doing so they translate the aims of the collectivity back into a more conventional formulation.

Within the collectivity, past episodes become the example to be followed, and conventional procedures become the mode of legitimation. Labor demonstrations and nationalistic displays have developed a few exemplary patterns. Lynchings have regularly borrowed such formalisms as a mock trial and provision for "last words."

Conventionalization of recurring forms of collective behavior takes place in connection with (1) use and exploitation and (2) instituting control and prediction. In the first instance, fashion and fad can only be understood as highly conventionalized and manipulated forms of collective behavior. The entire clothing industry is geared to the promotion and exploitation of fashion change. The strategy of marketing recreational devices is to promote and capitalize on fad. The popular recording industry counts on quick sale of "hits," and much real estate speculation is planned to capitalize on anticipated local "booms." In each instance predictability is incomplete, the collective behavior aspects remaining in a vital relationship with institutional efforts at exploitation. Organizations of various sorts employ the expressive crowd for the sake of the enthusiasm and *esprit de corps* which it develops. The political rally, the school pep rally, and the religious revival augment group feeling and lead people to set aside normal reservations to make greater personal commitments to the group than they would otherwise be prepared to do.

In the second case, the recurrent collective behavior which derives from indeterminacies in the social order and endemic strain constitute a continual threat to established leadership and orderly procedure. Hence procedures are normally developed over time to regulate these episodes and reduce their unpredictability. The election

public is such an effort to regulate the spontaneous publics which constantly arise as events create issues. The membership, periodicity, means of registering opinion, and the legitimate criterion of public opinion are formally defined. Organized interest groups assume primary control over communication in the public. The actual control remains limited, however, so that there is a continued interplay between formal procedures and the informal registrations of public opinion. Most societies have developed ritualized occasions on which considerable collective defiance of the mores is permitted. When the "orgy" is ritualized and compartmentalized, it becomes less of a threat to the mores and established authority.

FUNCTIONS OF COLLECTIVE BEHAVIOR

Enduring collective behavior which is directed toward change quickly becomes conventionalized in the framework of a social movement, and other recurrent collective behavior becomes conventionalized in the established order. The important functions of collective behavior must therefore be accomplished through conventional forms. Four major respects in which collective behavior contributes to the stable functioning of society can be enumerated.

Collective behavior contributes toward *legitimating decision* in areas in which the culture is insufficiently specific, and formal authority to render decisions is incomplete. The public is chiefly involved in this function, though the exemplification aspect of crowd behavior is regularly employed to justify decisions which minimize the likelihood of further episodes.

Collective behavior contributes to *solidarity* by countering the distance-provoking effects of formality in society. One of the endemic sources of strain in society is the antithesis between regulated order and interpersonal intimacy. One of the costs of orderliness and predictability, achieved through adherence to rules of interaction and atten-

tion to statuses, is the augmentation of reserve and segmentation in the relationships
between people. In the most highly regulated societies this development leads to the
exclusion of all but the most intimate
friends from the home, to severe restrictions
on spontaneous intimacies or even friendliness between strangers, to the restriction
of social interchange to noncontroversial
topics, and to cloaking interpersonal relationships in ritual politeness. As a consequence, intimate revelations are discouraged,
spontaneous friendship is inhibited, and all
relationships are marked by some anxiety
over who are really one's friends, and by
frustrated desires for impulsive sharing of
enthusiasms and disappointments. The re-
surgence of mechanical solidarity, with
freedom to address ingroup strangers and
opportunity to discover sentiments held in
common with one's fellows, revitalizes group
unity.

The penetration of reserve, evoking renewed solidarity, is one of the tasks of
ritually induced crowd behavior. It is doubtful that ceremonials effectively communicate the elaborate symbolization attributed
by Shils and Young (1953), for example,
to the British coronation. But by breaking
the daily routine and bringing people together in a situation in which customary
reserve can be suspended, some social revit-
alization can be achieved.

The third contribution of collective behavior is to the requirement for *action* in
the face of counterbalanced values and complex regulatory systems. The complexity of
society means that in many situations directives are contradictory, with values at hand
to justify contradictory courses of action.
The values are buttressed by interest groups,
and the individual is likely to owe allegiance
to groups which sponsor opposing directives
in some situations. The readiest consequence
of such cross-pressures is inaction or action
so compromised as to be ineffectual; an increased number of people with "no opinion"
is the consequence of pressures in contradictory directions (Kriesberg, 1949). The

surge of enthusiasm created through the
crowd in each of its many forms is a mechanism for periodically transcending these
blockages of action. The acting crowd
breaks the stalemate of inaction; the expressive crowd bursts the limits of qualified
commitment; the fad cracks the wall of resistance to innovation; the craze and boom
overcome the cautiousness of recognized
risk; and even panic may trigger covert desires to abandon a dangerous or unprofitable
mission.

Finally, collective behavior contributes to
the discovery of commitment in the absence
of experienced alternatives. A further cost
of effective regulation of behavior in a society is that conformities become empty, and
thoughtful persons are unsure of what they
genuinely stand for. The adolescent must
sometimes rebel a little before he discovers
through action how committed he is personally to the values which his parents have
taught him. The sophisticate must often experience the threat to his country's integrity
before he discovers how deeply committed
to patriotism he is. Recurrent opportunities
for collective action and struggle permit
people to penetrate the masks of their own
ritual attitudes.

Each of these four functions concerns the
need for balance in any social order. Regulated decision must be balanced by opportunity for more spontaneous collective
decision; the reserve associated with organization of society on the basis of status must
be balanced by opportunities for intimacy as
a contribution to social solidarity; cautious
action based on an intricate balance of contending values and interest groups must be
offset by enthusiasm which permits occasional action without concern for immediate
consequences; and devitalized conformity
must be countered by occasional opportunities to participate in attack or defense of the
established order to enable people to discover the nature of their actual commitments.
Each form of balance is an expression of the
antithesis between rigidity and flexibility
in society. The most general function of

collective behavior, then, is to maintain an element of flexibility in the workings of society.

REFERENCES

Allport, F. H. *Social psychology.* Boston: Houghton, 1924.

Allport, F. H., & Lepkin, M. Wartime rumors of waste and special privilege: Why some people believe them. *J. abnor. soc. Psychol.,* 1945, **40,** 3–36.

Allport, G., & Postman, L. *The psychology of rumor.* New York: Holt, 1947.

Asch, S. E. Effects of group pressure upon the modification and distortion of judgment. In H. Guetzkow (Ed.), *Groups, leadership & men.* Pittsburgh: Carnegie Press, 1951. Pp. 177–190.

Bagehot, W. *Physics and politics: Thoughts on the application of the principles of "natural selection" & "inheritance" to political society.* New York: Knopf, 1948 (first published 1869).

Baker, G. W., & Chapman, D. W. *Man and society in disaster.* New York: Basic Books, 1962.

Bauer, R. A., & Gleicher, D. B. Word of mouth of communication in the Soviet Union. *Publ. Opin. Quart.,* 1953, **17,** 297–310.

Belin-Milleron, Jean. Les expressions symboliques dans la psychologie collective des crises politiques. *Cahiers internationaux de sociologie,* 1951, **10,** 158–167.

Biderman, A. D., & Zimmer, H. (Eds.) *The manipulation of human behavior.* New York: Wiley, 1961.

Binet, A. *La suggestibilité.* Paris: Schleicher, 1900.

Blondel, C. *Introduction à la psychologie collective.* Paris: Librairie Armand Colin, 1952.

Blumer, H. Collective behavior. In A. M. Lee (Ed.), *New outline of the principles of sociology.* New York: Barnes & Noble, Inc., 1946 (first published 1939). Pp. 165–220.

Brown, R. W. Mass phenomena. In G. Lindzey (Ed.), *Handbook of social psychology.* Cambridge, Mass.: Addison-Wesley, 1954. II, 833–876.

Bucher, R. Blame and hostility in disaster. *Amer. J. Sociol.,* 1957, **62,** 467–475.

Cantril, H. *The psychology of social movements.* New York: Wiley, 1941.

Cantril, H. Public opinion in flux. *Ann. Amer. Acad. polit. soc. Sci.,* 1942, **220,** 136–150.

Cantril, H., Gaudet, H., & Herzog, H. *Invasion from Mars.* Princeton, N.J.: Princeton Univer. Press, 1940.

Caplow, T. Rumors in war. *Soc. Forces,* 1947, **25,** 298–302.

Danzig, E. R., Thayer, P. W., & Galanter, Lila R. *The effects of a threatening rumor on a disaster-stricken community.* Disaster study No. 10. Washington: National Academy of Sciences–National Research Council, 1958.

Dawson, C. A., & Gettys, W. E. *An introduction to sociology.* New York: Ronald, 1948.

DeFleur, M. L. Mass communication and the study of rumor. *Sociol. Inquiry,* 1962, **32,** 51–70.

Diggory, J. C. Some consequences of proximity to a disease threat. *Sociometry,* 1956, **19,** 47–53.

Disaster Research Group. *Field studies of disaster behavior: An inventory.* Disaster study No. 14. Washington: National Academy of Sciences–National Research Council, 1961.

Dollard, J., Doob, L. W., Miller, N. E., Mowrer, O. H., & Sears, R. R. *Frustration and aggression.* New Haven, Conn.: Yale Univer. Press, 1939.

Durkheim, E. *The division of labor in society.* G. Simpson (Trans.). Glencoe, Ill.: Free Press, 1947 (first published in French 1893).

Festinger, L., Cartwright, D., Barber, K., Fleischl, J., Gottsdanker, J., Keysen, A., & Leavitt, G. A study of rumor: Its origin and spread. *Hum. Relat.* 1948, **1,** 464–486.

Firth, R. Rumor in a primitive society. *J. abnorm. soc. Psychol.,* 1956, **53,** 122–132.

Form, W. H., & Loomis, C. P. The persistence and emergence of social and cultural systems in disasters. *Amer. sociol. Rev.,* 1956, **21,** 180–185.

Form, W. H., & Nosow, S. *Community in disaster.* New York: Harper, 1958.

French, J. R. P. Organized groups under fear and frustration. In K. Lewin, C. A. Meyers, J. Kalhorn, M. L. Farber, J. R. P. French (Eds.), *Authority and frustration.* Iowa City: Univer. of Iowa, 1944. Pp. 229–308.

Freud, S. *Group psychology and the analysis of the ego.* J. Strachey (Trans.). London: Hogarth, 1922.

Fritz, C. E., & Williams, H. B. The human being in disasters: A research perspective. *Ann. Amer. Acad. polit. soc. Sci.*, 1957, **309**, 42–51.

Halbwachs, M. *Les cadres sociaux de la memoire.* Paris: Librarie Félix Alcan, 1925.

Hovland, C. I., & Sears, R. R. Minor studies in aggression: VI, Correlations of lynchings with economic indices. *J. Psychol.*, 1949, **9**, 301–310.

Huizinga, J. *The waning of the middle ages.* New York: Doubleday, 1954 (first published 1924).

Jackson, M., Peterson, Eleanora, Bull, J., Monsen, S., & Richmond, Patricia. The failure of an incipient social movement. *Pacific sociol. Rev.*, 1960 **3**, 35–40.

Jung, C. C. *The undiscovered self.* R. F. C. Hull (Trans.). New York: Mentor, 1959 (first copyright 1957).

Killian, L. M. The significance of multiple-group membership in disaster. *Amer. J. Sociol.*, 1952, **57**, 309–314.

Kriesberg, M. Cross pressures and attitudes: A study of the influence of conflicting propaganda on opinions regarding American and Soviet relations. *Pub. Opin. Quart.*, 1949, **13**, 5–16.

Lang, K., & Lang, Gladys E. *Collective dynamics.* New York: Crowell, 1961.

LaPiere, R. T. *Collective behavior.* New York: McGraw, 1938.

Larsen, O. N., & Hill, R. J. Social structure and interpersonal communication. *Amer. J. Sociol.*, 1958, **63**, 497–505.

LeBon, G. *The crowd: A study of the popular mind.* London: Ernest Benn Ltd., 1896.

Lee, A. M., & Humphrey, N. D. *Race riot.* New York: Dryden, 1943.

Leighton, A. H. *The governing of men.* Princeton, N.J.: Princeton Univer. Press, 1945.

Lévy-Bruhl, L. *Les fonctions mentales dans les sociétés inférieures.* Paris: Librarie Félix Alcan, 1910.

Lind, A. *Hawaii's Japanese: An experiment in democracy.* Princeton, N. J.: Princeton Univer. Press, 1946.

MacCurdy, J. T. *The structure of morale.* New York: Macmillan, 1943.

McDougall, W. *The group mind: A sketch of the principles of collective psychology with some attempt to apply them to the interpretation of national life and character.* (2nd ed.) Cambridge: Cambridge Univer. Press, 1927 (first edition 1920).

Martin, E. D. *The behavior of crowds.* New York: Harper, 1920.

Medalia, N. Z. Who cries wolf? The reporters of damage to police in a pseudo-disaster. *Soc. Probs*, 1959–1960, **7**, 233–240.

Meerloo, J. A. M. *Patterns of panic.* New York: International Universities Press, 1950.

Miller, N. E., & Dollard, J. *Social learning and imitation.* New Haven, Conn.: Yale Univer. Press, 1941.

Mintz, A. Non-adaptive group behavior. *J. abnorm. soc. Psychol.*, 1951, **46**, 150–159.

Moore, H. E. Toward a theory of disaster. *Amer. sociol. Rev.*, 1956, **21**, 733–737.

Park, R. E., & Burgess, E. W. *Introduction to the science of sociology.* Chicago: Univer. of Chicago Press, 1921.

Peterson, W. A., & Gist, N. P. Rumor and public opinion. *Amer. J. Sociol.*, 1951, **57**, 159–167.

Prasad, J. The psychology of rumour: A study relating to the great Indian earthquake of 1934. *Brit. J. Psychol.*, 1935, **26**, 1–15.

Putney, S. W., & Cadwallader, M. L. An experiment in crisis interaction. *Res. Stud. State Coll. Wash.*, 1954, **22**, 94–102.

Quarantelli, E. L. A study of panic: Its nature, types and conditions. *Nat. Opin. Res. Center Surv. 308,* 1953.

Redl, F. The psychology of gang formation and the treatment of juvenile delinquents. *Psychoanalytic Stud. Child,* 1945, **1**, 367–377.

Rose, A. M. Rumor in the stock market. *Publ. Opin. Quart.*, 1951, **15**, 461–486.

Ross, E. A. *Social psychology.* New York: Macmillan, 1921.

Rudé, G. *The crowd in the French revolution.* Oxford: Oxford Univer. Press, 1959.

Schachter, S., & Burdick, H. A field experiment on rumor transmission and distortion. *J. abnorm. soc. Psychol.*, 1955, **50**, 363–371.

Sherif, M. A study of some social factors in perception. *Arch. Psychol.*, No. 187, 1935.

Shibutani, T. Rumors in a crisis situation. Unpublished masters dissertation, Univer. of Chicago, 1944.

Shibutani, T. The circulation of rumors as a form of collective behavior. Unpublished doctoral dissertation, Univer. of Chicago, 1948.

Shils, E., & Young, M. The meaning of the coronation. *Sociolog. Rev.*, 1953, 1, 63–81.

Smelser, N. J. *Theory of collective behavior.* New York: The Free Press of Glencoe, 1963.

Smith, G. H. Beliefs in statements labeled fact and rumor. *J. abnorm. soc. Psychol.*, 1947, 42, 80–90.

Sumner, W. G. *Folkways: A study of the sociological importance of usages, manners, customs, mores, and morals.* Boston: Ginn, 1940 (first published 1906).

Swanson, G. E. A preliminary study of the acting crowd. *Amer. sociolog. Rev.*, 1953, 18, 522–533.

Tarde, G. *L'opinion et la foule.* Paris: Librarie Félix Alcan, 1901.

Thomas, Dorothy S., & Nishimoto, R. S. *The spoilage.* Berkeley: Univer. of California Press, 1946.

Trotter, W. *Instincts of the herd in peace and war: 1916–1919.* (2nd ed.) London: Oxford Univer. Press, 1919 (first edition 1916).

Turner, R. H., & Killian, L. M. *Collective behavior.* Englewood Cliffs, N.J.: Prentice-Hall, Inc., 1957.

Turner, R. H., & Surace, S. J. Zoot-suiters and Mexicans: Symbols in crowd behavior. *Amer. J. Sociol.*, 1956, 62, 14–20.

Wolfenstein, Martha. *Disaster: A psychological essay.* Glencoe, Ill.: Free Press, 1957.

Young, Kimball, *Social psychology.* (2nd ed.) New York: Appleton-Century-Crofts, Inc., 1945.

Zaidi, S. M. H. An experimental study of distortion in rumor. *Indian J. soc. Work,* 1958, 19, 211–215.

CHAPTER 12 Social Movements

LEWIS M. KILLIAN

If one examines the history of any society, he will find that much of it consists of the story of the struggles of groups within the society to change some aspect of the culture. This is one reason why history books are filled with accounts of the careers of great leaders, the rise and fall of political movements, and the terrors of revolutions. The Crusades, the Reformation, the French and American revolutions, the antislavery movement, the labor movement, fascism, and communism—these, like many other social movements, have been accompanied by far-reaching changes in the societies which they touched. But are the efforts of the leaders of these movements and of the people who followed them really the causes of the changes or are they merely epiphenomena which accompany inevitable cultural changes? The writings of many sociologists have suggested the latter view.

Social movements are conventionally regarded as part of the subject matter of collective behavior, but they might just as well be viewed as an aspect of social change. The field of collective behavior, however, has been a neglected area of sociology, and in the study of social change, social movements have received relatively little emphasis. This is because men and groups have so often been regarded by sociologists as the creatures rather than the creators of social change. By and large, sociologists have looked to social or, more specifically, to cultural forces in their search for the dynamics of change, not to the actions and the interaction of men. This, in turn, has resulted from an implicit premise of determinism in sociology.

The evolutionary theories of Herbert Spencer, typical of the period of evolutionary theories or Social Darwinism, directed attention away from the deliberate, conscious efforts of men to change their societies. The early identification of "evolution" with "progress" suggested that such efforts, particularly revolutionary movements, were not only futile but antithetical to progress. In the United States, the conservative bias of William G. Sumner had a similar effect. While he did not adopt the organismic analogy, Sumner emphasized the slowness of change of the mores. He implied that it was not only futile but dangerous to attempt to force change. He directed the attention of sociologists to culture, but to culture as a force which persists and influences men rather than as something to be changed through men's purposive efforts.

The emphasis on culture rather than the group as the dynamic force in social change reached its peak in the writings of W. F. Ogburn (1922). Ogburn seemed to equate "social change" with "cultural change." His concept of culture was strongly influenced by the writings of the anthropologists, particularly A. H. Kroeber (1917), with his concept of culture as the "superorganic." He looked for laws of cultural change, including bases for prediction of when culture would change and of the effects of changes in one part of culture on other parts. During most of his career, furthermore, he emphasized material culture rather than ideas as the "lead" element in his famous "cultural lag" theory of change.

While evolutionism of various sorts dominated the early part of the history of sociology, it was later displaced by different forms of neopositivism emphasizing not only empiricism but quantification. The complex, long-lived social movement did not lend itself easily to the methods then in vogue. Social movements were more amenable to case studies and historical description. Such quantification as could occur would have to depend on the comparative analysis of many movements. The complex, dynamic interaction which characterizes a social movement was not an inviting subject for the data collection and field work which the empirical vogue demanded, particularly when the data sought were so often individual attitudes.

Finally, the pervasive approach described as "functionalism" has directed attention away from social movements as dynamic forces in social change. One consequence of this approach has been an overemphasis on "equilibrium" or "homeostasis." This has led, on the one hand, to a search for conditions conducive to equilibrium and, on the other, to the quest for dysfunctional aspects of culture which are presumed to upset the equilibrium and thereby produce change.

SOCIAL MOVEMENTS AS A FIELD OF SOCIOLOGY

R. M. MacIver emphasized the need for a distinction between "the cultural order," "the technological order," and "the social order."

The fact that cultural values are socially fostered need not blur the distinction of the cultural order, as a value configuration, from the social order, as a web of relationships. And similarly the fact that some aspects of social organization are specifically utilitarian need not prevent us from distinguishing a pattern of social relationships from a system of techniques (MacIver, 1942, p. 274).

The study of social movements is primarily a study of social change as well as cultural change, of a changing social order as well as of changing values and norms. In the words of Sherif and Sherif, "A social movement . . . is a formative stage of interaction in human relations. It expresses an on-going process" (1956, p. 724). Furthermore, "A social movement is always possessed by a sense of mission" (1956, p. 722). Hence, attention is focused on the interaction of conscious, striving human beings as part of an emergent collectivity which is the social movement. This is not the study of stable groups or established institutions, but of groups and institutions in the process of becoming. Cultural maladjustments are of interest, but only as conditions out of which the collective efforts of men to change their culture arise. The changes which take place in the culture are important as end-products of social movements and as features of the new milieu within which new movements develop.

These cultural changes are not regarded, however, as dependent variables to be predicted from independent variables which are themselves aspects of the culture. Social change is not simply a consequence of the intrusion of discordant elements into an otherwise stable system, nor are the efforts of men to bring about change mere symptoms of "cultural lag," "disequilibrium," or "social disorganization." Rather, change is a normal aspect of culture, and the social movement is one of the most important ways through which social change is manifest and cultural change produced.

EARLIER WRITINGS ON SOCIAL MOVEMENTS

In spite of the neglect of social movements and collective behavior in the main body of sociological writings, there has long been an interest in these subjects. Although he is often identified with a position of group realism and cultural determinism, Emile Durkheim adumbrated the study of social movements as a cause of social change. Culturalogical interpretations of Durkheim's work stress his emphasis on the independence of culture, its characteristics of "exteriority, priority and constraint," and his resemblance to the evolutionist school in his concept of the division of labor. But in his *Elementary Forms of Religious Life* (1915), he emphasized the importance of social interaction, or "psychosocial synthesis," which produces collective representations. As Parsons has pointed out, Durkheim finally shifted from a positivist orientation toward a voluntaristic approach which contrasts with the sort of cultural determinism often ascribed to him (1937, p. 450).

Gustave LeBon (1897) was another writer whose works pointed to the importance of the interaction which takes place in collective behavior as the factor producing social and cultural change. Although he wrote of "the crowd," his concept of the crowd was so broad that it included social movements. While we may find his explanations of the nature of "crowd psychology" mystical and psychologistic, he did suggest the importance of seeking an explanation of social change in the activities of those who make up the collectivity, not merely in the cultural forces which produced this activity. Although his influence was not felt in American sociology until relatively recently,

Max Weber represents a shift toward making the study of social movements a central rather than a peripheral concern. Weber's emphasis on the subjective element in social action was an important basis of the modern voluntaristic theory of social action which has challenged the deterministic theories which were a deterrent to the study of social movements. Of greater importance is his theory of charisma which, as Parsons points out, is not only a theory to explain the legitimacy of social order but is also a theory of social change. Weber did not emphasize only the charismatic leader who, as a "prophet," breaks free of and challenges the traditional order, he also stressed the "community" which thereby arises—"the social organization independent of the imminent development of the traditional order" (Parsons, 1937, p. 569). In his concept of the "routinization of charisma" he suggested how the new organization—the movement, if you will—constitutes not an alien disruption of the legitimate order but becomes the basis of it. Parsons declares, "Indeed, Weber's fullest treatment of legitimacy leaves no doubt that there is no legitimate order without a charismatic element" (1937, p. 665).

The greatest impetus to the study of social movements came from the early work of Robert E. Park. In *An Introduction to the Science of Sociology* (1924) by Park and Burgess, a section on "Collective Behavior" was included. Park and Burgess provided an early characterization of collective behavior as "[t]hose phenomena which exhibit in the most obvious and elementary way the process by which societies are disintegrated into their constituent elements and the processes by which these elements are brought together again into new relations to form new organizations and new societies" (pp. 924–925). These pioneers differentiated between the crowd, the public, and the mass movement. They pointed out the lack of systematic research on mass movements (p. 927), and they suggested various types of movements—revivals, reform movements, revolutions, and migrations.

Herbert Blumer carried on the interest of these sociologists in collective behavior, including social movements. Park and Burgess, influenced perhaps by the writings of LeBon (1897), Tarde (1903), and Wilfred Trotter (1920), overemphasized the factors of social contagion and circular interaction—the rapid, uniform spread of a single impulse through a collectivity under the influence of a strong emotion. Blumer sharpened and elaborated their conception of the subject matter of collective behavior and its position in the discipline of sociology, and focused attention on interaction rather than on imitation.

In his definitions, Blumer made explicit the close relationship of collective behavior, particularly social movements, to the study of social change, saying: "Sociology in general is interested in studying the social order and its constituents (customs, rules, institution, etc.) as they are. Collective behavior is concerned in studying the ways by which the social order comes into existence in the sense of the emergence and solidification of new forms of collective behavior" (Blumer, 1951, p. 169). He characterized social movements as "collective enterprises to establish a new order of life." Blumer stressed the importance of the career of the social movement, from collective behavior on the primitive level (milling, social contagion, circular reaction) through the stage at which it takes on the character of a society, with "a culture, a social organization, and a new scheme of life." In his discussion of the career, he suggested the importance of the interaction of different types of actors—different types of agitators and different types of leaders. Blumer distinguished between "*esprit de corps*" and "morale" and between tactics and strategy. He too undertook the development of a typology of social movements, suggesting as his three main types general social movements, specific social movements (with subtypes reform and revolutionary) and expressive movements (including religious movements and fashions). In distinguishing between the general and the specific movement, he made clearer the concept that a social movement is a collectivity of individuals characterized by a "we-consciousness" as distinguished from "the mass," individuals acting in the same way but on the basis of individual decisions and without a sense of membership.

Another American sociologist who has made the subject of social movements a topic of major interest is Rudolf Heberle. In his book, *Social Movements* (1951), his analysis is rather narrowly focused on political movements, and he specifically excludes from consideration any movements which he regards as of minor or local social significance. Yet his conception of "the social movement" is a broad one, and it is essentially sociological. He, too, emphasizes social movements as being central to social change, defining a social movement as "a collective attempt to reach a visualized goal, especially a change in certain social institutions" (1951, p. 6). Heberle sees social movements as groups or "social collectives," to be distinguished from social trends or tendencies, cultural changes which are merely "the aggregate effect of many individual actions" (1951, pp. 8–9). Finally, while contributing significantly to the analysis of what he calls the "social foundations" of social movements through his ecological studies, Heberle places at the center of his analysis the study of social movements as groups in the process of becoming organized.

A quite different approach to the study of social movements is represented by *The Psychology of Social Movements* by Hadley Cantril (1941). As the title suggests, this approach represents a return to a psychological mode of analysis in which the emphasis is placed on individual motivation. The author seeks to explain social movements in terms of "the mental context and motivation found in the individual who is adjusting himself to the social world" (1941, p. xii). This approach tends to oversimplify the variety of motives which may cause the many individuals involved to ally themselves to a social movement. More important, the approach neglects the developmental aspect of the social movement—the development of *esprit de corps* and morale within the movement, the roles of different types of leaders, the evolution of the structure of the movement, and the relation of the movement to other groups.

Efforts to extend and refine the line of analysis suggested by Blumer are found in two general treatments of collective behavior recently published, *Collective Behavior* by Turner and Killian (1957) and *Collective Dynamics* by Kurt and Gladys Lang (1961). A distinctly sociological approach is also utilized by C. Wendell King in *Social Movements in the United States* (1956). All three of these treatments rest on the analysis of the social movement as a collectivity with a career, an emergent structure, and a culture. The motives of the participants are assumed to be heterogeneous, their activities varied and interactive.

All of these treatments have been classified as "sociological" because, while they take account of the motivation of individuals to participate, they focus attention on the interaction which takes place within the social movement and the transformation of the behavior and the attitudes of persons as a result of this interaction. They seek the explanation of social change not in the personality of individuals but in the career of the social movement as a collectivity.

DEFINITIONS OF SOCIAL MOVEMENTS

Consider the similarities between the conceptions of social movements used by some of these sociologists. Blumer defines the movement simply as "a collective enterprise to establish a new order of life" (1951, p. 199). Heberle, in a similar vein, declares, "The main criterion of a social movement . . . is that it aims to bring about fundamental changes in the social order." He continues with the observation that a social movement is "a collective attempt to reach a visualized goal, especially a change in certain social institutions" (1951, p. 6). Lang

and Lang take a social movement to mean "large scale, widespread, and continuing, elementary collective action in pursuit of an objective that affects and shapes the social order in some fundamental way" (1961, p. 490). King proposes as his definition, "a group venture extending beyond a local community or a single event and involving a systematic effort to inaugurate changes in thought, behavior, and social relationships (1956, p. 27). Turner and Killian advance the most inclusive definition: "A collectivity acting with some continuity to promote or resist a change in the society or group of which it is a part" (1957, p. 308).

These definitions have two features in common. Central to all is the effort of men to intervene in the process of social and cultural change. Most of them emphasize the goal of bringing into being new social and cultural forms. Turner and Killian also included efforts to resist changes which appear imminent. But in either case, men are viewed as actors, not as passive responders to the flow of culture or the homeostatic tendencies of the social system. Also essential to these definitions is the notion that the men's acts are collective. They are not the discrete activities of so many scattered individuals, but of people acting together with a sense of engaging in a collective enterprise.

From these two features—action to promote or resist change, and behavior which is collective—the salient characteristics of social movements are derived:

1. The existence of shared values—a goal or an objective, sustained by an ideology.

2. A sense of membership or participation —a "we-ness," a distinction between those who are for and those against.

3. Norms—shared understandings as to how the followers should act, definitions of outgroups and how to behave toward them.

4. A structure—a division of labor between leaders and followers and between different classes of each. This is not a comprehensive structure, however, as Heberle points out (1951, p. 269).

The social movement is, then, a type of

collectivity; it is not a cultural trend or a precipitous cultural change. There is, of course, a close relationship between social movements and cultural change, but they constitute different aspects of social reality and of study. We may identify a series of related cultural changes which may be designated as a trend, invention, or even as a "revolution" (as in the case of the Industrial Revolution). We may describe the "culture base" out of which these changes emerge, and we may trace the derivative effects. But such changes do not necessarily grow out of social movements, nor does the analysis of the mechanisms and processes of cultural change elucidate the character of social movements. Cultural change may be brought about through the actions of many individuals reacting to and acting upon the culture which provides the common framework for their existence. Such changes may also occur as a result of the action of stable, organized groups which in the course of their existence produce inventions. For instance, the current trend in the automation of industry is a consequence of the collective activity of industrial and research organizations, but is not the consequence of a social movement.

Blumer has suggested that such changes—"cultural drifts"—provide the background out of which general social movements develop. He characterizes "general social movements" as follows: "General social movements take the form of groping and uncoordinated efforts. They have only a general direction, toward which they move in a slow, halting, yet persistent fashion. As movements they are unorganized, with neither established leadership nor recognized membership, and little guidance or control" (Blumer, 1951, p. 200).

The gradual and cumulative changes in culture which, together, constitute a cultural drift give currency to new self-conceptions, new desires and hopes. As many scattered individuals give expression to these ideas in a variety of ways, a general movement emerges, such as the woman's movement, the labor movement, or anticolonialism. But as Blumer emphasized, "the general social movement is dominated to a large extent by the mechanisms of mass behavior. . . . [It is] likely to be merely an aggregation of individual lines of action based on individual decisions and selections" (Blumer, 1951, p. 201).

General movements, in turn, constitute the soil out of which specific social movements may grow. The ideas expressed in the general movement may be perceived by some individuals as "the wave of the future," and these persons may be unwilling to be merely passive subjects carried on this wave. They may develop a program for hastening and directing these changes and rally around them like-minded people who collectively attempt to promote the change.

SOCIAL MOVEMENTS AND ASSOCIATIONS

Although the study of social movements as dynamic collectivities has been contrasted with the study of the structure and function of established, relatively stable associations, there is a constant and pervasive relationship between these two phases of social life. Social movements do not develop out of a vacuum or a state of complete social disorganization. The members of a social movement are members of a society and of one or more groups within that society, each with its own organization and norms. As the members attempt collectively to revise, preserve, or restore the social organization and the normative order of these relatively stable, pre-existing groups, they act as participants in a social movement. The social movement may be internal to a particular society or association, or it may cut across group boundaries. A social movement may encompass within itself associations whose members participate by virtue of their group membership rather than as discrete, unattached individuals. Finally, one of the most significant end-products of social movements is the emergence and stabilization of new institutions and new forms of social organization.

SOCIAL MOVEMENTS
AND OTHER COLLECTIVITIES

The other major forms of collectivities, the crowd and the public, must be differentiated from the social movement, but the relationship between the three forms is important. The crowd, compact or diffuse, differs from the social movement chiefly in its temporal duration and the breadth of its objectives. The crowd is of relatively short duration; its career is measured in hours or days, and its objective is limited. As a consequence, it fails to develop the complex and relatively stable structure, the broad program of change, and the elaborate ideology which characterize the social movement. The compact crowd is, unlike the social movement, also limited in space, consisting only of persons within sight and hearing of each other.

The crowd may be related to the social movement in a number of ways. The proximate cause of the development of the movement may be the excitement, the imagery, and the sense of unity which develops in a crowd. In this sense, the crowd may be a stage in the development of a social movement, growing out of the same condition and being concerned with the same issue. By the same token, the agitation which is part of the tactics of a social movement may be a stimulus to crowd behavior. More important, crowd behavior may be deliberately fostered and used by the leaders of a social movement, so crowds may constitute subordinate parts of the social movement.

The public may contain the seeds of a social movement. The public differs in that it includes people of different viewpoints who are engaged in discussion of an issue. But "if members of a public who have a common position concerning the issue at hand supplement their informal person-to-person discussion with some organization to promote their convictions effectively and insure more sustained activity," a social movement may develop (Turner & Killian, 1957, p. 307). Sometimes a segment of a public reaches the conviction that only its viewpoint is legitimate and that dissent should not be tolerated. As a result, it becomes a social movement devoted to promoting a program of action, not debating an issue. But even after the social movement is formed, the public may be co-existent with it. Public opinion concerning the issue may continue to develop; the social movement simply becomes a special part of the public. Moreover, a social movement may, through its activities, raise to the level of public controversy issues which have been of concern only to special interest groups.

Usually a social movement itself becomes an issue about which a public forms. When a movement's strategy envisions widespread acceptance both of its values and of itself as the legitimate promoter of these values, many of its activities will be directed toward creating a favorable public opinion. Hence, the leaders of a social movement may deliberately attempt to engender a public concerned with the values they seek to promote. In the present era of mass communications, such leaders jump at opportunities to appear on television programs or to present their views in magazine articles. The fact that hostility as well as sympathy may be aroused in the audience is not important—"a bad press is better than no press."

In summary, although the focus of study may be the social movement itself, the movement does not exist in isolation. A social movement develops within the framework of an on-going social order whose institutions and associations persist even as they are changing. The movement exists simultaneously with crowds, publics, and, most important, other social movements. Its relationship with all these other groups and collectivities must be considered.

THE GENESIS OF
SOCIAL MOVEMENTS

The most insistent demand on the social sciences is to explain the relationship between social order and social change. It is a fundamental premise of sociology that the social order develops to satisfy the needs of men, needs which they lack the instinctive mechanisms to meet. At the same time, the process of socialization creates other needs which are met by the social order. If the social order functioned perfectly to satisfy men's needs, biogenic and sociogenic, then there would be no social movements and no social change. If, on the other hand, man's biological nature could be shown to change significantly from time to time, the genesis of social movements would be simply man's changing innate needs. But since neither of these conditions has been shown to prevail, the genesis of social movements must be sought in the nature of the social order and the socialization process.

The social order in which men seek the satisfaction of their needs is not a spontaneous, biologically determined reflection of these needs. Nor is it a rationally planned, internally consistent order. Rather it is a constantly emerging system, much of which develops and is accepted without foresight. As societies merge, exchange members, or subdivide, the social order comes to have different components with diverse origins. Hence, not only values but value conflicts, not only group cohesion, but intergroup hostility, not only statuses and roles, but dilemmas and contradictions of status, are normal features of social life. Moreover, although human nature and man's motives are products of the process of induction into an on-going social order, no two human beings experience the socialization process in exactly the same way. The uniqueness of the individual, in spite of his similarities to his fellow humans, is a constant challenge to the stability and order of culture.

Hence, to say that the genesis of social movements and of all collective behavior is rooted in human frustration is not to say that culture and society are inevitably hostile and repressive to human nature. It is, rather, to say that social life is both satisfying and frustrating by its very nature. Faris suggested this in the statement, "All civilized societies, and perhaps most societies of any kind, are in a perpetual condition of change and partial disorganization so that persons experience conflicts and frustrations, divided loyalties, and failures of various kinds along with their good times in life" (Faris, 1952, p. 75).

The socialized individual seeks satisfaction of his needs in the social order. He looks to it for guidance as to what ends he should seek and what means he should use to gain these ends. If society fails to satisfy his needs and to provide a stable framework in which he can carry on his daily activities, he challenges the social order in some way. It may be through individual nonconformity which, depending on how his fellows evaluate it, may cause him to be punished as a criminal or hailed as a genius. But if his dissatisfaction is shared by, and communicated to, others in the society, a social movement may develop.

But frustration, even shared frustration, and the resultant random or rebellious behavior are not sufficient for the development of a social movement. They may lead only to short-lived crowd behavior in which an ephemeral organization is developed, along with short-range, immediate objectives which are soon forgotten when the crowd dissolves. For a social movement to develop there must be a vision, a belief in the possibility of a different state of affairs, and there must be an enduring organization devoted to the attainment of this vision. This is the active nucleus of the movement, the leadership group. "The nucleus consists of a group of individuals who are committed in varying degrees to the same mission and who stand in definite status and role relations to one another" (Sherif & Sherif, 1956, p. 726). Around it moves its following—participants whose relationship to the movement may range from formal membership to covert allegiance. The nucleus is the nerve center into which come the many impulses from the diffuse, loosely integrated following, to be synthesized into values and norms which, along with the organization, give the movement its identity as a collectivity. Like any but the most ephemeral collectivity, the social movement has as properties values, norms, and a structure.

THE PROPERTIES OF SOCIAL MOVEMENTS

Values

Every social movement has, as the standard around which the adherents rally, some value or set of values—a vision of a goal to be obtained by the voluntary striving of the members. On the surface, at any rate, devotion to the values is the *raison d'être* of the movement. These values are always of an ideal nature—they are "myths," in the sense that George Sorel used the term when he wrote, "The myth must be judged as a means of acting on the present; any attempt to discuss how far it can be taken literally as future history is devoid of sense" (1950, p. 144). This in no way reduces efficacy of the values, however, because it is the adherents' belief in them, not their "reality," which makes them important.

The stated values of a social movement may be of different types. One dimension depends upon their relationship to the existing social order. They may be forward-looking, or progressive, in that they purport to constitute a novel and better way of doing things. They may be reactionary, promising through their realization a restoration of a previous and better state of affairs. A movement with conservative values demands no significant change in the culture but merely advocates the preservation of existing features of the culture. Hence, the conservative movement usually constitutes a counter-movement, arising to oppose changes proposed by a progressive movement or sometimes by a reactionary movement.

The values of a movement may also be comprehensive or restricted. If they are comprehensive, they advocate changes in many aspects of a society, including its most important institutions—government, the family,

education, religion, and the economic system. A revision of the structure of the group is proposed. Restricted values call for changes in a limited area of culture, such as the manner of collecting taxes, appointing ministers, or caring for the aged, or the norms concerning the employment of children, the punishment of particular types of criminals, or the use of contraceptives. The strategy the movement adopts, the definition of the movement in the large society, and the type of opposition it evokes all depend, in part, upon the degree of comprehensiveness of its values.

The values of a social movement are not simple, clear, and specific, as the slogans which arise to express them may suggest. Instead they constitute a complex structure, part of which is more easily discernible than the rest. Without implying a clear-cut dichotomy, we may say that some values of a social movement are explicit while others are implicit.

King suggested this distinction when he discussed "goals," saying of "implicit goals" that they are ends about which the participants may be aware only tacitly or about which they may be quite ignorant. He explained, "Certain objectives may be nurtured by leaders who hope for great personal power and prestige, whether or not they sincerely believe in the explicit aims embraced by their followers. In other cases, the secrecy maintained by the functionaries simply reflects their fear that the participants are not yet 'ready' for, or will be alienated by, these goals" (King, 1956, p. 30). Gabriel Almond analyzed in detail what he calls the "esoteric" and the "exoteric" appeals of communism, showing clearly the distinction between them:

. . . at the level of mass appeals, the Communist movement portrays itself in ways which are adapted to specific social and political settings. Persons attracted to these external representations may later be systematically exposed to the esoteric or internal doctrine in the training schools and in the higher echelons of the movement (Almond, 1954, p. 66).

Heberle suggested, "The publicly proclaimed goals and ideas are not always the true and real aims. . . . Sometimes the goals are intentionally formulated in a very vague way, so as to unite masses of members who would not be able to agree on a more definite formulation" (1951, p. 25). That there is a diversity of values, some being more apparent than others, is not surprising when we remember that a social movement is a complex social system emerging through the interaction of equally complex individuals, each of whom may act in pursuit of a number of goals. It approximates what Sorokin described as an "inwardly antagonistic multibonded group" (1947, p. 238). Unless the antagonistic values are somehow insulated against direct conflict or are replaced by "solidary social compounds," the movement is likely to disintegrate. Inability either to eliminate conflicting values or to "keep the right hand from knowing what the left was doing" has brought many social movements to an early, abortive dissolution.

Moreover, the members of a social movement are concerned with presenting to others and to themselves an image which is socially acceptable. Since a movement develops within the context of the society which it seeks to change, and since the members are products of this society, it is constrained to reconcile its values with those of the larger society, no matter how revolutionary it may appear. Hence, it tends to develop explicit values, presented both to members and to nonmembers, which cloak the movement with a mantle of idealism and altruism, if not always of respectability. This is not mere duplicity or cynicism; the members come to believe, in varying degrees, in the primacy of these values. But it would obscure the analysis of the dynamics of a social movement to assume that these publicly emphasized values are the only values or even the most important ones. There are also implicit values which the members hesitate to emphasize to outsiders and may find difficulty in admitting to themselves.

The illustration which immediately suggests itself is the movement which has as one of its important goals the increase or preservation of the power and privileges of a particular segment of the society—a movement which asserts that this segment constitutes an elite which is rightly entitled to power. Turner and Killian (1957) differentiated such movements as "control" or "power-oriented" movements in contrast to "value-oriented" movements. Yet, even though the power orientations of such movements may be readily apparent to the outsider, the movements develop explicit values which serve to sanction the quest for power or privilege. While individual leaders may quite cynically propagate these seemingly altruistic values, the explicit values become a very real property of the movement as a collectivity and are believed in by many of the members. Thus, as naked a quest for power as his movement may have appeared, even Hitler argued that Nazism was a crusade for the welfare of not only the German folk but of all "Aryan" peoples. The judgment of psychiatrists that he was an "unmistakably neurotic personality seeking an outlet for his aggressions through political power" (Gilbert, 1950, p. 51) need not imply that he did not believe his own propaganda. Similarly, while it is obvious that "white supremacy" is an important value in the segregation movement, it is joined to "states rights," "Americanism," and other such values even though the theme of preserving the dominance of a racial elite is hardly concealed. On the other hand, movements which place more emphasis on altruistic values should be examined carefully for less broadly acceptable values. The American revolutionary movement crystallized the value system evolved through years of English history and expressed in the Declaration of Independence. Yet the explicit value of "liberty" integrated the implied values of economic equality for the colonial merchants and freedom from the Established English Church for religious dissenters.

As this suggests, the explicit values may consist of a congeries of values of widely divergent groups which come together in a movement under the banner of an abstract, explicit, manifest value. While all may subscribe to this general, abstract value, it has various specific meanings for them in terms of the implicit values. Thus the "far right" movement of the 1960's in the United States emphasizes publicly its dedication to freedom, Americanism, and resistance to communism. Yet there is abundant evidence that for one of its most powerful segments, these values really mean freedom of business from government regulation, high taxes, and harassment by strong labor unions. The movement constitutes, for this segment, a bid for economic and political power. For other segments, however, the movement and its explicit values represent an expression of the implicit values of religious fundamentalism, resistance to "socialized medicine," or preservation of white supremacy. Yet another segment which has joined in this movement includes certain people with a long history of anti-Semitic activity. This implicit value, which might seriously damage the public image of the movement if openly displayed, has been explicitly denied and officially condemned by many right-wing leaders. Nevertheless, the elements which cherish it have not been eliminated from the movement and anti-Semitism remains an implicit value which might become more evident were the movement to attain power.

Values have another dimension in that the conception of the ends of a movement carries implications for the means by which these ends can be achieved. These means, as intermediate steps to the achievement of the broader, more abstract values, may come to constitute values in themselves. One type of intermediate value is societal reorganization, the restructuring of the social system in order to bring about the realization of the ultimate values. Often the means of bringing about societal reorganization is the seizure of power, and this becomes an explicit goal of the movement. The other type of intermediate value is personal transformation, the conversion of a sufficient number of individuals to make the realization of the ultimate values possible. If this is the means-orientation of the values, then maximizing participation in the movement becomes a goal. Hence the values of a movement carry implications for strategy, and, as will be shown later, they impose normative limitations on tactics.

Finally, the value system of a movement encompasses the ideology—the justification of the values. The ideology is sometimes formalized in a vast body of literature produced by the intellectuals in the movement. But even if it is not formalized in this manner, it still develops through the informal interaction of the members and becomes a stable part of their belief system.

The ideology consists typically of four parts. The first is a version—a "revision"—of history which shows that the goals of the movement are in harmony with the traditions of the society. Thus American history has been reinterpreted to show that Tom Paine was the only patriot who really expressed the democratic values of the American Revolution, that the Germans in early America were really the founders of independence, that a Negro was the first casualty of the Revolution, and that Abraham Lincoln was a segregationist at heart, all in support of the values of specific movements of the twentieth century—communism, native fascism, the Negro protest, and the segregation movement. One of the most elaborate revisionist attempts has been the production of a large body of literature "proving" that the Fourteenth Amendment was never legally adopted.

The ideology also includes not one but two visions of the future—a vision of paradise and a vision of hell. George Sorel recognized the value of the utopian vision, or "myth," when he observed:

The framing of a future, in some indeterminate time, may, when it is done in a certain way, be very effective and have very few inconveniences; this happens when the anticipation of the future takes the form of those myths, which inclose with them, all the strongest inclinations of a people . . . (Sorel, 1950, p. 142).

At the same time, the necessity of the success of the movement is dramatized by a portrayal of the miserable conditions which would result if the movement were to fail. Thus the Nazis threatened the people of Germany with a Germany and a world ruled by Jews and Communists if they did not wholeheartedly support the party. In the United States, integrationists warn of an America gradually forsaking its democratic ideals, isolated from the other free nations and eventually succumbing to communism if full democracy is not extended to Negroes. Segregationists counter with a picture of a society dominated by Negro voting blocs, dragged down to the inferior moral and intellectual level of the Negroes, and "mongrelized."

Closely related to these myths is a set of stereotyped conceptions of the "heroes" and the "villains" of the struggle in which the social movement is involved. A new perspective on alignments of members of the society is developed, reflecting an evaluation of their orientations toward the values of the movement. Thus the very terms integrationists and segregationists are themselves part of the ideologies of the opposing movements. Leaders of the conservative movement see the United States as inhabited by "conservatives," "patriots," or "anti-Communists," who are opposed by "liberals," "comsymps," or "anti-anti-Communists." The "New Dealers" conjured up the image of "economic royalists" to identify their opposition. Even movements which emphasize participation rather than social reorganization develop these stereotypes—thus "beatniks" have to contend with "squares," and fundamentalist revivalists rail against "religious liberals" or "complacent Christians."

THE NORMS OF SOCIAL MOVEMENTS

One of the characteristic properties of a group is a system of norms governing the behavior of its members toward each other and toward members of outgroups. As a collectivity in the process of becoming a group, the social movement also develops norms. Since the movement is oriented basically toward conflict, these norms relate particularly to intramovement discipline. They require of the member behavior which will symbolize his loyalty to the movement, strengthen his identification with it, and, in some cases, set him apart from nonmembers.

In some movements, a norm of absolute, unquestioning obedience to the leaders develops. This is most likely to occur as control tendencies increase and the explicit values are pushed into the background. Thus, the loyal Communist is not expected to interpret the movement's values for himself; he is required instead to follow the "party line," the current interpretation of the values by the leaders. The requirement for obedience need not be so strict, however. For example, the Congress of Racial Equality, an association within the Negro protest movement, has an elite of "active members" who commit themselves to rigid discipline, particularly with reference to nonviolence. But it also has a class of "associate members" who support the goals of the organization but do not feel that they can submit to the discipline. Obviously the more diffuse and loosely organized a movement is, the less likely it is that such a stringent norm will develop.

Even in the absence of an explicit, formal interpretation of the values by the leaders, a movement develops norms which in effect constitute a "line"—a definition of specific things which members should favor or oppose. Again, the party line of the Communists is an obvious example of an explicit set of such definitions. But, without having the rigid discipline and the ideological formalism of the Communist movement, the "far right" movement in the United States has evolved a "line" which defines the "correct" position on a variety of issues. The norms include opposition to cooperatives, support of restrictive immigration policies, opposition to the World Council of Churches, "get the U.S. out of the U.N. and the U.N. out of the U.S.," denunciation of Walter Reuther, opposition to "Progressive Education," support for the House Committee on Un-American Activities, and positions on many other current issues. While these attitudes may correspond to the explicit or implicit values of the movement, they may also be viewed as reflections of norms in that there is pressure on the individual to adopt these positions even in the absence of knowledge of the issues. Expression of these views becomes a mark of identification with the movement and its central values; disagreement with them makes one at least suspect if it does not clearly mark him as an outsider.

Not just the activities which explicitly constitute "working for the movement," but the everyday activities of the members may come to be governed by norms. Religious movements may prescribe how their followers should dress, what movies they should or should not see, and what forms of recreation are sinful or worldly. In Fidel Castro's revolutionary movement in Cuba, the wearing of beards became a symbol of loyalty. In various types of "liberal" movements, the singing or appreciation of folk songs has come to be a mark of adherence to the movement. Indeed, a movement may develop an elaborate culture which guides its members in their selection of music, literature, paintings, and even foods. The leaders of Black Muslims, members of a Negro nationalist movement which claims to be a religion, prescribe what foods their followers may not eat. While the list of taboo foods includes items forbidden by Mosaic law, it also includes such delicacies as cornbread, lima beans, blackeyed peas, green cabbage, collard greens, rabbit, possum, and squirrel (Essien-Udom, 1962, pp. 205–206). The effort to set the "Blacks" apart from ordinary, plebeian "Negroes" is evident. At the same time, conformity to the cultural demands of a movement strengthens the feeling of belonging of the individual and reassures his fellow members of his loyalty.

The emergence of distinctive norms as the property of a social movement may be seen most clearly in the development of "special languages." The movement redefines the symbolic environment of the members; in the process, familiar terms take on new meanings, and neologisms arise. In the course of the prohibition or temperance movement in the United States, the term temperance came to connote "abstinence," not "moderation." The somewhat awkward phrase beverage alcohol developed as an inclusive concept to denote the members' opposition to all forms of "drinks." As a countermovement emerged to roll back the legal restrictions imposed at the behest of the "drys" or "tee-totalers," the words legal control became a slogan for the repeal of prohibition laws. In the far right movement, to refer to the United States as a "republic," not as a "democracy" has become a mark of identification, as has reference to one of the two major political parties as the "Democrat party" rather than the "Democratic party." More recently, this movement has contributed the term anti-anti-Communist to the language.

Particularly important are terms of self-reference which members of a movement develop. The "old-age movement" of this century has produced such euphemisms as "senior citizens" and "the aged" as substitutes for "old folks" or "old people." An extreme form of redefinition of self is found in the Black Muslims, who have dropped the designation "Negro" and given the adjective "Black" a positive rather than a derogatory flavor and have even required the members to drop their "slave" names. Similarly, members of various nationalist movements on the continent of Africa have given new emphasis to the name "African" and insist that it can be properly applied only to black men (it is taboo to call a black African a "*Negro*"), not to whites, even those born in Africa.

Values as a Source of Normative Restrictions

The most important and pervasive source of normative prescriptions and restrictions is the values themselves. As has been noted, values carry with them implications for the means by which they should be attained. The nature of the values carries implications both for the members and the public as to what sorts of tactics are congruent with the image of the movement. For members, and particularly for leaders, to resort to tactics which are inconsistent with the explicit, publicly-stated values may evoke opposition or suspicion from heretofore sympathetic members of the public and give the opposition ammunition. It may also sow dangerous seeds of doubt and dissatisfaction in the minds of individuals who are committed to the movement on the basis of these values.

Many of these normative limitations on tactics are negative. Members of a movement committed to nonviolence cannot be permitted to resort to violence, no matter what the provocation. A movement with strong participation orientation must avoid acts of arbitrary exclusion of friendly categories of recruits lest it be accused of snobbishness and insincerity. Thus the evangelist who preaches a message of reform through universal conversion must attempt to reconcile socially incompatible population elements if he is to be "all things to all men." Even a movement with strong power orientations must still give the appearance of attempting to gain power only through tactics which are consonant with the values it promises to promote when it gains control.

The values may also give rise to positive prescriptions for action by a movement. As a movement develops an image of aggressive, uncompromising pursuit of the values it espouses, the pressure increases for it to display this aggressive stance in relation to every issue. When, in 1959, a number of relatively unknown Negro youths chose to challenge segregation of lunch counters through "sit-ins," the NAACP was forced to support this phase of the Negro protest movement even though it had chosen neither the issue nor the tactics (Killian, 1962, p. 158). By the same token, the values of the segregation countermovement require that the leaders keep up a pretense of unyielding resistance even as they are in the act of accommodating to "tokenism."

In summation, as a movement endures, grows, and becomes more cohesive, it develops a culture, a set of norms which are binding on both followers and leaders. These norms prescribe behavior which sets the members apart from nonmembers in the society and strengthens their identification with the movement. They provide the adherents with guidelines as to how they should act with reference to a wide variety of objects. Most important, they exert a constant pressure to give the movement continuity and direction, a direction consistent with the values.

THE STRUCTURE OF SOCIAL MOVEMENTS

As important as the values which a social movement embodies are, it must still be remembered that the movement consists of people in interaction. As the members of the collectivity interact in the promotion of the values, a structure emerges. Roles are defined and differential evaluations are made of individuals and groups who are recognized as occupying different positions in the developing structure. Such evaluations are made not only by participants in the movement, but by outside observers. Indeed, it is as a structure develops, with leaders and their followers being identified as peculiarly and intensively concerned with the promotion of certain values, that the members of a society recognize that a social movement has arisen. It is for this reason that so many social movements are identified by the names of prominent leaders— the Townsend Movement, Garveyism— while the names of so many others immediately call to mind specific individuals who are regarded as personifications of the movements they led. The values of a movement are never entirely new nor exclusive to the movement. They have existed before in the society, perhaps for a long time, and may be shared by many members of the society. But as a structure develops, hitherto unrelated, unguided "believers" learn to look for guidance to certain individuals now defined as their leaders. Occupants of the leadership roles begin to count on various degrees of support for their proposals from various subleaders and types of followers. By the same token, these leaders begin to couch their declarations of principles and their appeals for action in terms of the anticipated responses of a following. "The leaders furnish an analysis of the situation. They formulate or specify an ideology containing their particular brand of explanation for problems and solutions which, explicitly or implicitly, states the values adhered to and the goals sought. They give short-cut expression to grievances . . ." (Sherif & Sherif, 1956, p. 726). It is the appearance of a structured, coordinated collectivity, not the values it promotes, which is novel and which constitutes the hallmark of the social movement.

The Leaders

Social movements are often identified with the name of a single outstanding leader, but it is more accurate to think in terms of a group of leaders, often a hierarchy, which plays a major part in guiding the movement from its very inception. Even the most dynamic, dedicated "messiah" must first gather around him a small group of devoted lieutenants to serve as a nucleus around which the larger, more dispersed body of followers may cluster. Not only do these lieutenants serve as agents to carry on the

work proposed by the leader, more importantly, they validate his leadership and thereby give the movement its initial unity and structure. Often these lieutenants have been leaders in their own right during the very earliest stages of the movement, each with his own following and a somewhat distinctive program. They may have vied with each other for influence and preeminence as spokesmen for the central values of the incipient movement. Out of such a nucleus of aspirants for leadership one may emerge to become the personal symbol of the movement and a figure around whom the others may rally, resolving or submerging their ideological and personal conflicts.

This is not meant to imply that all social movements are characterized by unity and centralization of leadership. Many movements are comprised of diverse segments, each with its own structure, loosely united only by their allegiance to the central, explicit values and by the tendency of outsiders to view them as parts of a single whole. Yet there is a strain toward centralization in any movement, and lack of a unified structure can be a source of weakness. Hence, the analysis of leadership in social movements will be couched in terms of the ideal type of a strong, unified movement with a well-defined leadership group. But no matter how centralized the leadership of a movement is, there is general agreement that different types of leaders are involved. Rex Hopper suggests that the types include the agitator, the prophet, the reformer, the statesman, and the administration-executive. In his "natural history" approach, he sees these types varying in importance in each of the four stages of the movement—the Preliminary, the Popular, the Formal, and the Institutional (Hopper, 1950). Lang and Lang also identify four similar kinds of leaders—the agitator, the prophet, the administrator, and the statesman (1961, p. 521). Heberle differentiates between "the leader" who takes the lead in group action, and "officials" or "functionaries" (1951, p. 132). Instead of suggesting that the types vary in preeminence during a life cycle of a social movement, he sees movements as tending either toward the charismatic type, in which the leader's authority is charismatic, or the rational type, in which the authority is institutional. Under either type of leadership, however, an administrative staff is likely to exist, but the authority of the members of this staff is conditioned by the types of leadership they serve (Heberle, 1951, p. 289).

Here we will consider three broad classes of leaders—the charismatic, the administrative, and the intellectual. The charismatic leader is the most prominently identified with the movement in the eyes of both the members and outside observers. As the concept "charismatic" implies, the preeminence and influence of this type of leader stem from personal qualities which his followers perceive as giving him extraordinary qualifications for leadership. Heberle says that "the typical charismatic leader is regarded as the creator of the movement and of its ideas, and he himself believes or pretends that this is so" (1951, p. 288). The personal qualities, experiences, or achievements which may give the leader the aura of charisma are diverse and difficult to define.

What is of more interest, however, is the style of his leadership activities. He tends to be bold, even impulsive, given to the dramatic gesture and the stirring appeal to emotions. He is both prophet and agitator. He states the movement's values in absolute terms, often through slogans. He exudes confidence and may propose novel, dramatic tactics which promise success for the movement against all odds. At the same time, he is a symbol of courage and of willingness to suffer martyrdom rather than compromise. This type of leader may appear impractical, idealistic, or even fanatical to the outsider. But he quickly assumes heroic proportions in the eyes of people already committed, even in part, to the values of the movement, and to many who are dissatisfied with the status quo but not yet committed to a specific program of change. He simplifies the issues, resolving the am-

bivalence which potential followers may feel.

King describes how this type of leader may serve to rally both confused, dissatisfied individuals and individuals possessing "a rigid set of convictions and ideas previously acquired" (1956, pp. 23-24). For the former, leaders of social movements explain the "real" basis of his trouble and show the way out. For the person who already "knows" the source of his problems, the leader who professes the same convictions confirms their validity and, particularly if means of mass communication are available, makes him aware of other people who, unknown to him, share these convictions.

With his confidence in the effectiveness of the solution which he advances, the charismatic leader allays the doubts of his potential followers as to whether anything can be done. Most important, as he gains their confidence, he wins their loyalty to him as the champion of their cause. The process is circular. As loyalty to the charismatic leader grows, so also does confidence in him and in the movement, for it is characteristic of him that he is beyond ordinary criticism. His inconsistencies, his vagueness, even his minor failures and temporary setbacks are overlooked.

An important variant of the charismatic leader is the martyr. By his "glorious suffering" for the cause he symbolizes full, unreserved commitment and makes lighter by comparison the burden of lesser demands on other followers. Like the slogans of the charismatic leader, the sacrifice of the martyr simplifies the issues and suggests a polarization of population segments into those who are fully committed to the cause and those who are "the enemy." At the same time, doubts as to the righteousness of the movement are resolved by the very demonstration of the wickedness of the opposition. Righteous indignation and compassion for the martyr serve as powerful emotional supports for theoretical convictions as to the rightness of the movement's values.

But the very qualities which make the

charismatic leader effective as a symbol of
the values of the movement—his idealism
and impulsiveness—handicap him in other
respects. A movement, to be successful, must
depend not only on inspiration and courage
but also on organization and strategy. E. A.
Shils says of "America nativism":

The failure of American nativism to organize its potential followers in the United States
has been a consequence of a lack of organization skill in its aspirants to leadership, by the
unstable and fluctuating relationships of the
anti-authoritarian and the authoritarian components in the personalities of their followers
and their consequent inability to sustain loyalty. They have had the necessary orientation
or *Ethos* but they have lacked the minimum
capacities to act in the roles necessary for a
movement or an institution (Shils, 1954, p. 45).

A social movement is a collectivity acting
with some continuity, not a short-lived collectivity like a crowd. Over its life span it
must develop some sort of structure; it must
often reconcile diverse elements and make
strange alliances; and it must act in terms
of expediency as well as of principle. Hence
leadership of another type, administrative
leadership, is needed.

The administrative leader in the social
movement tends toward pragmatism, whereas the charismatic leader tends toward idealism. This does not mean that the former
does not subscribe to the explicit values of
the movement, although it is not necessary
that he do so. But he does not view them in
such absolute terms as does the charismatic
leader, and he more readily tolerates compromises with these values as part of the
strategy for their ultimate attainment. He
is willing and able to concern himself with
the less dramatic and less heroic facets of
the movement, the mechanics of organization, finances, and diplomacy. Analysts of
the Nazi movement have pointed out the
importance in the rise of Hitler to the pinnacle of power of such "sophisticated real-
ists" as Von Papen, Von Ribbentrop, and
Hjalmar Schacht, who stood in sharp contrast to the fanatical "Old Fighters."

The administrative leader acts, on the one
hand, as a conservatizing force in the social
movement. In his concern for practical
strategy, he is likely to resist extravagant,
dramatic gestures which may symbolize the
values but which carry little promise of
strengthening the movement and which may
invite disastrous retaliation. At the same
time, he may be the source of a certain
recklessness and lack of discipline to the
extent that he will accept any means for
advancing the cause, even though it be inconsistent with the values. In a political
revolution, it is this type of leader who is
most likely to betray the ideals of the revolution in the effort to consolidate the power
following the initial victory.

A third type found in the leadership
group is the intellectual. The charismatic
leader simplifies and symbolizes the values;
the administrative leader promotes them;
the intellectual elaborates them and justifies
them. It has been pointed out that an important part of the values of a social movement is the ideology. The ideology may
exist in embryonic form in the folklore of
the movement in the form of beliefs, stereotypes, and aspirations. Burridge (1960), in
a study of cargo cults in Melanesia, showed
that among preliterate peoples, these fugitive
elements come to be elaborated and brought
together in a "myth-dream." The myth-
dream, he said, may be reduced to "a series
of themes, propositions, and problems which
are to be found in myths, in dreams, in the
half-lights of conversation, and in the emotional responses to a variety of actions and
questions asked." While he characterized
such a myth as "a community day-dream,"
he observed that "among literate peoples
portions of the myth-dream may be intellec-
tualized and set down in writing," adding,
"[e]ventually, such intellectualizations as are
made may become the definitive principles
upon which a group may organize themselves into a viable party or movement"
(Burridge, 1960, p. 148).

It is the task of the intellectual to elaborate the myth or ideology of the movement,

providing answers as to why the movement is right and what heights it may achieve. The intellectual is not an activist, as are the charismatic and administrative leaders. He is likely to present the appearance of being reasonable, logical, and well informed—in short, "intellectual," not "fanatical." Presenting this image to the unconverted, even to members of the movement's public, he is more likely to gain a respectful hearing. As King said of the ideology, the contribution of the intellectuals "adds a flavor of respectability and thus appeals to those thoughtful people whom obvious propaganda might not touch" (1956, p. 71). Although many members of the movement may not understand the writings of the intellectual, he still represents a prestige figure to whom they can refer in support of their position. Moreover, the ideology is a fruitful source of slogans, epithets, and stereotyped arguments which become part of the culture of the movement.

To describe the roles of the charismatic leader, the administrative leader, and the intellectual in ideal-typical terms does not mean that they may not be combined in the person of one leader, but this is unusual. Hitler observed this in *Mein Kampf* when he stated, "The combination of theorist, organizer, and leader in one person is the rarest thing to be found on this globe; this combination makes the great man" (1941, p. 849). The three types of leadership roles demand skills and attitudes which are not only different but are sometimes conflicting. An individual must be unusually versatile as well as talented to be able to reconcile these different roles.

The Following

While it may be relatively easy to identify the major leaders in a social movement, it is much more difficult to define the total membership, including the followers. The very nature of the movement as a collectivity rather than an association creates this difficulty, for membership need not be formal. Although the movement may encompass formal associations, many participants may be informally tied to it with varying degrees of commitment and involvement. Moreover, the following may be a shifting collectivity, expanding and contracting with the movement of individual participants in and out.

The simplest test of membership might appear to be acceptance of the movement's values. But those individuals defined as members by this criterion still may differ in the extent and the intensity of this acceptance and in the degrees of their activity in support of the values. A variety of terms have arisen to reflect these differences: the "active" versus the "passive" member, the "hard core" versus the "sympathizer," the "card-carrying member" versus the "fellow traveler," and the "radical" versus the "moderate." Pettee, in *The Process of Revolution,* identifies two types: "converts" and "adherents." The converts he describes as the "active membership—built around the doctrine." The adherents, he suggests, differ in that (1) they are "the passive membership"; (2) they generally are loyal only to parts of the doctrine rather than the whole; and (3) their loyalty and obedience are likely to vary from time to time (1938, pp. 77–83).

In his famous work on mass movements, Eric Hoffer analyzes the convert or fanatic as "the true believer" (1951). The fanatical members of all movements, he argues, share the general characteristics of being "frustrated," "disaffected," and "rejected." An assumption essential to his thesis is that "frustration of itself, without any proselytizing from the outside, can generate most of the peculiar characteristics of the true believer." The potential true believers may be disaffected for many reasons, however, and Hoffer proposes the following categories: (1) poor, (2) misfits, (3) outcasts, (4) minorities, (5) adolescent youth, (6) ambitious (whether facing insurmountable obstacles or unlimited opportunities), (7) those in the grip of some vice or obsession, (8) impotent (in body or mind), (9) inordinately selfish, (10) bored, and (11) sinners (1951, p. 30).

It may well be objected that this typology is so comprehensive that it excludes no one and thus renders the concept "the true believer" meaningless. But even if we accept the premise that fanatical converts are drawn only from categories who experience these states with unusual intensity, rarely if ever is a movement composed only of fanatics. Account must also be taken of those adherents whose psychological need for commitment to a cause is not so compelling.

While there must be some dissatisfaction with the status quo for an individual to seek to change it through a social movement, people still differ in degree of rationality of their commitment. In Parson's terms, the orientation of a movement member to the values may be cognitive or evaluative, not merely cathectic. Ironically, Hoffer's "true believer" is not a "believer" at all, for, in his words, "When people are ripe for a mass movement, they are usually ripe for any effective movement, and not solely for one with a particular doctrine or program" (1951, p. 25). But an important basis for interaction in a social movement would be overlooked were dedication stemming from ardent belief in a program equated with fanaticism arising from personality maladjustment. Both exist, and their coexistence creates a problem for the movement.

As a movement progresses, gaining success and recognition, it picks up adherents who may be neither fanatic or dedicated, but who see the movement as "the wave of the future." For them, joining is more of an act of conformity than of protest. They may join in response to the norms of their reference groups or from fear of negative sanctions from the movement itself. Early successes by a movement, as well as the constant repetition of its propaganda, may make its program appear more practical and plausible than it did in the earlier stages. Hence the movement may come to include

a growing proportion of "adherents" as opposed to "converts." These adherents may range from those who are active, although not with the vigor or consistency of the convert, through the nominal but passive member, to the sympathizer who contributes only his verbal support. As the Langs point out, even those people who are on the periphery of the movement may be crucial to its successes if only as a "cheering section" for the "active core" (1961, p. 520).

A social movement is what Sorokin has described as a "semi-organized group," organized in only a fraction of its potential membership. "When such a multitude has a nucleus of organized leaders it often gains spontaneous support, by virtue of its situation and aspirations, from the unorganized members" (Sorokin, 1947, p. 174).

Finally, those people must be counted as members who may care little or nothing for the movement's values but participate for their own private goals, attempting to "use" the movement even as they serve it. Hoffer characterizes them as "adventurers" who join in the hope that a movement will "give a spin to their wheel of fortune and whirl them to fame and power" (1951, p. 22). In somewhat the same category are members of other movements or associations who join forces with a new movement, seeing in the alliance an opportunity to advance their own cause.

The appeal of a movement to the self-interest of such allies "gives the movement access to the pre-established organization and communication networks of a group with some pre-existing homogeneity." But, by the same token, the movement can suffer drastically when the benefits it can offer to such a "carrier group" disappear (Turner & Killian, 1957, p. 35).

This brief typology of participants in a social movement is not intended to be exhaustive. Its importance lies in its suggestion that the members of a social movement are heterogeneous, not only as to age, sex, social class, and other objective characteristics, but also in their orientation toward the movement and its values. To attempt to account for the dynamics of a social movement in terms of common, pre-existing psychological states of individual members is to obscure the nature of the movement as a collectivity with emergent properties. What happens to the members as a consequence of their interaction within the movement is vastly more important than the reasons why they first came into the movement.

Herbert Blumer has contended that what is necessary not only to the success of a social movement in achieving its goal, but also to its very existence, is the development in the members of a sense of identification with each other within the movement—of *"esprit de corps"* (1951). Hence the essential test of membership is whether the individual comes to perceive himself as a member of the in-group which is the movement. Whatever else may be desired of the member, the minimum requirement is a willingness to make a confession of allegiance. He identifies himself not merely as a sympathetic member of a detached public; he sees himself as a supporter of the movement, if only a passive one.

But passive support is of no value unless there is a nucleus of active supporters whose identification with the movement is stronger, whose participation is more extensive. Hence one of the major tasks of a movement is to maximize the identification of the members of the active nucleus as well as to maintain discipline among them. Hitler worked on the principle that this distinction must be made between the active participants, "the members," and the passive supporters, "the followers." "As followership demands only a passive appreciation of an idea, while membership demands an active presentation and defense, there will be ten followers for every one or two members at most" (Hitler, 1941, p. 849). While warning that having too many members can dilute and weaken a movement by including individuals who, in his view, are fit only to be followers, he also defined the contribution of the "cowardly" followers to the success of the movement. "It is the task of propaganda," he said, "to win followers, and the task of organization to select from the followers the ablest to become disciplined, active members." At the same time, "Propaganda works on the community in the sense of an idea and it makes it ripe for the time of the victory of the idea . . ." (Hitler, 1941, p. 850).

Some types of movements, it is true, envision victory for the cause through personal transformation and the participation of the great majority of the people in the society. Hence they minimize the distinction between "members" and "followers," "converts" and "adherents" and endeavor to win an unlimited number of converts. But movements which have a stronger power orientation characteristically develop and maintain an elite, limited in numbers, strong in identification, and strict in obedience to movement discipline.

Blumer has suggested that there are three principal ways in which *esprit de corps* is developed in a social movement. These are the development of an in-group–out-group relationship, the formation of informal fellowship association, and participation in formal ceremonial behavior (Blumer, 1951, p. 206). Again, the extent and nature of involvement in these activities varies among different classes of participants. In particular, involvement in informal fellowship associations is more feasible for the small elite than for the larger number of adherents, while formal ceremonial behavior can involve much larger numbers, as in mass rallies and parades. Admission to the intimacy of the inner circle, where one may associate on an informal basis with the leaders of the movement, is an important step in transforming the adherent into the convert. The identification which is induced by participation in mass ceremonies is variable and uncertain. For instance, analysis of the enduring effects of the evangelistic services of Billy Sunday revealed that of the many people who made public commitments at these rallies, less than half subsequently showed any increase of religious activity (McLoughlin, 1955, pp. 203–215). This does not mean that such acts of public commitment, with the minimal degree of identification which they signify, are unimportant. It does emphasize again the need for the development of the active, strongly-identified nucleus through other means if the movement is to take positive, aggressive action in support of its program.

Blumer has also pointed out that *esprit de corps*, which he defines as essentially a psychological experience lodged in the individual, is insufficient to sustain the movement in the face of adversity. He comments, "Since the allegiance which it commands is based merely on heightened enthusiasm, it is likely to vanish with the collapse of such enthusiasm" (1951, p. 208). A kind of commitment which is deeper and more enduring than mere allegiance he calls "morale." Morale, he argues, is based on a set of convictions and takes on the character of a religious faith. The convictions on which it is based are of three kinds: (1) conviction of the absolute rectitude of the purpose of the movement, (2) faith in the ultimate attainment of the goal, and (3) belief that the movement is charged with a sacred mission. It is in connection with the development of morale that the charismatic type of leader assumes great importance. He comes to be viewed as endowed with miraculous powers, and his pronouncements acquire an aura of infallibility. Thus, as long as he can retain the faith and loyalty of his followers, he can explain away defeats and set-backs. When the lukewarm adherents drop away from the movement because of its apparent failure, he can inspire the faithful remnant to strive to achieve even greater heights. His own display of courage and confidence can turn disaster into a stimulus for renewed efforts on the part of his followers.

The creation of martyrs plays a particularly important part in the development of morale. The martyr, as stated above, by his sacrifice of self for the movement, makes the lesser sacrifices of other members seem smaller by comparison. To abandon the movement and allow his martyrdom to be futile becomes an act of betrayal. The movement is sanctified by his sacrifice, and the members are lifted out of their concern for themselves into a feeling of even stronger solidarity with a cause which must not fail. Moreover, the reaction against the agents who attacked the martyr or martyrs accentuates the in-group–out-group feelings of the movement members and binds them more inextricably to the movement.

Blumer has suggested that there are three types of morale—the practical, the romantic, and the sacred (1943). Practical morale rests on the conviction that achievement of the movement's values is necessary and essential to the members' mode of life. Romantic morale exists when the goal of the movement is portrayed in utopian style, offering tremendous rewards. Sacred morale rests on the conviction of the supreme righteousness of the movement's values. But whatever the type of the morale, it rests upon a conviction that the movement not only can, but must, succeed. The sharing of this feeling by the members, the reinforcement of it in each other, and the inducement in each individual of the feeling that he is part of something bigger and more important than himself combine to produce the kind of collective solidarity that does not diminish in the face of adversity, but may even increase.

INTERACTION IN SOCIAL MOVEMENTS

It has been argued above that although a social movement is not a group but a collectivity, it develops the properties of a group in a tentative and unstable form. It comes to be characterized by a sense of belonging, setting its members apart as an in-group. It develops values, norms, and a structure. This structure is not a formal one, and it is tentative and changing. Portrayed in sweeping strokes, it consists of a leadership group and a following. The leadership group includes charismatic, administrative, and intellectual types and, depending upon the size of the movement, may encompass an extensive hierarchy of major and minor leaders. The following includes both a nucleus of active members, strongly identified with the movement and obedient to its norms, and a vaguely defined body of passive adherents.

One of the salient differences between a social movement and an association lies in the way in which consensus is reached. As an emergent collectivity, the social movement cannot depend upon tradition, for it is in the process of making traditions, not following them. With its vaguely defined, unstable structure it lacks an orderly process for reaching decisions through a referendum or a parliamentary process. Instead, decisions are made for the most part by the leadership group, and sometimes by a single, powerful, charismatic leader. Only in the leadership group is there sufficient continuity and coherence for decisions to be made.

Yet the leaders of a movement do not direct its course in isolation and with complete freedom. They must be responsive to the reactions of the following, the movement's public, and the opposition.

A movement may be initiated by a handful of determined leaders who know the discontent and restlessness of the people to whom they appeal. But once the movement starts to acquire a definite leader-and-membership structure and gets under way, the leader is no longer free to stop or alter the course of action as his whims dictate (Sherif & Sherif, 1956, p. 738).

Hence, through the interaction of the leaders with one another and with these other elements, a social movement follows a tortuous, difficult-to-predict course, often involving changes in strategy and even in values. As Blumer expresses it, "A consciously directed and organized movement cannot be explained merely in terms of the psychological disposition or motivation of people, or in terms of a diffusion of an ideology. Explanations of this sort . . . overlook the fact that a movement has to be con-structed and has to carve out a career in what is practically always an opposed, resistant, or at least indifferent world" (Blumer, 1957, p. 147).

A social movement emerges out of a background of general dissatisfaction, concern, and unrest. This state is "general" in that it is shared by many members of the society or group in which the movement develops, yet has not been formulated into a specific program. Nor is a specific program likely to develop simply because of the existence of this general unrest. As Walter Lippmann observes, "Programs do not invent themselves synchronously in a multitude of minds. That is not because a multitude of minds is necessarily inferior to that of the leaders, but because thought is the function of an organism, and a mass is not an organism" (1946, p. 184). In the absence of leadership, the most that can be expected to arise from such mass dissatisfaction is sporadic crowd behavior, often simply expressive, through which people give vent to their feelings but do not really attempt to change the social order. A leader, or a number of leaders, is required to give the concerns of the many potential followers a unifying theme.

Many variables need to be examined in the effort to explain why, at particular times, a leader emerges to act as a catalyst for the crystallization of a movement. Certainly the personality characteristics of such leaders must be considered, but no matter how important these may be, the leader does not create the situation for the birth of a social movement; he only takes advantage of it. Of greater importance, therefore, is the identification of the circumstances in which such leaders arise. A particularly dramatic event which symbolizes the unsatisfactory conditions may be crucial in bringing social unrest to a head. On the other hand, the success of some minor or symbolic act of protest, or the knowledge of a successful protest by people in similar straits, may set the stage for the emergence of the leadership of an incipient movement. The precipitating incident need not be so specific, however. There may be a gradual and general worsening of conditions or there may be a gradual disillusionment with a process which had promised improvement. For instance, the failure of the Eisenhower administration, the first Republican administration in 20 years, to reverse completely the so-called socialistic trends of its predecessors may have been the stimulus for the emergence of the "far right" movement in the late 1950's. In a democracy, a social movement may develop when a segment of a public despairs of winning acceptance of its ideas through normal democratic processes and feels that it must launch a crusade which will silence its opposition. Pettee suggests the term "cramp," referring to the subjective sense of repression, as preferable to such concepts as "repression" or "frustration" (1938, p. 33). "Cramp" may be felt by a rising class just as well as by an objectively oppressed class.

Finally, as Blumer indicated in his discussion of types of agitation, a certain type of agitator may help to augment this cramp even before the movement appears as a visible force (1951, pp. 203–205).

When the early leaders of a social movement sound their rallying cry, the goals of the movement are usually ill-defined, and the strategy has not been formulated. There is a period of interaction between the leaders and other elements during which a sense of unity and strength in support of rather general values is developed. In this early stage, the values are likely to be negative, in the sense that they constitute a rejection of the existing order rather than a clear-cut vision of a new state of affairs. Also, it is during this period that Hoffer's characterization of the "true believer" as "the disaffected" and "the rejected" is most likely to fit most of the followers. The heterogeneity of these early members is reflected in the varied, sometimes contradictory, set of values. There is often a struggle between different leaders for ascendancy in a growing movement.

Two factors contribute most heavily to a clearer, more positive statement of the values of the movement. One is the evolution, through the struggle mentioned above, of a hierarchy of leadership. Dissonant viewpoints are suppressed and the charismatic leader begins to define an increasingly specific set of goals. The second factor, which limits even the most promising leader, is the response of the potential followers. As Lippmann describes the process:

So when a new policy is to be launched, there is a preliminary bid for community of feeling. . . . In the first phase, the leader vocalizes the prevalent opinion of the mass. . . . Finding that he is trustworthy, the multitude milling hither and thither may turn in towards him. He will then be expected to set forth a plan of campaign (Lippmann, 1946, p. 185).

No matter how strong his inspiration, how brilliant his vision, and how magnetic his personality, the leader must speak in specific terms as he seeks to recruit followers. In setting forth the objectives of the movement, he needs to portray two types—ultimate and intermediate objectives. The ultimate objectives constitute the grand vision, the utopian dream, the myth for which one may strive over a lifetime if need be. The intermediate objectives lack the grandeur of the utopian dream, but appear susceptible to earlier achievement. They serve to sustain the movement in the short run, allowing the members to enjoy some of the fruits of their struggle while awaiting the ultimate victory.

Concurrent with the clarification of the values there must be a formulation of strategy. The strategy of a social movement may take either of two general directions—societal manipulation or personal transformation. The first depends upon the exercise of power in the society in order to bring about the realization of the movement's values regardless of the extent of popular support for these values. The "exercise of power" can take a variety of forms—the military revolt, the *coup d'état*, the application of economic sanctions, even the invoking of legislative, judicial, or executive authority in support of unpopular "rights" in a democracy.

The movement which tends toward a strategy of personal transformation seeks success through widespread conversion of individuals. In some types of movements, particularly religious movements, all that the strategy requires is that the majority of the people in the society believe in and practice in their personal lives the precepts of the movement. In other movements, conversion of large numbers is expected to lead to concerted action to change the institutions of society. This is most likely to be true of social movements in democratic societies where the mechanisms for reform through popular action exist and the people still have faith in these mechanisms.

Which direction the evolving strategy takes may depend not only upon the nature of the values as initially formulated, but also on the sort of reception the movement gets as it proceeds. Values which incorporate some form of "the aristocratic fallacy," a belief in an elite, as described by MacIver (1950, pp. 130–131), may lead to an initial emphasis on power. So also may a belief that the structure and values of the existing society are overwhelmingly opposed to the values of the movement. In the first case, the masses are viewed as incapable of appreciating the values of the movement or, if they can be deceived into supporting them, of serving as anything more than tools for the movement. In the second case, the forces arrayed against the values are seen as so powerful, so ruthless, and so irreconcilably opposed to the movement's values that only equally powerful tactics have a chance to succeed. Thus, movements which arise in the more depressed or oppressed classes in a society are likely to develop control tendencies early in their careers. In some such cases, the movement may attempt to operate with as much secrecy as possible, limiting its following to a small, devoted band at least until the odds are more favorable. In others, a clear distinction is made between "converts" and "adherents," and rigid discipline is imposed on the relatively small body of converts. In either case, the followers are led to place blind faith in the ability of the leaders to create a better order once they have gained power. Hence the values may be vague, contradictory, or even shifting, and they do not exercise a severe restraining influence upon the tactics of the movement.

More often, however, the initial emphasis in a social movement is on the values themselves rather than on the achievement of power by the movement. The movement starts out as an idealistic, optimistic crusade to which large numbers are expected to rally. It creates an issue in support of which followers may align themselves and around which a public also arises. Thereafter, the interaction between the "charter members" of the movement and these other collectivities strongly influences the course which the movement takes.

One possibility is that the movement will attract followers, some of whom become leaders, whose primary commitment is to values somewhat different from those initially espoused by the movement. Some may even be adventurers who see in the burgeoning movement an opportunity for material gain or psychological satisfaction. Others may see in it the possibility for an alliance through which they may promote other values. In any case, implicit values are introduced which change the character of the movement and render the explicit values less determinative of the strategy.

Rapid growth in the number of followers may be followed by a shift toward either societal manipulation or personal transformation as the strategy. If rapid growth occurs, but determined opposition to the manifest goals is not encountered, the number of adherents rather than the actual changes in the society may come to be the measure of success. The program may continue to be vague and general, and compromises may be accepted and acclaimed as victories.

On the other hand, rapid growth combined with determined opposition, rather than tolerance, may embolden the leaders, encouraging them to resort to the shortcuts of power tactics. Instead of being called on to change their personal habits or to vote in a certain way, the followers may be called on to engage in strikes, boycotts, mass demonstrations, or even riots in order to force recalcitrant power holders to come to terms with the movement.

Whatever the influence of other variables, the influence of the nature of the opposition and of the public reaction to a movement cannot be overemphasized. The opposition includes established groups and counter-movements which actively oppose the movement. The public includes an unorganized, uncommitted collectivity of individuals who may look sympathetically on the movement but may also disagree with it or hold it up to scorn and ridicule.

If the movement is regarded as respectable, as an "honorable opponent" of certain features of the existing social order, not a sinister agent bent on destruction of its sacred values, it has greater freedom to depend on conversion as its strategy. In the freedom of public debate, the values may be clarified and even reduced to a detailed creed or "platform." They may be tempered somewhat at the behest of administrative leaders who are concerned with the practical aspects of "selling" them. Elements in the movement which resort to crude power tactics are restrained or repudiated because they create an image of the movement as unscrupulous and power-oriented. The greatest danger to the movement is that, as a result of this development, it may gain lip service from a large body of adherents but active support from few.

If the movement is defined as safe but "peculiar," the values are likely to become increasingly extreme. As these values are subjected to ridicule but not to serious examination and criticism, the members become more isolated from the main currents of thought in the society, and the values become more esoteric and bizarre. As Festinger et al. (1956) have shown, even the

disconfirmation of the prophecies of a movement, which usually leads to ridicule, can be followed by a greater fervor of belief and increased efforts to gain recruits. At the same time, the beliefs are revised to explain the apparent inaccuracies; these revisions may make the values seem even more ridiculous to the outsider.

If, on the other hand, a movement is publicly defined as dangerous and revolutionary and evokes violent opposition, then there are strong pressures for it to seek power through any means available. Denial of access to legitimate means of reaching a large number of potential converts forces adoption of coercive measures, subterfuge, and deception. Or, as Heberle observes, a movement which begins as an evolutionary reform movement may at times be compelled to abandon democratic tactics and resort to direct action when a ruling minority refuses to abide by the rules of democratic procedure in settling disputes (Heberle, 1951, p. 387). A different type of administrative leader, the conspirator rather than the statesman, may gain preeminence in formulating strategy. Opportunities arise for exploitation of the movement by leaders who suggest successful tactics even though these tactics are inconsistent with the explicit values.

The bitterness of a struggle against a hostile world and a vigorous opposition affects the values themselves and may increase the fanaticism of the charismatic leaders. The defense of the values leads to an oversimplification or "sharpening" of them into a dogma which is subscribed to with religious fervor. The opposing values appear increasingly demonic, the opponents of the movement ever more villainous. The Sherifs say of the effects of British opposition to the early expressions of the American revolutionary movement: "As the intensity of the crises grew, the contending groups became immersed in the self-righteousness of their own cause and deeds and were prone to accept wholesale even the most exaggerated imputations concerning the other's conduct" (Sherif & Sherif, 1956, p. 738).

Within the movement itself, there is growing intolerance of dissent. Arguments, proposals, and tactics which would have seemed radical in the earlier stages of the movement appear unassailable as the constant repetition of the ideology produces a new frame of reference in the followers. This polarization of ideas leads to such a fanatical belief in the righteousness not only of the values but also of the movement itself, that an "ends justify the means" philosophy develops. This belief in the absolute righteousness of the movement's values persists regardless of the success or failure of the movement. A familiar and oft-described feature of successful revolutions is the reign of terror, the period of consolidation of power once ascendancy is gained. During this period the ideals of the revolutionary movement seem to be suspended or even forsaken as the leaders and the more enthusiastic of the followers resort to whatever tactics seem expedient to stamp out all vestiges of the old order and to suppress any challengers for power in the new. Faced with the prospect of failure, such a movement may adopt a *Götterdämmerung* philosophy, turning to terrorism. The implication is that it is better that the society be destroyed than exist without realization of the sacred values of the movement.

Unless they represent the extreme cases of the conspiratorial revolutionary group or the evangelistic movement, which promises victory simply through conversion alone, social movements combine the strategies of societal manipulation, or control, and personal transformation, or participation. They still differ from each other and may vary at successive stages in the nature and the degree of emphasis on control versus participation. The connotations of the terms democratic and authoritarian are suitable for characterizing these tendencies. The movement which emphasizes participation may rely on changing the laws, the ruling groups, or the institutions of the society to attain its goals, but it attempts to do so by engendering widespread acceptance of these values. With such widespread support, the need for the exercise of power in support of the values is minimized and even radical changes in the culture can be effected with a minimum of conflict. Hence, while the movement may have as its goal institutional change, the production of attitudinal change is defined as the appropriate means.

The movement which emphasizes power implies that attitudinal change will come, by force if necessary, after institutional change has been effected. This does not mean that it neglects participation, but it seeks to engender consent or acquiescence, not support. Hitler expressed this principle of power when he wrote:

The most striking success of the revolution of a view of life will always be won whenever the new view of life is, if possible, taught to all people, and, if necessary, is later forced upon them, while the organization of the idea, that means the movement, has to embrace only so many people as absolutely necessary for the occupation of the nerve centers of the State involved (Hitler, 1941, p. 852).

Thus, as Cantril points out, "the terroristic methods so freely used by the Nazis after they attained power were part of their propaganda armament from the very beginning" (1941, p. 263). Whatever the explicit values of a movement may be, one sign of the ascendancy of control tendencies is the use of tactics designed to intimidate critics, whether by violence, boycotts, anonymous telephone calls, or public defamation. The movement which emphasizes personal transformation does not attempt to destroy the public which arises around it but regards it as a source of potential recruits.

A movement which is large and not rigidly controlled by a powerful hierarchy may be heterogeneous not only in membership but in tactics. Submovements or "wings" may arise, so that the social movement *in toto* resembles not a monolithic structure, but a tenuous alliance of smaller associations or collectivities. All may be generally oriented to the same explicit values but may employ different tactics and incorporate divergent implicit values. These submovements not only interact with each other but may even fight among themselves for dominance in the total movement. Such a struggle may be based on the personal aspirations of competing leaders, on differences in implicit values, or on disagreements as to the relationship of values to tactics. A submovement which emphasizes a democratic theme as part of the values is likely to rely heavily on a strategy of personal transformation. The resort to transparent power tactics by another segment of the movement will be perceived as a threat to the public definition of the entire movement and hence may be vigorously attacked. Ironically, the exigencies of the movement's career may, at a later time, lead the "moderate" wing to rely on the same type of tactics (Killian, 1959). Leaders who emphasize participation, persuasion, and respectability always find themselves at a disadvantage in competition with the power-oriented leader. The latter responds to and exploits the impatience of the followers. He offers them the opportunity for action, the promise of quick success, and the satisfaction of immediate, if only symbolic, accomplishments.

THE CONSEQUENCES OF
SOCIAL MOVEMENTS

The significance of social movements, of course, lies not in their careers but in their consequences for the larger society and its culture. Unless a social movement results in significant social change, it becomes merely an interesting sidelight to history, a curiosity.

It may be said that some movements do "fail" in that they leave little or no imprint upon the society. This may easily be the fate of a utopian movement with an almost purely participation-oriented strategy. It may be a chiliastic movement, such as the Millerite movement, or a movement which promises a more mundane utopia through social reform, such as technocracy. Such a movement may have a brief, active career marked by several flurries of proselyting. But as it

successively becomes defined as "peculiar," and then loses not only its public but most of its following, it comes to resemble a cult, if it survives at all. Its survival depends on a shift from emphasis on its initial missionary zeal to the personal satisfaction which a small group of people derive from mere participation.

Yet even a movement which "sputters out" in this fashion or is suppressed may have a profound effect on society. Mannheim argued that the utopian movements of the fifteenth and sixteenth centuries affected all the currents of the time and laid the foundation for an increasingly greater participation of the oppressed classes in the social process. On the one hand he said:

It is at this point [the emergence of the utopian mentality] that politics in the modern sense of the term begins, if we here understand by politics a more or less conscious participation of all strata of society in the achievement of some mundane purpose, as contrasted with a fatalistic acceptance of events as they are, or of control from "above" (Mannheim, 1946, p. 191).

At the same time Mannheim indicated:

This by no means implies that this most extreme form of the utopia mentality has been the only determining factor in history since that time. None the less its presence in the social realm has exerted an almost continual influence even upon antithetical mentalities. . . . The Chiliastic optimism of the revolutionaries ultimately gave birth to the formation of the conservative attitude of resignation and to the realistic attitude in politics (Mannheim, 1946, pp. 191-192).

A specific movement which itself "fails" and disappears may, within the framework of an enduring general movement, leave behind the seeds of another specific movement. For example, by the 1940's the Garvey Movement of the 1920's had come to be dismissed as a passing manifestation and an extreme expression of the "race consciousness and nationalistic sentiment which came into prominence during and following World

War I" among Negro Americans (Frazier, 1957, p. 530). Yet by 1960, a new movement embodying the same central explicit values had risen to prominence, the Black Muslims or "Nation of Islam." Essien-Udom saw not only an ideological kinship but a historical connection between the two, saying ". . . Muhammed also acknowledges Marcus Garvey as a forerunner of his movement" (1962, p. 63).

We can speak of the "success" of a social movement with several connotations, but rarely with the implication that its values have actually been realized. The values always have something of the character of a myth. But, as Mannheim so aptly expressed it, "The impossible gives birth to the possible, and the absolute interferes with the world and conditions actual events" (1946, p. 192).

One way in which a movement may contribute to social change is through forcing the established structure of the society to come to terms with it and its values, incorporating some features of its program into the existing institutions. This is best exemplified by the fate of "third party" movements in American history which, although failing to win political power, have at times forced the major parties to adopt modified versions of their programs.

Acceptance of the values of the movement as enduring parts of the culture may be accompanied by recognition of the personnel of the movement as legitimate custodians of these values. In such a case, the movement is institutionalized in the sense of being transformed into an association: "Institutionalization occurs when the movement is viewed as having some continuing function to perform in the larger society, as it is accepted as a desirable or unavoidable adjunct to the existing institutional arrangements. . . . Through institutionalization the environing society imposes additional stability upon the movement" (Turner & Killian, 1957, p. 481).

In this process, the movement becomes an association as the leadership is stabilized and endowed with greater responsibility, the membership is more formally and precisely defined, and the program made more realistic. The process of bureaucratization takes place. Since the values are modified in this process, new movements may subsequently arise in the society or even within the association to promote the same values ostensibly achieved already. Thus a religious denomination which has evolved from an earlier social movement, through the denominalization of a sect, may find itself under attack by a new movement within its membership seeking to promote the "primitive values." Similarly, as the labor movement in the United States became institutionalized with the A.F.L. as the chief custodian of its interests, the movement for industrial organization arose to undertake the unfinished business of the movement.

A movement which is sufficiently ambitious in terms of its goals and is strongly power-oriented may be successful in seizing control of the entire group or society—a revolution is effected. The movement is rapidly transformed into a particular type of association, a government. One of the most obvious conclusions to be drawn from the study of successful revolutionary movements is that the transformation of the values and norms continues and is even accelerated during this transition. Faced with the challenge of consolidating its gains, of defending a new regime rather than attacking an old one, the new government adopts many of the values and norms which it promised to replace. The explicit values are likely to survive primarily in the form of a set of abstract principles which are more often proclaimed than practiced. At the same time, the implicit values of the movement become more readily apparent at this time as the need for concealing them diminishes and the opportunity for achieving them increases. Hence they may have as great an influence on the actual nature of the new social order as do the explicit values of the movement.

Finally, frustration of the efforts of a strong, persistent movement to promote its values in the larger society may lead to the development of a secessionistic goal. A movement may, of course, incorporate secession into its program from the outset, as have many nationalistic or irredential movements. But a separatist theme may also develop in a movement which initially sets out to effect reforms within the society. Blocked in its efforts, it breaks away and starts a new career as an independent group or society. Paradoxically, one aftermath of the struggle may be that the group from which it seceded later adopts many of the values which were at issue, "locking the barn door after the horse is stolen." The Protestant Reformation, ending as a separatist movement, was followed by the Catholic Reformation which corrected many of the abuses which had led to the schism.

SOCIAL MOVEMENTS AND SOCIAL CHANGE

The intrinsic characteristics of culture which foster continuous change should not be discounted any more than the strivings of social movements should be dismissed as epiphenomenal. Culture changes continuously through the unwitting, uncoordinated actions of individuals who not only adjust to it, but change it in minute details. But changes in social structure and the normative order which, in retrospect, are seen as major changes, usually come about through a process of interaction within the society, with people struggling purposively and collectively to promote or resist change. In the course of cultural evolution, new ideas, visions of a new and different order, emerge in the minds of individuals. Yet, a social movement is not simply a creature of ideas. Its consequences are not a structure reflecting a blueprint drawn by the leaders and adhered to faithfully by the followers. Rather, throughout the course of the movement there is a continuous formulation, revision, and reformulation of the values and norms of the movement. There is constant interaction between various types of leaders, between the leadership and the following, within the following, between the movement and its public, and between it and its

opposition. As new values and norms become standardized as part of the culture of the movement, the members develop a commitment to them. The public develops an awareness of these values as issues. The opposition elaborates antithetical values and, in the synthesis, new ideas emerge.

At the same time, population segments are re-evaluated during the career of the movement. As participants in a movement, whole classes may find their role in society redefined, whether positively or negatively. New relationships are established as different population segments combine their efforts in the movement and evolve new and common identities. New roles are defined as the movement becomes a force which must be reckoned with by the larger society. Rarely does a social movement leave unchanged the structure of the group in which it arises.

Analysis of changes in culture, divorced from the activities of the men who create and use this culture, presses on us the conclusion that these changes are the inevitable result of inexorable laws of cultural change. The study of social movements reminds us of the irrepressible conviction of sentient men that they can collectively, if not individually, change their culture by their own endeavors. The fact that the changes which result are never those which are anticipated does not refute the evidence that it is interaction of men with each other, not their unwitting response to culture, which produces social change.

REFERENCES

Almond, G. *The appeals of communism.* Princeton, N.J.: Princeton Univer. Press, 1954.

Bell, D. (Ed.) *The new American right.* New York: Criterion, 1955.

Blumer, H. Morale in wartime. In W. F. Ogburn (Ed.), *American society in wartime.* Chicago: Univer. of Chicago Press, 1943. Pp. 207–231.

Blumer, H. Collective behavior. In A. M. Lee (Ed.), *Principles of sociology.* New York: Barnes & Noble, 1951. Pp. 167–222.

Blumer, H. Collective behavior. In J. B. Gittler (Ed.), *Review of sociology*. New York: Wiley, 1957. Pp. 127–158.

Brinton, C. *The anatomy of revolution*. New York: Norton, 1938.

Burridge, K. O. L. *Mambu: A Melanesian millennium*. New York: Humanities, 1960.

Cantril, H. *The psychology of social movements*. New York: Wiley, 1941.

Durkheim, E. *The elementary forms of religious life*. J. W. Swain (Trans.). New York: Macmillan, 1915.

Edwards, L. P. *The natural history of revolution*. Chicago: Univer. of Chicago Press, 1927.

Essien-Udom, E. U. *Black nationalism*. Chicago: Univer. of Chicago Press, 1962.

Faris, R. E. L. *Social psychology*. New York: Ronald Press, 1952.

Festinger, L., Riecken, H., & Schachter, S. *When prophecy fails*. Minneapolis: Univer. of Minnesota Press, 1956.

Frazier, E. *The Negro in the United States*. New York: Macmillan, 1957.

Gilbert, G. M. *The psychology of dictatorship*. New York: Ronald Press, 1950.

Greer, T. H. *American social reform movements: Their pattern since 1865*. Englewood Cliffs, N.J.: Prentice-Hall, Inc., 1946.

Grove, G. *Inside the John Birch society*. Greenwich, Conn.: Fawcett, 1961.

Heberle, R. *Social movements*. New York: Appleton-Century-Crofts, Inc., 1951.

Hitler, A. *Mein Kampf*. New York: Reynal & Hitchcock, 1941.

Hoffer, E. *The true believer*. New York: Mentor Books, 1951.

Hopper, R. D. The revolutionary process: A frame of reference for the study of revolutionary movements. *Soc. Forces*, 1950, 28, 270–279.

Killian, L. M. The purge of an agitator. *Soc. Probs*, 1959, 7, 152–156.

Killian, L. M. Leadership in the desegregation crisis: An institutional analysis. In M. Sherif (Ed.), *Intergroup relations and leadership*. New York: Wiley, 1962. Pp. 142–166.

King, C. W. *Social movements in the United States*. New York: Random House, Inc., 1956.

Kroeber, A. H. The superorganic. *Amer. Anthrogist*, 1917, 19, 163–213.

Lang, K., & Lang, Gladys. *Collective dynamics*. New York: Thomas Y. Crowell, 1961.

LeBon, G. *The crowd: A study of the popular mind*. London: Unwin, 1897.

Lincoln, C. E. *The Black Muslims in America*. Boston: Beacon, 1961.

Lippmann, W. *Public opinion*. New York: Pelican, 1946.

Lipset, M. L. *Agrarian socialism*. Berkeley: Univer. of California Press, 1950.

MacIver, R. M. *Social causation*. Boston: Ginn, 1942.

MacIver, R. M. *The ramparts we guard*. New York: Macmillan, 1950.

McLoughlin, W. G., Jr. *Billy Sunday was his real name*. Chicago: Univer. of Chicago Press, 1955.

Mannheim, K. *Ideology and utopia*. L. Wirth & E. A. Shils (Trans.). New York: Harcourt, 1946.

Ogburn, W. F. *Social change*. New York: Viking, 1922.

Park, R. E., & Burgess, E. W. *Introduction to the science of sociology*. (2nd ed.) Chicago: Univer. of Chicago Press, 1924.

Parsons, T. *The structure of social action*. New York: McGraw, 1937.

Pettee, G. S. *The process of revolution*. New York: Harper, 1938.

Reddich, L. D. *Crusader without violence*. New York: Harper, 1959.

Sherif, M., & Sherif, Carolyn. *An outline of social psychology*. New York: Harper, 1956.

Shils, E. A. Authoritarianism: Right & left. In R. Christie & M. Jahoda (Eds.), *Studies in the scope and method of 'the authoritarian personality.'* Glencoe, Ill.: Free Press, 1954. Pp. 24–49.

Sorel, G. *Reflections on violence*. T. E. Hulme & J. Roth (Trans.). Glencoe, Ill.: Free Press, 1950.

Sorokin, P. A. *Society, culture & personality*. New York: Harper, 1947.

Tarde, G. *The laws of imitation*. E. C. Parsons (Trans.). New York: Holt, 1903.

Trotter, W. *Instincts of the herd in peace and war*. London: Macmillan, 1926.

Turner, R. H., & Killian, L. M. *Collective behavior*. Englewood Cliffs, N.J.: Prentice-Hall, Inc., 1957.

Wolf, H. C. *On freedom's altar: The martyr complex in the abolition movement*. Madison: Univer. of Wisconsin Press, 1952.

CHAPTER 13　Norms, Values, and Sanctions

JUDITH BLAKE and KINGSLEY DAVIS

The meaning of "norm" in everyday usage is ambiguous. It often refers to a statistical regularity, as when we say that one's temperature is "normal" or that a man who has been sick has resumed his "normal" activities. On the other hand, it may indicate an accepted standard or model, as in the phrase "set the norm" or "conform to ethical norms." In sociology the same ambiguity is found, although ostensibly, at least, when a formal definition is given, the second meaning is stipulated. Thus the term is presumably employed, as is done in the present chapter, to designate any standard or rule that states what human beings should or should not think, say, or do under given circumstances.

In this strict sociological usage, the most important element is the *should*, for it clearly implies two important propositions: first, that actual behavior *may* differ from the norm; second, that it *will* differ from the norm unless some effort or force is exerted to bring about conformity. The sociological use of the term generally assumes, without always saying so, that norms are shared to some extent. A purely private, or indi-

vidual, view of what people should do or think is a norm, but unless it is shared by others, it has no social significance.

Anything in society which pertains to norms, including statements concerning their nature, rationalizations justifying them, and reactions to their violation, may be designated by the adjective "normative." Employed in this way, the word is seen to refer to an entire aspect of human society. It also refers to an element in individual behavior, as when we say that someone's actions are influenced by "normative" factors.

Construed in this way, the normative aspect of human society and human behavior is broad in coverage but conceptually distinct. It embraces, for example, the notion of "values," which are the goals or principles in terms of which specific norms are claimed to be desirable. For example, the rule that political officials should be elected is justified, or "explained," by saying that popular election is necessary if "democracy" is to be realized. The rule itself is the norm, but the value, democracy, is part of the normative reasoning. Disembodied values— i.e., values without any norms through

which they can be collectively achieved—
are, like purely private norms, sociologically
irrelevant.

The "normative" further embraces the
inner and outer compulsions (generally
called "sanctions") which tend to enforce
conformity. A banker who embezzles funds
must contend, even when he is successful,
with the efforts of others to catch him and
with his own ideas of the potential dangers
if he is caught. His behavior is therefore
"normatively oriented," not so much because of the sheer rule prohibiting em-
bezzlement as because of the sanctions
against violation of the rule.

WHY THE NORMATIVE PLAYS A CRUCIAL ROLE IN SOCIOLOGY

The reason that sociology has given a
great deal of attention to norms is clear.
Human society, as distinct from insect and
animal societies, is in part organized and
made possible by rules of behavior. By contrast, the intricate interactions of an ant
colony or a beehive, like those of a prairie
dog village, are governed mainly by instinctive reactions to natural and social stimuli.
Such interactions may involve learning to
some degree, but this learning, if it occurs,
is mainly a matter of habituation to (hence
remembrance of) particular environmental
stimuli, to which a stereotyped response becomes affixed. In human groups, on the
other hand, instinctive responses are channeled or even repressed by the enforcement
of behavioral rules that are transmitted by
symbolic communication. These rules differ
in character from one group to another,
and thus help to account for differences in
behavior among human societies. For insects
and animals, however, behavior tends to be
nearly identical from one group to another
within the same species, varying only with
external conditions. Obviously, then, if the
structure of human societies is to be understood, if human behavior is to be adequately
explained, the normative aspect must be
dealt with. A biologist, habituated to viewing behavior as a function of a physical
organism reacting to physical stimuli presented by the environment and other organisms, is apt to bring the same outlook to his
analysis of human conduct. If he does so
in the concrete sense of offering a complete
explanation of some social phenomenon, he
is "biologizing" human society. This fallacy
is no less bizarre than the opposite—namely,
an explanation of some aspect of insect or
animal society in terms of presumed norms
governing behavior.

Not only does the role of norms account
for the difference between human sociology
and biology, but it helps account for the
division of labor between sociology and economics. In general, economics assumes a
normative framework in terms of which the
process of production and exchange takes
place. Sociology, on the other hand, in trying to understand the way the entire society
works (not merely its economic system)
has to deal with the norms themselves.
For instance, a popular economics textbook
points out that in the United States the
distribution of income is influenced by the
fact that women and Negroes are kept out
of certain good jobs and are sometimes
paid less for the same job (Samuelson,
1961). If this fact were due to differences in
capacity between the races or the sexes, it
would come under the economic system of
explanation, because the "human resources"
available to enter into production would be
different. But, finding that "there are numerous jobs which either sex or race can do
equally well," the author attributes the discrimination to "prejudice" (pp. 126-127).
As an economist he is not obliged to explain why this prejudice occurs (the word
is not even in the index), although, as he
says, it affects something he is concerned
with, the distribution of income. He takes
the prejudice for granted, whereas the sociologist must explain its existence by accounting for the norms governing differential
hiring and pay. One way in which he does
this is by examining nonoccupational roles.
The norms governing women's participa-

tion in the labor force certainly have something to do with their particular role within the family.

If it be granted that social norms affect behavior, then the totality of norms, or at least the totality of major norms, within a society can be expected to have some consistency, or order. Otherwise, the social system would not approximate a "system," and the society would tend to fall to pieces and be absorbed by another one which was orderly. It follows that an important aspect of the study of social organization is the study of the "normative order."

VALUES AND NORMS

So far we have tried to distinguish the normative factor in behavior and to assess the reasons for its importance to sociology. Let us now admit that this "factor" is quite diverse in character and try to distinguish some of its elements or parts.

Probably the greatest single distinction within the normative realm is that between something variously called values, sentiments, themes, or ethical principles, on the one hand, and the specific rules of conduct, thought, and speech on the other. The line between the two is always fuzzy (Is the doctrine of freedom of the press, for example, a norm or a value?), but the attempt to separate them has been made again and again in sociological and philosophical thought. Apparently the reasons for this effort have varied, but two seem to stand out. Investigators have felt it necessary to probe beyond external behavior to the motives that impel behavior. In addition, since subjective phenomena seem bewildering in the number and variety of their expressions, observers have felt that it must be possible to reduce them to a few recurrent, underlying principles, or perhaps "real motives." In any case, the task of finding these subjective forces or entities has been complicated by the fact that human beings not only act but give reasons for their actions. An observer must therefore decide whether

to accept the reason given or to judge that, through ignorance or deception, it is not the real one. Not only do persons give private reasons, but there are official versions of what are the proper reasons for given kinds of conduct.

An early attempt to separate the essential values from the kaleidoscope of external manifestations was made by Vilfredo Pareto. In his general treatise on sociology (1935) he not only distinguished basic subjective factors but sought to use them in the analysis of social structure and social change. Underlying the countless rules and rites, verbal arguments and rationalizations (or "derivations"), he thought he could distill a few recurrent motives, or themes, which he called "residues," and which he thought responded to corresponding sentiments. The social system was, for him, a "social equilibrium" consisting of these sentiments acting as forces, and "social dynamics" was, in large part, a matter of the "circulation of the elite" in which differential strength of the various sentiments among the social classes was the main explanatory principle (pp. 509–519, 885–1120, 1740–1929).

Pareto was a student of advanced societies and therefore had to deal with the limitless sophistries of thought which came from the mouths and pens of priests, philosophers, statesmen, scholars, journalists, scientists, and other literate specialists and pleaders. He had to deal with conflicts and differences of opinion. For this reason he had particularly to wrestle with the problem of how to cope with the verbal arguments and explanations in getting to the actual motives hidden behind them. For William Graham Sumner, on the other hand, the problem was somewhat different. This great student of the norms drew his materials mostly from reports about primitive tribes. He therefore was required to pay little or no attention to written expressions of human thought as objects of study and did not need to consider seriously the supernatural and magical explanations that primitive people gave for their norms. In contrast to Pareto, therefore, he barely recognized anything like general principles or abstract values, and when he did, he saw them as consequences rather than determinants of the norms themselves, which he called folkways and mores.

All are forced to conform, and the folkways dominate social life. They seem true and right, and arise into mores as the norm of welfare. Thence are produced faiths, ideas, doctrines, religions, and philosophies, according to the stage of civilization and the fashion of reflection and generalization (Sumner, 1906, p. 38).

Both Pareto and Sumner refused to take the explanations people give for their norms or their conduct at face value. But Pareto sought to find behind the explanations a few basic motives or sentiments, while Sumner emphasized the norms themselves, simply regarding the verbal expressions of people as part of the normative system.

It seems that in general the literature dealing with norms has followed both men in certain respects, regardless of whether or not it was actually influenced directly by them. There has been a tendency to draw materials and inspiration, as Sumner did, from studies of preliterate villagers. Hence conflict, deviation, and the complexity of verbal statement and argument have been minimized. This line of treatment has of course been prominent among the social anthropologists, but it has been present too in the work of Talcott Parsons and some of his students. Due to the emphasis on *different* societies in anthropological thought, the search for values tended to take a new turn. It became a search for the particular underlying values, cultural themes, or ethos of each particular society. This development raised in turn the question of whether the values of one society had any relation to the values of another. In other words, is cultural relativity absolute, or is there a single set of values of which those of different societies are simply variant expressions? Pareto had made it clear that he regarded the sentiments as having "social utility"; Sumner thought that the folkways and mores were

adaptive, keeping the society in touch with reality and contributing to its survival. Presumably, in anthropological and sociological thought since Emile Durkheim and Bronislaw Malinowski, the values must have a *function* in society; but the question is obscure because, for many social scientists at least, what is taken as a value may be disfunctional, and what is functional may not be valued.

The search for a particular set of values which then explain or enlighten us concerning the social system is Paretian in character, all the more so if the values are considered to be a single set which may simply vary in strength from one group to another. This approach has apparently been followed by Parsons. Although his "value-orientations" are seemingly applicable to entire societies and appear relatively free from the complications of deviancy, group conflict, and deception (being to this extent Sumnerian), he does have, like Pareto, a single set which are then used as explanatory devices. It is perhaps an exaggeration to say so, but it does seem as if the ease of explanation provided by the value-attitudes is facilitated by the fact that, as "pattern-variables," their classification is given in pairs. If, in a given society or group, a phenomenon is not explicable in terms of "universalism," "achievement orientation," and "specificity," it surely will be explicable in terms of "particularism," "ascription," and "diffuseness."

An interesting addition to the literature on values arises from the attempt to investigate them empirically in complex rather than primitive societies (Carter, 1959; F. Kluckhohn & Strodtbeck, 1961; Rosenberg, 1951). When this is done by going to people and asking them about their attitudes and preferences, the old problem of what to do with verbal expressions, which may conceal as well as divulge, is raised again. For the most part it appears that these studies tend to construe values simply as expressions of opinion, feeling, or preference, accepting verbal statements of subjects more or less at face value. In doing so, the task of finding a few "underlying motives" which can be used for all mankind is given up, although the search may still be for a few values held to characterize the particular group or society. The reduction of "values" to verbally stated attitudes is illustrated by one study of "courtship values" which asked students what trait or quality they preferred in "dates" (Smith & Monane, 1953). The results showed, for example, that male students stress "desirable physical appearance" in their "dates."[1]

Empirical, quantitative research may prove the best antidote to the idea that there is a set of subjective entities or forces which, once posited, can be used to explain human behavior. This idea seems to be a trap, because the values, sentiments, or motives are always inferred, and hence have no better status for causal analysis than the observable phenomena from which they are inferred. Furthermore, since the implication is that there are only a few such entities—or even one, if the single "ethos" of a whole society is being depicted—the inferred items are so remote from the observed behavior that it is doubtful whether any two analysts working independently would reach the same results. Our skepticism is increased by what we take to be the lack of sociological usefulness in previous classifications of the motives of man. The most notable of these was the list of four wishes of W. I. Thomas (1927).

There is, of course, a distinction to be made between the standards involved in judgments, on the one hand, and the application of those standards in specific judgments, on the other. Thus, in regard to social behavior, it is one thing to say that parents prefer sons to daughters, and quite another to say that parents feel they should treat their daughters in a certain way under given circumstances. Presumably, a preference for sons is a value, but it says nothing

concrete concerning parental conduct and it has no sanctions. A norm, on the other hand, says that a given line of conduct must, or should, be followed. Thus a preference for sons in the United States does not mean that female infanticide is permitted or that boys are given more clothes. What, then, is the utility of the distinction between values and norms?

Whatever the utility may be, it surely is not that of designating cause and effect. Presumably a norm "exemplifies" a value, but this does not mean that the norm is *caused* by the value it exemplifies, or that the value is the motive and the norm simply the expression of this motive with respect to behavior. Such a mode of explanation is extremely tempting, not only because it is the way people think anyway—that is, the individual always has a reason for doing whatever he does—but also because it gives an unfailing mode of explaining norms and behavior. The flaw, however, lies in the question of logic and evidence. Can we accept as true people's verbal description of their values? These may be nothing more than a rationalization of the norms—as when, for instance, someone justifies the exclusion of married women from jobs on the ground that a woman's place is in the home. Can we adopt some indirect technique of getting verbal statements of values, thus deceiving the subject into revealing what he would not reveal if he knew our purpose? Such a technique still makes the assumption that the values are consciously held and are rationally connected with norms and conduct—an old-fashioned view controverted by voluminous evidence. Can we then take people's statements and *reinterpret* them to get at "underlying" values? Yes, provided we wish to make the questionable assumption that verbal statements inevitably reflect real values, and provided we admit that the process of symbolic reinterpretation in itself has no empirical controls and consequently may differ radically from one observer to another.

In practice, we tend to find the best

---

[1] The Index of the first 25 volumes of the *American Sociological Review* contains 45 articles under the heading of "values."

evidence of values in the norms themselves. If people manifest a dislike of cheating in examinations, of dishonest advertising in business, and of unnecessary roughness in sports, we infer something like a value of "fair competition." Such a process of reasoning may help us to insert the motivational linkages and thus integrate a body of diverse information. At bottom, however, it is a classification. Its usefulness does not extend to causal explanation, because the inferred value comes only from the specific norms themselves and hence cannot be used as an explanation of those norms. In other words, unless we have evidence independent of the norms themselves, we cannot logically derive norms from values. Independent evidence, if obtainable, may show that the so-called values are nonexistent, that they are consequences of the norms, or that they derive from a third factor which is also responsible for the norms.

It is the norms, not the values, that have the pressure of reality upon them. It is the norms that are enforced by sanctions, that are subject to the necessity of action and the agony of decision. It is therefore the norms that represent the cutting edge of social control. In this regard Sumner seems to have been more correct than some of his successors, for he emphasized the importance of the folkways and mores in understanding society rather than the vague, slippery ideologies, rationalizations, and generalizations people use in justifying their observance or nonobservance of norms.

A more satisfactory use of "values" in sociological analysis is to abandon them as causal agents and to recognize them frankly as sheer constructs by which we attempt to fill in the subjective linkages in the analysis of social causation. For example, the movement of peasants to cities during the process of industrialization is not "explained" by saying that they prefer the bright lights of the city to the drab monotony of the village. Only when the evolving economic and social situation in both the village and the city are taken into account can we begin to explain

this recurrent major social phenomenon. It helps us understand the process, however, if we can get some inkling of how the peasant's feelings and thoughts take shape in view of these conditions; and so we try to put together a model of his mental reactions and test it out against various kinds of empirical evidence, including his verbal statements.

THE FALLACY OF NORMATIVE DETERMINISM

We raise the question of causation with respect to values and norms because we believe that conceptual distinctions unrelated to empirical investigation are empty exercises. For the same reason, we wish to push on to the wider question of normative causation in general, apart from the distinction between values and norms. In doing so, we come to one of the most confused and at the same time basic issues in sociology and social anthropology. No one can doubt that norms exercise *some* influence on behavior, but the question of *how much* influence they exercise is highly debatable. At times, sociologists and social anthropologists have seemed to adopt an extreme view by treating the normative system as the sole object of analysis or as the sole determinant of social phenomena. This has usually been done by implicit assumption and careless overstatement rather than by deliberate doctrine, and it has been camouflaged at times by a seemingly broader position of cultural determinism. At any rate, it is a position that affords a good point of departure in analyzing the interrelation between norms and other factors in behavior.

At its most naive level, normative determinism takes the fact that norms *are meant* to control behavior as the basis for assuming that they *do* control it. The only task of social science is then to discover the particular norms in any given society. By this reasoning, nearly all social scientists in Latin America are trained in the law rather than in statistics and social research. The law, being the crystallization of the normative order, is assumed to be what one needs to know. At a more sophisticated level, the assumption is made that the independent variable consists in "cultural configurations," "basic value-orientations," or "the institutional system," which determines everything else in a society. This has a doctrinal side— e.g., in statements about the nature of man —as well as a methodological side. An anthropologist states with approval that national character studies assume that

each member of a society is systematically representative of the cultural pattern of that society, so that the treatment accorded infant or immigrant, pupils or employees or rulers, is indicative of the culturally regular character-forming methods of that society (Mead, 1953, p. 643).

C. Kluckhohn expresses a common dictum when he says that the constants in human life from one society to another "arise out of the biological nature of the species" and its fixed environment, whereas the variations arise from culture. Each culture, he says, has a "grammar." "The function of linguistic grammar is to control the freedom of words so that there is no needless congestion of the communication traffic. The grammar of culture, in general, likewise makes for orderliness" (1959, pp. 273–274).

According to this view, the avenue to understanding actual societies is to understand their cultures. The term culture has a bewildering and altogether too convenient variety of definitions. Sometimes it is used so broadly as to cover all material products of man, all social behavior, all ideas and goals. Used in this way, it includes society itself, and therefore the cultural determinism of social phenomena becomes a tautology. Frequently, however, the term culture is used primarily in the sense of a normative system. In this case we get what may be called a "blueprint theory" of society, namely, that there is a set of "culture-patterns" which are, so to speak, laid down in ad-

vance and followed by the members of the society. The determinism implicit in this view is indicated by such phrases as "handed down," "shaped by his culture," "ultimate values," "culture-bound," "way of life," and others.

The way of life that is *handed down* as the social heritage of every people does more than *supply* a set of skills for making a living and a *set of blueprints* for human relations. Each different way of life *makes its own assumptions* about the ends and purposes of human existence . . . (Italics supplied) (C. Kluckhohn, 1959, p. 247).

Similarly, Parsons and his followers have placed heavy emphasis on value-orientations as the key to sociological analysis. In the hands of some, this emphasis gets translated into dogma; for example, "Values determine the choices men make, and the ends they live by" (Stein & Cloward, 1958, p. 263).

Under the assumption of the supremacy of the norms and "dominant" value-orientations, the chief research method of the social disciplines becomes that of questioning informants. The investigator asks a member of the society what people are *supposed* to do, and hence the normative pattern will emerge. The informant necessarily knows the "culture," because he lives it and is determined by it.

Any member of a group, provided that his position within that group is specified, is a perfect sample of the group-wide pattern or which he is acting as an informant (Mead, 1953, p. 648).

Furthermore, with this reliance on norms and values as determinants of social phenomena, peculiar importance is naturally given to "socialization," normally interpreted to mean the acquisition, or "internalization," of the norms. According to Parsons:

There is reason to believe that, among the learned elements of personality in certain respects the stablest and most enduring are the major value-orientation patterns and there is much evidence that these are "laid down" in childhood and are not on a large scale subject to drastic alteration during adult life. There is good reason to treat these patterns of value-orientation, as analyzed in terms of pattern variable combinations, as the core of what is sometimes called "basic personality structure" . . . (1951, p. 208).

Most of the sociologists and anthropologists who stress culture, culture patterns, norms, value-attitudes, and such concepts would deny that they are determinists. They would say they are abstracting—treating behavior *as if* it were determined by the normative system. In practice, however, the emphasis on values and norms leads, as critics have been quick to point out, to deficiencies in the scientific understanding of real societies. The gravest deficiency arises, ironically, in the failure to deal adequately with norms themselves. As long as the cultural configurations, basic value-attitudes, prevailing mores, or what not are taken as the starting point and principal determinant, they have the status of unanalyzed assumptions. The very questions that would enable us to understand the norms tend not to be asked, and certain facts about society become difficult, if not impossible, to comprehend. For instance, an assumption of normative primacy renders it difficult to explain deviancy and crime, although the real world plainly exhibits a great deal of normative violation. If one is to understand deviancy, one must ask why societies frequently reward violation more heavily than conformity to the norms; why legitimate authority is one of the most widespread bases of illegitimate power; why ego and alter so frequently disagree on norms applicable to their relationship; why any action, no matter how atrocious, can be justified in terms of the verbal formulas in which norms and values are couched. Furthermore, the origin and appearance of new norms and their constant change—again facts of social existence—become incomprehensible under an assumption of normative sovereignty.

Worse yet, the deceptive ease of explanation in terms of norms or value-attitudes encourages an inattentiveness to methodological problems. By virtue of their subjective, emotional, and ethical character, norms, and especially values, are among the world's most difficult objects to identify with certainty. They are bones of contention and matters of disagreement. The assumption that for each society there is one norm or one value regarding a given aspect of behavior is in most instances untrue. Insofar as an investigator uses norms or values as explanatory principles for concrete behavior, he therefore tends to be explaining the known by the unknown, the specific by the unspecific. His identification of the normative principles may be so vague as to be universally useful, i.e., anything and everything becomes explicable. Thus, if Americans spend a great deal of money on "alcoholic beverages, theater and movie tickets, tobacco, cosmetics, and jewelry," the explanation is simple: They have a good-time ideology (C. Kluckhohn, 1949, p. 238). If, on the other hand, they devote themselves to hard work, it is because they have "an Evil-but-perfectible definition of *human nature*," in contrast to the fiesta-loving Mexicans (F. Kluckhohn & Strodtbeck, 1961, pp. 29–30). If "superficial intimacy is easy in America," it is "because of the cult of the average man" (C. Kluckhohn, 1949, p. 237). If, on the other hand, there is a lack of social intimacy between Negro and white, it is because of a "racism" value (Williams, 1960, pp. 466–468). The cynical critic might advise that, for convenience in causal interpretation, the values of a "culture" should always be described in pairs of opposites.

Explicit definitions, when given, demonstrate the nebulous character of "value." Here, for example, is the definition of "value-orientation" in a 437-page book on value-orientations:

Value orientations are complex but definitely patterned (rank-ordered) principles, resulting from the transactional interplay of three analytically distinguishable elements of the evaluative process—the cognitive, the affective, and the directive elements—which give order and direction to the ever-flowing stream of human acts and thoughts as these relate to the solution of "common human" problems (F. Kluckhohn & Strodtbeck, 1961, p. 4).[2]

We learn in the paragraphs explaining this definition that "value-orientations" differ from "basic values"! Also we are told that, instead of "amalgamating" the cognitive and affective elements, as do Hallowell, Whorf, and C. Kluckhohn, this definition "separates" them.

Presumably if one's interpretation is in terms of norms rather than values, one is on firmer ground. Yet the difficulty of proving the existence of the norm is great. As a consequence, there is a tendency to take regularities in behavior as the evidence of the norm. When this is done, to explain the behavior in terms of the norm is a redundancy. Seen in this light, statements such as the following are also redundant: "Knowledge of a culture makes it possible to predict a good many of the actions of any person who shares that culture" (C. Kluckhohn, 1949, p. 38). Why not simply say, "Knowledge of behavior in a society makes it possible to predict behavior in that society"? Of course, if norms are taken to be regularities of behavior, they have no analytical significance at all; they are then merely another name for behavior itself, and cannot contribute to an understanding of behavior.

TYPES OF NORMS

The blueprint theory of society does not fit the facts of social existence. Societies as we know them are highly active and dynamic, filled with conflict, striving, deceit, cunning. Behavior in a given situation tends to be closely related to that situation, to be strongly affected by individual interests, to be unpredictable from a knowledge of the

norms alone. Far from being fully determinant, the norms themselves tend to be a product of the constant interaction involving the interplay of interests, changing conditions, power, dominance, force, fraud, ignorance, and knowledge.

Furthermore, it is surprising how simplified the view of culture and of the normative system tends to be in the hands of many who emphasize their role. To show this, let us attempt a brief listing of the variegated aspects of the norms—aspects seldom all dealt with in the social science literature. We shall not deal with all these aspects either, but, in a treatment of the central question of the relation of norms to motives and behavior, we shall give consideration to one particular element—sanctions.

Some major aspects of norms, and ways in which they vary, are as follows:[3]

1. Content
   a. Societal requirement involved. (Norms ordinarily concern some functional requirement such as reproduction, division of labor, allocation of power. Norms clustered around a given functional requirement are often collectively designated as "institutions.")
   b. Whether the norm relates to a goal or to the means.
   c. How the norm is stated—whether put negatively (should not) or positively (should).
2. Types of Sanctions
   a. Maximum or minimum.
   b. Reward or punishment.
      Repressive or restitutive (in the case of punishment).
   c. Specific or diffuse (may be both).
3. Acceptance of the Norm
   a. Extent of acceptance (accepted as obligatory by virtually everyone or ac-

---

[2] In order to emphasize this succinct definition, the authors italicized it.

[3] This list is brought together from recent sociological literature. Some of the main references are Barton (1955), Linton (1936, Ch. 10), Morris (1956), and Williams (1960), Ch. 3.

cepted as obligatory by only certain groups, such as certain ethnic groups).

  b. Degree of acceptance (felt to be mildly obligatory or felt to be mandatory).

4. Mode of Transmission
  a. Primary socialization.
  b. Secondary socialization.

5. Source of Imputed Authority for the Norm
  a. Tradition.
  b. Law.
  c. A nonempirical or supernatural agency ("natural law," God, some member of a pantheon, ghosts, etc.).
  d. Public opinion.

6. Extent of Application of the Norm
  a. To which statuses does the norm apply? (The reader will note that the extent of application of a norm is different from the extent of its acceptance. A norm which applies only to the occupant of a particular status may nonetheless be accepted by everyone as the proper conduct for that status. Example: Everyone thinks a judge should be fair and impartial.)
  b. To what groups does the norm apply?

7. Mode of Origination
  a. Formal enactment.
  b. Informal, traditional accretion.

8. Formal Properties of the Statement of the Norm
  a. Explicit (a body of law, regulations, codes).
  b. Implicit ("gentlemen's agreements," rarely verbalized but understood ways of behaving and thinking).
  c. Vague, diffuse statement.
  d. Specific, detailed statement.
  e. Rigid (requires exact conformity).
  f. Flexible (latitude in the precision with which the normative demand must be met).

Clearly, these ways in which social norms can vary are interrelated. For example, a norm that is stated positively is, in effect, stated in terms of some *reward* for compli-

ance, whereas a negative normative statement implies punishment. Moreover, maximum sanctions—either rewards or punishments—typically imply that the norm involved is widely accepted (in the society, or group, or organization under consideration) and that strong sentiments support it. A norm of this type will also very likely be one that individuals have learned early in life at a time (the period of "primary socialization") when they must accept social rules in a more unreflective fashion than later. Further, norms carrying maximum sanctions are usually felt by people to be inherently right (natural) rather than simply legitimated by reference to law, tradition, or public opinion. Also, for maximum sanctions actually to be applied, the norm must definitely specify the relevant status. For instance, even a so-called universal in the United States such as the norm against killing another human being has so many legitimated exceptions that these must be clearly specified before sanctions can be brought to bear.

SANCTIONS

People not only conform to rules themselves but, by means of their sanctioning of others' behavior, motivate others to conform also. In most cases sanctions are informal—an approving or contemptuous glance, an encouraging or derisive laugh, a sympathetic or embarrassed silence. Such seemingly trivial but pervasive sanctions enable human beings to control informally a share of their own actions and reactions and the actions and reactions of others. However, it is also true that behavior is frequently controlled by formal sanctions as well—by a medal or a jail, an honorary dinner or an electric chair, a parade or a court-martial. In the ordinary course of our lives, we tend to be more aware of the explicitly sanctioning nature of formal than of informal rewards and punishments. Indeed, the relatively unruffled fashion in which informal sanctions operate constitutes one of their most important societal functions—they control behavior in a relatively painless manner before more formal measures are necessary.

Yet every viable society must develop supports to help individuals *resist* this type of informal pressure as well as to help them conform to it, for such pressures never are so finely geared to changing situations that it is socially advantageous for individuals always to respond with gusto to sanctions of this type. To be sure, the system is partially self-corrective in that what is negatively sanctioned by one individual may be highly rewarded by another. But this capacity for self-correction is limited, because individuals deal with one another in terms of social roles which, by definition, tend to be highly standardized sets of expectations. Hence, one of the problems that every society faces constantly is that of assuring itself role flexibility in the face of changing conditions.

Since so many sanctions are informal and applied continuously in the course of daily living, we are all in effect constantly "administering" the normative order. There must accordingly be mechanisms to keep individuals *cognitively* primed or "briefed" about the norms (what the norms are, to whom they apply, in what situations, etc.) and, in addition, to keep people *emotionally* primed respecting the *legitimacy* of norms. By and large, people must feel that behavior they are punishing or rewarding (either in themselves or others) is at least roughly the same as other people would punish or reward in similar situations. Yet, like any other set of rules, social norms are only approximations of how people should act. In specific situations, individuals must take many things into account, and, in particular, they are faced with the difficulty that adherence to the letter of a norm (or to the formal content of a number of different norms) may place them or others in situations having no apparent legitimacy at all. The result is that much of our lives is spent in seeking out the legitimacy of various courses of action and thereby inevitably redefining the legitimacy of specific norms—

an example of how the effort at conformity with social rules provides a dynamic source of social change.

A significant share of orderly conduct is, however, a result of assessing the consequences for nonconformity rather than a result of the "internalization" of the norms as just discussed. In fact, individuals' internalization of norms is doubtless differentiated and segmental in most societies. Individuals are emotionally committed to some norms and others they merely conform to, if they conform at all, out of calculation and rational assessment. Such a criss-crossing of commitment and objectivity toward norms gives societies another source of change and of stability. There are some people who regard certain rules as "outdated" and "unjust" and make efforts to change the rules, and there are people who, feeling that the same rules are adequate and legitimate, resist this change. Because of this criss-crossing, many societies can undergo remarkable social transformations, all the while retaining an adequate degree of social control.

Much of modern sociological thinking (such as that of Talcott Parsons and his students) has strongly emphasized the internalization of role expectations as the prime mover in social control, to the extent that the importance of calculation with respect to sanctions tends to be overlooked except as a last resort. Yet, we must never forget that social rules require doing what would ordinarily not be done if the rules did not exist. Since these rules therefore, by definition, have such a high nuisance value for human beings, it seems inconceivable that most people do not calculate extensively. Let us therefore turn to deviancy in relation to motives and sanctions, for this is the central question in the empirical theory of the relation of norms to behavior.

MOTIVES VERSUS BEHAVIOR IN THE SOCIOLOGY OF DEVIANCY

In the past 15 years of modern sociology, the etiology of the contra-normative has emerged as a complex and pressing theoretical issue. As Wrong (1961) has recently pointed out, critics from both the Marxian and the psychological camps charge that contemporary sociologists have either explained away or overlooked the reasons for group conflict and for the individual's personal conflict with normative demands. In their efforts to explain why human existence is not a war of all against all, sociologists like Parsons, Levy, Merton, Sutton, and Johnson are said to view "la vie en rose"—equating too glibly and readily people's desires and their obligations, and assuming a socialized, if not a natural, identity of interests among groups. Hence, Dahrendorf (1958), Lockwood (1956), Mills (1959), Wrong (1961), and others allege that the problem of social order (or disorder) has been ignored.

Stimulated by these complaints, we shall present here some answers that emerge from and are compatible with much of modern sociological thought. In doing so we shall confine ourselves to individual violation of norms that (for purposes of argument) we shall assume to be generally recognized as legitimate in ego's social circles. Thus, we shall ignore the subject of organized group conflict and differences in norms and interests resulting from subcultures, castes, religions, clans, or ethnic groups.

For our purposes, deviancy assumes the existence of a society or group in which there is some agreement on some norms from which the deviant's behavior can be said to diverge—otherwise the allegation of deviancy would not apply.[4] However, the discussion does not hinge on the validity of

assuming some overall consensus concerning a whole system of norms (although this is an important problem to consider in itself), but simply on the acknowledgment that some norms, although not necessarily the same ones, are strongly felt and widely enforced in all societies, and that sociological theory wants to explain why deviation from such norms occurs. Only if societies could be shown to be completely normless would the problem of deviancy in this sense be without scientific interest.

Whether an item of behavior is "deviant" can be decided only by referring to the norms in question, and these may vary greatly in content. Yet, much of the argument of critics of contemporary sociology like Dahrendorf and Wrong rests on the implicit assumption that norms (however else they may vary) are made up of demands for the peaceful, the static, and the homogeneous. The critics then are free to ask from whence come change, conflict, violence, war, the pursuit of power, and the like, if everyone is conforming to the norms (Dahrendorf, 1958, pp. 120–121; Lockwood, 1956, p. 136; Mills, 1959, pp. 32–33; Wrong, 1961, pp. 190–192). These writers overlook the intimate connection between norms and the incitement to, as well as the legitimation of, cruelty, horror, and violence. Equally, their confusion of the normative with the changeless and "utopian" overlooks the fact that many norms positively specify or prescribe constant change, growth, and development—that the dynamic is not equivalent to the disorganized or the random. In many highly organized spheres of existence (such as science), "conformity" consists in exhibiting dynamic and diverse behaviors, and "deviancy" in trying to inhibit change or in engaging in routinized activity. The fact that innovators and originators are also frequently conformists, and conformists *by virtue* of their innovating and originating behavior, is increasingly being evidenced by research on occupations where change and innovation are themselves obligations.

For example, Robert K. Merton says,

---

[4] There might still, in a theoretically normless society, be the problem of a struggle for power—Hobbes's problem—and the prospect of the group destroying itself in this struggle. It is important to remember that, logically, "deviancy" cannot exist in Hobbes's theory, because norms do not enter into the theory explicitly. Nonetheless, implicitly Hobbes is concerned with the desirability and necessity of political order and stability; therefore, in a sense, he is concerned with conflict as "deviant" (see Parsons 1949).

On every side, the scientist is reminded that it is his role to advance knowledge and his happiest fulfillment of that role, to advance knowledge greatly. This is only to say, of course, that in the institution of science, originality is at a premium. For it is through originality, in greater or smaller increments, that knowledge advances. When the institution of science works efficiently . . . recognition and esteem accrue to those who have best fulfilled their roles, to those who have made genuinely original contributions to the common stock of knowledge (1957b, p. 639).

The obligation to be "up to date" has been found to be of importance in the adoption of innovations by Marsh and Coleman (1956) (agricultural innovations), Menzel (1960), and Coleman, Katz, and Menzel (1957) (drug adoptions by physicians).

Any theory of sources of deviancy is faced with the fact that conscious motives (or desires) and behavior may or may not be congruent. Moreover, each of the two may be either conforming or deviant. The cross-tabulation of these possibilities gives us a fourfold table (Table 1) showing the interrelations between conformity and deviancy on the one hand, and motives and behavior on the other.

TABLE 1

DESIRE OR MOTIVE	BEHAVIOR	
	Conforming	Violating
Conforming	(1) ++	(2) +−
Violating	(3) −+	(4) −−

The table schematizes the motivational antecedents of deviant and conforming behavior, or the behavioral consequences of deviant and conforming desires. Cell (1) can be thought of as asking about the motivational background of conforming behavior. The answer (from this cell alone) is contained in conforming motives or desires. Cell (4) raises a question about the sources of deviant behavior and answers the question in

terms of deviant intent, or motive, or desire. But in cells (2) and (3) complications are seen to arise in the relationship between deviant motives and deviant behavior. Cell (2) indicates that, logically, deviant behavior is not necessarily preceded by deviant desires or intentions. Rather, such behavior can presumably occur in spite of a desire to conform. We are thus led to ask about an *additional* class of causes for deviant behavior over and above deviant desire and in spite of conforming motives—causes that do not appear explicitly in the table. Finally, cell (3) tells us that contra-normative motives or desires do not always result in deviant behavior—they may precede conforming behavior. Here again, some element not found explicitly in the simple interrelations of the fourfold table must be adduced to account for conforming behavior in the face of deviant desire.

In our discussion of these problems, let us for the moment ignore cell (1) and ask the following questions about deviant desires and deviant behavior.

a. What are the sources of unintentionally deviant behavior (cell 2)?

b. What are the sources of deviant motivation (cells 3 and 4)?

c. What prevents deviant motivation from emerging into deviant behavior (cell 3)?

We may now search for the answers to these questions in sociology today, and the reader can doubtless supplement what is said here from his own experience with the literature. Our purpose is not to offer a complete account, but to suggest the usefulness of the questions in systematizing many rather scattered concepts in sociology relevant to the problem of deviancy. When this is done even in a limited way, we see more clearly both the strengths and the weaknesses of our thinking about the contra-normative.

The Sources of Unintentionally Deviant Behavior

As we have seen, cell (2) tells us that, logically, deviant behavior may occur without an intention or desire to act contra-normatively. A moment's thought reveals that this relationship is not simply a logical possibility. Rather, it is a predicament with which everyone is acquainted. In this instance, the "cause" of deviancy may be said to lie not in desire but in *conditions*—factors over which the individual has no control. We are familiar with recognizing all sorts of *physical* and *environmental conditions* as causes of an individual's inability to meet normative demands. In some cases, to be sure, such hazards are taken into account by the norms, and the demands are temporarily abrogated. Thus, an acute illness may be an acceptable excuse for waiving ordinary demands until the person is well. But the situation is far less clear for many enduring conditional elements. For example, differences in physical stamina and energy are rarely taken into account by the norms except along the gross axes of age and sex. Consequently, a certain amount of deviant behavior seems to be clearly traceable to a mismatching of individual physique and temperament with social statuses. In such cases, relatively "low-powered" individuals may just barely fulfill normative demands no matter how hard they try; and "high-powered" persons in relatively undemanding life situations may exhibit pronounced aggression, restlessness, and dissatisfaction, thereby impairing the performance of even routine duties.

The role of physical and environmental factors in contra-normative behavior is so widely recognized that we will not elaborate on it further. Less systematically taken into account is the fact that the *normative system* itself is to some extent a condition. Although normative injunctions are seldom completely uncompromising or unconditional, they cannot by definition be manipulated at will, or refashioned freely to be more in line with either physical and environmental conditions *or* with each other. The fact that some norms are uncontrollable elements of the situation in which the individual must try to conform to other norms means that one

important source of unintentionally deviant behavior may be located, paradoxically, in normative demands themselves. Viewed in this way, we can readily find examples of sociology's conceptual recognition of the role of normative conditions in unintentionally deviant behavior.

Perhaps the best-known example is that of *status or role conflict*—the conflict experienced by the individual who occupies contemporaneous, but different and competing, roles or statuses that are normatively defined as "going together" but whose priorities are not clearly established. The individual is encouraged and even enjoined to occupy plural statuses without anyone considering it legitimate that the demands cannot all be fulfilled with the resources at his command. Caught in this situation, the person may exhibit some form of deviant behavior no matter how hard he tries to live up to his obligations, or how capable he is of performing in each of the statuses severally. Clearly, it is possible to think of statuses as completely separable from one another only on a conceptual level, because it is in the nature of social organization that statuses are articulated and imply one another in a complex chain of interrelationship. However, bearing this fact in mind, we can yet point to relatively "separate" status demands (attached to separate social locations and functional activities) that are in conflict. For example, although, for a man, having a family normally implies having an occupation, yet there can be severe conflict between the demands of his statuses as a husband and father and those of his status as a producer. There can also be conflict between his "father" status and his "husband" status, as there can be, for women, between the statuses of mother and mate.

A second well-known normative source of unintentionally deviant behavior (closely akin to the first but distinguishable from it analytically) is that of norms relating to the *same* status which make conflicting or competing demands on the resources of the status occupant. Such conflict or competition tends to arise for at least two reasons. On the one hand, it is impossible completely to formalize and integrate role obligations, because even within formal organizations these obligations also build up informally as *ad hoc* responses to conditions. It is hardly surprising, therefore, that those who have the authority to have significant expectations of a position will perceive others' role obligations in a poorly articulated manner. On the other hand, conflicting or competing demands will also arise because those with whom ego interacts by virtue of a particular status ("the role-set" in Merton's terms) are *motivated* to interpret his obligations in terms of their own statuses and interests— not only in terms of his or of each others' (Merton, 1957). This means that even where there is no profound cultural disagreement on norms, consensus about them tends to be modified because they are somewhat diversely understood and interpreted by persons in different social slots. Each person has some interests specially conditioned by his own status or statuses; he is motivated to emphasize the rights of his status, thereby inevitably emphasizing the reciprocal obligations of others. Thus, although management and workers view the status of "foreman" in terms similar enough to be recognizable when described by each side, they will diverge significantly in the facets of the foreman status they emphasize and in the priorities they assign to his obligations toward "his men" and "the boss." Similarly, the schoolteacher's rights and duties are not seen identically by parents, children, principal, or school superintendent.

A final normatively engendered source of unintended deviancy is that of *temporal* incompatibilities between statuses. A status at one life stage may be defined so differently from a later status that the individual is poorly prepared—socially, psychologically, and technically—to make the change. Such transitions appear to be stressful no matter whether they involve a major change in group affiliation or merely a change of status within the same group or organization.

Since retirement removes a man from his accustomed working group, it constitutes a fracturing of his life situation; but for him to remain in the organization with a lowered status more in keeping with his powers would also be difficult. The articulation of succeeding statuses can be so poor that some periods in the life cycle—e.g., adolescence in American society—are defined more in terms of conflict and adjustment than in terms of age or functional activity. For example, in a study of youthful Americans Hollingshead has written,

> Sociologically, adolescence is the period in the life of a person when the society in which he functions ceases to regard him (male or female) as a child and does not accord him full adult status, roles, and functions (Hollingshead, 1949, p. 6).

Temporal incompatibilities between statuses may arise because the meshing of succeeding statuses involves inherent difficulties (for example, childhood and the technical requirements of adulthood in industrial societies) or because the conception of what a status entails tends to lag behind what it actually entails. In the latter case, a status that the person expected to enter and was prepared to enter (old age, for instance) has changed radically in obligations and rights by the time it is actually reached. Such perceptual lags are tenacious because individuals define life-cycle statuses in the framework of their own parental and family models. The notion of "being a grandparent" often stems from one's actual experience with grandparents, an experience that may be outdated as a model for one's own grandparenthood.[5]

The Sources of Deviant Motivation

As our fourfold table illustrates, one may explain deviant behavior in terms of deviant

---

[5] The most explicit recognition of the "temporal incompatibilities" problem may be found in Benedict (1938). The problem has also received recognition by Parsons (1949a; 1949b).

motive or intent (cell 4). The question then arises, whence the motivation? A classic attempt at an answer has been by reference to man's biologically determined "human nature," and indeed such answers are still being proferred in the sociological literature. For example, Wrong's essay on the "oversocialized conception of man" falls back on drives, instincts, and needs ("forces in man that are resistant to socialization") to explain why people want to circumvent the norms (1961, pp. 191–193). The logical untenability of this position was ably demonstrated by Parsons almost 30 years ago, and it is widely recognized that the position is empirically unsound because it assumes some universal biological drive system distinctly separate from socialization and social context—a basic and intransigent human nature (1949, chs. 2–3). The invalidity of this assumption has received increasing empirical confirmation. For example, research on the effects of incomplete socialization does not show drive fortitude but rather human vulnerability to apathy, withdrawal, and extinction. In cases of physically adequate but otherwise impersonal mothering, what we see is not rampant drive expression but an amazing failure of drive mechanisms to operate at all in a manner appropriate to the physical organism. In this regard, René Spitz's (1945; 1946; 1949) well-known research on "hospitalism" in infants is still relevant despite numerous methodological caveats. Even more relevant to our point is William Goldfarb's (1943a; 1943b; 1943c; 1944a; 1944b; 1945a; 1945b) work on the later development of children cared for impersonally. This series of investigations found apathy and lack of emotional response to be a remarkably fixed result of impersonal early care—a result that is seemingly rarely reversible by improved mothering later in childhood. The earlier such deprivation begins and the longer it endures, the greater is the maladjustment likely to be. A recent evaluation by Yarrow (1961) points out that the apathy syndrome emerges as part of the "core of consistency" in the re-search on persons reared partially or wholly in institutional settings. Finally, although not directly relevant to humans, Harlow's studies of the later effects of emotional deprivation on infant rhesus monkeys is worth mentioning in connection with the notion that the sexual drive is in apposition to and separable from socialization. Inadequate socialization in infant monkeys resulted in a striking and apparently irreversible attenuation of sexuality among them. In addition, they exhibited a breakdown of the defensive response, attacking themselves in the face of possible danger rather than the danger source itself (Harlow & Harlow, 1962).

A related criticism concerns Wrong's failure to recognize that the repression of biological drives is merely an incidental part of normative control. The main role of norms relates to social organization and personality. Even when rules deal with bodily appetites or needs, they organize and facilitate satisfactions as well as repress them. In fact, satisfaction of a particular appetite would often not take place if competing drives were not hierarchically ordered and appropriate social contexts provided. For example, a recent study by the authors in Jamaica showed that relatively unregulated mating typically resulted in long periods of celibacy for women and thereby greatly reduced fertility over what it would have been had the women been stably married. Such tenuousness of sexual activity may also account in part for the badly impaired reproductivity of slaves in the New World (Blake, Stycos & Davis, 1961). Although few would deny that violations sometimes satisfy bodily desires, the same system of drives and needs is the raw material for all motivation and behavior, not simply the basis of the contranormative. Consequently, just as norms are not necessarily drive-repressive, neither are drives inherently deviant.

The same type of problem arises in regard to alcohol or drugs as causes of "deviant" motivation. Although use of such agents usually induces changes in motives and desires, such alterations are by no means wholly in a contra-normative direction. Drugs may have either an exciting or a tranquilizing effect, and either effect may conduce to socially preferred or socially condemned behavior, depending on the situation.[6] In fact, at least some of the medical prescription of tranquilizing drugs today would appear to be induced by the patient's need to adjust to a physically undemanding way of life while still in possession of the glandular make-up suited to man's recent history of hand-to-hand battles for survival, and to many, but not all, current situations. The successful football player who becomes an immobilized executive may require some "tranquilizing" if he is to remain civil and socially acceptable. In short, although drives, instincts, and man's neurological and glandular nature *may* constitute sources of deviant motives or intent, such elements are not specific to deviancy.

If we forego the assumption that deviant motivation is to be found primarily in drives and glands, we can focus on sociological sources of deviant motives. The normative conditions already discussed (role conflicts and others) typically represent a source of deviant desire as well as a possible source of unintentional deviant behavior. Individuals will inevitably react to conflicting intra- and interstatus demands with resentment and schemes for evading at least some responsibility. In other words, they will not unreflectingly continue forever trying to do the normatively impossible.

A further sociological source of deviant motivation lies in the means-end nature of human action. Here we must distinguish the possibility of deviant motivation respect-

---

[6] For an informative survey of recent research on sub-cortical centers of the brain from the time of Olds's early research to the present, the reader may find McGeer (1952) helpful. This article is particularly interesting because it discusses some of the neurological issues raised by the developments in neuropharmacology during the past few years.

ing goals (a desire for "illegitimate" goals) from deviant motivation with respect to means (the employment of illegitimate means, typically force and fraud) to reach goals that may or may not be legitimate. Let us begin with the latter possibility, and it is convenient to start from Merton's now classic explanation of deviancy in terms of differential access to means. "It is," Merton says, "when a system of cultural values extols, virtually above all else, certain *common* success-goals *for the population at large* while the social structure rigorously restricts or completely closes access to approved means of reaching these goals *for a considerable part of the same population,* that deviant behavior ensues on a large scale" (1957, p. 146. Italics original).

Applying his theory to differential crime rates by socioeconomic status in the United States, Merton claims that spectacular financial success is a "common goal" prescribed for all in America, and yet the social structure rigorously restricts access to legitimate means to this goal.

Of those located in the lower reaches of the social structure, the culture makes incompatible demands. On the one hand, they are asked to orient their conduct toward the prospect of large wealth—"Every man a king," said Marden and Carnegie and Long—and on the other, they are largely denied effective opportunities to do so institutionally. The consequence of this structural inconsistency is a high rate of deviant behavior (Merton, 1957, p. 146).

This deviant response is what he calls a "normal" or "expectable" one in the circumstances (pp. 131–132, 145). Finally, he accounts in two ways for individuals' willingness to utilize illegitimate means. On the one hand, "the culture," through its "emphasis" on the goal, tends to underplay (apparently by default) the satisfactions to be gained in the sheer pursuit of goals. The means are thus not experienced as ends in themselves (pp. 135–136). On the other hand, the users of deviant means are "imperfectly socialized" individuals—those who have never fully internalized the legitimate means in the first place. Persons more socialized will make different "adaptations," like that of "ritualism" (p. 149).

There are a number of difficulties with Merton's theory that preclude its acceptance and yet are relevant to our discussion. An initial drawback is a logical one brought out by our fourfold scheme. Although Merton's treatment apparently sets out to explain different types and rates of deviant *behavior* ("innovation" being the use of illegitimate means, for example), it actually addresses itself to a source of deviant *motivation,* and moves from this alone to an account of types of "adaptation" (behavior) and their probable distribution by social class. But, as we have seen, deviant behavior can occur without deviant motive or intent; and conscious deviant motives may well be present without any evidence in deviant behavior. The theory is thus logically incomplete in overlooking an important general cause of deviant behavior and in neglecting crucial intervening variables between motives and behavior. Merton himself has in later work recognized that his theory is principally one of motivation, or pressures on motives, and that there may be "countervailing social mechanisms" which prevent actual deviant behavior. However, he has not reformulated the theory in terms that would account for this recognition (1957a, p. 183).

Furthermore, Merton's thesis of "pressure" to use deviant means is tied to empirical assumptions about social location and cultural pathology in relation to means and goals that either have been disproved or seem incapable of being substantiated. First, we have no evidence that actual rates of deviant (or criminal) behavior, or rates of deviant motivation respecting means, are inversely related to social class (cf. Cloward, 1959). Second, the theory presupposes an absolute goal "held out" to all and internalized by all, irrespective of where the individuals are socially located. In regard to Merton's example of the success goal in the United States, Hyman (1953) has used public opinion data on the economic, educational, and occupational goals of different social classes to show with remarkable consistency a directly linear relationship between such goals and the respondents' present socioeconomic status. In fact, there is some evidence that lower-income groups entertain goals that are more modest than is realistically necessary. A part of their underprivileged condition is psychological rather than objective, and this lack of aspiration and knowledge is, through the family, self-reinforcing (Hyman, 1953, pp. 436–438; Knupfer, 1953; Lewin, Dembo, Festinger, & Sears, 1944).

Data such as Hyman's should not be too surprising, because as a rule the generation of mass commitment to common, undifferentiated goals is known to be very difficult. In a rejoinder to Hyman, Merton argued that even a modest *proportion* of the lower class having relatively high aspirations constitutes a large number of individuals, and that it is this absolute number that swells the ranks of lower-class deviants, thereby constituting the issue for his hypothesis. But this rejoinder is confusing, because his original article claimed to be discussing a higher rate of deviancy by class. That is, *using each class as a base,* the theory was explaining differential proportions deviant. It is unlikely that the original article was attempting to account for there being, *among all deviants,* more lower-class than upper-class ones. This finding would be more readily explained by the fact that there are more poor people than rich people, and hence more people at risk of any event occurring among the poor (1957a, pp. 170–176). Third, Merton's supposition of great "rigidity" in the American system of stratification has been shown to be unwarranted. Relative to other countries—even other industrial countries—the United States stands up well in overall levels of affluence, generational mobility, and the spread of available channels of mobility such as education (Anderson, 1956; Barber, 1957, Ch. 16; Chinoy, 1955; Kahl, 1957, Ch. 9; Lenski, 1958; Lipset &

Bendix, 1959; Petersen, 1953; Rogoff, 1953; Sjoberg, 1951; Warner & Abegglen, 1955). The type of "blocking" Merton postulates is more reminiscent of an experimental goal-box than a human society. It probably did not occur, as he assumes, even in caste societies like India, or in preindustrial Japan, much less in the United States at any point in its history.

Finally, the theory not only makes assumptions about social location in relation to means and ends, but it presupposes as well a "cultural overemphasis" on a particular goal or goals. Since Merton is not simply postulating an "emphasis" but an "*over*emphasis," the question naturally arises of how one would establish empirically that an "emphasis" is an "*over*emphasis." When does a hierarchy of differentially valued and rewarded goals become, to use Merton's term, "pathogenic"? Although it may be possible to devise ways of answering this question, the difficulties are well illustrated by Merton's own struggle to delineate an *over*emphasis on a goal. Almost inevitably, the evidence begs the question, for the evidence is in terms of a desire to use any means to attain the goal (the sentiment that the end justifies the means), but it is this desire that one is trying to explain. For example, in Merton's original article, failing independent evidence of an overemphasis on goals, he was reduced to treating the advent of deviancy itself as "symptomatic" of such a cultural excess.[7] Another article on the sociology of science attempts to explain sociologically the motives for fraudulent claims by scientists. Concern among scientists about recognition for priority in discovery results, Merton claims, from the high value placed on originality in the scientific community. He then concludes that scientific fraud is a consequence of a "great

cultural emphasis" on recognition for originality.[8] Yet, other than the fraud itself, Merton offers no independent evidence of an *excessive* emphasis on originality in science; the "pathogenic" nature of the culture of science is deduced from the existence of fraud, while the fraud is explained by the cultural pathology.[9] The general thesis of aberrant or pathological culture emphases therefore appears to be reduced to a claim that any hierarchy of differentially valued and rewarded goals (differential emphases) is "pathogenic," for all such hierarchies will "induce" or "exert pressure on" some individuals to employ deviant means.

Do these criticisms imply that the pressure toward goals is unrelated to the desire to use deviant means? On the contrary, Merton's formulation is not the only possible approach to locating sources of deviant motivation in the means-end situation. Even if one assumes that deviant motivation respecting means is independent of profound social imbalance or cultural pathology, one can still recognize that the means-end relation contains an intrinsic and universal tension. Let us consider this point.

We can begin by asking about the nature of unemphasized goals, or goals that do not exert pressure on the individual (if they are truly goals), or goals about which he does not experience some anxiety, uncertainty, or tension. Manifestly, by definition, goals are items that have received enough "emphasis" from somewhere to make them

---

[7] "It is, indeed, my central hypothesis that aberrant behavior may be regarded sociologically as a symptom of dissociation between culturally prescribed aspirations and socially structured avenues for realizing these aspirations" (Merton, 1957a, p. 134).

[8] ". . . great concern with the goal of recognition for originality can generate a tendency toward sharp practices just inside the rules of the game or sharper practices far outside" (Merton, 1957b, p. 649).

[9] "The great cultural emphasis upon recognition for original discovery can lead by gradations from these rare practices of outright fraud to more frequent practices just beyond the edge of acceptability. . . . Against this cultural and social background, one can glimpse the sources, other than idiosyncratic ones, of the misbehavior of individual scientists. The culture of science is, in this measure, pathogenic" (Merton, 1957b, pp. 651, 659).

desirable to, or mandatory for, someone. Moreover, and also by definition, goals are things that the individual does not now have, and that there is no absolute certainty of his having. Therefore, unless individuals are without impelling goals of some sort, there is always strong motivation to reduce risk and uncertainty by using means that are the most certain and foolproof regardless of their normative status. Individuals at all social levels and in all societies are in a state of *relative* deprivation regarding means to their goals, and it is this relative deprivation that provides the incentive to them all for using force and fraud. This is particularly true since illegitimate means have special advantages. Not only may they sometimes be the most technically appropriate methods of achieving a goal, but their efficiency is enhanced by the fact that, in a going society, most other people are inhibited from using them. Persons using such means have the advantage, therefore, of operating in a situation in which competitors are rendered gullible or impotent by virtue of their morality. This general formulation of the intrinsic nature of the means-end tension does not preclude extended sociological analysis of the desire to use deviant means, for many sociological variables (including social class) can doubtless be found to exacerbate and differentiate the tension. For example, differentially socialized personalities will presumably react variously to choosing among and balancing a system of cultural goals, as well as to choices among means. However, although such variables may influence the differential intensity of the means-end tension, they will not create this tension in and of themselves.

From motives with respect to means, we shall now turn to those with respect to goals, either in the form of cherishing illegitimate goals or eschewing mandatory ones. A useful beginning is to recall our earlier view that it is incorrect to reason solely in terms of the repressive nature of norms, with "all cultures" invariably doing "violence" to men's drives, as Freud (and

now Wrong, 1961, p. 192) claims. This view, which finds in man's biological nature the only important source of deviant goals, not only overlooks other sources for such ends but also fails to realize that organic drives contribute to the seeking of approved as well as disapproved objectives— that, in short, the normative status of the organically induced goal *varies* with social context and social situation. Typically, one finds social approval and prescription of desire (and behavior) in one context, and disapproval and proscription of the *identical* desire (or behavior) in another context. Murdock reminds us, for example, that all societies have strong rules of sexual obligation as well as restriction (1949, Ch. 9). Since sexual congress is a marital duty rather than simply a privilege, refusal of intercourse ("constructive desertion") is a ground for divorce, a form of marital deviancy. Plainly, it is not simply sexual desire per se that is an unsocialized aspect of man's nature, lack of such desire in a context demanding it may be deviant as well.

A second source of illegitimate goals may be their economy. Less effort or fewer resources may be required to attain them than to attain legitimate ones; consequently, choosing such an objective is a possible alternative to choosing an illegitimate means to a legitimate goal. Third, primary socialization may readily be a source of illegitimate ends in the direct sense that parents or guardians have such goals themselves and encourage or unwittingly induce their children to pursue them. Lastly, individuals are of course constantly vulnerable to socialization, because their dependency on others does not end with infancy or childhood. Thus, people may enter relationships because of personal interests or needs, but they readily become attached to or dependent upon persons who are sources of satisfaction, thereby becoming susceptible to the goals of these others. For instance, although delinquent gangs may be joined because the individual is *already* oriented toward delinquent objectives, this is not necessarily the case. He may become a member of these associations for otherwise compelling *legitimate* motives—a desire for companionship, for example. However, once he is a member of such a group (sometimes even a dyad), these very legitimate desires become the basis for his acceptance of the illegitimate goals of the gang or leader. The fact that this socialization process "works," and works very efficiently, regardless of the legitimacy of the goals, is the burden of the association theory of crime and delinquency so painstakingly documented by Shaw and McKay (1942), Sutherland (1937; 1949), and their students and followers. On a larger scale, the Nazi movement used the same mechanism to enlist support for goals, such as "the final solution," that few individuals would have subscribed to or aided had they not first been caught up in and supported by highly organized group activity and sentiment.[10]

Deviancy arises not only as pursuit of the wrong goals but also as failure to pursue the right ones. Merton has suggested in his discussion of "ritualism" and "retreatism" that the motive for withdrawal from proper goals lies in the blocking of means or channels to them. In terms of learning theory, the goal is "extinguished." An analysis of the validity of Merton's reasoning goes be-

yond the confines of this paper, but we can suggest a few of the issues involved.

First of all, for the withdrawal to be deviant the goal must truly be normative—something the individual is legitimately enjoined to pursue. Therefore, we cannot account as deviant the retreat or withdrawal from just any type of aspiration, such as the numerous ephemeral goals of youth. Second, since the hypothesis is in terms of mechanisms of reinforcement and extinction, it would be well before accepting it to take account of experimental evidence on the difficulty of extinguishing goals under conditions of deferred gratification and partial reward. It is perplexing, but apparently true, that partial and deferred gratification together with great effort in the learning process produce responses that are exceptionally durable.[11] Since human society is not a goalbox, individuals do not frequently experience the type of *total* blocking that Merton postulates. Instead, they are usually subjected to delayed reward and partial gratification, because they have diverse alternatives and group affiliations which roughly compensate for the "blocking" they experience in pursuing a particular goal. This compensation will not necessarily be merely an alternative form of satisfaction (another goal), it may actually be an alternative means or channel to reaching the same goal. For example, a young man from a poor Jewish family that has always encouraged and rewarded his particular talents, enhanced his ego, and scrimped to throw opportunities his way, can be said to have an important "means" or "channel" at his disposal. His means for reaching a high occupational goal may in fact be better than those of a rich Gentile boy with an overbearing father, an aimless mother, and the assurance of an education at Princeton or Harvard if he can "get in" and

---

[10] Trevor-Roper has called attention to the careful euphemisms used by the Nazis in referring to some of their activities. ". . . they used 'anodyne formulas,' 'disposal,' 'dispatch to the East,' 'final solution'; and even now they cannot be brought to admit that they actually harmed any human being. One will admit to passing an order; another to arranging transport; a third to superintending arrival; a fourth to selecting those fit to work; a fifth opened the doors of the 'disinfecting hall.' Then there is a pause, during which no one is responsible. After that a sixth removed the corpses, a seventh extracted the rings and teeth, an eighth fed the corpses to the flames. . ." (1961, p. 109). As Clinard has said, "Popular thinking about delinquency and crime is, for once, quite correct in its emphasis on the role of 'evil companions' in this behavior" (1957, p. 180).

[11] No one has explained this type of finding in a completely satisfactory manner, but Festinger's research on "cognitive dissonance" is of interest. See Festinger (1957) and Lawrence and Festinger (1962).

"stay in." This is not to say that it is more promising in this world to be poor and Jewish than rich and Gentile, but simply that the problem of "means" and "channels" is an empirical one of more complexity than is reflected in Merton's hypothesis. In short, although it is certainly possible that, with respect to a particular goal, complete blocking will result in extinction of the goal, normatively prescribed goals that are difficult to achieve will not necessarily be abandoned as long as some gratification is achieved.

We must therefore look elsewhere for sources of pervasive or generalized withdrawal. On the one hand, such withdrawal may be a feature of personality resulting from inadequacies in socialization. In fact, sustained withdrawal from all of the goals of one's society or group affiliation seems difficult to conceive of without accompanying psychic disorder. On the other hand, Durkheim's original formulation of the concept of *anomie* as a *courant suicidogène* is of relevance here, for it referred to the normative organization, limitation, and legitimation of goals, and not, as Merton implies, to norms regarding means.[12] The derangement Durkheim discussed is one of present goals (or lack of them) relative to past goals; not one of imbalance between normative injunctions regarding means and ends. Durkheim's famous example concerns the normatively enjoined economic goals of each social class. Great and sudden depression casts down such expectations to a point where the person sees them as totally im-

possible of achievement. He will need re-educating to acquire realistically lowered goals. Great and sudden prosperity upgrades the limits of the possible to a point where they seem infinite. But infinity is not a goal, and therefore individuals may experience a profound sense of futility until they get resocialized to their new-found wealth. In either case, according to Durkheim, the individual is vulnerable to suicide before his moral re-education takes place, because he is without goals (1951, Ch. 5).

Plainly, the idea of generalized goal withdrawal is so foreign to human activity that acceptable explanations of it entail the assumption of fairly extreme derangement either on a personal or a social level.

Inhibitions to Deviant Behavior

Given a conscious and established deviant desire, what prevents its eruption into deviant behavior? A systematic and complete answer to this question is not available in sociological literature, and this lack accounts for many criticisms of modern sociology. Wrong claims, for instance, that sociology of the Parsonian school relies completely on concepts of norm internalization, together with what Wrong calls "acceptance seeking" (a generalized sensitivity to community or public opinion), to explain the inhibition of deviant behavior.[13] But his criticism (and those of Dahrendorf [1958] and Lockwood [1956]) appears to be elicited more by lacunae in recent sociological formulations than by explicit statements that *only* internalization and "acceptance seeking" are of importance in controlling deviant behavior.

Actually, modern sociology recognizes at least five broad categories of inhibition to the acting out of deviant motivation in deviant behavior.

1. The internalization of norms. Norm "internalization" as an inhibitor of deviancy

---

[12] Merton's use of the term *anomie* bears little relation to Durkheim's, for Merton sees *anomie* as resulting from the use of technically appropriate (although deviant) means. He says, ". . . the sole significant question becomes: Which of available procedures is most efficient in netting the culturally approved value? The technically most effective procedure, whether culturally legitimate or not, becomes typically preferred to institutionally prescribed conduct. As this process of attenuation continues, the society becomes unstable and there develops what Durkheim has called 'anomie' (or normlessness)" (Merton, 1957c, p. 135).

[13] Wrong has not made a systematic distinction between the determinants of and inhibitions to deviant motivation and deviant behavior severally (1961, passim).

is, as Wrong and Dahrendorf complain, frequently used by sociologists in such a way as to imply that internalized norms blot out the individual's capacity to experience deviant motivation. Wrong (1961, pp. 185-196) cites statements such as the following by Sutton: "To a modern sociologist imbued with the conception that action follows institutionalized patterns, opposition of individual and common interests has only a very limited relevance or is thoroughly unsound" (Sutton et al., 1956, p. 304). A recent sociology text in the Parsonian tradition claims that, "Conformity to institutionalized norms is, of course, 'normal.' The actor, having internalized the norms, feels something like a need to conform. His conscience would bother him if he did not" (Johnson, 1960, p. 22, quoted by Wrong, 1961, p. 187). Equally unfortunate examples abound in the psychological literature, for example,

After this course of development, the successfully socialized individual emerges as the kind of person who can function effectively and happily in the society that formed him. Its outlets are his outlets, its anxieties his anxieties, its ways his ways. Having adapted himself to its demands, at considerable cost in spontaneity and personal pleasure, he now needs society in order to feel comfortable. It gives him a framework that makes the world meaningful, and as long as he remains within this framework he knows what to expect and what is expected of him. He knows how to attain satisfaction and how to avoid discomfort. He has learned to accept the society's secondary rewards, such as prestige and wealth, in place of the simple bodily pleasures and the immediate gratifications he has had to abandon. The outlets for guilt, anxiety, and repressed hostility which it offers are necessary for his comfort and well-being. As long as he stays within it, he functions well. Gratuities and deprivations dovetail neatly, and he is satisfied (Hartley & Hartley, 1952, pp. 335-336).

Not only does such usage, albeit implicit, violate our knowledge of actual human ex-

perience but, in addition, it theoretically excises altogether deviant motivation as a source of deviant behavior. Small wonder that critics like Dahrendorf and Wrong puzzle over some modern sociologists' accounts of the sources of deviancy.[14] Actually, the concept of internalization does not necessarily imply that the individual always, or typically, experiences no conscious desire for, or temptation to engage in, contra-normative activities. The concept loses none of its usefulness, and gains greatly in theoretical applicability, if it is confined to the connotation that social rules have become a part of the individual's motivational system in the sense that he is committed to them as being "right," or "legitimate," and, hence, "obligatory." It does not seem necessary to assume that "internalization" involves a blocking out of deviant motives such as would take place in sublimation and repression. Rather, we simply assume that *in the face of* temptation, one source of resistance to acting out deviant motivation in deviant behavior lies in the person's commitment to norms proscribing the behavior,

---

[14] Dahrendorf says, "what the social system can produce, however, is the well-known villain of the peace of utopia, the 'deviant.' Even he requires some considerable argument and the introduction of chance, or at least an undetermined variable—in this case, individual psychology. Although the system is perfect and in a state of equilibrium, individuals cannot always live up to this perfection." Dahrendorf quotes Parsons as saying, "Deviance is a motivated tendency for an actor to behave in contravention of one or more institutionalized normative patterns" (Parsons, 1951, p. 250). Dahrendorf then asks, "Motivated by what though?" He claims that Parsons looks to psychopathology or some unspecified disturbance in the social system for sources of deviancy (Dahrendorf, 1958, p. 120). In fairness to Parsons, had Dahrendorf read a few pages further in the same chapter, he would have found a section titled "Some Further Situational Aspects of the Genesis and Structuring of Deviance," which sketches out a few sources of deviant motivation. Nonetheless, Parsonian thinking about deviancy gives the impression of being poorly integrated with Parsonian statements about internalization. Wrong has joined in this criticism as well (1961, p. 187).

and in his ability to symbolize significantly to himself the moral reasons for not succumbing. It should perhaps be recalled at this point that the development of sociological thinking about internalization (inadequate as this thinking doubtless still is) was a response to empirical facts about nonrational and noninstrumental conformity.[15] Among other things, the concept provides a basis for thinking of individuals not only as the objects of moral enforcement, but also as enforcers. On the other hand, internalization is clearly not always successful as a source of self-imposed inhibition to deviant behavior. Consequently, there is wide latitude for the investigation of sources of *variation* in the effectiveness of internalization as a control mechanism. We are also moved to consider additional inhibitions to deviant behavior.

2. Desire for approval. In the case of internalization, the person is led to resist temptation by referring to his own evaluation. He asks, "Will I hate myself, if I do it?" Another inhibition lies in his anticipation of evaluations by significant others. However, the assumption of a desire or need for approval has (like that of internalization) been heavily overworked. From being one aspect of control over deviant behavior, the concept of sensitivity to opinion frequently becomes all-pervasive. Wrong's (1961, p. 188) quotation from Sutton is apt: "People are so profoundly sensitive to the expectations of others that all action is inevitably guided by these expectations" (Sutton et al., 1956, p. 264). No doubt approbation is enjoyable and necessary, but it is also frequently simply instrumental to other competing ends and interests, which limit how much one can invest in approval. As a result, it appears to be questionable that men are basically concerned with the maximization of favorable attitudes from others," as Zetterberg avers (1957, p. 189, quoted by Wrong, 1961, p. 189). It seems more realistic (and in accord with empirical evidence) to assume that men are concerned with the "optimization" of all satisfactions, including resistance to opinion pressures. The very notion of *statuses* implies norms relating to each status which, in effect, allow the incumbent to ignore the opinions of people who may try to influence him nonetheless. Not only is the status occupant protected from the righteous disapproval of the would-be influencer, but he is *a fortiori* protected from more extreme sanctions.

This point leads us to note that insofar as one finds widespread sensitivity to informal controls such as opinions, it may be interpreted as a sensitivity to "cues" of possibly more stringent consequences, not simply as a desire to bask in social approval. Depending on factors such as sociocultural backgrounds, personality, and intelligence, people in varying degrees understand that informal punishments (ridicule, gossip, criticism) are hints of possibly more unpleasant action. Let us now turn to this type of anticipation.

3. Anticipation of formal punishment. Formal punishment, whether by the state or other agencies, typically involves not only changes in the attitudes and responses of others toward the punished individual, but some concrete and drastic change in his life chances as well. He may, for example, be ostracized from his group, fired from his job, deprived of his citizenship, enclosed behind bars, or relieved of his life.

The importance we allow to formal punishment in controlling deviant behavior will, in part, be a function of the weight assigned to internalization and the desire for approval. Modern sociology's concern with "voluntaristic" controls has in fact led to an underplaying of the role of more formalized aspects of social control. In this, the discipline seems deficient for not looking more to actual empirical *variation* in the operation of different types of control as a

---

[15] See Parsons (1949c), particularly chs. 2–3 and 18–19. In Parsons' thinking, the internalization of values, as distinct from norms, is of primary importance. We shall discuss this briefly in the final section of this chapter.

normal part of social life. Given our knowledge of some of the elements in socialization and social situations that influence the operation of internalization and sensitivity to opinions, we must assume that the impact of these controls will vary among groups and among social contexts. Consequently, the importance of formal punishment (and its anticipation) cannot be axiomatically overlooked. Moreover, if in a particular instance such punishment and the threat of it are found to be of importance in controlling deviancy, we are not warranted in assuming that this finding is an indicator of social malintegration, or in Parsonian language, "strain."

The lack of a systematic distinction between sources of deviant motivation and sources of deviant behavior leads Parsons and many of his epigoni into a highly selective treatment of social control mechanisms. For instance, Johnson says, "One of the most general statements that can be made about deviant behavior is that it is a reaction to strain of some kind" (1960, p. 581). However, in actual fact Johnson turns out to be discussing deviant motivation and not deviant behavior, and this motivation is viewed as resulting from "strains" due to role conflicts and being overburdened by demands. The cure for strain is "therapy"— supportive, permissive, unreciprocating, and rewarding behavior on the part of some other role-player. Johnson's discussion thus glosses over sources of deviant motivation that are not due to strain, and only reluctantly mentions one type of formalized punishment—"branding and isolation" (e.g., putting criminals in prison). But few would deny that formalized punishments are a possibility in many types of social situations, punishments that go well beyond social disapproval and yet are not administered by the state.

4. Anticipation of nonreward. Since societies must influence the goals their members pursue, an important means of such control lies in the reward system. Conversely, nonreward as well as direct punishment is punitive. From the point of view of the observer, nonreward is milder than punishment because it does not deprive the individual of something he already has, but only of something he would have liked to have had. Thus, although the person may experience an acute sense of deprivation ("he had his heart set on it"), in his calculation of possible risks for deviant behavior, nonreward is far from the worst that can happen. Perhaps because of its objective mildness, and because it involves inaction rather than action, its role as a control mechanism in adult life is often overlooked by sociologists, although psychologists interested in learning processes have given it more attention.[16] Sociologically, nonreward has certain advantages over punishment in that it affords no source of glamour to the person punished and does not advertise the particular behavior that led to the punishment. Formal punishment arouses complex emotions in the society at large, not all of which are unsympathetic to the individual punished or to his deviancy. As a consequence, it is well known that criminals and delinquents gain status by means of the publicity they have received, the prisons they have been in, and so on. Furthermore, the type of deviancy itself may become fashionable if given enough notoriety. Nonreward carries no notoriety.

5. Lack of opportunity for deviant behavior. Finally, we should not forget that lack of opportunity may inhibit deviant behavior. At the broadest level, opportunity may be lacking because of the type of society. For example, in his analysis of why young adults did not openly rebel against their elders in traditional China, Levy (1949) does not rely on absence of deviant motivation. Instead, he alleges that traditionally there were sources of severe disaffection in the position of young Chinese adults, but that this kinship-based society

---

[16] The concept of nonreward is most often used in relation to the "extension" of "incorrect" responses in early learning.

offered no social and economic alternatives to young people except life in the family and its attendant obligation of filial piety. Although modern societies open up alternative modes of existence, all societies bind most individuals to time-consuming obligations which limit opportunities for deviant behavior. Such restrictions also operate on would-be partners in deviancy, thus limiting group deviation or deviancy that requires a partner. Naturally, lack of opportunity can sometimes be surmounted if motivation is high enough, but we are not claiming this to be the sole inhibitor.

Cloward (1959; Cloward & Ohlin, 1960) has recently called attention again to opportunity as a factor in deviant behavior. As he points out, we cannot assume that illegitimate means are readily available to the lower-class individual who finds that legitimate ones are scarce. A professional career in crime requires some training, contacts, and criminal facilities—some organization. As a result, the lower-class individual may fail in criminal as well as in legitimate activity. In other words, disadvantaged people may be restricted in both legitimate and illegitimate endeavors. Cloward goes on to raise the question of whether access to illegitimate means is unrelated to socioeconomic status, inversely related, or directly related. However, such a question presupposes that organized career crime constitutes the principal channel or facility for illegitimate means. The arbitrariness of this assumption is brought out by asking whether a bank president, if he wished to use illegitimate means to enrich himself, would need to become a pickpocket. Plainly, we must recognize that access to a wide range of effective means is part of the definition of high socioeconomic status, and whether these means are "legitimate" or "illegitimate" will vary with the context and manner in which they are employed. Therefore, whereas the low socioeconomic levels may be burdened by "double failure," the high levels have a relatively good chance for "double success," both legitimate and illegitimate.

Sources of Conforming Desires

Remaining in our table is cell (1), the case of conforming behavior *and* conforming intent. How may we explain, other than by chance, the absence of any conscious desire to deviate? The question exceeds our purpose, but we can suggest some answers drawn from the previous analysis. Clearly, internalization of norms per se does not account for an absence of deviant desire. Internalization of values, however, may mean that the individual regards many types of violation as not only immoral and illegitimate but also as undesirable. In such a case, the repugnance of an act makes its moral status irrelevant. On the other hand, although values may support norms in this manner, the ultimate and inflexible nature of values means that they may conduce to contra-normative behavior as well. The only exception is values pertaining to obeying norms in general. However, since there are no norms in general, such values are more theoretical than real. To follow out the value of "honesty," for example, would cause violation of numerous norms.

We may mention in addition that norm internalization can indirectly inhibit deviant desires through repression, sublimation, substitution, displacement, and projection. These mechanisms have in common the rejection from consciousness of motives and desires that threaten to overwhelm the ego.[17]

Although the internalization of values and the repression of deviant motives both may lead to conforming desires, they also entail risks and costs. Intense and pervasive value-internalization (or "cathexis") exposes the

---

[17] The essence of repression is, in Freud's words, ". . . in the function of rejecting and keeping something out of consciousness" (1924, p. 86). We may note here that in psychoanalytic theory, what is "repressed" is the symbolization (or conscious representation) of the desire or emotion in question. This leaves the presumed quantum of "affect" to some fate or other in "the unconscious"—perhaps "displacement" onto another object where symbolization and consciousness are not penalized or forbidden.

society to inflexibility and inability to adapt to changing circumstances. Repression creates much the same problem on a personality level. If, therefore, a society relied heavily on these two means of guaranteeing conformity, it would suffer social collapse rather than social change, mental breakdown rather than social control. Considerations of this nature explain many of the criticisms of Parsonian reliance on values and repressive internalization to explain social order. Indeed, the weight given in Parsonian theory to "value cathexis" seems justified as long as stability, integration, and cohesion alone are dealt with, but in the form presented by Parsons and men like Harry Johnson, it is inadequate for the analysis of social change and the realities of conflict and competition.

A final source of conforming motives rests in the fact that deviant desires may be caught "in the bud" (to use Parsons' phrase) and transformed by means of "therapy" (1951, pp. 299ff.; Johnson, 1960, pp. 581–585). In this case, the actor does not simply inhibit existing deviant desires, but is "cured" of them.

Summary of the Theory of Norms and Deviancy

In drawing from modern sociology the answers to numerous charges that the field lacks a theory of deviancy, we have confined ourselves to individual deviancy rather than to conflict among subcultures and groups (competing conformities) or to organized deviancy by professionalized criminal groups. Also, instead of assuming overall "consensus" on a whole system of norms, we have simply assumed that in each society and group *some* norms are operative. Our problem has been to explain why, given such norms, one finds the contra-normative as well. Defining the "deviant" as the contra-normative—that is, as violating concrete norms—we have rejected the a priori notion that some type of motive or behavior is universally undesirable or deviant.

Using the simple facts that behavior and motives may be either discrepant or similar, conforming or deviant, we have constructed a fourfold table showing that one cannot account for conforming or deviant behavior only by a corresponding motive, but must also account for them in the face of contrary motives. In particular, we have sought for the sources of unintentionally deviant behavior, the sources of deviant motivation, and the factors preventing deviant motives from erupting into deviant behavior. The answers can be found scattered in the sociological literature. Bringing them together in the organized fashion required by our fourfold table serves to pinpoint the weaknesses as well as the strengths of contemporary theory, just as it helps to understand without necessarily accepting the current all-or-none criticisms.

REFERENCES

Anderson, C. A. The social status of university students in relation to type of economy: An international comparison. In *Transactions of the third world congress of sociology*. Vol. 5. London: International Sociological Association, 1956. Pp. 51–63.

Barber, B. *Social stratification*. New York: Harcourt, 1957.

Barton, A. The concept of property-space in social research. In P. Lazarsfeld & M. Rosenberg (Eds.), *The language of social research*. Glencoe, Ill.: Free Press, 1955. Pp. 50–52.

Benedict, Ruth. Continuities and discontinuities in cultural conditioning. *Psychiatry*, 1938, 2, 161–167.

Blake, Judith, in collaboration with Stycos, J. M., & Davis, K. *Family structure in Jamaica: The social context of reproduction*. Glencoe, Ill.: Free Press, 1961.

Carter, R. E. An experiment in value measurement. *Amer. sociol. Rev.*, 1959, 21, 156–163.

Chinoy, E. Social mobility trends in the United States. *Amer. sociol. Rev.*, 1955, 20, 180–186.

Clinard, M. *Sociology of deviant behavior*. New York: Rinehart, 1957.

Cloward, R. A. Illegitimate means, anomie, and deviant behavior. *Amer. sociol. Rev.*, 1959, 24, 164–176.

Cloward, R. A., & Ohlin, L. E. *Delinquency and opportunity: A theory of delinquent gangs.* Glencoe, Ill.: Free Press, 1960.

Coleman, J. S., Katz, E., & Menzel, H. The diffusion of an innovation among physicians. *Sociometry,* 1957, 20, 253–270.

Dahrendorf, R. Out of Utopia: Towards a re-orientation of sociological analysis. *Amer. J. Sociol.,* 1958, 64, 115–127.

Durkheim, E. *Suicide.* J. A. Spaulding & G. Simpson (Trans.). Glencoe, Ill.: Free Press, 1951.

Festinger, L. *A theory of cognitive dissonance.* Evanston, Ill.: Row, Peterson, 1957.

Freud, S. *Collected papers.* Vol. 4. London: Hogarth Press, 1924.

Goldfarb, W. Infant rearing and problem behavior. *Amer. J. Orthopsychiat.,* 1943, 13, 249–266.(a)

Goldfarb, W. The effects of early institutional care on adolescent personality. *Child Develpm.,* 1943, 14, 213–225.(b)

Goldfarb, W. The effects of early institutional care on adolescent personality. *J. exp. Educ.,* 1943, 12, 107–129.(c)

Goldfarb, W. Effects of early institutional care on adolescent personality: Rorschach data. *Amer. J. Orthopsychiat.,* 1944, 14, 441–447.(a)

Goldfarb, W. Infant rearing as a factor in foster home placement. *Amer. J. Orthopsychiat.,* 1944, 14, 162–167.(b)

Goldfarb, W. Effects of psychological deprivation in infancy and subsequent stimulation. *Amer. J. Psychiat.,* 1945, 102, 18–33.(a)

Goldfarb, W. Psychological privation in infancy and subsequent adjustment. *Amer. J. Orthopsychiat.,* 1945, 15, 247–255.(b)

Hallowell, A. I. Culture, personality, and society. In A. L. Kroeber (Ed.), *Anthropology today.* Chicago: Univer. of Chicago Press, 1953. Pp. 597–620.

Harlow, H. F., & Harlow, Margaret K. Social deprivation in monkeys. *Sci. Amer.,* 1962, 207, 136–146.

Hartley, E. L., & Hartley, Ruth E. *Fundamentals of social psychology.* New York: Knopf, 1952.

Hollingshead, A. B. *Elmtown's youth.* New York: Wiley, 1949.

Hyman, H. H. The value systems of different classes: A social psychological contribution to the analysis of stratification. In R. Bendix & S. M. Lipset (Eds.), *Class, status, and power.* Glencoe, Ill.: Free Press, 1953. Pp. 426–442.

Johnson, H. M. *Sociology, a systematic introduction.* New York: Harcourt, 1960.

Kahl, J. A. *The American class structure.* New York: Rinehart, 1957.

Kluckhohn, C. *Mirror for man.* New York: McGraw, 1949.

Kluckhohn, C. Common humanity and diverse cultures. In D. Lerner (Ed.), *The human meaning of the social sciences.* New York: Meridian Books, 1959. Pp. 245–284.

Kluckhohn, Florence R., & Strodtbeck, F. L. *Variations in value orientations.* Evanston, Ill.: Row, Peterson, 1961.

Knupfer, Genevieve. Portrait of the underdog. In R. Bendix & S. M. Lipset (Eds.), *Class, status, and power.* Glencoe, Ill.: Free Press, 1953. Pp. 255–263.

Lawrence, D. H., & Festinger, L. *Deterrents and reinforcement: The psychology of insufficient reward.* Stanford: Stanford Univer. Press, 1962.

Lenski, G. Trends in intergenerational mobility in the United States. *Amer. sociol. Rev.,* 1958, 23, 514–523.

Levy, M. L., Jr. *The family revolution in modern China.* Cambridge, Mass.: Harvard Univer. Press, 1949.

Lewin, K., Dembo, Tamara, Festinger, L., & Sears, Pauline S. Level of aspiration. In J. McV. Hunt (Ed.), *Personality and the behavior disorders.* New York: Ronald Press, 1944. Ch. 10.

Linton, R. *The study of man.* New York: Appleton-Century, 1936.

Lipset, S. M., & Bendix, R. *Social mobility in industrial society.* Berkeley: Univer. of California Press, 1959.

Lockwood, D. Some remarks on the social system. *Brit. J. Sociol.,* 1956, 7, 134–146.

McGeer, P. L. Mind, drugs, and behavior. *Amer. Scient.,* 1952, 50, 322–338.

Marsh, C. P., & Coleman, A. L. Group influences and agricultural innovations: Some tentative findings and hypotheses. *Amer. J. Sociol.,* 1956, 61, 588–594.

Mead, Margaret. National character. In A. L. Kroeber (Ed.), *Anthropology today.* Chicago: Univer. of Chicago Press, 1953. Pp. 642–667.

Menzel, H. Innovation, integration, and marginality: A survey of physicians. *Amer. sociol. Rev.*, 1960, 25, 704–713.

Merton, R. K. Continuities in the theory of social structure and anomie. In *Social theory and social structure.* (rev. ed.) Glencoe, Ill.: Free Press, 1957.(a)

Merton, R. K. Priorities in scientific discovery: A chapter in the sociology of science. *Amer. sociol. Rev.*, 1957, 22, 635–639.(b)

Merton, R. K. Social structure and anomie. In *Social theory and social structure.* (rev. ed.) Glencoe, Ill.: Free Press, 1957.(c)

Merton, R. K. The role-set: Problems in sociological theory. *Brit. J. Sociol.*, 1957, 8, 106–120.(d)

Mills, C. W. *The sociological imagination.* New York: Oxford Univer. Press, 1959.

Morris, R. T. A typology of norms. *Amer. sociol. Rev.*, 1956, 21, 610–613.

Murdock, G. P. *Social structure.* New York: Macmillan, 1949.

Pareto, V. *General treatise on sociology.* (Mistrans. as *The mind and society.*) New York: Harcourt, 1935.

Parsons, T. Age and sex in the social structure of the United States. In *Essays in sociological theory.* Glencoe, Ill.: Free Press, 1949. Pp. 218–232.(a)

Parsons, T. Certain primary sources and patterns of aggression in the social structure of the western world. In *Essays in sociological theory.* Glencoe, Ill.: Free Press, 1949. Pp. 251–274.(b)

Parsons, T. *The structure of social action.* Glencoe, Ill.: Free Press, 1949.(c)

Parsons, T. *The social system.* Glencoe, Ill.: Free Press, 1951.

Petersen, W. Is America still the land of opportunity? *Commentary*, 1953, 16, 477–486.

Rogoff, Natalie. *Recent trends in occupational mobility.* Glencoe, Ill.: Free Press, 1953.

Rosenberg, M. *Occupations and values.* Glencoe, Ill.: Free Press, 1957.

Samuelson, P. A. *Economics: An introductory analysis.* (5th ed.) New York: McGraw, 1961.

Shaw, C. R., & McKay, H. *Juvenile delinquency and urban areas.* Chicago: Univer. of Chicago Press, 1937.

Sjoberg, G. Are social classes in America becoming more rigid? *Amer. sociol. Rev.*, 1951, 16, 775–783.

Smith, Eleanor, & Monane, J. H. G. Courtship values in a youth sample. *Amer. sociol. Rev.*, 1953, 18, 635–640.

Spitz, R. A. Hospitalism: An inquiry into the genesis of psychiatric conditions in early childhood. In Anna Freud et al. (Eds.), *The psychoanalytic study of the child.* Vol. 1. New York: International Universities Press, 1945. Pp. 53–74.

Spitz, R. A. Hospitalism: A follow-up report on investigations described in vol. 1, 1945. In Anna Freud et al. (Eds.), *The psychoanalytic study of the child.* Vol. 2. New York: International Universities Press, 1946. Pp. 113–117.

Spitz, R. A. The role of ecological factors in emotional development in infancy. *Child Developm.*, 1949, 20, 145–156.

Stein, H., & Cloward, R. A. *Social perspectives on behavior.* Glencoe, Ill.: Free Press, 1958.

Sumner, W. G. *Folkways.* Boston: Ginn, 1906.

Sutherland, E. H. *The professional thief.* Chicago: Univer. of Chicago Press, 1937.

Sutherland, E. H. *White collar crime.* New York: Dryden Press, 1949.

Sutton, F. X., et al. *The American business creed.* Cambridge, Mass.: Harvard Univer. Press, 1956.

Thomas, I. W., & Znaniecki, F. The Polish peasant in Europe and America. New York: Knopf, 1927.

Trevor-Roper, H. R. Eichmann is not unique. *N. Y. Times Mag.*, September 17, 1961. Pp. 13 et seq.

Warner, W. L., & Abegglen, J. *Occupational mobility in American business and industry, 1928–1952.* Minneapolis: Univer. of Minnesota Press, 1955.

Whorf, B. L. *Language, thought, and reality.* New York: Wiley, 1956.

Williams, R. M., Jr. *American society.* New York: Knopf, 1960.

Wrong, D. H. The oversocialized conception of man in modern sociology. *Amer. sociol. Rev.*, 1961, 26, 183–193.

Yarrow, L. J. Maternal deprivation: Toward an empirical and conceptual re-evaluation. *Psychol. Bull.*, 1961, 58 (6), 459–490.

Zetterberg, H. L. Compliant actions. *Acta sociol.*, 1957, 2.

CHAPTER 14 Theory of Organizations

W. RICHARD SCOTT

The title of this chapter represents a goal as yet unrealized. There does not yet exist a single, widely accepted theory of organizations. What does exist is a number of more or less well-developed conceptual schemes focused on varying aspects of organizations; a rapidly growing collection of empirical generalizations sometimes relevant to, but often uninformed by, the conceptual schemes; a handful of descriptive studies of concrete organizations or subunits of organizations; and, of least interest for present purposes, a voluminous body of materials which deplores or defends some aspects, or the very existence, of organizations or which offers how-to-do-it advice to the various types of organizational participants or aspirants.

Most of what is now known about organizations is based on materials collected by researchers in naturally occurring structures, and there is no dearth of subject matter. It is perhaps trite but nonetheless necessary to observe that organizations are a prominent if not the dominant characteristic of modern society. "Everywhere there is organization, everywhere bureaucratization; like the world of feudalism, the modern world is broken

up into areas dominated by castles, but not the castles of *les chansons de geste,* but the castles of Kafka" (Wolin, 1960, p. 354). Organizations being ubiquitous, sociological explorations in virtually every substantive area have been compelled to take account of their presence. While the analysis of organizations is the stock in trade of the industrial and military sociologist and, to a lesser extent, of the student of political sociology, the last two decades have seen the investigation of organizations or organizational phenomena in such diverse areas as criminology (Cressey, 1961), mental health (Stanton & Schwartz, 1954), medicine (Coser, 1962), secondary and higher education (Clark, 1960; Coleman, 1961), religion (Harrison, 1959), and social welfare (Wilensky & Lebeaux, 1958).

The mere prevalence of some phenomena, however, is not sufficient to justify its selection for scientific investigation. That decision should be based on an assessment of the potential contribution of such studies to the development of social theory. A case for the study of organizations can be made on two counts, both of which are suggested in the following statement: "the fact is that the organization of the large formal enterprises, governmental or private, in modern society is modeled on, is a rationalization of, tendencies that exist in all human groups" (Homans, 1950, pp. 186–187). To say that organizations exhibit "tendencies that exist in all human groups" is to suggest that organizations provide a setting within which many basic social processes occur—processes as diverse as socialization, communication, ranking, the formation of norms, deviance, or social control. It has been argued that organizations offer a particularly strategic setting for the examination of such phenomena in that their formal structure imposes limitations, controlling some aspects of the situation and allowing others to vary. In this sense, organizations can be said to constitute "natural laboratories" which facilitate the examination of certain social phenomena (Blau, 1956, pp. 23–25). The second contribution which the study of organizations can make to the development of sociological theory is suggested by Homans' statement that the tendencies which exist in all human groups *appear in a rationalized form* in organizations. This suggests that organizations are characterized by distinctive structures which modify the form in which the generic social processes are expressed. For instance, attempts on the part of one person to control the behavior of another may be investigated profitably in any social setting. But certain forms of control (for example, an authority structure) are best studied within organizations since they appear here in their most highly developed form. The nature of the difference between social phenomena occurring within and outside an organizational setting was suggested in general terms by March and Simon (1958, pp. 2–4), who point to the relative specificity of organizational processes as contrasted with the diffuseness which marks most social processes occurring outside the confines of organizations. The study of organizations, then, can contribute to the building of social theory by providing descriptive accounts and analytical formulations of generic social processes as they are modified by distinctive structural arrangements.

The Concept of Organization

This chapter is not devoted to an analysis of social organization, an extremely broad concept that encompasses all social groupings to the extent that their participants are linked by a network of relationships and share certain values and norms. Such a concept encompasses many kinds of diverse social arrangements from a street gang or a family at one extreme to the economy or an entire society at the other. Rather, the present discussion is limited to a particular type of social organization, a type which often carries some delimiting adjective such as "formal" or "complex" or "bureaucratic."

How is such a type of social organization to be defined? While many have wrestled with this problem, two men—Weber and Barnard—have been the primary shapers of a sociological conception of organizations. Weber approached the problem by first discussing the more general concept, "corporate group," which he defined in the following terms: "a social relationship which is either closed or limits the admission of outsiders by rules, will be called a 'corporate group' (*Verband*) so far as its order is enforced by the action of specific individuals whose regular function this is, of a chief or 'head' (*Leiter*) and usually also an administrative staff" (Weber, 1947, pp. 145–146). Three distinct criteria are apparent in this definition: (1) The corporate group is characterized by relatively fixed boundaries in the sense that certain persons are excluded or their participation is subject to specified conditions. In short, there are members and nonmembers. (2) There exists a body of rules or social norms—the legitimate order—supported by all members (for perhaps diverse reasons) which defines certain kinds of conduct as appropriate or desirable. (3) The order is "legal" (as opposed to "conventional") in that there is a differentiation of power among the participants, a subgroup being specifically empowered to exercise control and administer sanctions. A corporate group, however, is not an organization.

In Weber's view, an organization *(Betriebsverband)* is distinguished by two additional characteristics: (4) it is "associative" rather than "communal" in character; and (5) it is engaged in carrying out continuous purposive activity of a specified kind (Weber, 1947, pp. 136-139, 151-152). The fourth criterion relates to the orientation of members, the associative group furnishing participants with a means for pursuing common values or interests as contrasted with the communal group which brings together persons who share a feeling of belongingness, the members participating because of certain sentiments or because of a shared tradition (Bendix, 1960, p. 292). With this criterion, Weber excluded such groupings as the "national community" and the family from his concept of organization. Fifth, and finally, Weber noted that organizational activities are carried out without significant interruption and that the goals pursued by members are relatively specific ones.

Parsons' view of organizations appears to have been strongly influenced by that of Weber. His concept of "collectivity" seems closely analogous to Weber's concept of the corporate group (Parsons, 1951, pp. 39-41), and organizations are viewed as a subtype within this broader category. Parsons also distinguished between associative and communal collectivities, referring to the first type, where the goal is the result of common action, as "organizations" and the second, where the goal is inherent in the action, as *"Gemeinschaften"* (Landsberger, 1961b, p. 222). Major emphasis is placed by Parsons (1960, p. 17) on Weber's final criterion: "primacy of orientation to the attainment of a specific goal is used as the defining characteristic of an organization which distinguishes it from other types of social systems." Parsons did depart from Weber to some extent in the stress which he placed on the "shared" and the "collective" nature of the goals pursued by organizations (Parsons & Shils, 1954, p. 192). But if this focus led Parsons from Weber's camp, it drew him toward the tents of Barnard.

Like Weber, Barnard (1938) viewed organizations as a subtype of a more general class of phenomena which he labeled the "cooperative system." Cooperative systems provide a means for overcoming certain limitations—biological, physical, social—which restrict the effectiveness of individual activity although these systems are themselves subject to further limitations. An organization is "that type of cooperation among men that is conscious, deliberate and purposeful" (Barnard, 1938, p. 4). Organization is hence defined as "a system of consciously coordinated activities or forces of two or more persons" (Barnard, 1938, p. 73). This definition is meant to exclude persons and groups as such as well as all aspects of the physical environment, focusing attention on what is admittedly an analytical construct, "a field of personal forces," analogous to a field of electrical or magnetic forces. Barnard believed that abstracting and restricting the concept in this manner renders it useful over a wide range of concrete situations and permits investigation of the relationship of organization to related systems whether physical, biological, psychological, or social. The fundamental "elements" of organization are: (1) communication, (2) willingness to contribute, and (3) common purpose, all of which are required if an organization is to come into being. For an organization to continue to exist, either effectiveness (the accomplishment of the common purpose) or efficiency (the satisfaction of the motives of individual contributors) is also necessary (Barnard, 1938, p. 82). Given these elements, the essence of formal organization is the making of decisions—decisions to participate, choice of ends and selection among alternative means, and coordination of the various factors which together comprise the larger cooperative system. It is clear that Simon (1957), who adopted the decision premise as his central unit of organizational analysis, was strongly influenced by Barnard in his conception of organization.

The conceptions of Weber (1947) and Barnard (1938) are similar in some respects and different in others. Although neither used the terminology, both viewed organizations as a system of roles having definite boundaries, and both emphasized the pursuit of common, relatively specific, purposes. Weber distinguished organizations from communal groups while Barnard's conception was meant to include within its scope selected portions of these groups including families, communities, and entire societies. Perhaps the most important difference between the two views, however, is that Weber emphasized the existence of a system of power legitimated by the beliefs of its members, whereas Barnard focused on the communication structure which allows contributors to work together in the pursuit of common interests. More concisely, Weber focused on power, Barnard, on communication; Weber emphasized shared moral commitments, Barnard, rational self-interest (Hopkins, 1961).

Both of these conceptions have proved useful in the analysis of organizations, and both have their share of adherents. The two approaches, perhaps for historical reasons, have usually been viewed as conflicting. However, as Hopkins (1961) has argued, they appear to be essentially complementary rather than contradictory. Organizations are power *and* communication structures, and participants are motivated by self-interest as well as by shared values.

For the purposes of this chapter, organizations are defined as collectivities (in Parsons' [1951] sense of the term) that have been established for the pursuit of relatively specific objectives on a more or less continuous basis. It should be clear from the foregoing, however, that organizations have distinctive features other than goal specificity and continuity. These include relatively fixed boundaries, a normative order, authority ranks, a communication system, and an incentive system which enables various types of participants to work together in the pursuit of common goals.

The Emergence of Organizations

Organizations—in the sense in which the concept has just been defined—are not found in every known society but only in those with a sufficiently developed division of labor. The requirement that there be a group of persons who together engage more or less continuously in the pursuit of specific objectives implies a rather high level of differentiation in the society as well as some system of exchange; a person cannot make the required commitment to an organization unless he is assured that other specific goals are being pursued by other collectivities and that he may in some manner exchange a portion of his "product" for a portion of theirs. That organizations perform important functions in these societies has been emphasized by Parsons: "the development of organizations is the principal mechanism by which, in a highly differentiated society, it is possible to 'get things done,' to achieve goals beyond the reach of the individual" (Parsons, 1960, p. 41).

The emergence of the bureaucratic organization—the predominant type in all industrialized societies today—required, of course, a host of particular social conditions in addition to differentiation. Weber (1946, pp. 204–214) and Hintze (1908) made early attempts to describe these conditions, and Eisenstadt (1958), aided by some excellent descriptive and analytical accounts of both Western (e.g., Barker, 1944; Rosenberg, 1958; Tout, 1916) and non-Western (e.g., Furnivall, 1948; Kracke, 1953) societies, has turned his attention to this problem. His analysis suggests that the following conditions are among those of importance for the emergence of bureaucratic organizations: (1) a high degree of differentiation among roles and institutional spheres; (2) allocation of the crucial roles by universalistic rather than particularistic criteria; (3) extension of the boundaries of the community beyond that of any particularistic group; (4) the increasing complexity of social life; (5) the attempt by groups to develop and pursue political, economic, and social service goals which extend beyond the boundaries of any given particularistic group; and (6) the development of differences among groups concerning priority of goals and competition among them for scarce resources (Eisenstadt, 1958, p. 110).

These conditions are themselves the product of more basic changes in the structural foundations of the society which result in the gradual release of human and material resources from their moorings in ascriptive (e.g., kin and ethnic) groups, resources which become free-floating in the sense that they are subject to the competing claims of special-purpose groups (Eisenstadt, 1958; Parsons, 1961, pp. 242–249). Weber (1947, pp. 341–354) described these changes as occurring (in Western societies) over three stages: from primitive gerontocracy, through patrimonial, to bureaucratic forms of administration (Delany, 1963, pp. 460–468). One must beware, however, of the tendency to view present forms as everlasting. Weber himself apparently considered bureaucratic structures, based as they are on rational-legal authority, to be less stable than structures supported by traditional relations (Weber, 1947, p. 68). So many observers have reported contradictions in and transformations of bureaucratic structures that Delany (1963, pp. 474–479) chooses to speak of the emergence of various "post-bureaucratic" forms.

Levels of Analysis

While organizations furnish a common locus of research for many sociologists as well as members of sister disciplines, these investigators are by no means interested in finding answers to the same sorts of questions. Even apart from the variety of conceptual schemes which guide inquiry of the differences which prevail in methodological perspectives and tools utilized, investigators differ with respect to the *level* at which their analysis is placed.[1] For present purposes, the level of analysis is determined by the nature of the dependent variable, by whether the phenomena to be explained is the behavior of individual members, the functioning of some particular aspect or aspects of organizational structure, or the actions of the organization viewed as a total entity.

Some investigators are interested in explaining individual behavior within the context of organizations. At this level, the organization is viewed as "environment," and the investigator sets out to explore its impact—whether direct or contingent—on social psychological variables or processes as reflected in the behavior of individuals. Such a perspective is labeled "behavioral" and is best exemplified by the works of March and Simon (1958) and W. F. Whyte (1961).

A second approach takes as its major concern the explanation of the structural features and social processes which characterize organizations. The investigator taking this perspective may focus on the various subunits which comprise the organization (e.g., work groups, departments, authority ranks) or he may examine certain analytical variables (e.g., specialization, communication, hierarchy), attempting in both cases to account for their characteristics or values, and explore their interrelations. This level of analysis may be referred to as "structural," and examples of its use are to be found in the works of Seashore (1954) and Udy (1959b).

In the third level of analysis, the investigator focuses on the organization as an entity, viewing it as a unit in a larger system of relations. Within this perspective, the analyst may choose either to examine the relation between a specific organization and its institutional and cultural environment, as Selznick (1949) did in his study of the Tennessee Valley Authority, or he may wish

---

[1] For other discussions bearing on levels of analysis in the study of organizations, see Blau (1957), Duncan and Schnore (1959), Lazarsfeld and Menzel (1961), and Lipset, Trow, and Coleman (1956, pp. 421–425).

to examine the relations which develop among a number of organizations viewed as an interdependent system (Lieberson, 1961). This approach may be characterized as an "ecological" one.

Granting that the three levels which have been identified are somewhat arbitrary and are by no means completely unambiguous, they nevertheless are utilized to organize the main body of this chapter. Material relevant to the structural level is treated first at some length, followed by briefer discussions of the behavioral level (the individual in the organization) and the ecological level (the organization and its environment).

ORGANIZATIONAL STRUCTURE

Organizations are collectivities which have been established to achieve specific objectives. Given this definition, three foci of attention are possible, and, in fact, all three have been employed in the sociological investigation of organizational structure. First, it is possible to view organizations as *instruments* for the attainment of the specified goals. In this view, the predominant emphasis is placed on the rationality of the structure—that is, given certain goals, how effective is the organization as a means for realizing them? Second, it is possible to emphasize the fact that an organization is a *goal-directed structure* and that the specific goals pursued will determine in important respects the characteristics of the structure. Third, attention may be concentrated on the organization as a *social system* whose preservation becomes an end in itself. These three views are by no means incompatible; on the contrary, their joint consideration is essential to an understanding of any concrete organization as well as to the construction of a complete theory of organizational structure. Each of these perspectives will be examined as a means of surveying some of the current theory and research on organization, although it should be emphasized that their separation is completely artificial. Throughout the discussion, therefore, attempts are made to suggest the relevance of one perspective to the others.

THE ORGANIZATION AS INSTRUMENT

One important approach to the analysis of organizational structure is to view it from the standpoint of the contribution its various components make to rationality of action.[2] In this approach "the organization is conceived as an 'instrument'—that is, as a rationally conceived means to the realization of expressly announced group goals. Its structures are understood as tools deliberately established for the efficient realization of these group purposes" (Gouldner, 1959, p. 404). The nature of the goals served, as well as the decision-making processes involved in their selection, are outside the scope of this type of analysis. Not only is the organization as a whole expected to operate rationally, individual members of the organization are also expected to behave in a rational manner. "Such 'dual rationality' can be approximated in the case of formal organization," as Udy (1962, p. 300) points out, "only because the members of the organization are at the same time members of a larger society where integrative values can find expression independently of administrative structure." From this perspective, then, one primary organizational problem is that of seeing to it that an individual can achieve certain of his own goals most effectively by acting in such a manner that he contributes to the objectives of the organization.

While many analysts have viewed organizations primarily as rational structures, among sociologists it is Weber (1947) whose pioneering work is most closely associated with this approach, even though his anal-

---

[2] Rationality is to be understood in this context as indicating "that a series of actions is organized in such a way that it leads to a previously defined goal" (Mannheim, 1950, p. 53). Mannheim refers to this usage as "functional rationality," contrasting it with the more familiar "substantial rationality."

ysis was limited almost entirely to the administrative segments of an organization. His discussion of the characteristics of bureaucratic administration—or, more precisely, those characteristics which differentiate bureaucratic from patrimonial and patriarchal forms—can be viewed as an attempt to describe a set of elements which in combination constitutes a structure "capable of attaining the highest degree of efficiency" (Weber, 1947, p. 337) and is, therefore, technically superior to any other form of organization (Weber, 1946, p. 214). In short, he attempts to describe the most rational organizational structure.

Weber's (1947) analysis of the essential characteristics of bureaucratic structure is so well known that a brief statement of his position should suffice. He enumerated many specific structural characteristics but most important among them are the following. The organization is guided by a set of explicit and specific purposes from which a system of rules and regulations is derived that governs the operations of officials. The activities required to accomplish the purposes are distributed among offices so that each incumbent has a specified sphere of competence. The offices are arranged in a hierarchical authority structure, each official exercising and being subject to authority only in his capacity as office-holder and within the limits established by the rules. Officials are personally free, being bound to their offices by a contractual relationship and contributing their services in return for compensation, normally a salary. They regard the office as their primary occupation; on the other hand, officials cannot appropriate the office itself or any of the means of administration. Candidates for positions are selected on the basis of their technical competence, being appointed rather than elected. They are to carry out their functions in an impersonal manner (Weber, 1946, pp. 196–204; Weber, 1947, pp. 329–336). While Weber assembled these characteristics as a part of his ideal-type description of bureaucratic administration, his discussion

may be regarded as a complex hypothesis specifying the several major components of a rational administrative structure. Prior to considering some portions of this hypothesis, however, it would be well to recognize an important assertion that, in a sense, underlies Weber's discussion of the specific characteristics; namely, formalization of structure is functional for organizational rationality.

The Functions of Formal Structure

Formal structures are composed of sets of positions the relations among which are specified, at least in part, by explicit rules. When rationality of operations is desired, prescribing the rights and duties of positions independent of the characteristics of their occupants has numerous advantages over structures where these relations develop over time as a function of the interaction of particular persons. To begin with, the smooth functioning of the organization is not primarily dependent on the sentiments which members hold toward one another—on the sociometric structure. As Merton notes: "formality facilitates the interaction of the occupants of offices despite their (possibly hostile) private attitudes toward one another" (1957, p. 195). In fact, in the bureaucratic type of structure, the development of even positive sentiments among officials and between officials and clients is discouraged, emotional ties being considered the enemy of discipline and judgment.

Another functional consequence of formal structure is that the organization becomes less dependent on the participation of any particular person. Its fate is not tied to the life of a single individual inasmuch as its operating code includes rules for the replacement of officials at all levels. Grusky (1961, p. 267), noting a relationship between size of firm and stability and demonstrating that frequency of succession in top positions is positively related to size of firm, concludes that "the more bureaucratized the administrative component of an organization, the less the instability that is created

by administrative succession." A further and
related consequence is that the organization
need not depend on the recruitment of
"great men" for its key positions. While
superior leaders and technical experts may
improve the overall effectiveness of organizations, the survival of the latter is not made
to depend on the location of such superhuman talent. Wolin has pointed out that
organizational structure and scientific methodology perform similar functions in this
respect: "Method, like organization, is the
salvation of puny men, the compensatory
device for individual foibles, the gadget
which allows mediocrity to transcend its
limitations. On the one side organization,
by simplifying and routinizing procedures,
eliminates the need for surpassing talent.
It is predicated on 'average human beings'"
(Wolin, 1960, p. 383).

As might be expected, these same features
have been shown to have their negative side.
"If reserved detachment characterizes the
attitudes of the members of the organization
toward one another, it is unlikely that high
esprit de corps will develop among them"
(Blau, 1956, p. 33). Succession is rarely the
neutral process envisioned by the rational
theorist (Gouldner, 1954; Guest, 1962), and
the extent to which individual creativity
and leadership ability are important institutional requisites varies from one organization to another. If the nature of the tasks
to be performed by the organization demands creativity on the part of personnel,
then overly formal arrangements may interfere with or suppress this talent and be detrimental to organizational effectiveness. For
example, the same structures which render
effective the operations of clerical personnel
would play havoc if utilized to organize the
work of research chemists (Burns & Stalker,
1961), and, under some conditions, imaginative institutional leadership may not be a
luxury but a necessity (Selznick, 1957).

Some of the specific structural characteristics of organizations which Weber viewed
as contributing to rationality of operations
will now be examined. In each case, the
alleged contribution of a given characteristic
is briefly stated and some of the recent research and conjectures on the problem summarized.

Selected Structural Characteristics

Goal specificity. The presence of explicit
and specific objectives is fundamental to
the conception of the organization as a rational system. Parsons (1960), as has been
noted, regards this characteristic as so important that he made it the primary criterion
for differentiating organizations from other
types of social structures. This emphasis is
well placed. In the most rational case, the
organization is brought into being as a
means for attaining some specific objective.
The nature of the goal provides the criteria
to be used in the recruitment of personnel
and determines what resources are required
and the priorities for their acquisition. It
also furnishes a basis (relative contribution
to the attainment of the objectives) for
determining the amount of compensation
participants receive and, in part, for allocating authority among them. It should be
apparent, then, that to the extent that organizational goals are diffuse or lacking in
clarity and to the extent that multiple, possibly conflicting, goals are being pursued,
the organization will lack the rational basis
for making these critical decisions.

If organizations as a class are compared
with other kinds of social structures, their
objectives do appear to be relatively clear-
cut and explicit; yet, there is much variation
among organizations in this respect. Organizations differ, for example, with respect to
the specificity of their goals. Clark (1956)
notes that in some organizations the goals
are "undefined" and hence precarious, and
March and Simon (1958, pp. 156, 194) suggest that goals differ in the degree to
which they are "operational," that is, the
extent to which there is agreement on the
criteria for determining whether particular
activities do or do not contribute to the
goals. In universities and hospitals as com-

pared with factories or commercial establishments, for example, "the general goal of the organization specifies an area of activity instead of a specific activity and therefore is subject to wide differences in specific interpretations" (J. D. Thompson & Bates, 1957, p. 329). There exist differences, too, among organizations in the amount of consensus among members on the nature of the objectives of the organization. In a study of a large, general hospital, for example, Wessen (1958, p. 459) asked 75 respondents to list the basic aims of the institution and found considerable disagreement among them, the patterning of the responses being associated with membership in the various status groups in the hospital. If multiple objectives are being pursued, there exists the strong possibility that efforts to secure one objective interfere with the attainment of another. To use hospitals again as an illustration, the goal of providing optimal care for patients may at times interfere with the goal of furnishing medical students and other trainees with those experiences and responsibilities which will enable them to acquire the requisite skills of their trade.

Also, organizations differ radically in their need for consensus on goals, as Etzioni (1960, pp. 128–137) notes. Custody oriented prisons, for example, are expected to operate with little consensus between staff and inmates on objectives, but most voluntary associations, such as the Red Cross, could not long tolerate pronounced differences in goals between leaders and rank-and-file members.

Many investigators have reported that while an organization's objectives may be both specific and explicit, they often are not the actual objectives being pursued, that is, one must often distinguish between the professed and the operative goals of organizations (Selznick, 1943). The actual goals may be consciously concealed from the public by the organizational elite, as in the case of a subversive organization seeking popular support (Selznick, 1952), or they may have evolved over time in response to internal or external pressures without conscious action on the part of officials. A discussion of the conditions under which one set of organizational goals is displaced or succeeded by another is deferred to a later section.

Some specific evidence relating goal specificity to other organizational characteristics is contained in a study of 211 voluntary associations conducted by Simpson and Gulley (1962). Organizations pursuing specific objectives were found to possess a more centralized authority structure, be less concerned with the involvement of members, and put less emphasis on maintaining channels of internal communication than organizations pursuing diffuse goals. This suggests that goal specificity is associated with rationality of operations in the sense that less energy is expended in goal-specific organizations on self-maintenance.

Goal implementation. Organizational rationality, however, does not depend solely on the specificity and explicitness of the objectives pursued. Goals, after all, are only statements of valued or desired future states, and mechanisms must be established for their realization. The rational implementation of goals is a major concern of Herbert Simon who has been guided in his formulation of the problem by the pioneering work of Barnard (1938). Simon (1957, p. 102) argues that organizational rationality is achieved to the extent that individual members are subject to the influence of the organization in the decisions they make. Because every decision contains value as well as factual premises, it is not possible to characterize any given decision as being either "true" or "false"; however, if a decision is viewed as a means to the realization of some objective, it can be evaluated in terms of its effectiveness for reaching that goal. Rationality of behavior is dependent on the building of "means-ends chains" in which a given decision is viewed as a means to some end which in turn is considered a means to some further objective (Simon, 1957, p. 62). (The ultimate purposes cannot be evaluated on any objective basis but are determined by consensus or decree.)

Organizations enhance the rationality of action in two ways. First, they see to it that the aims (value premises) which govern the contributions of each organizational member and subunit function as means for the attainment of the larger organizational purposes. Thus, there is established a hierarchy of goals, in which each level is "considered as an end relative to the levels below it and as a means relative to the levels above it. Through the hierarchical structure of ends, behavior attains integration and consistency, for each member of a set of behavior alternatives is then weighed in terms of a comprehensive scale of values—the 'ultimate' ends" (Simon, 1957, p. 63). In an organization where the division of labor is "by purpose," this goal hierarchy can be identified with the organizational hierarchy so that any given subunit can be viewed as constituting the means for attaining ends set by the level above it and so on up to the policy-making level where the ultimate value decisions are made (Barnard, 1938, p. 137). Second, organizations "permit stable expectations to be formed by each member of the group as to the behavior of the other members under specified conditions" (Simon, 1957, p. 100). Such knowledge allows a given member to predict with some degree of accuracy the consequences of selecting one or another alternative course of action. One factor making for predictability is that organizations typically limit members not only in choice of goals to be pursued but also in their selection of instrumentalities. The mechanisms by which these controls over the actions of members are effected are precisely those one associates with bureaucratic structure: a division of labor, a set of general rules and procedures, a system of authority, regularized channels of communication, and training and indoctrination programs (Simon, 1957, pp. 102–103).

Simon's analysis deals with many aspects of organizational structure, some of which are discussed at greater length below. However, one problem which is directly related to his schema is that of subgoal formation. To the extent that general organizational purposes are subdivided so that they may be allocated among the various organizational units (e.g., one group assuming responsibility for production, another for sales, and another for the development of new products) there arises the danger that a given unit will pursue its objectives without regard for the welfare of other units or that of the larger organization. Dalton's (1959) investigation of the conflicts and power struggles that occur between staff and line officials and among various types of line officials in manufacturing concerns provides ample documentation of these tendencies. His descriptions emphasize the motivational aspects of these conflicts as a manager, guided by self-interest or by an identification with his unit, attempts to extend the functions and influence of his own department at the expense of his "competitors." March and Simon (1958, pp. 151–154), however, emphasize that such behavior has a cognitive as well as a motivational basis. Thus, at the individual level, they note that members will selectively perceive their "environment and attempt to rationalize away discordant information; at the group level, there is a reinforcement of these perceptions resulting from the selective content of in-group communication; and at the organizational level, there is again a reinforcement because of a selective exposure to environmental stimuli. Finally, Landsberger (1961a) argues that yet another basis for subgoal formation is the occurrence of objective dilemmas confronting organizations which pit the interests of one department against those of another.

Whatever its basis, the process of subgoal formation appears to be so pervasive a phenomenon as to call into question the usefulness of Simon's hierarchy of goals model. Eisenstadt, for example, has argued that organizational subgroups "may have entirely different conceptions of, and attitudes toward, the organization's goals and needs" and that the interaction among these groups "should be viewed as a continuous process of communication, of allocation of rewards, of adjustment of mutual perception, a process by which some—but only *some*—fusion (the extent of which necessarily varies from case to case and from period to period) between the motives and goals of different individuals and sub-groups and the overall organizational goals is effected" (Eisenstadt, 1958, p. 113).

The manner in which goals are implemented depends in part on the nature of the goals. The conventional bureaucracy functions best in circumstances where there is a large amount of routine work to be accomplished. Lower officials handle the bulk of the work by simply following regular procedures. It is only the exceptional case, one to which the regular rules do not apply, which must be called to the attention of superiors. Superiors make decisions about such cases—to change the rules, to make an exception to the rules, to ignore the case— which are passed down to subordinates. If virtually every case is exceptional in some sense, however, then the number of rules and their significance is small. Lower officials are expected to exercise discretion and, consequently, are usually better trained. Also, whereas officials in the former case can be evaluated on their basis of conformity to the rules, the latter officials must be evaluated on the basis of the results they achieve or, if results are difficult to evaluate, on the logic of their approach.

Division of labor. "Work division is the foundation of organization; indeed, the reason for organization," according to Luther Gulick (Gulick & Urwick, 1937, p. 3), an early student of administrative science. Obvious advantages are to be gained from a parceling out of the work of the organization so that a given individual does not perform all the tasks necessary for the accomplishment of the purposes of the organization, but some subset of them. Specialization of work force allows the organization to take advantage of particular skills a member may possess, and it also fosters the development of such skills through repetition and practice. Which particular sets of activities should be placed together to form a job and how persons should be allocated among these jobs is a problem to which such management scientists as Fayol (1930) and Gulick have devoted much attention. Implicit in this approach, however, has been a tendency "to view the employee as an inert instrument performing the tasks assigned to him" (March & Simon, 1958, p. 29) or, more brutally, in the case of factory workers, as an appendage to an incomplete machine (Bell, 1947; V. A. Thompson, 1961, p. 53). This view of man is not only morally unacceptable; it is administratively naive since it does not take into account the importance of motivational factors in job performance (Friedmann, 1955; March & Simon, 1958).

More clearly than in the case of any other organizational characteristic, the division of labor within an organization reflects the technological requirements of the tasks to be performed (Dubin, 1958, pp. 169–184). Sociologists, however, have not been particularly successful in building technological variables into their conceptual schemes. Notable exceptions to this generalization are the work of Cottrell (1955), J. D. Thompson and Bates (1957), Udy (1959b), and Woodward (1958). Thompson and Bates, for example, have identified two dimensions of technology having general significance for organizational structure. The first is the extent to which the technology is lodged in nonhuman rather than human resources, or the "ratio of mechanization to professionalization," and the second is the degree to which the technology can be adapted to serve various kinds of goals. These variables are expected to have consequences for many aspects of organizational functioning including policy formation, the management of resources, and the execution of policy. To give an example of the consequences of the first variable in the area of execution,

Thompson and Bates argue that "if the technology has a high ratio of mechanization, executing problems are likely to be of an engineering nature since specialization is largely in the machine, the bases for human differentiation are small, and the human 'zones of indifference' are great [whereas] if the technology has a low ratio of mechanization. . . . the coordination and integration of human activities will be a major administrative concern" (Thompson & Bates, 1957, p. 341), differentiation will be large, and the human "zones of indifference," small.

That specialization within an organization is in part a function of technology is clear; but that it has other sources is equally apparent. For example, data assembled by Udy (1959b; 1961) suggest that one basis for the division of labor within an organization may be the wish of those with power to escape from duties regarded as unpleasant (Blau & Scott, 1962, p. 210). V. A. Thompson has argued that the elaborate division of labor found in industrial situations is a reflection in part of management's "desire to avoid dependence on skilled workers; to keep workers docile by holding the threat of displacement over them and reducing their power" (1961, p. 56). More generally, one of Thompson's major theses is that much of the specialization to be found in organizations has no basis in the technical requirements of the task but is retained to bolster the hierarchical status structure. Udy is in substantial agreement, pointing out that the allocation of rewards by members of higher to those of lower authority constitutes "a mechanism whereby specialization can be 'artificially' institutionalized by management through its control over the reward system" (1962, p. 302).

It is apparent, then, that some but not all types of specialization may be viewed as contributing to organizational rationality. These examples, in which the status structure of the organization affects the division of labor among participants, provide clearcut instances of the intrusion of the organi-

zation as a social system on the organization as rational tool.

Rewards. Rewards must be allocated among participants in some fashion in return for their participation in the organization. Udy (1959b, p. 101) has indicated that reward systems can be viewed as fulfilling four general functions: (1) the assurance of adequate recruitment of personnel; (2) the maintenance of an acceptable level of performance on the part of participants; (3) the integration of the authority structure, such as occurs when higher officials control the distribution of rewards to subordinates; and (4) the assurance of adequate role differentiation, that is, the manipulation of rewards so as to support the division of labor required by technological and other determinants.

All four of these functions cannot be considered here, but the first, the assurance of adequate recruitment of personnel, is briefly discussed since it is the focal problem in the Barnard-Simon theory of organizational equilibrium (Barnard, 1938, pp. 139–160; Simon, 1957, pp. 110–122). The aim of this theory is to state "the conditions under which an organization can induce its members to continue their participation, and hence assure organizational survival" (March & Simon, 1958, p. 84). Briefly, the theory postulates that (1) each organizational participant receives inducements from the organization in return for his contributions to it; (2) each participant will continue his participation only so long as, in his view, the inducements offered to him are equal to or greater than the contributions required of him; (3) the contributions of one group provide the basis for the inducements offered another; and (4) an organization will continue to exist only so long as it receives sufficient contributions to cover the inducements it must offer (March & Simon, 1958, p. 84). To avoid being tautological, the theory requires independent measures of the behavior of the participants as they join, remain in, and leave the organization and of the balance of inducements and contributions as perceived by each participant. Measuring the latter variable is complicated if inducements-contributions utilities are to be directly observed or estimated. However, measurement is simplified if certain assumptions are made about the utility functions (e.g., that they change slowly, that they are similar for similar types of persons, etc.) (March & Simon, 1958, pp. 84–87).

Krupp (1961, pp. 105–117) has pointed to a basic difficulty with the inducements-contributions schema: The willingness of persons to make contributions to the organizations is not viewed as independent of organizational control. Barnard, for example, distinguished between organizational inducements—rewards offered by the organization in return for contributions—and organizational "persuasion" which he described in the following way: "if an organization is unable to afford incentives adequate to the personal contributions it requires it will perish unless it can by persuasion so change the desires of enough men that the incentives it can offer will be adequate" (Barnard, 1939, p. 149). Krupp (1961, pp. 107–108) argues that to talk of "inducements that win participation because they create satisfactions at a given level of willingness" and at the same time of "inducements that shift the level of willingness" leaves the analyst with an extremely complex view of organizational equilibrium. In fact, "an organization analysis that uses so complex a structure of equilibrium conditions and forces comes perilously close to establishing an equilibrium in which 'anything goes.'"

The authority structure. Perhaps the primary structural feature of organizations according to Weber (1947) is the presence of a hierarchy of authority. In the typical case, offices are arranged in a pyramid of ascending authority, each lower office being under the control and supervision of a higher one. Weber was particularly concerned with differentiating between authority and other types of control, such as power or influence,

and toward that end three criteria are employed (Blau & Scott, 1962, pp. 27–30; Weber, 1947, pp. 324–328). First, authority is distinguished from power in that under authority orders are voluntarily obeyed, that is, there exists under authority "a certain minimum of voluntary submission; thus an interest (based on ulterior motives or genuine acceptance) in obedience" (Weber, 1947, p. 324). Second, authority implies the a priori acceptance of a directive, and this criterion differentiates it from influence, in which one person controls another only to the extent that he is able to persuade him to change his own action premises. Simon makes this criterion the basis for his definition of authority: "a subordinate is said to accept authority whenever he permits his behavior to be guided by the decision of a superior, without independently examining the merits of that decision" (Simon, 1957, p. 11). Third, authority is present only to the extent that there exists a value orientation among persons subject to the control that defines the exercise of that control as legitimate. This criterion, which differentiates authority from both power and influence, was for Weber the crucial one, and he used differences in the types of beliefs—traditional, charismatic, legal—which attribute legitimacy to a system as the basis for constructing his well-known typology of authority systems (Weber, 1947, pp. 328–386). "Today," according to Weber (1947, p. 313), "the most usual basis of legitimacy is the belief in legality, the readiness to conform with rules which are formally correct and have been imposed by accepted procedure."

While Weber recognized the importance of other motives for compliance (e.g., self-interest) and other forms of control (e.g., coercion), he gave prominence in his discussion of organizations to the existence of a legitimate order. He argued that "no system of authority voluntarily limits itself to the appeal to material or affectual or ideal motives as a basis for guaranteeing its continuance. In addition every such system attempts to establish and to cultivate the belief in its 'legitimacy'" (Weber, 1947, p. 325).

It was Weber's belief that the presence of such a system of values provides the only sufficiently reliable basis for a stable and effective system of control. Simon (1952) has noted that legitimacy may be viewed as a psychological rather than a legal concept by being interpreted as an internalized attitude on the part of the individual which motivates him to accept his place in a system of authority. But legitimacy can also be viewed as a distinctly sociological concept (Blau & Scott, 1962, p. 29). To the extent that a value orientation arises among subordinates which supports the belief that the commands of a superior should be obeyed, then failure on the part of some member to comply may not only lead to sanctions applied by his superior but by his peer group as well. As Homans observes: "a leader's authority depends not only on his own relation with his followers but also his followers' relation with one another" (Homans, 1961, p. 295).

Some theorists have argued that the traditional focus on authority with its emphasis on control by consent has led to a studied neglect of the conflicts of interest which develop in all organizations and in the exercise of power as a widely-used mechanism of control. This imbalance, if it exists, is somewhat redressed by Etzioni's (1961) monograph, the principal focus of which is power. Types of power are differentiated in terms of the kinds of sanctions—physical, material, or symbolic—exercised to control the behavior of organizational participants. Of course, power becomes authority if the exercise of sanctions is viewed as legitimate by persons subject to them, and Etzioni argues that this will vary depending on the type of sanction employed: The use of symbolic sanctions is most likely to be viewed as legitimate, material sanctions less likely, and physical sanctions least so. In a strict sense, however, the use of sanctions of any kind by the superior is an indication of the erosion of the authority structure. As Blau has noted:

if a supervisor commands the voluntary obedience of subordinates, he need not induce them to obey him by promising them rewards or threatening them with punishment. In fact, the use of sanctions undermines authority. A supervisor who is in the habit of invoking sanctions to back his orders . . . shows that he does not expect unqualified compliance. As subordinates learn that he does not expect it, they will no longer feel obligated unconditionally to accept his directives (Blau, 1956, p. 76).

This is not to argue, however, that much of the compliance behavior that occurs within organizations is not a consequence of the application of power rather than the operation of an authority structure. If power— the ability to sanction—is an important basis for control within organizations, how is it that Weber (1947) and, consequently, his host of intellectual offspring, devoted relatively little attention to it? Several reasons may be advanced. First, as has been noted, Weber restricted his attention almost exclusively to the administrative staff as opposed to the "lower participants" (e.g., blue-collar workers, clients, students, enlisted men) of the organization, and it is undoubtedly the case that sanctions play a much larger role in effecting control over the latter than the former category. Second, and this is somewhat more speculative, it may be that officials in the particular bureaucracies with which Weber was most familiar, namely, the German governmental bureaus of the late nineteenth and early twentieth centuries, were more willing to accept as legitimate the legal order and the hierarchy based on it than is the case with members in many organizations today. This argument receives some support from the work of Bendix (1956) in which historical data are adduced to support the thesis that the ideologies which justify particular production arrangements differ from place to place and are subject to change over time. Third, Weber appears to assume the existence of a high, positive correlation between position in the hierarchy and technical competence—a circumstance which tends to strengthen authority—and it is possible that at the time in which he wrote, this relation was reasonably strong.[3] Today, however, with the proliferation of technical specialties and the acquisition of special skills by personnel in schools outside of the organization, it is frequently the case that a superior is less competent in a given specialty than are the employees he is expected to supervise. This growing discrepancy between position and competence is one of the most pervasive features of modern organization and necessarily undermines the stability of the authority structure. In fact, some observers have gone so far as to suggest that the hierarchical authority structure is an anachronism that is injurious to the rational operation of an organization (V. A. Thompson, 1961).

Cross-cultural data from 150 production organizations located in 150 different non-industrial societies as analyzed by Udy (1959a) indicate that a hierarchy of authority is not indispensable to and may, in some circumstances, interfere with organizational rationality. Udy identifies seven characteristics of organizations: (1) a hierarchical authority structure having three or more levels of authority; (2) a specialized administrative staff—in which persons are engaged in activities other than physical work; (3) rewards differentiated by office; (4) limited objectives with the organization being exclusively concerned with the production of material goods; (5) rewards differentiated by performance; (6) participation based on mutual limited agreements; and (7) compensatory rewards with members of higher authority distributing rewards to members of lower. In the sample of organizations examined, the first three characteristics were found to be positively interrelated (all relationships positive and significant by Yule's coefficient of association); the remaining four were likewise positively interrelated (all relationships positive and five of the six significant); but there was no association between the elements of the two clusters (9 of the 12 pairs were negative, but only 2 were significantly so, while none of the 3 positive relations was significant).[4] These data support the conclusion that a hierarchical authority structure with its related characteristics (the presence of a specialized administrative staff and the differentiation of rewards by office) is not invariably found in association with other organizational characteristics usually regarded as rational. The absence of any association between the hierarchical and rational elements is possibly the result of an inclusion within Udy's sample of a considerable number of organizations in which a previously existing political hierarchy had been imposed on a production situation (through "custodial recruitment"). In these situations, role assignment was based on ascribed political status, rewards were not likely to be distributed according to performance, and organizational objectives were more often diffuse rather than specific (Udy, 1959b, pp. 55-71). In such cases, it is not the hierarchy per se which impedes rationality, but the specific character of the hierarchy, an ascribed political order which in addition to its other functions is engaged in production. With organizations of this type in Udy's sample where the relation between hierarchy and rationality is assuredly negative, there must be others where the relation between these characteristics is positive in order to produce

---

[3] It must be noted here in passing that competence of officials does not constitute a basis for authority in the same sense as does incumbency in an office, although some have implied that this is the case. Rather, possessing competence is not unlike possessing sanctioning powers: both constitute potential means of rewarding or punishing others, and both can become transformed into authority through a process to be considered below in a discussion of the supervisor as leader.

[4] Udy interprets these data as indicating a negative association between the two clusters of variables. However, the data appear to be more in conformity with the interpretation that the clusters are unrelated.

the absence of association reported for the total sample.

Turning to data from an industrial society, Stinchcombe (1959), on the basis of research on the United States construction industry, concludes that, under certain conditions, a hierarchy which directs and supervises the performance of tasks may be unnecessary. Many of these conditions are peculiar to the construction industry, but one—the presence of a professionalized work force—is of general significance. It has long been recognized that certain characteristics of professional workers, in particular, their emphasis on internalized norms and standards reinforced by colleague surveillance, make them obstreperous organizational members (Goode, 1957; Hughes, 1958, pp. 131–138). So reluctant are most professionals to submit to the authority of any man, but especially a "layman," that in those instances where they possess sufficient power to control the conditions of their work they resist hierarchical regulation of any but the most peripheral aspects of their performance. In such circumstances, there usually develops a dual structure, one aspect of which is responsible for the "administrative" tasks and organized along traditional hierarchical lines, and the other performing the "professional" operations and organized at least partially according to collegial principles (Clark, 1961; Etzioni, 1959; Mary E. Goss, 1961; Kornhauser, 1962).

As the tasks performed by organizations become increasingly technical, one may expect more and more separation between what Parsons (1960, pp. 60–65) has referred to as the "technical" and the "managerial" authority structures. However, to jump to the conclusion that hierarchical control for all tasks and in all circumstances is detrimental to rationality of operations seems unwarranted. Stinchcombe (1959, p. 183) appears to agree with this conclusion since he regards both "bureaucracy" (the presence of a specialized administrative staff and supervisory hierarchy) and professionalization as two alternative methods of institu-

tionalizing rationality, the appropriate form determined by the nature of the work to be done and the characteristics of the work force.

Social insulation. Certain of the characteristics which Weber identified as contributing to rationality may be viewed as insulating the organization from its social context. For example, his stipulation that officials be appointed by free contract according to their technical qualifications and that they regard their office as their primary occupation (Weber, 1947, pp. 334–335) is intended to assure that the selection criteria are organizationally relevant and that the officials selected will be relatively free of conflicting social affiliations, whether religious, economic, political, or familial. Research conducted in non-Western societies, where organizations are less likely to be well insulated from other social institutions, indicates the importance of this characteristic for organizational rationality. In his study of a number of Japanese factories, for example, Abegglen (1958) suggests that both the bases of recruitment—education, which is primarily related to family status—and the type of contract between worker and management—what amounts to a life-time commitment on the part of both parties—impairs organizational flexibility in adapting to changing circumstances and, hence, rationality. Berger (1957, pp. 135–145), in a study of the Egyptian civil service based on a 16 per cent sample of officials in four ministries, reports that over 40 per cent of these officials believed that in addition to education and experience such criteria as family connections, wealth, and social background should be taken into account in the selection of civil servants. Berger indicates that the services offered by these officials to clients as well as the relations between superiors and subordinates within the service were frequently characterized by particularism, friends and relatives of officials more likely to receive favorable treatment.

The most conclusive study relating recruitment practices with organizational rationality is that reported by Udy (1962) based on a sample of 34 production organizations each located in a different nonindustrial society. Udy differentiated between five types of recruitment ranging from that involving "voluntary self-commitment and self-defined interest" (high insulation) to that "required by compulsory political ascription" (low insulation). Seven characteristics, including specific job assignment, the presence of specialization, and the distribution of rewards by members of higher authority to those of lower in return for the latter's participation, are taken as indicators of administrative rationality. Organizations with high insulation were more likely to exhibit rational characteristics than those marked by lower social insulation. Of course, as Stinchcombe (1961) has emphasized, the contribution made by social insulation to administrative rationality is particularly significant in societies characterized by ascriptive political and kinship structures, such as those which comprise Udy's sample. But regardless of the specific character of the society in which an organization functions, it would appear important that the organization retain control over the criteria by which its personnel are recruited for service.

Organizationally controlled recruitment criteria are, then, one important mechanism fostering insulation of the organization from its social environment. But Weber (1947) was also aware of the need for others. His insistence that officials, once recruited, should regard their office as their sole, or at least their primary, occupation indicates his recognition that other occupational affiliations of members may have consequences for their performance within an organization. However, it is not simply other occupational statuses which may have consequences for organizational performance. Diamond (1958), for example, in his analysis of the Virginia Company in the seventeenth century, shows how various kinds of statuses of company members acquired in the New World, such as landowner and renter, master and servant, old resident and newcomer, gradually came to take precedence over their affiliation with the company, undermining the legitimacy of organizational control and, eventually, transforming the organization into a society. Diamond's analysis indicates that, at one extreme, it is possible for the extra-organizational affiliations of organization members to assume such importance that they render inconsequential organizational statuses. At the other extreme, it is possible for an organization to restrict the outside affiliations of some of its members in such a way that the only significant status is that held within the organization. Organizations imposing such restrictions upon their members have been aptly labeled "total institutions" by Goffman (1961) and include such seemingly disparate units as mental hospitals, concentration camps, army barracks, and monasteries. Of course, the majority of organizations lie somewhere in between these polar situations exercising some control over the outside affiliations of their members but rarely being in a position completely to dominate or eliminate these relationships. In his recent popular work, W. H. Whyte (1956) argues that present-day organizations are rapidly (and inappropriately) extending their control to encompass more and more of the "private" lives of their participants. There has been, however, relatively little empirical research on this problem (but see the study by Schein and Ott [1962]), and even less attention devoted to such theoretical problems as: What are the consequences for organizations of various types of outside external affiliations on the part of its participants? Under what conditions does an organization attempt to extend its control over these relations? When is it likely to be successful in these attempts?

Communication networks. For adequate recognition of the contribution of communication channels to the effective functioning of organizations, it is necessary to turn momentarily from the work of Weber to that of Barnard. It is clear that Barnard (1938) viewed communication networks, carrying their freight of information, influence, and inducements, as the crucial component of organization structure. Several characteristics of effectively functioning channels were noted by Barnard, among them that the channels "should be definitely known," that there should be a "formal channel of communication to every member," that the lines linking members should be "as direct and short as possible," and that the "complete line of communication should usually be used," that is, a link should not be bypassed (1938, pp. 175–177).

The specification of explicit channels which link all members and the use of mediated links in which B communicates to A and C but not to D while C communicates to B and D but not to A are perhaps the central features of communication networks in formal organizations. Ideally, this system assures that each member will have access to the information he requires to perform his work and will be spared the burden of listening to matters that do not concern him. With an apparatus devised by Bavelas (1950), it is possible to simulate these features in an experimental setting in order to investigate the consequences of various patternings of communication networks. Numerous studies making use of the apparatus have shown that groups are more effective (perform assigned tasks faster and with fewer errors) if a hierarchical structure is imposed on or emerges within the group (Guetzkow & Simon, 1955; Leavitt, 1951). Blau and Scott (1962, pp. 116–134), however, cite numerous experimental and field studies which indicate that the hierarchical structuring of communication is only functional for the performance of tasks involving coordination (of persons, materials, information). If the task is one of generating new ideas or of working on difficult problems to which there is a single best solution, then a structure permitting a free flow of communication among all participants appears to be the more effective one.

Field studies of formal organizations indicate that the formal communication channels are always supplemented and often

replaced by informal channels which develop among members. The use of such informal channels may either inhibit or contribute to the organization's effectiveness. Simpson (1959), for example, in a study of communication in a textile mill, concludes that the organization benefited from the actions of first-line foremen who informally coordinated their efforts and settled their difficulties rather than referring all problems to their respective superiors and waiting for general solutions to be worked out and passed down. Also, Blau (1955, pp. 99–116) argues that agents in a federal investigation office made better decisions because they informally discussed their case problems with colleagues, although such discussions were prohibited by the rules. On the other hand, Georgopoulos and Mann (1962, pp. 525–531), analyzing data obtained from 10 general hospitals, conclude that there was a positive correlation between the quality of nursing performance and the use by nurses of formal rather than informal channels for the communication of task-relevant information. Of course, what is required at this point are attempts to examine the conditions under which informal channels develop and the circumstances which determine their consequences for the formal structure.

Investigators have long noted the close relation between the structuring of communication and the power or authority structure. A time-honored method of obtaining and retaining power in a system is to gain control over the communication channels. Thus, Lipset, Trow, and Coleman (1956) describe the advantages accruing to incumbent union officials from their control over the official media of communication, and McCleery's (1957) research shows how custody officials in a prison obtained power by gaining control over the communications system. (Leavitt's [1951] experimental studies found that persons occupying key positions in the communication network were more likely to be considered "leaders" by others in the network.) However, a study of communication and control contrasting a medical and a surgical ward of a general hospital by Rose Coser (1962) indicates that the two structures are not invariably congruent. According to her description,

while the line of communication on the medical floor is clear-cut and follows a scalar system, decision-making there generally proceeds through consensus. On the surgical floor, however, where the line of communication is not strictly adhered to, authority is not, as might be expected, diffused and shared, but tends to be concentrated and *arbitrary,* with decisions proceeding by fiat from the visiting doctor or the chief resident (Rose Coser, 1962, p. 15).

Circumscribed autonomy. The final set of structural characteristics to be considered are those that assure that members will have the proper degree of dependence on the organization. A delicate balance must be struck between autonomy and dependency, particularly in the upper levels of the organization. That is, officials must be willing to accept responsibility and exercise initiative but within overall limits imposed by the organization. Weber considered both the characteristics of officials and structural features of the bureaucracy which contributed to the attainment of this state of controlled autonomy. For example, the use of free men rather than slaves or serfs and the provision for tenure appointments were thought to encourage independence on the part of officials. On the other hand, the stipulation that officials were to be appointed rather than elected, that they were not to appropriate the facilities of their offices, and that they were to be salaried were features designed to assure their dependence on the hierarchy (Weber, 1947, pp. 330–336).

It is obvious that problems occur for the organization if the dependency-autonomy balance is upset in either direction. Merton (1957, pp. 195–206), in his classic paper on bureaucratic structure and personality, argues that many devices used to secure conformity to established rules and procedures (e.g., promotion by seniority, pensions, incremental salaries) have the unanticipated

consequence of fostering timidity, conservatism, and ritualism among officials. At the other extreme, the benefices and fiefs which allowed members of patrimonial bureaucracies too much independence from organizational authority have their present-day counterparts in modern organizations; for example, the research scientist whose ability to obtain grants frees him to some extent from organizational controls (Vollmer, 1963, pp. 99–103).

The Interrelation of Structural Characteristics

Several of the characteristics specified by Weber (1947) as contributing to organizational rationality have been considered and various problems associated with each have been noted. An important question that remains, however, is the extent to which these characteristics are interrelated so as to form a consistent system. Relatively little research has been done on this problem since most of the studies stimulated by Weber's conception have taken his characteristics en masse as a measuring stick to be held up to a specific organization in order to determine the "goodness of fit." The most important research examining the interrelation of characteristics is that conducted by Udy (1962) who has ingeniously exploited for theoretical purposes the variety of organizational forms found in preindustrial societies. His conclusion, based on data taken from the Human Relations Area File for a sample of 150 production organizations, is that while there are important exceptions, "relationships between many of the internal structural characteristics of production organizations exhibit a remarkable degree of consistency" (Udy, 1959b, p. 48). The data which best support this assertion are taken from his examination of a subsample of 34 "bureaucratic" organizations—organizations having three or more levels of authority (Udy, 1962). For this study, Udy specified seven characteristics which Weber and others have identified with administrative rationality:

TABLE 1
ADMINISTRATIVE RATIONALITY IN 34 NONINDUSTRIAL PRODUCTION ORGANIZATIONS[a, b]

Organization	Limited Objectives	Segmental Participation	Performance Emphasis	Specific Job Assignment	Specialization	Compensatory Rewards	Central Management
Iroquois	X	X	X	X	X	X	X
Navaho	X	X	X	X	X	X	X
Paiute	X	X	X	X	X	X	X
Sanpoil	X	X	X	X	X	X	X
Sinkaietk	X	X	O	X	X	X	X
Nambicuara	X	X	O	X	X	X	X
Otoro	O	X	O	X	X	X	X
Hopi	O	X	O	X	X	X	X
Tikopia	O	O	X	X	X	X	X
Kabyles	O	O	X	X	X	X	X
Jukun	O	O	X	O	X	X	X
Tallensi	O	O	X	X	O	X	X
Haida	O	O	O	X	X	X	X
Haitians	O	O	O	X	X	X	X
Dahomeans	O	O	O	X	O	X	X
Tarahumara	O	O	O	X	O	X	X
Turkana	O	O	O	X	O	X	X
Camayura	O	O	O	X	O	X	X
Betsileo	O	O	O	O	X	X	X
Trobrianders	O	O	O	O	X	X	X
Pukapukans	O	O	O	O	X	O	X
Malay	O	O	O	O	X	O	X
Bemba	O	O	O	O	O	X	X
Crow	O	O	O	O	O	X	X
Ifaluk	O	O	O	O	O	X	X
Ila	O	O	O	O	O	X	X
Kikuyu	O	O	O	O	O	X	X
Lobi	O	O	O	O	O	X	X
Papago	O	O	O	O	O	X	X
Sotho	O	O	O	O	O	X	X
Winnebago	O	O	O	O	O	X	X
Dogon	O	O	O	O	O	O	X
Tarasco	O	O	O	O	O	O	O
Tibetans	O	O	O	O	O	O	O

[a] Source: Udy, 1962, p. 303. For references, see Udy, 1959b, pp. 139–158 ff.
[b] Coefficient of reproducibility = .95.

(1) an orientation to limited objectives—the restriction of purpose to the production of certain products; (2) segmental participation —participation based on mutual contractual agreements; (3) a performance emphasis— rewards based in part on work contributed; (4) specific job assignments—the "continuous assignment by management of particular persons to particular roles"; (5) specialization —the concurrent performance of three or more different operations by different members; (6) compensatory rewards—the allocation of rewards by members of higher to those of lower authority; and (7) centralized management—the presence of a "single internal source of ultimate authority" (Udy, 1962, pp. 301–302).

The findings are presented in Table 1 where an X indicates that a characteristic is present in the organization, an O that it is not. (The crude nature of the original observations upon which Udy's study is based forced him to dichotomize what are in reality continuous variables.) The seven characteristics form a Guttman-type scale signifying that the structural elements of these organizations are indeed interrelated.[5] Udy (1962) argued that such a scale, while it does not indicate structural prerequisites— one element being required before a second develops—does suggest structural requisites —the emergence of one element creating pressures for the development of others. "For example, if specialization should be the first rational characteristic to develop in an organization, the scale implies that such an organization if it is to be stable must immediately develop a centralized management and compensatory rewards" (Udy, 1962, p. 307).

Weber assumed that the characteristics he described as making up a rational organizational structure were interrelated; Udy's data provide support for such an assumption, but at the same time indicate that for any given organization only a subset of these elements may be present. Many of the elements that Weber specified, including goal specificity, specialization, specific job assignment, and participation based on contractual obligations, appear to form a consistent system. While the presence of a well-developed authority structure is not an essential part of this system, it is clear that important facets of authority relations—compensatory rewards and centralized management—are necessary for motivation and control. The one apparent discrepancy between Weber's conception and Udy's findings concerns the distribution of rewards: Weber argued that rewards should be graded primarily according to hierarchical rank; Udy found that they must reflect at least in part the performance of participants.

[5] These data replicate the results of a previous study based on a sample of 12 organizations in which the interrelation of 4 of these 7 characteristics was examined (Udy, 1958). The patterning of characteristics was detected in a post facto analysis of the data from the first sample; the patterning was predicted in the replication.

Udy's (1962) data provide a suggestive but by no means definitive analysis of the interrelation of structural characteristics. However, the type of analysis employed, in which characteristics are examined across a widely varying sample of organizations, appears to be one well calculated to advance knowledge in the area. This also appears to be a particularly fruitful area for laboratory studies where investigators can better control the structural variables involved and therefore better assess the effects of one characteristic on another (Zelditch & Hopkins, 1961).

THE ORGANIZATION AS GOAL-DIRECTED STRUCTURE

Organizations are not simply structures; they are structures designed to do something. The importance of this characteristic of orientation to the attainment of specific goals is one recognized by most students of organization. There are numerous problems, however, in determining how the organizational goals are to be defined and in examining their consequences for organizational structure.

As already noted, it is important to distinguish between the official purposes of the organization as contained in formal statements of aims and objectives on the one hand and the actual or operative objectives on the other. The official statement of goals is not without significance. In providing an explicit statement of the values to be pursued, it furnishes (barring the case of duplicity) some general criteria for orienting the activities of organization members and for evaluating their contributions to the enterprise and also serves to legitimate the existence of the organization both for participants and the general public (Parsons, 1960, pp. 20–21). While the official goals do provide a general framework within which the activities of the organization are carried out, it is unrealistic to use them as the single standard for evaluating organizational performance. Since some discrepancy between goals and performance is inevitable, to do so foredooms the investigation to some variant of the following conclusions: "(a) that the organization does not realize its goals effectively, and/or (b) that the organization has different goals from those it claims to have" (Etzioni, 1960, p. 258). Social units are never perfectly effective in realizing their aims partly because much energy must be devoted to nongoal activities, such as the preservation of structure.

The operative objectives are those goals actually pursued. Their character can only be established "through intensive analysis of decisions, personnel practices, alliances and elite characteristics in each organization" (Perrow, 1961, p. 856). These objectives typically represent some sort of complex compromise between the official aims and purposes of the unit and the day-to-day pressures, both internal and external, which provide the context for decision-making.[6]

Structural Implications of Goal Attainment: General Considerations

What implications follow for the analysis of the structural characteristics of organizations from placing emphasis on the goal-directed nature of organizations? This question must be approached on two levels: First, what implications follow from the organization's primary orientation to the attainment of a set of objectives? and second, What implications follow from its pursuit of one type of goal rather than another?

Addressing himself to the first question, Parsons suggests that two consequences are fundamental. The first is that, although an organization must solve several basic problems if it is to continue to operate, priority is given to "those processes most directly involved with the success or failure of goal-attainment endeavors" (Parsons, 1960, p. 18). These processes have to do with the making

of decisions[7]—policy, allocative, and coordinating—which select and implement goals. In a more fundamental sense, these processes are concerned with the mobilization of power, legitimate power, to be sure, but power nevertheless, for the attainment of objectives (Parsons, 1960, p. 41). It is this characteristic of organizations coupled with the ruthless efficiency of the bureaucratic form of administration which led Weber to declare that "bureaucracy has been and is a power instrument of the first order—for the one who controls the bureaucratic apparatus" (Weber, 1946, p. 228). The question of who does, as well as who should, control and direct this power is a classic, much-debated problem in the study of organization which is examined in the final section of this chapter.

Many kinds of decisions are required in the operation of an organization, and a great variety of schemes has been proposed for their classification. One suggestive approach is based on Parsons' (1960, pp. 60–65) tripartite division of the hierarchical structure of an organization which associates responsibility for the carrying out of certain tasks and the making of certain decisions with different levels of the organization. The top or "institutional" level mediates between the organization and its larger environment, providing the necessary moral, and often the financial, support required for the establishment and continued operation of the organization. The middle or "managerial" level is responsible externally for the procural of specific inputs such as personnel and raw materials and for the disposal of the product; internally it is answerable for the allocation of resources among organizational subunits and for the coordination of their activities. The lower or "technical" level assumes responsibility

---

[6] For detailed examinations of the operative goals of particular organizations and the factors accounting for their emergence, see Clark (1958), Clark (1960), and Selznick (1949).

[7] A vast literature exists on decision-making both in general and as it functions within an organizational context. For two substantial reviews of this literature, see Edwards (1954) and Gore and Silander (1959). Simon (1957), of course, treats decision-making as the central organizational process.

tor turning out the organizational product and making the required technical or professional decisions. Elites within each of these levels make decisions concerning the operative goals to be pursued in the area of their concern.

Perrow (1961) has suggested that although in some cases these elites have approximately equal power, each making the decisions for which it is responsible and allowing considerable autonomy to the other levels, in other cases, one or another group will become dominant. Hence, which goals are given priority will in part be dependent on which elite group is dominant, and the relative power of elites is in turn dependent on such factors as the kind of work in which the organization is engaged and its stage of development. Perrow illustrates his thesis by focusing on the shifting power alignments in one type of organization: the voluntary general hospital. In the hospital's early stages of development, capital formation and legitimation problems were uppermost, and power was concentrated at the institutional level—in this case, the board of trustees. With important advances in medical technology, power tended to shift to persons making and implementing decisions at the technical level—the medical staff. As problems of coordination of activities and integration of diverse occupational groups come to the fore, members of the administrative level are gaining increasing influence. With each of these shifts, Perrow argues, a concomitant change has occurred in the operative goals of the hospital—from community welfare and the service of selected social groups under the trustees, to high technical standards of medical care with limited attention to general community welfare under the medical staff, and finally to financial solvency and overall efficiency under administrative domination.

The second consequence of dealing with systems giving primacy to the attainment of some goal is the need to focus on the relation between that system and others external to it. In attaining its goal, the organi-

zation produces some commodity or service, and what is a product for one organization is for another an input. Furthermore, since organizations are always subsystems operating within larger social structures, "what from the point of view of the organization in question is its specified goal is, from the point of view of the larger system of which it is a differentiated part or sub-system, a specialized or differentiated function" (Parsons, 1960, p. 19). An important analytical consequence of viewing organization as goal-attaining systems is, then, that this perspective forces the analyst to give some attention to the investigation of organizational-environmental relations. This is a particularly significant consequence in view of the past neglect of the topic by students of organization.

An organization requires many things from its environment: rather obvious things such as raw materials and equipment and markets (the input-output analysis techniques developed by Leontief [1951] have provided economists with a framework for systematically describing and analyzing these flows for industries) and less obvious things like political encouragement (for example, favorable tax laws and subsidies) and a socialized labor force. The relations between organizations and other societal sectors have only begun to be investigated (Parsons & Smelser, 1956) and cannot be developed with any precision here. However, it is clear that what an organization can hope to receive from its environment as well as the kinds of demands with which it will be confronted vary greatly depending on the type of goals the organization is engaged in pursuing.

Structural Implications of Goal Attainment: Specific Goals

In order to assess the consequences of varying kinds of goals for organizational structure, it is necessary first to have a typology of goals. Parsons (1960, pp. 44–47) has outlined one such typology, goals being classified in terms of the societal sector to which they contribute. In a scheme that parallels his description of system problems, Parsons identifies economic, political, integrative, and pattern-maintenance (cultural, educational, and expressive) goals. Since a given society differentially values its various functional sectors, organizations contributing to them will also be differentially evaluated. These judgments will have implications for the organization's claim to legitimacy and all of its manifestations with respect to the marshalling of resources, personnel, and so on. Parsons (1953, p. 106) has suggested that for American society, the functions are ordered as follows: (1) economic, (2) pattern-maintenance, (3) integrative, and (4) political.

To illustrate the structural differences which may attend the pursuit of varying goals, organizations oriented to economic goals will be compared with those oriented to cultural (pattern-maintenance) objectives. There are, of course, many differences among organizations within these broad categories, but it is, nevertheless, possible to indicate in a general way some of the characteristics which distinguish industrial and commercial enterprises from such organizations as universities and research institutes (Eisenstadt, 1958, pp. 116–119; Etzioni, 1961, pp. 71–88; Parsons, 1960, pp. 47–56).

To begin with, economic organizations are expected to "pay their own way" in a market situation whereas cultural organizations are very often supported in part by external sources, such as philanthropy and taxation. Different organs of adaptation are required by these two situations: A firm may need a host of white-collar salesmen to make contacts with potential customers, while a university may rely on a small number of top administrative officials—often including the president—who wheedle funds from dowagers, foundations, and legislatures. Employees in economic firms are expected to hold a "calculative" orientation toward the company, their compensation being governed by what their services are worth as determined by their market position. In cultural organizations, by contrast, the major group of employees are professionals who are not motivated primarily by material rewards, but who desire an opportunity to do work which they find intrinsically satisfying.

The two types of organizations differ drastically in their authority structures. Authority in economic organizations tends to be of the rational, legal type with each employee subordinate to a higher official. Policy decisions are made at the highest levels and implemented by the use of rules and directives which control the performances of lower-level employees. A high degree of specialization is present of a sort which makes for interdependence of units and requires sustained efforts at higher levels directed toward the coordination of activities. In cultural organizations, by contrast, employees tend to be of more equal status. Decision-making is decentralized, and employees demand maximum autonomy. While there is considerable specialization it tends to be of a parallel sort requiring little centralized coordination of activities. In such circumstances, authority is likely to be primarily collegial, although some hierarchical controls remain, and the control that is exercised based more on the competence of the person than on his formal position in the authority structure.

The preceding paragraphs describe in general terms some of the structural differences associated with the pursuit of two types of goals, but in no way account for these differences. A partial explanation is to be found in the nature of the tasks which must be performed in the pursuit of the goals. The tasks carried out by economic firms tend to be of the sort that can be routinized,[8] that is, the inputs (raw ma-

---

[8] Reference here is to the central tasks of economic organizations such as production and distribution. Other tasks—for example, research and development—have more in common with those performed by cultural organizations and the structure of units carrying on such tasks differs accordingly (cf. Kornhauser, 1962; Marcson, 1961; Shephard, 1956).

terials, customer requests, and others) are relatively standardized, the criteria for selecting the operations to be carried out are governed by a set of pre-existing rules, and the operations themselves are controlled by procedural regulations. Situations which cannot be handled within this framework (for example, unusual customer requests) are referred up the hierarchy where decisions are made on the disposition of the case. Changes in selection criteria and procedural rules are also initiated by higher officials. The routine nature of the tasks to be performed makes possible a high degree of both worker specialization and mechanization.

While the majority of tasks performed by economic organizations are routinized, the basic tasks performed by cultural organizations are exceptional in some sense. These organizations are primarily concerned with adding to or preserving some aspect of the cultural heritage. In the case of a research organization, the central tasks involve the solving of heretofore unsolved problems. While such work is governed by general scientific principles, the very nature of the tasks does not permit the use of routinized operations. Maximum autonomy must be accorded to the technical specialists as they creatively vary the definition of and the approach to the problems. Higher-level technical officials may provide expert advice but cannot expect to control the operations of the research team whose members may be more knowledgeable than they concerning the particular problems on which they are working. Administrative officials are chiefly concerned with facilitating the work of the research teams by supplying needed resources, although they may exercise certain budgetary controls over the work performed. Universities share these characteristics in so far as their primary members are engaged in research. The teaching function can be somewhat more routinized, but the changing character of the body of knowledge transmitted as well as the generally recognized need to adjust content and teaching method to differences among students (e.g.,

interests, capacity) set limits on the extent to which these tasks can be standardized.

This brief discussion has attempted only to establish the general proposition that the type of goal which an organization is engaged in pursuing exerts an important influence on its structural characteristics. Other consequences of an orientation to goal attainment, in particular the sorts of relationships which develop among organizations and between organizations and other aspects of social structure as a consequence of their pursuit of some specific objective, are examined in the final section of this chapter.

THE ORGANIZATION AS SOCIAL SYSTEM

Organizations as concrete social structures are made up of both rational and nonrational elements. Weber (1947) and his followers consciously emphasized the rational characteristics since, in their view, these were the elements that distinguished modern organizations from other types of collectivities. Gouldner, on the other hand, quite rightly points out that "the distinguishing characteristics of a bureaucratic organization are not its only characteristics; systematic attention must also be directed to those features of modern organizations, such as the need for loyalty, which they have in common with other types of groups" (Gouldner, 1959, p. 406). This statement could be interpreted as implying that the nonrational elements of organizations have been relatively neglected by social theorists in favor of the rational, but such does not appear to be the case. If anything, the reverse is true. Wolin's (1960) excellent historical survey of organizational theory emphasizes that there has never been a clear separation of the ideas of "organization" and "community," that from the earliest days of the industrial revolution to the present time men have "stubbornly refused to surrender the hope of community" and instead have "insisted on imputing its values to the stark and forbidding structures of

giant organizations" (Wolin, 1960, p. 366).
From Fourier (1890) to Mayo (1945) to
Selznick (1948) the talk has been of nonrational behavior and "informal" organization and of such communal values as integration, shared beliefs, traditional ways of
behavior, and group cohesiveness.

The conceptual model which is typically
employed to examine these nonrational features is that which views the organization as
a social system. Stated in its most general
form, the model assumes that a social unit
has certain "needs" which must be met if
it is to persist in its present form. The needs
are met by a set of elements which are
mutually interdependent so that variation
in one causes modification in the others.[9]
The analytical approach is characterized as
being structural-functional, the investigator
focusing on the consequences for the organizational system of a given structural element
or combination of them.[10] As applied to
organizations, the model emphasizes that an
organization has many needs, only one of
which is to attain its goals. Indeed, from
this perspective, the primary need is not goal
attainment but survival of the system, and
much of the organization's activity is interpreted as being directed toward assuring its
persistence, even at the sacrifice of its professed objectives.

[9] Such systems are often viewed as tending toward a
state of equilibrium, following the work of Pareto,
as interpreted by Henderson (1935). One of the earliest
empirical studies of an organization to utilize the equilibrium assumption was that conducted by Roethlisberger and Dickson (1939). Some of the numerous
dangers inherent in the use of this assumption are
discussed by Krupp (1961, pp. 20–50).

[10] Structural-functional analysis originated with such
social anthropologists as Malinowski and Radcliffe-
Brown, who wished to examine societies in which
there was a paucity of historical materials. However,
Merton's essay on functionalism (1957, pp. 19–84)
has been the most influential statement of this approach in sociology. Certain logical difficulties attend
the use of this model (cf. Nagel, 1956, pp. 247–283),
but if carefully employed it can be of value in the
analysis of self-regulating systems (Hempel, 1959).

The social system model is the one most
widely employed in the sociological analysis
of organizations. Although many studies begin by citing Weber's description of the organization as a rational instrument, the
investigator almost invariably turns to examine departures from this conception. Of
course, all discrepancies from the rational
model should not be viewed as irrational.
As Blau notes: "To administer a social organization according to purely technical
criteria of rationality is irrational, because
it ignores the nonrational aspects of social
conduct" (Blau, 1956, p. 58). Often the
analytical model underlying the discussion
of such discrepancies is implicit; however,
two influential students of organization
(Parsons, 1960; Selznick, 1943; Selznick,
1948) have formulated explicit social system
models. Selznick's canvas is somewhat narrower than Parsons' since he chose to concentrate on the nonrational ("adaptive")
aspects of organization to the exclusion of
their rational ("economic") structure. Parsons' conceptual model purports to encompass both aspects,[11] although his emphasis is
clearly on the organization's value system.

"The important point about organizations," according to Selznick (1949, p. 10),
"is that, though they are tools, each nevertheless has a life of its own." Selznick recognizes the existence of certain rationally
ordered structures within organizations but
sees their operation as being severely circumscribed by the various nonrational dimensions of their structure. The sources of these
nonrational dimensions are (1) individuals,
who participate in the organization as
"wholes" and not merely in terms of their
formal roles within the system; and (2) the
fact that the formal structure is only one

[11] "Broadly my aims have been, first to strike some
kind of balance between the more 'formal' emphases
of Weber and Barnard on the one hand, and the
emphasis on 'informal organization' which has been
more prominent in the tradition of industrial sociology
and the more recent 'bureaucracy' literature on the
other" (Parsons, 1960, p. 3).

aspect of the concrete social structure which must adjust in various ways to pressures brought to bear by its institutional environment (Selznick, 1948, pp. 19–20). In short, organizational rationality is constrained by "the recalcitrance of the tools of action": Persons bring certain characteristics to the organization and develop other commitments as members, which restrict their capacity for rational action; organizational procedures become valued as ends-in-themselves; the organization strikes bargains with its environment which limit future actions (Selznick, 1949, pp. 253–259). If the organization as conceived by Weber (1947) operates like a smoothly-functioning professional football team, Selznick's image corresponds more closely to Alice's efforts at croquet with equipment and competition provided by the Queen of Hearts. Alice swings her flamingo mallet but the bird may duck his head before the hedgehog-ball is struck; just so, the manager issues his directives but they may be neither understood nor followed by his subordinates.

As social systems, organizations must satisfy certain basic needs, such as ensuring their security and maintaining the stability of their authority relations. Taking his cue from Freudian psychology, Selznick (1948) proposes to focus on those organizational needs which are frustrated or blocked, that is, those that cannot be fulfilled within the approved avenues of operation. Such needs give rise to an informal structure based on personal relationships within the organization and to the use of certain defense mechanisms, such as co-optation, in dealing with the environment. Viewed over time, the specific decisions made to meet the basic needs result in the formation of a distinctive "organization character" (Selznick, 1957, pp. 38ff.). Such a focus may seem historical, and indeed Selznick and his students have been forced to rely for their data largely on the perusal of organizational documents from which the administrative history of the institution can be reconstructed. It is, however, sociological in that the anticipated product is knowledge of "the characteristic way in which *types* of institutions respond to *types* of circumstances" (Selznick, 1957, p. 142).

Parsons (Parsons, Bales & Shils, 1953) applies to organizations the same basic conceptual model he and his colleagues developed for the analysis of social systems in general. According to this model, all social systems are confronted by four basic system problems: adaptation, goal-attainment, integration, and pattern-maintenance or latency. In the case of organizations, the adaptive problems have to do with the need to mobilize resources (land, labor, and capital), goal attainment concerns the utilization of these resources in the service of goals, integration refers to the types of norms which commit the individual to the organization (for example, contractual and authority norms), and pattern-maintenance problems are those concerned with legitimizing the activities of the organization in the eyes of its members and the general public (Parsons, 1960, pp. 19–41). Organizations differ from other social systems primarily in the emphasis they give to the goal attainment sector. As Parsons uses these system concepts, they are also relevant for the investigation of suborganizational structures, that is, each sector is viewed as being composed of four subsectors which deal with analogous problems at this level, as well as for supra-organizational structures (it will be recalled that Parsons' classification of organizations discussed earlier allocates organizations according to the societal sectors to which they contribute). Finally, Parsons presses these same concepts into service in describing the connections ("boundary relations") between organizations and other aspects of the social structure (Parsons & Smelser, 1956).[12]

A large number of problems have been examined within the social system frame-

---

[12] A comprehensive presentation and critical evaluation of Parsons' theory of organizations is provided by Landsberger (1961b).

work. For illustrative purposes, three such problem areas will be briefly described and the findings of selected studies summarized. The first two topics—peer groups within organizations and supervisory behavior—have received much attention; the third—role impingement—is a relatively recent research focus within this tradition.

Peer Groups within Organizations

The power of the peer group as a source of worker motivation and control was "discovered" in the Hawthorne research (Roethlisberger & Dickson, 1939) and has been rediscovered in countless later studies. Whether the group consists of machine operators (Roy, 1952), prisoners (Sykes & Messinger, 1960), or medical students (Becker, Geer, Hughes & Strauss, 1961), normative standards develop which define the appropriate level and direction of effort for group members. Studies examining the effect of "group climate" have also demonstrated that the distribution of attitudes within a group can influence the behavior of individual members irrespective of their own particular attitudes on the matter in question (Blau & Scott, 1962, pp. 100–104). In general, the greater the cohesiveness of the group, that is, the more attractive membership in the group is to the participants, the greater will be the control exercised by the group norms and values over the members (Festinger, Schachter & Back, 1950). But whether or not this control will be utilized to aid or frustrate the goals of the larger structure depends upon other factors, such as the extent to which the group feels secure in its relation to the organization (Seashore, 1954).

Etzioni has argued that "the frequency with which workers are members of solidary work groups has been grossly overstated" (1961, pp. 165–166). He cites as evidence studies which show that blue-collar workers value extrawork relations over work group contacts and that a majority of several types of workers do not choose co-workers as close

friends. Such indicators, however, may not be the appropriate ones. Blau (1955) has suggested the necessity of distinguishing peer group relations, which develop among workers, from both friendship ties, on the one hand, and from impersonal categoric relations, on the other. In his study of a federal investigation agency, Blau describes cohesive work groups in which "the associations between particular individuals are valued, as in the case of friendships, which makes these associations integrative, but mutual obligations are definitely circumscribed, in contradistinction to those in friendships, which precludes unexpected personal services that would disrupt bureaucratic activities. This type of role expectation, which is clearly distinct from either *Gemeinschaft* or *Gesellschaft,* has probably become typical of work relationships in the highly bureaucratized societies of today" (Blau, 1955, p. 143).

The Supervisor as Leader

The supervisor or foreman is a man who holds the unenviable position of being between two relatively solidary groups. His job is a difficult one: He is expected to exercise control over his subordinates although he has little formal power over them, and he is expected to inspire them to more than minimal efforts, although he has few formal rewards to dispense (Bendix, 1956, pp. 212–215). It is because his success is dependent on the kinds of informal relationships he can develop with his subordinates and superiors that the supervisor has been such a popular research target for sociologists who view the organization as a social system. The empirical investigation of supervisory behavior has hence focused primarily on "leadership style." A series of studies conducted by the Survey Research Center, University of Michigan, and another carried out by the Personnel Research Board, The Ohio State University, have reached broadly similar conclusions regarding the characteristics of a good leader. The Michigan study classified work groups in various settings according to whether they were high or low on productivity and related these variations to differences in supervisory behavior. Supervisors of high production groups were more likely to be employee- rather than production-oriented, to spend time in planning and other supervisory ac- tivities, and were less likely to supervise closely (Kahn & Katz, 1953). The Ohio State studies were able to isolate two basic dimensions of leadership behavior: "consid- eration," the extent to which trust, friend- ship, and respect marks the relation between the supervisor and his men, and "initiating structure," the degree to which the super- visor is a good organizer who can "get the work out" (Halpin & Winer, 1957). These dimensions vary independently and, in gen- eral, the effective leader, that is, the leader whose work groups were high on produc- tivity and morale, scored high on both dimensions.

Such studies, which are based on a cross- sectional analysis, tend to obscure the proc- ess by which a supervisor gains control over his work group. One interpretation of this process is that the supervisor by his friend- liness and by his efforts to assist his men creates social obligations which they repay by complying with his requests and special demands. In short, by obligating his sub- ordinates to him, the supervisor is able to extend his influence over them. To the ex- tent that a belief (norm) develops among the subordinates which says in effect that "this man's requests are to be followed," his influence has become "authority," control being supported not merely by the super- visor's relation to his subordinates but by their relations with one another (Blau & Scott, 1962, pp. 141–145).

Further studies indicate that a supervisor's success is dependent at least as much on the quality of his relation with his own superior as it is on the kinds of relations he develops with his subordinates. Pelz (1952), for example, found that supervisors using "good" supervisory techniques were ineffectual unless they also had considerable influence with their superior; that is, to be effective, a supervisor needed to have suffi- cient influence with his own superior to be able to affect his decisions on issues critical to the work group. Fleishman, Harris, and Burtt (1955) suggest that the frequently reported failure of "human relations" train- ing programs to influence the behavior of supervisors once they return to their jobs may be a result of a lack of support for such practices from the supervisor's superiors.

The recent trend in the study of super- vision in formal organizations is away from simply examining the traits of the supervisor or even the character of his relations to others, such as his subordinates or superiors, to a consideration of the organization in more structural terms as a series of over- lapping groups. In such a conception, the supervisor is seen as performing a "linking- pin" function, although in effective organi- zations supervisors do not form the only link between their subordinates and the rest of the organization (Likert, 1961, pp. 97– 118).

Role Impingement

In the earlier discussion of social insula- tion, it was indicated that the roles which individuals enact outside the confines of the organization often have implications for their organizational performance. If an or- ganization is viewed as a social system or as a small society, to stretch a point, it be- comes apparent that the individual plays many roles and participates in many rela- tionships within the organization. This being so, it is possible that at times these roles will place conflicting demands on the individual. For example, Turner's analysis (1947) of the role of the navy disbursing officer reports that the incumbent was often unable to fulfill the demands of this role for impartiality of treatment because some of his "clients" were his superiors in rank and consequently held power over him in other relationships. Katz and Eisenstadt's

(1960) study of the relations between Israeli officials and new immigrants notes that bus drivers were often forced to teach immigrants how "passengers" are expected to behave. This circumstance not only adds a new dimension—that of teacher—to the traditional role of bus driver, but also changes this role "because the quality of interaction in the teacher-student relationships necessarily impinges on the more formal bureaucratic relationship" (Katz & Eisenstadt, 1960, p. 124).

The significance of the role impingement concept is that it provides a vehicle for the analysis of tendencies toward bureaucratization and debureaucratization within the organization.

If debureaucratization may be characterized in terms of the impingement of nonbureaucratic roles on bureaucratic ones, then overbureaucratization may be characterized as either the formalistic segregation of a bureaucratic relationship from all other role relations (even relevant ones) or, in its totalitarian form, as the imposition of the bureaucratic relationship on relations outside the scope of the bureaucracy (Katz & Eisenstadt, 1960, p. 119).

To the extent, for example, that friendship ties and other informal relations develop among workers or between workers and supervisors or clients and that these influence the conduct of individuals in these positions, the organization may be said to be debureaucratized. Bureaucratization and debureaucratization are terms usually reserved for the analysis of changes in the overall structure of the organization resulting from various kinds of environmental pressures (Eisenstadt, 1959). The concept of role impingement suggests that such processes occur in trickles as well as torrents.

In concluding this discussion of organizational structure, it must be emphasized again that the three approaches delineated are alternative ways of investigating a single structure. Each organization is to some degree a rational tool, a goal-oriented structure, and a social system, and any complete conception of organizational structures involves a consideration of all three aspects and their interrelations.

THE INDIVIDUAL AND THE ORGANIZATION

Organizations may be viewed not only as structures whose elements can be analytically examined, but also as environments within which persons live and work. March and Simon assume this perspective in their analysis of organizations: "taking the viewpoint of the social psychologist we are interested in what influences impinge upon the individual human being from his environment and how he responds to these influences. For most people formal organizations represent a major part of the environment" (March & Simon, 1958, p. 2). Many questions may be raised concerning the behavior of individuals within organizations, but attention here will be briefly focused on three problem areas: (1) the motivation of individual participants, (2) the reference group orientations of participants, and (3) the effect of the organization on the "personality" of participants.

The Motivation of Individual Participants

The term participant covers a wide variety of relationships with the organization. Blau and Scott (1962, p. 42) designate four groupings whose members vary in the nature of their association with the organization: (1) the members or rank-and-file participants, (2) the owners or managers, (3) the public-in-contact—persons technically outside the organization yet having regular direct contact with it, such as clients, and (4) the public-at-large—members of the society in which the organization operates. Persons in the fourth category are not usually regarded as organizational participants, although they may support the organization indirectly (e.g., through the payment of taxes) and may assuredly benefit from its activities. Persons in the third category may or may not be considered participants. One basis for making this determination has been proposed by Etzioni (1961, pp. 19–21), who suggests three dimensions along which "lower participants" may be found to vary: (1) the nature (direction and intensity) of their involvement in the organization; (2) the degree to which they are subordinated to organizational power; and (3) the amount of performance required of them by the organization. Etzioni proposes to define as participants "all actors who are high on at least one of the three dimensions of participation." Such a criterion would include as participants among the public-in-contact such categories as students and inmates, but would exclude such groupings as clients and customers.

Participants contribute to the organization in return for rewards or inducements.[13] The rewards available for distribution may be classified in many ways. Simon (1957, pp. 110–111) distinguishes three classes: Rewards are "direct" if "the goals set for the organization have direct personal value for the individual." This is the case for most members of the public-in-contact who contribute to the organization in return for obtaining its products or services. "Indirect" rewards are those personal inducements furnished by the organization to members in return for their participation. These may be of two types: They may or may not be directly related to the size and growth of the organization. Owners and sometimes managers are likely to receive the first type in the form of dividends, profits, and bonuses. Rank-and-file members typically receive the latter type in the form of wages and salaries. A more common classification scheme differentiates between financial and nonfinancial incentives, the latter including such rewards as attractiveness of work conditions and tasks to be performed, prestige associated with the work, and status in the organization.

Rewards and satisfaction. A number of surveys conducted in this country indicate that a large majority of the rank-and-file members of organizations—both blue- and white-collar—report general job satisfaction (Blauner, 1960, pp. 340–341). There are, however, systematic variations among types of employees in their degree of satisfaction, and these differences provide some indication of the kinds of incentives which affect worker satisfaction. Blauner's analysis (1960, pp. 343–352) indicates that, in general, workers, who have (1) high prestige, (2) some control rights, "control over the use of one's time and physical movement, which is fundamentally control over the pace of the work process, control over the environment, both technical and social, and control as the freedom from hierachical authority," (3) membership in an integrated work group, and (4) associations with fellow workers off-the-job as members of an occupational community, are more highly satisfied than are those who do not.

Such general patterns are of interest but can be misleading. Scarce rewards, such as prestige or control rights, may only be rewarding to the individual who feels he merits them; otherwise, they may bring guilt and discomfort rather than satisfaction. These considerations suggest that satisfaction is an expression of some sort of complex balance between what the worker believes he brings to and gives his job on the one hand and what he gets from it on the other. This formulation is the basis for Homans' "theory of distributive justice" (Homans, 1961, pp. 51–82, 232–264). The theory suggests, in its simplest form, that justice is realized when a man's profits—rewards less costs—are directly proportional to his investments. Applying the theory to an industrial situation, Homans would include in his category of rewards both financial and nonfinancial inducements—such things as pay, variety of work, and autonomy. Costs, then,

---

[13] Some types of participants, such as prison inmates, are not allowed to decide whether or not they will join the organization. However, once inside they contribute to it in return for rewards—even if the rewards are simply the withholding of punishment.

are simply low or negative values on these and similar job characteristics. Investments are the things a man brings with him to his job, for example, his age, sex, seniority, and skill-level. The theory is complicated by the fact that a person has many different kinds of investments, receives many kinds of rewards, and all of them may not be "in line" or congruent. Homans argues that this status inconsistency is itself a cost and that distributive justice is achieved by a person only when "each of the various features of his investments and his activities, put into rank-order in comparison with those of other men, fall in the same place in all the different rank-orders" (Homans, 1961, p. 264).

Rewards and productivity. There is no inherent relation between satisfaction and productivity. "One would not predict that 'satisfied' rats would perform best in a T-maze. Similarly, there is no reason for predicting that high satisfaction, per se, motivates a given individual to conform to the goals specified by the hierarchy" (March & Simon, 1958, p. 50). The relation between incentives and productivity is at best a complex one, as a recent empirical study indicates. Zaleznick, Christensen, and Roethlisberger (1958) distinguish between external and internal rewards, the former referring to incentives, such as pay, job security, status, and working conditions, provided by the larger organization, and the latter to such rewards as friendship and approval, which stem from membership in a work group. The authors believe that these two types of rewards are frequently in conflict in the modern industrial setting and that individuals differ in the value which they place on them. The relationship between incentives, employee satisfaction, and productivity was explored in one production department of a medium-sized industrial firm. Sociometric analysis revealed that some of the 50 employees were members of "regular" work groups while others participated in "deviant" groups—whose members interacted frequently with one another, as did

regular members, but did not share such values as generosity, helpfulness, and loyalty held by other members—or were isolates. In general, members of regular work groups could be said to receive favorable internal rewards: They tended to be satisfied and to produce in conformity with group output norms. Members of deviant groups and isolates—those receiving *un*favorable internal rewards—tended to be dissatisfied and to produce either above or below the output norm. Contrary to expectations, however, those producing above the output norm received relatively low external rewards and those producing below the norm, relatively high external rewards. The authors attempt to account for these results by noting differences in attitudes toward work and authority between the two types of producers, which in turn are related to differences in social background. Be that as it may, the significant finding is the lack of relation between external rewards and productivity for all department members.[14]

Reference Group Orientations

An important key to understanding the behavior of any organizational member is knowledge of the groups with which he compares himself or to which he looks for normative standards. Such groups have been labeled "reference groups" and may include both those to which the individual belongs (membership groups) and those to which he does not (Merton, 1957, p. 234). It should be recognized that reference group theory is not well developed and, at the present time, its notions are usually applied as post hoc interpretive concepts: An individual is observed to behave in a certain manner and his behavior is "explained" by noting his membership in or orientation to some group.

---

[14] For other discussions of the relation between types of incentives, worker satisfaction, and motivation to produce, see March and Simon (1958) and W. F. Whyte et al. (1955). For a study of executive compensation and performance, see Roberts (1959).

Since there are virtually no constraints on the use of the concept, the investigator can freely select from among the many membership and nonmembership groups the ones that seem most plausible in accounting for the behavior (B. P. Cohen, 1962). For example, Dalton (Whyte et al., 1955, pp. 39–49) suggests that "rate-busters" in a machine shop differed from "restricters" in their rate of productivity because of their orientation to divergent reference groups: They were raised in rural or urban lower-middle-class families as opposed to urban working-class families, they tended to be Republicans rather than Democrats, and, unlike restricters, they were not active church members. Such group memberships may have had an important impact on productivity behavior, but one does not know for certain that these groups were providing orientation for workers in this situation, and one does not know why these groups, and not others, were the salient ones.

The use of reference group concepts seems somewhat more defensible when the investigator specifies in advance a limited number of salient reference groups whose effects he wishes to explore. Thus, for example, one could determine whether or not a foreman is oriented toward management or toward his subordinates and then examine the consequences of these divergent orientations for his behavior as supervisor. This type of approach has been extensively used in the study of professional workers employed in bureaucracies. Here the assumption is made that such workers are confronted with a choice of two salient and partially-conflicting membership groups: the profession and the bureaucracy. Studies by Wilensky (1956, pp. 129–144), Gouldner (1957), and by Blau and Scott (1962, pp. 64–74), among others, have explored the consequences for work behavior of an orientation to one or the other group. Generally speaking, professionally-oriented workers, in contrast to their bureaucratically-oriented counterparts, have been found to be critical of bureaucratic rules and standards, reluctant to accept bu-

reaucratic supervision, and, in a majority of circumstances, lacking in loyalty to their organizational employer.

As reference group theory becomes more refined it can become a powerful tool in the study of organizations since a major problem in this setting is the analysis of conflicting group loyalties, both within the organization where the interests of subgroups often conflict and memberships overlap, and between the organization and its environment.

Organization and Personality

In approaching the broad topic of the effect of organizations on the personalities of their participants, a distinction must be made between what organizations consciously do, or attempt to do, to their members and what they do unknowingly. The former set of effects will be said to result from "manifest socialization" and the latter from "latent socialization" processes. It is also important to recognize that organizations not only change the personalities of their participants; they, in addition, select individuals with particular personality characteristics. (Such selection criteria may also be manifest or latent.) Any given personality type which is found in association with an organization is, of course, the product of both recruitment patterns and socialization processes.

Manifest socialization. Some organizations have as their primary goal the socialization of some subset of their members. As "forcing houses for changing persons" they share in common certain general characteristics. In their most extreme form they are "total institutions," segregating their members from all outside influences and stripping them of former statuses and possessions, placing all aspects of their lives under a single authority system of the echelon type, and regimenting all their activities in a tightly-scheduled, rational manner (Goffman, 1961, pp. 3–48). These features are shared, to a greater or lesser extent, by such organizations as prisons, mental hospitals, military academies, and monasteries. The nature of the socialization program varies according to whether members participate on a voluntary or an involuntary basis and whether or not members are committed to the goals of the organization. But irrespective of these dimensions, the effectiveness of socialization agencies is almost invariably diminished by the informal organization of their trainees, which often engages in the countersocialization of members, or, at least, sets limits on the formal socialization program (Becker, Greer, Hughes & Strauss, 1961; Coleman, 1961; Cressey, 1961; Dornbusch, 1955).

In the majority of organizations, the socialization function is a secondary one, necessary chiefly for assuring an adequate supply of trained personnel. Some organizations operate special training units where newcomers stay until they have acquired the basic skills, or, if the skills demanded are not great, workers may be trained on-the-job. Organizations that require highly-trained personnel, however, typically must rely on other agencies—socializing institutions such as universities and technical schools—for their supply, since they cannot bear the costs of elaborate and extended training programs. Because socialization always involves the learning of values, beliefs, and attitudes as well as information and skills, this separation between training and employment often poses difficult problems for the employing organization. (Note, however, that organizations differ in the extent to which they can exercise control over such external socialization units [Etzioni, 1961, pp. 148–149].) Recruits may arrive with the "proper" skills as viewed by the employer, but lack the "proper" attitudes: They, for example, may have acquired a professional orientation which brings them into conflict with organizational demands. The significance of location of training is illustrated by a study comparing nurses trained in degree (college controlled) programs with those trained in diploma (hospital controlled) programs (Corwin, 1961). Degree nurses were found more frequently to hold a professional self-conception than diploma nurses and consequently to suffer greater role conflict when placed in the bureaucratized hospital setting.

It must again be emphasized that socialization processes do not alone account for the nature of the end product. The better universities turn out more productive scholars partly because they are able to recruit brighter students. Also, according to Janowitz (1960, p. 241), the fact that the military officers who have attended war college hold more politically conservative views than officers who have not is primarily a function of "who gets selected" rather than of "the actual impact of the course of study." In order to evaluate the separate impact of these two influences, one has to examine the characteristics of those selected for admission in comparison to those who are not, as Janowitz (1960, pp. 79–103) did in his analysis of the background characteristics of military leaders. Also one must investigate changes over time in the characteristics of members as they move through the socializing institution, as exemplified by the study of changes in the political attitudes of Bennington students conducted by Newcomb (1943).

Selection criteria, even consciously adopted ones, sometimes have unanticipated consequences. Argyris (1954), in his study of a bank, found that the hiring procedures resulted in the selection of rather passive, introverted types which, while they made satisfactory employees, were ineffective bank officers when promoted.

The end product of a successful recruitment and socialization program is some degree of fit between the demands of an organizational role and the personality system of the occupant (Y. A. Cohen, 1962, pp. 187–198). Studies of successful business executives (Henry, 1949) and of various types of physical and social scientists (Roe, 1956) have attempted to identify the personality characteristics which occupants of these roles hold in common. Studies of this kind, however, tend either simply to describe these common characteristics without attempting to account for them, or to place emphasis on background factors shared by role occupants rather than on those characteristics acquired as a consequence of socialization undergone in preparation for holding the specific role.

Latent socialization. Just as everything that is taught is not learned, everything that is learned is not taught, at least, not consciously. Participation in an organization appears to have unanticipated effects on the personalities of the participants. There has been much speculation and conjecture about the nature of these consequences, but relatively little systematic research. Nevertheless, among scholars concerned with this topic, there appears to be considerable agreement that the effects of participation are, on balance, bad. The most sweeping indictment of organizations has come from Argyris (1957) who argues that the demands which organizations impose on participants are completely inconsistent with the needs of emotionally healthy individuals.

If the principles of formal organization are used as ideally defined, employees will tend to work in an environment where (1) they are provided minimal control over their workaday world, (2) they are expected to be passive, dependent, and subordinate, (3) they are expected to have a short time perspective, (4) they are induced to perfect and value the frequent use of a few skin-surface shallow abilities and, (5) they are expected to produce under conditions leading to psychological failure.

All of these characteristics are incongruent to the ones *healthy* human beings are postulated to desire. They are much more congruent with the needs of infants in our culture. . . . Frustration, conflict, failure, and short time perspective are predicted as resultants of this basic incongruency (Argyris, 1957, pp. 66, 74).

Merton (1957, pp. 195–206) has attempted to account for the development of two specific tendencies observed among bureaucratic officials: their timid, compulsive following of rules and their "arrogance" and "haughtiness" in relating to clients. He points to no special mechanisms in his explanation, but rather suggests that "the very elements which conduce toward efficiency in general produce inefficiency in specific instances" (Merton, 1957, p. 200). Specifically, incentives are geared to reward disciplined action and conformity to regulations, not innovation; "pride in craft" causes officials to resist changes in established routines; and norms of impersonality which govern relations with clients encourage officials to categorize clients and maintain their social distance. Such general factors, however, cannot explain why some officials become ritualists or martinets while others do not. Blau (1955), in his study of a state employment agency, found one factor which appeared to differentiate ritualists from other workers: status insecurity. "The instances of overconformity and resistance to change observed in the state agency were motivated by anxious concern with the attitudes and opinions of superiors" (Blau, 1955, p. 188). V. Thompson (1961) accepts status anxiety as the basic cause of "bureaupathic" behavior, but insists that this is not a limited but an extremely pervasive phenomenon brought about by the increasing discrepancy between the skill and the authority hierarchies.

Both Argyris (1957, pp. 76–122) and Presthus (1962) have suggested that individuals adapt in various ways to the demands of organizational life. Argyris has indicated several kinds of reactions, including attempted upward mobility, becoming apathetic and disinterested, and joining informal groups which support one's own attitudes and behavior, but does not attempt to specify what types of individuals select particular adaptive techniques. Presthus (1962), on the other hand, identifies three principal modes of adaptation—upward mobility, indifference, and ambivalence—the selection of which he attempts to relate to individual characteristics. The "upward mobile" tends to be of middle-class background and motivated by a strong fear of failure and respect for authority; the "indifferent" is of working-class origin and finds his chief satisfactions outside the work situation; and the "ambivalent," while of middle-class origin, tends to be introverted, intellectual, and incapable of giving his full loyalty to the organization.

ORGANIZATIONS AND THEIR ENVIRONMENT

Sociologists have sometimes viewed organizations as closed systems and have laboriously examined the interrelation of their internal characteristics without taking into account the extent to which these factors and the relations among them are influenced by external conditions (Krupp, 1961, pp. 60–61). It is relatively recently that most investigators have come to see that the line which separates organizations from their environment is an arbitrary one which must be drawn and redrawn to suit the purposes of specific investigations.

The preceding discussion has touched upon many of the significant points of contact between an organization and the larger society. For example, in discussing organizations as rational instruments, the importance of social insulation has been stressed: Organizations need to be sure that the external affiliations of their members do not come to determine their position and behavior within the organization. This, of course, is the rational ideal. In practice, the organization makes many accommodations to community values as they bear on the status of participants. The community's stratification system is usually reflected in the organizational hierarchy (Collins, 1946). Of course, the influence is reciprocal: Status in the organization is reflected in the community. The discussion of organizations as goal-attaining units pointed out that organizations pursuing goals defined by the public as socially significant were in a better position to obtain the resources necessary for their continued functioning. Also, in considering the or-

ganization as a social system, a primary focus is the survival of the organization within its environment.

Interorganizational Relations

Organizations do not relate to the environment in general but to specific aspects of it. More often than not, other organizations constitute the most salient features of the environment of a given organization. Thus, a business firm is directly affected by the actions of various federal regulatory agencies, suppliers, competitors, unions, banks, and customers, who may be other firms as well as individuals. Since organizations are simultaneously involved in a number of relations, inevitably there are conflicts between the demands of one group and those of another. A variety of mechanisms enables the organization to deal with these incompatible demands, including secrecy (agreements made with one group are concealed from others); publicity (the demands by one group are reported to others who may be affected); and the formation of mutual-benefit associations composed of organizations "in the same boat" for the purpose of determining their collective stance in relation to other organizations (Blau & Scott, 1962, pp. 195–196).

An organization may enter into a variety of relationships with others. J. D. Thompson and McEwen (1958) have distinguished four significant types: (1) competition, where there is no direct contact between the organizations although they share a common relation to some third party; (2) bargaining, in which there are limited agreements between the two parties concerning the exchange of goods and services; (3) co-optation, where leadership elements of one organization are taken into the other; and (4) coalition formation, in which organizations become formally committed to joint decisions. Viewed from one standpoint, the relationships are ranked in order of increasing support of one firm by the other; viewed from another, the relationships are ranked in order of decreasing sovereignty for each partner in the transaction.

Boundary roles. Managing the relations among organizations and between organizations and their various publics is often the responsibility of particular types of officials, who occupy what may be termed "boundary roles." These roles may occur at all levels of the organization but are typically concentrated at the top and the bottom of the structure and in some specialized departments, for example, public relations. At the top are those officials concerned with policy formation and the allocation of resources. While these officers are not usually thought of as occupying "boundary roles," it is clear that much of their attention must be directed toward the environment. At the highest level the leaders are charged with responsibility for defining the organization's "mission" and in doing so must, according to Selznick (1957, pp. 65–89), take account of both the internal state of the organization and the external demands placed upon it. To a large extent, the degree of receptiveness or hostility of the organization's institutional environment, together with the effectiveness of the organizational leadership in dealing with it, determines whether an organization is enabled to pursue its goals with such success that further objectives must be sought, or whether its history is one of retrenchment and goal displacement (Blau & Scott, 1962, pp. 228–230; Sills, 1957, pp. 253–268). Just below the highest level are those officers who must mediate between the organization and those who supply its resources and use its products. Dill (1958) has shown how the autonomy (freedom from both peer and superior control) of these officials is a function of the "task environments" with which they deal. For example, heterogeneous task environments increase the likelihood that officials will become differentiated in their functions and responsibilities and give each official exclusive access to a given type of information, thus increasing their autonomy within the organization.

Persons in the middle levels of the organization who occupy boundary roles are usually found in such specialized units as personnel, public relations, labor relations, and legal departments. Such "staff" departments are frequently composed of professional persons whose commitment to the organization is tenuous. Goldner (1960), however, in his analysis of the role of the labor-relations representative, suggests that some marginality in these roles may be functional for the organization. Some ambiguity of intentions is an ingredient of successful bargaining (J. D. Thompson & McEwen, 1958): If management presents its proposals to an outside group via marginal officials, it can, if necessary, protect itself against failures by denouncing its negotiators. Also, the marginality of a personnel officer may give him enough objectivity in the eyes of employees that he will be utilized as an arbiter of disputes when a "regular" officer would not do.

Members at lower levels in the organization often occupy boundary roles, since it is frequently at this point that the services or products of the organization are dispensed to customers or clients. J. D. Thompson (1962) has noted two important dimensions along which relations between lower members and nonmembers vary: The extent to which the organization has "programmed" (specified in detail the actions of) its representative; and the extent to which the nonmember is compelled to take part in the relationship. If the dimensions are dichotomized and combined, four types of relations are characterized: (1) member programmed-interaction mandatory, for example, clerical personnel in a governmental bureau issuing licenses; (2) member programmed-interaction optional, for example, salesmen selling mass-produced products under competitive conditions; (3) member heuristic-interaction mandatory, typical of a semiprofessional relation, such as occurs between a public school teacher and student; and (4) member heuristic-interaction optional, exemplified by a professional relation, such as that of doctor and patient. Thompson suggests that contact between an organizational representative and a nonmember may result in a transaction being completed in accordance with organizational norms, a breakdown of the relation before a transaction can be completed, or the completion of a side-transaction in which an exchange not sanctioned by the organization takes place. But the processes by which one or another of these results is arrived at differ for each of the four types of relations.

Another important dimension which affects relations between lower organizational members and nonmembers is the extent to which one or the other of them is part of a cohesive group. The Israeli officials, described by Katz and Eisenstadt (1960), sent out to become instructors in some remote village were far more likely to alter their behavior to accommodate the expectations of their clientele than were the state employment agency workers, described by Blau (1955, pp. 88–96), who laughed and joked among themselves about the "stupid" and "hostile" clients. In the former case where solitary officials were confronted by solidary clients, clients could force officials to carry out numerous side-transactions which led to the debureaucratization of the relationship; in the latter case where solitary clients were confronted by a cohesive group of officials, organizationally sanctioned transactions were completed. Since, however, the completed transactions often ignored relevant differences among clients, relations between workers and clients in this situation may be described as over-bureaucratized.

Organizational Autonomy and Its Limits

The effectiveness of a given organization is dependent upon its enjoying a degree of autonomy from its environment. The top authority level described by Parsons (1960, pp. 63–69)—the institutional level—has as its central function the creation of a set of conditions which allows the organization to pursue its goals without undue societal interference. Structures at this level, including

boards of trustees for educational and eleemosynary institutions and boards of directors for corporate concerns, must see to it that the organization's existence and activities are accorded legitimacy in the community, and they must marshall broad sources of support—moral, economic, and political. They also function as a buffer between the organization and its environment, protecting organizational officials from outside criticism and attempts to influence. Selznick and his students have provided numerous case studies of the torments that befall organizations unsupported by their institutional sectors (Clark, 1958) or not legitimated by their constituents (Selznick, 1949). Such organizations either fail to survive or enter into unfavorable bargains with sectors of their environment, sacrificing sovereignty in return for support.

The institutional level of the organization provides lebensraum to organizational officials not only by garnering environmental support, but also by themselves refraining from undue interference in administrative decision-making. Although board members may check compliance with overall policies, they must yield to appointed officials broad discretionary powers in the operation of the organization (Gross, Mason, & McEachern, 1958). Officials are granted such powers because they and not board members devote their full efforts to the organization, are considered to be expert in the particular type of administration, and are in close touch with the on-going operations of the organization. Second-guessing by board members of the administrator's decisions or too frequent evaluations of his performance (cf. Jaques, 1956) create tensions for the administrator both because they indicate a generalized lack of confidence in his abilities and because they interfere with his day-to-day decisions. In short, the administrator needs a free hand for maneuvering in the short run and expects to be judged on the overall quality of his performance.

To suggest that an organization requires some autonomy from its environment if it is to be at all effective in the pursuit of its goals is not to argue that organizations can or should be immune from all societal constraints. An organization is, after all, a unit of a larger social system, not an independent entity. Because every organization "in virtue of the services it performs, the areas it regulates, the interests between which it mediates, and its own structure and organization, develops into a centre of power which may become independent and unregulated" (Eisenstadt, 1958, p. 102), it is important to consider the appropriate limits of organizational autonomy.

Some conservative theorists are concerned with finding ways of curtailing the power of organizations in general. Such a program appears to ignore the differences among organizations in power and in their uses and misuses of it. To determine whether or not an organization is misusing its power requires some conception of what constitutes an appropriate use of it. One approach to such an analysis is suggested by a typology of organizations based on the question of who benefits from the organization's functioning (Blau & Scott, 1962, pp. 42–58). Four types of beneficiaries are distinguished: the rank-and-file members of the organization; its owners or managers; the public-in-contact, that is, persons not considered members but having regular, direct contact with the organization; and the public-at-large, composed of the members of the society in which the organization operates. Every organization has many types of beneficiaries, but the classification is determined by which class of participants is considered to be the primary beneficiary. The four resulting types of organizations are (1) "mutual benefit organizations," such as unions, political parties, and fraternal associations, where the rank-and-file members are the prime beneficiaries; (2) "business concerns," such as industrial firms and retail stores, where the owners or managers are the prime beneficiaries; (3) "service organizations," such as schools, hospitals, and clinics, where the clients are the prime beneficiaries; and (4) "commonweal organizations," such as governmental agencies, prisons, and armies, where the primary beneficiary is the public-at-large.

Misuse of power in mutual benefit associations typically takes the form of organizational resources being diverted from serving the interests of rank-and-file members to the interests of its officers or managers. As early as 1915, Michels (1949) provided a description of this process within political parties, and Lipset (1960, pp. 357–399) applied many of Michels' principles to the analysis of trade unions. The process, however, is not inevitable. A study of one union (the International Typographical Union) which has managed to retain power in the hands of members by preserving a two-party democratic structure, indicates that Michels' pessimistic "iron law of oligarchy" operates only under certain specific—albeit widespread—conditions (Lipset, Trow & Coleman, 1956). Whether or not rank-and-file members retain control of their unions is a problem of secondary importance to persons concerned with the increasing power of unions. Management has long been concerned with such developments, and since "there is no reason to believe that the self-interest of labor groups is any more closely identified with the public interest than that of General Motors" (Mason, 1960, p. 127), the public, through its elected representatives, has attempted to protect itself against some of the dangers inherent in the presence of trade union monopolies.

Owners and managers of business concerns, by the very nature of their position in the organization, are less likely to lose their place as prime beneficiaries to some competing group. It is true, however, that over the years, rank-and-file members of business concerns, through their unions and professional associations, and the members of the public, through governmental mechanisms, have gained increased power in relation to managers, so that the latter group has found its area of discretionary action reduced. In order to protect their position with the public, it has been necessary for managers to utilize the services of such specialists as public relations consultants, advertising firms, and lobbying groups. To shore up their control over rank-and-file members, many managers have turned to the use of "human relations" and similar techniques calculated to increase managerial influence.

Clients, who are expected to be prime beneficiaries of the activities of service organizations, are often in a relatively weak position and therefore have difficulty in protecting their interests. The inability of clients to evaluate the services proferred them by the technically skilled organization members is one source of their weakness, and their problems are compounded in those cases where their participation is involuntary, as it is, for example, in public schools and, to a lesser degree, in public welfare agencies. It would not do for clients directly to control the services offered to them; because of their relative ignorance, the wishes of clients should not be allowed to dominate the relation, although their interests should. Since only other persons with the same technical qualifications can adequately evaluate and control the performance of a given practitioner, clients typically "delegate" their control rights to the professional group of practitioners (Goode, 1957). In general, the higher the prestige of a professional group, the more likely it is that this delegation will take place. Professionals organize themselves into associations which evaluate the quality of newcomers, grant or withhold (with the backing of the state's authority) the right to practice, and pledge all members to uphold a rigid code of ethics. In the past, the bulk of professional services was dispensed by independent practitioners, and, although they were under some surveillance from their professional peers, there is some question of how much protection was afforded the individual client. As professionals have moved into organizations to dispense their services, other kinds of control techniques have been added. Since professionals

hold different ranks within the organization, the control function has become somewhat specialized by rank, higher officials reviewing the performances of lower. In addition, as Etzioni notes, "a large amount of control over professional performances has been transferred from the professional community to the professional organization" (1961, p. 259) not only to upper-level professionals but to lay administrators. Of course, such hierarchical control need not benefit clients; it may be directed toward serving the interests of the public-at-large (e.g., in their role as taxpayers) or it may be exercised to increase the power and line the pockets of the managers themselves.

Most commonweal organizations are the agencies of local, state, and federal governments. The tremendous growth of governmental functions over the past several decades has led to increasing concern with finding means of ensuring that the power vested in governmental agencies will be used to further the interests of the primary beneficiary, the general public, and not some special interest group. Kaufman (1956) has reviewed the history of attempts to make governmental agencies responsible to the public, identifying three central values stressed by reformers at various times in the life of this country. During the formative period, emphasis was placed on representativeness in government, with great powers being granted to legislatures and uncritical faith placed in the electoral principle. This value became somewhat tarnished with the appearance of the long ballot and the spoils system. As a remedy to these problems, reformers advocated that administration be taken out of politics, and the "quest for neutral competence" was underway by the middle of the nineteenth century.

The rationale was the now-familiar politics-administration dichotomy, according to which politics and administration are distinct and separate processes that should therefore be assigned to separate and distinct organs. The mechanisms were independent boards and commissions and the merit system, which were designed to insulate many public officials and public policies from political pressures (Kaufman, 1956, p. 1060).

The major limitation that became apparent with the implementation of this value was the tendency to fragmentation. Many agencies became too independent, with the result that contradictory policies, jurisdictional disputes, overlaps and gaps in services offered, and top-heavy organizations often developed. In response to this set of problems, there has developed a movement to strengthen the hand of the executive. This new emphasis on executive leadership—the third value—is indicated by such developments as increased use of the executive budget, greater interest in administrative reorganization, and increased size of the executive staff. This development, however, tends to return administration to its political origins and can be expected to raise new control problems for the public.

The changing fronts in the struggle to keep commonweal organizations from becoming indifferent to or dominating the public they were established to serve suggests that there is no final solution to the problems posed by the ubiquitous presence of large-scale public bureaucracies. In this struggle as in others, the price of freedom is eternal vigilance.

REFERENCES

Abegglen, J. C. The Japanese factory. Glencoe, Ill.: Free Press, 1958.

Argyris, C. Organization of a bank. New Haven, Conn.: Labor and Management Center, Yale Univer., 1954.

Argyris, C. Personality and organization. New York: Harper, 1957.

Barker, E. The development of public services in Western Europe, 1660-1930. New York: Oxford Univer. Press, 1944.

Barnard, C. I. The functions of the executive. Cambridge, Mass.: Harvard Univer. Press, 1938.

Bavelas, A. Communication patterns in task-oriented groups. J. acoustical Soc. Amer., 1950, 22, 725-730.

Becker, H. S., Geer, Blanche, Hughes, E. C., & Strauss, A. L. Boys in white. Chicago: Univer. of Chicago Press 1961.

Bell, D. Adjusting men to machines. Commentary, 1947, 3, 78-88.

Bendix, R. Work and authority in industry. New York: Wiley, 1956.

Bendix, R. Max Weber: An intellectual portrait. New York: Doubleday, 1960.

Berger, M. Bureaucracy and society in modern Egypt. Princeton, N.J.: Princeton Univer. Press, 1957.

Blau, P. M. The dynamics of bureaucracy. Chicago: Univer. of Chicago Press, 1955.

Blau, P. M. Bureaucracy in modern society. New York: Random House, Inc., 1956.

Blau, P. M. Formal organization: Dimensions of analysis. Amer. J. Sociol., 1957, 63, 58-69.

Blau, P. M., & Scott, W. R. Formal organizations. San Francisco: Chandler, 1962.

Blauner, R. Work satisfaction and industrial trends in modern society. In W. Galenson & S. M. Lipset (Eds.), Labor and trade unionism. New York: Wiley, 1960. Pp. 339-360.

Burns, T., & Stalker, G. M. The management of innovation. London: Tavistock, 1961.

Clark, B. R. Organizational adaptation and precarious values. Amer. sociol. Rev., 1956, 21, 327-336.

Clark, B. R. Adult education in transition. Berkeley: Univer. of California Press, 1958.

Clark, B. R. The open door college. New York: McGraw, 1960.

Clark, B. R. Faculty authority. Bull. Amer. Ass. Univer. Profs, 1961, 47, 293-302.

Cohen, B. P. The process of choosing a reference group. In Joan H. Criswell, H. Solomon, & P. Suppes (Eds.), Mathematical methods in small group processes. Stanford: Stanford Univer. Press, 1962. Pp. 101-118.

Cohen, Y. A. Social structure and personality. New York: Holt, 1962.

Coleman, J. S. The adolescent society. New York: The Free Press of Glencoe, 1961.

Collins, O. Ethnic behavior in industry. Amer. J. Sociol., 1946, 51, 293-298.

Corwin, R. G. The professional employee: A study of conflict in nursing roles. Amer. J. Sociol., 1961, 66, 604-615.

Coser, Rose L. *Life in the ward*. East Lansing: Michigan State Univer. Press, 1962.

Cottrell, F. *Energy and society*. New York: McGraw, 1955.

Cressey, D. R. (Ed.) *The prison*. New York: Holt, Rinehart & Winston, 1961.

Dalton, M. *Men who manage*. New York: Wiley, 1959.

Delany, W. The development and decline of patrimonial and bureaucratic administrations. *Admin. Sci. Quart.*, 1963, 7, 458–501.

Diamond, S. From organization to society: Virginia in the 17th century. *Amer. J. Sociol.*, 1958, 63, 457–475.

Dill, W. R. Environment as an influence on managerial autonomy. *Admin. Sci. Quart.*, 1958, 2, 409–443.

Dornbusch, S. M. The military academy as an assimilating institution. *Soc. Forces*, 1955, 33, 316–321.

Dubin, R. *The world of work*. Englewood Cliffs, N.J.: Prentice-Hall, Inc., 1958.

Duncan, O. D., & Schnore, L. F. Cultural, behavioral, and ecological perspectives in the study of social organization. *Amer. J. Sociol.*, 1959, 65, 132–146.

Edwards, W. The theory of decision making. *Psychol. Bull.*, 1954, 51, 380–417.

Eisenstadt, S. N. Bureaucracy and bureaucratization. *Curr. Sociol.*, 1958, 7, 99–163.

Eisenstadt, S. N. Bureaucracy, bureaucratization, and debureaucratization. *Admin. Sci. Quart.*, 1959, 4, 302–320.

Etzioni, A. Authority structure and organizational effectiveness. *Admin. Sci. Quart.*, 1959, 4, 293–302.

Etzioni, A. Two approaches to organizational analysis. *Admin. Sci. Quart.*, 1960, 5, 257–278.

Etzioni, A. *A comparative analysis of complex organizations*. New York: The Free Press of Glencoe, 1961.

Fayol, H. *Industrial and general administration*. London: Pitman & Sons, 1930.

Festinger, L., Schachter, S., & Back, K. *Social pressures in informal groups*. New York: Harper, 1950.

Fleishman, E. A., Harris, E. F., & Burtt, H. E. *Leadership and supervision in industry*. Columbus: The Ohio State Univer. Press, 1955.

Fourier, F. M. C. *Oeuvres choisies*. C. Gide (Ed.). Paris: Guillaumin, 1890.

Friedmann, G. *Industrial society*. H. L. Sheppard (Ed. of Eng. ed.). Glencoe, Ill.: Free Press, 1955.

Furnivall, J. S. *Colonial policy and practice*. Cambridge: Cambridge Univer. Press, 1948.

Georgopoulos, B. S., & Mann, F. C. *The community general hospital*. New York: Macmillan, 1962.

Goffman, E. *Asylums*. New York: Doubleday Anchor, 1961.

Goldner, F. H. Organizations and their environment. Abstracts of papers read at Fifty-fifth Ann. Meeting Amer. Sociol. Ass., New York, 1960.

Goode, W. J. Community within a community: The professions. *Amer. sociol. Rev.*, 1957, 22, 194–200.

Gore, W. J., & Silander, F. S. A bibliographical essay on decision making. *Admin. Sci. Quart.*, 1959, 4, 97–121.

Goss, Mary E. W. Influence and authority among physicians. *Amer. sociol. Rev.*, 1961, 26, 39–50.

Gouldner, A. W. *Patterns of industrial bureaucracy*. Glencoe, Ill.: Free Press, 1954.

Gouldner, A. W. Cosmopolitans and locals: Toward an analysis of latent social roles—I. *Admin. Sci. Quart.*, 1957, 2, 281–306.

Gouldner, A. W. Organizational analysis. In R. K. Merton, L. Broom, & L. S. Cottrell, Jr. (Eds.), *Sociology today*. New York: Basic Books, 1959. Pp. 400–428.

Gross, N., Mason, W. S., & McEachern, A. W. *Explorations in role analysis*. New York: Wiley, 1958.

Grusky, O. Corporate size, bureaucratization, and managerial succession. *Amer. J. Sociol.*, 1961, 67, 261–269.

Guest, R. H. *Organizational change*. Homewood, Ill.: Dorsey Press & Richard D. Irwin, 1962.

Guetzkow, H., & Simon, H. A. The impact of certain communication nets upon organization and performance in task-oriented groups. *Mgmt Sci.*, 1955, 1, 233–250.

Gulick, L., & Urwick, L. (Eds.) *Papers on the science of administration*. New York: Institute of Public Administration, 1937.

Haire, M. (Ed.) *Modern organization theory*. New York: Wiley, 1959.

Halpin, A. W., & Winer, B. J. A factorial study of the leader behavior descriptions. In R. M. Stogdill & A. E. Coons (Eds.), *Lead-*

er behavior: Its description and measurement. Columbus: Bureau of Business Research, The Ohio State Univer. Press, 1957. Pp. 39–51.

Harrison, P. M. *Authority and power in the free church tradition*. Princeton, N.J.: Princeton Univer. Press, 1959.

Hempel, C. The logic of functional analysis. In L. Gross (Ed.), *Symposium on sociological theory*. Evanston, Ill.: Row, Peterson, 1959. Pp. 271–307.

Henderson, L. J. *Pareto's general sociology*. Cambridge, Mass.: Harvard Univer. Press, 1935.

Henry, W. E. The business executive: The psychodynamics of a social role. *Amer. J. Sociol.*, 1949, 54, 286–291.

Hintze, O. Die Entstehung der modernen Staatsminsterien. *Historische Zeitschrift*, 1908, 100, 53–111.

Homans, G. C. *The human group*. New York: Harcourt, 1950.

Homans, G. C. *Social behavior: Its elementary forms*. New York: Harcourt, Brace & World, 1961.

Hopkins, T. K. Bureaucratic authority: The convergence of Weber and Barnard. In A. Etzioni (Ed.), *Complex organizations*. New York: Holt, 1961. Pp. 82–98.

Hughes, E. C. *Men and their work*. Glencoe, Ill.: Free Press, 1958.

Janowitz, M. *The professional soldier*. Glencoe, Ill.: Free Press, 1960.

Jaques, E. *The measurement of responsibility*. Cambridge, Mass.: Harvard Univer. Press, 1956.

Kahn, R. L., & Katz, D. Leadership practices in relation to productivity and morale. In D. Cartwright & A. Zander (Eds.), *Group dynamics*. Evanston, Ill.: Row, Peterson, 1953. Pp. 612–628.

Katz, E., & Eisenstadt, S. N. Some sociological observations on the response of Israeli organizations to new immigrants. *Admin. Sci. Quart.*, 1960, 5, 113–133.

Kaufman, H. Emerging conflicts in the doctrines of public administration. *Amer. pol. Sci. Rev.*, 1956, 50, 1057–1073.

Kornhauser, W. *Scientists in industry*. Berkeley: Univer. of California Press, 1962.

Kracke, E. A., Jr. *Civil service in early Sung China 960–1067*. Cambridge, Mass.: Harvard Univer. Press, 1953.

Krupp, S. *Pattern in organization analysis*. Philadelphia: Chilton, 1961.

Landsberger, H. A. The horizontal dimension in bureaucracy. *Admin. Sci. Quart.*, 1961, 6, 299–332.(a)

Landsberger, H. A. Parsons' theory of organizations. In M. Black (Ed.), *The social theories of Talcott Parsons*. Englewood Cliffs, N.J.: Prentice-Hall, Inc., 1961. Pp. 214–249. (b)

Lazarsfeld, P. F., & Menzel, H. On the relation between individual and collective properties. In A. Etzioni (Ed.), *Complex organizations*. New York: Holt, 1961. Pp. 422–440.

Leavitt, H. J. Some effects of certain communication patterns on group performance. *J. abnorm. soc. Psychol.*, 1951, 46, 38–50.

Leontief, W. W. *The structure of the American economy*. (rev. ed.) Cambridge, Mass.: Harvard Univer. Press, 1951.

Lieberson, S. The division of labor in banking. *Amer. J. Sociol.*, 1961, 66, 491–496.

Likert, R. *New patterns of management*. New York: McGraw, 1961.

Lipset, S. M. *Political man*. New York: Doubleday, 1960.

Lipset, S. M., Trow, M. A., & Coleman, J. S. *Union democracy*. Glencoe, Ill.: Free Press, 1956.

McCleery, R. H. *Policy change in prison management*. East Lansing: Governmental Research Bureau, Michigan State Univer. Press, 1957.

Mannheim, K. *Man and society in an age of reconstruction*. New York: Harcourt, 1950.

March, J. G., & Simon, H. A. *Organizations*. New York: Wiley, 1958.

Marcson, S. Organization and authority in industrial research. *Soc. Forces*, 1961, 40, 72–80.

Mason, E. S. Labor monopoly and all that. In W. Galenson & S. M. Lipset (Eds.), *Labor and trade unionism*. New York: Wiley, 1960. Pp. 119–149.

Mayo, E. *The social problems of an industrial civilization*. Boston: Graduate School of Business Administration, Harvard Univer., 1945.

Merton, R. K. *Social theory and social structure*. (rev. ed.) Glencoe, Ill.: Free Press, 1957.

Merton, R. K., Gray, Ailsa P., Hockey, Barbara, & Selvin, H. C. (Eds.) *Reader in bureaucracy.* Glencoe Ill.: Free Press, 1952.

Michels, R. *Political parties.* Glencoe, Ill.: Free Press, 1949.

Nagel, E. *Logic without metaphysics.* Glencoe, Ill.: Free Press, 1956.

Newcomb, T. M. *Personality and social change.* New York: Dryden, 1943.

Parsons, T. *The social system.* Glencoe, Ill.: Free Press, 1951.

Parsons, T. A revised analytical approach to the theory of social stratification. In R. Bendix & S. M. Lipset (Eds.), *Class, status and power.* Glencoe, Ill.: Free Press, 1953. Pp. 92–128.

Parsons, T. *Structure and process in modern societies.* Glencoe, Ill.: Free Press, 1960.

Parsons, T. Introduction to part two: Differentiation and variation in social structures. Vol. 1. In T. Parsons, E. Shils, K. D. Naegele, & J. R. Pitts (Eds.), *Theories of society.* New York: The Free Press of Glencoe, 1961.

Parsons, T., Bales, R. F., & Shils, E. A. *Working papers in the theory of action.* Glencoe, Ill.: Free Press, 1953.

Parsons, T., & Shils, E. A. (Eds.) *Toward a general theory of action.* Cambridge, Mass.: Harvard Univer. Press, 1954.

Parsons, T., & Smelser, N. J. *Economy and society.* Glencoe, Ill.: Free Press, 1956.

Pelz, D. C. Influence: A key to effective leadership in the first-line supervisor. *Personnel,* 1952, **29,** 209–217.

Perrow, C. The analysis of goals in complex organizations. *Amer. sociol. Rev.,* 1961, **26,** 854–866.

Presthus, R. *The organizational society.* New York: Knopf, 1962.

Roberts, D. R. *Executive compensation.* Glencoe, Ill.: Free Press, 1959.

Roe, Anne. *The psychology of occupations.* New York: Wiley, 1956.

Roethlisberger, F. J., & Dickson, W. J. *Management and the worker.* Cambridge, Mass.: Harvard Univer. Press, 1939.

Rosenberg, H. *Bureaucracy, aristocracy and autocracy.* Cambridge, Mass.: Harvard Univer. Press, 1958.

Roy, D. Quota restriction and goldbricking in a machine shop. *Amer. J. Sociol.,* 1952, **57,** 427–442.

Rubenstein, A. H., & Haberstroh, C. J. (Eds.) *Some theories of organization.* Homewood, Ill.: Dorsey Press & Richard D. Irwin, 1960.

Schein, E. H., & Ott, J. S. The legitimacy of organizational influence. *Amer. J. Sociol.,* 1962, **67,** 682–689.

Seashore, S. E. *Group cohesiveness in the industrial work group.* Ann Arbor: Institute for Social Research, Univer. of Michigan, 1954.

Selznick, P. An approach to a theory of bureaucracy. *Amer. sociol. Rev.,* 1943, **8,** 47–54.

Selznick, P. Foundations of the theory of organization. *Amer. sociol. Rev.,* 1948, **13,** 25–35.

Selznick, P. *TVA and the grass roots.* Berkeley: Univer. of California Press, 1949.

Selznick, P. *The organizational weapon.* New York: McGraw, 1952.

Selznick, P. *Leadership in administration.* Evanston, Ill.: Row, Peterson, 1957.

Shepard, H. A. Nine dilemmas in industrial research. *Admin. Sci. Quart.,* 1956, **1,** 295–309.

Sills, D. L. *The volunteers.* Glencoe, Ill.: Free Press, 1957.

Simon, H. Comments on the theory of organizations. *Amer. pol. Sci. Rev.,* 1952, **46,** 1130–1139.

Simon, H. A. *Administrative behavior.* (2nd ed.) New York: Macmillan, 1957.

Simpson, R. L. Vertical and horizontal communication in formal organizations. *Admin. Sci. Quart.,* 1959, **4,** 188–196.

Simpson, R. L., & Gulley, W. H. Goals, environmental pressures, and organizational characteristics. *Amer. sociol. Rev.,* 1962, **27,** 344–351.

Stanton, A. H., & Schwartz, M. S. *The mental hospital.* New York: Basic Books, 1954.

Stinchcombe, A. L. Bureaucratic and craft administration of production. *Admin. Sci. Quart.,* 1959, **4,** 168–187.

Stinchcombe, A. L. Comment on "Technical and institutional factors in production organization." *Amer. J. Sociol.,* 1961, **67,** 255–259.

Sykes, G. M., & Messinger, S. L. The inmate social system. In R. A. Cloward, D. R. Cressey, G. H. Grosser, R. McCleery, L. E. Ohlin, G. M. Sykes, & S. L. Messinger (Eds.), *Theoretical studies in social organi-*

zation of the prison. New York: Social Science Research Council, 1960. Pp. 5–19.

Thompson, J. D. Organizations and output transactions. *Amer. J. Sociol.,* 1962, **68,** 309–324.

Thompson, J. D., & Bates, F. L. Technology, organization, and administration. *Admin. Sci. Quart.,* 1957, **2,** 325–343.

Thompson, J. D., & McEwen, W. J. Organization goals and environment. *Amer. sociol. Rev.,* 1958, **23,** 23–31.

Thompson, V. A. *Modern organization.* New York: Knopf, 1961.

Tout, T. F. *The English civil service in the fourteenth century.* Manchester, Eng.: Univer. Press, 1916.

Turner, R. H. The navy disbursing officer as a bureaucrat. *Amer. sociol. Rev.,* 1947, **12,** 342–348.

Udy, S. H., Jr. "Bureaucratic" elements in organizations. *Amer. sociol. Rev.,* 1958, **23,** 415–418.

Udy, S. H., Jr. "Bureaucracy" and "rationality" in Weber's organization theory. *Amer. sociol. Rev.,* 1959, **24,** 791–795.(a)

Udy, S. H., Jr. *Organization of work.* New Haven, Conn.: HRAF Press, 1959.(b)

Udy, S. H., Jr. Technical and institutional factors in production organization. *Amer. J. Sociol.,* 1961, **67,** 247–254.

Udy, S. H., Jr. Administrative rationality, social setting, and organizational development. *Amer. J. Sociol.,* 1962, **68,** 299–308.

Vollmer, H. M. *Adaptations of scientists in an independent research organization.* Menlo Park, Calif.: Stanford Research Institute, 1963.

Weber, M. *From Max Weber: Essays in sociology.* H. H. Gerth & C. W. Mills (Eds. & Trans.). New York: Oxford Univer. Press, 1946.

Weber, M. *The theory of social and economic organization.* A. M. Henderson & T. Parsons (Trans.). Glencoe, Ill.: Free Press, 1947.

Wessen, A. F. Hospital ideology and communication between ward personnel. In E. G. Jaco (Ed.), *Patients, physicians and illness.* Glencoe, Ill.: Free Press, 1958, Pp. 448–468.

Whyte, W. F. *Men at work.* Homewood, Ill.: Dorsey Press & Richard D. Irwin, 1961.

Whyte, W. F., Dalton, M., Roy, D., Sayles, L., Collins, O., Miller, F., Strauss, G., Fuerstenberg, F., & Bavelas, A. *Money and motivation.* New York: Harper, 1955.

Whyte, W. H., Jr. *The organization man.* New York: Simon & Schuster, 1956.

Wilensky, H. L. *Intellectuals in labor unions.* Glencoe, Ill.: Free Press, 1956.

Wilensky, H. L., & Lebeaux, C. N. *Industrial society and social welfare.* New York: Russell Sage Foundation, 1958.

Wolin, S. S. *Politics and vision.* Boston: Little, 1960.

Woodward, Joan. *Management and technology.* London: H.M.S.O., 1958.

Zaleznik, A., Christensen, C. R., & Roethlisberger, F. J. *The motivation, productivity, and satisfaction of workers.* Boston: Graduate School of Business Administration, Harvard Univer., 1958.

Zelditch, M., Jr., & Hopkins, T. K. Laboratory experiments with organizations. In A. Etzioni (Ed.), *Complex organizations.* New York: Holt, Rinehart & Winston, 1961. Pp. 464–478.

CHAPTER 15 Social Differentiation

KAARE SVALASTOGA

THEORY

The Universality of Social Differentiation

The concept "social differentiation" refers to any differences between individuals, social positions, or groups, which evolve in the process of social interaction. Four major forms of such differentiation may be noted (see North, 1926). Functional differentiation, or division of labor, exists to the extent that people perform different jobs. Rank differentiation exists to the extent that whatever is scarce and desired is differentially distributed. Custom differentiation exists to the extent that the rules for proper behavior in given situations differ. Competitive differentiation may finally be said to exist to the extent that the success of one individual or group implies the failure of others.

The present chapter is focused on rank differentiation. A social system (group, organization, society) will in the following be referred to as rank differentiated, status differentiated, or stratified, these terms being treated as synonymous.

The fundamental character of systematic rank differentiation is suggested by its presence in all known human societies and in a wide range of animal societies.

The law of the peck-order, first formulated on the basis of research on the domestic hen (Schjelderup-Ebbe, 1921), was later confirmed for other species of birds, for many species of mammals, and for certain insects (Allee, 1949; Crawford, 1939; Schenkel, 1948; Svalastoga & Carlsson, 1961). Individual animals in close contact tend, according to the peck-order law, to constitute a hierarchy. Thus among three hens, the rule is that one will peck the two others, one of these will peck the other, who will peck no one. This hierarchy is highly stable and functions as a distributive system for the allotment of privileges, thereby further strengthening the hierarchy. Furthermore, once established, the hierarchy assures unequal distribution accompanied by a minimum of actual fighting.

The hierarchy of a gang (Whyte, 1943) resembles in important aspects the animal peck-order organization.

The proposition that rank differences are universal in human groups stands unchallenged by all research so far performed. In fact, researchers have frequently had to reject the counterhypotheses of complete equality postulated by group members. Murdock's world ethnographic sample provides excellent material for studying the distribution of certain more visible expressions of social rank (see below). However, it would be utterly fallacious to conclude the absence of rank distinctions from the absence of such features as slavery, nobility, and the like. Some anthropologists have the habit of referring to societies where the only obvious rank distinctions are those dependent upon age and sex as unstratified. Clearly, this does not imply that rank distinctions are absent, although it does imply that, barring sex distinctions, any person will normally pass through approximately the same cycle of rank as any other.

Rank distinctions may apply to individuals, to social positions, to groups, to institutions, or even to societies.

Since such distinctions seem to be universal, it is clearly a fairly unrewarding task simply to explain their existence. The absence of negative cases prevents the effective rejection of wrong hypotheses. Hence, only to the extent that explanatory attempts proceed to spell out the conditions conducive to more or less inequality do they achieve greater empirical relevance. Leaving out of consideration purely metaphysical explanations, all major attempts at explaining inequality seem to be reducible to three major types, that is:

1. Biological
2. Sociological, stressing cooperation
3. Sociological, stressing conflict.

Perhaps the oldest of all nonmetaphysical theories of social inequality is the biological explanation: People are differently rewarded in a society because they are unequally gifted. As Aristotle has it, "It is thus clear that there are by nature free men and slaves, and that servitude is agreeable and just for the latter" (Aristotle, 1959, p. 11).

The basic weakness of the biological explanation consists in its inability to account for the tremendous variation in stratification systems in time and space. Moreover, it does not account for the unequal rank of social positions. This is not to deny that certain systems of ranking of individuals may be chiefly accounted for in biological terms (race, sex, age), nor that the same factors are important in social selection.

In recent years, the most discussed theory of rank differentiation has been a sociological theory stressing the requirements of cooperation. This is the so-called functionalist explanation. Its main tenets, as set forth by Davis and Moore, are:

Rank differentiation is universal because it is necessary; i.e., no society could exist without it. Tasks that need to be executed in a society differ in importance, difficulty, and popularity. To ensure that vital and hard-to-do tasks, which are not necessarily popular, are performed, society is obliged to reward such performance more highly than less vital and less demanding tasks. By so doing, society creates a structure of differentially rewarded positions. As described by the authors, positional rewards will typically contain one economic component (e.g., income) and one noneconomic component (e.g., prestige, esteem) (Davis & Moore, 1945).

Few propositions have been as much debated as those just stated. At least one of them shares one basic weakness with many functionalist propositions. There is no way of proving or disproving it. Let us agree that inequality is universal. How shall it be decided whether it is universal and necessary or universal and unnecessary? Clearly there is no empirical procedure available for choosing between these two interpretations. It seems, in general, more fruitful to reformulate the problem as follows: Regardless of whether inequality is necessary or unnecessary, exactly what factors control the level of inequality of a given society? About these factors, it may be said that they must be of a highly general kind, referring to forces at work in any human and perhaps in many animal groups.

Another difficult concept in the functional theory of social stratification is the term functional importance. Davis and Moore express themselves as follows:

Unfortunately, functional importance is difficult to establish. To use the position prestige to establish it, as is often unconsciously done, constitutes circular reasoning from our point of view. There are, however, two independent clues: (a) the degree to which a position is functionally unique, there being no other positions that can perform the same function satisfactorily; (b) the degree to which other positions are dependent on the one in question. Both clues are best exemplified in organized systems of positions built around one major function. Thus, in most complex societies the religious, political, economic, and educational functions are handled by distinct structures not easily interchangeable. In addition, each structure possesses many different positions, some clearly dependent on, if not subordinate to, others. In sum, when an institutional nucleus becomes differentiated around one main function, and at the same time organizes a large portion of the population into its relationships, the key positions in it are of the highest functional importance. The absence of such specialization does not prove functional unimportance, for the whole society may be relatively unspecialized; but it is safe to assume that the more important functions receive the first and clearest structural differentiation (Davis & Moore, 1945, p. 244, fn 3).

It is also possible to consider, as does Parsons (1953), the social importance of an activity as a resultant of the values of a society. Parsons suggests in particular that there are four value sets that may be more or less prominent in a given society, a given organization, and a given activity. Although imperfectly defined, these value sets seem to correspond to different criteria of success, roughly as follows:

1. Economic success criteria; e.g., efficiency, productivity;
2. Political success criteria; e.g., decision-making, coordinating;
3. Familistic success criteria; e.g., solidarity;
4. Scientific or ideological (including religious) success criteria; e.g., fact finding;

promoting happiness, health, peace of mind, education.

Parsons asserts that the economic (adaptive) criteria tend to take first place in the United States, the political (goal achievement) in the U.S.S.R., and so on. Certainly it is commonly observed that societies differ in the composition of their value hierarchies. It is, however, somewhat problematic whether a reduction of the problem of the social importance of an activity to a theory of evaluational differences is the most productive strategy in view of the undeveloped state of the measurements of values.

One line of attack against the view that social positions differ in functional importance consists in referring to the indispensability to a factory of major categories of positions (e.g., "some labor force of unskilled workers," "some labor force of engineers" [Tumin, 1953]), regardless of their status. However, this hardly contradicts the highly observable fact that the manager of a firm is in a better position to make it succeed or fail than is the janitor, and hence that the former holds the more important position even if both are equally indispensible.

It does not follow from the functionalist theory that the differential rewards actually put out by society are adjusted so as to assure that the best talent is recruited for a given position (Davis, 1949). Hence, it is perfectly possible to endorse this theory and at the same time subscribe to Tumin's (1953) list of dysfunctions in stratification systems. The major dysfunction may be a reduction of the resilience of a society due to insufficient attention to the nurturing of creative talent and to a reduction of social integration.

Wrong's (1959) paper is the best available assessment of the strength and weakness of the functional theory of social stratification. In addition, it contains many new insights and references to much literature written by nonsociologists.

Wrong's main argument is that one main reason that the functional theory stands unrejected is that the theory is so general and affords only a limited opportunity for drawing deductions—these, furthermore, being so general that a wide array of empirical stratification systems is compatible with the theory.

In particular, he notes that the deduction, "rewards must be unequal," does not imply anything about the exact degree of inequality needed. It is perfectly possible that the inequality actually found may well be far above the amount considered necessary.

Furthermore, Wrong argues that inequality of opportunity by social origin is not necessarily dysfunctional. For certain occupations, it may be perfectly possible that those perform best who are born into families where the occupation is hereditary and hence where learning can begin early.

A variant of cooperation-centered explanation was put forth recently by Dahrendorf (1961), who points to the need for norms in cooperating groups. These norms are accompanied by rewards and punishment respectively for over- and underperformance. Hence, differential rewards between individuals appear, and, due to unequal chances of differentially located individuals to comply with the norms, inequality generalizes even to positions. It is not clear how one should account for variations in inequality according to this theory.

The conflict-centered type of explanation appears in various forms. Perhaps this type of theory could be more adequately described by saying that they either implicitly or explicitly assume a certain deficit of solidarity or integration between, as contrasted to within, primary groups (in particular nuclear families).

The theory is most explicitly stated by Gumplowicz. Davis and Moore ask, "who shall do the important work," and Gumplowicz asks, "who shall do the dirty work," i.e., work distasteful to most people.

The problem for a society is how to get this work performed. Gumplowicz contends that the standard solution is arrived at in a uniform way, which is related to the solidarity or integration of the social member:

Thus has nature herself, then, laid the foundation for such state construction by the manner in which she equipped men with desires and sentiments. She made men dependent upon the services of other men—implanted in their bosoms compassion with kinsmen and deadly hatred against strangers—and thus she forced men to subdue other men, strangers to them (Gumplowicz, 1885, p. 119, translation by writer).

Hence despised and defeated out-groups will perform the dirty work.

A variant of the conflict theory is Rousseau's hypothesis according to which private property is the determinant of inequality: "No private property, no inequality." As Dahrendorf (1957) has pointed out on the basis of a detailed study, Marx himself was rather strongly convinced that the abolition of private property would be the most important step toward the establishment of equality.

There may be few sociological hypotheses that have been tested at such a high human cost. The outcome as observed in Russia is noncontroversial. Inequality in the distribution of power and privilege continues to exist even after the abolition of major forms of private property (Inkeles, 1950). There is even reason to believe that the span of the stratification hierarchy has expanded rather than contracted in the process (see below).

In the opinion of the present writer, both the above-mentioned sociological theories contain elements that ought to enter into a more powerful theory of rank differentiation.

Activity, Differentiation, and Integration

Let a social system be defined as a set of social units (individuals, subsets of individuals, or subsystems) which maintain interaction in an environment. The relationship between the system and its environment is such that the system has to display activity to maintain its position in the environment. This activity affects the internal structure of the system in two ways. It affects its level of rank differentiation and its level of integration.

Postulates

1. An increase in the activity of the system increases rank differentiation.

2. The relationship between activity and social integration is curvilinear; i.e., integration increases with activity only up to a certain level of activity; with further increase in activity, integration decreases.

3. Rank differentiation is negatively related to integration, but the relationship depends on the activity level. At low levels, it is weak and hence easily damped by the much stronger relationship activity-integration. At higher levels, it is stronger and tends further to strengthen the negative relationship between integration and activity at these levels.

Let us next consider how a social system may increase its activity. There seem to be five major routes:

1. It may recruit more people by increasing fertility or immigration or by reducing mortality or emigration.

2. It may apply a more efficient technology.

3. It may institute longer hours of work or achieve more energetic application to work per time unit per worker.

4. It may design a more efficient functional differentiation.

5. It may improve its channels of communication.

Inferences (hypotheses)

1. Increasing technological efficiency increases rank differentiation (see Davis & Moore, 1945).

2. Increasing population size increases rank differentiation (Davis & Moore, 1945).

3. Increasing environmental resistance, to the extent that it increases the activity of the system, increases social differentiation, but only up to a certain level of resistance, whereupon the relationship becomes negative.

4. Increasing functional differentiation increases rank differentiation (see Homans, 1950, p. 406).

5. To the extent that integration may be affected by other factors than the amount of activity of the system, it is possible by varying integration to vary the rank differentiation.

6. Increasing technological efficiency, above a certain level, reduces integration.

7. Increasing population size reduces integration (Schermerhorn, 1961, p. 22).

8. Increasing environmental resistance increases integration up to a certain limit, at which point disintegration begins.

9. Increasing functional differentiation decreases integration.

The problem for a society desiring to maximize its resilience is to balance social rank differentiation against social integration so that the former is no more elaborate than needed for the task, but still sufficient to facilitate the upward flow of talent and the coordination of activity, the latter to be neither so high that it challenges efficiency nor so low that it threatens cooperation.

If this theory is sound, a society is faced with a double optimization problem, and, in the absence of relevant research regarding the critical limits, it is not possible to say whether the problem is soluble.

A partial support for hypothesis 1 is the absence of both nobility and slavery in the most primitive hunting societies. At the same time highly developed agricultural societies are the most likely to possess both nobility and slavery (Hobhouse, Wheeler, & Ginsberg, 1915). It remains for further research to show whether industrial society, characterized by absence of nobility and slavery, may be said to have a lower status span than agricultural societies or whether new rank distinctions may not have grown up so as to make the real status span in industrial societies larger than ever before. In particular, it should be pointed out that the lifting of the status floor does not contribute to a lower status span if the ceiling is at the same time lifted as much or more. Certainly the power elite seems vastly more influential than any previous elite. Also the scientific elite today seems to be vastly more efficient, and their skills further removed from common sense, than ever before.

The distinguishing mark between democracies and dictatorships cannot, according to this theory, be found in the presence or absence of inequality of power. Such inequality is universal. Rather the distinction should be found in the occurrence or non-occurrence of effective competition for the power to make social decisions by means of an appeal to the people's vote (see Schumpeter, 1952).

Massive, if still partial, support for hypothesis 2 comes from Table 1. It will be seen

the elaborate hierarchies of organizations presumably exposed to a particularly risky environment (the military organization, the ship, the hospital).

Hypothesis 4 gains indirect support from anthropological studies which show that there is a consistent logarithmic relationship between the size of the largest town of a society and the degree of functional differentiation (Naroll, 1956). A recent study reported a rank order correlation of .85 between technology and division of labor (Gibbs & Martin, 1962, p. 674). This suggests that hypothesis 4 may hold to the extent that hypothesis 1 holds and vice versa.

Hypothesis 5 suggests that it is always possible to soften a rigid status system, at

TABLE 1

SOCIAL STRATIFICATION AND SIZE OF SOCIETY[a]

Approximate Size and Political Organization	Level of Stratification[b]		Total	
	Higher	Lower	Per Cent	N
Larger state (10^5 and over)	100	0	100	77
Little state ($10^4 - 10^5$)	92	8	100	48
Minimal state ($1.5 \times 10^3 - 10^4$)	75	25	100	117
Autonomous community ($X \leq 1.5 \times 10^3$)	50	50	100	218
Family band (c. 10^2)	22	88	100	36

[a] Source: Murdock (1957). Table prepared by Erik Høgh.
[b] "Higher" stratification denotes presence of one or more of the following features: Complex stratification into three or more classes or castes, hereditary aristocracy, important wealth distinctions, slavery incipient or hereditary. "Lower" stratification denotes absence of all these features.

that with increasing size, at least up to 10, goes a regular increase in the percentage of societies possessing one or more signs of stratification (slavery, nobility, etc.).

Hypothesis 2 was expressed by Mosca (1939, p. 53) as follows: ". . . the larger the political community the smaller will be the proportion of the governing minority to the governed majority, and the more difficult will it be for the majority to organize for reaction against the minority."

Hypothesis 3 suggests a curvilinear relationship. Regarding the positive part of the relationship, suggestive evidence is found in

least for a time, by making room for the growth of love and charity.

Hypothesis 8 points to the integrative importance of maintaining a high level of talent utilization within a meaningful social scheme, and hypotheses 6, 7, and 9 suggest that this importance is increasing in so-called modern societies.

The first part of postulate 2 is similar to Homan's hypothesis (1950) that activity and sentiment are positively related. But the second part posits that for a sufficiently large activity increase, the relationship to integration (sentiment) is negative. The rationale for this part is the assumption that larger increases in activity will tend to make the group more highly differentiated in function, and thus it will, by hypothesis 4, experience an increase in its status span, and this in turn will, by postulate 3, reduce integration.

Criteria of Positional Rank

Since systems of positional rank distinctions evolve in the process of interaction, it is by the observation of this process that we can discover the criteria or values which constitute the bases of assigning differential status to individuals or to the positions they occupy in the social structure. If we apply an informal input-output analysis to this interaction, we may start by observing that the typical individual output consists in performing certain tasks, which may be more or less difficult, and which, when done, may influence other people more or less. The typical input consists in certain privileges of a social or economic nature which society permits him to enjoy.

It is hence suggested that a comprehensive analysis of the rank of a position should take into account:

1. Power or influence, whether socially acceptable or not
2. Information; i.e., skill or knowledge
3. Social status or deference
4. Economic status.

It may safely be said that economic status has been the favorite criterion used or suggested in older literature. Perhaps this is so because wealth, in comparison with the other criteria, enjoys an eminent degree of both visibility and transferability from father to son, at least so long as a minimum of social stability prevails. It is also the dimension most accessible to measurement.

At present, both power and social status are generally granted an important place in stratification literature, although power, because of the immature status of research on the subject, tends to be treated more superficially. In contrast, information is more

rarely accorded a place as a main criterion of rank. This is, in the writer's opinion, a serious defect because education seems increasingly to be becoming not only a major criterion of ranking, but also the most important means by which a person may change his other statuses.

Nor is the emphasis on education a novelty. Weber, who is commonly credited with only three stratification criteria—wealth, power, and honor (1948)—actually introduced education several times in one of his two discussions of social stratification (1947).

There are many discussions in the literature regarding the dimensionality of rank differentiation. One issue is whether stratification is unidimensional or multidimensional. But clearly, this depends upon what society we are considering. A society characterized by perfect correlation between all relevant criterion variables has a unidimensional stratification system. Conversely one in which the average correlation is lower will be multidimensional (see below). Furthermore, to the extent that it can be shown that only one rank factor varies markedly in a society whereas others are approximately constant, then again a unidimensional model will fit.

Another problem is whether the stratification variables should be regarded as discrete or continuous. Again, this will depend on the conditions governing in the society under study.

To the extent that vast differences in the possession of desired and scarce goods exist between the top people and those next to the top, a discrete model seems more adequate. Conversely, if it is possible to find people who differ minutely in rank at any point on the continuum, a continuous model seems more apposite (see Foote et al., 1954).

Criteria of Personal Rank

The problem posed by the concept personal rank is much more complicated than that posed by the concept positional rank. This is so because in the latter case, it was possible to limit attention to variables directly connected with task performance. In considering personal rank, it is necessary to introduce additional criteria which may be only loosely connected with task performance. Among these are the so-called ascriptive criteria: sex, age, and kinship (race, ethnicity, social origin). These criteria owe their importance to their central role in social selection (Linton, 1936). Some of these factors like race or ethnicity, for example, may weigh so heavily in the composition of a person's overall rank as to nearly delete the effect of positional rank.

A further complication introduced by the concept personal rank is that a person may engage in several tasks and hence be rewarded differentially in each. Conventionally, this problem is settled by limiting attention to his (primary) occupation.

This may suffice in a macrosocial approach but may be much too crude in a microsocial approach. In fact, several theorists have been concerned with the problem of combining into an index the specific positional prestige and personal esteem derived in the execution of a person's total set of positions (Hatt, 1950; Hyman, 1942; Linton, 1936).

For most purposes, it seems that the occupational position weighs so heavily that other positions only very weakly affect the social rank of a person in a society. But exceptions do exist. The modern emphasis on competitive sport has lifted the social rank of many young persons of modest occupation. Increasing professionalization again brings these positions under the general rule.

In social situations characterized by occupational homogeneity—e.g., small cohesive groups—a person's social rank will typically depend on "evaluated participation" (Homans, 1950).

An additional complication with individual social rank is that it varies for constant position or set of positions according to the excellence of role performance, thus giving each person a measure of personal esteem (Hatt, 1950) for each position he fills apart

from the prestige of the positions themselves. A further problem is the disturbing effect of status symbols. This effect is likely to increase with increasing social anonymity. To the extent that a person can appropriate the way of life of those above him, he is likely to be ranked higher except by those who know his other characteristics. This brings in the general problem of the effect of anonymity on personal rank. The best hypothesis seems to be that social ignorance is a damping factor, tending to reduce distinctions of social status and, furthermore, tending to make it possible to enlarge actual differences in other status dimensions without disintegrative effects (Moore & Tumin, 1949).

A fundamental theoretical problem is whether personal rank should be regarded as a sum of (weighted) scores on several variables, or as a product. Conventionally, indices have been constructed on the assumption of additivity. But is this a good sociological assumption? May a person achieve the highest rewards in a society by being sufficiently highly placed on only one or a few variables? Or does he drop down into the lowest levels only if the total set of relevant variables achieve their lowest values? Is it not rather the case that eminence requires many simultaneously present facilitating circumstances, and that a single false step may ruin a man's career?

An early student of eminence has this to say:

Eminence is always an exception produced by several favorable causes that rarely unite. For a man to become famous, great talent is insufficient, he needs in addition favorable circumstances, above all a readiness to act, to prove himself useful. Indifference, laziness of the body or the mind may arrest highly gifted persons, who without that would have been among the most illustrious (Candolle, 1872; here cited from Girard, 1961, p. 50).

The fact that many status criteria have approximately a log-normal distribution further strengthens the case for the multiplicative relationship between status criteria. The log-normal curve occurs in nature when events depend for their occurrence on the joint occurrence of several other events (Aitchison & Brown, 1957; see below).

Rank and Size

With increasing size, a group (society) becomes at the same time more differentiated and more anonymous. As a result, consensus will be harder to achieve in regard to positional rank and particularly in regard to personal rank. Thus, a differentiated national society will exhibit a high level of personal anonymity in its major cities and a high level of positional anonymity in the countryside (ignorance or insufficient knowledge about occupations, most of which are strictly urban).

Deductively, the small cities (of 2,000–19,000 inhabitants) should be most likely to exhibit ranking consensus. No test of this hypothesis has come to the author's attention. He has, however, shown that in Denmark such cities are definitely atypical insofar as they reveal a consistently higher tendency to stress status distinctions than does the rest of the country (Svalastoga, 1959).

These observations are particularly relevant in view of the tendency of the Warner school to assume that the nation is like the town: "All Americans are in Jonesville."

In contrast, it seems much safer, on the basis of the above arguments, to maintain not only that the nation is different from the town, but that, being larger, the nation will reveal much larger spans of power, wealth, and information and a stronger egalitarian bent. Thus, social status is perhaps made a more compressed variable, although the compression may be affected by efficient status symbolism (see Kornhauser, 1953; Pfautz & Duncan, 1950).

It may further be apposite here to draw upon the results of biological studies of the relative growth of an organism and its component parts. These results seem to point to an invariance, to the effect that given parts of a system (organism) tend to maintain constant relative growth rates as compared with the total system (the principle of allometric growth). Thus, within the class of mammalia it is found that the brain weight invariably grows slower than total body weight (inter-species comparison). More precisely, its relative rate of growth tends to be six-tenths of the relative growth rate of the total system. A parallel principle may obtain in social systems, as some research findings indicate. Of particular relevance may be the tendency of communities to grow faster the larger they are. To the extent that system parts are characterized by unequal growth rates, the larger system does not only contain more elementary units, but also displays a structure radically different from the smaller system (see Svalastoga, 1963, and sources cited there).

MEASUREMENT

Methods used for the measurement of social status vary according to: (1) the object of measurement—person or position; (2) the operational procedure used—self-rating (ranking), community- or other-rating (ranking), various indicators of interaction, so-called specific status indicators (education, income, etc.), or multidimensional indices.

Self-Rating and Community Rating

Self-rating of personal status has the advantage of wide applicability but suffers from the common disadvantage of interrogational data, that of dependence on the respondents' ability and readiness to give the desired information. Furthermore, several investigators have reported the observation of strong influence by the method of questioning. These handicaps are more serious in self-rating than in community rating because only one piece of information is obtained concerning each object of rating. In spite of these shortcomings, it is clear that under certain conditions the errors of the method may cancel each other. Besides, provided that respondent cooperation and ability is present, a person tends, according to social psychological theory, to see himself as others see him. Hence there will generally be a considerable correlation between the way a person is rated by others and the way he rates himself (r [tetrachoric] = .7 [Centers, 1949]; r = .6 [Svalastoga, 1959]).

Roper showed that Americans, when left free to label the class they belonged to, were more likely to choose the label "middle class" than any other (Cantril, 1951). Svalastoga (1959) reported a corresponding finding for Denmark.

At the same time, Centers (1949) in the United States, Benny and Geiss (1950) in England, Svalastoga in Denmark, and several European surveys reported that the use of a list of labelled classes among which both the label "middle class," and the label "working class" appeared, gave radically different results.

Scandinavians, Germans, Englishmen, and Americans, faced with such a list, tended to choose the "working class" label more frequently than the "middle class" label. The simplest explanation for this finding may be the existence of the combination of widespread middle-class aspirations and fairly low working-class solidarity among the upper levels of manual workers.

Through the pioneering efforts of William Lloyd Warner (Warner, Meeker, & Eells, 1949), a new method of measuring the status that a community allots to a group member was launched. His method—of evaluated participation—suffers from the defects of most pioneering attempts, but it has the virtue of being communicable, although it could be made more so.

The method consists in selecting a number of informants and conducting interviews with them with the purpose of (1) reaching a decision on how many strata or classes the population of the community recognizes and (2) establishing where in this stratification system a particular adult member of the community belongs.

A rather obvious weakness of the method

is its ambiguity. Clearly, in order to provide a reliable research tool, it is necessary to be precise about the way in which it should be used. This implies rules for deciding:

1. Composition of the rating group
2. Composition of the group rated
3. Questions to be posed
4. Scoring of the answers in respect to number of classes, the classification of persons, and the status interpretation of specific symbols, memberships, and so on.

Warner did not provide any of these rules. Furthermore, he did not give a precise operative technique for dealing with disagreement among raters. His own sampling suffered from numerical inadequacy and bias of selection (Kornhauser, 1953; Pfautz & Duncan, 1950). A considerable improvement of the method appears in the works of Hollingshead (1949) and Kaufman (1953).

Interactional Criteria

Social status differs from such other forms of status as power, wealth, or information by being completely determined by the nature of the social interaction of a person. Social interaction may, as with Homans, be regarded as an exchange of values. To the extent that the exchange transfers more deference to A than to B, A enjoys higher status. This will usually depend upon A's superior possibility for transferring desired assistance to B (Homans, 1961). Such regularly recurring and highly status-linked behavior as visiting, intermarriage, and occupational mobility are not convenient measures of social status.

In the absence of outside information, it is impossible to interpret correctly cases of low interactivity between two persons or groups, A and B. There are three possibilities:

1. A ranks much higher than B
2. B ranks much higher than A
3. There is no, or no major, difference in rank, but A and B interact infrequently because they live far apart, speak different languages, or for other reasons (cf. Barber, 1957).

In situations where the third and either the first or the second possibility may be excluded, measures of interaction frequency become important status measures.

Intermarriage is of particular relevance because of its high frequency, familial importance, and data accessibility (Beshers, 1962; see also G. Carlsson, 1958).

Status measurement in terms of interaction preferences is excellently illustrated in a study by Mahar (1960). Mahar documented that the rank order of castes in an Indian village could be determined with the precision of a Guttman scale on the basis of a set of questions dealing with the acceptability of directly or indirectly being touched by a member of a given caste.

Multidimensional Indices

Interest in multidimensional indices of social or socioeconomic status seems to have declined. One major reason for this may be that such indices conceal possible discrepancies between components and hence rule out the search for behavioral consequences of varying levels of correlations between such components (Gordon, 1958).

Of the many multiple item indices developed before World War II, very few are now in common use. The interested reader will find good surveys in Lundberg (1942; also Neff, 1938).

Still, at least two multiple indices of social status are frequently used or referred to. These are Warner's index of status characteristics (Warner et al., 1949), and Hollingshead's index of social position.

Warner's index has four components:

1. Occupations
2. Source of income
3. Type of house
4. Area lived in.

A person is ranked on a 1–7 continuum on each of the four components. The weighted sum is the final status score. The weights are derived from a linear regression equation, predicting an independent estimate of social status by means of the four above-mentioned factors. The following weights were used: occupation, 4; source of income and type of house, 3 each; area lived in, 2.

Hence the maximum and lowest ranking score is $7 \times 12 = 84$, and the minimum and highest ranking score is $1 \times 12 = 12$. The weakest link in this construction is the operational procedure indicated for scoring the four components.

As they are defined in *Social Class in America,* it seems rarely possible to obtain invariant ratings from different raters.

The occupational component is clearly a prestige variable, and it would probably be preferable in most applications to use prestige scales, based on the rating of representative samples, rather than researchers' single estimates.

The component, source of income, is, in the present writer's opinion, the most original and interesting contribution of the index. The ranking of income sources is as follows:

1. (highest) Inherited wealth
2. Earned wealth
3. Profits and fees
4. Salary
5. Wages
6. Private relief
7. Public relief and nonrespectable income.

Since Warner, in addition, gives rules for handling people on pension and people with multiple source of income, this scale is more precisely defined than the others. Its weakness arises from the difficulty of finding out about people who belong in the extreme categories.

Regarding house type and area lived in, the suggestions given by the authors toward operational definitions are highly insufficient. The scale for houses goes from "big" houses in "good" order to dilapidated dwellings regardless of size, leaving both big and good undefined. The neighborhood scale tries to capture the differential prestige attaching to urban neighborhoods (from the area for the best houses in town to the slum district), but again the implementation contains too large an element of researcher arbitrariness.

Hatt suggested that the Warner index might be made more generally useful by substituting rent for the two residential items in the index. This change would probably make the index more heavily loaded with purely economic weights. The recommendation has not, so far, appealed to any researchers (Hatt, 1950).

Hollingshead's (Hollingshead & Redlich, 1958) index of social position utilized three components:

1. Residence: a six point scale of residential areas

2. Occupation: a seven point scale from executives and proprietors of large concerns and major professionals at one end to unskilled workers at the other

3. Education: a seven point scale perfectly correlated with number of years of formal education.

The final index value was obtained by adding the three scores with weights as follows:

$$I = 6 \times \text{residence score} + 5 \times \text{education score} + 9 \times \text{occupation score}$$

The index ranges between 20 (highest social position) and 134 (lowest social position).

Thus, occupation is the dominant factor here just as in Warner's scale. Hollingshead's occupational classification clearly is highly correlated with a classification in terms of the single dimension of occupational prestige.

A definite advantage of the index is its incorporation of education, which is both a characteristic highly accessible to measurement and, as will appear later, one of the most predictive single variables used by researchers in this field.

Residence is a more dubious variable because it seems so difficult to arrive at ratings which are comparable from one community to another. Wherever possible, more direct and more comparable indicators of social status seem preferable (rental value of residence, income, wealth, etc.).

Actually, Scheuch and Daheim (1961) recently reported on German efforts to develop a multiple-item status scale. This scale was later found to depend mainly on three factors, viz., occupation and education, as in Hollingshead, but with income as a third factor.

Measurement of Occupational Prestige

Empirical work on occupational prestige began in 1925, when Counts (1925) had schoolchildren and teachers rank 45 occupations from most to least looked up to. Counts had many American followers who used institutional populations. An exception was Hartmann, who used samples of the normal village population also.

After World War II, two major expansions in research on occupational prestige took place: (1) prestige studies appeared, based on nationwide representative samples of respondents (in the United States, Holland, Sweden, and Denmark); (2) research on prestige spread to non-American parts of the world. In Europe, occupational prestige scales have been established for England (Hall & Jones, 1950), Germany (Bolte, 1959), Holland (van Heek & Vercruijsse, 1958), Italy (Pagani, 1960), Sweden (Carlsson, 1958), and Denmark (Svalastoga, 1959). Whereas the above studies use either representative regional or national samples or rather large and heterogeneous nonrepresentative samples, prestige ratings based on student samples are also available for some of the countries mentioned and for certain others. North and Hatt's study (1953) is the most important prestige scale for the United States. In addition, there is a study from Brazil by Hutchinson (1957) (student sample). Prestige scales are also available for Japan (urban sample), New Zealand (large heterogeneous sample), Australia (urban sample), the Philippines (heterogeneous sample), and, most recently, for Indonesia (student sample). In addition,

TABLE 2
INTERNATIONAL COMPARISON OF PRESTIGE MEASUREMENTS[a]

			Correlation Coefficients by Country				
Country	S	G	GB	USSR	USA	J	I
Scandinavia		.80[b]	.88		.90	.83	
Germany			.97[b]	.90[b]	.96[b]	.93[b]	.94[b]
Great Britain				.83	.94	.92	.92[b]
USSR					.90	.74	.94[b]
USA						.93	.94[b]
Japan							.94[b]
Indonesia							.92[b]

[a] The number of occupations compared seem to range between 10 and 30, except that comparisons involving the U.S.S.R. typically are based on fewer occupations. The sources for Scandinavia are Carlsson (1958), and Svalastoga (1959); the figures are either Danish or Swedish, or an average from the two countries. The Indonesian figures are from J. Thomas (1962). All other figures are taken from Inkeles and Rossi (1956).

[b] Rank correlations. All other correlations are product moment.

the Russian Research Center at Harvard has established a Russian prestige scale, covering 13 occupations with 2,100 Russian displaced persons as respondents. A Canadian scale of 18 occupations was presented by Tuckman (1947) (for a list of prestige studies up to 1959, see Svalastoga, 1959, Table 2.4, pp. 62–67; see also Davies, 1952; Hutchinson, 1957; J. Thomas, 1962).

Thus, there is available a considerable research base, which permits both intranational and international comparisons. Generalizations about prestige consensus and prestige determinants may thereby be presented with less risk of error than previously.

The most generally valid proposition in this field has to do with the degree of agreement between prestige raters. Rankings and ratings of occupations according to prestige produce an approximately invariant average prestige hierarchy, irrespective of the raters' nationality (see Table 2), sex, age, residence, education, or occupation.[1] In addition, and this is a finding of importance in mobility research, this invariance seems to hold re-

[1] Only one research report constitutes an exception to the consensus rule (Davis' comparison of American and Russian prestige ratings, 1927). In contrast Russian displaced persons after World War II revealed high consensus with American raters.

gardless of time within a span of one generation or less. Deeg and Paterson (1947) repeated Counts' (1925) study and reported a high correlation between the 1925 and the 1947 hierarchy.

The approximate invariance of the prestige hierarchy has several consequences. Theoretically, the results of a prestige investigation may be caused by respondent characteristics, by job characteristics, or by both. The invariance rule permits the conclusion that job characteristics are vastly more important than respondent characteristics. Prestige is a social reward accruing to the incumbent of an occupation. According to Davis and Moore (1945) it is therefore expected that prestige is related to two characteristics of the job—its functional importance and its difficulty. A test of this hypothesis gave a multiple correlation of .92, showing that the hypothesis might be accepted. Number of subordinates and level of schooling were used as indices of the two independent variables. Actually, a third variable was also used, but it was believed to contain a mixture of the two theoretical variables (see Svalastoga, 1959, p. 113). Furthermore, the rule of invariance implies that the so-called ethnocentric tendency, revealing itself in a tendency to place one's own occupation relatively high, is nowhere a major factor.

The above analysis was concerned with average results (prestige rating means). There is, however, considerable variation around these averages. This variation is produced by two respondent characteristics: (1) respondents' hierarchy of values, and (2) respondents' knowledge of the occupation rated.

The importance of differences in respondents' hierarchies of values was documented in a study of occupational prestige, executed in the Netherlands by van Heek and his associates (van Heek & Vercruijsse, 1958). Protestants allotted higher prestige to a Protestant minister, Catholics to a Catholic minister. There were also important differences among the Protestant respondents depending upon denomination.

A striking demonstration of the importance of information about the occupations rated comes from one of Hartmann's studies. Hartmann (1936) presented for rating a list of medical and semimedical occupations, including titles of several medical specialists. The general practitioner surpassed all medical specialists in attributed prestige, excepting only the surgeon. The best explanation seemed to be that medical specialist titles were too little known in the sample studied.

In spite of the fact that prestige ratings by now have been undertaken for more than a generation, surprisingly few methodological innovations have gained general acceptance.

The writer has elsewhere documented the importance of the questioning technique, the number of categories used, and the precision of the occupational stimulus (Svalastoga, 1954). Another important factor is the anchoring of the scale—i.e., the type of occupations at the top and the bottom of the scale. In some European studies, the university professor outranks all others simply because higher officials have not been included.

Attempts to prove that prestige scores for occupations conform to Guttman's scale criteria have, on the whole, been unsuccessful. The chief reason for this seems to be that occupations frequently differ from each other in regard to more than one prestige relevant factor (see Reiss, Duncan, Hatt, & North, 1961, p. 105).

One of the most promising methodological innovations may come from the statistician Kendall, who is engaged in an attempt to build interval scales by using repeated ranking—i.e., ranking items, ranking differences between ranks, etc. (Kendall, 1960).

Occupations rated for prestige constitute a small fraction of all existing occupations in Western societies. Hence, some scheme of estimation, from the known to the unknown, is called for. One frequently-employed method has been to allot the same prestige score to all occupations within a larger census category (e.g., the professions); the score used has been the average obtained by those (few) occupations inside the category submitted for rating.

Reiss submitted this use of the North-Hatt (1953) scale to closer scrutiny. He found that 65 of the 88 different (+ 2 duplicate) occupations rated accounted for 49 per cent of the civilian labor force, and that even for the total list, the figure could hardly be more than two or three percentage points higher. In addition, he documented that an average prestige score weighted by employment figures gave a slightly different rank order of major occupational categories from that based on the originally published unweighted average.

Under conditions of high value consensus and a high level of occupational information, occupational prestige will be largely determined by the two factors: social importance or responsibility, and difficulty (see above). A convenient, if not perfect, operational interpretation of the difficulty of an occupation is the amount of schooling required. Not so easily solved is the problem of measuring responsibility adequately, although Jaques's concept of discretionary time span is a challenging possibility (Jaques, 1956).

It may frequently be more convenient to use other more accessible occupational characteristics. In particular, the economic reward attached to an occupation deserves to be studied carefully with respect to its relationship to occupational prestige.

Duncan reported a correlation of .84 between a measure of occupational income and the North-Hatt prestige score of the occupation. Education and prestige gave a correlation coefficient of .85. Income and education were both defined so as to indicate probability of exceeding a given critical level. Thus, the income score of an occupation is the percentage of persons in that occupation who earned $3,500 a year or more in 1949. The educational score, similarly, is the percentage having 12 years or more formal education (high school graduates and more highly educated). The multiple correlation was .91, indicating that the two variables explain five-sixths of the variance in prestige scores. Duncan used 45 of the North-Hatt occupations in his analysis.

Duncan's critical levels are, however, rather lenient. On education, 35 per cent of the experienced civilian labor force for which information is available reach or surpass the critical level. On income, the corresponding percentage is 29.

This suggests that an index based on the two factors is incapable of discriminating within the top 10 per cent or more of the population when it is applied to more precisely defined occupations (Reiss et al., 1961).

MODELS

Parameters

It will be assumed that three sets of parameters are of eminent relevance in the analysis of any rank-differentiated social system. Distributive parameters give a parsimonious expression of the degree of inequality on a given stratification variable. Correlational parameters indicate the extent

to which rank changes have comprehensive implications. Parameters of rate of change, finally, may be the most important ones, because they may characterize both the stability of the rank system and the rate of individual movement within this system.

Pareto maintained that the income distribution of a society conforms to a simple formula. Let y denote number of persons with income X or larger. Then Pareto's "law" may be written: $y = aX^{-v}$, where a is a constant, v is approximately 1.5 (Davis, 1941). It only purports to hold for higher incomes, say, above the modal one.

The symbol v is a measure of equality, and the larger it is, the more egalitarian is the distribution of incomes. Values computed for several countries in 1945–1950 reveal in general considerably higher levels of equality than predicted by Pareto. Thus, the Pareto exponent v was 1.96 for the United States, 1947; 1.87 for Great Britain, 1948–1949; 2.13 for Denmark, 1949–1950; 2.32 for Australia, 1945–1946; and as high as 2.40 for Sweden, 1947 (Champernowne, 1952).

The index of inequality developed almost simultaneously by Gini, by Lorenz, and by others may be more convenient to apply. This index may be best visualized by means of a diagram:

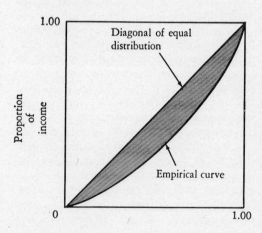

Fig. 1. Proportion of persons with income less than X.

The index is the ratio of the shaded area to the total area under the diagonal. It becomes zero when all incomes are equal, and it becomes unity when one person receives all income and all the rest receive nothing. For the case where the Pareto curve applies, there is a simple relationship between this index (p) and the Pareto exponent (v);

$$p = \frac{1}{2v-1}$$ (see Davis, 1941). Similarly for

the case where a log-normal curve applies to the income distribution, it may be shown that p is a monotonic function of the standard deviation of this distribution (Aitchison & Brown, 1957, p. 112).

Davis computed mean and standard deviation for the American income distribution in 1918. He reported a mean income of $1,543 and a standard deviation of $5,669. Whereas biological variables rarely spread more than 4 standard deviations from the mean, this income distribution showed a distance of 700 standard deviations between the mean and the maximum income.

The intercorrelation of major stratification variables has recently received considerable attention (see below). Such correlations tend to be positive, and this may be one of the conditions of system stability. Certainly situations are on record where the power elite was despised, ignorant, and not among the wealthiest (e.g., the Hitler gang), but such situations seem to be transient states of a system moving to a new equilibrium.

More important than either of the two above-mentioned sets of parameters are the parameters of rates of change because they by definition determine the stability of any state of the system or of subsystems. In particular, when a certain criterion of rank such as social status is chosen, the rate with which individuals change rank indicates the vertical mobility of the system or the permeability of any ranked stratum to any other. Permeability may range from a minimum, as when birth and death are the only legitimate modes of entrance and exit, to a maximum, as when entrance and exit are completely independent of birth and death.

A suggested hierarchy of stratification models in terms of increasing permeability is as follows:

1. Caste model: permeability zero
2. Estate model: permeability very low, but not absent
3. Class model: permeability about 40 per cent of maximum
4. Continuous model: permeability about 80 per cent of maximum
5. Egalitarian model: permeability perfect (maximum).

In these models, the general rule is that with decreasing permeability goes increasing tendency to reward the son as his father was rewarded. However, decreasing permeability also would result if there were a tendency to reward sons in inverse relationship to the way their fathers had been rewarded. This would merely indicate that birth still counted, except that the scoring system had changed.

Among these five models, the two extreme ones are least likely to be replicated in social experience.

Caste, Estate, and Class Models

A close approximation to a social system characterized by zero permeability of social layers, a perfect caste system, was found in India prior to the impact of Western culture.

A society organized according to the strict caste model is subject to severe internal and external pressures which tend to change the system. New employment opportunities, demographic imbalances resulting in deficits or excesses of certain castes, changes in the distribution of desired characteristics among castes, all these imperil the strict application of the model.

A caste system would seem to stand its best chance in situations of: (1) very slow technological change, (2) an economic surplus permitting fairly sizeable differences among members in respect to power and wealth, and (3) rather small differences in terms of life chances (in particular as measured by net reproduction) (see Gould, 1960).

Another characteristic of caste society seems to be a nearly perfect correlation of the four stratification variables. That is, the most respected tend to be the most powerful, the wealthiest, and those best trained in the lore of the society. Thus, Sivertsen (1962) reported from a study of an Indian village that the Brahmin caste owned nearly all land, and the outcasts held none. However, exceptions are on record. Thus, it is claimed that social power depended upon landownership, so that the Brahmins, who outranked others in ritual status, were "genuinely dominant only when they owned land" (Srinivas, Damle, Shahani, Beteille, & Caste, 1959, p. 140; compare also a similar view regarding the importance of landed wealth in Ceylon in Ryan [1953], and for a documentation on the Indian village level see Lewis & Barnouw [1956]).

At present, both India and Ceylon are moving away from the caste model under the impact of urbanization. This is indicated in India by such observable behavior as the loosening of the restrictions on interdining, the widespread violation of food taboos, a slight tendency to ignore intermarriage barriers, a gradual removal of untouchability, and the growth of social mobility (Davis, 1951). For Ceylon, Ryan (1953) noted that new occupations were increasingly becoming accessible irrespective of caste; whereas caste endogamy still was respected everywhere except in urban bohemias or slums.

An estate model should, to fit European medieval and early modern agrarian societies, definitely have a permeability above zero, although it should be very limited (Sorokin, 1947). The only quantitative datum on these societies that has come to the author's attention stems from a Swedish study (S. Carlsson, 1950). Carlsson's data from c. 1650 shows that Swedes, outside the

5 per cent strong elite, did enter the elite at the rate of about three per thousand per generation. Some 90 per cent of the population were ignorant, propertyless or nearly so, weak, and despised (cf. Fourastié, 1960, p. 27); this was perhaps a society in which rewards to most people seemed far less likely on earth than in heaven (see Painter, 1951, p. 55). Even in a caste society like India, the bottom stratum of outcasts does not seem to comprise more than 20 per cent of the population (K. Mayer, 1955).

Class models in the literature seem to differ mainly in two respects: (1) with respect to the criteria of hierarchical classification, and (2) with respect to the assumptions made regarding interaction within any class or between classes. Perhaps the most important dichotomy of criteria is that of economic and power criteria on one hand, and attitudinal or ability criteria on the other. This dichotomy appears in older sociology as a distinction between so-called objective and subjective criteria. Since, however, attitudes and abilities, when reliably measured, are objective to the same degree as any measurement with similar reliability, these older terms tend to create confusion.

Although Marx in various places stressed economic, political, and ideological criteria as class determiners, experts tend to agree that his favorite criterion was the economic one. In fact, Dahrendorf (1957) goes further by maintaining that to Marx the crucial class distinction variable was direct private ownership. Hence, Marx was led to conclude that the development of joint stock corporations (*Aktiengesellschaften*) was a step toward the abolition of classes.

The Marxian view of social classes included in its concept of class the idea of a solidary group sharply opposed to other social classes. This emphasis on within-class interaction appears with particular lucidity in Marx's discussion of the French small holders (*Parzellenbauern*) as of c. 1850 (Marx, 1869).

The permeability of the class model was

earlier somewhat arbitrarily characterized as about 40 per cent of maximum.

This characterization was based on what may be the oldest available European mobility data. Sundt (1864) collected information on the social class (farm-owner class, farm labor class) of rural Norwegians, who married in 1855–1856. The mobility observed was 42 per cent of what would have been observed in a society of perfect permeability. Reports from various regions of the world tend to support the conclusion that societies resembling the class model in terms of permeability are also characterized by a fairly high level of economic inequality. Thus in Chile, 1.4 per cent of the land holdings account for 68.2 per cent of the farm area, and in Brazil 1.5 per cent of the holdings include 48.4 per cent of the farm area (Schermerhorn, 1961, p. 47).

No information seems to be available on the level of intercorrelation among stratification factors in class societies. It is generally assumed that the average intercorrelation would fall between those of estate and continuous status societies (see below).

The Continuous Model

A general characteristic of the caste, estate, and class models is that the variable or variables used as criterion or criteria of stratification are discretely distributed. It follows that any plurel of persons is either equally placed or is obviously and sharply separated in status.

The continuous model drops the assumption of discreteness. It assumes that for any person of given status it is possible to find another as near him in status as desired without equalling him. Permeability in this model will be fixed at 80 per cent of maximum with a margin of deviation. Furthermore, the average intercorrelation between stratification factors will be about .5. Finally, it will be assumed that all stratification factors are log normally distributed.

The continuous model is the one which comes closest to representing present-day stratification and mobility experience in the industrialized parts of the world. Perhaps the strongest evidence in favor of the assertion that modern industrial society is distributing status more or less continuously along its major dimensions is found in the plight of research workers who desire to distribute social members into a few strata. In absolutely no case have researchers in these societies been able to show that their particular boundary lines denote discontinuities in the social hierarchy (see Hollingshead & Redlich, 1858; Kaufman, 1953; Lenski, 1952; Svalastoga, 1959).

A direct test of the continuity hypothesis is available in Kenkel's study of Columbus, Ohio (Cuber & Kenkel, 1954). Kenkel showed that whether his sample ($N = 300$) was distributed on the North-Hatt prestige scale (1953) or in terms of rental value of dwelling, no clear breaks in the distribution occurred. Kenkel was less convincing in his attempt to prove the same for residential prestige, due to the more impressionistic nature of his classification.

Another Ohio study, using the same sample size, addressed itself to the same problem with a different approach. Hetzler used graphic scales, on which a person rated himself by pencilling a point on a line, the end points of which were identified as the extremes of status. He was able to show that self-rating by this method, whether in terms of "social position" or "social class," produced distributions without larger breaks (Hetzler, 1953; see also Faris, 1954).

It is an empirical fact that the variables used as criteria of rank in modern societies uniformly have a skewed distribution. The maximum is much farther from the mean than is the minimum. The clearest illustration of such skewness is found in the distribution of economic status, whether measured in terms of income or total wealth.

Education, when measured in terms of years of formal education, also has a skewed distribution. The same seems to hold for power and social status as conventionally measured, although so far only ordinal measurements are available. It is also interesting to note that two additional variables, which are closely connected with social status in primary groups—viz., sociometric popularity, in terms of number of choices received, and discussion activity—likewise reveal a distribution resembling that of the log-normal curve (Hofstätter, 1958, p. 91; Homans, 1961, p. 157).

Schermerhorn suggested a skewed frequency distribution of social system states such that states in which power is exercised through charismatic leadership are rare, and those in which power is exercised through authority are most common, and those in which power is expressed through coercion are less common if not rare (Schermerhorn, 1961, p. 11).

Skewed frequency distributions are, moreover, quite widespread in nature. Thus it is reasonable to ask whether such distributions follow a certain mathematical law. A mathematical description of a distribution is generally better the closer it fits the fact and the more realistic its assumptions. Further, it is an advantage if its parameters possess clear empirical significance and if it is simple (Aitchison & Brown, 1957, p. 108).

The so-called log-normal distribution may well be one of the most suitable descriptions of the skewed distributions of sociological concern. It may be defined simply as the distribution of a variable whose logarithm obeys the normal law of probability (Aitchison & Brown, 1957, p. 1). If log X is normally distributed, then X has the log-normal distribution. There are two distinct ways in which log-normal distribution may be shown to be generated, giving dynamic and static models of generation.

The dynamic models proceed from the assumption that the value of a variable at a given time t is a random proportion of its value at time $t - 1$. This process generates a log-normal distribution, which, as time goes on, gives more and more inequality (increasing variance). Since this result may at times appear contrary to fact, static models seem preferable unless restraints are built

into the dynamic model. The static models depart from a multiplicative formulation of the central limit theorem. The theorem states that if X_j is a sequence of independent positive variates having the same probability distribution and a finite value, respectively, for the mean and variance of log X_j, then

$$Y = \pi_{j=1}^{n} X_j$$

shows asymptotically a log-normal distribution (Aitchison & Brown, 1957, p. 13).

In the static models, the more variates n are taken into account, the greater becomes the variance of the distribution.

According to Bjerke, various users of the static models have found that a log-normal distribution may result under certain conditions even if the original variables are not independent but positively correlated. Bjerke (1961) found on the basis of preliminary studies of 140 Danish trades: (1) that several homogenous trades revealed a tendency toward a log-normal distribution of income, this tendency being more pronounced than the tendency toward a normal distribution; (2) that the wage type exercised a decisive influence—in particular log-normality is favored by conditions of piece-work rates and minimum wages.

Several researchers have devoted themselves to the study of the relationship between different measures of status (Centers, 1949; Haer, 1957; Hollingshead & Redlich, 1958; Kahl & Davis, 1955; Lawson & Boek, 1960; Lenski, 1954; Reiss et al., 1961; Warner et al., 1949). Numerous measures have been compared. Here, only such measures as seem to reflect fairly adequately major stratification variables will be discussed. Hence, no attention will be paid to measures that are based on the estimate of one person only (self-rating, interviewer rating), and no measures will be discussed which do not directly refer to the person under investigation (parental social status, etc.). What remains to be considered are either scores derived from occupational information, years of formal education, amount or source of income, number of subordinates, or multidimensional indices.

As is the case in ecology, a distinction must be made between correlations based on individual persons and those based on groupings of persons. Generally the latter, when based on occupations, tend to run higher than the former.

When individuals are the units of measurement, the average intercorrelation of major stratification variables in the United States tends to range around a mean value of about .5, from a maximum of $+.6$ or $+.7$ for occupational prestige and education, to a minimum of $+.3$ or $+.4$ for education and income (see Table 3).

Since the interrelations between major stratification variables are rather loose, status discrepancy will be a frequent phenomenon in industrial societies. Many persons score high on one or more variables and lower on one or more others; however, because of the positive interrelationship, extreme discrepancies are rare.

Under conditions where such discrepancies are directly observable by group members, a strain toward status consistency tends to develop. Norms of fairness or justice tend to define status discrepancies as unjust (Homans, 1953).

Hughes focused attention on the fact that

TABLE 3

INTERCORRELATION OF MAJOR STRATIFICATION VARIABLES[a]

	Major Stratification Variables		
	Power	Information	Economic Status
Social status	C : .79 S : .67	W : .78 H_1 : .65 H_2 : .72 K : .65 S : .79 R : .83 D : .57	W : .89 H_1 : .50 C : .76 K : .52 L : .36 R : .85 D : .42
Power		S : .34	C : .65
Information			H_1 : .32 W : .59 K : .36

[a] The capital letter preceding the correlation coefficient denotes authors as follows:

C = Centers (1949)
D = Reiss et al. (1961, pp. 141, 142)
H_1 = Hochbaum et al. (1955)
H_2 = Haer (1957)
K = Kahl & Davis (1955)
L = Lawson & Boek (1960)
R = Reiss et al. (1961, p. 84)
S = Svalastoga (1959)
W = Warner (1949).

It should be emphasized that the operational definition of the variables changes somewhat from author to author. This may account for part of the differences observed in the table. More important, some authors work with occupations as unit of measurement (e.g., Reiss et al., 1961; Svalastoga, 1959) and some with individuals (e.g., Kahl & Davis, 1955).

the formal definition of the rights and duties of an occupation frequently is associated with a highly important informal set of expectations, e.g., a physician should be a white male person. Such informal expectations create nice problems of proper behavior when someone fills the formal role but does not possess the additional properties, as in the case of the Negro physician, or the female doctor. Isolation and segregation are frequently-used solutions. Negro sociologists will mostly teach in Negro universities and will do research on race, and female physicians will frequently be doctors of women (Hughes, 1945).

One of the most interesting and well designed studies in this field is that of Lenski (1954), who ranked a sample of respondents in terms of percentile scores along four dimensions: occupational prestige (North-Hatt scale, 1953), income, education, and ethnicity. He then proceeded to compute a status crystallization score for each person as follows:

$$y = 100 - \sqrt{\sum_{i=1}^{4} (x_i - \bar{x})^2}$$

where x_i for $i = 1 - \ldots 4$ refers to a person's percentile score on each of the four dimensions mentioned, and $\bar{x}$ denotes the mean value of the four scores. Next he dichotomized the sample into more and less status-crystallized groups, the latter constituting about 25 per cent of the sample. He was then able to document that persons who belonged in the less crystallized group, i.e., where the status scores were more unequal, rather consistently took a somewhat more liberal or radical stand on political issues. He also showed that this finding could not be explained by differences in mean status between the two groups (see also Lenski, 1956).

Inconsistency between a person's economic and educational ranks, and his social rank (Warner's revised occupational scale) was shown by Goffman (1957) to be directly related to a desire for change in power distribution.

A study by Jackson (1962) suggested the hypothesis that status inconsistency has differential behavioral outcome, depending upon whether status is ascribed or achieved. A combination of high-ascribed and low-achieved status (e.g., poor white in the United States) puts a person in a particularly difficult situation in modern society, since the nearly universal equality theme by definition rejects as unfair any tendency for ascribed status per se to influence achieved status. It was exactly in this high-ascribed–low-achieved category that Jackson found the highest incidence of symptoms of mental illness. In contrast, the combination high-achieved–low-ascribed status did not seem to affect mental health differentially; however, this category is the one that stands to gain most by an expansion of the influence of the equality theme, and it is therefore reasonable that Lenski (1954) found in this group the greatest tendency to favor liberal political opinions.

Of course, if status consistency also takes into account the paternal social status of a person, then discrepancy of status factors is a condition of most persons. The study of status inconsistency then becomes a problem regarding the effects of social mobility. A few studies suggest that the behavior of the mobile person is jointly determined by parental and own social status, tending to be intermediate relative to his father's and his own present stratum. At least this tendency has been observed both for fertility and political behavior (Berent, 1951; Svalastoga, 1959).

Many of the behaviors that political sociologists ascribe to "cross-pressures" may possibly be subsumed under the concept of *status discrepancy* (see Lipset, 1960).

Egalitarian Model

A society will be said to approach the egalitarian model to the extent that mobility between two positions proceeds independently of social origin. The egalitarian model seems most approachable in societies where economic production leaves little or no surplus beyond that essential for the maintenance of its members. Hence, this is the model that may fit the human societies that have existed over the major part of the history of man, i.e., the societies of collectors and hunters.

Mayer contends that, in all likelihood,

social stratification did not appear among prehistoric societies until the great innovations of farming and stock-raising occurred (K. Mayer, 1955).

It should be noted that Mayer differentiates between the existence of rank differences between people, which he deems to be universal, and the existence of a graded series of social positions, the occupants of similarly graded positions forming social strata. He assumes the existence of strata to depend upon the society's having passed a certain minimum size and having achieved a technology affording an economic surplus. Or, one might say that social mobility in pre-agricultural societies is expected to be independent, or nearly independent, of social origin.

It should be noted that although a society fits the egalitarian model, it does not follow that all persons are equally ranked in such a society (see above).

An excellent illustration of the difficulties involved in maintaining a condition of approximate social and economic equality is given by Talmon-Gerbier's (1952) account of the evolution of the Moshav cooperative settlements in Israel.

Direction and Rate of Change

Two characteristics of the modern technology trend may have far-reaching impact on the stratification system of modern societies: One is the increasing cost of energy and equipment; the other, the increasing rapidity of change. Both tendencies favor increase in scale: larger states, larger factories, larger newspapers, and so on. With advancing technology, the number of employers of men decreases. The vanishing servant, the plight of the small merchant, the crisis of small-scale farming increasingly dependent upon public support, the prolific growth of the activities of states and other already larger organizations all are evidence of the same general trend. The enormous productive capacity of modern technology may mean a future de-emphasis of the economic factor in stratification. Where nobody is ill, health tends to be taken for granted. In contrast, power may be rapidly becoming more unequally distributed, and of greater sociological relevance, in modern stratification systems.

Like power, information seems destined to be of increasing importance in future stratification systems. When power or information becomes extremely unevenly distributed, a society may face a threat not only to its integration but also to its efficiency. Hence, although dictatorships do occur, they are likely to be subjected to higher death risks than are less centralized governments. In contrast, social status—the amount of deference given and received—may not increase in importance, but rather be de-emphasized. This estimate is based on the assumptions that participation in the work process will continue to occupy a decreasing proportion of one's lifetime and that, outside the work situation, a trend toward despecialization is strong (the do-it-yourself movement) (see Chombart de Lauwe, 1956).

The increasing rate of change (Faris, 1961) seems slated both to further social mobility and to de-emphasize the behavioral implications of social status. The development of a class-specific style of life demands not only time, but also a certain slowness of technological change and social circulation.

BEHAVIOR

Interaction

Among the most important implications of social rank are the consequences for social interaction. It was noted above that many theorists have been sufficiently impressed by this relationship to include social interaction in their definition of social class.

Such variants of interaction as visiting, neighboring, and marriage all reveal a considerable dependence upon the social rank of partners. Such interaction increases in frequency with increasing rank equality.

(For visiting see, e.g., Warner & Lunt, 1941; for neighboring see, e.g., Loomis, 1946; for the relevant results of social area analysis, see, e.g., Shevky & Bell, 1955; intermarriage is illustrated in Table 7 below.)

Since massive and comprehensive interaction among status equals cannot very well be maintained unless mutual rewards are experienced in the process, it follows that interaction will be associated more often than not with social attraction. It should be noted that interaction among status equals seems to be more frequently rewarding per se, i.e., irrespective of consequences (see Zetterberg, 1962).

In contrast, interaction among persons of unequal status seems typically strainful and primarily instrumental (see Marris, 1960, on the plight of the budding new middle class in Nigeria).

The relationship between social rank and social interaction has far-reaching consequences, which increase with the tightness of the relationship. It adds to the differentiation of the social system. People of equal status interact more often, becoming thereby more similar in many respects and by inference more sharply set off from others (see Homans, 1950). It contributes to the perpetuation of the status of a family, thus reducing the permeability of the system (Beshers, 1962).

Thus, provided that the rate of change of the system is sufficiently slow, people differentially ranked will be subject to different life chances and will tend to evolve different life styles.

Life Chances

Villerme computed life expectancy by occupation in 1823–1834 for the French city of Mulhouse (Fourastié, 1960). At that time, Mulhouse was heavily industrialized but was in the phase of early industrialization characterized by long hours of work, poor hygienic conditions, child labor, etc., a fact which also could be read off from the data on life expectancy. The average figure

obtained for the city was 7.5 years, while for France as a whole, 20 years is the best estimate of life expectancy in that period.

Inside this unhealthy city, even the most well-to-do stratum was credited only with a 28-year life expectancy. But this figure was still more than 20 times the life expectancy of the children of simple weavers, which was given as one year and three months. Fourastié, who has reanalyzed Villerme's data, rejects the hypothesis that the results are subject to calculation error. Of 100 of these new-born children, 30 died within six months and another 20 in the following nine months (Fourastié, 1960, pp. 219–220).

In modern industrial societies, the average life expectancy is nearly 10 times higher, the difference between social classes is much reduced.

A. J. Mayer and Hauser (1953) have reported on life expectancy by economic class in Chicago over the period 1920–1940. For white persons in 1920, the difference between the highest and the lowest class in life expectancy was 10 years. Twenty years later, the same difference had been somewhat reduced to about eight years, suggesting a rate of decline of the order of one year per decade.

The maximum intersocietary difference in life expectancy is at present about 50 years. Hence, intrasocietary differences in life expectancy seem, at least in industrial societies, to be relatively modest.

Mean infant mortality is a very good predictor of average life expectation. In fact the line $Y = 75 - 1.8 X$, with $X =$ *infant mortality in percentages,* and $Y = $ *life expectation in years,* represents rather faithfully the data collected by the United Nations Population Division (1955). It follows that the data on status differences in infant mortality rates safely may be interpreted as differences in life expectancy.

Peller (1943) reported on the infant mortality rates among European royal families. For the seventeenth century, the infant mortality rate was 246 per 1,000, but it declined rather sharply and consistently in the ensuing centuries, to 41 per thousand in 1850–1899, and 8 in 1900–1930. These figures may be compared with the corresponding figure of 247 computed for the poorest district[2] of the city of York, England, in 1899 (Rowntree, 1901, p. 206).

Thus, it seems likely that in traversing the entire range of the British social hierarchy in 1900, one would find environmental extremes in regard to infantile life chances differing by a factor of about 10.

Although the span of the social hierarchy in Logan's studies of England was more moderate—from the bottom 13 per cent to the top 3 per cent he still found about four times as high risk of post-neonatal death (death between 2 and 12 months of life) in the lowest class as in the highest, and this held for all of three time periods between 1920 and 1950. It should be noted that post-neonatal figures generally show larger social differences than do figures for the complete first year of life because of the predominance of genetic factors in neonatal mortality (Logan, 1956). Thus, English data from 1946 showed infant mortality to be slightly less than twice as high in the lowest as in the highest social class. Differences of approximately the same order were reported by Lindhardt for Denmark in 1947 (Lindhardt, 1948).

Logan found that certain causes of death in England were rather consistently class linked. Thus, cancer of the stomach becomes increasingly rare as a cause of death with increasing social position. This regularity held in 1921–1923, 1930–1932, and 1950. Furthermore, the same rule holds for both men and married women (1921–1923 data not available for the latter). Bronchitis and respiratory tuberculosis obey the same regularity. In contrast, leukemia increases consistently as a common cause of death with increasing social status, although, as the author points out, class differences in the

quality of diagnosis may account in part for the finding.

The chief explanation for class differential mortality should be sought in the kind of home environment people of given status provide for themselves; their work environment appears to be a much less significant factor. Proof for this generalization comes from studies that give both male and female mortality differences by social or economic class. These studies reveal that the size of the differences is about the same regardless of sex (O. W. Anderson, 1958; Logan, 1956; A. J. Mayer & Hauser, 1953).

Still, it is well know that certain occupations involve serious risks to life (Dublin, Lotka, & Spiegelman, 1949). Most, but not all, such occupations are in the lower levels of the status hierarchy. Lasswell, however, has emphasized the high mortality risks of power elites at certain times in history (Lasswell, 1951, p. 296).

In preindustrial societies, the frequent positive association between social rank and polygyny renders plausible the hypothesis that fertility and social rank is predominantly positively related. Wrong has observed (1956, p. 76) that a positive correlation between socioeconomic status and fertility, on the whole, has often been observed for farm populations, being most characteristic of farm populations in nonindustrial societies.

Urbanism and, later, industrialization produced in the Western world a social environment less favorable to high fertility. In fact, as far back as reliable data for Western nations are obtainable, an inverse relationship between indicators of status and fertility is observed (Peterson, 1961, p. 218; Wrong, 1956, p. 72). An expansion of status differences in fertility developed in the late nineteenth and early twentieth centuries, because of differences by status in rate of adoption of birth control measures. In the between-war years, the expansion was followed by a contraction. Hence, while there still exists a negative relationship between social class and fertility, the relationship is weaker than it was a generation ago. This

---

[2] District population: 6,803, total urban population: 75,812.

is due to the increasing rate of adoption of birth control measures in the lower classes. A British survey on status differences over time in the use of contraceptives revealed a contraction corresponding to that observed generally for fertility, as follows (Glass, 1962, p. 260):

	Percentage points difference between nonmanual and manual workers in
Date of marriage	use of contraceptives
Before 1929	17
1930–1939	5
1940–1949	3

The lowest fertility rates typically occur not at the apex of the social hierarchy, but among certain lower-middle-class categories (Svalastoga & Carlsson, 1961; Wrong, 1956). Moreover, in Scandinavia, where contraction in the status fertility relationship has been particularly strong, data from the postwar period for certain occupational situses reveal a shift from negative to positive correlation with status (Svalastoga & Carlsson, 1961, p. 32).

At present, it seems impossible to predict whether the traditional negative correlation between status and fertility will generally shift to a positive correlation or whether the tendency is toward a lack of correlation. As Freedman points out with particular reference to income, this ignorance stems from insufficient knowledge regarding status elasticity in the demand for children (Freedman, 1962, p. 223).

Among couples who completely plan their families, the 1941 Indianapolis study reported a direct (not inverse), though weak, relationship between fertility and socioeconomic status (Kiser, 1962, p. 150; see Freedman, 1962, p. 222).

Berent (1951) investigated the relationship between social mobility and fertility. His study assesses the joint impact of own and paternal social status on family size after 20 years or more of marriage. With some exceptions, which may be due in part to insufficient sample size, the general result is fairly clear: The family size depends upon both present and past (paternal) social status. Hence, persons who are upwardly mobile tend to have families of a size intermediate between those of immobile persons in the stratum of origin and the stratum of arrival. A similar generalization holds for downwardly mobile persons (see Table 4).

TABLE 4

AVERAGE FAMILY SIZE BY PRESENT SOCIAL CLASS AND ACCORDING TO CLASS OF ORIGIN OF THE HUSBAND, IN MARRIAGES OF TWENTY YEARS OR MORE[a]

Social Origin of Husband	Average Family Size Present Social Class				
	I	II	III	IV	All
I Professional, managerial	1.74 (65)[b]	1.79 (43)	1.96 (23)	2.00 (11)	1.81 (142)
II Inspectional	2.05 (38)	2.14 (197)	2.51 (150)	2.97 (68)	2.38 (453)
III Skilled manual	1.87 (37.)	2.01 (154)	2.67 (431)	3.69 (244)	2.81 (866)
IV Unskilled	2.40 (5)	3.20 (45)	3.22 (162)	3.68 (220)	3.44 (432)
All	1.88 (145)	2.17 (439)	2.73 (766)	3.56 (543)	2.77 (1,893)

[a] Source: Berent (1951–1952).
[b] Numbers in parentheses are bases of averages (number in sample).
Family size = number of live births per couple.

Life Styles

Ample documentation shows that social rank differentiation tends to be accompanied by differences in styles of life—attitudes and behaviors. Space prevents a detailed treatment of this topic here, but the interested reader may refer to the many available research monographs and research summaries (see, Anastasi & Foley, 1949; Barber, 1957; Bendix & Lipset, 1953; Bronfenbrenner, 1958; Kahl, 1957).

Since the style of life characterizing the upper social strata typically appears attractive to many persons more modestly placed, one may ask how it comes about that life style differences are maintained. The mechanisms for conserving them are partly economic and partly noneconomic (see G. Carlsson, 1961). Certain life style items may be bought at market value, but price makes them inaccessible to persons below a given level of economic status.

Life styles of luxury are highly exposed to acquisition by those who are "merely rich," i.e., those whose social status is considerably lower than their economic status. Some economic status symbols are threatened by mass production of consumer goods and progressive taxation, and the raising of the economic level of persons in the lower strata makes them less inclined to accept personal service work.

Other life style characteristics are much less accessible to persons of lower class levels because they cannot be bought but have to be learned. Much, then, depends upon the time in life when such learning has to begin in order to be effective. To the extent that adult learning is impossible, or nearly so, a life style is protected from the intrusion of upstarts. The most important behavior of this type seems to be symbol manipulation. It is probably true that within broad limits, any normal adult can learn any speciality of symbol manipulation, but the energy expenditure required for perfection seems normally to be beyond the level of comfort for most people.

One of the most extreme theories in this field states that "the measureable interstatus linguistic differences between the lower working class and middle class . . . result from entirely different modes of speech, which are dominant and typical of these strata" (Bernstein, 1961, p. 289).

Certainly few distinctions stood out more sharply in the present author's Danish sample than that between the type of speech of the social elite and the lowest stratum (Svalastoga, 1959).

Various attempts have been made to associate distinctive life styles with the several social strata (Beshers, 1962; Kahl, 1957). It seems likely, however, that transitions between layers are gradual rather than sharp. Kahl characterizes the upper-class as emphasizing graceful living, the next lower levels as stressing career and respectability, and the lowest level as apathetic.

It is interesting to speculate on whether the two extremes are more similar than either of these and the middle levels. If, as Beshers suggests, a predominant old upper-class preoccupation is genealogy, then this interest may coexist with a disdainful apathy toward contemporary society. However, this point may easily be stretched too far. The impressive temperamental equilibrium built into the British model of a gentleman may possibly presuppose a self-confidence more easily nurtured from the deference granted a family member of high status than from the contempt bestowed upon persons of very low status (see Anastasi & Foley, 1949).

The Bible says: "For whosoever hath, to him shall be given, and he shall have more abundance: but whosoever hath not, from him shall be taken away even that he hath" (Matt. 13:12).

Some corroboration of this principle is available from studies by Hyman (1953), Knupfer (1947), and the Aberdeen team of researchers (Scott, Illsley & Biles, 1956). These studies center on the imputed effects of low status. It seems that a low status person's interaction with his environment sets in motion certain reactions which tend to preserve or further reduce his status unless checked by powerful outside factors. Thus, although this is the group among whom scientific information on maternity might be most helpful, this is also (according to Scott, Illsley & Biles, 1956) the group among whom an ostrich-like attitude of "I'd only worry, if I knew" is most prevalent.

The marked modesty of status aspiration in low status groups has been noted by Hyman (1953) and Svalastoga (1959). Genevieve Knupfer (1947) made a careful analysis of several American studies to portray the "underdog," the category of persons enjoying less than average status (the lower half or tenth), in terms of income, prestige, and the like. Such persons appeared regularly to be taking a less active part in social life, to have fewer associational memberships, to have fewer informal contacts, and to be more limited by physical distance in their choice of friends. They were also less likely to possess or even to seek such information as might reasonably be considered advantageous to themselves. By their greater tendency toward uncertain responses, even on questions of a purely preferential nature—that is, where no right or wrong answers exist—they reveal a more than average lack of self-confidence. As safeguards against frustrations they tend to set for themselves very modest levels of aspiration. In sum, it seems that their economic and educational handicaps may be severely intensified by an extreme psychological reaction to an underprivileged situation. Poverty of interests and ambition and a lack of self-confidence appear to a degree and extent harmful to this population (Knupfer, 1947; see Hyman, 1953; Scott, Illsley & Biles, 1956).

MOBILITY

Conceptualization and Measurement

Of the two major subforms of social mobility, the horizontal (involving no status change) and the vertical (involving status change) (Sorokin, 1927), the former occurs more frequently.

The concept of vertical mobility may refer to three main types which depend upon the unit of observation:

Unit of Observation	Type of Mobility
Individual	Career, intragenerational mobility: status change over the life cycle.
Family	Intergenerational mobility: status change of a family over two or more generations.
Collectivity (stratum, occupation, etc.)	Collective mobility: stratum (occupational) fluctuation in status.

Among these three types, intergenerational mobility has received most of the research attention. Therefore, in the following discussion, mobility will stand for intergenerational mobility unless otherwise specified.

In terms of the product moment correlation coefficient we may define minimum (caste), maximum, and equal chances of mobility very simply as referring to correlations of $+1$, -1, and 0 respectively between statuses of adjacent generations. Actual mobility in industrial societies seems to correspond to a correlation coefficient between $+.4$ and $+.5$.

It is much harder to solve the problem presented by the concept of optimum mobility. The concept presupposes a criterion variable, which, when correlated with mobility, is maximized for a given mobility level. This level is then, by definition, optimal mobility. The only research bearing on this topic to date is reported by C. Arnold Anderson and collaborators (C. A. Anderson, Brown, & Bowman, 1952). These authors calculated the amount of mobility that would be necessary to secure a perfect correspondence between social status and test intelligence. This amount was larger than that found in any industrial or agrarian society. At the same time, it was smaller than the mobility characterizing a society of equal chances.

If the correlation between paternal social status and paternal test intelligence is r_1 and the correlation between paternal and filial test intelligence is r_2, then under certain simplified conditions, $r = r_1 r_2$ will denote optimal mobility in the sense that there will be a perfect correlation ($r_3 = 1$) between filial social status and filial test intelligence.

To the extent that the simplified conditions (two-by-two tables with 50–50 split in both generations on both variables) are realistic (which they seem to be), optimal mobility on the criterion mentioned will, in modern society, be approximately $.5 \times .5 = .25$ (Anastasi & Foley, 1949; Svalastoga, 1958).

The multiplicity of criteria used for the measurement of status when dealing with one generation only contrasts sharply with the situation obtaining in mobility research. In fact, it seems that, without exception, mobility researchers use a classification of occupations as the instrument of measurement. This does not necessarily imply a high level of comparability among researchers because the classifications used are quite variable.

Intergenerational studies of social mobility may be based on documents or interviews. G. Carlsson (1958) subjected the problem of relative advantages of each source to a searching study.

Regardless of data collection procedure, three main types of studies may be distinguished: recruitment studies, community studies, and nationwide studies. Recruitment studies identify variations in the pattern of selection into given occupations or categories of persons, such as the *Who's Who* population, over some time interval. Such studies may provide good material regarding changes in the recruitment base of an occupation or other social category. Their findings are, however, often difficult to interpret because insufficient information is

available regarding the size and the social rank of the strata of departure and of arrival, and regarding the changes over time in these. Nationwide studies are costly; hence, to the extent that communities resemble the nation, local studies may save time, money, and labor force. The difficulty is that, so far, very little is known about which characteristics make a community approach the national average in terms of mobility. Most urban communities gain and lose more people by migration than do national societies, but it is not quite clear to what extent and how the vertical mobility within the community is affected thereby.

It is a convenient standard procedure to tabulate mobility data in matrix form to enable one to ascertain at a glance how many persons move from one place to another. However, both for intramatrix and intermatrix comparisons, the raw data must be transformed, but no consensus exists, as to the most suitable transformation.

Most researchers start by computing percentages based on row marginals, on column marginals, or on both. These are sometimes called inflow and outflow percentages. The outflow percentages show the chances of rise, fall, and immobility for constant social origin. The inflow percentages show how a certain stratum is composed in terms of relative contribution of persons from varying strata of origin. Together, these two sets of information characterize the permeability of each stratum. The use of these percentages becomes problematic whenever ascent or descent to strata of unequal size is compared. It is clear that a 5 per cent chance of reaching the top stratum means something different if the stratum contains 1 per cent of the population than it would if the stratum contained 10 per cent of the population.

In spite of this rather obvious shortcoming, most mobility studies have limited their analytical work to percentage calculation. Since about 1950, it has become increasingly common to relate the observed entries in a mobility matrix to the entries that would be expected if the two variables (parental status versus filial status) were independent. Clearly, this is a further step toward standardization, since both row and column marginals enter into the calculation of expected cell values.

The two most frequently used such expectation or association indices are:

1. The stability index $\dfrac{O}{E}$

2. The mobility index $\dfrac{\text{I}-O}{\text{I}-E}$

where $O = observed\ proportion\ stable$

$E = expected\ proportion\ stable$

and

$$E = \frac{\text{I}}{N^2} \ \Sigma \ M_{i.} \ M_{.j}$$
$$j = i$$

$N = sample\ size$

$M_{i.} = sum\ of\ entries\ in\ row\ i$

$M_{.j} = sum\ of\ entries\ in\ column\ j$

However, it is of course also possible to compute index values for single cells or any combination of cells in the matrix.

Instead of working with raw scores, X, denoting number of steps moved up or down, one may use standardized scores $\dfrac{X - \overline{X}}{\sigma_x}$. Here $\overline{X}$ refers to the arithmetic mean mobility of all sons whose fathers belong to one particular stratum, and σ_x similarly denotes the standard deviation of the scores of sons stemming from a particular stratum.

Tumin and Feldman (1961) seem to be the first and so far the only users of this procedure for measuring both intergenerational and intragenerational mobility. They list the advantages and disadvantages associated with the method (pp. 381–382). The most serious shortcoming for father-son comparison is that the distinction between

persons who rank respectively higher than, equal to, or lower than their fathers is lost. Instead we are invited to consider distinctions between persons in terms of deviation from the mean status achieved by those who had a similar start. It is a well established research finding that the former distinction is important. The importance of the latter remains largely to be proven. The authors report a correlation of .78 between the standardized score (termed by them $GOMS$) and occupational status. Since with but one exception, reported correlations with occupational status are higher than those for the standardized mobility score (Tumin & Feldman, 1961, p. 534), one is therefore left with the impression that the $GOMS$ score may be superfluous.

The Markov chain approach to social mobility analysis may be characterized as follows: A mobility matrix is denoted by P. Its typical element is the transition probability p_{ij}, denoting the probability that a son will arrive in stratum j if his father belonged to stratum i. The transition probabilities are assumed to be invariant over time: regardless of whether 2 or 10 generations pass, sons of fathers in stratum i will invariably have the chance p_{ij} of arriving in stratum j. Clearly, the risk of inaccuracy in applying a model with this built-in assumption increases with time.

However, over shorter generation ranges, the assumption of the Markov chain model is not particularly unrealistic. Thus, in Denmark the grandfather-father matrix shows approximately the same transition probabilities as does the father-son (respondent) matrix.

Under the assumption of father-son transition probability invariance, it follows deductively that the matrix, showing the relationship between the first generation and the n'th, may be obtained simply by raising the matrix P to the n'th power (Feller, 1950; Prais, 1955).

Social mobility may also be considered as a case of Leontief's input-output model (Allen, 1959). An analysis in terms of this model could provide the following type of information: Assume that a change in recruitment in the top stratum of a society is contemplated; if a reliable mobility table is given and a definite recruitment pattern is considered, the analysis reveals the exact effect on total mobility of this change of recruitment to the top stratum.

Outside of the field of economics, input-output analysis has been used in studies of migration (Löfgren, 1957) and in studies of social interaction in small groups (Glanzer & Glaser, 1959). It may also prove valuable in mobility analysis because it permits researchers to inspect mobility consequences of alternative assumptions regarding recruitment to a given stratum. So far, however, no study of social mobility has experimented with this approach.

There is a dearth of longitudinal studies of social mobility. Most long-range follow-up studies seem to have had biological or medical rather than sociological objectives (Kodlin & Thompson, 1958). Longitudinal work of a sociological nature seems to have progressed furthest in England and Scotland (Douglas & Blomfield, 1958; MacPherson, 1958).

Intragenerational Mobility

A comparison of studies measuring the rate of positional change with those measuring the rate of status change permits an assessment of the relative magnitude of the two rates.

Thus, for England and Wales, the following estimates of percentage change per year based on a sample investigation in 1948 (G. Thomas, 1951) is available:

	Percentage change per year (N = 3685)
Change of employer	13
Change of occupation	11
Change of industry	9
Change of town of residence in connection with employment change	7

There are clear indications of a long-time trend toward increasing mobility. This mobility arises from the slight and slow movement of many persons rather than from the swift movement of a few.

The high rate of change of employment shown above was confirmed by Lipset and Bendix (1959), who reported that 64 per cent of a sample from San Francisco had made more than two job changes per decade.

Regarding status change, Swedish census data on the period 1940–1945, as analyzed by G. Carlsson (1959), revealed an annual male upgrading from manual to nonmanual work corresponding to 2.5 per cent of the manual group or to 1.5 per cent of the total labor force. The corresponding downward move amounted to .8 per cent of the total labor force. The upward surge seemed thus to be roughly twice as strong as the downward movement. Upward mobility was barely more than one-third as strong each year in the depression period of 1930–1936 (.6 per cent per year). At the same time, downward mobility was relatively still more reduced (.1 per cent per year) (see C. A. Anderson, 1956, Table 1, p. 169; Sibley, 1942; Svalastoga, 1959, Table 5.3, p. 313).

For the Netherlands, Tulder arrived at estimates of annual vertical mobility between six strata for five subperiods between 1919 and 1954. These estimates varied between 1.6 per cent and 2.5 per cent (Tulder, 1962, Table 18, p. 103).

Hence, the best estimate for modern northwestern Europe is an annual rate of vertical mobility of about 2 per cent of the adult population, which probably does not correspond to more than about one-fifth of all occupational changes.

If Danish research results are representative, then to the average Westerner, the womb-to-tomb continuum is characterized by two waves (one complete and one incomplete, terminated by death). The womb-tomb continuum of status change resembles somewhat a sequence of two sinusoid curves, one having a periodicity of 32 years and amplitude of about .3 (on a status scale ranging from 1.0 to 9.0), and the other having a periodicity of 64 years and amplitude of about .4 and truncated by death.

Status loss between the age of 20 and retirement was rare. The simplest explanation is that the majority enter the occupational hierarchy at or near its bottom on starting their work career. Hence the dominant frustration engendered by the selective process is more a matter of the absence of ascent than of descent.

Repeated moves are also rare. Among Danish males aged 50 and over, only 16 per cent made two or more status moves after age 20, and only 2 per cent made three or more such moves (Svalastoga, 1959).

Intergenerational Mobility

The core of intergenerational mobility studies is a comparison of fathers and sons in terms of social status as assessed by their occupations. Typically, the data are collected by retrospective interviews, although documentary methods have been relied on in several studies. These studies aim to cover a given region (community or nation) and present some kind of overall assessment of the mobility of the region.

For such an overall assessment to be particularly valuable it should be repeatable in time and space. For this reason, it may frequently be advisable to expand mobility analysis so as to include intermarriage by status.

The findings on marital heterogamy or female marital mobility may, in many countries, be compared with marital records going more than a hundred years back in time. Similar comparisons for male occupational mobility is normally not possible. Marital mobility data are also frequently recorded on a day-to-day basis in sufficient detail to provide at least an estimate of trends. It is much more difficult to assess the magnitude of, and changes in, total mobility from the so-called recruitment studies. Still, recruitment studies are important, especially for the analysis of the changing permeability of elite occupations.

One of the most careful studies of intergenerational mobility was reported by Glass for England and Wales (1954, see Table 5 below). Table 5 reveals several characteristics of English society, which seem to be common features of industrial societies (see mobility tables in Miller, 1960).

1. Regardless of social origin, the majority is mobile. Measured by more refined means, a still larger majority would be so. Hence, the factors responsible for this mobility are sufficiently powerful and persistent to circulate most people in the course of 30 years to status levels other than those to which they were adjusted in childhood.

2. Mobility from one stratum to another becomes increasingly unlikely as the number of intervening strata increases, when size of stratum of arrival is taken into account. That is, most moves are short moves and long moves are rare. This holds both for upward and downward mobility. Hence, social mobility seems to obey a law of gravitation similar to the one formulated by various authors for the relationship between migration and physical distance. If such a law holds, it follows deductively that a decrease in the distance separating strata should increase mobility just as surely as a reduction of travel time, *ceteris paribus,* leads to more traffic (see below).

3. The marginal status distribution over the parental and the filial generation is approximately invariant. This is perhaps the most unexpected result, considering the velocity of technological changes. Still, when status is measured in terms of occupational prestige, this is the typical finding in recent national mobility studies.

The explanation should probably be sought in the fact that the two major shifts in the occupational structure over the last three generations have had opposite effects which approximately balance each other.

Thus, as of 1870, 53 per cent of the American population could be classified as workers, and in 1954, 56 per cent. But while the remainder in 1870 were mostly self-em-

TABLE 5
SOCIAL MOBILITY IN ENGLAND
DISTRIBUTION OF THE MALE SAMPLE ACCORDING TO SUBJECTS' AND SUBJECTS' FATHERS' STATUS CATEGORY[a]

Each cell shows two figures: the bottom-left figure (inflow percentage) followed by the top-right figure (outflow percentage).

Fathers' Status Category	Subjects' Present Status Category							Total
	1	2	3	4	5	6	7	
1	48.5 / 38.8[b]	11.9 / 14.6	7.9 / 20.2	1.7 / 6.2	1.3 / 14.0	1.0 / 4.7	0.5 / 1.5	100.0 (129)
2	15.5 / 10.7	25.2 / 26.7	10.3 / 22.7	3.9 / 12.0	2.2 / 20.6	1.4 / 5.3	0.7 / 2.0	100.0 (150)
3	11.7 / 3.5	22.0 / 10.1	19.7 / 18.8	14.4 / 19.1	8.6 / 35.7	3.9 / 6.7	5.0 / 6.1	100.0 (345)
4	10.7 / 2.1	12.6 / 3.9	17.6 / 11.2	24.0 / 21.2	15.6 / 43.0	10.8 / 12.4	7.5 / 6.2	100.0 (518)
5	13.6 / 0.9	22.6 / 2.4	34.5 / 7.5	40.3 / 12.3	50.0 / 47.3	43.5 / 17.1	44.6 / 12.5	100.0 (1510)
6	0.0 / 0.0	3.8 / 1.3	5.8 / 4.1	8.7 / 8.8	12.5 / 39.1	24.1 / 31.2	16.7 / 15.5	100.0 (458)
7	0.0 / 0.0	1.9 / 0.8	4.2 / 3.6	7.0 / 8.3	9.8 / 36.4	15.3 / 23.5	25.0 / 27.4	100.0 (387)
Total	100.0 (103)	100.0 (159)	100.0 (330)	100.0 (459)	100.0 (1429)	100.0 (593)	100.0 (424)	(3497)

[a] Source: Glass (1954, p. 183).
[b] Top right figure in a cell: outflow percentage showing percentage of sons given paternal category (stratum), who arrive in given stratum.
Bottom left figure in a cell: inflow percentage showing the percentage of sons of given present stratum, who stem from given paternal stratum.

ployed farmers and businessmen, they were mostly salaried employees as of 1954 (Table 6).

TABLE 6
STRUCTURAL CHANGE IN THE UNITED STATES
1870–1954[a]

Occupation	1870	1954
Self-employed	40.4	13.3
Salaried employees	6.6	30.8
Wage workers	52.8	55.8

[a] Source: K. Mayer (1956, Table 1, p. 70).

Hence, the reduction in upper- and middle-class positions due to the move from rural to urban employment and to the average growth in size of enterprise has been about equal in magnitude and velocity to the creation of new middle-class jobs.

It follows that upward and downward mobility from one generation to another must be approximately equal in magnitude. This relationship may not be as durable as the two first mentioned ones.

A further documentation for the second "law" of intergenerational mobility may be had from a study of Yugoslav marriages contracted in 1956–1958 (Table 7).

The imperfect correlation between economic and social status makes it possible that a loss in social status may sometimes accompany an increase in economic status, although on the whole the relationship is positive. One numerically important exemplification of such negative relationship is observed in the transition from farm to factory. Prestige scales reveal that even the small farmer, as long as he owns his farm, outranks the factory worker in the eyes of most people. Still, the income and general economic standard of the factory worker is often higher than that of the farmer. Since the factory worker also tends to live closer to institutions of higher learning and to health institutions than does the small farmer, his children may have higher health and educational standards. Hence, as pointed out by Sibley, many moves which are conventionally ranked as downward in terms of prestige, may by the subjects themselves be rated as upward (Sibley, 1942).

Pareto maintained that elite permeability moves in cycles. A new elite climbs to power, wealth, and privilege through revolution. Gradually thereafter the avenues to the elite are closed. Through inbreeding and

TABLE 7
MARITAL MOBILITY:
INDEX OF ASSOCIATION FOR YUGOSLAV MARRIAGES CONTRACTED DURING
1956–1958, BY OCCUPATION OF BRIDEGROOM AND BRIDE
$N = $ c.360,000[a]

Occupation of Bridegroom	Per Cent of All Bridegrooms[b]	Occupation of Bride						
		A	B	C	D	E	F	G
A	53	1.4	.1	.1	.1	.0	.0	.0
B	6	.8	4.5	1.1	1.3	.4	.2	.2
C	25	.6	2.1	2.8	2.3	2.0	1.4	.8
D	3	.5	1.7	1.6	4.2	2.7	2.3	2.0
E	2	.4	1.1	1.7	1.8	7.5	3.3	1.9
F	5	.4	1.0	1.3	1.6	2.2	4.6	2.7
G	6	.2	.4	.8	.7	1.8	4.0	8.0

[a] Source: Milić (1961).
[b] Cases where one or both parents were without occupation were omitted.
Explanation of symbols:

A = Farmers and farm workers
B = Unskilled workers
C = Semiskilled and skilled workers

D = Service workers
E = Salesmen and commercialists
F = Clerical and managerial workers
G = Professional and semiprofessional workers.

effeminization the elite deteriorates, while energetic talent accumulates below. In this way, another revolution is prepared, and the cycle is repeated (Pareto, 1935, vol. III, pp. 1429–1432).

Drawing upon the invariance suggested above, it follows that the larger an elite is relative to the total population, the more permeable it is. Furthermore, permeability is expected to increase when the mean status of the elite decreases, due either to a change of status distribution inside the elite or to a general contraction of the status hierarchy.

The first deduction may be compared with the empirical data on mobility assembled by Miller (1960). For such a comparison, it is important to hold constant the social origin of elite entrants because it might be that entrance to the elite is more frequent only because persons of middle status increase their elite representation in the filial generation, while persons of low status decrease theirs.

Considering then only variations in the accessibility to persons of manual origin as the elite changes in proportion, the following figures are obtained:

	Size A Per cent defined as elite	Per-me-abil-ity	Size B Per cent defined as elite	Per-me-abil-ity
France	8.5	.41	3.9	.36
Great Britain	7.5	.29	2.9	.21
Italy	6.6	.23	.9	0.00
Netherlands	11.1	.59	2.9	.41

Permeability is computed by dividing the percentage of the group of manual social origin who enter the elite, by the percentage figure for the size of the elite. The basic data are taken from Miller (1960).

The second deduction may not be easy to test at present, since prestige-rating data on occupations are not available for a sufficient time interval. It is presented here primarily as a warning to the effect that increasing permeability of a certain elite

occupation does not warrant the conclusion either that total mobility is increasing or that the avenue to occupations of given importance and difficulty has become more accessible.

Whether it is at all possible to increase permeability to an elite occupation without lowering its status is an unsolved problem. Mannsåker showed that Norwegian ministers have over the last hundred years been recruited increasingly from persons of non-elite origin. But, at the same time, considerable, though informal, evidence suggests a simultaneous lowering of the relative prestige of the occupation of minister in Norway (Svalastoga & Carlsson, 1961, p. 38).

Perhaps the most general proposition repeatedly validated by elite recruitment studies is that access to elite occupations is considerably more likely for those whose fathers are elite members than for those whose fathers are outside the elite, is less likely for persons of nonmanual origin, and is least accessible to persons of manual origin. This is, in fact, only a confirmation of the general rule stated above.

A study of recruitment to positions of top political leadership suggests that ascriptive factors (race, ethnicity, sex, and age) may be more important selective factors for entrance into the elite than they are further down in the hierarchy (Matthews, 1954).

Studies of recruitment into the American business elite do not seem to suggest any trend verified by all researchers. Rather, they suggest a fairly stable proportion of long distance climbers, with minor variations from decade to decade over the last hundred years (Lipset & Bendix, 1959). Moreover, students of eminence have generally found a similar absence of trend.

The study of social eminence has so far led to two generalizations:

1. That eminent men tend to be recruited predominantly from among the top-ranking strata of a society.

2. That they are more likely to be first-born or last-born than middle-born. (Levy-Leboyer, 1961).

While the first generalization squares well with findings regarding people who make more modest upward moves, the second generalization seems not to have received such support, except in the Dutch mobility study (Tulder, 1962).

Studies of recruitment to the professions or to educational levels appropriate for professional careers reveal a general tendency toward increased accessibility over time. Perhaps the most comprehensive tabulation of professional recruitment is found in a research study now in process in Norway (Aubert, Torgersen, Tangen, Lindbekk, Dollan, & Kjellberg, 1961–1962). It covers all professional categories and spans two hundred years or more.

International Comparisons

Outside Europe only three societies possess mobility tables of national coverage: United States, Puerto Rico, and Japan.

European countries are much better covered. This holds particularly for Western Europe; whereas in Eastern Europe only three countries possess mobility tables: U.S.S.R. (émigré sample), Hungary, and Yugoslavia.

For Western Europe, national mobility tables are available for 10 countries: Norway, Sweden, Denmark, Finland, Germany, Netherlands, Great Britain, France, Switzerland, and Italy.

Some countries have several mobility tables, Sweden, France, Germany, and the United States, thus permitting reliability checks or, as seems more useful, since differences in coverage and design are frequently important, a range of choice regarding the best particular table for international comparison.

For regions of the world not mentioned above, there may be severe difficulties in securing nationwide samples. In such case, samples of communities may be desirable substitutes. Geiger's study of the 100,000 Danish inhabitants of the city of Aarhus, when reanalyzed by the writer and later

compared with nationwide data, gave a surprisingly close estimate of the Danish national mobility rate (Svalastoga, 1959).

Miller includes four countries not mentioned above in his international mobility comparison, all of which are represented by urban community data only (Belgium, St. Martens-Latem and Mont-Saint-Guibert; Brazil, São Paolo; Australia, Melbourne; and India, Poona). Of these four, two are very deficient in regard to sample size—the Mont-Saint-Guibert study and especially the Melbourne study. Furthermore, because of a negative correlation in India between caste rigidity and urbanism, it would seem highly inadvisable to include the Indian data for the purpose of comparing nations. A parallel argument may weigh against the use of urban Brazil data to represent the entire country. Hence, among the community data mentioned, the only one that may tentatively be taken as nationally representative is Versichelen's careful study of the small Belgian town of St. Martens-Latem. It should be remembered that Belgium is a highly urbanized nation (Versichelen, 1959).

An important addition to community studies of social mobility was recently made available. Ganon (1961) published a report on social mobility in Montevideo, Uruguay ($N = 2,415$), which, since the city contains about one-third of the national population, is unlikely to be far removed from national figures.

The numerous problems posed by the international comparison of mobility data have been dealt with by several authors (see, e.g., Miller, 1960; Svalastoga, 1961, and the sources cited there).

Future mobility researchers may find it sufficient to characterize the mobility of a nation by means of one single measure. The material available at the present time is, however, too crude for such a procedure to be quite satisfactory. In particular, it seems important to take into account both the total volume of movement and some measure of the distance moved, with particular attention to long distance mobility. Table 8

TABLE 8

TENTATIVE CLASSIFICATION OF REGIONS ACCORDING TO
TOTAL MOBILITY AND LONG DISTANCE UPWARD MOBILITY

Total Mobility	Long Distance upward Mobility		
	Low	Middle	High
High	British	Scandinavian[a]	North American[b]
Middle	North Central European[d]	South Central European[e]	East European[c]
Low	South European[f]	None reported	None reported

[a] Inside Scandinavia (including Finland) the rank order from highest to lowest mobility is Sweden, Norway, Denmark, and Finland (see Ramsöy, 1961; Svalastoga & Carlsson, 1961).
[b] Only verified for the United States
[c] Only verified for Yugoslavia
[d] Germany and the Netherlands
[e] France belongs here, Belgium and Switzerland seem to belong here, Japan may also belong here
[f] Only verified for Italy.

represents a tentative two-dimensional classification of nations according to level of total mobility and the accessibility of their elites. The latter information is chiefly derived from Table 9 and the sources there cited; the former is taken from data in Glass (1954), G. Carlsson (1958), Svalastoga (1959), Bolte (1958), Janowitz (1958), Nisihira (1957), and Milić (1960). It should be emphasized that differences observed among these nations nowhere seem to be extreme.

It may be noted that Miller's indices of association for nonmanual and manual cate-

TABLE 9

LONG DISTANCE MOBILITY IN EUROPE AND AMERICA
BASED ON ORIGINAL MOBILITY MATRICES[a]

Country	1 A Elite Size, Filial Generation Per Cent	2 B Size of Lowest Ranking Category, parental generation Per Cent	3 Per Cent of B Reaching A	4 $\frac{3}{1}$
Scandinavia				
Denmark	3.3	22.2	1.1	.30
Sweden	6.6	41.7	2.1	.32
Great Britain	2.9	24.2	0	.00
Germany	4.6	36.1	.7	.15
Netherlands	2.9	37.4	.3	.12
United States				
(Indianapolis, 1940)	5.5	25.1	2.5	.45
France	3.9	29.1	1.4	.36
Italy	(a) 6.6	23.6	2.7	.40[b]
	(b) 6.6	64.8	1.7	.26

[a] Source: Miller (1960), G. Carlsson (1958), and Rogoff (1951).
[b] This figure is doubtful, because of results obtained in column B

gories respectively, when averaged for each country, give a partial, but only partial, confirmation of the mobility rank order listed in Table 8. It confirms the high rating of Great Britain, the United States, and Denmark, and the middle rating of Japan and Germany. But Miller's data seem to imply considerably lower mobility elsewhere in Scandinavia than in Denmark. This finding is contradicted by more detailed analysis (G. Carlsson, 1958; Svalastoga & Carlsson, 1961). Furthermore, Miller's indices seem to suggest a lower mobility in France than in Italy, which again contradicts previous and more detailed analysis by Glass and associates (1954).

Versichelen's (1959) study of the Belgian town St. Martens-Latem reveals a comparatively low level of mobility, suggesting that Belgium probably belongs in the same mobility category as France.

Miller and Bryce (1961) recently studied the relationship between certain macroeconomic variables and social mobility. Two such macroeconomic variables may demand special attention: (1) the proportion of nonagrarian persons in the labor force, and (2) the mean annual percentage change in total national product, 1900–1950.

It seems reasonable that high values on these two measures should be conducive to social mobility. Certainly a country like the United States, which admittedly enjoys a high mobility rate, is only surpassed by Great Britain in regard to the percentage in the nonagrarian labor force (United States, 89 per cent; Great Britain, 95 per cent), and is only surpassed by Sweden in rate of growth of national product (United States, 3.4 per cent; Sweden, 3.8 per cent).

Italy, placed in the bottom mobility category, is more agrarian than most Western European nations (29 per cent agrarian labor force). However, it has a surprisingly high rate of change of national product (2.2 per cent per year), exceeding that of Great Britain. It may be that high values on these factors are necessary, but not sufficient, to the achievement of high mobility.

Mobility Determinants

The main safeguard of high mobility is a high rate of social change (Lundberg, Schrag & Larsen, 1958, p. 508). In particular, four areas of change are of central importance: in technology, in differential reproduction, in abilities, and in attitudes (see Sorokin, 1927).

The most important attempt to measure the effect of technological change has been made by Kahl (1957, pp. 254–256), who concluded that about one-third of all cases of intergeneration mobility could be attributed to technological change. The instrument of measurement used was Edward's scale of socioeconomic status. Hence, the transition from rural to urban employment, which may frequently mean zero or near-zero change of occupational prestige, was included.

Technology may affect mobility more indirectly through two of its major effects—increase of scale and increase of functional differentiation. Data from American manufacturing industry support the hypothesis that the proportion of workers not directly engaged in production increases with the size of the organization (Caplow, 1956). Comparable findings were reported for school districts in California (Terrien & Mills, 1955). Other studies have failed to support the hypothesis (Hall, Haas, & Johnson, 1963). Hence, size may not be the only factor affecting the white collar proportion of a social organization.

Increasing functional differentiation implies that a wider range of talent may be rewarded. In certain preliterate societies a man who cannot hunt is useless. Even in some of the smaller European nations, persons with an uncommon occupational preference may face considerable hardships. In modern macrosocieties, however, the avenues to high social reward are typically manifold.

A stratum which fails to reproduce itself, or which does not reproduce itself as fast as does other strata, must accept mobile entrants to preserve its relative size. Thus, Glass (1954, p. 197) estimates that the 30 per cent nonmanual part of the English population as of 1950 had a net reproduction index of only .84, whereas the 70 per cent manual part had a net reproduction index of 1.07. This means that the ascending probability of the manual stratum obtains an increase of .064 because of differential reproduction only, or, otherwise expressed, 5 per cent of the total population will be mobile due to this factor.

This squares well with Kahl's estimate for the United States, which showed that 7 per cent of the labor force must be mobile to compensate for differential fertility, and of course not all mobility is vertical.

McGuire's estimate runs somewhat higher (11 per cent). McGuire (1950) is inclined to attribute a stronger total effect to the demographic factor than is indicated by the 11 per cent estimate. This is reasonable because most status changes are one-step changes on the status scale. To the extent that demographic surplus and deficit appear in strata that are far apart, it is safe to predict that more persons will move than would if such imbalances appeared in strata that were close to each other.

Mobility is favored, *ceteris paribus,* whenever the education of children departs from that of their parents. The actual correlation between parental and filial education in industrial societies is probably of the same order as that for parental-filial intelligence, i.e., about .5. However, the present author has not been able to locate relevant quantitative information. A preliminary assessment of his own data—Denmark, 1953–1954—dichotomized, gave a correlation coefficient of .4.

The effect of educational change, over generations, on social mobility may be reduced to the extent that the educational requirements for given social positions are stepped up in pace with the growth of educational attainment (G. Carlsson, 1958). Furthermore, education acts differently on persons of high as against low social origin.

To the former, education helps prevent or reduce downward mobility. To the latter, education increases the social distance moved. Glass and Hall reported a mean distance moved downward of 1.7 for persons of high[3] social origin and high (top 9 per cent) education. The corresponding drop for high origin persons with only elementary education was 2.5. Persons originating in one of the two lowest strata climbed on the average 2.3 units if they possessed high education as defined above, but only 1.3 units if they had only elementary education (Glass, 1954, Table 4, p. 301).

Comparable findings are reported in other studies. In England, Scandinavia, and probably in Europe generally, higher education is a fairly rare phenomenon, while upward mobility is not. It follows that the majority of cases of upward mobility in these countries cannot be explained through differences in formal education (G. Carlsson, 1958; Glass, 1954; Svalastoga, 1959).

Since social mobility is by definition the difference between two status variables differentially located in time, it is logical to consider the problem of predicting any one of these two variables. Thus, the question may be posed: Considering the variation in status at time *t*, what factors account for it?

This method has the advantage that factors like parental status and education may be compared in terms of predictive power or evaluated in combination. Using this approach, Duncan and Hodge (1963) reported, for a male, white, urban-origin Chicago sample in 1950, that the socioeconomic status of respondents, themselves, correlated only .3 with parental status on the same index. Hence, at most, 10 per cent of the total variation in respondents' status could be accounted for in terms of social origin. Adding education to the set of predictors, increased variation accounted for from 10 to 30 per cent. Hence, to the extent that parental influence determines filial education, this indirect effect of social origin is

---

[3] Strata 1 and 2 in Table 5.

more important than the direct one, i.e., the tendency to inherit paternal social status.

One side effect of superior education may be that of stepping up the rate of intragenerational mobility. If so, ascent should typically be slow among self-made people who lack higher education. This inference is amply confirmed in a recent study.

Porter noted that top Canadian banking positions were normally (in 22 of 23 cases) filled with persons lacking a university education. However, these people had, on the average, spent 38 years on "the long crawl" from the teller's cage to the directors' boardroom. Swifter moves seem possible only to persons who either possess an advanced education or originate at the top of the social hierarchy. Porter noted that among top corporation directors, persons in the latter category were much younger than the rest (Porter, 1961, pp. 490–491).

It seems a plausible hypothesis that sentiment and interaction tend to vary positively together as long as the interaction is mutually rewarding (Homans, 1950; Homans, 1961). Mobility is a macrosocial form of interaction and is usually positively valued. Hence, with more mobility should go a more favorable sentiment between persons differently placed in the social structure. Moreover, there is mutual dependence between these variables; a reduction of sentiment toward status unequals should result, according to the theory, in a reduced mobility rate. While no direct test of this derivation is available, it does receive indirect support from data dealing with the recruitment of university students (Geiger, 1955). Studies of university recruitment typically show that persons who identify themselves with the middle class but who are not better placed economically than the upper working class, still are more likely than people in the latter class to give their sons a mobility-favoring education.

Microsocial approach. The foregoing discussion of mobility determinants has been largely macrosocial, primarily addressed to

the identification of factors that may account for differences in rates of mobility between nations. A more microsocial approach attempts to identify factors that account for intrasocietary mobility differences between individuals.

Microsocial research has focused on such factors as conformity to upper-class norms, education, migration, career choice, and factors associated with family of procreation and family of origin (e.g., G. Carlsson, 1958; Lipset & Bendix, 1959; Svalastoga, 1959).

Talent Utilization

Societies seem to be able to survive with quite varied levels of social mobility. However, for a given technology, mobility level may affect prosperity. In particular, to the extent that the welfare of a society depends upon a high level of utilization of its collective talent, mobility becomes a vital concern to the society. This follows from the fact that the documented correlation between the abilities of fathers and sons, as observed in intelligence tests is only modest (Anastasi & Foley, 1949, Ch. 10, pp. 303–326).

Modern industrial society belongs to the category in which mobility affects prosperity. Sorokin posits reasonably that mobility, at least up to a certain limit, favors productivity in such societies (Sorokin, 1927, p. 533). The limit would perhaps be reached when a society, through the very rate of its mobility, would deprive itself of the informal training resources of the family (cf. Warner, Havighurst & Loeb, 1946). It does not seem likely that this limit has yet been reached or exceeded in any industrial society.

The physiological variables determining maximum ability in the individual are probably approximately normally distributed. However, as suggested in Faris' challenging paper (1961), "In most of the population, the levels of performance actually reached have virtually no relation to innate capacities." Zetterberg (1961) suggests that the level of mobilization of ability, i.e.,

$$\frac{actual\ ability}{maximum\ ability}$$ is generally kept at a low

level. Societies generally tend to look askance at higher mobilization of ability.

The effects of formal schooling are, to an important degree, reduced by braking systems that are located primarily in the nuclear family and in the local community and its peer-groups. In these social environments, a young person learns an appropriate level of aspiration, which is usually adjusted to the average level of attainment in the immediate social environment.

Perhaps the most serious defect of socially stratified systems is the low aspirational ceiling they tend to produce in the lower and numerically important strata. Thus, studies of the recruitment to universities reveal a consistent underrepresentation of youth of working-class origin—even when I.Q. is held constant (Boalt, 1954; Warner et al., 1946).

Glass recently pointed out that, in Britain, an I.Q. from the top 23 per cent at age 11, used as sole criterion of school admission, would result in a student body composed of 60 per cent from working-class backgrounds (Glass, 1961, p. 408n).

In contrast, the typical European situation may be fairly represented by the 1958–1959 figures from the Netherlands, showing that the upper 5 per cent in terms of occupational prestige of the population produces 45 per cent of all male students and 66 per cent of all female students; while the lowest 68 per cent produces only 9 per cent of all male, and 3 per cent of all female students (Heek, 1961).

In the United States around 1950, 58 per cent of those in the top 10 per cent in regard to I.Q. did not receive a college education (Wolfle, 1954, Table VI.I, p. 149; cf. Rogoff, 1961). Among Norwegian soldiers in the top 23 per cent on an I.Q. test at age 19, nearly one-half (48 per ecnt) had obtained only a maximum of 10 years of formal education as of 1950 (Ramsöy, 1961).

The combined operation of father's occupation and family residence was documented by Ramsöy (1961), who showed that the sons of fishermen who had grown up in small fishing villages had only 1 chance in 100 of obtaining more than 10 years of education, while the corresponding probability for sons of professional persons residing in the capital was 72 out of 100.

Such barriers to higher education as economy and distance may be less important than the counter attraction of occupations promising income, and hence an increase in independence, demanding no advanced education. Andresen (1962) reported that the most frequent explanation given for lack of higher education among Danish soldiers was, "I would rather start earning money, and be on my own."

In summary, the accumulated knowledge of social differentiation consists of many loosely connected facts and few principles. Further scientific work must advance the formulation of a set of invariances that, by their derivations, will explain the observed facts, effectively guide further research, and prove predictive. Tools of observation also must be refined.

REFERENCES

The *International Bibliography of Sociology,* edited first by UNESCO and now by Stevens & Sons, lists works on social stratification in a separate section. As of June, 1962, it covers the years 1951–1960 and is thus about one-and-one-half years behind.

Sociological Abstracts also devotes separate sections to social stratification, again with various degrees of lag.

Current Sociology devoted its second volume (1953–1954) to trend reports and bibliographies on social stratification: An international report by MacRae, and national reports by Wirth (United States), Boalt and Janson (Sweden), and by Odaka et al. (Japan). Volume 8, no. 3 (1959) was devoted to caste problems, and volume 9, no. 1 (1960) contains S. M. Miller, *Comparative Social Mobility,* a trend report and bibliography.

The *International Sociological Association* provided an important stimulus to work in this area by focusing two of its international meetings on the topics of social stratification and mobility. See *Transactions of the 2nd and 3rd World Congress of Sociology, International Sociological Association.* Its permanent committee on social stratification and mobility in cooperation with German scholars produced the volume, *Soziale Schichtung und soziale Mobilität,* edited by D. Glass and R. König, Cologne, 1961.

Another important bibliographic source is H. Pfautz. The current literature on social stratification, critique, and bibliography. *Amer. J. Sociol.,* 1953, 58, 391–418.

The most important textbooks are: P. Sorokin (1927) (reprinted under the title: *Social and cultural mobility,* 1959); B. Barber (1957); J. Kahl (1957); M. Gordon (1958).

Aitchison, J., & Brown, J. A. C. *The lognormal distribution.* Cambridge: Cambridge Univer. Press, 1957.

Allee, W. C., et al. *Principles of animal ecology.* Philadelphia: Saunders, 1949.

Allen, R. G. D. Mathematical economics. (2nd ed.) London: Macmillan, 1959.

Anastasi, A., & Foley, J. P., Jr. *Differential psychology.* (rev. ed.) New York: Macmillan, 1949.

Anderson, C. A., Brown, J. C., & Bowman, M. J. Intelligence and occupational mobility. *J. polit. Econ.,* 1952, 60, 218–239.

Anderson, C. A. Lifetime inter-occupational mobility patterns in Sweden. *Acta sociologica,* 1956, 1, 168–202.

Anderson, O. W. Infant mortality and social and cultural factors. In E. G. Jaco (Ed.), *Patients, physicians and illness.* Glencoe, Ill.: Free Press, 1958.

Andresen, A. Om intelligensreserven og dens udnyttelse. *Sociologiske Meddelelser,* 1962, 7, 93–108.

Aristotle. *Politics and Athenian constitution.* J. Warrington (Ed. & Trans.). London: Dent, 1959.

Aubert, V., Torgersen, U., Tangen, K., Lindbekk, T., Pollan, S., Kjellberg, F. The professions in Norwegian social structure 1720–1955. Oslo, Norway: Institute for social research, 1961–1962. 2 vols. (Mimeographed)

Barber, B. *Social stratification. A comparative analysis of structure and process.* New York: Harcourt, 1957.

Bendix, R., & Lipset, S. M. (Eds.) *Class, status, and power.* Glencoe, Ill.: Free Press, 1953.

Benny, M., & Geiss, P. Social class and politics in Greenwich. *Brit. J. Sociol.,* 1950, 1, 310–327.

Berent, J. Fertility and social mobility. *Pop. Stud.,* 1951–1952, 5, 244–260.

Bernstein, B. Social class and linguistic development. In A. H. Halsey, J. Floud, & C. A. Anderson (Eds.), *Education, economy, and society.* New York: The Free Press of Glencoe, 1961. Pp. 288–314.

Beshers, J. M. *Urban social structure.* New York: The Free Press of Glencoe, 1962.

Bjerke, K. Some income and wage distribution theories. *Weltwirtschaftliches Archiv,* 1961, 86 (1), 46–68.

Boalt, G. Social mobility in Stockholm. A pilot investigation. *Trans. 2nd World Cong. Sociol.,* 1954, 2, 67–73.

Bolte, K. Vom Umfang der Mobilität. *Kölner Zeitschrift für Soziologie,* 1958, 10, 49–55.

Bolte, K. *Sozialer Aufstieg und Abstieg. Eine Untersuchung über Berufsprestige und Berufsmobilität.* Stuttgart: Enke, 1959.

Bronfenbrenner, U. Socialization and social class through time and space. In E. E. Maccoby, T. M. Newcomb, & E. L. Hartley (Eds.), *Readings in social psychology.* (3rd ed.) New York: Holt, 1958. Pp. 400–425.

Candolle, A. de. *Histoire des sciences et des savants depuis deux siècles, suivie d'autres études sur des sujets scientifiques, en particulier sur la sélection dans l'espèce humaine.* Geneva: Georg, 1872.

Cantril, H. (Ed.) *Public opinion, 1935–1946.* Princeton, N. J.: Princeton Univer. Press, 1951.

Caplow, T. The effect of increasing size on organizational structure in industry. *Trans. 3rd World Cong. Sociol.,* 1956, 2, 157–164.

Carlsson, G. *Social mobility and class structure.* Lund: Gleerup, 1958.

Carlsson, G. Samhällsklasser och social rörlighet. In E. Dahlström (Ed.), *Svensk samhällsstruktur i sociologisk belysning.* Stockholm: Svenska Bokförlaget, 1959. Pp. 367–396.

Carlsson, G. Ökonomische Ungleichheit und Lebenschancen. In D. V. Glass & R. König (Eds.), Soziale Schichtung und soziale Mobilität. Cologne: Westdeutscher Verlag, 1961. Pp. 189–199. (*Kölner Zeitschrift für Soziologie und Sozialpsykologie, Sonderheft 5*).

Carlsson, S. *Svensk ståndscirculation 1680–1950*. Uppsala: Lindblad, 1950.

Centers, R. *The psychology of social classes*. Princeton, N. J.: Princeton Univer. Press, 1949.

Champernowne, D. C. The graduation of income distributions. *Econometrica*, 1952, 20, 591–615.

Chombart de Lauwe, P. *La vie quotidienne des familles ouvrières*. Paris: Centre National de la Recherche Scientifique, 1956.

Counts, G. S. The social status of occupations. *School Rev.*, 1925.

Crawford, M. P. The social psychology of the vertebrates. *Psychol. Bull.*, 1939, 36, 407–446.

Cuber, J. F., & Kenkel, W. F. *Social stratification in the United States*. New York: Appleton, 1954.

Dahrendorf, R. *Soziale Klassen und Klassenkonflikt*. Stuttgart: Enke, 1957.

Dahrendorf, R. *Über den Uhrsprung der Ungleichheit unter den Menschen*. Tübingen: Author, 1961.

Davies, A. Prestige of occupations. *Brit. J. Sociol.*, 1952, 3, 134–147.

Davis, H. T. *The analysis of economic time series*. Bloomington, Ind.: Principia Press, 1941.

Davis, K. *Human society*. New York: Macmillan, 1949.

Davis, K. *The population of India and Pakistan*. Princeton, N.J.: Princeton Univer. Press, 1951.

Davis, K., & Moore, W. Some principles of stratification. *Amer. Sociol. Rev.*, 1945, 10, 242–249.

Deeg, M. E., & Paterson, D. G. Changes in social status of occupations. *Occupations*, 1947, 25, 205–208.

Douglas, J. W. B., & Blomfield, J. M. *Children under five*. London: Allen & Unwin, 1958.

Dublin, L. I., Lotka, A. J., & Spiegelman, M. *Length of life. A study of the life table*. (rev. ed.) New York: Ronald Press, 1949.

Duncan, O. D., & Hodge, R. W. Education and occupational mobility. A regression analysis. *Amer. J. Sociol.*, 1963, 68, 629–644.

Faris, R. E. L. The alleged class system in the United States. *Res. Stud., State Coll. Washington*, 1954, 22, 77–83.

Faris, R. E. L. Reflections on the ability dimension. *Amer. sociol. Rev.*, 1961, 26, 835–843.

Feller, W. *An introduction to probability theory and its applications*. New York: Wiley, 1950.

Foote, N., et al. Alternative assumptions in stratification research. *Trans. 2nd World Cong. Sociol.*, 1954, 378–390.

Fourastié, J. *The causes of wealth*. Glencoe, Ill.: Free Press, 1960.

Freedman, R. American studies of family planning and fertility. A review of major trends and issues. In C. V. Kiser (Ed.), *Research in family planning*. Princeton, N.J.: Princeton Univer. Press, 1962. Pp. 231–261.

Ganon, I. Estratificación Social de Montevideo. *Boletim, Centro Latino Americano de Investigaciones en ciencias sociales*, 1961, 4, 303–330.

Geiger, T. Recruitment of university students. *Acta sociologica*, 1955, 1, 39–48.

Gibbs, J. C., & Martin, W. T. Urbanization, technology, and division of labor. *Amer. sociol. Rev.*, 1962, 27, 667–677.

Girard, A. La reussite sociale en France. *Institut nat. d'études demographiques. Travaux et documents*, No. 38. Paris: Presses Univer., 1961.

Glanzer, M., & Glaser, R. Techniques for the study of group structure I. *Psychol. Bull.*, 1959, 56, 317–332.

Glass, D. V. (Ed.) *Social mobility in Britain*. London: Routledge, 1954.

Glass, D. V. Education and social change in modern England. In A. H. Halsey, J. Floud, & C. A. Anderson (Eds.), *Education, economy, and society*. Glencoe, Ill.: Free Press, 1961. Pp. 391–413.

Glass, D. V. Family limitation in Europe. A survey of recent studies. In C. V. Kiser (Ed.), *Research in family planning*. Princeton, N.J.: Princeton Univer. Press, 1962. Pp. 231–261.

Goffman, I. W. Status consistency and preference for change in power distribution. *Amer. sociol. Rev.* 1957, 22, 275–281.

Gordon, M. M. *Social class in American sociology.* Durham, N.C.: Duke Univer. Press, 1958.

Gould, H. Castes, outcastes, and the sociology of stratification. *Int. J. comp. Sociol.,* 1960, 1, 220–238.

Gumplowicz, L. *Grundriss der Soziologie.* Vienna: Manz, 1885.

Haer, J. Predictive utility of five indices of social stratification. *Amer. sociol. Rev.,* 1957, 22, 541–546.

Hall, R., Haas, E., & Johnson, N. J. The size of the supportive component in organizations: A multi-organization analysis. Columbus, Ohio: Author, 1963. (Mimeographed)

Hall, J., & Jones, D. C. The social grading of occupations. *Brit. J. Sociol.,* 1950, 1, 31–55.

Hartmann, G. W. The relative social prestige of representative medical specialties. *J. appl. Psychol.,* 1936, 20, 659–663.

Hatt, P. K. Stratification in the mass society. *Amer. sociol. Rev.,* 1950, 15, 216–222.

Heek, F. van. Soziale Faktoren in den Niederlanden die einer optimalen Nachwuchsauslese für akademische Berufe im Wege stehen. In D. V. Glass & R. König (Eds.), Soziale Schichtung und soziale Mobilität. Cologne: Westdeutscher Verlag, 1961. Pp. 243–258. (*Kölner Z. für Soziol. und Sozialpsykol., Sonderheft 5*).

Heek, F. van, & Vercruijsse, E. V. W. De nederlandse berops-prestige-stratificatie. In *Sociale stijging en daling in Nederland.* Leiden: Steinfert Kroese, 1958——, 1 (1958), 11–48.

Hetzler, S. A. An investigation of the distinctiveness of social classes. *Amer. sociol. Rev.,* 1953, 18, 493–497.

Hobhouse, L. T., Wheeler, G. C., & Ginsberg, M. *The material culture and social institutions of the simpler peoples.* London: Chapman & Hall, 1915.

Hochbaum, G., Darley, J. G., Monachesi, E. D., & Bird, C. Socioeconomic variables in a large city. *Amer. J. Sociol.,* 1955, 61, 31–38.

Hofstätter, P. R. *Socialpsykol.* Stockholm: Svenska Bokförlaget, 1958. Trans. from German.

Hollingshead, A. *Elmtown's youth.* New York: Wiley, 1949.

Hollingshead, A., & Redlich, F. C. *Social class and mental disease.* New York: Wiley, 1958.

Homans, G. C. *The human group.* New York: Harcourt, 1950.

Homans, G. C. Status among clerical workers. *Hum. Organ.,* 1953, 12 (1), 5–10.

Homans, G. C. *Social behavior. Its elementary forms.* New York: Harcourt, 1961.

Hughes, E. C. Dilemmas and contradictions of status. *Amer. J. Sociol.,* 1945, 50, 353–359.

Hutchinson, B. The social grading of occupations in Brazil. *Brit. J. Sociol.,* 1957, 8, 176–189.

Hyman, H. H. The psychology of status. *Arch. Psychol.,* 1942, 38 (269), 1–94.

Hyman, H. H. The value systems of different classes. In R. Bendix, & S. M. Lipset (Eds.), *Class, status, and power.* Glencoe, Ill.: Free Press, 1953. Pp. 426–442.

Inkeles, A. Social stratification and mobility in the Soviet Union. *Amer. sociol. Rev.,* 1950, 15, 465–479.

Inkeles, A., & Rossi, P. National comparisons of occupational prestige. *Amer. J. Sociol.,* 1956, 61, 329–339.

Jackson, E. F. Status consistency and symptoms of stress. *Amer. sociol. Rev.,* 1962, 27, 469–480.

Janowitz, M. Social stratification and mobility in Western Germany. *Amer. J. Sociol.,* 1958, 64, 6–24.

Jaques, E. *Measurement of responsibility.* London: Tavistock, 1956.

Kahl, J. A. *The American class structure.* New York: Rinehart, 1957.

Kahl, J. A., & Davis, J. A comparison of indexes of socio-economic status. *Amer. sociol. Rev.,* 1955, 20, 317–325.

Kaufman, H. Prestige classes in a New York rural community. In R. Bendix & S. M. Lipset (Eds.), *Class, status, and power.* Glencoe, Ill.: Free Press, 1953. Pp. 190–203.

Kendall, M. G. From ranking to measurement. Lecture delivered at Copenhagen Univer., Sept. 30, 1960.

Kiser, C. V. The Indianapolis study of social and psychological factors affecting fertility. In C. V. Kiser (Ed.), *Research in family planning.* Princeton, N.J.: Princeton Univer. Press, 1962. Pp. 149–166.

Knupfer, Genevieve. Portrait of the underdog. *Publ. Opin. Quart.,* 1947, 11, 103–114.

Kodlin, D., & Thompson, D. J. An appraisal of the longitudinal approach. *Monogr. Soc. Res. in Child Develpm.* 1958, 23, Ser. No. 67 (1), pp. 1–47.

Kornhauser, Ruth R. The Warner approach to social stratification. In R. Bendix & S. M. Lipset (Eds.), *Class, status, and power.* Glencoe, Ill.: Free Press, 1953. Pp. 224–255.

Lasswell, H. D. *The political writings of.* . . . Glencoe, Ill.: Free Press, 1951.

Lawson, E., & Boek, W. Correlations of indexes of families' socio-economic status. *Soc. Forces,* 1960, 39, 149–152.

Lenski, G. E. American social classes: Statistical strata or social groups? *Amer. J. Sociol.,* 1952, 58, 139–144.

Lenski, G. E. Status crystallization: A non-vertical dimension of social status. *Amer. sociol. Rev.,* 1954, 19, 405–413.

Lenski, G. E. Comment on Kenkel's communication. *Amer. sociol. Rev.,* 1956, 21, 368–369.

Levy-Leboyer, C. Les determinants de la supériorité: État présent des recherches. In A. Girard (Ed.), La réussite sociale en France. *Institut nat. d'études demographiques. Travaux et documents,* No. 38. Paris: Presses Universitaires, 1961. Pp. 31–54.

Lewis, O., & Barnouw, V. Caste and the Jajmani system in a North Indian village. *Sci. mon.,* 1956, 83, 66–81.

Lindhardt, Marie. *Infant mortality in Denmark.* Copenhagen: Author, c. 1948.

Linton, R. *The study of man.* New York: Appleton, 1936.

Lipset, S. M. *Political man.* New York: Doubleday, 1960.

Lipset, S. M., & Bendix, R. *Social mobility in industrial society.* Berkeley: Univer. of California Press, 1959.

Löfgren, E. Mutual relations between migration fields. *Stud. Geography,* Ser. B., No. 13, 1957, 159–169.

Logan, W. P. P. Social class variations in mortality. In J. J. Spengler & O. D. Duncan (Eds.), *Demographic analysis. Selected readings.* Glencoe, Ill.: Free Press, 1956. Pp. 138–143.

Loomis, C. P. Political and occupational cleavages. *Sociometry,* 1946, 9, 316–333.

Lundberg, G. A. *Social research. A study in methods of gathering data.* (2nd ed.) New York: Longmans, 1942.

Lundberg, G. A., Schrag, C. C., & Larsen, O. N. *Sociology.* (rev. ed.) New York: Harper, 1958.

McGuire, C. Social stratification and mobility patterns. *Amer. sociol. Rev.,* 1950, 15, 195–204.

MacPherson, J. S. *Eleven-year-olds grow up.* London: Univer. of London Press, 1958.

Mahar, P. M. A ritual pollution scale for ranking Hindu castes. *Sociometry,* 1960, 23, 292–306.

Marris, P. Social change and social class. *Int. J. comp. Sociol.,* 1960, 1, 119–124.

Marx, K. *Der achtzente Brumaire.* (2nd ed.) Hamburg, 1869.

Matthews, D. R. *The social background of political decision-makers.* New York: Random House, Inc., 1954.

Mayer, A. J., & Hauser, P. M. Class differentials in expectation of life at birth. In R. Bendix & S. M. Lipset (Eds.), *Class, status, and power.* Glencoe, Ill.: Free Press, 1953. Pp. 281–292.

Mayer, K. *Class and society.* New York: Random House, Inc., 1955.

Mayer, K. Recent changes in the class structure of the United States. *Trans. 3rd World Cong. Sociol.,* 1956, 3, 66–80.

Milić, V. Osvrt na društvenu pokretljivost u Jugoslaviji. *Statističke Revije,* 1960, 10 (3–4), 184–235.

Milić, V. Some characteristics of marital mobility in Yugoslavia. *I. P. V. Conf.,* 1961, paper no. 72. (Mimeographed)

Miller, S. M. Comparative social mobility. *Curr. Sociol.,* 1960, 9, 1–172.

Miller S. M., & Bryce, H. Soziale Mobilität, wirtschaftliches Wachstum und Struktur. In D. V. Glass & R. König (Eds.), *Soziale Schichtung und soziale Mobilität.* Cologne: Westdeutscher Verlag, 1961. Pp. 303–315. (*Kölner Z. für Soziol. und Sozialpsykol., Sonderheft 5.*)

Moore, W. E., & Tumin, M. M. Some social functions of ignorance. *Amer. sociol. Rev.,* 1949, 14, 787–795.

Mosca, G. *The ruling class.* New York: McGraw, 1939.

Murdock, G. P. World ethnographic sample. *Amer. Anthropol.,* 1957, 59, 664–687.

Naroll, R. A preliminary index of social development. *Amer.. Anthropol.,* 1956, 58, 687–715.

Neff, W. S. Socio-economic status and intelligence. *Psychol. Bull.,* 1938, 35, 732–733.

Nisihira, S. Cross-national comparative study on social stratification and mobility. *Ann., Inst. statist. Math.*, 1957, 3, 181–191.

North, C. C. *Social differentiation.* Chapel Hill: Univer. of North Carolina Press, 1926.

North, C. C., & Hatt, P. K. National Opinion Research Center. Jobs and occupations. A popular evaluation. In R. Bendix & S. M. Lipset (Eds.), *Class, status, and power.* Glencoe, Ill.: Free Press, 1953. Pp. 411–426.

Pagani, A. (Ed.) *Classi e dinamica sociale.* Milano: Centro di ricerche economiche e sociali. Istituto di statistica dell' univercita di Pavia, 1960. (Mimeographed)

Painter, S. *Mediaeval society.* Ithaca, N.Y.: Cornell Univer. Press, 1951.

Pareto, V. *The mind and society. A general sociology.* London: Cape, 1935.

Parsons, T. A revised analytical approach to the theory of social stratification. In R. Bendix & S. M. Lipset (Eds.), *Class, status, and power.* Glencoe, Ill.: Free Press, 1953. Pp. 92–128.

Peller, S. Studies on mortality since the renaissance. *Bull. Hist. Med.*, 1943, 13, 427–461.

Peterson, W. *Population.* New York: Macmillan, 1961.

Pfautz, H. W., & Duncan, O. D. A critical evaluation of Warner's work in community stratification. *Amer. sociol. Rev.*, 1950, 15, 205–215.

Porter, J. The economic elite and the social structure in Canada. In B. Blishen et al. (Eds.), *Canadian society.* New York: The Free Press of Glencoe, 1961. Pp. 486–500.

Prais, S. J. Measuring social mobility. *Statist. J., Royal statist. Soc.*, 1955, Ser. A, 118, 56–66.

Ramsöy, Natalie E. Utdannelse og yrkesvalg i norsk samfunnsstruktur. *Tidsskrift for Samfunnsforskning,* 1961, 2, 217–237.

Reiss, A. J. with Duncan, O. D., Hatt, P. K., & North, C. C. *Occupations and social status.* New York: The Free Press of Glencoe, 1961.

Rogoff, Natalie. Recent trends in urban occupational mobility. In P. K. Hatt & A. J. Reiss, Jr. (Eds.), *Reader in urban sociology.* Glencoe, Ill.: Free Press, 1951. Pp. 406–420.

Rogoff, Natalie. American public schools and equality of opportunity. In A. H. Halsey, J. Floud, & C. A. Anderson (Eds.), *Education, economy, and society.* Glencoe, Ill.: Free Press, 1961. Pp. 140–147.

Rowntree, B. S. *Poverty. A study of town life.* London: Macmillan, 1901.

Ryan, B. *Caste in modern Ceylon.* New Brunswick, N.J.: Rutgers Univer. Press, 1953.

Schenkel, R. Ausdruckstudien an Wölfen. *Behavior,* 1948, 1, 81–129.

Schermerhorn, R. A. *Society and power.* New York: Random House, Inc., 1961.

Scheuch, E. K., & Daheim, H. Sozial Prestige und soziale Schichtung. In D. V. Glass & R. König (Eds.), *Soziale Schichtung und soziale Mobilität.* Cologne: Westdeutscher Verlag, 1961, 65–103. (*Kölner Z. für Soziol. und Sozialpsykol., Sonderheft 5.*)

Schjelderup-Ebbe, T. *Beiträge zur Sozial- und Individualpsychologie bei Gallus Domesticus.* Griefswald: Author, 1921.

Schumpeter, J. A. *Capitalism, socialism, and democracy.* (4th ed.) London: Allen & Unwin, 1952.

Scott, E. M., Illsley, R., & Biles, M. E. Some aspects of maternal behaviour. (A psychological investigation of primigravidae. Part 3). *J. Obstetr. & Gynaecol., Brit. Empire,* 1956, 63, 494–501.

Shevky, E., & Bell, W. Social area analysis. Stanford: Stanford Univer. Press, 1955.

Sibley, E. Some demographic clues to stratification. *Amer. sociol. Rev.*, 1942, 7, 322–330.

Sivertsen, D. Kasteskillene og kampen mot dem. *Forskningsnytt,* 1962, 3, 6–8, 16.

Sorokin, P. A. *Social mobility.* New York: Harper, 1927.

Sorokin, P. A. *Society, culture, and personality. Their structure and dynamics. A system of general sociology.* New York: Harper, 1947.

Srinivas, M. N., Damle, Y. B., Shahani S., & Beteille, A. Caste, a trend report and bibliography. *Curr. Sociol.*, 1959, 8 (3), 135–183.

Sundt, E. *Fortsatte Bidrag angående Sædelighedstilstanden i Norge.* Christiana. (Oslo): Author, 1864.

Svalastoga, K. Measurement of occupational prestige: Field techniques. *Trans. 2nd World Cong. Sociol.,* 1954, 2, 403–413.

Svalastoga, K. The family in the mobility process. In N. Anderson (Ed.), *Studies of the family.* Göttingen: Vandenhoeck, 1958. Vol. 3, pp. 289–306.

Svalastoga, K. *Prestige, class and mobility.* Copenhagen: Gyldendal, 1959.

Svalastoga, K. Gedanken zu internationalen Vergleichen sozialer Mobilität. In D. V. Glass & R. König (Eds.), *Soziale Schichtung und soziale Mobilität.* Cologne: Westdeutscher Verlag, 1961. Pp. 284–302. (*Kölner Z. für Soziol. und Sozialpsykol., Sonderheft 5.*)

Svalastoga, K. Size and system. On the social significance of change of scale. Copenhagen: Sociological Institute, Univer. of Copenhagen, 1963. (Mimeographed)

Svalastoga, K., & Carlsson, G. Social stratification and social mobility in Scandinavia. *Sociol. Inquiry,* 1961, 31, 23–46.

Talmon-Gerbier, Y. Social differentiation in cooperative communities. *Brit. J. Sociol.,* 1952, 3, 339–357.

Terrien, F. W., & Mills, D. L. The effect of changing size upon the internal structure of organizations. *Amer. sociol. Rev.,* 1955, 20, 11–13.

Thomas, G. Labour mobility in Great Britain 1945–1949. London: Social Survey, c. 1951. (Mimeographed)

Thomas, R. M. Reinspecting a structural position on occupational prestige. *Amer. J. Sociol.,* 1962, 67, 561–565.

Tuckman, J. Social status of occupations in Canada. *Canad. J. Psych.,* June, 1947, 1, 71–74.

Tulder, J. J. M. van. *De Beroepsmobiliteit in Nederland van 1919–1954: Een Sociaalstatistische Studie.* Leiden: Stenfert Kroese, 1962.

Tumin, M. M. Some principles of stratification. A critical analysis. *Amer. sociol. Rev.,* 1953, 18, 387–394.

Tumin, M. M., & Feldman, A. S. *Social class and social change in Puerto Rico.* Princeton, N.J.: Princeton Univer. Press, 1961.

United Nations Population Division. Age and sex patterns of mortality. *U.N. Population Studies,* 1955, No. 22.

Versichelen, M. Sociale mobiliteit. Een studie over differentiele levenskansen. Gent: Studie —en onderzoekcentrum voor sociale wetenschappen. Rijksuniversiteit te Gent, 1959. (*Verhandelingen van het studie—en onderzoekscentrum voor sociale wetenschappen.* Rijksuniversiteit te Gent. No. 1.)

Warner, W. L., Havighurst, R. J., & Loeb, M. B. *Who shall be educated?* London: Kegan Paul, 1946.

Warner, W. L., & Lunt, P. S. *The social life of a modern community.* New Haven, Conn.: Yale Univer. Press, 1941.

Warner, W. L., Meeker, M., & Eells, K. *Social class in America.* Chicago: Science Research Ass., 1949.

Weber, M. *The theory of social and economic organization.* (Trans. of Part I of *Wirtschaft und Gesellschaft*) T. Parsons (Ed.). London: Hodge, 1947.

Weber, M. *From Max Weber: Essays in sociology.* H. H. Gerth & C. Wright Mills (Ed. & Trans.). New York: Oxford Univer. Press, 1948.

Whyte, W. F. *Street corner society.* Chicago: Univer. of Chicago Press, 1943.

Wolfle, D. *America's resources of specialized talent.* New York: Harper, 1954.

Wrong, D. H. *Population.* (rev. ed.) New York: Random House, Inc., 1956.

Wrong, D. H. The functional theory of stratification: Some neglected considerations. *Amer. sociol. Rev.,* 1959, 24, 772–782.

Zetterberg, H. L. *Social theory and social practice.* New York: Bedminster Press, 1962.

CHAPTER **16** **Race and Ethnic Relations**[1]

FRANK R. WESTIE

In terms of volume of research material, the field of race and ethnic relations is one of the most developed in sociology. In terms of theoretical development, however, the field must be ranked among the least developed areas.

Simpson and Yinger observe that the "vast variety of situations within which people meet and the long list of variables that affect their interaction have led some writers, in recent years, to suggest that a general science of 'race relations' is impossible" (1959, p. 376). This statement is not cited to endorse the defeatism it contains; the complexity of the area should not induce a retreat from the classic goal of science. But the statement does document the fact that disillusionment regarding theory of race and ethnic relations is widespread.

Is the situation really this bad? Is there

not in this area an appreciable number of broad, abstract generalizations which have been derived through research and sustained by subsequent research? The answer is that there is an impressive number of such generalizations in the intergroup relations area, perhaps more than in most other areas of sociology. But these propositions, while general, abstract, and applicable to wide varieties of specific behaviors, are, at best, more or less discreet items of knowledge not meaningfully related to one another. At worst, they contradict one another.

THEORETICAL PROBLEMS

The reasons for this theoretical lag are many, but there are no empirically oriented *Wissensoziologen* around to tell us what they are or which are most important. Three contributing factors are, however, conspicuous and worthy of consideration: (1) ideological bias, (2) social action orientation, and (3) theoretical particularism. Although these are closely related, they will be discussed in order. The "complexity argument" will be ignored because it remains to be demonstrated that the significant variables

[1] Some of the material in this chapter will also appear in the author's forthcoming book on prejudice. Some previously unreported findings of the author's own research are also reported here. The assistance of Marcia T. Segal and Carl P. Wagoner, and the support of these projects by The Human Ecology Fund, The Social Science Research Council, and the Graduate School of Indiana University is gratefully acknowledged.

influencing intergroup behavior are any more numerous or complex than in most other areas of sociology.

Ideological Biases

Few people, including sociologists, psychologists, and anthropologists, are ideologically neutral on the subject of race and race relations. The biases of the citizen in the community are obvious and are in fact among the primary subjects of research in this area. The biases of the professional student of the subject are frequently just as intense and pervasive, albeit concealed behind scientific terminology and statistical tables.

Research from Action versus Research from Theory

The strengths and weaknesses of action research and theory in contrast to sociological research and theory are well understood in sociology. Social action research is, by definition, designed to derive social prescriptions; and such prescriptions, whether medical or social, are necessarily based primarily on value premises and only secondarily, if at all, on theoretical premises. It is embarrassing to pile up stock admonitions regarding the deleterious effects of ideology on the validity and theoretical utility of research, but if one despairs at these clichés, let him read Tumin's recent *Inventory and Appraisal of Research on American Anti-Semitism* (1961). The first half of this inventory summarizes objective and descriptive projects, many of them theoretically exciting. The second half emphasizes evaluational studies. The latter appear pale and weak in comparison to the former, and the money spent on the latter would have been better spent on the former. One may wonder if action research is even as significant as a guide to social policy as the theoretically guided studies.

Theoretically significant action-oriented research projects can of course be cited. Conspicuous among these are the studies preceding and following integration in particular units of the armed forces (Evans & Lang, 1956; Nichols, 1954; Stouffer, Suchman, DeVinney, Star, & Williams, 1949). These studies revised scholarly faith in cherished theories of the impotence of law in the face of contrary public attitudes and action preferences once cherished. Out of this research grew the most significant theoretical ideas to emerge in the intergroup relations area in the past 20 years. These are the theories of the relationship between attitudes, collective definitions of the situation, and overt acts. Nevertheless, such coincidental emergence of "social good" and "theoretical good" from projects designed within a social action frame of reference are exceptional. The dictum, "no research without action; no action without research," could well result, from the standpoint of the development of theory, in not much theoretically significant research.

Theoretical Particularism

While determinism has gone out of style in sociology, particularism remains. Particularism refers to the assignment of overwhelming importance to a particular factor or set of factors—leaving room, however, for the operation of other "less significant" factors. Particularism differs formally from its parent, determinism, in the casual nod given other factors and other theories. In practice, this difference is sometimes difficult to discern.

Like the problems of ideological bias and action orientation, the problem of particularism is in no way peculiar to the field of intergroup relations. Perhaps particularism survives most vigorously in areas with the longest history of determinism. Determinism, in turn, has been strongest in areas whose subject matter has characteristically been an object of emotional response. Race relations has certainly been such an area.

The two most common varieties of particularism in the intergroup relations area are the economic and the psychological (including the psychoanalytic). Many, but by no means all, who emphasize the role of economic forces in the development of prejudice and intergroup conflict take their cues from Marx. One seldom finds a Marxist interpretation of prejudice and intergroup conflict which is not clearly a species of old-fashioned determinism. Consider, for example, the following definition of prejudice:

Race prejudice is a social attitude propagated among the public by an exploiting class for the purpose of stigmatizing some group as inferior so that the exploitation of either the group itself or its resources may both be justified (Cox, 1948, p. 393).

Here we have a definition of prejudice which contains "*the* explanation" of the phenomenon. Research proceeding from this definition is likely to be a compilation of materials gathered to buttress the a priori explanation. Such is the nature of determinism.

While many psychological particularists see prejudice and intergroup conflict as an outcome of the conflict between Superego and Id, most such particularism is not of the psychoanalytic, "infantile experience" type. Theorists with a psychological bent, and they may be sociologists as well as psychologists, are inclined to view prejudice as a characteristic of particular personalities. The fact that prejudice is ultimately an attitude, and as such has its locus in the individual personality, has led many to look for the causes of prejudice (and ultimately of intergroup conflict in its various forms) within the individual personality. They have, in effect, individualized Durkheim's famous dictum: "The cause of a social fact must be sought in an antecedent social fact" to "the cause of a personality characteristic must be sought in another personality characteristic." Again, a definition serves to illustrate the approach in question:

Prejudice is a pattern of hostility in interpersonal relations which is directed against an entire group, or against its individual members; *it fulfills a specific irrational function for its bearer* (italics added) (Ackerman & Jahoda, 1950, p. 4).

Here again is a definition which includes an explanation in terms of an antecedent cause, if, as is frequently the case, one considers function and cause to be the same.

To say that the psychological approach tends to explain the psychological in terms of the psychological is not to imply that its practitioners are oblivious to the operation of external forces on the individual. But it is one thing to talk about an individual's social experiences and quite another to analyze the force of societal dynamics and culture on individual personality. Perhaps the most common shortcoming of the psychological approach is that it frequently is oblivious to both the concept and the phenomenon of culture. Although many behavioral phenomena can be analyzed by *starting with* the individual, as the psychologist is inclined to do, prejudice and intergroup relations are not among these.

To explain the consequences that prejudice, as an aspect of personality, has for another aspect of personality adds to our knowledge of prejudice, but such explanations fall far short of providing adequate understanding of either the psychology or sociology of prejudice. Again we would do well to heed an admonition of Durkheim:

Most sociologists think they have accounted for phenomena once they have shown how they are useful, what role they play, reasoning as if facts existed only from the point of view of this role and with no other determining cause than the sentiment, clear or confused, of the services they are called to render. This is why they think they have said all that is necessary, to render them intelligible, when they have established the reality of these services and have shown what social needs they satisfy (Durkheim, 1938, p. 89).

One final note on determinism: The most common lamentation regarding determinism and particularism, apart from the invalidity of monistic explanations of a multicaused society, is that such explanations lead to uncritical acceptance of particular doctrines which in turn results in the premature termination of curiosity and research. But the most serious consequence resides in the field's reaction to particular deterministic doctrines. Given the history of biological determinism sociologists have, for example, been inclined to negate, out of hand, the possibility of innate individual differences in temperament or aptitudes, even those of an artistic nature. By the same reaction formation, they have responded to economic determinism by devaluing the role of economic forces in the genesis and perpetuation of prejudice, discrimination, and intergroup conflict. This reaction formation is most conspicuous in the facile rejection, by many sociologists, of all psychoanalytic observations. Recognition is growing among sociologists that no *special* theories of prejudice, discrimination, or intergroup relations are necessary to the understanding of these phenomena. Significantly, the two best textbooks on the subject of intergroup relations take a multifactor approach to the subject: Simpson and Yinger (1954) and Gordon Allport (1954).

The relations between racial and ethnic groups do not differ basically from human relations in general. The social and psychological processes involved in race relations, for example, are no different from those prevailing between, among, and within families, communities, classes within communities, nations, or any other kinds of social groups and aggregates. Many of the processes which operate very subtly in other social situations become naked and obvious in the realm of minority-majority relations. It is sometimes useful to conceive of the area of race relations as an arena in which many social processes operate in exaggerated form. Obviously there will be differences in details; some social processes will be more pronounced in one area than another. In the relations between groups, however, regardless of the types, one finds differential

statuses, power differences, consciousness of differences, prejudices, differential and deferential treatment, situational constraints, competition, role definitions, and virtually the whole catalogue of sociological states and processes.

Consider, for example, the relations between peons and landed aristocrats in Latin America. On the highest level of abstraction, the sociological and psychological theories necessary to the explanation of the relations between these two groups are the same as those necessary to the understanding of race relations in the United States or anywhere else. The commonalities between the class systems in highly stratified societies and the race relations systems in prejudiced, though not-so-stratified societies are striking. Although the author knows of no systematic studies on the subject, conversations with particular Latin American sociologists suggest that the relations between peon and aristocrat are not distinguishable in kind from the relations between Negroes and whites in the United States. In both systems, the ascription of status at birth is paramount. While a degree of mobility is possible, it is sharply limited. It is doubtful that the peon's chances of taking a place in the inner social circles of the older, landed aristocracy are better than the American Negro's chances of acquiring membership in a top ranking, white country club in a North American community. Indeed, the Negro's chances may be better, considering differential rates of social change and the "pet Negro" phenomenon. In both systems, endogamy is stringently enforced, and both the American Negro and the Latin American peon are seen as possessing basic biological differences, "blood differences" which distinguish those in the lower stratum from those above, and the "lower blood" is seen in both systems as having a pernicious capacity to contaminate if permitted to flow upward.

A comparison such as this can easily be overdrawn; certainly there are points of dissimilarity between the two systems. But in the basic elements of race relations, the congruence is striking. This comparison is better appreciated if one recalls the formulation of the concept of "race relations" of Robert E. Park. Park emphasized that race relations are relations between people who are biologically different or *believed to be biologically different,* who are aware of these differences, and whose relations to one another are affected by this awareness. It makes no sense sociologically to define race relations as relations between biologically different groups or individuals. The relations between objectively quite different biological groupings may be, in particular times and places, unaffected by such differences; whereas interactions between groupings the world over are shaped by *believed* differences which do not in fact exist. W. I. Thomas' phenomenological view refers to the most important element in any conceptualization of race relations: "A situation defined as real is real in its consequences." By the same token, in Brazil, to the degree that people do not emphasize the "reality" of skin color differences, such differences may be said, *sociologically,* not to exist. (This is not meant to imply, however, that there is no race prejudice in Brazil.)

THE CURRENT STATE OF THEORY AND RESEARCH

Dennis Wrong has correctly observed that "Social theory must be seen primarily as a set of answers to questions we ask of social reality" (Wrong, 1961, p. 183). The sociologist, in his attempts to formulate theories in given areas, may, like the graduate student who falls in love with IBM machines and never finishes his thesis, become so enamored with the theoretical process that he loses sight of his original questions. The most general questions sociologists have asked in the intergroup relations area are really facets of even more general, "classic" questions sociologists and their antecedents throughout past centuries have asked about man and society.

The "classic" question has been: "How are men capable of uniting to form enduring societies in the first place?" (Wrong, 1961, p. 184).

When asked in the intergroup relations area, this question becomes: "What are the forces which contribute to cohesion (or solidarity, integration, harmony) between and among racially or culturally unlike groups within particular societies?" or conversely, "What are the forces which contribute to conflict (disintegration, disunity) between and among such groups?"

Another classic question: "Why and to what degree is change inherent in human societies and what are the sources of change?" (Wrong, 1961, p. 184).

And in the intergroup relations area, it becomes: "How do racially and ethnically prejudiced and discriminating societies develop these characteristics? Once developed, what are the possibilities for change, and what are the actual or possible sources of such change?"

Another classic question is: "What is the nature of the relationship between the individual and the group?"

And in the intergroup relations area, it is: "How and under what conditions do the prejudicial and discriminatory norms of a given social system become part of individual personalities occupying positions within that social system?" or conversely, "How do the psychological characteristics and status of individuals in a society affect cultural change?"

Of these basic types of queries, Wrong maintains, "They are not questions which lend themselves to successively more precise answers as the result of cumulative empirical research, for they remain eternally problematic." This writer agrees, but for a different reason. The basic concepts and relationships which are the stuff of these questions are so abstract and general (as they ought to be) and encompass such wide ranges of phenomena that to design a research project around any one of them would be the equivalent of an ichthyologic research on "the fish of the Atlantic Ocean." It is likely, however, that the second order of questions above, derived from the first and applying directly to intergroup relations, do suggest more specific (though still general) questions which can lead to researchable hypotheses.

For this reason, this discussion of research and theory does not include such concepts as "social solidarity," "integration," "harmony," and their opposites. Instead, it is built around the concepts of *prejudice* and *discrimination*, with greater emphasis on the former than the latter. Both of these concepts refer to phenomena which can be specifically conceptualized and observed. This is probably the reason why more research in this area has been built around the concepts of prejudice and discrimination than all of the other concepts in the area combined—with the possible exception of the concept "authoritarianism." In spite of disagreements among sociologists concerning the meaning of these concepts, they look sharp and precise beside many other concepts in the area.

Some sociologists disdain analysis of intergroup relations built around the concept "prejudice" because prejudice is regarded as an attitude; attitude is, to them, an objectionable concept. This attitude toward attitude largely stems from objections to attitude psychology as it existed in the 1920's and 1930's.

The following are basic questions in the area of intergroup relations, questions which can lead to testable hypotheses. They are on the level of abstraction below the two cited previously:

1. How does prejudice toward a particular object-group become part of the normative system(s) of a particular society? How is this aspect of the normative system(s) perpetuated?

2. What are the social functions of prejudicial norms in a given social system?

3. How do particular individuals in a particular society take as part of their personalities those aspects of their society's normative system(s) which define their relations to particular groups in prejudicial terms?

4. How does it happen that different people reared in the same neighborhood, in the same social class, in the same region, and in the same country can vary from one another in their attitudes toward particular racial and ethnic groups?

5. How does it happen that, in a social setting which has as one of its dominant themes the principle of race superiority, personalities occasionally develop in which the system's normative and cognitive imperatives regarding race and race relations are neither internalized nor even shallowly accepted? Conversely, how does it happen that a prejudiced personality occasionally occurs in a relatively nonprejudiced family in a relatively nonprejudiced community?[2]

A NORMATIVE THEORY OF PREJUDICE[3]

Of all the various sets of factors which work together to produce prejudice in

[2] The words relatively nonprejudiced are used because experience has shown that few persons can qualify as "unprejudiced" about race, ethnicity, or religion. Obviously, if the term prejudice is used in the general sense, everyone is prejudiced for and against many kinds of people, ideas, and objects. With regard to racial, religious, or ethnic prejudice, people who qualify as unprejudiced are very hard to find in the United States and probably in any other modern nation. In a study of "The Tolerant Personality" (Martin & Westie, 1958), the investigators experienced great difficulty in finding a sufficient number of tolerant persons to make the study feasible. Ultimately a smaller number of cases was used and the subjects were redefined as "relatively tolerant." Allport and Kramer (1946) maintain, "It would seem a sage estimate that at least four-fifths of the American population lead mental lives in which feelings of group hostility play an appreciable role."

[3] An expanded version of the normative theory is included in Spanish in Frank R. Westie, "Analisis Sociologia del Fenomeno del Prejuicio," *Estudios de Sociologia*, Buenos Aires, 1961. The qualifications of the normative theory, listed herein, will also appear in *Estudios de Sociologia*.

the society and the individual, none is more important than the normative, or cultural, factor. Yet of all the factors which produce prejudice, none has been more neglected.

One can but speculate regarding the reasons for this neglect. Perhaps the very obviousness of the role of the cultural process in the genesis of prejudice and discrimination has reduced what are essentially primary principles to the level of truisms. Moreover, the development of scientific knowledge of intergroup relations during the early decades of the present century was delayed by a premature, facile application of the normative pronouncements of William Graham Sumner. Prejudice and discrimination, in Sumner's sociology, were made right by the mores, and his adoption as the pet sociologist of the erudite segregationist made Sumner and all he stood for sociologically and politically wrong in the minds of many sociologists. It is the case, however, that a *qualified* application of Sumner, along with Boas, Linton, Leslie White, and others to whom sociologists owe their present understanding of culture, tells as much about the nature of prejudice in society and the individual as does any other approach. It goes without saying that the cultural approach does not and cannot explain all.

A simple statement may now be made of what is called "the normative theory of prejudice." Although some of these principles may have acquired the status of truisms in sociology, they are rarely enunciated by sociologists in systematic fashion. In observing the role of culture in the genesis and perpetuation of prejudice, they frequently go no further than Rogers and Hammerstein, whose song in *South Pacific* observes, "You've got to be taught to hate." Yet simple ideas of this kind are basic elements in the normative approach to prejudice, and the normative elements are the foundation of any overall theory of intergroup relations. Attempts to develop high-powered theories, however, have frequently lost sight of the simple truths that our sociological forebears painstakingly unravelled.

Sociologists frequently find it useful to view societies as consisting of two orders: the normative and the factual. The *normative* order consists of the systems of ideas held by people in a given society concerning "what ought to be." This includes notions of good, bad, right, wrong, what the good citizen looks like, and, most important for the analysis of prejudice, how people ought to behave in relation to one another. Viewed from a negative standpoint, the normative order includes all those ideas held by members of a society regarding what they ought not to be, ought not to do, and the like.

The *factual* order consists of the total system of actual behavior of a given society— that is, the patterns of behavior the members actually practice, regardless of what they think they ought to do.

Prejudice is a part of the normative order of the society in which it occurs. It is the part of the society's system of norms defining what "ought to be" which defines how the individual member of the society ought to evaluate and interact with particular groups within and outside of the society.

The normative order is, of course, part of the culture. Thus, if the normative order is crucially cultural, it is necessary to understand the nature of culture in order better to understand the normative order of society of which prejudice, on the social level, is a part.

Presented below are certain elementary principles regarding the nature of culture. In each statement one may parenthetically substitute the word prejudice for the word culture. This is intended to demonstrate that, because prejudice is, on the societal level, a part of culture, the accepted generalizations concerning the nature of culture become useful for understanding the nature of prejudice.

Culture (prejudice) is group behavior. Culture (prejudice) is learned, not inborn. Culture (prejudice) is transmitted through the learning experiences the oncoming generation has with the generation already on the scene. Cultural behaviors (prejudices) are shared by the members of the group—that is, they are practiced in common and are not peculiar to particular individuals in the society. These socially acquired patterns of behavior of a given group are organized into a system in which each part, including prejudice, tends to make sense, in relation to other parts to the extent that they are functionally related to one another. In simple terms, a given group's culture is the socially standardized "style of life" characterizing the group; socially shared prejudices are part of that style of life.

One of the first principles defining the relationship between culture and the individual is: *The culture of a particular generation in a given society is not a product of the people now living in that society so much as the men are a product of that culture.* The culture in which individuals find themselves completely immersed, which is as pervasive and penetrating as the air they breathe, existed ready-made for them at the time of their birth. The degree to which any one individual shapes or alters his culture is infinitesimally small. On the other hand, the way in which culture affects him is immeasurably huge.

However, no sociologist would claim that every individual personality in a given society is a perfect replica of his culture, nor would many substitute cultural interpretation for analysis of the role of psychological and societal dynamics.

The normative order is a part of culture; prejudice, if it is normative, has, like culture, the following characteristics:

1. Prejudice typically grows in the culture in spite of the wishes of particular men in any particular time or place.

2. Prejudice may, and typically does, persist long after the original factors which produce it cease to exist.

3. Prejudice is acquired by the individual through the involuntary, unconscious (on the part of the person being socialized) process of socialization. The individual has no more control, especially in his early years, of what prejudices he takes into himself than he has over his breathing. A young child can no more say to himself, "Should I or shouldn't I like these people?" referring to a particular culturally defined object of prejudice, than he can say, "Should I or shouldn't I eat?" The individual takes on his society's "people habits" in the same way he takes on its food habits. Just as not all foods are regarded as equally palatable, all peoples are not regarded as equally eligible for social acceptance. The child soon learns which people are "good" and which are "not so good" in the eyes of his society. Eventually these definitions come to assume the stature of moral principles.

4. This individual in turn passes on to his children and to others in the society his own prejudices toward the members of particular outgroups as right and proper—indeed, as moral. He may do this consciously, the child being told specifically and very early that it is highly improper to engage in certain kinds of interaction with members of particular outgroups. On the other hand, he may transmit his prejudice unintentionally through example, through his general demeanor in relation to the objects of his society's prejudices.

A person is prejudiced against racial, religious, and cultural groups for the same reasons and as a result of the same social processes which lead him to love and to feel loyalty toward his mother, his family, his nation, his school, his church (MacIver & Page, 1948, p. 410). The appropriate attitudes toward persons, things, and ideas are inculcated in the individual in the process of socialization.

The normative foundation of prejudice may be summarized as follows: *Individuals are prejudiced because they are raised in societies which have prejudice as a facet of the normative system of their culture. Prejudice is built into the culture in the form of normative precepts—that is, notions of "ought to be"—which define the ways in which members of the group ought to be-*

have in relation to the members of selected outgroups.

All this does not necessarily mean that it is perfectly normal to be prejudiced toward minorities and that this is the expected state of affairs in modern society. Though prejudice is normative in many modern societies, *nonprejudice may also be normative* in these *same* societies. Whereas there are group prejudices of various kinds in all modern societies, many of these same societies, at least in the Western world, have democratic and Christian traditions which diametrically oppose prejudice, discrimination, and intergroup conflict.

Contradictions between national ideals and specific practices are prevalent in most modern societies. Sociologists know that contradictions between the normative order of society and the factual order are a basic characteristic of all modern societies. Not only is there an American dilemma (Myrdal, 1962), there is also an English, a French, a German, and other European dilemmas, and a variety of Latin American dilemmas.

Qualifications of the Normative Theory

A monistic emphasis on the normative theory can lead to serious misunderstandings. A number of qualifications must be taken into account:

1. To say that prejudice exists in societies as normative propositions tends to place the problem on a moral plane. Thus, some people readily conclude that the solutions to problems of intergroup conflict are exclusively moral solutions. This view ignores political and economic realities. When minorities, through increased economic, educational, and cultural opportunities, become less distinguishable in their social and economic status, prejudice is more likely to decline. Perhaps what is experienced by many as a moral problem (which it is, if so defined) can be ameliorated through economic and political means (Crespi, 1945).

2. Exclusive attention to the normative

character of prejudice obscures the important psychological processes involved in the prejudices of those persons whose personalities are organized around consuming aggressions and hostilities toward outgroups (Adorno, Frenkel-Brunswik, Levinson, & Sanford, 1950).

3. A single-sided emphasis on the normative aspect obscures the fact that a large percentage of people in modern mass society make their decisions on how to behave on the basis of definitions provided for them in the immediate situations of particular groups to which they belong. Peer groups have a conspicuous influence on the individual's choice of action (Riesman, Glazer & Denny, 1950). Often peer groups define action for members in terms of the interests of the immediate group rather than in terms of the long-standing normative propositions (or mores) of the society at large (Killian, 1952; Lohman & Reitzes, 1952; Lohman & Reitzes, 1954; Reitzes, 1953).

4. The normative theory emphasizes the role of tradition, folkways, and mores and the perpetuation of these through the socialization process. Thus it leads to the mistaken conclusion that "you can't legislate prejudice and discrimination." The myth prevails that prejudice is so deeply ingrained and so personal that legislative actions cannot alter existing patterns of relations between groups (Lohman & Reitzes, 1952). While the acts of a legislative body may not appreciably alter the personal prejudices of the adult public, the fact remains that legislative actions in many nations have altered overt patterns of interaction between groups.

In North America, for example, discriminatory patterns of interaction have been changed by legislative, judicial, and executive actions in the areas of housing, education, employment, and public facilities. These changes in overt behavior need not await prior changes in attitudes or prejudices. The American experience of integration of the armed services is a case in point. During World War II, particular military units were integrated by simple administrative decree. Soldiers who were prejudiced toward Negroes and opposed to integration were required to serve in the same units as Negroes. Tests of the attitudes of prejudiced soldiers involved showed that their prejudices were appreciably modified by their combat experiences in integrated units. This is an instance of "legislative change," followed by interaction change, followed by attitudinal change. While there are limits to the degree that legislative action can be at variance with public attitudes, as the American experience with prohibition attests, it must be recognized that the public's attitudinal orientation is not a consistent whole.

5. In many Western nations, both pro-prejudice norms and antiprejudice norms frequently prevail simultaneously within the same society and within the same individual personality. Thus, an antidiscrimination legislative act may contradict certain prejudicial norms in the society and also be harmonious with the norms defining prejudice as undesirable. Moreover, it is possible for legislative bodies to demonstrate that conformity to prejudicial traditions is not in the best economic and political interests of the nation. And publics do respond to interests as well as to tradition.

6. Unqualified emphasis on prejudice as normative, and thus traditional, tends to picture societies as static. William Graham Sumner, the father of the normative view in American sociology, has been widely criticized for his dictum that "the mores can make anything right." To regard each individual and each generation of a particular society as a pawn in the hands of an omnipotent and unalterable system of traditions is to equate feudal and modern societies. While there remain primitive societies to which Sumner's analysis of the folkways and mores still applies, the feature which distinguishes modern societies from all of their predecessors is a rapid rate of structural change.

The normative theory in its emphasis on irrational force of tradition tends to obscure those subgroups within the society whose members may fully appreciate their own political and economic interests in the maintenance of prejudice and discrimination and who consciously work for the perpetuation of the race relations status quo. While this interpretation would be applicable only to the thought-ways and actions of a relatively minor subsegment of the population of the United States, the effect of such groups on community patterns of behavior is frequently out of proportion to their numerical size.

Despite these qualifications, all of which are valid to a degree, the fact that prejudice tends to be normative in the societies where it prevails remains a basic, primary datum.

A Comment on Normative Conflict

Gunnar Myrdal (1952) postulates the existence of an American dilemma resulting from the conflict between general valuations (normative precepts which apply to all Americans or, in some cases, to all men) and the specific valuations which define the nature of relations between Negroes and whites. He maintains that people bridge the contradictions between the two by calling forth beliefs (statements about the nature of reality) which exempt the specific Negro-white case from the more general statement. These beliefs are usually socially shared myths and stereotypes which are part of American culture.

The present writer's own research points to certain inadequacies in Myrdal's theory, but does not deny the existence of a basic conflict between the general and the specific self-involving valuations (Westie, 1964).

Myrdal's theory leads us to expect a series of responses which might look something like this: (1) "Yes, I believe in equality of opportunity"; (2) "No, I would not be willing to have a Negro as my supervisor in my place of work"; [because] (3) "Negroes are inferior to whites in their intellectual abilities." Some 50 per cent of a studied sample gave responses of this ideal-typical kind. Almost as many responses, however, did not conform to the Myrdal model, but involved the assertion of an additional valuation: (1) "Yes, I believe in equality of opportunity"; (2) "No, I would not be willing to have a Negro as my supervisor in my place of work"; [because] (3) "Negroes ought not to be supervisors."[4]

Myrdal maintains that Americans value rationality and seek to present a rational picture of themselves to themselves and to others. According to Myrdal, Americans are able to maintain this logical image in the face of the illogicality of their value conflicts through the process illustrated by the first example. However, many of the subjects in the above-mentioned study were not nearly as logical as Myrdal's theory suggests. The "logic" whereby conflicts were resolved was frequently of the childlike "just because" variety.

Some people who did not experience this particular value conflict because they accepted both the American Creed valuations and the specific democratic valuations regarding race relations manifested a different sort of conflict: They felt constrained to explain and justify their democratic preferences regarding race relations. Their conflict is clearly a consequence of the fact that they operate simultaneously within two contradictory normative systems, one of which (the general-national) expects allegiance to

the democratic tenets of the American Creed and the other of which (the specific-local) expects allegiance to local norms of prejudice and discrimination.

Despite these differences Myrdal's framework and the present writer's research indicate that society not only defines relations between Negroes and whites, but helps to provide ways out of the dilemma caused by the failure of race relations definitions to agree with other definitions of proper attitudes and behavior.

Evidence for the Normative View

In addition to the normative conflict findings, four other forms of evidence lend credence to the normative interpretation of prejudice: social distance studies, cross-cultural comparative studies, public opinion polls, and studies of the development of prejudice in children. These are discussed in order below.

Social distance and cross-cultural studies. Of all the evidence buttressing the normative proposition none is more convincing than the social distance findings of Bogardus (1959) and others using his scaling method. The normative nature of prejudice is dramatically demonstrated by the rankings of various racial and ethnic groups by samples widely separated both geographically and temporally.

Comparing samples of students (ages 18–35, predominantly) drawn from campuses across the country in 1926, 1946, and 1956, Bogardus (1958) found that "the races in the upper or nearest third of the total group of races toward which reactions are expressed are about the same for the three different dates, 1926, 1946, and 1956. They represent in the main the north European races and those lighter in color" (1958, p. 129). He hypothesized that "racial distances decrease very gradually, if at all, when embedded in deep-seated sentiments and traditions" (1958, p. 133). Significant changes over time seem to occur only in cases where major world events have thrown particular

---

[4] These statements are adapted from an article which reports the present writer's attempts to test the Myrdal theory empirically by asking respondents to express agreement or disagreement with a general Christian-democratic valuation and with a matched, specific, self-involving statement in the area of Negro-white relations. The respondent's spontaneous remarks were recorded, and the possible existence of a conflict was suggested to him if he made no mention of it himself.

Many of the questions in the Minard (1931) monograph are illustrations of this sort of conflict in children. A timetable for the learning of prejudice should include data on when the American Creed valuations are learned relative to when prejudicial norms are learned and at what age a conflict is apparent to the researcher and to the child.

nations and their nationals into the world spotlight.

Guilford (1931) reported that the social distance rankings of various groups made by students in seven widely separated colleges were highly similar (correlation coefficients ranged from .84 to .99). Hartley (1946) reported similar results for eight colleges in 1938 and 1939. Comparable findings are available for West Coast school teachers and businessmen, midwestern and eastern white college students, adult Negroes and American-born Jews studied between 1928 and 1946 (Simpson & Yinger, 1958, p. 159). Such evidence stimulated Hartley to conclude that "this pattern of prejudice is practically an American institution" (Simpson & Yinger, 1958, p. 159).

Social distance has also been charted in situations which would find no parallel in the United States, most notably in South Africa. The average American knows little or nothing of the Indian population of South Africa or the difference between rural and urban "Africans" (indigenous natives). Yet these are key distinctions in South Africa. Despite the fact that the groups from which distance is being measured are very different from those studied in America, Pettigrew found that his data "corroborate previous social distance and prejudice research [in America] on a number of points" (1959, p. 251). Among the points he considered are the fact that, in South Africa, Jewish students place less distance between themselves and nonwhites than do English and Afrikaner students. Nonetheless, in keeping with a Bogardus finding quoted above, Pettigrew's data show that each of the three light-skinned groups (English, Afrikaaner, and Jewish) draws a sharp social distance line between itself and the four dark-skinned groups (Indians, Coloured, and Urban and Rural Africans).

There are two fairly obvious interpretations for this similarity of social distance ranking across national and cultural lines: One is that there is something inherent in darkness of skin or the response to it which leads to its negative evaluation, but there is no scientific evidence to corroborate this interpretation; the other, which has substantial evidence to support it, is that both the South African and American national cultures are New World cultures that have in common many Old World antecedents.

Pettigrew's findings lend themselves to a cultural interpretation of social distance. Even within the white South African society there are sufficient cultural variations to produce social distance differences. Afrikaaners tend to place more distance between themselves and any dark-skinned people than do Jews or Englishmen. Moreover, Afrikaaners are more willing to accept rural Africans than urban ones; this finding is reversed for Englishmen and Jews. Pettigrew suggests that the Afrikaaner, coming from a rural culture, sees the urban African as an unknown quantity; whereas the urban English and Jewish students are better able to understand the urban African.

Van Den Berghe's (1961) study of students in Durban was undertaken with the Pettigrew study and an earlier one by MacCrone (1937; 1949) in mind. Van Den Berghe's findings are similar to Pettigrew's with one exception: He found a less negative attitude toward Indians on the part of his European subjects (predominantly British with a small proportion of Afrikaaners and Jews), but this difference can be explained in terms of the categories used to measure social distance. Van Den Berghe's questions were all framed in terms of business and social situations, and, given the economic structure of South Africa, no one there can avoid commercial associations with Indians. Thus willingness to accept Indians is not so much an indication of social acceptance as it is a reflection of objective reality.

Van Den Berghe also provides additional material in support of the normative theory. Pettigrew found that English women tended to place more social distance between themselves and other groups than did men. Possessing data on Indian and African women as well, Van Den Berghe makes the following comment:

In South Africa as in many other countries, the taboos and penalties for crossing the colour lines are stronger for women than for men. It is interesting to note that the sex differences [in social distance from Africans and Coloured] is [sic] greatest among Indians, the group among which women are most sheltered from outside contacts. The Indian taboo against gainful employment of women is strongest, and Indian women, both Hindu and Muslim, are still restricted to a greater extent than Europeans and Africans in their movements outside the home (Van Den Berghe, 1962, p. 62).

Indian culture, even in South Africa and among educated women, thus helps to shape the pattern of race relations.

Social distance studies have been conducted in a number of other countries. These studies demonstrate the relationship between the culture of the respondent and the various racial and ethnic groups they are asked to rate (Bardis, 1956–1957; Bardis, 1961; Bardis, 1962; Catapusan, 1953–1954; Dodd, 1956–1957; Gleason, 1932–1933; Hunt, 1955–1956; Lambert, 1952; Linton, 1945; Van Den Berghe & Colby, 1961; McDonagh, 1938–1939).

Public opinion polls. The findings of several nationwide public opinion polls provide a modest type of evidence of what the norms are and were regarding Negro-white relations in the United States.[5] The polls

most useful for this purpose are those which phrase the issue for the respondent in terms of what "ought to be" or "ought not to be." Hazel Gaudet Erskine (1962) performed an important service to the field of intergroup relations by bringing together the findings of a number of polls taken over the past 20 years. She correctly comments on the relevance of the earlier polls to present-day problems:

Every phase of prejudice and discrimination that is pertinent today was explored in these excellent investigations, in addition to the then pressing issue of integration in the armed forces. Most of these early questions were so timelessly conceived that they could be repeated with complete relevance today (Erskine, 1962, p. 137).

The timelessness of the questions may be evidence of the timelessness of race relations problems in the United States and of the relative stability of many of the norms defining the relations between Negroes and whites. "Relative stability," implies that normative changes have taken place only slowly. In light of this relative stability in most aspects of race relations, the changes in national opinion on school integration are striking.

Answers to questions on public transportation show a degree of normative change from 1942 to 1956. Analysis of a question comparing southern to nonsouthern re-

---

[5] The evidence is "modest" in that it is subject to limitations inherent in the public opinion poll method for gaining frank and valid responses to inquiries about the individual's race relations preferences. Immediate, initial responses to race relations questions are of doubtful utility. Frenquently the respondent gives an initial answer which is the socially approved, status-giving response, regardless of his true feelings on the issue in question. The socially approved response is often followed by the all-important "but," and the comments that follow are frequently more revealing than the simple "yes" or "no" response to the initial question. The public opinion poll-taker usually does not wait for the "post-but" responses. Polls also usually do not obtain depth data for interpreting the responses, and contain no cross-checks on the responses, thus allowing the wording of a question to have a considerable, but unmeasurable, effect. This is not to deprecate the general utility of public opinion polls or the method; the services they have rendered to the public and to social science, particularly in the case of studies of the type quoted here, are testimony to their achievements. Rather, it is desirable to observe that the employment of public opinion poll findings for sociological purposes requires caution. The establishment of normative preferences of people, even through lengthy interviews with provisions for recording open ended responses, is fraught with difficulty, and results must be seen as suggestive rather than conclusive.

sponses on this topic actually contrasts a proposed change in institutionalized norms with personal preferences. Outside the South, the proportion of people who do not think public transportation facilities should be segregated is higher, as is the proportion who have not formed an opinion. Southerners, living in a system in which segrega-

tion is normative, thus are more likely to support such a system.

The results of the two questions on transportation should be viewed together. One hardly knows whether to be impressed by the relative stability of the findings or by the degree of change which has in fact taken place. The percentages of respondents

TABLE 1
FINDINGS OF PUBLIC OPINION POLLS[a]

The U. S. Supreme Court has ruled that racial segregation in the public schools is illegal. This means that all children, no matter what their race, must be allowed to go to the same schools. Do you approve or disapprove of this decision? (AIPO, May 18, 1955; February 27, 1956; May 17, August 14, October 6, December 2, 1957; July 3, 1959; June 23, 1961)[b]

	Approve	Disapprove	No Opinion
		Per Cent	
National total:			
July, 1954	54	41	5
May, 1955	56	38	6
February, 1956	57	38	5
January, 1957	63	31	6
August, 1957	58	36	6
September, 1957[c]	56	38	6
October, 1957[d]	59	35	6
July, 1959	59	35	6
June, 1961	62	33	5
Outside the South:			
July, 1954	64	30	6
May, 1955	68	26	6
February, 1956	71	24	5
January, 1957	74	19	7
July, 1959	72	23	5
South only:			
July, 1954	24	71	5
May, 1955	20	73	7
February, 1956	22	72	6
January, 1957	27	67	6
August, 1957	20	75	5
September, 1957[c]	16	78	6
October, 1957[d]	23	72	5
July, 1959	22	71	7
June, 1961	24	69	7
Southern whites only:			
February, 1956	16	80	4
November, 1957	15	83	2
Southern Negroes only:			
February, 1956	53	36	11
November, 1957	69	13	18

Table 1 (Cont'd.)
FINDINGS OF PUBLIC OPINION POLLS

Generally speaking, do you think there should be separate sections for Negroes in street cars and buses? (NORC, June 20, 1952; April 20, 1956)

	Yes	No	Don't Know
		Per Cent	
White adults only:			
June, 1942	51	44	5
April, 1956	37	60	3

One of Truman's proposals concerns interstate travel. Do you think Negroes should or should not be required to occupy a separate part of a train or bus when traveling from one state to another? (NORC, June 20, 1942; April 20, 1956)

	Should	Should Not	No Opinion
		Per Cent	
National total:			
January, 1948	43	49	8
July, 1948	42	49	9
April, 1949	38	50	12
Outside the South:			
July, 1948	36	54	10
April, 1949	32	55	13
South only:			
July, 1948	84	12	4
April, 1949	79	14	7

[a] Reproduced from Erskine, Hazel G. The polls: Race relations. *Publ. opin. Quart.*, 1962, 26, 138–148. By permission.
[b] Source: The American Institute of Public Opinion (The Gallup Poll), Princeton, New Jersey.
[c] Before troops were sent to Little Rock.
[d] After the Little Rock incident.

in a national sample who thought there *should not* be segregated facilities were:

> 1942—44 per cent
> 1948—49 per cent
> 1949—50 per cent
> 1956—60 per cent

The 16 per cent change in only 14 years is impressive. In light of the length of the history of discrimination, this change should have a sobering effect on those who would use the normative argument in strictly Sumnerian terms. These changes should also be examined in the light of the argument that "you cannot legislate mores."

These and other findings presented in Table 1 demonstrate the democratizing effects of a war in which Nazi authoritarianism was the adversary and also the effects of Supreme Court decisions on segregation.

The responses to the question on school integration provide further evidence of the relative stability of norms defining race relations. Not surprisingly, they also demonstrate that this stability is much greater in the South than in the North. Seventy-one per cent of a southern sample disapproved of school integration in July, 1954. While variations occurred in the interim, 71 per cent of a similar southern sample disapproved in July, 1959. In the North 30 per cent disapproved in July, 1954, 23 per cent in July, 1959.

Studies of children. Taken collectively, studies of prejudice in children constitute a substantial literature, though much more needs to be done. The answers to many questions remain equivocal. To understand how people learn to be prejudiced and to discriminate, it is necessary to pay particular attention to the processes whereby these characteristics become part of particular personalities at the age period when these personalities are being formed.

Studies of development of prejudice in children lend support to the normative theory of prejudice to the extent that they show that: (1) Children start life without prejudice, (2) there is a systematic development in children of attitudinal orientations toward cognitive images of and interactional preferences for particular outgroups, and (3) these orientations, images, and preferences are shared among children of given age levels within the society at large and within particular subgroups within the society. All sociologists would agree with the first part of the statement. Concerning the last two parts, sociological knowledge is somewhat limited.

Several questions may be asked in an attempt to deal with the above statements: (1) At what age is prejudice first manifested? (2) Are there related attitudes and behaviors which are likely to be manifested *earlier* than actual prejudice? (3) Are there related behaviors which develop *after* the development of prejudice? (4) Are the racial and ethnic prejudices of children similar to those of adults—do children apply prejudices to the same outgroups, share the same stereotypes, and discriminate in the same manner as adults? (5) Where are prejudices learned—what contributions to prejudice are made by immediate groups such as the home, the school, the Sunday school and the peer group? (6) How are prejudices transmitted—to what extent are they conveyed deliberately or unconsciously and to what extent are they passed along by verbal instruction or through imitation of overt action?

Attempts to determine the process by which racial and ethnic prejudices are learned date back to Lasker's work in 1929.

With regard to the first question, research by the present author[6] and by Morland (1961) among other studies lend credence to the generalization that preschool children and even children in the early grades are, for the most part, unprejudiced and, in general, incapable of coherent, consistent stereotyping. It must be emphasized that, like all social generalizations, this one has exceptions. Some studies (which claim that well-developed prejudices exist on a preschool level) have made the exceptions the basis of generalizations. The vast majority of the 232 grade school children studied by this writer were as incoherent about their outgroup preferences and images as children are about almost any other social phenomenon. It is one thing to demonstrate that prejudice and stereotyping *can*, in some cases, develop in young children; it is quite another to say that they are characteristic of children.

Another difficulty with studies which conclude that prejudices develop in very early childhood is that the definitions of prejudice vary from study to study. Often the terms preference or attitude are used, and it is rarely made clear whether these terms are to be equated with prejudice or are related to them in some unspecified manner.

Clarke and Clarke (1952) found that Negro children as young as age three could distinguish between a "white doll" and a

---

[6] This discussion is based on a forthcoming monograph by the present author reporting a study of 451 children and young adults ranging from beginning grade school through high school and college. This study examines the development of awareness and of images of and attitudes toward various racial and ethnic groups. The present discussion deals with the findings for all grade school children. Table 2 reports some of the results with reference to the white subjects only; on pages 594–595 is a description of some of the techniques used.

"colored doll," but, not knowing what the word Negro meant, they could not distinguish between a "Negro doll" and a "white doll." The Clarkes imply that this ability to distinguish between the white doll and the colored doll indicates an ability to make racial distinctions. One wonders whether the term colored had any racial significance for the majority of three- or four-year-olds. What would the Clarkes have found if they had included a green doll and asked the children to pick out the "colored" doll?

Through the same technique, the Clarkes found that "the majority of these children prefer the white doll and reject the colored doll." It should be pointed out that this study was done in 1940–1941 before Negro dolls for Negro children came into vogue; because Negro children at this time probably had white dolls, they may well have selected the kind of doll most like their own.

Horowitz (1936) used three picture techniques to determine the preferences of white grammar school children in integrated schools in New York City and in segregated schools in Georgia and Tennessee. Preference for whites over Negroes was found to differ significantly from chance in all grammar school grades in both northern and southern schools.

Horowitz also provides some qualitative material pertinent to discussion of the normative nature of prejudice. He presents excerpts from the interviewer's conversations with some of the children which indicate that, particularly in the social situations test, some children did not make their choices on racial grounds but rather on the basis of the activity depicted. Other quotations show that the children were aware of the pattern of segregation and responded in terms of what was feasible, given their cultural milieu, rather than what they might have personally preferred (e.g., "Where I go swimming I don't think they allow colored people . . .") (Horowitz, 1936, p. 32).

Another type of evidence supporting the normative view was found by J. Kenneth Morland (1961). Working with both Negro and white children of nursery school age (three to six) in Lynchburg, Virginia, Morland used a picture technique similar to Horowitz' social situations test. Both Negro and white children accepted the whites as playmates. Whites were somewhat less likely than Negroes to accept Negroes but, significantly, 80 per cent of the white children did so. Children were also asked whether they *preferred* to play with the Negro or the white children pictured. When given this choice, both Negro and white children tended to prefer whites; however, when asked whether or not they *would* play with a Negro child (with no white choice given), a majority said they would. This suggests that these preferences are not internalized to any great extent and are hardly indicative of deep-seated aversion to Negroes as members of a racially different group or even as members of a socially inferior group. A child may prefer a banana split, but he is not likely to reject a dish of plain ice cream.

Morland also showed that verbalization was not prerequisite to preference:

Racial preference for whites by children of both races begins in the Lynchburg setting even before racial differences can be communicated. . . . Such results can be interpreted to mean that learning to prefer whites comes through indirect means rather than through direct verbal instruction (Morland, 1961, p. 22).

The study by Radke, Sutherland, and Rosenberg (1950) is among the better studies of children's *preferences*. They found that, as early as age seven, both white and Negro children tend to prefer whites. They also found that interracial choices on sociometric and projective tests were situation-bound. The children studied were from a low socioeconomic status area in Pittsburgh, where Negroes were a numerical majority in both the school and the neighborhood. Yet only in the classroom context were interracial choices common. Where both Negro and white teachers stressed the norm of amicable relations between Negroes and whites, interracial choices occurred. In the larger community, where parents perpetuated and enforced the traditional discriminatory norms, interracial choices were less common. Clearly these children were aware of what was expected of them in each situation and responded accordingly, despite the fact that the two sets of responses were diametrically opposed. Clearly, the Negro children tested were also aware of the behavior expected of them. When asked in realistic terms (i.e., with reference to classroom and neighborhood situations), the Negro children did not show more preference for whites.

Lundberg and Dickson (1952) gathered sociometric data in a large racially, ethnically, and socioeconomically heterogeneous Seattle high school. They found that the proportion of ingroup choices varied with the activity in question as well as with certain characteristics of the individuals making the choices. The authors suggest that ethnocentrism is a specific kind of thing, whereby members of the ingroup or various outgroups are preferred or not preferred for particular kinds of activities, not in general. This conception is somewhat akin to Bogardus' concept of social distance. Lundberg and Dickson also found that members of sororities and fraternities which had discriminatory membership norms were more ethnocentric than students who did not belong to such groups. Whether this is a case of selective recruitment, a consequence of belonging to such a group, or a case of mutual reinforcement is not clear. The relationship between the group norms and the individual's choices, however, is apparent.

Several researchers have concerned themselves with children's images and stereotypes of majority and minority groups. Radke, Trager, and Davis (1949) found that both Negro and white children assign unfavorable traits to Negroes. Blake and Den-

nis (1943), in a fairly comprehensive study of stereotypes, found that southern white children in grades four and five have a generally negative image of Negroes. Given a list of 60 traits, they tended to assign all culturally approved traits to whites and all negatively considered traits to Negroes. This resulted in an interesting "error" in stereotyping. Fourth and fifth graders assigned the trait "happy-go-lucky" to whites because they defined this as a positive trait. Tenth and eleventh grade subjects, however, had a full complement of adult stereotypes and showed more consensus in their judgments. This evidence indicates that even in a segregated southern community the conventional images and attitudes are learned slowly. The generalized negative attitude clearly precedes the stereotypes which are commonly invoked to justify the negative attitude.

A variety of studies have shown that Negro children prefer "white characteristics" to "Negro characteristics." Some authors have interpreted this as indicating a developing negative self-concept by Negro children. Seeman's (1946) findings, however, suggest a different interpretation. He found that, although Negro children in grades three to six tended to favor lighter-skinned Negro classmates, they did not, when asked to make three wishes, wish for lighter skin. This suggests that, while these children are aware of the positive evaluation of lightness in the culture, the judgment has not been internalized to such a degree that one could conclude that it is evidence of self-hatred.

Almost all studies of children and race and ethnic relations focus on Negro-white relationships. One significant exception is a study by Marian Radke-Yarrow (1953). Relevant to the present discussion is her finding that Jewish children as young as six are clearly aware of their minority status, but avoid stereotyping either Jews or non-Jews. Moreover, they exhibit no exclusive preference for friends from one group or the other.

Minard's (1931) early study of the attitudes of Iowa children remains one of the most useful in the literature. Though this study is quite old, the findings are of more than historical interest. They illustrate the impingement of multiple, though contradictory, normative systems on the children studied. Of Minard's 1,352 junior and senior high school students of Iowa communities of various sizes, only 9 per cent thought it was not all right for an American coed to be friendly with a Filipino boy who attended the same university. However, 71 per cent thought she ought to have broken off with him before they fell in love, thereby endorsing the normative precept that people should reserve romance for their own kind. When given the fact that the two were in love, 64 per cent thought it was right for them to marry (another normative precept, "one ought to marry for love"), but 62 per cent felt the girl's parents were right to object to the marriage (to enforce the norm that one should marry one's own kind). Here normative precepts proscribing miscegenation conflict with those prescribing romantic love as a prerequisite for marriage.

Returning to the six questions posed at the beginning of this section:

1. At what age is prejudice manifested? The literature indicates that adult patterns of stereotyping begin to develop at least as early as the fourth grade (around nine years) and are more or less completely developed by the time the child enters high school. A tendency to prefer whites over Negroes is manifested much earlier than is stereotyping, but there is no rigidity involved, the child as early as age three prefers the white, but does not reject the Negro. The present writer's own research indicates clearly that children have virtually no prejudice and are, for the most part, incapable of verbalizing outgroup images before the junior high school level.

2. Are there related attitudes or behaviors which are likely to be manifested earlier than actual prejudice? The "preferences" just discussed might be considered a pre-prejudice pattern because they apparently involve no highly developed categorical thinking. Ability to differentiate on some level between the ingroup and the outgroup must precede differential attitudes. Research to date, however, suggests that preferences can be measured before the child is able to verbalize the difference.

3. Are there related behaviors which develop *after* the development of prejudice? The present writer's research clearly indicates that stereotyping develops considerably later than prejudice, and the findings of Blake and Dennis and of Morland corroborate this finding.

4. Are the racial and ethnic prejudices of children the same as those of adults? The answer may vary according to the outgroup. Most researchers have, in general, concentrated on Negro-white relations, thus providing only a minimum of material on minorities in general, and religious minorities in particular. Available social distance data seem to indicate that the reactions of children to various ethnic groups are fairly stable over time and correspond roughly to the reactions of adults.

The three samples whose rankings are presented in Table 2 are very different in age and ethnic and educational composition; yet, allowing for the influence of world events (cf. the rankings of Russians and Japanese), the rankings are remarkably similar. The Cincinnati data are based on a sample from one public school in a "superior" socioeconomic status area; 82 per cent of the subjects were Jewish (Zeligs, Rose & Hendrickson, 1933). These data and those for the young adult sample are based on social distance questions. The Indianapolis data are from a study by the present author currently being prepared for publication. The children were from public schools and playgrounds selected to ensure a wide range of socioeconomic status backgrounds; all children reported on in Table 2 were white and most were gentile. After being asked to comment on a list of names and identify the ethnic background of the names,

TABLE 2
RANKING OF ETHNIC GROUPS BY CHILDREN[a]

200 Children Grade 6, Cincinnati, Ohio 1933[b]	322 Children Grades 1-12, Indianapolis, Indiana 1957-1961[c]	2,053 Young Adults Ages 18-35 Enrolled in College or Graduate Social Science Courses Nationwide, 1956[d]
American	American	American
English	English	English
(German) Jewish	Irish	Irish
Irish	Italian	Italian
Russian	Mexican	Polish
Japanese	Polish	Jewish
Polish	Jewish	Japanese (American)
Mexican	Japanese	Russian
Italian	Russian	Japanese (foreign born)
Negro	Negro	Mexican (American)
		Negro
		Mexican (foreign born)

[a] These lists have been altered to include only those groups represented in all three studies.
[b] Zeligs, Rose & Hendrickson (1933).
[c] Westie study.
[d] Bogardus (1959, p. 33)

the children were given the correct ethnic identifications if they had erred. Next they were asked: "If you could have chosen your own nationality and had to choose from these nine, which would be your first choice, your second choice. . . ?" They were then asked: "Where would you rank your own nationality?" This last question provided the data on "American." The designation "(German) Jewish" was included from the Cincinnati study because the Jewish name presented to the Indianapolis children was frequently identified as Jewish of probable German origin. Ranks for both American and foreign-born Japanese and Mexicans appear for the young adult sample because the Indianapolis children were told to consider a person with the name given who "lived in America."

Another aspect of this question is that of stereotyping. Ordinarily, the adult uses his stereotypes to buttress his prejudices and discriminatory behavior. If it is true that children acquire prejudices before they learn specific stereotypes, then it would appear that children's attitudes are, unlike adults', without cognitive support. This raises the question of whether children are bothered by the "American dilemma" and the normative contradiction it implies.

With reference to patterns of discrimination in children, some evidence indicates that the interaction preferences of children frequently reflect the demands and expectations of parents rather than internalized dispositions. Some research indicates that children would willingly deviate from the parental preferences if they could. Radke and associates (1950) found that children in a school where amicable race relations were encouraged made interracial sociometric choices in the classroom but made discriminatory choices in neighborhood activities. In both cases, these children seemed to be following the patterns approved and enforced by the adults who had authority in the situation in question. Lundberg and Dickson provide another case in point. The younger non-Jewish white students tended to make more outgroup choices than did the older students, suggesting that they had not yet learned the rules of the game.

5. Where are prejudices learned? Most writers believe that prejudices are learned

TABLE 3

SELECTED STUDIES INVOLVING ATTITUDES AND PREJUDICES IN CHILDREN

Author, date[a]	Sample	Aspect of attitude or action studied	Methods and techniques	Findings (with critical qualifications)
Ralph D. Minard (1931)	1,352 students grades 7–12 from Iowa communities of various sizes	General and specific valuations reflected in racial and ethnic preferences	A series of incidents was presented involving persons representative of one or more ethnic groups interacting with the majority group. Subjects judged the actions of the minority and majority group representative and stated their preferences or probable actions in the same situation.	Found that objective judgments became more tolerant and personal responses less tolerant with age. In Myrdal's terms, the American dilemma became more evident. (The questions presented following the statement of the situation were all more or less related to it, but were not precise or exactly comparable. Ideally, they should have represented a scale.)
Eugene L. Horowitz (1936) (representative of his work in this area)	Grammar school children: New York City: white in integrated schools, Georgia: urban and rural whites, Tennessee: urban whites, a few preschool children	Racial preferences in general and in specified social contexts	Picture tests: (1) Ranks—12 faces, 4 white; child indicates order of preference (2) Show me—same pictures, child asked which he would like to participate in various activities with, which were "nice," etc. (3) Social situation— a series of scenes paired so that one shot of each scene included a Negro and one did not; children specified which pictures they would like to be in.	Found an overall preference for whites. Only Ranks test showed this for the youngest (age 5). The author provided transcripts which indicated that some answers are based on nonrace considerations, and others showed that the child knew the pattern of segregation and failed to choose the Negro only because he did not feel the choice was really open to him. (Ability to recognize and/or verbalize racial difference is not necessarily evidence of prejudice or preference.)

Table 3 (Cont'd.)

SELECTED STUDIES INVOLVING ATTITUDES AND PREJUDICES IN CHILDREN

Author, date[a]	Sample	Aspect of attitude or action studied	Methods and techniques	Findings (with critical qualifications)
Kenneth B. & Mamie P. Clarke, (1952 [1940–1941]).	Negro children, 3–7 years, in nursery schools and kindergartens 134—South (segregated) 119—North (integrated)	Racial identifications and preferences	Dolls test (also coloring, questionnaire, & modified Horowitz line drawing results not reported here)	Found ability to identify increased with age but was present even in 3-year olds. Response to "give me the colored doll" was more accurate at a younger age than "give me the Negro doll." Light-skinned children were less accurate; i.e., identification was determined by the "concrete fact of their own skin color." The children tended to prefer the white doll. (Authors claim to corroborate Horowitz; they indicate that identification does not necessarily imply prejudice.)
Robert Blake and Wayne Dennis (1943)	324 white children, grades 4–11, consolidated public school, outskirts of Charlottesville, Va. (suburban and rural)	Development of stereotypes of Negroes	A list of 60 traits some of which are stereotypical of Negroes was presented. For each, the subject indicated whether he thought the trait: more common to the Negro, more common to the white, no difference, don't know	In grades 4 and 5, unfavorable characteristics were generally attributed to Negroes, but some favorable stereotypical characteristics (e.g., "happy-go-lucky") were attributed to whites. In grades 10 and 11 knowledge of stereotypes was clear. Consensus increased with age. (Presumably percentage of "don't knows" decreased with age; this possibility is somewhat obscured by statistical presentation; there were no tests of significance.)

597

Table 3 (Cont'd.)

SELECTED STUDIES INVOLVING ATTITUDES AND PREJUDICES IN CHILDREN

Author, date[a]	Sample	Aspect of attitude or action studied	Methods and techniques	Findings (with critical qualifications)
Melvin Seeman (1946)	81 Negro children grades 3–6	Skin color as a socially differentiating factor; color preferences	Sociometric questions and interview: "3 wishes test" Ohio recognition scale	Lightness of skin tended to be correlated with favorable sociometric choices, but this was not verbalized in terms of a "wish" for lighter skin. (The author suggests that light skin as a social value is part of the child's culture, but a part which he has not yet internalized.)
H. H. Remmers and N. L. Gage (1947)	7,000 high school students mostly from northern states	Attitudes toward Negroes, Japanese, and "minority groups in general"	Questionnaire allowing "yes," "no," and "undecided" responses	The percentage of "no" responses increased with the valuational specificity of the proposition. (Authors claim this illustrates the American dilemma in adolescents. Since specific and general propositions are not matched and since not all propositions are valuational, the claim must be considered very tentative.)
Else Frenkel-Brunswik (1946, 1948, 1954) (begun in 1941)	250 children, grades 6–8	Relationship between ethnocentrism and authoritarianism	Questionnaires and sociometric tests	Highly ethnocentric children were less often chosen as associates and more authoritarian. Pattern of authoritarianism similar but less developed than in adults.

Author, date[a]	Sample	Aspect of attitude or action studied	Methods and techniques	Findings (with critical qualifications)
Marian J. Radke, Helen G. Trager & Hadassah Davis (1949) & Marian J. Radke & Helen G. Trager (1950)	242 children, kindergarten–grade 2, mixed race and religion, Philadelphia	Knowledge of and reactions to Negroes, whites, Protestants, Catholics, and Jews	Projective tests (pictures, dolls, etc.)	Choices of "appropriate" clothing, housing, and activities for Negro and white dolls and reactions to pictures of potential racial or ethnic conflict situations led authors to believe that prejudice develops in early childhood. (Nature of the responses, small percentages, and failure to draw clear lines between ability to distinguish and prejudice makes this finding somewhat less meaningful than the authors claim.)
Marian Radke, Jean Sutherland, Pearl Rosenberg (1950)	475 Negro children, 48 white children, grades 2–6, ages 7–13, low SES, Pittsburgh	Subject's evaluations of personality characteristics of races and sociometric preferences	Projective picture tests and sociometric data	White children generally preferred whites. Interracial choices in classroom situations (the school was predominantly colored) were higher than in other situations (the neighborhood had same racial proportions). Negro children also preferred whites (on the wish level, not in classroom and neighborhood—i.e., more realistic situations). Both Negroes and whites assigned unfavorable traits to Negroes. (Authors see last point as "negative self-conception" on part of Negroes. This is open to question in terms of the normative theory—see text.)

Table 3 (Cont'd.)

SELECTED STUDIES INVOLVING ATTITUDES AND PREJUDICES IN CHILDREN

Author, date[a]	Sample	Aspect of attitude or action studied	Methods and techniques	Findings (with critical qualifications)
Mary Ellen Goodman (1952 [1943–1948])	103 nursery school children ages 4–5 in a northeastern coastal city and their parents	General awareness and response to Negroes and whites	Observation (participant and nonparticipant), interviews, tests, and play materials	Found 32 per cent high awareness, 52 per cent medium awareness, and 16 per cent low awareness and signs of bigotry in 4-year-old whites. (All measures are based on judgments rather than precise instruments and are relative within the group; therefore, we have no way of determining the meaning of these findings.)
George A. Lundberg & Leonore Dickson (1952)	Students in a racially mixed high school in Seattle	Racial and ethnic preferences	Sociometric questions relating to school and social situations	More in-group choices were made for friends and dates than for school-related activities. Minority group students also made choices from their own groups and exhibited different orders of preference for other minority groups. Members of social groups with discriminatory norms made fewer out-group choices. (Sociometric questions about more types of situations would have allowed conclusions about the norms governing the order of preference and degrees of social distance.)

Table 3 (Cont'd.)

SELECTED STUDIES INVOLVING ATTITUDES AND PREJUDICES IN CHILDREN

Author, date[a]	Sample	Aspect of attitude or action studied	Methods and techniques	Findings (with critical qualifications)
Margaret L. Hayes (1952–1953 [1945–1947])	103 boys, 106 girls, grade 10, in 4 schools, varied ethnic compositions and SES levels (public and private schools—one for girls only) in Albany, N.Y.	Attitudes toward Negroes	Mimeographed test from Bureau of Educational Research, Ohio State University; part of the Social Problems Analysis, advanced series	Attitudes toward Negroes are more favorable among: (1) girls, (2) old-stock Americans, (3) Jews, (4) children of normal age for grade, (5) children of higher than average intelligence, (6) children with higher SES. (Points 2–5 are more prevalent in high-SES schools; thus evidence is ambiguous.) Children from the one school with Negro students had lowest scores (unfavorable attitudes). (This school was low SES and low intelligence, too; thus this finding may have little to do with the presence of Negroes in the school.)
Marian Radke-Yarrow (1953)	114 Jewish children, ages 7–17, Greater Boston, low-middle to middle SES	Self-other attitudes and meaning of minority status	Picture test repeated after two weeks and questionnaire given with second picture test	Children of 6 and 8 years were aware of minority status, but awareness was most marked at 10 years and beyond. All tended to avoid stereotyping either Jews or gentiles, showed no preference for one group or the other. Minority status was increasingly frustrating. Most variations with age seem to be part of the general maturational pattern and unrelated to minority status.

Table 3 (Cont'd.)

SELECTED STUDIES INVOLVING ATTITUDES AND PREJUDICES IN CHILDREN

Author, date[a]	Sample	Aspect of attitude or action studied	Methods and techniques	Findings (with critical qualifications)
Donald L. Mosher & Alvin Scodel (1960)	(1) Original sample of 400 children, grades 6, 7; analysis of 161 whose mothers returned usable questionnaires (2) 161 mothers of children grades 6 and 7, middle-class suburb of Columbus, Ohio	Ethnocentrism in children and ethnocentrism and authoritarian child-rearing practices of mothers	Social distance type test given to children, mailed questionnaire based on E scale and child-rearing practices sent to mothers	A fairly strong correlation was found between ethnocentrism in mothers and children, and no correlation appeared between authoritarian child-rearing practices and ethnocentrism in children. There was some correlation between ethnocentrism and authoritarian practices *in mothers*. (The low percentage of return on the mothers' questionnaire may have impaired representativeness of the responses and, hence, the generalizability of the results.)
Kenneth Morland (1961 [1957–1959])	114 Negro children, 146 lower SES white children, 124 upper SES white children; age 3–6 (most 3–5); Lynchburg, Va., nursery schools	Acceptance and preference	A series of photographs of nursery school-age children in racially homogeneous and heterogeneous groups	Both white and Negro children preferred pictures of whites when given a choice but did not reject Negro group when no choice was given. SES level of whites made no difference.

[a] Studies are listed chronologically by publication date; where specified, the date of the research itself is also given in brackets. The publication date is important because it allows the reader to assess the study in terms of the theoretical developments which the writer may have drawn on. The date of the research permits the assessment of possible sociopolitical influences on the times (e.g., the comparison of studies of school integration before and after the Supreme Court ruling on separate but equal facilities.)

in the home. To some extent, this is because very young children have preferences (interpreted as prejudice) which could only have been learned at home; a three-year-old has very little contact with anyone other than his parents. However, if prejudices are learned in the home, they must be reinforced at school and in the playground if they are to persist and develop after the child reaches the age where teachers and peers have as much influence as parents. Mosher and Scodel (1960) demonstrate that ethnocentric children are likely to have ethnocentric mothers. One thing is clear: Prejudices are learned in some way other than experience with the object. Southern white children have clear-cut conceptions of and attitudes toward Negro children, even where contact with them is nearly nonexistent. This corresponds to the well-known principle that we acquire our prejudices through exposure to the attitudes of others rather than through experience with the object of the prejudice.

6. How are prejudices transmitted? The evidence here is limited. We would hypothesize that children do not learn prejudice as they learn arithmetic, primarily by deliberate and formal instruction, but more as they learn table manners, by the example of and occasional direct statements and object lessons from older people. If the teaching of prejudice were basically, rather than occasionally, formal and overt, children would be able to verbalize (or at least repeat by rote) reasons for choices and rationalizations for prejudicial behavior. Research shows that preschool and early grade school children are incapable of such verbalization.

THE PSYCHOLOGICAL APPROACH TO PREJUDICE

Although sociologists and psychologists approach the phenomenon of prejudice differently, they share many conclusions regarding the phenomenon. They agree that the personality characteristics an individual manifests, including his prejudices, are not generated within him independently of outside forces. Both concur that these outside forces are various kinds of exposures and experiences—such as contact with the culture of the society, the place the individual and his family occupy in the social and economic structure, early infantile experiences, the quality of relationships with parents and siblings, the degrees of deprivation, both physical and psychological, and satiation experienced, and other such forces. Great disagreement exists, however, on the question of which of these external forces is most important.

Sociologists see prejudice as a feature of culture which ultimately becomes a part of the individual personality through the processes of socialization. Psychologists, on the other hand, view prejudice as a characteristic of particular personalities. They seek to understand its relationship to other aspects of the personality and to the experiences the individual has in his relationships with others. Both views are correct and essential to overall understanding of the issue: Prejudice exists in cultures as social norms; prejudice is also an attitude, and, as such, is a characteristic of individual personality.

The Scapegoat Theory

The elements common to most psychological approaches are found in what has come to be known as the "Scapegoat Theory," which is restated here to make the subsequent criticisms more meaningful. This theory emphasizes the fact that a large number of our everyday activities are goal-oriented. Persons initiate various acts which they expect to lead to satisfaction of certain needs, desires, and motivations. These acts range all the way from strong sexual desires to simply wanting to get on a subway car before someone else. Of the many goal-oriented activities pursued each day, some do not culminate in the desired results, and thus dissatisfaction occurs. The psycholog-

ical experience of such blocks to goal-oriented behavior is "frustration." According to
the scapegoat theory, the individual's response to frustration frequently takes the
form of aggression.

Frustration might be classified in many
ways but, for purposes of understanding
the scapegoat theory, the following distinction is useful. There are two kinds of frustration: (1) those which are highly particular, nonrepetitive, and not characteristic of
a person's life or style of life (missing a
train and thus missing an important appointment); and (2) those of a continuous,
enduring nature experienced to the point
where they become an integral part of the
fabric of the daily and yearly round of life
(such as sexual incompatibility between husband and wife).

The particular immediate frustrations are
not nearly as important for understanding
prejudice as are the persistent, on-going
frustrations which sometimes come to affect
every aspect of the personality dealing with
them.

Although every adult has many little
frustrations, and, although most people have
at least some frustrations of the longer-
range variety, some people have an ab-
normally large number. Others, who may
not have as many of the serious kind, may
magnify those they do have or create new
ones in their minds. Real or imagined, the
results are the same.

There are, of course, many possible responses to frustration: objective analysis of
the causes of his frustration and behavior
designed to eliminate them; escape from
the situation by autistic retreat into a world
of imagination; and hostility manifested
in aggression. Group prejudice, in the case
of many persons, is a particular instance of
the latter.

There is disagreement about which type
of response to frustration is most common.
Many writers of psychoanalytic persuasion
readily assume that aggression, either expressed or repressed, is either the only response or the most common one. Gordon

Allport remarks, on the other hand, that
"the commonest reaction to frustration is
not aggression at all, but a simple and direct
attempt to surmount the obstacle in our
path" (1954). Both of these positions, however, assume empirical knowledge not yet
available.

When a person is frustrated by a particular event on a particular day, he may become momentarily angry, growl at his children or his wife, even throw something.
In such a case, both the frustration and the
aggression are particular and immediate. The
feeling of frustration and the aggressive
response may not be carried forward beyond the particular hour of the particular
day. Although immediate frustrations do
not typically result in long-lasting aggressions toward particular groups, they can
lead to immediate but somewhat transitory
aggressions toward outgroups.

Miller and Bugelski experimentally created frustration for a group of young men
and noted an increase in negative response
to particular minorities. It should be noted
that the particular, nonrepeated experiences
of the kind created for these subjects probably have little or no effect on the views
they will subsequently take toward the
group which may have been the scapegoat
in the immediate instance. If these transitory frustrations were sufficiently numerous,
and, if the object of aggression was always
available, they might have a long-range
effect. The outcome is different in the case
of those enduring frustrations more or less
built into one's life. Here the feeling of
frustration and the consequent aggression
seem to be cumulative.

Who becomes the target of aggression?
The first person or group one comes upon?
The most immediately available person or
group? Actually either may occur. Typically, a frustrated, aggressive, person does
not focus his aggressions on the most handy
person or object. According to some psychological theory, one condition must be satisfied: The object-person or object group—
that is, the scapegoat—must not be in a

position to strike back. The aggressors select not the strong as their objects of aggression but the weak, the defenseless, the dependent, and, above all, those who are defined by the aggressor's immediate groups or by his society as legitimate objects for aggression.

Minority groups provide a society and its majority group members with ideal objects for aggression. By sociological definition, a minority is a group that is less powerful than the majority. It is typically defenseless. The institutional protections of person and property are applied less rigorously in the defense of minority members. The way of life and the value system of the majority tend to be, or to become, the normative standards for the society as a whole, for minority persons as well as for the majority. To the extent that the majority's ways are the ways that "ought to be," the minority's ways (whether different in fact or in imagination) are "ought not to be" ways. Aggression against these "deviants" may thus be regarded by the aggressor as a moral imperative.

As previously observed, one of the most important features of the normative order of a society is its supply of definitions of how one ought to behave in relation to various categories of people inside and outside of the society. Thus, some aspects of the normative order of a society may tend to legitimatize aggression against particular minorities. Such aggression is not only sometimes not punished, it may be admired by fellow majority members. It is no surprise, then, that minority persons are objects of aggression. Against minorities one can, with impunity, pleasure, and even honor, perpetrate the kinds of aggressive acts that the society ordinarily permits only to little children. Obviously these actions occur not through a conscious, rational plan on the part of anyone in the society, past or present. Rather, they survive as features of the culture, sometimes precisely because they are useful. On the other hand, the sheer force of cultural inertia often results in the survival of useless, or even dysfunctional, forms.

Although aggression is not the private prerogative of majority groups, a perusal of the scientific literature does give this impression. Free-floating aggression is frequently generated in the minority group member as a result of life-long frustrations he experiences at the hands of the majority. Minority persons have a variety of prejudices, just as wide and virulent as do majority persons. This may be expected since minority groups have more reason to be prejudiced than the majority.

The prejudices of minority members have been virtually ignored in behavioral science research, though thousands of studies have investigated the prejudices of majority persons. This may result from the fact that sociologists and psychologists share a sympathy for the underdog prevalent in the society. Moreover, it is widely observed that intergroup prejudices and conflict are typically initiated by majority persons, and the prejudices of minorities are seen primarily as a similar and opposite reaction to majority action. However well intended this view may be, it has produced a literature which gives the impression that the minority person can "do no wrong."

In general, the minority person has three choices of objects upon which to vent his aggressions: (1) the majority group itself which is largely the source of his frustrations, (2) other minority groups in the society, and (3) his own minority or particular persons or subgroups within it.

Aggressions against the majority. The majority is the least available, psychologically, and the least significant object of minority aggression. Consequences for the aggressor are likely to be sure and swift. Direct, violent attacks on majority persons do occur, but these are relatively infrequent. Direct aggression may also be involved in organized political action designed to achieve political and social justice. The fact that such action may be the product of careful, rational planning in no way denies the fact that it may also satisfy the minority person's aggressive urges.

Indirect aggression against the majority may take many forms. Negroes and Jews, the two most conspicuous minorities in the United States, frequently use humor and satire in this way. Among Negroes, counter-aggression may also take the subtle form of "playing the part" assigned by the prevalent stereotypes. Some Negroes respond with exaggerated obsequiousness to whites, subtly communicating through satire just what they think of the role assigned to them. Perhaps the most common form of indirect aggression by minorities is antilocution, "talking against" the majority within the safe confines of the minority group. Research on direct counteraggression is meager, but a thorough cataloging of the many subtle, indirect ways in which counteraggression may be expressed would fill a book.

Aggression against other minorities. Direct aggression against other minorities is probably more common than direct aggression against the majority. It is convenient in two ways. First, other minorities are also weak, sometimes weaker than one's own group. Minority persons typically share many of the facets of the larger culture, and thus they too recognize the normative legitimacy of attack on other minorities despite the fact that this kind of thinking makes their own group a legitimate target for the majority and for other minorities. Second, through aggressive words and acts focused on another minority, the minority person borrows some measure of majority status. When an anti-Negro Jew and an anti-Negro gentile get together, they may experience a moment of brotherhood. (Studies of the relative degree of anti-Negro prejudice among Protestants, Catholics, and Jews, however, have found that Jews tend to be the least prejudiced.) A second generation immigrant who moves to the South from the North sometimes adopts the attitudes of the southern majority. Within a relatively short time he may exhibit more openly expressed anti-Negro attitudes than his hosts, thereby striving for acceptance in the majority group.

Some evidence suggests that there is an appreciable degree of anti-Semitism among northern urban Negroes. A study conducted in Detroit indicated that much of this feeling is focused on Jewish businessmen who cater to Negroes in segregated, all-Negro neighborhoods (Sheppard, 1947). This could be, of course, an instance of anti-white prejudice, the Jewish businessman in the Negro neighborhood simply being the most readily available white target.

Aggression toward one's own minority. It is a tenable hypothesis that aggression by minority members is directed most of all not on the majority or even on other minorities, but on their own group. While "inverted prejudice" may be directed toward the group as a whole, it is more often focused on other individuals or subgroups within the group.

Jewish self-hatred is both a group phenomenon and an individual phenomenon. In Europe, outstanding examples of a hostile sentiment in one Jewish group against another were those of the German or Austrian Jew against the East European Jew, and, more recently, the attitude of the French Jew toward the German Jew. That all the troubles the Jews had in Germany were due to the bad conduct of the East European Jew was an opinion not infrequently heard among German Jews. In this country [the United States], the resentment of the Spanish Jew against the immigrating German Jew, and the hostility of the latter to the East European Jew form a parallel to the European situation (Lewin, 1948, p. 186).

There thus exist, in a sense, "minorities within minorities." These consist of people who may be weaker than the average member of the larger minority. Frequently they are "visible," in the sense that they are distinguishable from others in the larger minority by virtue of particular cultural characteristics.

Sociologists and psychologists have been aware of the existence of inverted prejudice for a long time; nonetheless, few studies have investigated it since techniques are lacking with which to deal with inverted prejudice. Rare is the minority person who will openly admit prejudice against his own group. Not only is the person with inverted prejudice unlikely to express these feelings to researchers, he is unlikely to admit them to himself.

It is thus not a simple matter to decide when a particular attitude is an instance of inverted prejudice. Majority persons, particularly majority persons who are also sociologists or psychologists, frequently use the term inverted prejudice in an uncritical manner which suggests bias on their part. The person who accuses a minority person of inverted prejudice frequently makes certain tacit assumptions. If a Negro scholar criticizes in print a particular subgroup of Negro professionals and businessmen for spending too much time and money on frivolous activities and conspicuous consumption—activities designed to enhance their status—he is immediately charged with "inverted prejudice." He is criticized not only by Negroes, but by some sociologists and psychologists whose ideology permits no mention of the negative characteristics of any minority.

There is actually no large racial, national, or religious group in which all people are uncritically devoted to all others in the group. If a white American criticizes a particular category of white Americans, no one is likely to accuse him of being "anti-white." Vance Packard is not accused of inverted prejudice for criticizing American "status seekers," but E. Franklin Frazier (1957) has been accused of inverted prejudice for criticizing Negro status seekers. Inverted prejudice, it seems, is a phenomenon that is reserved by usage for minority members.

Another common assumption is that minorities are homogeneous. The homogeneity fallacy frequently operates in accusations of anti-Semitism among Jews, who are not as homogeneous as gentiles frequently imagine. The majority person who makes the accusation of "inverted prejudice" frequently fails to recognize the wide ranges of nationality, religious, and socioeconomic characteristics in the American Jewish population.

Inverted prejudice and self-hatred. Some instances of inverted prejudice are viewed as examples of a more general and more widespread phenomenon, self-hatred. The terms "inverted prejudice" and "self-hatred" are frequently used as synonyms; the quotation from Lewin (p. 606 above) is a case in point. A distinction, however, is useful: The term "inverted prejudice" might be used to refer to an attitude toward a group to which a person himself belongs; "self-hatred" might then be reserved for one's attitude toward oneself as an individual.

A common interpretation of self-hatred is derived from the psychology of Freud. It is simply a manifestation of the "drive to self-destruction." One need not, however, resort to instinct theory to understand self-hatred. Basic theory of social psychology provides interpretations of this phenomenon without seeking the "that's-just-the-way-people-are" refuge.

One may hypothesize that minority persons are more likely than majority persons to develop self-hatred for the simple reason that they receive more negative responses from others. No matter how winning his ways, how charming his personality, the minority person will not see an accurate reflection of himself as an individual in the responses of many others to him. Distortion is introduced by his minority group membership, and this can reduce the possibility of a healthy concept of self for the minority member. One result is that the minority person may have greater difficulty than others in determining his own identity. He cannot always separate the image of himself as an individual from the combined image of the group he is seen as representing. This is a persistent problem for minority persons. Everyone, of course, experiences this to some extent, since roles are a part of the personality, and people frequently respond to others in terms of particular roles. No person can ever succeed completely in making the separation for the simple reason that his roles are "him." "Did that man act that way because what I said was stupid or because I'm a woman?" The problem is, however, greatly compounded for the minority person. Many are incapable of accepting any response from a majority person as a response to them as individuals. These are people who minority members themselves criticize as "seeing the world through race-colored glasses."

Because all thinking is categorical, every person's reponse to every other person is categorical. But minority persons are typically victims of overcategorization. Some persons are more able than others to recognize overcategorical responses, and those who are least capable are probably the most likely candidates for self-hatred. They accept the total negative image as a valid image of themselves, and they come to dislike that image.

The concept of self of the most psychologically sophisticated minority member, no matter how good he is at recognizing prejudice when he sees it, is in no way completely ensured against damage. One is one's groups, and vice versa. One's roles in significant groups, such as the family, the clique, the church, the ethnic group, the nation, become internalized to form personality. If, then, others respond to the minority person as a member of a minority group rather than as an individual, even if the person realizes that this is going on, his concept of self is affected. Either through ascription by other or by personal identification, he is a part of the group, and whether it is he or the group that is insulted, his concept of self suffers. The person who can make no distinction between rebuffs to himself and rebuffs to his group is doubtless more vulnerable than the person who can.

Unlike most other theories of prejudice, which remain peculiarly the property of scholars hidden away in academic places, the scapegoat theory enjoys popularity in educated circles in the community at large. Perhaps this popularity is a result of the emphasis it has been given in popular interpretations of scientific literature. Then too, the theory is simple and refers to experiences many people feel can be validated by introspection.

Findings of research bearing on the scapegoat theory are contradictory. While the research of Miller and Bugelski (1948), Sherif and Sherif (1953), and Bettleheim and Janowitz (1950) tends to show the relationship between frustration, aggression, and prejudice indicated by the scapegoat theory, Lindzey (1950) found prejudiced men had higher scores than unprejudiced men using two measures of outwardly directed aggression. The prejudiced men reported more frustration than did the unprejudiced subjects, but they showed a smaller increase in aggression following frustration than did the unprejudiced men. Adorno and associates (1950) also found the relationship among the three factors far more ambiguous than the proponents of the scapegoat theory are ready to admit.

Although the scapegoat theory is understood and advocated in educated circles to a greater extent than any other theory of prejudice, the research testing it is hardly sufficient to constitute proof. The studies are either little experiments on a handful of subjects (e.g., Lindzey, 1950; Miller & Bugelski, 1948), or general theoretical statements of a qualitative nature (e.g., Dollard, Miller, Doob, Mowrer, & Sears, 1939). There is need for research and theory of the middle range. The well-known study of Bettelheim and Janowitz (1950) comes closest to this desideratum.

Qualifications of the scapegoat theory. Although the frustration-aggression phenomenon is a crucial factor in the genesis and perpetuation of prejudice in the society and the individual, it is far from a complete general explanation. The following qualifications of the scapegoat theory are abstracted from a more lengthy list compiled by Gordon Allport:

Frustration does not always lead to aggression. . . .

Aggression is not always displaced. Anger may be directed toward oneself, intropunitively. If so, scapegoating does not occur. . . .

Displacement does not, as the theory seems to imply, actually relieve the feeling of frustration. Since the displaced object is not, in fact, related to the frustration, the feeling continues . . . (Allport, 1954, pp. 350–351).

The scapegoat theory also erroneously treats the phenomenon of prejudice as though it is a consequence of the psychological characteristics of only the prejudiced person. The characteristics of the object-group are virtually ignored. Thus Zawadski maintains that the scapegoat theory does not answer, among others, the following questions:

Why, sometimes, a certain minority is selected to pick on where there are several to choose from.

Why there is sometimes a striking difference in intensity of dislike toward different minorities.

Why certain minorities are respected, if not liked, while others are disliked and despised (Zawadski, 1948, p. 132).

To this list must be added another important qualification made by Allport:

Finally, the theory itself overlooks the possibility of realistic social conflict. What seems like displacement may, in some instances, be an aggression directed toward the true source of the frustration (Allport, 1954, p. 351).

The scapegoat theory also virtually ignores the role of culture in the genesis, perpetuation, and expression of prejudice.

Whether or not aggression is overtly expressed depends on the degree to which the culture or subculture permits aggression. In some cultures, aggressive behavior is regarded as the mark of a "real man" and is not only permitted, but encouraged and rewarded. The Kwakiutl culture, as described by Benedict (1934), is a case in point. In other cultures, aggression is re-

garded as a force which seriously disrupts group harmony. The culture of the Zuni Indians is the most familiar example of this.

Of course it is not necessary to reach into far corners of the earth to find examples of situations in which aggression is not only tolerated but idealized. In many subgroups of the American population the "real man" is expected to aggress. Though the aggression may involve some personal risk and sacrifice, for some it is a high form of recreation. Certain immigrant groups, particularly of an earlier day, idealized physical interpersonal combat and to some extent lived up to the ideal. W. I. Thomas described Polish "warfare"; and the stereotype of the earlier male Irish immigrant as a ready, two-fisted type is not entirely unrelated to reality. Certain categories of sailors, marines, soldiers, lumberjacks, longshoremen, and oil field workers have participated in "he-man" subcultures which clearly endorse violent interpersonal aggression. The man who says "I don't believe in fighting" wins no popularity contests among them. Nor is it necessary to single out particular occupations to find cultural norms which encourage various forms of aggression. It is not rare in American society for a parent to look with disdain upon his son who comes home with a bloody nose.

Significant for race relations is the southern male who suffers from (or perhaps enjoys) the "one-hell-of-a-fellow" complex described by Cash in The Mind of the South (1954). This type, more rare today than in former times, idealizes violence and interpersonal aggression and is perpetually engaged in defending his easily offended honor or that of his "womenfolk." Another type (and to some extent a stereotype) of southerner, the "red neck" (the southern term for the poor, uneducated, rural man of violent disposition) was well represented in the reception committees which met the "freedom rider" buses.

On the other hand, some groups define overt aggression and fighting as sinful, or at least ungentlemanly or uncivilized. The majority religion in America, Christianity, defines aggression, physical or verbal, as un-Christian; however, some Christians believe in the teachings of the Sermon on the Mount, and others do not. Perhaps even more believe in these teachings and simultaneously believe in quite opposite precepts.

In brief, there are varieties of cultural settings in which aggression is expressed and even encouraged and others in which aggression is defined as improper or immoral. Whether or not one expresses his aggressions is not simply a consequence of the degree of psychological frustration. The definitions of appropriate behavior provided by the groups in which one acts are equally important in determining the outcome of frustration.

The failure to recognize prejudice as normative is the most serious defect in the scapegoat theory. Purely psychoanalytic theories of prejudice frequently give the impression that prejudiced people are psychologically sick, and behave differently from normal, mature citizens. In most cases, however, the prejudiced person is not sick, nor does he necessarily deviate from the response patterns of others in his community. Rather, it is the nonprejudiced or relatively unprejudiced person who departs from social norms defining the proper attitudes toward Negroes, Jews, Japanese, and others.

The majority of studies of prejudice have concentrated almost exclusively on prejudiced persons. Implicit in many of them is an attempt to understand the prejudiced person's "deviance." If one is interested in deviance, it would be just as logical to study tolerant persons and tolerant groups, to understand their tolerance, which is also an instance of deviance—deviance from the prejudicial norms of the society.

What, then, is the function of the scapegoat phenomenon and other psychological processes in the development and perpetuation of prejudice in the society and the individual? Persons whose prejudices are largely psychogenic are to be distinguished from persons whose prejudice is largely the product of socialization. One might say that their prejudice is provided with a "psychological boost." They find that society has provided them with ideal adjustment possibilities in the form of social norms which legitimate their essentially antisocial behavior. In summary, while group prejudice in general is a sociocultural phenomenon which occurs among normal and abnormal alike, the person who finds it psychologically useful is much more ready to conform to prejudicial norms.

Sociologists thus ask certain basic questions concerning the relationship between the normative and the psychogenic aspects of prejudice: To what extent is the group prejudice expressed by any person simply the result of his having been socialized to the prejudicial social norms of his society? What social norms exist in his region, his community, and his family defining the relation between his own ingroups and the outgroups which are the object of his prejudice? How important are these norms to other members of his community, to his peers, to his parents? Did others consciously attempt to make sure that he developed the "right" attitudes?

When answers to questions of this kind have been ascertained, it is then appropriate to move to the level of psychological analysis to ascertain the extent to which prejudices are functional for the individual in maintaining personality integration or a favorable concept of self. No such study has been done in either sociology or psychology, despite the fact that it would tell us more about the nature of prejudice than anything which has been done to the present. Thus far sociologists have, for the most part, been content to study the distribution and degree of prejudice in various communities and groups within communities. Psychologists, on the other hand, have limited their inquiries to the psychological functions prejudice performs for individual personalities, its place in particular personality types, and the ways in which prejudice is correlated with other personality attributes of the individual.

The Psychological Syndrome Approach

A strange amalgam of Freudian psychology, Gestalt psychology, and modern survey research has produced one of the more significant developments in the study of prejudice and intergroup relations—the syndrome or configurational approach. So conspicuous is the work of the "Berkeley group" which produced *The Authoritarian Personality* (Adorno et al., 1950) that their title phrase has come to assume the status of a designation of an area of specialization within social psychology.

The major premise upon which the theory and research on the authoritarian personality is based has been stated by Adorno and associates as follows:

the political, economic, and social convictions of an individual often form a broad and coherent pattern, as if bound together by a "mentality" or "spirit," and that this pattern is an expression of deep lying trends in his personality (1950, p. 1).

Their view is, essentially, that the person who has certain attitudes and cognitive orientations toward one aspect of the social system, say the economic, very likely holds certain functionally related and compatible orientations toward other aspects of the social system, for example, religion. Thus, these attitudes and beliefs about various aspects of his world form a coherent configuration.

The Berkeley group found that the man who hates foreigners is likely also to hate Negroes and Jews within his own country, is likely to be compulsively patriotic and highly nationalistic, and is likely also to be extremely conservative in his economic, political, and religious beliefs.

It would be impossible to enumerate the vast number of personality characteristics which have been found or hypothesized to be associated with the authoritarian syndrome. Perhaps the following thumbnail sketch in terms of the central characteristics of the syndrome will be sufficient to make criticisms and evaluations meaningful. The authoritarian loves power, he wants power, and he respects power. He idealizes power and authority in others and likes to think of himself in such terms. He has nothing but disdain for the weak, the soft, the deliberative person, and prefers situations in which decisions are made for him in which clear-cut answers to problems are readily available. He is intolerant of ambiguity; that is, he wants his world to be clearly separated into the black and the white, the good and the bad, the worthy and the unworthy; and where no such clear dichotomies are apparent, he makes them in his own mind. He wants to boss and be bossed and is impatient with the slow, deliberate, and often ambiguous democratic processes.

Hundreds of research projects on authoritarianism have followed the publication of the original work, and the body of material continues to grow. *Psychological Abstracts* for 1960 lists 56 entries under the heading "Authoritarianism." The most complete guides to this material are provided by Christie and Cook (1956), who cover the years from 1950, the date of publication of the original volume, to 1956, and by Titus and Hollander (1957), who cover the years 1950 to 1955. Christie and Cook list 230 articles, books, and monographs, not including unpublished theses and dissertations. The materials may be roughly divided into: (1) criticisms or elaborations of the original work or the theory propounded in it, (2) replications of tests in, or tests of hypotheses suggested by, the original work, including suggestions of alternative hypotheses based on empirical evidence, (3) employment of the F scale or a modified form of it as a research tool. The third class of materials presupposes acceptance of the F scale as a measure of authoritarianism.

Some of the syndrome research has attempted further to define various aspects of the authoritarian personality configuration and to develop instruments which correct the shortcomings of the original work. The work of Rokeach and his associates exemplifies this (1956). The theoretical framework of *The Authoritarian Personality* has also been applied to people's reactions to other groups and categories of people beyond racial or ethnic categories (Nadler & Morrow, 1959). The framework has also been used in studies of the responses of non-majority persons (Simpson, 1959) and of authoritarianism among people raised in societies other than the American (Diab, 1959). Srole and others have sought to determine the relationship between authoritarianism and other individual traits, especially anomie (Srole, 1956); and Lipset's theoretical discussion of working-class authoritarianism is outstanding among the materials which seek to relate authoritarianism to structural features of society (Lipset, 1960).

The Authoritarian Personality has been subject to widespread criticism by behavioral scientists. Most of these criticisms focus on research methods. The claim is made with some justification that the samples were not representative of any known group in the American population, that the scales for measuring degrees of prejudice and ethnocentrism were inadequate and many items ambiguous, that the scales for measuring the various characteristics of the authoritarian personality were not independent of one another, and that the correlations between these (and hence the syndromes themselves) artifacts of method rather than descriptive of relationships which actually prevail.

Edward Shils (1954) makes explicit the more serious consequences of the Berkeley group's tacit endorsement of the belief that all political, social, and economic philosophies can be classified on the "Right-Left" continuum.

What has been looked upon as a seamless unity was turning out to be a constellation of diverse elements which could be recombined into constellations which had not for many years been imagined. Hostility towards private property was now seen to be capable of combination with anti-Semitism, inequality, the repression of civil liberties, etc. Welfare legislation was seen to enter into combination with political oligarchy; the elimination of civil liberties was combined with an increase in equalitarianism. In short, what had once appeared to be a simple unidimensional scheme now turned out to be a complicated multidimensional pattern in which there were many different political positions. The attachment to private property was now perceived as compatible both with sympathy with humanitarianism and with a disapproval of welfare legislation, the respect for civil liberties could fit with either socialism or capitalism, equalitarianism could go with either democracy or oligarchy. But above all, the two poles of the continuum Right and Left which were once deemed incompatible and mutually antagonistic were discovered to overlap in many very striking respects (Shils, 1954, p. 27).

Among these consequences the following are perhaps most significant: For the most part only the "fascistic," "authoritarianism of the right" is studied directly; the "complete democrat" is defined residually as the direct opposite of the Fascists. The Berkeley Group not only failed to study the Communistic authoritarianism of the Left; they failed even to recognize its existence.

The authors of *The Authoritarian Personality* seemed to know little about the profile of "democratic" or "tolerant" person. For example, when it is found that the authoritarian is highly concerned with his own status, it is easy to reason that the democratic type of person is not particularly concerned with his status. Actually, the only way to determine the degree to which the democratic or tolerant type is concerned with his own status is to study him directly.

The criticisms presented above are but a few of those presented in the literature. Some important ones are omitted here because of the impossibility of covering them all in detail. For example, one can ask,

"What are the implications of Allen Edward's studies of the 'Social Desirability Factor' for the studies of the authoritarian personality?" Edwards (1957) and others (Hanley, 1956; Kenny, 1956; Rosen, 1956) have found that the endorsement of items in personality inventories can, to a considerable extent, be accounted for by the degree to which particular personality traits are regarded as socially desirable in a given population. In one instance, Edwards found a product moment correlation of .87 between probability of endorsement and social desirability scale value for a set of 140 personality statements. To the extent that the social desirability variable affected the endorsement of the various personality items used in the authoritarian personality studies, the findings of the latter must be questioned.

The research on personality syndrome is nevertheless one of the more significant developments in intergroup relations since World War II despite the fact that there are serious shortcomings in both the conception and the execution of the research.

INTERGROUP RELATIONS IN MASS SOCIETY

The development of mass society renders certain traditional theories of intergroup relations less appropriate than they used to be. Indeed, it appears that some sociologists would all but relegate the normative and psychological approaches to intergroup relations to the waste basket. The features of mass society most relevant to intergroup relations can be seen in the following quotations. Shils emphasizes that:

An important feature of that society [mass society] is the diminished sacredness of authority, the reduction in the awe it evokes and in the charisma attributed to it. This diminution in the status of authority runs parallel to a loosening of the power of tradition. Naturally, tradition continues to exert influence, but it becomes more open to divergent interpretations, and these frequently lead to divergent courses of action (Shils, 1961, p. 2).

C. Wright Mills lists what he regards as central features of a highly developed mass society:

At the opposite extreme [on the continuum from public to mass], in a *mass*, (1) far fewer people express opinions than receive them; for the community of publics becomes an abstract collection of individuals who receive impressions from the mass media. (2) The communications that prevail are so organized that it is difficult to answer back immediately or with any effect. (3) The realization of opinion in action is controlled by authorities who organize and control the channels of such action. (4) The mass has no autonomy from institutions; on the contrary, agents of authorized institutions penetrate this mass, reducing any autonomy it may have in the formation of opinion by discussion (Shils, 1959, p. 304).

Mills does not present this picture as a description of modern American society but as an ideal-typical construction of a society on the extreme end of the public-to-mass continuum.

Karl Mannheim emphasizes a feature of mass society which is particularly relevant for race relations theory:

. . . [individuals] are compelled to renounce their private interests and to subordinate themselves to the interests of the larger social units. . . . The attitude produced by competitive action between antagonistic groups is transformed into a new attitude of group solidarity though the groups from which it derives are not all inclusive. . . . The individual today . . . is gradually realizing that by resigning partial advantage he helps to save his own interests. . . . Today the individual thinks not in terms of the welfare of the community but in terms of that of his own particular group (Mannheim, 1940, pp. 69–70).

It is frequently difficult to determine whether such statements are intended to be ideal-typical constructions or empirical descriptions. None of the above-cited writers show evidence of the kind that would permit the elevation of their generalizations to the level of tested empirical relationships. Indeed, one wonders if it is possible to investigate scientifically anything so broad, heterogeneous, nebulous, and changing as "the American society" or "the American character." The basic query must be qualified: *If* the social reality continues to more closely approximate the ideal-typical construction of mass society outlined by writers such as Mannheim, Reisman and Mills, then what is the significance of this state of affairs for the understanding of prejudice and intergroup relations? Do people operate in terms of normative convictions instilled early in life through the socialization process? Or do they wander from one group to another opportunistically selecting the "convictions" and definitions for behavior provided by those immediately around them whose approval they so earnestly seek.

As stated earlier, the mass society argument virtually eliminates attitudes (including prejudice) and traditional mores as important variables affecting interaction between groups or individuals. Two papers, one by Lohman and Reitzes (1954) and the other by Herbert Blumer (1958) emphasize this mass society approach. Blumer maintains:

1. A knowledge of the racial feelings held by people is no safe guarantee of how they will act in racial situations, e.g., hostile racial feelings do not necessarily lead to hostile actions, and amicable feelings do not ensure amicable actions.
2. The social demands of a situation, particularly when supported by accepted authority figures, are effective determinants of individual action in racial relations.
3. Unambiguous declarations of institutional intention and firm efforts to implement the intentions are decisive means of shaping a given racial situation (Blumer, 1958, p. 432).

These observations and similar points made by Lohman and Reitzes are among the most important theoretical ideas to emerge in race relations theory since World War II. Sometimes, however, the case for the mass society view is overstated.

Lohman and Reitzes provide a detailed application of mass society theory to race relations:

Current research about racial relations is based on two dubious assumptions: that particularistic theories are necessary and appropriate and that human behavior in situations of racial contact is determined by individual attitudes. But in modern mass society individual behavior is increasingly controlled by deliberately organized collectivities. As concerns home ownership, wages and working conditions, and commercial transactions, the individual's racial attitudes are subordinated to and mobilized by definitions of the situation supplied by organizations (Lohman & Reitzes, 1952, p. 240).

Lohman and Reitzes further observe:

The reality is the social fact: the key to the situation and the individual's action is the collectivity, and in our time the collectivity is increasingly of the nature of a deliberately organized interest group. The collectivity even supplies the individual with a well-formulated rationale which makes meaningful and even personally justifies his activity; for example, in the acceptance and rejection of minority groups. Thus it is more frequently the policy, strategy, and tactics of deliberately organized interest groups, rather than the folkways, rather than the individual dimensions of personal prejudice or racial enmity, which control behavior in specific situations (Lohman & Reitzes, 1952, p. 242).

They go on to say that because of the power of these collectivities,

Individual behavior is, for all practical purposes, made a fiction. Hence a distinctly personal attitude toward minority groups may be of little consequence in explaining an individual's behavior (Lohman & Reitzes, 1952, p. 242).

The findings of Reitzes' (1953) research, based upon this conceptual framework, demonstrate the kind of personal inconsistency with which the mass society views postulates. He found that many people who accepted Negroes in the job situation qua members of a union that defines race relations in egalitarian terms also participated in a neighborhood Civic Club, the primary purpose of which was, as the members put it, to "keep up the bar against the colored element moving in here."

The same phenomenon has been observed by the present writer on northern campuses where white students from the South have lived in dormitory rooms adjacent to rooms occupied by Negro students from the South. From the standpoint of predicting overt behavior in this situation it is no doubt more important to know how the large, powerful, prestigeful university defines the situation than it is to know whether or not the individuals involved are prejudiced toward one another.

There can be no doubt that sociological understanding of twentieth-century race relations must be understood in terms of what we know about twentieth-century society. But sociologists must be wary of emphasizing these newest of their findings to the point where they relegate their basic knowledge of the cultural and psychological processes, which apply to people everywhere whether in mass society or not, to a place beside instinct theory in the museum of sociological artifacts.

Qualifications of the Mass Society Approach

The present chapter is not intended to be, nor is it, encyclopedic. To have attempted such would be an attempt to duplicate the works already extant. There are a number of excellent books and articles summarizing the research, writing, and theoretical propositions in the intergroup relations area. Among these are the following: Robin M. Williams, Jr., *The Reduction of Intergroup Tensions* (1947); Edward A. Suchman, John P. Dean and Robin M. Williams, Jr., *Desegregation: Some Propositions and Research Suggestions* (1958) and Melvin M. Tumin, *An Inventory and Appraisal of Re-*

search on American Anti-Semitism (1961). Among the better articles summarizing the field are: Robin M. Williams, Jr.,[7] "Racial and Cultural Relations" (1957); George E. Simpson and J. Milton Yinger, "The Sociology of Race and Ethnic Relations" (1954); Herbert Blumer, "[Recent research on racial relations in the] United States of America" (1958); Anthony H. Richmond, "[Recent research on racial relations in] England" (1958); Kripal S. Sodhi "[Recent research on racial relations in the] Federal Republic of Germany" (1958); and Barbara E. Ward, "[Recent research on racial relations in] East Africa" (1958).

REFERENCES

Ackerman, N. W., & Jahoda, Marie. *Anti-Semitism and emotional disorder.* New York: Harper, 1950.

Adorno, T. W., Frenkel-Brunswik, Else, Levinson, D. J., & Sanford, R. N. *The authoritarian personality.* New York: Harper, 1950.

Allport, G. W. *The nature of prejudice.* Cambridge, Mass.: Addison-Wesley, 1954.

Allport, G. W., & Kramer, B. M. Some roots of prejudice. *J. Psychol.,* 1946, **22**, 9–39.

Bardis, P. D. Social distance among foreign students. *Sociol. soc. Res.,* 1956–1957, **41**, 112–115.

Bardis, P. D. Social distance in southern Greece. *Sociol. soc. Res.,* 1961, **45**, 430–434.

Bardis, P. D. Social distance in a Greek metropolitan city. *Soc. Sci.,* 1962, **37**, 108–111.

Benedict, Ruth. *Patterns of culture.* New York: Houghton, 1934.

Bettelheim, B., & Janowitz, M. *Dynamics of prejudice: A psychological and sociological study of veterans.* New York: Harper, 1950.

---

[7] *Strangers Next Door,* by Robin M. Williams, Jr. (1964) is one of the most significant contributions to the scientific study of race and ethnic relations. Williams presents the results of the Cornell Studies in Intergroup Relations which were conducted over the past decade. While this work is a landmark in the area, its conclusions are not presented here because it appeared after the present chapter went to press.

Blake, R., & Dennis, W. Development of stereotypes concerning the Negro. *J. abnorm. soc. Psychol.,* 1943, 38, 525–535.

Blumer, H. [Recent research on racial relations in the] United States of America. *Int. soc. Sci. Bull.* (UNESCO), 1958, 10, 403–447.

Bogardus, E. S. Racial distance in the United States during the past thirty years. *Sociol. soc. Res.,* 1958, 43, 127–135.

Bogardus, E. S. *Social distance.* Los Angeles: Antioch, 1959.

Cash, W. J. *The mind of the south.* New York: Doubleday, 1954.

Catapusan, B. T. Social distance in the Philippines. *Sociol. soc. Res.,* 1953–1954, 38, 309–312.

Christie, R., & Cook, Peggy. A guide to published literature relating to *The authoritarian personality* through 1956. *J. Psychol.,* 1958, 45, 171–199.

Clarke, K. B., & Clarke, Mamie P. Racial identification and preference in Negro children. In G. Swanson, T. Newcombe, & E. Hartley (Eds.), *Readings in social psychology.* (rev. ed.) New York: Holt, 1952. Pp. 551–560.

Cox, O. C. *Caste, class, and race.* New York: Doubleday, 1948.

Crespi, L. Is Gunnar Myrdal on the right track? *Publ. Opin. Quart.,* 1945, 9, 201–212.

De Fleur, M. L., & Westie, F. R. Verbal attitudes and overt acts: An experiment on the salience of attitudes. *Amer. sociol. Rev.,* 1958, 23, 667–673.

De Fleur, M. L., & Westie, F. R. Attitude as a scientific concept. *Soc. Forces,* October, 1963, 50, 17–31.

Diab, L. N. Authoritarianism and prejudice in Near-Eastern students attending American universities. *J. soc. Psychol.,* 1959, 50, 175–187.

Dodd, S. C. A social distance test in the Near East. *Amer. J. Sociol.,* 1956–1957, 41, 194–204.

Dollard, J., Miller, N., Doob, L., Mowrer, O. H., & Sears, R. R. *Frustration and aggression.* New Haven, Conn.: Yale Univer. Press, 1939.

Durkheim, E. *The rules of sociological method.* Glencoe, Ill.: Free Press, 1950.

Edwards, A. L. Social desirability and probability of endorsement of items in the inter-personal check list. *J. abnorm. soc. Psychol.,* 1957, 55, 394–396.

Erskine, Hazel G. The polls: Race relations. *Publ. Opin. Quart.,* 1962, 26, 138–148.

Evans, J. C., & Lang, D. A., Jr. Integration in the armed services. *Ann. Amer. Acad. pol. soc. Sci.,* 1956, 304, 78–85.

Frazier, E. F. *Black bourgeoisie.* Glencoe, Ill.: Free Press, 1957.

Frenkel-Brunswik, Else. Abstract of a paper read at Western Psychological Association meetings, June 29, 1946. *Amer. Psychol.,* 1946, 1, 456.

Frenkel-Brunswik, Else. A study of prejudice in children. *Hum. Relat.,* 1948, 1, 295–306.

Frenkel-Brunswik, Else. Further explorations by a contributor to 'The authoritarian personality.' In R. Christie & Marie Jahoda (Eds.), *Studies in the scope and method of 'The authoritarian personality.'* Glencoe, Ill.: Free Press, 1954. Pp. 226–276.

Gleason, G. Social distance in Russia. *Sociol. soc. Res.,* 1932–1933, 17, 37–43.

Goodman, Mary E. *Race awareness in young children.* Cambridge, Mass.: Addison-Wesley, 1952.

Guilford, J. P. Racial preferences of a thousand American university students. *J. soc. Psychol.,* 1931, 2, 179–204.

Hanley, C. Social desirability and responses to items from three MMPI scales: D, Sc, and K. *J. appl. Psychol.,* 1956, 40, 324–328.

Hartley, E. *Problems in prejudice.* New York: King's Crown, 1946.

Hayes, Margaret L. Attitudes of high school students toward Negro problems. *J. educ. Res.,* 1952–1953, 46, 615–620.

Horowitz, E. L. Development of attitudes toward Negroes. In *Arch. Psychol., N.Y.,* 1936, 28 (194).

Hunt, C. L. Social distance in the Philippines. *Sociol. soc. Res.,* 1955–1956, 40, 253–260.

Kenny, D. T. The influence of social desirability on discrepancy measures between real self and ideal self. *J. consult. Psychol.,* 1956, 20, 315–318.

Killian, L. M. The effects of southern white workers on race relations in northern plants. *Amer. sociol. Rev.,* 1952, 17, 327–331.

Lambert, W. E. Comparison of French and American modes of response to the Bogardus social distance scale. *Soc. Forces,* 1952, 31, 155–160.

Lasker, B. *Race attitudes in children.* New York: Holt, 1929.

Lewin, K. *Resolving social conflicts.* New York: Harper, 1948.

Lindzey, G. Differences between the high and low in prejudice and their implications for a theory of prejudice. *J. Person.,* 1950, **19**, 16–40.

Linton, R. *The cultural background of personality.* New York: Appleton-Century, 1945.

Lipset, S. M. *Political man.* New York: Doubleday, 1960.

Lohman, J. D., & Reitzes, D. C. Note on race relations in mass society. *Amer. J. Sociol.,* 1952, **58**, 240–246.

Lohman, J. D., & Reitzes, D. C. Deliberately organized groups and racial behavior. *Amer. sociol. Rev.,* 1954, **19**, 342–344.

Lundberg, G. A., & Dickson, Leonore. Selective association among ethnic groups in a high school population. *Amer. sociol. Rev.,* 1952, **17**, 23–25.

MacCrone, I. D. *Race relations in South Africa.* London: Oxford Univer. Press, 1937.

MacCrone, I. D. Race attitudes: An analysis and interpretation. In Ellen Hellman (Ed.), *Handbook of race relations in South Africa.* Cape Town: Oxford Univer. Press, 1949. Pp. 669–705.

McDonagh, E. C. Asiatic stereotypes and national distance. *Sociol. soc. Res.,* 1938–1939, **23**, 474–478.

MacIver, R. M., & Page, C. H. *Society, an introductory analysis.* New York: Rinehart, 1948.

Mannheim, K. *Man and society in an age of reconstruction.* New York: Harcourt, 1940.

Miller, N. E., & Bugelski, R. Minor studies of aggression: II. The influence of frustrations imposed by the in-group on attitudes expressed toward outgroups. *J. Psychol.,* 1948, **25**, 437–442.

Mills, C. W. *The power elite.* New York: Oxford Univer. Press, 1959.

Minard, R. D. Race attitudes of Iowa children. *Univer. Iowa Stud. Charact.,* 1931, 4 (2).

Morland, K. J. Racial acceptance and preference among nursery school children in a southern city. Paper read at meetings of Amer. Sociol. Ass., St. Louis, 1961.

Mosher, D. L., & Scodel, A. Relationships between ethnocentrism in children and ethnocentrism and authoritarian child-rearing practices of their mothers. *Child Develpm.,* 1960, **31**, 369–376.

Myrdal, G. *An American dilemma.* (20th anniversary ed.) New York: Harper & Row, 1962.

Nadler, E. B., & Morrow, W. R. Authoritarian attitudes toward women and their correlates. *J. soc. Psychol.,* 1959, **49**, 113–123.

Nichols, L. *Breakthrough on the color front.* New York: Random House, Inc., 1954.

Pettigrew, T. F. Social distance attitudes of South African students. *Soc. Forces,* 1959, **38**, 246–253.

Radke, Marian J., Sutherland, Jean, & Rosenberg, Pearl. Racial attitudes of children. *Sociometry,* 1950, **13**, 151–171.

Radke-Yarrow, Marian J. Developmental changes in the meaning of minority group membership. *J. educ. Psychol.,* 1953, 44, 82–101.

Radke, Marian J., & Trager, Helen G. Children's perceptions of the social roles of Negroes and whites. *J. Psychol.,* 1950, **29**, 3–33.

Radke, Marian J., Trager, Helen G., & Davis, Hadassah. Social perceptions and attitudes of children. *Genet. Psychol. Monogr.,* 1949, **10**, 327–447.

Reitzes, D. C. The role of organization structures. *J. soc. Iss.,* 1953, **9**, 37–44.

Remmers, H. H., & Gage, N. L. Patterns of attitudes toward minorities among high school youth in the United States Middle West. *Int. J. Opin. Att. Res.,* 1947, **1**, 106–109.

Richmond, A. H. [Recent research on racial relations in] Britain. *Int. soc. Sci. Bull.* (UNESCO), 1958, **10**, 344–372.

Riesman, D., Glazer, N., & Denny, R. *The lonely crowd.* New York: Doubleday Anchor, 1950.

Rokeach, M. Political and religious dogmatism: An alternative to the authoritarian personality. *Psychol. Monogr.,* 1956, **70** (425).

Rosen, E. Self-appraisal, personal desirability, and perceived social desirability of personality traits. *J. abnorm. soc. Psychol.,* 1956, **52**, 151–158.

Seeman, Melvin. Skin color values in three all-Negro school classes. *Amer. sociol. Rev.,* 1946, **11**, 315–321.

Sheppard, H. L. The Negro merchant: A study of Negro anti-Semitism. *Amer. J. Sociol.,* 1947, **53**, 96–99.

Sherif, M., & Sherif, Carolyn W. *Groups in harmony and tension: An integration of studies on inter-group relations.* New York: Harper, 1953.

Shils, E. A. Authoritarianism: "Right" and "left." In R. Christie & Marie Jahoda (Eds.), *Studies in the scope and method of 'The authoritarian personality.'* Glencoe, Ill.: Free Press, 1954. Pp. 24–49.

Shils, E. A. Mass society and its culture. In N. Jacobs (Ed.), *Culture for the millions?* Princeton, N.J.: Van Nostrand, 1961.

Simpson, G. E., & Yinger, J. M. *Racial and cultural minorities.* (rev. ed.) New York: Harper, 1958.

Simpson, G. E., & Yinger, J. M. The sociology of race and ethnic relations. In R. K. Merton, L. Broom, & L. S. Cottrell, Jr. (Eds.), *Sociology today.* New York: Basic Books, 1959. Pp. 376–399.

Simpson, R. L. Negro-Jewish prejudice: Authoritarianism and some social variables as correlates. *Soc. Probs,* 1959, **7**, 138–146.

Sodhi, K. S. [Recent research on racial relations in the] Federal Republic of Germany. *Int. soc. Sci. Bull.* (UNESCO), 1958, **10**, 387–403.

Srole, L. Social integration and certain corollaries: An exploratory study. *Amer. sociol. Rev.,* 1956, **21**, 709–716.

Stouffer, S., Suchman, E., DeVinney, L., Star, Shirley, Williams, R., Jr. *The American soldier: Adjustment during army life.* Princeton, N.J.: Princeton Univer. Press, 1949.

Suchman, E. A., Dean, J. P., & Williams, R. W., Jr. *Desegregation: Some propositions and research suggestions.* New York: Anti-Defamation League of B'nai B'rith, 1958.

Titus, H. E., & Hollander, E. P. The California F-scale in psychological research: 1950–1955. *Psychol. Bull.,* 1957, **54**, 47–64.

Tumin, M. *Inventory and appraisal of research on American anti-Semitism.* New York: Freedom Books, 1961.

Van Den Berghe, P. L. Race relations in Durban, South Africa. *J. soc. Psychol.,* 1962, **57**, 55–72.

Van Den Berghe, P. L., & Colby, B. N. Ladino-Indian relations in the highlands of Chiapas, Mexico. *Soc. Forces,* 1961, **40**, 63–71.

Ward, Barbara E. [Recent research on racial relations in] East Africa. *Int. soc. Sci. Bull.* (UNESCO), 1958, **10**, 372–386.

Westie, F. R. Developmental study of attitudes in children. Unpublished monograph, 1964.

Westie, F. R. The American dilemma: An empirical test. Unpublished manuscript, 1964.

Westie, F. R., & De Fleur, M. L. Autonomic responses and their relationship to race attitudes. *J. abnorm. soc. Psychol.,* 1959, **58**, 340–347.

Westie, F. R., & Martin, J. The tolerant personality. *Amer. sociol. Rev.,* 1959, **24**, 521–528.

Williams, R. M., Jr. *The reduction of intergroup tensions: A survey of research on problems of ethnic, racial, and religious group relations.* New York: Social Science Research Council, 1947.

Williams, R. M., Jr. Review and assessment of research on race and culture conflict. *Conference on research in human relations.* New York: Rockefeller Foundation, 1953. (Typed)

Williams, R. M., Jr. Racial and cultural relations. In J. B. Gittler (Ed.), *Review of sociology: Analysis of a decade.* New York: Wiley, 1957.

Williams, R. M., Jr. *Strangers next door.* Englewood Cliffs, N.J.: Prentice-Hall, Inc., 1964.

Wrong, D. H. The oversocialized conception of man in modern society. *Amer. sociol. Rev.,* 1961, **26**, 183–193.

Zawadski, B. Limitations of the scapegoat theory of prejudice. *J. abnorm. soc. Psychol.,* 1948, **43**, 127–141.

Zeligs, Rose, & Hendrickson, G. Racial attitudes of 200 children. *Sociol. soc. Res.,* 1933, **18**, 26–36.

CHAPTER 17 Industrial Relations[1]

EDWARD GROSS

Industrial relations are work relations and sociologists study both because a man at work is no less a man. So one may learn something of why a man behaves as he does by looking at him as he goes about the task of earning a living. At times, his work enables him to stand apart from society; it is claimed that the same engineer took care of the water works in Paris before, during, and after the French Revolution. But such examples are not the rule. More often it is through his work that man is most intimately implicated in the human drama. It may not be his central life interest, but how he goes about it or even tries to avoid it tells us much about him. A man's work provides him with one of the major bonds through which he is united with his fellows. A few persons work alone, but most work with others on some common endeavor. The organization may be of the type illustrated by medicine, in which the physician is caught up in a network of relationships with medical schools, medical societies, health insurance societies, state licensing bodies, and hospitals, or the organization may be one of the types illustrated by modern government, commercialized recreation, education, the family business, or large-scale industry. Although our concern is mostly with industrial organizations, and particularly those in which persons gather to perform work tasks in a division of labor under one authority, it is clear that industrial organization is only one kind of organization. As such, a good deal of the research in the area draws upon findings made in other kinds of organizations. In turn, the general study of formal organizations in sociology leans heavily on the extensive research on industrial organizations. It is the fact of organization that produces the important sociological consequence that a man's work provides us with a funda-

---

[1] This chapter is limited to the sociological approach to industrial relations. The title "industrial relations" is often used in a broader sense by students of personnel administration and industrial organization to refer to general aspects of employment relationships and union-management relationships. So used, "industrial relations" includes the contributions of industrial psychology, industrial medicine, political science and other fields, as well as that of sociology. For examples of treatments of "industrial relations" from this broad point of view, see Wilensky (1954), and Yoder & Heneman (1959).

mental index of his status and self-respect. As place of origin and name have declined in significance, what a man does for a living has been elevated in importance. The question, "What do you do?" is immediately recognized as meaning what kind of *work* do you do. The answer one gets enables the questioner to place the man, at least approximately. The questioner can estimate how much the respondent's income is, whether he is likely to be married or not, the size of his family, where he lives, where he works, how he spends his leisure time, and to what clubs he belongs. From his estimates of these things, he can in turn make a judgment of how he should behave toward him—whether he should accord him respect, tolerance, or contempt; whether he should seek his help or offer him help; whether he wants him as a friend or not. At the same time, because persons do make judgments of a man on the basis of his work, it becomes important that those judgments be accurate. In brief, these considerations are the central concern of the study of industrial relations.

Some work organizations have received a great deal of attention, many no attention at all. Unlike the study of occupations in which the concentration has been on upper status occupations, particularly the professions, the study of organizations has tended to focus on the "lower participants" (Etzioni, 1961, pp. 16 ff.) in organization, and this may well present a distorted view. With the exception of studies such as Mills's (1948) of labor union leaders, Dalton's (1959) of industrial top management, and Janowitz' (1960) of military officers, most industrial studies have dealt with lower levels of employment, often with persons at the very bottom. The recent interest in white-collar workers has corrected this emphasis somewhat but here again the studies have tended to be of low-level clerical persons. The same has been true of the interest in professional persons in organizations. Although study of the latter has forced the researcher into relatively high level staff organizations, the concern is usually with the operating engineer or scientist and rarely with the top manager. Such a limitation reflects the difficulty of securing access to the inner councils of top management, but it may also reflect the long-sanctioned interest of the sociologist in the problems of the disadvantaged, as well as the fact that the sociologist is likely to be invited in by management to make a study of a phenomenon which is a "problem" to management. Such a problem the manager will usually see as concentrated in the people who work for him. If lower level persons could invite sociologists to make studies of *their* problems, we would have many more studies of top managers. Data on the unrepresentativeness of industrial research have been brought together in cogent form by Blauner (1962, p. 339).

PERSPECTIVES

A special problem in the study of work organization has to do with the definition and scope of industry itself. In its generic sense and for most writers the term is used to refer to productive processes in which mechanization is common and in which the formal organization that people associate with rational bureaucracy is most in evidence. In practice, discussions include craft, collegial, and other forms of organization, on the one hand, and extend to department stores, restaurants, railroads, shipyards, insurance organizations, military organizations, research laboratories, and hospitals, on the other. Although there is such a diversity of interest, it is often maintained that a common thread runs through such organizations and such branches of work because of the fact that they all tend to follow the "industrial" form of organization. A further task is the need to develop indices of industrialization so that areas of a country or whole countries may be compared with each other in terms of degree of industrialization, or of factors and variables associated with industrialization. For this purpose

Lipset (1959), Davis and Golden (1957), and Gibbs and Martin (1962) made use of the per capita consumption of energy, or of the per cent of males engaged in nonagricultural pursuits.

Inkeles (1960) criticized such broad measures as tending to generalize to the population as a whole characteristics which may be intensely developed in only one segment. Further, these measures provide approximations to the average level of response for an entire country and hence may mask the special influence of the industrial environment itself. Inkeles proposed instead the use of a structure of experience, attitude, and value which takes a special shape from the occupational structure. Wherever the factory or any large-scale organization exists, Inkeles claimed there will be a clearly stratified hierarchy of authority and of technical competence, and there will be a hierarchy of income, prestige, and other rewards as well. The attitudes, values, and perceptions of persons can be predicted by their *position* in such a hierarchy more accurately than by the sheer income or occupation that they happen to have. He presented data which show that for a variety of countries, including the Soviet Union, the higher a job is in power and prestige, the more often the incumbents of the job feel satisfied with their work. Only 23 per cent of the unskilled workers in the Soviet Union say they are satisfied with their jobs, whereas by contrast in the United States 72 per cent of the unskilled are satisfied with their jobs (a very high percentage indeed). If one were to compare these two percentages alone, he would simply conclude that there were striking differences between countries in the proportion of persons satisfied with their jobs when occupation is held constant. By taking the approach suggested by Inkeles, the conclusion is reached that, although such differences do indeed exist, it is equally striking to note that persons located near the bottom of the hierarchy are consistently less satisfied than those higher up. Therefore, such structural similarities as the strati-

ficational differences presumably associated with industrialization may be used to predict the order of satisfaction of persons with their jobs. He found similar kinds of generalizations possible for the degree of happiness of persons and for the mastery-optimism complex.

A structural approach was also used by Dunlop (1958) in the analysis of what he spoke of as "industrial relations systems." Such systems are analyzable into the following elements: the actors in a system and the contexts. The actors include a hierarchy of managers and their representatives in supervision, a hierarchy of workers and any spokesmen or representatives that they have, and specialized governmental agencies who are in any way concerned with workers or with relationships between workers and their enterprises.

These three groups of actors operate in a setting which includes three aspects, which Dunlop (1958) called the "contexts" of a system. These include the technological aspects of the work place and work community, the market or budgetary constraints on the actors, and the locus and distribution of power in the larger society. The actors in the contexts proceed to establish rules for the work place and work community. Such a "web of rules" consists of procedures for establishing rules, the rules themselves, and procedures for deciding on their application to particular situations. These rules become the center of attention in industrial relations systems. Examples of procedures include those in which the managerial hierarchy has a relatively free hand in setting rules, those in which a government agency may have a dominant role, and those in which the work hierarchy plays a major role in fixing rules. The substantive rules themselves are classified into rules relating to compensation of workers, to duties and performance expected from workers, and to defining the rights and duties of workers, including new or laid-off workers, on particular positions or jobs. Experts in the construction, manipulation, and administration of these rules operate to stabilize the rule-making and rule-administering process.

Work Shops

Of the major forms of work organization, guilds, household ("putting-out" system) types of organization, and the factory are among the most important. Guilds reached their climax in Europe in the thirteenth century although they were known considerably before then and indeed have not vanished from the world at present. The most important types of guilds were the religious fraternities (having mainly benevolent and protective functions), the craft guilds (including professional organizations), and the merchant guilds. The craft guilds concerned themselves with manufacturing goods or dispensing services, while the merchant guilds regulated conditions of sale and the economic life of the medieval town as a whole (Gross, 1890, pp. 46–47). The distinctive feature of the guild in contrast to other forms of work organization is the inclusion of both masters and workers in the same organization. Guilds existed partly for self-protection and partly to maintain social control over the membership and the process of manufacturing and distribution. As self-protective devices they made sure that they kept a monopoly of the available work, though there was competition from the monastic orders, rural craftsmen, and independent artisans (Moore, 1951, p. 19), controlling entry and limiting the number of masters permitted in a given guild activity and controlling trade with customers or with foreign sources. Control over the membership included determination of price, standards of craftsmanship, and other forms of behavior which in many cases went far beyond that strictly required by the work task. Mumford (1938) pointed out that the economic or occupational function of the guilds was only one of many tasks. The guild was a religious fraternity under the patronage of a saint, providing comfort and cheer and a decent burial. The "brothers ate and drank together on regular occasions: they formulated regulations for the conduct of their craft: they planned and paid for and enacted their parts in their mystery plays, for the edification of their fellow townsmen: and they built chapels, endowed chantries, and founded schools" (Mumford, 1938, pp. 29–30).

The structure of the guild related masters, apprentices, and journeymen to one another. The master owned the shop but usually not the tools that the workmen utilized. He was not a manager or a supervisor in the modern sense of the term, but rather the most skilled of the workmen present who assumed the responsibility for the final product. The relationship of apprentice to master was close. The apprentice was required "not to frequent taverns, commit fornication or adultery with the housemaids or in town, nor betroth himself without his master's permission. He [was] not to wear certain garments, play at dice, chequers, or any other unlawful game . . ." (Seligman, 1887, pp. 87–88). A journeyman was essentially a person who had completed his apprenticeship and was not yet a master in the sense of having a shop of his own, but rather worked for wages for various masters. The inability of journeymen to become masters reflected the essentially restrictive character of the guild form of organization and became much more pronounced as the guild form began to decline in the sixteenth century in Europe. By this time many journeymen had essentially become laborers for already established masters and had given up hope of ever becoming masters in their own right (Hauser, 1932). The power of certain masters meanwhile rose at the expense of others not so fortunate. Thus, some guilds became dominant over other guilds, and their masters assumed a dominant position of power in the town, hiring the services of other guild masters (Weber, 1950, p. 136). Perhaps most significant in the decline of the guild system as a whole was the emergence of new markets and the need for new products that arose with the coming of the period of discovery of the New World and the expansion of population, creating a demand for far greater production than the guilds were capable of (Schneider, 1957, pp. 35-36).

The *putting-out* system (Gay, 1932) overlapped the period of domination of the guilds and persisted into the factory period —somewhere between the fifteenth and eighteenth centuries—and it has certainly not vanished even now (Rosen & Rosen, 1941, Ch. XI). The merchant was often a former master in a merchant guild. He was able to take advantage of the surplus labor occasioned by population changes and by the enclosure movements in Europe. He took to the countryside outside of the cities, making use of depressed rural persons with few skills but with a strong need to find some type of income. To these persons, he supplied materials for work in the home, picking up the spun wool or cut cloth at a later period. For these services he paid in cash. In general the tools were simple and cheap enough to be owned by the workers and operated with little or no training. With wage payment the relationship became a wholly contractual one. As a method of organizing production it escaped the limiting controls on guild production, but proved difficult to supervise because of the absence of the merchant through most of the productive process. Eventually merchants attempted to bind the workers to them more closely by renting them tools and developing a debt bond between themselves and the workers. Entire families were employed in the putting-out system—typically for long hours—a pattern which then made it natural for whole families to think of working in the factories which came in later. Indeed much of the opposition to child labor under the factory system came not from the manufacturers themselves but from the parents of the children who had never known any other system than that of child labor (Bendix, 1956, pp. 36-37).

The factory form of production arose as a type of organization that was more efficient than both guild and putting-out systems and better adapted to the needs of a large, stable demand (Weber, 1950, Ch. XII). By bringing workers together in one place the expenses of transporting goods from rural cottage to cottage was eliminated together with the cost of the "entrepreneurial" services of the merchant himself. In addition, it became possible to supervise the activities of workers more closely and to enforce discipline. The existence of free labor made possible a contractual relationship in which persons were free from feudal, guild, and other traditional controls, although this freedom often was little more than formal insofar as the worker had no choice but to labor in the new mill. The enormously increased efficiency and productive output made possible by the factory was in part a consequence of the great demand created by the newly formed nation-states with their never ending need for more gunpowder, uniforms, and other instruments of national power and control. The state needed high productivity and high production and it needed dependable sources of materials and goods. Efficiency was also facilitated, as Weber (1950, Ch. XII) pointed out, by the large sources of capital, particularly of precious metals from the New World and, of course, was provided with its fundamental motivational force by the Calvinistic ethic. Not unimportant, too, was the need of the new states for taxes.

Along with the factory form of production the corporate form of organization became dominant. Although various types of corporations had existed previously, the distinctly modern corporation added special dimensions that the world had never before seen. The corporation, as it is known at present, appears to be of Germanic origin, apparently being first developed by the merchants of the Hanseatic League in order to finance the high cost of ships, warehouses, and the like and to spread the risk of loss in transit (Moore, 1951, pp. 42-43). The outstanding illustrations of corporations in the early period were the Dutch East India Company and the British East India Company. As Moore (1951, p. 43) pointed out, the British East India Company became the political government of India, a development which makes certain of the pretensions of modern corporations appear quite tame.

Berle and Means (1933) pointed out that the distinctive feature of the corporation is that it can sue and be sued as an entity in its own right, apart from the individuals in the organization. "From all this necessarily flowed a limited liability of the associates. Since only the entity was liable for debts, which did not attach to the various individuals, it followed that a stockholder was not normally liable for any of the debts of the enterprise; and he could thus embark a particular amount of capital in the corporate affairs without becoming responsible beyond this amount, for the corporate debts" (Berle & Means, 1933, pp. 128–129). It thus proved possible to gather together huge amounts of capital, enabling the corporation to grow large and enjoy the economic benefits of such size.

At the same time, Moore (1962) tells us, a whole set of questions is raised about the conduct of the corporation. It is not clear who may be said to be the owners of the corporation, because ownership of the stock is widely dispersed and many of the owners are banks or financial institutions rather than individuals. This dispersal of ownership means that most of the theoretical owners in fact have no interest at all in the actual conduct of the corporation, except that its conduct shall be of such a nature as to guarantee them a reasonable return on their investment. A relatively small group of investors who own only a small proportion of the stock may exercise effective control over the board of directors, who in turn will name the management. Such management, however, is expected to act both as a hired employee of the stockholders and at the same time as a trustee of the wealth which the stockholders have invested. In practice, management ordinarily

has a free hand in how it runs the corporation, subject to possible recall in case of dissatisfaction. Such relative looseness of day-to-day control over managers has meant that persons who do not own the corporation in fact control and direct it. It is not then surprising that much of what goes on in the corporation can hardly be justified in terms of the desires or the needs of the stockholders. Managers do things that they think are necessary for the good of the company or even for their own good. Moore (1962, pp. 14–15) hence raised the question of whether the very high salaries paid to top management can in any way be justified in the light of comparable duties expected of others, such as full generals and Supreme Court justices, who are paid much less.

Theoretical Approaches

Nine major theoretical approaches to the study of industrial relations may be distinguished.

Weberian theory. Much of current theoretical work consists of criticisms or refinements of Weber's (1950) major precepts. The theory focuses attention particularly on the bureaucratic elements in organizations—those elements which have the most directly to do with the maintenance of the organization as a going concern. As such, much of what Weber said has most meaning for the administrative officials of an organization, less to those at the very bottom who carry on the actual production or the service that marks off the organization from others. The major concepts that Weber used in describing the bureaucratic organizations (in contrast to organizations based on charismatic or traditional authority) are included in the following discussion (Gerth & Mills, 1946, pp. 196–264; Henderson & Parsons, 1947, pp. 324–423). Rationality is emphasized in the provision for explicit rules and for a maximization of dependence on knowledge rather than on tradition or ritual. Explicit rules are designed to ensure predictability, universalistic standards (for example, equality of treatment by superiors and equality of treatment of customers), and the definition of the limits of privacy (the official needs to know in advance what course of action a superior would take toward him in order not to feel that he must respond to every whim of his superior).

Weber (1950) was less explicit on the question of how the rules are made and how they are taught to officials. In a firm that he studied, Gouldner (1954) found that *representative* bureaucracy (for example, safety rules) differed from *punishment-centered* bureaucracy (for example, rules punishing persons for being absent from work) precisely on this point. In the first type of bureaucracy, rules were made in consultation with workers, but in the second they were simply imposed on workers. This point made a critical difference in the likelihood that these rules would be obeyed. Weber, however, tended to feel that rules are imposed from above. This hardly ensures obedience unless persons are accustomed to accept orders without question. The latter point was emphasized by Blau (1955, pp. 202–203) and by Friedrich (1952, pp. 30–31). In the Germany of Weber's day, the authoritarian tradition made it more likely that orders would be obeyed without question, and subordinates were not highly educated and generally had to be told what to do. In the United States, with a different tradition and a higher level of education, it may be more efficient to have frequent consultation about rules. Furthermore, the efficiency of explicit rules depends on the nature of the social situation or of the task. Thus Feld (1959) suggested that the character of rules differs in a military situation, depending on whether the rules are to be applied in the front lines or in the rear.

A similar point was made by Coser (1958) in a discussion of differences between rules in medical and surgical wards. Many sociologists (e.g., Gouldner, 1952) have called attention to the relation between over-emphasis upon rules and the general problem of red tape. To a client, such emphasis appears to be red tape, and he is likely to accuse the bureaucrat of excessive ritualism. But if the bureaucrat cuts too rapidly through red tape, he is likely to be accused of being arbitrary and of having too much power. There have been many criticisms also of the extent to which emphasis on rules gives a picture of an organization as being essentially impersonal. While this is true in the model, it leaves out the questions of how loyalty is to be induced (since men are loyal only to ideals or other men but not to rules as such), and of motivation for maximum positional performance. Weber felt that assurance to an official of a career in the organization would provide motivation, together with the class homogeneity that would result from the emphasis on educational qualifications. Yet the very fact of assurance of a career leads to the "old soldier" disease wherein men wait out the period until they can receive their pension.

The emphasis on maximization of dependence on knowledge was spelled out by Weber in terms of various kinds of knowledge. The organization may make maximum use of persons with extensive training such as lawyers, scientists, engineers, and other professional experts. Knowledge here includes concrete facts about social systems in which the organization is implicated; for example, the State Department employs experts on conditions in various parts of the world, and business firms employ persons with wide knowledge of market conditions or of the behavior of competitors. A third type of knowledge is embodied in the records of the organization's internal operations and in other checks on the efficiency of the firm. The emphasis on professionals and experts creates a dilemma, as Gouldner (1957–1958) and Parsons (1958) pointed out. Such professionals have ties to outside colleagues, as in professional associations, and these are necessary for the maintenance of professional standards. At the same time, such associational memberships and the ties that they involve enable the professional to resist some bureaucratic demands. In turn the bureaucracy has a counterweapon: It can threaten to expose incompetent professionals to their colleagues. Along with emphasis on knowledge, there may be an emphasis on secrecy necessary for efficiency (for example, for surprise in the case of an army attack or for keeping secret the new models to be sold in a business campaign), and this may help maintain internal morale (by, for ex-' ample, protecting government executive personnel from investigations by other branches of the government). Secrecy also helps maintain authority, since subordinates may obey superiors partly because they believe the superior has more knowledge than they do. It has been recognized by many, however, that such secrecy may be dysfunctional, for example, in so far as it prevents the dissemination of the results of research in business and military organizations. Without the possibility for other researchers to scrutinize research findings carefully, the basic test of scientific cross checking cannot be applied.

Weber emphasized that officials in a bureaucracy are appointed, rather than elected or. installed through hereditary succession. There are two marginal or exceptional situations: The man at the top is often not an appointee but may be elected, or may be in this position because of unique personal qualities (e.g., the first Henry Ford), and, of course, many "elections" are the functional equivalent of appointments. In the case, for example, of co-optation the members of a board of directors may simply add another man to their number. A question that is not so easy to answer is: Why are officials appointed? The obvious answer, "efficiency," is by no means easily proved, for much depends on how the appointment is made, the ease with which the job requirements may in fact be determined, and the ease with which the candidate's qualifications may be assessed. Sometimes, as Moore (1962, p. 42) pointed out, the tests themselves become self-confirming. Where it is difficult to measure job performance,

it is assumed that the worker who scored high on the qualification test must be performing well. Appointment, however, does have the effect of ensuring that the official is dependent upon his superiors and thus helps to ensure discipline and predictability of behavior.

Weber pointed to specificity in office (each man's job and responsibility limited to a specialty) and hierarchical control (each official reports to a superior who has authority over him). The result is a chain of command. Recent work (Blau & Scott, 1962, pp. 121–124; McGregor, 1960; Thompson, 1961) has cast doubt on the usefulness of the chain-of-command principle. In some organizations, there has been, instead, an increasing use of consultative and participative leadership. Weber's work has also been criticized for emphasis on the formal aspects of organization to the neglect of natural leadership and other informal phenomena and for tending to ignore the dysfunctions of organizations. In his defense, it must be pointed out that Weber was contrasting bureaucratic forms of organization with *earlier* forms, as exemplified by patrimonial and charismatic forms. In contrast with these earlier forms, Weber felt, bureaucracy was so much more efficient that, wherever in the world the bureaucratic form of organization came in, it tended to push out other forms.

Scientific management. "Scientific management" as a theory of industrial organizations was originated by the engineer Frederick W. Taylor in the late nineteenth century, a time of rapid industrialization in the United States. Taylor discovered gross inefficiencies in the way in which work was organized and in the motivation of workers and, in order to alter these conditions, proposed a point of view which embodied the following assumptions. He saw industrial man as an isolated individualist who related to his environment without regard to ties with other persons. The person to seek for any job was the person with the appropriate aptitude for the job. Hence, the focus was on relating the man to the job, with little attention to the relation of man to man. The primary motivation for man was money and consequently maximum productivity could be assured by paying the individual a piece-rate. Work should be simplified and standardized. The task of the industrial engineer was to study the job, find the "one best way," teach it to the worker, and then, by means of close supervision, make certain that the worker carried it out. Such a point of view allowed for little or no contribution from the workers, assumed to be ignorant and without originality.

This approach had an enormous influence and indeed is still regarded as valuable by a high proportion of persons in the general field of industrial relations. Its most important expression at the present time is in the emphasis on "needs" attributed to the worker. Although more sophisticated than Taylor's early notions of individual requirements, the concept of needs still places the focus on the individual and what one has to do to him in order that he be better able to do the job. The scientific management school, however, has been subjected to severe criticism by the human relations approach, a discussion of which follows.

Human relations. The human relations approach was initiated by the famous Western Electric experiments (Mayo, 1933; Mayo, 1946; Mayo, 1947; Roethlisberger & Dickson, 1939; Whitehead, 1936; Whitehead, 1938). These started as standard studies of the effects of working conditions on productivity, eventually expanding into the study of the effects of association of workers on their work behavior. The behavior of the women in the Relay Assembly Test Room, where they seemed to increase their productivity irrespective of how physical conditions were changed, led to an explanation in terms of the effect of experimentation itself (the Hawthorne effect, that is, the effect of having an observer present to ask the girls how they felt about every change) and the effect of differential treatment. The girls had no regular supervision,

and even vetoed ideas that the experimenters wanted to try out. This was then an early example of participation in the decision-making process. Critics of the Western Electric experiment (well discussed by Landsberger, 1958) have pointed out that the cooperation the women showed may well have been attributable to the fact that the depression of the 1930's had begun. The Western Electric studies also described in detail the phenomenon of restriction of output, a type of behavior which was difficult to explain except in terms of some type of group arrangements.

These experiments challenged the assumptions of Taylor and his followers at several points. Workers clearly did not respond simply as isolated individuals but were strongly influenced by the social relations they experienced. It was true that they worked for money, but there was strong evidence of restriction of output which kept their earnings well below what they might have earned if they had done their best. The experiments questioned the concept of mechanical aptitude, since individual aptitudes were found to be poorly correlated with productivity. The best predictor of the performance of men in the Bank Wiring Observation Room was their clique membership rather than their aptitude. Since those famous experiments, many other studies were conducted, by Warner and Low (1947) for example, in Yankee City, on the effects of the unionization of shoe workers and other phenomena involving union management and industry community relations.

Basically the human relations studies were negative; they were concerned with pointing out what was not true (Whyte, 1961, pp. 10–11). The "human relations" group under the leadership of Elton Mayo coined the term informal organization to describe the tendency of persons thrown together in organizations to develop relations with each other that are not specified by the formal organization structure and may even be in opposition to it. They emphasized that if one paid attention only to formal structure, one would get a misleading view. But they left open the question of the role that formal organization itself played.

The human relations approach led to the emphasis on face-to-face relationships. It was assumed that one could build harmonious relationships and reduce conflict by teaching persons how to deal effectively with one another. This led to an enormous expansion of supervisory training programs in human relations skills in the 1940's and the 1950's. Ignored in all of this were economic forces, technology, work flow, organization structure, and plant-community relations. In general it was felt that an increase in human relations skills would be effective under any conditions. Within recent years there has been a shift of emphasis from informal to formal relationships and a concern with the structure of work relations themselves as influencing work behavior.

Emphasis on technological imperatives and formal organization. It may be an exaggeration to characterize this as a theoretical approach but it does involve a set of distinct interests and sensitivities. The concern here is essentially with balancing the overemphasis of the human relations school on the impact of face-to-face relationships. Kerr and Siegel (1954) reported that conflict seems to be endemic to certain industries in country after country. Thus the longshore industry is strike-ridden in many countries whereas the railroad industry has few strikes. If conflict is related to human relations skills, one would have to assume that the longshoremen leaders are poorly skilled and railroad leaders are experts. There seems to be no reason to believe that this is true. Rather, the explanation must be sought in the special structure of the industries themselves. "Strike prone" industries are found to be those in which workers are in close proximity to each other on similar jobs and live in isolated communities cut off from other workers and from management. Peaceful union-management relations are found in industries characterized by job variety in which workers

are scattered throughout the community. Such a finding serves to emphasize the influence of job structure and community organization on the human relations context of the job. Whyte (1956) described two major pieces of research on the effects of supervisory training programs, which cast further doubt on the special importance of human relations. Fleishmann and others (1955) found that certain major supervisory training programs either had no effect or that the effect was not as anticipated. In a program at Detroit Edison, it was found that, in a division in which the supervisory training program was successful, the foreman had supervisors who supervised them according to the human relations principles being taught in the course. By contrast, in a division in which the supervisory training program was not effective, it was found that foremen had supervisors who directed them in ways just the opposite of how superiors were supposed to supervise according to the human relations course. This suggested that the success of the program depended not on the principles themselves but on whether or not the program was supported at high levels (Maier, 1952, pp. 184–192). One is driven, therefore, to examine the structure of the industry, the character of the technology, and the kinds of pressures the organization itself imposed on persons to explain the relative frequency of conflict in the parts of the organization.

Reciprocity theory. A recent approach with much promise is that of describing relationships in terms of exchange (Homans, 1958; Lévi-Strauss, 1949; Mauss, 1954). Gouldner (1960) contrasted complementarity with reciprocity in the context of the relation between rights and duties in role relationships. In the sense that a right always implies a duty, then, by complementarity, one will do as expected only if one has been socialized to the role, a process which clearly requires training and time. A second means of starting social relationships is through exchange, in which there is the notion of a return for one's efforts. One will then maintain a relationship not necessarily because one has been taught to or because one feels that one ought to but because it pays one to do so. Such a relation is self-enforcing. Reciprocity relationships, although entered into originally because of some idea of narrow gain, if continued for any length of time usually undergo alteration and reach a point where each party to the exchange develops an obligation of reciprocity, or a feeling that he *should* return what has been given to him. In time a bond develops which the exchange symbolizes. Seeing the tip to the waitress as a reward for output explains little of the relationship, particularly since rigidities may make this into a straight service charge (some customers always tip, others never do, and the tip may also be standardized). In time, the tip comes to have a second meaning—the symbolic gift. It becomes an expression of feeling for the restaurant as a whole, coming to mean that the customer likes the restaurant and the way he is treated. By contrast, "stiffing" (leaving no tip at all) may mean just the opposite. It also symbolizes the customer's superior position since he can tip or not as he pleases, making the waitress dependent on him. The amount exchanged and who makes the initial overture also become symbolic of the relative positions of the parties to the exchange. Zaleznik, Christensen, and Roethlisberger (1958), in a study of a department that machined and assembled small rotating equipment and miscellaneous utility equipment, described a lottery in which workers participated. On one occasion, the amount of money to be won was unusually large. Excitement was high and comments were made that whoever won the pool was not going to be liked. Yet when the pool was won by the lottery treasurer, there was hardly any protest at all for it was felt appropriate that she should win. She was the informal leader of the entire department, distinguished by her willingness and capabilities in accepting respon-

sibilities. The study raises the whole question of the principles underlying the exchange of valued goods. A major contribution was made by Homans in the delineation of a set of "rules of distributive justice" (Homans, 1961, Ch. 12). An example is: The value of what a member of a group receives from other members should be proportional to his investments. This he illustrates with data from the Western Electric study. An "investment" refers to what a person brings with him to the situation which affects his status in that situation and which cannot, for the time of the interaction at least, be altered. Examples are seniority, skill, age, sex, and race. In a discussion of girls employed as cash posters, ledger clerks, and address file clerks, he further developed the idea that a person's rewards should be proportional to his investments (and to the costs he assumes as well as the contributions he makes), but that in addition the various rewards that he gets should all be "in line" with one another. A person who has a great deal of authority is typically one to whom others go for advice. Therefore, if one sees a person who has high authority seeking out a person with less authority for advice, there is felt to be an incongruity, with the accompanying feeling that the person's authority is thrown into question. Therefore, persons will try to bring the various status positions they have in line if they can. Thus Whyte (1948, Ch. 6), in comparing the chef and waitress in a restaurant, pointed out that the former is higher on many statuses. He has more skill and seniority, he is older and more highly paid, and he is typically a man. But in one respect the waitresses have a position above that of chef—they give orders to the chef, and since customers are often hungry, the waitresses must often put pressure on the chef. Therefore, one would expect from the chef attempts to maintain superiority on this one dimension—authority. This is precisely what Whyte found, leading in some cases to the institution of a high counter to separate the chef from the waitresses and to the installation of a spindle so that waitresses could write out the order, place it on the spindle for the chef to read, and thus avoid any talking at all. Other studies have concluded that status congruence or crystallization (Lenski, 1954) is related to sociability on the job (Clark, 1958) and work effectiveness (Adams, 1953–1954).

Functional theory. Functional theory describes industrial organizations in terms of the model of a social system—a set of elements in a state of interdependence. In Parsons' (Parsons, 1953, pp. 395–397; Parsons, Bales, & Shils, 1953, pp. 183–186; Parsons & Smelser, 1956, pp. 46–51) view, all systems must solve certain basic problems in order to survive. The major problems, described in many places, are these: adaptation, goal attainment, integration, and pattern-maintenance and tension-management. Further, the various levels in industrial organizations are specialized in terms of these problems. The *technical* level, where the product of the organization is made or the service provided, is concerned with attaining the goals of the organization and adapting it to its environment. The *managerial* level integrates the organization, while the top or *institutional* level (board of directors) relates the organization to the larger society, thus legitimating it and providing for pattern-maintenance. The consequence is that each of these levels does not, in fact, "supervise" the next lower level, for each deals with problems of a wholly different order. Functional theory, in its many forms, Parsonian and other, has been highly influential in industrial relations research.

Interaction theory. Interaction theory is distinguished by its concentration on direct, face-to-face relationships in industrial organizations. In part, the approach is a legacy of human relations theory, but a distinctive perspective has been developed. Whether face-to-face nonmediated relationships are the major forms that relationships take in industrial organizations or not, and whatever the extent to which they can be generalized to mediated relationships, there is no question that a great many relationships are of this form, and consequently generalizations may be developed for them. Goffman's work may be conceived of as interactional since its concern is, for the most part, with what happens when persons directly encounter each other. He described an "establishment" as analyzable in terms of five distinct perspectives (Goffman, 1959, pp. 239–242): "technical" (seeing the organization in terms of efficiency and inefficiency), "political" (the deprivations, indulgences, and other means of social control), "structural" (the horizontal and vertical status divisions), "cultural" (the values relating to ultimate ends and normative restrictions on means), and "dramaturgical" (the techniques of impression management, and the means used by persons in the organization to establish identities). The dramaturgical perspective occupied Goffman's attention most. Whatever a person's intentions may be, he must somehow communicate those intentions to relevant others. Thus, the person who would be sincere cannot assume that his sincerity will simply shine through by virtue of the intensity of his feelings. He must express this sincerity in a perceptible manner and this means that part of what he does will be a performance. It may, of course, be "natural" and unconscious. So, too, power, in order to be effective, will have to be made visible to be sure that the possibility of its use is evident.

Another variant of interaction theory with special applicability to industrial relations is offered by a scheme used by Whyte (1951; 1959; 1961, Ch. 2) and Homans (1950; 1961). Three major elements—activities, interaction, and sentiments—are seen as a system, acting and reacting on each other. Activities include the things done while at work, Whyte giving particular attention to the question of who initiates or begins an activity. Interaction, it is claimed, can be observed and quantified (amount, frequency, and distribution). In addition, one can describe the person who initiates inter-action, a subject of importance in studying delegation of authority (Lawrence, 1958). To Whyte, sentiments make up a personal frame of reference through which the person perceives, interprets, and evaluates the world around him and his place in it. Homans uses the term sentiments to refer to emotions, feelings, and other internal states of the body. Whyte gave particular attention as well to the role of symbols in mediating human interaction. Symbols may activate sentiments (for example, pride in a company product), they may directly trigger activities (paying particular attention when a supervisor enters the room), or they may activate certain kinds of interaction (treating persons in different positions differently). Such social characteristics as sex, age, seniority, ethnicity, race, religion, and education are described in terms of their symbolic effects. There are also symbols of organization such as a uniform or insignia or the special foods for which a restaurant may be famous.

Though Whyte was usually at pains to find out how activities, interaction, and sentiments may each affect each other, much of his research has been concerned with showing how sentiments may be the dependent variable. If one desires to alter workers' sentiments toward management (as in an incentive system), a useful approach is not only to work on those sentiments directly through propaganda or other appeals, but to change the activities in which persons engage or to change their pattern of interaction. For example, he showed how sentiments toward an incentive system have been altered by bringing the time-study man into the structure of the suggestion-making process (Whyte, 1955). Homans treatment of the relationship among the three sets of variables is rather different from Whyte's. In an earlier work Homans (1950) gave attention to the "external system," by which was meant the relationships among the variables necessary for system survival. Whyte criticized this idea and Homans himself has since abandoned it.

Interaction theory, when applied to small groups, has led to much experimentation under controlled conditions since the smallness of the groups makes it possible to bring persons together in a laboratory. Other influential interaction theories were described by Bakke (1950; 1951; 1953; 1959), Argyris (1957; 1959; 1962), Likert (1961), and their colleagues.

Decision-making theory. Although not widely used by sociologists, decision-making theory (Barnard, 1938; Cyert & March, 1963; March & Simon, 1958; Simon, 1947; Simon, 1957; Simon, Smithburg & Thompson, 1950) has affected much of their work in industrial relations. A decision is not simply a choice among alternatives, but a conclusion drawn from premises. If a person makes a decision *for* somebody else, he states the premises which the other person must accept as given and from which the other may then infer what his own line of action should be. A decision also differs from a simple choice in the explicitness with which the possible alternatives are thought through and spelled out. In Simon's (1947; 1957) view, the organization is conceived of as a mechanism designed to maximize the likelihood of *rational* decision-making. But there are a variety of types of rationality.

. . . a decision may be called "objectively" rational if *in fact* it is the correct behavior for maximizing given values in a given situation. It is "subjectively" rational if it maximizes attainment relative to the actual knowledge of the subject. It is "consciously" rational to the degree that the adjustment of means to ends is a conscious process. It is "deliberately" rational to the degree that the adjustment of means to ends has been deliberately brought about by the individual or by the organization. A decision is "organizationally" rational if it is oriented to the organization's goals; it is "personally" rational if it is oriented to the individual's goals (Simon, 1947, pp. 76–77).

An industrial concern attempts to maximize

the probability that *organizationally* rational decisions will be made. The organization does this in a variety of ways: It limits the responsibilities of each person so that the area in which he is expected to make rational decisions is curtailed, it provides guidelines such as information and formal rules so that the official need not seek alternatives outside those broadly specified, and it seeks persons who are already trained to make organizationally rational decisions, such as professionals, or it may seek to indoctrinate persons through its own on-the-job training programs.

Decision-making theory has lent itself particularly well to mathematical analysis of organizations, for example, through the use of Markov chains, and with computer simulation. As Blau and Scott (1962, p. 38) point out, the net effect of this point of view is to focus attention on the individual rather than on social structure. It has, however, led to important insights into the structure of authority in organizations.

Conflict theory. Although far from being a dominant approach in sociology at present, conflict theory assumes particular importance as a corrective for other approaches, especially functional theory which is criticized for its neglect of problems of social change and for ignoring conflict itself. Berger (1962) attempted to explain the continuing wide appeal of Parsons' approach by suggesting that the approach ". . . gives to one a sense of the essential orderliness of society and culture with their profound resources for containing and absorbing disruptive forces, a sense of the adaptive genius, the 'wisdom,' inherent in the organization of social and cultural systems" (Berger, 1962, p. 513). Hence conflict and change are interferences with order or temporary stages on the road toward order. By contrast, conflict theory sees any order as a temporary equilibrium or shaky peace which may be upset by new forces at any time.

Conflict theory has a venerable history in sociology, being exemplified by the works of such men as Marx, Sumner, Bagehot, Ratzenhofer, Gumplowicz, Small, and Oppenheimer. Representative conflict views applicable to industrial relations have been offered by Dalton (1959), Boulding (1962), Krupp (1961), and Coser (1956). The various elements in organizations are viewed as empires under the domain of chiefs, each of whom struggles to increase his own power and the power of the department under him. Rules and other structural elements are essentially the laws of war, useful mainly for predicting what the opponent may do next. An organization sets goals but is usually uncertain as to what is the most effective way of attaining them. For example, it may not be at all clear whether it is to the organization's interest to be sales-oriented or production-oriented. Persons in positions of power in the organization may make a decision that the organization shall move in the direction of emphasizing sales. It then becomes the task of the production men to prove that production is at least as important as sales, if not more so. Consequently, such a decision is simply the signal for the production-oriented personnel to show that the decision was incorrect or should be abridged or restricted in some way.

Organizations, therefore, are seen as places in which men battle for their share of the scarce goods or other valued products which the organization produces. Coser (1956) presented a rather paradoxical attempt to blend the points of view of functionalism and conflict theory. Conflict, he insisted, is not only a way of looking at an organization or society as a whole, but in fact is functional for the survival of the society. He pointed out that conflict increases identification with the group and that conflict is in many cases (for example, the courtroom) institutionalized as the major method whereby issues may be brought out into the open and squarely faced. Such a view of conflict is most evident in the collective bargaining process.

A somewhat similar position was taken

by Dubin (1958, Ch. 8) when he spoke of constructive aspects of industrial conflict. Consequently, issues that divide labor and management, such as the question of worker control over decision-making rights and the portion of the returns that will accrue to labor, will inevitably be subjects of dispute and will not be eliminated by increasing understanding between the two parties. Mediators may point out wherein the conflict dividing the two parties is nonrealistic, but the effect will be to bring the actual differences into the open rather than to eliminate the conflict itself. From this point of view, ". . . the strike in present-day American society is a component of the collective bargaining system, which in turn is an essential feature of the enterprise system. Collective bargaining would have little meaning were it not for the possibility of a strike, with attendant losses on both sides, since there would be little pressure on the parties to modify their positions and reach agreements" (Kornhauser, Dubin, & Ross, 1954, p. 12).

The recent (early 1960's) pressure in the United States on labor and management to decrease strike activity on the grounds that strikes are "barbaric" and that they may hamper the United States in its ability to compete with other countries, raises the question, however, of how "natural" strikes themselves are. The statutory strike, for example, has been proposed as a way of having the benefits of the strike without the cost to the consumer. In such a strike, a daily fine equivalent to the estimated daily cost of a strike would be levied on the two parties, but work would go on as usual. Such a device is intended to encourage a speedy settlement of the dispute. If the strike or its functional equivalent were done away with, however, the conflict theorist would maintain that the issues that divide labor and management would remain and that the conflict would be shifted to another area. Governmental intervention does not settle disputes but only changes the locus of their occurrence.

IMAGES OF MAN AT WORK

Identity and Work Life

To some persons, their occupation is a large component of their identity. Such an identification is often spoken of as a "vocation" and refers to the situation in which the person sees his work as a burden and feels an obligation to try to be especially good or proficient. It is not surprising that the term is used most commonly among the clergy, although persons in some of the professions take a similar attitude. A special problem is presented by situations in which the hoped for enthusiasm gets out of hand. Thus, Barrett (1927, p. 327), an ex-Jesuit, described how the Order punished him for getting overexcited about his research on psychoanalysis by assigning him to teach spelling, reading, and recitation to little country boys in an out-of-the-way village in Ireland.

At the other extreme is the casual attitude. The individual looks upon the occupation for its money and prestige and would change readily to a different job if a higher wage or other inducement were offered. His work does not enter much into his personality. Most workers fall somewhere in between the two extremes. Bakke (1939) described the situation among unemployed skilled workers. When they first became unemployed, they did not immediately seek any job but preferred to wait a while before accepting a job very different from the one they regarded as their own. For such skilled workmen, with some identification with their craft, changing occupations meant changing self-conceptions.

The extent to which one's work enters into one's identity was examined empirically by Dubin (1956) through the use of a "central life-interests" schedule. He asked a number of industrial workers in three midwestern plants a set of 40 questions. For example, What would the respondent hate most: "missing a day's work, missing a meeting of an organization he belongs to, missing almost anything he usually does?" If a person checked the first of these, this was considered a job-oriented response. If he checked the second, it was considered to be a non-job response, and the third, an indifferent response. When Dubin summed up the pattern of responses to all of his questions, he found that only 24 per cent of all workers were job-oriented in their life interest. He wrote: "Three out of four of this group of industrial workers did not see their jobs and work places as central life interests for themselves. They found their preferred human associations and preferred areas of behavior outside of employment" (Dubin, 1956, p. 135). The Central Life Interests questionnaire tapped four areas. The first referred to informal group experiences, with questions such as whether he would rather take his vacation with his family, with work friends, or by himself; whether it hurt him more to be disliked by "the people at work," by "the people around town," by "anyone I know." Dubin found that only 9 per cent of the industrial workers in the sample prefer the informal group life that is centered on the job.

A second group of questions dealt with activities that gave the worker pleasure, satisfaction, or general rewards. They were asked about "the most important things I do," "my worries," and the like. In this case only 15 per cent of the workers gave job-oriented preferences. The work place, therefore, seems to be relatively unimportant as a place of preferred primary human relationships and, in addition, does not seem to be able to evoke significant sentiments and emotions from workers. On the other hand, Dubin (1956) did find that the work organization itself was preferred over other organizations that the person belonged to. Sixty-one per cent chose their companies as the most meaningful context when their life experiences in organizations were brought into focus. Finally, the questionnaire probed the extent to which the work experience was their most important contact with the technical aspects of their environ-

ment. For example, a question asked whether noise bothers them most: "when working at home," "when working at the plant," "hardly ever." Here 63 per cent of the respondents were scored as job-oriented. Dubin concluded:

Industrial man seems to perceive his life history as having its center outside of work for his intimate human relationships and for his feelings of enjoyment, happiness, and worth. On the other hand, for his experiences with the technological aspects of his life space and for his participation in formal organizations, he clearly recognizes the primacy of the work place. In short, he has a well developed sense of attachment to his work and work place without a corresponding sense of total commitment to it (Dubin, 1956, p. 140).

Orzack (1959) examined the applicability of Dubin's (1956) generalizations to a group of 150 professional nurses. He speculated that professionals would be expected to have a greater interest in their work and that it should therefore occupy a more central position in their life's interest. The findings partially confirm his expectations. On the questions dealing with the importance of the organization one works for and the importance of work as providing contact with the technical environment, his results parallel those of Dubin. Nurses, like industrial workers, regard their work organization as the most important formal organization they belong to and the technical contacts at work as the most important contacts they have with the technical environment. On informal relations, the results for nurses are in the direction of Dubin's results, but they are not as striking. Whereas 91 per cent of Dubin's industrial workers felt their most important informal relations were off the job, only 55 per cent of the nurses did. Finally, whereas 85 per cent of Dubin's workers received their important personal satisfactions in nonwork areas, two-thirds of Orzack's nurses found theirs in their work. He speculated that training as professionals helps instill deeply felt motivation toward seeking personal satisfaction in work. Orzack (1959) also speculated that study of other kinds of professionals may not yield the same results. For example, in fields such as optometry or dentistry, in which persons practice in a setting outside of large organizations and where one's co-workers are typically not colleagues, the optometrists or dentists may prefer to relax with persons who are neither professional peers (whom they do not interact with much anyhow) nor nonprofessional work associates. Such persons might show much less orientation to their work than was shown by the nurses.

Within recent years the concept of alienation in work, as early developed by Marx (Fromm, 1961), has become highly popular (Arendt, 1958; Bell, 1960, Ch. 16; Pappenheim, 1959). Marx described alienation in an objective sense, referring to company rather than worker ownership of machines and tools, company rather than worker ownership of the total product, company ownership of the plant itself, and the relatively small contribution of the worker to the actual product. Recent discussions of alienation have turned attention to the subjective aspects of the subject.

Blauner (1962) applied certain distinctions made by Seeman (1959) to a variety of industrial settings. Blauner saw alienation as a fragmentation in which the person is used as a "thing." It includes five major dimensions: powerlessness, meaninglessness, normlessness, isolation, and self-estrangement. Blauner maintained that simply asking whether any particular group of workers is "more alienated" than any other group ignores the types and degrees of alienation by industry. He, therefore, examined the research on a craft industry, in particular printing (other examples would be building construction, aircraft manufacturing, and shipbuilding), a machine or machine-tending industry, in particular textiles (other examples would be the apparel industry and leather goods manufacturing, especially of shoes), assembly-line industry, in particular automobile assembly (other examples would

be the electrical equipment industry, electronics, canning, meat-packing, and processing of dairy products), and continuous process industry, in particular the chemical industry (another example would be oil refining).

On the dimension of powerlessness, Blauner (1962) found that printers are hardly alienated at all. They control the pace at which they work, select the tools and techniques to carry out the job, control the quality and even the quantity of work output, within limits. The degree of freedom and control of workers in machine industry is much less. Here the pace and rhythm of work is set by the machine or the organization of the tasks. Supervision is typically close and there is little opportunity to vary the manner in which the work is done. As celebrated in many studies, this kind of powerlessness reaches an extreme in the case of the assembly-line technology of the automobile worker, although it should be noticed that the control here comes from an impersonal line rather than from a personal supervisor. The situation, however, reverses itself in the case of automated continuous process technology. Workers are free to carry on routine monitoring tasks at their own pace, providing everything is going well. Process operators feel that they control the technology rather than that the technology controls them.

On the dimension of meaningless, the printers again feel little if any alienation. The skilled compositor works on the whole product rather than a small part of it. In machine industries the portion of the product is much reduced and here the alienation is greater. The tendency again reaches its extreme with the automobile worker, whose sense of purpose and function is reduced to a minimum. In the case of the chemicals industry, the work becomes meaningful again. Attention focuses on the process rather than the individual job. The worker's role changes from that of providing a needed skill to that of accepting a responsibility.

On the third and fourth dimensions,

normlessness and isolation, Blauner (1962) found the four industrial types differing not only in degree but also in basis. The degree of normative integration and cohesiveness decreases as one moves from craft to assembly line technologies but rises again with the continuous process of technology. The differences are not so great on this dimension, in part because other bases of integration exist. In textiles the location of the plant in a small town and the persistence of traditional paternalistic relationships between workers and management preserve strong integrative forces, whereas in the assembly-line technology unionization and bureaucratic structures provide strong links between workers and the organization. In regard to self-estrangement, industries clearly differ. Craft technology allows for self-expression and personal growth. In machine technology, monotony is a problem. Blauner, however, found that the self-estranging tendencies are in fact minimal because much of the unskilled work is taken over by women, and women, he suggested, are less likely to have aspirations for challenging and creative *work* activity. In addition, the worker's integrated role in the life of the community and its institutions helps reduce self-estrangement. Automobile assembly-line technology is the most self-estranging of all, he found, but in continuous process technology, the curve reverses. There are periods of routine, but these are followed by periods of frantic intense activity whenever breakdowns occur.

Blauner (1962) concluded that the burden of proof is on the investigator who claims that the modern manual worker has become alienated from his work. Certainly, he suggested, there are major variations in type of industry and degree of alienation as well as in kind of alienation. He did not find much evidence of a widespread normlessness, or isolation. Powerlessness is more common, but he raised the question of its significance, for although the person may not own his tools or the product, he may not be particularly interested in doing so. The problem of

meaninglessness is more serious, and the same is probably true of self-actualization.

Research has also concerned itself with the identities that conflict with work identity. Persons may develop loyalties to a cause, to an outside group, to the organization in which they work, and to their clients. Identification with a cause frees a person from the controls of the colleague group. Consequently, persons who are in the forefront of new developments in occupations are in continuous danger of being thought of as quacks. If one identifies with one's colleagues, one learns to keep certain silences, and one of the most important of these concerns new developments in the field. The accepted procedure is to let one's colleagues pass judgment on new things. If one takes the new idea or technique to the public, as, for example, did Nurse Sister Kenny, one is rejecting one's colleagues and their opinions. The resulting criticism may be harsh, and this should not be surprising. Identifications with groups altogether outside one's occupation include ethnic or racial identifications, feminist identifications, and identifications with labor unions.

Ethnic or racial identifications often turn up with the entry of ethnic or racial groups into an occupation previously pre-empted by another ethnic or racial group. For example, the first Negro personnel man in a factory must face the question: What is he, a personnel man or a Negro? Often he has had to fight to receive this position and consequently his identification with his colleagues is strong. What should he do when he discovers that all of the "race" questions are automatically referred to him, or what if he discovers that there is in fact a quota on Negroes on certain jobs? Should he notify Negro leaders in the community? If he does not and he is found out (as he is likely to be), he will be accused by the Negroes of deserting them. On the other hand, if he does inform them, it is likely that his colleagues will reject him as a person who cannot be trusted to keep his mouth shut. So, too, the woman in personnel work is usually hired because there are a large number of women in the plant, and she is to provide "the woman's point of view." Should she be a feminist and fight for the rights of women or identify with her personnel colleagues?

Certain union leaders come to think of themselves primarily as unionists rather than as workers, and the identification with the union may become a ladder of its own which some people will elect to try to climb. Identification dilemmas may revolve about position in the organization. Many studies have pointed to the foreman's marginal role as the workers' representative to management and as the first line of management to the workers (Roethlisberger, 1945; Strauss, 1957; Walker, Guest & Turner, 1956; Whyte & Gardner, 1945; Wray, 1949). In the case of identification with the client, one gets a distinction like that found by Hall (1948) between "colleague type" physicians and "individualistic type" physicians. This is a distinction between the man oriented to his colleagues and the man oriented to his patients (often because he has no alternative). The former does not have to be aggressive about getting patients since the referral system keeps him busy; the latter must attract patients directly, a much more difficult job. Among college professors one gets, occasionally, "the student man," who spends much time counseling students or helping them put on dances, to the possible neglect of teaching or research. Finally, attention is called to the fact that incentive systems are closely related to identities. Hence, their relative success or failure is often contingent on the extent to which identities are in fact tapped.

The Moral Structure of Work Relationships

Mills (1951) divided all philosophies of work into two categories: The various forms of Protestantism (and their secular derivatives) which saw work as a means to salvation (or to some external reward) and the Renaissance view which saw work as intrinsically meaningful, creative, and satisfying in its own right. Work is neither of those to present-day workers. "If there is little Calvinist compulsion to work, among propertyless factory workers and file clerks, there is also little Renaissance exuberance in the work of the insurance clerk, freight handler, or department store saleslady" (Mills, 1951, p. 219). Nevertheless, the kinds of meaning which work comes to have for persons have shifted rather than vanished. Work retains a distinctive moral structure.

The view of work as essentially instrumental or contractual suggests a picture of the worker as offering a segment of his personality to his employer. He does what is expected of him—no more, no less—and in exchange receives income or other compensation. However, although he be only paid for his behavior in one of his roles, he takes his whole self with him to the work situation. When he asks for a raise, it is likely to be not only on the basis of his competence or the job he has done, but also on the basis of family or other personal needs. Industry itself does not really behave as economically as it claims it does. Persons are chosen for positions not only on the basis of competence but on the basis of race, sex, religion, and other criteria which have little relationship to the job itself, but which have become traditionally attached to the job. Thus, Williams (1946), in a famous study of the preferences of patients for physicians by race and sex, found both men and women, white and Negro, preferring that their physician be a white male. So, too, Malinowski pointed out long ago that when the Trobriand Islanders were preparing a canoe for a voyage on the open sea, they insisted that certain magic had to be performed or the canoe might sink. They were not, however, so stupid as to go out in a canoe that had been properly blessed but had a hole in it.

So one thinks, then, of the requirements of a job as referring to technical qualifications on the one hand and moral qualifications on the other. Industry presents the paradox that it respects the moral conceptions of its employees, its customers, or imposes its own. But the logic of industrialism forces it to be much less discriminating than it might prefer. It must have large numbers of workers, and they must be competent. Consequently, it is forced to take persons of every race, religion, and sex. Industry has helped to break up castes in India, change the pattern of race relations in the United States, and dissolve cultures wherever it goes.

The moral connection never vanishes entirely; it only changes. A striking example is provided by the sex-typing of occupations. It has become a commonplace to point out that an increasing proportion of women are working and that women are invading more and more traditionally male areas. When such invasion occurs, however, the net effect is usually to make these jobs into "women's jobs"; when women move into an area they take it over. The concentration by sex in occupations is one of the most striking of all the demographic characteristics of the labor force (National Manpower Council, 1957, pp. 58ff.). Approximately 20 occupations account for nearly three-quarters of all employed women; over one-half of the women are in 8 occupations. In addition, the occupations in which women are found tend to be dominated by women: Nearly one-half of all working women are in occupations in which three-quarters or more of the workers are women. Sex-typing goes even further since the figures for a whole occupation often understate the amount of concentration. For example, while one-quarter of all teachers are men and three-quarters women, there is segregation within the occupation. Most men teach in high schools and most women in elementary schools. Within the high school the discrimination goes on: The physical sciences and some of the social sciences are usually taught by men, while languages and literature are mainly the concern of women. Even more difficult to explain in rational or instrumental terms is the fact that what is regarded as a man's job in one city is considered a woman's job in a nearby city. In 1950, 43 per cent of the persons who waited on tables in New York City were men, whereas 85 per cent in Philadelphia were women.

A special form of the moral structure of work is provided by the stratification of work activities. Specific attention will be given to this subject below. Here attention will merely be called to the fact that specialties are stratified in strange ways. Under the law, all physicians are physicians, but this fact does not prevent the formation of a college of surgeons or an association of pediatricians which are then ranked with reference to one another. In the ministry or priesthood one finds "church-builders," "clean-up men" (clergymen skilled in arranging the settling of church debts), "peace-men" (who know how to patch up splits and cleavages), "example-setters" (for those clergymen who have not quite lived up to moral expectations), and "funeral preachers." So, too, in an academic department of sociology there are the specialties that are publicly visible (criminology, social theory, the family) and these may sometimes be stratified. But there are also informal specialties (the scholar, the outstanding teacher, the good administrator, the research operator) and, these, too, differ in standing. From these specialties it is but a step to others which are a consequence of segregation by race, religion, sex, or any other category valued by the society. Thus, the notion that Negro physicians treat Negro patients does not describe the facts, for the division of labor between Negro and white physicians includes also the handing on to Negroes of cases of whites suffering from venereal or other shameful diseases. The Negro lawyer gets very little white practice and not much more Negro practice.

To the poor Negro, the law is trouble to be got out of. A lower-class Negro wants to win an insurance case against a utility or an employer. A Negro woman has a son in jail and wants to get him out. They often believe that a white lawyer can manipulate all these institutions better than a Negro lawyer could: it is, after all, a white man's world. . . . On the other hand, the middle-class Negro wants a divorce which has already been agreed upon; he wants a deed, articles of partnership or incorporation, or advice regarding a contract. It is "friendly" law. He goes to the Negro lawyer and feels very loyal to his race (Hughes & Hughes, 1952, pp. 96–97).

So, too, the middle classes of many ethnic and racial minorities achieved their place by earning a living serving their own peoples. So they are sometimes accused of having a stake in continued segregation. Such phenomena give credence to the concept of a moral division of labor in society. Further support for the concept may be secured by examining the strenuous attempts of industrial managements everywhere to seek a justification for their right to command others. Such justification is not sought merely to quiet their consciences. For if their power can be legitimized, the probability of obedience to their commands is increased (Bendix, 1954; Bendix, 1956, Ch. 7; Berliner, 1957; Kerr, Dunlop, Harbison, & Myers, 1960; Moore, 1962, pp. 8–10). Thus are moral and technical elements blended.

INDUSTRY IN SOCIETY: THE WORK COMPLEX

Goal Definition

That which is a goal or an end, to persons inside an organization, is a means or facility to those outside. Customers, for example, make use of the industry's product to satisfy needs of their own or, if the outsiders are other organizations, the industry's products may provide the raw materials with which they work. Viewed thus, defining the goal of an industrial organization is essentially a matter of "determining a relationship of the organization to the larger society, which in turn becomes a question of what the society (or elements within it) wants done

or can be persuaded to support" (Thompson & McEwen, 1958, p. 23). As such, goal setting is a dynamic problem since goals are being continually altered in the light of changes in the organization's environment or society or, often, of changes in the organization itself (Perrow, 1961). If a goal is the means by which an organization relates itself to the environing society, this raises the question of the legitimation of the organization. For business organizations in America the major legitimating circumstance has been the ability to make a profit and stay in business. Many businesses producing luxury products, goods which could only be sold with a high-pressure advertising campaign or even products that are directly harmful, could still remain in business if they passed this test. Yet even to make a profit a business organization must pay some attention to the state of public attitudes to their products or to the company itself, else it might face the danger of governmental control. Consequently, the general question of the feelings of customers and of the general public toward business firms is not irrelevant to the process of goal definition.

It is not known whether popular conceptions of business have changed or not. The fictional literature of the past is full of "robber barons" and "money changers." Jones (1953) felt that, although the present literary conception of the businessman is not flattering, he is depicted less as evil than as frustrated and unhappy. The results of the many polls which have attempted to tap opinions have not been unfavorable to business. During the depression, a poll (conducted in 1937) found that 75 per cent of the persons with an opinion gave favorable answers to a question asking whether big business concerns were good or bad for the country (Cantril & Strunk, 1951, p. 335). A careful study by the Survey Research Center (1951) of the University of Michigan in 1950 reported similar results. Seventy-six per cent believed that the advantageous effects of business outweighed the disadvantageous effects. When asked to give their conception of the actual power position of big business in comparison to small business, labor unions, state government, and national government, only 13 per cent felt that big business was the most powerful of this group, although most persons were not eager for business to become any more powerful than it was; 46 per cent believed that big business pays higher wages than smaller business; 53 per cent felt that it provided more job security; while 78 per cent believed that it helped create jobs. There was considerable public skepticism regarding the fairness of business profit. Seventy-one per cent found profits excessive.

This finding has been confirmed in other polls. Special polls directed at farmers report that more than half of the respondents maintained that prices were set according to the manufacturer's pleasure rather than by free and open competition (Hickman & Kuhn, 1956, pp. 118–119). Clergymen were asked in a poll how well they felt business met its obligations and responsibilities. The businessmen came out fairly well; only 24 per cent believed that business did not discharge its responsibilities adequately. Over half of the clergymen, however, believed that most businessmen try to keep prices as high as they can (Hickman & Kuhn, 1956, pp. 119–120). Such findings suggest that business occupies an accepted place in American society but this acceptance is not enthusiastic. Business remains suspect because of memories of the depression of the thirties, because of the ethic of "let the buyer beware," and because business has been subjected to legal and governmental control in a number of striking cases (Glover, 1954).

An important kind of legitimation takes place through the ties of business organizations with one another. Thompson and McEwen (1958) described relationships among organizations in terms of four strategies: competition, bargaining, co-optation (in which threatening elements are added to the leadership of the organization), and coalition. Each form of strategy is a way of securing the support of the other organization, but as one moves from bargaining through coalition there is less and less independence of operation. The examination of relationships between organizations raises the question of how organizations interact with one another. Overlapping memberships exist on boards of directors and in interlocking directorships. A study by Goldner (1960) of labor relations representatives conceived of those representatives as playing "boundary roles." Though members of the firm, their continued interaction with unions leads to their being viewed by line management as representing the union's viewpoint. The unions also regarded them with suspicion, feeling that they knew a great deal about the union but obviously could not be counted upon to support it. This marginal position is used by labor relations men in performing their duties. They are able to carry trial balloons back and forth in order to get a reaction from the other side without committing either management or the union.

Interorganizational analysis is one of the most needed types of inquiry in industrial relations. Litwak and Hylton (1962) suggested that key variables are awareness, standardization, degree of interdependence, and number of organizations. Where there is great interdependence between organizations, the tendency is toward organizational merger. On the other hand, where there is little standardization but high interdependence and awareness, professionalistic models (for example, a hospital) develop. Where interdependence is moderate, they see a variety of possibilities. In the case of a large number of organizations with high awareness and high standardization, one will get the development of fair price laws, directories of agencies, and the like. Under the same conditions but where standardization is low, one will get permanent arbitrators for grievances. In the case where there is moderate interdependence but low awareness and high standardization, one may get informal cooperation between members of different organizations handled as friendship favors. Should there be a high degree of awareness, numbers remaining small, one gets the situation found in dental care or unemployment, where information is handled by a family agency in a small community by informal telephoning rather than through the use of directories. Although one would expect that relationships among business organizations would be determined by commercial advantage, in time a structure would be expected to develop in which relationships would be controlled by norms other than business norms. Business firms, like other kinds of organizations, desire predictability and dependability of supplies. Also one may be able to use friendship and the ties of tradition in order to secure more favorable terms than one could otherwise secure. Durkheim's (1947) well-known discussion of such noncontractual elements in contracts has been further developed by Macaulay (1963).

Industrial and Occupational Trends

The major trends over the last half-century are clear. Clerical and professional workers have shown striking proportionate increases. Semiskilled workers showed a similar trend until recently (they actually declined proportionally between 1950 and 1960). Skilled workers have increased their proportion of the working force more slowly, failing to keep pace with the total increase between 1950 and 1960. Proprietors, managers, and officials have barely held their own, and unskilled workers have been declining in numbers (Fichlander, 1955; Gross, 1958, Ch. 3).

The great increase in clerical workers has been a result of two main influences: increase in the complexity of administrative activity (including business accounting and the emphasis on promotional and sales activity), and increase in complexity and growth of governmental services. The clerical workers are now a large part of the working force—approximately one-seventh (nearly one-fourth if one includes sales

workers)—and, as their numbers have increased, their prestige has declined. Because the machines that clerical workers make use of are relatively small and inexpensive, it is possible for this group, perhaps more than any other, to be trained in separate vocational schools. This produces a profound contrast with a great deal of factory work where unions may act as a control on the entry of the workers. There are comparatively few controls on the increase of clerical workers.

Although clerical workers constitute one of the largest of the categories of the labor force, they are among the most impotent politically. Not only are they poorly organized, but there remains strong among them a lingering hope of upward mobility because of their traditions and because of their closeness to management. Attempts to organize white-collar workers have not so far been as successful as they have been among factory workers, although in some places where unionization is strong (Seattle, for example) the proportion of unionized white-collar workers may also be high. Another reason for the lack of organized power in this group is its sex composition. Females make up a large proportion—60 per cent in 1962—and the position of females in the work situation remains ambiguous. Child-bearing may cut short or seriously limit a woman's earning ability, and normally a wife is expected to supplement the family income rather than to be its sole or main provider. Consequently, she is not so likely to have as strong a feeling of job identification as does her husband. But the situation is changing. The many labor-saving devices in the home, the marked decline in the birth rate (at least over the last half century), and the rise in facilities for looking after children have tended to change the work status of women. An increasing number of married women are taking permanent jobs (Nye & Hoffman, 1963, chs. 1–3).

The role of clerical workers in our society has not been sufficiently studied. They are not yet a powerful group, but they represent a great potential. It is this group which, as Corey (1945) pointed out, Marx underestimated. Rather than disappearing, it has grown even larger.

The striking increase in professional workers can be attributed to two major factors. The actual number of persons in traditional professions has increased, reflecting a greater emphasis on education, growing public awareness of the need for expertly trained persons, and greatly increased technological complexity of professional activities. Also, wholly new professions have emerged in such areas as public health, teaching, accounting, engineering, and social work. The largest increase within professional ranks has been among the professions related to industry—technical engineer, chemist, designer, and draftsman—many of which hardly existed in the nineteenth century.

The failure of proprietors, managers, and officials to do little better than hold their own as a proportion of the labor force can be traced to the inclusion in this category of disparate groups. A declining group has been the farmers, both owners and tenants, who have been making up a smaller and smaller proportion of all workers. As long ago as 1920, not only did the farmers decline proportionately but in actual number. A second reason for the slow growth of this category has been the lack of increase in self-employment. Owners of many small businesses have become skilled or semiskilled workers in someone else's employment. Members of middle management—the executives and the organization men—have become numerically more important with the growth of large-scale organization.

The changes in manual workers are closely interrelated. Those changes can be traced largely to the mechanization of work over the last half-century. The skilled worker has tended increasingly to become a machine operator who is classified as semiskilled, although the trend in this direction has not been sufficiently great to prevent a moderate increase in the proportion of skilled workers in the population. The unskilled worker who depends primarily on his muscles is actually declining in sheer numbers as his work is taken over by machines. Here the effects of the decline in craftsmanship and the rise of industry as a mode of organizing work are seen. The whole conception of "craft" is becoming obsolete. The company advertises not for a tailor but a sewing machine operator, not for a mechanic but a riveter or a punch-press operator. The extent to which this is true is illustrated in the United States Census classification of operatives. Some illustrations are: operatives in electric light power plants; operatives in gas works; operatives in lime, cement, and artificial stone factories; operatives in paint factories. One sees here the emergence of the industry, rather than the occupation, as the distinguishing feature.

As a consequence, the craft becomes less and less the unit of organization and is replaced by the industry, the process, or the machine. One finds the United Automobile Workers including within their ranks persons who have nothing at all to do with the making of automobiles. The Teamsters unions include clerks, employees of Boeing Aircraft, and salesmen. This trend gives an entirely new dimension to social organization. There is greatly decreased interest in beauty or fine workmanship—the machine takes care of those matters. Interest shifts to uniformity, the correct operation of the machine.

One gets, therefore, a picture of skills being increasingly transferred to the machine and less skill being required to operate it. This in turn means a decrease in the need for skilled workers and an increase in the need for semiskilled workers. The *designing* of these machines, however, becomes a highly complex activity and an activity of the *professional* group, producing the engineer and designer. The fact that a worker spends much of his time before a machine also raises questions of boredom and efficiency, requiring emergence of personnel men and other persons concerned with efficiency who also belong to the professional group.

Where crafts decline and work becomes uniform, the worker finds that his job yields little personal satisfaction or pride in workmanship—a familiar lament of observers of the industrial scene for half a century. Not so well known is the emergence of an increasing amount of data casting doubt on the *efficiency* of finely subdivided work (Friedmann, 1961). Some firms are beginning to reverse the trend, deliberately enlarging jobs which have reached what seemed to be a point of diminishing return in the division of labor. Still another trend has been for the finely subdivided job to disappear in the face of automation. Insofar as a job can be broken up into small units and the human contribution removed from it, it becomes that much easier to mechanize it and submit it to the control of the computer.

The *Manpower Report of the President* (1963) emphasized three main recent changes. First, the shift from goods-producing to service-producing industries has accelerated since 1957. The proportion of all workers in the goods-producing industries (agriculture, mining, manufacturing, and construction) dropped from 51 per cent in 1947 to 42 per cent in 1962. In contrast, growth has increased in the services (transportation and public utilities; trade; finance, insurance, and real estate; service and miscellaneous industries; and government). The most spectacular growth has been shown by government employment. The numbers rose from 5.5 million in 1947 to 9.2 million in 1962, a rate which is more than 2.5 times the rate of growth of all nonfarm employment. This growth has been chiefly in state and local government, which now employs about three-quarters of all government workers. The growth of government employment at the state and local level has been concentrated mostly in hospitals, sanitation services, and, most of all, education.

Farm employment continues its long-range drop, reaching a proportion of about 7 per cent of the labor force at present in contrast to the approximately 50 per cent of the labor force involved in agriculture in 1870. The picture for manufacturing is not clear. In 1870, the number of workers was less than half as great as those in agriculture. With each census year as agriculture lost numbers manufacturing registered gains until it reached the peak in 1920 of approximately 30 per cent of the working force. It has not gone appreciably above that percentage since, although it has continued to register numerical gains. In 1962, the number in manufacturing was 16.8 million, representing about 23 per cent of the labor force (27.7 per cent of employed persons). The fact that a constant or even a declining percentage of the labor force has been able to provide manufactured goods for a rapidly increasing population is a testimony to the enormous productivity of manufacturing. At the same time, the inability of manufacturing to exceed the 1920 proportion suggests that it has only been able to maintain its position as the largest industry division by virtue not only of the overall population increase but by the increased demand of that population for manufactured goods. Its continued growth will undoubtedly depend on the magnitude of that demand.

The second major shift has been the much faster growth of white-collar occupations over blue-collar occupations, not only in manufacturing but in the economy generally. In 1956, for the first time in United States history, professional, managerial, clerical, and sales employees actually outnumbered employees in manual occupations. In fact, the increase in white-collar workers accounted for most of the employment increase in all fields of work over the period since 1947. The third shift is the continued growth of the professions and other occupations requiring education and training while employment in unskilled jobs continues to drop. No important changes in these overall trends are anticipated for the near future.

The data on size of business organizations presents a paradox. Woytinsky (1953, p

342) estimated that no more than one-seventh of the farmers and one-half of the nonagricultural employers hire as much as one man-year of labor during a year. Data supplied by Spaulding (1961, p. 148) enable us to assess the distribution of firms by size. These data are provided in Table 1. From

TABLE 1

EMPLOYER FIRMS REPORTING TO OLD AGE
AND SURVIVORS INSURANCE,
AND THEIR EMPLOYEES,
BY SIZE OF FIRM, JANUARY–MARCH 1953
(in per cent)[a]

Size of Firm (number of employees)		Employers (firms)	Employees
0–	3	59.8	6.9
4–	7	20.4	7.4
8–	19	12.1	10.2
20–	99	6.4	17.7
100–	999	1.2	21.1
1,000–	9,999	0.1	18.6
10,000– or more		0.1	18.0
Total		100.00	100.00

[a] Source: Data provided by the Bureau of Old Age and Survivors Insurance, upon request. Taken from Spaulding (1961, p. 148).

this table a striking fact emerges. On the one hand, it is clear that the United States is a nation with many small firms. Over 90 per cent employ fewer than 20 workers, whereas those employing over 100 make up a trifle over 1 per cent of all firms. However, the 90 per cent of the firms that are small employ less than one-quarter of the employees, whereas the small group that have more than 100 employees employ close to 60 per cent of all workers. Hence, though firms are small on the average, most employees work for large firms. The various sizes of firms are distributed differentially in different industries. Smaller concerns predominate in farming, construction, retail trade, and services; larger organizations are found in manufacturing, utilities and communications, banking and finance, and insurance.

Trend data on size of businesses is not easy to secure, in part because of differences of definition of small business. Taking advantage of the fact that unincorporated businesses are nearly all small, McKean (1958) used trend data on unincorporated firms to give an indication of the relative changes in the proportion that small firms make of the total number of firms. He found that between 1900 and 1955, unincorporated business units constituted from 84 to 90 per cent of all businesses. Although not increasing the proportion of employees that they account for nor increasing their power in other ways, the data clearly indicate a persistence of small business in United States society. Data on assets, income, and earnings support this conclusion.

Industry and the Family, the Community, and Government

The impact of industrialism on the Western family has been described by many researchers. Industrialism, it has been shown, helped to break the ties of peasant families to their farms and to stimulate the movement to urban living. At the same time it separated place of work from place of family and produced a division of labor and separation of roles between the various members of the family. The man became the breadwinner and the woman a housewife. As time went on, appropriate legislation and changed cultural emphases restricted children to the status of incompetent minors. By the time children were old enough to work they were also old enough to leave the family and establish their own household. The separation of generations in family roles thus became almost complete. The resulting dependence of the family on the economic efforts of the father consequently means that the social class level of the family is usually determined by the economic and class position of the father, and it is customary to assign every member of the family to the same social class. Children may rise above or fall below their parents' social class, but when they do so it is as heads of independent families. The extended family becomes less important, as a result in part of increased mobility and in part of the costs of land in the city, so that the various parts of a family are unable to afford to live under one roof. Since the family rests much less than formerly on ties of property or other claims of the extended family, its stability depends increasingly on compatibility of husband and wife, a consequence which leads to greater emphasis on the romantic complex and young people's independence than was the case previously in Western society.

Recent research has cast doubt on the extent to which some of these developments are characteristic of industrial society. Aldous (1962), Axelrod (1956), Young and Willmott (1957) and others suggested that the lending, visiting, and helping pattern among extended kin has not vanished even in the modern, industrial city. On the other hand, Greenfield (1961) presented data from Barbados which show that the small nuclear family can diffuse without industrialization or urbanization. Abegglen (1958) and Johnson (1960) described the way in which the unifying structure of the extended family can be neatly integrated with the industrializing process in Japan. Lenski (1963, pp. 219–220), while discussing data showing that strength of family ties is generally inversely related to occupational success, pointed to the paradox of Jewish families for whom the reverse is true. The explanation, he suggested, lies in the high incidence of family-owned and operated businesses among Jews. When working for a fellow member of the family, strength of attachment may enhance one's chances of success in the firm. Many writers have called attention to dynastic uses of the family to keep investment capital freely available to family members.

While it is true that the modern Western family is more mobile than families in other historical periods, migratory laborers have developed a pattern by which entire families, including extended kin, may migrate together. A similar picture was presented by Davis (1946) in his examination of lower-class families. For them the extended family is the major means of surviving individual catastrophes, such as loss of employment or loss of support. A member of such a large family expects that his kin will take care of him should he fall in need, and he in turn expects to take care of others should he be lucky enough to have a good job. Hence the family survives as a large unit when it could not survive as a set of small nuclear families.

Whyte (1955) pointed out that one of the main distinctions between the corner-boys and the college-boys in Cornerville was that the college-boys saved their money but the corner-boys shared theirs. In order to go to college they had to take any extra money and put it to one side for the future. From one moral point of view this was simply a provision for the future, but from the point of view of the corner-boys it was a selfish act which indicated a lack of concern for peers. Consequently, the tendencies of the college-boys to isolate themselves from the other boys was reinforced by the corner-boys themselves. It has also been claimed by researchers that the separation of the father from the family makes it more difficult for him to serve as a role model for his sons, since the type of work he does may be unknown to his son and impossible to explain. While this claim can easily be exaggerated (many occupations such as those in the building trades and others carried out in the open are not esoteric), even for cases where it is true, the father may be as important as ever. Faris (1947) suggested that the most important thing transmitted may be a set of drives and ambitions or a set of attitudes, and this surely is as likely to occur whether the son understands what the father does for a living or not. With rapid change in needed skills these attitudes may well be the most important things that the father can transmit to his son.

Considerable attention has been given to

the increasing number of married working women. Approximately one-third of married women are working, a figure that actually understates the true proportion since there is a tendency for most women to work in the early years of marriage, to stop working when their children are young, and then to come back into the labor force when their children begin to go to school and become able to take care of themselves for at least part of the day. Therefore, for married women in the older years, particularly in the thirties and forties, the proportion employed approaches one-half. It is still true that there is an inverse relationship between the likelihood of a wife's working and the economic level of her husband. The motives for working, Schneider (1957, pp. 441–442) suggested, probably vary by social class. In the upper- and upper-middle classes the wife works to relieve boredom, to fulfill some creative need, or to satisfy interests. She is likely to choose an occupation appropriate to her social class. Among women of lower socioeconomic levels, motives for working are likely to be more strongly economic, though the tradition of working may also be decisive. At the same time, ability to hold a job is made more difficult by virtue of the fact that the lower-class woman is unable to call upon domestic help such as the upper-class woman can.

Although the proportion of children working has greatly declined, it has not vanished even in the United States. The frequency officially employed between the ages of 10 and 15 is around 6 per cent for boys and about 3 per cent for girls, a high proportion of whom are found on farms. The extent of concealment of facts on employment of children has never been accurately measured, however, and these percentages may represent a considerable understatement. Indeed the emphasis in the middle-class family on early acquisition of appropriate attitudes toward business and salesmanship provides a justification for pushing youngsters into the labor market at tender ages. Among adolescents, there is a split between those who remain in school and those who drop out, the latter being by far the higher proportion. Jaffe and Stewart (1951, p. 123) reported that in 1950 close to one-half of the boys between the ages of 16 and 17 were already employed. The largest group of employed male adolescents (ages 14 to 19) is concentrated in operatives and kindred workers, while the largest number of girls is concentrated in clerical and kindred workers. These are the jobs with the poorest futures because they are most subject to technological displacement.

The role of the aged in industrial society has received increasing attention. Although the proportion of the population over 65 has been increasing, there has not been a corresponding increase in the proportion of older persons who are working. In fact, the trend has been the reverse. Thus, the average working life of white male workers is now about the same as it was 50 years ago (around 41 years), but the period in retirement has been extended from 9.5 years to 15.9 years. The proportion of persons 65 or over who are working has dropped from around two-thirds in the year 1900 to the present figure of just under 40 per cent. On the other hand, female employment participation among the elderly has been steady.

The distribution of the elderly in the various occupational groups is by no means even. Among the males, the older persons make up 6.5 per cent of managers, officials, and proprietors (except farm), but only 2.7 per cent of operatives and kindred workers. While the lower rates of retirement in the higher ranking occupations may possibly reflect greater life expectancy in those occupations, it is more likely, as Schneider (1957, p. 450) suggested, to reflect the ability of higher status men to control the age of their retirement. The increasing speed of technological change and the increasing emphasis on education produces further pressure on the tendency of industry to retire persons early. At the same time the prospect for large-scale programs of reeducation in the middle years becomes better.

Industry relates itself to the community in a variety of ways. Of importance to many industries are the traditional family work arrangements of people in the vicinity of the industry. Industries whose labor needs fluctuate may require a family system in which members of a family are willing, and accustomed, to shift rapidly from one type of work to another. Arensberg (1942) pointed out how the stability of plastics manufacturing plants in New England depends on a readiness of the working population to shift to farming when the demand for factory labor falls.

The location of industry has been much studied. The most crucial needs of industry are for an adequate source of power and cheap raw materials. If these two resources happen to be located near each other, the industry can be located there with minimum costs. Such was the case of Slocum's Hollow, which was a quiet Pennsylvania village until extensive coal deposits were discovered in 1840. Mine barracks were erected, tunnels dug, and the name changed to Scranton. Whether towns based on extractive industries survive depends largely on the value and extent of the resources. Some become ghost towns whereas others, such as Kimberley, South Africa, with its extensive diamond deposits, and Sudbury, Canada, with its enormous nickel resources, continue to maintain themselves. Besides being near raw materials and power, it is usually desired to locate near a good supply of labor, a market, and a source of capital. The latter three usually mean establishing in or near a city, and most factories are so located. Within the city, manufacturing firms tend to be found in two locations: near the center of the city and near the outskirts in industrial suburbs. The division is likely to be one between light manufacturing near the center, and heavy manufacturing in the outskirts because of the greater need of the latter for large amounts of space. Along with light manufacturing one also finds storage, wholesaling, and other kinds of industrial activities in which the machinery is light and can be located on the second or third floors of older buildings.

Industrial suburbs are of value not only because of low land costs, but also because the various industries can together do things which no one of them would be able to do by themselves. They can arrange for common parking space, power lines can be shared, and common arrangements made for the disposal of industrial waste products. Several industries can present a united front against protests of residents of the area against noise, smoke, and other noxious accompaniments of industrial production. The resistance of residential dwellers may lead to zoning ordinances so that industrial owners discover that they must locate near the old ones even if they do not wish to. With a large group of industries it becomes worthwhile for railroads to build spur lines into the suburb, so that the disadvantages of being far from the downtown freight depots are eliminated. The existence of such suburbs suggests a caution in viewing all suburbs as composed of middle-management people on their way up. The working-class suburb has been examined in works by Berger (1960) and Dobriner (1958; 1963).

One-industry towns, whether the one industry is a college, a gambling casino, the national government, or a manufacturing concern, though becoming less common, are still of interest sociologically. Their most striking feature is the antagonism and resentment between the industry and the town. Members of the community resent the hold the industry has on the fortunes of the town, and members of management resent the apparent lack of gratitude for the great boon the industry represents. Occasionally management will try to make its point by paying all workers in silver dollars. As these flood the community, it is hoped that merchants and businessmen will realize how much they owe to the industries present. Such symbolic devices are only likely to produce a sense of outrage. Forced awareness of dependence rarely produces gratitude.

When all business in the United States was small, local customs acted as major regulators of industrial affairs. Business tended to dominate the community not by a definite ideology which countenanced such dominance, but rather because government did not counterbalance business control. The great changes in the latter half of the nineteenth century in size of industry and growth of international markets led to a breakdown of local controls over business. Government became more important as the only institution capable of controlling industry in the interest of the community. Health hazards caused by smoke and dumping industrial waste were modified, and laws were enacted regulating working conditions. Nor was it entirely a matter of control. Expanding industry required and even demanded increased services from government, such as gas, sewage disposal, employment bureaus, educational facilities, transportation, and other kinds of special services. As time went on the government took an increasing role in the form of workmen's compensation and other wages and hours laws, control of labor-management relations, vehicle licensing, and other types of regulations such as those in interstate commerce, monopoly, and international trade. Form and Miller (1960, p. 147) pointed out that the view that all government regulation is simply interference with business is only partially valid, because many regulations are imposed at the request of industry. These include laws to ensure free trade, limit monopoly, provide tariff protections against foreign competition, and limit union power. Form and Miller predicted that business will inevitably find itself caught up in politics, since business will wish governmental services to continue, will want the costs of those services to be kept down, will want the government to be sympathetic to business, and will want to limit the power of organized labor. Business also has a stake in the role of the government as a major consumer of goods and services.

Industries, therefore, have found it necessary to form associations, such as the National Drygoods Association, the Association of American Railroads, the National Steel Institute, and the National Association of Manufacturers. Correspondingly, organized labor has from the beginning interested itself in politics, and in its early period made attempts to create a definite labor party and other types of radical parties. Since Gompers, labor has in general not advocated a third party, but this does not mean that it has not continued its interest in politics. The Political Action Committee of the Congress of Industrial Organization, Labor's League for Political Education of the American Federation of Labor (LLPE), and the Committee on Political Education (C.O.P.E.) of the AFL-CIO indicate labor's involvement in politics. Organized labor in the United States has become increasingly identified with the Democratic Party and has striven for power within that party.

Form and Miller (1960, p. 152) pointed to two important and sometimes contradictory roles that the government may play in the area of industrial relations. On the one hand, it acts in the public interest, intervening in disputes to assure a continued flow of goods and services. On the other hand, the government can and does swing its weight on one side or the other. It is also, as stated above, one of the major purchasers of goods and services and can by the threat of withdrawal of those services greatly influence the context of union-management relations.

Industrialization as Process

The increasing spread of industrialization to new countries has led to concern with the question of whether there may not be a distinctive form and structure which industrialism assumes all over the world irrespective of the particular society or the culture in which it may be found. Kerr, Dunlop, Harbison and Myers (1960), after a careful examination of the data, concluded that there is a "logic of industrialism." The industrialization process, they suggested, utilizes a level of technology far more complex than that of earlier societies. This requires that it have the support of research organizations such as universities, research institutes, laboratories, and specialized departments of enterprises. The industrial system requires a wide range of skill and professional competence broadly distributed throughout the work force. The creation of such a highly skilled professional labor force is one of the major requirements of the society in transition to industrialism, and its shortage is no less serious than a shortage of capital goods. The science and technology that go with industrialization in turn force continuing change on the society. The work force is confronted with repeated lessons in the general futility of fighting these changes. The industrial society thus tends to be an open society in which assignment to occupations takes place more according to ability and appropriateness than to caste, race, sex, or family status. "There is no place for the extended family in the industrial society; it is on balance an impediment to requisite mobility" (Kerr et al., 1960, p. 35). Other generalizations relate to the role of education, occupational differentiation, regularized discipline, government, the military, rules relating managers to subordinates, and a set of values (high value being assigned to science, education, mobility, pluralism, production, and hard work) (Kerr et al., 1960, Ch. 2).

Other students of industrialization have questioned the existence of a single logic of industrialism, suggesting instead that there may be several roads to industrialization. A frequently cited case is modern Japan which succeeded in building an industrial society while maintaining many traditionalistic elements, particularly the central position of the joint family. Belshaw (1960, p. 106) questioned the emphasis on rationalism, asking whether production may not be greater if the working force develops a sense of positive identification with the prosperity of the work organization. The need to adopt any particular set of values was questioned by Singer (1960, pp. 259–263), who pointed out that the late arrivals on the industrial scene are confronted by a different situation from their predecessors. The late arrivals can take advantage of an already developed industrial technology which can often be imported, can avoid the mistakes of the past, and can use new sources of energy such as nuclear and solar and hydroelectric dams, rather than duplicating the coal-based economy of the textile industry in early England. Furthermore, the state, having a more important role than formerly, may enable the society to avoid many of the experiences of the earlier industrializing countries. Hoselitz (1960, p. 228) found no evidence for a necessary incompatibility between the joint family and industrialism. The burden of proof would appear to be on those who insist that this family is incompatible with industrialism. In a reply to these criticisms, Kerr (1960) conceded that, at least for a time, there will be many differences among industrializing societies but insisted: "They will be much more nearly alike than preindustrial societies" (Kerr, 1960, p. 349).

Automation

Automation is not simply mechanization writ large. It adds two principal elements: continuous process, whereby parts move themselves along from one operation to the next, and self-control, in which machines feed information back so that the programed computer can make decisions, including those otherwise performed by inspectors and maintenance men. Although the most famous examples are provided by automatic data processing, other forms of information handling are coming to be used. Numerical control, a device which is well adapted to short-runs of materials, is a means whereby programs may be prepunched onto tape and the tape changed as the requirements change. Process control is used to handle problems in which persons must read many hundreds of dials or in which there are many changes taking place one after the other, such as shifts in traffic on different air strips or different roads. Information retrieval systems provide scientists with means for searching the literature in their area, compiling, editing, and analyzing statistical information, and providing the basis for translation machines for foreign languages.

The labor displacement effect of automation has become a subject of major national concern. The most vulnerable activities are the subdivided repetitive jobs, the most common of which are held by operatives and semiskilled workers in offices (filing and accounting) and factories. Many of the displaced employees no doubt shift to nonmechanized industries where they become semiskilled workers in service industries. Whether automation leads to an actual decline in employment is not clear. In the short run it may not, since automation is introduced not only to cut labor costs but also for two other reasons. It is often introduced to expand output without adding workers, and many firms that have been automating are able to report no loss of working force, sometimes even expansion. Of course, the ability to increase output depends on a rising demand for products over an indefinite future. Automation will also not produce a reduction in workers where it is used to do things humans cannot do, such as handling radioactive materials, or running an automatic pilot for a jet airplane.

Where genuine displacement occurs one may expect certain changes. First, the company is confronted with the choice between hiring new workers with proper training or retraining as many as possible of their present workers. Because of union pressure, community pressure, and management's own desire to reward loyalty, it usually tries to retrain existing workers. The experience so far with retraining efforts, carried on

either by industry or under the auspices of the government, has not been encouraging. A large part of the problem has been a low level of worker motivation to participate in the programs at all and perhaps a tendency for selection to be overly strict. There is also a problem of developing new self-concepts in persons who are forced to adopt a new career in their middle years. Another possible effect is that, since the company will not be able to keep all of its employees, its retirement and security benefit program will not be as strong an incentive as it has been in the past. Because of shrinking labor demands there will be a tendency for teen-agers to stay in school longer and probably for older persons to retire earlier. The net result would be a reduction in the length of the work life. With the increase in leisure time, and in the number of nonworkers, continued growth of the entertainment and leisure industries is to be expected. Whether employment in these latter industries will take up the slack created by displacement elsewhere will depend on the extent to which these industries are also mechanized.

Most of the new occupations created by automation appear to be professional or highly skilled. These are the occupations of persons who design the machines and service and repair them. Drucker (1957, p. 26) speculated that the factory of the future will have few workers on the floor, already seen in power generation and oil refining; workers will have done their tasks in advance (machine building, installation) or will be called in when breakdowns occur. The number of programers and controllers is not likely to be large. Servicing will not consist of the simple "fixing" as done by present-day maintenance crews; such maintenance will be built into the machine. Rather, servicing will require complete taking-apart of the line and its reconstruction —clearly a highly skilled task. Because of increasing need for such highly-trained and professional persons, pressure will be put on educational institutions to supply them. One result may be mechanization of teaching and other changes to equip schools to supply the need. This emphasis will also accentuate the tendency for persons to stay in school longer.

Management itself is likely to change under the impact of automation, which provides management with far more data than it ever had before. The Sylvania Electric Company, for example, maintains a decentralized operation but has all its files in St. Louis. Many activities that are now a part of management, such as scheduling and scrap disposal, will be among those that will be automated. This may have the effect of making management a more exacting form of work. Managers will only do those things that machines cannot do (or cannot do at present), such as motivating workers. Whisler and Schultz (1962, pp. 83–84) suggested that middle management will be most affected. Mann and Hoffman (1960, pp. 55–60) showed how the automation of an oil plant led to a considerable increase in the power of the first-line foreman, in part because second-level managers were removed. If middle management is removed, where will candidates for top management come from? The problem arises because middle management has often been the training ground for top management. There may occur an increase in the tendency to select top-level managers from outside. Since automation leads to the increased use of professionals, there may be more line-staff conflict.

The whole development also raises the question of changes in the power of labor and management. If automation displaces the traditional crafts and operatives, it may well hurt the unions, at least in numbers, even though their control over key industries may remain. It does not follow, however, that management's power will increase. Automation means a shift to complex self-operating machinery which is enormously expensive. Therefore automation typically implies a 24-hour shift operation. Breakdown or interruption can be financially disastrous. A study by Faunce (1958) reported that men whose jobs had been automated felt that the foremen became more tense, presumably because they were concerned that there might be a breakdown in the line. Consequently the foremen and the whole organization were more than ever dependent on the men in the organization to keep the line operating. This means that the labor which does remain may be enormously powerful whether organized or not. The paradox may be that even though labor unions may be smaller in size, their reduced power may be compensated by an increase in the power of still-employed labor.

The impact of automation on particular industries is difficult to forecast. Diebold (1955) expected that manufacturing of agricultural equipment will become much more automated but agriculture itself will not. Buckingham (1955) sees automation most likely in "continuous flow" industries such as oil refining, flour milling, and chemical production, and least likely if the product is "highly individualistic," if personal service is needed, if there is special advantage in small scale units, or a "vast space" is required. Such analyses make sense but contain a flaw, for they assume present-day models of the processes whose future they are attempting to forecast. To rule out the possibility of automating agriculture because vast spaces are required assumes that they will always be required. In view of expanding food needs and the rising standard of living, surely there will be pressure to use less space in the future, through already existing hydroponic or "factory agriculture," wherein plants grow on shelves, one above the other, taking no more space than agricultural machinery plants. To rule out automation for activities where personal or individual service is "needed" is surely begging the question, for all one is saying is that personal service is now needed. Such forecasts are only guesses. The major restricting factors will probably be need and expense.

MANAGEMENT OF INDUSTRY

Administration and Leadership

Commons (1959, p. 284) conceived of the wage bargain as involving the sale by the worker of his "*willingness* to use his faculties according to a purpose that has been pointed out to him." Such a legal contract is quite limited. Blau and Scott (1962, p. 140) pointed out that the worker can leave his job if he can find a better one, and his employer can dismiss him unless tenure provisions or union agreements specifically prohibit dismissals. The very legal nature of the contract necessarily obligates the employee to perform only a specified set of tasks and does not provide for his striving to achieve optimum performance. In order to increase its influence, management usually seeks to have results beyond such legal understandings and to exert "administrative leadership." It is the fact that different managers employ different styles of leadership that gives the study of management a sociological appeal. Otherwise a mere reading of the procedures manual would suffice (Blau & Scott, 1962, p. 141).

Organizational leadership goes further than the motivation of unusual work behavior. It refers to the kind of behavior to be applied when the structure of the organization needs alteration and the degree of alteration is such that the organization has little previous experience to decide what is to be done. The task of the leader is to judge that the organization does need such alteration and to direct the changes. In contrast, administration, in the strictly technical sense, is concerned with maintaining the structure when the shape of the structure itself can be taken for granted. Chapple and Sayles (1961) said administrative action (which they called "management") is required in those situations that involve "deviations from normal operating conditions" (Chapple & Sayles, 1961, p. 64). They do not include all such deviations but only those which recur often enough to have

their limits be predictable. If the organization itself is sufficiently predictable that the manager can function as an administrator, he can focus on efficiency and the reduction of costs. The model of the organization as simply a tool for getting the work done is applicable. But when the tool itself cannot be taken for granted, then how efficient it is is irrelevant. It must be changed, and this is the task of the organizational leader. Selznick (1957) saw leadership as being necessary even in such activities as recruitment or training when these activities are designed to produce a fundamental change in the structure of the organization. If one wishes to change the character of a business firm from one which emphasizes sales more than production, leadership is called for in the design of the recruitment process.

Although organizational leadership may be called for anywhere, there appear to be certain key organizational problems where leadership is particularly likely to be evident, namely, goal definition and goal implementation. In the case of goal definition, a special problem requiring leadership occurs when the organization attains its goals, as Sills (1957) showed in the case of the National Foundation for Infantile Paralysis. The organization had built up a particular set of abilities, interests, and sensitivities with reference to a particular disease and was highly successful in achieving its goal. It was then faced with the task of shifting its goals or ceasing to exist.

The problem of shifting goals may sometimes have a tragic aspect. An army, for example, is designed to achieve victory. The better the army does its job, the sooner its goal is reached, and some of the need for the army vanishes.

Selznick (1957, pp. 25–28) called attention to the various ways leaders may default when confronted with goal-setting problems. They may fail to set goals because of a desire to avoid hard work and because of the desire to avoid conflict with persons threatened by sharp definition of purpose and may take refuge in a vaguely stated goal, such as "profit" or "readiness." The goal may also be defined as "survival," which is not really a goal since it does not provide guidelines for behavior. Among the consequences of failures to define goals are opportunism and utopianism (Selznick, 1957, pp. 74ff.)

Goal implementation describes the process of spelling out the specific ways of fulfilling the mission of the organization and the infusion of the organization with the values implied by the goals. A private hospital as compared to a teaching hospital has both a different set of goals and a different set of values.

This implementation process has been described by Lipset (1950) in the case of the coming to power by the CCF in Saskatchewan, where a bureaucracy was able to frustrate the ideological goals of a socialist political party. Organizational leadership may also be called for in other problem areas faced by industrial organizations, in particular the definition and clarification of means, task assignment and coordination, motivation, integration, and what may be spoken of as the "sparking function," which refers to the need for someone who knows when to press the button, for someone in an army platoon to raise his hand and shout "charge." This is a scheduling function in one sense but more broadly it is a matter of timing. It means sensing the psychological moment when motivation is at a maximum, supplies are available, communication is right, and goals are clear (Gross, 1961).

A recent development that seems promising for research is the examination of cross-national as well as cross-cultural variations in management, since organizational leadership is most evident in new industries. Important work has been brought together by Harbison and Myers (1959), who also offer a framework for the examination of management by conceiving of it as a resource, a system of authority, and a class. They concluded that there is no evidence to support the claim that a managerial elite is gaining power in industrializing countries. On the contrary, they suggested that the power of management is counterbalanced by strong trade unions and governments, even in advanced industrial countries.

Supervision as a Social Process

There has been much research in recent years on the role of the supervisor and on effects of differing styles of supervision on work behavior and attitudes. One type of research has focused on the foreman, seeing him in a variety of roles. Davis (1962, pp. 123–126) described five views of the foreman's role: key man in management, man in the middle, marginal man, simply another worker, and human relations specialist. Strauss (1957) summarized research dealing with the working, or first-line, supervisor. The authority of this official has been reduced as a consequence of increased authority given to foremen, increased distance between the supervisor and the foreman as foremen are hired directly from universities and as their sphere of interest shifts to human relations leadership, and as the authority of both foreman and working-supervisor are abridged by the increased power of the union.

Extensive research has been carried on over the last 15 years by the Survey Research Center of the University of Michigan on the effects of supervisory practices on productivity and morale (Likert, 1961). In a study of office workers it was found that six out of nine employee-oriented supervisors had high-productivity groups, and seven out of eight of the production-oriented supervisors had low-productivity groups. There was also evidence of more favorable sentiment toward the supervisor among workers under the employee-oriented supervisors (Katz et al., 1950). Hence one could conclude that the supervisor who thinks of his men gets better production as well as favorable sentiment directed toward himself. Whyte (1961, p. 552) questioned such a conclusion on the ground that the direction of causation is not clear. The supervisors of low-productivity sections may give more direct attention to production because it is so low and may be resented because of the need to pressure the men. Further, subsequent studies did not completely confirm the office-worker study. The Survey Research Center studies also suggested that closeness of supervision is related to productivity: Supervisors practicing general supervision get better production results than those who supervise closely. However, data from a railroad section gang did not confirm this finding, a consequence which the investigators attributed to differences in the nature of the jobs. It was felt that since the office workers were involved in routine clerical jobs of little skill, the supervisors knowledge of operations could contribute little to employee performance. Consequently close supervision would be resented. This was less likely to be the case for the section-gang operation, however. A study by Pelz (1952) suggested that the relation between employee-orientation and satisfaction with the supervisor is conditioned by the power that the supervisor has with his superiors in turn. Those foremen who had high power with superiors showed a positive correlation between employee orientation and satisfaction with supervisor. Such a relationship was not obtained when the foreman had low power. Whyte (1961, pp. 556–557) suggested that the somewhat inconclusive results of the Survey Research work may result from the fact that an attempt is being made to explain too much on the basis of interpersonal relations. One would have to take the perspective of the whole department, or of the influences emanating from the whole organization, in order to get higher predictive accuracy. Nevertheless, Likert (1961) was much more optimistic that the findings of the Survey Research Center can in fact be fitted together. He attempted to state the overall conclusion in the following principle: "The leadership and other processes of the organization must be such as to insure a maximum probability that in all interactions and in all relationships with the organization each member will, in light of his background, values, and expectations, view the experience as supportive and one which builds and maintains his sense of personal worth and importance" (Likert, 1961, p. 103). Blau and Scott (1962, pp. 151–153) reported contradictory findings in studies of two social work agencies. Work group productivity as measured by the number of visits to recipients per month was not found to be related to authoritarianism. They suggested that perhaps in a service organization, in contrast to factories and private offices, employees do not react to authoritarian supervision by reducing the effort that they devote to their work. Blau and Scott (1962, pp. 153–159) also examined studies dealing with other aspects of the relationship between supervisor and subordinate, in particular emotional detachment, consistency, and hierarchial interdependence —dimensions which have been ignored by many researchers. They found that these three characteristics were most closely related to the ability to command the loyalty of subordinates. Worker productivity in the welfare agencies that they studied was largely associated with factors that were related to loyalty, perhaps because supervisors who had won the loyal support of their subordinates were most successful in commanding willing compliance with their directives and in stimulating interest in their work groups.

Another kind of research has to do with the traditional problem of span of control in industry: the number of persons that should be supervised by any manager. Worthy (Whyte, 1961, pp. 88–90), basing his views on studies he conducted on the Sears Roebuck organization, concluded that flat organizations (many subordinates under each manager) have higher productivity and contribute more than their share of persons with management potential to the organization than do tall organizations. He attributed these results to the fact that when the manager of a store with a flat organization was faced with the task of supervising the work of some 30 department managers, he was forced to let each of them run his department in his own way since he could not supervise them closely. As a consequence these men developed initiative and became persons with greater managerial potential because they in effect had to train themselves in the management process. By contrast in tall organizations the store manager would supervise about six second-level supervisors who in turn would each supervise about six department managers. As a consequence each was able to give close supervision, resulting in the subordinate's lack of opportunity to develop his own initiative. Whyte (1961, pp. 91–92), in reexamining Worthy's work, suggested that more attention should be paid to the fact that Worthy only secured such results in the medium-sized Sears stores and that the larger stores, particularly those with mail order sections, typically did not exhibit this difference and in fact were tall organizations. Whyte felt that the notion of providing each supervisor with a large number of subordinates will work only in situations such as the Sears small stores where departments are essentially independent of one another. Should the candy department be poorly run, no adverse effects will be suffered by the men's clothing department. In time the poor management of the candy department will come to the attention of the supervisor through cost reports or in other ways, and he can take appropriate action. This differs from the case in a factory, in which the poor management of the rivet department spreads out in the form of insufficient supplies of rivets, or badly made rivets, in a variety of departments and hence may bring the entire production process to a halt. In such a situation one needs another level of supervision to relate the rivet department to the departments that make use of rivets. Similar problems arise in connection with situations where the technology is complex, or where it is not easy to measure the result of a particular department and therefore to attribute changes in its cost or income position to what went on in that department alone. This research casts doubt on traditional assumptions that there is a particular number of persons that a supervisor can effectively supervise.

Managerial Succession

An important new direction of research concerns the structural consequences of managerial succession. A study by Gouldner (1954) of a gypsum plant and a study by Guest (1962b) of an automobile plant may be directly compared. In the gypsum plant the succession resulted in sharp increases in tension and stress and (presumably) a falling off of performance, whereas in the automobile plant there was a decrease in cost, betterment of output, less absenteeism and turnover, fewer labor grievances and improvement in other measures. Guest (1962a) suggested important factors that account for the differences in results. Peel (the successor in the gypsum plant) encountered two problems which Cooley (the successor in the automobile plant) did not have to face. In the gypsum plant the tradition to promote from within had been violated in the appointment of Peel, who came to the organization from the outside. Consequently, the legitimacy of Peel's succession was questionable. Peel's predecessor, who had left behind him a corps of personally loyal men, had also created an "indulgency pattern" which permitted considerable variation from the rules. Consequently, Peel could not count on automatic loyalty. In the automobile plant, on the other hand, the men were accustomed to a change in managers once every three to five years. Managers typically came from other plants in the division and, because the plant was in a large metropolitan area, there was no sense of a close association between a manager and a local community (as had developed in the gypsum plant). Thus Cooley was not breaking any precedent, nor were there a number of persons personally loyal to him. Since Peel could not initiate contact with the organization through informal means because of the pattern of loyalty to his previous successor, he was forced (or believed he was forced) to tighten up control and to destroy the indulgency pattern which had formerly existed. Without such a tradition Cooley initiated a series of meetings in which he placed himself in the role of learner. Cooley's predecessor had in fact behaved much as Peel now did and had maintained a relatively rigid, tight, rule-enforcing type of organization. Hence it was relatively easy for his successor to relax rules. In commenting on the two cases, Gouldner (1962) summed up by suggesting that a successor who follows a situation in which rule-emphasizing bureaucracy prevails has an opportunity to recharge subordinates' motivations by withholding or reducing the constraints previously in effect. Otherwise, he has little alternative but to tighten up.

The evidence on the relationships between size of organization and the relative size of the administrative component bears on the problems of succession. Though the evidence is not conclusive, it appears to be true (Anderson & Warkov, 1961) that as organizations increase in size their complexity increases. Caplow (1957) offered data indicating that the greater the size of the organization the greater is its stability. Taking note of these data, Grusky (1961) called attention to the fact that most studies of succession in organizations (such as those previously discussed) have been concerned with small organizations. He asked whether the stress created may not be peculiar to small organizations. Perhaps large organizations are better able to weather storms created by succession because their greater complexity is a reflection of greater bureaucratization. Using data provided by *Fortune* magazine on the 500 largest corporations in the United States, he took the top 26 and the bottom 27 of those corporations as his

sample of "large" and "small" firms. With data from *Moody's Industrial Manual,* 1959, and *Poor's Register of Directors and Executives,* 1949, he secured data on changes in the names listed in key jobs in the firms over the 10 year period from 1949 to 1959. His data show that frequency of succession at the top was positively related to size of firm, even when age was held constant. This result suggests that the greater degree of bureaucratization in the larger firms acts to nullify, or at least cushion, the otherwise disruptive consequences of succession. By contrast, in small unbureaucratized firms the chief executive is more likely to be the founder or related to the founder and to be closely identified with the organization as a whole. Any change will have unsettling consequences for the firm. Since highly-bureaucratized firms are staffed mainly by professional managers, they routinize the succession process by establishing rules regulating retirement, rotation, and promotion of officials.

In a further test of Grusky's generalization on a sample of heads of state public health departments, state, community, and institutional mental health programs, local (city, county, or regional) public health departments, and local mental health departments or centers, Kriesberg (1962) confirmed Grusky's conclusion. Such confirmation is particularly striking in view not only of the totally different kinds of organizations in which he made the tests but also because the organizational sizes were far smaller than those Grusky was dealing with. Hughes (1956) distinguished between "itinerant" and the "home-guard" career lines: "The home-guard are the people who make their careers with little or no itinerancy; the itinerants progress by moving from one place or institution to another" (Hughes, 1956, p. 25). Kriesberg (1962, pp. 356–357) suggested that perhaps the larger departments are likely to recruit itinerants (persons who have national reputations), who then continue to advance by moving to other places or institutions. The likelihood of succession is thus shown to be related to the career pattern. Perhaps large organizations attract persons to whom succession or movement from firm to firm is appropriate to the sorts of careers that these individuals follow.

As implied by the studies described, most research on managerial succession has dealt with changes at the top. Whyte (1961, Ch. 23) presented one of the few case studies of succession at the lower levels, in a restaurant organization.

Intramanagerial Relations

Most discussions of management deal with the relations of managers to the managed, or to important power groups outside of the organization, such as government, managers of other firms, or labor union leaders. Some research has focused on the relations of the managers to one another within the same firm.

One of the most important changes that has taken place in the structure of managerial activities has been the great growth of staff organizations which are supposed to act in an auxiliary capacity to the line. The legal department is expected to tell the company how to handle patents, the inspection department checks the quality of goods produced, and the purchasing department acquires supplies from outside vendors. Such a picture is not necessarily simple. In fact, as Etzioni (1959) suggested, the roles of staff and line may be reversed in certain kinds of organizations. For example, the physicians who cure patients in the hospital are on the professional staff of the hospital and are not a part of the line administration.

Strauss and Sayles (1960, pp. 397–399) described three stages that personnel departments have gone through. At first they were concerned mainly with keeping records, a task which has still by no means vanished. In the 1920's, they instituted employee services. This involved a vast expansion in response to new theories of industrial rela-

tions. Many managers believed that the threat of union organization and the success of the Russian Revolution required a frontal attack on employee discontent. Consequently they attempted to beat organizers to the punch by paternally providing benefits. These took the forms of cafeterias, better restrooms, company stores, counselors, medical aid, and so forth. Next came the personnel decision-making stage, which increased the personnel department's control. During the 1930's, in many companies, the personnel department, renamed the department of industrial relations, was asked to take direct charge of all employee and union relations. It was often given full responsibility for hiring, firing, wage determination, union grievances, and transfers and promotions. Partly this was because the unions, which had been only a threat, now began to make progress in organizational drives. Also the government began to insist on standards. In unionized plants, some members of the personnel department became full-time negotiators and others spent their time justifying promotions to the union. Still others found themselves in charge of developing fringe benefit programs in response to union pressures.

A major effect of these changes was to abridge the power of the line supervisor. He found he could no longer hire, fire, reward, discipline, or handle grievances, yet he was likely to be blamed for any employee discontent that did occur. In this new situation officials of the personnel department, as well as other staff departments, found themselves expected to give advice and counsel to the line. The problem is how a personnel department, for example, can be expected to help a line supervisor make important decisions and at the same time maintain harmonious relations with him. Theoretically, the personnel department gives information and advice and the line actually makes the decision. Actually this distinction is not realistic, since the person receiving the advice is in the uncomfortable position of ignoring the advice at his peril. In such a case the advisor comes actually to make some decisions for the line supervisor. Further, the staff, as experts, have access to knowledge the line manager does not have and as trained persons have a natural desire to use this knowledge. Therefore it is easy for them to slip from an advisory role into a decision-making role. They may be aided in this process by the capitulation of line organizations, which "assign" them the responsibility for all of the "personal" problems.

Dalton (1950), drawing upon research in three large manufacturing firms, reported continuous line-staff conflict. Staff personnel were found to be ambitious, restless, and mobile, partly because they were younger than line personnel. There was also an unwillingness on the part of older line officers to accept instructions from younger men. Staff persons, often better educated, had expected that their knowledge would carry authority. Nor did the formal structure or hierarchy of statuses offer sufficient opportunities for mobility of staff persons, consequently a staff incumbent who desired to move up found that the only way he could do so was to move into a line position, and that required being able to get along with line personnel. Staff persons were status conscious, placing great emphasis on dress and appearance—another fact which served to create a gulf between line and staff persons. Line officers also feared innovations which staff persons could bring in at any time. They feared being "shown up" for not having thought of the changes themselves and feared the changes in methods or personnel that might result, as well as changes which would expose established though forbidden practices and departmental inefficiency. In this situation Dalton reported that staff and line had much to contribute to each other by making what he called "accommodations" (1950, pp. 348–350) which sometimes resulted in sabotage of company policies.

In a later work Dalton (1959) focused on conflict among line officers themselves. He found that the most effective managers were goal-oriented rather than method-oriented. They fought for expansion of jurisdiction of their departments, in part to increase their own power but in part to help maximize departmental objectives. Since such expansion often led to disputes, many power struggles developed, in which the less aggressive managers and their departments lost. Dalton regarded such power struggles as functional for organizational change, since without them the organizations would be too slow to adjust their structures to changing conditions. Such a picture of a continuous battle between managers contrasts sharply with the picture offered by W. H. Whyte (1956) of the "organization man."

Blau and Scott (1962, pp. 175–176) referred to an unpublished study by Crozier of the French tobacco monopoly. Interviewing revealed that maintenance workers were very satisfied with their situation, production workers were less satisfied, and supervisors were quite dissatisfied. A similar pattern was found at the managerial levels where technical engineers were more satisfied than top managers, their superiors. Crozier suggested that bureaucracy has the effect of eliminating many areas of uncertainty and that power accrues to those who can control the remaining areas of uncertainty. In the tobacco plants, machine breakdown was the main remaining area of uncertainty, hence the unofficial power of maintenance workers, and particularly of engineers, in charge of these activities increased. In contrast to Weber, who saw expertness as the *basis* of formal authority, Crozier saw it as an alternative to it that becomes manifest in areas that are not yet fully bureaucratized. Furthermore, the power that rests on expertness in areas of uncertainty is not stable, since "the expert's success is constantly self-diminishing" (Blau & Scott, 1962, p. 176). That is, as their knowledge increases, the areas that were formerly uncertain become areas which can be routinely handled.

INDUSTRIAL ORGANIZATION

Types of Industrial Organization

Blauner (1962, p. 8) pointed to the existence of a consistent bias in the selection of types of organization in industrial sociology. Most studies have been restricted to highly regimented assembly line industries, particularly automobile manufacturing and food, to industries with particularly militant and strike-prone labor forces, such as coal mining, to grievance-ridden or backward industries with severe social problems, such as steel and textiles, and to those with strong socialist traditions in convenient locations near urban centers and major universities, for example, the garment industry and automobile manufacturing. Blauner urged development of a sociology of *industries* which would take into account important variations in structure that exist between industries, rather than attempting to treat all as if the findings from any one could be generalized to the others. His own classification is based on variations in technology. Etzioni (1961) made the same point and proposed a typology which goes beyond industrial organizations, based on compliance structures—coercive, utilitarian, and normative. Other classifications have been based on the extent to which an organization is manned by volunteers, employees, or conscripts, the type of institutional area in which the organization falls (economic, political, religious, etc.), the type of decision-making strategy used (Thompson & Tuden, 1959), the distinction between production and service, and the criterion of who benefits (Blau & Scott, 1962, pp. 42–57).

While each such classification has its merit, and future research will settle the question of their relative fruitfulness, the limited concern of this chapter with industrial organization results in a classification of such organizations into three main forms, which describe the major types of industry that have in fact been studied. These are the bureaucratic, collegial, and paternalistic forms.

Bureaucratic forms have been most intensely studied and probably make up the bulk of industrial studies. Bureaucratic organizations are particularly well illustrated by manufacturing firms and may be described in terms of the distinctive characteristics of bureaucracy that Weber (1950) outlined—specialization, hierarchical coordination, the dominance of rules, and impersonality. The structure is divided into a technical and social organization. Technical relations in turn are often divided into two main kinds of organizations—the shop and engineering organizations. The shop organization carries on the line activity—the conversion of raw materials into finished products or provision of the service the firm provides. The engineering organization plans the shop's technical procedures and the tools and machinery that it uses. Such a sharp distinction, however, is often not maintained. One finds chemists or engineers at the job level who assist with shop technical problems, and engineering organizations, in turn, may become so large that they include some persons who perform shop activities for the engineering departments, such as making blueprints, special planning, and others. The formal social organization of the industry is usually described in terms of three interlocking organizations: the supervisory organization, the line organization, and the staff organization. The supervisory organization makes up the formal authority structure. Each individual reports directly to his superior and is directly responsible to him; each superior usually has a number of subordinates who report to him. The result is the familiar branching type of organization one sees on company organization charts. Orders and information are expected to flow along these lines. Cutting across both technical and formal organizations in some industries is the labor union, a type of organization which excludes supervisors and is not directly concerned with facilitating the manufacturing process (although it may in fact do so).

The whole structure is integrated through a communication network which involves face-to-face communication, nonface-to-face oral communication (telephone, interoffice communication), and written communication. This communication network is usually discussed in terms of direction of the communication: vertical or horizontal. In the case of vertical communication orders presumably go down the line and information comes up the line. The significant element here is the extent to which orders are interpreted (and therefore altered) as they go down and the extent to which information becomes similarly interpreted or generalized as it moves up. Of particular importance are cost control and union information since they need not go up the line step-by-step. Such information is gathered at the bottom, summarized, mimeographed, and distributed simultaneously to several levels considerably higher up, but not to the first and second line of supervisors. The information therefore puts great pressure on the supervisors, and a part of their time is spent attempting to determine what form this information will take and in preparing for it.

Horizontal communication is theoretically simple but in fact becomes extremely complicated. From a purely formal point of view any interaction between persons on the same level should take place through a common supervisor. In fact this is so time-consuming that shortcuts take place. Such shortcuts save time and trouble for the person bypassed, but at the same time this means the information is kept from him. In a study of a spinning department, Simpson (1959) found that communication was predominantly horizontal rather than vertical. The ease with which horizontal interaction takes place may depend on structural variables, or it may depend on the nature of the interpersonal relationships prevailing. For example, if the shop is a product shop, horizontal relationships are restricted to those departments that supply the shop with its raw materials and to those departments to whom it delivers its raw materials. On the other hand, in the case of a functional shop (a rivet shop or a paint shop), a single activity is carried out for a large number of shops and consequently there may be a large number of departments with which this shop will have relationships. Although the bureaucratic form of organization has been subject to much criticism and although its admirers have tended to underestimate dysfunctional consequences (as pointed out above), it remains the most efficient method for the accomplishing of large-scale tasks that has yet been discovered by man.

Collegial organizations are committees with task assignments, case conferences, university departments, R and D organizations, many kinds of craft and professional organizations and others. Much research has taken place on small groups and the forms of structure which affect their productivity. Sociological research on task-oriented groups has focused on the kinds of roles which persons bring with them to such meetings and the kinds of roles that they then assume. It is recognized that each person's behavior results in the building-up of a set of role expectations and that such expectations eventually lead to a stable structure in the small group. The roles which persons assume at meetings were described by Beane and Sheats (1948) as content roles (initiator, information seeker, blocker, expert, and others), and process roles (summarizer, task-setter, encourager, mediator, playboy, and so on). Research has examined the relative productivity of having the chairman play both content and process roles on the one hand, or restrict himself to process roles on the other.

There has been much research on leaderless groups. Maier and Solem (1952) showed that groups with formal leaders were better at solving mathematical problems than those without such leaders, because formal leaders made sure that minority opinions were expressed, and often those were the correct ones. After a careful examination of much of the research in this area, Blau and Scott concluded: "By providing social support, challenging stimulation, error correction, and a *laissez-faire* competition for respect among participants, the free flow of communication contributes to finding solutions to problems, to making decisions, and to creative thinking. But the battleground of ideas generated by such a free flow makes coordination more difficult" (1962, p. 139). Thus one might have to pay for some control and coordination by giving up some of the potentially fruitful results of allowing a free flow of communication in a task-oriented group.

In a comparison of the organization of construction and mass production industries in the United States, Stinchcombe (1959) found that the former are much less bureaucratized though just as rationalized as the latter. This result is attributed to seasonal variations in the construction industry. In addition, the greater professionalization of its labor force enables the construction industry to do without much of the administrative staff required by mass-production industry, as may also be the case in many kinds of professional organizations as well. Both collegial and bureaucratic forms of industrial organization are combined (although in an unstable form) in research and development organizations in industry. Howton (1963) pointed out that in order to be able to avoid "dirty work" (work that is demeaning or hurtful to the professional self-image) the scientists he observed had to spend a great deal of their time securing acceptable work assignments, which left them with less time to carry on the work itself. Special problems presented by professionals in large organizations are further treated below.

Paternalistic forms of industrial organization often reflect a feudal tradition in which the lord of the manor had responsibility for the welfare of his subordinates in return for their loyalty and services. In exchange for housing, food, medical care and social services, the worker is expected to be productive.

Kerr and his associates (1960) found this form of organization common in the early stages of industrial development in many societies. Particularly in small establishments, where the proprietor may hire his relatives as workers, such a pattern enables the family to remain intact while the society begins the slow process of industrialization. It has been a common form in countries such as Germany and Japan, where the members of pre-existing dynastic elites were the first to move toward industrialization. One finds it also in India.

Management may provide services for reasons other than those stemming from a sense of moral obligation. "Malnutrition may force managements to provide free lunches in the interest of productivity. Other services or payments in kind may be required in enterprises which operate in areas remote from centers of population. The oil producing companies in Saudi Arabia, Iraq, and Kuwait are good examples, as are the sugar plantations and mills in the sparsely inhabited coastal deserts of Peru or the copper mines of Rhodesia" (Kerr et al., 1960, p. 152). These paternalistic organizations have by no means departed from the United States where it has been and still is a part of the personnel policies of International Business Machines, Eastman Kodak, and the Hershey Chocolate Corporation. It is also clearly of importance for the approximately 85 per cent of all United States business firms which are small.

Teaching and Learning

Teaching and learning are not only means whereby persons acquire skills or ideas which are related to work performance, but are also means whereby persons assume the status of industrial colleague. Consequently, particular interest focuses on the standards and values which students in training, whether in a separate educational setting or on the job itself, are exposed to. At the same time it is recognized that one of the most important controls on the make-up of work colleague groups may be provided by restricting the number of persons permitted to learn the occupational skills. Each of these two controls in the would-be worker will be examined, considering first techniques for restricting the number permitted to learn.

Restrictions on entry to the learning situation may be either formal or informal. Formal restrictions include such devices as prerequisites for admission to dental, law, or engineering schools. The sheer length of the occupational education itself will stop many persons even after they have begun their course of study. Many occupations require internships, and there are good and poor internships. A Negro physician may be prevented from entering practice on the same level as a white by inability to secure an internship in a good hospital. Where much of the learning must take place on the job, still other devices are used. The factory personnel office screens persons, and the union may use the device of the hiring hall or the closed shop, if legal, or other controls on the hiring process. This becomes a circular process whereby persons are unable to learn the skills the job requires except by taking a job, but are unable to secure the job because they do not have the skills. Informal obstacles may include race, religion, age, and sex and these may operate in various ways. A popular technique is the informal quota in schools. Another is the use of a performance test, as in dentistry. As is well known the requirement of a photograph on the application form may be used to restrict Negroes and other populations.

Other powerful controls are present in the learning situation itself. Where the learning consists in part of a formal education, control is exercised by having accepted members of the occupation do the teaching. Accountants teach accounting students, and engineers teach engineering students. In this manner there is assurance that appropriate attitudes are being transmitted along with skills.

The most important control on learning is the control that occurs on the job itself, however much formal education the occupation requires. The things learned on the job are of three kinds: regular technical skills, tricks of the trade, and social skills.

The teaching of regular technical skills is distinguished from the teaching of such skills off-the-job by the realism of the on-the-job situation. In addition a great deal of the learning is informal, so that persons may be unaware of the fact that learning is taking place until some time has lapsed. This in turn may lead to the growth of myths about the length of time required to produce a skilled member of the trade, as in the case of the boy apprentice in the building trades (Myers, 1948).

By a "trick of the trade" is meant a device which saves a person from his own mistakes. The most important are tricks that save time, save energy, and prevent injury. All occupations have short-cuts and a part of the efficiency of experienced workers can be attributed to them. In some occupations, one must learn how to lift heavy weights without strain; in others one learns to avoid cutting oneself or hitting one's thumb with a hammer. Matthews (1950) described how a rookie fireman must learn never to look up when scaling a ladder lest burning material fall on his face. The fireman also learns to put on his helmet before he buttons his fireman's coat so that if he falls off the "rig" his head will be protected, and he learns to change from his street shoes to his firemen's boots, one shoe at a time, so that if the alarm should go off, he will never have more than one shoe to put on. Perhaps the most ingenious is the trick of the "smoke eater" (who can stay in a smoke-filled room for a long time) of getting breaths of fresh air from the nozzle of the hose before water is pumped through it. Sutherland (1937, pp. 44-45) described the trick of the pickpocket of stationing himself next to a sign saying "Beware of pick-pockets" to take advantage of the tendency of persons, on reading the sign, to feel for their wallets, thus revealing where the wallet is kept.

Last are social skills. The worker must learn how to get along with fellow workers. To do this he must learn of their social world and their code. One of the commonest ways of teaching social skills is by horseplay, including all the legendary devices for making the novice look foolish—tripping him as he passes, hiding his tools, sending him for a nonexistent tool. Such devices have the function of letting the individual know that there is a group and that the individual cannot regard himself as a member until he has been accepted by that group. Acceptance, in turn, means learning how to behave. The individual must learn what is considered to be a day's work and to restrict his output to that amount. He must learn when to keep his mouth shut and what it is safe to talk about. He must learn whom he can talk to and whom he must avoid. The importance of these considerations led Merton and his colleagues (1957), in their intensive study of the student physician, to describe the process of learning in terms of socialization, the process by which persons "selectively acquire the values and attitudes, the interest, skills and knowledge—in short, the culture—current in the groups in which they are, or seek to become a member" (Merton et al., 1957, p. 287). On the other hand, Becker et al. (1961) disputed the socialization approach, maintaining instead that medical students do not take on a professional role while they are students, largely because the system they operate in does not allow them to do so. Students are made painfully aware of the fact that they are students, that they know very little, and that they can only play at being doctors. They are forced to come to terms with the immediate problem of pleasing their instructors and of doing well in medical school if they ever wish to be physicians at all. There remains, however, no question that values— in this case the culture of the student group —must be learned. Clear indices of the presence of this culture is "student talk," distinct clothing, favorite haunts, and rebellious behavior.

Systems of Work Control

There are two main sorts of work controls: those that come from within the work situation (folkways, mores, and sanctions) and those that come from outside. In any new work situation there is considerable floundering around at first. Since persons do not know which situations are likely to recur, they do not know which situations should be subjected to group control and definition. But gradually persons come to know what to expect of one another. Bendix (1956, pp. 203–204) described this process in the early industrial period in England. It took a considerable length of time, he pointed out, for workers to develop what he called "an internalized ethic of work performance." Gradually folkways and mores develop that define duties and obligation. Among occupations with pretensions to become professions a code develops. The code often becomes formal and as such may get further and further away from the actual work situation until it becomes a creed or faith, a statement of what occupational members are supposed to live up to. Such a code functions as an *apologia* which states what the industry does for the world and justifies its contribution. In back of this code there remains a real working code which guides work behavior.

Sanctions may be imposed in many ways. One of the best is to make them appear to come from the outside, like the schoolboy technique of punishing a fellow pupil by getting him in bad with the teacher. The rate-buster may find rejected pieces slipping into his work pile, or the group may work at top speed in order to cause the rate-buster to get behind in his work. As the pieces pile up on his desk, the foreman wonders about him, and he may get a reputation for being a slow worker and then be shifted out of the work group. In most professions referral is a major source of clients. One of the ways one can hurt an individual is to stop referring clients to him—a powerful informal control.

There are, of course, formal sanctions. The individual may be rejected from the occupation, the priest may be excommunicated or reprimanded or unfrocked, the lawyer may be disbarred. These happen but are much less common than is informal exclusion from an inner circle. If legal sanctions are applied at all, they are likely to come from a group outside the professional body. Informal sanctions are applied first and formal sanctions only if the person gets far out of line. At the same time in order that informal sanctions shall work effectively, the person must identify with the group, that is, his status in the work group must be his most important status. If the person has an escape into another status, however, group sanctions may not hurt him much at all. Illustrations of those with status escapes are minority groups: Negroes, Jews, Mexicans, Japanese, women. It is possible for members of minority groups to escape the impact of group sanctions if they believe that the sanction is being imposed on them because of their minority group membership rather than because of work group membership. The question is: Who can insult you? To be an insult it must hurt. Only if a person values the opinion of the group will he be much upset by group disapproval of his behavior.

Controls from outside the work situation include those from clients, other professions and occupations, and public opinion in general. Such control is typically mediated through an authority structure (for example, work duties of electricians employed in a factory), the market price mechanism (charges self-employed electricians are able to collect for their services), governmental controls (building codes, licensing), and the general control of custom (few electricians would refuse to respond to an urgent night call from a householder whose electricity had failed for no obvious reason). Nonoccupational controls are particularly

strong among the professions yet no occupation escapes some control. People allow the playwright and actor some license to satirize society and be risqué, but the censor is never far away.

Controls in industrial organizations may take a variety of forms that are related to the kind of organization one is examining. Thus Blau and Scott (1962, pp. 169-170) pointed out that, in the welfare agencies that they studied, the work of case workers was continually interrupted by emergency requests from clients and by supervisors who felt free to disrupt their work when they thought it necessary. Less of this sort of interruption occurred in higher levels of the organization. Jaques (1956) analyzed the time between interruptions or, more generally, between evaluations of employee performance, feeling that this time provides a measure of responsibility. He found that financial rewards are correlated with the relative span of discretionary responsibility.

Also affecting the way in which work is evaluated are physical factors, such as the distance separating the supervisor from the subordinate. Clark (1958, pp. 71-72) suggested that geographical dispersion of centers of adult education in a metropolitan area give the officials more autonomy than they might otherwise have. Of importance in industrial organization are impersonal mechanisms of control. These have been examined by Walker and Guest (1952; 1956) in their studies of assembly-line production. In an assembly line there is no need for close supervision, as the line itself dictates the pace of work. The foreman spends his time assisting men who are having difficulty, since the latter are unable to leave the line. Consequently the foreman may not be perceived as exercising close supervision. In automated operations one might expect a further reduction in the closeness of supervision, but this result is not in fact what happens, as research by Faunce (1958) and Walker (1957) has shown. Blau and Scott (1962, pp. 181-183) interpreted this finding as meaning that as long as automation does not require a higher level of skill, it will not result in increased discretion. On the other hand, a study by Blauner (1962) of a chemical firm in the Bay area of California reported a reduction in closeness of supervision and a greater sense of responsibility on the part of the workers, although they were not noticeably higher skilled persons. Blauner cast doubts on the utility of the concept of skill for operators in automated settings, preferring to look on such operators as "responsible" for chemical processes. Nor do such workers feel the machines are "controlling" them.

WORK GROUPS AND COLLEAGUESHIP

Work Cliques and Interest Groups

A distinction may be made between persons who are marginal to the work situation and those who are full colleagues. For example, one may distinguish between those who are "occupied" and those who are "preoccupied" (Burke, 1935, pp. 303-316), the latter illustrated by women who work but whose primary identification is with their families. Another class of marginal persons is made up of those who attempt to gain employment but are opposed because of race or religion. Such persons may have to content themselves with doing the dirty work of their colleagues: an upper-class white law firm maintains its reputation by diverting its shady cases to Negro lawyers, who have no choice but to accept. On the other hand, work activities which were once marginal may become caught up in the central work organizations themselves. Midwifery, nursing, pharmacy, surgery, and eye-measuring were all historic trades or mysteries which once existed outside of medicine and have since been brought in as specialties, or their practitioners have become subordinates or auxiliaries to physicians. Yet the position of specialties remains unstable (Wardwell, 1963). The accountant is the creature of capitalistic industry and continues to serve it. But the certified public accountant, articled by the state and responsible only to his colleagues, is a man whose prestige and power are at the point where the businessman who "employs" him regards him with respect and not a little fear. So, too, the increasing tendency to add lawyers, scientists, and other professionals to the staffs of corporations is motivated not only by the need for their talents but also by the desire to enlist their sympathy and understanding of corporation problems. It is well enough to seek out a lawyer when one needs legal advice, but it is even better if the lawyer can be counted on to understand the special problems that the corporation faces, and such understanding is more likely when he is on retainer for the corporation.

Considerable research has been done on means of building colleagueship. An important means is developing some control on the entry of new members. The most serious problem is illustrated in occupations such as harvest work, where there is a reservoir population from whom large numbers may be drawn, such as women, youngsters, and minority group members, who compete with regular harvest workers. Professionals within organizations will often resist the entry of such persons and hence find themselves at odds with the desire of the work organization for willing and cheap help. Professions provide the most striking examples of work organizations which carefully control entry and consequently are able to develop a high degree of colleagueship.

A second means for developing colleagueship is to attempt to develop occupational consciousness. The attempt is made to develop an image of the practitioners as the unique purveyors of a service to a world that would be much the worse without them. As Riley (1963) and others showed, corporations spend a great deal of their time attempting to develop such an image. The image cannot long be maintained unless it is believed in by the members them-

selves. In order to achieve this, obligations
to the organization must stand high in
priority over obligations to others and particularly to clients. Hence the continuous
tension on the part of service workers and
professionals over their loyalty to the controls of their colleagues on the one hand
and the needs of their clients on the other.
The extent to which members of an occupation highly value their services is illustrated
at all levels. Hughes (1951), referring to
research among Negro industrial workers
who had lowest status jobs, wrote:

It was from these people that we learned that
the common dignifying rationalization of people in all positions of a work hierarchy except
the very top one is, "We in this position save
the people in the next higher position above
from their own mistakes." The notion that one
saves a person of more acknowledged skill,
and certainly of more acknowledged prestige
and power, than oneself from his mistakes appears to be peculiarly satisfying (Hughes, 1951,
p. 316).

The fact of high evaluation of one's own
occupation appears to develop colleagueship
more when there goes with it a sense of
rejection of other occupations and of superiority over clients. Lipset, Trow, and Coleman (1956), in a study of the International
Typographical Union, advanced the "marginal status hypothesis." Printers regard
themselves (as they always have) as the
elite group among the manual workers.
They are literate, better educated, and tend
to have a stronger middle-class orientation
than do other manual workers. Consequently, they would be expected to prefer to
associate with middle-class persons, but, if
that were not possible, they would associate
with other printers. Colleagueship may also
be developed by deliberately facilitating informal interaction among colleagues. Lipset
and associates (1956) pointed out that printers have an extensive "occupational community" which takes the form of voluntary
associations and informal visiting with one
another. Those most active in this com-

munity were also found to be most interested in and informed about union political
affairs. In addition, the night work broke
up the normal pattern of family and recreational life and threw the printers into one
another's company. A fourth factor contributing to colleagueship is the development of "rules of the game" to control
competition among members. Examples are
provided by the ethics of professional
groups, work rules among industrial workers, and the controls of informal groups.

Through such means as these colleagues
make their demands on one another, and
these demands may reach deep into one's
life. This raises the question: Which actions
do a man's colleagues have the right to be
concerned about? The answer seems to be:
They have a right to be concerned about
any actions which affect the welfare of the
work group. As a consequence, one finds in
every work organization the development
of a set of expectations or obligations toward
one another which, in time, become work
mores. One of the most important obligations of colleagueship is the obligation of
secrecy. Of course one keeps the client's
affairs secret but, at a deeper level, secrecy
includes the obligation to double talk—to
talk in one frame of reference to one's
clients or society at large, and a different
frame of reference to one's colleagues. This
is not simply a matter of "fooling the
client," for if the chemist were to tell the
line manager the plain truth in scientific
language he would tell him very little or
simply alarm him. Consequently, he learns
to tell the manager in language he will
understand. The professional faces the most
difficulty here, for he is forced to deal routinely with the crises of others. As a consequence, he must develop a language for
discussing objectively the affairs of clients
and of those he serves, though such objectivity may appear to the client very much
like callousness.

One wishes for colleagues who are more
than technically competent; one wants persons with whom one feels one can com-

municate, and who can be counted upon to understand. This work and client talk, being esoteric, is expressed in an argot or work language. Elkin (1946) called attention to the fact that the soldier's language is related to his image of solidarity (G.I., or "Mac"), to his freedom from customary social restraints (the omnipresent obscene word prefix), to his belief in his strength ("sweat out"), and to his attitude toward authority ("sad sack"). When such an argot is fully developed it not only identifies colleagues and facilitates communication among them, it also symbolizes the strength of the ties between them.

One of the earliest objects of research in industrial relations was the informal work group. To some scholars these groups are unimportant because they are natural. What, after all, is more natural than a few friends meeting for coffee or chatting informally around the water cooler? To workers themselves, such small group behavior is not worthy of discussion. On the other hand, management often takes the reverse position, regarding such groups as not merely a waste of time but as actual threats to the attainment of organizational work goals. The persistence and universality of such groups suggest that they must perform important functions for their members. The major functions seem to be the following:

First, they provide protection and assistance to their members. They will take over one another's work in emergencies, make excuses for one another, put in a good word with the supervisor, and in general support one of their members if he is attacked, maligned, or accused.

Second, informal groups have communication functions. Particularly in office situations, small groups are likely to be made up of persons from different parts of the organization. A small group may be composed of clerks from the sales department, accounting department, complaint department, and filing department. It is then possible for persons in different parts of the organization to learn what is going on in other parts. This arrangement may result in the discovery of forthcoming decisions, so that the individual may be better prepared for them. On the other hand, a person who is not a member of an informal group is without this protection and must depend on the formal channels for his information. A third function of informal groups is the control of members' behavior. It is in the informal group that standards of proper behavior are taught, and where sanctions for deviations from them are imposed.

Still a fourth function of such groups is the provision of personal satisfactions. In the company of persons he trusts, the member secures a haven from the impersonal, rationalized relationships within which he must move in the work situation. Here he gets intimate response, understanding, and recognition. It is here he finds persons who understand him, who are interested in his problems, and want to hear him talk about them. Every kind of work involves performance up to a standard. Therefore, every worker is confronted with the possibility of failure and of developing means for handling failure. In medicine, no matter how skilled the physician is, some of his patients die. In religion, no matter how hard the priest tries, some of his charges go to hell. In teaching, no matter how skilled the instructor is, some of his students fail. In industrial organizations, no matter how skilled the chemist is, process runs may fail, costing the company thousands of dollars. On the assembly line, no matter how experienced a worker is, he may unintentionally drop a wrench into the line. It is the work group of one's colleagues that comes in at such times to give the individual a sense of assurance, so that he will not crack up in the face of such failure. Here is the only group in which it is safe to let one's hair down and recount one's mistakes. The members of the group can then tell him of similar mistakes of their own, or reassure him so that he gets back his faith in himself.

The presence of such a colleague group

is an intimate part of the whole phenomenon of self-confidence. A major reason why the new teacher, the new lawyer, the new counselor, or the new executive feels anxiety and self-doubt is not simply that he lacks experience; it is also because a new worker is not admitted to colleague groups until others feel they can trust him. When he has earned that trust, then he may experience the powerful group support that his colleagues have to offer.

The manifold functions of such friendship cliques has earned for them a lion's share of research attention. Their significance may even have led to overattention. Mayo and Lombard (1944), in the heyday of human relations research, were able to conclude that high turnover in aircraft plants in California was a consequence of lack of such friendship groups. It began to be evident, though, from many studies that such groups never include all of the workers in any organization. It was recognized that "rate-busters," after all, were not members of such groups. A study of British longshoremen revealed that a high proportion of them deliberately avoided what they felt were overly close personal involvements in work gangs (*The Dock Worker*, 1954, pp. 61ff.). The research of recent years does not support the claim that there is any necessary relationship between group cohesiveness and productivity. In a study of a large number of work groups, Seashore (1954) concluded that the effect of high cohesiveness was a narrowing of the range of individual outputs, but that average output might be either high or low, depending upon whether the work groups were oriented toward management goals or opposed to them. Many scholars have felt that satisfaction should be positively related to productivity. Homans (1961, p. 282), after a survey of data on this old question, concluded that the relationship between the two depends on the frequency with which the activity is rewarded. Often the more satisfied a man is the less productive he is.

A recent focus of interest has been on the factors accounting for the formation of such groups, and their effects on work methods. James (1951), Mack (1954), and Sayles (1958) investigated the relation between work groups and the layout of physical work facilities. In a summary of a large number of industrial studies which he and his associates conducted, Sayles (1958, Ch. 3) found that all of the following were important in explaining the presence or absence of groups and differences among them: relative position on the promotional ladder of the plant, relative size and importance of the group (with the more solidary groups often being the larger rather than the smaller ones), similarity of jobs within the group, essentiality of the work, and the precision with which management can measure work load and pace. On the other hand, the repetitiveness of the task, the hours of work, the density of the work force, and the sex distribution within the group seem to be of considerably less importance. Informal association may lead to work methods changes, as when workers on repetitive jobs exchange jobs with one another or where, as in the automobile industry, a worker takes over a colleague's job and thus enables him to enjoy a rest. So, too, Gross (1953) found that informal occasions were often used by supervisors to size up the job abilities of members of their departments.

Sayles (1958) suggested that the study of the friendship clique has limited attention to the stabilizing functions of small groups. He drew attention to another type of group, characterized as an *interest group*. Instead of protecting the status quo, holding tight to work standards, resisting rule enforcement and the like, interest groups seek to improve the relative position of the members of the group. Such improvements can take the form of looser standards, better seniority, more overtime, better supervision, better equipment, and the like. Sayles developed a typology of such work groups, which relates to their participation in the grievance process. (1) *Apathetic* groups are the least likely to develop grievances or engage in concerted action to pressure management and the union, although they are not ranked highest by management for productivity or cooperativeness. Leadership is dispersed among the members with relatively little cohesiveness. (2) *Erratic* groups exhibit no relation between the seriousness of their grievances and the intensity of their protests. Issues that both management and the union consider minor, and which could be settled by brief discussions, suddenly erupt into a major grievance. At the same time deep-seated grievances might exist for a long time with no apparent reaction. Management regards this type of a group as dangerous because it is unpredictable. Such groups have highly autocratic leaders, who might just as easily be converted into favorable relationships with management as to any other kind of relationship. (3) *Strategic* groups are shrewdly calculating pressure groups who demand constant attention to their problems and have the ability to back up their demands by group action. These are highly cohesive, with leadership consisting of a small corps of very active and influential group members. They make up the heart of the union as well as the grievance activity in their respective plants. The men have what are considered good jobs (though not the best) in the plant and maintain good production records over the long run in many such groups, though not necessarily in all of them. (4) *Conservative* groups are the least likely to use concerted action without warning (as well as less likely to participate in union affairs). The strength of these groups is ensured by their possessing a monopoly of critical scarce skills. They are self-oriented groups interested in improving their position in the work organizations. They would not engage in unpredictable walkouts, but a quick stoppage is always a possibility. Aware of their latent strength, they do not demand the immediate service that the erratic or strategic groups do.

Sayles (1958) found a close relationship between the type of work that was done and the likelihood of membership in one of these four types. What is distinctive of such a classification is that these groups are seen to be "free enterprise units," attempting to increase their share of the goods and favors which the organization has to offer. They are self-oriented, even turning against other fellow workers if it will suit their own group better. They are not limited to those in direct day-to-day interaction with each other but may contain a hundred or more workers who share common objectives. The result may be not a system tending toward equilibrium, but rather an increasing instability, as groups continue to battle for what they think they deserve.

Professionals in Industry

Much of the research on the professions in sociology has used the model of the free (self-employed) professional. Yet as far back as one hundred years ago there were only about one-half as many free professionals as there were salaried professionals. Whereas, as has been said above, in many "old" professions, such as teaching and the ministry, independent practice has never been the norm. The trend has continued. Randle (1959, p. 128) showed that in the 12-year period after World War II, when the number of production workers increased by 6 per cent in the United States, the number of scientists and engineers in industry increased fourfold. The increase in the proportion of salaried professionals is due in part to the demand for wholly new services, particularly research and development, and in part to the increased hiring by organizations of members of "old" professions (lawyers, physicians) as staff members. Professional and bureaucratic orientations to work have much in common (Blau & Scott, 1962, pp. 60–62). Both emphasize universalistic standards, specificity of function, affective neutrality, and evaluation of competence on the basis of performance rather than ascribed characteristics such as sex or birth order.

In at least two basic respects, however, the

professional and the bureaucratic orientation clash. The bureaucratic orientation, as expressed in the modern business corporation, is directed toward the increase in the self-interest of the corporation. The professional is expected to be oriented toward service to his client. This does not mean that the professional is expected to be uninterested in improving his own position. Rather, the relations in the profession are so structured that only by serving his client does he serve himself. The professional in the organization is expected to regard the organization as his "client." At the same time, since he may be involved in product research or in activities which relate the firm to the outside world, he will be equally interested in serving the public at large as an outside client, an orientation which may run afoul of the organization's desire to have him serve the organization only.

A second important contrast is in the structure of authority. In the organization, decision-making is hierarchically organized; in the profession, colleague control is decisive. Kornhauser (1962) summarized the major issues as conflicts in the attainment of goals, conflicts over controls, and conflicts over incentives and influence in industry. The scientist, whether he is in an organization or not, seeks to carry on research and make contributions to knowledge. In industrial organizations he finds himself strongly pressured to orient his research to "practical" concerns, or to those that may have some possible future use to the organization. At the same time, there is a continuing dilemma, for organizations are repeatedly confronted with "useless" types of research which later turn out to be enormously profitable. Yet putting one's money on research activities means taking long-range risks.

The major conflict occurs over the difference between bureaucratic authority and colleague (or professional) authority. Kornhauser (1962, Ch. III) saw these problems of control becoming crystallized about the issues of recruitment, organization, supervision, and communication. The problem

of the loyalty of the professional—whether to one's professional colleagues or to the organization that employs one—has long been recognized, although only recently has any research been directed to it. Reissman (1949) used the term functional bureaucrat to refer to the type of bureaucrat who is oriented toward his professional group rather than to the bureaucracy itself. Wilensky (1956, pp. 129-144) similarly found that the "professional service" labor union intellectual is oriented to his colleagues outside the union and might even be induced to go to work for company management. Caplow and McGee (1958, p. 85) described the scholar's orientation to his institution as sometimes operating to disorient him to his discipline. Professionally-oriented scholars may regard their institutions as "a temporary shelter" where they can continue to pursue their careers. These orientations were intensely studied by Gouldner (1957-1958) in a small private liberal arts college with results which are likely generalizable to industrial organizations. Using the three criteria of loyalty to the employing organization, commitment to specialized role skills, and reference group orientation, he drew a distinction between "cosmopolitans" and "locals." "Cosmopolitans" have a more strong outer reference group orientation and a relatively high commitment to specialized role skills, but low loyalty to the employee organization. Factor analysis reveals certain clusters. The "locals" were found to be divisible into the "dedicated" (who support organization values), the "true bureaucrats" (who support the security of the organization against outside criticism and who tend to be oriented to the local community), the "homeguard" (mostly middle administration persons who got their degrees at that college and now are back), the "elders" (old-timers who know many people and who have a strong peer group reference). "Cosmopolitans" were of two types: the "outsiders" (who are in but not entirely of the university), and "empire-builders" (who have a departmental orientation). The "locals" as a whole characterized by loyalty, and the "cosmopolitans" as a whole by emphasis on competence. Blau and Scott (1962) suggested a modification of the Gouldner conclusions because of contradictory findings reported by Bennis, Berkowitz, Affinito, and Malone (1958) in a study of nurses. They suggested that "commitment to professional skills will be associated with low organization loyalty only if professional opportunities are more limited in the organization under consideration than in others with which it competes for manpower" (p. 71).

The conflict over professional incentives arises from the fact that scientific professions judge a man by his contributions through research papers and attendance at professional meetings and the like, whereas the employing organization evaluates a man on the basis of his contributions to production and sales or to new or improved devices, and it rewards the man through promotions, income, and increased power. Many firms are attempting to utilize professional incentives by giving their scientists and other professionals time off to attend professional meetings, paying their professional dues for them, giving them tuition refunds for further professional training, allowing publication of research results under certain conditions, and providing double ladders of advancement so that a man can remain a scientist yet still advance in the company.

Four kinds of professional organizations may be distinguished: the learned society, the professional association, the trade union, and the professional union. Only the last three are of importance for the professional in organizations. Professional associations are oriented to the improvement of the welfare of their members. As such they usually include members of management as well as scientists and others who are not involved in administrative activities. Trade unions such as the American Federation of Technical Engineers (AFL-CIO) attempt to follow the model of the standard trade union in emphasizing the special advantages of trade union membership and bringing pressure to bear on members of management to improve the lot of engineers, architects, chemists, bacteriologists, and other professional employees. Often membership is open to technicians and engineers who perform no research or scientific functions, but it is closed to those in managerial positions. The professional union, as exemplified by the one-time national union, the Engineers and Scientists of America, is something of a hybrid organization. It stresses the special needs of professionals and at the same time gives direct attention to the employee status of its members and engages in collective bargaining. On the whole the collective bargaining principle has not made spectacular gains among engineers and scientists. Within recent years it may actually have declined in the face of increasing influence of professional associations. Thus, one finds a typical meeting of industrial professionals including both members of management and of the staffs who work under them. Special problems in the development of solidarity are therefore presented, particularly since one of the main problems, as was pointed out, is the conflict over authority.

CONCLUSION

The principal concerns in this chapter have been with types of work shops, identity and the moral structure of work relations, goal definition, the family and community, industrialization and automation, management, status and authority, work groups, and professionals in organizations. Although usually dealt with in industrial sociology, space limitations and the fact that they are partly dealt with in other chapters, forced omission of detailed consideration of the social structure of labor markets, careers, labor unions, and the motivation of work behavior.

It is useful to conclude by pointing to eight major issues in the study of industrial relations in sociology. The first five involve choices among differing strategies in scientific procedure. The remaining three were described by Blau and Scott (1962, pp. 242–250) as "dilemmas of formal organization." These latter are more a matter of the generic character of organizations than a matter of choice in scientific procedure.

1. An important controversy revolves about the question of the degree of attention that should be given to internal or microsociological problems as compared to industry-community or macrosociological problems. The former emphasis is illustrated by the "human relations" interest in the relations of the worker to his fellow worker at the work bench, and the latter emphasis is illustrated in studies of union-management relations, or the impact of legislation on worker rights.

2. There is a cleavage between sociologists interested in the study of power and those interested in the study of values in industrial organizations. The students of power focus attention on the major decisions of owners or top managers and on the legitimation of the decision-making powers which managers have. Those who emphasize values place greater emphasis on the integrating beliefs and ideas in various parts of the industrial organization and the role of common understandings in reducing conflict.

3. Related to the previous issue, but having a distinctive character, is concern of some with harmony and of others with conflict. While the students of either problem freely admit that the other exists, there is a strong difference in the direction of interests. One group of researchers is keenly sensitive to the elements that knit employees together on the one hand, and managers and workers on the other, while other researchers focus attention on the elements that divide these persons.

4. A fourth issue is the general question of whether industrialization takes similar forms wherever it develops, or whether there are "several roads" to industrialism. Some point to the similarities of industrialism everywhere in the world in the form of a distinctive discipline and of various relationships between managers and managed, oth-

ers point, for example, to the special variations introduced by Japan in the course of her industrialization.

5. The fifth issue is methodological. The point here is whether one should do intensive case studies in which one examines intimately one particular industry, or whether one should gather more extensive data about many industries. Partly the problem is simply the extreme difficulty of studying more than one industry at one time without necessarily reducing the intensity of focus. At the same time it is recognized that special research tools are necessary for the study of industrial organizations. For example, sampling takes different forms from that used in house-to-house surveys. One may be uninterested in random sampling because of the peculiar structure of an organization. Though there be only one manager, it is usually essential to include him in the interviewing. Also an interview has ramifications in an organization that it may not have in a house-to-house survey. If the interviewer structures his own role unsuccessfully in a house-to-house survey, the worst that may befall him is that the door may be slammed in his face, or an irritated phone call made to the research headquarters. Whatever the result, the next person on the list will usually be unaware of the previous difficulty and one gets a fresh start. By contrast, in organizations the first interview affects all subsequent ones. If the first encounter is successful, the interviewed persons carry the word to others and one's task becomes easier. If unsuccessful, the respondents become more and more difficult, and it may become impossible to carry on the study at all. Such problems may lead organizational researchers to make use of indirect approaches, or to use records or documents indicative of the total organization.

6. There is the dilemma of the strain between the need for coordination and the equal need for communication in organizations. The free flow of communication, Blau and Scott (1962) suggested, improves problem-solving but stands in the way of coordi-

nation. With free communication many solutions may be proposed but coordination may require that a single solution be agreed upon.

7. There is a conflict between the requirements of bureaucratic discipline, on the one hand, and of professional expertness on the other.

8. Finally, the need for centralized planning conflicts with the need to provide for individual initiative in organization. This is perhaps a special form of the more general problem of the conflict between order and freedom. One wishes a maximum of initiative from the members of the organization but one wishes that this freedom be somehow organized and focused on the limited goal of the organization and consequently that it be disciplined in the service of the industrial objective.

The eight issues just discussed are far from being settled at the present writing. Some, such as the last three, represent what seem to be inherent dilemmas in the nature of industrial and indeed of all formal organizations. Nevertheless, the polarization of positions concerning these eight major issues has helped to carve out a distinctive area of industrial relations for the sociologist and has helped to motivate him in his studies of them.

REFERENCES

Abegglen, J. C. The Japanese factory. Glencoe, Ill.: Free Press, 1958.

Adams, S. N. Status congruency as a variable in small group performance. Soc. Forces, 1953–1954, 32, 16–22.

Aldous, Joan. Urbanization, the extended family, and kinship ties in West Africa. Soc. Forces, 1962, 41, 6–12.

Anderson, T. R., & Warkov, S. Organizational size and functional complexity. Amer. sociol. Rev., 1961, 26, 23–28.

Arendt, Hannah. The human condition. Chicago: Univer. of Chicago Press, 1958.

Arensberg, C. M. Industry and the community. Amer. J. Sociol., 1942, 48, 1–12.

Argyris, C. Personality and organization. New York: Harper, 1957.

Argyris, C. Understanding human behavior in organizations: One viewpoint. In M. Haire (Ed.), Modern organization theory. New York: Wiley, 1959. Ch. 5.

Argyris, C. Interpersonal competence and organizational effectiveness. Homewood, Ill.: Dorsey Press and Richard D. Irwin, 1962.

Axelrod, M. Urban structure and social participation. Amer. sociol. Rev., 1956, 21, 13–18.

Bakke, E. W. Citizens without work. New Haven: Yale Univer. Press, 1939.

Bakke, E. W. Bonds of organization. New York: Harper, 1950.

Bakke, E. W. Adaptive human behavior. New Haven, Conn.: Labor and Management Center, Yale Univer., 1951.

Bakke, E. W. The fusion process. New Haven, Conn.: Labor and Management Center, Yale Univer., 1953.

Bakke, E. W. Concept of the social organization. In M. Haire (Ed.), Modern organization theory. New York: Wiley, 1959. Ch. 2.

Barnard, C. I. The functions of the executive. Cambridge, Mass.: Harvard Univer. Press, 1938.

Barrett, E. B. The Jesuit enigma. New York: Boni and Liveright, 1927.

Becker, H., Geer, Blanche, Hughes, E. C., & Strauss, A. L. Boys in white. Chicago: Univer. of Chicago Press 1961.

Benne, K. D., & Sheats, P. Functional roles of group members. J. soc. Iss., 1948, 4, 41–50.

Bell, D. The end of ideology. New York: The Free Press of Glencoe, 1960.

Belshaw, C. S. Adaptation of personnel policies in social context. In W. E. Moore & A. S. Feldman (Eds.), Labor commitment and social change in developing areas. New York: Social Science Research Council, 1960. Ch. 6.

Bendix, R. Bureaucratization in industry. In A. Kornhauser, R. Dubin, & A. M. Ross (Eds.), Industrial conflict. New York: McGraw, 1954. Ch. 12.

Bendix, R. Work and authority in industry. New York: Wiley, 1956.

Bendix, R. Industrialization, ideologies, and social structure. Amer. sociol. Rev., 1959, 24, 613–623.

Bennis, W. G., Berkowitz, N., Affinito, M., & Malone, M. Reference groups and loyalties in the out-patient department. *Admin. Sci. Quart.*, 1958, 2, 481–500.

Berger, B. M. *Working class suburb.* Berkeley and Los Angeles: Univer. of California Press, 1960.

Berger, B. M. On Talcott Parsons. *Commentary*, 1962, 6, 507–513.

Berle, A. A., & Means, G. C. *The modern corporation and private property.* New York: Macmillan, 1933.

Berliner, J. S. *Factory and manager in the USSR.* Cambridge, Mass.: Harvard Univer. Press, 1957.

Blau, P. W. *The dynamics of bureaucracy.* Chicago: Univer. of Chicago Press, 1955.

Blau, P. W., & Scott, W. R. *Formal organizations.* San Francisco: Chandler, 1962.

Blauner, R. Alienation and freedom: The manual worker in industry. Unpublished manuscript, Berkeley, Univer. of California, July, 1962.

Boulding, K. E. *Conflict and defense.* New York: Harper, 1962.

Buckingham, W. S., Jr. *Testimony in Automation and technological change.* Washington: Government Printing Office, 1955. Pp. 29–37.

Burke, K. *Permanence and change.* New York: New Republic, 1935.

Cantril, H., & Strunk, Mildred (Eds.) *Public Opinion 1935–1946.* Princeton, N.J.: Princeton Univer. Press, 1951.

Caplow, T. *The sociology of work.* Minneapolis: Univer. of Minnesota Press, 1954.

Caplow, T. Organizational size. *Admin. Sci. Quart.*, 1957, 1, 484–505.

Caplow, T., & McGee, R. J. *The academic marketplace.* New York: Basic Books, 1958.

Chapple, E. D., & Sayles, L. R. *The measure of management.* New York: Macmillan, 1961.

Clark, B. R. *Adult education in transition.* Berkeley: Univer. of California Press, 1958.

Clark, B. R. *The open door college.* New York: McGraw, 1960.

Clark, J. V. A preliminary investigation of some unconscious assumptions affecting labor efficiency in eight supermarkets. Unpublished doctoral dissertation, Boston, Harvard Graduate School of Business Administration, 1958.

Commons, J. R. *Legal foundations of capitalism.* Madison: Univer. of Wisconsin Press, 1959. (First published, 1924.)

Corey, L. Problems of the peace: IV. The middle class. *Antioch Rev.*, 1945, 5, 68–87.

Coser, L. *The functions of social conflict.* Glencoe, Ill.: Free Press, 1956.

Coser, Rose Laub. Authority and decision-making in a hospital. *Amer. sociol. Rev.*, 1958, 23, 56–63.

Cyert, R. M., & March, J. G. *A behavioral theory of the firm.* Englewood Cliffs, N.J.: Prentice-Hall, Inc., 1963.

Dalton, M. Conflicts between staff and line managerial officers. *Amer. sociol. Rev.*, 1950, 15, 342–351.

Dalton, M. *Men who manage.* New York: Wiley, 1959.

Davis, A. The motivation of the under-privileged worker. In W. F. Whyte (Ed.), *Industry and society.* New York: McGraw, 1946. Pp. 84–106.

Davis, K. *Human relations at work.* New York: McGraw, 1962.

Davis, K., & Golden, Hilda H. Urbanization and the development of preindustrial areas. In P. K. Hatt & A. J. Reiss, Jr. (Eds.), *Cities and society.* (rev. ed.) Glencoe, Ill.: Free Press, 1957. Pp. 120–140.

Diebold, J. *Testimony in automation and technological change.* Washington, D.C.: Government Printing Office, 1955. Pp. 6–29.

Dobriner, W. M. (Ed.) *The suburban community.* New York: Putnam, 1958.

Dobriner, W. M. *Class in suburbia.* Englewood Cliffs, N.J.: Prentice-Hall, Inc., 1963.

The dock worker. Liverpool, Eng.: Univer. Press of Liverpool, 1954.

Drucker, P. F. *America's next twenty years.* New York: Harper, 1957.

Dubin, R. Industrial workers' worlds: A study of the "central life interests" of industrial workers. *Soc. Probs,* 1956, 3, 131–142.

Dubin, R. *Working union-management relations.* Englewood Cliffs, N.J.: Prentice-Hall, Inc., 1958.

Dunlop, J. T. *Industrial relations systems.* New York: Holt-Dryden, 1958.

Dunlop, J. T. Structural changes in the American labor movement and industrial relations system. In W. Galenson & S. M. Lipset (Eds.), *Labor and trade unionism.* New York: Wiley, 1960. Pp. 102–116.

Durkheim, E. Some notes on occupational groups. In G. Simpson (Trans.), *The Division of Labor in Society*. Glencoe, Ill.: Free Press, 1947. Preface to second edition.

Elkin, F. The soldier's language. *Amer. J. Sociol.*, 1946, 51, 414–422.

Etzioni, A. Authority structure and organizational effectiveness. *Admin. Sci. Quart.*, 1959, 4, 43–67.

Etzioni, A. *A comparative analysis of complex organizations*. New York: The Free Press of Glencoe, 1961.

Faris, R. E. L. Interaction of generations and family stability. *Amer. sociol. Rev.*, 1947, 12, 159–164.

Faunce, W. A. Automation in the automobile industry: Some consequences for in-plant structure. *Amer. sociol. Rev.*, 1958, 23, 401–407.

Feld, M. D. Information and authority: The structure of military organization. *Amer. sociol. Rev.*, 1959, 24, 15–22.

Fichlander, T. C. The labor force. In J. F. Dewhurst & Associates (Eds.), *America's needs and resources*. New York: Twentieth Century Fund, 1955. Pp. 721–734.

Fleishmann, E. A., Harris, E. F., & Burtt, H. E. *Leadership and supervision in industry: An evaluation of a supervisory training program*. Columbus, Ohio: Bureau of Educational Research, The Ohio State University, Monograph No. 33, 1955.

Form, W. H., & Miller, D. C. *Industry, labor and community*. New York: Harper, 1960.

Friedmann, G. *The anatomy of work*. New York: The Free Press of Glencoe, 1961.

Friedrich, C. J. Some observations on Weber's analysis of bureaucracy. In R. K. Merton, A. P. Gray, B. Hockey, & H. C. Selvin (Eds.), *Reader in bureaucracy*. Glencoe, Ill.: Free Press, 1952. Pp. 27–33.

Fromm, E. *Marx's concept of man*. New York: Frederick Ungar, 1961.

Gay, E. F. Putting-out system. In *Encyclopedia of the social sciences*, 1932, 13, 7–11.

Gerth, H., & Mills C, W. (Trans.) *From Max Weber: Essays in sociology*. New York: Oxford Univer. Press, 1946.

Gibbs, J. P., & Martin, W. T. Urbanization, technology, and the division of labor: International patterns. *Amer. sociol. Rev.*, 1962, 27, 667–677.

Glover, J. D. *The attack on big business*. Cambridge, Mass., Harvard Univer. Press, 1954.

Goffman, E. *The presentation of self in everyday life*. New York: Doubleday, 1959.

Goldner, F. H. Organizations and their environment: Roles at their boundary. Paper read at Amer. sociol. Soc., New York, 1960.

Gouldner, A. W. Red tape as a social problem. In R. K. Merton, A. P. Gray, B. Hockey, & H. C. Selvin (Eds.), *Reader in bureaucracy*. Glencoe, Ill.: Free Press, 1952, Pp. 410–418.

Gouldner, A. W. *Patterns of industrial bureaucracy*. Glencoe, Ill.: Free Press, 1954.(a)

Gouldner, A. W. *Wildcat strike*. Yellow Springs, Ohio: Antioch Press, 1954.(b)

Gouldner, A. W. Cosmopolitans and locals: Toward an analysis of latent social roles— I and II. *Admin. Sci. Quart.*, 1957–1958, 2, 281–306, 444–480.

Gouldner, A. W. The norm of reciprocity: A preliminary statement. *Amer. sociol. Rev.*, 1960, 25, 161–178.

Gouldner, A. W. Comment on "managerial succession in complex organizations," *Amer. J. Sociol.*, 1962, 68, 54–56.

Greenfield, S. M. Industrialization and the family in sociological theory. *Amer. J. Sociol.*, 1961, 67, 312–322.

Gross, C. *The gild merchant*. Oxford: Clarendon, 1890.

Gross, E. Some functional consequences of primary controls in formal work organizations. *Amer. sociol. Rev.*, 1953, 18, 368–373.

Gross, E. *Work and society*. New York: Crowell, 1958.

Gross, E. Dimensions of leadership. *Personnel J.*, 1961, 40, 213–228.

Grusky, O. Corporate size, bureaucratization, and managerial succession. *Amer. J. Sociol.*, 1961, 67, 261–269.

Guest, R. H. Managerial succession in complex organizations. *Amer. J. Sociol.*, 1962, 68, 47–54.(a)

Guest, R. H. *Organizational change: The effect of successful leadership*. Homewood, Ill.: Dorsey Press and Richard D. Irwin, 1962.(b)

Hall, O. Types of medical careers. *Amer. J. Sociol.*, 1948, 53, 327–336.

Harbison, F., & Myers, C. A. *Management in the industrial world, an international analysis*. New York: McGraw, 1959.

Hare, A. P. *Handbook of small group research.* New York: The Free Press of Glencoe, 1962.

Hauser, H. Journeymen's societies. In *Encyclopedia of the Social Sciences,* 1932, **8**, 424–427.

Henderson, A. M., & Parsons, T. (Trans.) *The theory of social and economic organization.* Glencoe, Ill.: Free Press, 1947.

Hickman, C. A., & Kuhn, M. H. *Individuals, groups, and economic behavior.* New York: Dryden, 1956.

Homans, G. C. *The human group.* New York: Harcourt, 1950.

Homans, G. C. Human behavior as exchange. *Amer. J. Sociol.,* 1958, **63**, 597–606.

Homans, G. C. *Social behavior: Its elementary forms.* New York: Harcourt, 1961.

Hoselitz, B. F. The market matrix. In W. E. Moore & A. S. Feldman (Eds.), *Labor commitment and social change in developing areas.* New York: Social Science Research Council, 1960. Ch. 12.

Howton, F. W. Work assignment and interpersonal relations in a research organization: Some participant observations. *Admin. Sci. Quart.,* 1963, **7**, 502–520.

Hughes, E. C. Work and the self. In J. H. Rohrer, & M. Sherif (Eds.), *Social psychology at the crossroads.* New York: Harper, 1951.

Hughes, E. C. The making of a physician. *Hum. Organ.,* Winter, 1956, **14**, 21–25.

Hughes, E. C., & Hughes, Helen M. *Where peoples meet.* Glencoe, Ill.: Free Press, 1952.

Inkeles, A. Industrial man: The relation of status to experience, perception, and value. *Amer. J. Sociol.,* 1960, **66**, 1–31.

Jaffe, A. J., & Stewart, C. D. *Manpower resources and utilization.* New York: Wiley, 1951.

James, J. Clique organization in a small industrial plant. *Res. Stud., State Coll. Wash.,* 1951, **19**, 125–130.

Janowitz, M. *The professional soldier.* New York: The Free Press of Glencoe, 1960.

Jaques, E. *Measurement of responsibility.* London: Tavistock, 1956.

Johnson, E. H. The stem family and its extensions in modern Japan. Paper read at Amer. Anthropol. Ass., Minneapolis, 1960.

Jones, H. M. Looking around. *Harvard Bus. Rev.,* 1953, **31**, 133–142.

Katz, D., Maccoby, N. & Morse, Nancy C. *Productivity, supervision, and morale in an office situation.* Ann Arbor: Survey Research Center, Univer. of Michigan, 1950.

Kerr, C. Changing social structures. In W. E. Moore & A. S. Feldman (Eds.), *Labor commitment and social change in developing areas.* New York: Social Science Research Council, 1960. Ch. 19.

Kerr, C., Dunlop, J. T., Harbison, F. H., & Myers, C. A. *Industrialism and industrial man.* Cambridge, Mass.: Harvard Univer. Press, 1960.

Kerr, C. & Siegel, A. The interindustry propensity to strike—An international comparison. In A. Kornhauser, R. Dubin, & A. M. Ross (Eds.), *Industrial conflict.* New York: McGraw, 1954. Ch. 14.

Kornhauser, A., Dubin, R., & Ross, A. M. (Eds.), *Industrial conflict.* New York: McGraw, 1954.

Kornhauser, W. (with the assistance of Hagstrom, W. O.). *Scientists in industry.* Berkeley and Los Angeles: Univer. of California Press, 1962.

Kriesberg, L. Careers, organization size, and succession. *Amer. J. Sociol.,* 1962, **68**, 355–359.

Krupp, S. *Pattern in organization analysis.* Philadelphia: Chilton, 1961.

Landsberger, H. A. *Hawthorne revisited: Management and the worker, its critics, and developments in human relations in industry.* Ithaca, N.Y.: Cornell Univer. Press, 1958.

Lawrence, P. *The changing of organizational behavior patterns.* Boston: Harvard Univer. Graduate School of Business Administration, 1958.

Lenski, G. Status crystallization. *Amer. sociol. Rev.,* 1954, **19**, 405–413.

Lenski, G. *The religious factor.* New York: Doubleday, 1963.

Lesieur, F. G. (Ed.) *The Scanlon plan.* New York: Wiley, 1958.

Lévi-Strauss, C. Le principe de réciprocité. In C. Lévi-Strauss (Ed.), *Les structures élémentaires de la parenté.* Paris: Presses Universitaires de France, 1949. Ch. V.

Likert, R. *New patterns of management.* New York: McGraw, 1961.

Lipset, S. M. *Agrarian socialism.* Berkeley and Los Angeles: Univer. of California Press, 1950.

Lipset, S. M. Some social requisites of democracy: Economic development and political legitimacy. *Amer. polit. Sci. Rev.,* 1959, **53,** 69–105.

Lipset, S. M., Bendix, R., & Malm, F. T. Job plans and entry into the labor market. *Soc. Forces,* 1955, **33,** 224–232.

Lipset, S. M., Trow, M. A., & Coleman, J. S. *Union democracy.* Glencoe, Ill.: Free Press, 1956.

Litwak, E., & Hylton, Lydia F. Interorganizational analysis: A hypothesis on co-ordinating agencies. *Admin. Sci. Quart.,* 1962, **6,** 395–420.

Macaulay, S. Non-contractual relations in business: A preliminary study. *Amer. sociol. Rev.,* 1963, **28,** 55–67.

McGregor, D. *The human side of enterprise.* New York: McGraw, 1960.

Mack, R. W. Ecological patterns in an industrial shop. *Soc. Forces,* 1954, **32,** 351–356.

McKean, E. C. *The persistence of small business: A study of unincorporated enterprise.* Kalamazoo, Mich.: W. E. Upjohn Institute for Community Research, 1958.

Maier, N. A. *Principles of human relations.* New York: Wiley, 1952.

Maier, N. R. F., & Solem, A. R. The contribution of the discussion leader to the quality of group thinking: The effective use of minority opinions. *Hum. Relat.,* 1952, **5,** 277–288.

Mann, F. C., & Hoffman, L. R. *Automation and the worker.* New York: Holt-Dryden, 1960.

Manpower report of the president and a report on manpower requirements, resources, utilization, and training. Washington, D.C.: Government Printing Office, 1963.

March, J. G., & Simon, H. A., with the collaboration of Guetzkow, H. *Organizations.* New York: Wiley, 1958.

Matthews, T. J. The urban fire station: A sociological analysis of an occupation. Unpublished master dissertation, Department of Sociology, Washington State Univer., 1950.

Mauss, M. *The gift.* I. Cunnison (Trans.). Glencoe, Ill.: Free Press, 1954.

Mayo, E. *The human problems of an industrial civilization.* New York: Macmillan, 1933.

Mayo, E. *The social problems of an industrial civilization.* Boston: Harvard Univer. Graduate School of Business Administration, 1946.

Mayo, E. *The political problems of an industrial civilization.* Boston: Harvard Univer. Graduate School of Business Administration, 1947.

Mayo, E., & Lombard, G. F. F. *Teamwork and labor turnover in the aircraft industry of southern California.* Boston: Harvard Univer. Graduate School of Business Administration, 1944.

Merton, R. K., Reader, G. C., & Kendall, Patricia L. *The student physician.* Cambridge, Mass.: Harvard Univer. Press, 1957.

Mills, C. W. *The new men of power: America's labor leaders.* New York: Harcourt, 1948.

Mills, C. W. *White collar.* New York: Oxford, 1951.

Moore, W. E. *Industrial relations and the social order.* New York: Macmillan, 1951.

Moore, W. E. *The conduct of the corporation.* New York: Random House, Inc., 1962.

Moore, W. E. *Man, time, and society.* New York: Wiley, 1963.

Mumford, L. *The culture of cities.* New York: Harcourt, 1938.

Myers, R. C. Myth and status systems in industry. *Soc. Forces,* 1948, **26,** 331–337.

National Manpower Council. *Womanpower.* New York: Columbia Univer. Press, 1957.

National Opinion Research Center. Jobs and occupations: A popular evaluation. In R. Bendix & S. M. Lipset (Eds.), *Class, status, and power.* Glencoe, Ill.: Free Press, 1953. Pp. 411–426.

Nye, F. I., & Hoffman, Lois W. *The employed mother in America.* Chicago: Rand, 1963.

Orzack, L. H. Work as a "central life interest" of professionals. *Soc. Probs,* 1959, **7,** 125–132.

Pappenheim, F. *The alienation of modern man.* New York: Monthly Review Press, 1959.

Parsons, T. A revised analytical approach to the theory of social stratification. In R. Bendix & S. M. Lipset (Eds.), *Class, status, and power.* Glencoe, Ill.: Free Press, 1953. Pp. 92–128.

Parsons, T. Some ingredients of a general theory of formal organization. In A. W. Halpin (Ed.), *Administrative theory in education.* Chicago: Univer. of Chicago Midwest Administration Center, 1958. Ch. III.

Parsons, T., Bales, R. F., & Shils, E. A. (Eds.) *Working papers in the theory of action.* Glencoe, Ill.: Free Press, 1953.

Parsons, T., & Smelser, N. J. *Economy and society.* Glencoe, Ill.: Free Press, 1956.

Pelz, D. C. Influence: A key to effective leadership in the first-line supervisor. *Personnel,* 1952, **29,** 209–217.

Perrow, C. The analysis of goals in complex organizations. *Amer. sociol. Rev.,* 1961, **26,** 854–866.

Randle, C. W. Problems of research and development management. *Harvard Bus. Rev.,* 1959, **37,** 128–136.

Reissman, L. A study of role conceptions in bureaucracy. *Soc. Forces,* 1949, **27,** 305–310.

Riley, J. W., Jr. (Ed.) *The corporation and its publics.* New York: Wiley, 1963.

Robinson, H. A. Job satisfaction researches of 1958. *Personnel guid. J.,* 1959, **37,** 669–673.

Roethlisberger, F. J. The foreman: Master and victim of double talk. *Harvard Bus. Rev.,* 1945, **23,** 283–298.

Roethlisberger, F. J., & Dickson, W. J. *Management and the worker.* Cambridge, Mass.: Harvard Univer. Press, 1939.

Rosen, S. M., & Rosen, Laura. *Technology and society.* New York: Macmillan, 1941.

Sayles, L. R. *Behavior of industrial work groups.* New York: Wiley, 1958.

Schneider, E. V. *Industrial sociology.* New York: McGraw, 1957.

Seashore, S. *Group cohesiveness in the industrial work group.* Ann Arbor: Survey Research Center, Univer. of Michigan, 1954.

Seeman, M. On the meaning of alienation. *Amer. sociol. Rev.,* 1959, **24,** 783–791.

Seligman, E. R. A. *Two chapters on the mediaeval guilds of England.* Baltimore: American Economic Ass., 1887.

Selznick, P. *TVA and the grass roots.* Berkeley: Univer. of California Press, 1953.

Selznick, P. *Leadership in administration.* Evanston, Ill.: Row, Peterson, 1957.

Sills, D. L. *The volunteers.* Glencoe, Ill.: Free Press, 1957.

Simon, H. A. *Administrative behavior.* New York: Macmillan, 1947.

Simon, H. A. *Models of man.* New York: Wiley, 1957.

Simon, H. A., Smithburg, D. W., & Thompson, V. A. *Public administration.* New York: Knopf, 1950.

Simpson, R. L. Vertical and horizontal communication in formal organizations. *Admin. Sci. Quart.,* 1959, **4,** 188–196.

Singer, M. Changing craft traditions in India. In W. E. Moore & A. S. Feldman (Eds.), *Labor commitment and social change in developing areas.* New York: Social Science Research Council, 1960. Ch. 14.

Spaulding, C. B. *An introduction to industrial sociology.* San Francisco: Chandler, 1961.

Stinchcombe, A. L. Bureaucratic and craft administration of production: A comparative study. *Admin. Sci. Quart.,* 1959, **4,** 168–187.

Strauss, G. The changing role of the working supervisor. *J. Bus. Univer. Chicago,* 1957, **30,** 202–211.

Strauss, G., & Sayles, L. R. *Personnel.* Englewood Cliffs, N.J.: Prentice-Hall, Inc., 1960.

Survey Research Center. *Big business from the viewpoint of the public.* Ann Arbor: Univer. of Michigan Press, 1951.

Sutherland, E. H. (annotated and interpreted), *The professional thief.* Chicago: Univer. of Chicago Press, 1937.

Thompson, J. D., & McEwen, W. J. Organizational goals and environment: Goal-setting as an interaction process. *Amer. sociol. Rev.,* 1958, **23,** 23–31.

Thompson, J. D., & Tuden, A. Strategies, structures, and processes of organizational decision. In J. D. Thompson (Ed.), *Comparative studies in administration.* Pittsburgh: Univer. of Pittsburgh Press, 1959. Pp. 195–216.

Thompson, V. A. *Modern organization.* New York: Knopf, 1961.

Walker, C. R. *Toward the automatic factory.* New Haven, Conn.: Yale Univer. Press, 1957.

Walker, C. R., & Guest, R. H. *The man on the assembly line.* Cambridge, Mass.: Harvard Univer. Press, 1952.(a)

Walker, C. R., & Guest, R. H. The man on the assembly line. *Harvard Bus. Rev.,* May–June, 1952, **30,** 71–83.(b)

Walker, C. R., Guest, R. H., & Turner, A. N. *The foreman on the assembly line.* Cambridge, Mass.: Harvard Univer. Press, 1956.

Wardwell, W. I. Limited, marginal, and quasi-practitioners. In H. E. Freeman, S. Levine, & L. G. Reeder (Eds.), *Handbook of medical sociology.* Englewood Cliffs, N.J.: Prentice-Hall, Inc., 1963. Ch. 9.

Warner, W. L., & Low, J. O. *The social system of the modern factory.* New Haven, Conn.: Yale Univer. Press, 1947.

Weber, M. *General economic history.* Frank H. Knight (Trans.). Glencoe, Ill.: Free Press, 1950.

Whisler, T. L., & Schultz, G. P. Automation and the management process. *Ann. Amer. Acad. polit. soc. Sci.,* March, 1962, **340,** 81–89.

Whitehead, T. N. *Leadership in a free society.* Cambridge, Mass.: Harvard Univer. Press, 1936.

Whitehead, T. N. *The industrial worker.* Cambridge, Mass.: Harvard Univer. Press, 1938.

Whyte, W. F. *Human relations in the restaurant industry.* New York: McGraw, 1948.

Whyte, W. F. *Pattern for industrial peace.* New York: Harper, 1951.

Whyte, W. F. *Money and motivation.* New York: Harper, 1955.(a)

Whyte, W. F. *Street corner society.* (enlarged ed.) Chicago: Univer. of Chicago Press, 1955.(b)

Whyte, W. F. Human relations theory: A progress report. *Harvard Bus. Rev.,* 1956, **34,** 125–132.

Whyte, W. F. *Man and organization.* Homewood, Ill.: Dorsey Press and Richard D. Irwin, 1959.

Whyte, W. F. *Men at work.* Homewood, Ill.: Dorsey Press and Richard D. Irwin, 1961.

Whyte, W. F., & Gardner, B. B. The man in the middle: Position and problems of the foreman. *Appl. Anthro.,* Spring, 1945, **4,** 1–28.

Whyte, W. H., Jr., *The organization man.* New York: Simon & Schuster, 1956.

Wilensky, H. L. *Syllabus of industrial relations.* Chicago: Univer. of Chicago Press, 1954.

Wilensky, H. L. *Intellectuals in labor unions.* Glencoe, Ill.: Free Press, 1956.

Wilensky, H. L. Orderly careers and social participation: The impact of work history on social integration in the middle mass. *Amer. sociol. Rev.,* 1961, **26,** 521–539.

Williams, Josephine J. Patients and prejudice: Lay attitudes toward women physicians. *Amer. J. Sociol.,* 1946, **51,** 283–287.

Woytinsky, W. S., & Associates. *Employment and wages in the United States.* New York: Twentieth Century Fund, 1953.

Wray, D. E. Marginal men of industry: The foremen. *Amer. J. Sociol.,* 1949, **54,** 298–301.

Yoder, D., & Heneman, H. G., Jr. *Labor economics and industrial relations.* Cincinnati, Ohio: South-Western Publishing Co., 1959.

Young, M., & Willmott, P. *Family and kinship in East London.* Glencoe, Ill.: Free Press, 1957.

Zaleznik, A., Christensen, C. R., & Roethlisberger, F. J., with the assistance and collaboration of Homans, G. C. *The motivation, productivity, and satisfaction of workers: A prediction study.* Boston: Harvard Univer. Division of Research, Graduate School of Business Administration, 1958.

CHAPTER 18   Family, Marriage, and Kinship

MORRIS ZELDITCH, JR.

If the family is universal, it ought to be possible to say just what property universally characterizes all families and only families. Yet such an eminent scholar of the subject as Leach (1955, p. 183) claims that there is no such property. Some of the most obvious definitions are clearly unsatisfactory. While every family now known permits sexual access of husband to wife, it is not sufficient to define a family as the institution which regulates sexual access, since in the first place the family is never solely concerned with sexual access and in the second place sexual access is often not confined solely to the family. Murdock (1949), for example, in a comparative study of family and community structure, found that only 39 per cent of a sample of 250 societies disapproves entirely of sexual access among unrelated partners before marriage; as many as 24 societies permit great sexual freedom after marriage; and 83 permit sexual freedom after marriage among certain related partners, such as a woman and her husband's brother (Murdock, 1949, pp. 5, 270). Nor is it sufficient to identify the family as the institution that is universally concerned with the biological facts of birth. If it is

fatherhood with which the family is concerned, it is sociological and not biological fatherhood that matters. The biological father of a child may be called its *genitor*. In a number of societies in Australia and Africa the genitor is distinguished from the *pater,* the person in a society through whom a child's jural rights and obligations are transmitted, and who is recognized as responsible for his conduct until he is mature. Among Australian tribes a child is socially fathered by the husband of its mother, regardless of its genitor (Radcliffe-Brown, 1930). Among some African tribes, a sterile male may even consciously delegate the conception of his child to some other man. The resulting child belongs legally to the former as pater and is indistinguishable from his own begotten child not only in law but even in sentiment—the pater feels all the emotions and pride of fatherhood even though he is not the genitor (Fortes, 1949). In some societies it is even possible to coöpt a female as pater. A female marries another woman who takes the role of father to her children, and in that society the legal and sociological definitions of a family are satisfied, though this is never the predominant family type in the society (see for example, Evans-Pritchard, 1951).

DEFINITIONS AND FUNCTIONS OF THE FAMILY

One possible definition is the following: A *family* is a social group in which sexual access is permitted between adult members, reproduction legitimately occurs, the group is responsible to society for the care and upbringing of children, and the group is an economic unit at least in consumption. This definition is the result of influential—and controversial—research by the American anthropologist G. P. Murdock (1949). Murdock argued that in each of 250 societies for which he had evidence in 1949 (he has since added more than twice that number to his sample) a small social unit, consisting of husband, wife, and children (and called a *nuclear* family) exists that satisfies this definition. While no one of the four criteria alone is sufficient, all four are necessary and together they are sufficient.

While no scholar has yet questioned that the four "functions" attributed by Murdock (1949) to the family are universal, the identification of these functions with a concrete social unit, the nuclear family, has been attacked sharply. Levy and Fallers (1959) objected that for no other institutional sphere has anyone discovered either a universal concrete structure or one which invariably performs the same functions, and they did not believe such a structure exists among family institutions. They believed that sexual access, procreation, socialization, and economic cooperation are universal, that they are universally found to be functions of some kinship-based unit, that this is universally a relatively small unit (like the nuclear family). What they objected to is the view that this is invariably the nuclear family composed of husband-father, wife-mother, son, and daughter. Levy (1955), Spiro (1954), and E. Kathleen Gough (1959) have offered counterexamples from China, Israel, and the Malabar coast of India. In each case, though the nuclear family performs one or more of the Murdock functions, at least one of them is performed by some other social group. For example, in an Israeli *Kibbutz,* the husband-wife unit neither raises and instructs its children nor is it the basic economic unit in the Murdock sense (Spiro, 1954). The Indian Nayar (a warrior caste) separate the husband-wife unit so that it is not a stable residential cohabiting group, nor does it raise and instruct the children it reproduces. The co-residential unit is a brother-sister-sister's-child group (E. Kathleen Gough, 1959). In China the nuclear family may be indistinguishable as an economic and educational unit within the extended family (Levy, 1955).

If there is no concrete group which can be universally identified as "the family," is there at least some institutionalized norm that can be universally identified with it? Malinowski (1930) proposed that legitimacy is such an institution. Legitimate birth is a concept that places the newborn child in appropriate jural relations with members already socialized into a given society; it regulates both the social relations of members with the newborn and the rights of the newborn to care, succession, inheritance, and instruction. More exactly, according to this definition, a family exists if, and only if, there is a pater role, and a pater role is one that (1) determines the jural status, rights, and obligations of a child recognized as the pater's child and (2) is charged by members of the society with responsibility for the child's conduct.

The definition is subtle, partly because of what it does not say. It does not imply that the pater must be a male; it does not imply that only one person may be a child's pater; it does not even imply that, because he is responsible for a child's conduct, the pater must himself instruct the child. It only implies that he must in some way supervise his child and is held to account by society for misconduct. (This is an elaboration of Malinowski's original definition, but is probably consistent with it; see Malinowski [1930].)

This definition is not less open to attack than Murdock's (1949), because it surely presumes that every society has some conception of legitimate birth. Where societies exist, such as that of Haiti, which may have illegitimacy rates of as much as 85 per cent of all registered births, it is open to serious question whether illegitimacy is everywhere defined, or everywhere defined as morally wrong. Among the Caribbean countries, in fact, at least eight have illegitimacy rates of over 60 per cent (Goode, 1960, p. 22).

Goode (1960) rescued the definition, however, by a careful survey of Caribbean courtship and marriage. He argued that high rates of illegitimacy are not a result of the absence of legitimacy norms, nor even of sanctions for illegitimate birth; they follow from family disorganization among lower-class families, particularly a breakdown of traditional courtship practices without any corresponding growth of new regulative structures. That marriage and legitimate birth are preferred is shown by the fact that women enter consensual unions when they have too little power to bargain for immediate marriage in a gamble that eventually the unions may be converted into marriages. Though often very late, almost everyone does get married. By that time, however, the number of births out of wedlock is high. The original courtship institutions depended on chaperonage and parental supervision, which in the contemporary period have deteriorated. Among the middle and upper classes of the Caribbean societies consensual union and illegitimate birth are not found. For the moment, therefore, the single property that seems universally identified with a structure that one would intuitively recognize as a family is the legitimacy principle.

THE IMPORTANCE OF THE FAMILY: THE SOVIET EXPERIENCE

Between 1917 and 1926 the Soviet Union enacted a sweeping series of family reforms which some of its most radical, though not most official, ideologists believed would lead eventually to the "withering away" of the family. Between 1936 and 1944 the Soviet Union enacted an equally sweeping series of family reforms marking a radical reversal of policy, which its ideologists explained were necessary to strengthen the family, because a strong family was crucial to the stability of the new Soviet society. The evidence is not conclusive, but the Soviet experience provides an instructive example of the importance of the family to society.

The fundamental ideological document is Engels, *The Origin of the Family, Private Property, and the State,* first published in 1884. Relying on Morgan's (1870) evolutionary theory, Engels traced the family through history, arguing that the bourgeois, capitalist family was essentially an economic arrangement in which love was less important than property, the wife was enslaved and exploited by the husband, the husband's authority was enforced by Church and State (which prohibited divorce), and, in any case, the wife was made economically dependent on her husband (her "provider") so that she could not leave him even if she came to hate him. In the Socialist society, Engels then argued, the female would be liberated and the family as an economic unit of society abolished. Women would work equally with men, property inheritance would cease to play a decisive role because property would not exist, and there would be no other motive left for marriage except "mutual inclination." Since the woman would be economically independent of the male, if she ceased to have the inclination she would simply part from the husband. "If only the marriage based on love is moral, then also only the marriage in which love continues . . . and if an affection definitely comes to an end . . . separation is a benefit for both parties as well as society . . ." (Engels, 1884, p. 89). Engels was not, perhaps, as extreme as some of the more radical feminists of the early Bolshevik movement. Though never official, Sabsovich (1929) and

Aleksandra Kollontai (1920) (in Marxist terms "Leftist-deviationists" in family matters) saw the family as altogether withering away. Sabsovich said in an early tract on the future of the Soviet society: ". . . the elimination of the individual household is not only a task whose achievement would be desirable . . . but a task whose satisfactory solution is an unavoidable necessity, one of the most important prerequisites for a realization of other fundamental objects of the general plan . . ." (Sabsovich, 1929, p. 170). Kollontai described the Soviet society as destroying the three main props of the capitalist family: the husband's role as provider, the wife's role in regulating home consumption (feeding and clothing her family), and the parents' role in bringing up their children. In the Soviet society women would be economically independent of men, the duties of the household would be taken over by public agencies (public kitchens and dining halls, public factory-made clothing, public baths, public nurseries and schools that would take the child in from birth), and what would be left would be "a union of affection and comradeship" (Aleksandra Kollontai, 1920).

Lenin, it is true, was considerably more conservative than Sabsovich (1929) or Kollontai (1920). He did not approve of casual sexual unions and did not refer to the withering away of the family (Lenin, 1949; Schlesinger, 1949, pp. 14, 22n). What he was more concerned with was destroying the traditional Russian family as an institution. His conception of the family was much like the family as Burgess and Locke (1945) described it when they referred to the historical change in our society from "institution" to "companionship." But the attack on the family by the early Bolsheviks, nevertheless, was thorough and remarkable. It was a three-pronged attack, aimed at the family as an economic unit; the family as a traditional, patriarchical institution; and the family as a conserver of traditional anti-Soviet values. Not only the heritage of radical feminism, but also the immediate

and practical interests of the new regime, were at stake. The family, it recognized, was the basic agent for the transmission of cultural values, and these values were clearly prerevolutionary and potentially counter-revolutionary. Therefore, added to ideology were concerns for sheer power (see Geiger, 1955; Geiger, 1956; Inkeles & Bauer, 1959, pp. 219–298).

From 1918 to 1926, when a comprehensive family code was published, the Bolshevik regime enacted laws and sought to implement their program in practice by making abortion legal; recognizing de facto marriages as having the same legal force as registered marriages; making divorce a purely private matter, not subject to court inquiry or decision; abolishing community property rights of the husband over the wife's income or dowry; abolishing the legal distinction between legitimate and illegitimate children; insisting on evidence that a marriage was voluntary on both husband and wife's part before recognizing it legally; giving women equal legal rights and equal education in the same institutions as men; and "collectivizing" household duties through a series of communal nurseries, kitchens, and baths. There was a concentrated effort to attack both the authority of husbands over wives and the authority of parents over children (Berman, 1946; Geiger & Inkeles, 1954; Hazard, 1939; Hazard, 1953; Schlesinger, 1949).

One can only infer the effects from later discussions that led to new family reforms. Having focused attention so closely on male exploitation of women and family transmission of conservative political traditions, the Soviet jurists and ideologists discovered that they had freed not only women and children, but also men. The ease of divorce and abortion, the state responsibility for the upbringing of children, and the fact that the household functions of women were not necessary to men apparently led to considerable male "irresponsibility" (Krilenko, 1937). This irresponsibility, in the new party line, was of course recognized as a survival of the old capitalist, exploitative attitude of males, in a new guise.

All survivals of this kind are a result of the extreme viability of the exploiting attitude towards women which has been fostered by the bourgeoisie for centuries. . . . The Capitalist plunderer regards woman above all . . . as . . . property. . . . The freedom given to the family by the revolution of the proletariat, the liberation of men and women from the fetters of compulsory life-long association, was taken by some morally unstable elements to confer a right to unbridled sexual debauchery, to caddishness and irresponsibility in family relations (Wolffson, 1936, p. 304).

In part the failure of the family to wither away, described below, was the result of a failure of the State to provide sufficient facilities for the collectivization of households. Thus, Wolffson wrote, "The breaking up of a family means in the overwhelming majority of the cases that children are left without adequate care and the necessary educational influence . . ." (Wolffson, 1936, p. 305). In part this may result from the inadequacy of the nursery as a substitute for the family. But more likely it simply follows from the fact that there were never enough nurseries, at least up to 1936 when the new conservative trend began, to accommodate more than a small part of the potential nursery population. The evaluation of the Soviet experience is made difficult by the inadequate and unreliable statistics available, but by the most conservative estimates there could not actually have been available more than 14 per cent of the places needed to care for children in 1936. From 1928 to 1939 the best estimates give an average annual increase in population of 2 million (Eason, 1953; compare U.S.S.R., 1957 & Lorimer, 1946). The Soviet yazli took children from about two months to three years of age (later four years). The kindergartens and preschool institutions took them from that time until about seven years of age. In any given year, therefore, about 6 million places in yazlis and 8 million places in later preschool institutions would be required to absorb all children seven and under. Estimates of actual places open in either type of institution are unreliable, but in 1950 there were 777,000 places in yazlis and 1.16 million places in nursery schools (U.S.S.R., 1957). Despite the intervening war years, a conservative estimate (i.e., one that would inflate the number of places) of the number of places available in 1936 would be that a total of about 1.9 million places were available. The ratio of places available to places needed, 1.9 million/14 million, is about one in seven, or 14 per cent (contrast Susan Kingsbury & Mildred Fairchild, 1935).

The child-care institutions, however, were certainly the most successful of the efforts at state performance of family functions. The so-called communal dining halls turned out to be inexpensive cafeterias and restaurants in which one would buy a meal and eat it in the restaurant or take it home (Susan Kingsbury & Mildred Fairchild, 1935); the public provision of clothing turned out to be the factory production of ready-made clothing, to be purchased by the family. The public baths failed to attract much attention. Coeducation, indeed, did become fact, and the proportion of the labor force that was female did increase markedly, so that women became more independent. State aid to families did increase sharply, though it seems always to have been expected that families would support their aged dependents.

From 1936 to 1944 the Soviet Union reversed many of these policies in an effort to "stabilize" the society. Abortion was made illegal; divorce was made more difficult; de facto marriages were no longer recognized; a wife was given rights to her husband's property; alimony and maintenance of children were enforced on divorced husbands; paternity suits were abolished, thus making for a factual recognition of illegitimacy though the state undertook the support of illegitimate children; coeducation was abolished; and parental responsibility for the conduct of children was re-established. The family, further, was no longer regarded legally and ideologically as a matter only of "private" concern. The State's interest was reasserted on the ground that a stable society depended on a stable family (Geiger & Inkeles, 1954; Hazard, 1939; Hazard, 1953; Inkeles, 1949; Schlesinger, 1949).

The implications of this experience are not conclusive, in the sense that they do not establish the fact that the family is universally required for the stability of a society. For one thing, on a much smaller scale the same policies—and for the same reasons— have been more successfully implemented in the Israeli Kibbutzim (see p. 698). It cannot, however, be argued that the Soviet experience shows only that old habits die hard. There have, clearly, been marked changes in Soviet family structure. The regime did succeed in destroying the traditional Russian family. A change apparently occurred to a family type most commonly found in other European societies and in the United States and is probably to be associated with industrialization. The counterrevolution in the family did not alter the requirement that marriage be voluntary, nor did it alter the changing legal and economic status of women more than is consistent with other Western nations. The Soviet experience probably does show that in a large-scale society the family is a crucial economic and social institution and that it is not easily destroyed without consequences for other social institutions of a society.

MARRIAGE AND DIVORCE

Romantic love, as a motive for marriage, is a relatively uncommon institution. It implies an intense affective involvement to a particular person, so that only that person could conceivably be one's mate; it implies that the mate is chosen without regard to the wishes of anyone else and certainly without regard to the wishes of the parents of those involved; and it implies that instrumental issues—questions of money, power, rank, or any calculated advantage—play no part in the choice.

Marriage and Instrumental Interests

Post-famine Ireland. A more common attitude is an old Kerryman's observation that ". . . marriage is just a business like buying or selling a farm of land." In Ireland, between the time of the famine and a relatively recent present, "up and down the country love-matches were laughed at" (Connell, 1962, p. 503). The purpose of an Irish farmer's match was not to gratify a couple's desire for companions, for sex, or for children; it was contemplated not when a man needed a wife, but "when the land needed a woman" (Connell, 1962, p. 503). When a man's mother got so old that she could not carry out her household functions, then it was time to bring in a daughter-in-law to replace her. One result was that the average age at marriage, for an Irish farmer, was slightly over 38 years. Another was that, because it was a matter of farm economy rather than personal inclination that determined marriage, the match was arranged by the father, who took great care to see that the needs of the land were served. A girl was chosen who had good health, and who brought in a good dowry. As to her appearance: "there's not the difference of a cow . . . between any two women in the world." If a girl were particularly unattractive a slight addition to her dowry would recompense her mate. The dowry was no mean economic addition to a man's resources; in the 1880's it might come to equal 10-12 years of farm rents (Connell, 1962, p. 505). Often the dowry was paid in installments, since it was so large, with the result that a woman brought to her husband a substantial income. It could be, and usually was, used to provide for brothers and sisters of the groom who were not to be settled on the land. From the girl's point of view, the purpose of the dowry was to buy her a place on the land. The matter was a serious economic adventure, and to calculate the girl's advantages a party of "viewers" was sent to "walk the land" of the prospective groom before a match was made. The viewers carefully examined the land, investigated searchingly the groom's title to the land, and checked also the good nature of the groom's mother, for it was with the mother that the girl was likely to have much of her future work relationships. Marriage was associated with a transfer of property from father to son; the viewers had to make particularly certain that their girl married the son who was to inherit the property. They might even require a written deed to the place ensuring the boy's claim before permitting marriage. Since in the Irish system of succession only one son inherited the land, one result was the high proportion of men and women in Ireland who in that period never married at all. In 1951, 34 per cent of the males and 26.5 per cent of the females in the Irish Republic as a whole (including urban areas) were still unmarried between 40 and 49 years of age, and, of farmers between 65 and 74, 25 per cent were still unmarried (Connell, 1962, p. 502).

Because the transaction was essentially an economic bargain, because it was the land, not personal desire, that determined the match, and because the land was the father's, at least until his son should marry, it was the father who determined both when and whom a boy should marry. Many fathers, "until their dying day saw no sufficient reason for bringing in a daughter-in-law; and until the old man died, many a son was unable to marry because he owned no land" (Connell, 1962, p. 512). If the father was no longer living, the match was arranged in some other way. But it was seldom a matter of individual choice, because, even if the prospective groom took the initiative, it was usually his prospective bride's father with whom he had to deal in his "courting."

Because of the conventional association between property and authority, when the son finally did marry the father retired from active farming, some fathers retiring more gradually than others.

Records and documents from before the time of the potato famine show that individual choice and an early age at marriage then predominated. Contemporary sources suggest that in very recent years the arranged match is again declining. The period of the arranged match, then, with its associated late and low rate of marriage, is confined to the years between the famine and the present. It is not so much that the basic determinants of Irish marriage have changed —land, as always, has determined marriage —but agricultural conditions have changed considerably. Before the famine, although the Irish did not have partible inheritance, they did subdivide their land to provide for new generations; because of the nature of the potato crop it seemed possible to do so without endangering the farm economy. Young men and girls, when they chose to marry, could readily do so because new land could be found: ". . . they need wait neither for dead men's shoes, nor for the dowry that purchased them" (Connell, 1962, p. 521). Fathers in such a situation "were ill-placed to dictate their children's marrying," and indeed marriage was one means of escaping a parent's authority. But subdivision proceeded to a point of diminishing returns, and after the famine subdivision was no longer seen as possible. If a man wanted to marry, then, he had to wait for his father's land; if a girl wanted to marry, she had to find a man on whom a father was willing to settle his land and then needed to find the money to buy this man. Most recently, apparently, the desire to emigrate has replaced the early abundance of land, so that the desire to wait for the father's transfer of land has again declined.

Arranged marriage. Arranged marriage is found where the consequences of marriage concern whole groups of kinsmen. Kinsmen usually have three kinds of interest in a marriage. The marriage is often conceived as an alliance between two kinship groups, not simply as the relation of the two partners to the marriage, and the group is anxious to select allies carefully. Significant economic interests are usually involved, both in the exchange of goods that accompanies the marriage and in the effect of the marriage on the dispersal or concentration of inherited property, wealth, and resources. Where the kinship unit as a whole is the unit of the stratification system, so that a "poor marriage" lowers the social rank of the whole group, the kinsmen are concerned to protect the family name.

The significance of the arranged marriage can be seen from two points of view: (1) that of the marriage choice itself, in which all the considerations just mentioned are important, and (2) that of the solidarity of the conjugal bond after the marriage, as against the parent-child bond that is important to the descent group. Because of the latter fact, where corporate descent groups (see chart 1 for the definition of this and other technical terms.) are found, arranged marriage is important because it ensures that personal attachments do not so develop that they destroy lineal bonds.

Looking at the matter from the first point of view, where not much wealth or property is at stake or not much reputation is to be lost, freedom of choice is greatly increased. Hence freedom of choice is correlated with class position within societies and with subsistence level between societies (Driver & Massey, 1957, p. 394). This may be seen, for example, by contrasting the Central African Bemba with South Eastern Bantu tribes (Audrey I. Richards, 1940). The Bemba are close to the subsistence level, do not have permanent, inheritable possessions, and are seminomadic shifting cultivators—they move every four or five years—so that no hereditary claim to any particular plot of land is established. No extensive bride-wealth is exchanged. When a man marries no great economic involvement of his kinsmen is entailed, and he is relatively free to choose his wife as he wishes. In any case, since kinsmen do not provide him with bride-wealth, they cannot enforce authority over him even if they should wish to do so. The pastoral Bantu have much more inheritable wealth, and extensive exchanges of economic goods accompany marriage. There is therefore a network created between the marry-ing kin groups of credits, debts, future obligations, and instrumental concerns, and the system of payment and repayment binds individuals together for two to three generations (Audrey I. Richards, 1940, p. 14).

But the solidarity of the conjugal bond is also important. The Bemba are matrilineal and matrilocal. Therefore, although the husband's kinsmen care little about his choice, the wife's kinsmen care a great deal. The man may marry without his parents' consent, the woman may not. According to Richards (1940), Bemba women are famous for rebelling and even succeed in their rebellion some of the time; they are, however, much more restricted than men, because their father's and their mother's brothers (the latter are the authority figures in Bemba matrilineages) care who is going to become their working partner or who is going to threaten the solidarity of the descent group, respectively. In Africa generally, as Gluckman (1955) observed, the bonds of conjugal solidarity are suspect. Among the Barotse, for example—and they are typical in this respect—if a man becomes too devoted to his wife his family claims that his wife and her family used illegitimate magic to bewitch him out of his senses (Gluckman, 1955, p. 60). The representatives of the descent group are particularly jealous of inmarrying of "strangers."

Where the exchange between kinship groups becomes very important, it is usually expressed in marriage payments or bride-wealth. The bride-wealth represents two things: the cement of an instrumental alliance between groups; and the exchange of wealth for the rights to a woman's offspring, and hence the heir necessary to perpetuate the descent group. It is not viewed as payment for chattel or as payment for rights to treat the wife as a slave—indeed the wife's family often views it as insurance of good treatment, since in the event of divorce the bride-wealth must be returned. In patrilineal societies, the association of bride-wealth with jural rights to a woman's offspring is indicated in the importance of bride-wealth as a criterion of legitimacy. If a woman bears a child to a man who has not paid bride-wealth, the child is often not legitimate, and payment is required to validate the child as heir to the father. Bride-wealth is most likely of all when residence is patrilocal and does not occur at all when residence is neolocal.

Mechanisms of Mate Selection

If the marriage of a boy and girl can so drastically influence their parents' and relatives' instrumental and social interest, then love is a dangerous thing (Goode, 1959). Even if laughed at, once experienced it can endanger the kinship group. Some means of containing its effect, therefore, is associated with the arrangement of marriage. One such means is the child marriage in which a marriage is arranged much before romantic attachments are likely to lead individual youth to the wrong choice. Another is the seclusion of women, preventing them from meeting marriageable, and more important, unmarriageable men before a match is arranged for them. A third method is the preferential marriage system, in which the choice of a mate must be within some stipulated class of relatives. Thus one preferential marriage rule is that a male must marry, if possible, only a female who is either his mother's brother's daughter, or who is classified by his society as equivalent to the mother's brother's daughter.

All these mechanisms tend to prevent romantic love from intruding on the carefully calculated advantages of the right marriage. But even where mate selection is free, and instrumental calculations are unconscious if they operate at all, some mechanisms of mate selection tend to ensure that mates are at least of similar social rank. The control mechanisms are to some extent managed by parents, to some extent the results of the way in which a society's system of stratification affects interaction, and to some extent the results of peer group control over the dating process (Goode, 1959, pp. 44–46;

Sussman, 1953b; Waller, 1937). Dating, which Americans perhaps take somewhat for granted, is a system of mate selection with three important properties: (1) choice of a date is formally free of instrumental considerations; (2) actual dating behavior is not directly supervised by parents or other adults; (3) to be seen alone in public with a woman does not automatically imply to others that a male is committed to marry her. Because of the latter norm, which is rather an important institution of American society (Marsh & O'Hara, 1961), a certain amount of exploration of the market is possible. This exploration, however, is not completely unregulated.

Stratification and mate selection. The observed distribution of marriages in a society at some given time is a result of four decision steps: (1) some initial contact must take place; (2) there must be a decision by a man and a woman to consider one another as a potential sexual object; (3) sexual association must lead to marriage; (4) the marriage must be stable. All four appear to be affected by the class origin of the two mates. In most societies the observed distributions of marriages are *homogamous* in social and status characteristics (for the United States, see Burgess & Wallin, 1943; Centers, 1949; Hollingshead, 1950). That is, husband and wife come from approximately the same social backgrounds. This is partly a result of the fact that initial contacts between two social classes are restricted in certain ways; partly an effect of the fact that once the persons are in contact cross-class unions are not intimate, and if they are they are regarded as "illicit" and hence not marriage worthy; and partly a consequence of the fact that nonhomogamous marriages are less stable. In every society, however, there are some stable nonhomogamous marriages. In a few they are an institutionalized form of marriage. Among the Kachin of Burma, for example, the daughters of chiefs regularly marry lower-ranking subchiefs and the union is legal (Leach, 1957). The available data suggest that *hypergamy* is more common than *hypogamy,* that is, females tend to marry males of higher social rank more often than males tend to marry females of higher social rank.

There is a great deal of evidence to show that more intimate, equal-status contacts between persons tend to occur between persons of equal social rank. This is reflected in the data on residential propinquity of couples before marriage (Bossard, 1932; Clarke, 1952; Davie & Reeves, 1939; Koller, 1948). Considering the great geographical mobility within American society and the great opportunity to meet in various voluntary associations, it is remarkable how many newly married urban couples seem to have lived only a few blocks apart before marriage. On the average, married couples live only about seven blocks apart before marriage, in other words in the same neighborhood. Since in most modern urban communities neighborhoods are class-segregated, the simple fact of differential association should produce a distribution of marriages in which males and females come from about the same social background.

But differential association does not seem to be the only mechanism assuring homogamy. Where the marriage market is not regulated by adult supervision, it seems that control over it is exercised by peers. Waller

(1937), for example, described how adolescents and young adults consider the evaluative criteria of their community in "dating," so that one wants to date only males or females who are equal or higher in evaluation. These homophilous choices are reinforced, perhaps enforced, by peer-group responses. The cross-cultural distribution of this peer-group control of dating seems very widespread (Goode, 1959). It also seems to be true that cross-class liaisons, where formed, are often defined as "illicit," exploitative, and not presuming marriage; they are purely for sexual pleasure and cannot result in legitimate children. This is particularly noticeable with cross-caste unions. The amount of Negro-White miscegenation in the United States seems at one time to have been great and perhaps still is. White male–Negro female unions seem to be the more frequent type. Most of them, however, are forms of concubinage rather than marriage.

The data in tables 1 and 2 come from a national sample of the United States in 1945 (Centers, 1949). Except for the highest-ranking males (businessmen and professionals), about 75 to 80 per cent of all marriages are in one's own or the next adjacent classes. For females, the overall tendency to homogamy is slightly less; but, about 60 to 80

TABLE 1

URBAN MARRIAGES OF URBAN MALES:
UNITED STATES, 1945[a]

Occupational Stratum of Male	No.	Percentages Married to Women of Various Occupational Strata[b]							
		Business Executive	Professional	Small Business	White Collar	Skilled Manual	Semiskilled Manual	Unskilled Manual	Total (per cent)
Business executive	40	15	15	33	13	20	2	2	100
Professional	44	7	25	30	2	23	13	—	100
Small business	78	3	8	40	8	25	10	6	100
White-collar	88	—	5	32	23	24	13	3	100
Skilled manual	81	—	1	14	9	46	24	6	100
Semiskilled	85	—	2	12	8	27	41	10	100
Unskilled	33	—	—	3	12	9	36	40	100

[a] Source: Centers (1949, p. 532).
[b] The occupational stratum of the woman is defined by her father's occupation.

TABLE 2
URBAN MARRIAGES OF URBAN FEMALES:
UNITED STATES, 1945[a]

Occupational Stratum of Female	No.	Percentages Married to Males of Various Occupational Strata							
		Business Executive	Profes-sional	Small Business	White Collar	Skilled Manual	Semi-skilled Manual	Un-skilled Manual	Total (per cent)
Business executive	11	55	27	18	—	—	—	—	100
Professional	30	20	37	20	13	3	7	—	100
Small business	108	12	12	29	26	11	9	1	100
White-collar	50	10	2	12	40	14	14	8	100
Skilled manual	123	6	8	16	18	30	19	3	100
Semiskilled	92	1	6	9	12	21	38	13	100
Unskilled	35	3	—	14	9	14	23	37	100

[a] Source: Centers (1949, p. 533).

per cent of all marriages are within the same or the next adjacent class. The proportions married into a given class decline as one moves farther from one's own class, so that the nonhomogamous marriages decrease as the magnitude of rank difference increases. There are, however, many males and females who do marry outside their own class; in these cases, males seem more likely to marry down while females seem more likely to marry up. About 85 per cent of the males who are business executives marry down, whereas only 45 per cent of the females whose fathers are business executives marry down. On the other hand, of unskilled males about 24 per cent marry outside their own or the next adjacent class, while of females with unskilled fathers, about 37 per cent marry outside the skilled or semiskilled classes.

Davis (1941) and Merton (1941), in separate papers, offered theories about hypergamous and hypogamous marriage which attempt to explain such data. Their theory assumes that for reasons having to do with the nature of stratification, a family is a unit treated by outside evaluators as having a common social rank. In many societies, for example, the male's rank determines the rank of his nuclear family. Therefore, if a high-status male marries a low-status female, after marriage she and her children may

take his status. Therefore, a male may marry down without much loss of status, so long as there is not much instrumental cost, and a woman may marry up and gain status. If hypergamy exceeds homogamy, of course, the system of stratification cannot remain very rigid or clearly defined; but from the point of view of individuals marrying, the loss in rank is minimized by hypergamous as against hypogamous unions. Note that the theory associates marriage with a gain or loss in social reputation and assumes those involved will minimize loss of rank, which accounts for the fact that where marriage is not into one's own class it is most likely to be in the next adjacent class.

So far the theory also assumes that females take the male's status; but there is one kind of stratification system in which this does not take place. In racial castes, the status of the family unit is determined by whichever partner is from the lower caste, and the child born to them belongs either to the lower caste or to some intermediate group. This radically alters the exchange involved in marriage, so that hypergamy is not nearly as likely. In fact, the observed evidence shows hypogamy more common between racial castes. Here the allocation of rank to the nuclear family unit is determined by the fact that racial caste is visible and indelible, so that the marks of caste remain after mar-

TABLE 3

Parties to Negro-White Marriages 1914–1938, and Gainful Workers in the Total Population 1930, by Sex, Color, and Occupation, Boston[a]

Occupation	Intermarriages								Gainful Workers[b]			
	Grooms				Brides				Male		Female	
	Negro		White		Negro		White		Negro	White	Negro	White
	No.	%	No.	%	No.	%	No.	%	%	%	%	%
Professions	19	8.4	3	6.1	1	2.6	14	8.7	3.8	5.2	3.7	13.2
Proprietors, managers, and officials	7	3.1	2	4.1	—	—	—	—	1.7	10.0	0.5	1.4
Clerks and kindred workers	13	5.7	4	8.2	1	2.6	24	14.9	6.0	20.9	4.3	40.4
Skilled workers and foreman	42	18.6	8	16.3	—	—	1	0.6	9.9	22.6	0.3	1.4
Semiskilled workers	52	23.0	12	24.5	7	17.9	20	12.3	18.1	22.2	29.7	27.8
Unskilled workers	93	41.2	20	40.8	30	76.9	103	63.6	60.4	19.0	61.5	15.7
Total gainfully employed	226	100	49	100	39	100	162	100	100	100	100	100
Not gainfully employed	1	—	—	—	10	—	65	—	—	—	—	—
Total	227	—	49	—	49	—	227	—	—	—	—	—

[a] Source: Wirth and Goldhamer (1944, p. 290).
[b] U.S. Bureau of the Census. A socio-economic grouping of gainful workers in cities of 500,000 or more: 1930. Washington: March 11, 1938. Mimeographed supplement.

TABLE 4

NEGRO GROOMS IN NEGRO-WHITE MARRIAGES BY OWN OCCUPATION AND
OCCUPATION OF BRIDE, BOSTON, 1914–1938[a]

	Occupation of bride					
	I	II	III			
Occupation of Groom	Professionals, Proprietors, Managers, Clerks	Skilled and Semi-skilled Workers	Unskilled Workers	Total Gainfully Employed	Not Gainfully Employed	Total
I. Professionals, proprietors, managers, clerks	16	3	13	32	7	39
II. Skilled and semiskilled workers	11	11	46	68	26	94
III. Unskilled workers	11	7	44	62	31	93
Total gainfully employed	38	21	103	162	64	226
Not gainfully employed	0	0	0	0	1	1
Total	38	21	103	162	65	227

[a] Source: Wirth and Goldhamer (1944, p. 293).

riage and change in rank of the wife is not nearly as possible. Furthermore, if rank did not always remain at the lowest level, there would be no racial caste system. It is not that males do not form sexual associations with lower-caste females, but only that these do not end in marriage. Marriages that do occur seem to be between upper-caste females and lower-caste males. The ratio of hypergamous to hypogamous interracial unions, for example, is between 1:5 and 1:4 (Wirth & Goldhamer, 1944, p. 282). What, nevertheless, would compel an upper-caste woman to lose caste by marriage? So far, this discussion has only suggested that she has more power than the lower-caste woman and therefore can compel a lower-caste male to marry her. Merton (1941) and Davis (1941) both suggested that caste hypo-gamous unions are class hypergamous. That is, the upper-caste females should come from

the lower class, and the lower-caste males should be from the higher class of their caste. It seems to be true that if one compares the occupational distributions of males and employed females who intermarry with the occupational distributions of their respective color castes (see Table 3), the Negro grooms come disproportionately from professional and managerial classes whereas the white brides come disproportionately from unskilled workers. Table 4, however, which shows the occupations of pairs that married among the caste-hypogamous unions in Boston from 1914–1938, reveals that the greater proportion of marriages are still homogamous, even though hypergamous unions exceed hypogamous unions. This is not what Merton (1941) specifically predicted, and Wirth and Goldhamer (1944) concluded that his hypothesis is disconfirmed. The failure, however, seems largely a result of the fact that the observed marriage distribution is the outcome of a complicated process in which the rank exchanges involved in the marriage affect only one

from the present data to test exactly the Davis-Merton theory.

It is possible, however, to find data from studies of divorce that specify the last step.

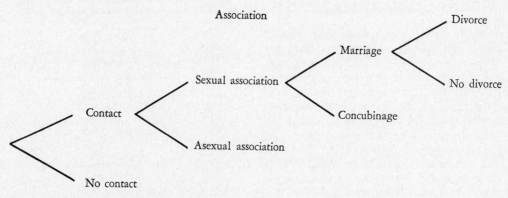

Fig. 1. Decision steps in intermarriage process.

step in the process (see also, Golden, 1953; Golden, 1959). The Davis (1941) and Merton (1941) theory focuses mainly on the probability that, given contact and sexual interest, the match ends in marriage. Merton did allow other processes, such as rebellious-

Goode (1956), for example, showed that the tendency to divorce is greater for non-homogamous unions than for homogamous unions, and that hypergamous unions less often end in divorce than hypogamous unions (Table 5).

TABLE 5
DIVORCED AND MARRIED, BY TYPE OF UNION
(occupation as index)[a]

	Homogamous	Type of Union Hypergamous (wife marries upward)	Hypogamous	Totals
Divorced sample (Goode)	48%	23%	30%	101%
Married sample (Centers)	55	24	21	100

[a] Source: Goode (1956, p. 101).

ness or anomie, to affect frequency of marriage; but probably the homogamy found in Negro–White intermarriages results from differential contact in work settings. It is lower-class white females who are mostly involved in intermarriages, and their most likely interracial contacts are with lower-class Negro males. Hence it is not possible

One should discover, of course, that where the rank of a group in society changes, the rates of intermarriage also change. Thus, as immigrant groups become assimilated they seem to increase in rank, and intermarriage becomes more common. Religious differences, however, do not seem to erode as much as do ethnic differences, and most interethnic marriages do not cross the Protestant-Catholic-Jewish lines (Ruby J. R. Kennedy, 1944).

American Divorce Rates

In 1860 there were 1.2 divorces for each 1,000 marriages in existence in that year. (Note: this is not the rate per 1,000 marriages contracted in that year, a frequently quoted statistic, nor even the rate per 1,000 population, which is the most frequently quoted of all.) In 1956 the estimated rate per 1,000 marriages in existence was 9.3. In 1945 it was even higher—18.2. Thus at a peak period of divorces after World War II, the divorce rate was about 15 times greater than it had been just before the Civil War (Jacobson, 1959).

A large proportion of these divorces occurs within the earliest years of marriage among childless couples, and most of the

TABLE 6

DIVORCES AND ANNULMENTS: UNITED STATES, 1860–1956[a]

Year	Divorces per 1000 Existing Marriages[b]
1860	1.2
1870	1.5
1880	2.2
1890	3.0
1900	4.0
1910	4.5
1920	7.7
1930	7.4
1940	8.7
1950	10.2
1951	9.9
1952	10.0
1953	9.9
1954	9.5
1955	9.3
1956	9.3

[a] Source: Jacobson (1959, p. 90).
[b] Includes annulments for the years 1920 and after.

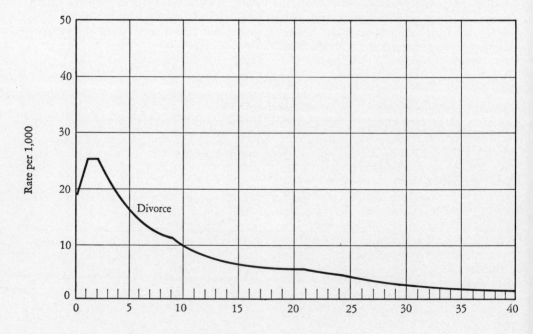

Fig. 2. Divorce and the duration of marriage: United States, 1955 (Source: Jacobson, 1959, p. 147).

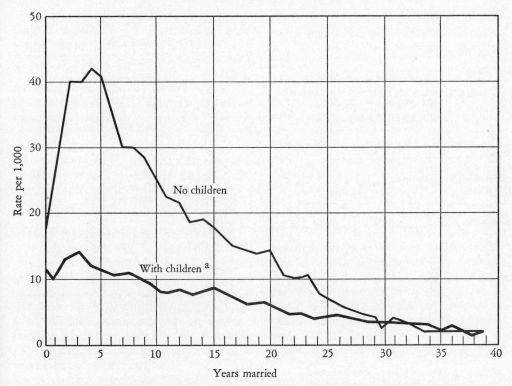

Fig.3. Divorce, duration and childlessness: United States, 1948 (Source: Jacobson, 1959, p. 134).

divorced remarry (compare Goode, 1956). The peak period of divorce is in the second year of marriage (see Figure 2), after which the rate drops precipitously. Actually such marriages break up even sooner, since it is often a year or more after divorce is decided on before a decree is granted (Goode, 1956). It is probably the correlation of childlessness with brief duration that explains the high proportion of divorces that occur to childless couples. But even with duration-specific rates, such as are shown in Figure 3, childless couples are more likely to divorce than are couples with children. This is most true in the early years of marriage, and the difference declines sharply after the fifth year.

Exhaustive research has discovered that divorce is affected by a great number of factors, among them: urban background, early marriage (between the ages of 15 and 19 years), short courtship and short engagement, mixed marriages, disapproval from friends and relatives, dissimilar backgrounds, and unhappy parental marriages (for an extensive survey and bibliography, see Goode, 1961). The greatest instability appears to be in urban working classes and particularly in Negro urban working classes. Careful investigation and analysis by Goode, for example, has shown a marked inverse relationship between occupation and divorce rates, both nationally and in a sample of metropolitan Detroit. In Detroit the "proneness to divorce," which is the proportion of divorced husbands in any given occupational class to the proportion of all males in that occupational class, is slightly more than 2.5 times greater in the unskilled class than in the professional-proprietor class. Lower white-collar occupations have slightly greater proneness to divorce than do upper blue collar, but otherwise the trend is unbroken, increasing sharply between upper and lower blue-collar occupations (see Table 7).

TABLE 7

INDEX OF PRONENESS TO DIVORCE,
BY OCCUPATION:
DETROIT, 1948[a]

Professional and proprietary	67.7
Clerical, sales, service	83.2
Skilled, foremen	74.1
Semi-skilled, operatives	126.1
Unskilled	179.7

[a] Source: Goode (1956, p. 47).

The divorce rate for Negroes has historically been lower than for whites, because many marriages that end in separation do not reach the courts and are not counted as divorces. Recently, however, the Negro and white divorce rates have been converging, reflecting the greater use of legal divorce by Negroes (Kephart & Monahan, 1952).

Cross-Cultural Divorce Rates

Most Americans, alarmed at the rapid increase in their divorce rate, seem to regard it as unusually high. Many other societies have an even higher rate, however. Nor is this just a result of their correspondingly greater "disorganization" as they become more "civilized."

Japan and the Arab countries, for instance, provide an interesting contrast with United States rates. Before 1900 both Japan and Algeria had rates over six times the United States rate (see Goode, 1961). After 1900 their rates decreased markedly, while the United States rate increased markedly. At the present time their rates are lower than the United States rate. Evidently changes in the United States family have led to increasing divorce, while changes in Japanese and Arab families have led to decreasing divorce. Yet all three countries have supposedly been experiencing modernization and industrialization.

Both Japan and the Arab countries traditionally had a strong patrilineal descent group. Is this related to their initially higher divorce rates? Gluckman (1950; 1953) supposed that, on the contrary, the strong patrilineal descent group is correlated with lower divorce rates. Observing first that expensive bride-price is often correlated with low divorce rates, he suggested that this is the result of a spurious correlation of both bride-wealth and family stability with strong patrilineages. The strength of the patrilineage produces family stability, which in turn makes possible the elaboration of bride-wealth.

In fact there are many patrilineal societies —the Zulu is one—where the divorce rate is negligible. This does not mean that strains are lacking in the marriage relationship which produce instability of a sort. Schneider (1953) pointed out that one must distinguish clearly three kinds of stability: (1) stability of the conjugal pair itself; (2) stability of the jural bond of marriage; (3) stability of a marriage system. Instability of the jural bond itself does not imply either instability or stability of the other two. Many divorceless patrilineal societies have a good deal of separation. But marriage is a matter of jural relationships, of rights to a woman's offspring, and a couple can separate without disrupting these legal rights. Particularly where these jural relationships are between large kinship groups, and elaborated and ensured by bride-wealth, disruption of the jural bond is rare. Nor do high divorce rates imply instability of marriage systems. A marriage system is unstable when the norms institutionalizing one kind of marriage and courtship behavior change. But it is possible for divorce rates to be very high, as for example in many matrilineal societies, without any change over time in patterns of marriage or courtship.

There are, then, two kinds of patrilineal societies: those with high divorce rates and those with low divorce rates. The difference appears to depend on the relation of the wife to her husband's lineage. In some societies she is assimilated into it completely. Her legal ties and even many of her social ties to her own lineage are severed, and she belongs solely to her husband's lineage. In such societies the divorce rate is negligible. In other patrilineal societies, although all her children's legal rights are with her husband's lineage, she herself retains membership and important ties to her own (her father's) lineage. In such societies the divorce rate is very high.

Both Fallers (1957) and Leach (1957) advanced the above hypothesis. Fallers observed that among the patrilineal Soga (Africa), between 25 per cent and 50 per cent of marriages contracted end in divorce, even though bride-wealth must be repaid on divorce. This, he believed, is because Soga wives are not completely assimilated into their husband's lineages. Leach contrasted three south Asian marriage systems, the Gumsa Kachins, the Guari Kachins, and the Lakher. All three have complicated and expensive bride-price, matrilateral cross-cousin marriage, and hypogamy; all three have a feudal vassal relation of son-in-law to father-in-law; all three are patrilineal; and all three prefer the levirate. Divorces, however, are not permitted among the Gumsa, permitted though not common among the Guari, and frequent among the Lakher. Contrasting the two extremes, the Gumsa absorb a woman wholly into her husband's patrilineage, never legally to return to her own lineage which has no rights over her. The sibling tie (which is a way of expressing the tie to the descent group) is weaker than the marriage tie, and in a conflict the sibling tie gives first. But among the Lakher, although a woman's children are legally the husband's lineage's property, the wife herself is not. Legally she is still a member of her father's lineage, and the sibling tie is strong.

The same hypothesis accounts for the exceedingly high rates of divorce often found in matrilineal societies. A matrilineage is so structured that it cannot, unlike some patrilineal societies, ever completely divorce either males or females legally from the matrilineage (Schneider, 1961). Females are the line through which descent is counted; males are the line through which, despite popular impressions to the contrary, authority in the matrilineage is exercised. In marriage, males are always a threat to their wives' matrilineages and always strongly rooted in their own matrilineages. Divorce is almost always easy—a man just walks off, or a woman puts her husband's few personal possessions outside the door. The marriage system is stable, however, even though the conjugal bond and jural ties are very unstable.

One might interpret the time trends in United States and Japanese divorce rates, assuming that both are undergoing industrialization, to mean that the conjugal family, a family in which the conjugal tie is the primary solidarity relative to larger kin groups, has an intermediate level equilibrium divorce rate. If it were true that Japanese family structure is changing as a consequence of industrialization (a hypothesis to be examined below), then a shift away from strong patrilineages of the Lakher type—in which women partly retain ties to their own lineage but in which the husband's tie to his own lineage is stronger than his tie to his wife—would lead to an increasingly strong conjugal bond, with the effect that the divorce rate would be reduced. On the other hand, a "traditional" American family in which the conjugal bond was less strong (if such a family ever existed historically, which is still an open question) and which under the impact of industrialization increased the importance of the conjugal tie, would possibly increase its divorce rate. The argument, however, should be treated as pure conjecture.

THE NUCLEAR FAMILY

When father, mother, and child form a recognizable unit within a society, this unit is referred to as a nuclear family. It is a recognizable entity when it is an acting unit with respect to some task or function and when treated as a single unit by persons outside the nuclear family for at least some, though not necessarily all, purposes. Commonly the nuclear family acts as a distinct unit in socializing children, in regulating sexual access of adults, in reproducing children, and in distributing economic resources to its members. These may be called the *Murdock functions*.

The Universality of the Nuclear Family

It has already been seen that Levy (1955), Levy and Fallers (1959), Spiro (1954), and E. Kathleen Gough (1959) objected to Murdock's (1949) assertion that the nuclear family, as a concrete acting unit, is universal. The nuclear family roles—father, mother, son, daughter, husband, wife, brother, sister —are, so far as is now known, universally found. The question is: Do they always form a recognized acting unit distinct from other units, and do they always perform at least the four Murdock functions?

Both Gough (1959) and Spiro (1954) reported cases in which the nuclear family unit is not, in their view, the relevant acting unit for all of these four functions. Among the Nayar (E. Kathleen Gough, 1959), the intact household unit is made up of the brother, sister, and sister's son or sister's daughter; husbands "visit" their wives. At a very young age a woman is ritually married to a man chosen by her family and within days is ritually divorced from him; the woman is then free to take "lovers," although these may be more or less regular. These lovers give her gifts but do not provide her support. If a child is born, one of the woman's lovers, not necessarily the genitor, pays a fee that legitimates the child and is thereby legally recognized as the father. The husband-wife relationship satisfies Malinowski's criterion of a family because without out the ritual marriage of the woman or public recognition by a putative father no child born is legitimate. But socialization,

economic cooperation, and household composition are structured around the brother-sister relation. (There is always a misleading aspect to such a statement, because the status "brother" may be occupied by someone who is not biologically the woman's actual brother. What is important is that some male member of the matrilineage exercises authority over the female's household.)

In an Israeli *Kibbutz,* or collective farm (Spiro, 1954), the acting units are the husband-wife unit, where again sexual access and legitimation of the child are regulated; nurseries for children who live apart from their parents, where socialization is regulated; and the *Kibbutz* as a whole, which is the unit of economic cooperation. Thus, although the children have some of the same feelings that most children do for their specific parents, they only "visit" them in their room, much as Nayar husbands visit their wives. And the economic activities of the husband and wife are in and for the *Kibbutz* itself, not for the "family." In return the *Kibbutz* provides meals, allowances, and clothes. The children in the nurseries, furthermore, come to think of themselves as siblings in the same family; for example, an incest taboo spontaneously develops among them.

Because the Nayar and *Kibbutz* families actually live apart, they are relatively easily recognized as exceptions to Murdock's (1949) rule. The Chinese family poses more difficult problems of interpretation (Levy, 1955). Levy argues that the nuclear family unit is not the unit of economic cooperation; rather, husband and wife contribute services to the extended family, within which the nuclear family is completely (for economic purposes) unidentifiable. In socialization, furthermore, for many phases of that process the relevant units are the females of the extended family as a whole and the males of the extended family as a whole. Except for sexual relations, in fact, Levy does not see any set of nuclear family bonds as acting units distinct from the extended family. Many family systems in Murdock's sample are probably like the Chinese family in these respects, so that the difference between Levy and Murdock turns on how they interpreted the structure of an extended family. Murdock viewed it as an aggregation of component and distinct nuclear families. Although in many societies the conjugal bond is a secondary and subordinate solidarity, Murdock did not see the nuclear family as ever quite completely obscured. Levy, on the other hand, believed it incorrect to see the extended family, in cases like the Chinese family, as an aggregation of nuclear families; the solidarity of the larger unit is so paramount that the nuclear family cannot be said to exist as a distinct unit for any purpose at all (also Levy & Fallers, 1959, p. 649).

Actually it is not entirely clear how either Levy (1955) or Murdock (1949) intended their argument. Levy might, for example, have wanted to say any of the following:

1. The nuclear family in China is for no purposes an acting unit.

2. The nuclear family in China is for most purposes not an acting unit.

3. The nuclear family in China is for many purposes an acting unit, but is for most purposes not the unit of paramount importance. Probably he meant at least the second, and possibly the first. It is of course equally unclear what Murdock wanted to say, in the sense that he might have meant that the nuclear family is with respect to sex, procreation, socialization, and economic actions, always the acting unit, or that for most socialization and economic purposes it is an acting unit, or even that for his four functions it is always the paramount unit. It is clearly wrong to say that the nuclear family is always paramount, or even always an acting unit. Not only is there the Nayar and *Kibbutz* to account for, but in many societies the nuclear family is clearly so subordinated that for many purposes it is not the acting unit and for equally many purposes not the paramount unit. On the other hand, it has yet to be demonstrated that, except for the Nayar and *Kibbutz* and

perhaps the Minangkabau (deJong, 1951), there is not at least one purpose or activity, in many societies and perhaps most, with respect to which the nuclear family is sometimes an acting unit.

Types of Nuclear Family Role Structure

Any concrete social structure is a very complicated thing, but the nuclear family, considering how few the number of its roles, has so far proved more complicated than the concepts yet invented by sociologists to describe it. If one looks only at conjugal roles and oversimplifies to an absurd degree, there are still at least eight possible nuclear family structures that might be found (see Figure 4). Until the early 1950's sociologists, like laymen, talked rather simply of matriarchal, patriarchal, or egalitarian (companionship) families, which probably meant to most people that there was a single monolithic power structure in the family; either father made all the decisions, or mother did, or both did equally. Parsons and Bales (1955), however, argued that there were actually multiple power structures in the family that were independent of each other; while the husband might be more influential in some decisions the wife would be in others. There is still the question of the role played by the less powerful member, who may either participate in decision-making or be excluded. Finally, there is the question of balance of power; husband might be more, less, or about equal in influence to his wife if there is a single power structure. If there are multiple power structures, one might still assess the balance of power by counting the number of decision-areas in which each has most influence, or by weighting their importance.

Assessing the balance of power in differentiated families, of course, would reduce their complex power structure to one of the single-power-structure types. A "colleague" family (Miller & Swanson, 1958), for example, is one in which there is role-differ-

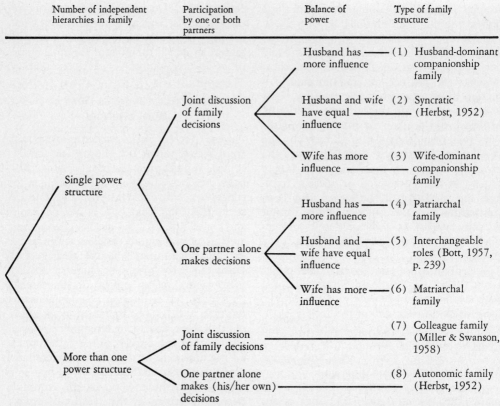

Number of independent hierarchies in family	Participation by one or both partners	Balance of power	Type of family structure

Fig. 4. Some types of nuclear family role structure. Compare Herbst, 1952; Elizabeth Bott, 1957, Appendix A; and Wolfe, 1959.

entiation and joint participation. If the more important decisions were made by the husband, it might be classified as a husband-dominant colleague family. There are actually not 8 but 12 logically possible nuclear family structures, if one takes into account 3 types of colleague and 3 types of autonomic family (see Figure 4). Because few investigators like to deal with 12 types of social structure in any one study, various ways of reducing this family typology have been employed, no two of which are exactly comparable. It is partly because of the problem of typological reduction that there are so many and such confused concepts, measures, and results in the study of nuclear family structure. The story begins, properly, with Herbst's (1952) study of urban Australian

families. Herbst's typology first distinguished four activities of the family: household duties, child care, social activities, and economic activities. He then distinguished actual execution of a task from making decisions about it and classified each of these dimensions by who decided or who did what was required. This yielded 36 logically possible patterns, which he reduced to 4 as follows:

1. The autonomic pattern. Given by the sum of areas in which husband or wife decide and do tasks by themselves.

2. The husband-dominant pattern. Given by the sum of areas in which the husband decides alone what is to be done, and either both together or wife alone executes the task.

3. Wife-dominant pattern. Given by the sum of areas in which wife decides alone, but both together or husband alone execute task.

4. Syncratic pattern. Given by the sum of areas in which both decide, and either both execute task together or husband or wife execute task alone.

This classification strongly influenced Elizabeth Bott's (1957) study of London families, and Wolfe's (1959) study of power structure, but each combined the logical possibilities in somewhat different ways. Bott, for example, finally distinguished only (1) joint families (husband and wife decide things together, do them together, or either could interchangeably perform the same functions if not together); (2) independent families (husband and wife perform different, independent tasks without discussion with each other—Herbst's [1952] "autonomic" family); and (3) complementary families (husband and wife perform differentiated, but complementary or interdependent functions, but perform them apart from each other) (Elizabeth Bott, 1957, pp. 238–240). Wolfe (1959) distinguished the same types as Herbst but used somewhat different operations to measure them. He dropped the question of whether the activity is performed together or not, and defined for any one activity whether the husband has greater power, equal power, or less power than the wife. If equal, husband and wife are said to share power. The ratio of husband's power areas to wife's power areas gives the relative balance of power. The autonomic family is, then, that family in which husband and wife have a relative balance of power ratio of close to 1.00 (i.e., equal power) but a shared power score of less than .50 (i.e., less than half the areas of decisions are shared). The syncratic family has also a balance of power ratio of close to 1.00 but a shared decision area of more than .50. The husband-dominant family has husband's power in relation to wife's power greater than 1.00, and a shared region less than .50, while the wife-dominant family

has a balance of power ratio of less than 1.00, and the shared region is less than .50.

Not only is there a confusing number of ways in which to reduce possible family types to a manageable number, but, if the family has more than one power structure (and it will be shown that it has), the measurement of the number of husband-dominant, wife-dominant, etc. families in a sample will obviously depend on the sampling of family decision-making tasks. If one observes the family on tasks $1,2,3...n$ and counts the number which are husband-dominant in structure and assumes that some tasks are husband's tasks and other tasks are wife's tasks, then the proportion of families in a sample that are "husband-dominant families" is a direct function of the number of husband's tasks which were sampled in making the observations. Blood and Wolfe (1960), for example, asked families such questions as: Who makes decisions about what car to buy, whether or not to buy life-insurance, what house or apartment to get, what job the husband should take, whether or not the wife should work, what amount of money the family can afford for food, what doctor to call, and where to take a vacation? Much of their succeeding analysis measures family power structure by the average husband-power score over these eight items. Any different selection of items should give a different average husband-power score, although of course there is no objection to making comparisons on a given dimension. Nor is it compelling to argue that for comparisons within a given sample it makes no difference, since it may be that different dimensions are correlated differently with such factors as income, education, race, whether the wife works or not, and so on. While one can criticize, one can only feel compassion for any investigator who wants an overall power score of some sort. For as Bott (1957) found, ". . . I tried to define the major tasks of families and to classify activities according to their contribution to the tasks. . . . But at this stage it was impossible to work out satisfactory criteria of the importance of activities and tasks . . ." (Bott, 1957, p. 239).

To problems of concept formation and measurement, one can add even greater difficulties in obtaining reliable responses to questions about power structure. Ferber (1955) found great differences between husband and wife reports of who had greater influence over various consumer decisions; Bott (1957, p. 238) found most families totally unable to describe how they arrived at decisions; Kenkel (Kenkel & Hoffman, 1956; Kenkel, 1957) found that families observed in a standard observational setting and task neither predicted accurately who would influence whom ahead of time, nor were able to describe at all accurately who had influenced whom after decisions had been made. Actual reports on husband-wife reliability vary from study to study, where the investigator takes the care to check at all, but probably most survey data reviewed below are moderately to extremely unreliable. Much of the unreliability, however, is in the direction of overestimating how "equilitarian" the family is, and this can be taken into account in interpreting the results.

If survey data are so unreliable, could one depend on observational data and avoid the problem of verbal reports? Aside from the fact that there are very few to rely on as yet, observational studies have problems of their own which make them difficult to interpret. These arise not so much from inherent defects of the method as from the current state of disorder in concepts and measures. Power, for example, can be taken to mean: (1) Who participates most in discussion? (2) Who had the ideas that were finally adopted by the family? (3) Who had the right to make the final decision, regardless of who originated the idea adopted? (4) Who received the most deference or agreement from whom? (5) Whose ideas were adopted if husband and wife initially disagreed? And perhaps more. Possibly all of these are correlated and possibly not. The problem arises partly from the

absence of clear conceptualization of the process by which power is exercised, so that it is not clear how these concepts are related. For example: Suppose one argues that the position of power in a group, given that members recognize the right of one particular person to make a final decision, is maintained by forcing all other members to express their opinions before the most powerful member expresses his own views. The power figure then simply determines the final decision without ever having first committed himself to an initial stand. In this way he is never overruled and never decreases in power. But the effect of his power is to decrease his total output of acts, and he has originated no ideas. The revealed differences technique, invented by Strodtbeck (1951), partly avoids this problem by forcing couples to make an initial choice and also forcing them to discuss their disagreements. But it is not enough to score whose choice becomes the final choice; one must also consider who made the final choice. If one could agree on how the process works, so that one could assure careful attention to all the relevant behavior, one probably could also agree on what is important and what irrelevant in the setting of the observation and in the task. At the moment there is no such agreement, so that what appears to be small differences in procedure—whether couples are forced to disagree initially or not, whether they are forced to come to a group decision or not, whether the task is veridical (objective) or not, whether the task is one which husband and wife, as a family, regard as an important common goal or not, and so on—may or may not be theoretically significant differences. Every present indication, however, is that they are important differences and different results are obtained as each of these conditions varies. The experimental results, therefore, do not represent much cumulative information; since not just one, but usually more than one, of these conditions varies at the same time, and comparisons of one observation with another are not valid.

Evidently no conclusive results are going to come from reviewing the literature on family roles; nevertheless the following undertakes to survey what there is.

Is there a single power structure? A Parsons-Bales role structure, as it may conveniently be called, actually involves four distinct ideas: (1) power within a family becomes differentiated, so that some members have more influence than others; (2) there is not one, but at least two, distinct power structures; (3) one of these two power structures focuses more on instrumental performance (such as making economic decisions, providing support for the family, managing the family farm or business) and the other focuses more on expressive leadership (such as nurturant behavior, child-rearing, expression of affiliation); and (4) that the two forms of power are allocated according to sex and age, the husband-father being more instrumental, the wife-mother more expressive, and the children subordinate in both dimensions. Parsons and Bales saw the processes that lead to the first three properties of nuclear family structure, as inherent in any group, whether a family group or not. They are produced by the requirements of decision-making situations. That is, if there is disagreement within the group and a decision must be made, then someone must influence someone else; and, as a result, one gains and the other loses power. As this process continues power may stabilize around a given figure in the group. A by-product of this process, however, is the separation of the task leader from the expressive leader. Disagreement, forced decision, and submission to another tend to focus both aggression and fear on the more powerful member. If he avoids this by not forcing his point, the disagreements are less and the decision not coercive, but the accomplishment of the system's goal is endangered. Thus, as the process continues, expressive behavior may become specialized in the hands of some member of the group other than the task leader (Bales & Slater, 1955). The conditions that seem relevant, in this argument, are the commitment to the system goal, the development of disagreements, the necessity of making a decision, and the interest in maintaining the group in the face of disruption, which seems to account for the expressive members' behavior.

There may, of course, be more than two such hierarchies in more complex groups. Parsons and Bales (Parsons, Bales & Shils, 1953) saw instrumental leadership at least as capable of much further differentiation. That instrumental tasks and decision-making are differentiated into subareas, with some family members regarded as responsible for some but not others, is shown by several studies. Sharp and Mott (1956) found that in 749 Detroit families, wives reported they had more influence than their husbands in deciding how much to spend on food, for example, while the husband had much more influence on deciding what car to get. Vacations and what house or apartment to get were decided by both together. But the wife more than the husband kept track of money and bills. Elizabeth Wolgast (1958) found that decisions about savings and furniture were joint more often than not, but in about 25 per cent of families the wife made such decisions alone. In the only available panel study of the problem, Wolgast showed that after one-and-one-half years the wife's plans are more likely to be fulfilled than the husband's, which Wolgast interprets to mean only that wives are more realistic budgeters than husbands. The results of Blood and Wolfe's (1960) research are shown in Table 8. The husband's mean power score is close to the maximum score of 5.00 for job decisions and not far off for what car to buy, is slightly in favor of the husband for insurance and vacation decisions but is rather close to equal balance, and is markedly low for decisions about the food budget and what doctor to call.

But does this suggest any regular pattern of instrumental-expressive differentiation? Results here are more mixed. A cross-cultural study of conjugal roles in 56 societies

TABLE 8

ALLOCATION OF POWER IN DECISION-MAKING AREAS
(731 Detroit families)[a]

Who Decides?	Decision							
	Husband's Job	Car	Insur-ance	Vaca-tion	House	Wife's Work	Doctor	Food
(5) Husband always	90%	56%	31%	12%	12%	26%	7%	10%
(4) Husband more than wife	4	12	11	6	6	5	3	2
(3) Husband and wife exactly the same	3	25	41	68	58	18	45	32
(2) Wife more than husband	0	2	4	4	10	9	11	11
(1) Wife always	1	3	10	7	13	39	31	41
N.A.	2	1	2	3	1	3	3	3
Total	100	99	99	100	100	100	100	99
Husband's mean power[b]	4.86	4.18	3.50	3.12	2.94	2.69	2.53	2.26

[a] Source: Blood and Wolfe (1960, p. 21).

[b] The mean for each column is computed on the basis of the weights shown at the left end of the Table, e.g., "husband always" = 5 . . . , "wife always" = 1.

(Zelditch, 1955, p. 320) found that 46 of them had a Parsons-Bales role structure. The most universal property of the nuclear family was the subordination of children to parents; next was the expressive content of the wife-mother role; the least constant property was the instrumental authority of the husband-father, which tended to vary with kinship structure. Kenkel (1957) also, in a study of families in a Bales observational setting, found that husbands specialized more in ideas and suggestions (husband more than wife in 64 per cent of families) and wives specialized more in social-emotional acts (agreements, praise, smiling; wife more than husband in 80 per cent of families), where the task was to spend $300, leaving nothing over and not spending it on anything previously planned.

A careful investigation by Kohn and Carroll (1960), however, cast some doubt on the hypothesis. They divided responsibilities in child-socialization into support, measured by encouragement of the child and the child's predisposition to turn to one parent as readily or more readily than the other, and constraint, or limit-setting, measured by who is the stricter on several behavioral control items. Among middle-class families, mothers report that the son turns to the father for advice and reassurance, and the father is as encouraging as the mother in about half the families (Kohn & Carroll, 1960, p. 378). In almost a third more the father is as encouraging as the mother, although the son turns more readily to the mother. In only one-fifth of the middle-class families is the father sharply differentiated from the mother in support.

In working-class families the differentiation is more marked, but nevertheless only about two-fifths of the fathers are as low as the two lowest scale scores on support. The meaning of encouragement and "turning to father for advice" is somewhat different in the two social classes. Middle-class mothers are more likely to consider the father "encouraging" when he does not play a major part in setting limits and see son turning to father as more likely when father has less to do with constraint. Working-class mothers are more likely to call their husbands "encouraging" when they also report that husbands set limits and also are more likely to perceive their sons as turning to father when he sets limits, although working-class sons, when interviewed, in fact were less likely to turn to father for advice and re-assurance when he was high in constraint.

Middle-class fathers, finally, almost always help the mother with child care and spend some leisure time with children, while working-class fathers spend much less time in child care, but still participate in sub-stantial proportions. Thus 61 per cent of working-class fathers and 93 per cent of middle-class fathers relieve wives of some child-care functions and 78 per cent of working-class fathers and 93 per cent of middle-class fathers participate in leisure-time activities with a son. The most marked differentiation found by Kohn and Carroll (1960) actually was by sex of child. Fathers tended to be much more involved with sons than daughters, mothers much more with daughters, particularly in the working class.

Segregation of conjugal roles. If roles of husband and wife are differentiated it is possible for them to perform their functions relatively independently of each other so that in some societies they live in virtually segregated worlds. In others they distribute influence differently over different tasks, but decision-making is nevertheless a joint proc-ess. Elizabeth Bott (1957) made perhaps the best known contribution to this problem, correlating segregation of conjugal role with what she referred to as the "connectedness" of social networks. What appears to be go-ing on in her data is that when husband and wife live close to friends and relatives with whom they have many prior associa-tions, one tends to find segregated conjugal roles. In part this may be because the worlds were separate before marriage and the couple is not cut off from these worlds after marriage. Townsend (1957, p. 76), however, suggested that the correlation is really with the strength of the kinship net-work. Man's world and woman's world are more sharply distinct and apart, according to this hypothesis, when man's and woman's relatives have a stronger hold over them. It both weakens the conjugal solidarity and brings the inherently conflicting interests of the two kinship groups more sharply into juxtaposition if the two worlds are not kept separate.

A review of the problem by Mirra Komarovsky (1961) included among its hypotheses the effects on joint decision-making of planning for the future, the strength of consanguine ties, and, partic-ularly, the importance of the decision from the point of view of its capacity to rule out some other alternative choices the family might have made. This led her to the hypothesis that joint decision-making has a curvilinear correlation with social class; in the lower-income class most income is spent on routine purchases which the wife makes more or less without consultation; while in the higher-income class there is sufficient income so that committing it to one choice does not so completely rule out other alter-natives. In addition, she reasoned that as income increases more specialized technical knowledge is required to decide its invest-ment and this is more likely to be husband's knowledge. Finally, she argued that mobil-ity aspirations are greatest in the middle-income class, and hence more planning and orientation to the future leads to greater joint consultation. The most significant con-firming evidence has been reported by Wilkening (1958), who, indeed, originally suggested the hypotheses that are most im-portant in Komarovsky's reasoning. Wilken-ing, from interviews (with 614 Wisconsin farm operators and their wives), about par-ticipation in decisions to plant crops, buy home appliances, make changes in the home, make changes in the farm, and buy machinery, found that there was low joint involvement in decisions for the lower-income farmers, high joint involvement for the middle-income farmers, and low joint involvement again in the high-income group (Wilkening, 1958, p. 189). Wilkening, sur-veying his results on effects of wife's education, participation in mother's clubs, level of living, income, and indebtedness, reformulated his hypothesis:

. . . joint decision-making . . . is a function of the extent to which farm and family decisions are viewed as having joint consequences for both farm and home. In other words, when decisions pertaining to the expenditure of major sums of money or other family resources are viewed by either husband or wife as having consequences for the farm for which the husband is primarily responsible, or for the home, for which the wife is primarily responsible, there will be an attempt to arrive at some consensus concerning decisions which affect both (Wilkening, 1958, p. 191).

He also pointed out that indebtedness indicates the degree to which family resources must be extended in order to add equipment to the house or farm. Decisions, therefore, become more crucial for the family in debt and more so as income decreases. Thus, joint decision-making increases with increasing indebtedness; but, with income level held constant, indebtedness has less effect as income increases.

Balance of power. Wolfe (1959) developed the following theory of power in the nuclear family: Power is the capacity to induce a change in another's behavior. The amount of power of a person A over a person B is a function of B's needs and A's resources. Needs include, for example, needs for economic support, social rank, love, and affection, while resources include income to support B, social rank to give B, or capacities for love and affection. Needs are best understood as goals of B, including those goals of the family to which B is committed. Resources are best understood as characteristics of A that satisfy needs of B or bring the family closer to attainment of its goals. If A has resources instrumental to B's goals he has power over B, and the more resources are concentrated in the hands of one member, for a given set of needs, the more that member has power over others in the family.

This theory conceives power as a kind of exchange and does not depend on how cultural values define family roles. Thus, if the "patriarchal" family exists at all, it is not, in this theory, because of cultural traditions as much as because inheritance, succession, economic resources, social status, and skills in managing enterprises are all concentrated in the hands of male heads of households. If social changes occur that concentrate less of these things in the hands of male heads and more in the hands of wives or sons, then the structure of the family should show corresponding changes in power structure. The theory, being an exchange theory, depends as much on what B needs as it does on what A can provide. Thus if either B needs less or A can provide less, equivalent losses occur in A's power over B.

While the exchange theory does not base its arguments on any particularly important part played by cultural role-traditions, it does admit the possibility that traditionally defined diffuse characteristics influence competence expectations. That is, such characteristics as sex and age may be associated, in a given social structure, with expectations of competence sufficiently generalized that in the absence of other cues or prior direct experience in interaction between A and B, A and B may believe that A has more ability than B if A is of higher social status, is male, is older (but not yet senile), or has some other relatively diffuse characteristic associated with subordination. In that case, at least until much disconfirming data alter the structure, one can expect decision-making in a given relatively new structure to be partly determined by these characteristics (see Strodtbeck & Mann, 1956). Hence any new family should for a time be influenced by them, and probably the more visible, more common, and more ascribed characteristics are the more commonly institutionalized.

Researches by Wolfe (1959), Blood and Wolfe (1960), Blood and Hamblin (1958), Nye (1961), Heer (1958), Lois Hoffman

(1960), and Gold and Slater (1958) investigated the effects on the wife's power of the husband's social rank, her own social rank, her working, and her ability to contribute to the husband's social rank. These studies find, in general, that:

1. The higher the husband's income, the higher the husband's relative power in the family (Blood & Wolfe, 1960; Gold & Slater, 1958; Heer, 1958; Wolfe, 1959).

2. The contribution of an independent income by the wife increases the wife's power in the family (Blood & Wolfe, 1960; Heer, 1958; Wolfe, 1959; but contrast Blood & Hamblin, 1958; Nye, 1961).

3. The higher the wife's education relative to her husband's education the greater her power in the family (Blood & Wolfe, 1960).

4. The Negro husband has less power than the white husband even after his occupation, income, and general social rank are controlled (Blood & Wolfe, 1960).

5. The more the wife contributes to her husband's ability to increase social status, the more power she has in the family (Gold & Slater, 1958).

It must be recalled that all these studies have methodological weaknesses, so that the findings are not definitive. Each defined balance of power in a somewhat different way —Heer (1958), for example, asked who makes "major" decisions, Blood and Wolfe (1960) take the husband's mean power score over eight decision areas—although presumably one is reassured that they agree. A very interesting hypothesis, but one which has not been investigated, is that if the balance of power is in the husband's hands and the wife makes decisions in decision-area *D,* then *D* will become regarded as not a major decision area. Suggestive evidence is found in investigations of who makes financial decisions for the family which is often found not to correlate with the balance of power (e.g., Wolfe, 1959).

An instructive negative finding was reported by Frances Scott (1962). Making a small variation in Strodtbeck's (1951) re-vealed-differences technique, Scott observed families making decisions and found that in husband-wife-aged-parent families the wife has the greatest total participation and receives the greatest total amount of support (agreement, praise); in husband-wife-aged-parent and adolescent-child families, the husband has the greatest participation, but the support intake is greatest for the child; in husband-wife-aged-parent-two-child families, the oldest child has the highest participation, and support intake is greatest for aged parent and youngest child (Scott, 1962, pp. 221–223). Granting both that the numbers are small and indicators probably invalid measures of power, Scott, nevertheless, reconsidered the differences in procedure between herself and Strodtbeck and concluded that had the family been involved in a "true" decision-making situation the power structure would have corresponded more closely with the age-sex structure. In her case the family was not confronted with decisions that had any important consequences for them as a family, nor were they forced to make a final decision (Frances Scott, 1962, p. 216). Thus, the properties of the task and decision-making situation are critical conditions in observing family power structures.

The Negro Matrifocal Family

The American and Caribbean Negro family has been described by Frazier (1939), Henriques (1953), M. J. and Frances Herskovits (1947), and others as unstable and, because husband-fathers are often absent from the household, as matrifocal. That is, because of frequent desertion, high rates of illegitimacy, early male mortality, and similar factors, the dominant authority in households is exercised by mothers rather than fathers. Careful analysis of quantitative data (R. T. Smith, 1956) for British Guiana Negro communities shows that actually the grandmother-mother-daughter family is not the typical family type; but, nevertheless, there is a family type that can be called

"matrifocal" in which, even where the husband-father is present in the household, he
is not the dominant authority. The matrifocal family, Smith showed, is actually one
phase in a cycle that begins when a couple
sets up a household, has children, who in
time begin various extraresidential unions
that might or might not become stable. The
father sometimes dies or deserts, the daughter's children from extraresidential unions
become part of the household. Finally the
daughters form more stable unions and
leave the household to begin the cycle again.
For most of a woman's child-bearing career,
once she has set up a new household, the
husband-father is in that household. He is
the primary source of its support, although
he may gradually be replaced by sons or, if
he deserts, by new lovers of the mother
(who do not necessarily live in her house).
Father is also active in early socialization.
But, "Whether they leave or not, the focus
of authority and control gradually shifts to
the wife-mother, so that irrespective of
whether there is a husband-father present,
the household at this stage can be referred to
as 'matrifocal' " (R. T. Smith, 1957, p. 70).

The matrifocal family pattern is not prevalent throughout the society in which it is
found, however. It is predominantly determined by class and color. R. T. Smith
(1956) interpreted this as a result of the
following:

1. Among lower-class Negroes there is
little internal differentiation in rank, no
property, no upward mobility, and uncertain wages.

2. Therefore, the male is "marginal" in
the sense that he contributes nothing to the
social status of the family, and his support
of it cannot be counted on.

3. Therefore, one can interpret variations
in the authority of the husband-father as
resulting from his position in the economic
and rank structures of the larger society.
The more marginal he is the weaker his
authority.

Smith supported this argument further by
observing that the husband-father role is
more important where ecology or class increases his contribution to the status and
support of his family. Among middle-class
Negroes in British Guiana there is more
differentiation of status, and the husband's
occupation can increase (or decrease) the
family's status. "So long as the man's income provides the basis for the style of life
that is important in maintaining the whole
group, then there is a point beyond which
his position in the family is unlikely to
deteriorate" (R. T. Smith, 1957, pp. 72–73).
Among Negro families in Orange Grove,
Jamaica (Edith Clarke, 1953) the husband-
father is the manager of a medium-sized
farm, a position which confers status on the
family, and the husband-father role is correspondingly greater in authority. This analysis has been challenged by M. G. Smith
(1962) who instead argued that alternate
forms of mating, themselves products of
the particular past histories of different
communities, account for variations in
Caribbean family structures.

The Husband in the Matrilineage

In patrilineal descent groups, the line of
authority and the line of descent are coordinate; that is, descent is from father to
son, and authority is of father over son. The
effect is to increase the authority of husbands and fathers when the nuclear family
is patrilocal and descent is patrilineal due to
the fact that authority in the nuclear family
is added to the authority inherent in extended family headship. While younger the
husband-father is actually subordinate to his
own father and very often exercises less
authority even over his own family than the
head of the extended family; but because he
will in time be the successor his authority
is still great. In patrilineal, patrilocal cases
the husband-father is ordinarily an instrumental authority figure, regardless of degree
of strength of the larger kinship group.

But in matrilineal descent groups the
line of authority and the line of descent are
not coordinate (Audrey I. Richards, 1950;

Schneider, 1961), because males are as much in authority in matrilineal societies as in patrilineal societies. The result is what Richards (1950, p. 246) called the "matrilineal puzzle," the problem of reconciling authority of husband-father versus brother-mother's brother. The effect on the husband-father's role depends on how strong the matrilineage is and how completely the nuclear family is subordinated to it. In the Trobriands, for example, the content of the husband-father role is almost as expressive as the mother's role, with most authority and instrumental functions allocated to the wife's brother. This is not, however, always the case.

Comparing a number of matrilineal tribes in Central Africa, Richards (1950) found three common solutions to the matrilineal puzzle, though this does not exhaust the possibilities. Among the Mayombe, for example, the residential unit is the avunculocal extended family. This means that typically the matrilineal descent group is localized around its male members, maximizing their authority. At puberty Mayombe males move from their mother's to their mother's brother's household, and it is to the latter household that they bring their wives when they marry. Their own children move away when they, in turn, reach puberty. As in patrilineal systems, the wife is subordinate to her husband, but authority over children is divided between father and mother's brother. The father tends to have substantial domestic authority, exercised over his children when they are at home, while the mother's brother has the overriding jural rights over those activities that are important to the descent group, such as regulating mate-selection or determining inheritance and succession. When the sister's children are transferred to his household he acquires also the primary domestic authority over them.

Among the Bemba, the residential unit was described by Richards (1950) as the "father-daughter-grandfamily"; that is, the typical household consists of a grandfather, his married daughters and their husbands,

and their unmarried children. This structure develops out of matri-patrilocal residence, or perhaps more exactly as a result of bride-service. A young man lives in the compound of his wife until gradually he validates his position as a husband, after which he moves, with his wife, back into his own village. The domestic authority of the grandfather is great and that of the husband-father gradually increases as the marriage stabilizes. But the overriding jural rights are still the mother's brother's.

Among the Ila, residence is patrilocal, so that the typical household consists of a grandfather, his married sons, and their children. The wife is subordinate to her husband—domestic authority resembles that of a patrilineal, patrilocal household. The jural rights over the child are divided between father and mother's brother. The father, for example, legally may keep his children if he is divorced by his wife, even though they belong still to her descent group. The Ila differ from both the Bemba and Mayombe in having substantial inheritance through fathers to sons, in addition to matrilineal succession to offices; cattle and homesteads may both be inherited from fathers.

Thus there is a pattern of divided authority rights, in which the following must be distinguished from each other: (1) a husband's authority over his wife; (2) a father's domestic authority over his own children; (3) a mother's brother's jural rights over his sister's children; (4) not described very much in Richards (1950), but often found elsewhere, the mother's brother's rights to discipline, direct, and socialize his sister's sons. In 18 of 19 matrilineal societies for which data on role differentiation have been examined (Zelditch, 1955, p. 331), the husband role was more important than the brother role in economic support of the household; in 19 out of 19, husband was more instrumental in this respect than wife; in 15 of the 19, however, mother's brother had greater *jural* authority than father;

though, in 10 of these 15, father had the greater *domestic* authority.

Strodtbeck (1951) observed Navaho, Mormon, and rural Texan families in a standardized Bales (Parsons, Bales, & Shils, 1953) setting, first forcing disagreement among the couples and then forcing them to come to a decision. Measuring decisions won by family role, the proportion of decisions won by the husband varies with his position in his society. Mormon husbands are traditionally fairly "patriarchal" and won most decisions; rural Texans are more like the average American family, and husbands won just slightly more decisions than wives; Navaho husbands are most subordinate to their wives and won fewer decisions than did their wives.

The argument concerning Navaho husbands is interesting, though Strodtbeck (1951) did not carry it far. Navaho are matrilineal, counting descent through females and inheritance is partly associated with descent. Ownership of stock or land is in the female's hands, in the sense that it belongs to the woman's kinship group rather than her husband's. Actually no matrilineage, so far as is now known, institutionalizes power in the female's hands; the difference between matrilineages and other kinship systems is that authority and power are in the hands of "brothers" rather than "husbands." Had brother-sister pairs been observed, then, one should expect brothers to win more decisions. It is likely also that had unrelated male-female pairs been observed, more decisions would have been won by males. Thus the Strodtbeck data probably reflect the peculiarly powerless position of the husband in a matrilineal system, as distinct from other male roles.

Dynamic Changes in Balance of Power

In *Families in Trouble,* Koos (1946) showed that, "If in the opinion of the family, the father failed to meet the demands of a trouble situation, a loss of dominance

followed in every instance . . . (Koos, 1946, p. 94). Koos's study, in which 62 low-income New York families were studied over more than a year's time, provides longitudinal evidence that is useful in trying to see "power" as a process over time. An illustration of what Koos meant is given in Figure 5, which shows changes in balance of power within a single family in which the father was blamed by the family for not hospitalizing the daughter early enough when she became ill:

The old man was always boss in our place. That's OK, he got a right to be the boss. But Christ, he wasn't boss after he belted that one around. When he raised hell and wouldn't let Agnes go to the hospital . . . everybody forgot he was the old man. None of us paid any attention to what he said. . . . Yeah, he's boss again, but not the way he was before . . . he wasn't worth two cents in our family for a while (Koos, 1946, p. 95).

After the initial loss of power, the mother in this family assumed dominance. The daughter recovered, and the father recaptured some authority. After 18 months, however, he had still not regained his former position. The effects, furthermore, are cumulative. In families with a succession of crises ineffectively dealt with, each crisis brings about a perceptible decrease in authority (Koos, 1946, p. 96).

On the other hand, a crisis successfully handled increases authority. Koos (1946) illustrated this process with the following case: A slightly dominant husband, with an aggressive wife, unexpectedly got his family out of debt. His wife thereafter thought of him as "a bigger man" (Koos, 1946, p. 97), as a "more important man," and the effect on both wife and children was stable over the following 11 months of observation.

Koos (1946) found that loss in dominance during a crisis occurred in every type of family; but the recovery pattern varied with the "adequacy" of the family's organization and the basis of the husband's dominance. By "adequacy of organization" he meant

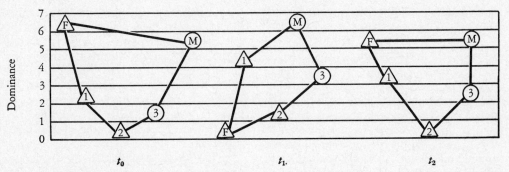

Fig. 5. Changes in power structure after failure to deal with crisis. From t_0 to t_2 is 18 months. The scale at left is intended to measure degree of dominance of each member of the family (see Koos, 1946, p. 94).

the acceptance of roles by family members, their sense of common goals, and the satisfactions they found in the family. He found that adequacy in this sense was correlated with the basis of the husband's dominance, which he classified as institutional (acceptance of authority as traditionally right), personal (love, affection, personal needs, admiration), or instrumental (fear, need for economic support). In the most "adequate" families, the original level of family organization was recovered after crisis in 4 out of 5 cases; in the moderately adequate families the original level of organization was recovered in 23 of 62 cases; but in the least adequate families the original level was recovered in no case out of 42 cases. A second important conditional factor is the attribution of blame for how a crisis is handled.

In time of trouble there appeared to be an inverse relation between responsibility for the action initiating the trouble and the evaluation of the individual's roles, but only where there was a real or implied responsibility for the initiating cause. The sharp division between troubles that are the *fault* of someone and those "that happen because we have to live the way we do" was . . . apparent . . . (Koos, 1946, p. 102).

With more or less detail, the same sort of findings had been reported in earlier studies of the effects of the depression on the family. Mirra Komarovsky (1940), for example,

obtained detailed interviews with husband, wife, and child in 59 families in Newark in which the husband was unemployed because of the depression. She found that 44 out of 59 did not change in power structure. Classifying the bases of power as primary (love, admiration, or tradition) and instrumental (fear, utilitarian needs), she found that 8 out of 12 of the instrumental-based family power structures changed, whereas only 2 out of 35 of the primary-based family power structures changed. Mixed family power structures did not change in 8 out of 11 cases. Among instrumental and mixed families, a second factor that was crucial was whether or not the husband's behavior deteriorated as a consequence of his unemployment. While deterioration had little effect among primary families, among mixed and instrumental families 8 out of 11 cases in which the husband did not "deteriorate" in behavior did not change in husband-dominance, whereas among those that did deteriorate only 3 out of 11 did not lose authority. The tendency among primary families was not to blame the husband for loss of employment and to positively evaluate his efforts to do something about the family's condition.

My husband looks for work mighty hard. He is never home except when it rains real hard. . . . He handles everything—the relief and the creditors. Believe me, I'm mighty thankful for that. If it hadn't been for him and his calm ways, I don't know what I would have done . . . (Mirra Komarovsky, 1940, p. 56).

Between fathers and children, relations with younger children were not affected by loss of job. Among older children deterioration of father's behavior and reversal of roles—child employed, father not—accounted for loss of authority over the child, which was accentuated where husband-wife dominance had also shifted (Mirra Komarovsky, 1940, p. 114).

Earlier studies by Ruth Cavan and Katherine Ranck (1938) and Angell (1936) also stressed the prior organization of the family as a factor in reorganization in the face of depression-crisis. Cavan and Ranck, studying 100 Chicago families, on which they obtained predepression records, showed that "well-organized" families, meaning families with a unified purpose to which individual goals were subordinated and in which reciprocal roles were accepted, were most vulnerable to the crisis because they had most to lose, but also had greater probability of satisfactorily reorganizing. The loss in these families, which were largely middle class, was more a loss of status than of economic security, since many had resources sufficient to ensure the necessities of life. Angell's study, usually regarded as the pioneer in this field, is somewhat obscure regarding the process by which power in the family changes. His conceptualization of the problem involves three key ideas:

1. The effects of the depression should be classified according to degree of change they cause in the prior family organization. If the father is no longer the primary support of the family and his wife or child is employed and contributes most to the family's support, the pressure of the depression is a maximum. If there is no real change in relative roles, despite curtailed income, the pressure was a minimum. If the depression modified family positions but did not actually reverse them, pressure was moderate.

2. Consequent changes in the family should be classified according to both the role-changes that occurred and the success of the family's readjustment. If a family did not change at all it was "firmly invulnerable," if it successfully changed it was "readjustively invulnerable," and if neither of these it was vulnerable or yielding, i.e., either disintegrated or offered no resistance to pressure.

3. The prior organization of the family was classified according to degrees of prior integration and adaptability. Where there is minimum pressure on family positions, change occurs in only the least adequate organizations—the low adaptable or low integrated families. Where pressure is maximum, only the most integrated and adaptable families are invulnerable, and these survive only by changing their role-structures. Where pressure is moderate, moderately integrated and adaptable families change their role-structures and reorganize successfully, while unadaptable or unintegrated families disorganize.

The Incest Taboo

Incest and *exogamy* are institutions that respectively prohibit sexual relationships and marriage within certain kinship relationships. The analysis of the incest taboo, which is the primary concern here, is complicated by the fact that incest and exogamy are often confused, so that some theories of incest actually explain only exogamy, while some theories of exogamy actually explain only incest. The basic empirical regularities in application of the incest taboo are:

1. Incest taboos apply universally to all persons of opposite sex within the nuclear family except husband and wife.
2. They do not apply universally to any relatives outside the nuclear family.
3. They never apply only to the nuclear family.
4. In application to persons outside the nuclear family, incest taboos fail to coincide with actual nearness of biological relationship.

5. They apply with diminished intensity outside the nuclear family.

6. They are highly correlated with conventional groupings of kinsmen (such as the descent group) (Murdock, 1949, Ch. 9).

Most theories of the incest taboo make it depend on the role-structure of the nuclear family (Davis, 1949, pp. 401–404; Parsons, 1954; Brenda Seligman, 1929, p. 35). Since the theories of parent-child and brother-sister incest are somewhat different in detail, they will at first be considered separately. If socialization requires that children be subordinate to parents and that parents cooperate in raising them, then father-daughter or mother-son incest would disrupt the socialization of the child (Parsons, 1954). The child will become more equal to the parent, so that it is problematic who socializes whom, and the parents will compete for the favors of the child, so that it is problematic who is in coalition with whom. The same, of course, is not true for brother and sister. Here the critical problem arises if a child is born and the brother becomes both father and mother's brother to it while the sister becomes both mother and father's sister. To the degree that these are statuses the roles of which are different, the result is confusion (Davis, 1949, p. 403). They are frequently different, the difference lying in the relative distribution of affection and respect. Thus, the theory claims:

1. Sexual relations of parent and child tend to make parent and child more equal.

2. Sexual relations of brother and sister tend to put one or the other in a role which simultaneously involves both affection and respect, if a child is born.

3. A role that is both superordinate and not superordinate is incompatible.

4. A role that is both affective (based on affection) and neutral (based on respect) is incompatible.

5. Incompatible roles are unstable.

Such a theory is extremely difficult to disprove. Appeal is usually made to the universality of the incest taboo, but what is required is some evidence of the actual effects of incest on roles in the family. Because the evidence is scarce, it is difficult to find a clear trend in the available data, and what there is shows the effects only on families where the incest taboo already exists. Therefore the possible effects if there were no taboo are confounded with the effects of the violation of any taboo. Riemer (1940), analyzing 58 cases of father-daughter incest in Sweden, found that, "The daughter simply replaces the mother, and this becomes possible only under the strain of intense sexual desire, combined with a number of environmental circumstances which tend to destroy social responsibility" (Riemer, 1940, p. 573). The circumstances referred to are the work history—high turnover and declining careers—of the fathers and interrupted sexual relations with the wife.

Where the incestuous relation becomes stable, Riemer (1940) found that the daughter assumes the mother's role—performing her household duties and child care functions (Riemer, 1940, p. 575). This suggests that, if role confusion is not exactly a consequence of incest, it is certainly associated with it. On the other hand, there is no question of sexual relations with daughter decreasing the father's authority over her; on the contrary, Riemer found that the power of the father remains great. He even interpreted the frequencies with which various kinds of incest are known (father-daughter incest is the most frequently detected, brother-sister next, and mother-son least detected) as consequences of power differences in the family. Father-daughter incest may become a stable relation because the father's power over the daughter is great. Brother-sister incest occurs less and is less stable, because the brother's power position is weaker. Mother-son incest is rare because the mother does not have the same dominance as the father.

Weinberg (1955), studying 203 cases of incest from Illinois (159 were father-daughter cases, 2 were mother-son cases, the remainder were brother-sister cases, except for 5 cases of multiple incestuous relations) obtained rather similar findings. The fathers had social backgrounds similar to Riemer's cases, and power was an important factor in father-daughter incest. Only 8.6 per cent of daughters claim to have willingly participated, compared to 51.4 per cent of sisters. Like Riemer, he also found that daughters frequently played the role of mothers in incestuous families, while mother (in some, not all cases) "shirked maternal responsibility or was . . . bent upon having a good time and in avoiding household duties . . ." or was away, ill, insane, or alcoholic and so could not assume her duties.

In brother-sister incest none of the consequences supposed in the Davis (1949)-Seligman (1929) theory were found, since most violations were detected before a child was born and in no case was a child being raised. This type of incest was found frequently when the father did not have the kind of dominant position found in father-daughter cases.

At the onset of brother-sister incest, the father was absent from, subordinate in, or indifferent to the family; or he was incapacitated, old, and weak, overworked or concerned with earning a living. . . . Frequently he was removed from the family through death or desertion (Weinberg, 1955, p. 73).

Weinberg does believe that father-daughter incest creates a "conflict of marriage and the family" in which the father becomes a lover. Brother-sister incest was usually more transitory, and only 6 pairs of siblings out of 37 cases seem to have thought of themselves as marriage partners. He also noted that mother and daughter often became rivals for the father, as did siblings. In very detailed case interviews with 11 daughters, Kaufman, Peck, and Tagiuri (1954) found that the mothers were very dependent, did not wish to assume their maternal responsibilities, trained one of their daughters to assume the maternal role, and frequently withdrew or unconsciously encouraged the daughter to play not only the mother but the wife role.

One of the typical cases in our study was June Smith. She was 11 years 2 months old at the time of her referral. . . . When [Mr. and Mrs. Smith] quarreled, Mrs. Smith went upstairs to sleep with the maternal grandmother, leaving the children with Mr. Smith who often was drunk at these times. . . . [Mrs. Smith] said that June seemed more like her mother than her daughter . . . taking over much of the care and responsibility of the home and children. . . . Mrs. Smith never had her own opinions; she always consulted the maternal grandmother. June often told her mother that she wasn't grown up. June had to take care of the little ones and made her father's lunch . . . (Kaufman, Alice Peck, & Consuelo Tagiuri, 1954, pp. 271–273).

By "unconscious encouragement" of the incest, Kaufman, Peck, and Tagiuri (1954) meant such behavior as "[one mother said that] she could not tolerate her husband's snoring and went to sleep in another room. Then out of concern that he would feel lonely she put the daughter in her place in bed with the husband" (Kaufman, Peck, & Tagiuri, 1954, p. 275).

Cross-cultural data on the consequences of incest are scarce, but since the theory is so dependent on processes in the nuclear family, it should be useful to examine incest taboos in cases where the nuclear family (in the Murdock [1949] sense) does not exist.

Gough (1952a) reported on incest taboos among the North and South Malabar Nayars. The North Malabar Nayars are matrilineal but patrilocal, paternity is important, the father brings up the children. Incest with either father or mother is regarded as horrible and incest taboos are extended to the father's kin, such as his sister and his brother's daughter. The South Malabar Nayars have the "visiting husband" union described earlier, are polyandrous with relatively unstable conjugal bonds, and the mother's brother raises the sister's son. Mother-son and brother-sister incest are regarded as horrible, but father-daughter incest, though prohibited, is regarded only as amusing. It is prohibited, according to Nayars, because it would make mother and daughter co-wives, which would contradict their asymmetrical relation. Nor is the incest taboo extended to the father's relatives. In more recent times, though, as paternity has become increasingly important and the father raises the child, father-daughter incest has excited more sense of horror.

Fox (1962) objected to the teleological structure of the Davis (1949)-Parsons (1954) argument, preferring to discover the causes of the incest taboo in early childhood experiences. His argument is applied largely to brother-sister incest and makes use of Spiro's (1958) data from the *Kibbutz,* where again the nuclear family is not, in the Murdock (1949) sense, present. Fox distinguished a "Westermarck" effect, in which early constant contact leads to aversion, which leads to brother-sister avoidance (though not external prohibitions), from a Freud effect, in which early separation of brother and sister leads to repression of desire which leads to great horror at the thought of incest and strong taboos.

Spiro (1958) found evidence that both effects exist. In the *Kibbutz,* for example, children of a number of families are raised in coeducational dormitories, take mixed showers, and are permitted considerable sexual freedom from birth through adolescence. But Spiro found no evidence of actual sexual intercourse within peer groups that grow up together and no desire to marry each other. That is, they spontaneously develop rules of incest and exogamy. When asked why, they report that they feel like siblings. There are, however, societies in which great horror—not just indifference —does accompany the idea of brother-sister incest, and these are also societies in which brother and sister are separated early. Unfortunately, it is still unclear why brother and sister are separated—it is usually argued that this is to prevent their sexual attraction —or why the thought of their sexual attraction should frighten parents.

Middleton (1962) also objected to the theory, on the grounds that incest taboos are not universal (see also Slotkin, 1947). Reviewing evidence on brother-sister marriage in Egypt he pointed out that historians now have strong indications that brother-sister marriage was not only a royal affair, but, at least in Roman Egypt, commoners sometimes, possibly often, resorted to it. Thus in Arsinoe during the Roman period, out of 52 marriages for which documentary evidence has been discovered, 20 were consanguine (Middleton, 1962, p. 607). In other Egyptian communities the rate was less, but of 124 total marriages, 38 were consanguine. The most plausible conjecture, Middleton believes, is that because daughters inherited family property as well as sons, brother-sister marriage developed as a way of maintaining property and estate intact. Thus, he argued, although role confusion may be a problem, incest taboos should be seen as part of the total balance of forces in a family system. Marriage is a matter of the preservation of interests and privileges of kinship groups, and these interests may combine to override the interests in nuclear family stability. It may be observed, of course, that Middleton confused incest and exogamy, but that hardly seems to matter to his argument. If Middleton is right and Fox (1962) not conclusive, it remains an open problem why the brother-sister incest taboo is so nearly universal.

KINSHIP STRUCTURES

A glossary of the most common terms used in the study of kinship is found in Chart 1. This glossary follows most common usage, and where competing usages are common it mostly follows Murdock (1949). The definition of a few terms (e.g., clan) differs from Murdock in order to conform to more common usage, but in general it is advisable to have some standard, and Murdock provides the most acceptable one. Sociologists, for example, are either ignorant of, careless of, or have their

CHART 1

Glossary of Some Technical Terms in the Study of Kinship

Affine: In-marrying person from the point of view of a given descent group.

Ambilineage: A bilateral descent group in which descent is counted from a given ancestor or founder through either male or female descendants.

Avunculocal extended family: An extended family in which nephews bring their wives to live with them at their uncle's home after marriage.

Bilateral descent: A system in which descent is traced through both males and females.

Bilocal residence rule: Residence rule permitting either matrilocal or patrilocal residence after marriage.

Clan: A unilineal descent group in which genealogical connections are fictional or traditional but cannot actually be traced.

Compound nuclear family: A nuclear family with two or more mothers, or two or more fathers.

Corporate descent group: Two usages exist: (1) a descent group that acts as a unit with a differentiated authority structure; (2) a descent group capable of standing before the law as a single person with undying legal personality and undying transmission of rights to office and estate.

Deme: Localized bilateral descent group, including affines as members, in which not all genealogical connections can actually be traced but in which all members assume such ties exist.

Descent group: A group of persons related according to some specified rule of descent.

Double descent: A system in which both matrilineal and patrilineal descent groups exist.

Endogamy: A rule requiring marriage within some given kinship (or other) unit.

Exogamy: A rule requiring marriage outside of some given kinship (or other) unit.

Extended family: Two or more nuclear families forming a single household and single economic unit, spanning two or more generations, and including *all* the married children of one sex, with their spouses and families.

Fraternal polyandry: Polyandrous marriage of two or more brothers to one wife.

Incest: A rule prohibiting sexual associations of given relatives.

Inheritance: Transmission of legal and customary rights to persons and things.

Kindred: A bilateral descent group which includes all relatives recognized by a given ego.

Lineage: A unilineal descent group in which genealogical relations can actually be traced.

Localized descent group: A descent group localized in a given territory. Includes affinal members.

Matrilineal descent group: A descent group in which the rule of relationship is that ego (male or female) belongs to mother's descent group.

Matrilocal extended family: An extended family in which the daughters bring their husbands to live with them at their father's (or mother's) home after marriage.

Matrilocal-patrilocal residence rule: Residence rule requiring a couple to live first with the wife's family and then with the husband's family after marriage.

Neolocal residence rule: Residence rule requiring that couples establish an independent household after marriage.

Nuclear family: An acting unit of father, mother, son, daughter roles.

Polyandrous family: Compound nuclear family with one wife-mother and two or more husband-fathers.

Polygynous family: Compound nuclear family with one husband-father and two or more wife-mothers.

Patrilineal descent group: A descent group in which the rule of relationship is that ego (male or female) belongs to father's descent group.

Chart 1 (Cont'd.)

GLOSSARY OF SOME TECHNICAL TERMS IN THE STUDY OF KINSHIP

Patrilocal extended family: An extended family in which the sons bring their wives to live with them at their father's home after marriage.

Primogeniture: A rule of inheritance by which the eldest son inherits his parents' entire estate.

Residence rule: Institutionalized norm determining residence after marriage.

Sororal polygyny: Polygynous marriage of two or more sisters to one husband.

Stem-family: Two nuclear families forming a single household and single economic unit in which one is a father-mother and unmarried children and the other is one (and only one) married child and that child's family; other married children leave the household.

Succession: Inheritance of office or status.

Ultimogeniture: A rule of inheritance by which the youngest son inherits his parents' entire estate.

Unigeniture: A rule of inheritance by which only one among a group of siblings inherits their parents' estate.

Unilineal descent: System of either patrilineal or matrilineal descent.

Unilocal residence rule: Residence rule requiring matrilocal, patrilocal, or avunculocal residence.

---

own usage of, the term extended family; the glossary definition follows both Murdock and almost universal usage by specialists in kinship. No further comment is added to the glossary definitions except in the case of the corporate kinship group, which is the fundamental unit of kinship systems in many parts of the world, and in the case of bilateral kinship units, since the topic is of immediate interest in the study of contemporary Western societies. Greater detail on the study of kinship, particularly the properties of matrilineal and patrilineal descent groups and of corporate kinship groups generally, will be found in Zelditch (1964) and Mogey (1964).

Corporate Kinship Groups

The birth of a new child in any society inevitably affects the rights and privileges of other members. Some are compelled to assume new obligations. Others may gain new rights. The prospects of others are altered with respect to such matters as inheritance, succession, and marriage. In short, jural relations are modified in various ways, and everyone must know how his own are affected (Murdock, 1949, p. 43).

One knows how his rights and duties are affected by applying a rule of descent. A rule of descent affiliates a person with a group of relatives who have certain rights and obligations with respect to him. That the various rules of descent are matters of social recognition of rights and not different theories of biology was shown very early by Rivers (1924).

Radcliffe-Brown (1935) classified the rights that are transmitted as: (1) rights in personam, which impose duties on a given person; (2) rights in rem, which impose duties on the rest of the world in respect to its behavior toward that person; and (3) rights over things, which are fundamentally the same as (2), but establish the duties of other persons toward things in which one has some vested interest. The three classes of rights taken together Radcliffe-Brown called an estate. Thus an estate in this sense involves not only property rights in the usual sense, but also what the Romans meant by one's "status." Succession is the transmission of this estate.

The estate can be held in three ways: (1) in common, which means that two persons,

A and *B,* with respect to a person or thing *C,* have equal rights—as two hunters might equally use the same hunting ground and have the same rights over it; (2) jointly, which means that *A* and *B* constitute from the outside a single rights-holding unit, the rights of which they jointly exercise over *C;* and (3) divided, which means that *A* exercises one class of rights and *B* another. Where rights are jointly exercised by a collection of persons one may speak of a corporation (Radcliffe-Brown, 1935). If the corporation is kinship group, and succession is based on kinship, then continuity in succession of these rights depends on developing a unilineal rule of descent.

Such groups are called corporate descent groups. Current usage follows either Maine (1861) or Weber (1947), or sometimes both (Fortes, 1953; Fried, 1957). Maine meant by a corporation a group capable of acting as, and being treated as, a single legal person which could have rights defined independently of any particular members of the group—as stockholders or directors are legally not the same as a corporation in our society. Such a group can be perpetual in that death of members does not imply extinction of the rights-exercising "person." Weber meant by a corporate group (a Verband) a group capable of acting together as a unit and having a differentiated authority structure. Such a group has a "leader" who directs its activities. The principal properties of the corporate descent group are:

1. All members are jurally equivalent before the law—they have collective responsibility. This follows from their legal identity.

2. Boundaries of the descent group are unequivocal and do not overlap other descent groups. The boundary is the same for all members. The result is the segmentation of society into concrete, mutually exclusive groups each with structurally unchanging rights over estates.

3. While the exercise of control over production, distribution, and similar economic activities requires the localization of the lineage, many activities of the lineage

as cult, as property-owner, and as marriage-regulator can be carried out even if the lineage is dispersed.

4. Because rights are vested in the corporation itself, not simply transmitted to particular members, the rights lapse if the "ancestors" are not fertile, rather than simply gravitating to other groups linked by other kinship ties. The lapse of rights is usually regarded with horror and despair, and various fictitious devices exist to recruit members into the group if procreation itself fails.

The corporate descent group, however, may be stronger or weaker, in the sense either that it encompasses more or less of the life of its members or is more or less solidary (Schneider & Roberts, 1956). The strong descent group tends to be a multifunctional unit, through which political, economic, and ritual functions may be organized in place of differentiated structures such as the state (Bohannan, 1957; Evans-Pritchard, 1940; Fortes, 1945; Middleton & Tait, 1958), the market (Firth, 1929; Firth, 1939; Audrey I. Richards, 1932), or the church (Hu, 1948). For example, stateless societies of considerable size (called segmentary societies) can exist because of the possibility of organizing territorial and judicial relations through the genealogical relations of lineages. The strength of the descent group, as has already been seen, correlates with ease of divorce, the significance of marital ties, the conflicts and tensions within a society (between the descent group and other groups), and the structure of both the extended family and the nuclear family. The range of functions it performs, however, depends partly on its localization. Although not all localized descent groups are strong (Kroeber, 1917; Schneider & Roberts, 1956), most descent groups that are not localized are relatively weak (Fried, 1957, p. 17). If they are not localized, of course, conflicts over transmission of the estate between descent group and residential kinship units are greater, and acting as a single decision-making unit is more difficult.

Murdock (1949, p. 71) found that localized descent groups with a definite organization and corporate activities are present in 87 societies and absent in 131 out of 218 for which he was able to assemble definite information. Of the 131 societies which do not have organized local descent groups, 56 have unilinear descent (Murdock, 1949, p. 71). There are 33 matrilineal societies with either matrilocal or avunculocal residence (Murdock, 1949, p. 59), but only 15 with matrilocal or avunculocal localized descent groups (Murdock, 1949, p. 71). There are 92 patrilineal societies with patrilocal or matri-patrilocal residence (Murdock, 1949, p. 59), but only 72 localized patrilineal descent groups. Of the 56 societies that have unilinear descent but no localized descent groups, 30 are matrilineal and 23 are patrilineal. The remaining 3 have double descent (Murdock, 1949, p. 75).

Bilateral Kinship

About one-third of the societies of the world are bilateral, but only recently have the concepts necessary to analyze bilateral kinship been developed and its properties examined with any care. There appear to be two fundamentally distinct forms of bilateral kinship groups. One is the kindred, in which descent is counted from a given person (referred to as ego) through any connection, male or female, up to some stipulated collateral range. The other is the ambilineage (also called ramage, or non-unilineal descent group) in which descent may be through either a male or female, but the focus on which the group is defined is an ancestor. The difference is quite fundamental, the ambilineage having more in common with unilineal descent groups than with the kindred.

A kindred, because it is structured around ego, has the following properties (Freeman, 1961; Murdock, 1960).

1. It is never the same for two individuals except full siblings. Ego and his father,

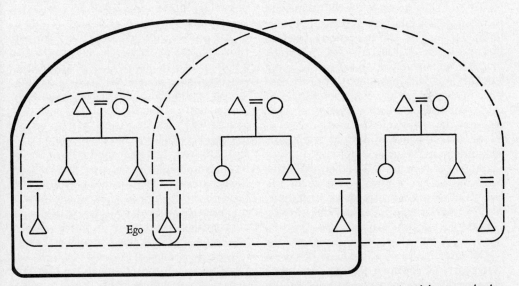

Fig. 6. Structure of the bilateral kindred. Part of ego's kindred is shown enclosed by an unbroken line. His brother's kindred would be the same. His father's kindred excludes some of the members of ego's kindred—ego's mother's father, for example. His cousin (mother's brother's son) has a third, though still overlapping, kindred. It includes the cousin's own mother's father and mother's mother who are not in ego's kindred. Thus for every two individuals except siblings the kindred is different, though the kindreds of relatives overlap; and in every generation old kindreds disappear and new ones appear.

for example, have different kindreds (see Figure 6).

2. Hence kindreds of different persons overlap, so that discrete, united collectives are not formed, and they have no common sense of identity, no collective interests, and no well-developed structure of authority common to all members.

3. Though never a regular corporate group, a kindred can be activated on specific occasions for specific purposes. It may, for example, be active at weddings, funerals, and other rites de passage. But again these are always focused on a specific ego. They are not corporate activities of a distinctive descent group.

The kindred seems everywhere to be correlated with a small, bilaterally constructed domestic family and never with a uniform unilocal residence. Murdock (1960) identified three domestic family types associated with it: (1) the independent nuclear family (including the polygamous family); (2) the stem family (Le Play, 1879), in which one child remains in the household at marriage but the others leave; (3) the lineal family, in which several brothers remain in the household after marriage, but the household is split up when the parents die (Murdock, 1960). Where children do remain in the house of their parents, residence is bilocal, usually depending on the relative economic needs or resources of the husband's and wife's parents. The usual range of kindreds, Murdock found, is between second and fourth cousins. Kindreds are known which count collaterals in the sixth-cousin range, and some, such as the Ifugao kindred, can include as many as two thousand persons (Barton, 1919).

The ambilineage, because it is based on descent from a common ancestor, has many properties of the corporate descent group, differing from the unilineal descent group mainly in the flexibility with which membership is determined. By emphasizing the founder rather than ego, it is possible to construct discrete collectivities all of whose members have the same descent group in common. Such a group can be named, own land in perpetuity, transmit status and titles, and otherwise act as a single entity (Goodenough, 1955). There is a considerable range of types possible (Davenport, 1959; Murdock, 1960), depending on:

1. The range of choice permitted: A child may (a) be assigned at birth by his parents to one or the other of their groups; (b) choose at the time he is married from groups to which his parents belong; (c) choose any group to which parents, grandparents, sometimes even great-grandparents have belonged.

2. Exclusiveness of membership: A person may (a) be required to choose one and only one ambilineage, giving up rights in other possible choices; or (b) allowed to retain claims on and membership in more than one at a time.

A kindred, although fundamentally different in structure from an ambilineage, can approach it in form under certain conditions. Davenport (1959) pointed out that if land-holding rights are separated into rights of use and control versus rights to alienate property, use and control can be vested in a title which is inherited by a member of the title-holder's kindred. So long as there is any patterned rule of succession, the "ownership" of the land will be continuous and action with respect to it may be collective. Davenport referred to this as the stem kindred. The stem kindred will always have certain rights in the land that the title-holder must respect; for example, it has the right to forbid him to alienate any part of the estate. Title, of course, will not be allowed to pass out of the kindred. Persons born outside the recognized collateral range in any given generation, however, will lose their rights and their claim to the title. The stem kindred will resemble a single genealogical line for many generations in the past, but be a kindred in the present. Like the ambilineage, such a group is not ego-centered. Its focus is clearly governed by the present and past title-holders.

Kinship in Preindustrial England

Consider the aims of the fifteenth century Englishman. He lived . . . not for himself, or for God, but for the family. Not to make the family rich or comfortable, but to raise its status—a status that might be illustrated by wealth . . . , but to which comfort must certainly be sacrificed . . . . Children were . . . creatures whose sole purpose was, when grown up, to help forward the family (Trevor-Roper, 1957, p. 30).

To that end, life, marriage, career, everything was openly subordinated. The great motive was to expand if possible, to reunite if necessary, the inheritance of one's ancestors. Not that all England had the same family structure, because there were hundreds of local variations and great changes from the thirteenth century, when it is first possible to look closely at the family, to the middle of the eighteenth century when the industrial revolution is often supposed to have begun. Manorial England proper, traversing the center of the country from the south almost to the Scottish border, was predominantly primogenitary, lived in stem-family households, and was dominated by the dynastic impulse. Thirteenth-century Kent, East Anglia, and perhaps other counties outside the manorial "champion" country had both the independent nuclear family and the joint family. The custom of inheritance in those counties was gavelkind, or partition. A group of coheirs might ask the lord to disgavel their lands at the death of the previous tenant. Or again they might not. If they did, each took an equal share and operated his holding independently of his coheirs. If they did not they were joint tenants, living in the same household and working their inheritance cooperatively. About the time of Henry III, half of unfree holdings and all but four of free holdings were held in joint tenancy (Jolliffe, 1933). By the fifteenth century less than one-fifth of holdings were held jointly. At that time gavelkind was associated in the minds of crown magistrates with individualism, fragmentation, and the decay of great estates.

The ambition to transmit the family holding undivided was the motive alike of the greatest territorial magnates and the most modest English villagers (Holmes, 1957; Homans, 1941). It can be seen clearly as the dominant purpose of the land and inheritance laws of Edward I (Plucknett, 1949). The cardinal principle was the protection of reversions. English family and inheritance law, basically bilateral, endangers the undivided transmission of an estate in many ways; but in just as many ways countermeasures were found to protect the estate from division and dispersal, and these measures had mostly crystallized by the thirteenth century.

One such measure, for example, was unigeniture—typically but not always primogeniture, for ultimogeniture and other forms existed. But, originally connected with fiefs held in military service and apparently intended to prevent fragmentation of an estate to the point where it could no longer support a knight, unigeniture did not apply to female coheirs when male heirs were lacking. An estate would then be divided. It would revert, however, should the female heirs themselves fail of heirs of the body. If the female had an heir, that heir could unite its mother's inheritance with its father's inheritance, producing a new and expanded estate. But if the female's heir himself died without heirs of the body, the estate inherited from his mother reverted to his mother's family whether or not there were closer collateral heirs on the father's side (Paterna paternis, materna maternis). Furthermore, within collaterals on the mother's side, the heir had to be of the blood of the original donor. Thus a fragment that had been for some time lost could be reunited to the estate (Holdsworth, 1909, Vol. 3; Pollock & Maitland, 1905, Vol. ii).

Portions of the estate could also be recaptured from grants settled at marriage or grants made in wealthier families and settled on the younger sons, To marry off his daughters a father had to provide dowry, which in the thirteenth century meant a grant of land, called a maritagium. This grant, joined to a grant settled by the groom's father, helped to establish the new family. If the daughter had no heirs of the body, however, it reverted to the original donor. It was said to be entailed, held in fee tail. Provisions for younger sons, always a problem in primogenitary families, were usually made from minor titles and assart, or recently acquired, lands held by a family—subsidiary titles and lands acquired so recently that one did not have the sense that they were part of the traditional inheritance which must pass to the eldest son. These, too, were entailed, so that failing heirs of the body, or sometimes more strictly male heirs of the body, they reverted to the original donor's estate. By the fourteenth century even such restricted grants were thought dangerous, and the maritagium gave way to life-interests in rents; the grant to the younger son gave way to life-interests from trusts (Holmes, 1957, p. 57).

The lord, too, was a danger to the estate. By ancient feudal tradition estates were not in fact inherited at all; they escheated to the lord who then regranted them to anyone he chose. By the thirteenth century, when rights of inheritance had been firmly institutionalized, the conflict of family with lord was confined largely to the fate of the estate either on failure of heirs or, particularly, during minorities. If the heir succeeded while under age, he was ward to the lord. To support the ward the lord was entitled to farm one-third of the estate. But, more serious, he could sell the ward's marriage. Since marriage was an economic exchange it was a valuable commodity. If the lord did not himself want to arrange the marriage, he could sell it to a second party for resale to a third party. The family lost the value received (it was that, not the barbarism of selling wardships which disturbed the family of the thirteenth century

[Stone, 1960]), and the estate might be farmed rapaciously by the lord or the guardian. In the thirteenth century child marriage was frequently used to rob the lord of his rights of marriage and wardship. By the fourteenth century, trusts and executors were turned to this end. Indeed in that century, "It seems that the magnates were claiming, and to some extent obtaining, a greater control over the destiny of their inheritance" (Holmes, 1957, p. 51).

It was from the lord that this destiny was most threatened in the fourteenth century; the dynastic impulse was too strong to fear future depredations of heirs themselves (Holmes, 1957, pp. 44-45). But by the seventeenth century the dynast feared his heirs sufficiently that he bound them by the classical entail in perpetuity. The classical entail was part of the "strict" marriage settlement made at the first marriage of the eldest son of the family. This settlement determined the future land policy of the family, divesting both father and son of any right other than life-interests in the estate and limiting its inheritance to primogenitary heirs. This settlement bound both father and son not to sell or mortgage the land, stipulated exactly how much could be raised from it for dowries and portions settled on younger sons (for this one purpose mortgages were permitted), and settled also jointures and portions for the children of the heir (Habakkuk, 1950; Stone, 1960).

But already the provisions of the fourteenth century had "made it possible for the tenant to bypass the operations of feudal law with almost as much efficiency as an undying corporation . . ." (Holmes, 1957, p. 57). What can be seen throughout the period, in fact, is something very like Davenport's (1959) stem kindred. The estate itself—continuity enhanced partly by the fact that it was administered by a council that survived the death of any given holder —was like an undying person with a personality before the law and perpetual succession. What perhaps more exactly describes the structure is the term heir-centered ambilineage.

How such ambilineages functioned can be best seen in the economic and political life of the eighteenth century. The parliament of 1701, for example, consisted not so much of parties called Whigs and Tories, though such labels existed, but of "family connexions" (Namier, 1929; Namier, 1952; Pares, 1953; Walcott, 1956; Wiggin, 1958). The great territorial magnates controlled nomination to many of the seats since voting rights were vested in land and land in the family; a seat was one way of providing for younger sons; it was also a way of acquiring the crown's patronage with which other younger sons or relatives could be settled. For a younger son to advance in the army, navy, church, or civil service the family had to have patronage, since no other kind of advancement existed except in emergency situations such as war. The crown was willing to grant livings, commissions, and custom houses to those in parliament who were powerful.

A strong family connexion was essential to power. One built a strong family connexion by nominating one's more dependent relatives, and one's dependent clients, to seats. Even the clients—nonrelatives—seem to have looked on the connexions as family matters, since they in turn persuaded the lord to nominate their nephews, sons, and sons-in-law. Almost half of the 513 seats of the parliament of 1701 were held by such family-client connexions, and, of these, 97 seats were held by actual relatives of territorial magnates. Membership in a connexion was through either males or females and might even be affinal. Thus the elder Pitt, though he could have allied himself with the dozen other Pitts in various parliaments of the mid-eighteenth century, counted himself instead a member of the Grenville-Lyttleton connexion into which he had married. One could and did change connexions, however, and when they did not conflict one could count oneself a member of more than one.

Similar structures have been described by Bailyn (1955) among seventeenth-century merchants in the triangular Boston–West Indies–London trade. There they are of interest because apparently without such family connexions capital formation and credit arrangements were inhibited. One dealt with or employed a cousin, brother, uncle, or son-in-law as an agent, factor, or correspondent because only a relative was reliable. If one wanted to trade in the Barbados one could acquire a trustworthy agent by marrying off a daughter and sending the son-in-law to live there. Family and entrepreneurial policy were thus closely linked (Bailyn, 1955).

As for structures larger than these ambilineages, present evidence indicates that, in the champion country, villages were not themselves kinship groups or demes (Homans, 1941, p. 218). In the class of notables, also, impartible inheritance favored downward mobility of cadet branches so that after a few generations many were lost without trace, while others had established themselves as essentially separate families with only tenuous attachments to the main branch (Wagner, 1960, Ch. 5). But in the far north and in traditional Wales the deme existed, and possibly also in Kent (Jolliffe, 1933). Rees, for example, in contemporary Welsh villages found everyone "tied up like a pig's entrails," and anyone who cannot at least say, "his cousin is married to my cousin" is a stranger in the village no matter how long he has lived there (Rees, 1950; Williams, 1956).

Kinship in Industrial Societies

Are the bilateral kindred and independent nuclear families today found in most Western societies in some way connected with the fact that these societies are industrialized? Owing to considerable conceptual confusion, this question has had a somewhat complicated history. The names most closely associated with this history are Ogburn (Ogburn, 1928; Ogburn & Tibbitts, 1933), who showed that the American family has become progressively more differentiated from structures with economic, religious, welfare, and other nondomestic functions; Burgess (1926), who contrasted the relatively small family, "emancipated" from control of the wider kinship group, with an older, larger kinship group in which individuals were subordinate to extended family authority, surviving, for example, in recent immigrants; and Parsons (1943) who identified industrial economies and open-class stratification with the "isolated conjugal family," a nuclear family that is not incorporated into a unilineal corporate descent group to the authority of which it is subordinate.

Attempts to verify the hypotheses of Ogburn (1928), Burgess (1926), and Parsons (1943) have confused descent groups with extended families, interpersonal interaction with authority structures, "structural" isolation with sociometric isolation. To shifting terms can be added shifting statements of the hypothesis, for sometimes industrialization is supposed to be a necessary condition of the kindred or independent nuclear family, sometimes sufficient though not necessary; and sometimes neither necessary nor sufficient, but they are still found to facilitate industrialization.

Industrialization is clearly not a necessary condition of either the kindred or the isolated conjugal family. In the first place, the kindred was found in the most ancient Frankish, Anglo-Saxon, Celtic, and other traditions of Western Europe. In the second place, independent nuclear families were found at least in Kent in the fifteenth century and probably in other areas of partible inheritance before industrialization (Jolliffe, 1933). In the third place, some of the most primitive hunting-gathering cultures are organized around the independent nuclear family (Nimkoff & Middleton, 1960; Steward, 1938).

If it existed before industrialization, did kindred and nuclear family facilitate that process? Evidence here is less conclusive. In the first place, ambilineages like those described by Bailyn (1955) could well have stimulated industrialization more than the nuclear family, since they were bearers of the expansive dynastic tradition and since they were important mechanisms in capital formation and credit arrangements. In the second place, one finds modern ambilineages that do not retard either geographical or social mobility among New York City Jews (Hope Leichter, 1961; Mitchell, 1961b; Mitchell & Hope Leichter, n.d.). But here the crucial property is that they are divorced from the occupational structure (Mitchell, 1961b). The work of Levy (1949) and Landes (1951) suggests that fusion of economic and family structures does retard industrialization, both by substituting familial obligation for efficient production criteria and by encouraging safe, nonventuresome investment policies. In the third place, one finds that the nuclear family can actually retard industrialization, where family and economy are not differentiated from each other and where the economy is agricultural. In areas of partible inheritance in Northern Europe, geographical mobility and social mobility were encouraged less than in impartible areas (Habakkuk, 1955), since in partible areas every child could look forward to owning his own land on which he could settle his own nuclear family. In such circumstances, the stem family probably facilitated the development of an industrial labor force more than the nuclear family tied to the land. What is important, evidently, is the segregation of kinship and occupational systems.

Industrialization is not necessary to produce the nuclear family or the kindred; given that they exist already, they do not necessarily facilitate industrialization. But perhaps industrialization is sufficient to cause some other kinship system to change into one of kindreds and nuclear families. Spoehr (1944; 1947), for example, showed that the Seminole, Creek, Cherokee, and Choctaw matrilineages have become more bilateral and their extended families have broken down into independent nuclear families. More compelling, since changes in

American Indian social structures might have resulted from acculturation alone, Dore (1958, p. 157) found that the urban Japanese family is moving in the direction of conjugal solidarity.

Still, one may ask if it is really industrialization that causes the disintegration of the descent group and extended family. That the factor might really be urbanization is ruled out by Sjoberg (1960), who showed that many urban, preindustrial communities are organized in extended families. Comhaire (1956) and Agarwala (1955) reported similar findings in Africa and Lewis in Mexico (1952). Nor is geographical mobility alone sufficient, as Dore (1958), Hu (1948), and again Comhaire (1956) showed, for often close bonds remain within the descent group after migration. But Greenfield (1961) was able to show that it is not industrialization per se, but only certain features that are presumably associated with it that are important. The Barbadian economy (Greenfield, 1961) is based on commercial export agriculture. Labor is paid a wage, it is achievement oriented, there is open-class stratification. As in industrialized societies a man's occupational status determines his nuclear family's status, though otherwise kinship and occupation are differentiated systems. In Barbados Greenfield found the isolated conjugal family. Kathleen Gough (1952b), too, found that the Nayar matrilineage began to disintegrate before industrialization, as a result of commercial and political changes that both opened new occupational opportunities and divorced these from the kinship structure. Apparently the process that occurs begins with the differentiation of occupational and kinship structures, industrialization being a sufficient (Smelser, 1959) but not necessary condition of this effect; as a result, the power and patronage on which the corporate descent group and extended family depend for their authority erode; after which their authority, in turn, erodes; and what is left is a primarily expressive kindred in which relatives continue to find personal

reasons for liking each other and helping each other but without the same compelling subordination to a common goal and common authority. This process is described by Aileen Ross (1962) in India and by Dore (1958), who believes that

the Japanese *doozoku* holds its original authority over its members, even though geographically mobile, so long as it retains its "economic stranglehold" over them. But . . . as soon as the economic implications of the traditional main-branch family relations cease to hold good, main and branch status are mutually recognized and visiting is continued only so long as there are personal affective links between members of the two families. . . . The stress is now on personal links whereas it was formerly essentially a question of relations between family units (Dore, 1958, pp. 148–149).

One sees the same process, independent of industrialization, described by Wiggin (1958) in eighteenth-century English politics. The Pitt-Grenville-Lyttleton cousinhood was in its "youth" solidary, because through the family connexion patronage was dispensed. When first George Lyttleton, then William Pitt, and finally George Grenville each began to be powerful and courted by the crown's ministers, they each acquired independent access to other sources of patronage. The purely personal ties of the three main figures of the cousinhood were not sufficient to hold the group together. Though there was still the old impetus to dispense patronage to one's dependent relatives, there was not the impetus to ally with those relatives who now had their own sources of patronage.

That "kinship" was not completely obliterated by the industrial revolution, however, is shown by a large number of recent investigations. In the first place, extended families or ambilineages have been discovered in many kinds of subcultures of industrial society: in working-class neighborhoods (see tables 9 and 10) (Firth & Judith Djamour, 1956; Mogey, 1956; Townsend, 1957; Willmott & Young, 1960; Young and Will-

TABLE 9

PROXIMITY OF MARRIED CHILDREN TO
PARENTS: BOROUGH OF BETHNAL GREEN,
LONDON, 1955[a]

Parent's Residence	Married Men	Married Women
Bethnal Green	50%	59%
Same house or flat	14%	28%
Same street or block of flats	14%	23%
Elsewhere in Bethnal Green	72%	49%
Total of those in Bethnal Green	100% = 97	100% = 102
Adjacent borough	18%	16%
Elsewhere	32%	25%
Total Sample	100% = 195	100% = 174

[a] Source: Young and Willmott (1957, p. 21, tables 4 & 5).

TABLE 10

CONTACTS OF MARRIED MEN AND WOMEN:
BOROUGH OF BETHNAL GREEN,
LONDON, 1955[a]

	Men	Women
With fathers		
Percentage of those with father alive who saw him in previous 24 hours	30%	48%
[(n) = number of respondents with father alive]	(116)	(100)
With mothers		
Percentage of those with mother alive who saw her in previous 24 hours	31%	55%
[(n) = number of respondents with mother alive]	(163)	(155)
With brothers		
Percentage of brothers seen in previous week	27%	42%
[(n) = number of brothers]	(755)	(701)
With sisters		
Percentage of sisters seen in previous week	35%	52%
[(n) = number of sisters]	(769)	(750)

[a] Source: Young and Willmott (1957, pp. 29 & 58, tables 6 & 9).

mott, 1957); in ethnic communities (Gans, 1962; Garigue, 1956; Garigue & Firth, 1956; Hope Leichter & Candace Rogers, 1962; Mitchell, 1961a; Mitchell, 1961b; Mitchell & Hope Leichter, n.d.); among small business men who want to "keep the business in the family" (Margaret Stacey, 1960). The working class extended families that have been discovered have been in relatively stable, old communities, however, and appear to disintegrate if members are mobile (Mogey, 1956; Margaret Stacey, 1960; Willmott & Young, 1960).

What is left is the expressive kindred. This group, or more properly, this network, since the structure consists of sets of linked families that may never, as a whole, act as a group, has proved to be extraordinarily viable (Sussman & Burchinal, 1962a; Sussman & Burchinal, 1962b). It survives, even facilitates, social (see tables 11 and 12) and

TABLE 11

THE OCCUPATIONALLY MOBILE ARE AS
LIKELY AS OTHER GROUPS TO HAVE
FAMILY VISITS[a]

	Percentage Receiving One or More Family Visits a Week
Stationary upper class	36 (249)[b]
Upwardly mobile class	34 (288)
Downwardly mobile class	37 (142)
Stationary manual class	39 (245)

[a] Source: Litwak (1960b, p. 15).
[b] Numbers in parentheses indicate population upon which the percentage is based.

geographical (see Table 13) mobility (Hope Leichter, 1961; Litwak, 1960a; Litwak, 1960b; Streib, 1958). The ties are variable—Millicent Ayoub (1959) reported even in a rural area, for example, a range of between 49 and 268 recognized kin for female ego—and often predominantly personal (Schneider & Homans, 1955) rather than determined by the kinship statuses themselves. Between parent and child, furthermore, some of the instrumental functions of the family also

TABLE 12
OCCUPATIONALLY MOBILE GROUPS ARE MODERATELY IDENTIFIED WITH THEIR EXTENDED FAMILY[a]

	Percentage Extended Family Orientation	Percentage Nuclear Family Orientation	Percentage Nonfamily Orientation	Population
Stationary upper class	26	55	19	100 (247)[b]
Upwardly mobile class	22	55	23	100 (284)
Downwardly mobile class	17	52	31	100 (147)
Stationary manual class	15	51	34	100 (242)

[a] Source: Litwak (1960b, p. 17).
[b] Numbers in parentheses indicate population upon which the percentage is based.

survive. Sussman (1953a; 1954) found that, although the authority structure of an extended family did not exist, in a sample of 97 New Haven middle-class families, partially concealed subsidies were given the family of the child at marriage in order to establish it at the same class level as the parents. And kindred more generally exchange services, such as baby-sitting, help during child-birth, help during illness (Bellin, 1961; Sharp & Axelrod, 1956). Nor do some of these services and exchanges decrease with mobility. For example, data collected during the depression of the 1930's show that coresidence of relatives was greater among middle-class households than among working-class households, suggesting that mobility, by increasing resources, increases the obligation to help (Zelditch, 1956).

Viable as it is, however, the expressive kindred is not altogether invulnerable to mobility. Although evidence to date is incomplete, the kindred will probably turn out to be segmented into minimal, medial, and maximal levels, like the unilineal descent group. It is likely that it is the minimal kindred that is invulnerable to geographical and social mobility, but not the more distant relationships (Reiss, 1962). By minimal kindred is meant here kindred within the sibling range—parents, their children, their siblings—although even between parent-child and sibling-sibling bonds there are differences in vulnerability to mobility (Bellin, 1961). Present evidence suggests that, if anything, mobility increases rather than decreases contact between parents and children, has virtually no effect on siblings, but is negatively correlated with contacts among

TABLE 13
GEOGRAPHICAL DISTANCE DOES NOT LEAD TO A LOSS OF EXTENDED FAMILY IDENTIFICATION[a]

	Percentage Extended Family Oriented	Percentage Nuclear Family Oriented	Percentage Nonfamily Oriented	Total
Relatives living in town	20	52	28	100 (648)[b]
Relatives living out of town	22	58	20	100 (272)

[a] Source: Litwak (1960a, p. 389).
[b] Figures in parentheses indicate the population base for a given percentage.

cousins (Zelditch, Anderson, Takagi, & Whiteside, 1963). Thus the range of the kindred is probably reduced by mobility.

REFERENCES

Agarwala, B. R. In a mobile commercial community. *Sociol. Bull.*, 1955, 4(2).

Angell, R. C. The family encounters the depression. New York: Scribner, 1936.

Ayoub, Millicent R. American children and their relatives. Unpublished manuscript, Fels Research Institute, 1959.

Bailyn, B. *The New England merchants in the 17th century.* Cambridge, Mass.: Harvard Univer. Press, 1955.

Bales, R. F., & Slater, P. E. Role differentiation in small decision-making groups. In Parsons & Bales (Eds.), *Family, socialization, and interaction process.* Glencoe, Ill.: Free Press, 1955. Pp. 259–306.

Barton, R. F., *Ifugao law.* Chicago: Univer. of Chicago Press, 1919.

Bellin, S. S. Extended family relations in later years of life. Unpublished doctoral dissertation, Columbia University, 1961.

Berman, H. J. Soviet family law in the light of Russian history and Marxian theory. *Yale Law J.,* 1946, 56, 26–57.

Blood, R. O., & Hamblin, R. L. The effect of the wife's employment on the family power structure. *Soc. Forces,* 1958, 36, 347–352.

Blood, R. O., & Wolfe, D. M. *Husbands and wives.* Glencoe, Ill.: Free Press, 1960.

Bohannan, P. *Justice and judgment among the Tiv.* London: Oxford Univer. Press, 1957.

Bossard, J. H. S. Residential propinquity as a factor in marriage selection. *Amer. J. Sociol.,* 1932, 38, 219–224.

Bott, Elizabeth. *Family and social network.* London: Tavistock Publishers, 1957.

Burgess, E. W. The family as a unity of interacting personalities. *The Family,* 1926, 7, 3–9.

Burgess, E. W., & Locke, H. J. *The family.* New York: American Book Co., 1945.

Burgess, E. W., & Wallin, P. Homogamy in social characteristics. *Amer. J. Sociol.,* 1943, 49, 109–124.

Cavan, Ruth S., & Ranck, Katherine H. *The family and the depression.* Chicago: Univer. of Chicago Press, 1938.

Centers, R. Marital selection and occupational strata. *Amer. J. Sociol.,* 1949, 54, 530–535.

Clarke, A. C. An examination of the operation of residential propinquity as a factor in mate selection. *Amer sociol. Rev.,* 1952, 17, 17–22.

Clarke, Edith. Land tenure and the family in four selected communities in Jamaica. *Soc. econ. Stud.,* 1953, 1, 81–118.

Comhaire J. L. Economic change and the extended family. *Ann. Amer. Acad. pol. soc. Sci.,* 1956 (305).

Connell, K. H. Peasant marriage in Ireland: Its structure and development since the famine. *Econ. His. Rev.* (2nd series), 1962, 14, 502–523.

Davenport, W. Nonunilinear descent and descent groups. *Amer. Anthro.,* 1959, 61, 557–572.

Davie, M. R., & Reeves, R. J. Propinquity of residence before marriage. *Amer. J. Sociol.,* 1939, 44, 510–517.

Davis, K. Intermarriage in caste societies. *Amer. Anthro.,* 1941, 43, 376–395.

Davis, K. *Human society.* New York: Macmillan, 1949.

De Jong, P. E. De Josselin. *Minangkabau and Negri Sembilan.* Leiden: E. Ijdo, 1951.

Dore, R. P. *City life in Japan.* Berkeley: Univer. of California Press, 1958.

Driver, H. E., & Massey, W. C. Comparative studies of N. American Indians. *Trans. Amer. phil. Soc.* (new series), 1957, 47, Part II.

Eason, W. W. Population and labor force. In A. Bergson (Ed.), *Soviet economic growth.* Evanston, Ill.: Row, Peterson, 1953. Pp. 101–122.

Engels, F. *The origin of the family, private property and the state.* (orig. ed., 1884) In K. Marx & F. Engels, *Selected works.* Moscow: Foreign Languages Publishing House, 1955. Vol. ii.

Evans-Pritchard, E. E. *The Nuer.* Oxford: Clarendon Press, 1940.

Evans-Pritchard, E. E. *Kinship and marriage among the Nuer.* Oxford: Clarendon Press, 1951.

Fallers, L. A. Some determinants of marriage stability in Busoga: A reformulation of Gluckman's hypothesis. *Africa,* 1957, 27, 106–123.

Ferber, R. On the reliability of purchase influence studies. *J. Market.,* 1955, 19, 225–232.

Firth, R. *Primitive economics of the New Zealand Maori.* New York: E. P. Dutton, 1929.

Firth, R. *Primitive Polynesian economy.* London: George Routledge, 1939.

Firth, R., & Djamour, Judith. Kinship in South Borough. In R. Firth (Ed.), *Two studies of kinship in London.* London: Univer. of London, 1956. Pp. 33–63.

Fortes, M. *The dynamics of clanship among the Tallensi.* London: Oxford Univer. Press, 1945.

Fortes, M. *The web of kinship among the Tallensi.* London: Oxford Univer. Press, 1949.

Fortes, M. The structure of unilineal descent groups. *Amer. Anthro.,* 1953, **55,** 17–41.

Fox, J. R. Sibling incest. *Brit. J. Sociol.,* 1962, **13,** 128–150.

Frazier, E. F. *The Negro family in the United States.* Chicago: Univer. of Chicago Press, 1939.

Freeman, J. D. On the concept of the kindred. *J. Roy. anthro. Inst.,* 1961, **91,** 192–220.

Fried, M. H. The classification of corporate unilineal descent groups. *J. Roy. anthro. Inst.,* 1957, **87,** 1–29.

Gans, H. J. *The urban villagers.* New York: The Free Press of Glencoe, 1962.

Garigue, P. French Canadian kinship and urban life. *Amer. anthro.,* 1956, **58,** 1090–1101.

Garigue, P., & Firth, R. Kinship organization of Italianates in London. In R. Firth (Ed.), *Two studies of kinship in London.* London: Univer. of London Press, 1956. Pp. 67–93.

Geiger, K. Deprivation and solidarity in the Soviet urban family. *Amer. sociol. Rev.,* 1955, **20,** 57–68.

Geiger, K. Changing political attitudes in totalitarian society: A case study of the role of the family. *World Polit.,* 1956, **8,** 187–205.

Geiger, K., & Inkeles, A. The family in the USSR. *Marr. fam. Living,* 1954, **16,** 397–404.

Gluckman, M. Kinship and marriage among the Lozi of Northern Rhodesia and the Zulu of Natal. In A. R. Radcliffe-Brown & D. Forde (Eds.), *African systems of kinship and marriage.* London: Oxford Univer. Press, 1950. Pp. 166–206.

Gluckman, M. Bridewealth and the stability of marriage. *Man,* 1953, No. 223.

Gluckman, M. *Custom and conflict in Africa.* Oxford, Eng.: Basil Blackwell, 1955.

Gold, M., & Slater, Carol. Office, factory, store —and family: A study of integration setting. *Amer. sociol. Rev.,* 1958, **23,** 64–74.

Golden, J. Characteristics of the Negro-White intermarried in Philadelphia. *Amer. sociol. Rev.,* 1953, **18,** 177–183.

Golden, J. Facilitating factors in Negro-White intermarriage. *PHYLON,* 1959, **20,** 273–284.

Goode, W. J. *After divorce.* Glencoe, Ill.: Free Press, 1956.

Goode, W. J. The theoretical importance of love. *Amer. sociol. Rev.,* 1959, **24,** 38–47.

Goode, W. J. Illegitimacy in the Caribbean social structure. *Amer. sociol. Rev.,* 1960, **25,** 21–30.

Goode, W. J. Family disorganization. In R. K. Merton & R. Nisbet (Eds.), *Contemporary social problems.* New York: Harcourt, 1961. Pp. 390–458.

Goodenough, W. A problem in Malayo-Polynesian social organization. *Amer. Anthro.,* 1955, **57,** 71–83.

Gough, E. Kathleen. A comparison of incest prohibitions and the rules of exogamy in 3 matrilineal groups of the Malabar Coast. *Int. Arch. Ethnogr.,* 1952, **46,** 82–105.(a)

Gough, E. Kathleen. Changing kinship usages in the setting of political and economic change among the Nayars of Malabar. *J. Roy. anthro. Inst.,* 1952, **82,** 71–87.(b)

Gough, E. Kathleen. The Nayars and the definition of marriage. *J. Roy. anthro. Inst.,* 1959, **89,** 23–34.

Greenfield, S. Industrialization and the family in sociological theory. *Amer. J. Sociol.,* 1961, **67,** 312–322.

Habakkuk, H. J. Marriage settlements in the 18th century. *Trans. Roy. hist. Soc.* (4th series), 1950, **32,** 15–30.

Habakkuk, H. J. Family structure and economic change in 19th century Europe. *J. econ. Hist.,* 1955, **15,** 1–12.

Hazard, J. Law and the Soviet family. *Wis. Law Rev.,* 1939, **1939,** 224–253.

Hazard, J. *Law and social change in the U.S.S.R.* Toronto: Carswell, 1953.

Heer, D. Dominance and the working wife. *Soc. Forces,* 1958, **36,** 341–347.

Henriques, F. *Family and colour in Jamaica*. London: Eyre & Spottiswoode, 1953.

Herbst, P. G. The measurement of family relationships. *Hum. Relat.*, 1952, **5**, 3–35.

Herskovits, M. J., & Herskovits, Frances S. *Trinidad village*. New York: Knopf, 1947.

Hoffman, Lois W. Effects of the employment of mothers on parental power relations and the division of household tasks. *Marr. fam. Living*, 1960, **22**, 27–35.

Holdsworth, W. S. *A history of English law*. London: Methuen & Co., 1903.

Hollingshead, A. B. Cultural factors in the selection of marriage mates. *Amer. sociol. Rev.*, 1950, **15**, 619–627.

Holmes, G. A. *The estates of the higher nobility in fourteenth-century England*. Cambridge, Eng.: Cambridge Univer. Press, 1957.

Homans, G. C. *English villagers of the thirteenth century*. Cambridge, Mass.: Harvard Univer. Press, 1941.

Hu, Hsien Chin. *The common descent group in China and its functions*. New York: Viking Fund Publ. in Anthro. No. 10, 1948.

Inkeles, A. Family and church in the postwar U.S.S.R. *Ann. Amer. Acad. pol. soc. Sci.*, 1949, **263**, 33–44.

Inkeles, A., & Bauer, R. A. *The Soviet citizen*. Cambridge, Mass.: Harvard Univer. Press, 1959.

Jacobson, P. H. *American marriage and divorce*. New York: Rinehart, 1959.

Jolliffe, J. E. A. *Pre-feudal England: The Jutes*. London: Oxford Univer. Press, 1933.

Kaufman, I., Peck, Alice L., & Tagiuri, Consuelo K. The family constellation and overt incestuous relations between father and daughter. *Amer. J. Orthopsychiat.*, 1954, **24**, 266–277.

Kenkel, W. F. Influence differentiation in family decision-making. *Sociol. soc. Res.*, 1957, **42**, 18–25.

Kenkel, W. F., & Hoffman, D. K. Real and conceived roles in family decision-making. *Marr. fam. Living*, 1956, **18**, 311–316.

Kennedy, Ruby J. R. Single or triple melting pot? Intermarriage trends in New Haven, 1870–1940. *Amer. J. Sociol.*, 1944, **49**, 331–339.

Kephart, W. M., & Monahan, T. P. Desertion and divorce in Philadelphia. *Amer. sociol. Rev.*, 1952, **17**, 719–727.

Kingsbury, Susan M., & Fairchild, Mildred. *Factory, family, and woman in the Soviet Union*. New York: Putnam, 1935.

Kohn, M. L., & Carroll, Eleanor E. Social class and the allocation of parental responsibilities. *Sociometry*, 1960, **23**, 372–392.

Koller, M. R. Residential propinquity of white mates at marriage in relation to age and occupation of males, Columbus, Ohio. *Amer. sociol. Rev.*, 1948, **13**, 613–616.

Kollontai, Aleksandra M. *Communism and the family*. London: Workers Socialist Federation, 1920.

Komarovsky, Mirra. *The unemployed man and his family*. New York: Dryden, 1940.

Komarovsky, Mirra. Class differences in family decision-making on expenditures. In N. Foote (Ed.), *Household decision-making*. New York: New York Univer. Press, 1961.

Koos, E. L. *Families in trouble*. New York: King's Crown Press, 1946.

Krilenko, N. V. The family in Soviet Russia. *Pol. Quart.*, 1937, **8**, 204–226.

Kroeber, A. L. Zuni kin and clan. *Amer. Mus. nat. Hist. Anthro. Papers*, 1917, **18**, Part II.

Landes, D. French business and the businessman: A social and cultural analysis. In E. M. Earle (Ed.), *Modern France*. Princeton, N.J.: Princeton Univer. Press, 1951. Pp. 334–353.

Leach, E. R. Polyandry, inheritance and the definition of marriage. *Man*, 1955, **55**, No. 199.

Leach, E. R. Aspects of bridewealth and marriage stability among the Kachin and Lakher. *Man*, 1957, **57**(59).

Leichter, Hope J. Kinship values and casework intervention. In *Casework Papers—1961*. New York: Family Service Association of America, 1961. N. p.

Leichter, Hope J., & Rogers, Candace L. Laterality and conflict in kinship ties. Unpublished manuscript, Family Service Association of America, 1962.

Lenin, V. I. Letters to Inesse Armand. In R. Schlesinger (Ed.), *The family in the U.S.S.R.* London: Routledge & Kegan Paul, 1949. Document No. 1.

Le Play, F. Les ouvriers Europèens. Paris, 1879. S. Dupertius (Trans.). In C. Zimmerman & M. Frampton (Eds.), *Family and society*. New York: Van Nostrand, 1935.

Levy, M. J. *Family revolution in modern China.* Cambridge, Mass.: Harvard Univer. Press, 1949.

Levy, M. J. Some questions about Parsons' treatment of the incest problem. *Brit. J. Sociol.,* 1955, 6, 277–285.

Levy, M. J., & Fallers, L. A. The family: Some comparative considerations. *Amer. Anthro.,* 1959, 61, 647–651.

Lewis, O. Urbanization without breakdown: A case study. *Scient. mon.,* July, 1952, 75, 31–41.

Litwak, E. Geographical mobility and extended family cohesion. *Amer. sociol. Rev.,* 1960, 25, 385–394.(a)

Litwak, E. Occupational mobility and extended family cohesion. *Amer. sociol. Rev.,* 1960, 25, 9–21.(b)

Lorimer, F. *The population of the Soviet Union.* Geneva: League of Nations, 1946.

Maine, Sir H. J. S. *Ancient law.* London: J. Murray, 1861.

Malinowski, B. Parenthood—the basis of social structure. In V. F. Calverton & Schmalhausen (Eds.), *The new generation.* New York: Macaulay, 1930. Pp. 113–168.

Marsh, R. M., & O'Hara, A. R. Attitudes toward marriage and the family in Taiwan. *Amer. J. Sociol.,* 1961, 67, 1–8.

Merton, R. K. Intermarriage and the social structure: Fact and theory. *Psychiat.,* 1941, 4, 361–374.

Middleton, J., & Tait, D. *Tribes without rulers.* London: Routledge & Kegan Paul, 1958.

Middleton, R. Brother-sister and father-daughter marriage in ancient Egypt. *Amer. sociol. Rev.,* 1962, 27, 603–611.

Miller, D. R., & Swanson, G. *The changing American parent.* New York: Wiley, 1958.

Mitchell, W. E. Descent groups among New York City Jews. *Jew. J. Sociol.,* 1961, 3, 121–127.(a)

Mitchell, W. E. Lineality and laterality in urban Jewish ambilineages. Unpublished manuscript, Family Service Association of America, 1961.(b)

Mitchell, W. E., & Leichter, Hope J. Urban ambilineages and social mobility. Unpublished manuscript, Family Service Association of America, n.d.

Mogey, J. M. *Family and neighborhood.* London: Oxford Univer. Press, 1956.

Mogey, J. M. Family and community. In H. Christensen (Ed.), *Handbook of marriage and the family.* Chicago: Rand, 1964. Pp. 501–534.

Morgan, L. H. Systems of consanguinity and affinity of the human family. *Smithsonian Contribution to Knowledge,* 1870, 17, 2–570.

Murdock, G. P. *Social structure.* New York: Macmillan, 1949.

Murdock, G. P. Cognatic forms of social organization. In G. P. Murdock (Ed.), *Social structure in South East Asia.* Chicago: Quadrangle Books, 1960.

Namier, L. *Structure of politics at the accession of George III.* New York: Macmillan, 1929.

Namier, L. *Monarchy and the party system.* Oxford: Clarendon Press, 1952.

Nimkoff, M. F., & Middleton, R. Types of family and types of economy. *Amer. J. Sociol.,* 1960, 66, 215–225.

Nye, F. I. Maternal employment and marital interaction: Some contingent conditions. *Soc. Forces,* 1961, 40, 113–119.

Ogburn, W. F. The changing family. *Publ. Amer. sociol. Soc.,* 1928, 23, 124–133.

Ogburn, W. F., & Tibbitts, C. The family and its functions. In President's Research Committee on Social Trends, *Recent social trends in the United States.* New York: McGraw, 1933.

Pares, R. *King George III and the politicians.* Oxford: Clarendon Press, 1953.

Parsons, T. The kinship system of the contemporary United States. *Amer. Anthro.,* 1943, 45, 22–38.

Parsons, T. The incest taboo in relation to social structure and the socialization of the child. *Brit. J. Sociol.,* 1954, 5, 101–117.

Parsons, T., & Bales, R. F. *Family, socialization, and interaction process.* Glencoe, Ill.: Free Press, 1955.

Parsons, T., Bales, R. F., & Shils, E. A. *Working papers in the theory of action.* Glencoe, Ill.: Free Press, 1953.

Plucknett, T. F. T. *Legislation of Edward I.* Oxford: Clarendon Press, 1949.

Pollock, F., & Maitland, F. W. *The history of English law.* (2nd ed.) Cambridge, Eng.: Cambridge Univer. Press, 1905.

Radcliffe-Brown, A. R. The social organization of Australian tribes. *Oceania Monogr.,* 1930, 1.

Radcliffe-Brown, A. R. Patrilineal and matrilineal succession. *Iowa Law Rev.,* 1935, 20 (2), 286–303.

Rees, A. D. *Life in a Welsh countryside.* Cardiff: Univer. of Wales Press, 1950.

Reiss, P. J. The extended kinship system: Correlates of and attitudes on frequency of interaction. *Marr. fam. Living,* 1962, 24, 333–339.

Richards, Audrey I. *Hunger and work in a savage tribe.* London: George Routledge, 1932.

Richards, Audrey I. Bemba marriage and present economic conditions. *Rhodes-Livingstone Papers,* No. 4, 1940.

Richards, Audrey I. Some types of family structure amongst the central Bantu. In A. R. Radcliffe-Brown & D. Forde (Eds.), *African systems of kinship and marriage.* London: Oxford Univer. Press, 1950. Pp. 207–251.

Riemer, S. A research note on incest. *Amer. J. Sociol.,* 1940, 45, 566–575.

Rivers, W. H. R. *Social organization.* New York: Knopf, 1924.

Ross, Aileen D. *The Hindu family in its urban setting.* Toronto: Univer. of Toronto Press, 1962.

Sabsovich, A. M. The U.S.S.R. after another 15 years. Moscow, 1929. In R. Schlesinger (Ed.), *The family in the U.S.S.R.* London: Routledge & Kegan Paul, 1949. Document no. 8.

Schlesinger, R. *The family in the U.S.S.R.* London: Routledge & Kegan Paul, 1949.

Schneider, D. M. A note on bridewealth and the stability of marriage. *Man,* 1953, 53(75).

Schneider, D. M. The distinctive features of matrilineal descent groups. In D. M. Schneider & E. Kathleen Gough (Eds.), *Matrilineal kinship.* Berkeley: Univer. of California Press, 1961. Pp. 1–29.

Schneider, D. M., & Homans, G. C. Kinship terminology and the American kinship system. *Amer. Anthro.,* 1955, 57, 1194–1208.

Schneider, D. M., & Roberts, J. M. Zuni kin terms. Lincoln: Univer. of Nebraska Laboratory of Anthropology. *Note Book* No. 3, 1956, 1–23.

Scott, Frances G. Family group structure and patterns of social interaction. *Amer. J. Sociol.,* 1962, 68, 214–228.

Seligman, Brenda Z. Incest and descent: Their influence on social organization. *J. Roy. anthro. Inst.,* 1929, 59, 231–272.

Sharp, H., & Axelrod, M. Mutual aid among relatives in an urban population. In R. Freedman, A. Hawley, G. Lenski, W. S. Landecker, & H. Miner (Eds.), *Principles of sociology.* New York: Holt, 1956. Pp. 433–439.

Sharp, H., & Mott, P. Consumer decisions in the metropolitan family. *J. Market.* 1956, 21, 149–156.

Sjoberg, G. *The pre-industrial city.* Glencoe, Ill.: Free Press, 1960.

Slotkin, J. S. On a possible lack of incest regulations in old Iran. *Amer. Anthro.,* 1947, 49, 612–617.

Smelser, N. *Social change in the industrial revolution.* Chicago: Univer. of Chicago Press, 1959.

Smith, M. G. *West Indian family structure.* Seattle: Univer. of Washington Press, 1962.

Smith, R. T. *The Negro family in British Guiana.* London: Routledge & Kegan Paul, 1956.

Smith, R. T. The family in the Caribbean. In Vera Rubin (Ed.), *Caribbean studies: A symposium.* Jamaica: Institute of Social & Economic Research, Univer. College of the West Indies, 1957. Pp. 67–75.

Spiro, M. E. Is the family universal? *Amer. Anthro.,* 1954, 56, 839–846.

Spiro, M. E. *Children of the Kibbutz.* Cambridge, Mass.: Harvard Univer. Press, 1958.

Spoehr, A. The Florida Seminole camp. *Field Museum of nat. Hist. Anthro. Ser.,* 1944, 33(3).

Spoehr, A. Changing kinship systems: A study in the acculturation of the Creeks, Cherokee, and Choctaw. *Field Museum of nat. Hist. Anthro. Ser.,* 1947, 33(4).

Stacey, Margaret. *Tradition and change: A study of Banbury.* London: Oxford Univer. Press, 1960.

Steward, J. H. *Basin-plateau aboriginal sociopolitical groups.* Washington: Bureau of American Ethnology Bull., No. 120, 1938.

Stone, L. Marriage among the English nobility in the 16th and 17th centuries. *Comp. Stud. Soc. Hist.,* 1960, 3, 182–206.

Streib, G. F. Family patterns in retirement. *J. soc. Issues,* 1958, 14(2), 46–60.

Strodtbeck, F. Husband-wife interaction over revealed differences. *Amer. sociol. Rev.,* 1951, 16, 468–473.

Strodtbeck, F. L., & Mann, R. D. Sex role differentiation in jury deliberations. *Sociometry,* 1956, 19, 3–11.

Sussman, M. B. The help pattern in the middle class family. *Amer. sociol. Rev.*, 1953, 18, 22–28.(a)

Sussman, M. B. Parental participation in mate selection and its effect upon family continuity. *Soc. Forces,* 1953, 32, 76–81.(b)

Sussman, M. B. Family continuity: Selective factors which affect relationships between families at generational levels. *Marr. fam. Living,* 1954, 16, 112–120.

Sussman, M. B., & Burchinal, L. Kin family network: Unheralded structure in current conceptualizations of family functioning. *Marr. fam. Living,* 1962, 24, 231–240.(a)

Sussman, M. B., & Burchinal, L. Parental aid to married children: Implications for family functioning. *Marr. fam. Living,* 1962, 24, 320–332.(b)

Townsend, P. *The family life of old people.* Glencoe, Ill.: Free Press, 1957.

Trevor-Roper, H. R. Up and down in the country: The Paston letters. In H. R. Trevor-Roper, *Historical essays.* New York: Macmillan, 1957. Pp. 30–34.

U.S.S.R. Council of Ministers. *The U.S.S.R. economy: A statistical abstract.* London: Lawrence & Wishart, 1957.

Wagner, A. R. *English genealogy.* Oxford: Clarendon Press, 1960.

Walcott, R. *English politics in the early eighteenth century.* Cambridge, Mass.: Harvard Univer. Press, 1956.

Waller, W. The rating and dating complex. *Amer. sociol. Rev.,* 1937, 2, 727–734.

Weber, M. *The theory of social and economic organization.* A. M. Henderson & T. Parsons (Trans.). London: Oxford Univer. Press, 1947.

Weinberg, S. K. *Incest behavior.* New York: Citadel Press, 1955.

Wiggin, L. M. *The faction of cousins.* New Haven, Conn.: Yale Univer. Press, 1958.

Wilkening, E. A. Joint decision-making in farm families as a function of status and role. *Amer. sociol. Rev.,* 1958, 23, 187–192.

Williams, W. *Gosforth: The sociology of an English village.* Glencoe, Ill.: Free Press, 1956.

Willmott, P., & Young, M. *Family and class in a London suburb.* London: Routledge & Kegan Paul, 1960.

Wirth, L., & Goldhamer, H. The hybrid and the problem of miscegenation. In O. Klineberg (Ed.), *Characteristics of the American Negro.* New York: Harper, 1944. Part V.

Wolfe, D. Power and authority in the family. In D. Cartwright (Ed.), *Studies in social power.* Ann Arbor: Univer. of Michigan Press, 1959. Pp. 99–117.

Wolffson, S. Socialism and the family. Moscow, 1936. In R. Schlesinger (Ed.), *The family in the U.S.S.R.* London: Routledge & Kegan Paul, 1949. Document No. 14.

Wolgast, Elizabeth H. Do husbands or wives make the purchasing decision? *J. Market.,* 1958, 23, 151–158.

Young, M., & Willmott, P. *Family and kinship in East London.* Glencoe, Ill.: Free Press, 1957.

Zelditch, M., Jr. Role differentiation in the nuclear family: A comparative study. In T. Parsons & R. F. Bales (Eds.), *Family, socialization, and interaction process.* Glencoe, Ill.: Free Press, 1955. Pp. 307–352.

Zelditch, M., Jr. Doubling rates and family structure in the United States. Unpublished manuscript, Columbia Univer., 1956.

Zelditch, M., Jr. Cross-cultural analyses of the family structure. In H. Christensen (Ed.), *Handbook of marriage and the family.* Chicago: Rand, 1964. Pp. 462–500.

Zelditch, M., Jr., Anderson, B., Takagi, P., & Whiteside, D. Fission in the bilateral kindred. Unpublished manuscript, Stanford Univer., 1963.

CHAPTER 19 Sociology of Education[1]

BURTON R. CLARK

The fascination of education in the modern era lies in its combination of enlarging importance and diminishing clarity. The growing importance follows from new and expanding functions that place education in the center of society, a position that, with some lag, has been heralded by heightened public concern and scholarly interest. Citizens and scholars alike perceive that nations and civilizations depend increasingly for their viability upon the mental capacity required for technological innovation and development, together with the informed wisdom necessary to control that technology within preferred social and political frameworks. The requisite intellectual capacities imply "Education," since training up to advanced skills and complex social perspectives falls largely within the realm of the formally differentiated organs of teaching and learning.

Mass education also now takes the stage as one of the major revolutionary forces of the twentieth century, especially in traditional societies undergoing modernization where the effects of education in transforming the social structure are critical in national development. Mass education involves the populace in the operations of the schools and extends concern about the effects of schooling on individual fate. At the same time that men care more, however, education grows more opaque to the quick and easy glance. The conventional wisdom of the casual observer falls behind as the augmenting size and deepening complexity of education mask many of its characteristics. The understanding of education that everyone possesses from the remembrance of things past, already distorted by sentiment and myth, is confounded by the changing nature of the educational enterprise. As casual observation and memory of one's experience weaken as guides to even the simple empirical realities of education, the belief grows that more men ought to work at the understanding of education and to engage in specialized and systematic investigation. Thus rising concern is coupled with

[1] This chapter draws heavily upon Clark (1962; 1963b). For other statements of the scope and problems of this field of study, or that cover work in a major part of the field, see Brim (1958), Brookover (1955), Floud and Halsey (1958), Gross (1959), Halsey, Floud and Anderson (1961), Havighurst and Neugarten (1957), and Mercer and Carr (1957).

a turn to the social sciences, and it is hardly in doubt that education will soon become a major interest of all the social sciences. The sociology of education, long manned by only a thin Regular Army, now has volunteer scholars flocking to its cause, and sociological analysis is expanding and intensifying. To match the intellectual challenge, however, research needs to quicken at a rapid pace. In having assumed a place beside the economy, the state, and the military establishment as a shaper of men and mankind, education has become an awesome institution whose comprehension demands sustained and diversified inquiry.

There are many fronts on which sociological effort might construct perspectives, accumulate data, and extend knowledge to illumine the educational condition. Limiting the definition of education to formally differentiated systems of instruction, the broadest sector of inquiry lies in the connection of education to the external social structure: to other major institutions (economy, politics); to such features of the encompassing society as its structure of population, its class and ethnic patterns; and to the intersecting groups of family, neighborhood, and age peers that help to define the educability of the young. The connections between education and its environment constitute a network in which influence flows both ways, with education performing as the shaper of other institutions and the general social structure as well as being shaped by external social conditions and forces. This "education and society" interest, extensive in scope within a single society, becomes world-wide in character as investigation turns to cross-cultural comparisons. The second major and often overlooked sector of sociological attention is the educational institution taken whole, or in major segments larger than the individual agency of education. Considered as a social institution, education is among other things a web of organizations and associations, a network characterized in modern society by a growing division of tasks that both differ-

entiates organizations and knits them dependently in interlocking functions. And, taken whole, education is also a labor force, an occupation, a segment of the world of work in which the phenomena of recruitment, job status, occupational orientation, mobility, and career, affect the educational process and the capacities of schools and colleges to perform social tasks.

A third center of attention in the sociology of education, one now developing rapidly, is the internal life of the educational organization. The school or college is (a) a formal organization, with bureaucratic and professional features; (b) a subculture, or a set of interrelated subcultures of students and faculty; and (c) a series of interactions of teachers and students centered on the formal instruction of the classroom. Within the organization as a whole, or the subculture, or the classroom, socially emergent patterns as well as planned relations condition the educational process. In turn, educational practices affect the value orientations and social structure of the school and help to determine the social fate of individuals and segments of the population.

For a fourth sector, sociological inquiry needs to define and comprehend education outside of Education, especially that which emerges as sizeable organized components of other major institutions. The growth and spread of educational work is leading to substantial educational subsystems in the military and in business as well as in the church. The future promises great spread of formal instruction outside of the regular line of schools and colleges, and a grasp of the common and uncommon functions of these educational subsystems would measureably extend understanding of the changing roles of education in the social structure.

Thus there are four sectors of concern: education and society; the educational institution; the educational organization; and the educational subsystems of other institutions. These analytical distinctions are not categories for containing research, for inquiry will normally spill over their boundaries.

To analyze features of school organization, one often considers their environmental determinants; to comprehend interpersonal relations in the classroom, one may need to consider the articulation of the school with the labor force. These categories serve simply to delineate major areas of the relation of education to social structure and to suggest the scope and promise of a more developed sociology of education. Little will be said about the fourth sector, the educational subsystems of other major institutions, about which least is known; and the more anthropological definition of education as a general human activity which in undifferentiated form is present in most relations between generations will also be left aside. The regular formal agencies of systematic instruction constitute in themselves a large and varied subject whose social contours, however intriguing, remain partially veiled and distant to the intimate touch.

EDUCATION AND SOCIETY

In relatively undifferentiated societies, education is blended with other activities of the family and the larger social groupings of tribe, clan, estate, and community within which the young are raised, and, hence, education is part of the socialization that takes place in these contexts. Education gradually emerged as a separate institution as Western social organization developed from a homogeneous society to one characterized by increasing division of labor. In the advanced industrial society, education is extensively differentiated, internally complex, and elaborately connected with other features of society. Its proliferating social and cultural functions radiate in all directions, and the forces that shape it are almost without end. From out of this tangled profusion, certain relations of education to the economy, the stratification system, the culture, and the general integration of society are selected for this chapter. The family as a locator of the individual in the social structure will be touched only briefly, leaving aside such apparently important matters as child-rearing practices and family size, and religion and leisure are entirely omitted. A final major topic not developed here is the relation of education to the political order, a matter destined to receive increasing attention along at least two major lines of concern: the administration of schools and colleges, public and private, in relation to the major levels of government; and the effects of education on politics, from alteration of political attitudes while in school and college to the revolutionary role of student movements in the politics of some societies undergoing modernization. For recent discussions of education and politics, and references to the literature, see Key (1961), Litt (1963), Orlans (1962), and The Economics and Politics of Public Education Series (1962–1963).

Education and Economy

The change in the economy from agriculture to manufacturing and then to service industry that takes place with advancing industrialism affects deeply the nature of the educational institution, for the shift in labor from manual to mental and from low to high degree of skill markedly alters the educational requirements of work. Literacy is required for the mass of workers, at first a literacy of the most elementary reading and writing, and then at later stages of industrialism a rising "functional literacy" of more advanced capability, for example, the reading ability necessary to comprehend employment forms, written tests, and blueprints. For a constantly growing sector of the labor force, work requires educational preparation measureably beyond this minimal level, including lengthened general education for the sophistication useful in much white-collar work and particularized education in an occupational specialty. In short, as industrialism advances, the educational threshold of employment rises across the labor force, and educational preparation is markedly lengthened for fields based on advanced mental skills.

With industrialism, therefore, education becomes more necessary for the economy and is linked more closely and extensively to it. Thus bound to the economy, education becomes the major institutional mediator between manpower demand and supply. Men become part of the potential labor force by qualifying for the work required, and, increasingly, capability is defined by formal schooling. Advanced education offers competence; little schooling defines occupational incompetence. Thus occupational achievement is prefigured by education. Those who remain on the educational escalator are carried to the jobs for which their general education and specialized vocational training have earmarked them, while the early leavers are designated, in the aggregate, for unskilled work and unemployment.

In equipping men with the capabilities necessary for the modern economy, education becomes a way of investing in human capital. This investment takes place across all levels of skill, but it has its most significant effects at the highest reaches, and its most burdensome and difficult problems at the lowest levels. At the top, education has developed a particularly forceful role in the economy through its part in the production and distribution of knowledge. Machlup (1962), using a generous definition of knowledge production, identified five major knowledge industries: research and development, education, media of communication, information machines (e.g., computers), and information services (e.g., legal advice, accounting, and auditing). The knowledge industries, together employing nearly one-third of the labor force, are segments of the economy that are heavily dependent on brainpower and are either identical with education or closely linked to it.

The most dynamic element in the knowledge industries complex is research and development, the activity centered on the production of socially-new knowledge. Located in industry, governmental agencies, universities, and nonprofit organizations, research and development constitutes a massive effort of innovation, a commitment of large numbers of scientists and highly trained technologists in large laboratories to the search for new knowledge and inventions and to the subsequent development of the new for practical use. The scientists and engineers working in research and development laboratories approximated 7,000 to 10,000 in 1920, 85,000 in 1941, 150,000 in 1950, 225,000 in 1954, 325,000 in 1958, and 425,000 in 1962 (Machlup, 1962, pp. 159–161). With the enormous growth of research and development, the creation of knowledge is strongly institutionalized and, hence, is less of a by-product of other functions, such as cultural transmission, than it was in the past. This full-time, specialized, and differentiated concentration on production and utilization of knowledge also transforms technical invention from amateur tinkering to systematic inquiry and development based on expanding scientific theory. It also shortens the time lag between new idea and practical use, and hence accelerates technical and social change.

Higher education is deeply involved in the working of the new economic prime mover, partly as a location for much scientific and technological work and especially as the agency that trains the scientists and engineers who man the laboratories. Higher education has a monopoly as the supplier of scientists and engineers and is thus in a position to retard or accelerate technological advance. A constricted output of technologists reduces the amount of effort sustained in research and development; an enlarged flow of highly trained men into this unusual sector of the economy, on the other hand, makes possible a large and varied research and development establishment and may accelerate the growth of the economy. An industry that creates socially-new knowledge and puts it to work may be more subject to a principle of acceleration than the older forms of industry. The new knowledge is the base for new technologies which lead to new industries and the revamping of others.

In short, the dynamic impact of higher education on the economy in particular lies in the determination of the supply of people with advanced education, especially scientists and engineers, for this supply increasingly determines the pace of economic growth (O.E.C.D., 1963).

Research and development is a special case of a general phenomenon: Brain workers of an ever-higher calibre are *the* economic need of societies in advanced stages of industrialism. The possibility has emerged that education cannot overtrain and overproduce for the economy. If increased supply of high competence means more and varied innovation leading to economic growth, then a rising supply constantly accelerates the demand for trained personnel.

If education possibly cannot overtrain for an expanding, job-upgrading economy, it can certainly undertrain, and with results that are increasingly disastrous for the individual and malintegrative for society. As suggested earlier, persons who receive little formal schooling are subsequently likely to find themselves in unskilled work. The undereducated are also more prone to unemployment: In March, 1959, 8.5 per cent of the workers who had not graduated from high school were unemployed, compared to 5 per cent among high school graduates, and 2.5 per cent among those with some college education (U.S. Department of Labor, 1960, p. 17). The unemployment rate among school dropouts—the young just entering the ranks of the unskilled—was an estimated 27 per cent in 1961, compared with 18 per cent among that year's high school graduates (U.S. Department of Labor, 1963, p. 41). In another study, over one-third of the workers who had not graduated from high school reported that they had been unemployed at some time during the previous five years, while only 7 per cent of those with college degrees were similarly affected (Morgan, David, Cohen & Brazer, 1962, pp. 350–352).

With unemployment rates showing a close, inverse relationship to level of education, there is increasing likelihood that a low amount of education defines a man as unemployable. Linked to the rising curves of skill and knowledge, the unemployability of the uneducated is a new phenomenon. Always before, the uneducated man constituted cheap labor. But now the productivity of the educated man is expanded manyfold by the knowledge and technology at his command, and the gap between the productivity of the skilled and unskilled is widening to the point where the unskilled are driven from work. The unskilled are no longer cheap labor, especially since ideals of social justice (e.g., minimum wage) do not permit their wages to shrink ever lower. It is economically efficient to mechanize the unskilled work and retire the unskilled positions from the occupational structure. Then the young with little education and no skill have no place to go; the "problem of the school dropout" is largely defined by the problems of school dropouts in the labor market. The potential for unemployment that is created by education's sizeable output or seepage of undereducated youth constitutes a major dysfunction for the economy and society.

The rapid change in jobs and occupations endemic to advanced industrialism also causes skills to become obsolete more quickly, necessitating more retraining at all levels of skill. Blue-collar workers need retraining for a different occupation as machines and new processes replace them in their original line of work; a new pipeline carrying coal in a liquid stream may require only 5 to 10 men trained in handling computer controls in place of 1,200 railroad men whose jobs were dependent on the coal traffic. Engineers need to go back to the classroom to maintain competence; with the growth in new knowledge, the engineer of 10 years experience who has not engaged in substantial re-education may have less value than a new engineering graduate. Teachers at all levels of education face a growing need for periodic retraining. The accelerating obsolescence of skill and knowledge is a pressure to extend education over the adult years of work, to diversify education in such forms as the governmental manpower training program, and to move educational work into such locations as the work shop and the union hall. The retraining and readjusting of adults apparently must become a major educational mission as societies move deeper into the modern technological stage.

Education's expanding role in occupational preparation, which thrusts it into the economic order, is the aspect of modern education that has greatest influence in changing its nature and altering its relations to society. Higher education is directly affected as it becomes in greater degree the pre-employment arm of the world of work, providing training and certificates—sometimes only the certificates for jobs where the educational requirements have been inflated beyond any functional need. The growth in the college population takes place largely in fields that represent specialized preparation for work rather than education as a cultivation. The number of graduates in business, education, and engineering increased in the late 1950's at a rate almost twice as fast as the whole population of college graduates—49 per cent compared with an increase of 27 per cent in all bachelor's and first professional degrees between 1954–1955 and 1957–1958 (Clark & Trow, 1960). Two out of three college students were, in 1956–1957, in occupational as compared to liberal arts programs (Pierson, 1959, p. 6). The shift toward the vocational does not mean, however, that undergraduate enrollment will necessarily continue to swing toward the occupational curricula. Specific training tends to shift upward among the levels of education, especially enlarging graduate education; and the liberal arts disciplines are sometimes defined as occupationally relevant. Thus the professional preparation of elementary and secondary teachers in the United States is shifting toward the graduate level, with their undergraduate work in the liberal arts, as more emphasis in teacher education is placed on command of subject-matter.

The connection of education to the modern economy alters the relation of education to government. There is rising concern on the part of governmental bodies as it is increasingly realized that expenditures on education constitute investment. Education is drawn more into the political process, especially at the national level, and receives more scrutiny by public officials. It becomes to a greater extent than in the past a part of political economy.

Education and Social Stratification

Wherever formally differentiated agencies of education exist, their general social function of training the young for adult roles entails also some part in the assignment of status to individuals and groups. This part grows as education connects more closely to the economy: Education's mediation between the demand and supply of workers entails an expanding mediation in the assignment of social position and status from one generation to the next. Education links forward and backward to the stratification system, forward through the effects of schooling on the adult placement of upcoming generations, and backward in time to a prior system of stratification through the ways that access to the school and achievement in it are affected by the social origins of the young. These links often join over time to form a circle of low social status, little education, or of high status leading to favorable educational opportunity and then on to high status. In other cases, however, education breaks the status linkage of successive generations. The central problem in the relation of education to stratification is the relative weight of education as an institution of social inheritance, stabilizing social class positions across generations, compared to its weight as an institution of social mobility, appointing sons to statuses different from their fathers'.

The forward link to adult placement.

TABLE 1

OCCUPATION AND EDUCATION
(Labor force of the United States, 1959)[a]

Occupation	Amount of Education			
	Less than High School Graduation	High School Graduation	Some College Education	Median School Years Completed
	(In per cent)			
White-collar workers:				
Professional and technical workers	6	19	75	16.2
Proprietors and managers	38	33	29	12.4
Clerical or sales workers	25	53	22	12.5
Blue-collar and service workers:				
Skilled workers	59	33	8	11.0
Semiskilled workers	70	26	4	9.9
Unskilled workers	80	17	3	8.6
Service workers	69	25	6	9.7
Farmers and farm workers	76	19	5	8.6

[a] Source: U.S. Department of Labor. *Manpower: Challenge of the 1960s* (1960. Pp. 11, 17).

Education's contribution to occupational placement across the labor force is suggested in part by the amount of education that typifies different occupations and the distribution of occupations within levels of educational attainment. Table 1 reviews the educational level of major categories of occupations in the United States in 1959. In manual work, whether skilled, unskilled, or farm, a majority of workers had not graduated from high school. In occupations based on mental labor, most workers had a high school education or higher, and professional and technical workers constituted a largely college-educated group. Among the white-collar workers, the managerial group was most diverse in educational attainment, largely because of divergent patterns for proprietors and salaried officials: "about one-half of those in business for themselves had not received a high school diploma," while "only about one-fourth of the men who were managers had less than a high school education" (Berry, 1961, p. 144). Warner and Abegglen (1955, p. 108) showed that top executives in the largest firms in the United States are much better educated now than a quarter of a century ago: In 1952, 4 per cent had less than a high-school education, compared to 27 per cent in 1928; 57 per cent in 1952 were college graduates, compared to 32 per cent in the earlier group.

The median years of schooling completed by workers in the various major categories of occupations (Table 1) has such a large range that the figure at one end is nearly double that at the other—over 16 years for professional and technical workers, now the fastest growing of the major occupations, compared to 8.5 years among those in the dwindling labor force of agriculture and unskilled nonfarm workers. A growing skill differential is stretching the educational differential.

The distribution of occupations within categories of educational attainment was shown by Morgan, David, Cohen, and Brazer (1962) for the first occupation of the worker upon entering the labor force. Few workers without a college degree entered into professional and technical work; few without a high school diploma entered clerical and sales occupations; more than 70 per cent of those with less than high school educations entered semiskilled and unskilled work. Subsequent careers are heavily dependent on the first occupation, and thus education influences strongly both the first occupation and the subsequent career.

Education also firmly connects to later income. The average annual income of American men, age 45–54, in 1958, by amount of education received, showed the following wide differences (Miller, 1960):

Some elementary schooling	$3,008
Completed elementary school	$4,337
Some high school	$4,864
Completed high school	$6,295
Some college	$8,682
Completed college	$12,269

The differences in estimated life-time income, from age 18 to death, were also great: The estimates were $182,000 for those with only an elementary education, $258,000 for high-school graduates, and $435,000 for those with four or more years of college, producing an elementary-secondary differential of approximately $75,000 and a secondary-college differential approximating $175,000. These differences have been increasing: The elementary-high school differential widened between 1949 and 1958, and the high school–college differential widened even more in both annual and life-time income (Miller, 1960, pp. 975–983).

The backward link to social position. Education is differentially distributed among the young by the social attributes that most sharply differentiate and stratify their families of origin, their neighborhoods and communities, and their schools. One important set of factors is class linked; another is bound to race.

Research on social class and education has shown a strong relation between parents' class position and educational attitudes, aspirations, opportunities, and achievements. The social status of the family correlates inversely with school dropout (Davie, 1953; Havighurst, Bowman, Liddle, Matthews, & Pierce, 1962). Family position correlates with aspirations to go to college. Its weight relative to the ability of the student, however, has varied greatly in studies of different populations: A Boston study (Kahl, 1953) showed the family to be almost twice as influential as ability; a Wisconsin study (Sewell, Haller, & Straus, 1956) showed ability to be almost three times as important as the family; and a nationwide study of 35,000 seniors in over 500 high schools (Rogoff, 1961) showed family status and student ability playing about an equal role.

Family status is probably decreasing in relative importance, primarily because of the trend in modern society from ascription to achievement and the closer bond between education and the economy. Yet even if family status were reduced to little influence, the impact of social origins might still be significant. Educational aspiration, opportunity, and achievement are conditioned not alone by family of origin and student ability, but also by the larger social contexts of state, community, and neighborhood within which the student is located, and the schools through which he passes. The 50 states in the United States vary greatly in educational opportunity and achievement; 55 per cent of the young men of draft age in South Carolina in 1961 could not pass the Selective Service mental test, compared to 5 per cent in Utah (N.E.A., 1963b). That communities differentially facilitate academic achievement and aspiration was shown by Rogoff; the proportion of high school seniors planning to attend college varied by type of community, from 33 per cent in independent towns of less than 2,500, to 50 per cent in surburban cities of 10,000 to 50,000

(Rogoff, 1961). Havighurst and his colleagues (1962) suggested that children tend to follow the educational values of the neighborhood. Wilson (1959) showed that schools within a large city are characterized by different climates of aspiration— climates linked to the segregating of youth of different social strata in the process of assigning schools to neighborhoods. These school climates affect attitude, accounting for some of the variation in aspirations among youth within a single class. Middle-class youth attending a predominantly lower-class school have their aspirations depressed; lower-class youth in predominantly white-collar schools have their aspirations raised. Where home and school are similar in class characteristics, they have cumulative enhancing or depressing effects on the education of youth.

The conditioning of aspiration and achievement by such extra-familial features of social context as the community and the school means that there is a "continuing but ever-changing link between ecological processes that lead to spatial patterns of residence and work [and schooling] on the one hand, and the processes through which persons are allocated to positions in the social-class structure, on the other" (Rogoff, 1961, p. 243). The significant move in research on social class and education is toward the analysis of interaction over time between the characteristics of the person and his family and the larger contexts of neighborhood, community, and school (and peer group) which intersect as an environment of socialization. Neighborhood, peer group, and school climate are likely to have cumulative effect on the education of the young, since the school climate reflects the neighborhood and its youth subcultures more closely than it reflects the climate of socialization found in the family. The rationalization and bureaucratization of the school also enter into the processes of social mobility, a point discussed below in considering the school as a formal organization.

Education, therefore, is now the common way to climb in the social structure or maintain high inherited position and appears a more important determinant of occupational achievement than class as measured by father's occupation. The weight of education is increasing, both in influence apart from level of origin and in its role as a factor intervening between origin and adult destination (Duncan & Hodge, 1963). Education constantly raises its price for mobility, however, for as the occupational structure is upgraded in skill and required education, the young need to secure more education than their parents merely to keep even with their status (Havighurst et al., 1962).

The educational system may work for the racial minority as it does for the class structure, either as a servant of the status quo or as an instrument of change. If the schools provide inferior education for the members of a minority group, they restrict the chances of the sons improving beyond the lot of the fathers. If the schools offer educational opportunity for the minority, they act to change the existing distribution of the minority members in the social structure.

The recent history of the education of the Negro in the United States has shown three ways in which minority-group membership may depress educational attainment through social assignment. First, the individual is assigned to an inferior school directly because of his race or ethnicity; second, he is assigned to an inferior school indirectly because his race or ethnicity places him in lower-class neighborhoods which have inferior schools; third, he is assigned to an inferior school indirectly because his race or ethnicity together with his lower-class status assign him to segregated housing and then to schools which are both lower class and segregated. The first pattern has characterized the American South, where Negroes have been assigned to separate schools noteworthy for their lower quality of facilities and personnel and a sense of inferiority of school and self that affects motivation. The second and third patterns have been characteristic of the racially-mixed and racially-segregated urban areas of the North, where the assignment of inferior status in itself does not enter decisively in assignment to schools. Here the racial assignment to class and residence become the critical determinants. One study has found that the "overall differences in educational aspirations between Negroes and Whites are 'explained' by the predominantly working-class and low educational status of the Negroes" (Wilson, 1959, p. 838). The process of the second pattern is that a Negro child lives in a lower-class family and becomes subject to class-linked effects, including a school climate that depresses aspiration even when it does not inculcate a sense of inferiority. In the third pattern, where the combination of inferior status and lower-class position assigns the young to housing separate from other races and other classes and to a neighborhood-related separation along the same lines in the schools, the process is that the Negro child begins with a lower-class family position and a lower-class Negro neighborhood and is assigned to a school whose climate is shaped both by a lower-class ethos and the sense of inferiority cultivated by racial attitudes.

These patterns of direct and indirect linkage between race and schooling do not, of course, exhaust the possibilities since when race makes a difference it is generally across the board, affecting every aspect of the location of the individual in society. For example, in quantity of education relative to that of whites, one of the most important accidents of birth for a Negro in the United States has been what state he was born in and reared in. The discrepancy between the education of whites and Negroes 25 years and older in 1960 ranged from less than one year in nine states (e.g., Rhode Island, Kentucky) to over four years in eight states (e.g., South Carolina, Mississippi) (N.E.A., 1963b). Race is a particularly potent determiner of education and adult status where it has cumulative effect not only with class,

but also with urban-rural and regional differences in educational provision. In the United States, these spatially-linked differences are extended by the decentralization of control, with local decision-making based on local sentiment and resources.

The discussion of education and stratification may be concluded with three points:

1. There are a number of intersecting social environments that shape the motivation and aspiration of the school learner. The family, which in turn is shaped by class and ethnic location; the province or state, community, and neighborhood—larger spatially-based environments that vary in educational impulse; the peer groups of the young, which are linked to the above social and geographical locations but are also affected by quasi-autonomous cultures of youth; and the succession of schools through which the child moves. These shaping environments may have cumulative or canceling effects. Extensive analysis of the interaction of these environments and of how they change under the impact of the larger social trends of urbanization and industrialization is needed.

2. The school is a battleground of ways of defining status. The "prior" social environments tend to define the child in ascriptive and particularistic terms; the future environments that the school anticipates for the student will define him more on achievement and universalistic criteria. The past and future intrude to produce a conflict in the present: Will the ascriptive and particularistic definitions of the prior environments dominate in the relation of school and student or will the achievement and universalistic standards that anticipate the future be stronger?

3. Differences among the young that are associated with social status are the crux of the barriers between a society's "pool" of ability and the development of ability in the major training institution. The pool of ability is socially as well as biologically defined and "talent" is a function of social strata and educational provision

Education and Culture

Core values and education. Educators are
agents of cultural indoctrination, a segment
of the adult population set apart to work
full-time at the socialization of the culturally
unformed. The work of these socializers is
conditioned by the core values of society in
two principal ways: The values help to
determine the personal ends of the "clients,"
and hence what these members of the
public-in-contact expect as they enter the
school; the values affect the institutional
means themselves, or what educational agencies are ready and able to offer.

First, cultural values help to set the aspirations of parents for their children and of the
young for themselves. The American value
system contains an ethnic of personal
achievement that motivates the young to
take an instrumental attitude toward education, stressing economic return and individual mobility (Williams, 1952). The value
system of a traditional, colonial society now
undergoing modernization may stress that
educated gentlemen enter public administration and the esteemed professions, causing
those fortunate enough to gain admittance
to the university to bunch up in oversupply
around the curricula that lead to the civil
service, while avoiding promising opportunities in engineering. In addition, values
differentiated by class or ethnicity also influence the pursuit of education. Lower-class
youth in the United States often lack desire
as well as money for advanced education,
and the attitudes of their parents toward
education may be ambivalent or hostile
(Gans, 1962; Hyman, 1953; Kahl, 1953). In
brief, the values of society and the focal concerns of class and ethnic subcultures affect
education by defining the motives of the
young.

Core values also shape the socially structured avenues of education. The educational
structure reflects general definitions in the
community and society of who shall be
educated, how long, and in what way. These
definitions, although affected by changes in
the economy and the class system, have
some independent force of their own and
may advance or restrain the educational impulses that follow from economic and social
demands. The ideals of egalitarianism characteristic of modern democratic societies encourage schooling for all, especially in childhood and early adolescence, in order that
the young may begin on near equal footing.
The democratic societies then differ among
themselves in how far they wish this mass
schooling to go. The late formal selection
characteristic of the American educational
enterprise reflects the American definition
of equal opportunity as open admittance at
even the more advanced levels, a propensity
that gives a strong normative thrust to the
trend of mass higher education. The nations
of Western Europe in contrast have much
normative resistance to mass education,
stemming from elitist traditions of advanced
education for the few and an interpretation
of equal opportunity as fair competition for
limited admittance. The economic and
social demands for mass education have
thus been favored in the one case, and restricted in the other, by the value system
of society.

Beside helping to define who shall be
taught, and hence how many and what kind
of schools and colleges are needed, basic
values also help define what is taught (e.g.,
national legends have long colored the
teaching of history in the schools) (Walworth, 1938). The effect of values on educational content is a large and intricate topic
on which little is known in any systematic
detail. Values also help to define the personnel by entering into the status of the
teaching occupation and hence into recruitment and motivation. Some aspects of who
teaches and why are considered below in a
discussion of education as an occupation.

The impact of values on the structure of
education as well as on the motives of youth
does not ensure an articulation of the personal ends of the individual and the means
of achievement available to him. There is
conflict among the shaping values, as in the

case of concentration on top talent clashing with emphasis on education for all—"elite" versus "mass" conceptions. The educational structure is also shaped by the availability of resources, and the organizations of education generate their own traditions that are not in a one-to-one alignment with general values. As a result, disjunctures appear between the ends that are culturally prescribed for the individual and the avenues available for achieving those ends. The most important case of this discrepancy in democratic educational systems is the inconsistency between universal encouragement to achieve and the realities of limited opportunity. To this blocked opportunity or cultural deprivation, there are various styles of personal adaptation (Merton, 1957) and modes of organizational accommodation (Clark, 1960).

Cultural functions of education. Education's broadest function has long been to act as caretaker and dispenser of certain cultural funds of society. In cultural transmission, educators work with essentially two populations, a minor one composed of adult immigrants ignorant of the culture of a society, and a major class composed of barbarians born within the gates whose untutored state, if allowed to remain, would threaten the continuity of the culture and the stability of the social order. The raising of the culturally innocent to the state of cultured man is the activity on which the formal institution of education was founded, an effort to do systematically and effectively what family and community had long done in an undifferentiated fashion before they were rendered incompetent by societal differentiation and complexity.

One may distinguish three aspects of culture transmitted in schools and colleges: norms, knowledge, and skills. There may be important differences in the relative primacy of each at different educational levels, in different kinds of schools, and in different particular schools. The lower-educational levels are more heavily involved in transmitting the normative components of the general culture, while higher levels incline toward knowledge and skill. The higher levels (e.g., the professional school) are likely to combine a normative orientation based on the specific value system of an occupation with the imparting of knowledge and training in skills. Within higher education, there is much variation by kind of college. A private, residential liberal arts college is more concerned about character and attitude than is a public nonresidential city college combining an array of occupational fields with the traditional liberal arts. Then, of course, within many colleges and universities there is wide variation in emphasis on style of life, knowledge, and skill. The subcultures of the faculty and the students that are based increasingly on departments and professional schools reflect these emphases (Clark, 1963a; Clark & Trow, 1960).

Of all the relations of education to society, the primordial function of cultural transmission is the one most seriously disturbed by modern social forces, the connection whose strength and shape is most thrown in doubt. Society continues to invest ever more heavily in schools and colleges in order that this function be performed adequately; the broadening of educational opportunity represents cultural as well as economic investment. But the work of cultural transmission in the educational institution is being sharply altered in at least two ways: through slippage to new institutions, and through specialization within education.

Some of the work of cultural transmission which in the past has shifted from family and community to the schools is now flowing out of the hands of educators into other agencies. This shift takes the form in part, as mentioned earlier, of educational subsystems emerging or becoming more extensively developed in the institutions of adult work, including the military. This form represents diffusions of systematic, formal instruction into the other spheres of society, as instruction lengthens in years and adapts to the specialization of work and the variety of requirements of differentiated institutions. In a sense, all institutions of work tend also to become institutions of training. The shift in cultural transmission away from the school also occurs in a second major form in the rise of new agencies in society that blend cultural instruction with noneducational activities. The most important of these agencies are television, radio, movies, and the record industry, where the teaching of the young is blended with entertainment and commerce. This blend, competitive with the school, is relatively new, especially in its near-universal coverage. In 1900, the child heard and saw the teacher—often a single teacher in the one-room elementary school—and was told about life outside the school by a small number of surrounding adults and peers. He read a few books and perhaps an occasional newspaper or magazine. Now the situation is qualitatively different, for the child is tuned in—hours daily—to a national network of entertainment and information. The television tube is the arm of central taste-molders—agents of the culture selected for purposes other than systematic transmission. Some part of the core culture, especially the normative components, but also much knowledge and skill, is surely now transmitted through these new channels. The problem for research is what part of the imagery and knowledge of youth is transmitted in these extraeducational ways and what alterations in the content of core culture are made. One plausible hypothesis holds that "low-brow" aspects of the general culture are transmitted in greater volume as the new methods of mass communication take their place with "the custodians of superior culture and its mediocre variants" who formerly had a near monopoly of the means of communicating from the center to the periphery of society (Shils, 1960, p. 295). The lowest common denominator is the norm when advertising ideas linked to mass production and consumption dominate communication (Mannheim, 1951).

The emergence of certain of the mass media as transmitters of lore and molders of taste represents an important shift in the location of cultural indoctrination in the social structure. One can delineate three major locations: (1) the family, church, and neighborhood in which cultural instruction is blended with other activities in webs of primary or quasi-intimate relations; (2) the school, college, and formally designated subsystems of education in other spheres in which cultural instruction is a differentiated activity with its own work force and its own institutional features; (3) the mass media in which cultural instruction for the young as well as the old is again a blended activity, but in a context of largely secondary relations normal to the roles of spectator, customer, and citizen in a large society. The shift to the third location relates the child to national centers of cultural instruction in a pattern little mediated by surrounding adults. The mass media reach directly to the peer groups of early childhood and adolescence, serving and shaping the subcultures of youth (Coleman, 1961). The cultural materials handled in this fashion are primarily selected by the universalistic criteria of commercial mass appeal.

The second major alteration in the function of cultural transmission in schools and colleges stems from the increasing specialization of culture. The weight of educational work shifts toward transmission of variant values and norms, as compared with common values, as the upper end of education is both extended and differentiated to prepare men for an elaborating structure of skilled occupations. General education for all, traditionally located in the early years of schooling, has indeed been extended upward in number of years of schooling for a larger segment of the population, constituting a major component of secondary education. But the extension and differentiation at the higher level of education causes a relatively greater growth in the transmission of perspectives and knowledge that are special to different occupations and various rather than common across adult statuses. The professional schools in particular, but even the disciplines of the liberal arts, in part are now purveyors of specialized culture. Men are differentially socialized to the spreading variety of adult locations.

As indicated in the discussion of education and economy, education's relation to the general culture is greatly broadened in modern society, since to the traditional role of transmitting a heritage there is added the fateful expansion in the role of creating knowledge. In the past, the conservation of knowledge intermittently and modestly has led to the development of knowledge. In the present, the commitment to research means that this historically minor role of creating knowledge moves rapidly toward dominance in higher education. This role is a critical change; the expansion in creation of knowledge makes education an active, intrusive force in cultural affairs, pushing scientific knowledge to the fore, and this dynamic relation to culture constitutes part of the awesomeness of the educational enterprise in modern times.

Finally, modern education decides in some measure the fate of ideas, as well as the fate of individuals. The "culture" is not evenly and uniformly transmitted, but is selectively handled, especially as the fund of culture becomes so large that all agents of instruction must be cultural specialists in some degree. With a variety of traditions and of new perspectives competing for a place in men's minds, there is a competitive determination of the fate of ideas in which such aspects of education as teacher training have important influence. If teacher training emphasizes sociability over intellectuality in the training of the young, the understanding of history is weakened. If the schools of a region sieve historical facts and current events with a fine mesh of racial prejudice, they strengthen a traditional racial philosophy while weakening alternative styles of explanation such as the modern anthropological understanding of the nature of man. In the extreme of totalitarian control of education, cultural selection is made extreme; educational instrumentalities are used to break contact with the past so that new values may

ascend rapidly to dominance. Since values, ideas, and other aspects of culture move around horizontally from one location to another in society, and ascend or descend in prestige and influence in the structure of culture, one may speak of horizontal and vertical cultural mobility. Research on cultural mobility, already begun through the study of the diffusion of information and innovation and the study of changes in attitudes and values over the college years, may measureably extend our understanding of the support given by major elements of the social structure, such as the school system, to the major value systems of society.

Education and Social Integration

The sociological study of a particular institution must ultimately face the question of the relation of that institution to the integration of society. The answers to this query are among the most difficult of all sociological explanations to obtain, requiring first a comprehension of the major social and cultural functions of the institution—in the case of education, its effects on the culture, the class system, the economy, the political order—and second a weighing of the balance of the functions (and dysfunctions) for integration. The contribution of education to integration has been a major problem only in the last century or a little longer. While formal instruction has long existed for certain political and religious elites, the dominance of a differentiated institution in the task of bringing the young to adult ways is a product of the modern era. One historian has estimated that in colonial America, "the span of pedagogy in the entire spectrum of education remained small," for "family, community, and church together accounted for the greater part of the mechanism by which English culture transferred itself across the generations" (Bailyn, 1960, pp. 18–19). Even as late as the first stages of the industrial revolution, formal education was a negligible factor, with widespread illiteracy in the working classes

(Ashby, 1958). The structural differentiation of educational work accelerated in the late nineteenth and the twentieth century and its present differentiation in the United States is roughly indicated by the fact that it is the locus of daily activity for over one-fourth of the population—approximately 2 million adults and 46 million students in a population of 180 million in 1960.

The greater the differentiation of the educational institution, the more complex and problematic is its relation to social order. Critical is the increasing diversity and magnitude of the activities and functions education assumes as industrialism advances in a society. The related trends of industrialization, urbanization, and multiplication of secondary groups disturb and attenuate the relations between individuals and the wider society, and the schools and colleges are asked to "undertake broad educative functions for the mass of the people which were formerly fulfilled by the now weakened 'primary groups' of family, neighborhood, and church" (Floud, 1962b, pp. 521–522; Mannheim, 1951). To education accrues a larger share of the "preparatory" activities basic to consensus and integration—the activities that lead to instilling of culture and training for adult roles. Also, it has been emphasized earlier that with the higher levels of technical training and cultural competence needed for work in the modern economy, education is particularly required to play an ever-larger role in the prework instruction of the labor force and the allocation of individuals, according to talent and training, to the occupational structure. How, and how well, these tasks are performed affects the integration of a society and its viability in the international order.

Education's central relation to integration in societies characterized by advanced industrialism appears to lie not in the continuity of a traditional moral consensus but in the allocation of men to positions in the social structure. This prevails because the educational system has become the central mechanism of society for systematic and orderly change, across generations, in the class location of individuals and cultural groups, as well as for the stabilized transmission of status and power, while its role in transmission of common culture is increasingly attenuated. This central link defines a critical danger: Changes in occupational structure and group demands will move ahead of the capacity of the educational institution to adjust its schedules for training and assignment. The threat of malintegration in this regard appears at the high and low ends of skill and social competence, particularly at the low end, where education relates to the segments of the occupational structure that are being demolished. As unskilled work diminishes and semiskilled work is made subject to rapid obsolescence, educators need not only train the mass of the population up to an ever-rising threshold of functional literacy, but must also, above that threshold, educate for ever-rising levels of versatility and retrainability. Preparatory education needs to articulate with the requirements of adult re-education.

In the modern era the rapidity of social change in itself presents problems of unparalleled depth and intensity in the relation of the major training institution to social integration. Mannheim (1951) maintained that the school of the past was "a training ground for imitative adjustment to an established society," while the school is (or ought to be) "an introduction into an already dynamic society" (Mannheim, 1951, p. 248). Rapid social change means that the appropriate ways of behaving for the next generation may differ extensively from the ways of the past; hence to instill only traditional forms of culture in the schools is potentially malintegrative. No one knows ahead of time, however, what will be the functional behavior patterns of the future. Rapidity of change, then, to the degree it is perceived and responded to, is likely to be a pressure on the schools to educate for "adaptability"; i.e., educating the young to be perceptive and understanding of the social environment and flexible and imaginative in dealing with it, with little control by the patterns of the past. If rapid change tends to promote a more open form of preparation, however, it opens up a Pandora's box of risks: Ambiguous criteria may lead to weak transmission of the cultural heritage and perhaps then to cultural discontinuity; there may be a general weakening of standards of conduct; and men may be educated to adjust easily and passively to group and institutional demands. Education for flexibility is likely to lead to confusion, and may even lead to chaos, "the archenemy of Democracy" (Mannheim, 1951, p. 243). Social and cultural integration is, therefore, dependent on the capacity of the school to blend anticipation of a changing future with imitation of the past, avoiding both extreme individualism and cultural orthodoxy.

THE EDUCATIONAL INSTITUTION

The growth in size and expansion of functions, characteristic of education in societies that have undergone substantial industrialization and modernization, affect markedly the internal structure and processes of the educational institution. Already differentiated externally from other activities, education is ever-more differentiated internally. Major and minor sectors (levels of education, types of schools and colleges) form around permutations of program, personnel, clientele, and control; the growing array of sectors intensifies the problems of division of labor among organizations, articulation of specialized lines of work, and control and influence in the institution at large. Since the modern functions of education render it more important to the national economy and to other interests of national government, the more decentralized educational institutions, particularly the American system, are under pressure to alter their structure of control so as to admit greater national influence in the decision-making process. New indirect and subtle patterns of influence emerge. It is to such considerations

of organization and control within education that this section first turns. Then certain occupational characteristics of educational personnel, features of the work force of this major institution that have extensive and deep effects on performance and function, will be considered.

The Institutional Web

The large, decentralized complex of schools and colleges in the United States consisted in 1960 of 92,000 elementary and 26,000 secondary public schools, grouped in 40,000 public school districts; and 13,000 elementary and 4,000 secondary private schools; together with 140 universities, 760 liberal arts colleges, 200 teachers colleges, 50 technological schools, 520 junior colleges, and about 300 assorted theological schools, art schools, and detached professional schools, that added up to a known population of nearly 2,000 units in education beyond the secondary school (U.S. Department of Health, Education, and Welfare, 1961; U.S. Department of Health, Education, and Welfare, 1962). In addition, there are an unknown number of pre-elementary nursery schools and two- and three-year semiprofessional schools and technical institutes that prepare students for work without earning credit toward a degree. *Associations* of schools and colleges and of teaching and administrative personnel are also large in number and represent the interests of various educational strata, from college admissions officers to elementary teachers to Catholic colleges. There were over 1,100 of these associations in 1960 at national and regional levels alone, offering to the public and to government an exceedingly pluralistic interpretation of the interests of education.

Sources of diversity. The diversity of organizations in American education has been produced by the interaction of a variety of educational tasks with a wide dispersion of authority. The tasks of education are everywhere diversified as education is extended to a larger share of the population, lengthened to occupy more years in the life cycle, and linked more closely to the allocation of status. In countries characterized by central control in educational policy, national authorities attempt to allocate the various tasks systematically and to institute some system-wide standardization of schools, programs, and requirements of entry, transfer, and completion. In the United States, however, where control is decentralized to local and state levels and further fractured by the pluralism of private sponsorship, the thousands of schools and colleges have been established under diverse public and private auspices—local, state, and national government, churches, foundations, private entrepreneurs, groups of parents. With task variety attacked by private initiative and by dispersed public authorities, the formal tools of education exhibit uncommon variation. The public school systems alone vary widely in quality within a single state, because of their separate financial bases and differing value orientations of local authorities. The public systems of the states vary greatly within the country, from regional and urban-rural differences, causing among other things great inequality of opportunity. The private sector admits the widest possible variety, for the private groups can establish schools more narrowly tailored to group interest. The personnel of schools and colleges, particularly the private ones, also have some discretion to give their own agencies a character distinct from other units, adding emergent variety to the diversity that ensues from planned allocation of tasks within local and state systems. This differentiation allows individual agencies to develop particular capabilities and serve particular publics, while the institutional complex as a whole has many capacities and serves the increasingly varied educational requirements of a heterogeneous population.

Comprehensive versus specialized organization. Schools and colleges vary widely in degree of specialization, with some organized around a single task and others grouping a range of activities. The American public high school, specialized in grade level and students of a certain age, is comprehensive in placing the major lines of study available to students of this level and age under one roof. The secondary school in European countries generally specializes in curriculum as well as grade level and age group, with the major programs allocated to separate schools. This difference in division of labor among organizations is not accidental nor innocent; it reflects the linkage of the internal structure of an institution to dominant values and social patterns in society, and it has fundamental consequences for the educational process. The American comprehensive school reflects commitment to an achievement orientation and universalistic standards of status, together with a somewhat open social class system that offers support for these values greater than that found in Western Europe. The European tradition has held more strongly than the American that the higher academic training—the secondary level in this case—is for the few, and class-linked elites have had greater influence in Europe, in part through centralized control, in holding policy to this tradition. The consequences are fundamental: With specialized secondary schools, critical steps in selection must be taken early—age 11 or 12, for example—in order to assign students to different schools. The earlier the selection, the greater the impact of social origins. Selection for advanced education and high-status career is moved closer to the differences in environment of home and neighborhood that are linked to class and ethnicity, to the settings that form motivation before the child enters or proceeds far in school. With comprehensive secondary schools, selection to curricular streams is formally delayed, leaving the critical judgment open to influences of school and personal development that may modify or override the influence of social origins. On the basis of its later formal streaming, the comprehensive secondary school offers greater scope for the play of universalistic standards and achievement criteria (Turner, 1960).

The curriculum is not the only basis, however, beside grade level and age of student, on which schools are specialized. The universality of the comprehensive school can be severely limited by other features of social structure and school operation. A single high school in a small town takes in all students as well as all curricula and hence is comprehensive across social strata, but the many high schools of the metropolis specialize in types of students. Urbanization has caused the American comprehensive secondary school to become increasingly differentiated by neighborhood, specialized in social class and ethnicity and in such correlates of class and ethnicity as aspiration and sophistication of the young. The policy of a door open to all now no longer causes students of all classes and races to mix on common ground, but assures specialized assortment on other than the universalistic criteria of ability and achievement. Neighborhood of origin, an ascriptive factor for the individual, weighs ever more heavily in the educational process, wherever the internal differentiation of the metropolitan area—the slums from the suburbs—outruns the efforts of school systems to provide equal opportunity for students unequal in social origins. In short, urban differentiation turns the "comprehensive school" into a specialized school, a school specialized not only by neighborhood and clientele but also by the practices and curricula adaptive to clientele. The link to social origins is forged anew. To reverse this ironic transformation, students have to be selected and assigned to schools on grounds other than the geography of neighborhoods. Changing population patterns alter the relation of school structures to cultural values and social strata.

The urge to generalize magnificently about critical educational differences between comprehensive and specialized schools is also restrained by the realization that the "late" selection of the common school may be a formal ratification of selection made earlier by educational personnel. When selection does not take place at the door of an educational agency, it may well begin soon after entry, and one must allow for the possibility that it is done early and announced late. Some processes of internal classification and sorting, discussed below in the section on formal organization, diminish the difference between systems that are formally selective or unselective, and formally early or late in assigning students to futures.

Centralized versus decentralized systems. Diversified agencies of education may exist as a network of organizations within either centralized or decentralized systems of control, although a higher degree of diversification is favored by decentralization. Diversification can be planned by central authorities; and since schools left to their own devices may narrow their differences by converging on prestigeful models (Riesman, 1956), an unplanned free market can conceivably lead to less differentiation than a planned and enforced division of functions among schools.

Centralization of educational control in a national ministry, or, at a lower level, in a regional or state department, serves certain ends and presents certain institutional problems, while decentralization serves other ends and leads to problems of a different order. Centralization serves integration, orderly procedure, the uniform application of standards, and innovation from the top. It allows for redistribution of resources across a large system—"equalization"—to reduce the disparity between the poor and the rich, the backward and the advanced, among local units of education. The problems posed by central control are ones particularly of rigidity and the lessening of initiative in the provinces.

Decentralization allows for widespread initiative. It also encourages adaptation to the immediate social context, rendering the school more sensitive, often subservient, to local interests. Decentralized control in education may also encourage innovation. Ben-David (1960) suggested that competition among independent universities encourages scientific innovation; when academic scientists move among agencies free of central allocation of personnel and central control of facilities and incentives, famous men are attracted or kept from leaving by higher rewards in the form of laboratories, assistants, scientific jobs, and recognition of new disciplines. The innovative effects of competition within a decentralized system, however, obtain only under certain conditions. Among these may be extended visibility of men and agencies and the dependence of organizational prestige on the reputation of individuals. Top scientists and major universities are highly visible; the prestige of star scientists is critical to the prestige of the university. Where these (or functionally equivalent) conditions are absent, however, decentralization may lead to isolation, local adjustment, and inertia. In the case of American public schools, the school and the teacher do not have national visibility, and academic stars are not critical to the school's performance and prestige. Competition has been weak, and decentralized authority has meant "innovation" chiefly in the form of adjustment to local interests. In this context, major educational innovations have stemmed mainly from the efforts of national agencies (Ford Foundation, National Science Foundation), private reform groups (Physical Science Study Committee), or from the few elite, experimental schools that do have national visibility and care about their status as national pacesetters. The salutory effects of talent competition on innovation might become stronger in the American system, however, if state and national tests were used to identify publicly the quality of work in school systems, and community pride—a functional equivalent to institutional pride—were to become invested in the ranking of the schools.

The great problem of a decentralized educational institution in modern society is uncoordinated, piecemeal response to needs and interests that extend across society. The tendency of a locally-adaptive system to drift is not a disturbance when the other aspects of society remain oriented toward local and state levels of action and when education's tasks bear little on national interests. But educational drift develops into a social problem as authority moves upward in other institutions, e.g., as national corporations and state regulatory agencies come to dominate the economy, and as the tasks of education relate closely to the national economy and such "interests" as the technology of national advance and protection. Drift in American education now calls out efforts to insert some direction, to intervene sufficiently that national outcomes will not be the sum of unconnected decisions made only with local ends in view. Thus, foundations, study committees, and single individuals, as well as the federal executive agencies, constitute themselves as national voices offering some unifying direction. The perceived costs of drift and the insensitivity of local authority to national concerns promote the effort to centralize control, or to construct and strengthen national mechanisms for influencing the scattered authorities who retain formal control. Subsidized research and development in instructional materials, evidenced in the work of the Physical Science Study Committee and other national curriculum study committees, and teacher training institutes sponsored by the National Science Foundation are but two of the means emerging to exercise a concerted influence in a formally decentralized system.

Institutional cohesion. Bureaucratic coordination is an important source of cohesion in the more centralized educational institutions. In addition, integration normally has other supports, and in decentralized systems of education cohesion is strictly dependent on other aspects of social structure and value orientation. Critical in cohesion is the relation between specific values and specific social segments of an institution. Values held in common throughout the system are for the most part integrative, e.g., the consensus in the United States on free elementary and secondary education. But variant values may also serve integration, in indirect and complex ways, a relation of some moment in view of the growing internal differentiation of institutions in modern times. A hypothesis of cohesion through variant values may be stated as follows: Orientations to different values in the parts of a structurally differentiated institution promote integration by (1) giving normative support and protection to specialized persons, and (2) legitimating a variety of activities so that each segment in the system has a socially-valued function and does not collapse the division of labor by converging on a particularly prestigeful activity. This formulation is derived from a diverse literature on the relation between differentiation in social structure and differentiation in values, especially Durkheim (1933), Hughes (1958), Kluckhohn and Strodtbeck (1961), and Turk (1963). Sharp conflict occurs within an institution when the constituent groups orient to the same activities and fight for jurisdiction.

The import of legitimate, specialized values for specialized activities and groups can be seen in state systems of higher education, in the United States, that have attempted to plan a division of work among colleges. A tripartite structure (e.g., state university, state college, junior college) depends on orienting the three segments to different purposes and gaining broad social acceptance for each of the missions. The planned differentiation flounders when one segment refuses the function assigned to it and seeks to take on the mission of another. The most important instance in American higher education is the common refusal of state colleges to occupy and stabilize a role different from that of the state university and instead seek to become more like the university, indeed sometimes becoming a university. The proposed state-college mission of four- and five-year programs in the liberal arts and occupational training lacks the legitimacy of the university's manifold purposes, which include the prestigeful elements of research and advanced graduate

programs. Thus, a consensus among college personnel on the prestige ranking and the social value of educational programs may disturb integration, through promoting group conflict, while differentiated valuation of programs may aid integration by legitimating the parts of a differentiated structure and reducing jurisdictional convergence and warfare.

Teaching as an Occupation

Teaching is by far the largest of the advanced white-collar fields defined, in the United States, as professions. Education's large participating clientele, a fourth of the population, required in 1960 a work force in excess of 1.75 million in elementary and secondary education, and 200,000 in higher education. One-third of all college graduates —a staggering proportion—expect to enter primary and secondary education as a career field (J. A. Davis, 1963). This work force has a distinctive social composition and certain unusual patterns of career at the elementary and secondary level, that, one may conjecture, affect deeply the educational process.

Division by sex. Education is two occupations, one for women and one for men. At the elementary level, education is a woman's occupation; in higher education, it is a man's work. At the secondary level, it is mixed but inclined toward a woman's occupation by the wedding of secondary to elementary education in the organization of school districts and in the publicly-defined field of "school teaching" in which 70 per cent are women. In elementary education, approximately 85 per cent of the teachers are women; less than one out of three of the men who teach in the schools teach at this level, and they are outnumbered six to one. In secondary education, where two out of three of the men teachers are located, women number about one-half of the teaching force. In higher education, about one-fifth are women. There is a relatively high proportion of women on the staffs of teachers colleges, liberal arts colleges, and junior colleges (over 30 per cent) and a relatively low proportion (13 per cent) in the universities and professional schools (NEA, 1957; U.S. Department of Health, Education and Welfare, 1957–1958).

A predominance of women has characterized American school teaching since at least 1870 (Lieberman, 1956). This feminization has made education an attractive occupation for women and an unattractive one for men. Men suffer degradation in status from working in what others perceive as a women's occupation; the male elementary teacher is particularly prone to the feeling that he is in a feminine role (Mead, 1951). Men are also relatively deprived in financial rewards, compared both to men in other advanced white-collar work and to women teachers. Under the principle of equal pay for equal work, men and women teachers have been paid increasingly under the same salary schedules. But since most women teachers are either single, or represent a second income in the family, while the men must look to their salary for supporting a family, equal pay means attractive salaries for women, especially in light of their almost total exclusion from many professions (women number 3 per cent in law, 6 per cent in medicine), and unattractive salaries for men. Men teachers must accept women's pay, or at best a pay which is a compromise between what it takes to recruit women and to recruit men (Mason, 1961). As a result of their relative deprivation in status and remuneration, men are less satisfied. When teachers were asked in 1956 if they would re-enter teaching, more than 80 per cent of the women indicated they would, while among the men only 54 per cent were pleased with their work, 17 per cent were not sure, and 29 per cent said they would do something else (NEA, 1957). An earlier study reported that only about one-third of male elementary teachers professed to liking their work and even fewer (27 per cent) would enter elementary teaching if they were to start over again (Kaplan, 1948).

Occupational instability. Teaching is an unstable occupation in either its male or female form. Women perceive and use teaching as an in-and-out career. Two out of three (65 per cent) beginning women teachers, for reasons extrinsic to the work itself, expect to leave teaching within five years. Both single and married new women teachers anticipate, or hope, to begin their own families, which will leave them preoccupied for awhile: 70 per cent of the new women teachers hope to be "homemakers," and 5 out of 6 of these want also to return to teaching (Mason, 1961). Three out of four of all female school teachers are or have been married (NEA, 1963a), two out of three married school teachers do indeed break their service, and a fourth of the married women report two or more extended absences (NEA, 1957).

For men, the anticipated career in education is up-or-out, rather than in-and-out: They go into teaching hoping to advance up the school ladder into administration, or permanently leave education to take employment in another field. Among beginning men teachers, over one-half hope for a non-teaching position in education, and an additional one-fifth expect to move to another occupation, leaving only 3 out of 10 who plan at the outset to teach until retirement (Mason, 1961). Among men teaching in 1956, less than 10 per cent had been away from teaching for five or more years since beginning to teach, compared to one-third of the women then teaching (NEA, 1957). Thus, men persist in their teaching careers better than do the women, but they persist with the intent of getting away from the women's work of teaching into the men's work of administration. Two-thirds to three-fourths of elementary school principals are men, and the proportion is higher in the junior and senior high schools (Lieberman, 1956). Advancement to administrative positions may be 7 to 10 times greater for men than for women (Morris, 1957).

The patterns of women leaving and returning and of men leaving the classroom for other work are reflected in age differentials. In 1956, the median age of men was 35, and of women 45; the distribution of the men and women within age brackets was as follows (NEA, 1957):

Age	Men	Women
Under 26	19.6	80.4
26–35	51.4	48.6
36–45	26.7	73.3
46–55	15.8	84.2
56 and over	17.4	82.6

The unstable nature of the educational work force below the college level relates to its feminization, and teaching has the following characteristics of a women's occupation: short-term work, large turnover, discontinuities in career, fleeing of men, and a general lack of occupational solidity (Caplow, 1954; Lieberman, 1956).

The instability of this occupation extends to the fleeing of recruits at the time of decision to enter the field. The general magnitude of mortality, early as well as late, is suggested by the following information drawn from a study of University of Illinois graduates over a 10-year period: 40 per cent of those qualified to teach never took public school jobs; of those who began teaching, one-half had dropped out by the end of 2 years; for every 1,000 prepared to teach, only 150 were still teaching after 5 years and less than 100 were teaching after 10 years (Charters, 1956). Entry and retention rates markedly below those of other fields (engineering, medicine, dentistry, law, social work) are also indicated by the conclusions of other studies and reviews of research; e.g., one-third of all persons trained for education do not enter the field; not more than two-fifths of those prepared are at any one time actually teaching (Brim, 1958; Morris, 1957; Wolfle, 1954).

Observers of the occupational characteristics of education have also noted a great amount of horizontal mobility of teachers, who move to other schools within the same or neighboring districts in search of better conditions of work, higher status, and shorter commuting distances (Becker, 1952a; Brim, 1958; Havighurst & Neugarten, 1957). Since the odds of moving vertically are heavily against women, the pattern of moving from school to school within the status of classroom teacher is, for them, an important consolation prize, especially since the horizontal move is generally to a school higher in social status and thus constitutes some equivalent of vertical mobility. It would therefore appear that vertical and horizontal mobility are heavily differentiated by sex, and, further, that the different patterns may be extensions of the men's and women's status trajectories in society. Men teachers are from somewhat lower social origins than are the women (46 per cent compared to 30 per cent from blue-collar families) and thus are more often upwardly mobile in general social status, particularly so when teaching leads to administration; while women are more frequently from white-collar families (51 per cent compared to 38 per cent for men) and thus more often remain on a status level close to that of their parents (Mason, 1961). There is some tendency for the teaching career to serve a status maintenance function for women both within and outside the school, while operating for men as a mechanism of general status change.

These characteristics of the educational labor force are attributes of the education institution whose effects radiate in every direction, affecting the quantity and quality of teaching, the temper of educational administration, the climate of the school, and interaction in the classroom. Five possible effects will be mentioned. First, the quantity of labor available for elementary and secondary teaching is reduced sharply by low retention of personnel, and any shortage of labor at these levels is primarily a result of this low retention. A "shortage of teachers" is actually a "man year" shortage produced by low survival and discontinuity in the occupation (Charters, 1956). Men who stay in teaching contribute more man-hours of teaching than do women; women who combine teaching and marriage contribute more than do women "who view marriage and a career as mutually exclusive alternatives, with marriage as the highly preferred" (Charters, 1956, p. 255).

Second, the quality of labor in low-status schools is markedly lowered by teacher career patterns, particularly the horizontal movement of teachers within districts in which experienced teachers move to schools of their choice. With this pattern, the low-status school is staffed by experienced hands who have made their adjustment (including a downward adjustment in expectation of student performance) and by new teachers who are learning to teach through apprenticeship in "Siberia" (Becker, 1952a). The harsh effects of the transfer privilege on low-status schools confronts urban school systems with the dilemma of maintaining the transfer system and suffering the resultant inequalities of education, or of abolishing the transfer system in order to improve quality of low-status schools and thereby risk lower reward and morale and an even lower rate of retention of personnel.

Third, the professionalization of educational work is retarded. The in-and-out and up-or-out career patterns help to keep the field a place for amateurs. The turnover of teachers restricts identification, commitment, and expertness, necessary ingredients of advanced professionalism. It is to the interest of the women to have teaching as an occupation in which the gain in skill achieved by continuous experience is slight, in which loss of skill during long periods of inactivity is relatively small, and in which re-entry is easy (Caplow, 1954). In addition, turnover that is linked to tours of duty in "homemaking" helps to keep the field feminine as well as amateur. The constant exchange of women between the school and the home is a bridge across which the nurturant and affective norms of the role of mother are transported into the school. Thus the mobile teacher-mother-teacher serves to tie the school to the home; a major segment of the staff in education, she may be an important

counterforce to the orientation of the school away from the home and toward impersonal universalistic criteria that grows stronger under the impulse of education's tightening connections to national economic and political concerns.

It may also be the case that the teacher's tour of duty in the home as mother is an important ingredient of in-service training for keeping up with a rapidly changing world. Margaret Mead stressed that age and experience for teachers in the modern world become not orienting factors but disorienting ones, as the young early incorporate into their thinking new ideas that many older persons never fully assimilate (1951). The time spent in the role of mother, according to this interpretation, is an orientation excursion to the playground and nursery school as well as the home, acquainting the teacher with the new perspectives, interests, and activities of the young. However that may be, the feminization and intermittent employment patterns of teaching greatly reduce the autonomy and the organizability of the occupation (Lieberman, 1956). Entry to the field, early or late, is relatively easy, and numerous backdoors to employment exist in the form of temporary and emergency credentials. Since such patterns lead to cheap labor and docility in the work force, they are consonant with certain interests of school boards and administrators in economy and management.

Fourth, the psychological and financial deprivation of men in teaching, which helps to sustain the career pattern of men moving upward into administration, probably adds to the rigidity of school administration. The gap between the rewards of teaching and the rewards of administration is especially wide for men, possibly making them reluctant to return to the ranks—analogous to the reluctance of union officials to return to the factory floor when the gap between the status of the official and the status of the rank-and-file member is large (Lipset, 1954). School administrators in the American system of decentralized, lay-board control are in the first instance made cautious by their vulnerability to lay approval and influence. They have additional cause to administer conservatively, in order to avoid mistakes and friction, as they glance over their shoulders at the role and status of teacher that they have left behind.

Fifth, the sex and career patterns of the teaching force contribute to distinctive problems of socialization. Students move from a women's world to a men's world as they move up the grades. The shortage of men in the elementary school may contribute to tendencies of boys to define education as feminine, to identify with peers (and against the school), and to become behavior problems. The shortage of women in most sectors of higher education, on the other hand, may contribute to the young woman's problem of reconciliation of home and career. The models of reconciliation are in short supply, appearing on some campuses only as visiting missionaries. In brief, critical problems of identification and identity are probably related to the markedly uneven distribution of men and women in the labor force of society's main formal agency of socialization.

THE EDUCATIONAL ORGANIZATION

The internal life of the school or college can be analytically constituted on various planes and from several sociological perspectives. The present discussion will provide only limited illustration of the analytic possibilities, skipping over such major concerns as the social psychology of classroom interaction. Several features of the structure of the school and college will be connected to the previous discussion of education and society and the nature of the educational institution.

The Educational Agency as Formal Organization

Organizational place. The particular place in the general institutional web that is allotted to, seized by, or accidentally found by a school or college is an important, but generally overlooked, determinant of its character, often having decisive effect on the status of the organization and its members. A school is judged and rated by public perception of its main task or tasks, which have high or low status according primarily to their connection with occupations and social status. Among the specialized schools of English secondary education, the grammar school leads to the university and high-status occupations and is assigned high status, while the secondary modern school, which for the most part does not lead to the lofty places, is generally awarded lower status (Banks, 1954). The staff and the students in the modern school labor under the stigma of lower status, stimulating concern about how to achieve a parity of esteem for schools performing different educational and social tasks. The realization that this is virtually impossible lends support to the effort to group the secondary "streams" within comprehensive schools, somewhat similar to the American form.

The resources—money, staff, students—available to a school or college are heavily influenced by its place within education and society. The social hierarchy of the major types of English secondary schools affects recruitment; the proportion of teachers from middle class homes increases and the proportion from working class homes decreases, as one moves from the lower- to the higher-status schools (Floud & Scott, 1961). In the United States, there is a noticeable self-selection of students to Ivy League colleges because of their high status and the realistic belief (Havemann & West, 1952) that these colleges promote allocation to high positions. The geographical location of a school or college can in itself be decisive, as the introductory pages of college catalogs have long recognized in their glowing prose about rural charm and urban convenience. To place a college in the American South is to intensify greatly the problems of staff recruitment, since for reasons of racial problems and anti-intellectual climate all other regions of the country are preferred by Ph.D. candidates, and a large proportion of advanced graduate students will not consider teaching at any college in five of the southern states (Middleton, 1961). Such examples make the point that organizational analysis of a school or college must frequently begin with an understanding of its location in organizational space, and its specific social and cultural functions, as these are perceived and defined by other educators and the public. Actual and perceived location among other organizations becomes increasingly important as schools and colleges grow in number and variety.

Internal structure. With educational work becoming more varied and complex, the school or college does not escape the growing specialization found elsewhere in modern social organization, but rather becomes more of a system for coordinating a growing array of unlike specialties. Expanding knowledge militates sharply against efforts to maintain educational work in an undifferentiated state. Academic disciplines proliferate, and professors specialize in and within disciplines, fragmenting the campus and deepening the problems of communication and coordination. The teacher in the elementary and secondary school is less affected by the intense specialization that occurs along the edges of advanced knowledge, but he also moves toward specialization in subject matter and grade level. The teacher who could handle all subjects for six to eight grades in the small school house has been rendered incompetent, and the changes underway in the 1960's in the curriculum of the elementary school (e.g., foreign language instruction, new mathematical and scientific materials) accelerate the trend toward specialization that has replaced the old schoolmarm with teachers who possess a particular strength and prefer to handle only a small part of the subject matter. The internal array of specialties is also widened by expertness in administration, as the administrator acquires respon-

sibility for such tasks as purchasing, budget control, public relations, counseling, and student activities.

When new duties are added to the work of a school or college, they may be located in newly differentiated roles or added to the traditional ones. One interpretation of the modern American university professor, congruent with the feeling of distraction and overwork common among academics, holds that his position of work is undergoing considerable strain because "the academic role has been gradually redefined to embrace the variety of diverse tasks that the university has assumed" (Gross, 1963, p. 62). To undergraduate teaching and advising, academia has added graduate teaching, research, consulting, and extensive committee work. This formulation calls attention to the burdens of new and expanded tasks, but one needs also consider what duties and expectations have been lifted from the professor and what tasks added to the modern university have been assigned to other roles. In the nineteenth-century college the professor spent a great deal of effort in student discipline: "Faculty members and administrators in virtually all American colleges spent almost as much time trying to cope with the behavior of the adolescents entrusted to them as with their studies" (Schmidt, 1957, p. 76). The little hellions were to be supervised from morning to evening, including the overseeing of prayers, rendering the old-time professor the regulator of student conduct virtually around the clock, and the object of student rebellion. There is little wonder that in the transformation of American colleges from single to multipurpose organizations the American professor has been willing to allow the supervision of student behavior and counseling to be detached from his role and placed in the hands of deans and other student personnel officials. And, of course, various tasks have been added and assigned to administrations, separated from teaching and internally differentiated.

Thus an alternative interpretation is offered to the hypothesis of the inclusive role: The proliferation of work activities in education, as elsewhere, induces a differentiation of roles. The professorial role has shed some major tasks as others have been added. The role itself is currently undergoing much internal differentiation, with a string of roles appearing in the guise of one. Some professors only teach, particularly in small four-year colleges and junior colleges; some teach and serve as part-time counselors; some teach and do research and consult; some only do research; some in professional schools are nearly full-time consultants. These patterns are structural adjustments to task diversity. Such role differentiation in its early stages develops without much formal recognition in titles and status ladders. That the formal will follow to codify the emergent is now exemplified by the case of academics in university laboratories and institutes, whose differentiated work is leading to titles, salary scales, and career ladders distinguishable from that of their fellows in the departments.

Authority. The exercise of authority takes radically different forms in American schools and colleges, the critical divide lying between the college and the lower schools. Each of these two major levels will be briefly considered.

In higher education, the increased specialization of work and differentiation of roles extend the need for bureaucratic coordination, and there is a pronounced trend toward formal codification of rules, accompanied by a weaker trend toward the fixing of responsibility in a higher and wider hierarchy of administrative positions. Rule-making proceeds at a rapid rate as faculties and administrators seek to apply universalistic criteria across large, complex staffs. But the attempt to fix authority in a single structure within which salaried experts are accountable to superiors is countered and somewhat contained by the authority of the faculty. With its origins in the self-rule of the teacher and student guilds that comprised the medieval university, faculty authority his-torically has been collegial, hence antibureaucratic, in form. Faculty authority is now evolving away from its traditional collegial form, under the impact of modern expertness and the growing size and complexity of the campus, but the form to which it tends is also largely antibureaucratic. As the campus moves from the characteristics of a community to the characteristics of a loosely-joined federation, faculty authority moves from the meeting of the assembled faculty and the informal interaction of a small body to the numerous, dispersed units (departments, subschools, subcolleges) that are the foci of the disciplinary interests of the faculty and to a more formal representative government in which there is greater differentiation between those who participate and those who do not. Faculty authority tends toward an order whose main function is to protect the autonomy of experts—similar to the function of professionalism in other organizations. A growing literature depicts the clash of bureaucratic and professional authority in the modern large-scale organization (Blau & Scott, 1962; Caplow & McGee, 1958; Clark, 1961; Gouldner, 1957–1958; Janowitz, 1960; Kornhauser, 1962; Marcson, 1960; L. Wilson, 1942). The faculty man is a professional in the sense of the specialized expert whose competence has considerable intellectual content and who has a strong commitment to a career based on his special competence (Kornhauser, 1962). Academic man occupies a role that has much in common with the position of other experts in other organizations, particularly the scientist in industry and the physician in the hospital, where the demands for extensive personal and group autonomy are high. Modern faculty control is different from professional authority in other places, however, in its extensive fragmentation, its tendency to group around the interests of a large variety of groups of roughly equal status and power. The experts—chemists, linguists, historians, professors of marketing—identify with their separate disciplines, and the overall academic profession comes off a poor second. As an organization of professionals, the campus is decentralized and multiple, rather than a close-knit group whose members see the world from one perspective. In short, faculty authority tends toward professional authority in federated form. The combination of professionalism and loosely-joined structure functions to protect the autonomy of the work of experts amid extensive divergence of interest and commitment.

Bureaucratization and professionalization in modern higher education both stem from the same basic trends in the relation of education to society. A widening array of educational tasks for an expanding population leads to increase in size, complexity, and internal specialization in educational organizations. With higher education's commitment to research and scholarship—the frontiers of knowledge—the increased specialization takes the form, in large part, of intense pursuit of specialized knowledge. The need for personal and group autonomy grows, and there is a pronounced move toward professionalism, with authority based on technical knowledge and located in the individual expert and semiautonomous clusters of experts. At the same time, the differentiation and proliferation deepens the need for administrative coordination, and so the campus moves toward some bureaucratic arrangements. The modern campus is too large and complicated for professional or collegial direction to provide the overall coordination, and this task is performed largely by bureaucracy. But bureaucracy cannot provide or adequately protect the exercise of judgment by diverse experts, and this task is performed largely by a federated professionalism.

With academic disciplines and professional fields constituting the natural bases of academic federalism, the academic tasks that move toward marginal status are those that cut across disciplines and require attention, commitment, and consensus from the faculty as a whole (e.g., general education), or are little rewarded in the career

patterns of the separate fields (e.g., undergraduate teaching). General education for the undergraduate stands in double jeopardy, and general educationists have sought to reverse this situation by utilizing the principle of federated structure for their own ends, by arranging the campus in the form of a federation of small colleges and residential houses organized around undergraduates.

In elementary and secondary education in the United States the authority structure takes a markedly different form from that just described. There is less expertness, less impulse toward federated professionalism protective of teacher autonomy. The public school systems are more characterized by a vulnerable bureaucracy. The authority structure of the school takes the form of a single hierarchy, rather than of the dual and multiple governments of the college, with teachers as employees under supervision of administrators. The critical feature of this authority is its amenability to external control. Vulnerability stems in part from the decentralization of control to local lay boards, with job security of administrators closely dependent on lay approval. The vulnerability is extended by the correlated ideology of local lay control that has been a sacred component of the American conception of educational governance. In addition, the ideologies of public school administration have adjusted to this vulnerability, with administration often guided by conceptions of service to lay demands, and efficient operation of the schools in line with community dictates (Callahan, 1962; Clark, 1956; Lieberman, 1956). The vulnerability does not mean total dependence on lay interests, since many matters, one of which is considered below, are shielded from public view or only dimly perceived, and others are so latent that even school personnel are not aware of them. Increasing size and complexity has masking effects, and school personnel work out some defenses against external demands (Becker, 1953). But on issues of major concern to laymen, the

American school administrator is highly vulnerable to external pressure, compared with his counterpart in the democratic industrialized societies of Europe where educators are protected by centralization, close ties to the educated elites, and an accepted posture of superior judgment.

Leaving aside the vulnerability primarily characteristic of the American schools, the bureaucratization of the school is a general phenomenon that has significant bearing on social mobility. Bureaucratization increases the weight of the formal apparatus of education in determining the future of the young; it renders careers more dependent on classificatory and treatment processes of the school (Cicourel & Kitsuse, 1963; Clark, 1960; Goslin, 1963; Schelsky, 1961; Sexton, 1961). A modern school system initiates a dossier on the student in the lower grades, adds information to the file from time to time, and passes the records along through channels as the student moves to the next step in the organizational treatment. The file provides the information which officials interpret to classify the student as an academic-social type, and from the classification follows efforts to assign students to different treatments. The typing process increasingly runs through the office of an official, the counselor, who specializes in student classification. Is the student to be defined as bright, average, dull; overachiever, normal achiever, underachiever; well-adjusted, neurotic; a good boy, a delinquent? Given the nature of his case, what careers are possible and what courses and class assignments are therefore appropriate?

The criteria of classification are shaky and often differentially interpreted and applied. But increasing specialization among occupations and longer formal instruction make hit-and-miss and late identification of capability seem more costly for both the individual and the society. The effort to locate and train talent in order to enhance the manpower of a nation also adds to the pressures to develop and apply methods for identifying the attributes of students, meas-

uring their progress, and steering if not controlling their choices. In secondary and higher education, the counselor also needs an apparatus of records, grades, and interviews to "cool out" or socially demote the student whose aspirations are markedly out of line with ability. The within-school selection characteristic of mass democratic systems of advanced education is heavily dependent on bureaucratization.

In short, modern trends in the organization of schools and colleges have the broad social consequence of partially bureaucratizing and rationalizing the processes of social mobility. Parental and student orientations must interact with the increasingly more systematized institutional means of achievement. Their orientations are sometimes defined, sometimes redefined, and always processed by the everyday activities of a school bureaucracy. These activities differentiate and distribute the student population among major lines of future career development (Cicourel & Kitsuse, 1963).

Educational Subculture

A school or a college has certain normative and symbolic features not readily subsumed under formal organization, as in the case of student traditions passed down through the generations and supported by cliques, clubs, and living groups that are partly independent of the official scheme. Waller pointed out that one need not cross the seas to find strange customs: "Folklore and myth, tradition, taboo, magic rites, ceremonials of all sorts, collective representations, *participation mystique,* all abound in the front yard of every school . . ." (Waller, 1932, p. 103). To some degree, any school or college has or partakes of a subculture of society. These subcultures vary extensively in content, however, and they may be unified or fragmented, strong or weak, dependent on or largely independent of the greater society. Research that has begun to identify the common and variant features of educational subcultures and suggest their determinants and effects is found in Becker, Geer, Hughes and Strauss (1961), Caplow and McGee (1958), Clark (1963a), Clark and Trow (1960), Coleman (1961), Goldsen, Rosenberg, Williams and Suchman (1960), Gordon (1957), Gouldner (1957–1958), Hollingshead (1949), Newcomb (1943), Sanford (1962), Sussman (1960), Waller (1932), and Wenkert and Selvin (1962). A fuller discussion than is here presented may be found in Clark (1962). The analysis below is limited to several changes now occurring in the structure of these subcultures.

Change in educational subcultures. There is a pronounced trend toward fragmentation of normative systems within schools and colleges linked to increasing size, complexity, and specialization. The monolithic culture characteristic of the one-room schoolhouse and the residential liberal arts college of several hundred students gives way in the modern era to a multiplicity of values and perspectives. In the college faculty, paralleling the trend in authority, a culture of the whole gives way to a set of subcultures based on disciplines or clusters of related disciplines. Specialized lines of work, professional perspectives, even different vocabularies, induce subculturing within the faculty. In faculty-student contact, there is also a pulling apart. Faculty members are now busy with nonstudent matters, live off campus, and spend more time away in the line of duty, reducing the interaction with students that is necessary to fuse student and faculty values into a unified culture. In the student body, the larger campuses exhibit a further multiplicity of subcultures. Alongside the collegiate or "Joe College" style of life, the value system dominant among students on many campuses since the 1880's but now in decline, there exists a variety of vocational, academic, and nonconformist orientations. Some students orient primarily to job training and a certificate; others are little "Dons" imitating faculty perspectives even before they get to graduate school; still others are routine grade-getters; some, who

are in college simply because it is easier to remain in school than to break the habit, are characterized by lack of any commitment; and there are tiny bands of nonconformists or detachers who cluster around politics, art, music, and mountain-climbing. Mass higher education contains many definitions of college and uses of the college years, and these variant definitions and uses are core elements for more general but variant subcultures. So, too, in the larger secondary schools, a variety of subcultures exists, sometimes competing sharply for hegemony. Cultural heroes of the high school vary from the brilliant student who represents brains and serious study, to the star athlete who epitomizes sports and glamour, to the "hood" who models delinquent behavior. The social control of students over each other may in small schools render one subculture supreme; but, unless the surrounding environments of socialization are unusually monolithic, the larger schools are more like pluralistic societies. Students who choose one style of life in the school can support one another and establish some isolation and protection from the controls of students attached to other styles.

The trend from single to multiple subcultures within the school and college is accompanied by some attenuation of group supports. Particularly in higher education, some subcultures tend to become orientations without distinctive, unified social locations. The collegiate subculture of the past had a firm social base in fraternities and sororities and in the dormitories that imitated the life of fraternity and sorority row, and this base continues in weakened form. The vocational orientation, widely extended by mass higher education and found in considerable strength in public colleges and universities, has relatively little organized support. Its upholders live in dispersed, isolated places off campus and often have little time for campus interaction as they bolt for the parking lot and their outside jobs and families. So, too, within the faculty, the interests and styles of work that have gathered strength in recent decades are less supported by stable, unified groups than are the more traditional cultures. The cosmopolitanism of the modern researcher and professional consultant involves orientation to distant places, less time on the campus, less association with other faculty members, and a shorter duration at the college, compared with the more traditional localism in which men make a college a career (Gouldner, 1957–1958). Locals derive strength in campus politics by not only out-sitting the cosmopolitans on committees, but also by remaining longer at a college and interacting more frequently with others of similar orientation. Hence, locals are more likely to have a group-supported subculture, while cosmopolitans have an orientation that gains in popularity but is less grounded in a stable social base within the college. In short, the interests of the faculty that move toward dominance are inherently divisive of the campus culture and receive their strength from their prestige in the college and society, rather than from group interaction.

Determinants of campus subcultures. The determinants of campus orientations lie in the larger society and the larger organization (Clark & Trow, 1960) as well as in the quasi-independent ways that students perceive and respond to the special problems they face in the student role (Becker et al., 1961). In this section, the interest is in the extent to which the internal subcultures are determined by and reflect the larger society. Critical factors in this determination are the autonomy-dependence of the school or college and the isolation-amalgamation of student and nonstudent roles. The subcultures are heavily determined by the external social setting when the control of the school or college is not autonomous, but is dependent on immediate environment, and interaction is not isolated, with the students and faculty spending much time in other social locations. Typically, elementary and high school subcultures reflect values of the neighborhood if not the home, more than do the subcultures of college, because the schools are dependent on the local environment and the student role is exposed to the influence of roles in the age group and the home. Student subcultures at these levels are particularly influenced by wider adolescent subcultures that exist in part outside the school and are supported by subsocieties of youth that are served and shaped by the mass media. Colleges manage to operate at somewhat greater distance from lay supervision, occasionally achieving a remarkable degree of autonomy, and pull the student away from family and neighborhood groups. The colleges vary greatly, however: The commuter college controlled by local lay authorities is likely to reflect community sentiments; the private residential college has its culture or subcultures affected in greater degree by its own character, developed somewhat independently. If a residential college develops a distinctive character, it may approach total encapsulation, evidenced among students and faculty by a two-world definition of reality—"our" world and the world of the unlucky outsiders—and by a campus-wide ethos that is objectively different from, even opposed to, the prevailing sentiments in the larger society. The gaining of a distinction that characterizes the whole campus frequently cuts the bond of campus subcultures to the general culture. Any selection of students by a college represents a pulling out of individuals of particular orientations and interests from a vast pool of potential students. Screening is greatly extended when the college also has a reputation as a particular kind of place, for then self-recruitment goes to work—the fun-oriented boy to the "country club," the brainy boy to the "tough" school, and so on. The effect of formal selection and self-recruitment is to draw somewhat similar students out of different backgrounds. Thus, the lower-class students who end up at leading private colleges are more like the upper-middle-class students who predominate there than they are like lower-class students in state colleges. Hence, selection and reputation modify the impact of social origins and outside culture on the campus subcultures. The college's own character sets the terms of existence for the student subcultures.

The Classroom

A developed sociology of the classroom, now barely on the horizon, will understand classroom interaction in the context of larger social structures that encompass and shape it. The structure of the labor market and its articulation with the school, a case in point, help determine the details of interpersonal relations in the classroom (Stinchcombe, 1960). The young to some degree estimate and orient to future adult status, and their anticipation of what lies in store in the world of work conditions their approach to schooling and their interaction with teachers. Suspicion of a dismal job future seems to play a part in apathy and rebellion. Thus, anticipated status as well as social origins set the stage for the classroom drama, and it is often the impact of differential orientations to the future among the youth of given social strata that reduces the correlation of social background and classroom attitude. Teachers in turn are also oriented to the futures of the young, especially in the secondary school, since they must attempt to define the young person in terms of his future and make him aware of where he stands in the light of universalistic standards. The classroom is an arena in which forces of the past, present, and future converge to shape the educational process.

Critical in the social structure of the classroom is the authority of the teacher. The socialization process is bound up in how students and teachers perceive, use, and control one another. Durkheim (1956) maintained that moral authority was the dominant quality of the educator, an ascendance of the teacher over his pupils deriving from superiority of experience and culture. Recognizing that Durkheim's account of teacher authority was only a part of the story, even in France at the turn of the century (Floud,

1962a), the authority he depicted may be denoted as "traditional authority," where the power of the teacher in relation to his young "charges" is based largely on moral and intellectual grounds. The teacher knew more, represented society, and it was therefore right, especially in the eyes of the parents, that he should be obeyed. But changes in the relations of education to society tend to undermine this form of authority, reducing the relevance of the Durkheimian thesis. The teacher's position shifts toward the power of an arbiter of one's fate, based on the teacher's location as gatekeeper to the bureaucratized channels of social mobility (Floud, 1962; Schelsky, 1961). Even with this new institutional source of influence, however, the authority of the teacher apparently has diminished. The reign of the peer groups and subcultures of youth has extended ever more fully into the classroom— charges have become chargers; the rising educational level of the population has produced a larger proportion of adults whose knowledge is equal or superior to that of the teacher; and adults seek from the teacher not morality and discipline, but help in keeping the kids busy and safe and in making progress toward a career. School books have shown a steady decline in moral teaching (De Charms & Moeller, 1962), and school systems move toward neutrality in many matters of values in the face of their dependence on a heterogeneous public.

The authority of the teacher in the classroom varies greatly between countries, since authority within this smaller system is affected by the prestige and authority of the teacher in the educational structure and society; on these grounds, the school teacher in England has considerably more authority than his counterpart in the United States. He has less need to seek the consensus of his students, and "parents are either active or passive supporters of teachers in their disciplinary problems" (Baron & Tropp, 1961, p. 554). The American school teacher has less prestige, and the bases of his authority are shaky and more open to definition by the interaction of the classroom. Bright students may grant power only to bright teachers; gang members may grant it only when the teacher grades work and maintains discipline in ways the gang sees as legitimate:

(What do you do when you discover that the teacher has been grading you unfairly?) Lots of time we just get up and walk out. Like you say, "Oh man, I'm tired of this class." You just jump up and walk out and shut the door. (What do the teachers do?) Mostly they just look at us and then resume with the rest of the class and don't say nothing. (Why don't they report you?) I guess they be glad for us to be out of their class (Werthman, 1963, p. 55).

A crisis of authority may be a fair characterization of the role of the teacher in much American education.

A second critical feature in the social structure of the classroom, one interactive with authority, is the teacher's response to student characteristics. Whatever their own social backgrounds, teachers in keeping with all workers other than missionaries and crusaders like to work with promising materials in pleasant surroundings, and wish to see results. In the United States, lower-class children, especially Negroes, are likely to repel the teacher, since they more often are ill-prepared for school, have low or indifferent motivation, are harder to control, and have offensive personal characteristics (Becker, 1952b). Their schools are less attractive and the results of teaching are relatively low. Teaching that would accomplish the normal amount of work is more difficult. Unless above-average resources are committed to the lower-class school, the teacher response to such students is typically comprised of greater emphasis on discipline and a lessening of expectation of achievement. The flouting of teacher authority that often occurs adds to the inclination to make the best of a bad situation. Performance in the classroom is lowered and, as the grades go by, performance slips further and further behind that of pupils in middle-class schools.

Performance can be so close to zero that, with automatic promotion, the high-school classroom contains students who "cannot read, write, or spell the names of the streets they live on" (Werthman, 1963, p. 40).

CONCLUSION

The contest among men and ideas over the nature of society is reflected throughout the educational institution in modern times, as the formal agencies of cultural transmission and socialization enter ever more intimately and decisively into economic, political, and social affairs. The demands on education range from the mounting of morality to the making of technicians, from the maintenance of the small community to the exploration of space. The effects of education on other institutions and society, large as they currently appear, are undoubtedly more complex and substantial than has yet been imagined. Social science has attended little to education, and rapid change has moved empirical reality out of reach of perspectives brilliantly applicable to the societies and social problems of 1850 or 1900. Fortunately, social scientists are becoming aware that the society characterized by technology and expertness is an educative society, a place where man is to be conceptualized as Educational Man as well as economic and political man. So, too, in the case of the traditional society undergoing industrialization, attention swings toward man in his educational aspects and to society in its educational forms. The sociological imagination has long grasped the general idea that he who forms the child and dispenses cultural funds also maintains and changes society and culture. That imagination is now moving closer to the astonishing implications of locating much cultural transmission and socialization in a separate major institution, there to be shaped by different processes and forces, there to pose distinctive problems of performance and function. This modern perspective dictates that he who would write a general sociology need understand educational affairs. Who says society, says education.

REFERENCES

Ashby, E. *Technology and the academics: An essay on universities and the scientific revolution.* London: Macmillan, 1958.

Bailyn, B. *Education in the forming of American society.* Chapel Hill: Univer. of North Carolina Press, 1960.

Banks, Olive. *Parity and prestige in English secondary education.* London: Routledge & Kegan Paul, 1954.

Baron, G., & Tropp, A. Teachers in England and America. In A. H. Halsey, Jean Floud, & C. A. Anderson (Eds.), *Education, economy, and society.* New York: The Free Press of Glencoe, 1961. Pp. 545–557.

Becker, H. S. The career of the Chicago public school teacher. *Amer. J. Sociol.,* 1952, 57, 470–477.(a)

Becker, H. S. Social-class variations in the teacher-pupil relationship. *J. educ. Sociol.,* 1952, 25, 451–465.(b)

Becker, H. S. The teacher in the authority system of the public schools. *J. educ. Sociol.,* 1953, 27, 128–141.

Becker, H. S., Geer, Blanche, Hughes, E. C., & Strauss, A. L. *Boys in white: Student culture in medical school.* Chicago: Univer. of Chicago Press, 1961.

Ben-David, J. Scientific productivity and academic organization in nineteenth century medicine. *Amer. sociol. Rev.,* 1960, 25, 828–843.

Berelson, B. *Graduate education in the United States.* New York: McGraw, 1960.

Berry, Carol A. White collar employment: II–characteristics. Special Labor Force Reps, No. 12. *Mon. Labor Rev.,* 1961, 139–147.

Blau, P. M., & Scott, W. R. *Formal organizations.* San Francisco: Chandler, 1962.

Brim, O. G., Jr. *Sociology and the field of education.* New York: Russell Sage Foundation, 1958.

Brookover, W. B. *A sociology of education.* New York: American Book Company, 1955.

Callahan, R. E. *Education and the cult of efficiency.* Chicago: Univer. of Chicago Press, 1962.

Caplow, T. *The sociology of work.* Minneapolis: Univer. of Minnesota Press, 1954.

Caplow, T., & McGee, R. J. *The academic marketplace.* New York: Basic Books, 1958.

Charters, W. W., Jr. Survival in the profession: A criterion for selecting teacher trainees. *J. teacher Educ.,* 1956, 7, 253–255.

Cicourel, A. V., & Kitsuse, J. I. *The educational decision-makers.* Indianapolis: Bobbs, 1963.

Clark, B. R. *Adult education in transition.* Berkeley: Univer. of California Press, 1956.

Clark, B. R. *The open door college.* New York: McGraw, 1960.

Clark, B. R. Faculty authority. *Bull. Amer. Ass. Univer. Professors,* 1961, 47, 293–302.

Clark, B. R. *Educating the expert society.* San Francisco: Chandler, 1962.

Clark, B. R. Faculty culture. In *The study of campus cultures.* Boulder, Col.: Western Interstate Commission for Higher Education, 1963. Pp. 39–54.(a)

Clark, B. R. (in collaboration with Broom, L., & Selznick, P.). In L. Broom & P. Selznick, *Sociology.* (3rd ed.) Evanston, Ill.: Row, Peterson, 1963.(b)

Clark, B. R., & Trow, M. A. Determinants of college student subculture. Unpublished manuscript, Center for the Study of Higher Education, University of California (Berkeley), 1960. (Mimeographed)

Coleman, J. S. *The adolescent society.* New York: The Free Press of Glencoe, 1961.

Davie, J. S. Social class factors and school attendance. *Harvard educ. Rev.,* 1953, 23, 175–185.

Davis, A. *Social class influences upon learning.* Cambridge, Mass.: Harvard Univer. Press. 1948.

Davis, J. A. *Great aspirations.* Vol. 1. *Career decisions and educational plans during college.* Chicago: National Opinion Research Center Rept No. 90, 1963.

DeCharms, R., & Moeller, G. H. Values expressed in American children's readers: 1800–1950. *J. abnorm. soc. Psychol.,* 1962, 64, 136–142.

Duncan, O. D., & Hodge, R. W. Education and occupational mobility: A regression analysis. *Amer. J. Soc.,* 1963, 68, 629–644.

Durkheim, E. *The division of labor in society.* G. Simpson (Trans.). Glencoe, Ill.: Free Press, 1947 (copyright, Macmillan, 1933).

Durkheim, E. *Education and society.* D. Fox (Trans.). Glencoe, Ill.: Free Press, 1956.

The economics and politics of public education series. Syracuse, N.Y.: Syracuse Univer. Press, 12 monographs, 1962–63.

Floud, Jean. Teaching in the affluent society. *Brit. J. Sociol.,* 1962, 13, 299–308.(a)

Floud, Jean. The sociology of education. In A. T. Welford, M. Argyle, D. V. Glass, & J. N. Morris (Eds.), *Society: Problems and methods of study.* London: Routledge & Kegan Paul, 1962.(b)

Floud, Jean, & Halsey, A. H. The sociology of education: A trend report and biblography. *Curr. Sociol.,* 1958, 7.

Floud, Jean, & Scott, W. Recruitment to teaching in England and Wales. In A. H. Halsey, Jean Floud, & C. A. Anderson (Eds.), *Education, economy, and society.* New York: The Free Press of Glencoe, 1961. Pp. 527–544.

Gans, H. J. *The urban villagers.* New York: The Free Press of Glencoe, 1962.

Goldsen, Rose K., Rosenberg, M., Williams, R. M., Jr., & Suchman, E. A. *What college students think.* Princeton, N.J.: Van Nostrand, 1960.

Gordon, C. W. *The social system of the high school.* Glencoe, Ill.: Free Press, 1957.

Goslin, D. A. *The search for ability: Standardized testing in social perspective.* New York: Russell Sage, 1963.

Gouldner, A. W. Cosmopolitans and locals: Toward an analysis of latent social roles. Part I. *Admin. Sci. Quart.,* 1957, 2, 281–306.

Gouldner, A. W. Cosmopolitans and locals: Toward an analysis of latent social roles. Part II. *Admin. Sci. Quart.,* 1958, 2, 444–480.

Gross, N. The sociology of education. In R. K. Merton, L. Broom, & L. S. Cottrell, Jr. (Eds.), *Sociology today.* New York: Basic Books, 1959. Pp. 128–152.

Gross, N. Organizational lag in American universities. *Harvard educ. Rev.,* 1963, 33, 58–73.

Gross, N., Mason, W. S., & McEachern, A. W. *Explorations in role analysis: Studies of the school superintendency role.* New York: Wiley, 1958.

Halsey, A. H. The changing functions of universities in advanced industrial societies. *Harvard educ. Rev.,* 1960, 30, 118–127.

Halsey, A. H., Floud, Jean, & Anderson, C. A. (Eds.) *Education, economy, and society.* New York: The Free Press of Glencoe, 1961.

Havemann, E., & West, Patricia Salter. *They went to college.* New York: Harcourt, 1952.

Havighurst, R. J., Bowman, P. H., Liddle, G. P., Matthews, C. V., & Pierce, J. V. *Growing up in River City.* New York: Wiley, 1962.

Havighurst, R. J., & Neugarten, Bernice L. *Society and education.* Boston: Allyn and Bacon, 1957.

Hollingshead, A. H. *Elmtown's youth.* New York: Wiley, 1949.

Hughes, E. C. *Men and their work.* Glencoe, Ill.: Free Press, 1958.

Hyman, H. The value systems of different classes: A social psychological contribution to the analysis of stratification. In R. Bendix & S. M. Lipset (Eds.), *Class, status and power.* Glencoe, Ill.: Free Press, 1953. Pp. 426–442.

Jackson, B., & Marsden, D. *Education and the working class.* London: Routledge & Kegan Paul, 1962.

Janowitz, M. *The professional soldier.* New York: The Free Press of Glencoe, 1960.

Kahl, J. A. Educational and occupational aspirations of "common man" boys. *Harvard educ. Rev.,* 1953, 23, 186–203.

Kaplan, L. More men for elementary schools. *Phi Delta Kappan,* 1948, 29, 299–302.

Key, V. O., Jr. *Public opinion and American democracy.* New York: Knopf, 1961.

Kluckhohn, Florence R., & Strodtbeck, F. L. *Variations in value orientations.* Evanston, Ill.: Row, Peterson, 1961.

Kornhauser, W. *Scientists in industry: Conflict and accommodation.* Berkeley: Univer. of California Press, 1962.

Lieberman, M. *Education as a profession.* Englewood Cliffs, N.J.: Prentice-Hall, Inc., 1956.

Lipset, S. M. The political process in trade unions: A theoretical statement. In M. Berger, T. Abel, & C. H. Page (Eds.), *Freedom and control in modern society.* Princeton, N.J.: Van Nostrand, 1954. Pp. 82–124.

Litt, E. Education, community norms, and political indoctrination. *Amer. sociol. Rev.,* 1963, 28, 69–75.

Machlup, F. *The production and distribution of knowledge in the United States.* Princeton, N.J.: Princeton Univer. Press, 1962.

Mannheim, K. *Freedom, power and democratic planning.* London: Routledge & Kegan Paul, 1951.

Marcson, S. *The scientist in American industry.* New York: Harper, 1960.

Mason, W. *The beginning teacher: Status and career orientations.* Washington: Office of Education, U.S. Department of Health, Education and Welfare, 1961.

Mead, Margaret. *The school in American culture.* Cambridge, Mass.: Harvard Univer. Press, 1951.

Mercer, B. E., & Carr, E. R. (Eds.), *Education and the social order.* New York: Rinehart, 1957.

Merton, R. K. Social structure and anomie. In *Social theory and social structure* (rev. ed.). Glencoe, Ill.: Free Press, 1957 Pp. 131–160.

Middleton, R. Racial problems and the recruitment of academic staff at southern colleges and universities. *Amer. sociol. Rev.,* 1961, 26, 960–970.

Miller, H. P. Annual and lifetime income in relation to education, 1939–1959. *Amer. econ. Rev.,* 1960, 50, 962–986.

Morgan, J. N., David, M. H., Cohen, W. J., & Brazer, H. E. *Income and welfare in the United States.* New York: McGraw, 1962.

Morris, C. N. Career patterns of teachers. In J. Stiles (Ed.), *The teacher's role in American society.* New York: Harper, 1957. Ch. 18.

National Education Association. *The status of the American public-school teacher.* Washington: Author, 1957.

National Education Association. *NEA Res. Bull.,* 1963, 41(1).(a)

National Education Association. *Rankings of the states, 1963.* Washington: Author, 1963. (b)

Newcomb, T. M. *Personality and social change.* New York: Dryden, 1943.

Organisation for Economic Co-operation and Development. *Higher education and the demand for scientific manpower in the United States.* Paris: O.E.C.D., 1963.

Orlans, H. *The effects of federal programs on higher education.* Washington: The Brookings Institution, 1962.

Parsons, T. The school class as a social system: Some of its functions in American society. *Harvard educ. Rev.,* 1959, 29, 297–318.

Pierson, F. C. *The education of American businessmen.* New York: McGraw, 1959.

Riesman, D. *Constraint and variety in American education.* Lincoln: Univer. of Nebraska Press, 1956.

Rogoff, Natalie. Local social structure and educational selection. In A. H. Halsey, Jean Floud, & C. A. Anderson (Eds.), *Education, economy and society.* New York: The Free Press of Glencoe, 1961. Pp. 241–251.

Sanford, N. (Ed.) *The American college.* New York: Wiley, 1962.

Schelsky, H. Family and school in modern society. In A. H. Halsey, Jean Floud, & C. A. Anderson (Eds.), *Education, economy and society.* New York: The Free Press of Glencoe, 1961. Pp. 414–420.

Schmidt, G. P. *The liberal arts college.* New Brunswick, N.J.: Rutgers Univer. Press, 1957.

Sewell, W. H., Haller, A. O., & Straus, M. A. Social status and educational and occupational aspiration. *Amer. sociol. Rev.,* 1957, 22, 67–73.

Sexton, Patricia C. *Education and income.* New York: Viking Press, Inc., 1961.

Shils, E. Mass society and its culture. *Daedalus,* Spring, 1960, 288–314.

Stiles, L. J. (Ed.) *The teacher's role in American society.* New York: Harper, 1957.

Stinchcombe, A. L. Social sources of rebellion in a high school. Unpublished doctoral dissertation, Univer. of California (Berkeley), 1960.

Sussman, Leila. *Freshman morale at M.I.T.* Cambridge: Massachusetts Institute of Technology, 1960.

Trow, M. The second transformation of American secondary education. *Intern. J. comp. Sociol.,* 1961, 2, 144–166.

Trow, M. The democratization of higher education in America. *Arch. Europ. sociol.,* 1962, 3, 231–262.

Turk, H. Social cohesion through variant values: Evidence from medical role relations. *Amer. sociol. Rev.,* 1963, 28, 28–37.

Turner, R. H. Sponsored and contest mobility and the school system. *Amer. sociol. Rev.,* 1960, 25, 855–867.

U.S. Department of Health, Education and Welfare, Office of Education. *Biennial survey of education in the United States, 1956–1958, statistics of higher education: Faculty, students, and degrees, 1957–1958.* Washington: Government Printing Office, 1958.

U.S. Department of Health, Education and Welfare, Office of Education. *Higher education*. No. 17. Washington: Government Printing Office, 1961.

U.S. Department of Health, Education and Welfare. *Health, education and welfare trends, 1962 edition*. Washington: Government Printing Office, 1962.

U.S. Department of Labor. *Manpower: Challenge of the 1960s*. Washington: Government Printing Office, 1960.

U.S. Department of Labor. *Manpower report of the president and a report on manpower requirements, resources, utilization, and training*. Washington: Government Printing Office, 1963.

Vaisey, J. *Britain in the sixties: Education for tomorrow*. Middlesex, Eng.: Penguin Books, 1962.

Veblen, T. *The higher learning in America*. New York: B. W. Heubsch, 1918; and Stanford: Academic Reprints, 1954.

Waller, W. *The sociology of teaching*. New York: Wiley, 1932.

Walworth, A. *School histories at war*. Cambridge, Mass.: Harvard Univer. Press, 1938.

Warner, W. L., & Abegglen, J. C. *Occupational mobility in American business and industry, 1928–1952*. Minneapolis: Univer. of Minnesota Press, 1955.

Warner, W. L., Havighurst, R. J., & Loeb, M. B. *Who shall be educated? The challenge of unequal opportunity*. New York: Harper, 1944.

Wayland, S., & Brunner, E. de S. *The educational characteristics of the American people*. New York: Bureau of Applied Social Research, Columbia Univer., 1958.

Wenkert, R., & Selvin, H. C. School spirit in the context of a liberal education. *Social Probs,* Fall, 1962, 9, 156–168.

Werthman, C. Delinquents in school: A test for the legitimacy of authority. *Berkeley J. Sociol.,* 1963, 8, 39–60.

Williams, R. M., Jr. *American society*. New York: Knopf, 1952.

Wilson, A. B. Residential segregation of social classes and aspirations of high school boys. *Amer. sociol. Rev.,* 1959, 24, 836–845.

Wilson, B. R. The teacher's role—a sociological analysis. *Brit. J. Sociol.,* 1962, 13, 15–32.

Wilson, L. *The academic man*. London: Oxford Univer. Press, 1942.

Wolfle, D. *America's resources of specialized talent*. New York: Harper, 1954.

CHAPTER 20 Problems in the Sociology of Religion

LOUIS SCHNEIDER

Sociology of religion is a rapidly growing field of inquiry which involves a large variety of sociological impulses. Like many other fields of sociology, it has numerous points of contact with various studies by persons who are not professed sociologists, and it would be unwise for the sociologist of religion to ignore work being conducted by historians, anthropologists, and others. Much that now seems peripheral to the sociology of religion, a newly developing and in many ways amorphous field, may in a short while appear to be rather central. This, of course, makes it difficult to present the field within the compass of a relatively short chapter. It would be easy to succumb to the temptation to catalogue work done and in process or to provide a bibliography with an overlying froth of comment. It would be easy to persuade one's self of the utility of presenting a mass of factual matter on, let us say, sex and age differences in church participation, on the relation of religious affiliation to voting, on religion and fertility patterns, on variant religious opinion and belief, and on a large number of other things for which statistical data of some sort are available for at least a handful

of Western countries. The temptations thus suggested have here been resisted. This chapter has been entitled "Problems in the Sociology of Religion," and the title has been chosen as suitable for a statement designed to cover a number of issues that seem to the writer to be of considerable importance and at the same time to give rough coverage of a number of main preoccupations in the field. No pretense is made that anything like a full statement or one that does justice to all significant concerns in the field has been achieved. Sociological-historical concern with religion and science, with religion and polity, with sect-denomination–church contrasts, for example, could, regrettably, be given only slight or virtually no attention. Numerous worthwhile pieces of work have had to be bypassed. It would be extremely difficult or impossible for anyone to present this field briefly today in the hope that others would acknowledge that he had afforded the essence of the matter. Selection and an author's own sense of the significant must in any case be operative.

The most economical way of organizing this statement on problems in the sociology of religion is to present, in succession, some observations on religion and functional analysis, on religion and culture, on religion and society. A certain arbitrariness cannot be avoided, and some matters discussed under one rubric might conceivably have been discussed under another.

An initial word on definitions of religion is not amiss. The relevant literature shows a considerable preoccupation with definitions. Thus, Carrier (1960, pp. 36–37) notes that Leuba (1912) presented a collection of some 48 of these (and added 2 of his own), but did not achieve a satisfactory generic formula; that a symposium in the *Journal of Religion* in 1927 failed to suggest a hoped-for minimum of agreement on definition of religion; that Walter H. Clark reported in 1958 that he had obtained exceedingly varied answers from 63 social scientists to the question of what constitutes religion. Williams and others (1962) show continuing preoccupation with the problem of definition or delimitation. It may be suggested that the problem is less serious than it appears to be to a number of social scientists.

There are obviously many terms used by social scientists for which there is less than "perfect" delimitation, whatever that might be, and less than thorough agreement, whatever that might mean. Perhaps the term society is as good an example of this as any. Moreover, there is still obvious merit in the implication of the first sentence of Weber's (1922) section on the sociology of religion in his major work: "A definition of what religion 'is' cannot possibly stand at the beginning but could perhaps stand at the conclusion of an inquiry such as the following" (Weber, 1922, p. 227). It is true that another initial sentence, also by a notable contributor to the sociology of religion (Durkheim, 1898–1899), reads: "Since the sociology of religion treats religious facts it must begin by defining them." But this assertion by Durkheim does not put him so far from Weber in this matter as might immediately appear, for at a later point (p. 16) Durkheim writes that the fault common to the various definitions of religion he has

reviewed and rejected is that they seek to determine the content of religion at a single stroke, at once. Such an effort he regarded as useless, for determination of the content of religion in some "definitive" sense will be feasible only with the advancement of knowledge. His own definition, he indicated, was guided by the notion that "only the exterior and conspicuous form of religious phenomena is immediately available to observation." Let it be added that if agreement on definitions seems important, one line of advance toward it and toward greater strictness of definition than is now feasible may be looked for in a more careful scrutiny than has yet been made of what different students of religion actually "do" when in their own view they study religion. It is, at any rate, a plausible notion that there may be more implicit agreement than appears from explicitly presented definitions. While it is admittedly not always easy to specify what comes within "the mass of data which are alleged by serious students to be religious" (Williams), it is very hard to doubt that there is such a "mass" or to believe that it is so "massive" as to make the basic category of the religious hopelessly inclusive. Again, little profit might be had from too "strict" a definition at this stage of study, by way of premature and inept resolutions as to what should be called religion and what not. There is also no occasion to think that delimitation of the general field of religion must be a task for sociology alone; other disciplines have evident interests and competences in the matter. It would appear that for some time patience will be necessary with a variety of observations to the effect that religion deals with the "sacred," the "transcendent," the "ultimate," or the like, and even a degree of tolerance when a student of Javanese religion, for instance, informs us that "the three major foci" of the Hindu strain in the religion of Java are "etiquette, art, and mystical practice" (Geertz, 1960, p. 238), although this may seem, especially when taken out of context, unusually lax. None of this should be taken to deny that looseness about the term religion results in part from inadequacy of knowledge (although it may also be due to a relatively "adequate" knowledge) and does sometimes prove handicapping in analysis and research. But neither need a certain looseness create despair about scientific aspirations in the study of religion.

Definitions of the *sociology* of religion are no more a source of intellectual comfort than one might at present expect. Wach (1944, p. 11) writes of studying "the interrelation of religion and society and the forms of interaction which take place between them" and gives it as an assumption basic to the sociology of religion that "religious impulses, ideas, and institutions influence and, in turn, are influenced by social forces, social organization, and stratification" (Wach, 1944, pp. 11, 205). This seems to suggest little more than that religion can in principle be studied sociologically, an unobjectionable but not very revealing view. The prevalence of "definitions" such as these suggests that there may be some merit in holding to the view that the sociology of religion is as it does, that is, that the field consists in what is actually done by those who profess to be working in it. A definition of this latter type is bound to have some appeal, especially where it seems likely to put a stop to verbal futilities, but if taken too seriously it could obviously inhibit efforts to conceive a field more profoundly or more generously than it is conceived at a particular time. Maître (1958, pp. 105–106) has noted how much of Le Bras (1955; 1956) is concerned with estimation of obedience to the precepts of the Catholic church and with data of social history as casting light on variations in this obedience. (In principle or by intention, however, Le Bras' interests are very broad. Of the numerous indications of this, it is enough to point to his suggested outline [1956, pp. 807–812] for "sociological inquiry into all religions.") Catholic parish studies show strong preoccupation with the same topics. Nothing is necessarily wrong with this, and some of the parish studies are excellent. But it would seem an injustice to the potential scope and significance of the sociology of religion to confine it to such things as, say, the "parish sociology" with which a fair number of practitioners in the field may be concerned at some special time. The sociology of religion is, in this light, not only what it does but also what it *might* do, under the guidance of well conceived notions of the place and significance of religion in social life. The following selective presentation of problems is not intended to support any narrow and constricting conception of the field.

RELIGION AND FUNCTIONAL ANALYSIS

What has come to be known as functional analysis of religion continues to represent a large and complex body of thought, from which four elements are chosen for emphasis here. The first has to do with religion as nonrational; the second with religion and the postulate of unity or interconnection; the third with the view of religion as effecting social "integration"; the fourth with the "uses" of religion and with problems bearing on the becoming manifest of latent functions of religion. (The manifest-latent distinction is made by Merton, 1957, Ch. 1.)

1. In connection with religion as nonrational, it is well to revert to some older anthropological and sociological studies whose significance is now too often not well understood. A crucial element in the meaning of a functional view of, or approach to, religion may be suggested by an initially stark contrast between an outlook on religion that takes it primarily as an intellectual elaboration which is fundamentally mistaken and an outlook that takes it primarily as a set of rites or practices whose main significance lies in their consequences for the society or the members of the society in which they occur. The starkness of this contrast may be relieved with refined analysis,

but it is well to have matters thus put initially.

The intellectualist or rationalist view is well represented in the tradition of Tylor (1924), Spencer, and Frazer. For Tylor, who may be taken as representative of the tradition, it will be recalled, the building of an animistic world-view is basic for the rise and development of religion. The belief in spiritual beings, which constitutes animism, arises in a context of primitive experience and interpretation that typically elaborates such phenomena as dreams on the line of "explaining" by way of the notion of an etherealized double the circumstance that in dreams one is vividly aware of being "away" while at the same time one realizes that one could not possibly have been away. Tylor's primitives are strong reasoners, and from their explanations of dreams and other phenomena arises the entirety of the animistic structure; a well enough reasoned structure indeed, but one based on incorrect premises and bound, in time, to prove intellectually quite insecure. Broadly, then, for Tylor, in the beginning was the word or the thought. Word or thought is historically primary; religious action, religious establishment or institution, religious feeling are secondary and follow upon word or thought. It may be acknowledged that Tylor, in making animism his great concern, touched something important for religion at large. The point is neither to deny the significance and wide prevalence of animistic notions nor to repudiate without qualification Tylor's rationalism. It is to suggest that that rationalism does have notable weaknesses and easily leads to a view of religion that misses much of its sociological sense.

On the other side of the contrast, the stress, as has been noted, is on rite or practice. One of the best known instances of this stress is given by Robertson Smith's (1956 [1889]) work on the religion of the Semites. Smith's emphasis on rite is so cogently set out and so strikingly put to use that it is tempting, even today, to quote him at length, as Radcliffe-Brown (1961, pp. 155-

156) aptly does in his own analysis of "Religion and Society." A few lines must suffice here. "In all the antique religions," writes Smith, "mythology takes the place of dogma," but this mythology is "no essential part of ancient religion," for it has "no sacred sanction and no binding force on the worshippers." There follows this significant comment: "The myths connected with individual sanctuaries and ceremonies were merely part of the apparatus of worship; they served to excite the fancy and sustain the interest of the worshipper; but he was often offered a choice of several accounts of the same thing, and, provided that he fulfilled the ritual with accuracy, no one cared what he believed about its origin." Smith affirms "with confidence"—probably with too much confidence—that "in almost every case . . . myth was derived from . . . ritual, and not . . . ritual from myth; for the ritual was fixed and the myth was variable, the ritual was obligatory and faith in the myth was at the discretion of the worshipper." The contrast with the Tylor tradition is forcefully brought out in these assertions: "But it is of the first importance to realize clearly from the outset that ritual and practical usage were . . . the sum-total of ancient religions. Religion in primitive times was not a system of belief with practical applications; it was a body of fixed traditional practices, to which every member of society conformed as a matter of course" (Smith, 1956, pp. 17, 18, 20).

The relations of myth and ritual continue to be a problem in anthropological literature. Thus, Kluckhohn (1942) presents the relations of the two as variable and inclines to the view that they are better regarded as interdependent than in terms suggesting that either generates the other. Even so, he is evidently not unsympathetic to the view that, broadly, one may contend for a primacy of ritual over myth or that "behavioral patterns" alter first more frequently. (For an instance of stress on ritual as strong as Smith's, see Lord Raglan's paper in Sebeok [1955, pp. 76-83].)

Smith thus opens the way to consideration of religion as a set of practices with distinctive consequences, or functions. Religion in this view does *not* appear as in the first place a faulty intellectual construction from which dubious secondary practices have been derived: dubious precisely because of their poor intellectual foundation and secondary both because following upon (defective) thought and because of their but minor interest to the anthropological or sociological analyst who "understands" their intellectual derivation. "Primitive religion," writes Jane Harrison (1927), in a work that has strong affinities with Smith's and was much influenced by Durkheim, "was not, as I had drifted into thinking, a tissue of errors leading to mistaken conduct; rather it was a web of practice emphasizing particular parts of life, issuing necessarily in representations and ultimately dying out into abstract conceptions." Harrison's view on myth and ritual (here all too briefly resumed) is that "myth arose out of or rather together with . . . ritual, not the ritual out of the myth," and that myth is not at first etiological or explanatory: "it does not arise to give a reason; it is representative, another form of utterance, of expression." Indeed, "the ritual act . . . is prior to the divinity." Harrison's perspective on magic is enlighteningly similar. In its psychologically most "primitive" forms, magic has a foundation of emotion or desire and carries with it no special sophistication or explanatory load: "You get a letter that hurts you, you tear it up instantly. You do this not because you think you are tearing up the writer, but just because you are hurt, and hurt nerves seek muscular discharge." Harrison avers: "The simplest case of all is Mr. Marett's famous bull. A man escapes from an enraged bull leaving his coat; the bull goes on goring the coat. Of course, as Mr. Marett prudently observes, 'it is very hard to know what is going on in the bull's mind,' but one may guess that the bull does not act in obedience to a mistaken application of the laws of association; he is simply letting loose his rage on something that happens to be goreable."

Despite Harrison's disavowal of "any theory of magic which starts rather from the intellect than from the will," she also holds that "it would be a great mistake to suppose that magic contains nothing of intellectual effort, no theory whatever." Characteristically, however, she asserts of a primitive Australian ceremony that "at the back of the whole grotesque performance" lies not so much a process of reasoning as "an intense desire for food, issuing in a vivid representation." She writes of "the old rationalist fallacy that saw in primitive man the leisured and eager enquirer bent on research, all alive *rerum cognoscere causas.*" Her discussions of the points indicated, her development of the distinction of dromena ("things done") and legomena ("things said"), her notions of the emergence of deity from chorus and on the "essence" of religion set out views whose imaginativeness and perceptiveness make them still worthy of consideration (Jane Harrison, 1927, pp. 13, 16, 29, 45ff., 83, 84, 329–330, 485–486, *passim*).

Harrison's (1927) "behavioral" bias has been shared in at least some degree by other modern classical scholars, as by Dodds (1957), who was plainly partial to the view that "the belief in survival was not originally arrived at by any process of logical thought (as Tylor and Frazer had assumed)" but by "the turning of a blind eye" to evidence that was emotionally unacceptable (Dodds, 1957, p. 157).

The stress on rite or practice coalesces readily, in functionalist writing, with stress on emotion and sentiment, as Harrison's views well indicate. And accordingly it is not surprising that there is a *strand* in functionalist thought that is prepared to look upon "things said," so-called intellectual content (although "things said" is here employed as if it excluded sheer utterances and strongly emotionally conditioned expressions quite different from readily intelligible assertions—and Harrison's usage was not so simple as this), as derivative or secondary, as contingent on things done or things felt. There is much in Durkheim's (1926 [1912]) work to support this outlook. The outlook may be said to invert the intellectualist or rationalist view. In the latter view, rite and practice (and emotion or sentiment) are not intelligible except as their putative intellectual derivation becomes known. In the inverted view, intellectual content is not intelligible except as its grounding in rite and practice and emotion is uncovered. In the latter view, "things said" are often merely symbolic of the level of things done or felt. Thus, Durkheim (1926), in discussing the primitive Australian conception of the spirit of a newly dead man as malevolently disposed and noting that this conception changes after the performance of mourning rites, proposes an explanation of the change that must be amply quoted:

The foundation of mourning is the impression of a loss which the group feels when it loses one of its members, but this very impression results in bringing individuals together, in putting them into closer relations with one another, in associating them all in the same mental state, and therefore in disengaging a sensation of comfort which compensates the original loss. Since they weep together, they hold to one another and the group is not weakened, in spite of the blow which has fallen upon it. Of course they have only sad emotions in common, but communicating in sorrow is still communicating. . . . The exceptional violence of the manifestations by which the common pain is necessarily and obligatorily expressed even testifies to the fact that at this moment the society is more alive and active than ever. In fact, whenever the social sentiment is painfully wounded, it reacts with greater force than ordinarily: one never holds so closely to his family as when it has just suffered. This surplus energy . . . dissipates the feeling of coldness which death always brings with it. The group feels its strength gradually returning to it; it begins to hope and to live again. Presently one stops mourning, and he does so owing to the mourning itself. *But as the idea formed of the soul reflects the moral state of the society, this idea should*

change as this state changes. When one is in the period of dejection and agony, he represents the soul with the traits of an evil being, whose sole occupation is to persecute men. But when he feels himself confident and secure once more, he must admit that it has retaken its former nature and its former sentiments of tenderness and solidarity (italics supplied) (Durkheim, 1926, pp. 401–402).

The symbolic, projective nature of "ideas" as reflecting actions and feelings could hardly be more strongly affirmed. The conception of the dead that precedes the mourning rites reflects one social and emotional state; the post-mourning rite conception reflects another. The "ideas" entertained of the soul tell us, not of the soul, but of the state of the society and the feelings of its members. There is a "language" here in need of translation by sociological cues, so that one might say, for example, that the primitive assertion, "The soul of X is ill-disposed," has the meaning—"*We* feel saddened and diminished." It is worth noting that assertions of this kind, thus interpreted, have an unequivocally poetic flavor and could not conflict with scientific assertions, since as poetry they are bits of metaphor and not to be taken literally, and after "translation" they have no content that would oppose them to scientific assertions. (On relations of religion and poetry, see Santayana, 1936; Santayana, 1957.) But we have nothing like a systematic and reliable "symbology" of religion in the sense that all this might suggest, and the rather simple kind of relation that Durkheim claimed to find in the case cited does not carry us very far. Even in many primitive (to say nothing of nonprimitive) religious frameworks, it is difficult to develop the kind of analysis he presents, and it seems very likely that there are autonomous religious ideas and values that will simply not lend themselves to any "translation." Even in Durkheim's thought, the symbolic bias is only a *component,* if an important one. Bellah (1959) remarks: "Unfortunately, Durkheim never undertook a full-scale study of the place of religion in modern society. He believed that traditional religion was on its way out, essentially because it conflicts with science." Here, clearly, another aspect of Durkheim's thought is marked, one that allows a conflict that the aspect rehearsed above would by implication disallow (Bellah, 1959, p. 460).

By way of review and extension, certain aspects of a functional outlook on religion may be stated as follows: If religion involves things said and things done (and things felt; and the addition of this last and this entire vocabulary still leave us with much, if convenient, simplification), a functional approach, minimally, makes their relations *problematic*. A strongly intellectualist or rationalist approach in the tradition of Tylor does not. For the latter approach, things done, rites and practices (and sentiments) follow upon or are derived by human agents via reflection and inference from things said —myths, beliefs, dogmas, or the like. An intellectualist approach takes an emphatically and exaggeratedly cognitive view of religion. Once it is "clear" that the foundations of religious thought are scientifically insecure, religious practice, which, as suggested, is supposed to be based on or derived from that thought, becomes a set of ineptitudes or futilities of no great interest to the analyst of religion. A functional approach is more biased toward getting hold of religion on the side of rite or practice or sentiment in the first place. It takes religious practice seriously, that is, it is willing in principle to give painstaking attention to its social consequences or functions, which are indeed given much stress.

It should be clear, however, that, historically, functionalism *had* to stress rite and practice, very nearly in order to show that religion was a social phenomenon at all, in opposition to a view that represented it as primarily an intellectual aberration. This does not mean that functionalism must as a matter of principle regard ideas or values in the religious (or any other) sphere as necessarily "secondary"—as derivatives or reflections or symbolizations of practice or

sentiment—once it has made some essential points against the intellectualist outlook. On the other hand, not all elements in modern sociological thought, including thought about religion, need be conceived as readily reconcilable. Points of tension certainly exist. If the historical background of functionalism still induces a bent toward getting hold of religion on the side of practice and sentiment today, this may itself function as a salutary reminder of a position won in a struggle against an excessive rationalism, or it may conceivably conflict with a valuable and no longer naively rationalistic bent toward getting hold of religion on the side of central ideas and values.

For a functional approach it is important to allow the view by which religion becomes a set of organized social and cultural activities which are in themselves neither "stupid" nor "smart" nor "rational" nor "irrational." They are specifically nonrational, and no more rational or irrational than the sexual drive in the human male, a handshake between old friends, the ceremonial activities of the Kula ring, or a baseball game played for its own sake. This outlook encourages and directs inquiry, not toward questions about, say, the truth-value of religious propositions that may occur within the entire complex of activity, but toward questions about the consequences of any or all portions of the activity undertaken. The outlook may, again, induce a tendency to regard religious ideas and values in particular as "no more than" a part of activities that function in distinctive ways. This is well exemplified in Durkheim's (1951) argument that the idea- and value-components (as such) of different religions are not crucial in the (differential) suicide-inhibitive effect he attributes to the various religions: "The beneficent influence of religion is . . . not due to the special nature of religious conceptions. If religion protects man against the desire for self-destruction, it is not that it preaches the respect for his own person to him . . . but because it is a society. What constitutes this society is the existence of . . . beliefs and practices common to all the faithful . . . (Durkheim, 1951, p. 170). (Yet it must be added that for many purposes it may be vital to allow primacy to ideas and values. The various tensions and different perspectives thus suggested cannot here be adequately treated or reconciled. It remains a large task in the sociology of religion to achieve theoretical statements that will do justice to well founded criticism of excessive intellectualism and nonrational dimensions of social life while they also allow proper scope and significance to ideas, values, and meanings.)

In a functional view, also, religious activity will have its consequences or functions even if what the practitioners "say" about those consequences is quite erroneous and repeatedly refuted. The situation is admittedly more complicated than this flat assertion suggests, but what is intended may be conveyed by a convenient illustration from magic. One of Malinowski's Trobriand magicians may say that his magic averts an unwanted, feared storm. No doubt, the magic does nothing of the sort. It may nevertheless do something else (as it may give magician and beneficiaries of his work a set of traditionally prescribed actions to perform in a situation wherein sheer inaction would intensify a feeling of helplessness in the face of contingencies they conceive as threatening) and do this regardless of what the magician says. Endless refutation by an outsider of what the magician says (insofar as that comprises intelligible assertions) would in principle leave the functions of the magic intact. Attempted refutation, then, of assertions in magical or religious context can in this sense be quite idle, since they leave unaffected the functions of magical or religious activity which magical or religious practitioners themselves may not know or may not be able to state with any clarity. (This suggests, in turn, questions about "coming to know"—about the becoming manifest of latent functions— which will be taken up later.)

There are other possible relations between things said and things done (just now omitting things felt) than those that have been indicated above. One may thus try, not to derive either from the other, but to postulate unity or interaction between them. Such postulation is considered in the next section. In the interim, it may be said that the issues presented in this section are admittedly complex and tangled and often hard to set in such fashion that evidence may clearly and unambiguously be brought to bear upon them. This hardly means that the effort to clarify them and make them more susceptible of check by evidence is not worthwhile. And it may be suggested that the idea, at least reinforced by functionalism, that religion contains elements of practice and sentiment neither "refutable" (because they are not propositions but nonpropositional "realities") nor necessarily pale reflections of errors in thought remains permanently valuable.

2. Functionalism also has tended to emphasize the "interconnection of things" in society, sometimes perhaps even to the point of uselessness suggested by the notion that everything is connected with everything else. The postulate of the functional unity of society, as Merton (1957, p. 25) labels it, remains a significant guiding conception even if, as Merton notes, the degree of unity is definitely an "empirical variable." The stress here will be on that aspect of the conception of functional unity that highlights closeness of relationship of units or parts of a system (sensitivity to "interconnection" is, of course, not of itself a unique feature of functionalism among sociological theories, but there is no occasion in this chapter to analyze its points of resemblance to and difference from other theoretical structures), their interdependence, their possible mutual reinforcement—and not on that aspect in particular that comes to some form of the view that what is functional or dysfunctional for one unit of a system must be functional or dysfunctional for all the units. In Durkheim's definition (1926, p. 47) of religion, the latter is a *unified* system of

beliefs and practices; and when functionalism is in the intellectual mood of "unity," it looks for interaction and mutual reinforcement of components of a religious system, as of things done, said, and felt.

The view from which functionalism starts when it stresses unity in religion may be put thus: Looking at religion from the standpoint of actors involved in a religious system, it is clear that, as long as the religion they adhere to is more or less intact, its dogmas or beliefs, to start with these, do not appeal solely on their own ground as dogmas or beliefs. The dogmas are charged with the appeal that comes from practices in turn charged with emotion, the whole system exhibiting interaction of its parts, so that no part has an "independent" or merely intrinsic appeal but each is constantly affected by the others. Argument and evidence bearing on this view are not ideally full and good, but, at least as regards belief and practice, some may be adduced. Groethuysen (1927, Ch. 3) argues that the Catholic church came under certain disadvantages in the modern world when consideration of dogma or doctrine as such became an *abstract* affair, that is, drawn away from the actual life of the church and the traditional practices of believers. Practice and belief may be presumed to reinforce one another and establish one another's inevitability and "obviousness." When dogma is taken in abstraction from practice, it cannot have the same significance and force it once had. Two "abstractions" thus occur for the man who questions the church outside the profoundly conditioning and constraining life of the church itself: the abstraction of dogma and the abstraction of the church conceived as an institution that lays claim to authority. Once this doubling of abstraction occurs, the church cannot deal with unbelief or with skeptical questions on the same terms and with the same advantages as before.

This argues for the broad point of unity of belief and practice. But at least the matter of the degree of unity remains in question. Carrier (1960, pp. 233–238) in effect contends that this degree is in fact variable. He notes that there is reason to think that adherence to doctrines and dogmas, on the one hand, and church practice on the other, are rather closely connected. At the same time, this appears to be particularly true for Catholics. Data from a 1958 French Institute of Public Opinion survey of 18-to-30-year-old French youth indicate that 97 per cent of practicing youth accepts the dogma that Christ is the Son of God, while only 59 per cent of nonpracticing youth does so; that 90 per cent of practicing youth believes in the Trinity and immortality, while only 43 per cent of nonpracticing youth believes in these. This in itself is hardly startling, although the discrepancies do appear on the face of them considerable. (It has been noted, however, by Maître, 1958, p. 119, that in the work of the French Institute of Public Opinion sampling problems have occasioned very considerable difficulty.) But Carrier further cites the work of Brown and Lowe (1951), who found (among students at the University of Denver) that divergence in belief in traditional Christian doctrines was about twice as great between practicing and nonpracticing *Catholics* as it was between practicing and nonpracticing *Protestants*. Carrier notes: "Catholics who have abandoned all contact with the Church seem . . . more alienated from their co-religionists than religiously unattached Protestants are from Protestants who show church adherence" (Carrier, 1960, p. 235). Faith in a predominantly Catholic milieu may well "mean" Catholic practice, and Catholic practice "means" faith, so that faith in any sense independent of Catholicism tends in such a milieu not to seem feasible or even "meaningful" at all. Clearly, this suggests particularly strong solidarity, for Catholics, between faith or adherence to doctrine and religious practice.

Carrier adds reference to an earlier French survey, of religious opinion, conducted in 1947 (*Sondages, 10,* February, 1948, pp. 31–33) for 12 countries and posing the question, "Do you believe in God?" and "Do you believe in the immortality of the soul?" In countries like Australia, Great Britain, and Sweden, there was considerable divergence in the percentages of affirmative responses to the two questions. Thus, in Great Britain, 84 per cent of those asked affirmed belief in God, but only 49 per cent affirmed belief in immortality. In overwhelmingly Catholic France (where Léonard [1955, p. 82] estimates no more than eight hundred thousand Protestants today and Dansette [1957, p. 17], a 3 per cent non-Catholic population), on the other hand, while only 66 per cent affirmed belief in God, 58 per cent affirmed belief in immortality. Data such as these are undoubtedly precarious. Yet there remains for further investigation the suggestion of an interesting Catholic belief-solidarity. Belief, indeed, on the basis of Carrier's argument, seems to be both internally solidary or unitary *and* solidary with practice, within the Catholic framework. Carrier marks "the need for the sociologist, when he studies changes in religious attitudes, to discriminate carefully the religious confession he has to do with," since religious attitudes are differently "anchored" in different religious communities and "divergences between faith and affiliation occur in different modes" (Carrier, 1960, p. 238). If one cannot be sure that Carrier's evidence adequately sustains his remark by way of summary (p. 241) that "the relation between faith and institutional affiliation is much closer for the Catholic than for the Protestant; so that a Catholic abandoning his Church will be more liable to abandonment of his faith itself," nevertheless his materials do suggest this and they are of considerable interest for the possibility they foreshadow of close and careful scrutiny of such broad notions as that of the unity of society.

Thus far, unity *within* the context of religion (and with respect to a limited set of problems) has been touched upon. There are far more pertinent problems in the relations of religious and nonreligious phe-

nomena than can here be noted. Writers on primitive religion in particular have often given the impression that religion in the societies they study is highly "pervasive," so that all of social life is profoundly touched by it. But in the history of nonprimitive societies religion has of course also often seemed pervasive, and this has suggested to the historian and others the need for study of the relations of religion to economy, science, art, and so on. It is clearly not enough for the sociologist (just as it is not enough for the historian) to note historical events. His analytical bent constrains him to try for much more than this. The entire matter of modes or types and mechanisms of connection and disconnection of religious and nonreligious phenomena plainly presents a challenge to him. One relevant line of inquiry has to do with the ways and means of various kinds of secularization (understood for the immediate purpose as the mitigation or elimination of the pervasion by religion of nonreligious spheres of thought or activity) in the modern world. Merton's (1938) study of seventeenth-century science can be read as an attempt to probe the character of a significant secularization (an attempt that in its "dialectical" character is suggestive of mechanisms that work beyond the special sphere of historical application to Puritanism and science). In Merton's view, Puritanism involved a practical-ethical emphasis that encouraged science, a value bias that aided in the development of the latter. Thus far, indeed, one may read his material as demonstrating *pervasion* or penetration of science by religion. But ultimately a developed and ambitious science reacted upon the religious forces that had originally stimulated it and challenged some of the essential bases of these forces. Merton accordingly remarks that "the realization of values may lead to their renunciation" (p. 460), for, again, the science that had been nourished by religion came to question religion itself and sever its connection with it. The religious seed, so to put it, nourished a scientific flower that came to react adversely upon the seed. The secularization process thus involved has a distinctly dialectical appearance, and it is not inappropriate to refer to a self-destroying unity or solidarity or pervasion. A greater sensitivity to the relations of religion and other cultural or social spheres in the light of the notion of unity or pervasion may well lead us in time to concentrate more on the developmental detail of those relations in an effort to define with considerable precision mechanisms whereby pervasion or unity is built or destroyed.

None of the above, it may be remarked, should be taken as sustaining any particular thesis with regard to the secularization of the modern world in a broad sense, a topic that poses problems too large to be dealt with in detail here. But it may be said that pervasion of Western society and culture by religious values and influences has been and continues to be a goal of various significant groups and movements. The inclination that the leaders of the American Social Gospel movement had to "Christianize the social order" is well known. Pervasion is a major and ambitiously conceived aim of a sector of today's French clergy, including a number of Catholic sociologists of religion who are most eager to "Christianize" religiously disaffected elements in French society and are especially desirous of influencing the French working class. Christian Democracy is a more or less highly self-conscious effort by laymen not directly ecclesiastically controlled to infuse with "Christian principles" the running of such organizations as political parties, trade unions, and farmers' unions; while Christian Action organizations seek a similar infusion as direct auxiliaries of the clergy (Fogarty, 1957). The members of these organizations undoubtedly see themselves as confronting an uncongenially secularized world. Fogarty writes: "In Britain and on the Continent alike, the problem for the Christian believer today is more likely to be to attract attention in an indifferent environment than to beat off the assaults of

militant anti-clericals" (Fogarty, 1957, p. xvi). The presence of "militant anti-clericals" would at least suggest a continuation of emotional involvement; indifference plainly does not. Dansette (1957) observes in a similar vein, with special reference to the French worker: "As for the Church, if it does not arouse a violent anticlericalism directed against its power of oppression and its obscurantism, that should be a source of regret: that hatred still derived from respect" (Dansette, 1957, pp. 61–62).

Certainly, all this (and much more) suggests secularization (as well as effort to combat it), and it would seem impossible to deny that religious influences decreasingly pervade various important spheres of social life. But the whole matter of secularization in the large presents considerable difficulties with regard to essential points of fact and interpretation. La Bras (1960), taking a world-wide perspective, observes that, despite a "general tendency toward secularization," there are signs of religious reawakening in contemporary Hinduism, in the land of Israel, and in Catholicism, particularly the Catholicism of England and France (Le Bras, 1960, p. 83). Parsons (1963) has recently raised some provocative questions that indicate need for closer examination of the degree of "Christianization" of Western society itself. Data on church attendance, lapse of self-announced religious commitment or church membership, and decline followed by claimed revival in church affiliation in recent years (as for Britain and the United States) do not "speak for themselves." They need critical appraisal and interpretation. It is no doubt easier to reach conclusions about specific cultural and organizational areas than it is to decide about secularization in an overall sense, for a country, for the West, for the entire world. The term secularization is itself susceptible of much refinement, and terms like Christianization, in theological as well as sociological perspective, are not always unambiguous.

3. Functional analysts of religion have un-

questionably been disposed to stress "integration." This is to be understood with a rather different accent from that above given to "unity." The accent now falls on specifically human solidarity, on the "cohesion" of the humans participant in a religious system, on the mitigation of hostility among them, on the affirmation and validation for all of common values. It is possible that integration so understood is more readily effected in primitive than in nonprimitive societies. What is quite certain is that here, too, not to make the integrative function of religion problematic—merely to assume it—would be intellectually disastrous. Clarification of the term itself would again undoubtedly be helpful, as would clarification of the intention of various propositions that bear on presumed integrative functions of religion.

It does seem evident that some of the criticism of theories that stress integrative functions misses intentions or intimations of delimitation. Thus, when Bergson (1935) in his peculiar, tendentious language remarks that "religion is . . . a defensive reaction of nature against the dissolvent power of intelligence" (in italics in original) (p. 112), the context makes it clear that he has in view a "model" of presocial individuals who would be guided by a shrewd (although in the long run not a sufficiently shrewd) self-interest to act to obtain a pleasant life for themselves, quite regardless of the welfare of others. "Before" individuals can so act, religion intervenes and sets up norms backed by sanctions that provide barriers within and outside of particular individuals to inhibit such selfish action. Taken from this standpoint, writes Bergson, primitive religion is "a precaution against the danger man runs, as soon as he thinks at all, of thinking of himself alone," and religion in this sense, in Bergson's teleological style of discourse, becomes "a defensive reaction of nature against intelligence." Religion, or primitive religion, is also thus, in a clear meaning of the term, "integrative" (Bergson, 1935, p. 113). But all this can and should be taken as stressing certain aspects

of religion, not as unqualified assertion about all religion at all times and places. The same religions may well be "integrative" in some aspects and "disintegrative" in others. Granted that even as Bergson apparently intends his propositions about religion they call for more care in formulation than he gives them and for further evidence bearing on them, it is plainly unprofitable to take them in an unqualified sense that occasions loss of such insight as they do provide and a spate of irrelevant criticism.

If we do take the notion of the integrative functions of religion in unqualified fashion, it is extremely easy to show that religion is not always integrative. Should we understand "disintegrative" to refer to strife among religions, the chronic reality of such strife in the history of the West is known to schoolchildren. The history of the Orient, while somewhat different in this regard, is also similar in significant respects. Sansom (1958) writes that "a spirit of compromise in matters of faith is visible throughout the history of Japan," yet contrasts the harmony between Buddhism and Shinto with "the hostility between Buddhism and Confucianism or Buddhism and Taoism in China." Even as regards Japan itself, it is clear that there were significant elements of strife. The Lotus or Hokke sect protested against all other forms of Buddhism. The Hokke evangelist, Nichiren, was thoroughly intolerant and insisted until his death in 1282 that "the government must condemn and suppress all heresies and unite Japan under his Church." Something of Nichiren's character may be inferred from the circumstance that in connection with a population estimate of something over four and a half million for medieval Japan ascribed to him, he comments that all these millions will go to Hell if they do not follow his teaching— a provocative addendum to a sort of primitive census. Sansom does write that Nichiren and Hokke introduce into Japanese religion "an entirely new spirit of intolerance and national pride." Yet, if, as he also avers, "most of the numerous sects of Buddhism in Japan were tolerant to the point of indifference in matters of doctrine," they were still quite jealous in matters having to do with their rights and privileges (Sansom, 1958, pp. 76, 120, 428, 486, 427; Sansom, 1961, p. 153).

Should we understand "disintegrative" to refer to strife or disharmony between religion and civil authorities, the history of Japan again affords good enough materials for the rudimentary point involved. At the end of the eighth century, the Buddhist church "threatened the stability of government by reason of the political ambitions of its leaders and the fiscal immunities which they abused. The absorption of public lands into ecclesiastical domains deprived the state of revenue which it badly needed. . . ." Bodies of armed men, marked less by piety than by brawn, yet more or less on the order of servitors and lay brothers in Christian monasteries, became attached to medieval Japanese monasteries and would periodically get out of control and occasion or increase disorder in the capital. They were evidently not militarily genuinely formidable, but they were "religious," and controlling them was an awkward problem to rulers not disposed to risk supernatural sanctions. (The soldier-monks of different monasteries would also conflict.) Oda Nobunaga, the sixteenth-century warrior and dictator, hated the interference in political matters of the Buddhist churchmen and was antagonistic to their employment of military strength (Sansom, 1958, pp. 270, 273, 399; Sansom, 1961, p. 295).

Should we understand "disintegrative" to refer to elements within religion itself that tend to cut men off from their fellows, it is far from difficult to find such elements. The Buddhist stress on the evil of desire and on detachment has at times occasioned the sort of observation that a monk in Ceylon made to Pratt's wife: "I have mother and father and sisters but leave them all to themselves and think of myself only and my salvation. . . . To love your husband or your father very dangerous. If you live pure

life without attachments you will be young and good-looking when you will attain eighty or one hundred years." This hardly does justice to the strong element of compassion in Buddhism, but it is evidently not invariably easy to blend detachment and compassion, to wander "alone like a rhinoceros" and yet be profoundly sympathetic to others (Pratt, 1928, pp. 137, 176–177). Pratt adds in a footnote: "The difficulty in question is not in principle confined to Buddhism; it presents itself to every religion and every individual that would cultivate both spiritual freedom and social sympathy. In Buddhism the difficulty comes more sharply to the attention than elsewhere because of the Buddhist extreme dislike of inner disturbance" (Pratt, 1928, p. 177).

It has often been remarked that the integration of a religious group may be increased by persecution, by a split or "disintegration," that is, within the larger social framework within which it exists. In such cases, integration paradoxically becomes a function of disintegration, and "religion" simultaneously integrates and disintegrates. Thus, Scoville (1960) contends that persecution of the French Huguenots long before the Revocation of the Edict of Nantes "strengthened Protestantism as fire strengthens steel," and argues that Huguenot religious convictions and courage were fortified around the time of the Revocation. This at least suggests "integration." (He also argues that persecution nourished the economic aptitude and devotion of the Huguenots) (Scoville, 1960, pp. 2, 228, 445). And Poland (1957) holds that "the tempered persecution" of French Protestantism in the eighteenth century had actually been one of the chief sources of strength for the Protestant Church. Relaxation of this persecution, Poland contends, even more clearly to the present point than Scoville, brought "anarchy and dissension." A more thoroughgoing persecution might have wiped out French Protestantism; "tempered persecution," in this view, gave it a certain vitality (Poland, 1957, pp. 221–222). (This is incidentally illustrative of the theme that "evil things" may work eufunctionally, though the specification of context within which they so work must of course always be made. Toynbee [1956] quotes the following from Bayle: "There are people who maintain that it was necessary for Luther, Calvin, Farel, and some of the others to be hot-tempered, choleric, and full of bile. Without this, so they say, they never could have overcome the resistance [that they encountered]" [Toynbee, 1956, pp. 175-176]. Norbeck [1961, Ch. 11] treats witchcraft and ritual rebellion in a fashion relevant to this theme [see, also, Kluckhohn, 1962].)

Some partial, restricted evidence suggests that church attendance on the part of Protestants is more marked where Protestantism is a minority religion and less marked where it is dominant. Fogarty (1957, pp. 353-354) estimates that two-thirds of French Protestants may be "in some sense practicing," as compared with about 40 per cent of French Catholics who are regular Sunday churchgoers. The Dutch Gereformeerde churches, with some 10 per cent of the population nominally adherent to them, "have a high standard of practice," but the Dutch national church, the Hervormde Kerk, "has shown till recently a marked lack of solidity in its own ranks" and has been the main source of those enumerated as "churchless." Fogarty notes that a study made by J. P. Kruijt about 1930 (presumably the 1933 "thesis" by Kruijt "on the growth of indifference in the Protestant churches" to which Fogarty refers, p. 444) showed church attendance among Hervormde adherents as from 5 to 20 per cent of church members in the mainly Protestant regions of Holland (and as low as 4 per cent in Amsterdam) but as high as 60 per cent in the predominantly Catholic areas. One could reasonably argue that a sense of vulnerability, if not of outright persecution, in some circumstances, enhances the integration of those feeling vulnerable.

Whatever turns of analysis the consideration of integration may involve us in, there is no excuse whatever for lack of clarity on a last point—the point that integration is not necessarily "good." Obviously, a band of murderers could show high solidarity, be highly integrated.

4. The notion of the social "usefulness" of the gods, of belief, of religion is frequently bound in with the notion that religion has integrative functions or functions of social control. Gibbon (1932, Ch. 2) does not expand in functional style his well known statement that the modes of worship prevalent in the Roman world "were all considered by the people as equally true; by the philosopher, as equally false; and by the magistrate, as equally useful," but, since it is magistrates in particular to whom he imputes the last outlook, it seems a fair inference that he had in view functions of religion as keeping men within the bounds of order. Writing of the eighteenth century, Manuel (1959) remarks that "the idea that religion was a mechanism which inspired terror, but terror useful for the preservation of society, was a wide-spread conviction even among sceptics and atheists" (Manuel, 1959, p. 240). Groethuysen (1927, pp. 167-169, 225, 308-309; 1930, pp. 213-216, 313-315) notes that the eighteenth-century French bourgeoisie, once it had begun to realize some of its cherished goals, was visited with a sense of social responsibility and impressed with the need not to represent the deity's punitive powers over-gently, lest the imagining of the last judgment become too feeble a thing to preserve social order by keeping men within bounds by fear. Conservatives and radicals are often at one in assessing the integrative and control functions of religion. Writing of the emergent bourgeoisie in modern England, Engels (Marx & Engels, 1955) remarks that it had a "common interest" with "the ruling classes" in "keeping in subjection the great working mass of the nation" and that it soon discovered the opportunities religion offered it for making the masses "submissive to the behests of the masters it had pleased God to place over them" (Marx & Engels,

1955, p. 303). Thus there is evident justification for Merton's (1957) observation that "it is in the *evaluation* of . . . functions of religion, rather than in the logic of analysis . . . that . . . functionalists and . . . Marxists part company" (Merton, 1957, p 45).

It would not be difficult to put together a considerable anthology of views (from various times and places) such as those indicated in the above paragraph. As instances of relevant items: Frederick the Great considered religion "necessary as a discipline of the masses" and would have reserved scepticism for the "elite only," as Nicholls (1956, p. 51) puts it. Cross (1958) writes: "Mark Hanna was supposed to have said that the only two safeguards against anarchy in the United States were the Supreme Court and the Roman Catholic Church. William Howard Taft, under attack for allegedly discriminating in favor of the Church, sturdily retorted that he considered Catholicism 'one of the bulwarks against socialism and anarchy in this country, and I welcome its presence here' " (Cross, 1958, p. 35). Baltzell (1958) notes: "The fabulous railroad baron, James Hill, took a realistic view of the Catholic Church in American society. Hill, himself a Protestant, when asked why he had suddenly donated a million dollars for the establishment of a Roman Catholic theological seminary in St. Paul, Minnesota, quickly replied: 'Look at the millions of foreigners pouring into this country for whom the Catholic Church represents the only authority they fear or respect' " (Baltzell, 1958, p. 224). Baumer (1960), drawing on the Rowntree-Lavers study of English life and leisure, records a voice from the lower ranks, that of a working-class housewife averring of "the nobs" that they "try to make working folk believe (religion is true), so that they won't kick up a fuss" (Baumer, 1960, p. 7).

The significance of these views for the present purpose is that they show not only a measure of recognition of some of the functions of religion, on the lines of its making for integration or preserving social order, but also an *instrumental* attitude toward the functions, an attitude prepared to utilize or exploit the functions precisely in the interest of preserving a certain order. (The working-class housewife quoted, for her part, obviously responds negatively to what she perceives as an instrumentalization of religion on the part of "the nobs"). Functions of religion that were once latent thus become manifest to particular persons in particular strata and are then instrumentally regarded or treated. But this represents only one of a number of significant modes in which the process of recognition of functions and subsequent instrumentalization thereof has taken place.

A somewhat different mode is ostensibly more "high-minded," by intention less obviously bound in with the interests of a stratum or class, and pointed toward the interests of an entire community. Comte (1877) affords a good example of this. In his *Positive Philosophy* he had already shown keen awareness of functions of religion, and his own brand of instrumentalization of functions appears full blown in later work. It will be recalled that in Comte's view man is eminently a creature prone to the pursuit of selfish interests and that it is vitally important to make an "altruistic" being of him. Religion is indispensable to this end, and the Religion of Humanity, specifically, will "combine" and "regulate" individuals; provide ample "altruizing" rituals modeled on, though in detail different from, those of Catholicism; translate men beyond themselves via worship of women to adoration of the Great Being of Humanity; cleanse the Great Being itself of dross, so that it will in the end feature a kind of hypostatized "best" of all humanity. The intention to "use" religion as a major instrument of social policy and social reformation is beyond doubt. Harrison (1913), Comte's English follower, wrote that Catholic and Protestant divines "recognize how deeply . . . Comte has seen to the foundations of all religion, has apprehended what religion *really has to do*"

(Harrison, 1913, p. 233). The italics are Harrison's, and the context makes it quite clear that he thinks in positivist terms of manipulating and fashioning religion so that its "true functions" may be realized in a recasting that makes them goals consciously striven for, at least by a significant sector of society, for the ostensible benefit of all sectors. To Huxley's familiar comment that Comte's religious construction "might be compendiously described as Catholicism *minus* Christianity," Richard Congreve (1874) responded that he would rather recommend the characterization, "Catholicism plus Science" (Congreve, 1874, p. 275). The positivist instrumental bias toward "scientific utilization" of religion is again made very clear. One of the more obvious doubts it generated bore on the dangers of "manipulation" by a positivist pontificate. Perhaps somewhat more subtle are questions on the line of whether it is possible to continue to "be religious" while making a deliberate "use" of religion.

A third mode of recognition-cum-instrumentalization has evident theological roots. One of the most striking aspects of religious phenomena in "developed" religions is the constant tension of opposed religious principles. Particularly relevant here is the tension between the principle of a hard and impenetrable or inscrutable God who pursues His own ways to which man must submit, no matter how humanly unjust they may seem, and the principle of a softer, more humanized and more humanly understandable God—as in the historic oppositions of Jansenists and Jesuits (Groethuysen, 1927, pp. 135–147, 148–158). The tension may be stated in extreme form as being between a principle which asserts that God's existence is for God's "benefit" regardless of men and one which asserts that God's existence is for men's benefit regardless of God. Knox (1961) notes that "some of the Quietists seem to have spent their whole lives under the conviction that they were destined to be lost." He adds that "perhaps we must not quarrel with the eccentric

legacy by which a disciple of Père Piny endowed a series of Masses, not for the welfare of her soul, but in thanksgiving to God for having decreed her salvation or damnation, as the case might be," but then wonders "what you were to do when you were summoned to the death-bed of a young priest who asked God in set terms to send him to hell, so that the Divine justice and the Divine glory might be more fully manifested" (Knox, 1961, pp. 272, 273). This is obviously on the side of the principle that God's existence is for God's benefit regardless of men. Its tension with the opposed principle richly affects a great deal of religious history. Significantly, either principle alone (insofar as either has ever been adhered to alone) has constantly generated difficulties for the religious or religiously interested, and the blending of the two principles constantly threatens to be unstable.

Groethuysen (1927, pp. 187–188), in writing of the Jansenist version of God versus an emergent humanized version in eighteenth-century France, notes that the more humanized, just, or fair, by human standards, the deity became, the less men believed in Him. As He lost his inscrutability and infinite remoteness and became more of a "good sport," then, the price of this humanization proved to be His very divinity, for, accommodated and adapted to human standards, He ceased to appear divine. But, when He continued to be upheld as the old God of mystery whose election and reprobation of men is not ultimately comprehensible by the latter, He also suffered repudiation by educated laymen and bourgeois who could no longer believe in Him in this form. Humanized, He lost the regard of humans; unhumanized, He repelled the human sense and feelings of many. The dilemma thus presented is not unique to eighteenth-century France.

If God's existence is for His benefit, many things may evidently be demanded of men that do not conduce to their worldly comfort or welfare. It is a matter of *"Thy* will be done." If the opposed principle holds sway without opposition or reservation, then men may expect endless divine benefits for themselves. Theological (and pastoral) stresses on the latter principle have co-existed with stresses on the former. Unstable though a blending of the principles be, one at least tends to hover in the background when the other is to the fore. Even grim predestinarians have not been unmindful of their own salvation, and the most unrestrained advocates of the notion that religion is "for man" have at least had to face the criticism from others that they were forgetting or abandoning God in the interests of man. The phenomenon of special interest here emerges with realization of the existence of a theological stress on religion as being "for man," awareness that this functions to encourage a strain toward making religion respond to human needs, and the taking of a final step toward instrumentalization with the more or less deliberate exploitation of religion for human uses.

Recognition-cum-instrumentalization in the first mode noted above involves the tendency of members of a stratum or class to utilize religion for special stratum or class interests; and in the second mode, the bias toward utilizing religion for the ostensible benefit of an entire community or society. In the third mode (granted that there may be points of overlap with the others), the bent has been not so much toward the deliberate enhancing of the interests of either a stratum or community but rather toward exploiting a variety of particular functions of religion, first recognized and then of course recast as goals, and with frequent stress on the psychological benefits of religion. The latter stress within the third mode has been evident in much American writing on the psychology of religion. James (1936, p. 497) cites Leuba's view that "so long as men can *use* their God, they care very little who he is, or even whether he is at all," and further quotes him: *"God is not known, he is not understood; he is used*—sometimes as meat-purveyor, some-

times as moral support, sometimes as friend, sometimes as an object of love. If he proves himself useful, the religious consciousness asks for no more than that. . . . Not God, but life, more life, a larger, richer, more satisfying life, is, in the last analysis, the end of religion . . ." (James, 1936, p. 497). James's own views, as set out in *The Varieties,* hardly indicate hesitancy in the matter of making use of deity or religion. And his entire discussion makes it plain that he had become keenly aware of the possible psychotherapeutic functions of religion in particular and was minded to develop a psychology and philosophy of religion at least in part designed to exploit those functions, now recognized and recast as goals. There arises again the question, among others, of the extent to which it is possible to hold an instrumental view and yet adhere to authentic "faith"—a question that might also be put by asking whether (or to what extent) instrumentalization may not be self-defeating. Subsequent American popularization of views like those of James at the hands of writers like Peale, with a very generous extension of once-latent-functions-become-manifest and re-set as goals, so that peace of mind, prosperity, happy human relations, and the like may all be attained via a religious technology has been treated elsewhere (Schneider & Dornbusch, 1958). (The instrumental attitude toward religious faith that has had considerable support in American psychology of religion is analyzed by Pratt (1920, *passim*) in a fashion as cogent today as when he originally made his analysis.)

A continued tension between instrumentalization and the "Thy will be done" principle (if the matter may be thus roughly put) may be necessary for instrumentalization to "work" at all. And a continued tension between the two may also be necessary for the "Thy will be done" principle to make appeal. Plainly, more knowledge about these matters than is now available is needed; it is also plain that this is one of the many fields in which a sociology of religion willing to pose significant questions must take some account of theological positions. (The variety of occasions for this necessity cannot be elaborated. An instance of another contrast—of church as "protestant" and as "catholic"—which strongly suggests the necessity is given by Niebuhr [1956, p. 25].) In the interim, a certain scepticism about instrumentalization may be allowed to generate or reinforce some of the questions sociologists are constrained to ask in this entire context. H. R. Niebuhr (1937) has contended relevantly: "The instrumental value of faith for society is dependent upon faith's conviction that it has more than instrumental value. Faith could not defend men if it believed that defense was its meaning. The godliness which is profitable to all things becomes unprofitable when profit rather than God comes to be its interest" (Niebuhr, 1937, p. 12). If "heresy promotes business spirit," as a Spanish proverb has it (Scoville, 1960, p. 150) or if "piety and industry generally go hand in hand," as Sweet (1950, p. 114) contends, it does not follow that a deliberate cultivation of "heresy" or piety with a view to promoting one's group's business spirit or bent for industry would achieve its object.

Functional approaches to religion undoubtedly have their limitations. At times, although certainly not always, they suggest an apparatus rather exclusively designed to analyze a primitive brew of tribal rituals, oracles, witchcraft, and the like, and not pointed toward analysis of "high" religion. They often appear not to get beyond the creation of sensitivity to significant problems. But, granting these and other limitations, it is especially appropriate, given the subject of this chapter, to recall the words of the sage who commented that we do not throw to the dogs everything that is not fit for the altar of the gods.

RELIGION AS CULTURE

The element in religion that structures the cosmos and gives it meaning so that it is conceived, say, that a cosmic struggle goes on between two ultrahuman entities respectively representing good and evil, or that a benevolent deity desirous of redeeming a humanity involved in sin assumes human form to mediate effectively between himself and man and thereby alters the course of all history, or that existence is a round of incarnations and associated sufferings whose root is desire or ignorance—this element, unequivocally cultural, is slighted by sociologists of religion only at the risk of trivializing their discipline. The well known older works of Weber (1922; 1930; 1951b; 1952; 1958; 1963) and Troeltsch (1950) gave considerable, even major, attention to the cultural content of religion—to religion as meaning or value or symbolic form. It is as well to stress the significance of that content at a time when numerous studies tend to take it for granted or deal with it in peculiarly thin forms. In the following sections, a few general remarks are made on the study of cultural content and typologies; one area is set out in which further work on content might well be done; attention is given to the notion of degeneration of religious culture through vulgarization.

1. The sociology of religion is evidently not comparative religion, but it can certainly draw on the latter, and the latter affords the former ample raw material for analysis of religious culture. Comparative religion indeed constantly presents perspectives that suggest the possibility of useful typological work that could be turned to sociological ends. Thus, when it is noted (Mensching, 1947, p. 91) that Buddhism rejects the world on grounds of asceticism, that primitive Christianity did so because of its belief in the nearing end of the world, and that Islam affirms the world but seeks to impregnate it with religious principles and outlooks to the end that the human community may be constituted as a new and specifically *religious* community, the dimensions of "rejection" and "affirmation" of the world are plainly suggested. The question easily arises as to what other dimensions

it may be analytically profitable, for various purposes, to combine with rejection and affirmation, set out in terms of types, and relate to human interaction. Typology is hardly an end in itself, and it must be admitted that rather pointless typologizing has been something of a plague in the sociology of religion, as for example, in the endeavor to construct a typology of Catholic parishes by Bodzenta (1960) or (perhaps a somewhat more excusable endeavor) Honigsheim's (1958, pp. 132–135) effort to piece out typological work by Weber and Troeltsch. Nevertheless, typologies can be and have been helpful in the field. Weber's typological efforts remain stimulating, and revealing typological work has been done since his day, as in the case of H. R. Niebuhr's (1951) *Christ and Culture,* the work of a theologian, to be sure, but containing much that is most suggestive sociologically.

In this whole context, much of course depends on the purposes of analysis. Lacking firm purpose, one is likely enough to end with still another formalistic exercise in the elaboration of types of some sort. It is certainly feasible, however, to construct some simple typologies of select phenomena of religious culture which have, minimally, a shorthand or summarizing function, whose relevance to the material they purport to condense is plain, and which are so set out that they would lend themselves readily to elaboration and to rudimentary comparisons with the content of a number of other religio-cultural phenomena. An effort at a typology of this kind is instanced in Schneider and Dornbusch's (1958) categories for analysis of the content of American inspirational religious literature—characterized as instrumentally radical if it stressed the use of religion to achieve wealth, health, or other worldly goods and instrumentally conservative if it stressed goods such as wealth and health only as by-products of religious activity undertaken for other reasons; characterized further as medico-psychologically radical or conservative, depending on the literalness and seriousness with which it

took the view that religious faith alone can heal all bodily and mental ailments; characterized finally as socially radical or conservative depending on whether or not it inclined to condemn an existing social order in the light of absolute religious ideals of love and charity. The simplicity of this typing is evident. It was constructed for quite limited purposes. Much more ambitious schemes, involving more dimensions and types, are obviously possible. The simple schemes with few terms will not carry very far and will not present a large number of logical possibilities that might be empirically significant. Yet at the same time, as intimated above, heavy elaborations of typological schemes and combinations and permutations of the elements that go into their making may turn out to be largely idle games, neither actually nor potentially culturally or socially relevant.

But the point is not especially to advocate typological work or to express reservations about it. Typology has been stressed because it has been a prominent device for organizing and analyzing the cultural content of major religions, and the effort to do this *and* at the same time relate that content to social interaction is what is crucial. (New and more subtle modes of apprehending religio-cultural content than typologies, however helpful, afford may conceivably be found and may be needed even if they are not likely to be available. Well-conceived statistical work often is called for to supplement typological endeavor in any case. Swanson's [1960] recent work, which is partly relevant to the concern with religion as culture here set out, may foreshadow significant developments, even if at present it seems more interesting technically than substantively.) The current relative lack of effort by sociologists to compare, and bring to bear on the sphere of social relations, cultural components of major religions is one of the most telling signs of the absence of theoretical imagination and scope in the sociology of religion. It is undoubtedly a sense of this relative lack that prompts Schreuder (1961) in his recent pithy summary of the field to aver that the "classical" contributions to it are still the major ones.

2. A very large heritage of problems in the sociology of religion was left by Weber. Documentation of this heritage is a huge enterprise in itself. Only a few present-day continuities in it can even be referred to. Historians like the Georges (1961) and Nelson (1949) continue to wrestle with problems sharply posed by Weber, as on the lines of the connections of Calvinism and capitalism and of universalism in economic relations. Sociologists, economists, and psychologists (Bellah, 1957; Hagen, 1962, Ch. 13; Lenski, 1961, Ch. 3; Lipset & Bendix, 1959, pp. 48–56; McClelland, 1961, pp. 319–322, 356–364, 406–411) continue to be concerned with matters clearly suggested to them by Weber, as on the lines of the relations between Japanese religion and Japanese economy, the broad relations between religion and economic innovation, the relations between Protestantism and Catholicism and social mobility, differences in Protestant and Catholic education and achievement need, and the influence of conversion to Protestantism on achievement need.

Many of the problems set by Weber appear most unlikely to be "exhausted" for at least some time to come. Among them is a set suggested by those portions of Weber's work that bear on what may be called a religious theory of signs. The reference to a religious theory of signs is intended particularly to call attention to Weber's concern with such things as profitableness and prosperity and the character of the conduct of life insofar as these were historically construed to have a transcendental or symbolic significance. In what follows no more than a crude sketch is attempted of the issues raised by a religious theory of signs in some special directions. The object of the sketch is to reinforce the theme of the need for a well developed sociology of religion to investigate in detail important religio-cultural content (whose importance for social in-

teraction in the case of the materials presented is broadly evident and cannot here be developed). If this reinforcement is achieved by way of indicating the possibility of further fruitful work on some matters of old interest, that is all that can be expected.

Weber (1930) averred that Calvin himself held that "the elect differ externally in this life in no way from the damned" (p. 110). McNeill (1954) has accordingly contended that "the now popular notion that Calvin held the prosperity of believers to be proof of their election is a perversion of Weber and an inversion of Calvin" (McNeill, 1954, p. 222). And he asserts further in regard to the notion that Calvin gave free rein to "an individualistic business activity, sanctioned by the view that worldly prosperity is evidence of the favor of God," that this "actually called forth from Calvin the most emphatic words of condemnation" (McNeill, 1954, p. 418). McNeill, however, also makes this significant concession: "Certainly the bourgeois heresy of wealth as a mark of divine approval entered into late Calvinism, though always under the restraints of insistence upon charity and service. It may have broken in during the era of Puritan individualism, with the triumph of the Independents and the growth of foreign trading interests. Cromwell saw in his military victories the manifest favor of God . . ." (McNeill, 1954, p. 419). Similar notions on the line that prosperity argues divine approval or election (and with a hint or more than a hint that poverty argues disapproval or reprobation) have been imputed to the Puritan creed by other historians (as Hauser, 1931, Ch. 2; Tawney, 1947, Ch. 4). On the other hand, the Georges (1961) (who, incidentally, have some critical remarks about the term Puritan that need not be considered in this place), while they record from their study of Protestant thought in the English Reformation from 1570 to 1640 that "a remarkably friendly attitude toward the possession, acquisition, and enjoyment of property" prevailed among the divines of this period, nevertheless hold that "all possibility of ultimately viewing worldly prosperity as a reliable indicator of divine favor or the soundness of one's spiritual state is forestalled by the fundamental insistence (nagging common sense!) that the blessings of the world are distributed indiscriminately to the good and to the bad." They do not deny the existence of "a tendency to see worldly prosperity as a likely accompaniment of Christian zeal," but write that "the much more usual and emphatic judgment is that by far the gifts of best quality and most quantity that the world can offer fall to the share of the wicked rather than the virtuous" (C. H. George & Katherine George, 1961, p. 161). This is close enough, for present purposes, to suggesting some serious reservations about simple connections between prosperity and divine approval.

The Georges (1961), it may be noted by the way, afford one of a number of instances of rather severe critics of Weber who are nevertheless disposed to make certain concessions to his views on Calvinism and capitalism. After expressing various reservations about Weber's work and choosing, as they put it, "to see religion in any social or historical situation as simply one among many conditioning factors and itself conditioned far more than it conditions" (C. H. George & K. George, 1961, p. 75), they end their discussion (p. 173) with the observation that "the association of Protestantism with capitalism is nevertheless a unique and doubtless important historical fact." The remainder of the paragraph in which this observation appears leaves some uncertainty as to just what they mean by the observation itself. Léonard (1955) affords another instance of a skeptical view of Weber in which nevertheless an interesting concession is made. He writes that "it does not seem that the first French Protestants . . . showed any particular love for business" and interprets the development of French Protestant finance in a way having nothing to do with Weber's views. This does not prevent him from noting that Protestants played crucial innovative and executive roles in seventeenth-century France or from remarking that "the spirit of initiative and the taste for profit are certainly . . . fruits of the Calvinist reform in its adherents." He observes parenthetically with regard to this last remark that it affirms "nearly all that one can grant Max Weber" (Léonard, 1955, pp. 44, 50–52, 86). Although this grants little in one sense, it still allows a connection of religion and economic activity that calls for further probing.

But let us return to the matter of signs. The sociologist not an expert in sixteenth- and seventeenth-century theological thought must obviously proceed with care in this matter. Yet despite disagreements (and reservations such as those of the Georges) there seems to be some solid consensus that there was a *strain* of acceptance in Protestant thought (especially after the earlier decades of the Reformation) of a religious theory of signs in the specific sense that worldly conditions like prosperity and poverty symbolize or prefigure transcendental conditions. In a simplified and evidently extreme "model" of this religious theory of signs, prosperity would argue or imply salvation or election, just as salvation or election would imply or involve a prosperous worldly condition, while poverty would argue or imply reprobation and reprobation would imply or involve a worldly condition of poverty. On this model, the world is plainly given transcendental or symbolic meaning in certain directions and heavenly and earthly realms are in symbolic contact. The model affords points of reference for a theory of signs that was in flux for a long time and was adopted in varying degrees and with varying qualifications by groups adhering to theologies that differed in a good many respects. A few aspects of this flux and variation may be noted.

The model constitutes an obvious simplification and intensification, and at various times and in different groups, as just suggested, there were unquestionably inconsistences and reservations that destroyed its simplicity. The Georges' suggestion that "nagging common sense" would enforce the view that "the blessings of the world are distributed indiscriminately to the good and to the bad" is at any rate plausible. Moreover, there are strong indications that the model was at times broken by impulses of charity (as suggested by McNeill). This is very clear in the case of the Quakers, for example. The Quakers may seem a curious group to choose for this purpose, in view of their rejection of predestination, their avowal of the view that every man is "enlightened by the divine light of Christ" and that every man has been given, as Barclay (1827) puts it, "a day or time of visitation, wherein it is possible for him to be saved" (in italics in original) (Barclay, 1827, p. 153). But the model has its points of application in the case of the Quakers. Tolles (1948) notes, in his study of the Quaker merchants of colonial Philadelphia: "If one kept one's inner eye solely to the Lord and labored diligently in one's calling, one could expect that God would show His favor by adding His blessing in the form of material prosperity. And conversely business success could be regarded as a visible sign that one was indeed living 'in the Light'" (Tolles, 1948, p. 56). Yet, although business success was construed as a sign of living "in the Light," Quakers were strongly committed to works of charity, for every man was truly "a vehicle of the seed of God" and merited sympathetic help in case of misfortune; "nothing" Tolles remarks, "could have been further removed from the Puritan view of poverty as a crime and a disgrace, a visible sign of God's displeasure" (Tolles, 1948, p. 65). In terms of the model, there was a Quaker bias toward accepting the prosperity-argues-or-implies-salvation formula and the salvation-implies-or-involves-prosperity formula, but not toward accepting the poverty-or-failure-implies-no-salvation formula (or its inversion).

If there is reason to think that there were inconsistencies in the model from the time of initial adherence to at least some of its elements, questions are readily suggested about the *extinguishment* of formulas of the kind included in the model. How does the model perish and how do its formula-elements get dissolved? Alternatively, how does the world become *de-symbolized,* deprived of meaning in certain particular directions, so that there ceases to be, say, a backward and forward reference whereby prosperity argues salvation and salvation prosperity? There is room for more exact and detailed knowledge than we have on courses and processes of de-symbolization and on the emergence of substitute sustainments for economic activity (insofar as it is in fact true that Protestantism gave stimulation to economic activity through insistence on the verity of certain formulas). We can witness courses of *attenuation* of formulas of the type proposed in the model. Bates and Dittemore (1932) write of Augusta Stetson, Mary Baker Eddy's follower: "From the fundamental principles of Christian Science she boldly drew certain inferences. . . . Evil being error, and poverty being an indubitable form of evil, Mrs. Stetson argued, it followed that poverty must be error and indicated a wrong state of mind in its victims. Prosperity was a result of spirituality, its symbol and unerring accompaniment. 'To demonstrate prosperity' was an important part of the Christian Scientist's duty" (Bates & Dittemore, 1932, p. 381). This still *perhaps* harks back to a significance for prosperity and poverty that is "religious" or "spiritual" in a more or less traditional sense of these terms. (But no effort can be made to trace historical links between the religio-philosophical background of Christian Science and the religious theory of signs in its European home.) It also points forward, however, to a radical psychologizing of signs (common enough in American cultist thought) whereby prosperity argues no more than "right thinking" or "positive thinking" and poverty no more than "wrong thinking" or "negative thinking." (To insist that this is still "religious" or "spiritual" is at least to do some violence to traditional senses of these terms.) The phenomenon of attenuation suggests possibilities of better understanding of processes of extinguishment or radical de-symbolization than is now available, since, plainly, it holds out some chance of witnessing extinguishment on its way. In turn, all this suggests a dimension of study of sects and cults that might well give additional significance to work being done on them.

It is instructive, in connection with a religious theory of signs, simply to remark how different symbolic significance may be attached to a similar *core* of conduct. Thus, ascetic conduct is very plainly a strong element in the Christian tradition. It may be noted, after Groethuysen (1930, pp. 190–206), that hard work, renunciation of pleasure, self-conquest, repudiation of sinful impulses and of the mode of life of those who seek ease were valued in the Christian tradition in eighteenth-century France, as before and elsewhere. But in strictly Christian terms, they were valued for themselves as giving evidence of Christian disposition (or they were valued as lending strength to the "order" of society which calls for the conviction that work is obligatory but that its reward is not to be looked for in this life). The rising bourgeoisie, for its part, could and did agree on the worthwhileness of asceticism, of hard work, of renunciation of self-indulgence and idleness, but there was the crucial difference that the bourgeois asceticism was pointed toward success in *this* life, "to an intensification of life-energy, to a new affirmation of the values of this life" (Groethuysen, 1930, p. 193). The symbolic value of asceticism thus shifted radically. Asceticism as indication of sober Christian temperament (and as a useful prop for the ordering of society) is clearly one thing; while asceticism as activity designed to further one's success and progress in this world is clearly something else. Asceticism may be a sign of Christian other-worldliness. It may be a sign of wholehearted commitment to success-values in

this world. It may, for that matter, also be a sign of Protestant inner-worldly orientation, in accordance with Weber's thesis. This does not deny that close investigation of these several kinds of asceticism would quickly reveal not merely a similar core of conduct and values but also highly significant *variant* elements.

Since asceticism has thus been referred to, it may be further noted by the way that this has been even a richer cultural phenomenon than the above might suggest. It is of interest to remark the value struggles that have occurred within it. Léonard (1955, p. 111) notes that the Mennonites of Eastern France, although they abandoned certain affectations of clothing regarded as too rich, at the beginning of this century, nevertheless compensated themselves by the *quality* of the fabrics they wore. Tolles (1948) writes: "Wives and daughters of the Quaker grandees compensated for their self-denial in the matter of ornaments by having their garments made only of the finest and most expensive stuffs. Christopher Sower, the Dunker printer, observed in 1724 that plainness was still noticeable in Quaker garb 'except that the material is very costly or even velvet'" (Tolles, 1948, pp. 126–127). Peter Kalm, a quarter of a century later, wrote of Quaker women who "pretend not to have their clothes made after the latest fashion, or to wear cuffs and be dressed as gaily as others," but who "strangely enough have their garments made of the finest and costliest materials that can be procured." McClelland (1961) remarks that "the famous ascetic 'Quaker gray' could be, and was, converted into a luxurious dress of costly material to be worn by the wife of a wealthy Quaker merchant" (McClelland, 1961, p. 313).

It may be reaffirmed that serious and substantial investigation of the content of major religious cultures is indispensable for a sociology of religion that seeks scope and significance. Historical work can be of great and obvious aid in this, but the sociology of religion need not for that reason relinquish its distinctive analytical concerns and dissolve into the history of religion.

3. Another kind of concern with religion as culture is to be found in the works of writers like Sorokin (1962) and Mensching (1947; 1959), who mark a process of what might be called the degeneration of "high" religious culture by way of "vulgarization." This stress, in Sorokin, is indeed part of a larger theme of cultural degeneration through vulgarization. "Qualitatively," he writes, "the greatest religious, philosophical, ethical, scientific or artistic systems are at their best and purest when their followers are limited to a small group of faithful, competent, and understanding apostles. When they are diffused among vast millions, their purity, verity, adequacy, is lost, disfigured, and vulgarized" (Sorokin, 1962, vol. 4, p. 84). The threat of destruction or degeneration is thus realized as "success" via gain of adherents comes about.

The "purity" of religion, for Sorokin, it should be added, may be impaired in other ways, as in the shift from Ascetic to Active Ideationalism as this reduces the asceticism of men who become taken up with organizational imperatives that thrust them increasingly into the circumstances of "this world" (Sorokin, 1962, vol. 1, p. 135).

A view much like Sorokin's has been presented by Mensching (1947, pp. 132–160, 215–218; 1959, *passim;* argument that might be used in favor of the view had also been presented by Weber, 1922, as at pp. 266–267). For Mensching, an "inner dialectic" of universal religion also exists. The claim to universality made by such religion must be validated through expansion and incorporation of the masses, but this is achieved at the cost of the "depth and distinctiveness" of the universal religion. The analysis largely runs, then, in terms of the bafflement of "high" by "low" religious impulse. The masses are credulous and possessed of crude and rigid perceptions and understanding. They are impatient of the deviant outlooks of independent individuals. They demand authority. They look to religion for favor-

able practical effects in the way of good fortune, happiness, and the like. They have a powerful and ineradicable bias in favor of magic, charms, amulets, and mysteriously virtuous candles and bells, conjuring, and processions to enhance the fertility of the earth. The religion they sustain is markedly animistic. They demand that the powers they revere or propitiate be close to them, vivid, specialized, or differentiated. They want gods or spirits to preside very palpably over particular areas of human concern. They even adapt the higher religious conceptions to their own uses. The notion of Tao thus afforded a point of attachment for mass magical tendencies that ultimately built into a "vulgar Taoism" concerned with the making of elixirs to prolong life and produce gold. In brief, the masses have a notable power to transform the metaphysical, spiritual, deeply conceived, into the superficial, magical, and shallow. Religious meanings, values, and symbols are thus repeatedly subjected to stultification and again the universal religions suffer degeneration of their highest components precisely as they succeed in the effort to universalize their message.

This "pessimistic" representation of the spiritual potential of the masses has strong points of resemblance to the picture of the inhabitants of French villages within zones of urban influence painted by Schmitt-Eglin (1952). By the "simple" peasants in these villages, nuances and qualifications are neither understood nor regarded without suspicion. The "good" priest is one who is readily understandable, who simplifies and makes vivid, who is kindly and "easy," whose demands are light. The simple "love to be confirmed in their moral routines, but balk at the preacher who would shake their torpor . . . and make them go forward to a higher spirituality" (Schmitt-Eglin, 1952, p. 94). The theme is developed with a call for a kind of heroic work on the part of the Catholic priesthood that may well seem unlikely to have much success to anyone convinced by the descriptive-interpretive portions of Schmitt-Eglin's own book. (The "mass man" in the sense of the "atomized" man, as for Mensching, below, also is discernible in Schmitt-Eglin's work.)

The view of Sorokin and Mensching applies to masses in the sense of those who, within the framework of a high religion such as Christianity, maintain the elements of a folk or collectivistic religious outlook. (Mensching, however, distinguishes mass in another sense, that of large numbers uprooted by modern technology, out of contact with more "primitive" religious and social frameworks, concerned solely with material welfare and lacking individuality because "atomized" and not because "collectivized." Corresponding to mass in the first sense is the term folk belief; to mass in the second sense, "superstition." Folk belief is naive and primitive and may be said to recall earlier forms of a subsequently evolved high religion. It remains connected with a sense of the "holy." Superstition, in Mensching's view, is "outside all religion"; it is secular and shows no feeling for the holy and no sense of the metaphysical.) The general representation of degeneration by way of vulgarizing given by Sorokin and Mensching undoubtedly has a measure of validity (and the problem is to determine how much). It has particular importance for the dialectical view it proposes, and for its intimation of mechanisms in religious development which, as will be stressed later, are important for the prospect they hold out of connecting the sociology of religion with sociological analysis at large. And it is the kind of representation that readily generates valuable questions for detailed research. It may still be asked whether it does not, as it stands, tend too much to presume a more or less eternally identical mass, ever and equally ready to degenerate high religious (and other) values. The social contexts of masses are hardly always identical; the groups that "environ" them are not always of the same sort and do not necessarily have the same kinds of contacts with them. There is warrant for the view that these different mass contexts are a source of variant mass responses.

Two other perspectives on religion as culture should be given brief mention. One has to do with ambitious speculations about the meaning-value-symbol content of religion as *congruous* with the content of other areas of "total" cultures. The character of such proposed congruities was well enough suggested by Marx (1936) when he asserted that "for a society based upon the production of commodities, in which the producers in general enter into social relations with one another by treating their products as commodities and values, whereby they reduce their individual private labour to the standard of homogeneous human labour— for such a society, Christianity with its *cultus* of abstract man, more especially in its bourgeois developments, Protestantism, Deism, etc., is the most fitting form of religion" (Marx, 1936, p. 91). Speculations on such lines are often intriguing but plainly have to be scrutinized for the possibility that they may rest on verbal play and in any case tend to present difficult problems of marshaling evidence. Very different from this is the matter of culture in its aspect of transmission from generation to generation. Studies of sects have been significant in this connection as they have presented questions about maintenance or breakdown in subsequent generations of the values of original members of sectarian groups. Both blood descendants of sect founders and recruits from outside often miss unique and vivid incidents experienced by the original members (such as the undergoing or witnessing of martyrdom). The distinctive values of the latter, unsustained in a new time by such experiences, are liable to a certain disintegration. Or it may be that these values appear to have little foundation left in the light of a changing environment. Or the sect values of original members may have been subjected to a dialectical kind of development whereby they have become "internally" changed. Thus, Weber (1930, pp. 174–176) suggests a process whereby wealth, once accumulated through the exercise of the virtues of thrift, industry, and frugality, reacts upon those same virtues. Under the "bombardment of interests and appetites," as Parsons (1937, p. 685) puts it, those virtues begin to give way, failing to withstand the enticements brought about by their own effects. However the threat to the old values comes, it is likely to pose problems in the socialization of both blood descendants and recruits from the outside. It may occasion uneasy compromises or initiate a desperate search for isolation from an uncongenial environing larger culture. It may also induce schism and strong and even fanatical reaffirmation of original sect values. Variously suggestive in this whole matter are studies by Niebuhr (1954), Pope (1942), and Boisen (1955). (On somewhat different lines, problems of cultural transmission are suggested by Herberg [1956].)

RELIGION AND SOCIETY

The variety of matters that might be included under this heading are here reduced to two: some aspects of religion and social stratification, and religious and generic "nonreligious" social phenomena. These two matters, however, present strategic problems for the sociology of religion.

1. Isambert (1962, p. 495) begins a recent paper by observing that it is well known that in the Latin countries of Western Europe the classes of common people ("les classes populaires") are estranged from the Catholic church. He adds that this circumstance of estrangement goes well beyond the geographical area of these countries and poses "the question of the existence of a general phenomenon."

Birnbaum (1960, pp. 49–65) suggests that the modern sociology of religion began in Great Britain with a church attendance count in 1851, the report dealing with which indicated in detail the alienation of the working class from the churches. This alienation indeed existed before the middle of the last century. A good instance of specific

documentation of it in a large city is afforded by Wickham's (1957) investigation of Sheffield. That it is alienation that was historically involved, in the sense of working classes actually staying away from the churches and holding distinctive feelings that the churches catered not to their interests but to interests of members of other strata or that workers were effectively excluded from church by the expenditures involved in such things as owning or renting scarce pews—there evidently can be no doubt. Even with national losses from the church in the past two generations coming "substantially from the middling classes of society" ("industrial and professional middle classes, the inhabitants of suburbia, shopkeepers, black-coated workers, superior craftsmen, foremen. . . ."), Wickham concludes that "despite the losses, the middling groups are still more easily embraced by churches of all denominations than working-class groups" (Wickham, 1957, pp. 218–219; see also, Birnbaum, 1960). "Alienation" or "estrangement" will be retained in the following to apply in general to relative working-class nonattendance at church (or nonparticipation in churchly or church-related activity), it being understood that this nonattendance is accompanied by varying (as by country) intensity and diffusion of feeling on the part of members of working class or "lower stratum" groups that they are excluded or unwelcome or do not belong (or even would be ill advised in the light of their interests to seek to belong).

A variety of American studies (e.g., Lazerwitz, 1961b; Lazerwitz, 1962a; Lazerwitz, 1962b; Lenski, 1961, p. 44; Lenski, 1962, p. 313) suggest some alienation on the American scene, although as Lenski notes (1962, p. 313) "by comparison with other groups, the churches in the United States have an excellent record of attracting members of the working classes to their services" (Lenski, 1962, p. 313). Lenski (1962) sees "the problem" as not that of why American workers attend church so rarely but "why . . . they avoid formal organizational activities generally, even the churches to some extent" (Lenski, 1962, p. 313). This way of seeing the matter may well be most useful, although Lazerwitz (1962a) has recently argued that, while there is some association between regularity of church attendance and totality of activity in voluntary organizations, the relationship is complex and it is unlikely that church attendance results from the same factors that affect voluntary activities. In raising the question whether the criterion of frequency of church attendance may not exaggerate differences in class *religious* commitment, Lenski (1962, p. 314) is quite justified. In principle, the distinction between church attendance or activity and religious commitment should be kept in view for all countries, although the degree of coincidence between the two is undoubtedly variable for different countries.

Winter's (1961) study of the suburbanization of American churches presents the whole matter in a distinctive way by documenting an "escape" of middle-class churches to the suburbs, an escape Winter regards as motivated by "status panic" and one that leaves working-class (and lower-middle class) elements of the large urban populations to cope with a variety of social problems without the aid of middle-class church resources. Further, and in any case, the suburban churches deliberately address themselves to a set of problems bearing on leisure and family values and well removed from the problems of the working class left in the central cities. Physical removal and social and psychological irrelevance to lower strata thus sustain or enhance the alienation of the latter.

Relevant data for Germany appear to be harder to find, but also suggest working-class alienation. A table presented by Fogarty (1957, p. 239) "from an estimate by K. von Bismarck," drawn from a "cyclostyled report of a lecture in Berlin, January 9th, 1954," on church and working class, indicates that, for one hundred Evangelical churches in Westphalia in 1953, workers comprised 45 per cent (35 per cent "settled"

and 10 per cent "casual and refugee" workers) of "baptised Evangelicals known as such to the ministers." These same workers constituted only 5 per cent of churchgoers and none of the elders (church council members). On the other hand, the "lower middle class" (including "tradesmen, craftsmen, and more established workers") made up 25 per cent of baptised Evangelicals, but 65 per cent of churchgoers and 85 per cent of elders, and an "upper middle class" group comprising 5 per cent of baptised Evangelicals constituted 15 per cent of churchgoers and 15 per cent of elders. (But a group of "intermediate 'intellectual' grades," including, for example, journalists, comprised 5 per cent of baptised Evangelicals, but only 2 per cent of churchgoers and none of the elders.) At least for these one hundred Westphalian churches, the data, if they are valid (and their general trend is at any rate certainly credible), suggest church alienation as characteristic of the "lower" ranks of workers. Tenbruck (1960, pp. 122–132) reports an investigation of the small town of Reutlingen in Württemberg (conducted in 1955 and 1956) in which the working class showed "the lowest participation in, the most careless attitude toward, and the earliest separation from the church" (Tenbruck, 1960, p. 127; see also, Höffner, 1960, p. 48; Luckmann, 1960, p. 143).

Belgium, Italy (at least Central and Southern Italy), Spain, and the countries of Latin America evidently present a similar phenomenon (Isambert, 1961, p. 47). If there are exceptions among Catholic countries, such as Poland and Ireland, where nationalistic and religious sentiment coalesced in opposition to enemies of different religion (Pin, 1962, p. 515), the larger trend still remains clear. But it is notably in France among main modern countries that the entire problem of the church estrangement of the working classes has aroused attention. The historical circumstances of the estrangement in France are not such as to allow of easy generalization (Isambert, 1961). The sheer outcome of estrangement, however, is a matter of strong consensus. Le Bras (1962) has recently reaffirmed "the extremely low workers' rate of participation in Catholic worship in present-day France." Dansette (1957, p. 21), in a convenient summary of pertinent materials, indicates the very low level of attendance at mass by workers in the larger cities and their outskirts. In the three parishes of the poor sector of Rouen which Quoist (1952, p. 194) studied, he found the percentage of workers attending Sunday mass to be less than a third that of other inhabitants and—a striking datum—he found a lone docker attending out of a total of 661 dockers. In one of the very best parish studies made to date, Pin (1956) found in Lyons the usual worker alienation from the church. The wealth of Pin's data cannot be reproduced here, but a sketch of some of his findings will be useful for this account. It is well to recall, in connection with his work, that the French clergy and other Catholic groups have sought recently to increase the appeal of the Church to the working class. Numerous Catholic leaders after World War II "wanted to associate the Church more closely with progressive forces in France, to convince the masses that the Church was no longer an institution of the French bourgeoisie" (Bosworth, 1962, p. 57). The course of clerical progressivism and leftism has not run smooth, but considerable study of the working class and religion has been undertaken.

Pin (1956) found education to be "a variable with which religious practice is more closely associated than with any other" (Pin, 1956, p. 219; the point is interestingly taken up by Labbens, 1959, pp. 61–63). Both amount and type of education were relevant. Persons with little education tended to less religious practice or attendance at mass than others; and the technically educated also tended to lower religious practice than the nontechnically educated. But if education is a highly important variable, it is seen nevertheless by Pin as the mark and symbol of a culture proper to a stratum or class. Pin's mode of stress on class as culture and

his finding that religious practice goes along with "a style of life which presupposes a minimum income, but which, beyond this minimum, is but slightly dependent on variations in income" (Pin, 1956, p. 161) are reminiscent of Weber's apprehension of the subtlety of connection between stratum and religious outlook. (The latter's sense of this subtlety is rather neatly indicated in a single sentence in which he sums up in a "slogan-like way" those "strata that were carriers and propagators of the so-called world religions," and, after specifying them or their leading figures in Confucianism, Hinduism, Buddhism, Islam, Judaism, and Christianity, indicated that they are to be regarded "not as representatives of their occupations or of material 'class interests,' but as ideological carriers of an ethic or doctrine of redemption such as had an easy affinity with their social situations" [Weber, 1922, p. 293].)

The working class expectably has the lowest level of education and the lowest standard of living. Manual workers constitute most of it, but Pin also includes such employees as caretakers, janitors, and domestics, so that the occupational criterion is not the sole one. The rate of religious practice in this class is so low that one may say that the class simply does not practice. Pin avers that "non-integration into urban society appears to us to summarize best" the traits of this class and adds that "this absence of integration is shown not only by exclusion from the concrete group constituted by the 'bourgeois,' that is by the authentic citizens of urban society, but still more by the feebleness of a cultural level which does not allow for understanding, for mastery of the complex world of technical, juridical, economic, and administrative mechanisms of urban life" (Pin, 1956, pp. 225–226).

The working class is thus above all characterized by "lacks," for Pin—lack of comprehension of the modern world, lack of ability to foresee, lack of means to integrate into urban society. Magical notions play a large role in the idea-system of the members of the class, and non-Catholic "sects" have found some favorable hearing among them. The prime demand of the class, however, Pin sees as a community that will engage in "action for justice." The Communist Party has held out the hope of such a community, has offered primary group contacts, and has operated in terms of a style and a language that shrewdly make appeal (in the terms of an oversimplified radical doctrine) to immediate experience, which members of the working class can understand. Pin's own view is that this class can adhere only to "a religion which shows its capacity for creating a just world" (Pin, 1956, p. 402). He argues accordingly that estrangement from the Church on the part of the working class is connected precisely with the sentiment that the Church has little to offer toward attainment of social justice and that this estrangement is therefore a mass estrangement. In elevated bourgeois circles (consisting of such persons as business heads [in Lyons, particularly heads of silk factories], business managers, and higher civil servants. Family origins are of some importance, especially for the professionals and officials), on the other hand, departure from the Church, where it occurs, is connected with the sentiment that the Church is critical of individual moral (and perhaps especially sexual) lapses, and this departure is manifested in the form of abstention from Church participation on the part of particular individuals. Bourgeois culture nourishes critical reflection, bias toward individual autonomy that constitutes an easily understood reaction to a complex urban life threatening anonymity, but also bias toward maintenance of acquired privilege, while on the working class side recourse to the immediacy of contacts and feelings, bias toward action together, and demand for justice are all marked. And in all this, the Church has moved in spheres and affected a style remote from the working class. It is, indeed, as if there were a "secret affinity" between the bourgeois cultural world and the Catholic church (Pin, 1956, p. 232).

This résumé omits numerous nuances and reference to various "middling" groups, but this much may be added: In Pin's view, small tradesmen and artisans are scarcely more "integrated" into urban life than workers and scarcely have a better understanding of its complexities. He believes this may help to account for their similar attitude toward religious practice. Their rate of practice hardly exceeds that of workers. But there are differences between workers and this group. The small tradesmen have their aspirations, and, while the workers have more or less renounced the attempt to integrate themselves into or become part of urban society, this is not the case for the other (small tradesman-artisan) group. However, both lack the intellectual equipment needed to understand an urban mode of life (Pin, 1956, p. 227). There are "middle groups" which are more "integrated" than either the workers or small tradesmen and that show higher religious practice, while the bourgeoisie shows the highest religious practice.

Pin's views, which are certainly not his alone, suggest an advocacy of elements of a religio-political philosophy (that would make the liturgy more comprehensible to the working class, encourage the clergy in certain distinctive attitudes toward various classes, and so on) that goes well beyond a sociology of religion in a strict sense. Whether French Catholicism can ultimately in any large sense "win" the working class is a question outside the scope of this chapter. It may be noted, however, that Dansette (1957) observes in broad terms that Catholicism may attempt via social action to realize the Kingdom of God here below, in which case it "runs the risk of allowing itself to be seduced by Marxism"; or it may leave room for hope only in another world, in which case it risks addressing itself to a restricted audience (Dansette, 1957, p. 468). Authentic problems are pointed to by the dilemma. A sharp contrast between "bourgeoisie" and "proletariat" has been relatively highly justified in France. Thus, Bosworth remarks: "The French working class retains in 1961 many of the anticapitalist and 'proletarian' reflexes that characterized most Western workers' movements a century ago" (Bosworth, 1962, p. 114). Such a description is not justified everywhere else, and certainly not in the United States. Continuing French economic prosperity and political changes may in time greatly alter portions of Pin's picture. But his effort to portray class as culture and, moreover, as religiously relevant culture, remains notable (even if it is to some extent based on surveys of opinion whose representativeness is uncertain and on data for a single parish). It has been remarked, also, that in his view "nonintegration into urban society" is crucial in understanding the working class, and the whole notion of nonintegration is significant well beyond Pin's particular French contexts.

Nonintegration as it is now to be used refers to the phenomenon of being "outside" a certain community or class—a phenomenon with which distinctive personal traits of character and modes of conduct are likely to be associated. (Relative lack of comprehension of the social world, emphasized by Pin, could also easily be accommodated in the view of nonintegration here adopted.) Lipset (1960) has noted the "isolation" of members of the "lower strata" from "the activities, controversies, and organizations of democratic society" (Lipset, 1960, p. 112). Nonintegration in this sense might also be called nonincorporation, and, if this is considered from a "community" point of view, then the change in traits that is correlated with incorporation may be labeled "civil"-izing; if it is considered from a class point of view, the change may be labeled "bourgeoisfying." The latter term is used in the sense of "middle-class-izing" and refers (to follow Faris, 1960) to the emergence of "ambition, industry, thrift, long-range goals with deferment of immediate gratification, individual responsibility, effective performance . . . effective manners and personal relations, and . . . respect for property." (It should be remarked that there is no inten-

tion to suggest an assessment of class virtues in this context, and, in particular, no intention to impute greater virtue to some classes than to others. The statements made here must be made within strict space limitations, but it has to be said that class self-exaltation considerable virtues of generosity and felis only too easy to achieve and that defenders of the workers have, at any rate, at various times claimed to find among them very lowship [see, for example, Isambert, 1961, p. 207].) This brief statement may well pass too glibly over the contrast of "community" and "class" points of view. But the problems that might arise in this connection will not be considered. In what follows, reference will be made to civil-izing or bourgeoisfying religious influences.

That religious influences can civil-ize or bourgeoisfy is quite evident. As is well known, Methodism gained considerable support from the industrial working classes of England, reducing the nonintegration of the latter. Methodism brought a measure of education to miners and their children. Miners who went to Chapel found it "necessary to appear decent there," obtained new clothes, and "became what is termed respectable." Guns and dogs and fighting cocks were discouraged by the Methodists, but not such things as hymns in place of "public house ditties" or prayer-meetings in place of "pay-night frolics." The Methodists inculcated "earnestness, sobriety, industry and regularity of conduct" (Wearmouth, 1937, p. 227, with special reference to Northumberland and Durham). Methodist traveling preachers in the eighteenth century were urged to express disapprobation of "Sabbath-breaking, dram-drinking, evil speaking, unprofitable conversation . . . contracting debts without due care to discharge them" (Wearmouth, 1945, p. 246). In accounts of the work of the Salvation Army, it has repeatedly appeared that a person of working class or lower stratum origin is "down and out," addicted to drink, neglectful of family. He is affected by the Army, "gets religion," obtains steady work, stops drinking, develops an interest in family and the education of his children. The spiritual conversion is thus paralleled by a civil-izing or bourgeoisfying development. Religion appears as a kind of starting-mechanism for new patterns of conduct and thought. American Negro cults show a tendency to be decidedly restrictive of sexual activity (Fauset, 1944). It is possible that sexual laxity among lower stratum Negroes "re-quires" initially powerful persuasion to make sexual standards conform to "higher" norms, although for lack of adequate evi-dence any such imputation of function to the "wilder" cults must remain for the time being no more than an imputation, if a plausible one. Essien-Udom's (1962) study of the Black Muslims "suggests rather strongly that upwardly mobile lower-class Negroes join and remain" in the Muslim movement, and Essien-Udom notes the Muslim encouragement "to practice and assimilate habits that we associate with the middle class" (Essien-Udom, 1962, pp. 104, 105). On certain conditions, the Muslims might conceivably "integrate" out of their hostility to white society—but this is ad-mittedly a complex matter.

Obviously, "religion" need not always have a civil-izing or bourgeoisfying or inte-grating influence. Evidently, also, other than religious agencies may have similar func-tions, as when workers' unions enforce a discipline on lines of punctuality and scrup-ulousness about debts. Where religious in-fluences have been important, however, special interest attaches to processes whereby styles of "responsibility," "earnestness," "punctuality," sexual and other kinds of restraint, and so on, achieve functional autonomy and can continue without reli-gious reinforcement where this has lapsed. Life histories and family histories could sup-ply pertinent materials. It is possible that religion in the West is no longer of great significance as a starting mechanism in breaking out of lower-stratum patterns of life, but little should be taken for granted here and the extent to which religion ever worked in the fashion indicated itself re-mains a matter for fuller investigation.

A further aspect of the field of religious and social stratification is the relationship of class and sect. Pope's (1942, pp. 122–124) listing of the transitions that occur in move-ment from sect to church marks one im-portant kind of development of sects which has class aspects. The transitions include a movement from poverty to wealth, from a negative or indifferent attitude toward existing culture and society to a positive or affirmative one, from fervor to restraint in worship. A pattern reminiscent of Pope's work is noted by Wilson (1961, p. 312) who observes that, while first-generation British Christadelphians came from the ranks of the poor, subsequent generations have experienced some social mobility and there has been a corresponding shift in specific religious emphases (in the Christa-delphian case, toward concern with devo-tional life and away from concern with the establishment of God's kingdom on earth). But this is not a necessary pattern. Wilson writes that "modern sects do not necessarily express the needs of the lower classes" and that "socioeconomic position is not the only determinant of sectarian development, if it ever were" (Wilson, 1961, p. 327). Sects may achieve a certain stabilization without a full following through of the movements described by Pope or Boisen (1955, as at pp. 89–90, 231–232). Even Boisen, in describing the origin of sects, writes of "little groups of like-minded persons, *nearly* always of the struggling, underprivileged classes" (italics supplied). The reservation suggested by the adverb is important. With-in the sect or sectlike group, a prestige hier-archy based on some order of sacredness or sanctification is evidently hard or perhaps even impossible to avoid. Poll (1962, pp. 59–60) notes that within the Hasidic commu-nity of Williamsburg social stratification is genuine, although it is based upon fre-quency and intensity of religious observ-ance. (The association of particular religious affiliation with class status has not been treated above. Some factual aspects of this, for the United States, are reviewed in Lazerwitz [1961a].)

2. Since religion has features that mark it as a product of human activity and the work of men associated in groups, it has sociocultural aspects, and the sociological mode of abstraction from the total religious phenomenon is accordingly a perfectly legitimate one. But insofar as religion is a social reality, it may be expected to share characteristics with a variety of nonreligious phenomena that happen also to be sociocultural. It is suggested in this section that it is theoretically profitable to stress that phenomena roughly "within" the sphere of religion often share dialectical form and dialectical modes of development or change with social phenomena outside the religious sphere; that, further, there are mechanisms that unite or bind the religio-social with the generic-social spheres; that, finally, there is a set of phenomena—on the lines of organizational reality, dilemmas, oppositions of principle, and broad social processes—that, again, unite the religio-social and generic-social.

Dialectical development has been alluded to earlier, in connection with Merton's work on seventeenth-century science and religion, Sorokin's and Mensching's views on the vulgarization of high religion, Weber's suggestion of the process whereby wealth produced by virtues of industry, thrift, and frugality "bombards" and jeopardizes the very virtues from which it has emerged. (In his later work, Mensching [1959] also affords "dialectically" most pertinent discussion of selected religious phenomena.) As regards dialectical form, it may be noted that one of the most striking aspects of dialectical representations of development or change is stress on the emergence of "opposites" as development or change occurs—a stress that lends a strongly paradoxical aspect to such representations. The stress may indeed be exemplified in the cases just referred to. Science, at least partly nurtured by "good" Puritan theological

premises, produces the "bad" effect of serious challenge to those very premises. High religion, seeking the "good" of further diffusion of itself, produces the "evil" of its own vulgarization even as it succeeds in being diffused. Protestant asceticism seeks or practices the "good" by way of industry, thrift, and frugality and inadvertently produces the "bad" when the products of industry and cognate virtues corrupt the virtues themselves. (These assertions are of course not to be taken as final statements of unqualified truths. Study of the matters that Merton, Sorokin and Mensching and Weber have considered is presumably far from finished.) This phenomenon of the emergence of "opposites" in a course of development or change is very far indeed from being confined to the "religious" sphere. In the economic field, quite outside religion, it is an old and very well known observation that the "bad" (selfish) pursuit of private interest can lead to the "good" result of public welfare. Weber (1951a, p. 33) was as thoroughly aware of the emergence of such opposites in the economic field as he was aware of it in the religious arena.

It has been characteristic of dialectical thought to stress that systems carry within themselves the sources of their own destruction and that the same "elements" that initially prosper a system also generate effects that bring about its decline or elimination. Many developments in religion can be read according to this pattern, as, once more, it may be contended that Puritan religion helped rear a science which in turn "came back" in developed form to challenge premises of the religion that helped rear it. Outside the religious sphere, the same pattern of development or change can be, and has been, argued to occur in very many social phenomena (to emphasize the pervasiveness of dialectical modes of change, incidentally, is not at all to presume that all change must be of dialectical type) (cf. Schneider, 1964). The intimation of the value of a perspective that binds religious and nonreligious social spheres by noting the circumstance that both spheres exhibit susceptibility to dialectical constructions may be strengthened by consideration of the working of mechanisms of dialectical movement.

Representations of dialectical development can be made sharper by specification of mechanisms indispensable to that development or movement. An indispensable agency in the movement in the situation wherein industry, thrift, and frugality produce a wealth that reacts disintegratingly on those very virtues is a boomerang mechanism. Without the return effect (or, if one will, "feedback," which in this case works the "wrong way") or boomerang from the wealth-product of the virtues, the movement would not take place. If, in the same general situation, we note a response whereby some persons, outraged by the spectacle of the corruption of others by wealth, reaffirm the more strongly the virtues of industry, thrift, and frugality and practice them the more strenuously (thereby helping to ensure the recurrence of the same problem of threat to virtue through virtue-produced wealth) and if we allow this response also to be implicated in a dialectical movement, a mechanism that works by way of intensification of the valuation and practice of virtue through reaction to observed rejection of virtue may be discriminated. This mechanism has some points of resemblance to the process described by Festinger, Riecken, and Schachter (1956), wherein proselyting for a system of belief is under certain conditions enhanced after the belief has been clearly disconfirmed.

This necessarily abbreviated consideration of dialectic and mechanisms at least allows the view that there are most significant resemblances in the workings of "social matter" qua religious and qua nonreligious. The mechanisms have been noted in the context of dialectical movement and are taken to be operative in dialectical movement both within and without the religious sphere. But even if the dialectical context is removed, and special reference to dialectical movement is dropped, it is clear that mechanisms of the kind indicated operate without as well as within religio-social spheres. The boomerang mechanism is thoroughly familiar to social psychologists and sociologists in areas outside the socio-religious sphere. The other mechanism referred to above has perhaps received less formal recognition in sociopsychological and sociological literature, but outraged or indignant reaffirmation of old ways of life and cherished virtue against the spectacle of a rejection of those virtues because of effects coming from their very exercise is a broad human phenomenon that cannot be confined to religion and has some affinities with absolutistic or "fanatical" attitudes that, again, are well outside "religion" even if that is very broadly defined.

It may now seem that the stress on the second mechanism indicated, in particular, involves special attention to psychological rather than social phenomena. This should occasion no discomfort. The psychological and social are in any case notoriously intertwined, and reduplicated psychological phenomena in which numbers of persons have much the same kinds of reactions, with opportunity for mutual reinforcement of sentiments bearing on values and conduct, easily shade into social phenomena. And there is no need at all to deny that mechanisms may have very significant psychological aspects. It is very likely, indeed, that increased knowledge of distinctive psychological phenomena would improve knowledge of certain mechanisms. Knox (1961, *passim*) has brilliantly described how, time and again in religious history, antinomianism has arisen out of perfectionist movements. The aspirant to perfection in his own view can become so perfect that he is not liable to corruption even by the corrupt. Hence perfectionism makes room for "contempt for the decencies" and the super-pure often get involved in an impurity which, since *they* are involved in it, cannot be impure. The "elect" in the sense of the perfect come to have, in the area of their moral conduct, a surprising affinity with the damned and the wicked, and movements that initially aim for special holiness or the like may end by becoming peculiarly unholy. (The point is also developed and documented by Cohn [1961], who writes:

The core of the heresy of the Free Spirit lay in the adept's attitude to himself: he believed that he had attained a perfection so absolute that he was incapable of sin. Although the practical consequences of this belief could vary, one possible consequence was antinomianism. The "perfect man" could always draw the conclusion that it was permissible for him, even incumbent on him, to do whatever was commonly thought of as forbidden. In a Christian civilization, which attached particular value to chastity and regarded sexual intercourse outside marriage as particularly sinful, such antinomianism most commonly took the form of promiscuity on principle [Cohn, 1961, p. 152].)

There is a suggestion of dialectical movement here also, and a dialectical flavor is certainly rendered by the emergence of the opposite of "purity" from the very heart of what purports to be "purity" or perfection itself. But there is a challenge in this to the specification of the precise ways and means or mechanism(s) whereby the pure converts into the impure, and there are most certainly psychological problems involved in penetrating the mechanism(s). The entire process seems roughly "understandable," but there is surely room for better comprehension of it. Once again, there are undoubtedly nonreligious parallels to both whole process and mechanism(s). Totalitarian political movements, if these may be taken as quite nonreligious for the immediate purpose, have generated appreciably similar phenomena. The theme that great "purity" at least need not be contaminated by most "impure" experiences is strikingly suggested by words of Himmler's bearing on the destruction of the European Jews, in an address to his top commanders in 1943: "Most of you know what it means when 100 corpses lie there, or when 500 corpses lie there, or when 1000 corpses lie there. To

have gone through this and—apart from a few exceptions caused by human weakness —to have remained decent, that has made us great. That is a page of glory in our history which has never been written and which is never to be written . . ." (as reported by Hilberg, 1961, p. 648).

Certain fairly obvious additional phenomena that unite or bind the religio-social and the generic-social may be noted. Churches, to say nothing of other kinds of religious associations, are societies and, in particular, organizations, and thereby comparable with other societies or organizations. They undoubtedly have features quite their own, but also share a great many with other organizations, and the apparatus of analysis applied to organizations thus has important points of application to them. "The Church is *earthen*—of the stuff of natural and historical life," as one writer puts the matter (Gustafson, 1961, p. x). Being "earthen," or like other organizations, it is constantly confronted with problems, not the least of which is its involvement in dilemma. The general dilemma of the church, in a very wide sense, that Wiese and Becker (1932, Ch. 44), among others, have stressed may be recalled. In the simplest terms, the church is an organization and at the same time embodies distinctive principles and ideals. As an organization, it is subject to organizational imperatives and may become involved in coercion and a variety of stratagems to ensure its own organizational health and survival. Its principles or ideals are not always compatible with such imperatives. "The church combines, after a fashion, the water of the religious and the oil of the social" (Wiese & Becker, 1932, p. 617). For Gustafson (1961), who prefers other metaphors, it puts "treasure" in "earthen vessels." The dilemma consequently steadily regenerated for the church, with due allowances for differences of content in principle or ideal and the like, also appears for other organizations, although that of the church has its unique aspects. This points to but one of a number of possibilities of analyzing church and other organizations in more or less common terms (on dilemma, see also O'Dea, 1963).

Readily suggested by dilemma is opposition of principles, which is as plainly a religio-social as it is a generic-social phenomenon. Conflict between prophetic and priestly principles, between principles that sustain enthusiasm and those that support more restrained kinds of religious expression, between principles that stress religion "for God" and those that stress religion "for man"—these are thoroughly familiar in religion; just as conflict of principles with other kinds of content (although there can be subtle resemblances to the content of *religious* principles-in-conflict) is to be found in labor unions, political parties, academic bureaucracies, and so on. Dilemma and conflict, incidentally, both frequently suggest the utility of dialectical modes of thought in analyzing religio-social and generic-social phenomena.

Various broad social processes are also at work within and outside the religious sphere. Reference need be made only to cyclical processes for illustrative purposes. Schismatic groups have repeatedly sought to return to what they regarded as original Christian inspiration and then have gone through phases of development that ultimately put their endeavor back in the fold of "institutionalized" religion, whereupon the whole course may be gone through again. Details of the cycle vary, but the fact of its frequent repetition is plain. Lapse of original fervor, entanglement and compromise with "the world," and other features of these cyclical movements are duplicated in cyclical developments outside formally religious movements. Dilemmas, oppositions of principle, and dialectical play accompany the unfolding of the cyclical course, but the stress now is also that these are caught up or contained within a cycle of development. The theory of the circulation of elites long ago formulated by Pareto, with its theme of recurrence, its unmistakable dialectical bias, its concern in particular with the succession of leaderships (with different value orientations) whose very triumph prepares their downfall, and its scrutiny of the intrusion of "alien" elements into leaderships, may well have in some respects a peculiar relevance to certain cyclical developments in the religious sphere. And if this particular juxtaposition initially seems somewhat odd, it is designed to reinforce the point of this section—that the sociology of religion, whatever the unique problems it has, is in many crucial respects "merely" sociology. It does no harm whatever for the point to be insistently stressed—and it could have been stressed with a larger range of materials than it has been possible to mention in this section.

Increased knowledge of matters of interest in the sociology of religion should certainly bring increased knowledge of matters of interest to sociology in general, just as sociology in general should be helpful to the sociology of religion in particular. A lively sense of the connections and problems in common of the sociology of religion and sociology at large is indeed surely one of the conditions for the prospering of the religion subfield. If, further, the subfield maintains close contact with relevant work in history, anthropology, psychology, philosophy, and the rich theological writing of the present day, and at the same time keeps firm hold of the thoroughly indispensable empirical tradition in sociology, it may yet turn out to be something better than a thing of shreds and patches and become a most significant area of intellectual concern.

REFERENCES

Baltzell, E. D. *Philadelphia gentlemen*. Glencoe, Ill.: Free Press, 1958.

Barclay, R. *An apology for the true Christian divinity*. New York: Samuel Wood & Sons, 1827.

Bates, E. S., & Dittemore, J. V. *Mary Baker Eddy: The truth and the tradition*. New York: Knopf, 1932.

Baumer, F. L. *Religion and the rise of scepticism*. New York: Harcourt, 1960.

Bellah, R. N. *Tokugawa religion*. Glencoe, Ill.: Free Press, 1957.

Bellah, R. N. Durkheim and history. *Amer. sociol. Rev.*, 1959, 24, 447–461.

Bergson, H. *The two sources of morality and religion.* New York: Holt, 1935.

Birnbaum, N. Soziologie der Kirchengemeinde in Grossbritannien. In D. Goldschmidt, F. Greiner, & H. Schelsky (Eds.), *Soziologie der Kirchengemeinde.* Stuttgart: F. Enke, 1960. Pp. 49–65.

Bodzenta, E. Versuch einer Sozial-religiösen Typologie der Katholischen Pfarren. In D. Goldschmidt, F. Greiner, & H. Schelsky (Eds.), *Soziologie der Kirchengemeinde.* Stuttgart: F. Enke, 1960. Pp. 179–195.

Boisen, A. T. *Religion in crisis and custom.* New York: Harper, 1955.

Bosworth, W. *Catholicism and crisis in modern France.* Princeton, N.J.: Princeton Univer. Press, 1962.

Brown, D. G., & Lowe, W. L. Religious beliefs and personality characteristics of college students. *J. soc. Psychol.,* 1951, 33, 103–129.

Carrier, H. *Psycho-sociologie de l'appartenance religieuse.* Rome: Presses de l'Universite Grégorienne, 1960.

Cohn, N. *The pursuit of the millenium.* New York: Harper, 1961.

Comte, A. *System of positive polity.* London: Longmans Green, 1877.

Congreve, R. *Essays: Political, social, and religious.* London: Longmans Green, 1874.

Cross, R. D. *The emergence of liberal catholicism in America.* Cambridge, Mass.: Harvard Univer. Press, 1958.

Dansette, A. *Destin du Catholicisme Français.* Paris: Flammarion, 1957.

Dodds, E. R. *The Greeks and the irrational.* Boston: Beacon Press, 1957.

Durkheim, E. De la définition du phénomène religieux. *L'Année sociologique,* 1898–1899, 2, 1–28.

Durkheim, E. *The elementary forms of the religious life.* New York: Macmillan, 1926.

Durkheim, E. *Suicide.* Glencoe, Ill.: Free Press, 1951.

Essien-Udom, E. U. *Black nationalism.* Chicago: Univer. of Chicago Press, 1962.

Faris, R. E. L. The middle class from a sociological viewpoint. *Soc. Forces,* 1960, 39, 1–5.

Fauset, A. H. *Black gods of the metropolis.* Philadelphia: Univer. of Pennsylvania Press, 1944.

Festinger, L., Riecken, H., & Schachter, S. *When prophecy fails.* Minneapolis: Univer. of Minnesota Press, 1956.

Fogarty, M. P. *Christian democracy in West-ern Europe.* London: Routledge & Kegan Paul, 1957.

Geertz, C. *The religion of Java.* Glencoe, Ill.: Free Press, 1960.

George, C. H., & George, Katherine. *The protestant mind of the English reformation.* Princeton, N.J.: Princeton Univer. Press, 1961.

Gibbon, E. *The decline and fall of the Roman empire.* New York: Modern Library, 1932.

Groethuysen, B. *Die Entstehung der Bürgerlichen Welt-und Lebensanschauung in Frankreich.* Halle-Saale: Niemeyer, 1927–1930. 2 vols.

Gustafson, J. M. *Treasure in earthen vessels.* New York: Harper, 1961.

Hagen, E. E. *On the theory of social change.* Homewood, Ill.: Dorsey Press, 1962.

Harrison, F. *The positive evolution of religion.* London: Heinemann, 1913.

Harrison, Jane Ellen. *Themis: A study of the social origins of Greek religion.* (2nd ed.) Cambridge: The University Press, 1927.

Hauser, H. *Les débuts du capitalisme.* Paris: Alcan, 1931.

Herberg, W. *Protestant-Catholic-Jew.* New York: Doubleday, 1956.

Hillberg, R. *The destruction of the European Jews.* Chicago: Quadrangle Books, 1961.

Höffner, J. (Ed.) *Jahrbuch des Instituts für Christliche Sozialwissenschaften.* Münster: Regensberg, 1960.

Honigsheim, P. Religionssoziologie. In G. Eisermann (Ed.), *Die Lehre von der Gesellschaft.* Stuttgart: F. Enke, 1958. Pp. 119–180.

Isambert, F. A. *Christianisme et class ouvrière.* Tournai, France: Casterman, 1961.

Isambert, F. A. Christianisme et Stratification Sociale. *Soc. Compass,* 1962, 9, 495–513.

James, W. *The varieties of religious experience.* New York: Modern Library, 1936, originally 1902.

Kluckhohn, C. Myths and rituals: A general theory. *Harvard theological Rev.,* January, 1942, 35, 45–79.

Kluckhohn, C. *Navaho witchcraft.* Boston: Beacon Press, 1962.

Knox, R. *Enthusiasm.* New York: Oxford Univer. Press, 1961.

Kruijt, P. J. Die Erforschung der Protestantischen Kirchengemeinde in den Niederlanden. In D. Goldschimdt, F. Greiner, & H.

Schelsky (Eds.), *Soziologie der Kirchenge-meinde*. Stuttgart: F. Enke, 1960. Pp. 35–49.

Labbens, J. *L'Eglise et les centres urbains*. Paris: Spes, 1959.

Lazerwitz, B. A comparison of major United States religious groups. *J. Amer. statist. Ass.*, 1961, **56**, 568–579.(a)

Lazerwitz, B. Some factors associated with variations in church attendance. *Soc. Forces*, 1961, **39**, 301–309.(b)

Lazerwitz, B. Membership in voluntary associations and frequency of church attendance. *J. scient. Stud. Rel.*, 1962, **2**, 74–84.(a)

Lazerwitz, B. National data on participation rates among residential belts in the United States. *Amer. sociol. Rev.*, 1962, **27**, 691–696.(b)

Le Bras, G. *Etudes de sociologie religieuse*. Paris: Presses Universitaires, 1955–1956. 2 vols.

Le Bras, G. Problèmes de la sociologie des religions. In G. Gurvitch (Ed.), *Traité de Sociologie*. Paris: Presses Universitaires, 1960. Vol. 2, pp. 79–102.

Le Bras, G. Review of Isambert, *Christianisme et classe Ouvrière*. *Arch. de Sociologie des Religions*, 1962, **14**, 180–181.

Lenski, G. *The religious factor*. New York: Doubleday, 1961.

Lenski, G. The sociology of religion in the United States. *Soc. Compass*, 1962, **9**, 307–337.

Léonard, E.-G. *Le protestant français*. Paris: Presses Universitaires, 1955.

Lipset, S. M. *Political man*. New York: Doubleday, 1960.

Lipset, S. M., & Bendix, R. *Social mobility in industrial society*. Berkeley: Univer. of California Press, 1959.

Luckmann, T. Vier Protestantische Kirchengemeinden. Bericht über eine Vergleichende Untersuchung. In D. Goldschmidt, F. Greiner, & H. Schelsky (Eds.), *Soziologie der Kirchengemeinde*. Stuttgart: F. Enke, 1960. Pp. 122–132.

McClelland, D. C. *The achieving society*. Princeton, N.J.: Van Nostrand, 1961.

McNeill, J. T. *The history and character of Calvinism*. New York: Oxford Univer. Press, 1954.

Maître, J. Les sociologues du catholicisme français. *Cahiers internationaux de sociologie*, 1958, **24**, 104–124.

Manuel, F. E. *The eighteenth century confronts the gods*. Cambridge, Mass.: Harvard Univer. Press, 1959.

Marx, K. *Capital*. New York: Modern Library, 1936.

Marx, K., & Engels, F. *On religion*. Moscow: Foreign Languages Publishing House, 1955.

Mensching, G. *Soziologie der Religion*. Bonn: Ludwig Röhrschied, 1947.

Mensching, G. *Die Religion*. Stuttgart: C. E. Schwab, 1959.

Merton, R. K. Science, technology, and society in seventeenth-century England. *Osiris*, 1938, **4**, 360–632.

Merton, R. K. *Social theory and social structure*. Glencoe, Ill: Free Press, 1957.

Nelson, B. *The idea of usury*. Princeton, N.J.: Princeton Univer. Press, 1949.

Nicholls, J. H. *History of Christianity, 1650–1950*. New York: Ronald Press, 1956.

Niebuhr, H. R. *The Kingdom of God in America*. Chicago & New York: Willett, Clark, 1937.

Niebuhr, H. R. *Christ and culture*. New York: Harper, 1951.

Niebuhr, H. R. *The social sources of denominationalism*. Hamden, Conn.: Shoe String Press, 1954.

Niebuhr, H. R. *The purpose of the church and its ministry*. New York: Harper, 1956.

Norbeck, E. *Religion in primitive society*. New York: Harper, 1961.

O'Dea, T. F. Sociological dilemmas: Five paradoxes of institutionalization. In E. A. Tiryakian (Ed.), *Sociological theory, values, and sociocultural change: Essays in honor of Pitirim A. Sorokin*. New York: The Free Press of Glencoe, 1963. Pp. 71–89.

Parsons, T. *The structure of social action*. New York: McGraw, 1937.

Parsons, T. Christianity and modern industrial society. In E. A. Tiryakian (Ed.), *Sociological theory, values, and sociocultural change: Essays in honor of Pitirim A. Sorokin*. New York: The Free Press of Glencoe, 1963. Pp. 33–70.

Pin, E. *Pratique religieuse et classes sociales*. Paris: Spes, 1956.

Pin, E. Hypothèses relatives à la desaffection religieuse dans les classes inferieures. *Soc. Compass*, 1962, **9**, 515–537.

Poland, B. C. *French protestantism and the French revolution*. Princeton, N. J.: Princeton Univer. Press, 1957.

Poll, S. *The Hasidic community of Williamsburg.* New York: The Free Press of Glencoe, 1962.

Pope, L. *Millhands and preachers.* New Haven, Conn.: Yale Univer. Press, 1942.

Pratt, J. B. *The religious consciousness.* New York: Macmillan, 1920.

Pratt, J. B. *The pilgrimage of Buddhism.* New York: Macmillan, 1928.

Quoist, M. *La ville et l'homme.* Les Editions Ouvrières. Paris: Economie et Humanisme, 1952.

Radcliffe-Brown, A. R. *Structure and function in primitive society.* Glencoe, Ill.: Free Press, 1961.

Raglan, Lord. Myth and ritual. In T. A. Sebeok (Ed.), *Myth: A symposium.* Philadelphia: American Folklore Society, 1955. Pp. 76–83.

Sansom, G. *A history of Japan to 1334.* London: Cresset Press, 1958.

Sansom, G. *A history of Japan, 1334–1615.* Stanford: Stanford Univer. Press, 1961.

Santayana, G. *Reason in religion.* New York: Scribner, 1936.

Santayana, G. *Interpretations of poetry and religion.* New York: Harper, 1957.

Schmitt-Eglin, P. *Le mécanisme de la déchristianisation.* Paris: Alsatia, 1952.

Schneider, L. Toward assessment of Sorokin's view of change. In G. K. Zollschan & W. Hirsch (Eds.), *Explorations in social change.* Boston: Houghton, 1964. Ch. 15.

Schneider, L., & Dornbusch, S. M. *Popular religion.* Chicago: Univer. of Chicago Press, 1958.

Schreuder, O. Religionssoziologie. Vol. 6. *Staatslexikon.* Freiburg im Breisgau: Herder, 1961.

Scoville, W. C. *The persecution of Huguenots and French economic development.* Berkeley: Univer. of California Press, 1960.

Smith, W. R. *Lectures on the religion of the Semites.* New York: Meridian Library, 1956.

Sorokin, P. A. *Social and cultural dynamics.* Vols. 1, 4. New York: Bedminster Press, 1962.

Swanson, G. E. *The birth of the gods.* Ann Arbor: Univer. of Michigan Press, 1960.

Sweet, W. W. *The story of religion in America.* New York: Harper, 1950.

Tawney, R. H. *Religion and the rise of capitalism.* New York: Penguin Books, 1947.

Tenbruck, F. H. Die Kirchengemeinde in der Entkirchlichten Gesellschaft. Ergebnisse und Deutung der "Reutlingen-Studie." In D. Goldschmidt, F. Greiner, & H. Schelsky (Eds.), *Soziologie der Kirchengemeinde.* Stuttgart: F. Enke, 1960. Pp. 122–132.

Tolles, F. B. *Meeting house and counting house.* Chapel Hill: Univer. of North Carolina Press, 1948.

Toynbee, A. J. *An historian's approach to religion.* New York: Oxford Univer. Press, 1956.

Troeltsch, E. *The social teaching of the Christian churches.* New York: Macmillan, 1950. 2 vols.

Tylor, E. B. *Primitive culture.* (7th ed.) New York: Brentano's, 1924. 2 vols.

Wach, J. *The sociology of religion.* Chicago: Univer. of Chicago Press, 1944.

Wearmouth, R. F. *Methodism and the working-class movements of England: 1800–1850.* London: Epworth, 1937.

Wearmouth, R. F. *Methodism and the common people of the eighteenth century.* London: Epworth, 1945.

Weber, M. Religionssoziologie. In M. Weber (Ed.), *Wirtschaft und Gesellschaft.* Tübingen: J. C. B. Mohr (Paul Siebeck), 1922. Pp. 227–363.

Weber, M. *The protestant ethic and the spirit of capitalism.* London: Allen & Unwin, 1930.

Weber, M. *Gesammelte Aufsätze zur Wissenschaftslehre.* Tübingen: J. C. B. Mohr (Paul Siebeck), 1951.(a)

Weber, M. *The religion of China.* Glencoe, Ill.: Free Press, 1951. (b)

Weber, M. *Ancient Judaism.* Glencoe, Ill.: Free Press, 1952.

Weber, M. *The religion of India.* Glencoe, Ill.: Free Press, 1958.

Weber, M. *The sociology of religion.* Boston: Beacon Press, 1963.

Wickham, E. R. *Church and people in an industrial city.* London: Lutterworth, 1957.

Wiese, L., & Becker, H. *Systematic sociology.* New York: Wiley, 1932.

Williams, J. P., Friess, H. L., Binkley, L. J., Hick, J. H., Cohn, W., & Klausner, S. Z. Symposium: The problem of attempting to define religion. *J. scient. Stud. Rel.,* 1962, 2, 3–35.

Wilson, B. R. *Sects and society.* Berkeley: Univer. of California Press, 1961.

Winter, G. *The suburban captivity of the churches.* New York: Doubleday, 1961.

CHAPTER 21 Political Sociology

SCOTT GREER and PETER ORLEANS

Political sociology would seem to be, simply, the sociological study of politics. But what is politics? As usual, when we venture into a new area for the application of sociology, we begin with definitions from folk thought. Generally, "politics" is seen as the separated realm of government and its behavior. This is what we mean when we "talk politics." At the same time, we talk of "politics" in everyday, nongovernmental, contexts. In office, shop, and school, behavior is explained by being called, rather vaguely, "politics." Some major studies, purporting to be political sociology, have focused upon private organizations (Greer, 1959; Lipset, Trow, & Coleman, 1956; Wilensky, 1956). But is *private* government not a contradiction in terms? If it is not, then the study of politics is simply the study of control systems and contention for control, and the family is political. For control systems are universal attributes of groups; such a political sociology is simply general sociology which is focused upon social control, and control can be studied in many ways, of which sociological analysis is only one.

The analytical theory at the base of soci-

ology today has developed within a frame-of-reference which sees social structure as a limit on and director of behavior. The resulting explanatory theory sensitizes us to certain problems as units, and it also supplies acceptable (because sociological) solutions. Thus a specialized conceptual vocabulary abstracts the sociologically relevant aspects of a given situation, allowing a basis for meaningful analysis and the integration of subunits into a "sociologically" whole picture of the event. If such a derived picture, or interpretation, is scientifically adequate it should, of course, allow prediction and control. Sociology is, then, one way of abstracting from the aesthetic and concrete whole.

Men sometimes speak of "the political, economic, and social aspect" of any given problem that concerns them. Such a trichotomy represents a serious misunderstanding; a sociology which did not include economic and political behavior would be utterly ineffectual. Sociological analysis cannot, however, be an eclectic summation of existing economics and political science. What is needed is real concern with that requirement of systematic theory which demands that concepts be internal to the same system. If this rule is taken seriously, we must translate the vocabulary of politics, both folk and specialized, into the vocabulary of sociological analysis. In the process we can see if any light is shed upon sociological theory and knowledge and whether sociological analysis adds any power to the interpretive schemes now used in understanding politics, government, and the state.

Several strategies may be distinguished in contemporary sociological analysis. (1) The existing social structure is seen as producing individual variables; the structure determines rates for the class, though within the class the individuals who make up the rate may be random from the sociologist's viewpoint. Thus Durkheim explained rates of suicide by the state of the overall national society. (2) Individual variables may be studied as conducive to the production of a social structure in a specified situation. From interaction of personalities one sees the emergence of a constraining group with a normative system. This is the specific concern of such microsociologists as George Homans. (3) Social structure may be seen as self-constraining within the unit; one regularity forces the other. This is the notion of the mutually adjustive system in which deviations from regularity produce responses which restore regularity (though it need not be the previous "state of the system"). (4) The social structure may be seen as a unit interacting with a significant environment. The environment may be organizational, communicational, or the non-human given. Structure and environment interact, with consequent mutual modification. Students of contemporary social change have used this strategy most consistently.

Each of these strategies has been used in the sociological study of politics. The first is evident in the study of voting as an outcome of social differentiation—ethnicity, social class, community type, participation in the parapolitical structure (Berelson, Lazarsfeld, & McPhee, 1954; Campbell, Converse, Miller, & Stokes, 1960). The second approach occurs in studies of the self-selection of elites (Bell, Hill, & Wright, 1961; Hyman, 1959; Lane, 1959). Social structure as self-constraining in the unit underlies several important studies of governmental bureaucracy (Blau, 1955; Kriesberg, 1955; Selznick, 1949), while interaction of the social unit and its environment is the object of studies as disparate as those concerned with the change of leadership in labor unions (Wilensky, 1956), the shift in ethnic background of precinct leaders (Rossi & Cutright, 1961), and the preconditions for national democracy (Lipset, 1960).

Any of these strategies may be applied to behavior singled out as important by folk thought, policy, or sociological theory. The specialized segment of societies called "government" may be so approached. On the other hand, each strategy can be applied to the study of control systems in general, and to contention for control. Here the unit of observation, the site of the problem, is as varied as the groups in the society; the generic approach of the sociologist does not differ.

But the *state* is a type of concrete group that differs in kind from all other groups, and that difference is as important as its similarity. Here the sociologistic fallacy implicit in reducing the larger unit of action to the rules of the smaller (a parallel to the psychologistic fallacy) may create serious difficulties in explaining the simplest social fact. For the state, one of the overwhelming aspects of our historical period, cannot be treated either as an extensive business enterprise or as a small group.

The state differs from other social systems by its inclusiveness. The population of the earth today is entirely included, as citizens, fiefs, or captives of nation-states, and each state is inclusive of both persons and behaviors. One cannot act outside the boundaries of a state, and one's actions must conform to what is permitted by the state under pain of probable sanction. Even birth is a matter of state, an automatic membership. The importance of this fact lies in the relative decline of alternative inclusive systems, those of kin, guild, enterprise, locality group, ecclesia (cf. Nisbet, 1953). The state has become the chief custodian of overall social order; it is monitor, comptroller, arbitrator. For the first time in history the implicit overall order, the "loose confederation called a society," has an explicit formal structure with formal responsibility. At an extreme, this leads to the "totalitarian state," which is simply the completely politicized society.

There are two major sociological definitions of the state, that of Max Weber (1947) and that of Emile Durkheim (1960). Weber, fascinated with the history of complex societies and bearing in mind theories of conquest as the origin of the state, defined it as the monopoly of legitimate violence over a given territory. This definition has limits and implications. It does not, for instance, allow us to discuss nonterritorial or superterritorial units as states. Nor does it allow us to consider the partial cases, the situations in which there is no monopoly, but oligopoly or even a partialed market. Revolution is an attribute of a stateless society in this definition, for a large portion of the population does not accept the legitimacy, and so attacks the monopoly. On the other hand, a family may be a state if it is territorially dominant.

Durkheim (1960), with his interest in primitive societies and societies as wholes, placed a greater emphasis upon the problems of maintaining inner order. His state is a legalist's construction—it is the order which controls interunit relations, within a structure from which there is no appeal. In such a definition two requisites stand out: There must be problems of interunit relations, and there must be a containing structure from which appeal is impossible (Durkheim, 1933; Durkheim, 1958). States, in this view, are not to be identified with territories; the emphasis is upon the social group and its social bonds. Thus nomads may be considered to have a state. Nor is the emphasis upon the monolithic, the

monopolistic, character of the state; attention is directed, instead, to the plurality of contending groups and the emerging order.

Both definitions are useful. The monopoly of legitimate violence yields a clear category in wide use today. Territoriality, however, is not intrinsic to the concept. The powers of states range far afield, and their strength is not a matter of statute miles. An acceptable reconciliation of the definitions might run as follows: A state is a social organization exercising a monopoly of legitimate force, within an inclusive aggregate made up of contending subunits. In this definition the territorial aspect is subordinate to the sociological aspect.

The major empirical problem of political sociology today would seem, then, to be the description, analysis, and sociological explanation of the peculiar social structure called the state. This leads to concern with the structure of this social organization; the nature and conditions of legitimacy, the nature of the monopoly and its exercise, the nature of the subunits and their contention, and the addition or loss of subunits. For in the state we find the contemporary focus of control, the largest and most inclusive unit within which control is exercised, and a system which dominates and legitimates those subgroups which also exercise controls. In the process of studying the state, however, we must keep in mind the contending groups as well as the dominating and legitimate order—the monopoly of legitimate violence, the court from which there is no appeal (Bentley, 1935).

In the remainder of this paper we will discuss each of these areas of inquiry—consensus and legitimacy, participation and representation, and the relationships between economic development and political change. We cannot hope to be definitive, for the more immature a branch of inquiry the more discursive and unsummarized its conclusions. We do hope to indicate major propositions and research accomplishments, as well as problem areas which demand inquiry whether they have received it or not.

CONSENSUS AND LEGITIMACY

The questions of how shared definitions, rules for behavior, and norms defining what ought to be are sustained, transmitted, and changed in a complex society have been at the source of writings concerned with legitimacy. (For a discussion of the historical basis of modern sociology traced through the theorists of the mass society, see Bramson, 1961.) For these questions taken together comprise the problem area of "consensus," the agreed upon definitions of the situation which allow action toward common goals.

Theorists of the "mass society," such as Mannheim (1950), Wirth (1938), Lederer (1940), and Arendt (1954), have viewed modern society with concern. They saw the breakdown of old ties, the development of large scale means of communication, and the aggregation of people in cities as setting the groundwork for totalitarianism, with the manipulative potential of the mass media as its handmaiden. Indeed, early research on the city, the site and essence of the mass society, was promulgated on the assumption that individuals were detached and isolated. Research and thinking about the mass media of communication was to some extent centered on the deleterious effects of manipulation and propaganda.

As Shils (1951) and Bramson (1961) have pointed out, the strength of this view of contemporary society diminished when sociologists "rediscovered the primary group." Beginning in the area of industrial social psychology (Roethlisberger & Dickson, 1939), spreading into the domain of mass communications and voting behavior (Lazarsfeld, Berelson, & Gaudet, 1948), and finally appearing in studies of social organization in the metropolis (Axelrod, 1956; Janowitz, 1952; Wright & Hyman, 1958), sociologists found that modern men were not isolated, but worked, played, came to political decisions, and attended to mass media, in group contexts. Influence on masses was discovered to flow through interpersonal contacts, with opinion leaders in-

terpreting and transmitting information to their publics (Coleman, et al., 1957; Katz & Lazarsfeld, 1955).

The current view of modern complex society is pluralistic, based in large measure on the earlier Durkheimian emphasis on organizations which mediate between the citizen and the state (Durkheim, 1960). This view must still be tempered, however, by the question which prompted the writings of the mass society theorists in the first place: How is it possible, given the proliferation of subgroupings within society, to maintain a viable polity based on consensus?

A first answer to the question derives from the view of social organization as patterned interdependence fashioned by interconnecting lines of communication. It is the economic and social interdependence of the subgroups within society which, through the agencies of communication and cultural transmission, generates and sustains the consensus at the foundations of political order. Insofar as citizens are subjected to the same kinds of experiences, substantive consensus increases, together with support for the procedural norms of pluralistic politics.

Although varying social and economic conditions (and specific membership groups) modify the effects of exposure, individuals are subjected to common experiences by the media and by the educational system. Sociologists have neglected to explore the full extent to which the media transmit and inform general perspectives. Similarly, little research has been done on the transmission of political ideologies, beliefs, and techniques through the public schools. The few studies available indicate that a very simple vocabulary does exist, one which flattens, blurs, and personalizes public issues, resembling strongly the results of experimental rumor diffusion (Allport & Postman, 1952; Greer, 1963; Merton, 1957). It has been left primarily to the political scientist to emphasize mass culture as a source of symbols which inform, as well as shape, the consensus which cuts across the subgroups of society (De Sola Pool, 1959; Key, 1961; Lang &

Lang, 1959). This consensus may be no more, as V. O. Key suggested (1961) than an agreement on the legitimacy of authority; to a sociologist this is an important consensus.

The perspectives transmitted by public agencies of communication are more general than those which have been the subject of research in political behavior—the specific issues concerning elections and party affiliation. Following Parsons' (1959) discussion of consensus and cleavage in the polity, we think these general and abstract norms, which are transmitted by the media and the other common elements of "mass culture," should be distinguished from the specific rules of political behavior and knowledge relevant to the political issues of the day. The former constitute the broad bases of the political system. Thus, for example, there are norms supporting the competitiveness of the two-party system but limiting the extent to which competition has free reign. This type of consensus provides the basis on which agreement about competing political alternatives may finally be achieved. Such norms are formally similar to the "norm of reciprocity" which Gouldner (1960) discussed. Other norms are those which generate specific perspectives relating to party affiliation, provide information concerning issues of current interest, and information concerning the operations of government.

Public Agencies

By providing the groundwork for a "universe of discourse," public agencies of cultural transmission—mass media and public education—perform an integrating function in multigroup society. They also play an informing role and, regardless of the number of steps from the media to the individual citizen, these channels transmit definitions proferred by those in power and developed through public discourse. They also provide feedback from the citizens in the form of "public opinion." Studies such as Warren Breed's (1955) "Social Control in the News-

room," focusing on the social organization of the media, have major implications for the study of political communication and culture. Research is needed to determine more precisely what is communicated to the public and how the social organization of the media, as well as the place of the media in the total complex of society, influences the public's access to the relevant political information.

Walter Lippmann (1922) did much to demonstrate how uninformed the public is. More recently Hyman and Sheatsley (1950) presented a survey on the status of public opinion, indicating that "in almost every instance where the polls have tested public information, at least twenty per cent of the population have revealed complete ignorance." Greer found that only 20 per cent of a suburban sample knew any major provision of a Charter for which they voted in referendum (Greer, 1963). Janowitz, Wright and Delaney (1958), in a study of public perspectives on public bureaucracy, also found a considerable amount of ignorance about the functioning of governmental bureaucracy, and they raise some major questions about its implications for democratic consent. Research is needed to determine where obstructions occur in the communication process.

The role of the public schools in the political process has received even less attention than the mass media. An exception to this is a study by Litt (1963) which analyzed civic education texts and attitudes of students exposed to the courses in communities differing in socioeconomic status. Litt found that regardless of socioeconomic status all tests stressed the basic tenets of democracy, but differed in the extent to which political participation was encouraged and the political process portrayed as a mechanism for ameliorating conflict. Attitudes of students exposed to the courses indicated that the effects of the texts were to level differences among communities in support for democratic processes, but the texts apparently did not affect attitudes toward citizen participation. As Litt suggested, attitudes toward political activity are so affected by other agencies that the civic education program had little independent effect.

Other studies dealing with education and political behavior indicate that the better educated persons are more politically active, attend to the available information, and exhibit greater political awareness and interest than persons with less education. The processes by which education politically activates citizens are yet to be explored. Lipset (1959) presented evidence indicating that better educated people are less prone to extremist politics, regardless of the direction of the extremism. He suggested the proposition that the lack of a "rich, complex frame of reference" explains the relationship between low social status and predisposition toward authoritarian political systems. Other data indicate that the better educated are more tolerant of nonconformity (Stouffer, 1955).

Studies such as *The People's Choice* (Lazarsfeld et al., 1948) and *Voting* (Berelson et al., 1954) indicate that the media heighten public interest in political campaigns. By presenting the campaign, the media stimulate public awareness of candidates and issues (even though they apparently do not directly influence voting intentions) and heighten partisanship. As Lang and Lang (1959) suggested, by presenting the issues of the campaign the media can indirectly influence the outcome of the vote. For example, the authors of *Voting* state that the "salience of class issues was brought home through the mass media." Apparently socioeconomic issues were also crucial to the outcome of the national election in 1948 (Berelson et al., 1954).

Riesman (1950) observed that the media sometimes create public opinion through presenting test cases of norms in conflict. The responses of citizens to the pollster then represent an objective gauge of the legitimacy and popularity of public decisions. The "feedback" of media effects through the findings of the sample survey is already

a major aspect of our political process. It has been discussed at some length by Key (1961), but is seldom the focus for sociological research (Mosteller, 1949; Rogers, 1958; White, 1961). In general, investigators tend to specialize in one arc of a circle which leads from action to media to poll findings and back to the modification of action by the political elite. (As a result, a true "check list of operative democracy" is difficult to score.) Yet if Speier (1950) was correct in tracing the origins of "public opinion" to the growth of the newspaper and other media, a logical extension would include the public opinion poll as a major mechanism in the creation of public opinion.

The Family as an Agent of Political Socialization

Hyman's (1959) survey of the research literature on political socialization points to the importance of family influence on political activity. A series of studies examining the relationship between politically relevant attitudes of children and their parents yielded, in the main, coefficients of correlation of around .5. Research on party preference yielded even greater coefficients, and one study (Weltman & Remmers, 1946) yielded a median correlation value of .9. Similarly, the Elmira Study (Berelson et al., 1954) indicated that family voting tradition was a better predictor of the political allegiances of respondents than either socioeconomic position or religion, while Maccoby, Matthews and Morton (1954) found that in 86 per cent of the cases in which parents are of the same party, their child chooses that same party. Even the coercive influences of the work situation do not appear to alter familial influence on voting preference. Shepard and Kornhauser (1956) interviewed members of the United Automobile Workers living in Detroit. Presumably, all the respondents were exposed to the strong pro-Democratic influences from the union, yet these researchers found that of those whose fathers were Democratic,

84 per cent reported voting for the Democratic presidential candidate, whereas only 49 per cent of those whose fathers were Republican voted for the Democratic candidate. Lipset, Trow and Coleman (1956) noted that the influence of the family on political affiliation appeared to carry over into union politics. Although they did not have the data to test the hypothesis that men brought up in Democratic families, and with Democratic allegiances, would be more likely to develop a liberal ideology with respect to union politics than those brought up as Republicans, they did find that, holding constant all other relevant background variables, political party allegiance was correlated with ideological convictions on union matters.

One of the interesting findings in Hyman's (1959) analysis of research on political socialization was that the correlations between the general ideological perspectives of parents and children were usually lower than those pertaining specifically to party preference. In his analysis of patterns of differentiation in preadult life, Hyman found that the relationships between socioeconomic status, sex, and the like, and political interest and affiliation were much the same for adults and high school students. Ideology (authoritarianism, tolerance for nonconformity), however, was not clearly differentiated among children. Hyman (1959) suggested that "Party loyalty, because of the simplicity of symbols involved or because of greater direct indoctrination or the lesser range of alternatives available, is more readily transmitted in the course of socialization." Apparently, then, broader political perspectives develop via the mechanisms of adult socialization, in the confrontation of the adult and his social environment. Little work has been done to explore the processes of adult socialization.

The relationship between political and economic ideology and party affiliation has been noted in studies of voting behavior. It is not, however, until one becomes a political actor that the congeries of perspectives woven into an amorphous ideology become relevant. But how are such perspectives shaped and how do they become differentiated by party affiliation? We would suggest that the media play an important role in the adult socialization process. Information relevant to political action, the everyday reporting of national and international events, is presented within a party context. For example, when a representative states his opinion on an issue, the media generally indicate the representative's party affiliation. As noted previously, the media serve to heighten interest in political campaigns. They dramatize politics and hand the citizen some ready-made topics for discussion. Reasons for supporting one candidate or another, one party versus another, become sharpened and further shaped in the citizen's conversations with his friends and work associates.

Interpersonal Influences and Parapolitical Structures

As noted before, studies of voting behavior and studies on patterns of influence indicate that the small group, and the network of a person's social relationships, intervene between the mass media and the individual. This was a finding of the Lazarsfeld, Berelson and Gaudet (1948) study of the 1940 election. In a study of opinion leaders, Merton (1957) added to the growing body of evidence underlining the importance of the social context for political influence. He found that opinion leaders acted as channels of information, filtering the material offered by the media and providing a standard against which the information was to be judged. He isolated two types of leaders—the "local" and the "cosmopolitan." Each was influential in its special domain, and each had characteristic modes of influence.

Janowitz (1952), in his study of the community press, identified the ways in which the press and networks of social relationship interact to form the basis for integration of communities in the metropolis. The study of opinion leadership in Decatur, Illinois, was an elaboration of this same tradition of research; Katz and Lazarsfeld (1955) sought to determine the structural position of opinion leaders and the nature of the flow of influence. They found that leaders tended to specialize in particular domains, but opinion leaders tended to be found in all social groups and strata. Only in the area of public issues was there a concentration of leaders in the highest status, but the evidence indicated that influence probably flows from this group to people of lower status. (It is important to remember, however, that the "flow" was weakest in the domain of public affairs; indeed, it was a mere trickle. This may have been partly because the sample was composed of females.) In the Elmira Study (Berelson et al., 1954) opinion leaders were distributed in every status level, and conversations about the campaign took place predominantly among people of similar social backgrounds. In the study of a referendum cited earlier, Greer found political conversation most commonly occurring with relatives, friends, work associates, and neighbors in that order. Agreement between the "opinion group" and respondents declined in the same order (Greer, 1963). Studies of diffusion of information concerning new drugs indicated that both integration in a network of social relationships and access to information are of crucial importance.

These studies all emphasize the importance of social integration through interpersonal relationships. They raise the question of how variations in the structure of interpersonal relations mediate access to the flow of information. Although everyone has access to the mass media, there is variation in access to interpersonal relations through which information generated by the mass media is interpreted and imbued with political significance. Thus variation in the structuring of interpersonal relations (we may call these opportunity structures) may have significance for the political efficacy and attachments of different portions of the population, for integration may take a number of forms. Greer and Orleans (1962) showed that differences in the characteristics of residential areas are associated with differences in access to what they termed the parapolitical structure—the network of social relationships which transmit politically relevant information even though they are not manifestly political in their functions. These differences in access to the parapolitical were then shown to have consequences for political behavior. Specifically, where access to both the media and personal relations existed, political competence and the likelihood of participation in the political process were higher.

A wealth of studies shows that people of lower socioeconomic status, the more poorly educated, and those in lower-status occupations have lower levels of social involvement than people of higher socioeconomic status (Wright & Hyman, 1958). They are less likely to be involved in formal and informal associations, and less likely to be politically active. Although it is possible that there is something resembling a general factor of involvement or activity, these studies of personal influence and social and political involvement suggest that social integration is a precondition for political involvement.

The picture of the United States given in this research literature shows little resemblance to a mass society of isolated and manipulated individuals. Rather it appears that certain segments of the society do not have access to the opportunities of social and political participation necessary for a viable polity based on democratic consent. Attention of political sociologists to structural sources of cleavage would seem to be a logical next step.

It is within such a context that the question of political and social alienation becomes relevant. Here the work of Kornhauser (1959) or Grodzins (1956) and the research of Trow (1958) and Lipset (1960) point to a relationship between weak social attachmnts and susceptibility to extremist politics. In their major study of propensity to strike, Kerr and Siegel (1954) reach congruent conclusions: Strike-prone industries are those which isolate their workers from the society at large. "Differential association" theory, developed for the study of criminal etiology (Cohen, Lindesmith, & Schuessler, 1956), seems applicable to any area of cultural genesis and transmission. If we focus squarely on political culture as a result of within-group versus between-group interaction, we may develop adequate tools for solving problems of consensus and legitimacy. The mass political culture, the variant subcultures, the syncretisms and incomplete political cultures, as well as the erratically enculturated, the indifferent, the alienated, and the culture heroes, all seem most logically approached in this manner.

VOTING

An exhaustive survey of the literature on voting is not necessary, since several articles devoted to this task are available (Eldersveld, 1956; Lipset, Lazarsfeld, Barton, & Linz, 1954; Rossi, 1959). Instead of summarizing and reviewing this literature we will try to place it in perspective with contemporary political sociology.

Why should the political sociologist be concerned with voting at all? And, what information yielded by research on voting is relevant to a sociology of politics? As Robert Wood (1959) pointed out in his critical review of *American Voting Behavior*:

Able minds reviewing the same data find little agreement as to the prime factors influencing voting choices, the conclusions to be drawn from such a study, or the relevance to central theories (of various disciplines). . . . Inferences to be made for more general propositions about political behavior are similarly divided. . . . For some, voting evidence contains abundant implications for the general study of human behavior; for others, it is barren of utility beyond the act of voting itself.

This confusion derives from the multiplicity of questions posed by researchers who, presumably, are concerned with a single research topic. The reason for this state of affairs lies in the bare empiricism of many studies; what has motivated research into voting is usually only implicit.

It can no longer be considered novel to suggest that much of this research has been biased in the direction of equating "the people's choice" with individual choice. Still it is appropriate to ask what has been done to supplement the psychological determinism which has been so prevalent in the study of voting behavior and what is the proper role of the political sociologist in this endeavor. In other words, given the groundwork laid by the formative investigations of voting behavior, where should we go from here?

If the proper domain of the political sociologist is to be an analysis of the social organization of the state, with all it entails, then the theoretical orientation of voting studies needs revision. Questions of the representativeness of electoral decisions, the dimensions of electoral consensus, and the legitimacy of authority must be directly addressed instead of being dragged in as an afterthought. They must become the focus of attention. This requires that voting research be oriented not so much to an analysis of the determinants of individual electoral choice as to an analysis of variation in the voting of different segments of the electorate and the basis of variation in the social structure.

The electoral process is one of the principal mechanisms through which consensus and cleavage within a modern democratic polity is expressed. Yet, as Lipset (1959b) noted, studies of voting behavior have rarely been designed as investigations of consensus. (One such major effort is the Janowitz and Marvick analysis [1956] of the 1952 national election.) It should be remembered that overt consent is not the only means by which a political organization secures consensus. As McCleery (1957) noted, a common definition of the situation is necessary, even for authoritarian organizations based on force. The conditions for consensus may then be expected to vary with the organization of the polity, though the relationship between the two is complex. At the same time, the mode of consensus within a society is independent of the extent to which a society is integrated (Etzioni, 1961). Voting behavior is, then, only one kind of political activity which may be examined in an analysis of consensus. Particularly in non-democratic forms of political organization, other types of political activity may be more salient, but even in democratic systems consensus results from membership in committed groups, the generalized compliance to agreed upon norms, the "peasant" acceptance of a passive role (Greer, 1961b).

For the majority of citizens in the United States, voting is the only direct political act. How then can voting be used in an analysis of the nature and degree of consensus which obtains in the polity, and what kinds of questions does a consideration of consensus raise for voting behavior?

There is an inherent danger in any pluralistic society of groups proliferating in isolation from one another, co-existing without shared norms. Gusfield (1962) spoke of "superimposed segmentation" when membership in one group requires membership in another. We shall refer to the type of consensus which obtains under these conditions as segmental consensus, and under these conditions one expects serious cleavage between different segments in the polity.

Thus, for example, sociologically distinct segments of a society tend to occupy geographically distinct areas, according to their own volition or as the consequence of structural constraints. Individuals sharing common life styles congregate together, and those possessing certain skills or disabilities are forced together by circumstances beyond their control (Greer, 1962a). Thus localities become the basis for social interaction among relatively homogeneous segments of the population which are differentiated from one another. At the same time, political order is defined by locality. Thus in smaller communities, we should expect less segregation by social type and less segmentation in the polity. Support for this proposition is found in several studies (Campbell & Cooper, 1956; Ennis, 1962; MacRae, 1955), where social class was found a less important source of cleavage within smaller communities. The metropolitan area should produce a highly segmented kind of consensus, one in which interests not held in common might outweigh commonalities. This seems to be the case in many areas studied (Schmandt, Steinbicker, & Wendel, 1961; Sofen, 1963).

A theoretical scheme which allows for the comparative analysis of various enclaves within the society facilitates an assessment of the extent to which the society is characterized by segmental consensus. If extreme segregation is conducive to the genesis of extremist politics, then a structural analysis of voting which locates the sources of cleavage among segments of the electorate should allow us to delineate the points at which extremist politics are most likely to be found.

Political Ecology

Ecological studies of voting behavior provide one means for assessing the degree of segmental consensus which characterizes a given society. Heberle's (1945) analysis of voting in the Schleswig-Holstein region of Germany, focused upon the rise of the Nazi Party, and his reinterpretation of Rice's (1928) analysis of voting behavior in the middle western United States suggest that the chances for extreme parties are greater in one-crop grain-producing agricultural regions than in areas where the agriculture is diversified; his reasoning is congruent with the conditions stated above. Lipset's (1950) analysis of agrarian socialism in Canada further substantiates Heberle's interpretation.

A current formulation of the problem of differential social contexts, and their influence on voting, is found in competing hypotheses concerning suburbanization and voting. The question is whether latent cleavages within the electorate are accentuated by the geographical segregation of redistributed populations, since changes in the boundaries of political divisions do not keep up with shifts in the population. As the population redistributes itself both students of politics and practical politicians are becoming more interested in the question: Do political prejudices (which will eventually be translated into votes at the polls) get transplanted as voters move to the suburbs, or does political conversion occur (Campbell et al., 1960; Lubell, 1956a; Wood, 1958)?

Before definitive answers to these questions can be proffered, information about the selective nature of the migration to the suburbs must be collated with our knowledge of the relationship between social attributes of voters and their voting and with analyses of the mediating effects of different social environments. (Parenthetically, while migration from the farm to the city, which is now of a lesser scale, has attracted less attention, a parallel set of questions regarding the voting behavior of these migrants might also be examined.)

Where the groups which constitute a pluralistic society are interconnected with one another (when there is "linked-segmentation" in Gusfield's [1962] terms) political cleavage is minimized. Overlapping memberships integrate the community by accentuating the commonality of norms. At the same time, however, individual voters may be enmeshed in a network of inconsistent norms. Viewed from this perspective the "cross pressure" (Lazarsfeld et al., 1948) may be seen as a mechanism which alleviates possible discord in the polity, although it may do so by discouraging the voter from casting his ballot. Such an interpretation lends some credence to the argument that a certain amount of electoral apathy is functional for the stability of the polity, but it is the cross-pressure, not the apathy, which is functional. Because social segregation mediates against a viable system of

partially congruent groupings, the extent of segregation should signal the danger of cleavage in the polity. To the extent that physical segregation conditions social segregation, ecological studies of voting provide means of assessment.

Studying the consequence for voting of variation in structural attachments, Pinard (1963) stressed this point of view. He found that in closely knit communities (i.e., those with linked-segmentation) there is greater unanimity of electoral decisions and a greater likelihood that politics endorsed by the formal leadership will be supported than is the case in loosely attached communities. He also found that where turnout is high the result is the increased voting of less attached people (while the electoral decision is likely to be less clear-cut). Consistent with this finding are the results obtained by Horton and Thompson (1962) and Schmandt, Steinbicker, and Wendel (1961). They find increased voter turnout where referenda are defeated and a consistent pattern of negative voting among the economically deprived segments of the population— segments which usually contribute disproportionately to the nonvoters. Their evidence indicates the protest to have come from those most weakly tied to any group in the community (cf. Lederer, 1940).

Levels of Political Community

Voting studies cannot confront questions of the representativeness of the vote or the legitimacy of authority until the social and political context of the vote are considered. Thus it is when the majority-minority status of the voter is considered (as is the case in Ennis' [1962] research), or when the relation of the voter to the existing power structure is recognized and made the focus of analysis (as is the case with the work of Horton & Thompson, 1962; Pinard, 1963), or when economic and demographic characteristics of the electorate are considered (as with the work of Key, 1949; Key & Munger, 1959), that the analyses of electoral behavior transcend the particular historical exigencies and gain a more universal theoretical relevance. When this happens voting studies are elevated from the status of descriptive enumeration to the status of analytical explanations.

A further shortcoming of recent research on voting in this country is its usual restriction to the analyses of presidential elections. One major exception is *Public Opinion and Congressional Elections* (McPhee & Glaser, 1962). While this restriction must be partly attributed to the fact that the presidential election is the one election which directly concerns the total population, and is therefore particularly amenable to survey research sampling techniques, it also reflects a certain disinterest in the phenomena of local government. Where sociologists have concerned themselves with local government, they have chiefly been concerned with "community power structure." The role of the individual citizen is conspicuously absent from such studies, and where he is included it is merely as an observer or assessor of the structure of community power.

As a result of this orientation, our conception of political man may be distorted through the analysis of one small portion of the voter's relationship to a total political situation. It may be that differences in voting between presidential elections and other types of elections are differences in kind rather than differences in degree. However, if the portion of the electorate attracted to the polls by different types of elections varies substantially (i.e., if the occasional and the chronic or committed voters constitute significantly large and distinct portions of the total electorate), then generalizations about voting behavior derived from a single type of election would be open to serious question.

Because of local variations in the electoral system, local elections are particularly difficult to analyze. Differences in the timing of local elections, the form of the ballot, the criteria for election, the nature of the offices involved, the quality of the public records,

and the configuration of contests from community to community present serious problems for comparative analyses (Orleans, 1964). The sheer amount of effort involved in establishing the comparability of different electoral situations is almost prohibitive. Nevertheless, once these problems are surmounted the investigator has at his hands a rich source of material.

The most obvious difference between national and local elections is the difference in turnout; decline in the vote is randomly distributed in the electorate, but systematically related to the nature of the election (Orleans, 1964). The rate of nonvoting becomes much higher in local elections. The implications for the state of political consensus, and thus the legitimation of authority in local government, are serious. Glaser (1962), in a study of fluctuations in turnout, found, however, that certain groups are more likely to fluctuate than others, while Hastings (1956) stated that nonvoters in local elections are the least politicized and most politically fickle element in the electorate. They are also least committed to the local community and the parapolitical structure, according to a study by Greer (Bollens, 1961). Measured by length of residence, commitment was found to predict voting more consistently and effectively than conventional measures of social rank in both local and national elections.

In this perspective the local election may provide a bedrock measure of the state of political consensus, a consensus diluted in the case of more glamorous elections. But uncommonly high turnout in local elections is sometimes indicative of protest voting by the most detached segments of the electorate and, because they often constitute a larger proportion of a smaller vote, the potential for disruption of consensus and continuity is great. A few investigators have analyzed referenda for the creation of "metropolitan governments," and their findings are generally congruent with Horton's thesis. Referenda on complex and novel issues strain the existing consensus and result in a "massification of issues" (Greer, 1963). We have noted that Schmandt found the referendum for the Metropolitan District Plan in St. Louis was overwhelmingly defeated because the ethnic and working-class neighborhoods voted proportionately, rather than abstaining as usual (Schmandt et al., 1961). Salisbury interpreted this as follows: A working system of agreement allows partial and substantive issues to be resolved by "reason," but a basic structural change in the St. Louis polity activates the "class war" (Salisbury, 1961).

Another type of local election which has been systematically probed in recent years is the referendum on fluoridation. Studies indicate the potential value of examining specific political issues, common to a variety of communities, as a way of assessing the state of the political order, the local polity. Particularly important is Coleman's (1957) hypothesis (derived from these studies among others) that communities unused to political controversy are the ones most likely to suffer violent and lasting schism when it does occur. This flexibility, or tolerance for contention, seems to vary, however, with the social characteristics of the community. One study documents a violent and unprecedented conflict which had few lasting effects on the community (Greer, Holderman, & McHugh, 1960).

Until recently, one of the most neglected areas of research on voting was the effect of partisanship, but Adrian's (1952) prospectus on the characteristics of nonpartisan elections and Lee's (1960) study of the politics of nonpartisanship have done much to correct this. Increasingly, however, discrepancies in the reported findings point to the need for further work. Williams and Adrian (1959) and Agger and Goldrich (1958) found that the nonpartisan ballot tends to favor "main street," the most highly organized segment of the electorate in small communities. Orleans (1964), however, found just the reverse in his analysis of nonpartisan elections in two major metropolitan communities. The discrepancy suggests that the organization of electorates varies from setting to setting. These findings, and those of Glaser and Kadushin (1962), suggest that further analyses of voting in different types of elections are needed.

Is it reasonable to assume that elections to local offices (in which participation is known to be greatly reduced) are comparable to presidential elections? How do referenda and bond issue elections compare with candidate elections? What are the effects of uncontested elections? At-large elections? Nonpartisan elections? Special elections? Primary elections? Glaser and Kadushin's (1962) study of "Political Behavior in Midterm Elections" represents an attempt to assess the generality of propositions about voting, derived mainly from presidential elections. Retesting the original propositions developed in *Voting* (Berelson et al., 1954) in the context of midterm elections, they found that most of the findings hold true in the midterm election data as well as in the presidential election data in which they were first discovered. But important differences as well as continuities were discovered, and these differences require further investigation. For example, differences in community contexts were found to affect the solidarity of different segments of the electorate. The meaning of various religious and ethnic statuses was found to vary among the samples, with the consequence that each correlated with electoral participation differently, depending upon the characteristics of ethnic and religious groups and the social contexts in which they were found. In addition to locational differences in voting, Glaser and Kadushin found that with the passage of time the concrete indicators of status change in their significance. Although high or low social status correlated at all times with voting, income was once the most adequate predictor of social status, but occupation has become a more powerful predictor. They reasoned that occupation has become relatively more instrumental as a tie to social groupings that influence individual political behavior (Wilensky, 1961).

Although the purpose of the comparative analysis carried out by Glaser and Kadushin (1962) was to assess the effect of varying type of election on voting behavior, their principal finding pertains to the effects of differences in social context. Otherwise the only major differences between presidential and midterm elections were related to the fact that the latter represent fewer strong stimuli, and therefore the electorate is less interested and less active, and there are few pressures inducing the voters to make consistent decisions.

REPRESENTATION AND PARTICIPATION

The mechanisms of consensus have major implications for the achievement of a political role and behavior in that role. They lead to representation and participation. The concept of participation is meaningless unless it implies influence on the delegate; the concept of representation demands delegation and accountability of some sort and thus participation by the represented. The two principles add up to communication and cooperation in policies backed by the compulsion of the state.

Such communication may take various forms, however, of which the *vox populi* registered by voting machines is only one— thus the controversy over popular versus representative "democracy." The former emphasizes the agreement of the electorate in detail and as a whole with the actions of the state, the delegates merely summarizing popular sentiment. (The mechanisms of initiative, referendum, and recall were intended to produce such results in the states where they were introduced.) The latter emphasizes the commitment of the delegate to the general goals of the community and his responsibility for finding ways to implement those goals. In a normatively heterogeneous community, popular democracy tends to prevent governmental action of any sort, while representational democracy tends to allow action at the price of dominance by one group. Thus the paper ballot election repeatedly urged on leaders of the new nations is frequently rejected precisely because they prefer a legitimacy based on popular acclaim and the police rather than allocation of power by vote: It allows greater effectiveness (Lipset, 1960). The specific norms controlling participation and representation determine the place of a state on the continuum between incapacity (anarchy) on the one hand and the self-perpetuating elite (tyranny) on the other. The ideological heat surrounding the issue sometimes obscures the underlying constraints: In a heterogeneous society the norms of cooperation may not be adequate to the facts of interdependence. At the same time, the organized minority, when it controls the apparatus of state, has a great advantage over the divided and unorganized majority (Mosca, 1939).

The topic of representation has been approached from two separate viewpoints. On one hand, some political scientists have asked: How far does the system of representation deviate from the implied or stated norms of the democratic constitutions? They have analyzed the apportionment of votes to representatives, assuming that arithmetical equality satisfied the norms. They have been criticized, in turn, by others who note that the process of representation is not guaranteed by equal numbered voting districts, that it relies on communication between delegates and citizens.

Others approach the topic by asking: What is the structure of constraints on a representative resulting from the participation of his constituents? Here data are scanty, though the question is central to the study of political systems. Sample survey studies indicate that only a very small proportion of the electorate ever acts to communicate with a representative, other than by voting (Campbell, Converse, Miller, & Stokes, 1960). Various studies of specific interest groups which lobby for their corporate interests indicate that such tactics are sometimes successful, particularly when the interest group represents a large body of voters in the district—prohibition legislation was carried through the state legislatures in this fashion (Garceau & Silverman, 1954). A number of investigators have studied the patterning of roll-call votes and find regularities and even scalability in such behavior (Derge, 1958; Key, 1949; MacCrae, 1952; Truman, 1959). In general, party policies predominate when they do not come into basic conflict with regional norms or interests in the representative's district. Thus Key (1949) found that southern congressmen were consistent supporters of the national Democratic party on most New Deal and foreign relations bills, but not on actions relevant to race relations.

Such findings move from the social characteristics of the voting district (and, in some cases, the delegate) to the assumed significance of the policy at issue for such persons. They indicate that certain "sacred schisms" in the electorate (race, religion, class) have great and continuous constraining power on the behavior of elected representatives. Presumably this is a result of political wisdom, which interprets the issue through a knowledge of the voters' probable reaction, although these studies cannot demonstrate it, and one observer has recently suggested that it is only partially true. After several years experience as an observing participant in state government, he concluded that the delegates act in a situation of very incomplete information, observing political "rules" by default because they have no others, and seldom testing their utility (Long, 1963). The key question, the nature of feedback from the actions of the electorate to the actions of their representatives, is not, at present, answerable.

We have discussed only American representation, and have emphasized the problem of communication and influence between electors and delegates. A general question which can be answered only through comparative studies is: What difference does the franchise make to the fortunes of groups and the operation of the state? This question, whose assumed answer underlies various approaches to representation, has not been empirically investigated, except in a major study of Negro representation in the American South (Matthews & Prothro, forthcoming). Studies of decision-making in the Soviet Union yield some clues as to the politics of a state without contention at the polls; these indicate fierce, underground political struggles between representatives of different bureaucratic segments—the state, the party, the army, and so forth. Formal compliance of the electorate does not abolish representation and participation in politics, it simply transforms them (Inkeles, 1959).

The legitimate, representative government brings the schisms and struggle in the larger society into the small-scale arena of the parliamentary assembly. The latter constitutes a social system in its own right, one which changes the meaning of "public issues" as it turns them into the parliamentary game. Legislative behavior has been studied, recently, by a number of investigators: Meyerson and Banfield (1955) traced the career of an issue through the Chicago City Council; Sayre and Kaufman (1960) analyzed policy-making in New York City; Banfield (1961) traced all major issues over a two-year period in Chicago; and Walter (1962) studied the natural history of several issues in a small southern city. State legislatures have been studied in a comparative framework (Wahlke, Eulau, Buchanan, & Ferguson, 1962) and through time. Congress has been the subject of several specialized studies (Bailey, 1950; Key, 1949; Robinson, 1961; Truman, 1959), and Alger (1961) analyzed the United Nations General Assembly as a parliamentary body.

The Behavior of Representatives

An important finding is the remarkable stability of the indigenous, partially unwritten, "rules of the game." Another is the tendency for prolonged face-to-face interaction to produce close personal relations across lines of party, race, region, and other social differences. A high degree of cooperation occurs in the working task forces of a legislature, and there is considerable stability in leadership. New roles continually emerge, based upon variations in technical competence among legislators; these are frequently accompanied by "bridging roles" between legislature and administrative agencies.

Dependable regularities are, however, not common to all legislatures. In some cases, the average representative is part of a "mass," manipulated by a few leaders and acting in ignorance of the issue (Garceau & Silverman, 1954); in some countries fisticuffs are common in the Chamber of Deputies; even the United States Senate has been the scene of mayhem. The conditions under which the assembly develops and maintains controlling norms that cross parties and continue through time are not spelled out. One would hypothesize the following at a minimum: an underlying stability in the normative system of the society and its party system; effective consensus on norms relevant to contention for control; a dependable degree of insulation of representatives from electors; a constitution which forces agreement on a range of basic decisions. Legislative assemblies vary from stasis and deadlock (or dictatorship by a self-perpetuating minority) to anarchy and deadlock; the reasons for such variation demand comparisons and types of analysis not yet brought to bear in an adequate fashion. We have been able to assemble the results of scattered studies facing some sociologically relevant problems of a peculiar type of group—one which is a space-binding unit, yet frequently a strong, concrete, localized group; one which is highly organized, yet miscast as any sort of bureaucracy; one which is an organization of leaders, yet organized with its own leaders; one which may have a very high turnover of personnel, yet a very great continuity of organizational structure. We have been unable to find a study by a sociologist of such groups.

Equally relevant is the task of describing and analyzing, in its relation to the structure of the state, the role of the political head. Most sociological discussion (e.g., in elementary texts) has paralleled Weber's (1946) essay on the presidency. Using his typology of authority, he noted the extreme importance of charisma in the office of the American President. His shrewd observation of the freedom this yields our political head versus the party system still seems a fertile lead (though he overestimated the bureaucratic organization of our parties). It indicates, for one thing, the importance of the public to which the delegate must appeal (in this case, the entire national electorate), and therefore the heterogeneity of groups which must be tendered some sort of access. Sociologists, however, tend to use the political terms of Weber as adequate explanation, attempting little in the way of their reformulation and empirical test.

The word charisma would seem to be freighted with surplus meaning. In Weber's terms it is unusual quality *imputed* to the leader, but is this not true to a degree of anyone who succeeds in achieving the presidency? And what of the "charisma of office"? Is such a term usable, and if so what separates the three sources of authority? Is it possible that all three aspects of authority are conferred in the American electoral system, with its emphasis upon the sanctity of party affiliation and presidential office (tradition), the relevance of complex, technological issues (legal-rational), and the unusual qualities of a man (charisma)? If this were a plausible contention, we should use a logic more complex than simple Aristotelian types.

The political head has been studied in a framework which emphasizes both the bridging function of the role and the potentiality for instigating action. Thus the common approach to the presidency uses "game theoretical" terms (with very little rigor) and biographical or historical data (Laski, 1940; Rossiter, 1956; Wilson, 1916). Some observers concentrate upon the organizational constraints of the office; Lubell (1956a) emphasized, for instance, the overweening importance of the balance of power in the Congress, while Seligman (1955) documented the sheer growth in size and complexity of the office of President itself. At other levels of government, Banfield (1961) created an organizational portrait of the big city political head, the mayor of Chicago. What emerges from analysis of issue determination, in six major Chicago issues, is a picture of the leadership role rigorously limited by the possibilities of consensus among a heterogeneous collection of interest groups and a leader who will validate anything the major interests can agree on. Sayre and Kaufman (1960) described a "weak mayor city," New York, and their picture is congruent with that of Chicago, modified by a powerful, nonresponsible, executive committee which makes the major fiscal decisions for the city.

It may be that political sociology is most useful in analyzing the constraints upon the political head. Certainly, the few empirical studies cited lean heavily in that direction. On the other hand, the almost completely jettisoned approach called "the study of social action" might yield additional power to sociological analysis. Organizational analysis, with its emphasis on the ruthlessly simplified system of structural constraints, may contain a hidden bias which prevents any freedom or innovation on the part of even the head of a polity. Giving our social actor more choice, within his cage of constraint, might improve our empirical power (Long, 1963; Wrong, 1961). This topic, however, requires a re-examination beyond the scope of our paper.

Participation and Interest

Participation, with its consequence in representation, is usually conceived as a device for translating the effective societal interests into political power. The legislative assembly is, then, the mechanism for the ordering of those interests and the allocation of costs and benefits in the use of the state's authority. Participation has generally been studied through either a comparison of rates for different social categories, or analysis of the organized groups which take action at some stage in the policy-making process.

Differential participation in politics has been the subject of widespread and careful study, partly because it is amenable to sample survey techniques. As we noted earlier, participating in the vote is highly correlated with social rank, modified by stability and familism. This higher rate of voting is accompanied by better knowledge of the political process and the political topics at issue, as well as a much more consistently positive response to Campbell's Sense of Political Efficacy scale (Campbell et al., 1960; Greer, 1962c; Janowitz, Wright & Delaney, 1958; Sykes, 1951). In summary, persons more educated, higher paid, and with more highly regarded jobs are more likely to be better informed and interested in politics.

Does high participation result in greater influence upon the political system? Donald Matthews (1954) documented the disproportionate number of elected representatives, at every level of government, who come from the same social categories as the high participators. This cannot be interpreted as a direct result, however; intervening is the process controlling the selection of candidates. Even the more "working class" Democratic Party tends to select "middle class" candidates. It seems plausible that the same characteristics which are associated with voting are associated with running for office. (Thus the poorly educated, poorly paid, unskilled worker would still be a striking deviant in most electoral contests in the United States.) Indications are that this is true elsewhere, but not nearly as much so; stronger party systems and working-class parties tend to open the political arena to the lower socioeconomic categories (Matthews, 1954; Miller, 1958). Whatever the social background of political officials, however, Matthews warned us against the easy assumption that it provides any automatic predictor of either ideology or their political behavior. That connection is also loose. More important is the make-up of the political public and the kinds of issues that will "sell." Here the poor would seem to be particularly without political access in a nation with a majority of its voters relatively well educated, well paid and with major stakes in the *status quo* (The plight of the "poverty stricken" in America today stems in part from the general prosperity of the mass of citizens. They have few allies.) (Harrington, 1962).

There are other organized groups which allow access, indirectly, to the political actors. These parapolitical organizations include the entire spectrum of voluntary organizations, are widespread, and are generally open to almost anyone (Greer & Orleans, 1962). When we look at the evidence concerning these organizations, however, we find that the same disproportion in participation by social class is evident although mediated by the type of local community. Within organizations the leaders are disproportionately from the higher social ranks (Bell, Hill, & Wright, 1961; Hausknecht, 1962). Even in the one common working-class organization, the labor union, elected leaders tend to come from the more highly regarded and rewarded jobs (Greer, 1959). Thus the class difference in participation and representation holds at every level of social organization. It varies somewhat by levels, however; wherever the organization requires activation of the lower social ranks and ethnic minorities, their representation increases proportionately—in labor unions, in city government, and, in general, at the local level (Bell et al., 1961; Greer, 1958).

Differential access to elective power is reflected in appointive power. The court system is also predominantly staffed by white middle-class men; the grand jury presents an extremely biased sample of American citizenry (Lemert, 1945; Robinson, 1950). And the actions of the courts are equally biased: The best predictor for length of sentence for the same offense was, in one study, racial background (Lemert & Rosberg, 1948), while the differential treatment of the poor and the ethnic citizenry by the police has also been documented for various cities (Reckless, 1950; Westley, 1953). Such differences in the administration of justice are at the very base of politics, for the protection of person and property is a major power of government, that "monopoly of legitimate violence."

Howard Brotz (1959) recently attempted to frame the question of representation and participation in terms of "first class citizenship." Whose concerns are paramount, whose interests count, in American politics? Such a question subsumes both the difference in access to policy formation, and the question of citizenship. The latter asks, in sociological terms: What are the minimal rights and duties of membership in the polity? How do these vary by categories of citizens? The classic answer is that of the Lynds (1929; 1937) echoed by many community studies carried out in the three decades since their work: The middle class of Main Street are the norm of the first-class citizen. The question of citizenship is distinct from that of influence, however. It is a question of legal power allocated to the individual in a certain category; it becomes a question of public determination only when traditional role assignments are called into question (as in Germany under the Nazis, or in the American South today).

Both meanings of "first class citizenship" are involved, however, in the shift of community structure that has taken place since "Middletown" was written. Although Main Street is over-represented at all levels of government, it has ceased to be the model; instead, the enormous urbanized area with concentration and segregation by social class and race is the norm. The consequent separation of social categories has accompanied (and probably helped produce) a fragmentation of the prestige system and, consequently, the definition of a first-class citizen (Goldschmidt, 1950). As legislative voting districts come to coincide with the settlements of the poor and ethnic, there is an increase in their representation at the level

of city, state, and federal politics. Within
the central city, the increasing proportion
of the voters made up of ethnics and the
working class results in a striking increase
in their legislative power. As a result, the
pressure for a polity in which their interests
are recognized grows, including pressure for
minimal equality of rights and duties
(Greer, 1963; Watson & Romani, 1961).
Increased participation in the vote, relative
to such voting districts, brings increased
representation, while the representatives of
minorities, in turn, are forced to fight as
"race men."

We have discussed representation and participation by social characteristic as *distributive* phenomena. As Blumer (1948) noted,
little significant action, aside from voting
and shopping, occurs outside a group context. A major emphasis in the sociological
analysis of politics has been the participation
and representation of corporate groups.
Arthur F. Bentley (1935), a political sociologist largely unknown to sociologists, insisted on a wholly corporate vision of
politics; in his approach there were only
groups as usable units. Groups were, in
turn, organized on the basis of interest, and
politics was their contention for control.

This has been the major task taken by
students of corporate participation and representation. A wide range of studies has
portrayed the politics of agriculture, medicine, veteran's benefits, water resources, and
others (Garceau, 1941; Kile, 1948; Ostrom,
1953). The emphasis has been upon identification of the groups which do (or do not)
get through to the policy-making process,
how they do it, and what the consequences
are. This "pressure group" approach to politics has emphasized the discrepancy between
the electoral consequences of action and
the substantive consequences; interest groups
exploit both "grass roots" support, on one
hand, and the indeterminacy of the voters'
response on the other. The response of the
electorate between elections, aside from letters
to congressmen, is typically the presentation
of a point of view at a congressional hear-

ing. The self-selected representatives of the
people are not unrepresentative per se, but
the "noise" possible in the communication
system has fascinated analysts. It is a long
time between elections, and sample survey
data are not available on many issues—in
fact, the voters have no opinion on many
issues. The arguments of self-selected spokesmen in face-to-face confrontation probably
weigh heavily in the decisions of legislators,
for argument, threat, reward, in more or
less tangible form, can be brought to play.
The major sociological question, then, becomes the relative weight to assign different
media of influence in predicting the response of the representatives.

Many of those who espouse the interest
group theory of politics also emphasize the
efficacy of specific groups in controlling
major policy decisions. C. Wright Mills
(1956), a major spokesman, emphasized an
image of a unified "power elite," a holding
company of big business, labor, and the
military, which ran the government. Relying on data concerning the social background of major decision-makers, he inferred from this a kind of solidarity and
influence which monopolized the decision-
making process. Brady (1943) sketched out
a monolithic control system among business
firms, with implications that it is directly
translated into political power, while Hunter
(1953) and others described the dictatorship
of business in the smaller arena of the city.
In this extreme "interest group" approach,
the only interests represented are a few,
well organized, oligarchically controlled segments of the economy, work force, and
citizenry; they, and they only, really participate in government.

Other scholars, equally committed to an
interest group approach, emphasize the
proliferation of interest groups and the
uneasy balance among them which frequently results in stalemate. Riesman (1950)
coined the term veto groups to summarize
this state of affairs. Lubell's picture of the
American polity since the 1940's is one
which emphasizes an even balance in the

Congress and the consequent immobility of the government (Lubell, 1956a; Lubell, 1956b). At the local level, Banfield (1961) argued for the *inability* of local government in a great city, one supposedly dominated by the most powerful "machine" in the United States, while Sayre and Kaufman (1960) analyzed a city government which resembles Byzantium in its complexity, inertia, and scale.

The image of government as holding company for the interests of the economic elites is clearly presented in Floyd Hunter's (1953) study of "community power structure." Using an approach which identified power by reputation, he isolated several dozen men whom he considered to be the executive committee of Atlanta. This has been criticized by those who insist that power must be demonstrated through the analysis of specific issues and their outcome (Kaufman & Jones, 1954). Empirical studies of issues do not seem to support Hunter's contention; Dahl (1961) indicated there is a separate elite controlling each kind of issue; Scoble (1961) demonstrated bifurcation and lack of cohesion in one local elite; Banfield (1961) and others emphasized the looseness of organization and high rate of turnover among "civic leadership." On the other hand, reputational studies using similar methods identify similar clusters of highly visible persons to whom control is imputed (Miller, 1958; Pellegrin & Coates, 1956).

These two points of view are hardly reconcilable, yet it is difficult to disprove either. To demonstrate the existence of a "power elite," one would have to show a social organization (1) being formed by delegates from private interests, (2) persisting through time, (3) attacking the major issues of the day, (4) and determining the outcome of those issues, through internal coordination of resources and the application of pressures to the formal decision-makers. General agreement between the organizational aims of these delegates and the outcome of governmental decisions is not sufficient proof of effective power. To disprove Mills's contention, however, is equally difficult; one must demonstrate that one or the other of the four conditions does not hold.

The conflicting findings and interpretations have a number of possible explanations. It is likely that the method is so weak that the conclusions are built into the research design in either or both of these approaches. It is also, however, likely that community control systems vary greatly by the scale of the local community. The size and nature of its population and economic base are reflected in segmentation and the resulting problems of integration for the polity. So some cities, probably the smaller and more parochial, may have a "community power structure" while others do not. Finally, it is possible to reconcile the two views, that of the unitary power structure versus that of shifting coalitions selected from "influentials," if one sees them as indicating different, but complementary, aspects of the local polity.

As Schulze (1961) demonstrated, some of the "mystery of power" can be dispelled if we place the local community in a framework of social change. His study of Ypsilanti shows a developing schism between political control and the major economic elites of the city; this resulted from the merger of local firms with large corporations and the transformation of the city into a "branch-plant town." Such processes affect not only smaller cities but the great metropolitan conglomerates as well. The vulnerability of economic elites to purely local threats diminishes with merger in national systems; so does their commitment to the state of the local polity (Banfield, 1961; Greer, 1962b; Long, 1962). In consequence, the formal agencies of the government and the political leaders dominate public decisions in the metropolis.

Again, it is worth remembering that the nature of decisions may determine the kind of control possible. The allocation of resources to national defense is a kind of decision on which there is general, overall agreement in times of national tension. Since the outbreak of World War II, through six presidential terms, money has been regularly appropriated at about the level requested. The already established tasks of government have the same status: They are continued, their resources rising with population and gross national product. But when we look to innovation, governmental invention in the face of new conditions, we find little indication of capability at any level of government. And here we must remember Lubell's (1956a; 1956b) emphasis on the even balance of power on each issue and, behind that, the balance of interest groups. These are the veto groups whose joint product is stalemate. It is highly significant that Mills (1956) devoted very few paragraphs to the United States Congress in his description of "the power elite"; the powerful roles in Congress interlock and form the stalemate.

Many interest groups, organized and corporate bodies sharing common requisites, participate in governmental decision-making and are thus represented in the polity. They participate, however, within the framework of the given balance of political power and the established programs of government. They are represented at every level: in the choice of nominees and the campaign for office, in the elected representatives and the action of the congressional body, in the hearings before new law is considered, and in the deliberations of the agencies which administer the laws. The range is wide—consisting of economic producers, distributors, and consumers; ethnic groups, professional guilds, and occupational societies; and regional organizations with specific regional interests.

Their representation is, however, a function of the overall structure of the state. When such groups are permitted, they emerge; their points of access vary, however, by the location of legislative power and administrative discretion. (Thus the opponents of metropolitan government in greater Lon-

don cannot go to the electorate or the local political heads; decision is in Parliament.) The hearings of an appointed committee of nongovernmental persons is the major arena of contentions (Smallwood, 1964). Their effectiveness in controlling decisions, as the organization of the state varies, is hardly known, and is a major subject for inquiry. Approaching their behavior in Durkheim's (1960) framework, we may ask: Are these the subgroups which, controlled by the state yet exercising a veto power over the state, allow for a maximum of choice on the part of the citizen? If so, can they exist in a fully politicized state? Some theorists of the mass society answer no (Lederer, 1940; Nisbet, 1953). Comparison across polities, across time, across groups, and across issues is the only way to settle, empirically, some of the polemical questions raised by Mills (1956), Riesman (1950), and others.

The state, as the explicit organization responsible for the inner order of the society, may be conceived as an organization, a super group. It is one in which organized segments have distinctive roles—rights and duties specified by law and custom. There is interdependence among these subgroups, the kind that Durkheim (1960) called "organic" at the least; there is also communication among them and a consequent ordering of behavior. Their communication and mutual influence is multifarious and diverse, but when it deals with rights and duties guaranteed by law (or threatened by change of law) it is carried out through the organization of the state. The party is the entrepreneur of their interests, and the new party rises when no existing party exploits the demands of threatened or expanding segments of the society.

Thus Heberle (1945) demonstrated the close connection between the threatened interests of the small farmers and businessmen and the rise of national socialism in Schleswig-Holstein. Neither the conventional parties nor the Communists spoke for the interests of these economically endangered populations and, as in other countries, they moved toward political entrepreneurs who stood for radical counterattacks on the "modern" trends. (Lipset's [1960] interpretation of extremists groups is similar in outline.) Heberle points out, however, that this was more than a defense of economic interests: It was an effort to defend a way of life and a normative system based upon the small-scale rural society which is everywhere in collapse today among the more prosperous nations. In explaining this peculiar combination of radicalism and piety, he emphasized Tönnies distinction between *Gemeinschaft* (primary society) and *Gesellschaft* (secondary society). A major theme is that of pseudo-*Gemeinschaft,* the evocation of norms appropriate to a rural or small town way of life for the purpose of manipulating the citizens of a large-scale state. Merton (1957) documented such appeals in his study of a bond selling campaign; while Lerner's (1958) study of rapid change in the Middle East, *The Passing of Traditional Society,* presents the cultural discontinuity in dramatic terms. The careers of such American political entrepreneurs as Huey Long, "Pappy" O'Daniel, and "Gene" Talmadge are cited as examples of the same process (Key, 1949; Larson, 1963). Such careers are notably more common in the South, the area in most rapid transition from rural and small-town society to large-scale urban society.

Participation as Ritual

Such phenomena call attention to the ritual functions of participation and the ritual nature of the representative (Lubell, 1956b; Parsons, 1959; Warner, 1963). Elections may be seen as ceremonial affirmation of solidarity. In Durkheim's terms, the collective representations are intensely communicated and the population coheres, first around its respective political moiety, then, after the ceremonial battle, around the resulting unified leadership. Such a viewpoint demands that we pay attention to the modes

of behavior in elections. Robinson (1952) demonstrated the sharply different types of participators, from those involved actively in contention to those who are chiefly spectators of the campaigns, and Riesman (1950) spoke of politics as an article of consumption. Lazarsfeld, Berelson, and Gaudet (1948) demonstrated, however, the increasing polarization of the electorate as the campaign progresses and the decreasing tolerance for the opposition; the indifferent spectator is relatively rare among those who vote.

In general, however, the persuasive efforts of the campaign rarely find the enemy; they are addressed to the loyal troops. Lazarsfeld (1948) spoke of the two contending parties as talking past each other. This is congruent with another finding—the consistency of voting by family lineage through time. Party affiliation is almost a hereditary membership in the moiety, and voting for the party of one's family an act of filial piety.

In this respect it resembles religious identification, as interpreted by Herberg (1955). He saw the continuing and increasing importance of religion as the result not of "religious" factors, but of the utility of a denomination in establishing social identity and membership. When two pieties coincide, as with the Catholic voters and the Democratic party, there results a social regularity with great staying power (Greer, 1961c). There are, however, fairly consistent ideological differences between the two major United States parties, and it seems likely that the campaign functions to exaggerate the differences. The polarization of the electorate during the campaign may be the reason why elected leaders of the two American parties present much sharper ideological differences than do the voters. Their task is in part to increase polarization and thus commitment to the party.

The intensification of schism might be expected to endanger the very grounds of consensus for the polity. Certainly elections are viewed in many countries as dangerous to public order. In the United States and

Great Britain, on the other hand, this effect occurs rarely. At the basis of overall procedural stability probably lies the two-party system (Schattschneider, 1942). Two parties, competing for control over the same voters, tend toward "antagonistic cooperation" as they appeal to the same array of social segments. When a third party appears it tends to increase radical conflict; not only does it clarify the social differences in the bases of the older parties, but it has an obvious strategic interest in augmenting their disagreements. So overwhelmingly popular are the older parties, however, that the new party cannot win. The older parties in their competition then coopt the ideas of the third party, destroying some of its social base in the process. Thus the party vote is a reaffirmation of the state, and the party system has become an informal part of the basic constitution.

The nature of the party organization would, then, produce different sorts of piety and affirmation. In certain cases it would reflect commitment to social class, race, or religion; in others adherence to a sacred ideology strengthened in combat; or in still others a marginal choice reflecting merely family and community norms (Lubell, 1956a). So loose and heterogeneous is the American party system that each type of loyalty seems relevant. Discrimination among the electorate by this criterion should greatly increase an understanding of the meaning of the vote and party changing.

Because of the ritualization of party loyalty, the candidate is, for many voters, relatively unimportant. Voters are represented through a traditional identification with party and the mechanism of social trust seems to consist in delegation through this symbolic membership. But partisan membership is not perfectly inherited; each new generation is a problem for each party as the overall social condition of the electorate shifts and, with it, economic interests, ways of life, and normative structures. Both the voters and the party change. This is apparent in the rise of a charismatic top level

political head (Roosevelt in the Democratic Party, DeGaulle in France, Eisenhower in the Republican party) who may have a dynamic effect on the rituals. Voters may move around party solidarity to national solidarity.

This raises again the question of kinds of representation. The most commonly discussed is representation through a party, a holding company for a more or less wide and diverse range of interests. This is complemented by legislative representation through proportionate vote in the districts— it is a sort of arithmetical weighting. There is also, however, "virtual representation," in which the delegate is trusted as representative because he shares the same interests and norms as the constituency, regardless of how he is chosen. (The largely self-selected elites of suburban municipalities are often representatives of this sort [Greer & Orleans, 1962].) There is also representation through the "culture hero," the charismatic leader who is trusted on the grounds of his imputed character. Several observers have noted the rough outlines of charisma in various American campaigns (Campbell et al., 1960; White, 1961), and content analyses have been used in efforts to sketch in "heros of the popular culture" (Lowenthal, 1956). The major types of hero in American society have been tentatively described (Klapp, 1962), and most politicians have definite notions of what an electable social type is. Still, the findings are scanty and usually unrelated to major sociological relevancies. It would be most useful if we knew the basis, in norms and role-systems, of the American political charismas. Knowledge of regional, class, and ethnic variations, as well as the nature and strength of common norms, would help greatly in understanding the dynamics of elections which, when they are national, create a temporary and intermittent national system of communication. Electronic media make possible a form of political communication which is, in some ways, more similar to that of the Athenian democracy than to the American democracy of the nineteenth and early twentieth centuries.

Though the electronic mass media constitute the central arena for the creation of "imputed qualities," the exact implications of these for the inherited party system are difficult to see. One hypothesis is that, by-passing the party system, they increase the importance of direct communication between national contenders and the range of voters. They involve a wider array of voters than the earlier media, and they probably allow a contender to penetrate across party lines more easily than before. As topics of conversation, political programs on television are probably more widely shared, and therefore more conducive to the informal discussion of politics, than the printed word. Thus the political culture is blurred and melded, flattened and stereotyped (Bennett & Tumin, 1949; Berelson et al., 1954; Greer, 1963; Wirth, 1948). Conversation, however, still tends to occur within politically homogeneous groups.

Participation and Cooptation

If the state is the explicit organization of subunits, whose regular and predictable relations are necessary for the persistence of control, then the party system can be seen as one method of *cooptation*. This term, first used seriously as a research tool by Selznick (1949) in his study of TVA, indicates the mechanisms of committing necessary subgroups to the dominant group and the ongoing enterprise. In terms of the state, then, the party system and the right to participate through the vote controls new and politically unbounded social movements. These movements arise through collective behavior, the unanticipated consequences of distributive regularities in the society. They are granted representation in the state through the party system, and the cost is their becoming, in a way, representatives of the state. Thus the American polity has seen, in succession, the entry of European immigrants (from the Irish and Germans to the Italians and Poles), of farmers and manual laborers, of white southerners (after Reconstruction) and, today, of Negroes, into the controlling organizations of the parties, thence to shared control of the state.

As societies increase in scale, the extent and intensity of interdependence also increases (Durkheim, 1933; Wilson & Wilson, 1954). Whether this takes place through formal delegation, "the primal act of organization" (Selznick, 1948), or whether it results from the necessity of assuming steady states in the division of labor, it produces a world in which subgroups must be able to predict gross regularities in the behavior of other groups. At the same time, as the chain of organization lengthens, the possibilities of error, noncooperation, and sabotage increase. One solution to this problem is the increasing internal inclusiveness of the society, cooptation through the universal grant of "first class citizenship" and the widening definition of legitimate interests (Bell et al., in press; Marshall, 1950).

Complex, large-scale societies continually create technological monopolies; this is the gist of the "Durkheim dilemma," as Moore (1951) has called it. These monopolies permit objective alternatives to the subgroups making up the nation, and the practical problems which ensue produce a crude sort of participation by the active group. This remains problematic and disorganizing, however, and citizenship is one solution to this state of affairs. But citizenship, in turn, produces further problems in participation and representation—practical, intellectual, and sociological.

THE STUDY OF ELITES

The term elite is heavily loaded with surplus meaning. An old concept given new currency by Pareto, it has both physical and metaphysical meanings. Pareto (1935) used it in both senses, frequently confusing his discourse beyond explication. By metaphysical connotations is meant the tendency to confuse the given roles in society, the elite roles, with the proper nominees for those roles in the judgment of the speaker. If the elite is defined as the best, without regard to social definition, the term is simply a value judgment, a statement of personal aspiration, disguised as social analysis. On the other hand, the term can have a clear meaning and, therefore, provide grounds for discourse. Such a meaning will be somewhat arbitrary, for usage is confused.

It is here proposed to use elite as a term designating those roles which include the right and duty to exercise direct control over the relevant system. As such, they will be entered in specified ways and will be subject to orderly succession, which is predictable through a knowledge of the role-system and its environing society. An organized structure with a scalar dimension, assigning disproportionate control over collective decisions to some actors, is the basic precondition for elites. Elites can, then, be found in any organized group, and the content of the group action is irrelevant while the judgment of quality in performance is another subject entirely. There can be elites of business, labor, city government, or organized sports, but they need not include spectacular performers in any of their realms. In fact, the relation between control and quality of performance varies considerably among organized systems and is itself a serious problem for sociological analysis.

Because this chapter is a discussion of political sociology, it is primarily concerned with the elite roles in government. Insofar as the parties are a part of the machinery of state, the party elites are also relevant. Such roles never include all who may possibly be significant for the political process; it is more useful to see others as potential elites, as actors exercising power on the elite, and as elites in systems related to the state. This allows us to raise the important question: What other elites are significant for the political elites? Further, what are the relations among elites in general? How are the elites of, e.g., the educational system, the mass media, the economy, and the state,

related? One can approach these problems through many avenues, but the questions are possible only through a rigorous limitation of terms.

The class of roles called, collectively, "political elites," has been approached from two directions. The "circulation of elites" was Pareto's (1935) chief contribution to the metaphors of sociology. Analogous to the metabolism of the physical body, such a circulation was seen as a causal explanation for changes in the character and policy of the state. There has also been a broader concern with the shift in the structure of control and consequent shifts in the elite "table of organization." The distinction is analytically clear but empirically difficult, for a change in the sources of recruitment to the political elite usually accompanies a change in the organization of control within the society as a whole, as well as changes in significant subsegments. Examples would be, in the first instance, the rise of a labor movement; in the second, the widespread corporate merger of firms. Either would change the profile of party elites and would most likely be accompanied by circulation of individuals and of social types.

Circulation of Elites

The circulation of elites implies movement into positions of political control of persons and social types not heretofore eligible; it also implies the outflow of incumbents of the same positions. Considering the elective national offices of the Federal government as a relatively stable set of positions, one can study the changing ethnic composition of that body, shifts by race, nationality of original immigration, and religion. (One can also study the changing social class composition; except for a decline in the category "farmer" there has been remarkably little change [Matthews, 1954].) Henry Adams (1931) spoke eloquently of the circulation of elites in the Federal government of the nineteenth century. An heir to the New England dominants, he saw his political career destroyed by the decline of his class and region and the succession of political tradesmen from the hinterlands.

The conditions for circulation of elites and for different rates of circulation for different classes of elites are not well understood. The two most general propositions hinge around access and self-selection. Thus, in the relatively stable political orders recorded by historians and anthropologists, there is a range of "openness" which seems to vary with the degree of integration among the various elites of a society. The interlocking elite system is one in which the same class of persons produces leaders in the polity, the economy, the ecclesia, and the army. This class of persons (Romans of the Republic, from equestrian status upward; the English gentry of the eighteenth century) is typically hereditary, so family becomes the major transmission belt for the recruitment of the various elites. At the same time, control of the various command posts allows self-perpetuation of the class, while class-endogamy creates, from a set of elites in heterogeneous activity, a defensive social group with common norms and sanctions.

At the other pole are the elites which emphasize recruitment by the demands of the control system for specific learned abilities, rather than by access through family. Impure as the cases are, the Catholic Ecclesia of the medieval period, the Mandarin bureaucracy of Imperial China, and various military orders are most frequently cited as cases of the circulation of elites in stable societies. Each is, notably, a bureaucratic organization, functionally set apart from other organizational segments of the society and insulated from the class system through specific requirements which may be class-correlated but are not class monopolies. The Catholic church, for example, reduced the possibility of class dominance through requiring celibacy.

In complex societies these functionally specialized and segmented organizations multiply (this is implied by the definition of complexity), with a consequent increase in the access of various classes of persons to the office. American sociologists have concentrated, for the most part, on the study of economic elites, and their findings indicate a large and rather constant rate of circulation (Anderson & Davidson, 1940; Bendix & Lipset, 1957; Rogoff, 1953; Warner & Abegglen, 1955). Even controlling for shifts in the job distribution, the rates remain substantial (Rogoff, 1953), and there seems little reason to question them. Studies of political elites and their "circulation," however, are rare; a few pioneer studies have described the higher civil servants, elected officials (Matthews, 1954), and the "power elites" of small and middle-sized cities (Form & Miller, 1960; Hunter, 1953). Mills assembled data which indicate the dominance of certain training institutions in producing the American military leadership (1956), and others have documented the dominance of attorneys in the political process (from Weber on), but no adequate comparative study of the problem area is available, even at a descriptive level. It is likely, however, that the more complex the society the weaker will be hereditary elites, with a compensating continuity of *social type*.

This brings up the question of self-selection, as against access. Interlocking elites which require family lineage for entry are rare today, but many of the advantages which basically guaranteed their continuity still exist and are class correlated. That is, the family as the vehicle for the social placement of the child greatly affects his opportunities in general, including political opportunities (Sibley, 1949; Sorokin, 1927). On the other hand, the production of large numbers of persons qualified in principle for access to the elite positions in the state raises the question: Who chooses this line of endeavor? Lasswell (1948) attempted to sketch a theory of a "political personality," and others have concerned themselves with "political socialization" (Hyman, 1959; Lane, 1959). Beyond a few broad and crude findings we know little. Lawyers are disproportionately included in the elites of the state, as are college graduates, sons of the middle class, "old Americans" by family lineage, and men. The changing backgrounds of political elites in elective versus appointive office, in specifically skilled versus unskilled (or socially skilled) roles, at the national and the local level, these are some unknowns. Therefore we can only speculate on what produces variable rates across elites and time, and what the consequences of those rates are. Certainly matters discussed earlier (police protection, the ability to raise issues and defend interests, the requirements of charisma and the rules for its use) would be involved in adequate answers to these questions and, until we answer these questions, we cannot know if Pareto was correct in his contention that circulation of elites alone accounts for a substantial degree of variation in the character and policy of the state.

Shifts in Elite Structure

A shift in the elite structure means a basic reorganization of control in the society, resulting in a new distribution of dominance among roles and a new method of integrating control. This could occur with no change in the "political class," but empirically it seems always to produce some circulation of elites. (Even the Latin American revolution is accompanied by some seepage of new personnel into the state from the army, the university, the higher civil service, or other organizations relevant to control of the nation.) Such shifts are the main source of massive elite circulation.

The basic sociological argument used in accounting for shifts in elite structures begins with a consideration of the distribution of advantage among subgroups. The pre-existing elite structure reflects the dominance of certain roles, their high social valuation, and a rigorous selection of incumbents (through, e.g., education, "proper" family, and the like). Thus argued Davis and Moore (1945) in their classic essay on the functional bases of stratification. Since control is necessary, such stratification is socially

useful and, indeed, inescapable. The contrary argument, made by Tumin (1953), underscores the disjunction between what is necessary to maintain an elite structure and what is necessary to maintain a society. The argument can degenerate into a question of terms, but should not do so; both of the major propositions are necessary for a description of a control system.

For, although a control system of some minimal efficacy is necessary for a state to remain in being, there may be many functional alternatives to the existing structure. They are prevented to the degree that the existing organized elites are capable of perpetuating the dominance of their lineage or their social category, either preventing the rise of new "command posts," or capturing them for their own purposes. The closure of elites, however, tends to make easier the first alternative—the prevention of change—for the normative system common to the elite and diffused through relevant publics also tends to closure, with a consequent devaluation of new processes, organization, and roles. The further outside the elite class's habitual concerns the new organizations lie, the less likely their leaders to be coopted by the pre-existing elite.

The most spectacular shifts in the elite structure are those produced by political revolution. The monopoly of legitimate violence is broken and the very structure of legitimacy dissolves. Contending subgroups no longer accept the accommodation forced by the state and turn against the state the organizational weapons forged through intergroup contention (Selznick, 1952). The state may be reformulated through including the effective dissident groups in the political elite, or it may be captured and reorganized by the dissidents; in either case, a massive "circulation" accompanies such a shift.

Studies of revolution emphasize the shifts in age, in social background, and in normative systems, which accompany this transfusion of leadership from subgroup to state. Revolutionaries are younger and have more diverse social backgrounds (and more often are commoners or working class); they are committed to norms which make the state clearly separate from the society (and make legitimacy a product of the latter) and the nature of the state problematic (Bell et al., in press; Matthews, 1954; Moskos, in Blanksten & Mack, in press). The sharper the break in continuity of elites, the more pronounced are such changes. The new nations of the twentieth century evidence a wide range of types, from the peaceful revolution in the West Indies (Bell et al., in press), where the elites after Independence were almost identical to those before, to Algeria, where a completely new cadre took the command posts of the state.

Political revolution is possible only when radical schisms exist in the politically relevant populations. Such faults run along lines of economic interest, ways of life, and religion; they are inevitable accompaniments, at least in the short run, of expanding scale (Nisbet, 1953; Shevky & Bell, 1955; Wilson & Wilson, 1954). The processes which create large-scale society bring together diverse peoples, differentiate them further by social rank, and assure their interdependence in the orderly carrying out of necessary tasks. Their interdependence may not be accompanied, however, by organization—the coordination through a normative system whose effectiveness supports sanctions, positive and negative. Further, organization at one level may not be accompanied by organization at another and equally crucial level; thus the Wilsons interpret the racial conflicts of South Africa as results of a radical disjuncture between the scale of the polity and that of the economy. The former allocates partial citizenship on the basis of race, the latter allocates full participation at crucial points in the economy (Wilson & Wilson, 1954). Sociologists have often pointed out a similar disjuncture in the American South (Myrdal, 1944), and the drive for Negro political equality can be traced in large part to the increasing inclusion of Negroes in the economy.

Thus, increasing scale forces an increasing internal inclusiveness of the polity (Bell, in press). This, in turn, creates organizational leverage for the economically and ethnically disadvantaged. Such is, in truth, the basic assumption of a democratic polity; the state is conceived as the arena in which particularistic conflict can be resolved authoritatively, and the state must then be inclusive of all conflict capable of destroying the authority system. Bendix and Lipset (1957) stated that "Societies are characterized by unresolved tensions among the groups comprising them, as well as by a basic consensus concerning the rules of the game which govern. . . ." Should the tensions be unamenable to the game, the rules may well be changed.

Unresolved tensions are not likely to disappear in rapidly changing societies. Max Weber (1947), with his shrewd analysis of history as the succession and solution of practical problems, illuminated the causes of the major organizational transformation of our time, the bureaucratization of work. Noting that the princes who survived were those who "ruthlessly bureaucratized," he saw bureaucracy as the retention of organizational forms which yield advantage in competition, conflict, expansion. The differential rate of bureaucratization in different realms of the society, conflict between the interests of the various bureaucracies, and conflict between what can be bureaucratically organized and what cannot, create continual strains upon the order maintained by the state.

With increasing bureaucratization, elites become organizational commanders and staff men. Thus the conditions for entry and success in the bureaucratic order become a prerequisite for attaining elite role, and the diploma, the organizational career, and the specialized role are attributes of elites in economy, church, and governmental agency. This is less true of newly organized contenders for power; labor movements and ethnic protest movements draw upon a wider range of social types, for they present

opportunities for the organizational entrepreneur. One can own his "means of production" in such movements during their
days of organization and violent contention.
As they become fixed and legitimate parts of
the control system, however, their regulation
by the state, accompanied by their participation in the business of state, result in a regu-
larizing of roles within the organization.
The protest movement becomes the bureaucratized agency of representation, with increasing dominance by a professional staff
showing diplomas, organizational career,
and specialized competence (Wilensky,
1961). Though American sociologists seem
to have been chiefly interested in the imperfections of bureacracy, it has survived as the
most common method for the twin goals of
keeping the organization in business and
maintaining control over its policy.

Such a temporal trend suggests change in
the base for political authority. The increasing public concern with the economic prosperity of the society and its external safety,
translated into changing definitions of what
is legitimate for the government to do, results in a heavy emphasis upon technical
competence—and this is very near the notion of "rational-legal" authority. Changing
norms of legitimacy are reflected in the
changing criteria for recruitment to high
political office: The expert becomes a person
with quasi-governmental influence.

The dominance of bureaucracies is a product of organizational evolution, accompanying increased scale of the society. It does not,
as Weber (1947) was careful to note, imply
any given economic order or any given
political order. Nor does it imply a necessary
increase in the rational efficiency of the state
(though the government may be finally
judged by the consequences of its policies
for the citizens). Instead it implies specified
criteria supposedly relevant to the problems
of economic order and defense in complex
society. Such problems as inflation of currency, the nature of armaments requisite for
military safety, the balance of trade and
payments, and spending for consumption

goods as against capital investment, for the
public sector as against the private, are
major questions of policy in all contemporary states. Each of them requires a decision
based upon a kind of knowledge accessible
only to persons specifically trained for the job.

The operation of the state is not, however,
contingent only upon such technical problems and their solutions. The state as an
explicit and encompassing social order must
gain and maintain the support of the variety
of citizens and contending subgroups, and
this is maximized in a democracy. In this
task the public personality is crucial and,
for this reason, the mechanisms of social
trust and delegation are the basis for a
technology peculiar to politics. The eliciting
of ritual affirmation (whether or not it takes
place through the Australian ballot) is a
major part of the role for heads of state in
all contemporary nations.

Between the task of maintaining support
on the one hand and solving the massive
practical problems on the other, there is no
necessary relationship—particularly if the
consequences of the wrong solution take
many years to unfold. The great bureaucracies do not control the head of state, nor
does he necessarily control them. Meanwhile
the basis of his appeal to the citizens may
be a set of norms continuously traduced by
the necessary workings of the machinery of
state. Under such circumstances "pseudo-
Gemeinschaft" may be expected to thrive
at the price of increasing institutional vulnerability (Selznick, 1951). When symbols
become irrelevant to the major problems of
a society, yet their use in political discourse
remains effective, they act as blocks to communication. In this situation the head of
state stands between the people and the
bureaucracies (Williams, 1960).

The possibilities of enlightened self-
government are greatly reduced by this
circumstance. Specialization of knowledge
produces intellectual disenfranchisement,
sometimes openly acknowledged by most
citizens (as in the problem of choosing
necessary armaments) and sometimes muted

by a general belief that every man has a right to an opinion. In the latter case the provision of protection from the citizenry for elites whose assigned task requires that they violate the conventional wisdom or sacred norms is a major part of the role of the political head. The assumption that expertness is requisite to leadership, a basic norm in, for example, the Soviet or British political culture, is much more conducive to its free use, with the concomitant danger of poor communications from the society in general.

PRIVATE ORDER, PUBLIC ORDER, AND THE POLITY

Much of the ordered behavior requisite for a complex society results from multitudinous groups and systems not overtly political in their focus or aims. The state is, for them, a set of limiting conditions, of ground rules, which they usually accept. It is the encompassing and dominant structure for intergroup order, an instrument for forced accommodation among groups. Arbiter and enforcer, it supplies in its role system the proper rights and duties for categories of actors, including corporate actors.

This entire system of groups, politically relevant but not political in their legitimacy and everyday task, has been dubbed "the parapolitical structure," in analogy to the paramilitary (Greer & Orleans, 1962). Grounded in significant participation, since their everyday utility is derived from the functional requirements of occupations, business enterprises, households, and neighborhoods, these groups may become important representatives of societal interests not so clearly expressed elsewhere. Galbraith (1956) spoke of "countervailing forces" in the American economy—consumers versus producers of labor and goods—and from the basic balance of power adduced increased freedom for the totality. Nisbet (1953) and Lederer (1940), disturbed by the vision of the totalitarian state, placed their confidence in these groups as the basic bulwarks against uncontrolled national dominance.

Such groups are related to the polity, for persons who are active participators in them are also active in the political realm (Greer & Orleans, 1962). They are also significant as training grounds for political action and as representatives before the legislative bodies and administrative agencies. They provide categories for organizing the vote, categories which may supplement or modify party categories, and they may turn the substance of an election from a judgment of a man to a referendum on a policy. (Thus "right to work" laws in some states have turned elections for state governing personnel into referenda on the legitimate rights and duties of labor versus management in those states.)

The internal order of such groups (often called their "private governments") has fascinated social scientists for some time. Michels (1959), in his classic study of the German Social Democratic party, set the major theme. Taking what he considered to be the group most committed to widespread democracy, he demonstrated that its control system was best described as a self-perpetuating oligarchy. He concluded that effectiveness in such groups requires organization, and "whoever says organization says oligarchy." Lipset (1956) and his associates, however, studying a major American trade union, demonstrated the possibility of continuous and responsible democratic political processes. They state some preconditions in the social-economic function and structure of the group and in its constitution, which result in a two-party system and a competitive democracy. Similar findings result from a comparative study of union locals in Los Angeles, though the major emphasis in the latter study is upon integration of work group and union group as the precondition for viable subgroups within the membership (Greer, 1959). One cannot quarrel with Michels' contention that complex, persisting groups require delegation and some degree of continuity in control; the key question is, What are the possibilities for delegation? How does the communication system between representatives and the membership function?

Studies of the internal organization of interest groups indicate a widespread condition of staff dominance (Brady, 1943; Garceau, 1941; Greer, 1959; Messinger, 1955). That is, the paid, full-time employees tend to dominate the policies of the group through their day-to-day surveillance and responsibility for operations. In Simon's (1957) terms, technical decisions without review are identical in their consequences to "line command." At the same time, the more demanding the work of the staff roles, the greater the reliance must be upon the incumbents, and the stronger their bargaining power. Thus they achieve a degree of job security which reinforces their influence. The counterpart of their expert knowledge is the relative ignorance and incompetence of the rank and file. The communication flow between staff and membership requires a high level of education in the members, great simplification of issues, or, most common, skillful use of delegation by charisma, together with pseudo-*Gemeinschaft* (Gouldner, 1954; Greer, 1959; Mills, 1948).

The nature of interorganizational relations is at present the despair of anyone who goes to sociology with questions about the real world. There are studies of intergroup relations (race and, to some degree, social class) which focus upon individuals in isolation or merged with an aggregate, and there are intensive studies of behavior within one formal organization, but the relations between these organized units remain subject largely to speculation (see also Moore, 1951). It is clear that large segments of behavior are organized by "peak associations" of one sort or another—labor federations, councils of churches, trade associations, regional councils, and national councils. What is not clear is the precise nature of control so generated, its origins, and its consequences. Brady (1943) spoke at length of business as a system of power; Ross (1949) indicated that the degree of organized agreement among employers and among unions is an

important determinant of collective bargaining outcomes; the economists have demonstrated the reasons for oligopoly and some consequences (including such "scandals" as the General Electric et al. practice of fixing prices for governmental purchases); nowhere do we have an explicated theory of relations among complex formal organizations.

Williams (1960), in a penetrating discussion, emphasized the importance of such relationships; "as the size and power of organizational units increase, the consequences of decisions increasingly outrun the limits of the unit in which they originate." His approach emphasizes the basic importance of an organizational calculus in interpreting such relations. Problems of power, policy, and tactical outcomes are more important controls than folkways and prejudices, because a language of organizational technology allows abstract generality, universal administrative applicability, and concrete definitions for classification. Such an approach has been used in accounting for the various policies of labor unions with respect to ethnic minorities (Greer, 1959).

These organized segments of the parapolitical structure are important because they have major effects on the internal order of the constituent groups. The ability of trade union leaders to marshall the power of other unions through the boycott has sometimes disenfranchised members of the leaders' own locals (Greer, 1959). The "higher level" organization may, in fact, be a major basis for continuing oligarchy in the parapolitical group, while such oligarchy bolsters the order within the peak organizations. The latter, in turn, seem to be logical solutions to emerging problems of large-scale society. The need for predictability in, say, market and resources sometimes leads to merger—lateral and vertical integration—but it need not do so when a larger order allows accommodation, hence predictability. Moore has indicated the possibility of a spectrum, from warfare for organizational survival through forced accommodation by formal sanctions, bargaining and agreement by contract, basic consensus, and merger (Moore, 1951). The requisite outcome, for firm or union local, as well as the economy as a whole, is known: minimal predictability. The precise determinants of outcomes and the variety of solutions are unknown.

Such intergroup relations have been sporadically studied in the field of union-management relations (Dubin & Harbison, 1947). The railroad industry, for example, is often likened to a syndicalist system in which government, union, and management are so agreed that no sharp boundaries separate the three systems (Cottrell, 1962). This is predicated, however, upon a control of market and resources which deteriorates as competitive segments develop, i.e., automotive and air transport. Similar relationships among building contractors and unions have been reported, with an alliance of the two management groups against the "craft brotherhood" of the workers. One suspects a long-run pressure for merger between the interdependent components of major significance in the society, with a final goal of mutual protection against time, chance, and the outside world. Threatening such merger, however, are technological innovation, uncontrollable shifts in market or resources, and violent competition which does not fit within the existing order.

In the view of some observers the parapolitical structure is the overall determinant of the polity. At an extreme, we have Marx's belief that government was simply the "executive committee of the bourgeoisie." Such a view is supported by a casual acquaintance with the interpenetration of economic and political enterprises, but discouraged by careful analysis of these relations. We have already noted the tendency toward stalemate in the legislative assemblies of the United States. Such stalemate indicates, not a unified and monolithic control, but a highly fragmented pattern in which political officials represent diverse and contradictory interests. And indeed, as Banfield (1961) pointed out, the very heterogeneity of interest among major business enterprises almost

guarantees that they will fail to consolidate their forces in political battle. If one may hazard a guess, it seems that the government, rather than being identified as their executive committee, is seen as a mortal enemy by the businessmen of America (Sutton, 1956). From city council to Federal Senate, businessmen exert an erratic and divided pressure upon the legislator. The latter, however, depends upon a separate means of production from the ones controlled by business; where the vote is not purchasable the politician has a high degree of autonomy (Greer, 1962b). The enormous triumvirate of the military, industry, and the government in the developed nations results from a political task, the national defense, and allocation of contracts is more predictable through a knowledge of foreign threat than a knowledge of the profit statements of firms. To be sure, economic enterprises are the vehicles for production and therefore beneficiaries of war orders. While it is difficult to imagine an alternative, still, as Weber (1947) carefully pointed out, indispensability is not the same thing as power.

The concept of the "managerial revolution," devised by Burnham (1941), is useful, however, if we remember Weber's (1947) caution. One impressive aspect of the big business executive role today is the dominance of the legal-rational ethos. This is concurrent with the "evaporation of the substance of property" and the bureaucratization of business. As Schumpeter (1942) said, "the true pace-makers of socialism were not the intellectuals or agitators who preached it but the Vanderbilts, Carnegies, and Rockefellers," who destroyed the world of small, family-owned firms. Thus the American business executive lives today by rules similar to those of any other bureaucratic head, and the state is to him a necessary but not controllable (or completely predictable) condition for his firm's existence. Nor do things appear very different abroad. The prestige and role of the executive are, if anything, more modest in Germany, England, and

Russia (Inkeles, 1959; Lewis & Stewart, 1961).

At the same time, the increasing complexity of the society and increasing demands for protection by the citizens also result in closer relations between government and the economy. Much of this structure resulted from mass supported demands opposed by business interests. These demands are chiefly for social and economic security on, between, and after the job and for control of private enterprises in the public interest. Thus a kind of shadow staff exists in certain parts of the economy—a staff made up of governmental investigators and regulators. As this evolved (and the first major example was the railroad industry, crucial to a wide range of interests), the civil servants who were delegated the task of safeguarding the public interest (while safeguarding the industry) tended to become identified with the norms and practices of their wards and clients. The differential association theory would lead us to predict this outcome, while the practice of recruiting the governmental personnel from the industry would be expected to maximize the commonality of outlook and norms. Consequently, each regulatory agency attached to a given industry tends to become a representative of that industry in the national government (Bernstein, 1955). Selznick (1949) demonstrated the close tie between the National Farm Bureau and the Department of Agriculture, and the important effects this tie had upon the original character of TVA. Similar ties have been demonstrated for the Federal Communications Commission, the Interstate Commerce Commission, the Railway Commission, and others (Bernstein, 1955).

The pressures upon government to regulate private enterprises are a direct result of the increasing need and political demand for protection of the general welfare against the welfare of specific firms. In short, the tangible value of citizenship has increased, *pari passu* with governmental powers. At the same time, this increasing importance of political rules and surveillance has forced business enterprises to take initiative in governmental realms. Despite their ideological suspicion of governments, the requirements of national policy force American business enterprises to take government into partnership. Their leverage upon the government, however, aside from the occasional bribe, is limited to their ability to use either technological monopoly or influence with the voters. The first is dangerous for the firm in the long run and the latter varies greatly with the type of issue considered. It is probably greatest when pious and highly simplified interpretations of economic fact, broadcast among the citizens, can be used to achieve the immediate interests of the businessman.

TOTALITARIANISM AND THE DURKHEIM DILEMMA

The diffusion of control among many parapolitical and nonpolitical groups, with government as a separated bureaucracy, is what Durkheim (1933) meant by organic solidarity. Each one of many groups is essential to the health and persistence of others and, hence, to the whole society; thus the pressure for accommodation. However, with increasing specialization, "mechanical solidarity" based on uniform life chances, culture, and position, declines precipitously for the society as a whole. Thus the Durkheim dilemma: Interdependence among organized parts requires, but does not guarantee, predictability. Durkheim spoke of a component of morality which cuts across the major segments of the society, one which guarantees the ground rules of contention and forced accommodation. But the guarantee must finally reside in the capability of the national state, for norms without sanctions are not dependable for serious business.

Since Durkheim's (1933) first statement of the problem, the trend in every society of expanding scale has been consistent with his prediction. The effort to maintain a sharp distinction between economy, polity, and the remaining ("social") aspects of society, characteristic of nineteenth-century liberalism, has collapsed before powerful demands for national coordination. These, in turn, result from the dangers of modern warfare and economic depression. Facilitated by increasing energy transformation and a declining space-time ratio, economy and polity are reintegrated on a national basis. We have already noted the increasing politicization of the economy, almost as marked in "capitalist" America as in "socialist" Britain. This is not the only consequence of increasing national integration. As the state increases in its relative importance for a wide range of activities, the elites who make the crucial decisions become concentrated in the national capitol. Since these decisions affect most radically the life of the entire array of citizens (from economic policy to foreign relations) significant discourse of the society also becomes nationally based and focused upon the capitol. The locality unit, from city to state to region, declines in its autonomy and significance. Many major choices affecting its future are made outside its borders, at the headquarters of giant corporation, labor union, and government. The result is a bifurcation between powers locally organized by the smaller polity and powers organized by the national organizations and polity.

Durkheim (1933) saw clearly the possibility of the totalitarian state in the emerging dominance of the nation. Committed as he was to maximizing freedom within an adequately coordinated society, his solution was a further extension of the balance of power metaphor. The conditions required are the existence of partially autonomous, parapolitical groups, which exercise constraint upon the state, and a concomitant regulation of these groups by the state. In short, the balance should allow the parapolitical to protect the citizen from the state and the state to protect him from the tyranny of the parapolitical system—that "tyranny of democracy" which De Tocqueville (1945) so dreaded. As a good "Federalist"

Durkheim agreed with Madison and Monroe that the constituent groups must have real sanctions against the state, otherwise they can protect no values and enforce no norms. Thus his prescription is for a society in a continual state of tension between action generated in various spheres and tolerated or reinforced or resisted by other organized groups and the State.

Federalism: Dilemmas of Durkheim's Solution

The classical political device for assuring such a system is Federalism, a basic aspect of the American polity. The allocation of major realms of legitimate action to the states and, through them, to the local communities is a system remarkably congruent with Durkheim's (1933) prescription. The further effort, to keep legally separate the economy and polity, is equally in accordance with the doctrine. When this is combined with a "cross-cutting" of memberships and social categories the American society would appear to be a test of Durkheim's notions. But, if this is so, the Durkheimian solution appears to produce dilemmas almost as painful as the original problem.

The widespread dispersion of authority forces the cooptation of various subordinate but partially autonomous groups, if anything at all is to be accomplished by the state. Their cooperation, however, depends upon the consent of local political elites which may be indifferent, if not hostile, to the larger problems which national policy is designed to solve. The history of the metropolitan problem is replete with such opposition; in truth, local elites are not accountable for problems whose solution requires their cooperation (Greer, 1963; Jones, 1942; Schmandt, 1961; Sofen, 1963). Should such elites assume responsibility, however, they are stringently limited by the requirement of voter approval through referenda. At state and local levels this tool of direct democracy sometimes results in political decisions by roulette wheel.

The dilemmas of dispersed control are dramatically evident in large metropolitan areas. Decentralization of work and residence, combined with rigidity of governmental boundary lines and powers, result in a proliferation of loosely integrated segments. The exploding metropolis has produced a congeries of separate, incorporated suburbs, what Banfield and Grodzins (1961) termed "the present Balkanization of government in the metropolitan area." The development of semiautonomous subunits has resulted from a free market in urban land and private enterprise in the incorporation of local governments that has, at the same time, facilitated the resurrection of (some) local community life. Yet it has prevented the development of a responsible polity for the urban area as a whole.

Meanwhile, real problems accumulate for the governors of the various jurisdictions within the metropolis. The segregation of the poor and ethnic citizens in the central city results in serious political pressure on the government of the older center for improvements in housing, policing, education, and occupational opportunities. There is also pressure on the governments of new suburbia for major facilities—roads, schools, parks, and the like. Both pressures are combined with conservative norms which militate against increased powers for local government, whether the powers in question are fiscal, police, or control of land use. The ubiquity of the referendum allows full expression of these conservative norms.

There are two major mechanisms for avoiding this dilemma. The local government increasingly tends to pass its problems upward to the state and the federal government. Federal tax collectors furnish the basis for new capital investment, for highways and urban renewal, for local transportation and university campuses, for welfare and unemployment relief, for aid to the handicapped and control of waterways. The fragmentation of jurisdictions without respect for the nature of governmental services leads, in another strategy, to reintegration through single-purpose special district governments.

These solutions produce further dilemmas. Federal agencies operate on a national scale and independently of one another. Thus they have neither the desire nor the need to coordinate their actions and take into account the total effects of their work upon the local community. While the effort is made to renew the central city (at a high cost in the destruction of cheap housing), the highway programs underwrite dispersion (Wood, 1961). Control of special districts is also largely beyond the polity of the general government. The solutions to the problems of fragmented powers thus increase fragmentation of policy, taking control completely out of the community most affected.

As this occurs, the local polity begins to resemble in its true role the local union steward. The federal system requires a degree of consent at the state and local level for programs originated in Washington. This consent is the mayor's bargaining tool. As representative of the local electorate he can bargain for advantages, and even withdraw from the program. But his power is chiefly that of the veto. Innovation in ideas and financial resources are the dynamics, and they tend to be the monopoly of outsiders. The origins of problems, in the unanticipated consequences of organization outside the polity, are now combined with solutions which also come from abroad. This redefinition of local government has reached its most extreme form in the "Lakewood Plan." Named for the municipality in Los Angeles County where it originated, this plan results in a large municipality which performs no governmental tasks; all are contracted out to the Los Angeles County government. The City Manager is the official bargaining agent, with the Council as his bargaining and grievance committee (Ostrom, Tiebout & Warren, 1961). As Ostrom and his associates pointed out, this is a version of suburban government which allows a wide range in residential choice for the citizen, for he can shop in the market for suburbs, buying the level of services he wants. It allows a certain representation of the citizen through delegation to the bargaining committee. While it does not encourage a high degree of participation, the value of participation is a matter of individual choice. It requires little in the way of responsible citizenship beyond payment of the taxes, the "union dues."

In short, the conflict between the market and the polity is resolved by the Lakewood Plan through the development of a polity much like a market. As such, it is hardly the "laboratory for democracy" envisaged by Jefferson as the chief value of local communities. It is, in truth, a conservative polity —one which preserves a steady state of neighborhoods, adding amenities as they become fashionable and avoiding the problems of the metropolis as a whole. Meanwhile, in the central city, the outward flow of the new, white, middle-rank families and the growth of the nonwhite electorate produce major anticipated consequences.

Similar difficulties exist where the nation must secure the cooperation of economic enterprises. Although these enterprises take little responsibility for the public weal, the rigid separation of economy and polity maintained in a given program may require that all constructive action be instigated by them. The problems of urban renewal and housing, for example, are in large part a result of this dilemma (Greer, 1964; Haar, 1960). The requirement that national policy be coordinated with the behavior of local groups and nonpolitical groups results in a maximization of the need to predict. National policy is, after all, limited by the kinds of action permitted the state, and, if coercion of necessary actions is not permitted, prediction must do. The diffusion of power and the multiplication of possible veto groups has resulted in the increasing importance of the "public entrepreneur," the man who is a specialist at persuasion and prediction and who puts together the enterprise which is to carry out the national policy. His task is, in Long's phrase, to involve some of the players of many different games in his, the public game (Duggar, 1961; Long, 1958; Wood, 1961). An appointive official, he frequently bears the responsibility and the power of an elected representative.

At many points in the society the intercalation of the elected representatives is not possible on a scale, and at a pace, to allow action at all. When stalemates occur, the usual tactic is a sort of bypassing of the inactive structure, with an accompanying decline in accountability to the citizens. Thus the major response to pressure for an extension of first-class citizenship to Negroes has come from the Federal judiciary. The solution of many problems accompanying urban expansion has been the creation of special district governments (called "ghost governments" by one observer), whose officials are frequently unknown and whose decisions are unmonitored by the citizens (Bollens, 1957). The regulation of business enterprise in the public interest has been the task of administrative agencies which combine the functions of legislature, administrator, investigator, and court (Bernstein, 1955). Efforts to control land use, to plan transportation systems, and to renew cities have been the responsibility of higher civil servants in the Housing and Home Finance Agency (Greer, 1964). Everywhere the national polity has bypassed the local polity and returned in the guise of the public entrepreneur who achieves through cajolery, threat, bribe, and persuasion. The roots of this situation lie in the incapacity of the parapolitical to take (or at least tolerate) innovative action.

In summary, then, the multiplication of necessary parties to an agreement is positively correlated with legitimacy and negatively correlated with efficacy (Lipset, 1960). The result has been, in the United States, a tendency to use mere extrapolation as a basic framework for confronting the future. The powers, fiscal and otherwise, of state and local governments are used to increase expenditures in old ways as population and economic activity rise. Though the national government is limited in a similar manner, the relative insulation of the national political elite from the pressures of the local community allow the maintenance of radical programs inherited from the New Deal and the occasional introduction of novelties in response to crisis. These are accompanied by a patterned evasion of norms (Williams, 1960)—the bypassing of local government. But such innovation in procedure seems to be necessary for innovations in substance.

The diffusion of control to subgroups is not the only solution to Durkheim's (1933) dilemma. His original formulation included the possibility of a uniform commitment of significant actors to a moral component, a set of norms which could also act as a modifying influence upon the power of the nation-state. It is likely that, in such a nation as Britain, this condition prevails, with the national political parties as the major representatives and safeguards of individual freedom. Whether the American society will ever approach such a polity is highly questionable. The basic ground rules here assume and protect that diffusion of control which prevents the development of a national party organization. As societies increase in scale one must delegate beyond immediate surveillance and control; the dichotomies of private firm and public agency, federal union and local community are the dimensions of that delegation in America's ideal political culture. As these units become ineffective, their place is taken by others—the federal judiciary, the administrative tribunal, the special district government, and, above all, the public entrepreneur with his skill in building coalitions among business firms, city governments, federal agencies, and the public.

An End to Ideology?

Reviewing the relatively placid and slow-moving course of political contention and change in the United States, some observers have declared an end to "ideology" (Bell,

1960). Lipset (1960), reviewing the present state of the polity and the comity, saw no major domestic grounds for significant political conflict and suggested that the major focus of political efforts in the United States for the foreseeable future may be the politics of the emerging nations. Such a view seems time-bound, parochial in perspective, and contrary to the observable trends in the society. On every hand the burdens of government and the dominant responsibility of the state increase. The nation, today, is guarantor and promoter of full citizenship, and as the society increases in scale this means an increasing internal inclusiveness for peoples who are only partially included, a fuller participation in the total range of the society.

New schisms are created wherever the rights of a category of citizens fall below those the norms prescribe. Such schisms, with increasing political expression, foreshadow the kinds of political tension, contention, and mobilization we can expect in the future. It is clear, for example, that Negro Americans have achieved a degree of political organization which will be expressed at the polls for decades. It is also clear that the rapid introduction of machinery and nonhuman energy into work will create enormous displacements in the labor force. In a nation which has no means of allocating income save through the business enterprise and the dole, this presages a massive schism in the body politic. Some economists estimate that, within 25 years, only one in six Americans will be employed at the kind of tasks Adam Smith would have regarded as productive. (Meanwhile even many white-collar jobs are in danger of massive displacement.) A further consideration, difficult to weigh but striking in some manifestations, is the rapidity of change in job, community, and way of life, which sees small-town and country people turn into suburbanites in a few years. Their traditional political cultures are hardly relevant to the metropolitan world, and their faith healers operate in abandoned movie houses next door to the headquarters of international petroleum companies. They have the vote, and that vote is hardly an expression of the urbane views held by former ideologists.

While there seem to be many sources for a continued domestic politics, and such a politics will operate in a vocabulary of ideology, it is likely that vocabulary will be far different from the nineteenth-century terms of sociopolitical struggle. The grand utopias and deterministic evolutionary schemes of the past seem to be dying under the impact of empirical test and developing social science. Still, some of the unfinished revolutions will continue to press, through the organized resistance of populations to second-class citizenship and the insistence of the disprivileged on the assumption of responsibility by the state. The counterforces of existing parapolitical organization exhibit norms which may change easily into a fighting ideology, a protection against threats to prestige, power, and self implicit in a further leveling. In this struggle social science itself assumes the guise of an ideology—which may explain the exaggerated reports of "the end of ideology."

REFERENCES

Adams, H. *The education of Henry Adams.* New York: Modern Library, 1931.

Adrian, C. R. Some general characteristics of nonpartisan elections. *Amer. polit. Sci. Rev.,* 1952, 46, 766–776.

Agger, R. E., & Goldrich, D. Community power structures and partisanship. *Amer. sociol. Rev.,* 1958, 23, 383–392.

Alger, C. F. Non-resolution consequences of the United Nations and their effect on international conflict. *J. conflict Resolution,* 1961, 2, 128–145.

Allport, G. W., & Postman, L. J. The basic psychology of rumor. In G. E. Swanson, Eleanor E. Macoby, T. M. Newcomb, & E. L. Hartley (Eds.), *Readings in social psychology.* (3rd ed.) New York: Holt, 1952. Pp. 54–65.

Almond, G. A., & Coleman, J. S. *The politics of the developing areas.* Princeton, N.J.: Princeton Univer. Press, 1960.

Anderson, H. D., & Davidson, P. E. *Occupational trends in the United States.* Stanford: Stanford Univer. Press, 1940.

Arendt, H. *The origins of totalitarianism.* New York: Harcourt, 1954.

Axelrod, M. Urban structure and social participation. *Amer. sociol. Rev.,* 1956, 21, 13–18.

Bailey, S. *Congress makes a law.* New York: Columbia Univer. Press, 1950.

Banfield, E. C. *Political influence.* Glencoe, Ill.: Free Press, 1961.

Banfield, E. C., & Grodzins, M. The desirable and the possible. In E. C. Banfield (Ed.), *Urban government: A reader in administration and politics.* Glencoe, Ill.: Free Press, 1961. Pp. 82–88.

Bell, D. *The end of ideology.* Glencoe, Ill.: Free Press, 1960.

Bell, W. Changing elites and evolutionary theory. In G. Blanksten & R. Mack (Eds.), *Social science and the underdeveloped areas: A revival of evolutionary theory?* New York: Wiley, in press.

Bell, W. (Ed.) *The democratic revolution in the West Indies: Studies in nationalism, leadership, and the belief in progress.* Berkeley: Univer. of California Press, in press.

Bell, W., Hill, R. J., & Wright, C. R. *Public leadership.* San Franscisco: Chandler Publishing Company, 1961.

Bendix, R., & Lipset, S. M. Political sociology. *Curr. Sociol.,* 1957, 6, 79–99.

Bennett, J. W., & Tumin, M. *Social life: Structure and function.* New York: Knopf, 1949.

Bentley, A. F. *The process of government.* Evanston: The Principia Press of Illinois, Inc., 1935.

Berelson, B. R., Lazarsfeld, P. F., & McPhee, W. N. *Voting.* Chicago: Univer. of Chicago Press, 1954.

Bernstein, M. *Regulating business by independent commission.* Princeton, N.J.: Princeton Univer. Press, 1955.

Blanksten, G., & Mack, R. (Eds.) *Social science and the underdeveloped areas: A revival of evolutionary theory?* New York: Wiley, in press.

Blau, P. M. *The dynamics of bureaucracy.* Chicago: Univer. of Chicago Press, 1955.

Blumer, H. Public opinion and the public opinion polls. *Amer. sociol. Rev.,* 1948, **13,** 542–549.

Bollens, J. C. *Special district governments in the United States.* Berkeley: Univer. of California Press, 1957.

Brady, R. A. *Business as a system of power.* New York: Columbia Univer. Press, 1943.

Bramson, L. *The political context of sociology.* Princeton, N.J.: Princeton Univer. Press, 1961.

Breed, W. Social control in the newsroom: A functional analysis. *Soc. Forces,* 1955, **33,** 326–335.

Brotz, H. M. Social stratification and the political order. *Amer. J. Sociol.,* May, 1959, **64** (6), 571–578.

Burdick, E., & Brodbeck, A. J. (Eds.) *American voting behavior.* Glencoe, Ill.: Free Press, 1959.

Burnham, J. *The managerial revolution.* New York: John Day, 1941.

Campbell, A., Converse, P. E., Miller, W. E., & Stokes, D. E. *The American voter.* New York: Wiley, 1960.

Campbell, A., & Cooper, H. C. *Group differences in attitudes and votes.* Ann Arbor, Mich.: Institute for Social Research, 1956.

Cohen, A., Lindesmith, A., & Schuessler, K. (Eds.) *The Sutherland papers.* Bloomington: Indiana Univer. Press, 1956.

Coleman, J. S. *Community conflict.* Glencoe, Ill.: Free Press, 1957.

Coleman, J. S., Katz, E., & Menzel, H. The diffusion of innovation among physicians. *Sociometry,* 1957, **20,** 253–270.

Cottrell, F. *Technological change and the future of the railroads.* Evanston, Ill.: Publication of the Northwestern University Transportation Center, 1962.

Dahl, R. A. *Who governs? Democracy and power in an American city.* New Haven, Conn.: Yale Univer. Press, 1961.

Davis, K., & Moore, W. E. Some principles of stratification. *Amer. sociol. Rev.,* 1945, **10,** 242–249.

Derge, D. R. Metropolitan and outstate alignments in Illinois and Missouri legislative delegations. *Amer. polit. Sci. Rev.,* 1958, **52,** 1051–1065.

De Sola Pool, I. TV: A new dimension in politics. In E. Burdick & A. J. Brodbeck

(Eds.), *American voting behavior.* Glencoe, Ill.: Free Press, 1959. Pp. 236–261.

De Tocqueville, A. *Democracy in America.* New York: Knopf, 1945.

Dubin, R., & Harbison, F. *Patterns of union-management relations.* Chicago: Science Research Associates, 1947.

Duggar, G. The politics of urban renewal: Suggestions for a conceptual scheme. Paper read at Amer. Polit. Sci. Ass. Meetings, St. Louis, 1961.

Durkheim, E. *The division of labor in society.* (2nd ed.) G. Simpson (Trans.). Glencoe, Ill.: Free Press, 1933.

Durkheim, E. *Socialism and Saint-Simon.* A. Gouldner (Trans.). Yellow Springs, Ohio: Antioch Press, 1958.

Durkheim, E. *Professional ethics and civic morals.* Cornelia Brookfield (Trans.). Glencoe, Ill.: Free Press, 1960.

Eldersveld, S. J. Theory and method in voting behavior research. In H. Eulau, S. J. Eldersveld, & M. Janowitz (Eds.), *Political behavior: A reader in theory and research.* Glencoe, Ill.: Free Press, 1956. Pp. 267–274.

Ennis, P. H. The contextual dimension in voting. In W. N. McPhee & W. A. Glaser (Eds.), *Public opinion and congressional elections.* New York: The Free Press of Glencoe, 1962. Pp. 180–211.

Etzioni, A. *A comparative analysis of complex organizations.* Glencoe, Ill.: Free Press, 1961.

Form, W. H., & D'Antonio, W. V. Integration and cleavage among community influentials in two border cities. *Amer. sociol. Rev.,* 1959, **24,** 804–814.

Form, W. H., & Miller, D. C. *Industry, labor, and community.* New York: Harper, 1960.

Galbraith, J. K. *American capitalism: The concept of countervailing power.* Boston: Houghton, 1956.

Garceau, O. *The political life of the American Medical Association.* Cambridge, Mass.: Harvard Univer. Press, 1941.

Garceau, O., & Silverman, C. A pressure group and the pressured. *Amer. polit. Sci. Rev.,* 1954, **48,** 672–691.

Glaser, W. A. Fluctuations in turnout. In W. N. McPhee & W. A. Glaser (Eds.), *Public opinion and congressional elections.* New York: The Free Press of Glencoe, 1962. Pp. 19–51.

Glaser, W. A., & Kadushin, C. Political behavior in midterm elections. In W. N. Mc-Phee & W. A. Glaser (Eds.), *Public opinion and congressional elections.* New York: The Free Press of Glencoe, 1962. Pp. 251–272.

Goldschmidt, W. Social class in America—A critical review. *Amer. Anthrogist,* 1950, 52, 483–498.

Gouldner, A. W. *Patterns of industrial bureaucracy.* Glencoe, Ill.: Free Press, 1954.

Gouldner, A. W. The norm of reciprocity: A preliminary statement. *Amer. sociol. Rev.,* 1960, 25, 161–178.

Granick, D. *The red executive: A study of the organization man in Russian industry.* New York: Doubleday, 1961.

Greer, S. Individual participation in mass society. In R. Young (Ed.), *Approaches to the study of politics.* Evanston, Ill.: Northwestern Univer. Press, 1958. Pp. 329–342.

Greer, S. *Last man in.* Glencoe, Ill.: Free Press, 1959.

Greer, S. Catholic voters and the Democratic party. *Publ. Opin. Quart.,* 1961, 25, 611–625. (a)

Greer, S. Citizen participation and attitudes. In J. C. Bollens (Ed.), *Exploring the metropolitan community.* Berkeley: Univer. of California Press, 1961. Pp. 181–316.(b)

Greer, S. *The emerging city: Myth and reality.* New York: The Free Press of Glencoe, 1962. (a)

Greer, S. *Governing the metropolis.* New York: Wiley, 1962.(b)

Greer, S. The social structure and political process of suburbia: An empirical test. *Rural Sociol.,* 1962, 27, 438–459.(c)

Greer, S. *Metropolitics: A study of political culture.* New York: Wiley, 1963.

Greer, S. *Urban renewal: A sociological critique.* Indianapolis: Bobbs, 1964.

Greer, S., Holderman, J., & McHugh, P. The social and political structure of Winnetka. Evanston, Ill.: Center for Metropolitan Studies at Northwestern University, 1960. (Mimeographed)

Greer, S., & Orleans, P. The mass society and the parapolitical structure. *Amer. sociol. Rev.,* 1962, 27, 634–646.

Grodzins, M. *The loyal and the disloyal.* Chicago: Univer. of Chicago Press, 1956.

Gusfield, J. R. Mass society and extremist politics. *Amer. sociol. Rev.,* 1962, 27, 19–30.

Haar, C. M. *Federal credit and private housing: The mass financing dilemma.* New York: McGraw, 1960. ACTION series in Housing and Community Development.

Harrington, M. *The other America.* New York: Macmillan, 1962.

Hastings, P. K. The voter and the non-voter. *Amer. J. Sociol.,* 1956, 62, 302–307.

Hausknecht, M. *The joiners: A sociological description of voluntary association membership in the United States.* New York: Bedminster Press, 1962.

Heberle, R. *From democracy to nazism: A regional case study on political parties in Germany.* Baton-Rouge: Louisana State Univer. Press, 1945.

Heberle, R. *Social movements: An introduction to political sociology.* New York: Appleton-Century-Crofts, Inc., 1951.

Herberg, W. *Protestant-Catholic-Jew.* New York: Doubleday, 1955.

Horton, J. E., & Thompson, W. E. Powerlessness and political negativism: A study of defeated local referendums. *Amer. J. Sociol.,* 1962, 67, 485–493.

Hunter, F. *Community power structure.* Chapel Hill: Univer. of North Carolina Press, 1953.

Hyman, H. H. *Political socialization: A study in the psychology of political behavior.* Glencoe, Ill.: Free Press, 1959.

Hyman, H. H., & Sheatsley, P. B. The current status of American public opinion. In J. C. Payne (Ed.), *Twenty-first yearbook* National Council for the Social Studies, 1950. Pp. 11–34.

Inkeles, A. *The Soviet citizen.* Cambridge, Mass.: Harvard Univer. Press, 1959.

Janowitz, M. *The community press in an urban setting.* Glencoe, Ill.: Free Press, 1952.

Janowitz, M., & Marvick, D. Competitive pressure and democratic consent. In H. Eulau, S. J. Eldersveld, & M. Janowitz (Eds.), *Political behavior: A reader in theory and research.* Glencoe, Ill.: Free Press, 1956. Pp. 275–285.

Janowitz, M., Wright, D., & Delany, W. *Public administration and the public—Perspectives toward government in a metropolitan community.* Ann Arbor: Bureau of Government, Institute of Public Administration, Univer. of Michigan, 1958.

Jones, V. *Metropolitan government*. Chicago: Univer. of Chicago Press, 1942.

Katz, E. The two-step flow of communication: An up-to-date report on an hypothesis. *Pub. Opin. Quart.*, 1957, 21, 61–78.

Katz, E., & Lazarsfeld, P. F. *Personal influence*. Glencoe, Ill.: Free Press, 1955.

Kaufman, H., & Jones, V. The mystery of power. *Pub. admin. Rev.*, 1954, 14, 205–212.

Kerr, C., & Siegel, A. The interindustry propensity to strike—An international comparison. In A. Kornhauser, R. Dubin, & A. M. Ross (Eds.), *Industrial conflict*. New York: McGraw, 1954. Pp. 189–212.

Key, V. O., Jr. *Southern politics*. New York: Knopf, 1949.

Key, V. O., Jr. *Public opinion and American democracy*. New York: Knopf, 1961.

Key, V. O., Jr., & Munger, F. Social determinism and electoral decision: The case of Indiana. In E. Burdick & A. J. Brodbeck (Eds.), *American voting behavior*. Glencoe, Ill.: Free Press, 1959. Pp. 281–299.

Kile, O. M. *The farm bureau movement: The farm bureau through three decades*. Baltimore: Waverley Press, 1948.

Klapp, O. E. *Heroes, villains, and fools*. Englewood Cliffs, N.J.: Prentice-Hall, Inc., 1962.

Kornhauser, W. *The politics of mass society*. Glencoe, Ill.: Free Press, 1959.

Kriesberg, L. Occupational controls among steel distributors. *Amer. J. Sociol.*, 1955, 61, 203–212.

Lane, R. E. *Political life*. Glencoe, Ill.: Free Press, 1959.

Lang, K., & Lang, G. E. The mass media and voting. In E. Burdick & A. J. Brodbeck (Eds.), *American voting behavior*. Glencoe, Ill.: Free Press, 1959. Pp. 217–235.

Larson, A. Southern demagogues: A study of charismatic leadership. Unpublished doctoral dissertation, Northwestern Univer., 1963.

Laski, H. J. *The American presidency*. New York: Harper, 1940.

Lasswell, H. *Power and personality*. New York: Norton, 1948.

Lazarsfeld, P. F., Berelson, B., & Gaudet, H. *The people's choice*. New York: Columbia Univer. Press, 1948.

Lederer, E. *The state of the masses*. New York: Norton, 1940.

Lee, E. C. *The politics of nonpartisanship*. Berkeley: Univer. of California Press, 1960.

Lemert, E. M., & Rosberg, J. The administration of justice to minority groups in Los Angeles County. *Calif. Univer. Publ. Cult. Soc.*, 1948.

Lerner, D. *The passing of traditional society: Modernizing the Middle East*. Glencoe, Ill.: Free Press, 1958.

Lewis, R., & Stewart, R. *The managers: A new examination of the English, German and American executive*. New York: New American Library, 1961.

Lippmann, W. *Public opinion*. New York: Harcourt, 1922.

Lipset, S. M. *Agrarian socialism*. Berkeley: Univer. of California Press, 1950.

Lipset, S. M. Democracy and working-class authoritarianism. *Amer. sociol. Rev.*, 1959, 24, 482–501.(a)

Lipset, S. M. Political sociology. In R. K. Merton, L. Broom, & L. S. Cottrell, Jr. (Eds.), *Sociology today: Problems and prospects*. New York: Basic Books, Inc., 1959. Pp. 81–114.(b)

Lipset, S. M. *Political man*. New York: Doubleday, 1960.

Lipset, S. M., & Bendix, R. *Social mobility in industrial society*. Berkeley: Univer. of California Press, 1960.

Lipset, S. M., Lazarsfeld, P. F., Barton, A. H., & Linz, J. The psychology of voting: An analysis of political behavior. Vol. II. G. Lindzey (Ed.), *Handbook of social psychology*. Cambridge, Mass.: Addison-Wesley, 1954. Pp. 1124–1176.

Lipset, S. M., Trow, M., & Coleman, J. *Union democracy*. Glencoe, Ill.: Free Press, 1956.

Litt, E. Civic education, community norms, and political indoctrination. *Amer. sociol. Rev.*, 1963, 28, 69–76.

Long, N. E. The local community as an ecology of games. *Amer. J. Sociol.*, 1958, 44, 251–261.

Long, N. E. After the voting is over. *Midwest J. pol. Sci.*, 1962, 6 (2), 183–200.(a)

Long, N. E. *The polity*. Chicago: Rand, 1962. (b)

Long, N. E. The political act as an act of will. *Amer. J. Sociol.*, 1963, 49, 1–6.

Loomis, C. P., & Loomis, Z. K. *Modern social theories: Selected American writers*. Princeton, N.J.: Van Nostrand, 1961.

Lowenthal, L. Biographies in popular magazines. In W. Petersen (Ed.), *American so-*

cial patterns. New York: Doubleday, 1956. Pp. 63–118.

Lubell, S. *The future of American politics.* (2nd ed.) New York: Doubleday, 1956.(a)

Lubell, S. *The revolt of the moderates.* New York: Harper, 1956.(b)

Lynd, R. S., & Lynd, H. M. *Middletown: A study in contemporary American culture.* New York: Harcourt, 1929.

Lynd, R. S., & Lynd, H. M. *Middletown in transition: A study in cultural conflicts.* New York: Harcourt, 1937.

McCleery, R. H. *Policy change in prison management.* East Lansing: Governmental Research Bureau, Michigan State Univer., 1957.

Maccoby, E. E., Matthews, R. E., & Morton, A. S. Youth and political change. *Publ. Opin. Quart.,* 1954, **18**, 23–39.

McPhee, W. N., & Glaser, W. A. (Eds.) *Public opinion and congressional elections.* New York: The Free Press of Glencoe, 1962.

McRae, D. Jr. The relation between roll call votes and constituencies in the Massachusetts House of Representatives. *Amer. polit. Sci. Rev.,* 1952, **46**, 1046–1055.

McRae, D., Jr. Occupations and the congressional vote, 1940–1950. *Amer. sociol. Rev.,* 1955, **20**, 332–340.

Mannheim, K. *Man and society in an age of reconstruction.* New York: Harcourt, 1950.

Marshall, T. M. *Citizenship and social class and other essays.* Cambridge, Mass.: Cambridge Univer. Press, 1950.

Matthews, D. R. *The social background of political decision-makers.* New York: Doubleday, 1954.

Matthews, D. R., & Prothro, J. *Negro voting in the South.* New York: Wiley, forthcoming.

Merton, R. K. *Social theory and social structure.* (rev. & enlarged ed.) Glencoe, Ill.: Free Press, 1957.

Messinger, S. L. Organizational transformation: A case study of a declining social movement. *Amer. sociol Rev.,* 1955, **20**, 3–10.

Meyerson, M., & Banfield, E. C. *Politics, planning, and the public interest.* Glencoe, Ill.: Free Press, 1955.

Michels, R. *Political parties.* New York: Dover Publications, Inc., 1959.

Miller, D. C. Industry and community power structure: A comparative study of an American and an English city. *Amer. sociol. Rev.,* 1958, **23**, 9–15.

Mills, C. W. (with the assistance of H. Schneider). *The new men of power: America's labor leaders.* New York: Harcourt, 1948.

Mills, C. W. *The power elite.* New York: Oxford Univer. Press, 1956.

Moore, W. E. *Industrial relations and the social order.* New York: Macmillan, 1951.

Mosca, G. *The ruling class.* New York: McGraw, 1939.

Moskos, C., Jr. Social transformation of the Albanian elite: From monarchy to communism. In G. Blanksten & R. Mack (Eds.), *Social science and the underdeveloped areas: A revival of evolutionary theory?* New York: Wiley, in press.

Mosteller, F. (in collaboration with L. Doob and others). *The pre-election polls of 1948.* New York: Social Science Research Council, 1949.

Myrdal, G. *An American dilemma.* New York: Harper, 1944.

Nisbet, R. A. *The quest for community.* New York: Oxford Univer. Press, 1953.

Orleans, P. Partisan and nonpartisan politics in the metropolis: An analysis of the social contexts of political participation. Unpublished doctoral dissertation, Northwestern Univer., 1964.

Ostrom, V. A. *Water and politics: A study of water policies and administration in the development of Los Angeles.* Los Angeles: The Haynes Foundation, 1953.

Ostrom, V. A., Tiebout, C., & Warren, C. The organization of government in metropolitan areas: A theoretical inquiry. *Amer. polit. Sci. Rev.,* 1961, **55**, 831–842.

Pareto, V. *The mind and society.* New York: Harcourt, 1935.

Parsons, T. "Voting" and the equilibrium of the American political system. In E. Burdick & A. J. Brodbeck (Eds.), *American voting behavior.* Glencoe, Ill.: Free Press, 1959. Pp. 80–120.

Pellegrin, R. J., & Coates, C. H. Absentee owned corporations and community power structure. *Amer. J. Sociol.,* 1956, **61**, 413–419.

Pinard, M. Structural attachments and political support in urban politics: The case of fluoridation referendums. *Amer. J. Sociol.,* 1963, **68**, 513–526.

Reckless, W. *The crime problem*. New York: Appleton-Century-Crofts, Inc., 1950.

Rice, S. A. *Quantitative methods in politics*. New York: Knopf, 1928.

Riesman, D. (with N. Glazer & R. Denney). *The lonely crowd*. New Haven, Conn.: Yale Univer. Press, 1950.

Robinson, J. A. The role of the rules committee in regulating debate in the U. S. House of Representatives. *Midwest J. polit. Sci.*, 1961, 1, 59–69.

Robinson, W. S. Bias, probability and trial by jury. *Amer. sociol. Rev.*, 1950, 15, 73–78.

Robinson, W. S. The motivational structure of political participation. *Amer. sociol. Rev.*, 1952, 17, 151–156.

Roethlisberger, F. J., & Dickson, W. J. *Management and the worker*. Cambridge, Mass.: Harvard Univer. Press, 1939.

Rogers, L. Political philosophy in the twentieth century: An appraisal of its contribution to the study of politics. In R. Young (Ed.), *Approaches to the study of politics*. Evanston, Ill.: Northwestern Univer. Press, 1958. Pp. 189–214.

Rogoff, N. *Recent trends in occupational mobility*. Glencoe, Ill.: Free Press, 1953.

Ross, A. *Trade union determinants of industrial wage policy*. Berkeley: Univer. of California Press, 1949.

Rossi, P. H. Four landmarks in voting research. In E. Burdick & A. J. Brodbeck (Eds.), *American voting behavior*. Glencoe, Ill.: Free Press, 1959. Pp. 5–54.

Rossi, P. H., & Cutright, P. The impact of party organization in an industrial setting. In M. Janowitz (Ed.), *Community political systems*. Glencoe, Ill.: Free Press, 1961. Pp. 81–116.

Rossiter, C. L. *The American presidency*. New York: Harcourt, 1956.

Rostow, W. W. *The process of economic growth*. New York: Norton, 1952.

Salisbury, R. H. The dynamics of reform: Charter politics in St. Louis. *Midwest J. polit. Sci.*, 1961, 5, 260–275.

Sayre, W. S., & Kaufman, H. *Governing New York City: Politics in the metropolis*. New York: Russell Sage Foundation, 1960.

Schattschneider, E. E. *Party government*. New York: Farrar & Rinehart, Inc., 1942.

Schmandt, H. J., Steinbicker, P. G., & Wendel,

G. D. *Metropolitan reform in St. Louis*. New York: Holt, Rinehart & Winston, 1961.

Schulze, R. O. The bifurcation of power in a satellite city. In M. Janowitz (Ed.), *Community political systems*. Glencoe, Ill.: Free Press, 1961. Pp. 19–80.

Schumpeter, J. A. *Capitalism, socialism, and democracy*. New York: Harper, 1942.

Scoble, H. Leadership hierarchies and political issues in a New England town. In M. Janowitz (Ed.), *Community political systems*. Glencoe, Ill.: Free Press, 1961.

Seligman, L. G. Developments in the presidency and the conception of political leadership. *Amer. sociol. Rev.*, 1955, 20, 706–712.

Selznick, P. Foundations of the theory of organization. *Amer. sociol. Rev.*, 1948, 13, 25–35.

Selznick, P. *TVA and the grassroots*. Berkeley: Univer. of California Press, 1949.

Selznick, P. Institutional vulnerability in mass society. *Amer. J. Sociol.*, 1951, 56, 320–331.

Selznick, P. *The organizational weapon*. New York: McGraw, 1952.

Shepard, H., & Kornhauser, A. *When labor votes*. New York: University Books, 1956.

Shevky, E., & Bell, W. *Social area analysis*. Stanford: Stanford Univer. Press, 1955.

Shils, E. A. The study of the primary group. In D. Lerner & H. Lasswell (Eds.), *The policy sciences*. Stanford: Stanford Univer. Press, 1951. Pp. 44–69.

Sibley, E. Some demographic clues to stratification. In L. Wilson & W. L. Kolb (Eds.), *Sociological analysis*. New York: Harcourt, 1949. Pp. 642–650.

Simon, H. A. *Administrative behavior*. (2nd ed.) New York: Macmillan, 1957.

Smallwood, F. *The government of Greater London*. Indianapolis: Bobbs, 1964.

Sofen, E. P. *The Miami metropolitan experiment*. Bloomington: Indiana Univer. Press, 1963.

Sorokin, P. *Social mobility*. New York: Harper, 1927.

Speier, H. Historical development of public opinion. *Amer. J. Sociol.*, 1950, 55, 376–388.

Stouffer, S. A. *Communism, conformity, and civil liberties: A cross-section of the nation speaks its mind*. New York: Doubleday, 1955.

Sutton, F. X. *The American business creed*.

Cambridge, Mass.: Harvard Univer. Press, 1956.

Sykes, G. M. The differential distribution of community knowledge. In P. K. Hatt & A. J. Reiss (Eds.), *Cities and society*. Glencoe, Ill.: Free Press, 1951. Pp. 711–721.

Trow, M. Small business, political tolerance, and support for McCarthy. *Amer. J. Sociol.,* 1958, 64, 270–281.

Truman, D. B. *The congressional party*. New York: Wiley, 1959.

Tumin, M. Some principles of stratification: A critical analysis. *Amer. sociol. Rev.,* 1953, 18, 387–394.

Wahlke, J. C., Eulau, H., Buchanan, W., & Ferguson, L. C. *The legislative system: Explorations in legislative behavior*. New York: Wiley, 1962.

Walter, B. Political decision making in Arcadia. In F. S. Chapin, Jr. & S. F. Weiss (Eds.), *Urban growth dynamics in a regional cluster of cities*. New York: Wiley, 1962. Pp. 144–187.

Warner, W. L. (Ed.) *Yankee City* (abrid. ed.) New Haven, Conn.: Yale Univer. Press, 1963.

Warner, W. L., & Abegglen, J. C. *Big business leaders in America*. New York: Harper, 1955.

Watson, R. A., & Romani, J. H. Metropolitan government for metropolitan Cleveland: An analysis of the voting record. *Midwest J. polit. Sci.,* 1961, 5, 365–390.

Weber, M. Politics as a vocation. In H. H. Gerth & C. W. Mills (Eds.), *From Max Weber: Essays in sociology*. New York: Oxford Univer. Press, 1946.

Weber, M. *The theory of economic and social organization*. A. M. Henderson & T. Parsons (Trans.). Glencoe, Ill.: Free Press, 1947.

Weltman, N., & Remmers, H. H. Pupils', parents', and teachers' attitudes—Similarities and differences. *Stud. higher Educ.,* 1936, 31, 1–52.

Westley, W. A. Violence and the police. *Amer. J. Sociol.,* 1953, 39, 34–41.

White, T. H. *The making of a president: 1960*. New York: Atheneum Publishers, 1961.

Wilensky, H. *Intellectuals in the labor unions*. Glencoe, Ill.: Free Press, 1956.

Wilensky, H. Orderly careers and social participation: The impact of work history on social integration in the middle mass. *Amer. sociol. Rev.,* 1961, 26, 521–539.

Williams, O. P., & Adrian, C. R. The insulation of local politics under the nonpartisan ballot. *Amer. polit. Sci. Rev.,* 1959, 53, 1052–1063.

Williams, R. M., Jr. *American society*. New York: Knopf, 1960.

Wilson, G., & Wilson, M. *The analysis of social change*. Cambridge: Cambridge Univer. Press, 1954.

Wilson, W. *The president of the United States*. New York: Harper, 1916.

Wirth, L. Urbanism as a way of life. *Amer. J. Sociol.,* 1938, 44, 1–24.

Wirth, L. Consensus and mass communication. *Amer. sociol. Rev.,* 1948, 13, 1–15.

Wood, R. C. *Suburbia: Its people and their politics*. Boston: Houghton, 1958.

Wood, R. C. Review of American voting behavior. E. Burdick & A. J. Brodbeck (Eds.). *Amer. sociol. Rev.,* 1959, 24, 719–720.

Wood, R. C. (with C. V. Almendinger). *1400 governments: The political economy of the New York metropolitan region*. Cambridge, Mass.: Harvard Univer. Press, 1961.

Wright, C. R., & Hyman, H. H. Voluntary association memberships of American adults: Evidence from national sample surveys. *Amer. sociol. Rev.,* 1958, 23, 284–294.

Wrong, D. H. The oversocialized conception of man in modern sociology. *Amer. sociol. Rev.,* 1961, 26, 183–193.

CHAPTER 22 Sociology of Science

NORMAN KAPLAN[1]

A quarter of a century has passed since Merton (1938) first published his pioneering study of science and technology in seventeenth-century England. More than a decade has passed since the appearance of the first textbook, by Bernard Barber (1952), wholly devoted to the sociology of science, and some years have passed since Barber's (1956b) discussion of the trends in the sociology of science. In his Foreword to Barber's text, Merton (1952) noted and analyzed the relative neglect by sociologists of the sociology of science. The present review shows that sociologists continue to neglect this field. The sociology of science itself, however, has been literally blossoming in this past decade.

The virtual neglect of the field by sociologists is amply evident throughout this chapter, primarily by the scarcity of studies. No further detailed documentation is necessary but a few items might be noted in passing. For example: (1) The number of American sociologists explicitly interested in the sociology of science is extremely small: The hard core consists of perhaps a dozen, with another score or so interested in a peripheral fashion. (2) The introductory sociology textbooks, often considered (rightly or wrongly) a reflection of developments in the field, have practically ignored the sociology of science. Chinoy (1961, Ch. 16) stands as the sole major exception. A review of the major texts which have appeared in recent years shows almost no awareness at all of the existence of science as a social institution. In many of the leading texts there is not a single reference to the existence of science. (3) A review of the Ph.D. thesis titles listed in the *American Journal of Sociology* during the past decade suggests that, even with the broadest definition

[1] Grateful acknowledgment is made to the U.S.P.H.S. (United States Public Health Service), National Institutes of Health for a series of research grants (the current one being GM 09225—03) which have made it possible to explore some of the facets of the sociology of science discussed here. I also wish to acknowledge the help and critical suggestions of Harold J. Bershady, Beverly F. Porter, and Brenda R. Silver.

In addition I wish to thank the following colleagues who read the draft copy and sent in many valuable suggestions and comments: Stevan Dedijer, Gerald Gordon, Warren Hagstrom, Walter Hirsch, Norman Storer, Christopher Wright, and Conway Zirkle. Unfortunately, many came too late to be incorporated but, needless to say, all errors and omissions are the sole responsibility of the author.

of what constitutes the sociology of science, no more than an average of one dissertation per year could reasonably be classified as devoted to the sociology of science. (4) A review of the articles published in the major journals of sociology during the past decade shows a very small number devoted primarily to the sociology of science. In short, a review confined primarily to the contributions of sociologists to the sociology of science would not only be a very brief one, but would also omit most of the contributions that have been made to the field during the past decade.

What is the sociology of science? In the broadest sense, the sociology of science is concerned with the interrelations of science and society. How has science influenced values, education, class structure, ways of life, political decisions, and ways of looking at the world? How has society, in turn, influenced the development of science itself? These questions loom so large on the horizon today that many scholars have been unwilling to wait until the sociologists themselves become interested in the sociology of science.

There is no readily available and acceptable conceptual scheme which defines the boundaries or lays out the major theoretical questions and hypotheses in the sociology of science. Barber (1959, p. 223) suggested that Talcott Parsons' (1951, Ch. 8) discussion is perhaps the best available conceptual scheme, but even as "a guide to theoretical fundamentals" this treatment is considered unsatisfactory as a general framework for the whole of the sociology of science, however adequate it may be for some portions of it. Despite the absence of a unifying conceptual scheme, a review chapter such as this must implicitly suggest one, for the categories used to organize the material reviewed reflect decisions to include as well as exclude materials. The scheme is certainly a rudimentary one. It divides the review that follows into four major categories: (1) the nature of science; (2) the nature of scientists; (3) the organization of

science; and (4) the interrelationships of science and society.

In the first section, the emphasis is primarily on science as a social system or social institution with its own distinct values, roles, and intra- as well as interinstitutional relationships. In the second category, a review will be presented of what is known of the social background, personality, motivation, socialization, and other social psychological aspects of the scientist.

The organization of science is subdivided into two categories. The first deals with the organization of scientific research at the laboratory level. Here are included studies of the increasing complexity of research organization, the development of new organizational roles such as that of the research administrator, and the growing concern to develop organizational environments which will promote productivity and creativity. The second part treats some of the new problems encountered and studied with respect to national patterns of scientific organization in different societies. Especially important are the problems of the support, planning, and control of science at the national level.

The final section reviews some of the more significant developments in the increasingly intimate relationship between science and society. Science is rapidly losing its former insulated status. It is now in the forefront of many of the major decisions made in the political, economic, military, and social spheres. Whether one is concerned with the newly developing nations, the cold war, or the population explosion, one is actively concerned with the role of science and scientists.

Before proceeding it should be noted that this review departs from traditional practices, for it does not include an explicit section on the historical antecedents of the sociology of science. These are described in the various works of Barber (1952; 1956a; 1956b; 1959). To discuss these antecedents in a brief space would hardly do justice to the richness of the available material. One

point should be mentioned, however: The
continued neglect by sociologists of the sociology of science has inevitably resulted in
the neglect of some of the more important
contributions of its earlier sociologists. While
the author would agree with Barber about
the significance of the contributions of Weber (1946), Marx (1935), Mannheim (1936),
Znaniecki (1940), and others, he can only
add that their suggestions and fruitful hypotheses have yet to be fully exploited in
much of the work currently in progress.
Rather than pay the usual lip service to
the founding fathers, it will be left to the
reader to judge for himself whether the
sociology of science has benefited, and
would benefit, from a closer reading of
some of their works.

THE NATURE OF SCIENCE

Scientists actively engaged in research are
not concerned particularly with the nature
of science as such. They have been largely
content to leave such broad questions to
the historians and philosophers of science.
Many scientists have argued that too much
self-awareness and self-consciousness in following the formal description of how science
is conducted would inevitably impede the
progress of the research. Whether this is
so or not, anyone who would study science
from a sociological perspective must have
some working conception of the nature of
science.

One must be able to distinguish between
the ideal pattern and the actual patterns
which exist. It should be superfluous to
point out that scientific research does not
progress as it is described in a scientific
publication. The textbook description of
scientific method which leads one to expect an orderly progression from the recognition and definition of the problem, to
the framing of hypotheses, to the empirical
testing of these hypotheses, to their subsequent verification (or not), followed by the
reformulation of hypotheses, and their reintegration with existing theory, and so on

does not occur so neatly in real life laboratory situations. We all know that it is not so
and yet sometimes we behave as if it were
—a situation which may be all right for the
man conducting the research but is less desirable for one who would *study* the man
who is conducting the research.

Science has often been viewed as a monolithic entity, especially the corpus of the
physical and natural sciences. Social scientists are well aware of the usual distinction
between the developed and less-developed
sciences, but sometimes forget that there are
vast differences between some of the highly
developed natural sciences and some of the
newer and considerably less well-developed
ones. Moreover, they tend to forget about
the significant differences within a single
broad science, such as physics, in which
some of the newer subfields are as much
underdeveloped as some of the social
sciences.

Another problem is the question of basic
versus applied research. This has played a
large role in the discussion of scientists
(Wolfle, 1959b), in the development of adequate statistics on the scientific effort, and
in the formulation of national policies (National Science Foundation, 1957; Naval Research Advisory Committee, 1959), but has
been largely unexplored by social scientists.
The distinction is most frequently made in
terms of the motivations and attitudes of
the scientist—whether he does research for
its own sake or to attain some particular
end considered useful; e.g., a cure for a
disease or a new clean bomb (Kidd, 1959b).
Despite this large social component, most
social scientists have been content to accept
this distinction without much question and
certainly without the considerable analysis
required.

Sociologists and others who would study
science as a phenomenon in its own right
need to have a far more accurate picture of
the reality of scientific endeavor. They do
not need to become physicists or chemists,
nor even to acquire the entire corpus of
knowledge of a contemporary physicist or

chemist, any more than they would need to become juvenile delinquents or lawyers or unemployed housewives to study any of those populations.

Those who would study science or scientists from a social perspective must know something about the technical aspects of science. Whether they lean most heavily on the philosopher of science (Nagel, 1961), the historian of science (Kuhn, 1962b), the scientist himself, or some combination of these is immaterial. Kuhn's (1962b) work is an especially important contribution in this context since he raised many new questions concerning the traditional views of science and its development. He challenged the usual notions of the cumulative nature of science, and, even more important, his distinctions between "normal science" and the revolutions in science have enormous, but as yet barely explored, implications for the sociology of science. The important thing is not to neglect the technical aspects of science in order to be able to decide how these affect and are affected by social and other "external" conditions and factors.

Science as a Social System

Just as Durkheim (1933) did for the division of labor, and Weber (1930) for the rise of capitalism, so Merton (1938) attempted to explain the origins of modern science. The development of modern science was aided and abetted by changes in religious and other values of the society. Behind the rules that developed for the conduct of science stood a system of moral imperatives, sanctions, and interrelated roles which helped to support and maintain the purely technical aspects of science as an ongoing activity. While the technical aspects are exceedingly important, as was noted above, one must also be alert to the extremely and equally important nontechnical factors which are often sociological in nature.

The work of Merton (1938; 1957b) and Parsons (1951) in laying out some of the distinctive features of science as a social system has probably exerted the most influence on contemporary research in the field. Barber (1952) not only brought them together and added some of his own comments, but also was instrumental in bringing their work to the attention of a wider audience.

In his now classic paper on "Science and the Social Order," Merton (1957b) suggested that there were four basic institutional imperatives for science. These were: universalism, communism, disinterestedness, and organized skepticism. All of these, Merton argued, were derived from, or related to, the technical demands of science. But these were singled out because of their moral aspect which gave them the characteristic of being more than technical norms. Merton readily admitted that these imperatives were derived largely from the writings and documents of the seventeenth century. Implicit in Merton's formulation of his four institutional imperatives is the idea that these have remained relatively unchanged from the time of their early origins. But this hypothesis needs to be reexamined (Kaplan, 1963b). West (1960), for example, found substantial departures from the classical position on moral values governing scientific research among a small sample of academic scientists.

Parsons (1951) treated the normative system of science in three different categories, some of which overlap Merton's (1957b) institutional imperatives. Parsons posited four basic norms relevant to scientific knowledge: empirical validity, logical clarity, logical consistency, and generality of the principles involved (Parsons, 1951, p. 335). These are primarily "technical" norms. When Parsons discussed the scientist's occupational role he did so in terms of his pattern variable configuration: universalism, affective neutrality, specificity, achievement orientation, and collectivity orientation (Parsons, 1951, p. 343). Parsons also talked of two norms which bind the scientist as researcher, namely, tentativeness and the acceptance of the validity of scientific findings which have been adequately demonstrated (Parsons, 1951, p. 353). The latter are clearly equivalent to Merton's organized skepticism and to universalism. Merton's other two imperatives may be found amongst Parsons' pattern variables.

It is, or course, possible to separate theoretically the values or norms of an institution from those of the participants involved, at least at an abstract conceptual level. The four basic norms of scientific knowledge posited by Parsons (1951) are binding on the man of science. His work must be empirically valid, logically clear and consistent, and general in terms of the principles involved. These are more or less technical rules simultaneously constituting limiting conditions and goals for the activities called science. They are also the desirable and, indeed, required attitudes which a scientist should display toward his work. In addition, these basic norms provide the criteria by which one's work is judged and evaluated.

The pattern variables, on the other hand, define the expectations specific to the role. So long as the basic norms of producing scientific knowledge are accepted, the role configuration is in some senses superfluous. For example, one would judge a work according to its empirical validity, logical clarity, and so on, without reference to the man's color, class, or other social attributes. Perhaps, though, the specific role attributes are essential because any particular individual has to be "reminded" of the need to be universalistic, affectively neutral, and so on, in his role as scientist, since in other roles these same criteria might not apply with equal force. One might also question Parsons' (1951) distinction between the scientist's occupational role (to which he attached a particular pattern variable configuration) and his designation of the scientist as researcher, to which he adds two additional norms discussed previously.

A general question which emerges is the extent to which the norms posited by Parsons (1951) or Merton (1957b) are explicitly tied to the occupational role, or to some facet of that role. Is it possible to view these norms as essentially "free floating"? To what extent is the researcher role different from the occupational role of scientist? Is Parsons referring particularly to the occupational role within an institutional context, such as the role of the university professor? Questions may be raised also about the interrelations of a set of values for the system and for the participants within that system. Is one to assume, for example, that these particular values are the more strongly held by a scientist the more strongly he is integrated into the scientific social system? Is the scientist more or less integrated into the system at different points in time? Is the scientist more or less integrated in the period immediately after initial socialization or at a much later stage in his career? Are there differences in the way in which these values are accepted by participants in relation to differences in "the stage of development" of a science itself—for example, are sociologists more likely to overconform (or underconform) to these values (say, compared with physicists) because sociologists are relative newcomers to the world of science? Finally, one must question the strong suggestion that all scientists are peers, with an almost total neglect of the internal hierarchical structuring and the resulting relationships which occur whether these be in a university, industrial, or government laboratory.

A further point concerning the value system posited by Merton (1957b), Parsons (1951), and others is the extent to which these values are presumed to have remained unchanged since the seventeenth century. Merton in particular argued that they have hardly changed and pointed to certain deviations, and the reactions to these, which occurred during World War I, for example, as evidence of the continued strength of these norms. There have been few attempts either to study these values and norms in some broad systematic way or to develop them further along theoretical lines. In general, there seems to be unqualified acceptance of them by scholars who study science and scientists. For example, two recent books, one by Marcson (1960b) and the other by Kornhauser (1962), are based largely on the hypothesis that these values are still in existence and strong. In both books the central problem is viewed as the conflict between the values of science and the values of the organization, more specifically those of industrial organizations. Though the terms employed are not identical, in general the conflict is seen to be between the requirement for autonomy of the social system of science versus the requirement of control of the industrial organization. Further, the specific institutional imperatives of science are viewed as being threatened by those of industry. This applies particularly to the norms of communality (as Barber [1952] rechristened Merton's imperative of communism) and disinterestedness. Whether their analysis is correct or not, the point to be stressed here is that the values posited by Merton and Barber and Parsons have been fully accepted as those which prevail today, without any additional empirical verification or theoretical analysis.

The Communications System in Science

The institutional imperative of communism obliges the scientist to communicate his results freely and to abhor secrecy. Aside from the problems of restricted communication in matters of military security and in industry, where possibly a competitive advantage may be gained by withholding technical data, the imperative against secrecy appears to be superfluous. Scientists, especially those in the universities, seem well aware of the increasing significance of the "publish or perish" theme. The current "publications explosion" is viewed by many observers as an indication that too many scientists are rushing into print much too often (cf. Calder, 1961).

Surprisingly, there has been little discussion about the norms surrounding publication. A major exception has been the series of papers by Merton (1957a; 1961; 1963) on the conflicts over priority rights among scientists. But there has been no known systematic study of the norms pertaining to the precise timing of a scientific communication in relation to the stage of the research project; to the arrangement of names in multiple-authored papers; or to the assignment of publication credit where the original idea may have come from one man, but where the actual research experiment has come from several others, the analysis has been done by another, and the major writing job has been done by yet another man. A physicist (Reif, 1961) recently suggested that the competition is becoming much more intense in this arena, even for the "pure" scientist.

Clearly, the whole area of communications is a vital part of the social system of science. It is essential to remind oneself of this fact in the light of the tremendous upsurge of interest in the technical aspects of communication resulting from the continuing publications "explosion." For example, as a recent government report stated:

Chemical Abstracts in 1930 contained 54,000 abstracts; a private subscription cost $7.50 per year, an institutional subscription cost $12 per year. In 1962 *Chemical Abstracts* published 165,000 abstracts and the 1963 price will be $500 to American Chemical Society members and to colleges and universities, and $1000 per year to all others (President's Science Advisory Committee, 1963, p. 18).

Some have estimated the total number of papers published annually in the sciences in the early 1960's as over 2 million. In addition to published papers it was estimated that in the United States alone some 100,000 informal government reports are published annually, of which 75,000 are "unclassified" (President's Science Advisory Committee, 1963, p. 19).

This communications explosion within

science has given rise to concerted efforts to deal with the problem on the basis of new technological advances. Through the use of computers and a variety of other technical devices, an effort is being made to facilitate the storage and retrieval of information. Considerable progress is being made along these lines, but at the same time questions have been raised about the changing function of scientific communication and a host of other quasi-technical and nontechnical aspects of the communications process. It is in the latter terms that a discussion of communications is relevant within the general topic of the nature of science and its social system.

In his recent book, D. de S. Price (1963) reviewed briefly the history of the scientific paper. He suggested that it came into being originally because there were "too many books." The scientific journal, born around the middle of the seventeenth century, came into being with the function of "digesting the books and doings of the learned all over Europe. Through them the casual reader might inform himself without the network of personal correspondence, private rumor, and browsing in Europe's bookstores, formerly essential" (D. de S. Price, 1963, p. 63). According to Price, the original purpose of these journals was primarily the social one of finding out what was being done and by whom, rather than the scholarly one of publishing new knowledge (1963, p. 63). Price, relying heavily on Barber's (1961) paper, went on to state, "original publication of short papers by single authors was a distinct innovation in the life of science, and, like all innovations it met with considerable resistance from scientists" (D. de S. Price, 1963, p. 63). It was not until about the middle of the nineteenth century that the short paper as an independent unit began to appear. In addition to communicating new knowledge, one of the prime factors in the establishment of the scientific paper as the mode of communication is the necessity to maintain and establish one's intellectual property—as Derek Price put it, "the never-

gentle art of establishing of priority claims" (D. de S. Price, 1963, p. 65; cf. Merton, 1957a; Merton, 1961; Merton, 1963).

Publications have assumed still another function which has played an increasingly important role in modern times. The number of publications a man has produced is generally accepted (despite the usual reservations) as a measure of a man's scientific worth. The fact that this is so has "moved people to publish merely because this is how they may be judged" (D. de S. Price, 1963, p. 40). Until the 1950's or so these judgments were primarily those of deans, chairmen of departments, research directors, and the like, in evaluating a man's promotion or salary increase within his own institution (see, for example, Caplow & McGee, 1958). Recently, however, with the growth of the project grant system and the expansion of federal aid for research, it has become almost as necessary to publish papers simply to continue to receive research support, irrespective of whether one is in line for promotion or salary increase at that time.

In a development related to the changing social organization of research, the number of multiple-authored papers has risen sharply since the beginning of this century. Moreover, in recent years it has been possible to find articles with as many as a dozen authors listed. Some (e.g., D. de S. Price, 1963, p. 90) see the beginning of a new trend wherein none of the authors is listed; instead the name of the research team or organization is listed as the author of the scientific communication.

One of the best examples of pioneering social research in the science communications area is the series of studies conducted at the Bureau of Applied Social Research (1958; 1960). In an exploratory study at a single university, Menzel and his associates conducted intensive interviews with 77 scientists in biochemistry, chemistry, and zoology to learn about their communications behavior. They were interested primarily in the following kinds of questions: (1) What are the scientists' communications channels

for exchanging and gathering information?
(2) What are the varying functions of scientific communication? (3) What are communications' "needs" and how well are these satisfied? (4) What are the situations in which the exchange of information takes place? (5) What are the conditions and opportunities which influence information needs and information-gathering habits?

On the basis of this exploratory study, Menzel (Bureau of Applied Social Research, 1958, p. 132) raised a number of important research questions. In particular, he pointed to the range of functions, both manifest and latent, as well as the range of possible means, of communications. He noted the importance of a variety of informal channels, some of which D. de S. Price (1963, Ch. 3) later aptly labeled the "invisible colleges."

Since that study Menzel (Bureau of Applied Social Research, 1960) has also published a review of related studies and has been concerned with a series of other studies which would build on the initial exploratory work already completed. Parenthetically, it might be noted that this work on the communications behavior among scientists can be traced back fairly directly to some of the early communications studies done at the Bureau in the 1940's and 1950's. In particular there seems to be a direct line from the Decatur study (Katz, 1957; Katz & Lazarsfeld, 1955) to the more recent and somewhat more closely related studies of diffusion of knowledge among physicians, especially concerning new drugs (Coleman, Katz, & Menzel, 1957; Coleman, Menzel, & Katz, 1959; Menzel, 1957; Menzel, 1960). In this, and in subsequent studies undertaken at the Bureau, the scientific communications process is viewed as part of a larger social system. While professional information experts, librarians, editors, abstractors, and others seek a variety of ways to improve communications by electronic and other devices, sociologists are making, and will make, their contribution by pointing to the network of social relationships in which

communication is embedded and to the inadequacy of restricting attention solely to formal means of communication.

As Menzel (Bureau of Applied Social Research, 1958) pointed out, and as others have increasingly begun to recognize, face-to-face and interpersonal communication plays a role of ever-increasing importance in scientific communication. As the number of scientists has increased and specialization has been intensified and as the time lag between the publication of a paper and its submission for consideration has increased, so the need for alternative modes of communication has arisen. In this situation it is less than surprising that interpersonal communications have come to the fore. In addition there has arisen what is now institutionalized as the "preprint" (the mimeographed or dittoed document) which is privately circulated. As one observer recently put it, "with respect to preprints, science faces a real danger of reverting to the privacy of the 17th century: some biologists think this has already happened to molecular biology, where preprints are often circulated only to one's friends" (Weinberg, 1963, pp. 68, 71). This quotation is from an article which summarized a part of a recent report of the President's Advisory Science Committee, chaired by Dr. Weinberg, on "Science, Government, and Information." As this report noted,

Transfer of information is an inseparable part of research and development. All those concerned with research and development . . . must accept responsibility for the transfer of information in the same degree and spirit that they accept responsibility for research and development itself.

The later steps in the information transfer process, such as retrieval, are strongly affected by the attitudes and practices of the originators of scientific information. The working scientist must therefore share many of the burdens which have traditionally been carried by the professional documentalist. The technical community generally must devote a larger share than heretofore of its time and resources to the discriminating management of the ever increasing technical record. Doing less will lead to fragmented and ineffective science and technology (President's Science Advisory Committee, 1963, p. 1).

Not only does the report urge the technical community to recognize the importance of handling information adequately, stressing that it is an integral part of the scientific process (one wonders why it should be so necessary to stress this), but it also urges that new techniques and methods be explored for what it calls "switching," by which is meant devices for connecting the user with the information (as contrasted with the documents) he needs. Among the suggested methods are: specialized information centers; central depositories; mechanized information processing; and the development of what is termed "software," which indicates the panel's recognition that hardware alone is inadequate for coping with the problems of information retrieval. In the panel's view, software includes methods of analyzing, indexing, and programing for successful information retrieval. Although Weinberg (1963), a nuclear physicist by training, and the other physical scientists on the panel are undoubtedly aware of some of the social aspects of this communication process, it is regrettable that so little of this shows in their report and recommendations.

While it can be said that a start has been made toward the study of many aspects of the scientific communications process, almost nothing has been done about yet another aspect, namely, the scientific convention or meeting. Sociologists themselves know about it primarily because they are participants in this process and are likely to hear jokes, sarcastic remarks about "living it up," and other such informal characterizations of the changing nature of scientific conventions. For example, the following item appeared in *The Observer:*

Dr. William H. Pickering, the president of the American Rocket Society, says that the space industry spends, directly and indirectly, 150 million dollars a year on attending and exhibiting at technical conferences. . . . The same technical papers, thinly disguised, are presented again and again . . . (and) many people spend most of their time shuffling from one conference to another (*The Observer,* November 5, 1961, p. 4).

One specialist told of an international scientific conference at which some seven hundred papers were "read" by title only. In other words, there was no communication of scientific findings at all (except what might be gleaned from a brief title). For many scientists, however, international congresses and other large gatherings are not as valuable only for the formal papers as they are for the opportunity to interact face-to-face with a number of fellow specialists. Except for anecdotal reports, then, there have been no studies of the changing functions of scientific congresses, as well as of the different kinds of scientific meetings which have sprung up.

The communications area has been treated in some detail to provide examples of the kinds of research questions which may emerge from considering one important facet of the social system of science. The field of scientific communications is an interesting case where applied interests and new technical developments spur research efforts from which may come new basic knowledge. As more social scientists delve into these problems, it is highly likely that more of the total social system of science will be opened up to fruitful inquiry. One such direction of obvious importance is the individual scientist as a subject for further study.

THE NATURE OF THE SCIENTIST

Shortly after World War II, it was estimated that altogether there were 140,000 people engaged in science in the United States (*Fortune,* 1948). Of these only some 25,000 held the Ph.D. in one of the natural or physical sciences. By 1960 it was estimated that there were 1.4 million scientists, engineers, and teachers of science of whom 87,000 had a doctorate (National Science Foundation, 1961). Who are these people? What is known about this increasingly important yet tiny fraction of the population?

Strangely enough, little is known today about the social characteristics of American scientists. It is highly unlikely that a study of America's scientists in the mid-1960's would find (as the post World War II studies found [*Fortune,* 1948; Steelman, 1947, Vol. III, Appendix III]) that a large proportion of biologists came from a rural farm background, while physical scientists were more likely to have come from a middle-class, Protestant, small-town or urban background. The social background of today's scientists is different not only because of changing population patterns within the country, but also because of the broadening of the recruitment base for many of the sciences. It seems strange that so little is known because this is probably the one area in which sociologists have the greatest immediate capability in conceptual and methodological tools. This is especially true for the sociologists of occupations and professions.

The Creative Scientist

Much of the existing knowledge about the nature of scientists derives from a small number of studies by psychologists interested in the creative scientist. Perhaps the most widely known, most influential, and most frequently cited one is the study by Anne Roe (1953). Although she chose a total of 64 outstanding scientists in 4 different fields and made no attempt to generalize to all scientists, her work is frequently cited in support of various statements made about scientists in general.

McClelland (1962) listed the following characteristics of physical scientists that seem to him to have been confirmed in various studies, recognizing the difficulty and danger of making generalizations based on the varied and small populations studied.

One way of minimizing the difficulty is to try to select only those characteristics which are so striking that they apply (with variations, of course) to all scientifically oriented subjects but in greater degree to those who are more creative or eminent. Another way of minimizing the danger of too-sweeping generalizations is to focus on experimental physical science—in particular on physics and chemistry. Theoretical physics and mathematics shade off in one direction from such a focus and the biological sciences in another so that any statements made need not apply as fully to scientists in these areas. With these guidelines in mind the following generalizations would appear to summarize fairly well the characteristics of physical scientists as they have been uncovered by investigations up to the present (McClelland, 1962, pp. 143–144).

McClelland's (1962) generalizations are as follows: (1) Men are more likely to be creative scientists than women. (2) Experimental physical scientists come from a background of radical protestantism more often than would be expected by chance, but are not themselves religious. (3) Scientists avoid interpersonal contact. (4) Creative scientists are unusually hard working to the extent of appearing almost obsessed with their work. (5) Scientists avoid and are disturbed by complex human emotions, perhaps particularly by interpersonal aggression. Scientists react emotionally to human feelings and try to avoid them. (6) Physical scientists like music and dislike art and poetry. (7) Physical scientists are intensely masculine. (8) Physical scientists develop a strong interest in analysis, in the structure of things, early in life (McClelland, 1962, pp. 144ff).

In a study of 40 scientists, Eiduson (1962) suggested the following list of personality characteristics:

(a) The scientist has strong emotional leanings to intellectual activities; (b) he is independent in his thoughts and actions, and does not mimic others; (c) he is challenged by frustration and anxiety-producing situations; (d) curiosity is likely to be the major determinate in his work; (e) strong ego involvement and conflict are expressed in work; (f) he does not use parental ideals to set up his own goals; (g) he shows a strong capacity for sensual gratification; (h) he is motivated by a desire to master or interpret natural forces or reality; (i) he is sensitive to the moods and feelings of others; (j) he is sensitive to his internal environment, needs, wishes, desires; (k) he values his work primarily as permitting expression of inner personality (Eiduson, 1962, pp. 86–87).

Such lists could be multiplied almost endlessly. The interested reader is referred to two major sources in addition to the ones already mentioned: Taylor and Barron (1963), which contains selected papers from the first three Utah Conferences on the Identification of Creative Talent; and Stein and Heinze (1960), which is a detailed annotated bibliography of the more important works in this field.

Fascinating and important as the study of creativity may be, a detailed review, especially of the psychological and psychiatric studies, would be out of place here. This subject will be returned to again in the next section, where some of the studies of organizational and other social factors which may influence the creativity of scientists are reviewed.

Many of the psychologically-oriented creativity studies were designed to ascertain the characteristics of creative scientists in order to devise effective selection procedures for potential recruits to science. This follows the traditional psychological strategy of determining attributes of "successful" people and designing standardized tests which attempt to tap those particular attributes. The reader now comes to the more general area of the recognition, recruitment, and selection of scientists.

Selection and Recruitment of Scientists

Perhaps the best recent summary of the state of available knowledge about the characteristics of the scientist in general is contained in a volume by Super and Bachrach (1957). The aim of this review was to summarize what was already known about scientific careers, the characteristics of the natural and physical scientist, the mathematician, and the engineer, together with recommendations about further research which seemed advisable.

As the authors of this volume noted: "The portrait of the successful natural scientist which emerges from the general literature is that of a paragon" (Super & Bachrach, 1957, p. 1). According to these studies the scientist is capable of rigorous and abstract thinking and of a high level of achievement; he has good verbal reasoning ability, a high level of reading speed and comprehension, an extensive vocabulary, a facility of expression; he has superior scholarship, superior quantitative aptitudes, good spatial visualization, high mechanical comprehension, superior manual dexterity. He is also said to be ingenious, curious, industrious, full of initiative, strongly inner directed, enthusiastic, energetic, exceptionally honest, imaginative, and he possesses originality and high analytic ability. The authors state that "the stereotype of the scientist as a lonely, socially inadequate, and somewhat withdrawn individual, curious, self-disciplined, unemotional, tolerant of others, and intensively devoted to his work finds considerable support in the research literature" (Super & Bachrach, 1957, p. 3). The potential scientist is likely to become interested in science rather early in life, often around the age of 10. He comes from an upwardly mobile middle-class family background which can be characterized as intellectually stimulating and well endowed.

But the authors noted in their conclusions: "Research has been based largely on trait-and-factor theory, derived from the psychology of individual differences and from a static approach to social factors" (Super & Bachrach, 1957, p. 6). A large proportion of the studies reviewed are concerned with success in college, with the main criterion often that of success in college courses. The authors stated: "There is an overemphasis on intellectual factors and other easily measured characteristics, but there are too few studies investigating such less easily assessed and quantified factors as personality traits and motivation" (Super & Bachrach, 1957, p. 7). One particularly promising exception to this kind of approach may be found in Cooley (1958). Many of the studies are relatively static in design instead of longitudinal and rarely use carefully selected samples of chemists, biologists, and the like, as opposed to relatively heterogeneous samples of "scientists."

Fortune magazine (1948) reported on one of the first nationwide sample surveys of American scientists and continued its pioneering ways with a series of articles in 1960 on the "great American scientists" (Editors of *Fortune*, 1961). While not adding much to our systematic knowledge of scientists in general, these perceptive articles brought together the personal life histories of some of the great scientists, together with a discussion of the work they had accomplished in the development of a number of specific scientific fields.

Some information about scientists as well as about the academic institutions which produced them is to be found in the classic studies by Knapp and Goodrich (1952) and by Knapp and J. J. Greenbaum (1953). They showed that the smaller, liberal arts, middle- and far-western colleges were much more effective producers of scientists than other academic institutions. This so-called institutional productivity hypothesis was reexamined in the light of certain studies connected with the National Merit Scholarship program. It was suggested that "institutional productivity" was "a function of the differential college attendance, paternal vocational motivations, and their implied correlates among high aptitude students" (Holland, 1957, p. 437).

Some notions of the characteristics of the American scientist have been derived especially from studies among high school and college students of their images of the scientist. Mention should be made in particular of the study by Margaret Mead and Rhoda Metraux (1957) and the study by David C. Beardslee and Donald D. O'Dowd (1961). However important these images are for the recruitment of new scientists, they obviously tell much more about images than about the actual characteristics of scientists in America today.

Because of limitations of space it is necessary to omit a number of manpower and recruitment studies, as well as studies in a number of related areas (e.g., Brown & Harbison, 1957). Many of these have grown out of the pre-Sputnik concern with the shortage of engineers and the post-Sputnik concern with the shortage of scientists generally. In addition, there have been a number of studies which have attempted to add to the knowledge of the early recognition of potential scientists, selection procedures, aptitudes and motivations, and measures of potential ability.

In summary, little is known of the sociological aspects of the nature of the scientist in America today. As noted earlier, there have been no nationwide surveys of scientists since 1947–1948. The *Reader in the Sociology of Science* by Barber and Hirsch (1962), for example, does not have a single selection on the current characteristics of scientists. It does have selections from some of the sources mentioned earlier on high school and college student images of scientists, as well as the Knapp and related studies. There have been several Ph.D. dissertations, for example, Krohn (1960; 1962) and Merz (1961) which, although confined to relatively local and small samples, suggest that there have been enormous changes in the characteristics, values, and attitudes of the men being recruited into science today. Until new comprehensive studies are completed, knowledge of such matters remains unsatisfactory.

THE ORGANIZATION OF SCIENCE

There are still some scientists among the 4 million or so in the world who work

alone at the bench. There are no accurate
figures, but it is highly probable that few
of the world's scientists now do so. Even
where they are directing their own projects,
they are likely to have a number of collaborators and assistants. And even the minority who work alone are likely to be part
of an organization devoted to research.

Recently, sociologists have become increasingly interested in studying a variety of
large-scale organizations (Barton, 1961;
Etzioni, 1961). But few of these studies,
as will be seen below, have been concerned
with scientific research organization, whether in universities, government, or industry.

The first part of this section will discuss
the internal organization of research; the
second part will focus on the external. By
"internal" is meant the organization of the
laboratory, or of larger units, engaged directly in the conduct of research. Since most
such organizations are themselves a part
of still larger organizations, the interrelationships of these to each other is included.
Conceptually, these "parent" organizations
(a university, an industrial company, a government agency) might well be treated as
part of the external system (Kaplan, 1959a;
Vollmer, 1962). So little has been done to
develop this potentially promising distinction, however, that most of the discussion
of this topic is included in the first section.

The external organization emphasized in
the second part is the larger national context in which research activities are carried
out. Increasingly, it is the national governments, in the United States and in every
other scientifically developed society, which
are influencing and supporting the conduct
of research. This influence is becoming more
direct and more overt and is surely affecting the internal organization of research
(Whitney, 1960). To understand why laboratories in a certain country are large or
small, permanent or temporary, bureaucratic or not, it is necessary to know something about that country (Kaplan, 1961).
To understand whether differences observed
result from the internal nature of science

or from characteristics of the larger society,
more comparative studies are needed. These
issues are raised in the latter part of this
section. First, however, one should review
recent developments in order to learn more
about the internal organization of research.

The Organization of Research

The literature on research organization
is enormous. The discussion which follows
is more of a guide to a few of the varieties
available than it is a general review. A
recent bibliography of the literature by
Rhenman and Svensson (1961), which is
labeled as "selected" and confines itself to
recent literature, contains nearly four hundred references. One of the first bibliographies on research administration, Bush
(1954), contains over 1,100 references, most
of them since 1945. There is almost no overlap between these two bibliographies.

With the trend toward increasingly larger and more complex research organizations,
a host of problems, many of which are not
necessarily inherent in the research process
itself, has arisen to interest, as well as
plague, scientists and administrators. Scientists and others have been particularly fear-
ful of the effect of what they see as the
bureaucratization of the scientist and of
scientific research (Speyer, 1957; Tuve,
1959; Whyte, 1956). Organizations have
struggled to maintain an environment in
which research could be as free as possible,
while at the same time imposing what are
considered necessary organizational restrictions and regulations. Attempts have been
made to standardize criteria both for the
effectiveness of research organizations and
for its individual scientists (Quinn, 1958;
Randle, 1959; Rubenstein, 1957b). The
problems calling for study of research organization are myriad (Rubenstein, 1959;
Shepard, 1956a). Recent reviews of particular parts of the literature may be found in
Peters (1957), Folger and Gordon (1962),
and Vollmer (1962), to mention just a
few sources.

Studies of research organization have followed a wide range of orientations. So, for example, there have been studies essentially in the human relations tradition (Pelz, 1956b; Pelz, Mellinger, & Davis, 1953; Shepherd & Weschler, 1955), the industrial management tradition (Anthony, 1952; Dinsmore, 1958; Hirsch, Milwitt, & Oakes, 1958), the formal-informal organizational tradition (P. Brown, 1954; Marcson, 1960b), morale studies of scientists in relation to supervisory practices (Shepard, 1955), and the interrelationship of professionals on different hierarchial levels within large-scale organizations (Shepard, 1956c; Shepard, 1958).

One sample of the kinds of problems studied and the results obtained follows. Task-oriented interaction is greater among development groups than it is among research groups (Shepard, Pitkin, Simmons & Moyer, 1954). There is also the suggestion in these studies that the tradition of leaving scientists alone is not as effective as that of encouraging scientists to interact with one another. On the basis of a study of a large government medical research laboratory, Pelz (1956b) and his associates concluded that daily contact with colleagues who do not share one's values leads to better performance. Pelz also suggested, on the basis of the same study, that when the main colleague contact and contact with the supervisor is analyzed, higher performance results when one of these two contacts is with a man in a different field from the respondent.

Many studies have been directed largely to applied and immediate problems, often those set by the organizations being studied. In this vein are the studies concerned with the problem of whether the laboratory should be organized along functional or project lines (Ashcroft, 1959; Pelz, 1956b). There is the problem of the role of administration (Gargiulo, Hannoch, Hertz, & Zang, 1961) and the role of various supporting personnel (Pelz, 1959). Research has been directed not only to ex post facto measures of effectiveness but to trying to anticipate whether one project will succeed over another and whether one will be more profitable than another, regardless of its technical "success." Various attempts have been made to assign financial and other quantitative measures to different choices which might be made (Freeman, 1960; Horowitz, 1960; Johnson & Milton, 1961).

Many of the investigators are former physical scientists who have become research administrators and are thus directly concerned with such problems; some have been operations researchers employed on a permanent or consulting basis; and others have been men with backgrounds in industrial psychology, industrial management, and allied fields, called upon to make studies of this kind in order to answer pressing applied problems. But, increasingly, social scientists have begun to turn their attention to some of these problems, too. What kinds of problems have they attacked? What kinds of results have they achieved?

Some have focused on problems of leadership and supervision in the laboratory. The Michigan studies (Pelz, 1956b), following in a Lewinian tradition, found that "participatory" leadership tends to be more effective than either directed or laissez faire types of leadership. In a more detailed analysis, Baumgartel (1956; 1957) concluded that the leader who is most effective is one who is both technically competent and a good administrator.

Using data from the Michigan studies (Davis, 1956) regarding the National Institutes of Health, scientists were divided into those primarily oriented toward science and those oriented toward the institution. The latter were much more interested in helping people, especially by finding a cure for disease. As it happens, this is also the official goal of the National Institutes of Health. But the Michigan study found that only the science orientation was related to performance as judged by peers. The best performance seemed to occur where there was a high science orientation combined with a low institutional orientation (Davis, 1956).

This suggests, among other things, that the ratings by peers were based on the values of general science, rather than medical values which might stress the cure of patients. For another example of the effect of scientists' orientations on research in an agricultural research setting, see Storer (1961; 1962a).

One of the first full-scale published case studies of a research and development organization was by Marcson (1960b). The central theme of this work is the conflict between traditional business ideology, organization, and concepts of authority, and the traditional values of the scientist.

Marcson (1960b) made a contribution in his careful description and analysis of both the formal and informal organization of the laboratory. This is scarce in the literature, and even where it does appear there is little appreciation of the subtleties of the interrelationship between the formal and informal, such as are treated in the Marcson volume (see especially Ch. 3). The scientist finds himself typically in the work group rather than alone, and these work groups, according to Marcson, become informal networks of interpersonal loyalties which not only help in the conduct of research but, presumably, satisfy some of the scientist's demands for interpersonal recognition and colleague relationships.

These many suggestive observations and interpretations point up how much there is yet to learn about scientists and their research organizations. When single case studies of large industrial or other organizations first began to appear in sizeable numbers in the sociological literature, a clamor sounded for something more. Valuable and necessary as these are at the outset of an attack on the problem, they emphasize the need to go on to comparative studies in which many more precisely defined variables are systematically examined.

Kornhauser's study (1962) was much more concerned with the general problem of the strains and adaptations between professions (with science as the prime example) and organizations. Although Kornhauser studied six industrial laboratories, a trade association laboratory, a government laboratory, and an independent research institute, he made little attempt to compare systematically the different laboratories or to discern the differences among them. One should recognize, he argued, that professionals are increasingly employed by large organizations and hence should not try to rescue the earlier stereotype of the independent professional. Although there is inescapable tension between the values of the professional and the values of the organization, Kornhauser saw the end accommodation as one in which organizations will become more professionally oriented and the professionals more organizationally oriented. Whether one wants to quarrel with this conclusion or not, one of the main difficulties is the undifferentiated nature of both "professional" and "organizational" in this analysis.

Using a somewhat different approach Kaplan (1959b) tried to analyze the formal structure of a research organization through a study of the roles which had been developed. The role of the research administrator was selected as particularly crucial because of its newness and because it did not have an exact counterpart in other types of organizations. The research administrator was seen as a role in which the conflicting policies and demands of the organization on the one hand, and the scientists, on the other, were focused. The growing importance of this role in research laboratories in the United States seemed to indicate the increasing bureaucratization of research laboratory organization. But, in a companion piece on the role of the research administrator in Soviet medical research organization, Kaplan (1961) suggested that increasing bureaucratization is not a necessary result or by-product of the creation of such a role.

In almost all cases the dependent variable, or the factor which most investigators sought to explain, was labeled as productivity or performance. The studies reviewed here suggest that there are in fact many organizational, social, and other "nontechnical" factors which influence scientific productivity, but the results are still ambiguous or contradictory. Moreover, there is still considerable work to be done with the dependent variable. So far, investigators have relied on the following indicators of scientific productivity or performance: (1) the number of papers published or the number of patents issued (Ben-David, 1960b; Lehman, 1954; D. de S. Price, 1963); (2) the number of citations received by a paper as an index to the quality of the paper, on the assumption that the higher the quality the more often it will be cited in other people's works (Comrey, 1956; Garfield, 1955; Meltzer, 1956; Platz & Blakeloch, 1960), this latter standard being introduced because of the general discomfiture with simply counting the number of publications and equating, in effect, the paper by Einstein in which he developed his theory of relativity and the one by Mr. Jones reporting a replication of a trivial experiment; (3) other ratings of productivity—such as self-ratings, ratings by one's peers, ratings by a specially selected group of seniors in one's organization, ratings by immediate supervisor, ratings by middle-level supervisors, and ratings by the chief of the research organization (Pelz, 1956a; Pelz, 1960; Pelz & Andrews, 1961; Pelz & Andrews, 1962).

Some relationships have been found with all of these methods of determining scientific productivity. No relationships have been consistently strong in one direction or the other. Nor is any investigator entirely happy with any of these measures. Clearly, the development of new concepts and techniques to measure research productivity will aid the study of research considerably. One intriguing hypothesis, which Pelz (1960) suggested, is that when there are factors in the scientist's social or job environment which jostle him intellectually, his performance becomes higher. This jostling or uncertainty was labeled "dither" (following

Weaver's [1959] use of this term). The general notion was that uncertainty and anxiety go together in promoting creativity and high performance for a scientist, but each of these factors should be operating in opposite directions at any given time. Thus, when uncertainty is high, anxiety should be low. Pelz (1963) now seems to feel that an atmosphere of intellectual "dither" is more functional for the scientist engaged in research, while experience or cumulative wisdom is more valuable for the man in development work.

Despite the apparent lack of a common framework, two general problems stand out. The first is concerned with the effects of the research atmosphere or environment on scientific performance. The second might be put roughly in reverse terms: The effects of expanded research activities on the traditional nature of the parent organization.

Both problems make sense theoretically, but neither has stemmed primarily from theoretical concerns. It is largely because these have been applied, policy-seeking research undertakings that there has been a peculiar balance in the resulting empirical work. Thus, studies of the effects of the research environment have been concentrated in industrial laboratories, occur to a lesser extent in government laboratories, and are least likely to be found in university laboratories. The reverse holds for the study of the effects of the research activities on the organization.

While all three institutional sectors have been faced with the problem of how to cope with a considerably expanded, complicated, and much more expensive research operation than had ever been known, each sector chose to focus on a different set of problems. One of the best recent series of descriptive papers emphasizing the role of basic research in each of the different institutional sectors may be found in Wolfle (1959b). In part, this arose from a set of untested assumptions. The first holds that the university is really the "natural" home for research. The second holds that research is a set of activities sufficiently different from all others performed in the organization (especially in industry), that it must be differently organized, or, at the very least, that there are special problems in trying to organize research. The suitability of the academic model to some research organizations has been questioned, and the so-called project form of organization has been substituted in whole or in part. Herbert A. Shepard (1957) has been among those social scientists who have devoted considerable attention to this particular problem. The first two assumptions are often compounded with a third, namely, that scientists are essentially different from most other employees and consequently have to be "handled" differently. Randle (1959) is one of a number of industrial consultants beginning to question these assumptions.

In part, the different emphases have arisen from certain inherent differences in orientation characteristic of each sector. In the era of the cost accountant in industry, each activity, each department of the company, must not only pay its own way, but show a profit, and one of the main problems for industrial research was to devise ways of attaching costs and profits to the research operation (National Association of Cost Accountants, 1955; Rubenstein, 1957a). But it was generally recognized that other means had to be devised (quantitative if possible) to evaluate the effectiveness of the research program and operation. This gave rise to a variety of approaches to the study of the problems of appraising research.

In industry, the search has been concentrated on devising a formula, or some other precise indicators, which would help management decide on which of a number of proposed projects should be selected and how to evaluate progress of on-going projects. For a general review of some of the problems involved, see Rubenstein (1957b); for a review of some of the actual approaches tried, see Rubenstein (1957a).

Neither government nor the universities seem to have been as concerned with these sorts of appraisals. This is probably not the case for a considerable part of the government's military research effort, but practically nothing is available for study because of security restrictions.

Still another concern of some investigators has been the relationship between the organizational environment or atmosphere and the yearning for creative (as well as productive) research. Stein (1955; 1959) conducted an elaborate series of studies which seek to explore the interaction of purely psychological characteristics with organizational and general environmental factors. A series of volumes will report the final results. Stein is one of the leading exceptions to the generalization that most of the psychological studies of creativity have disregarded organizational environment (Taylor & Barron, 1963). Some of the factors which have been overlooked in these studies are discussed by Kaplan (1960b; 1963a), in which an effort is made to specify factors in the different institutional environments in which research is conducted.

Although there are a number of studies with the words organizational atmosphere and organizational environment in the title, very few treat the matter in a genuinely analytical way (Orth, 1959). For example, Pelz and Andrews (1962) relied primarily on the goals of the laboratory, and dominance by Ph.D. scientists, as the distinguishing characteristics of atmosphere. Gordon, Marquis, and Anderson (1962) considered the possible range of freedom and control and their combinations in different settings. Since it is obvious that there are some industrial laboratories (e.g., Bell Laboratories) where there may be considerably less restriction on the scientist's freedom than may be found even in some university organizations, Gordon and his colleagues advanced the hypothesis that it is the immediacy and specificity of research goals rather than the institutional context which varies directly with the controls exerted on the scientist, although there tends to be some relationship between these two factors.

During the early 1950's the prime concern of most educational institutions centered on problems of financing research (The Committee on Institutional Research Policy, 1954). Kidd (1959a) was the first to publish a full-scale study of the changing interrelationships of the federal government and the universities as a consequence of increased federal support for research. Kidd was especially concerned with the effects (at that time largely unrecognized by the academic community or, more precisely, the academic hierarchy) of large-scale university research on teaching and on the other goals and practices of the university.

Since that time there have been an increasing number of studies of various facets of this new problem. Rivlin (1961) analyzed the developing financial relationships between the federal government and the universities and raised questions about outright subsidization of higher education and research. Orlans (1962) studied 36 institutions of higher learning to assess the impacts of federal support on the quality of education, the organization and administration of the universities, and a host of other factors. The Carnegie Foundation for the Advancement of Teaching (The Carnegie Report, 1963) sponsored "self-studies" at 26 selected campuses, centering inquiry on many of the same problems as the Orleans study. The entire issue in which this report appears is devoted to "Partners in Search of Policies: Higher Education and Federal Government."

Finances continue to occupy the attention of many educators, although there seems to be less overt fear of federal "control" as a concomitant of federal support (Kaplan, 1960a).

These studies indicate that the major research orientation still tends to be applied and practical rather than theoretically directed. One of the best examples of the kind of research needed may be found in a series of articles by Ben-David (1960a; 1960b; Ben-David & Zloczower, 1962). Although these have been concerned mainly with the nineteenth century, there is every reason to believe that the same sort of sophisticated sociological analysis of the contemporary situation is possible. It would be necessary to take into account not only the structural and other features of the universities themselves, but, also, and more important, the value system which guides them, the larger social systems in which they operate, and the interaction of various parts of the social system (Kaplan, 1961). So far, the purely practical studies have not succeeded in casting such a wide net.

National Organization of Science

Aside from the specific interest in the role of the larger environment as a factor in the internal organization of research, there is a growing interest in the total organization of science within any given society. Until recently such interests were manifested primarily in historical studies, for example in Dupree (1957) and in Cardwell (1957). But it has only been recently that the overall organization of science has been viewed as a significant contemporary problem.

Up to World War II science continued to expand mainly as a result of a series of individual decisions made in the universities and in other laboratories and by individuals attracted to pursue science. Competition within a particular nation and among the several nations served to correct major imbalances in the total scientific effort, although not always effectively or successfully (Ben-David, 1960a; Ben-David, 1960b). This was in many senses a much better example of a true system of laissez faire than the economic system ever was.

The failure of the laissez faire system can be seen in the shift of leadership in scientific pursuits from Europe to other countries, chiefly the United States. The rapid rise in the number of Nobel prizes won by scientists who are residents of the United States is but one of many such indices.

The increasing emigration of European scientists to America is another (Dedijer, 1961; National Science Foundation, 1962). Some of the factors involved in the decline of European science are also apparent from such recent papers as those by Renée Fox (1962), Consolazio (1961), and Kaplan (1962). The underlying theme of these papers might be summed up as a concern with the manifest inadequacies of the old system, concentrated in, but not confined to, the university, to cope with the development and promotion of modern science in the world of today.

One of the best indices of the failure of the laissez faire system for science lies in the scope and amount of effort currently being exerted to reorganize and revitalize the organization of research in much of Western Europe. Accompanying this reorganization is the recognition, for the first time in many instances, that almost no systematic information and data on the organization of science at the national level existed previously. Social scientists in Europe, no less than in the United States, have remained unaware of the rapidly changing nature of the organization of science and have laid little of the groundwork necessary to enable the practitioners to make decisions concerning the various facets of the total organization. To cope with this gap in information a number of *ad hoc* studies have been instituted by specially created commissions of scientists and government officials and by other national agencies. But almost everywhere there was explicit recognition of the necessity for systematic data on the state of the present system before proceeding to recommend changes and modifications.

In recent years the American Association for the Advancement of Science sponsored a symposium which resulted in a series of papers on the overall organization of science in Great Britain by Hiscocks (1959), Major (1959) on Norway, Ballard (1959) on Canada, and Don K. Price (1959) on a comparative summary. Korol (1957), DeWitt (1960;

1961a; 1961b; 1961c; 1962a; 1962b), and Vucinich (1956) all contributed studies of the organization of various aspects of the Soviet research organization. Orleans (1961), Lindbeck (1961), and Thompson (1963) studied the scientific research organization of mainland China. There is also an excellent short study, by a Belgian sociologist (Molitor, 1960), of the United States national organization of science, done under a Ford grant while he was still Secretary General of the Belgian National Research Council. Finally, there are a number of studies by a variety of government agencies, as well as international ones such as the Office of European Economic Co-operation (1954; 1960a; 1960b), and in the last year or so by the International Office of the National Science Foundation (Watson, 1962).

Despite the inadequacies of many of these studies and the variability in the local situations, a number of common themes are readily evident. They may be summarized as a concern with the complexity of the existing organizational arrangements. This includes arrangements for financing research, for conducting research, for promoting specific programs of research, and for advising on new directions which scientific research should take. Coupled with this is the obvious fact that science is no longer a small, self-contained, autonomous, self-governing community. Although each of these points cannot be treated in any detail in this chapter, it should be pointed out that the sheer change in the size of the scientific endeavor is bound to have ramifications far beyond the increase in the number of people involved. The role of scientists in exerting some control over their efforts and products is also changing as a result. Whether the new scientific establishment which emerges in the years ahead can ever maintain some semblance of self-government is an open question. Some of the lines being followed in an effort to answer this question are discussed in the next section.

SCIENCE AND SOCIETY

The new scientific establishment is much more intimately related to society than ever before. In fact, one could ask whether it is still possible, except for theoretical purposes, to speak of modern science without society, or of a modern society without science. Certainly, the recent studies reviewed in this section attest to the growing interdependence of science and society.

The impact of science on society has always been far better developed and explored than the impact of society on science (Merton, 1952). Today this distinction is quite blurred; American society is a scientific society. One used to conceive of the impact of science on society in much the same way as one would regard Newtonian forces—where an external force exerts pressure on an object and causes it to move in a certain way. The topic is no longer clearly restricted to its effects on employment and unemployment, or on new technological developments (Waterman, 1962). Science is making it possible either to revolutionize or to destroy society as it has been known, and the choice is now largely a matter of social and political arrangements.

In the last decade or two the interrelations of science and society have become more intimate, overt, and direct. For example, the "market place of ideas" as a major mechanism determining choice of scientific problems is rapidly being replaced by a deliberate attempt to link the goals of society with the research goals of science. Scientists are not forced to work in these socially approved fields; they may still disregard these and work on problems of their own choosing, no matter how "irrelevant" the society may consider them. There is no question, however, that it is generally easier to obtain financial support and facilities, and especially to obtain a more adequate share of these, if one chooses to work in the areas defined as socially desirable. For a most perceptive discussion

bearing on some of the newly developing patterns for doing research, the work of a physicist, Holton (1962), is especially important.

The "traditional autonomy" of science is being modified from yet another direction. Political, military, economic, and social policies have become so intertwined with, and dependent upon, science that scientists are increasingly being called upon to act as advisors upon political matters which often have some technical aspects.

Conceptually, it is simple to distinguish between two types of science advisors: One is concerned with what happens inside the world of science, while the other is supposed to bring his scientific knowledge to bear on political and other types of nonscientific questions. But, practically, it is difficult to separate these roles (Lang, 1963; Sayre, 1961).

Wohlstetter (1962), a RAND analyst, has criticized a number of physicists for their role during the fallout and testing controversy in the late 1950's. Wohlstetter took the scientists to task for speaking out as "experts" on subjects which he defined as essentially nonscientific and political. Since equally prominent and respected scientists were on opposite sides of many of these political issues and since both sides seemed to rely on scientific data, the problem of which scientist to believe, and on what basis, was magnified.

A recent study by a political scientist, Gilpin (1962a), analyzed the changing role of the scientist as political advisor and as political activist since the end of World War II. Each of these roles is new for most American scientists, and there are undoubtedly many scientists who still wish they could stay out of politics. In Gilpin's view the end of political innocence for many scientists came with the Oppenheimer case (Gilpin, 1962a). Whether or not one dates the loss of innocence then, Gilpin's review of the scientist's role in shaping early United States' policy on nuclear weapons, the control of atomic energy, the development of the H-bomb, through many other military-political decisions of the cold war decade, must be contrasted with the United States scientist's political innocence prior to the war. These problems deserve more intensive study than they have so far received.

Wohlstetter's (1962) open attack on the scientists as political advisors may perhaps be viewed as an index of the early stages of the institutionalization of this new role for scientists. The awesome decisions scientists are being called upon to help formulate, privately and secretly (Snow, 1961), are of concern to all. Fortunately, many of the scientists involved have not taken their responsibilities lightly and have openly discussed (within security restrictions) some of the key issues involved.

In the early years after World War II, the *Bulletin of the Atomic Scientists* provided a forum primarily for the physical scientists. But in more recent years the forum, the participants, and the audience have all expanded. The "Arms Control Issue" of *Daedalus* (1960) was rightly hailed as the best available collection of papers on the subject which had appeared to that date. The decision to develop the H-bomb, as well as many of the other aspects of the nuclear arms race, has gradually been opened to analysis by physical and social scientists alike (see, for example, Dupré & Lakoff, 1962; Gilpin, 1962b; Schilling, 1961; Zuckerman, 1962). As a sign of the times, physical scientists now write about foreign policy not only for other scientists (Kistiakowsky, 1960), but also for foreign policy specialists (Haskins, 1962).

Of special interest in this connection is a conference of both physical and social scientists sponsored by the Council for Atomic Age Studies of Columbia University late in 1962. Some notion of the scope of topics covered can be gleaned from the titles of the papers presented: Gilpin (1962b), *Civil-Scientific Relations in the United States;* Wood (1962), *Scientists and Politics: The Rise of an Apolitical Elite;* Gilpin (1962c),

National Policy and the President's Science Advisors; Kreidler (1962), *National Science Policy and the President's Science Advisors;* Wohlstetter (1962), *Scientists, Seers and Strategy;* Brodie (1962), *The Scientific Strategists;* and Wright (1962), *The Establishment of Science Affairs.* As a "summary" statement Wright is quoted: "With the benefit of hindsight we now know that we have been living in an age of science for twenty years or more without understanding the implications of this fact" (Wright, 1962, p. 4).

The second type of science advisor is concerned primarily with the internal organization and development of science, insofar as it is possible to separate this from some of the external issues just discussed (Storer, 1962b). The first formal American science advisor (outside of wartime), known officially as the Special Assistant to the President for Science and Technology, had the double duty of "strengthening science" and relating it "more effectively to policy-making" (Killian, 1959a).

Since that time, the President's Science Advisory Committee (1958; 1959; 1960; 1962a) reviewed and made recommendations on a wide variety of problems bearing on recruitment, education, the universities, and the federal government.

Some other sources which should be mentioned in connection with the development of a science policy are Brozen (1962); Price, Dupré, and Gustafson (1960); the text by Dupré and Lakoff (1962); and Don K. Price's (1954) earlier work which anticipated many of these problems by almost a decade. Kidd (1959a), in a first-rate study of the interrelations of the federal government and the universities, and Wolfle (1959a), drawing on his experience as executive officer of the American Association for the Advancement of Science, raised many of the questions which will have to be explored by anyone interested in studying the problems of a developing science policy.

The increasing support for science by

Congress and the national government has inevitably affected the relations of scientists to nonscientists. Whether or not one accepts C. P. Snow's (1959) "two cultures" thesis, there is little question of the increasing need for the public and congressmen along with politically influential laymen, to understand something of what is happening within science. Lamson (1960) documented in detail some of the substantial gaps and differences in orientations and attitudes between scientists and congressmen. The need to inform the public on the developments of science has been recognized, and diffusion of knowledge has been accelerated, by such organizations as the National Association of Science Writers. Much more needs to be done to determine how much and what kind of information the public needs in order to inform itself intelligently about scientific developments (Withey, 1959).

Various other steps have been taken and many others have been suggested to strengthen American science. Most of these, characteristically, have involved direct as well as indirect action by the federal government. For example, the suggestion has been made, especially by Senator Humphrey (1960), to create a new Department of Science. This has met with mixed reactions from the scientists (for a summary of some of these, see, Dupré & Lakoff, 1962, pp. 69–73; Stover, 1962). Others have argued that most governmental actions have been "relatively minor adjustments in the administrative machinery" and that more basic changes are needed in government, science, and society to cope with the new challenge (Honey, 1960). (An entire issue of *The Annals* [Wengert, 1960] covered a wide range of views on the changing interrelations of science and society—a subject which deserves a more detailed analysis than can be afforded here.)

The tremendous expansion of the physical and natural sciences has had an impact on the development of the social sciences. Although there was controversy, the final version of the National Science Foundation Act did not explicitly prohibit support for the social sciences (Alpert, 1955; Alpert, 1957; Alpert, 1960). A social science program was established quite early, but had a small budget and operated under a cautious set of rules which eliminated many potential applicants. By the early 1960's the social science section was established as a formal division—almost an equal among equals. As significant as the change in National Science Foundation attitude and policy toward the social sciences is, it doubtless reflects a general change in public attitude. The President's Science Advisory Committee, which in 1963 still had no social science representatives, did establish a special panel to study the behavioral science situation. The panel in turn recommended considerably more encouragement for the rapid expansion of the behavioral sciences (President's Science Advisory Committee, 1962b). Undoubtedly the social sciences have benefited some from the "halo-effect," surrounding science generally, though in the view of many hardly enough.

The present discussion has touched upon some aspects of newly emerging problems of the advisor for science and of the increasing recognition of the need to formulate public policies for science at the national level (Hailsham, 1963). But already there are indications that such policy-making is unlikely to stop at national borders. The scale of Big Science is such that cooperative research ventures among a number of nations, such as CERN (European Organization for Nuclear Research) for nuclear energy research and the newly formed European Space Research Agency, are essential if smaller nations are to participate at all in certain fields of scientific research.

The Organization for Economic Cooperation and Development, whose work in this area has been mentioned earlier (King, 1962), has had an *ad hoc* advisory group on science policy (1963) which reviewed the possible roles of the OECD (Organiza-

tion for Economic Co-operation & Development) in promoting science and cooperation on policy among the member
nations. Kramish (1963) conducted an extensive comparative analysis of available
data on scientific manpower and effort in
relation to economic indices in the Common Market countries, the United States,
the United Kingdom, and the Soviet Union.
Such a report could serve as a basis for
an eventual Common Market policy for
science, inconceivable as such a step would
have been to most observers even a few
years ago.

Yet another aspect of the external science
policy has been the emergence of various
national and international efforts to help
promote the growth of science in the newly
developing nations of the world. Both the
highly industrialized and the industrializing
nations have become increasingly aware of
the significance of science for accelerating
economic productivity.

Ben-David (1962), contrasting the development of science in a new and small nation like Israel with that of the United
States, offered some suggestions about the
directions which might be followed by
smaller and less industrial nations. Stevan
Dedijer (1957; 1959; 1962a; 1962b), a physicist turned sociologist of science, has written a number of papers outlining the dimensions of trying to develop science and a
science policy in the new nations. Recently
there has been an enormous increase of
interest among scientists (Blackett, 1962)
and statesmen (United Nations, 1963) in
the exploration of these problems.

The first international conference devoted
to science and the developing nations was
held in 1960 at the Weizmann Institute of
Science in Rehovoth, Israel (Gruber, 1961).
Scientists and politicians came together to
discuss the role of science—from solar energy to chemical fertilizers to the kinds of
physics courses needed in universities of
the new states. This was followed early in
1963 by a much more comprehensive conference in Geneva, sponsored by the United

Nations, at which over 2,000 papers were
presented by scientists and politicians representing 87 nations. The list of papers is
in a United Nations (1963) document of
360 pages. The United States contributions
were published in 12 volumes, the most
relevant in this context being Volume IX
(United States, 1963) on scientific planning
and policy. For the social scientist, not only
the conference papers, but the conference
itself is worthy of further study.

This section began by noting how much
science and society have become intertwined. In the process, new problems have
arisen and new ways of viewing these have
become necessary. As has been seen, physical scientists and the whole range of social
scientists have become increasingly concerned, as they must, for this new revolution concerns everyone. The natural scientists can hardly speak of the future of science without touching upon the larger implications for man's life span, his health,
and well being (DuBos, 1959; Weaver,
1960). It is up to the social scientists to
contribute their share toward a greater
understanding of these revolutionary implications.

For the scientist, the changes he faces in
his way of conducting research pose many
questions and problems for the study of
research. The effects of Big Science, the
changing role of the government, the deliberate attempts to plan and formulate policies for the development of science, and a
host of other related changes, have barely
been outlined. The changing roles of the
scientist outside of the research laboratory,
the emerging scientist-statesman and the
statesman-scientist have implications which
have hardly been touched upon. For the
sociologist to ignore these central problems
of the time would be a loss for both science
and society.

CONCLUSION

The sociology of science is beginning to
show signs of rapid development, but it is

plainly evident that sociologists have much more to contribute. The majority of works by nonsociologists reviewed here would have benefited greatly from the collaboration of sociologists.

On balance, much has been accomplished recently by scientists whose technical training has been in almost all the sciences. The major progress has been to call attention to the quiet revolution now in progress in and around science and to raise some of the questions which must be asked before answers can be sought.

This review has attempted to raise only some of the questions of all the possible ones which already have been, or still remain to be, asked. The main goal has been to bring forth issues about which sociologists have been less active, and possibly less familiar. The traditional concerns of sociologists with stratification, power, social change, and the other areas covered in this Handbook, are now inextricably a part of the activities of many scientists—those inside the laboratories as well as those outside the laboratories in the capitals of the world.

Sociologists have long argued about the importance of studying social change. Leading sociologists of the nineteenth century, such as Max Weber (1930) did not argue about its importance; they studied change. Science is changing internally even as are views of its earlier developments. The traditional conceptions of the role of scientist as scientist need also to be changed radically. But the new role of the scientist in the forefront of political and economic change implies an even more drastic reappraisal of present views of social processes. The technical expert was always supposed to be "on tap but not on top" and this may still be true of the scientist advisors today. But in the not too distant tomorrow, the scientist may also be called on to be on top, as scientist and statesman become blended into a new role. And where will the sociologists be on coronation day?

REFERENCES

Ad Hoc Advisory Group on Science Policy. *Science and the policies of governments.* Paris: OECD, 1963.

Alpert, H. The social sciences and the National Science Foundation: 1945–1955. *Amer. sociol. Rev.,* 1955, **20**, 653–661.

Alpert, H. The social science research program of the National Science Foundation. *Amer. sociol. Rev.,* 1957, **22**, 582–585.

Alpert, H. The government's growing recognition of social science. *Ann. Amer. Acad. polit. soc. Sci.,* 1960, **327**, 59–67.

Anthony, R. N. *Management controls in industrial research organizations.* Boston: Harvard Univer., Graduate School of Business Administration, Division of Research, 1952.

Ashcroft, A. G. The industrial problem of product growth. The project team approach. *Research Admin.,* 1959, **2**, 119–134.

Avery, R. W. Enculturation in industrial research. *IRE Trans. engin. Mgmt,* 1960, **EM-7**, 20–24.

Ballard, B. G. Organization of scientific activities in Canada. *Science,* 1959, **129**, 754–759.

Barber, B. *Science and the social order.* Glencoe, Ill.: Free Press, 1952.

Barber, B. Sociology of knowledge and science, 1945–1955. In H. L. Zetterberg (Ed.), *Sociology in the United States of America: A trend report.* Paris: UNESCO, 1956. Pp. 68–70.(a)

Barber, B. Sociology of science: A trend report and bibliography. *Curr. Sociol.,* 1956, **5**, 91–153.(b)

Barber, B. The sociology of science. In R. K. Merton, L. Broom, & L. S. Cottrell, Jr. (Eds.), *Sociology today.* New York: Basic Books, 1959. Pp. 215–228.

Barber, B. Resistance by scientists to scientific discovery. *Science,* 1961, **134**, 596–602.

Barber, B., & Hirsch, W. (Eds.), *The sociology of science.* New York: The Free Press of Glencoe, 1962.

Barton, A. H. *Organizational measurement and its bearing on the study of college environments.* New York: College Entrance Examination Board, 1961.

Baumgartel, H. Leadership, motivations, and attitudes in research laboratories. *J. soc. Iss.,* 1956, **12** (2), 24–31.

Baumgartel, H. Leadership style as a variable in research administration. *Admin. sci. Quart.*, 1957, 2, 344–360.

Beardslee, D. C., & O'Dowd, D. D. The college-student image of the scientist. *Science*, 1961, 133, 997–1001.

Ben-David, J. Roles and innovations in medicine. *Amer. J. Sociol.*, 1960, 65, 557–568. (a)

Ben-David, J. Scientific productivity and academic organization in nineteenth century medicine. *Amer. sociol. Rev.*, 1960, 25, 828–843.(b)

Ben-David, J. Scientific endeavor in Israel and the United States. *Amer. behav. Scient.*, 1962, 6 (4), 12–16.

Ben-David, J., & Zloczower, A. Universities and academic systems in modern societies. *Archives Européennes de Sociologie*, 1962, 3 (I), 45–84.

Blackett, P. M. S. Science, technology and world advancement. *Nature*, 1962, 193, 416–420.

Brodie, B. The scientific strategists. New York: Columbia Univer., Council for Atomic Age Studies, 1962, No. 7. (Mimeographed)

Brown, J. D., & Harbison, F. *High-talent manpower for science and industry.* Princeton, N.J.: Princeton Univer., Industrial Relations Section, 1957.

Brown, Paula. Bureaucracy in a government laboratory. *Soc. Forces*, 1954, 32, 259–268.

Brozen, Y. The role of government in research and development. *Amer. behav. Scient.*, 1962, 6 (4), 22–26.

Bureau of Applied Social Research. *Flow of information among scientists.* New York: Columbia Univer., Author, 1958.

Bureau of Applied Social Research. *Review of studies in the flow of information among scientists.* New York: Columbia Univer., Author, 1960. 2 vols.

Bush, G. P. *Bibliography on research administration.* Washington: The Univer. Press of Washington, D.C., 1954.

Calder, N. Science notebook. *New Statesman*, 1961, 62, 858.

Caplow, T., & McGee, R. J. *The academic marketplace.* New York: Basic Books, 1958.

Cardwell, D. S. L. *The organisation of science in England: A retrospect.* London: William Heinemann, Ltd., 1957.

The Carnegie Report. Twenty-six campuses and the federal government. *Educ. Rec.*, 1963, 44 (2), 95–136.

Chinoy, E. *Society: An introduction to sociology.* New York: Random House, Inc., 1961.

Coleman, J., Katz, E., & Menzel, H. The diffusion of an innovation among physicians. *Sociometry*, 1957, 20 (4), 253–270.

Coleman, J., Menzel, H., & Katz, E. Social processes in physicians' adoption of a new drug. *J. chronic Diseases*, 1959, 9 (1), 1–19.

The Committee on Institutional Research Policy. *Sponsored research policy of colleges and universities.* Washington: American Council on Education, 1954.

Comrey, A. L. Publication rate and interests in certain psychologists. *Amer. Psychogist*, 1956, 11, 314–322.

Consolazio, W. V. Dilemma of academic biology in Europe. *Science*, 1961, 133, 1892–1896.

Cooley, W. W. Attributes of potential scientists. *Harvard educ. Rev.*, 1958, 28 (1), 1–18.

Daedalus (Arms Control Issue), 1960, 89.

Davis, R. C. Commitment to professional values as related to the role performance of research scientists. Unpublished doctoral dissertation, Univer. of Michigan, 1956.

Dedijer, S. Research and freedom in undeveloped countries. *Bull. atomic Scient.*, 1957, 13, 238–242.

Dedijer, S. Windowshopping for a research policy. *Bull. atomic Scient.*, 1959, 15, 367–371.

Dedijer, S. Why did Daedalus leave? *Science*, 1961, 133, 2047–2052.

Dedijer, S. Measuring the growth of science. *Science*, 1962, 138, 781–788.(a)

Dedijer, S. Research and the developing countries—problems and possibilities. *Tek. Vetenskaplig Forskning*, 1962, 33 (1), 1–20.(b)

DeWitt, N. Soviet science: The institutional debate. *Bull. atomic Scient.*, 1960, 16, 208–211.

DeWitt, N. *Education and professional employment in the U.S.S.R.* Washington: Nation Science Foundation, 1961.(a)

DeWitt, N. Reorganization of science and research in the U.S.S.R. *Science*, 1961, 133, 1981–1991.(b)

DeWitt, N. The Soviet student: Profile and prediction. *Teacher's Coll. Rec.*, 1961, 64, 91–98.(c)

DeWitt, N. Politics of Soviet science. *Amer. behav. Scient.*, 1962, 6 (4), 7–11.(a)

DeWitt, N. Soviet brainpower. *Int. Sci. Tech.*, 1962 (1), 33–38.(b)

Dinsmore, R. P. Improving the professional

environment of research people: Human relations are important. *Res. Mgmt*, 1958, 1, 101–112.

DuBos, R. J. Medical utopias. *Daedalus*, 1959, 88, 410–424.

Dupré, J. S., & Lakoff, S. A. *Science and the nation*. Englewood Cliffs, N. J.: Prentice-Hall, Inc., 1962.

Dupree, A. H. *Science in the federal government*. Cambridge, Mass.: Harvard Univer. Press, 1957.

Durkheim, E. *On the division of labor in society*. New York: Macmillan, 1933.

Eiduson, Bernice T. *Scientists: Their psychological world*. New York: Basic Books, 1962.

Etzioni, A. *Complex organizations: A sociological reader*. New York: Holt, Rinehart & Winston, 1961.

Folger, Anne, & Gordon, G. Scientific accomplishment and social organization: A review of the literature. *Amer. behav. Scient.*, 1962, 6 (4), 51–58.

Fortune. The scientists. 1948, 38, 106–112, 166–176.

Fortune, Editors of. *Great American scientists*. Englewood Cliffs, N.J.: Prentice-Hall, Inc., 1961.

Fox, Renée C. Medical scientists in a château. *Science*, 1962, 136, 476–483.

Freeman, R. J. A stochastic model for determining the size and allocation of the research budget. *IRE Trans. engin. Mgmt*, 1960, EM–7, 2–7.

Garfield, E. Citation indexes for science. *Science*, 1955, 122, 108–111.

Gargiulo, G. R., Hannoch, J., Hertz, D. B., & Zang, T. Developing systematic procedures for directing research programs. *IRE Trans. engin. Mgmt*, 1961, EM–8, 24–29.

Gilpin, R. *American scientists and nuclear weapons policy*. Princeton, N.J.: Princeton Univer. Press, 1962.(a)

Gilpin, R. Civil-scientific relations in the United States. New York: Columbia Univer., Council for Atomic Age Studies, 1962, No. 1. (Mimeographed) (b)

Gilpin, R. National policy and the president's science advisors. New York: Columbia Univer., Council for Atomic Age Studies, 1962, No. 4. (Mimeographed) (c)

Gordon, G., Marquis, Sue, & Anderson, O. W. Freedom and control in four types of scientific settings. *Amer. behav. Scient.*, 1962, 6 (4), 39–42.

Gruber, Ruth (Ed.) *Science and the new nations*. New York: Basic Books, 1961.

Hailsham, Lord. *Science and politics*. London: Faber & Faber, 1963.

Haskins, C. P. Technology, science and American foreign policy. *For. Aff.*, 1962, 40, 1–20.

Hirsch, I., Milwitt, W., & Oakes, W. J., Jr. Increasing the productivity of scientists. *Harvard Bus. Rev.*, 1958, 36, 66–76.

Hiscocks, E. S. Organization of science in the United Kingdom. *Science*, 1959, 129, 689–693.

Holland, J. L. Undergraduate origins of American scientists. *Science*, 1957, 126, 433–437.

Holton, G. Scientific research and scholarship: Notes toward the design of proper scales. *Daedalus*, 1962, 91, 362–399.

Honey, J. C. The challenge of government science. *Ann. Amer. Acad. polit. soc. Sci.*, 1960, 327, 1–9.

Horowitz, I. Regression models for company expenditures on and returns from research and development. *IRE Trans. engin. Mgmt*, 1960, EM–7, 8–13.

Humphrey, H. H. The need for a department of science. *Ann. Amer. Acad. polit. soc Sci.*, 1960, 327, 27–35.

Johnson, E. A., & Milton, H. S. A proposed cost-of-research index. *IRE Trans. engin. Mgmt*, 1961, EM–8, 172–176.

Kaplan, N. Research atmospheres in two different institutional contexts. Paper read at Amer. Sociol. Ass., Chicago, August, 1959. (a)

Kaplan, N. The role of the research administrator. *Admin. sci. Quart.*, 1959, 4, 20–42. (b)

Kaplan, N. Research overhead and the universities. *Science*, 1960, 132, 400–404.(a)

Kaplan, N. Some organizational factors affecting creativity. *IRE Trans. engin. Mgmt*, 1960, EM–7, 24–30.(b)

Kaplan, N. Research administration and the administrator: U.S.S.R. and U.S. *Admin. sci. Quart.*, 1961, 6, 51–72.

Kaplan, N. The western European scientific establishment in transition. *Amer. behav. Scient.*, 1962, 6 (4), 17–21.

Kaplan, N. The relation of creativity to sociological variables in research organizations. In C. W. Taylor & F. Barron (Eds.), *Scientific creativity: Its recognition and development*. New York: Wiley, 1963. Pp. 195–204.(a)

Kaplan, N. Science and the democratic social structure revisited. Paper read at Amer. Sociol. Ass., 58th Ann. Meeting, Los Angeles, August, 1963.(b)

Katz, E. The two-step flow of communication: An up-to-date report on an hypothesis. *Publ. Opin. Quart.*, 1957, 21 (1), 61–78.

Katz, E., & Lazarsfeld, P. F. *Personal influence.* Glencoe, Ill.: Free Press, 1955.

Kidd, C. V. *American universities and federal research funds.* Cambridge, Mass.: Harvard Univer. Press, 1959.(a)

Kidd, C. V. Basic research—description versus definition. *Science*, 1959, 129, 368–371.(b)

Killian, J. R., Jr. Science and public policy. *Science*, 1959, 129, 129–136.(a)

Killian, J. R., Jr. Strengthening American science. *Amer. Scient*, 1959, 47, 264–287.(b)

King, A. Toward a national science policy. *Impact Sci. Societ.*, 1962, 12, 157–176.

Kistiakowsky, G. Science and foreign affairs. *Bull. atomic Scient.*, 1960, 16, 114–116.

Knapp, R. H., & Goodrich, H. B. *Origins of American scientists.* Chicago: Univer. of Chicago Press, 1952.

Knapp, R. H., & Greenbaum, J. J. *The younger American scholar.* Chicago: Univer. of Chicago Press for Wesleyan Univer., Middletown, Conn., 1953.

Kornhauser, W. *Scientists in industry: Conflict and accommodation.* Berkeley: Univer. of California Press, 1962.

Korol, A. G. *Soviet education for science and technology.* New York: Technology Press of Massachusetts Institute of Technology and Wiley, 1957.

Kramish, A. Research and development in the Common Market vis-a-vis the U.K., U.S., and U.S.S.R. Santa Monica, Calif.: RAND Corporation, P-2742, 1963. (Mimeographed)

Kreidler, R. N. National science policy and the president's science advisors. New York: Columbia Univer., Council for Atomic Age Studies, 1962, No. 5. (Mimeographed)

Krohn, R. G. Science and social change: The effects of new institutional locals on the transitional structure of science. Unpublished doctoral dissertation, Univer. of Minnesota, 1960.

Krohn, R. G. The scientist: A changing social type. *Amer. behav. Scient.*, 1962, 6 (4), 48–50.

Kuhn, T. S. Historical structure of scientific discovery. *Science*, 1962, 136, 760–764.(a)

Kuhn, T. S. *The structure of scientific revolutions.* Chicago: Univer. of Chicago Press, 1962.(b)

Lamson, R. Scientists and congressmen. Unpublished doctoral dissertation, Univer. of Chicago, 1960.

Lang, D. Profile of Jerome B. Wiesner—A scientist's advice. *New Yorker,* January 26, 1963, 38, 38–71.

Lehman, H. C. Men's creative production rate at different ages and in different countries. *Scient. Mon.*, 1954, 78, 321–326.

Lindbeck, J. M. H. Organization and development of science. In S. H. Gould (Ed.), *Sciences in Communist China.* Washington: American Association for the Advancement of Science, 1961. Pp. 3–58.

McClelland, D. C. On the psychodynamics of creative physical scientists. In H. E. Gruber, G. Terrall, & M. Wertheimer (Eds.), *Contemporary approaches to creative thinking.* New York: Atherton Press, 1962. Pp. 141–174.

Major, R. Organization of scientific activities in Norway. *Science*, 1959, 129, 694–700.

Mannheim, K. *Ideology and utopia.* New York: Harcourt, 1936.

Marcson, S. Role adaptation of scientists in industrial research. *IRE Trans. engin. Mgmt*, 1960, EM–7, 159–166.(a)

Marcson, S. *The scientist in American industry: Some organization determinants in manpower utilization.* New York: Harper, 1960. (b)

Marx, K. *Selected works.* Vol. 1. Moscow: Co-operative Publishing Society of Foreign Workers in the U.S.S.R., 1935.

Mead, Margaret, & Metraux, Rhoda. Images of the scientist among high school students. *Science,* 1957, 126, 384–390.

Meltzer, L. Scientific productivity in organizational settings. *J. soc. Iss.*, 1956, 12 (2), 32–40.

Menzel, H. Flow of information on current developments in three scientific disciplines. *Fed. Proc.*, 1957, 16, 706–711.

Menzel, H. Innovation, integration, and marginality: A survey of physicians. *Amer. sociol. Rev.*, 1960, 25, 704–713.

Merton, R. K. Science, technology, and society in 17th century England. *Osiris*, 1938, 4, 360–632.

Merton, R. K. Introduction. In B. Barber (Ed.), *Science and the social order.* Glencoe, Ill.: Free Press, 1952. Pp. xi-xxiii.

Merton, R. K. Priorities in scientific discovery: A chapter in the sociology of science. *Amer. sociol. Rev.,* 1957, 22, 635–659.(a)

Merton, R. K. *Social theory and social structure.* (rev. ed.) Glencoe, Ill.: Free Press, 1957.(b)

Merton, R. K. Singletons and multiples in scientific discovery: A chapter in the sociology of science. *Proc. Amer. phil. Soc.,* 1961, 105, 470–486.

Merton, R. K. The ambivalence of scientists. *Bull. The Johns Hopkins Hospital,* 1963, 112, 77–97.

Merz, Louise E. The graduate school as a socializing agency: A pilot study of sociological aspects of graduate training in the physical sciences. Unpublished doctoral dissertation, Cornell Univer., 1961.

Molitor, A. La recherche scientifique aux U.S.A. Rapport sur un voyage d'études effectué sous les auspices de la Ford Foundation. Bruxelles, 1960. (Mimeographed)

Nagel, E. *The structure of science: Problems in the logic of scientific explanation.* New York: Harcourt, Brace & World, 1961.

National Association of Cost Accountants. Accounting for research and development costs. *Nat. Ass. Cost Acctants Bull.,* 1955, Research series No. 29.

National Science Foundation. *Basic research: A national resource.* Washington: Author, 1957.

National Science Foundation. *Investing in scientific progress, 1961–1970.* Washington: Author, 1961.

National Science Foundation. *Scientific manpower from abroad.* NSF 62–24. Washington: Author, 1962.

Naval Research Advisory Committee. *Basic research in the Navy.* Washington: U.S. Department of Commerce, Office of Technical Services, 1959. 2 vols.

Office of European Economic Cooperation. *The organization of applied research in Europe.* Paris: Author, 1954. 3 vols.

Organization for European Economic Co-operation, Office for Scientific and Technical Personnel. *Forecasting: Manpower needs for the age of science.* Paris: Author, 1960.(a)

Organization for European Economic Co-operation, Office for Scientific and Technical Personnel. *Producing scientists and engineers.* Paris: Author, 1960.(b)

Orlans, H. *The effects of federal programs on higher education.* Washington: Brookings Institution, 1962.

Orleans, L. A. *Professional manpower and education in Communist China.* Washington: National Science Foundation, 1961.

Orth, C. D. The optimum climate for industrial research. *Harvard Bus. Rev.,* 1959, 37 (2), 55–64.

Parsons, T. *The social system.* Glencoe, Ill.: Free Press, 1951.

Pelz, D. C. Relationships between measures of scientific performance and other variables. In C. W. Taylor (Ed.), *The 1955 University of Utah research conference on the identification of creative scientific talent.* Salt Lake City: Univer. of Utah Press, 1956. Pp. 53–61.(a)

Pelz, D. C. Some social factors related to performance in a research organization. *Admin. sci. Quart.,* 1956, 1, 310–325.(b)

Pelz, D. C. Interaction and attitudes between scientists and the auxiliary staff: I. Viewpoint of the staff; II. Viewpoint of scientists. *Admin. sci. Quart.,* 1959, 4, 321–336, 410–425.

Pelz, D. C. Uncertainty and anxiety in scientific performance. 1960. (Mimeographed)

Pelz, D. C. Dither and time in the motivation of scientists. *Chemist,* 1963, 40, 139–149.

Pelz, D. C., & Andrews, F. M. *Organizational atmosphere, as related to types of motives and levels of output.* Analysis Memo No. 9, Study of Scientific Personnel. Ann Arbor: Univer. of Michigan, Institute for Social Research, Survey Research Center, 1961.

Pelz, D. C., & Andrews, F. M. Organizational atmosphere, motivation, and research contribution. *Amer. behav. Scient.,* 1962, 6 (4), 43–47.

Pelz, D. C., Mellinger, G. D., & Davis, R. C. Human relations in a research organization. Ann Arbor: Univer. of Michigan, Institute for Social Research, 1953. 2 vols. (Mimeographed)

Peters, H. W. Human factors in research administration. In R. Likert & S. P. Hayes, Jr. (Eds.), *Some applications of behavioral research.* New York: UNESCO, 1957. Ch. 4.

Platz, A., & Blakelock, E. Productivity of American psychologists: Quantity versus quality. *Amer. Psychogist,* 1960, 15, 310–312.

President's Science Advisory Committee. *Strengthening American science.* Washington: Author, 1958.

President's Science Advisory Committee. *Education for the age of science.* Washington: Author, 1959.

President's Science Advisory Committee. *Scientific progress, the universities, and the federal government.* Washington: Author, 1960.

President's Science Advisory Committee. *Meeting manpower needs in science and technology.* Washington: Author, 1962.(a)

President's Science Advisory Committee. Strengthening the behavioral sciences. *Science,* 1962, 136, 233–241.(b)

President's Science Advisory Committee. *Science, government, and information.* Washington: Author, 1963.

Price, D. De S. *Little science, big science.* New York: Columbia Univer. Press, 1963.

Price, D. K. *Government and science. Their dynamic relation in American democracy.* New York: New York Univer. Press, 1954.

Price, D. K. Organization of science here and abroad. *Science,* 1959, 129, 759–765.

Price, D. K., Dupré, J. S., & Gustafson, W. E. Current trends in science policy in the United States. *Impact Sci. Soc.,* 1960, 10, 187–312.

Quinn, J. B. The measurement and evaluation of research results. Unpublished doctoral dissertation, Columbia Univer., 1958.

Randle, C. W. Problems of R & D management. *Harvard Bus. Rev.,* 1959, 37 (1), 128–136.

Reif, F. The competitive world of the pure scientist. *Science,* 1961, 134, 1957–1962.

Rhenman, E., & Svensson, S. *Research administration: A selected and annotated bibliography of recent literature.* (2nd ed.) Stockholm: Aktiebolaget Atomenergi, 1961.

Rivlin, Alice M. *The role of the federal government in financing higher education.* Washington: Brookings Institution, 1961.

Roe, Anne. *The making of a scientist.* New York: Dodd, 1953.

Rubenstein, A. H. Looking around. *Harvard Bus. Rev.,* 1957, 35, 133–146.(a)

Rubenstein, A. H. Setting criteria for R & D. *Harvard Bus. Rev.,* 1957, 35, 95–104.(b)

Rubenstein, A. H. Research on the research process. *IRE Trans. engin. Mgmt,* 1959. EM-6, 87–88.

Sayre, W. S. Scientists and American science policy. *Science,* 1961, 133, 859–864.

Schilling, W. R. The H-bomb decision: How to decide without actually choosing. *Polit. sci. Quart.,* 1961, 76 (1), 24–46.

Shepard, H. A. Some studies of laboratory management. *Armed Forces Mgmt,* 1955.

Shepard, H. A. Nine dilemmas in industrial research. *Admin. sci. Quart.,* 1956, 1 (3), 295–309.(a)

Shepard, H. A. Patterns of organization for applied research and development. *J. Bus.,* 1956, 1, 52–58.(b)

Shepard, H. A. Superiors and subordinates in research. *J. Bus.,* 1956, 29, 261–267.(c)

Shepard, H. A. Organization and social structure in the laboratory. In R. T. Livingston & S. H. Milberg (Eds.), *Human relations in industrial research management.* New York: Columbia Univer. Press, 1957. Pp. 185–196.

Shepard, H. A. The dual hierarchy in research. *Res. Mgmt,* 1958, 1, 177–187.

Shepard, H. A., Pitkin, D., Simmons, H., & Moyer, June. *Field studies in the organization and management of research.* Progress report, Sloan Research Fund Project No. 504. Cambridge: Massachusetts Institute of Technology, 1954.

Shepherd, C., & Weschler, I. R. The relation between three interpersonal variables and communication effectiveness: A pilot study. *Sociometry,* 1955, 18, 103–110.

Snow, C. P. *The two cultures and the scientific revolution.* New York: Cambridge Univer. Press, 1959.

Snow, C. P. *Science and government.* Cambridge, Mass.: Harvard Univer. Press, 1961.

Speyer, E. Scientists in the bureaucratic age. *Dissent,* 1957, 4, 402–418.

Steelman, J. R. Science and public policy. A report to the President. Washington: The President's Scientific Research Board, 1947. 5 vols.

Stein, M. I. A transactional approach to creativity. Paper read at Univer. of Utah Res. Conf. on the Identification of Creative Scientific Talent, Brighton, Utah, August 27–30, 1955.

Stein, M. I. Problems involved in predictors of creativity. Paper read at Midwestern Psych. Ass. meetings, Chicago, May, 1959.

Stein, M. I., & Heinze, Shirley J. *Creativity*

and the individual: Summaries of selected literature in psychology and psychiatry. Glencoe, Ill.: Free Press, 1960.

Storer, N. W. Science and scientists in an agricultural research organization: A sociological study. Unpublished doctoral dissertation, Cornell Univer., 1961.

Storer, N. W. Research orientations and attitudes toward teamwork. IRE Trans. engin. Mgmt, 1962, EM–9, 29–33.(a)

Storer, N. W. Some sociological aspects of federal science policy. Amer. behav. Scient., 1962, 6 (4), 27–29.(b)

Stover, C. F. The government of science. A report for the Center for the Study of Democratic Institutions, Santa Barbara, California, 1962.

Super, D. E., & Bachrach, P. B. Scientific careers and vocational development theory. New York: Columbia Univer., Teacher's College, Bur. of Publs, 1957.

Taylor, C. W., & Barron, F. (Eds.), Scientific creativity: Its recognition and development. New York: Wiley, 1963.

Thompson, H. W. Science in China. Int. Sci. Tech., 1963, 18, 86–95.

Tuve, Merle A. Basic research in private research institutes. In D. Wolfle (Ed.), Symposium on basic research. Washington, Amer. Ass. for the Advmt of Sci., 1959. Pp. 169–184.

United Nations Conference on the Application of Science and Technology for the Benefit of the Less Developed Areas. List of papers. New York: United Nations, 1963.

United States Papers Prepared for the United Nations Conference on the Application of Science and Technology for the Benefit of the Less Developed Areas. Science, technology, and development. Vol. IX. Scientific and technological policy, planning, and organization. Washington: U.S. Government Printing Office, 1963.

Vollmer, H. W. A preliminary investigation and analysis of the role of scientists in research organizations. Technical Report—Phase 1. Stanford: Stanford Research Institute, 1962.

Vucinich, A. The Soviet academy of sciences. Stanford: Stanford Univer. Press, Hoover Institute Studies, Series E, No. 3, 1956.

Waterman, A. Integration of science and society. Amer. behav. Scient., 1962, 6 (4), 3–6.

Watson, E. C. Organization of scientific activities in India. Washington: National Science Foundation, Office of International Science Activities, 1962.

Weaver, W. Dither. (Editorial) Science, 1959, 130, 301.

Weaver, W. A great age for science. The Report of the President's Commission on National Goals, Goals for Americans. New York: Columbia Univer., The American Assembly (Prentice-Hall, Inc.), 1960.

Weber, M. From Max Weber: Essays in sociology, H. H. Gerth & C. W. Mills (Eds.). New York: Oxford Univer. Press, 1946.

Weinberg, A. M. Scientific communication. Int. Sci. Tech., 1963, 65–74, 102–104.

Wengert, N. (Special Iss. Ed.) Perspectives on government and science. Ann. Amer. Acad. polit. soc. Sci., 1960, 327.

West, S. S. The ideology of academic scientists. IRE Trans. engin. Mgmt, 1960, EM–7, 54–62.

Whitney, V. H. Science, government, and society. Ann. Amer. Acad. polit. soc. Sci., 1960, 327, 50–58.

Whyte, W. H., Jr. The organization man. New York: Simon & Schuster, 1956.

Withey, S. B. Public opinion about science and scientists. Publ. Opin. Quart., 1959, 23, 382–388.

Wohlstetter, A. Scientists, seers and strategy. New York: Columbia Univer., Council for Atomic Age Studies, 1962, No. 6. (Mimeographed)

Wolfle, D. Science and public policy. Lincoln: Univer. of Nebraska Press, 1959.(a)

Wolfle, D. (Ed.) Symposium on basic research. Washington: Amer. Ass. for the Advmt. of Science, 1959.(b)

Wood, R. C. Scientists and politics: The rise of an apolitical elite. New York: Columbia Univer., Council for Atomic Age Studies, 1962, No. 2. (Mimeographed)

Wright, C. The establishment of science affairs. New York: Columbia Univer., Council for Atomic Age Studies, 1962, No. 8. (Mimeographed)

Znaniecki, F. The social role of the man of knowledge. New York: Columbia Univer. Press, 1940.

Zuckerman, Sir S. Judgment and control in modern warfare. For. Aff., 1962, 40, 196–212.

CHAPTER 23 Social Aspects of Economic Development

WILBERT E. MOORE[1]

The claims—or, as some would say, the pretensions—of sociology to be the generalizing science of human behavior in social aggregates have been poorly matched with the predominant actual concerns of sociological research and writing. For the most part the literature of sociology, rapidly expanding in quantity and occasionally improving in quality of investigation and of subjects explored, has been built on the observation of contemporary social phenomena and especially of social behavior in the United States.

The circumstance that a very large majority of the world's sociologists are to be found in the United States provides a kind of spatial or ecological explanation for the emphasis on American social structure. A large, complex, and in many ways heterogeneous society provides extensive opportunities for the study of uniformities and differences in social processes. Yet few so-

[1] The theoretical orientation of this chapter owes much to joint work with Professor Arnold S. Feldman (1962). The conception of society as a tension-management system was mainly developed by Feldman, and other parts of the attempt to develop a defensible dynamic model grew out of our extensive discussions.

ciologists would explicitly claim that the American social system is typical or representative of the whole range of social experience. Indeed, general texts if not research reports increasingly reflect an interest in comparative materials. A growing minority of sociologists use historical as well as contemporary data, attend to change as well static coexistence, and even conduct their field investigations of social processes in exotic places.

One major manifestation of broadening temporal and spatial horizons in sociological research is to be found in the studies of the "social aspects of economic development." Interest in comparative studies of social change was scarcely evident until after World War II, except for scholarly works following the intellectual heritage of Karl Marx and Max Weber in analyzing the historical rise of industrialism in the Western world. As science and society always interpenetrate to some degree, it is not surprising that the influences that prompted scholarly attention to the modernization of traditional societies were only partly those of intellectual evolution. The first of those influences was the gross fact that the cultural isolation of tribal societies and archaic civilizations was being rapidly dissipated, and in its stead there appeared indigenous spokesmen, often with strident voices, clamoring for inclusion in the modern world. A second influence stemmed from the first, namely, a growing demand for both information and advice, a demand that arose in the councils of government in the United States and the European metropolitan powers disassembling colonial empires, and in the United Nations and its specialized agencies.

It would be an improper exaggeration of the social determinants of scientific interests to stop with these external influences. Scientific disciplines also develop in part from their own internal logic. Knowledge accumulates and techniques of investigation become refined. Conceptual models or "approaches" are pressed to their limits and, proving too limited, are discarded or modified. One major development within sociology after World War II, somewhat independent of the sweep of larger events, was a growing measure of dissatisfaction with the relatively narrow focus of empirical studies, whereby "culture-bound" became a derogatory comment on generalizations, and also with the lack of attention to sequence and change in social patterns. It is not possible, and fortunately not important, to assess the relative influences of the external and the internal developments, the pragmatic as compared with the theoretical. The intersection has resulted in a relatively new and rapidly growing field of specialized study which broadens the geographical and temporal scope of sociological inquiry. Starting as an extension and application of established sociological approaches, the analysis of the social aspects of economic development has come to be a major source of empirically-grounded generalizations about the patterns of social change.

It is instructive, however, to trace out in some detail how the problems presented in the study of modernization of traditional societies have interacted with the ways sociologists have sought to order social phenomena and with theory, in the restricted sense of a body of predictive propositions.

THE PROBLEM OF CONCEPTUAL MODELS

As sociologists sought predictive answers to the multitude of questions posed by rapid social transformation in "underdeveloped areas," or were asked to provide answers for the use of agencies concerned with advisory policies, they naturally first turned to the kinds of intellectual equipment commonly used in their other studies. This equipment proved to be unsatisfactory in several respects, though often serving to develop and order principles and generalizations that were both sound and, occasionally, useful. The evolution of the systematic way problems were formulated—which is one way of characterizing "conceptual models" —will serve to introduce the extent and boundaries of reliable knowledge about the aspects or consequences of economic development. It may also serve as an illustration of the way scientific theory grows and changes under the impact of novel problems.

The "Three-Stage" Model and Its Difficulties

By far the most common sociological approach to the transformation of underdeveloped areas of the world has rested upon a kind of model of change that was rarely made explicit. By exclusive attention to societies "in transition," students of economic development implied a preceding, traditional stage and a succeeding, industrial or advanced state (Feldman & Moore, 1962). The premodern stage was taken to be essentially static, the social structure persisting through a balance of interdependent forces and actions. Even more unrealistically, the fully modernized society was also taken to be static, though this assumption had to remain implicit because of its patent falsity.

Now what is initially interesting and instructive about this approach is not its crudity but its utility. By concentrating on the manifold sources of contemporary evidence, by formalizing the kinds of structural changes to be expected from changes in so essential a societal feature as its system of production, scholars have compiled an impressive list of predictive principles, along with a partial accounting for variations. Many of the principles that will be summarized later in this chapter derive precisely from this approach.

The virtues and failures of each part of this conceptual model merit scrutiny. The conception of societies prior to modernization has not been so naive as to assume that they were or are alike. Sociologists have been in sufficiently close touch with anthropologists, if not with historians, to be aware of cultural diversity. Indeed the general texts commonly emphasize the range of social patterns and leave to the chapter headings the inferential fact that these are variations on themes rather than a random assembly of odd social practices. No, the mischief has arisen not primarily from the assumption of uniformity among traditional societies, but from the static connotations of the very term traditional. Traditional they may be in the sense of commonly justifying present practices in terms of precedent, and even in the extended sense that change in the past has not been rapid, continuous, and pervasive. Yet change is an intrinsic characteristic of all societies (Moore, 1963b), and the historic paths to the present inevitably and significantly affect the continuing paths to the future.

Ironically, one of the major dividends of the studies of economic development has been to diminish the emphasis on the diversity of tribal and agrarian societies by turning attention to the common functional features of societies everywhere. In a sense, this advance in the claims of sociology as a generalizing science was a by-product of the analytic necessity of having a uniform set of rubrics—a kind of taxonomy of essential functions—for the analysis of just what was "in transition."

The lack of historical perspective, however, has proved embarrassing. At the extreme this conceptual model has led to the *sociologistic fallacy,* the assumption that history began yesterday, if not early this morning. This kind of temporal myopia has neglected not only the intrinsic sources and courses of change in all societies but also the important circumstance that most of the world has been under some form and degree of "Western" influence for periods of years and in some instances (such as, say, Latin America) for over four centuries. The results of this prolonged contact have been a great intermixture of cultural forms and social organizations. This intermixture of civilization in turn has built new barriers to modernization or raised old ones while obviously starting the slow process of modernizations in some other sectors of social life (Moore, 1954). The imposition of a radical "racial" or ethnic distinction between managers and the managed, for example, has in many places added an irrational barrier to labor mobility on top of the real impediments of simple lack of trained skills. On the other hand, the commercialization of subsistence economies has clearly started them "on the way" to full participation in modern forms of production and distribution.

Modernization itself takes on a deceptively simple character. The organizational forms of "advanced" societies are introduced as a set of patterns to which the pre-existing features of the "traditional" societies must either adapt or surrender. The logical model of this argument is the utmost in simplicity: A common and highly interrelated set of causes produces a common set of results, virtually independent of admittedly variable conditions. The important sources of variation in both procedures and consequences are traced out below in the discussion of dynamic models. Again, however, there has been sufficient validity to this approach to permit a fairly precise identification of what structural changes must accompany economic modernization and what characteristics of traditional societies clearly cannot survive the impact of industry and its associated structural features.

The identification of consequences and of impossible inconsistencies in the social order environing a modernized economy has been greatly aided, again paradoxically, by the unrealistic assumption that industrial societies are both static and homogenous among themselves. This assumption has had sufficient proximity to fact in certain major respects to permit the use of the generalized features of industrial societies as a predictive destination for those now in the process of modernization. "This particular history gets written mainly from the future into the present—what is currently happening comes from what is to be. The future is the cause and the present is the effect" (Kerr, 1960, p. 358).

Yet the future is still being created and at an accelerating pace of change in industrial societies. As they change, their resemblance to each other increases in some respects and scarcely at all in others. To match the unrealistic timelessness of the sociologistic fallacy there is a kind of determinism of social structures that may be called the *functional equilibrium fallacy*. The useful and indeed essential conception of social action as taking place in interdependent systems can be carried to the improper extreme of assuming not only that nothing changes from intrinsic sources, but also that any feature of the system is a key to all others. Societies are far looser aggregates than any biological organism, and at least the more complex animal species permit considerable ranges of structural variation and of individual differences. What the future imposes on the present for the developing areas is a resemblance but not a replication. It can be expected, for example, and for reasons to be delineated in subsequent discussion, that the administrative structure of the national state will more nearly approach a common form than will the allocation of effective political power. Similarly, the forms of market organiza-

tion are more intimately connected with a highly specialized system of production than are the forms of supernatural belief and religious ritual. The specification of the order of "requiredness" of major features of the institutional system is another valuable by-product of the systematic comparison of social systems, though this can be and is done (Levy, 1952; Murdock, 1949) without the specific impetus of tracing out the social aspects of economic development. The advantage of the focus on change is that it provides, or seems to provide, a causal order and not a mere correlation or lack of it. Given economic development, the question runs, what other changes will then ensue? If one took the implications of the three-stage model absolutely seriously, the answer would be simple and comforting. The peoples of the world would all become "just like us," and the fragmentary studies of American society would turn out to be general sociology after all.

Economic Change as Prime Mover

Taking economic change as given is a procedure of dubious validity, as it appears to be a form of "economic determinism," long and properly discredited in sociological theory. Clearly, modernization involves more than changes in methods of producing goods. Practices and organizations ranging from sanitation to state administration, from the training of teachers to the improvement of accounting systems may require attention. Yet it should also be noted that virtually every improvement in individual welfare or social organization carries some kind of a price tag. To a marked degree, their possibility is created or enhanced by increasing the economic yield of the society.

It is the very instrumental character of the economy that justifies primary attention to economic change. It is the relevance of the economy for virtually every other aspect of social organization that warns against viewing economic change as primary in a

temporal or causal sense. The goals of economic development, the uses to which goods
and money will be put, have a manifest
priority both logically and temporally. The
mere fact that the goals may be now pretty
much taken for granted, since economic
growth has been articulated as a major
aspect of public policy virtually everywhere,
does not remove the importance of the priority of values over instrumental arrangements. The point is worth insisting on because of one intellectual tradition in sociology. This tradition, usually traced to Karl
Marx (1904) and modified by Thorstein
Veblen (1919) and William F. Ogburn
(1936), views economic organization, and
especially its associated technology, as the
prime mover in social change. Now this
theory is of doubtful validity anywhere,
unless technological change is viewed as
essentially accidental or animated by something mysteriously intrinsic to technology
itself and independent of human goals and
aspirations. The clear though variable importance of technical change in all societies
is more properly interpreted as a manifestation of a universal "environmental challenge"—that is, that the adaptation of human societies to their nonhuman settings
is never complete, and it is the gap between
the actual and the ideal that permits the
acceptance of accidental innovations or the
fostering of deliberate ones (Moore, 1963b).
     In the present context, however, there is
an additional point of crucial importance.
In the underdeveloped areas it is precisely
the economy (or technology) that is lagging. The recognition of this backwardness
of the productive system prompts deliberate
efforts at modernization. Since simultaneous
change of other, interdependent, elements
of the social structure cannot be expected,
once economic change occurs there may be
extensive examples of lag throughout the
society.
     Once more, then, a contrary-to-fact con-
ceptual model—that of economic primacy in
social change—turns out to have some utility
in the analysis of social change accompanying economic modernization. The prior step
of goal identification is not highly problematical, and the widely instrumental value
of economic growth gives it a strategic value
for the start of a sequential chain of social
consequences.

The Development of a Dynamic Model

     The conceptual models or approaches al-
ready discussed have a number of weaknesses that can now be recapitulated: (1)
Though permitting a number of generalizations of a high order concerning social
aspects of economic development, they have
served also to exaggerate the uniformity of
antecedent conditions, of the very transitional processes that form the major empirical basis for comparison, and of the end
results. (2) The treatment of economic
change as the "prime mover" not only
started the analysis of a causal chain in
the middle, but also had tended to understate the extensive interplay between the
economy and other aspects of social organization by exclusive emphasis on economic
organization as a sovereign variable. (3)
Though dealing with social changes of great
magnitude and extent, the analyses have
remarkably little information to offer on
processes of transformation, on the sequence,
rate, and mechanisms whereby major social
institutions and organizations adapt to the
altered conditions of life that economic
growth entails.
     Each of these demerits deserves a little
further comment. For example, the assumption of uniformity among premodern societies must overlook manifold differences
or treat them as essentially inconsequential.
It must also incur the dangers of the sociologistic fallacy by neglecting all sorts of
cross-currents in the history of colonial and
other societies that have experienced various
external influences for various periods of
time. The argument tends to go, however,
that these variations, even if otherwise significant, wash out under the homogenizing
influence of a compact and uniform set of

requirements imposed by economic modernization. Feldman and Moore (1962) persuasively argued against this view, maintaining that the way barriers to modernization are overcome not only affects the course of social change for a transitional period but also leaves a lasting residue in the social structure as a consequence of the measures taken for dealing with the problem. If, for example, underutilized land in large estates such as the Latin American haciendas gives rise to political discontent as well as low levels of agricultural production, the development measures will sooner or later include a land reform, and the kind of land reform will have enduring consequences for income distribution, capital formation, and labor recruitment (Moore, 1951, Ch. 9). Though such examples might be regarded as a tedious attention to detail, their significance is somewhat deeper, for they bear on a major theoretical (and practical) question in the contemporary world: namely, the degree to which "advanced" societies are becoming alike. The legacy of history is one major reason for introducing a cautionary note in the recitals of the manifold ways in which industrialized societies resemble one another.

Perhaps the major variable affecting the route or trajectory of change is the era or stage at which a political unit enters on a course of rapid economic change. Latecomers have available several models of historical transformation and of forms of political regime. They are bound neither by the rate nor by the sequence established by their predecessors in adding products and processes, forms of social organization, strategies of communication, or scientific knowledge. The new (or newly modernizing) nation might be compared with the shopper in an extensive and well-stocked supermarket. The shopper can select products from the shelves with virtually no regard to the date or order at which the goods entered the market's inventory.

The metaphor is exaggerated, of course, because a random or whimsical selection of the components available will violate all sorts of principles of interdependence and the functional relation of elements in social systems. Nevertheless, atomic power may be introduced before coal, radios before telephones, antibiotics before aspirin, and airfields before highways. And the supermarket analogy can be translated into somewhat more austere and significant terms. For some purposes it is useful to regard the entire world as a single social system, marked by extensive internal disharmonies but marked also by extensive transit of ideologies, knowledge, and products across conventional political boundaries.

Now the manner in which history prevents its own replication creates difficulties in generalizations that will unite historical and contemporary experience and deal with the diversity that optional paths of change introduce. The situation is by no means desperate, as subsequent discussion of highly general patterns will demonstrate. It is, however, sufficiently serious not to be brushed aside lightly.

In addition to minimum, required sequences and results what is needed, and is mostly not at hand, is the construction of limited-alternative or typological sequences where total generalization is improper. The first part of the desiderata can be partially fulfilled by the distinction between social preconditions of economic modernization and the concomitants and consequences of modernization. A summary of the reliable propositions relating to these components of social organization and its changes comprises the second and third sections of the chapter. Even here the state of knowledge is far from satisfactory, for it provides little information on processes and rates of change and virtually nothing on the interplay among variables as they change. The "before and after" comparison is no mean achievement but it does not provide a clear map or timetable for the journey from one to the other.

It is unnecessary to repeat the explanation for the inhibitions imposed by a static model of social systems. What is more to the point is the way the problems posed by the attempt to order the phenomena of contemporary change that are refractory in their diversity has led to a recognition of kinds of ignorance that were previously ignored. An example is in order. It is generally assumed that a rising level of adult literacy and an increase in the average number of years of school completed and in the proportion of secondary school and college graduates in the population are somehow associated with economic development. The functional needs for literacy and for specialized training can be persuasively argued. Yet the historic course of changes in literacy and education levels in the older industrial societies is virtually unknown. Is education to be viewed primarily as a capital investment, a prerequisite for other changes, or as a consumption good that a prosperous economy can provide? The answer clearly has practical implications for the plans of developing countries (Anderson, 1963) as well as theoretical interest for the sequences and rates of social transformation. A before-and-after model will not answer that kind of question; actual information on the timing of trends is required. The question was not likely to be asked except as a result of the interplay between policy questions and the evolution of conceptual models used by scholars.

The uncertainty concerning trends in education as they relate to other changes illustrates both the difficulty in assuming the primacy of "economic" change and the relative paucity of propositions that will simultaneously indicate the order and processes of social change.

The actual diversity of newly developing areas and indeed of advanced industrial societies and the theoretical problem of accounting for change have led to a substantial modification of the very conception of society. Much of modern sociology has been built upon the conception of society as a system characterized by functional interdependence of major elements and relationships, and characterized by an orderly and persistent balance, a kind of equilibrium. In the hands of skilled theorists (e.g., Levy, 1952; Merton, 1957, Ch. 1) it was not assumed that the fit of each element with the balance of the system was perfect, or the best possible arrangement under the circumstances. Dysfunctional consequences of particular patterns of action were recognized and even identified as potential sites of change. A further step is to view tensions as pervasive in social systems, arising from both intrinsic and extrinsic sources. A society persists not only through orderly continuity of established patterns but also through tension-management and change (Moore & Feldman, 1962).

This conception of society has certain advantages in terms of the "fit" of the model to observed characteristics, even those of a persistent or recurrent quality, such as social deviation. It has overwhelming advantages in dealing with the phenomena of leads and lags in situations of rapid transformation. An outstanding way in which both industrializing and industrial societies differ in social structure is in the allocation of power and the political structure of the state. If societies differ in their characteristic tensions, because of varying historic legacies and the ways these intersect with current problems of achieving social goals, then it is readily understandable that the principal agency functionally responsible for tension-management for the system as a whole, the state, will differ in its structure and forms of action.

The tension-management model also permits explicit recognition of a grossly evident fact difficult to reconcile with a kind of self-balancing mechanical system. That fact is the widespread use of deliberate change both in the attempted solution of identified problems and in the attempted achievement of goals associated with, say, economic development. A principal kind of tension, in other words, is the failure to achieve social ideals, whether those ideals be simply those of reliable conformity with norms or the approximation to new standards and aspirations.

What one learns from "functional" models includes the partial structural convergence of industrial societies. This mode of generalization is not trivial and indeed comprises most of the solidly established principles that current knowledge affords. Although when this model is applied to economic development the predictable structural changes are called "consequences," the conceptual model is really that of comparative statics, before-and-after.

What one learns from the incompletely developed dynamic models includes both the common and typological sequences of change, on the one hand, and the persistent (not temporary) modes of tension-management and prospective change, on the other. Thus the claims of sociology for generality are somewhat enhanced by the demands for sociology to be particular about social transformations in exotic places.

The Meaning of "Economic Development"

The rather extensive excursion into problems in sociological theory has postponed direct and systematic attention to economic development and its relation to other aspects of societies. It is now time, or perhaps a trifle late, to identify the key variable, economic development. In the broadest sense economic development might be viewed as any growth in real income per capita, from whatever source. The meaning here is substantially narrower: The extensive application of inanimate power and other technologies to the production and distribution of economic goods. In this sense economic development is practically equivalent to industrialization if that term in turn is taken to include the application of rational productive techniques throughout the economy and not just in manufacturing. Though there has been some theoretical argument to the effect that industrialization in the narrow sense is neither possible nor necessary for many underdeveloped areas, there is no historical precedent for substantial increases in per capita income without diversion of both capital and labor out of agriculture (Kuznets, 1957).

Conceptual problems reappear if the characterization of economic development is made very broad—including, for example, labor mobility or a national currency or an extensive educational system—for many of the changes that are more properly viewed as conditions and consequences of the implementation of a rational productive technology would be lost to view by assimilation into the key variable. Unless many structural elements are purely simultaneous and dependent variables, permitting no leads and lags, no independent variability, and thus no strategic problems in identifying areas of social action, it is important to keep an extended array. The empirical evidence for some measure of independent variability, particularly in a temporal sense, is overwhelming. It is simply ridiculous to assume that everything changes at once, yet that is the kind of conclusion that flows from a functional equilibrium model.

An extended illustration from an otherwise sensible and valuable research monograph (Jaffe & Stewart, 1951) may serve to point up the difficulty of packaging variables too quickly. The authors first divided the countries of the world into two categories—developed and under-developed—principally on the basis of per capita income. (The dichotomy, a division of variable phenomena into two mutually exclusive categories, is a frequently useful and uniformly dangerous procedure. Most of nature varies in terms of scales, not neatly by division into presence or absence of an attribute.) A rather extensive series of statistical comparisons is then presented. Developed countries turn out to have high expectation of life at birth, low fertility, high literacy and average educational achievement, high production of kilowatts of electricity per capita, low proportions of the labor force engaged in agriculture, and so on. The underdeveloped countries exhibit contrasting quantities of these statistical dividers. Because of the high intercorrelations among the statistical indicators for which data could be assembled, the authors jumped to the "logical" conclusion: Economic development entails changing "everything at once" (Jaffe & Stewart, 1951, pp. 410–414). The conclusion is not justified. It is the product of a simplifying procedure and not the result of an analysis of social change as it occurs. Until one knows the timing and rate at which various characteristics of a modernized economy and society have occurred, one is permitted to say precisely nothing about the order of social changes.

Economic development, then, will be taken to mean the "rationalization" of economic production, and its proximate measure will be taken as an increase in real income per capita. All other changes are subject to scrutiny, to analysis in terms of degree of requiredness, and to examination in terms of the order in which they may be expected.

THE SOCIAL FRAMEWORK OR "PRECONDITIONS"[2]

The identification of the social preconditions of economic development aptly illustrates the importance of some dissection of functionally related systems. The principal components of the social framework that will be examined are values or ideology, institutions or normative complexes, organizations, and motives. Now with the possible exception of organizations all of these may appear to be simply differing ways of stating "attitudinal" factors as related to social action. In a perfectly integrated social system there would be complete consensus on the goals of human activity and indeed on the general perception of the meaning of life and its setting. Also in such a system the rules of conduct, the morally sanctioned

---

[2] This section follows closely the organization presented in Moore (1961).

prescriptions for behavior, would be unanimously accepted and followed, and the rules would assume achievement of the goals. Finally, this unproblematical integration would come about and be preserved because the social actors would have "internalized" both the values and the procedures; their motives would be uniform and coincident with social expectations. An inquiry into social values or individual motives would yield the same answers, and the behavioral manifestations of values and motives would be both conscientious on the part of the actor and elicit only approval by others. All enduring systems must approximate this state of affairs in some degree, and virtually none exemplifies it fully. In particular, it neglects the evident tensions and dissidence in all societies, and it does not provide much insight into the sources and mechanism of change. It is especially with regard to change that the somewhat "attitudinal" elements are viewed as having some independent variability, along with the ways that certain activities are organized in a more or less deliberate fashion.

Values

When the problems of economic growth in underdeveloped areas began to engage the attention of various social scientists, there appeared a fairly sharp division of opinion between economists on the one hand and anthropologists and sociologists on the other. With respect to questions of values or goals of economic growth the economists were on the whole optimistic or untroubled. Starting from the kind of hedonic psychological assumptions that underlay classical theories of economic behavior, they saw no reason to view human nature differently in other settings. Impediments to growth were more likely to be identified as lying in archaic social structure than in any absence of acquisitiveness. If attitudinal barriers were identified at all, it was in the shortage of entrepreneurial innovators but not in social values generally. Anthropologists and sociologists had ample reason to emphasize the dissimilarity of human nature as it emerged from cultures and societies displaying a great diversity of values and customs. They therefore tended to emphasize all sorts of traditional values as impediments to social transformation.

The simple fact is that the economists were more nearly right than their "better informed" antagonists. By any evidence at hand, populations throughout the world will, given the option, prefer food to hunger, comfort to discomfort, health to sickness, and life to death. The preference may not hold at all costs, and the costs here and there include cherished customs and even transcendental values of the very sort the pessimists had in mind. Yet economic growth, as previously noted, has become an explicit goal of political policy virtually everywhere, and the opposition or apathy that may be encountered among those not in power is much more likely to represent a lack of enthusiasm for particular instrumental changes than it is to indicate a kind of rejection of economic benefits (Feldman & Moore, 1960, pp. 4–8).

Economic development then becomes a social value that is a strategic requirement for actual plans of implementation. The apparently unproblematical character of this value might seem to argue for checking it off and moving on speedily to others. A few cautionary statements are in order, however. It is important to underscore the instrumental character of the economy. Expanded production does not necessarily mean expanded consumption, if, for example, the expansion is entirely devoted to military production or to capital construction. The goals as set by political officials may not correspond to the aspirations of others. In fact it is commonly noted that the rapid rise in aspirations on the part of the general population (unlike their historic predecessors who had no prosperous models to emulate and envy) is more than slightly embarrassing to economic planners, who seek to maximize savings for invest-

ment rather than increasing current consumption to the point that continued growth is imperiled. Then, too, the distribution of benefits is of some consequence, for the rich may well become richer and the poor become poorer (at least relatively) and the normal polarization of social strata in early industrialization become accentuated.

The goal of development cannot be separated from the necessary means. The remaining merit of the functional equilibrium model—but indeed of any system model—is the reminder that the economy does not stand apart from the society. As previously noted by Moore (1961):

The "means" turn out to be new patterns of daily existence, and thus in conflict with an intricately interrelated social structure. These patterns of behavior and their normative sanctions in turn relate to goals and values other than economic development or material well-being. Since material well-being is not the sole goal of any society, and could not be if it is to survive as a viable system, the value conflict is not trivial or simply based on temporary ignorance or misunderstanding (Moore, 1961, p. 62).

In a sense therefore the anthropologists or sociologists were right all along, except that these systemic complications might have been identified more properly as retarding influences, sources of strain, and challenges to the specific strategies of innovators. Even so, a totally negative view of tradition is unwarranted. Hoselitz (1961) observed that some traditional values may be favorable to economic growth rather than a barrier. Even the values associated with an extended family system (commonly assumed to be an impediment) may encourage a pooling of capital resources for business expansion where the more formal commercial credit system operates ineffectively.

Nationalism as a social value is second only to the goal of economic growth itself as an apparently essential precondition for economic development. This statement, however, needs qualification by adding the designation "rapid." Slow and halting improvements in output may take place without a strong and focused national identification and without any substantial political impetus. In the situation of the underdeveloped countries today, however, it is only the state that can command both the resources and the loyalty for radical transformation in the patterns of social existence. Davis (1955) observed that

nationalism is a *sine qua non* of industrialization, because it provides people with an overriding, easily acquired, secular motivation for making painful changes. National strength or prestige becomes the supreme goal, industrialization the chief means (Davis, 1955, p. 294).

Though Weber's (1948) famous thesis on the relation between protestantism and capitalism is clearly not applicable to other cultures and civilizations today, Smelser (1963, pp. 38–39) thought that other ideologies, including nationalism, serve a comparable function. He wrote:

Because the existing commitments and methods of integration are deeply rooted in the organization of traditional society, a very generalized and powerful commitment is required to pry individuals from these attachments. The values of ascetic and this-worldly religious beliefs, xenophobic national aspirations, and political ideologies (like, e.g., socialism) provide such a lever (Smelser, 1963, p. 38).

Even in the historic development of capitalism, which was both slower and more decentralized than the massive and integrated effort to "catch up" in underdeveloped countries today, the state was of considerable importance both as an agency of economic decision and as a focus of loyalties. A very considerable proportion of technological change has been related to military concerns, and wars have served to stimulate economic growth as well as to destroy its products.

The subject of values should not be concluded without some further comment about their general functions in a social system.

The principal elements of order in social relations derive from the general and predictive compliance with norms, that is, rules of conduct. Some such compliance may be merely habitual, and some may be constrained by the threat of external sanctions, but a great deal of the integration of social systems arises from conscientious behavior, behavior in accordance with norms because they are "right." Now norms stand to values approximately as means to ends, and the rationale of institutions (complexes of norms relating to a major aspect of social organization) or of particular rules is generally some more ultimate value-orientation. Thus rules relating to property, or status in the family, or the uses of time rest on various basic values. As operating codes are changed to conform with new organizations and patterns of activity, a new set of value premises are needed if old ones are not to become impediments (Herskovits, 1961). Even in a revolutionary state, where a whole new legal code may be adopted, these more everyday matters of social conduct are likely not to be provided for completely. As strains appear from value conflicts they are likely to be resolved with any success only if a kind of "change ideology," related in turn to economic growth and national welfare, becomes a value premise of fairly wide acceptance.

Institutions

The institutional order of society provides the rules and procedures for social action and social relationships within and between various concrete organizations and contexts of action. Values may remain as unspoken assumptions except as they are made explicit by leaders or become articulated because challenged. Institutions, on the other hand, provide the procedures by which virtually every action is governed. Actions and procedures become "institutionalized" when they are endowed with moral significance and thus subject to approval or disapproval on the part of an actor's "significant others."

Although, in interdependent systems, institutions of all sorts may be affected by so crucial a social change as economic modernization, certain normative complexes have a logical and temporal priority as mediating conditions for development. Rights in scarce values (property), for example, must be transferable in order to make possible the assembly of capital goods, raw materials, and power sources for production. Impediments to transfer inhibit shifts from unproductive or less productive to more productive uses. Nationalization or "socialization" of productive property avoids some questions of changing ownership, but does not alone solve the questions of effective control and responsibility by particular agents of the collectivity. The Soviet factory manager who cannot get delivery on repair parts because of some bureaucratic complication is no better off than his free-enterprise counterpart who cannot get the rights to extract minerals from a family estate that must be preserved intact for heirs.

Labor, too, must be mobile. This is in minor degree a problem of knowledge of opportunities and sheer geographical movement, and in major degree a problem of a set of procedures for assigning tasks and filling positions radically different from the primarily ascriptive basis of status in most traditional societies (Moore, 1951). Whether the institutionalization of labor mobility is viewed as providing "freedom from traditional restraints" or more positively as a set of norms relating to technical competence, merit placement, functionally specific role relationships, and impersonal judgments of performance, it is clear that mobility is a crucial condition for even the beginnings of a rationalized economic system.

Exchange, too, requires a set of norms relating to the operation of a money-mediated market (Feldman & Moore, 1960, Ch. 3; Hoselitz, 1960). Other types of exchange relationships are by no means uncommon even in tribal societies (Smelser, 1959), and monetary markets have existed for long periods in many nonindustrial societies. The establishment and extension of relatively impersonal exchange relationships is absolutely crucial to a productive system that involves extreme specialization of productive roles. Services and fairly "nonmaterial" values are subject to commercialization along with goods as markets expand. Though many market transactions are virtually instantaneous, and subject only to the norms of honesty (which may be rather flexible) and an expectation of prudence and rationality, business markets are likely to involve contracts, promises of future delivery, credit arrangements, and a great variety of quality standards and specifications. Thus predictability, trust, and the availability of sanctions for fraud or noncompliance with contractual agreements become important ingredients of the norms of the marketplace.

The availability of sanctions highlights another essential condition for economic development: a high measure of political order. At the minimum, fixed capital installations must be protected from destruction in civil disturbances and goods or energy assured of safe transit. It is, however, especially with regard to the enforceable rules of conduct that the state figures crucially, and its political stability is essential to provide the predictability of future action that a complex economy entails. Laws and institutions are not exactly coterminous, but there is a very large overlap in complex societies. Not all laws have a pronounced moral content, as some are essentially matters of administrative convenience—some rule is preferable to none. Many rules of conduct are either fairly peculiar to a specific organization and thus constitute a kind of "private law" or are "informally sanctioned" but not supported by the full coercive power of the state. Yet the state is the principal agency of rule-making and rule-enforcing for the economy, and some durability of rules and reasonable reliability in their interpretation and enforcement are fairly essential if a highly interdependent and temporally phased system is to operate.

The institutional preconditions of economic development include, paradoxically, the necessary normative order for the encouragement of technology, mistakenly identified as a "prime mover" in Marxist (1904) and other "materialist" interpretations of structure and change. The probability of some accidental or even deliberate technical innovation is widespread, as previously noted. However, for rapid economic development rationality must be institutionalized and, along with it, deliberate change as manifested in science and technology (as well as elsewhere). Now rational action—the use of verifiable fact and logical inference in relating means to ends—is characteristic of the human species and not of modern man alone. Man, sometimes called the tool-using animal, is more properly characterized as the problem-solving animal. Yet the horizons of knowledge are always limited, and deliberate effort to expand those horizons is rare in the whole range of human experience. For most people in most of man's history standard problems of life had conventional solutions, and novelty was not encouraged. Even accidental discoveries and innovations might be discredited by the conventional wisdom. The situation in the modern world differs sharply, at least in degree. New knowledge and superior (less costly, more reliable) techniques are positively encouraged; indeed, large resources are devoted to deliberate change. Spengler (1961) viewed the rationality and rational technology essential for economic development as a problem of the suppression of "ideology," which he defined narrowly as nonrational beliefs; he argued that ideology is always inhibiting. A somewhat different interpretation, the one adopted here, is that a positive ideology favoring purposive change is required and given efficacy by normative codes that make rational action expected and irrational action penalized.

There is a kind of "technology of technology," of learning how to make inventions. The advantage of "late-comers" in borrowing technology should not be exaggerated. The technology must still be understood and, most importantly, adapted. Though a few modern equivalents of the tribal magician may supply the necessary mechanical knowledge, a rational, technical orientation is appropriate throughout the labor force, and with reference to such critical matters as social organization as well as, say, organic chemistry and metallurgy. It may well be, as Moore (1958) suggested, that what he called the "rise of the rational spirit" in the recent history of the Western world owes much to the earlier development of expanded knowledge of and control over man's nonhuman environment. (It also is worth noting, of course, that during the present century the same Western world has produced some of the wilder irrationalities in man's experience.) Deliberate change in major aspects of the social structure implies the extensive application of rational orientations to the social order. What was perhaps a consequence rather than a cause of historic economic growth has now become a condition for effective development, in view of the importance of planning and implementing programs of change in underdeveloped countries.

Organizations

Values and institutions find their chief manifestations in patterns of action and particularly in concrete organizations. Such organizations have evolved or have been more or less aptly designed to further human interests according to regular (and regulated) procedures. Economic development generally requires quite novel organizational forms, or such radical adaptations of existing structures that the continuity that maintains identity may be small and superficial.

It is impossible to generalize concerning the precise strategic and temporal priority of essential organizations, since many underdeveloped areas are not in their "pristine" stage, and, in any event, the premodern social systems differed widely. In most areas of the world, for example, there is at least some modern banking system and commercialized distribution, but these may be a very thin overlay on a predominantly traditional economic system. Banks may not be sufficiently extensive and well-established to attract the small savings that are likely to exist even in very poor countries. Markets may represent a mixture of traditional barter and modern exchange at prices determined by supply and demand. Organizations providing various financial and transfer functions may have as their chief assets the personal contacts with governmental officials or hereditary elites rather than the rational efficiency of their operations.

The ancillary and mediating structures mentioned in the preceding paragraph clearly are essential to a modern economy and have a high priority if they do not exist, or if they function in an incomplete or distorted fashion. To these may be added transportation and communication, both necessary for any substantial unification of a country's economic life.

The typological organization of an advanced economy is, of course, the manufacturing concern, with its elaborate specialization of work assignments, strongly influenced by technological considerations. Among the many features of such organizations (Moore, 1962) several are of critical importance because of the contrast they provide to typical organizations in preindustrial societies. Such organizations have a narrowly defined mission (or function), which in turn is subdivided into complementary and sequential operations assigned to organizational units and, finally, to individual positions. The position is precedent to the person, and occupants are selected in terms of technical qualifications for the tasks as specified. Relationships are impersonal and affectively neutral, communication is predominantly indirect, and authority is limited and specific to the organizational setting. The manufacturing organization displays some additional characteristics. The production worker in particular and other participants in varying degrees are caught up in a complex system of interdependence, some of it strictly reciprocal, some of it sequential. Temporal coordination involves both synchronization and sequential rates.

The fact that pure cases of the rationally organized structure do not exist "in nature" is not of great moment, as long as they are approximated. It is important to note, however, that certain modifications are highly probable in early industrial establishments, since new industrial recruits are likely to be both unskilled and uncommitted (Feldman & Moore, 1960). The supervisor is likely to have to be far more of a leader, and especially a teacher-demonstrator, than is common in advanced industrial societies. The problem of discipline is likely to occupy a substantial portion of the supervisor's time and energy, since rules may not be understood and will not have been internalized.

For the worker and indeed for many of the managers and technicians the requisite work organization may be depicted as a kind of social machine, with cooperative results essentially a mechanical by-product of performing individual assignments. At higher levels of administration the organization is more aptly characterized as a decision-making operation. The necessary decisions involve the handling of internal problems and uncertainties, but also keeping the organization in a viable relationship to a changing and not always benign environment. Whether the control of enterprises is public or private, and in the latter case whether it is under concentrated family control or only moderately responsible to dispersed stockholders will make some difference in the details of administrative organization, but the main features and problems are likely to be very similar.

As the case of Japan illustrates, economic development may take place on the basis of small-shop production in substantial sectors of the economy (Lockwood, 1954), with productive organization departing very substantially from the ideal model sketched above. Yet the significance of this special case is often exaggerated (for example, Abegglen, 1958) by neglect of the large-scale organizations that were a critically important feature of the economic landscape.

Another organizational condition for economic development represents a very different type of social structure—namely, the urban community. To consider urbanization a condition rather than a consequence of industrialization requires some comment, and indeed the establishment of any relationship is not obvious. Cities and industry have had historically a somewhat independent and somewhat intersecting course. Preindustrial cities were probable sites for some new manufacturing establishments, but other industries were established in rather small communities that became larger as a consequence of the influx of factory workers and the many service trades that a large community requires. International comparisons confirm the close association between industrialization and urbanization. Kuznets (1963, p. 102) concluded, ". . . the association of urbanization, industrialization, and per capita income is definitely positive and marked." On the other hand the pace of urbanization in underdeveloped countries is much more rapid than the pace of industrialization as measured, say, by the expansion of employment in manufacturing (Hauser, 1961; Hauser, 1963).

In a sense, therefore, the discussion of the importance of urbanization for industrialization is academic. The cities exist and are growing, even without much industrialization in the narrow meaning. Yet modernization in the extended sense is perforce occurring in the growing cities, as at least some measures are taken to provide the public services appropriate to urban life, and the new city-dwellers somehow survive on the fringes of a commercial system. And a city with very little local manufacturing cannot be said to be "independent" of in-

dustrialization if the products of industry carry its food supplies, power, and population, provide a livelihood for vendors, alleviate the suffering of the sick, and arm the keepers of the peace.

Cities are the likely sites for the expansion of manufacturing, since they offer, in addition to supplies of underemployed labor, transportation and communication facilities, residential facilities and various public services, and local consumer markets. In addition, as Hoselitz (1953) noted, the city acts as a major source of contact with the international world and a point of diffusion for the novel products and ideas that characterize contemporary civilization.

As with other elements of the social framework of economic development, the organizational features that have been identified constitute necessary but not sufficient conditions. In their absence little growth is likely to occur. Their presence may still not assure that other necessary measures will be taken to change the way resources are used to yield a larger product.

Motives

The simple preference for higher standards of health and physical well-being can be assumed virtually everywhere, as noted previously with reference to values and ideologies. What remains in question is the strength of these preferences and the willingness and energy to alter the conditions of life. It is in this special sense that particular motives and attitudes constitute conditions for sharp and rapid departures from conventional forms of economic activity.

The particular personality structure that will engage in creative innovation is characterized by a high "need achievement" orientation, according to McClelland (1961; McClelland, Atkinson, Clark, & Lowell, 1953). Persons with such personalities get satisfaction from tackling and solving problems and, of course, from positive achievements. The prevalence of such personality types, McClelland argued from a variety of direct tests and indirect evidence, is uneven within societies and markedly different between societies. If very few such individuals are to be found, McClelland (1963) did not expect much by way of rapid economic transition. McClelland's psychological interpretation has been related to social structure by Hagen (1962), who viewed economic growth as being instigated by innovational as distinct from authoritarian personality types. These personalities, Hagen argued, are likely to appear among the children of social groups that have suffered a "withdrawal of status respect" (Hagen, 1962, pp. 185–199). Parents may well react primarily in terms of "retreatism," following Merton's (1957, pp. 131–160) designation of such behavior deriving from rejection of both the standard cultural goals and prescribed means for achieving them, but mothers, Hagen believed, will act with their children in such a way that the children develop what might be called "constructive anxiety."

Though the theories of McClelland and Hagen are scarcely to be rejected out of hand, both suffer from a common defect in one important particular. Both deal exclusively with personality formation in early socialization. Now, if attitudes or "orientations" can be formed only in infancy, the system is essentially closed to change, since there is no way parents (especially mothers) can adopt new attitudes and thus influence their children. In view of the overwhelming evidence for adolescent and adult socialization—the internalization of values and norms appropriate to contexts of social action that could not possibly be learned in infancy—exclusive attention to infant socialization represents a radical distortion of the interaction between the individual personality and the social order. Yet it would be improper to deny the importance of "marginal" and even "disaffected" groups as initiators of social change. Unmitigated frustration is unlikely to produce creative innovation, and apathy is somewhat more likely than destructive or criminal innovation. If, however, social circumstances provide a measure of

both opportunity and immediate rewards for novelty, then the structure and personality may interact in ways that produce useful novelty.

The theses expounded by McClelland (1963) and Hagen (1962) may be viewed as simply more sophisticated versions of a doctrine popular with economists, namely, that economic growth depends on "entrepreneurship." For many economists entrepreneurship is the little black box that contains the magical remedy for economic stagnation. This notion is of very little use either for analysis or for economic policy, unless it is possible to specify the conditions under which entrepreneurship will occur. Otherwise, the emphasis on the entrepreneur could be translated: "Things will continue pretty much as they are unless someone takes the trouble to change them." Older economic doctrines, summarized and criticized by Hoselitz (1952), emphasized profit-seeking. To this Schumpeter (1934) added the innovating role of the entrepreneur in seeking profits. Though such motivational patterns may have been appropriate in the historical development of capitalism and may be appropriate in the private sectors of "mixed" economies in developing areas now, they scarcely fit the predominantly socialist states. Moreover, and regardless of economic regime, the innovation "needs" are far wider than simply those of new productive enterprises (Harbison, 1963). For industrial administration Harbison and Myers (1959) concluded that "as industrialization advances, the *proportion* of managerial resources in the labor force of the industrial society must increase" (Harbison & Myers, 1959, p. 38), noting as reasons the increasing complexity of organization and the increasing importance of innovation. Harbison (1963) argued that constructive innovators are likely to be drawn chiefly from "high-level manpower," meaning by that term primarily those with advanced and technical training. With respect to educational policies for developing countries, therefore, Harbison recommended the concentration of limited resources for educational investment on increasing the number of these strategic skills and associated attitudes in the labor force.

The argument is a reasonable one if not overstated. Feldman and Moore (1960) warned:

The importance of managerial skills . . . should not be exaggerated into a doctrine of "entrepreneurial determinism," which would imply that the notable barriers to effective labor supply of all types could be erased by the comparatively simple expedient of training managers with appropriate leadership and even manipulative talents. The supply of executives and coordinators depends on educational and motivational qualifications. *The same is true for other occupations* (Feldman & Moore, 1960, p. 45).

A reluctant and uncommitted labor force, willing to seek new employment opportunities only because more traditionally acceptable means of gaining a livelihood are not available, will clearly require greater attention to demonstration and teaching and also to discipline and close supervision by managers than will better trained and more committed workers. The shortage of skilled managers in developing areas is thus doubly exacerbated—the skills required are somewhat broader and the relative numbers somewhat greater than is the normal case in countries with established industrial relations. Though there is no ideal solution to the problem of what part of the labor force planning strategists ought to be concerned about in educational policy, short of an unrealistic attention to "all," it is by no means clear that the production of high skills and innovating attitudes among the few at the cost of providing no education for the many is even sensible. It appears more reasonable to argue that some trained persons will need to be imported from abroad and some nationals sent abroad for training, while local educational systems are expanded in the most strategic ways possible. One important occupation, as Harbison (1963) noted, is that of qualified teachers and, especially, teachers of teachers.

Functional literacy and the command of ordinary arithmetic are of critical importance throughout the labor force of a commercial-industrial economy. Yet the primary concern in the discussion at this point is with motives, and the efficacy of the school as an agency of change in attitudes is not well known anywhere. Certain formal characteristics of the secular school and its curriculum permit some hypothetical inferences, however. The elementary school based on any model from Western Europe or the United States has certain common and significant characteristics (Moore, 1963b). The child is expected to adjust to orderly change, by the hour, day, week, and year. The child is also expected to compete and is given fairly immediate information and sanctions according to his relative success or failure. At some point, probably variable among schools, he is asked to take a "constructive," problem-solving orientation to tasks and not simply a mechanical apprehension and memorization process of accumulating information and skills.

Now these characteristics imply habits and even attitudes of mind that are highly appropriate to a social order that is not only very competitive and changeful but also provides opportunities for rational innovation. For an industrial society the most valuable product of the schools is not a matrix of particular skills but a population accustomed to uncertainty and positively oriented to continuous learning and creative problem-solving. No society has come very close to optimal "human resource utilization" in this sense, but no society is going to achieve much economic (or any other) modernization without effective education in the attitudinal sense among fairly broad sectors of the population.

A kind of hard-bitten realism, emphasizing elite leadership and severe constraints (if not outright coercion) in extracting performance from others appears on close examination to be another black box, containing perfectly spurious magical solutions. Unless a positive attitude toward change and a measure of creativity in bringing about change at various levels and types of skills are rather broadly distributed in the population, the social order will remain essentially static—indeed one might properly say "stagnant."

This is not to deny the importance of leadership in bringing about constructive change but to note that its potential availability in various walks of life is radically misrepresented by exclusive attention to a thin layer of highly trained talent.

Realism may, however, indicate that the schools of a poor country will be unevenly distributed in terms of both location and quality, as Anderson (1963) suggested. It is probably true that a year or two of elementary education has little, if any, lasting effect. What is impressive in the developing countries is the way that education and its visible manifestation in schools are popularly regarded as symbols of a new and better social order. It is doubtful that any political regime, however authoritarian its structure, could survive conspicuous failure to provide schools and teachers. If the arguments advanced here have merit, this "common sense" or "public opinion" may be a sounder basis for policy than some of the expert opinion that neglects the importance of attitudes and motives.

The popular support for education is one important example of another feature of human motivation that is of major importance in contemporary efforts at economic development. The chances of change being accepted and even actively sought are markedly increased if new avenues of positive participation are opened.

The most stringent system of coercive political control to be found in industrialized and developing societies is that of the Communist states. These countries provide a dual paradox. First, an equalitarian ideology is coupled with a ruthless minority dictatorship. But, second, that dictatorship emphasizes a degree of popular participation —manipulated and restrained but still real —that is scarcely to be matched in those developing countries that have followed a more pluralistic model of social organization. In terms of ideological appeals and organizational inventiveness, the leaders of Communist states have correctly understood that followers, too, are important and that a sense of positive participation in the creation of a new social order is an important condition for rapid and successful modernization.

THE IMPACT OF INDUSTRY[3]

By the somewhat arbitrary convention of distinguishing between conditions and consequences of economic development, the discussion now turns to the ways a modernizing economy affects various other components of operating societies. The tracing out of such consequences is one of the major uses of the conception of societies as constituting "systems." It seems appropriate, however, to reiterate some qualifications and add one or two more. First, the conception of social systems as static and "in equilibrium" is peculiarly inappropriate for the analysis of the consequences of industrialization, since continuous and rapid change is especially marked in societies undergoing modernization and, as far as is now evident or predictable, forever after. Next, the before-and-after model provides no guidance as to rates and sequences and (paradoxically for a theoretical approach utilizing the notion of functional relations) understates the interplay among social elements in the process of transformation; this deficiency derives in the main from exaggerated attention to economic change as a unique "prime mover." Also, the emphasis on what might be called "congruence" among structural elements tends to neglect the substantial and persistent conflicts and tensions that are in-

---

[3] This section represents a selective reorganization of the extensive summary survey presented in Moore (1963a).

trinsic to all societies and especially prominent, both as cause and effect, where change is extremely rapid. To these points that are essentially restatements of considerations previously advanced, another should be added. Though sociologists commonly opperrate under the brave and challenging assumption that "everything is related to everything," the nature of complex societies (and in some degree all societies) warrants a kind of disarming caution. A society can persist with fairly high degrees of functional autonomy and independent variability in various aspects of its social organization and particularly in its cultural orientations and values. Thus the social terrain may be marked by open areas and somewhat isolated settlements along with the intricate web of structures that lends comfort to the seeker after relationships. The selections of consequences discussed here therefore implies a judgment that some characteristics of societies are more directly related to the economic system (or any other part of the central web) than are others not discussed, such as art forms or the substantive content of supernatural beliefs. This does not mean that the topics discussed below are offered as definitive, for such pretensions have a sad record of premature closure, but only that the current evidence provides few maps beyond the settled area, and the possibility that the unknown territory is empty must be entertained.

Changes in Economic Structure

Aside from changes in the way productive activities are organized, already discussed as a condition of development, the most evident alterations in the economic structure consequent on modernization relate to the distribution of economic activities among the productive population or labor force. The now-classic formulation of Clark (1940) was to the effect that with economic growth the labor force underwent a major shift out of primary production (agriculture and extractive processes) into secondary production (chiefly manufacturing) and thence to tertiary production (services of various kinds). The main outlines of this generalization are approximately valid (Kuznets, 1957), though some modifications with regard to services need to be made. Domestic service workers tend to decline in numerical proportions in the process of economic growth because more lucrative and prestigeful employments become available. As noted with reference to urbanization, underdeveloped areas now are often marked by a rapid expansion of rather low-level service activities as the increase of employment in manufacturing fails to keep pace with the rural exodus. Nevertheless, there is no exception to the rule that the proportions, and usually even the numbers, of the population dependent on agriculture or gainfully occupied in farm production declines as economic growth occurs. (Total agricultural production is likely to rise meanwhile, despite the reduction of labor input, as production becomes more highly capitalized and various technological improvements are made.)

Several other occupational changes are important. One is that of occupational specialization. Differentiation of positions and skills in the productive system is not a single, once-for-all transformation as an economy becomes modern, but a continuing process for which no terminus is discernible (Smelser, 1963).

The literal *division* of labor—the breaking up of craft or professional skill combinations into narrower component units—is only one side of the process of specialization. It may or may not lead to a kind of status degradation. The other side of specialization is the creation of new occupations requiring new skills and their combination. The frequent inability of persons whose skills have been technologically displaced to qualify for the new occupations is one of the individual and social costs of continuous changes of occupational structures.

Though part of the coordination of specialized activities may be accomplished through a market system of exchange, according to the "classical" economic model, much of it requires administrative organization and the development of both reciprocal and sequential relations among occupational activities. Thus managers, coordinators, and intermediaries of all sorts will increase disproportionately to other occupational functions.

The shift from agriculture to industry on the part of the new industrial recruit is likely to be relatively neutral with respect to status mobility (Moore, 1960)—that is, the change neither involves much advance in a skill hierarchy, since the worker will be essentially unskilled at his new job, nor does it normally involve a substantial "degradation" of status, contrary to a long line of critics of industrialism. Some craftsmen who have lost their markets by inability to compete with cheap manufactured goods may indeed seek factory employment. Generally, however, the first workers will be drawn from the landless poor of the countryside or from the urban slums. The mobility involved is essentially lateral, a "situs" change, rather than a marked change of status (Hatt, 1950).

Subsequent changes in industrial processes lead to a rising average level of skills required and probably a rising minimum level also. In fact, in the United States and other highly industrialized countries those workers who, for whatever reason, have not kept pace with the general increase in educational and skill levels are those most difficult or impossible to place in useful employments. In the United States and to a somewhat lesser extent in other industrial countries there are two further indications of the broad validity of Clark's (1940) formulation with respect to the increase of services. Services of all types account for over half of the labor force—that is, more than agriculture and manufacturing combined (Kuznets, 1958). By broad occupational classifications, "head" or "white-collar" workers now outnumber "hand" or "blue-collar" workers.

The labor mobility associated with eco-nomic development is of several types that are analytically and often concretely distinct. Geographical mobility represents the human side of the location of economic activities. Is is often, though not necessarily, associated with changes in employers and with changes in industry or economic sector —situs mobility. Status mobility—changes in relative rank, income, or skill level—is commonly divided into that occurring between generations and that marking an individual career. Both kinds of status mobility will be affected by changes in the occupational structure itself—for example, the relative increase of administrative and professional positions—and by changes in the degree of openness in the system in terms of recruitment and promotion—for example, the extent to which educational opportunities are relatively equal on the basis of merit (Rogoff, 1953). About the only characteristic that these various kinds of mobility have in common, other than uniformly representing some sort of change in position in the economy, is that all are likely to increase in association with economic development.

Changes in occupational structure of course are consequences of economic development and a condition for continuous growth. Skill shortages are a persistent characteristic of growing economies, along with the steady obsolescence of other skills.

A very comparable situation prevails with respect to savings and investment. Clearly new investments are necessary if the economy is to modernize at all. The pent-up demand for consumer goods, particularly in very poor countries, can impede continuous growth, if part of current production is not in the form of capital for further expansion.

One of the principal organizational features of a modernized economy is the creation of banks, securities markets, and other means of tapping and channeling private savings. Partly because currently underdeveloped areas are generally poorer than were Western economies prior to industrialization and partly because of the desire on the part of officials for speedy transformation, it is very likely that the state will figure prominently as an agency of gathering and disbursing capital. Taxation, foreign grants and loans, and domestic bond issues provide sources of capital, along with whatever private profits are available for reinvestment. Though in economies with a large private economic sector the proportion of savings rises with income, viewed cross-sectionally, it does not appear that savings increase proportionally through time as the economy becomes more prosperous (Kuznets, 1953).

With respect to consumption, on the other hand, it does appear that cross-sectional differences also operate through time. That is, the time-honored principle ("Engel's Law," see Holton, 1960) that the proportions of family income spent on food will decrease at higher income levels also operates as between poor and rich countries (Kuznets, 1963) and through time as average income increases (Kuznets, 1962).

The commercialization of an economy means an extension and complication of markets and distribution, and an apparently unlimited expansion of the total variety of goods produced and consumed. An especially interesting feature of economic development is the commercialization of services, whereby various forms of "self help" or mutual aid come to have a market value and indeed to be fulfilled primarily by financial transactions. These two trends taken together yield a paradoxical result: Materialism may be increasingly indulged as an economy prospers, but so may all sorts of nonmaterialistic services and benefits. The quest for money cannot be equated with mere materialism under these circumstances.

The social limits of the market as a means of allocating services and establishing reciprocities are not precisely known from empirical evidence. There is, however, some theoretical and empirical basis for supposing that the nominally impersonal market (where only money talks) will have little or no importance where affectivity is a major and normatively sanctioned component of the relationship (Feldman & Moore, 1960, pp. 42–43). Thus financial allocations may be made within the family, but on the basis of individual needs, not primarily on the basis of services at market value. Economic development does tend to increase the relative importance of economic transactions in the whole web of social existence, a trend that led Tumin (1956) to criticize "institutional imbalance," yet economic actions remain primarily instrumental to the functions of the family, church, or state and not really final or superordinate.

Demographic and Ecological Structure

One of the early and major advantages of modernization is that of a sharp reduction of the risks of dying. And it is precisely this advantage that presents developing countries with one of their major problems, namely, the achievement of a pace of total growth that will outrun the expansion of population.

The grim predictions of Malthus (1806) concerning the consequences of the capacity of human population to grow more rapidly than the means for their subsistence were essentially negated by the dual circumstances of physical expansion of European populations into lightly settled areas and the phenomenal growth of the technology of production (Kuznets, 1960). Neither of these solutions to rapid reproduction provides much help to the underdeveloped areas. The problem, indeed, is increased by what is normally an advantage of late-comers to modernization—it is now possible through public health measures and the use of insecticides and drugs to reduce death rates at a precipitous pace. This permits the normally high fertility of traditional societies to prevail unchecked, for a time, and bring about an extremely rapid population growth (Keyfitz, 1963). Recent and current rates of population growth may run as high as 3 per cent a year, and since children soon become parents a continuation of so rapid a growth rate may double the population about every 25 years (United Nations, 1953, pp. 71–97).

The practical, short-range consequence of rapid population growth is the necessity for economic planners seeking a rise in per capita income to attempt to produce growth rates in excess of population increase. Otherwise, plans successfully completed may achieve virtually no increase in material welfare (Coale & Hoover, 1958). Over the longer term it is clear that space is finite and that the capacity of an economy continuously to provide increases in per capita income is distinctly depressed by rapid growth in the population to be supported.

In general, the advantage of late-comers in being able to take advantage of the end-products of technological evolution is substantial. The paradox of the population problem is that the short-run benefits of a readily borrowed technology may have nearly disastrous consequences for the possibility of sustained growth.

Though urbanization and industrialization have been credited with providing the appropriate environment for voluntary restriction on child-bearing (Davis, 1958), particularly through the efficacy of mobility orientations of parents for themselves and their children, it appears that birth rates, like death rates, may be subjected to rather deliberate attention by agencies of public welfare in order to avoid a kind of confirmation of the dire predictions of Malthus in other places and other times (Notestein, 1950).

The interposition of "rational" control of fertility, an aspect of human behavior long thought to be relatively immune to rational considerations, is closely associated with education. This adds evidence to the view expressed earlier that a wide extension of education, which is partly a condition and partly a consequence of economic development, is one of the more important aspects of social change accompanying rapid growth in a society's productive system.

Rapid population growth—and here there is another paradox—creates a very large pro-portion of young dependents and thus makes more difficult precisely the expansion of elementary educational opportunities that a modernizing society requires (United Nations, 1953, pp. 262–287).

No doubt demographic expansion is a major factor in the rapid pace of urbanization noted earlier. Very little is actually known of the selectivity of urban in-migrants except that they are predominantly young adults, and it may be presumed that the failure of the rural economy and social system to provide them with an adequate place prompts their search for better opportunities in the cities. The city's opportunities may prove disappointing over the short run, and the short run may last long enough that full incorporation of the migratory family into urban life will await the maturity of the children.

The record of cities in the more economically advanced countries in fully "assimilating" migrants (or their own populations) to the tensely competitive yet impersonal world of urban life is not wholly encouraging to those who seek change without problems. The new migrants may behave very much as transplanted villagers, though their children may have neither the effective informal controls provided by kinsmen and meaningful neighbors nor a new fabric of relations consistent with the law and norms relating to urban social relations. Alienation and apathy appear to be endemic in the urban way of life, along with a degree of creativity ranging from the instrumental and technological to the arts of civilization (Hauser, 1963).

The recurrent pattern of population distribution in the course of economic modernization appears to be one of initial concentration, to the degree that land values and incomes permit, followed by decentralization or "suburbanization" on the part of those who can afford the investment of time and transportation costs in return for less congestion. One of the transitional stages evident in the urban centers of countries with a newly prosperous set of city dwellers is the close juxtaposition of luxury apartments, and even single dwellings, with the "shanty-town" slums on the urban fringe, a "ring of poverty" typical of most poor but developing countries.

The ecological patterns of urban development will be affected by administrative policies of political agencies with respect to land use, subsidized housing, public transportation, and so on. Yet not even totalitarian regimes have been able, or seen fit, to control urban growth and residential locations in ways and degrees that prevent slums, sprawl, and lack of synchronization of population densities and community services.

Characteristic Aspects of Social Structure

The ramifications of a modernized economic order through other modes and patterns of social relations are far-reaching, but probably not total. Historical continuities may persist, and certain cultural systems may be relatively immune to mere changes in the fundamental conditions of life and the way it is organized. Yet it is clearly possible, and proper, to identify the characteristic changes in the principal forms of social organization and the way universal survival functions are performed.

One could not do better than to start with the impact of economic modernization on the family and kinship systems, a universal structural feature of human societies. The exclusive emphasis of some anthropologists on the kinship system as virtually coextensive with society cannot be taken seriously. Given the universality of the "incest taboo" and therefore some requirement of exogamy —marriage outside the group—some form of super-familial order must prevail. Nevertheless, the range of social activities that revolve around familial and kinship relations in many societies is very large. This means, among other things, that social positions are likely to be ascriptive—owing to predetermined "accidents" of birth—rather than based on individual performance criteria. Hereditary status is likely to be the

norm, extreme individual successes or failures the exceptions. Now it can be seen readily that a system that assigns adult position at birth and emphasizes the unity of an extended group of kinsmen is unsuited to the geographical and social mobility required by a modernized economy. One of the surest generalizations about economic development is that it is destructive of extended kinship systems (Goode, 1963; Levy, 1949; Nash, 1960).

Yet the functional fit between industrialism and the small "nuclear" or "conjugal" family—parents and their immature children—is a little too neat. More extended kinship relations at least in the form of mutual aid may exhibit hardy survival powers (Goode, 1963; Hoselitz, 1960a; Hoselitz, 1960b; Hoselitz, 1961; Nash, 1960). On the other hand, the Western ideal of substantial separation of the generations and of adult siblings may well have antedated the industrial revolution by centuries (Lorimer, 1954). The mobility and subsequent prosperity of industrial societies may have made possible a pre-existing ideal, and the same circumstances in other areas may make necessary a substantial departure from ideals.

Though reliable evidence is lacking, it appears proper to speculate that the initial impact of modernization on extended kinship structures is much more severe than the long-range effect. The development of easy transportation and communication may reduce the significance of geographical separation of nuclear units, and the kinship system itself may accommodate to the social inequality of its single familial units. This is clearly the case in the contemporary United States.

The social controls characteristic of the traditional community also tend to be undermined by the greater knowledge and new alternatives available to the young (Moore, 1951); by the intrusion of such external influences as the nationally responsible political leader, the development technician, and the school; and by the pervasive influence of a market economy (Loomis, 1953; F. W. Young & Ruth C. Young, 1960).

In the urban environment, novel to the in-migrants, a substantial loss of affiliation with significant others may be coupled with the frustration of unrealistic expectations. The sins of the cities may well be exaggerated because they come to formal notice, but the diversity of populations assembled in urban areas and the predominance of social interaction with strangers cannot provide a complete social existence and may well result in heightened rates of personal and social disorganization, partly transitional but partly enduring. The integration of traditional communities should not be exaggerated, but sheer size and diversity of social origins tend to reduce the efficacy of informal social controls in the city for those cast loose from familial and other significant sources of both emotional support and restraint. The relatively unrecorded incidence of apathy and alienation may well exceed the recorded incidence of crime and acts of overt deviation.

The effects of the city in furthering constructive change in the economy and in the forms of social organization are not to be dismissed, however. It is probable, though not conclusively demonstrated, that the urban in-migrants include a disproportionate share of the more creative and intelligent members of the youthful population, and it is clearly the case that "constructive" talents have more opportunities in the competitive and changeful urban environment than in the small and traditionally organized community where unusual talents are likely, and properly, to be regarded as disruptive.

The historic course of social change in the older industrial societies has been characterized by urbanization in the strict ecological sense of the growth of cities and diminution of rural populations (Hauser, 1963) and also in the extension of an "urban way of life." The radical disparity between the sophisticated city-dweller and the country bumpkin, between the burgher and the peasant, was gradually but inexorably reduced by the spread of the market and especially of communications. The special province of "rural sociology" as the study of a distinctive type of social organization peculiar to an agricultural setting has tended to disappear in highly industrialized societies, just as finding uncontaminated tribal societies has become a kind of technologically doomed profession for ethnographic anthropologists.

The availability of modern telecommunications in developing areas radically foreshortens the pace of this transition. Radios in the household or at least in the village square may well precede functional literacy (like antibiotics before aspirin). The pervasive influence of a mass culture is greatly aided by mass communication. Standardization of messages is hopefully pursued by political authorities as a way of securing undivided allegiance and a sort of national identity. The results of such integrated communication systems cannot be dismissed lightly, but like all propaganda everywhere the efficacy of both informational and ideological messages is partly dependent on conformity with pre-existing capacity to understand and with special attitudes consistent with the novel elements fostered (Doob, 1935).

There is no question that standardized and centralized communications media and the existence of a mass audience for all sorts of literary and cultural expression radically alters the pattern of communication between the communicator or artist and his public. Many "folk" arts may be degenerated by standardization and commercialization. The arguments along this line are, however, mostly tendentious and patronizing. It is not necessarily true that a "mass" culture is inferior to one peculiar to an elite, that a wide audience is automatically a low-level and undiscriminating one, or that popular appreciation automatically degrades the quality of expression—intellectual or esthetic.

The outstanding characteristics of an industrialized society is not uniformity but diversity. The typically organized or bureaucratic form of work organizations does not diminish the diversity of occupations but rather takes advantage of diversity and adds to it, within a system of coordination that suppresses but does not stifle individuality (Moore, 1962). Outside the work place a host of old interests that were more or less taken care of by the familial and community organization and a host of new interests not previously imagined form the rationale for specialized associations. If the auspices for economic modernization are unitary and totalitarian, the creation of special-interest associations will be hesitant and controlled (Inkeles & Bauer, 1961). If liberal, pluralistic traditions prevail, specialized associations may be more numerous and will be predominantly voluntary. In either situation, strictly occupational and economic interests are certain to take organizational form (Bendix, 1956; Moore, 1960) along with organized expression of like interests in the diversity of "cultural" activities that a modernized society both implements and creates (MacIver & Page, 1949, pp. 437–452).

The relation of religion to economic modernization presents a mixed picture. On the evidence, the worldly asceticism of Calvinistic protestantism is not a necessary condition for contemporary development, whatever its historic role with respect to industrial capitalism (Weber, 1948). The essentially religious elements in nationalism and communism may be interpreted as fulfilling comparable ideological functions. Traditional religions, on the other hand, may well survive the radical transformations attendant on economic development, particularly in their supernatural beliefs and cosmology. Science has no teaching on the nature of life after death or the ultimate meaning of man's destiny. Yet traditional religions do face the erosive force of *secularization,* since the extensive and normatively sanctioned rationality of a modernized society will certainly undermine (but not necessarily destroy) confidence in mundane

magic which virtually all religions countenance. The use of prayers and incantations, amulets and rituals, to alter the course of empirical events can scarcely vie with rational technology over the long run (Moore, 1963b). Even strictly religious convictions may encounter substantial agnosticism, though religious explanations of life's meaning are virtually certain to endure in some form or degree.

Religious justifications for the forms of social inequality—as in the Hindu rationale for the caste system in India—can scarcely survive the mobility of a modernized society (Davis, 1955). In fact virtually all pre-industrial forms of social stratification, whatever their rationales, are subject to major alteration as new social positions and new modes of recruitment and mobility are established (Tumin, 1960). For some transitional period it is approximately accurate to refer to the existence of competing systems of stratification. The qualifier "approximately" is used, for the forms of social differentiation and social inequality characteristic of an industrialized society are scarcely rectilinear and tidy. "Classes" tend not to be unambiguously identifiable as to number, boundaries, or membership. The relevance of lineage is unlikely to be completely erased, while a great variety of positional and performance criteria are subject to differential valuation. Not all of the forms of inequality are directly linked to social stratification in the narrow sense of a generalized social rank with tendencies to become hereditary through inequalities of opportunity for children (Tumin, 1963).

The system of stratification associated with industrialism is actually least ambiguous during the earliest stages of rapid development. Marx's (1904) perception of polarization between capitalists and workers was essentially correct for the middle of the nineteenth century. His extrapolation of total polarization, incorporating and destroying anachronistic segments of the pre-industrial order, was diametrically wrong. Yet at comparable stages of development, and conspicuously including communistic states, a similar duality of social strata appears: the innovators and the reluctant followers, the managers and the managed, the commissars and the unskilled workers, the educated and the ignorant (Moore, 1960). As skill levels increase and become increasingly differentiated (Feldman, 1962) and a great variety of service functions are created, the neat polarization is destroyed and indeed on most measures of status the "middle groups" predominate. Marx simply did not understand the dynamics of the industrial society, which, however, are somewhat easier to comprehend in retrospect than in prospect.

Of the major structural and institutional features of complex societies, the nature of political organizations offers the greatest difficulty in generalization. The administrative structure of the state—some variant of the basic forms of bureaucracy—is likely to be fairly common to all developing and industrial societies (Eisenstadt, 1963). The political structure proper, however, the concentration and distribution of power and responsibility and the forms of political recruitment, is on the evidence widely variable. That the state in a country now seeking rapid economic revolution will exercise a major degree of control by comparison with the earliest models of industrialization seems clear, and this forms another basis for generalization (Smelser, 1963). It is probable that some form of popular political participation will be widely tolerated or encouraged, but perhaps more often manipulated and supportive of a unitary party than genuinely democratic in the sense of representation of diverse and even divisive interests (Apter, 1960).

Popular political participation is a mode of "tension management" amidst rapid and disruptive change, along with the more formal agencies of political power. Feldman and Moore (1962) argued that, although the major organizational features of industrial societies are similar, the conspicuous exception of the state as a political organiza-

tion is to be explained by the peculiar function of the state as the principal instrumentality of tension management. Since there are ample reasons, previously reviewed, to expect the characteristic tensions of societies to differ between societies and through time, political parallelism and absolute structural stability are not to be expected. Moreover, because of the high utility of nationalism as an instrumentality of internal integration, the problems of managing international tensions become exacerbated in the process of economic development. The record to date of neither bilateral diplomacy nor international organization leads to optimistic conclusions about the orderly persistence of a competitive international system.

CODA

The tenuous prospects for peace in the contemporary world provide a depressing reminder that the virtually universal effort at improving man's material conditions of life has serious and perhaps disastrous costs as well as obvious benefits. The unity of the contemporary world is based on like interests rather than common ones, on the competitive quest for the magic instrument of economic development, not on shared ultimate values and a common and binding moral order. If the world's cultures had remained as distinct as they appeared to be through the first four decades of the twentieth century, comparisons among them would have remained a challenging and sticky problem for the social scientist but would not have got into the auditoriums and corridors of international agencies, the offices of embassies and heads of state, or the deliberations of legislative bodies. The gross inequalities in national incomes per head provide a basis of comparison as well as sources of tension, an instrument of international policy second in noise level only to the rattle of rockets.

The "cold war" may provide at least a temporary advantage to uncommitted countries because of the gamesmanship opportunities for playing both sides and receiving competitive assistance. But prosperous countries are more terrifying potential foes than poor ones. Peace and prosperity seem to have a random or perhaps even negative relation. The problem of poverty is at least receiving major attention, though the difficulties of finding a rapid cure are great. The growing unity of the world in its material standards illuminates its disunity in the levels of well-being and especially in its failure to manage the relations among national states.

REFERENCES

Abegglen, J. G. The Japanese factory: Aspects of its social organization. Glencoe, Ill.: Free Press, 1958.

Aitken, H. G. J. (Ed.) The state and economic growth. New York: Social Science Research Council, 1959.

Almond, G. A., & Coleman, J. S. (Eds.) The politics of the developing areas. Princeton, N.J.: Princeton Univer. Press, 1960.

Anderson, C. A. The impact of the educational system on technological change and modernization. In B. F. Hoselitz & W. E. Moore (Eds.), Industrialization and society. Paris and The Hague· UNESCO & Mouton, 1963. Pp. 259–278.

Apter, D. C. Political organization and ideology. In W. E. Moore & A. S. Feldman (Eds.), Labor commitment and social change in developing areas. New York: Social Science Research Council, 1960. Pp. 326–347.

Barclay, G. W. Colonial development and population in Taiwan. Princeton, N.J.: Princeton Univer. Press, 1954.

Bendix, R. Work and authority in industry. New York: Wiley, 1956.

Clark, C. The conditions of economic progress. London: Macmillan, 1940.

Coale, A. J., & Hoover, E. M. Population growth and economic development in low income countries. Princeton, N.J.: Princeton Univer. Press, 1958.

Davis, K. The population of India and Pakistan. Princeton, N.J.: Princeton Univer. Press, 1951.

Davis, K. Social and demographic aspects of economic development in India. In S. Kuznets, W. E. Moore, & J. J. Spengler (Eds.), Economic growth: Brazil, India, Japan. Durham, N.C.: Duke Univer. Press, 1955. Pp. 263-315.

Davis, K. The demographic consequences of changes in productive technology. In International Social Science Council, Social, economic and technological change. Paris: International Social Science Council, 1958. Pp. 193-227.

Davis, K., & Golden, Hilda H. Urbanization and the development of pre-industrial areas. Econ. Develpm. cult. Change, 1954, 3, 6-26.

DeVries, E. Man in rapid social change. New York: Doubleday, 1961.

Doob, L. W. Propaganda. New York: Holt, 1935.

Eisenstadt, S. N. Problems of emerging bureaucracies in developing areas and new states. In B. F. Hoselitz & W. E. Moore (Eds.), Industrialization and society. Paris and The Hague: UNESCO & Mouton, 1963. Pp. 159-174.

Feldman, A. S. The interpenetration of firm and society. In International Social Science Council, Social implication of technological change. Paris: International Social Science Council, 1962. Pp. 179–198.

Feldman, A. S., & Moore, W. E. Spheres of commitment. In W. E. Moore & A. S. Feldman (Eds.), Labor commitment and social change in developing areas. New York: Social Science Research Council, 1960. Part I, chs. 1–4, pp. 1–77.

Feldman, A. S., & Moore, W. E. Industrialization and industrialism: Convergence and differentiation. Trans. fifth World Congr. Sociol., 1962, 2, 151–169.

Goode, W. J. Industrialization and family change. In B. F. Hoselitz & W. E. Moore (Eds.), Industrialization and society. Paris and The Hague: UNESCO & Mouton, 1963. Pp. 237-255.

Hagen, E. E. On the theory of social change: How economic growth begins. Homewood, Ill.: Dorsey, 1962.

Harbison, F. The prime movers of innovation. Paper read at Conf. Educ. Econ. Develpm. sponsored by Committee on Economic Growth, Social Science Research Council, and Comparative Education Center, Univer. of Chicago, Chicago, April, 1963. (Mimeographed)

Harbison, F., & Myers, C. A. *Management in the industrial world*. New York: McGraw, 1959.

Hatt, P. K. Occupation and social stratification. *Amer. J. Sociol.,* 1950, 55, 538-543.

Hauser, P. M. (Ed.) *Urbanization in Latin America*. Paris: UNESCO, 1961.

Hauser, P. M. The social, economic, and technological problems of rapid urbanization. In B. F. Hoselitz & W. E. Moore (Eds.), *Industrialization and society*. Paris and The Hague: UNESCO & Mouton, 1963. Pp. 199—217.

Heintz, P. (Ed.) *Soziologie der Entwicklungsländer*. Koln and Berlin: Kiepenheuer & Witsch, 1962.

Herskovits, M. J. Economic change and cultural dynamics. In R. Braibanti & J. J. Spengler (Eds.), *Tradition, values, and socio-economic development*. Durham, N.C.: Duke Univer. Press, 1961. Pp. 114-138.

Holton, R. H. Changing demand and consumption. In W. E. Moore & A. S. Feldman (Eds.), *Labor commitment and social change in developing areas*. New York: Social Science Research Council, 1960. Pp. 201-216.

Hoselitz, B. F. Entrepreneurship and economic growth. *Amer. J. Econ. Sociol.,* 1952, 12, 97-109.

Hoselitz, B. F. (Ed.) *The progress of underdeveloped areas*. Chicago: Univer. of Chicago Press, 1952.

Hoselitz, B. F. The role of cities in the economic growth of underdeveloped countries. *J. polit. Econ.,* 1953, 61, 195-208.

Hoselitz, B. F. The market matrix. In W. E. Moore & A. S. Feldman (Eds.), *Labor commitment and social change in developing areas*. New York; Social Science Research Council, 1960. Pp. 217-237. (a)

Hoselitz, B. F. *Sociological aspects of economic growth*. Glencoe, Ill.: Free Press, 1960.(b)

Hoselitz, B. F. Tradition and economic growth. In R. Braibanti & J. J. Spengler (Eds.), *Tradition, values and socio-economic development*. Durham, N.C.: Duke Univer. Press, 1961. Pp. 83–113.

Inkeles, A., & Bauer, R. A. *The Soviet citizen*. Cambridge, Mass.: Harvard Univer. Press, 1961.

Jaffe, A. J., & Stewart, C. D. *Manpower resources and utilization*. New York: Wiley, 1951.

Kerr, C. Changing social structures. In W. E. Moore & A. S. Feldman (Eds.), *Labor commitment and social change in developing areas*. New York: Social Science Research Council, 1960. Pp. 348-359.

Kerr, C., Dunlop, J. T., Harbison, F., & Myers, C. A. *Industrialism and industrial man*. Cambridge, Mass.: Harvard Univer. Press, 1960.

Keyfitz, N. The impact of technological change on demographic patterns. In B. F. Hoselitz & W. E. Moore (Eds.), *Industrialization and society*. Paris and The Hague: UNESCO & Mouton, 1963. Pp. 218-236.

Kuznets, S. *Shares of upper income groups in savings and investment*. New York: National Bureau of Economic Research, 1953.

Kuznets, S. Quantitative aspects of the economic growth of nations. II. Industrial distribution of national product and labor force. *Econ. Develpm. cult. Change.* 1957, Suppl. to 5 (4).

Kuznets, S. Quantitative aspects of the economic growth of nations. III. Industrial distribution of income and labor force by states, United States, 1919-1921 to 1955. *Econ. Develpm. cult. Change,* 1958, Suppl. to 6 (4).

Kuznets, S. Population change and aggregate output. In National Bureau of Economic Research, *Demographic and economic change in developed countries*. Princeton, N.J.: Princeton Univer. Press, 1960. Pp. 324-340.

Kuznets, S. Quantitative aspects of the economic growth of nations. VII. The share and structure of consumption. *Econ. Develpm. cult. Change,* 1962, Suppl. to 10 (2).

Kuznets, S. Consumption, industrialization, and urbanization. In B. F. Hoselitz & W. E. Moore (Eds.), *Industrialization and society*. Paris and The Hague: UNESCO & Mouton, 1963. Pp. 99–114.

Levy, M. J., Jr. *The family revolution in modern China*. Cambridge, Mass.: Harvard Univer. Press, 1949.

Levy, M. J., Jr. *The structure of society*. Princeton, N.J.: Princeton Univer. Press, 1952.

Lockwood, W. W. *The economic development of Japan*. Princeton, N.J.: Princeton Univer. Press, 1954.

Loomis, C. P. *Turrialba: Social systems and the introduction of change*. Glencoe, Ill.: Free Press, 1953.

Lorimer, F. *Culture and human fertility*. Paris: UNESCO, 1954.

McClelland, D. *The achieving society*. Princeton, N. J.: Van Nostrand, 1961.

McClelland, D. The achievement motive in economic growth. In B. F. Hoselitz & W. E. Moore (Eds.), *Industrialization and society*. Paris and The Hague: UNESCO & Mouton, 1963. Pp. 74–95.

McClelland, D., Atkinson, J. W., Clark, R. A., & Lowell, E. W. *The achievement motive*. New York: Appleton-Century-Crofts, Inc., 1953.

MacIver, R. M., & Page, C. H. *Society*. New York: Rinehart, 1949.

Malthus, T. R. *An essay on the principle of population*. (3rd ed.) London: Johnson, 1806.

Marx, K. *A contribution to the critique of political economy*. New York: International Library, 1904.

Meier, G. M., & Baldwin, R. E. *Economic development: Theory, history, policy* New York: Wiley, 1957.

Merton, R. K. *Social theory and social structure*. (rev. ed.) Glencoe, Ill.: Free Press, 1957.

Moore, W. E. *Industrialization and labor*. Ithaca, N.Y.: Cornell Univer. Press, 1951.

Moore, W. E. Problems of timing, balance, and priorities in development measures. *Econ. Develpm. cult. Change*, 1954, **2**, 239–248.

Moore, W. E. Measurement of organizational and institutional implications of changes in productive technology. In International Social Science Council, *Social, economic and technological change*. Paris: International Social Science Council, 1958. Pp. 229–259.

Moore, W. E. Notes for a general theory of labor organization. *Industr. labor Relat. Rev.*, 1960, **13**, 387–397.

Moore, W. E. The social framework of economic development. In R. Braibanti & J. J. Spengler (Eds.), *Tradition, values and socio-economic development*. Durham, N.C.: Duke Univer. Press, 1961. Pp. 57–82.

Moore, W. E. *The conduct of the corporation*. New York: Random House, Inc., 1962.

Moore, W. E. Industrialization and social change. In B. F. Hoselitz & W. E. Moore (Eds.), *Industrialization and society*. Paris and The Hague: UNESCO & Mouton, 1963. Pp. 299–370.(a)

Moore, W. E. *Social change*. Englewood Cliffs, N.J.: Prentice-Hall, Inc., 1963.(b)

Moore, W. E., & Feldman, A. S. Society as a tension-management system. In G. W. Baker & L. S. Cottrell, Jr. (Eds.), *Behavioral science and civil defense*. Washington: National Research Council, Disaster Research Group Study No. 16, 1962. Pp. 93–105.

Murdock, G. P. *Social structure*. New York: Macmillan, 1949.

Nash, M. Kinship and voluntary association. In W. E. Moore & A. S. Feldman (Eds.), *Labor commitment and social change in developing areas*. New York: Social Science Research Council, 1960. Pp. 313–325.

Notestein, F. W. The reduction of human fertility as an aid to programs of economic development in densely settled agrarian regions. In Milbank Memorial Fund, *Modernization programs in relation to human resources and population problems*. New York: Milbank Memorial Fund, 1950. Pp. 89–100.

Ogburn, W. F. *Social change*. New York: Viking, 1936.

Rogoff, Natalie. *Recent trends in occupational mobility*. Glencoe, Ill.: Free Press, 1953.

Schumpeter, J. A. *The theory of economic development*. Cambridge, Mass.: Harvard Univer. Press, 1934.

Shannon, L. W. (Ed.) *Underdeveloped areas*. New York: Harper, 1957.

Smelser, N. J. A comparative view of exchange systems. *Econ. Develpm. cult. Change*, 1959, **7**, 173–182.

Smelser, N. J. Mechanisms of change and adjustment to change. In B. F. Hoselitz & W. E. Moore (Eds.), *Industrialization and society*. Paris and The Hague: UNESCO & Mouton, 1963. Pp. 32–54.

Spengler, J. J. Theory, ideology, non-economic values, and politico-economic development. In R. Braibanti & J. J. Spengler (Eds.), *Tradition, values, and socio-economic development*. Durham, N.C.: Duke Univer. Press, 1961. Pp. 30–56.

Taeuber, Irene B. *The population of Japan*. Princeton, N.J.: Princeton Univer. Press, 1958.

Tumin, M. M. Some disfunctions of institutional imbalance. *Behav. Sci.,* 1956, 1, 21–223.

Tumin, M. M. Competing status systems. In W. E. Moore & A. S. Feldman (Eds.), *Labor commitment and social change in developing areas.* New York: Social Science Research Council, 1960. Pp. 277–290.

Tumin, M. M. On inequality. *Amer. sociol. Rev.,* 1963, 28, 19–26.

United Nations, Department of Social Affairs, Population Division. *The determinants and consequences of population trends.* New York: Author, 1953.

Veblen, T. *The vested interests and the state of the industrial arts.* New York: Huebsch, 1919.

Weber, M. *The theory of social and economic organization.* New York: Oxford, 1947.

Weber, M. *The Protestant ethic and the spirit of capitalism.* London: Allen & Unwin, 1948.

Williamson, H. F., & Buttrick, J. A. (Eds.) *Economic development: Principles and patterns.* New York: Prentice-Hall, Inc., 1954.

Young, F. W., & Young, Ruth C. Social integration and change in twenty-four Mexican villages. *Econ. Develpm. cult. Change,* 1960, 8, 366-377.

CHAPTER 24 The Development of Sociological Thought

WILLIAM R. CATTON, JR.

The history of sociological thought includes more cumulative development than is revealed by the manner in which it is usually presented. Either it is presented as a chronological account that avoids generalization, or it is merely biographical, dealing with great sociologists of the past, perhaps classified by nationality but presented in relative isolation from main developmental trends. When such history emphasizes theory, it tends to be overly facile in classifying past sociologists into schools that become reified and regarded as mutually exclusive rather than complementary.

Sociologists inevitably and properly differ in the specific directions of their scholarly and research interests. Some are concerned with demography, others with social psychology, criminology, the family, and other fields. But the differences do not necessarily represent disagreements and need not produce disputes. Content specialties need not be treated as schools of thought.

There are also differences among sociologists in the emphasis given to various concepts and methods apart from their content specialties. These differences seem to have been greater in the past than now. It is doubtful that Znaniecki was justified in declaring as recently as 1945 that the original idea of a unified science of sociology had lost influence and that "sociology seems to be disintegrating into a number of separate disciplines with little, if any, logical connection among them" (Znaniecki, 1945, p. 514). Znaniecki felt that this was happening partly as a result of conflicts between various schools of sociological thought.

As a scientist, the sociologist finds it necessary to devise classification schemes for establishing order in his data. If the behavior he studies happens to consist of the theoretical writing of colleagues and predecessors, the need to classify and abstract is as strong as in the case of any other human behavior that interests him. In studying behavior other than the writing activities of sociologists, sociologists have learned not to take persons as their only units. The act may also be taken as the unit. One may study the act in terms of a context of social structure exhibiting continuity and change and of culture, as well as in terms of personalities. When attention does focus on personality, it is seen as a moving structure of smaller, interrelated components.

TABLE 1

COMPARISON OF LISTS OF "SCHOOLS OF SOCIOLOGICAL THOUGHT"

Hankins, 1925	Sorokin, 1928	Timasheff, 1955	Martindale, 1960
1. Geographical determinists	1. Mechanistic school	1. Sociological pioneers	1. Positivistic organicism
2. Biological determinists	2. Frederic Le Play's school	2. Social Darwinism	(a) Classical (b) Bio-organismic (c) Voluntaristic
3. Psychological determinists	3. Geographical school	3. Evolutionism (a) Psychological (b) Economic (c) Technological (d) Demographic (e) Religious	(c) Voluntaristic
4. Cultural determinists	4. Bio-organismic school		2. Conflict theory (a) Conflict ideologies (Marxism, Social Dar-
5. Social philosophers, idealists and reformers	5. Anthropo-racial, selectionist, and hereditarist school	4. Organicism (non-evolutionary) 5. Analytical sociology	winism) (b) Sociological conflict theories
	6. Sociological interpretation of the "struggle for existence" and the sociology of war	6. Sociological real-ism (Durkheim) 7. Russian subjecti-vism 8. Neo-positivism	3. Sociological formalism (a) Neo-Kantian branch (b) Phenomeno-logical branch
	7. Demographic school	9. Psychological sociology	4. Social behaviorism (a) Pluralistic behaviorism
	8. Sociologistic school (a) Formal branch (b) Economic branch	10. Functional soci-ology 11. Institutional sociology 12. Phenomenological sociology	(b) Symbolic interaction-ism (c) Social action theory
	9. Psychological school	13. Historical sociology	5. Sociological functionalism (a) Macro-functionalism
	10. Psycho-sociologistic theories	14. Neo-evolutionism 15. Formal sociology	(b) Micro-functionalism

The act is taken as a developing process, rather than a discrete event (Miyamoto, 1959).

When one chooses to write about the intellectual activities of sociologists, however, for some reason he tends to abandon his sociological thoughtways and revert to the practice of considering each person a nearly indivisible unit. Instead of classifying a person's acts, and looking for sequences, he classifies *men* in a search for schools of thought. When this leaves the appetite for knowledge of how sociology came to be what it is unappeased, one some-

times crudely approximates the study of sequences by framing hypotheses of an order of succession among the alleged schools. The image thus created is one of scholastic discontinuity—of a perpetual theoretical cold war. To say that this image is inaccurate and misleading is not to assert that there have been no cases of interpersonal rivalry or outspoken theoretical debate among sociologists. But it is incorrect to characterize the history of sociological thought, even inadvertently, as primarily a tooth-and-claw struggle for existence among antagonists, or to imply that today's sociologists must ult:

mately "choose sides" for a theoretical play-off between irreconcilably different schools.

Various attempts have been made to compile lists of schools of sociological thought. A comparison of four such lists is shown in Table 1. It is apparent that the four classification schemes do not sort out sociological theories in the same way. Nor is there enough closer agreement within the later decade than within the earlier decade to permit any hopeful inference that a reliable taxonomy of sociological theories or theorists is emerging. Neither the number of pigeon-holes, their arrangement, nor the labels applied to them show any appreciable stability. A detailed inspection of the contents of the categories would bring one no closer to consistency. Even a single taxonomist often has to assign the same theorist to more than one school, thus failing to make the categories mutually exclusive.

In view of the unreliability so readily apparent from the above comparison, there is little justification for the author of the fourth of these lists, having cited two of the three earlier works in his own book, to reify his own categories so fully as to conclude, "After all, there are five major schools of sociological theory. None of them has less than two branches" (Martindale, 1960, p. 538). It is even more astonishing that he could claim to have "established beyond any doubt" that "the schools are true alternative formations of theory" forming "independent systems of concepts that cannot be arbitrarily intermixed" (Martindale, 1960, p. 538).

Sociology, according to Martindale (1960), has nevertheless established itself as a field of study by investigating problems in an area whose boundaries are more or less agreed upon by all of the schools. It has institutionalized and professionalized itself. It has emancipated itself from its early reliance on second-hand data, now tests its propositions against data of its own, and has come to share a common pool of terms, concepts, and even empirical generalizations, he said. One can agree with Martindale

that these things have been accomplished to a considerable extent. It can be argued, however, that classifying sociological theorists into schools obscures the above trends more than it reveals them.

THE CHANGING GOALS OF SOCIOLOGY

Prescientific Goals

Sociology began as little more than an inspiration. In retrospect it seems pretentious of Comte to have labelled his joint essay with Saint-Simon (1822) proclaiming the feasibility and necessity of a science of society the "discovery of 1822." But his appraisal of his inspiration is understandable. To have at last perceived that the very nature of explanation had, in regard to certain nonsocietal phenomena, changed from theological to metaphysical to positive, and to have extrapolated this conception to reach the conclusion that a similar transition in social thought could be the basis for establishment of a stable and felicitous social order must have been, for Comte, truly a "religious experience."

This is not to say that Comte's "discovery" was without precedent, or that it must be attributed to direct revelation. Precedents existed. In the intellectual climate that nurtured him, the doctrine of progress was already well developed. Social contract theory had made familiar the notion that a social order could be deliberately established, and for some scholars this had come to mean that it could be deliberately modified and improved. Utopian visions had claimed the attention of a number of writers ever since Sir Thomas More (1516). And the impressive accomplishments of natural science in liberating itself from religious dogma and reducing the varied phenomena of the universe to a mechanical order were much in the minds of eighteenth- and nineteenth-century intellectuals. These factors, and the focusing effects of the French revolution together with the beginnings of the industrial revolution, made articulation of the "law of three stages" and hierarchical ordering of the sciences probable.

To Comte (1830–1842), man's recent intellectual history seemed to consist of the successive building of one science on top of another—first mathematics as the foundation of all the sciences, then astronomy, then physics, then chemistry, then biology (including psychology). It was apparent to him that one more level must yet be added to this edifice—the scientific study of social statics and social dynamics, or sociology. Each of the domains represented in the other sciences, before they came to be studied scientifically, had been subjected first to theological and then to metaphysical explanations. Social phenomena still tended to be explained in these outmoded ways, Comte recognized. He contended this was the heart of the problem facing mankind. The social disorder he saw all around him was "abundantly accounted for by the existence, all at once, of three incompatible philosophies—the theological, the metaphysical, and the positive" (Comte, 1830–1842, p. 36). The only cure for such disorder was to achieve a unified, and preferably positive, philosophy. This was why sociology had to be established.

Once created, however, sociology would actually assist the other sciences, according to Comte. Since scientific discovery is a social phenomenon, if the laws of social development can be discovered, one can thereby predict future scientific discoveries (Comte, 1830–1842, pp. 495–496). It was in this sense that sociology could be called "queen of the sciences." This was but a gratifying by-product, however. Sociology's principal purpose, for Comte, was the reorganization of society (Timasheff, 1955, p. 16). The positive philosophy would provide an anchor for men adrift in a transitional society without consistent convictions. It would prevent the unsound speculations and dangerous actions to which moral uncertainty could lead (Martineau, 1856, p. 5).

The makers of policy in the Positivist society, as envisioned by Comte, were to be a sociological priesthood—those having closest acquaintance with the principles of sociology on which enlightened social policy must be based (Barnes, 1948, p. 100).

These aspects of Comte's (1822) dream have become largely obsolete. Sociologists today do not generally embrace the priesthood concept. Even the most dedicated sociologists would put quotes around the "queen of the sciences" phrase, and it is doubtful that Comte's Positive Philosophy has high priority on the reading list of most graduate students. When one does get around to it, however, it is still a rewarding book to read; Comte's encyclopedic interests are stimulating, and some of his statements blocking out the research tasks and suggesting aspects of sociological method show considerable foresight and make reasonably good metasociological sense even today. At the least, Comte's coinage of the word sociology was a contribution. By giving the discipline an identity, it gave initial impetus and helped sustain the young science in the face of early intellectual opposition and competition.

Comte was by no means alone among early sociologists in assigning to the discipline the function of recreating society. The other pioneers of sociology—Spencer, Ward, Morgan, Sumner, and even the gloomy conflict-theorist, Gumplowicz—were all motivated by a combination of the ameliorative motive and interest in social evolution. Ward, and to some extent Morgan, like Comte, regarded the main lesson of sociology to be the feasibility of wisely guided social change. Spencer, Sumner, and Gumplowicz took the opposite position— that the lesson of sociology was the necessity for noninterference with spontaneous processes of social evolution. Sociology was to facilitate social evolution by teaching men to let it happen without their meddling. But all six of these pioneers were in agreement that "the main justification of sociology is to be found in the generalizations that it can offer with respect to social change and social reform" (Barnes, 1948, p. 81).

Spencer is regarded as almost a co-founder of sociology, with Comte, despite the fact that they never collaborated. Without the attention called to sociology by Spencer's writing, the works of Comte might have been to no avail. At a time when evolutionary doctrine was spreading for a variety of reasons, Spencer integrated it into sociology and thus attracted a following for sociology, particularly among those who saw in the principles of evolution, as he did, complete scientific justification for political laissez faire.

Spencer's famous statement of the general evolutionary principle emphasized: "Evolution is an integration of matter and a concomitant dissipation of motion during which the matter passes from a relatively indefinite, incoherent homogeneity to a relatively coherent heterogeneity and during which the retained motion undergoes a parallel transformation (Spencer, 1862, p. 396). One might translate this to read: The structural complexity of things tends to increase and the behavior of their parts becomes more specialized, but also more coordinated. While sociologists today seldom concern themselves with such highly general statements, some of the corollaries stated by Spencer have manifested themselves in later sociological work. His conclusion that differentiating factors spread in a geometric ratio is reflected in studies of cultural growth in exponential and even log-log curves (Hart, 1959, pp. 196–238), and in studies of technological growth (Allen, Hart, Miller, Ogburn & Nimkoff, 1957; Ogburn, 1946) and of invention (Gilfillan, 1935). Spencer's expectation that differentiated parts of a social organism will become segregated, through a clustering of similar units, is reflected in the principles of human ecology, a flourishing branch of modern sociology. His statement that evolutionary changes culminate in a state of equilibrium has its modern counterpart in applications of the (asymptotic) logistic growth curve to social change data.

Spencer's organic analogy was used as a powerful conceptual argument for laissez faire, and it is difficult to avoid inferring that this use was a major motivation of Spencer's interest in sociology and was responsible for the interest of many of his readers. Certainly Spencer's sociological writing had ideological overtones and served an ideological function. Under the misleading label of "Social Darwinism" the evolutionary ideas of Spencer came to be embraced by some political and economic leaders of the late nineteenth century whose interests were given the appearance of scientific legitimation thereby. Social dislocations of the time could be written off as simply the inevitable price of progress. What *is* became defended as that which has survived and therefore is *fittest*. Dominant persons, groups, or nations could assert that their dominance was justified; they had simply come out the strongest in the universal struggle for existence. Evolution was a cosmic process, not to be resisted or even redirected by little men. It was to be the function of sociology to demonstrate the folly of any such defiance.

Sumner, though not really a "disciple" of Spencer, admired him for demonstrating the possibility of social *science* and approved his method. He disagreed with Spencer theologically, but was able to separate theological and sociological considerations. Like Spencer, Sumner ardently adhered to a laissez faire position. Much of his sociological writing seems to have revolved around a desire to show that human attempts to make the world over are absurd (Sumner, 1934). Even his theory that folkways evolve by trial and error out of interaction between hedonistic human beings and surrounding environmental conditions (Sumner, 1906) seems partly to have been a rejoinder to those about him who believed in social telesis. By lavishly documenting the proposition that "the mores can make anything right," Sumner was, in effect, depriving his political opponents' values of any element of finality or absolute validity. Sumner was not opposed to social progress, but he was opposed to what he regarded as naive efforts to decree progress by legislative fiat—efforts which he felt, in agreement with Spencer, could only delay true progress or aggravate its painful side-effects.

If a substantial part of the early impetus of sociology arose from the desire for scientific legitimation of the doctrine of laissez faire, another substantial part stemmed from its opposite, the desire for scientific knowledge to be used in social engineering. Ward, who gave scholars the phrase "social telesis," now seldom used, regarded sociology as essentially the study of the methods of "collective conation." Its aim was to improve collective effectiveness in the pursuit of happiness by giving one the knowledge with which to control "social forces" as he controls other forces of nature. "Conation" was derived from Latin *conatio,* an endeavoring. For Ward, the lesson of sociology was clearly *not* that individuals must keep hands off the evolutionary process, but rather that they must discover and universally disseminate all possible knowledge.

For Ward (1883; 1897), there were "social forces" that were included within the general category of "forces of nature." In principle, then, if man can learn to manipulate to his advantage the nonsocietal forces of nature, he should be able to do so with forces of society as well. The failure of well-meant attempts in the past, Ward felt, resulted from the willingness of men who would readily confess their ignorance of physical principles to presume more knowledge than they actually had of sociological principles. Admitting incompetence to devise physical inventions, they nevertheless made bold to create social (i.e., legislative) inventions that were ill-conceived. In response to Spencer's (1862) arguments for laissez faire, Ward admitted that legislative efforts for progress had often turned out badly, proving, however, that man's endeavors do have effects. If man's endeavors

were more knowledgeable, the effects would be more desirable.

Like Comte (1830–1842), Ward (1897) saw the sociological fraternity as something of a new elite. Unlike Comte, he did not conceive it as a priesthood. It was to be more of an academy of scientists available for consultation on social problems and social policies.

Scientific Knowledge as the Goal

Durkheim was not the first to urge that sociology must study its subject-matter scientifically, but his own participation in the growth of sociology represents a turning point of considerable importance. Bringing to sociology his family's heritage of rabbinical scholarship and his own acquired distaste for dilettantism, he entered the sociological scene during the early years of the Third Republic in France. The ideals of liberty and progress which had motivated two previous French Republics were still in men's minds, but their realization had been repeatedly postponed by Napoleon, Louis XVIII, Charles X, Louis Philippe, a second revolution, Napoleon III, and the Franco-Prussian War. Comte's dream of a humane and stable society founded on positivism had not materialized. Durkheim was attracted by that dream and believed sociological knowledge could be socially useful. But he realized, better than Comte had, that a great deal of careful empirical research would be required if a body of positive sociological knowledge were to be built up.

Early in his academic career, Durkheim surveyed the German university world and met Wilhelm Wundt in Leipzig. Durkheim strove to infuse into sociology some of the specificity and concreteness exemplified by the work of Wundt's psychophysical laboratory. Durkheim's own researches had a common theme. Taken together, his major works can all be said to constitute a thorough study of the nature of the social bond. In *The Division of Labor in Society* (1893) he described the transition from mechanical to organic solidarity. Mechanical solidarity is based on similarity among a society's members, while organic solidarity is based on their functional dissimilarity. There is a resemblance to Spencer's (1862) notion of evolution from homogeneity to heterogeneity, but for Durkheim the focus is not on evolution but on the fact of cohesion. In *Suicide* (1897) he showed how the individual is sustained as well as constrained by social cohesion. Apart from "altruistic" suicide which is induced by social solidarity, suicide rates tend to vary inversely with the strength of the social bond, because "egoistic" suicide results when a society is not strongly integrated and "anomic" suicide results from gaps in the normative system. In *The Elementary Forms of Religious Life* (1912) he examined totemism and found that religious symbols are representations of the group itself. Sacred objects personify society. It is a function of religion to establish and maintain solidarity.

These researches were important for sociology in two ways. First, they were carefully reasoned analyses of empirical evidence pertaining to a specific sociological problem. Durkheim was not attempting to formulate a comprehensive sociological "system" as had been the fashion of the earliest sociologists; he was building substantive sociological knowledge, piece by piece. Second, Durkheim practiced what he preached about sociology being an "independent" science of social facts. He did not find it necessary, as had Comte (1830–1842), to survey the whole domain of positive knowledge, including mathematics, astronomy, physics, chemistry, and biology, in order to draw sociological conclusions. Comte had even said that sociology would be in some respects subordinate to such disciplines as, for example, chemistry, because of its "immediate and manifest connection with physiology" and because, social phenomena being the most complex and particular of all, "their laws must be subject to those of all the preceding orders, each of which mani-

fests, in social science, its own peculiar influence" (Comte, 1830–1842, p. 258). It seems audacious for Durkheim to have commenced his sociological studies on such a fundamental topic, when sociology was yet so far from scientific maturity. The nature and conditions of chemical union could only begin to be understood after knowledge of chemistry was detailed, comprehensive, and advanced; Linus Pauling's *The Nature of the Chemical Bond* was published as recently as 1939, and it was nearly half a century prior to that that Durkheim had begun to try to determine the nature of social bonds. Though his conclusions may have been considerably less definitive for sociology than Pauling's were for chemistry, it is nevertheless clear that Durkheim's audacity was justified by his achievements.

Had he lived in a more stable society, Durkheim might not have chosen to study so fundamental a topic so soon. His work thus shows something of the same faith that had motivated his sociological predecessors —the belief that sociological knowledge would be socially useful. The difference was that Durkheim more clearly perceived science as a collective and crescive enterprise. By choosing not to try single-handedly to write a complete *Principia Sociologica,* undertaking instead to concentrate on a few specific research topics related to one fundamental aspect of sociology, Durkheim helped to change the nature of sociological thought. Sociological knowledge came to be viewed as having ultimate rather than immediate policy implications and was pursued increasingly for scientific rather than ideological or ameliorative reasons.

Several major lines of sociological thought since Durkheim have continued to augment the knowledge of the nature of social bonds. Functional analysis is one, human ecology is another. Functional analysis is based on the pioneering contributions of Durkheim, and many studies of human ecology have shown at least a methodological resemblance to Durkheim's (1897) study of varying suicide rates.

To Durkheim (1895), sociology was a natural science, and this implied the applicability of causal analysis to social phenomena. But in addition to adducing causes (i.e., antecedent conditions) the full explanation of social phenomena required analysis of functions as well, according to Durkheim. Division of labor was explained partly by antecedent conditions such as the growing complexity of technology and by increasing population and increasing "moral density," but it was not fully explained apart from its function, the reduction of competition. Durkheim insisted that neither causes nor functions could be reduced to individual volitions.

Though it also draws upon developments in cultural anthropology, functional analysis in sociology may be considered an elaboration of Durkheim's (1893) conception of organic solidarity. The parts of a system are held together by their interdependence rather than by their similarity through what Giddings (1896) called "consciousness of kind." The participants in a society and a culture do not always recognize the ways in which their lives and the continuity of their activities depend on various institutional features; hence the concept of "latent functions," suggested by Merton (Merton, 1957, pp. 19–84). The distinction between manifest and latent functions is, in part, an extension of Durkheim's recognition that the functions of a social practice could be distinguished from the individual volitions that men felt in engaging in the practice. But if the basic premise of functional analysis is to be sustained—that the functions of an institution explain its persistence—functional theory must show how men can be bound to a practice by its *latent* functions (of which, by definition, they are not aware). Otherwise, if all functions that actually tend to maintain the system are manifest functions (i.e., recognized by the participants) there ceases to be any real difference between functional analysis and causal analysis.

It has sometimes been asserted that func-

tional analysis leads to a static view of society and culture and tends to become a conservative ideology (Moore, 1963). Its advocates have denied this (Davis, 1959; Merton, 1957). It may be that persons with conservative leanings tend to be receptive to functional analysis, just as people of an earlier time were receptive for ideological reasons to Darwin's (1859) scientific and not intentionally ideological theory of natural selection. But sociological studies that can be classified as functional analyses seem clearly to be attempts to add to objective knowledge rather than attempts directly to influence social policy.

The same can be said for research in human ecology. Though ecological studies obviously can have significance for community planning and other policy matters, studies of processes of centralization, segregation, invasion and succession have added to objective knowledge. Observations of symbiotic relationships between functionally differentiated components of human communities have added another dimension to the knowledge of social cohesion. The growth of literature on human ecology abundantly manifests the change in sociology's goals from society-building or progress-promoting to the development of objective, scientific description of social structure and social processes. Human ecology was brought into being by Park, for whom the purpose of sociology was to seek "natural laws and generalizations in regard to human nature and society" (Park & Burgess, 1924, p. 11). These ought ultimately to be useful, but their application, Park felt, should be left to nonsociologists.

This change in the goals of sociological thought was also evident in the changing content of scholarly publication in the first 50 volumes of the *American Journal of Sociology*. From 1895 to 1945, 2,373 articles were published. Ethel Shanas (1945) classified these into 16 categories. The relative frequency of articles in the categories fluctuated through time, with only two of the categories showing nearly linear trends.

There was a decline in articles about social reform and a not quite so steady increase in the proportion of articles on research methods (Shanas, 1945). These two trends together indicate a shift from humanitarian to scientific concerns among sociologists.

THE CHANGING STRATEGY OF SOCIOLOGY

From the Cosmic to the Specific

In the first generation, sociology was the product of encyclopedic minds. Comte's lectures resulted in a multivolume system of positive philosophy, containing a comprehensive survey of not only sociology but the sciences preceding it. It was all meant to hang together systematically in a hierarchy of sciences. The detailed prescriptions for the reorganization of society and the creation of the religion of humanity which Comte subsequently set forth in his *Positive Polity* (1851–1854) imply that in his own view he had not merely laid the epistemological foundations for a new science, but rather that he had brought forth a mature and virtually complete sociological system. Spencer, too, incorporated his sociology into an ambitious, multivolume system of "synthetic philosophy." His *Principles of Sociology* (1876–1896), taken together with volumes on biological, psychological, and ethical principles and on the philosophical foundations of it all, gave the impression of a finished theory of the world in its human aspects, exhaustive in scope and synthetic in character. A number of others wrote in a similar vein.

This has clearly ceased to be the strategy of sociological investigation or theorizing in the present time except in the work of an occasional individual like Sorokin (1937). The change can be attributed to a number of factors. Some are indigenous to sociological thought; others follow from historical circumstances.

A major departure from the cosmological style of thought in sociology occurred in the work of Georg Simmel. As a founder of "formal" sociology, he advocated sociological thought that was, in effect, more nearly analogous to geometry than to cosmology. His approach has often been characterized as study of the forms of sociation irrespective of content. Taken literally, this would only mean that he wanted to work on a higher level of abstraction than the historian. This was the case, and part of his concern was to establish a distinction between history and sociology, as well as between sociology and other cognate disciplines. But this misses part of the point. Simmel's study of forms influenced the subsequent character of sociological thought precisely because the particular forms he studied were rather specific in scope. (Spencer's abstract statement of the principle of evolution could also be regarded as a proposition about "forms" irrespective of content, but this resemblance to Simmel was less important for the growth of sociological thought than were their differences.) In a series of essays translated into English by Small and published in the early issues of the *American Journal of Sociology* (1896; 1898; 1902; 1904; 1906), Simmel analyzed such phenomena as superordination-subordination, secrecy and secret societies, conflict, group persistence, and effects of group size on group structure. Unlike the earlier sociologists who had tried to formulate complete and exhaustive theories of social evolution, Simmel concerned himself with such very general but compact problems as the character and conditions of sociability (Simmel, 1950, pp. 40ff.). He anticipated the researches of a number of American sociologists when he analyzed the negative character of collective behavior, the role of the stranger, and the psychological impact of life in a metropolis (Simmel, 1950, pp. 396ff.).

Like Durkheim, Simmel was interested in the nature of the social bond. In Kantian (1893) fashion, he addressed himself to the question "what makes society possible." It was in order to answer this question that he stressed the study of forms of sociation. If sociological thought today is disinclined to limit itself to a priori concepts, the kinds of problems with which it deals both theoretically and empirically are nevertheless closer to those outlined by Simmel than to those with which his predecessors were preoccupied.

The reader has seen how Durkheim, in order to investigate the nature of social bonds, defined several specific research problems for himself. Instead of writing volumes of sweeping generalizations about social progress, he concerned himself with the specifics of sociological research methods, with empirical studies of the growth in division of labor and concomitant changes in legal rules, with variations in suicide rates and their implications, and with the social functioning of religious symbolism. This, too, was sociology of the type that has become conventional today. It was not conventional in Durkheim's day. It had to be pioneered.

Even the study of societal evolution underwent transformation. Publication of Ogburn's (1922) book on *Social Change* was another contribution to making sociological thought concrete. It was part of Ogburn's purpose to show that a social order and a way of life could change greatly without presupposing any biological modification of the human species, and this was a necessary challenge to the assumptions of the Social Darwinists. But two other aspects of Ogburn's book were crucial. It substituted the concept of "change" for the earlier, often value-loaded, concept of "evolution," and it employed quantitative, tabular data to clarify and support one of its key notions, "cultural lag."

The shift from "evolution" to mere "change" may have been partly a result of the disillusionment following World War I. It was no longer so easy to assume that progress was inevitable and natural. While Ogburn (1922) did talk about the growth of material culture from paleolithic times to the present (partly in connection with re-

jection of biological determinism and partly to show that cultural growth can be cumulative), his book was otherwise unlike the works of Comte (1830–1842), or Spencer (1862). Cultural lag was found in such concrete quantitative data on contemporary affairs as the higher ratio of policemen to population in declining cities compared with growing cities, or the time interval between growing industrial accident rates and workmen's compensation laws. The cultural lag hypothesis has been strongly debated in the four decades since, but the practice of arguing either for or against a sociological hypothesis in terms of specific quantitative data has been firmly established. Most sociologists since Ogburn have more or less specialized, as he did, in a particular kind of sociological problem.

Specialization by sociologists, and research focused on compact problems, was doubtless facilitated (and thus fostered) by establishment of sociological journals. Specialization has become increasingly apparent ever since the American Sociological Society departed, in 1921, from its previous custom of organizing the annual program around a single topic to be dealt with in a series of solicited papers. Since that time, various sessions at each annual meeting have been organized by committees concerned with an assortment of specialized subject-matter areas. This pattern had become so strongly institutionalized that some resistance was encountered in 1962 when "The Uses of Sociology" was proclaimed by President Paul Lazarsfeld of the renamed American Sociological Association as the program theme for the fifty-seventh annual meeting. While more than half of the sessions were devoted to various aspects of the uses and potential uses of sociology and a joint session with the International Sociological Association (opening its Fifth World Congress of Sociology) was devoted to "The Sociologists, the Policy-Makers, and the Public," there were 20 "traditional" sessions scheduled for presentation of the usual research papers on methodology, family, criminology, social organization, human ecology, social psychology, stratification, social change, etc.

In addition to the fragmentation of sociological thought into an assortment of specialties, the quest common to all of these specialties changed in the twentieth century from an attempt to discover "natural laws" to something more like attempts to invent concepts and formulas that would serve as *ad hoc* descriptions of more or less recurrent aspects of interhuman behavior. When it is said that sociology reduced emphasis on theory in the interval between the two world wars, this is what is meant: Numerous generalizations about data were made, but less attention was given to deriving one generalization from others. There continued to be effort to show that sociological generalizations could not be derived from (or reduced to) generalizations of other disciplines like psychology or economics, and the antireductionist premise came to be generally taken for granted. A heightened scientific modesty came to prevail, for a time, and few sociological writers cared to refer to their generalizations as "laws." The term theory was still permissible, but it was apparently widely assumed that the theories of nineteenth-century sociologists were either incorrect or obsolete, and a considerable backlog of factual knowledge would have to be accumulated before much in the way of new and better theories could be expected.

Since World War II, however, a renewed interest has developed in nomothetic explanation, derivation of theorems from axioms, and particularly in examining "isomorphism" or structural similarity between theories. While no stigma has been attached to "theory," another word has come into abundant use—"model," with or without the modifier, "mathematical." This word is used, unfortunately, with considerable ambiguity. It is sometimes nothing more than a synonym or substitute for "theory." Sometimes it refers to a certain kind of theory, especially one that is untested, or one that involves some obvious fictions

(e.g., ideal types, or other abstractions without empirical referents). Sometimes it has a slightly more specific meaning, implying a quantified theory. In none of these usages is a new term really necessary: "Theory" would suffice.

Brodbeck (1959) suggested that an appropriately limited meaning of "model" would be the case in which one theory has different empirical concepts but the same structure as another and can thus be said to serve as a model of the other (Brodbeck, 1959). An example would be the use of a theory of epidemiology as a model for a theory of cultural diffusion. Taking one theory as a model for another is useful only insofar as confirmed generalizations about one area may suggest hypotheses about another area—to be tested, of course, by data obtained from that second area. There has clearly been a trend toward consciously employing this technique in sociological thought. Equally important, it is now almost fully recognized, as it was not in the nineteenth century, that sociological laws must be accepted or rejected on the basis of their degree of congruence with sociological data. Models may only be used to suggest such laws and not to establish their truth. Their truth is not confirmed by the mere fact that they are isomorphic with laws of another science. That this is now so well appreciated as to make the arguments of certain nineteenth-century writers appear painfully naive is a token of the growing scientific maturity of sociological thought.

The Natural Science Trend

The scientific maturation of sociology is revealed also by the abandonment of a so-called comparative method, that in practice was employed to support doctrine, and could more appropriately be labeled illustrative. Comte (1830–1842) imagined that he had arrived at his law of three stages and his hierarchy of the sciences by inductive examination of historical data on the growth of the several sciences. The so-called law of three stages purported to be a generalization based on comparative study—i.e., comparison of the histories of the various sciences arranged in a chronological and logical order. His division of sociology into the twin fields of statics and dynamics was a "deduction" from the supposedly induced generalization that all positive sciences are so divided. Thus Comte used an allegedly comparative method to arrive at a body of metasociological propositions.

Spencer (1862) stated a universal law of evolution from incoherent homogeneity to coherent heterogeneity on the basis partly of deduction from some postulates borrowed from physical mechanics and partly from a supposedly comparative study of the several sciences describing the inorganic, organic, and superorganic realms, respectively. His sociological laws, in turn, were in part derivations from the universal evolutionary principle and its corollaries and in part conclusions drawn from comparative study of ethnographic materials. In his comparative studies, however, Spencer cavalierly ignored chronological sequence and cultural context when so doing suited his preconceptions about the order of evolutionary stages. Both Comte and Spencer specifically mentioned "comparison" as a desirable method for sociologists. Both cautioned against the biased perceptions and inductions of others, but both seemed largely oblivious of the selectivity of their own perceptions and inductions.

Ward (1883), too, confused patchwork with comparison, and confounded this with a borrowing of concepts and hypotheses from presociological sciences that was hardly systematic enough to merit the label "model." The borrowings from biological and other sciences will be considered further in another context.

In *Folkways,* Sumner (1906) employed a comparative method that at times tended toward the merely illustrative. He had given Spencer credit for a genuinely scientific method both in the search for basic philosophical principles among the various sciences and in the use of ethnographic data. In his own use of ethnographic literature, however, Sumner differed from Spencer in one important respect. He was less concerned with showing the evolution of mores from most primitive to most advanced (i.e., most like those of Spencer's Britain) than he was in showing that "the mores can make anything right." The fact of great cultural variability can be satisfactorily demonstrated with less rigorous use of a genuinely comparative method than would be required to demonstrate a unilinear evolution of culture. The prevalence of ethnocentrism might not be too greatly exaggerated by reliance on an illustrative method that would hardly suffice to demonstrate a long-range trend toward its increase or its decrease. The hypothesis that there is a "strain toward consistency" in culture does involve time and may therefore have been given exaggerated support by the illustrative method.

When Thomas and Znaniecki (1918–1920) made their study of the impact of cultural relocation on Polish peasants transplanted to America, the comparative method was applied to a more narrowly circumscribed class of phenomena—the experience of individuals as represented by "human documents," rather than the practices of societies as described in ethnographic literature. Though unrigorous in many ways in analyzing their documentary data, and certainly nonquantitative, Thomas and Znaniecki made a genuine attempt to be inductive. Twenty years after publication, a critique by Blumer (1939) contended that their theoretical conclusions were not adequately tested by their data and that such documentary data were probably less than adequate for validation of theories of any kind. Blumer nevertheless concluded that such documents could serve as invaluable sources of hunches and hypotheses, perspectives and insights. Thomas and Znaniecki were transitional, then, between the early speculative and philosophical kind of sociological thought that was too self-assured, and the now standard practice of trying to distill generalizations from rigorously sampled and systematically observed data.

The study of the Polish Peasant was followed by a long series of other investigations by Chicago sociologists. Many of these continued to be exploratory and not methodologically rigorous, but they all manifested the concern for keeping close to concrete data and studying in depth a problem of limited scope.

Ogburn went to the University of Chicago in 1927 and carried on a series of studies of social change, technology, and cultural lag. Increasingly these studies made use of quantitative data and statistical techniques. In spirit, they fitted in with two other lines of thought and research for which the Chicago department became noted: social psychology, and social structure and community organization.

It was at Chicago that sociology most clearly became concerned with the study of interhuman behavior (rather than with the study of society as an evolving entity). Social psychology, as a specialized division of sociology, developed out of some of the work of Thomas and Znaniecki (1918–1920), together with the ideas about symbolic interaction developed by John Dewey (1930) and George Herbert Mead (1934), both Chicago men, and the concepts of primary group and the looking-glass self devised by Cooley (1902) (of Michigan). These have become such standard parts of the sociological perspective that it is misleading to speak of symbolic interaction*ism,* as if one still had to choose whether to go along with this "school" or to align oneself with some other.

The turning point in the development of social psychology came with the devastation of the once popular instinct theories. The effective case against the instinct concept was stated by Ellsworth Faris (E. Faris, 1921), in a paper entitled, "Are Instincts Data or Hypotheses?" He argued from ethnological data that behavior patterns have no constant relationship to alleged instincts and concluded that so-called instincts in humans were mere hypothetical constructs, too often reified by users of the concept. Social scientists should abandon the concept and instead study the socialization process, he concluded. Definitive destructive criticism of the instinct theories came three years later in a book by L. L. Bernard (1924) (a Chicago Ph.D.). Bernard examined some 2,000 books in biology, neurology, psychology, education, sociology, and other disciplines and found over 15,000 separate instincts listed. These were classified into some 6,000 types. The instinct concept was thus shown to be far too cumbersome and inconsistent to serve as a scientific tool for explaining or predicting human behavior. Many so-called instincts clearly were actions learned in the process of socialization, and it was made apparent that a theory of personality development need not include the instinct concept at all (Bernard, 1924).

Sociology became committed to the study of community organization and social structure under the influence of another Chicagoan, Robert E. Park, an ex-newspaperman whose main sociological explorations were in three fields: human ecology, collective behavior, and race relations. Park took up some of the concepts of formal sociology—the so-called social processes—and combined them with the biological model of the "web of life" to formulate a theory of human ecology. Land-use patterns emerge, he noted, apart from deliberate planning, through processes of competition, concentration, segregation, invasion, and succession, and these processes produce "natural areas" within a human community. Park sent his students out to study these natural areas, one by one, and in relation to each other. The impact of ecological structure on suicide rates, divorce rates, and juvenile delinquency rates was studied. Special studies of hotel life, the life of the hobo, the Ghetto, the gang, the Gold Coast and the slum, and social distance and the marginal man were undertaken. In collaboration with Burgess, Park (1924) assembled an introductory textbook that was immediately and widely influential. It helped spread and establish the new approach to sociology as close-up empirical investigation and conceptual analysis of all phases of interhuman behavior.

The Chicago department was also influential, of course, because under Small's leadership it had started to publish the *American Journal of Sociology*. Despite the aversion of sociologists to any sort of great man theory of history, it is difficult to avoid the conviction that sociological thought today would be appreciably different had events in the lives of a few key individuals been slightly altered. Had Small heeded the counsel of certain academic friends and remained president of Colby College rather than responding to the challenge of pioneering a new department of sociology in the brand new University of Chicago; or had Ellsworth Faris been able to remain a missionary in Africa, or preferred subsequently to remain Director of the Iowa Child Welfare Research Station, rather than shift from psychology to sociology to become successor to Thomas at Chicago; or had Park remained a journalist or continued as Booker T. Washington's secretary rather than responding to persuasion by Faris to return to Chicago, the transformation of sociology into an empirically oriented science might have occurred much later. What is sociologically instructive about these events, despite their apparent defiance of the sociologist's habitual distaste for great man theories, is that the influence of these individuals depended on an organization and a situation. They shaped sociological thought not just as isolated individual theorists but as members of the first (and for a considerable time, the leading) graduate department of sociology. Their influence might have been much less, or at least quite different, had that department not been located in a rapidly growing city in the American

Midwest in which a heterogeneous population was undergoing conspicuous social change.

While the work of the Chicago sociologists was helping to make sociology concrete, it was also inadvertently providing fuel for a major methodological controversy. Followers of Thomas and Znaniecki (1918–1920), who emulated their use of personal documents to trace out life histories, felt that this was a way that sociologists could objectively get at the inner, mental life of social human beings. They further felt that it was essential to obtain knowledge of these inner phenomena if sociological explanation of social behavior was to be adequate and valid. There was thus a temptation to become doctrinaire about life history studies as *the* method of sociology. Followers of Park, in their studies of natural areas, were virtually creating *collective* case histories as a means of understanding the "metabolism" of the community. But meanwhile, interest in statistical methods was growing. At Chicago, Ogburn, a student of Giddings, and Stouffer, a student of Ogburn, pushed in this direction, and at various places the growth of sociological interest in demographic studies was helping to promote interest in quantitative reasoning. A number of sociologists began to insist in the 1920's that quantification was a prerequisite to the achievement of scientific maturity by sociology. Rather than regarding these different currents of methodological thought as complementary, or even as mere matters of varying personal predilection or specialization, some writers began to treat them as mutually exclusive alternatives.

In 1929, the quantification argument was forcefully and instructively presented in Lundberg's *Social Research* (1929). A decade later, in his *Foundations of Sociology* (1939), he elaborated on the metasociological postulates underlying objective, quantified sociological theory and research and argued for regarding sociology as a natural science of human behavior. He characterized human behavior as fundamentally communicative. Together with a number of journal articles and a published body of professional correspondence, these books established Lundberg as both a leader and a symbol of the movement to make quantification and objective procedures customary among sociologists. Between the appearance of these two books, Znaniecki's volume on *The Method of Sociology* (1934) presented a counter argument. Znaniecki outlined and advocated the method of "analytic induction," adapted to the use of human documents as data. Adequately applied, he argued, it could lead to definitive statements of causal relations and leave no real problem for "enumerative induction" (i.e., statistical methods) to solve. Its merit was supposed to be that it would isolate the "essential" characters which determine the occurrence of the phenomenon being studied.

Znaniecki's (1934) method was a refinement of the procedures he and Thomas (1918–1920) had employed in their Polish Peasant study. It consisted, in a sense, of letting a working hypothesis interact with some documentary data and thereby undergo successive modifications. First, the phenomenon to be explained is roughly defined. A working hypothesis is formulated which tentatively explains this phenomenon. Then a case is examined to see whether the hypothesis fits. If it does, then another case is examined, and so on. Whenever a case does not fit, either the hypothesis is revised to make it applicable to that case and all those previously examined, or the phenomenon is redefined so as to exclude the recalcitrant case. By a series of such revisions and redefinitions, the investigator finally arrives at a hypothesis which perfectly explains all retained cases. It is this perfection which led Znaniecki to believe there would be nothing left for statistical research.

After explicit use by various sociologists in connection with a variety of problems, the method of analytic induction came in for sharp criticism in the 1950's. By this time, statistical methods had become commonplace, and logical weaknesses in the analytic induction method could be readily pointed out from a statistical frame of reference. As a procedure for refining hypotheses prior to subjecting them to statistical test, the method of analytic induction seems quite useful. As *the* method of sociology, it falls short of Znaniecki's aspirations for scientific rigor and finality, because it ordinarily neglects to study an explicit control group. Moreover, so far as this writer knows, no test of the reliability of the method has ever been made, or even suggested. It would be instructive to see whether two different sociologists working with the same set of human documents and starting with the same initial hypothesis would arrive at equivalent final hypotheses. It would also be interesting to discover whether permuting the sequence in which cases were considered would alter the kind of hypothesis finally arrived at.

If the outline of the method of analytic induction is taken not as a prescription for the work of an individual sociologist, but as a description of the collective enterprise of sociology, it is more nearly apt. Whenever an accepted hypothesis in the sociological literature encounters data from a new sample which call it into question, however many previous studies may have supported it, sociologists have two alternatives. They revise the hypothesis to include the new data without impairing its congruence with the old data, if possible, or they redefine certain variables in the hypothesis so as to exclude the new and contradictory data from its range of applicability. The latter alternative does not, as it might seem to, give the sociologist complete license to ignore all negative findings. If he chooses to redefine certain variables so as to exclude disconfirming data, he may discover that he has thereby also excluded some of the previous data that had tended to confirm the hypothesis within previous definitions. It turns out to be possible, then, to regard the analytic induction paradigm as, in a sense, the method of sociology (and perhaps of science in general), but not of the individual sociologist. It is an emergent quality of cumulative scientific work.

Procedures followed in the conduct of individual projects of sociological research have come to resemble closely, by now, the method advocated a generation ago by Lundberg (1929). By 1955, Lundberg felt justified in speaking of a "natural science trend" in sociology. He identified the elements of the natural science orientation as quantitativism, behaviorism, and pragmatism. Quantitativism facilitates corroboration and generalization, and these are essentials of scientific work, he said. He rejected, "in common with all natural scientists," the notion that some phenomena are intrinsically quantitative while others are not and noted that scholars who object to quantification in sociology find it necessary to use terms that imply quantity without precision—like "more" and "less" anomie, or "higher" and "lower" status. The behavioristic sociologist, according to Lundberg, is as interested as any other in making full use of attitudinal or mental data, so long as the implied "subjective" phenomena are reliably represented by objective behavioral indexes. Natural science sociology is pragmatic in its emphasis on the sensory basis of knowledge. Operationism is a means of facilitating the specific and reliably communicative use of sociology's technical concepts (Lundberg, 1955).

Opponents of the "natural science trend" in sociology have argued that some phenomena simply cannot be quantified. Moreover they seem to have misunderstood the advocates of operationism. They have supposed that those who favor defining variables operationally are rejecting from sociological consideration all variables not defined in terms of observational procedures. But as a metasociological norm, operationism can be creative rather than restrictive. If theory says a certain variable is important, it says the steps necessary to make it ob-

servable and measurable (or at least objectively inferrable) are essential steps, worthy of the investment of great intellectual effort. A number of theorists have proclaimed the importance of attitudes in social phenomena. A psychologist, Thurstone, made an operational breakthrough by showing that "Attitudes Can Be Measured" (Thurstone & Chave, 1929). Others, in both psychology and sociology, have gone on to devise a variety of ways of conceiving and measuring attitudes.

The metasociological issues in this controversy have reflected broader issues of epistemology. The institutionalization of a natural science orientation in sociology was given some philosophical aid and comfort by the "unity of science" movement and the doctrines of logical positivism emanating from the Vienna Circle. The trend was indigenous to sociological thought, however, and the logical positivists should be regarded primarily as reinforcing it, rather than initiating it.

Important as such controversies were, they never were really characteristic of American sociological thought, and they are also bound to disappear from sociological thought in Europe and elsewhere as sociology becomes academically established and the growth of professional associations facilitates effective communication among sociologists. The establishment of courses and departments of sociology in colleges and universities in the United States, the growth of sociological associations, and the proliferation of sociological publication were described in considerable detail by Odum (1951). Similar trends seem to be accelerating in other countries, though in most instances they were later in starting. The result of such trends has been in America (and will be elsewhere) the collectivization of sociological thought. That is, as R. E. L. Faris (1946) pointed out, after World War I it was no longer fashionable in the United States for an individual sociologist to try to father a school of thought. The development of sociology was no longer governed by the logic of classification of sciences or by any individual's decision but was established by tentative and exploratory efforts in many directions, some of which were rewarded by success. Schools of thought do not survive well in this stage of development, and such schools as were once characteristic of American sociology have been steadily withering away, or perhaps it would be better to say the differences have been dissolving (R. E. L. Faris, 1946, p. 546).

The growth of valid sociological theory will be expedited neither by sociologists seeking, nor becoming, disciples. It follows that sociology is done a disservice when the history of sociological thought is interpreted in ways that seem to imply the inevitability of discipleship. Due recognition that discipleship has occurred ought to be divorced from any implied suggestion that it is desirable or that theoretical convergence is illusory or impossible.

THE CHANGING CONTENT OF SOCIOLOGY

From Ethnocentrism to Cultural Relativism

Early sociological thought was almost always ethnocentric. Each sociologist had absorbed something of the doctrine of progress that was prevalent in the intellectual climate of the mid-nineteenth century. He tended to see the way of life that existed (or which he thought was about to come into existence) in his own time and place as higher or more advanced than previous or alien ways of life. Whether the mission of sociology was to show how to hasten progress or to show the necessity for allowing progress to happen without bungling interference, it was scarcely doubted that human societies progressed through a series of stages, each of which was morally superior to those which preceded it. If the past was seen as mere prologue, it was easy to see other peoples as mere children who would someday grow up to be like members of one's own civilization. Early theories, then, sought to enumerate the

stages of evolution, the forces that advanced a society from stage to stage, and the historical factors accounting for the differential advancement of different societies.

This is no longer the principal content of sociological theory. Even the recent renewal of interest in formulating theories of social change, evoked by the political concern about "underdeveloped" or "emerging" countries, has not revived the ethnocentrism or the preoccupation with unilinear evolution once so characteristic of sociological thought. Hughes (1961) suggested that there is grave danger of slipping back into an ethnocentrism that would leave much of the world unstudied by either the sociologist or the anthropologist. At the moment it can at least be said that ethnocentrism is a viewpoint which sociologists are expected to avoid.

Cultural relativism has become a basic working conception in sociological thought. It is not that the sociologist as a person has no values; he makes an effort to suspend his values which he knows are absorbed from his own culture and subcultures. He makes this effort because he recognizes that his values, the values of his culture, operate as perceptual filters. If he is to make accurate observations of social and cultural phenomena, he knows he must penetrate these filters. He realizes, of course, that he can never wholly succeed, but his observations can only contribute to a science of sociology if the efforts are at least partially successful and are augmented by the partially and differently successful efforts of his colleagues.

Cultural relativism is not a sudden contribution of a single theorist. It evolved and had presociological antecedents. Montesquieu (1748), for example, often regarded as little more than a geographic (or climatic) determinist, concluded that institutions are relative to the conditions in which a society exists. The institutions most adaptive for one society may not be most suitable for another that is situated in a different environment. He, of course, did not mean that any arbitrarily designated set of institutions is just as suitable as another for a given society, as is sometimes asserted in sophomoric vulgarizations of cultural relativism.

In the *Positive Philosophy,* Comte (1830–1842) wrote that "the relative character of scientific conceptions is inseparable from the true idea of natural laws . . ." (Comte, 1830–1842, p. 453). Spencer (1873), too, expressed a relativist attitude, in spite of the highly ethnocentric implications of his evolutionary theory. He wrote, for example, "Recognizing what truth there is in the great-man theory . . . if limited to early societies . . . its immense error lies in the assumption that what was once true is true for ever . . ." (Spencer, 1873, p. 32).

The idea of cultural relativism is probably most strongly associated with Sumner (1906), however, because he defined and named its opposite, ethnocentrism. He provided abundant instances of ethnocentrism from many cultures, implying that it is a universal human phenomenon, and he suggested its functions for society—its exaggeration of in-group uniqueness so as to promote identification with and control by the in-group. But Sumner came to be interested in the concept apparently for ideological reasons. He was ardently in favor of a thoroughly laissez faire doctrine and supported his political and economic opinions with Social Darwinist principles. Progress, he felt, depended on unrestricted competition, since any restrictions would tend to interfere with natural selections. To the extent that his contemporaries were promoting such restrictions in the name of humanitarianism, democracy, and an American ideal of equality, Sumner was ready and willing to denounce such values. Denunciation could be most effective if it appeared scientific. By arguing that democracy was only possible under certain conditions— when population density is not too high and the struggle for existence is not too severe —Sumner was able, in such essays as "Earth Hunger" (1934), to imply with the apparent authority of science that American customs generally regarded as immutable were mere phases in on-going cultural evolution. The values held by his opponents, then, were not absolute and eternal, but relative and ephemeral.

It is not intended here to accuse Sumner of deliberate deception. He was undoubtedly sincere in his espousal of the theory of natural selection, and he deserves credit for continuing to rethink the theory and thus to move from believing at first in survival of the fittest groups or persons to believing later in survival of the fittest folkways. Many others who were enticed by Social Darwinism made no such advance. What one learns from Sumner's approach to the idea of cultural relativism is that a sound scientific insight may have somewhat unscientific origins. An ideology is potentially a scientific theory as truly as a scientific theory (e.g., natural selection) is a potential ideology. If it was for ideological reasons that Sumner chose to call the customs accepted as right at a given time by a given people "folkways," introduction of this word was nonetheless a valuable scientific contribution. As Hughes has pointed out, "It enabled people to speak with detachment of matters which, in ethics, they would have argued about with heat" (Hughes, 1961, p. 1).

Arriving at the concept of ethnocentrism and finding the reverse orientation—cultural relativism—useful in undermining his adversaries' assumptions, Sumner was then able to make penetrating generalizations about folkways, mores, and institutions. Thus out of an ideological interest, he contributed substantive sociological knowledge. His own laissez faire convictions remained unshaken, even though consistency might have required that they too be regarded as a passing phase in cultural evolution. It is common for sociologists to acquire the capacity to recognize others' ethnocentrism without seeing it in themselves. Both Sumner and Spencer remained largely oblivious of the beam in their own eyes while correctly discerning the vision-impairing motes in nonsociological eyes. At the close of World War II, Znaniecki (1945) expressed the conviction that to be theoretically objective, the sociologist must "investigate all valuations and actions of human agents (by whatever standards and norms they are guided) as facts, refraining from any evaluative and normative judgments of his own" (Znaniecki, 1945, p. 515). But he acknowledged that because students of culture are themselves active participants in a culture this is difficult to do.

Harriet Martineau (1856) had written, half a century before Sumner's *Folkways* (1906), "The theological world cannot but hate a book [like Comte's *Positive Philosophy*] which treats of theological belief as a transient state of the human mind." She had predicted that "preachers and teachers, of all sects and schools . . . contemplating and judging of the universe from the point of view of their own minds, instead of having learned to take their stand out of themselves . . . must necessarily think ill of a work which exposes the futility of their method, and the worthlessness of the results to which it leads" (Martineau, 1856, p. 9). But Sumner seems to have meant what he said when he epitomized cultural relativism with his trenchant observation that "The mores can make anything right," and yet he did not forthwith abandon his theology. He had long since left the Episcopal ministry to assume his professorship at Yale, but it was because he felt his personal qualifications more suited to the latter role. His relativism never led to indifference or to moral nihilism, and his adherence to Christian morality did not preclude his comprehending and accepting cultural relativism as a working scientific orientation.

In the years following World War II, much nonsense was written about the immorality (or the impossibility) of adhering to cultural relativism. Anthropological literature, especially, had previously gone to excess and sometimes construed cultural relativism as implying the equal validity and desirability of all cultures without regard to the circumstances in which they exist. Those who had come to think that cultural relativism meant that "anything goes" would understandably suppose that cultural relativism would require them to approve of Nazism and Hitler's way of solving "the Jewish problem." In their revulsion against genocide, they felt compelled to deny cultural relativism. But even if genocide could properly have been called a part of the German culture, its approval would not have been required by cultural relativism. One does not become a cultural relativist by approving out-group mores but by acknowledging that they exist and regulate behavior. Ethnocentrism makes us see out-group behavior as deviation from in-group mores rather than as adherence to out-group mores. The scientific function of cultural relativism is to enable us to perceive alien customs, not to make us approve them. This is an old idea but we still have to struggle to grasp it. Comte wrote that "all antecedent experience shows that in other departments of natural philosophy, scientific ideas have not become arbitrary by becoming relative, but have, on the contrary, acquired a new consistence and stability by being implicated in a system of relations which is ever extending and strengthening, and more and more restraining all serious aberration. There is therefore no fear of falling into a dangerous skepticism by destroying the absolute spirit, if it is done in the natural course of passing on toward the positive state" (Comte, 1830–1842, p. 454).

In his role as scientist, the sociologist has increasingly found it desirable to take the stance of cultural relativism. He need not take the same attitude in his role as citizen. The force of his socially acquired conscience need no more be destroyed by recognition that what is right in his own culture is wrong in another than the force of gravity is destroyed for him by recognition that the direction called "down" in one place would be "up" to a person at the antipodes.

From Study of Society to Study of Association

The shift from ethnocentric to relativistic sociology was accompanied by a change from being principally concerned with societies as the basic unit of study to being concerned with generalizations about groups of all sizes and types and generalizations about abstract social processes. A number of sociologists around the turn of the century began to make this transition partly on the basis of such influences as Tarde's (1890) formulation of "laws of imitation." Small (1905), whose influence was amplified by his position at Chicago, showed vestiges of the older preoccupations, but in transplanting the sociological conflict theory of Ratzenhofer to the American scene, Small somewhat played down inter-societal conflict, emphasized processes of conflict between interest groups of lesser magnitude, and stressed the tendency of conflict to resolve itself into cooperation. Over all, then, Small offered the study of association rather than the study of society as the subject-matter of sociology. For a whole generation, the work of the department he founded served to implement this reorientation.

Giddings (1896), famous for the term consciousness of kind, implied by it a concept rather similar to the reflective sympathy which Adam Smith had recognized as socially important. Despite Giddings' lingering interest in social evolution, this concept required him to regard the social human being, rather than society, as the basic unit to be studied by sociology. As an evolutionist, he coined odd terms, in a manner reminiscent of Ward's practice, and spoke of evolution through four stages: "zoogenic," "anthropogenic," "ethnogenic," and "demogenic." But he also distinguished between two forms of social organization— social composition and social constitution— which were very much like the *Gemeinschaft* and *Gesellschaft* patterns distinguished by Tönnies (1887). Such concepts represented a phase in the transition from sociology as the study of societies to sociology as the study of social acts. As the transition occurred, the old tendency to inject biological, economic, political, and even cosmological matters into ostensibly sociological writing subsided. Tönnies did a little of this at first, but he has been credited with helping "to establish a purely sociological approach that might be applied to any and all social phenomena" (Boskoff, 1957, pp. 18-19).

Even Gumplowicz (1899), embittered Social Darwinist who believed in the "polygenetic" origin of the various human races as an explanation of their supposedly inevitable hatred for each other, contributed to this transformation of sociology. Because he became interested in processes of internal differentiation of human groups, as well as in conflict processes, Gumplowicz "shifted the study of sociology from society in general to relations between specific societies, and thence in part to the interaction of differentiated groups in politically organized societies" (Boskoff, 1957, p. 13).

Ross, writing on social control, distinguished between "internal" and "external" processes by which personal behavior is controlled by groups and thereby also participated in this transition. He later wrote a pioneering book on social psychology. Without the infusion of social psychological concerns into sociological thought, the transition could hardly have been consummated. The consummation was achieved in the works of Cooley (1902; 1909; 1918), on human nature, social organization, and the social process; in the posthumously published lectures of Mead (1934) on social development of the self through communication; and in the tersely illuminating analyses by Ellsworth Faris (1937) of the nature of human nature. The organismic orientation of the earliest sociologists was not so much abandoned by these developments as it was reconciled with the individualistic and voluntaristic attitudes so deep-seated in American culture. The individual and society were described as "twin-born"—each as real and each as much an abstraction as the other. The reconciliation took time, of course, and a debate over whether groups are real lasted for two or three decades.

Completion of the redefinition of sociology as the science of interhuman behavior rather than only the science of society is perhaps best dated from the time sociological theory began seriously to try to account for deviant behavior in the same terms by which it explained approved behavior. Sutherland's (1940) theory of differential association, by no means either the first or the final word on the subject, brought scholars to the concept of a deviant subculture within which acts would be normal that were regarded in the larger society as deviant. Proliferation of research on deviant subcultures, and further development of theory in this realm, would have been impossible without the achievement of at least some degree of cultural relativism by sociologists.

One peril involved in the shift from the sociology of societies to the sociology of interaction was a temporary tendency to forget or drift away from the originally strong recognition in sociology of the operation of impersonal social forces. Evolutionary theories had, whatever their flaws, this virtue: They saw that social change (and concrete historic events) could happen without awareness and without the intention of the participating persons. This was an incidental but important respect in which society was indeed like an organism, whose parts are all caught up in a process that shapes them at least as much as they shape it. As the content of sociology became redefined, however, it was a great temptation to construct theories that presupposed rational men interacting with full awareness of the conditions of their interaction.

Max Weber is supposed to have intended his "ideal types"—both his "Protestant ethic" and "spirit of capitalism," and his three types of authority—as baselines against which actual behavior could be compared, with full expectation that there would be

discrepancies. In his formulation of the characteristics of the ideal bureaucracy, Weber was saying what organizational behavior would be like if it were maximally rational. Subsequent research findings, sometimes said to have "rediscovered", the primary group by showing the universal tendency for sentiments to assert themselves so that informal structures emerge within the populations involved in a formal organization, would not have surprised Weber. But partly because one of the topics he studied was rational-legal authority and bureaucratic (or "rationalized") organization and partly because his method was the rational assessment of cognitive similarities between ideal types, Weber's work has been taken to imply that sociological thought is more concerned with rational than nonrational aspects of interhuman behavior.

When the shock of World War I weakened faith in human rationality, an intellectual climate was created in which many thinkers would be tempted to go to the other extreme and discount human rationality altogether. Pareto's analyses of "nonlogical" behavior thus met a receptive audience upon translation into English at a time when the Great Depression of the 1930's had aggravated the shock of World War I.

Parsons' conviction that Pareto and Weber could be integrated has led to a theory of "action," which can be regarded as a worthy attempt to restore a proper balance in the postulates about the rationality or nonrationality of human conduct, even though in this writer's view action theory assumptions about the nature of social human beings are too hedonistic, too voluntaristic, and too individualistic. But in spite of World War II followed by a continuing Cold War and chronic unemployment, systematic analysis of the rational aspects of human interaction is still not unfashionable. Game theory is a sophisticated analysis of contingent probabilities and action strategies in a framework which assumes that each interacting party is rational—and that he imputes rationality to the other. Recognition hat game theory is the answer to some, but not all, theoretical needs is evidence of the rationality of sociologists.

Outgrowing Conceptual Distractions

Before sociological thought could come close to establishing an agreed-upon set of fundamental concepts with agreed-upon definitions, certain major conceptual blind alleys had to be recognized as such. The one which distracted attention from genuinely sociological matters most effectively was the attempt to explain societal phenomena largely within a biological framework. Social Darwinism is a label often applied to an assortment of ideas on this topic.

In *The Rules of the Sociological Method* Durkheim (1895) declared that a social fact would always be best explained by relating it to other social facts, not by relating it to facts of a different order—psychological or biological. Sociology has a real subject-matter; society is more than a mere aggregate of individuals, it is prior to the individual and constrains his acts. Before, and even after, Durkheim stated this position, many sociologists persistently tried to explain social facts in terms of nonsociological factors and frameworks.

Sociology started when evolution was the big, new, fascinating, inescapable idea. Spencer asserted that everything on earth and in the cosmos—inorganic, organic, and superorganic—evolves from incoherent homogeneity to coherent heterogeneity. Deductively, society had to evolve because everything evolves. This idea would have been practically useless in the formulation of meaningful theory, but by itself it might also have been innocuous. It quickly became misleading; the evolution idea was promptly identified with Darwin, who had shown the main outlines of the mechanism of biological evolution, natural selection. The temptation to generalize this mechanism as an explanation of the evolution of other entities than organic species was ap-

parently too strong for many nineteenth-century minds to resist. Spencer had pointed out some obvious and rather cogent points of similarity between a society and an organism: Society was therefore taken to be an organism. It was easy to conclude that it is because organisms evolve that society evolves and that it must evolve in the same way that organisms do, by natural selection. Though easy to reach, this conclusion was flagrantly wrong in that it misunderstood what it is that evolves by natural selection, even in the biological world. It is not an organism that evolves, but a species of organisms, whose trait *distribution* is altered from generation to generation. Individual organisms may remain unchanged, but if fewer organisms without a given trait than those possessing that trait survive to reproduce themselves, then that trait will become increasingly frequent in successive generations.

Social Darwinism in its boldest form was misleading not because it said there was social evolution, or because it applied natural selection to the human species. The greatest error was not even the obscuring of the difference, important though the difference is, between genetic transmission of traits, subject to natural selection, and social transmission of cultural elements, subject to quite different evolutionary mechanisms. The tragedy of Social Darwinist thought was that, as Ross (1920) pointed out, it asserted a statement to be true in sociology because its equivalent was true in biology, regardless of whether the statement was supported by sociological data.

This had the effect of making sociology just a branch of biology, and Social Darwinism is sometimes deplored in these terms. Being regarded as a branch of biology, however, at first probably helped sociology more than it hurt it. It helped give sociology apparent scientific status. In the fetal stage, it was perhaps necessary that sociology be somewhat parasitic. But it would have been stillborn if it had remained so too long. To be viable and begin to grow up as a science, sociology had to begin to test its hypotheses by comparison with data rather than just with analogous propositions from an older science. Isomorphism would not have been enough, even if the theory of social evolution really had been isomorphic with Darwin's theory of biological evolution, which was not the case.

But Social Darwinism was not entirely abortive. The reader has seen how, in Sumner, it stimulated clarification of cultural relativism and how the crude version which supposed that the fittest groups or persons survived gave way to a subtler version which asserted that the fittest folkways survive. The latter version was no longer a biological explanation of societal evolution, but a genuinely sociological explanation of *cultural* evolution. It still was not to be taken as true just because of its similarity to a biological proposition, and its tautological character would prevent it from being testable against data. But it could suggest further hypotheses regarding what kinds of folkways are fit to survive. Sumner described two distinct dimensions of fitness: Folkways survive insofar as they are adaptive to the conditions of the environment, but also insofar as they are compatible with other folkways. There is, he said, a "strain toward consistency" among folkways in a given culture. Since the same needs of the human species might be equally well served by various alternative folkways, selection must sometimes be based almost entirely on relative congruence with the rest of the culture. To say the folkways are subject to a "strain toward consistency" is thus to say in a positive way what sounds merely negative when expressed as the relativism of right and wrong to a cultural context.

Social Darwinism, then, tended to be a conceptual blind alley not just because it was biological and not even just because of reasoning by analogy. Sumner reasoned by analogy from biology and created some genuinely sociological hypotheses. Analogy can be exceedingly useful so long as it is not mistaken for proof. Hypotheses obtained analogically need to be tested empirically, and it was the tendency not to bother doing so that was the Social Darwinists' unpardonable sin.

Another conceptual blind alley, deriving some measure of respectability for a time from its biological connotations, but basically a psychological distraction, was the attempt to explain human interaction in terms of instincts. This alley was blind because it was wholly tautological. Tautologies, as such, are not always sterile. Newton's three laws of motion are tautological but conspicuously fertile. Though not testable themselves, quantitative predictions could be derived from them regarding motions of physical bodies, and there were observational facts which these fitted. There was already substantial consensus on what motions of what bodies required explanation, and there were abundant data of high precision. In sociological thought, however, the tautology of explaining an act, by attributing it to an instinct inferred from it, was sterile for two reasons. First, to the extent that certain asserted instincts led to predictions that could be tested (e.g., the expected universality of an act alleged to be instinctive) either the predictions were not factually correct, or they were as readily derivable from some alternative theory. Second, consensus was never achieved on a definitive list of instincts.

But the notion that one is driven to do things by some finite list of innate and qualitatively different urges was hard to escape. There were introduced a number of related concepts, implying something less than the rigidity of instincts, but presupposing that interhuman behavior can be resolved into combinations of a few elements that reside in human individuals: the "interests" of Ratzenhofer and Small (1905), the "four wishes" of Thomas (1918–1920), the "residues" of Pareto (1916), and some versions of the "values" lists that have claimed increasing attention in recent years. Of course there were also the "needs" and the "drives" of the psychologists. The fundamental defect of all such theories was not their quest for parsimony, even though they generally were premature and excessive in this respect. Basically, where they went wrong was in assuming that the individual is prior to the group, neglecting what should have been clear at least since Durkheim's work, that every individual is born into an already existing group which molds his behavior at least as much as he can mold the group.

Premature and excessive parsimony was also manifest in the various single-factor theories, of which economic determinism is a persisting example. There can no longer be any reasonable doubt that economic variables are among the important determinants of interhuman behavior, but there certainly are others. Sociologists were not the first to say, "Man does not live by bread alone," but they have had occasion to agree with it and reassert it. Once again the importance of cultural relativism is apparent; sociology happens to have flourished in a society whose cultural focus has been its economic institution, and it takes imagination and effort to transcend the easy hypothesis that economic variables are the key to all social phenomena everywhere. Economic determinism did have one attribute which tended to offset some of its disadvantages. It did at least posit the dependence of interhuman behavior on a variable external to the individual—a stratification system arising from his relation to the means of production. Oversimplified it was, but nevertheless remindful of what must be virtually an axiom of sociology.

One by one, these and other conceptual blind alleys have been discovered to be such, and sociological thought has turned away from them. In a wandering search into the heart of a conceptual wilderness, sociologists have finally formed a pretty clear idea of the lay of the land. With use, conceptual pathways have become more clearly marked out, and it has become easier to tell where they are leading. At times, the routes are devious, but as the paths are extended they increasingly intersect and multiply each other's significance.

Approaching Conceptual Clarity

Two examples of the trend toward conceptual clarity will be described. One of them has to do with a cluster of concepts that are approaching, but have not yet achieved, complete clarity; consensus on their definitions is still over the horizon. These are the concepts analyzing the position-status-role phenomena. The other example is the culture concept, on which near consensus has been reached, but only after a genuinely evolutionary process. Both examples indicate past growth in the scientific stature of sociology, and a careful recapitulation of the manner in which such stature has been achieved may help to augment it still further.

Tracing the evolution of scientific concepts is more than an exercise in etymology (where the interest would be in locating the original form or the original meaning of some word). The purpose rather is to try to discern where the concept stands now and where it is going, rather than where it started. In three incisive books, Max Jammer (1954; 1957; 1961) showed how greatly the meanings of three basic concepts of physical science—space, force, and mass—have evolved. There is certainly no implication that their original meanings were their truest meanings. Force, for example, was animistic in its meaning when it first entered the vocabulary of science. Galileo, Kepler, and Newton helped transform it. It was further reinterpreted by Leibniz, Kant, Mach, Hertz, and others, until today it is almost purely mathematical in its meaning. Science now seems to be moving in a direction that someday may even eliminate force as a concept having any physical referent, but this is hardly to be regarded as backsliding toward animism. Sociologists evidently need feel no embarrassment that their fundamental concepts have not always meant what they now mean, or have meant different things to different men.

Components of social structure. Two terms that are so common in sociological writing today as to be almost universally regarded as indispensable to sociological thought are "role" and "status"—with or without the redundant prefix "social." Their meanings are still undergoing adjustment and clarification. Sometimes they are used almost or quite interchangeably, but even when a more or less clear distinction between them is maintained, they are used in close association. For every role, it is said, there is a corresponding status, and for every status there is a corresponding role.

The usage which is thus far most nearly conventional is not yet fully consistent; there is room, in other words, for additional improvements in this portion of sociology's conceptual apparatus. Some writers, responding to this need, have begun to use the additional terms position and rank to denote concepts closely allied with role or status. The cluster of phenomena being variously dealt with by such terms is of undoubted importance to sociology, but sociologists have tried various ways of dissecting this cluster. Tracing the history of this set of concepts should make it apparent that the sociological vocabulary, like the terminology of older sciences, tends to be evolved rather than invented. New semantic wine is constantly being poured into old linguistic bottles, and old wine is sometimes put into new bottles. It will become apparent that the main struggle has been to free the conceptualization of the units of social structure from its originally invidious implications. The observational perspective called cultural relativism, essential if one wants clear perception of social facts, was not easily attained, as has been seen. It has been just as difficult to learn to describe social structure in terms that are not value-loaded.

The first sociological reference to these concepts used neither the word status nor the word role. In discussing the field of social statics in *The Positive Philosophy,* Comte (1830–1842) had roughly anticipated the modern concepts of role and status when he asserted that social organization tends to allocate its members to "employments" according to their qualifications, including their "own nature (which however is seldom very distinctly marked)," their "education," and their "position" (Comte, 1830–1842, p. 454). In this context, the word employment seems to approximate the concept of roles, and position seems to refer chiefly to social class.

Herbert Spencer used the term position similarly. In describing the difficulties confronting the sociologist wishing to make objective observations, Spencer mentioned the prejudicial effect of "the position occupied in respect to the phenomena to be generalized." The meaning intended for the word position is suggested by his use of "place" and "relationships" as apparent substitutes for it: ". . . the citizen's life is made possible only by due performance of his function in the place he fills . . ." and he can not "cut himself off in thought from all his relationships of race, and country, and citizenship . . ." (Spencer, 1873, p. 67). It is interesting that Spencer used "function" where one would now say "role." Today one tends to speak of people having roles, while institutions have functions.

Nowadays the textbooks often use the word position to define the term status. While Comte's and Spencer's use of "position" is not unrelated to the modern meaning, it is not identical, and they clearly were not offering it as a technical term in a specialized vocabulary. "Status," which more or less took the place of "position" as a technical vocabulary emerged, has changed meaning greatly. Sociology seems to have acquired the word status from Sir Henry Sumner Maine, who wrote in *Ancient Law* (1861) and again in *Popular Government* (1885) of man's progress from a social order based on "status" to one based on "contract." His distinction was similar to that expressed later by Tönnies in *Gemeinschaft und Gesellschaft* (1887) and to Durkheim's (1893) distinction between "mechanical solidarity" and "organic solidarity." Roughly speaking, societies had shifted from a mode of organization based on persons' identity to a mode of organization based on what they can do. "Status" referred to the first style. To "have status" was to "be somebody," and the word is still widely used in this sense.

In an 1899 paper by Charles Horton Cooley, adapted and reprinted in the classic introductory textbook by Park and Burgess (1924), Maine's term status was employed in a slightly modified sense and contrasted with "competition." Cooley clearly intended "status" to refer to "ascribed status" as the phrase is now used, and by "competition" he meant a process by which persons acquire what has since been termed "achieved status." Max Weber (1946) used "status" and "class" to denote a distinction rather similar to this.

Ralph Linton (1936) recast this distinction in the now familiar terms of "ascribed status" and "achieved status" and set the example for the general usage of "status" as such which has followed. He defined "status" in terms of the word previously used by Comte (1830–1842) and Spencer (1873) when he wrote, "A status . . . is a position in a particular pattern" of reciprocal behavior between individuals or groups" and went on to say, on the same page, "A status . . . is simply a collection of rights and duties" (Linton, 1936, p. 113). Linton, and nearly all other sociological writers since, have used the word role to refer to the duties portion of this collection. "Role" had, of course, been used earlier in much this same sense by Mead (1934), and a similar concept had been implied by Georg Simmel's use of "vocation" as a link between self and society (Simmel, 1950).

Simmel had also used "position" as early as the 1890's in connection with his discussions of superordination-subordination. Simmel (1896) was referring primarily to position in some system of vertical differen-

tiation, but there were repeated hints in his writing that he recognized that positions could be related to each other in terms of a structure more complex than some single vertical continuum. It was clear, moreover, that "position" had a more general meaning for Simmel than it had had for Comte (1830–1842), and it was beginning to be a genuinely technical term. In illustrating and emphasizing the fundamental difference between "personality" and "position" as determinants of behavior, Simmel spoke of an "office" (*Amt*) as an instance of position, and there were indications that offices involve more than mere prestige or social class relationships. In the recent literature, too, there are indications that "position" has been taking on a meaning more general than mere altitude on a prestige ladder.

Park (1925) had used "position" in his presidential address in a purely spatial sense. Distance and proximity between persons both influence and reflect their social relations, he noted, and held out the hope that social phenomena could be "measured and described in mathematical formulas" because "social structure can be defined in terms of position" and "social changes may be described in terms of movement" of people from one position to another in physical space. He concluded his plea for the new field of human ecology by suggesting its relevance to other phases of sociology, asserting, for example, that changes in people's spatial positions can result from the "struggle for status" in which every individual is involved, "a struggle to preserve his personal prestige, his point of view, and his self-respect" (Park, 1925, pp. 2, 9, 13). It is clear that Park was not using "status" and "position" as synonyms. He was recognizing that even in the physical spatial sense, position could be an *indicator* of status. With frequent use, the indicator came to be identified with its referent.

Kingsley Davis (1949) acknowledged his dependence on Linton (1936) and appraised the treatment of "role" and "status" therein as "An excellent presentation which has had

wide influence." Davis, however, took "identity" as the basic term, rather than "position"
and then equated both "position" and "status" with it. A person's identity, or position,
or status in a social structure "establishes his
rights and obligations with reference to others holding positions within the same structure" (Davis, 1949, p. 86). The rights and
obligations are defined by the normative
system. A right is a legitimate expectation
which a person in one position may hold
toward the behavior of a person in another
position. One person's right is another's
obligation. This much of Davis' terminology
seems quite value-free.

Davis (1949) defined "role" not in terms
of the behavior prescribed for a given position, but the behavior actually performed
by a person in a position. In a footnote he
pointed out a parallel between this relation
of "role" to position-obligations and Mead's
(1934) view of the relation of the "I" as
actual behavior in a position and the "me" as
the internally perceived position (Davis,
1949, p. 90). Other writers, however, have
tended to use "role" to mean prescribed
behavior associated with a position, or the
positional behavior prescriptions themselves
(duties).

In the paragraphs immediately following
Davis' (1949) initial definition of "position"
or "status" as identity, it seems fairly clear
that while positions may differ in degrees
of prestige, that is not the only variable on
which they vary, and he did not initially
intend "status" to mean social rank. But
this meaning crept back in after he attempted a distinction resembling Maine's
(1861) "status" versus "contract" dichotomy.
Davis suggested that some positions are defined by the general folkways and mores,
while others are defined by the special rules
of a specific organization. He proposed a
special usage of the term status, then, to
refer to the former, and "office" for the
latter. As he then went on to cite examples
and state some tentative generalizations
about these two kinds of position it began
to be apparent that "status" was going to

connote social rank after all. One example:

A general and a private both occupy a niche
in the army, but because of the great difference
of rank their respective positions give them a
quite different status with the public at large.
Furthermore, in wartime when the function of
the army is supremely important the prestige
attached to all army positions tends to rise,
whereas in peacetime it usually falls again
(Davis, 1949, p. 89).

Davis (1949) employed an additional
term to refer to the whole constellation of
positions one person may hold simultaneously in the overall social structure—one's
"station." To refer to a large number of
persons in a given society enjoying roughly
the same station, he used the word stratum.
Although he went on to make explicit
statement of the empirical fact that various
stations are publicly felt to be unequal, just
his choice of the word stratum rather than
such words as category or class for such a
set of similar stations seems to imply that
he saw vertical differentiation as almost the
defining characteristic of "stations" and
hence of "status" or "position."

This reluctant muddying of the conceptual waters after he had so nearly settled
them was partly offset by his recognition
that degrees of value can become associated
with persons in positions in two distinct
ways (Davis, 1949, pp. 93–94). "Prestige"
refers to value attached to the position itself.
"Esteem" refers to value attached to performance of the position's obligations. This
is part of the reason that it has seemed
impossible for "position" or even "status"
to be used *consistently* to denote social
rank even though it usually has had a social
rank connotation. Davis (1949) also noted
that "All positions carry a certain amount
of prestige, either high or low. But it does
not follow that between any two positions
there is an invidious distinction; they may
carry the same amount of prestige" (Davis,
1949, p. 94).

Since the tendency has been to define
"role" and "status" in terms of "position,"

the clarity of the two defined terms depends on what "position" itself is taken to mean. Bates (1956), in a critical article, began as usual by acknowledging indebtedness to Linton (1936) and defined "position" in a manner which seemed to use Park's (1925) spatial framework in a metaphorical sense that had become commonplace and appeared to require little or no departure from Linton: ". . . a position is a location in a social structure which is associated with a set of norms called rights and duties and to which is attached a certain amount of prestige." That this actually involved a radical break with the Linton conceptualization only became apparent when Bates went on to define "role" as "A part of a social position consisting of a more or less integrated or related sub-set of social norms which is distinguishable from other sets of norms forming the same position" (Bates, 1956, p. 314). In going on to develop a theory of group structure based on position conceived as a constellation of roles (each role being a set of norms), Bates clearly ceased to use position as connoting social rank.

Though it has become rather conventional to define "status" as position as Linton (1936) did, the concept of position apart from its implications of social rank has been exceedingly difficult to grasp. Textbooks *define* "status" as position and then *use* "status" to refer chiefly to differentiation of people on some vertical continuum (e.g., prestige, or esteem, or power). Merrill (1957) noted that "status" is commonly applied "only to the position of the individual in the prestige systems of his society" (Merrill, 1957, p. 190). He spoke of this as erroneous usage, however, and specifically deplored the tendency to talk of some people as having "more status" than others. Some writers have begun to introduce the term rank as a separate concept, apparently to solidify the gain in clarity toward which Merrill was moving.

The evolution of sociological terminology is not yet complete, and these problems are not settled. In another textbook of similar vintage (Freedman, Hawley, Landecker, Lenski, & Miner, 1956, p. 206), the term role is defined the way most texts define the term status, as "the position an individual occupies" in "a system of relationships. . . ." These authors, however, did use the term rank to refer to the "hierarchical ordering of comparable social positions on the basis of variations in the degree of power vested in them by the group" (Freedman et al., 1956, p. 232). Each position *has* a rank, and it is clear that "position" is not here being used as a synonym for rank.

Homans (1950) also had used "rank" and distinguished it from "status" as well as from "role." His terminology was based on somewhat similar considerations. Homans went out of his way to explain his decision to use "rank" in discussing the Norton Street Gang rather than retaining "status" as it had been used by William Foote Whyte (1943) in the original study of that group. Perceptively, Homans wrote:

When a sociologist says that a man has high status in an organization, he may mean any or all of the following: (a) the man is close to the center of the web of communication in the organization; (b) he is carrying on a particular kind of activity or maintaining a certain level of activity; and (c) by reason of his position in the web of communication and the kind of job he does he is highly ranked or valued. . . . We do not want to lump all three aspects of his position together under the name of *status,* but to separate them and see the relations among them. And of the three aspects, we give the name *rank* to the evaluation or prestige aspect . . . (Homans, 1950, p. 179).

It is worth noting the nature of the challenge confronting Homans (1950): *Research* had yielded results whose theoretical implications could only be developed with the aid of clearer concepts. Homans felt it necessary to isolate the rank aspects of what Whyte (1943) had simply called status, and give these aspects a separate name. At about the same time, other research developments began to lead to other clarifications of concepts. In laboratory experimentation with small *ad hoc* groups, Bavelas (1948) and others assigned subjects to locations in variously structured communication nets and studied the effects of structure on their behavior in collectively solving certain information-processing problems (Bavelas, 1948; Bavelas, 1953; Leavitt, 1951). The spatial-behavioral parallelism noted earlier by Park (1925) was here being used as a basis for experimental manipulation. The experimentation in turn would change the connotations of social structure terminology.

For example, when five subjects were situated in booths that were connected by communication channels forming a pattern like this

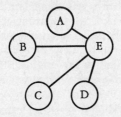

it was found that the person in booth *E* tended to acquire a leadership role. In a pattern like this, however,

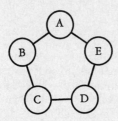

the person in booth *E* had no greater tendency than persons in the other booths to become a leader. Although such findings may not seem surprising, as such research began to become familiar the concept of position became increasingly neutral with regard to value-connotations. The subject who was randomly assigned to booth *E* (in the first pattern) was thereby put into a

position in a contrived social structure, and that position would shape his behavior. As relations between his behavior and position and the behavior and positions of the other subjects began to become apparent to all of them in the course of the experiment, roles began to be defined by them. The role associated with position *E* differed from the others in such a way that it could be accorded a higher rank. By experimental creation of positions that could be represented spatially rather than by verbal labels carrying connotations of rank, the sociological concept of position was sharpened.

Another line of research leading to conceptual clarification in this area consisted of studies of role conflict. Stouffer (1949) studied the problems confronting persons for whom two positions are simultaneously salient but involve contradictory duties or obligations. Almost a decade later, Gross, Mason, and McEachern (1958) made a detailed study of an instance in which conflicting expectations attached to a single position—that of school superintendent. Thus, in addition to regarding positions as elements in a social structure, it became meaningful to analyze the internal structure of a position.

Textbooks, meanwhile, continued to juggle the familiar terms, gradually redefining and realigning them in ways that more or less reflected the impact of these researches. A comparison of successive editions of several leading textbooks will be instructive.

Ogburn and Nimkoff, in their first edition (1940), defined "status" as "the position of the individual in the group" and said this has two aspects, one being "rank" or "group standing," and the other being "role" or "formalized behavior." They noted that each person typically has several statuses, and argued that status (in the singular) is not an amalgam of these but some particular one of them which the group selects for emphasis. In discussing class status, and ascribed versus achieved status, they virtually equated "status" with the notion of category. In their second edition (1950) all this was repeated, unchanged. In their third edition (1958), they changed the definition of "status" and equated it with rank. First they asserted that the division of labor is functional for a group. Then they used "position" in a division of labor framework, to define role: ". . . a role is a set of socially expected and approved behavior patterns, consisting of both duties and privileges, associated with a particular position in a group" (Ogburn & Nimkoff, 1958, pp. 153–154). Next, instead of distinguishing (as they had in the first two editions) between ascribed and achieved status, they distinguished between ascribed and achieved roles. Finally, they defined "status" as "the rank-order position assigned by a group to a role or to a set of roles." Thus, the meanings of "status" are reduced from two to one, between the first and third editions, but at the expense of giving "position" the burden of dual meanings.

In the first two editions of their *Sociology* (1955; 1958), Broom and Selznick used both "status" and "role" without explicitly defining them. "Status" was used in connection with stratification, and the distinction between ascribed and achieved status was discussed. In their third edition (1963) they inserted definitions of these terms. "Role" was defined as "a pattern of behavior associated with a distinctive social position" but it was further asserted that a role specifies *both* the rights *and* duties belonging to a position. "Status" was acknowledged to have two meanings: First, it can "refer simply to a person's social position. Each role in society is associated with a social position or status. . . . In this meaning, status does not necessarily have any connotation of 'higher' or 'lower.'" Second, it can also designate "an individual's place within a system of social ranking. . . . This second meaning is narrower than the first, and is focused on the idea of rank" (Broom & Selznick, 1963, pp. 16, 42). They went on to talk about differences between society based on status and society based on contract, with specific citation of Maine (1861), and they concluded that a society based on status "emphasizes rank."

The concept of rank is not yet firmly fixed in the lexicon of sociology, however. Although in their third edition, Broom and Selznick (1963) used it as mentioned above and also spoke of "formal ranks" and a "formal ranking system" in their chapter on "Associations," "rank" was apparently not considered significant enough to be listed in the index.

Bredemeier and Stephenson (1962) did adopt the term rank. They initially equated "status" with position, as has been conventional, but went on to speak of status as "a set of cultural definitions that specify how a person is supposed to perceive and respond to objects and people when he is in a particular relationship with them." "Status rights" were then distinguished from "status obligations," and "rank" was used to refer to the evaluation of statuses in a graded series (Bredemeier & Stephenson, 1962, pp. 30, 37).

Larsen and Catton (1962) presented separate definitions of the four terms: position, status, role, and social rank. The key concept, "position," was defined as the "location of a person or a category of persons in a set of social relationships," reflecting the influence of the Bavelas (1948; 1953) experiments. "Status" was defined in a way that paralleled the "status rights" notion of Bredemeier and Stephenson (1962): "The rights, privileges, and perquisites accorded to persons while they occupy a given social position." "Role" paralleled "status obligations" and was defined as "A pattern of collectively held expectations which define appropriate behavior for persons in a given social position." Finally, "social rank" was taken to mean the "relative degree of prestige or honor accorded to persons while they occupy a given social position."

In the first two editions of the influential textbook by Lundberg, Schrag, and Larsen (1954; 1958), the "role" and "status" concepts were used very much in the manner defined by Linton (1936). However, the phrasing of the definition of "status" did change somewhat. The first edition said, "Social status is the position accorded an individual by the various members of his group" and then explained that when people are "accorded status" this means that others behave toward them in ways that reflect "different degrees of dominance and superiority or subordination and inferiority" (Lundberg et al., 1954, p. 243). In the second edition, "position" was not used in defining "social status," which was said to denote "the comparative degrees of prestige, deference, or respect accorded persons who have been assigned different roles within a group or community" (Lundberg et al., 1958, p. 761). In the third edition (1963), a definition was given for "position" as a concept in its own right: "Location of a person or a category of persons in a set of social relationships" (Lundberg et al., 1963, p. 764). The way it was used in several parts of this edition makes it clear that "position" no longer meant rank for these authors. Now, instead of defining a single concept of "role," separate definitions of "role anticipation," "role expectation," "role performance," and "role prescription" were given, with "role requirements" also used to include both role expectations and role prescriptions. The work of Gross, Mason, and McEachern (1958) seems to have had considerable impact here. Finally, "social status" was defined in this third edition exactly as "social rank" had been defined by Larsen and Catton (1962): "Relative degree of prestige or honor accorded to persons while they occupy a given social position" (Lundberg et al., 1963, p. 766). Clearly, status and position were now viewed as separate concepts, though rank and status were still equated.

In their first edition, Lundberg, Schrag, and Larsen (1954) made the distinction Linton had made between ascribed status and achieved status (Lundberg et al., 1954, p. 245). In the second edition (1958), they modified this slightly, and distinguished ascribed role and status from achieved role and status (Lundberg et al., 1958, p. 315). In the third edition (1963), this became the distinction between ascribed positions and roles and achieved positions and roles (Lundberg et al., 1963, pp. 150ff.).

The final way of dissecting this conceptual complex has doubtless not yet occurred. To sum up what has happened so far: Considerable change in meaning has taken place with regard to a closely interrelated set of concepts that have a great degree of centrality in sociological thought; the change has been evolutionary and clarity seems to be emerging. This emerging clarity could be expressed in the following way. In a system of social relationships, a person will hold a position, which entails duties or obligations (his role) and rights, privileges, and perquisites (his status). The various positions in the system will be graded in a hierarchy of prestige or esteem (their respective social rank). The rank of a person in a position will depend partly on the adequacy of his performance of its role, partly on the nature of the duties or obligations incumbent on him and how these are socially evaluated, and partly on the value attached socially to the rights, privileges, and perquisites given him by the position. These conceptual relations are schematically represented in the following diagram.

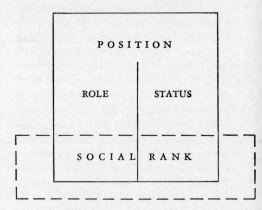

Operationally, a position can only be inferred from observing how a person behaves toward others in the group and how others behave toward him. "Position" is, then, simply the logical sum of "status" and "role," where each of these terms refers to a cluster of normative patterns inferrable from observed behavior. Hence the earlier difficulty in disentangling these terms, and hence such a makeshift solution as was adopted by Parsons (1951) who has used the hyphenated term status-roles. (Like other sociologists, Parsons regarded the "status" half of this composite term as referring to a person's "location" or "position," while "role" refers to what he does in that location.)

The rank of a position must likewise be inferred from the apparent deference or honor implied in the reactions of others to both the role and status aspects of a position (and to performance by its incumbent). It is because *both* roles and statuses can be ranked that Merrill (1957) was on sound ground in referring to the equating of "rank" with "status" as erroneous usage.

Early sociologists, as has been seen, had started to make occasional use of the word position. They had in mind the division of labor, but there was often a strong connotation of rank. The word was potentially more free of evaluative meaning than "status," but the latter came into the literature at a time when sociologists were not yet strongly concerned to separate value-judgment from observation. Sociological thought still tended to be highly ethnocentric; sociologists were concerned with progress rather than change, with discovering the ideal social order rather than analyzing the diversity of viable social systems, and often with proving their own culture to be the highest yet attained if not actually the ultimate. They were thus not especially alert to the perils of the word status. It had the advantage of jargon, and until its ambiguity was fully recognized it remained a standard part of the sociological vocabulary.

"Position" came back into the literature, at first as a convenient primitive term with which to go through the motions of defining the technical term status, later as a concept

in its own right, value-free, and sharpened in meaning by its geometrical representation in small-group research. "Role," at first defined as an aspect of status, has tended repeatedly to displace "status." In its theatrical origins, "role" refers to the part played by an actor, and sociologists seem to have been able to use it in a more consistently value-free sense than has been the case with "status." The drift from thinking of status ascription versus achievement, to thinking of role ascription versus achievement, seems to reflect the theoretical advantages of noninvidious terminology.

But invidious distinctions among men do occur, as part of the social behavior the sociologist studies, and he therefore needs a word that refers to this phenomenon alone. "Rank" seems to be gaining recognition as a suitable term for that purpose. The trouble with "status" was that it confounded the division of labor idea with the idea of rank, and the trouble with the sociological analysis of these matters has been that it took so long for sociologists to see that this was happening. Perhaps it would have been apparent sooner if it had been customary to write the history of sociological thought in terms of conceptual development rather than in terms of rivalry between schools of thought.

Concepts of culture. As early as the end of the eighteenth century, "Cultur" (or "Kultur") was part of the German language and meant cultivation of man's moral or intellectual capacities. German usage evolved rapidly until, early in the nineteenth century, the word had already come to mean the processes and forms of social life and their spiritual and material products. In a book published in 1843, with the term in its title—*Allgemeine Culturwissen geschichte der Menschheit*—Gustav Klemm used "Cultur" to mean the customs, arts, skills, and style of life of a people. Edward B. Tylor (1865) tried out the word and cited Klemm's work as a source. By 1871, Tylor was ready to commit himself to the concept and began a book entitled *Primitive*

Culture by defining culture as "that complex whole which includes knowledge, belief, art, law, morals, custom, and any other capabilities and habits acquired by man as a member of society." This would almost suffice today, but the irony is that sociology (and even anthropology) had to undergo considerable groping with other words and definitions before adopting "culture" with almost the precise meaning Tylor had given it. It was not until the 1920's that the word became firmly established in the sociological vocabulary. The derived concept of "cultural lag" which found such a receptive audience when it was set forth by Ogburn (1922) may have provided the necessary reinforcement.

Meanwhile many sociologists had more or less perceptively described cultural phenomena, using various other terms. The lesson to be gained from this period of groping is not that sociologists were blind to the relevant facts, or even that they were unwilling to read each other's works and adopt each other's terminology. After all, "culture" did break into sociological literature before its technical meaning began to penetrate public consciousness or to appear in standard English dictionaries. Rather, the lesson is that until a number of people have begun to use the same word in the same way, there is no communicative reason for preferring one name over any other reasonably plausible name for the same concept. The ascendency of one term over its competitors almost has to be accidental or circumstantial. However, until a common terminology does begin to crystalize it is difficult to tell whether various terms really do refer to "the same" concept.

Spencer's (1862) organic analogy pointed to a complex of phenomena that certainly included much of what is now meant by culture. His references to the "superorganic" can often be read just as meaningfully if "cultural" is substituted. Of course, Spencer is remembered for his evolutionary theory which asserted that superorganic phenomena undergo the same kind of evolution as do organic (and inorganic) phenomena. In this, he obviously missed one of the main implications of the culture concept.

Ward (1897), on the other hand, clearly did grasp this implication, even without adopting culture as a key term. One of his main theses was the fundamental difference between organic evolution and social evolution. Much that he wrote about the difference between "genesis" and "telesis" had to do with the advantages a culture-bearing species has over other kinds of creatures. Even his phrase "collective conation" implies the operation of a number of aspects of culture.

Bagehot (1872), of course, used the phrase "cake of custom" to mean almost exactly what Tylor (1871) meant by "culture." However picturesque this phrase, it had no particular scientific advantage over any of its competitors.

Durkheim (1893) perceived culture even if he did not adopt that term as a standard name for it; he insisted that individual behavior is subject to social constraint, that the standards of conduct exist, and that social facts are things. He referred to the *conscience collective,* a term which might have taken root had "culture" not been available and had sociology not happened to find in English-speaking America, rather than France, its most receptive environment.

When Sumner (1906) wrote about folkways, mores, and institutions, and the strain toward consistency among folkways, in all this the culture concept was almost fully developed, but not given that name. He preferred to avoid the term, and according to Kroeber and Kluckhohn (1963, p. 55) said once that the word culture was one that illustrates "the degeneracy of language" because "it has been stolen by the dilettanti and made to stand for their own favorite forms and amounts of attainments." This was in answer to literary usage of the word.

Similarly, Giddings' (1896) use of the term social mind and Cooley's (1902: 1909) discussions of traditions, institutions, and conventions came close to the culture concept. Many writers, of course, used "civilization" to mean approximately what is now meant by "culture," and there were even references to "primitive civilizations." Civilization is now thought of as a special type of culture, more advanced than others, but any implicit ethnocentrism in this usage is deplored and therefore the attempt is made to avoid it. There was a period in which yet another distinction between "civilization" and "culture" was attempted. Kroeber and Kluckhohn (1963) showed that "culture" once meant to some writers approximately what is now called "material culture" while "civilization" meant nonmaterial culture. But there were others who made the same distinction with the labels reversed, and both usages have died out (or perhaps cancelled each other out).

Sociologists, of course, share the culture concept with other social scientists, particularly anthropologists. In their definitions, sociologists have sometimes emphasized different features of culture than have the anthropologists, but there is little indication that the difference between disciplines has expressed itself in the form of rivalry, though by the assumptions implicit in the "schools of thought" approach this should have been the case. The concept has developed in such a way that it has achieved abundant usage in both bodies of literature, and members of each discipline have freely cited the writings of the other. For brevity, however, consideration of the anthropological literature as such will be omitted here, and only the highlights in the sharpening of the culture concept in sociological thought will be noted.

Small (1905) defined "culture" as "the total equipment of technique, mechanical, mental and moral, by use of which the people of a given period try to attain their ends . . ." (Small, 1905, pp. 344–345). He said people of a given *period* rather than of a given *society,* and this reflects the concern still prevalent at that time for the study of social evolution, a concern that tended

toward expressions of ethnocentrism by the sociologist.

Several definitions offered subsequently showed close resemblance to Small's (1905). The idea that culture is a "total," a "sum," or a "sum total" recurred in many sociological texts: Park and Burgess (1924), Sumner and Keller (1927), Young (1934), Reuter (1939), LaPiere (1946), Broom and Selznick (1955; 1958; 1963). Another element was included in the Park and Burgess definition, however, and this element has gained increasing emphasis in later writings. This was the idea that culture is organized, or is a system. "The culture of a group is the sum total and organization of the social heritages which have acquired a social meaning" for that group (Park & Burgess, 1924, p. 72). This important modification of the concept was going to require further clarification, however. As recently as 1939, Reuter (1939) used it in a context that reflected vestiges of the obsolete sociological pontification on social progress:

The term *culture* is used to signify the sum-total of human creations, the organized result of human experience up to the present time. Culture includes all that man has made in the form of tools, weapons, shelter, and other material goods and processes, all that he has elaborated in the way of attitudes and beliefs, ideas and judgments, codes and institutions, arts and sciences, philosophy and social organization (Reuter, 1939, p. 191).

This was not yet the idea of a distinctive, organized culture characterizing the way of life of each autonomous society.

Sutherland and Woodward (1940) referred to culture as a "complex whole"—a term with connotations of organization or system. In the same year, Ogburn and Nimkoff (1940) quoted in their textbook the early definition by Tylor (1871) and another from unpublished lectures by Redfield. Then they enumerated the traits they themselves wanted to include under the term culture, argued the case for classifying traits into "material culture" versus "nonmaterial culture," and concluded that in a given culture the various institutions "are interlinked to form a pattern which is unique for each society" (Ogburn & Nimkoff, 1940, p. 63). Their second and third editions (1950; 1958) changed little of this, except to omit the argument about including material traits as part of culture, implying that this was now accepted usage not requiring further debate.

Another element in the modern culture concept is communication. Ward (1883) emphasized the difference between the mechanism by which culture traits are transmitted to the next generation and the mechanisms of transmission of the biological heritage, but without using the terminology familiar to sociologists today. Sutherland and Woodward (1940, p. 19) defined "culture" as "everything that can be communicated" including the method of communication itself. Davis (1949) made communication the main element in his definition of "culture" as "all modes of thought and behavior that are handed down by communicative interaction—i.e., by symbolic transmission—rather than by genetic inheritance" (Davis, 1949, pp. 3-4).

There is not quite enough parallel between changes from one generation to another and changes from one textbook edition to another to permit one to say that among sociologists "ontogeny recapitulates phylogeny." Since textbook revision is intended to reflect improvement or advancement, however, it may be regarded as a part of the conceptual development process. In their first edition, Lundberg, Schrag, and Larsen (1954) defined "culture" as consisting of "(1) the systems of social behavior observed among the members of a society and (2) the symbolic and nonsymbolic products of such behavior" (Lundberg et al., 1954, p. 162). Their second edition elaborated this definition by bringing in the communication process: "The systems of learned behavior that are observed among the members of a society and are communicated from one generation to the next

through processes of socialization, including standards of judgment, belief, and conduct, as well as the material products of these behavior systems" (Lundberg et al., 1958, p. 755). In the third edition this was shortened, and the implication that culture is behavior (rather than inferred normative patterns underlying behavior) was avoided: "A system of socially acquired and socially transmitted standards of judgment, belief, and conduct, as well as the symbolic and material products of the resulting conventional patterns of behavior" (Lundberg et al., 1963, p. 761).

In the history of sociology, the word culture first had to compete with other candidate labels for the same concept. Once adopted, its definition had to undergo evolution. It seems reasonable to say that sociologists have now achieved near consensus on the culture concept. All use the term and remaining differences of definition are quite minor. There is substantial agreement on what is meant when sociologists refer to man as the culture-bearing species, though they may disagree on whether this is a conclusion or a point of departure as far as research on cultural change is concerned. The most recent definition of "culture" offered by Lundberg and his associates (1963) seems fully compatible with the conceptualization employed by Sorokin (1937–1941) or in any of his later and briefer treatises on the same subject. It is also thoroughly compatible with Parsons' (1952) usage. If there are differences that seem to be enormous between Lundberg and Sorokin or Parsons, this only emphasizes the error of conceiving the history of sociological thought as rivalry between schools or between men; to do so can only make one insensitive to the important degree of conceptual agreement that has been achieved by sociologists of diverse backgrounds and diverse research interests.

From the foregoing account of the history of the culture concept, and the account of the history of the status and role conceptual complex, it is apparent that conceptual clarification in sociology proceeds in a crescive manner. Conceptual clarity is not likely to be achieved through enactment. The point is, though, that clarification does happen. One need not despair by imagining that present ambiguities and imprecisions are permanent, or that concepts must forever be merely "sensitizing." Nor need one revert to a Spencer-like attitude of laissez faire as the only alternative to vain efforts to decree final definitions. One can at least participate actively as a contributor in an interpersonal process of conceptual evolution.

CONCLUSION

The history of sociological thought consists of more than scattered, unconnected, incompatible writings. There has also been constant advancement and coalescence. The goals have changed so that where once the mission was ideological, and sociologists were divided between those who favored social telesis and those who considered it a dangerous illusion, today they are united in the pursuit of knowledge as such and in the implicit expectation that it will have at least ultimate social utility. Research strategy has also changed, so that almost all sociologists are now empirically oriented, and in research activity tend to specialize in some limited phase of sociology, confidently expecting their contributions to complement those of colleagues with different specialties. Differences between interhuman behavior and behavior studied by other sciences are acknowledged, but the strategy of natural science in its broadest terms is now widely accepted as the effective strategy in sociology. The quest for precise measurement and rigorous testing of quantitative hypotheses is no longer a matter of great controversy. There has also been change in the content of theories, so that they deal less with describing and explaining what societies do or how they evolve, and more with how people associate and groups organize, interact, perpetuate themselves, and develop structured ways of controlling their

members' behavior. Sociologists are now convinced of the reality of groups. Their theories are less ethnocentric than they used to be, and despite occasional backsliding they are resolving an earlier ambivalence about the perceptual advantages of cultural relativism and learning to distinguish the value-free scientific role from the value-commitments involved in their other roles as persons. They have tried and rejected various abortive theoretical frameworks and have learned to be their sociological selves without having to be defensive. Concepts have begun to stabilize, and with a recognition that clarity is a crescive rather than an enacted accomplishment, still further clarification will be achieved.

Sociological thought has come a long way, but its impressive progress involves certain present hazards. If the early ethnocentric sociologists framed evolutionary theories that made the past seem nothing but prologue for the present, there is a danger that sociologists could become ethnocentric in their conviction that sociological thought has evolved in a progressive direction. If there is merit in studying where the discipline came from so as to know how it got where it is, it is in order to learn how to go farther yet, not in order to indulge in self-congratulation. Sociological concepts are not yet *wholly* value-free. Useful though it is for clear perception, cultural relativism is still difficult to achieve and maintain. There is a need to apply it in the study of the intellectual behavior of sociologists just as seriously as in the study of other human conduct. The scholar must resist the temptation to identify with an in-group of only *some* sociologists, whose purity may be thought to be endangered by communication with those in the out-group. He must also resist the temptation to define only sociologists as the in-group, excluding contact with theories and concepts from other disciplines, for history permits the conclusion: Sociological thought has sufficiently come of age so that it can afford to lower its protective intellectual tariffs.

REFERENCES

Allen, F. R., Hart, H., Miller, D. C., Ogburn, W. F., & Nimkoff, M. F. (Eds.) *Technology and social change*. New York: Appleton-Century-Crofts, Inc., 1957.

Bagehot, W. *Physics and politics*. (Orig. ed. 1872) New York: Knopf, 1948.

Barnes, H. E. *An introduction to the history of sociology*. Chicago: Univer. of Chicago Press, 1948.

Barnes, H. E., & Becker, H. *Social thought from lore to science*. (2nd ed.) Washington: Harren Press, 1952.

Bates, F. L. Position, role and status: A reformulation of concepts. *Soc. Forces,* 1956, 34, 313–321.

Bavelas, A. A mathematical model for group structures. *Appl. Anthro.,* 1948, 7, 16–30.

Bavelas, A. Communication patterns in task-oriented groups. In D. Cartwright & A. Zander (Eds.), *Group dynamics: Research and theory*. Evanston, Ill.: Row, Peterson, 1953. Pp. 493–506.

Bernard, L. L. *Instinct: A study in social psychology*. New York: Holt, 1924.

Blumer, H. *An appraisal of Thomas and Znaniecki's the Polish peasant in Europe and America*. New York: Social Science Research Council, 1939.

Boskoff, A. From social thought to sociological theory. In H. Becker & A. Boskoff (Eds.), *Modern sociological theory*. New York: Dryden, 1957. Pp. 3–32.

Bredemeier, H. C., & Stephenson, R. M. *The analysis of social systems*. New York: Holt, Rinehart & Winston, 1962.

Brodbeck, M. Models, meaning, and theories. In L. Gross (Ed.), *Symposium on sociological theory*. Evanston, Ill.: Row, Peterson, 1959. Pp. 373–403.

Broom, L., & Selznick, P. *Sociology*. Evanston, Ill.: Row, Peterson, 1955.

Broom, L., & Selznick, P. *Sociology*. (2nd ed.) Evanston, Ill.: Row, Peterson, 1958.

Broom, L., & Selznick, P. *Sociology*. (3rd ed.) New York: Harper & Row, 1963.

Comte, A. *The positive philosophy*. Harriet Martineau (Trans.) (3rd ed. Orig. ed. 1830–1842). New York: Calvin Blanchard, 1856.

Comte, A. *System of positive polity*. J. H. Bridges & F. Harrison (Trans.) (Orig. French ed. 1851–1854). London: Longmans, Green, 1875–1877.

Comte, A., & Saint-Simon, H. Plan of the scientific operations necessary for the re-organization of society. (1822) Reprinted in appendix, *System of positive polity*. J. H. Bridges & F. Harrison (Trans.) (Orig. French ed. 1851–1854). London: Longmans Green, 1875–1877.

Cooley, C. H. Personal competition. *Econ. Stud.,* 1899, 4, 78–173.

Cooley, C. H. *Human nature and the social order*. New York: Scribner, 1902.

Cooley, C. H. *Social organization*. New York: Scribner, 1909.

Cooley, C. H. *Social process*. New York: Scribner, 1918.

Darwin, C. *On the origin of species by means of natural selection*. London: J. Murray, 1859.

Davis, K. *Human society*. New York: Macmillan, 1949.

Davis, K. The myth of functional analysis as a special method in sociology and anthropology. *Amer. sociol. Rev.,* 1959, 24, 757–772.

Dewey, J. *Human nature and conduct*. New York: Modern Library, 1930.

Durkheim, E. *The elementary forms of the religious life*. J. W. Swain (Trans.) (Orig. French ed. 1912). London: Allen, 1915.

Durkheim, E. *The division of labor in society*. G. Simpson (Trans.) (Orig. French ed. 1893). New York: Macmillan, 1933.

Durkheim, E. *The rules of the sociological method*. Sarah A. Solovay & J. H. Mueller (Trans.) (Orig. French ed. 1895). Chicago: Univer. of Chicago Press, 1938.

Durkheim, E. *Suicide*. J. A. Spaulding & G. Simpson (Trans.) (Orig. French ed. 1897). Glencoe, Ill.: Free Press, 1951.

Faris, E. Are instincts data or hypotheses? *Amer. J. Sociol.,* 1921, 27, 184–196.

Faris, E. *The nature of human nature*. New York: McGraw, 1937.

Faris, R. E. L. American sociology. In G. Gurvitch & W. E. Moore (Eds.), *Twentieth century sociology*. New York: Philosophical library, 1946. Pp. 538–561.

Freedman, R., Hawley, A. H., Landecker, W. S., Lenski, G. E., & Miner, H. M. *Principles of sociology*. (rev. ed.) New York: Holt, 1956.

Giddings, F. *Principles of sociology*. New York: Macmillan, 1896.

Gilfillan, S. C. *Sociology of inventions*. New York: Follett, 1935.

Gross, N., Mason, W. S., & McEachern, A. W. *Explorations in role analysis.* New York: Wiley, 1958.

Gumplowicz, L. *Outlines of sociology.* F. W. Moore (Trans.). Philadelphia: American Academy of Political and Social Science, 1899.

Hankins, F. H. Sociology. In H. E. Barnes (Ed.), *The history and prospects of the social sciences.* New York: Knopf, 1925. Pp. 255–332.

Hart, H. Social theory and social change. In L. Gross (Ed.), *Symposium on sociological theory.* Evanston, Ill.: Row, Peterson, 1959. Pp. 196–238.

Homans, G. C. *The human group.* New York: Harcourt, 1950.

Hughes, E. C. Ethnocentric sociology. *Soc. Forces,* 1961, **40,** 1–4.

Jammer, M. *Concepts of space.* Cambridge, Mass.: Harvard Univer. Press, 1954.

Jammer, M. *Concepts of force.* Cambridge, Mass.: Harvard Univer. Press, 1957.

Jammer, M. *Concepts of mass.* Cambridge, Mass.: Harvard Univer. Press, 1961.

Kant, I. *Critique of pure reason.* J. M. D. Meiklejohn (Trans.). London: G. Bell, 1893.

Kroeber, A. L., & Kluckhohn, C. *Culture: A critical review of concepts and definitions.* New York: Vintage, 1963.

LaPiere, R. T. *Sociology.* New York: McGraw, 1946.

Larsen, O. N., & Catton, W. R., Jr. *Conceptual sociology.* New York: Harper & Row, 1962.

Leavitt, H. J. Some effects of certain communication patterns on group performance. *J. abnorm. soc. Psychol.,* 1951, **46,** 38–50.

Linton, R. *The study of man.* New York: Appleton-Century-Crofts, Inc., 1936.

Lundberg, G. A. *Social research.* New York: Longmans, 1929.

Lundberg, G. A. *Foundations of sociology.* New York: Macmillan, 1939.

Lundberg, G. A. The natural science trend in sociology. *Amer. J. Sociol.,* 1955, **61,** 191–202.

Lundberg, G. A., Schrag, C. C., & Larsen, O. N. *Sociology.* New York: Harper, 1954.

Lundberg G. A., Schrag, C. C., & Larsen, O. N. *Sociology.* (rev. ed.) New York: Harper, 1958.

Lundberg, G. A., Schrag, C. C., & Larsen, O. N. *Sociology.* (3rd ed.) New York: Harper & Row, 1963.

Maine, Sir H. *Ancient law.* (Orig. ed. 1861) New York: Dutton, 1960.

Martindale, D. *The nature and types of sociological theory.* Boston: Houghton, 1960.

Martineau, Harriet. Preface. In A. Comte, *The positive philosophy.* Harriet Martineau (Trans.) (3rd ed.). New York: Calvin Blanchard, 1856.

Mead, G. H. *Mind, self and society from the standpoint of a social behaviorist.* Chicago: Univer. of Chicago Press, 1934.

Merrill, F. *Society and culture.* Englewood Cliffs, N.J.: Prentice-Hall, Inc., 1957.

Merton, R. K. *Social theory and social structure.* (rev. ed.) Glencoe, Ill.: Free Press, 1957.

Miyamoto, S. F. The social act: Re-examination of a concept. *Pacific sociol. Rev.,* 1959, **2,** 51–55.

Miyamoto, S. F. The impact on research of different conceptions of role. *Sociol. Inquiry,* 1963, **33,** 114–123.

Montesquieu, Baron de. *The spirit of laws.* T. Nugent (Trans.) (Orig. French ed. 1748). London: G. Bell, 1914.

Moore, W. E. *Social change.* Englewood Cliffs, N.J.: Prentice-Hall, Inc., 1963.

More, Sir T. *Utopia.* R. Robinson (Trans.) (Orig. Latin ed. 1516). London: G. Bell, 1910.

Odum, H. W. *American sociology.* New York: Longmans, 1951.

Ogburn, W. F. *Social change.* New York: Viking Press, Inc., 1922.

Ogburn, W. F. *The social effects of aviation.* Boston: Houghton, 1946.

Ogburn, W. F., & Nimkoff, M. F. *Sociology.* Boston: Houghton, 1940.

Ogburn, W. F., & Nimkoff, M. F. *Sociology.* (2nd ed.) Boston: Houghton, 1950.

Ogburn, W. F., & Nimkoff, M. F. *Sociology.* (3rd ed.) Boston: Houghton, 1958.

Pareto, V. *The mind and society.* A. Bongiorno & A. Livingston (Trans.) (Orig. Italian ed. 1916). New York: Harcourt, 1935.

Park, R. E. The concept of position in sociology. *Publ. Amer. sociol. Soc.,* 1925, **20,** 1–14.

Park, R. E., & Burgess, E. W. *Introduction to the science of sociology.* (2nd ed.) Chicago: Univer. of Chicago Press, 1924.

Parsons, T. *The structure of social action.* New York: McGraw, 1937.

Parsons, T. *The social system.* Glencoe, Ill.: Free Press, 1951.

Parsons, T., & Shils, E. A. (Eds.) *Toward a general theory of action.* Cambridge, Mass.: Harvard Univer. Press, 1952.

Reuter, E. B. Race and culture. In R. E. Park (Ed.), *An outline of the principles of sociology.* New York: Barnes & Noble, Inc., 1939. Pp. 171–217.

Ross, E. A. *Social control.* New York: Macmillan, 1901.

Ross, E. A. *The foundations of sociology.* (5th ed.) New York: Macmillan, 1920.

Shanas, Ethel. The *American Journal of Sociology* through fifty years. *Amer. J. Sociol.,* 1945, 50, 523–533.

Simmel, G. Superiority and subordination as subject-matter of sociology. *Amer. J. Sociol.,* 1896, 2, 167–189, 392–415.

Simmel, G. The persistence of social groups. *Amer. J. Sociol.,* 1898, 3, 662–698, 829–836; 4, 35–50.

Simmel, G. The number of members as determining the sociological form of the group. *Amer. J. Sociol.,* 1902, 8, 1–46, 158–196.

Simmel, G. The sociology of conflict. *Amer. J. Sociol.,* 1904, 9, 490–525, 672–689, 798–811.

Simmel, G. The sociology of secrecy and of secret societies. *Amer. J. Sociol.,* 1906, 11, 441–498.

Simmel, G. *The sociology of Georg Simmel.* K. H. Wolff (Trans. & Ed.). Glencoe, Ill.: Free Press, 1950.

Small, A. W. *General sociology.* Chicago: Univer. of Chicago Press, 1905.

Sorokin, P. A. *Contemporary sociological theories.* New York: Harper, 1928.

Sorokin, P. A. *Social and cultural dynamics.* New York: American Book, 1937–1941.

Spencer, H. *Social statics.* (Orig. ed. 1850) New York: Appleton-Century-Crofts, Inc., 1883.

Spencer, H. *First principles.* (Orig. ed. 1862) New York: Appleton-Century-Crofts, Inc., 1892.

Spencer, H. *The principles of sociology.* (Orig. ed. 1876–1896) New York: Appleton-Century-Crofts, Inc., 1910.

Spencer, H. *The study of sociology.* (Orig. ed. 1873) Ann Arbor: Univer. of Michigan Press, 1961.

Stouffer, S. A. An analysis of conflicting social norms. *Amer. sociol. Rev.,* 1949, 14, 707–717.

Sumner, W. G. *Folkways.* Boston: Ginn, 1906.

Sumner, W. G. The absurd attempt to make the world over. In A. G. Keller & M. R. Davie (Eds.), *Essays of William Graham Sumner.* New Haven, Conn.: Yale Univer. Press, 1934. Pp. 234–247.

Sumner, W. G., & Keller, A. G. *The science of society.* New Haven, Conn.: Yale Univer. Press, 1927.

Sutherland, R. L., & Woodward, J. L. *An introduction to sociology.* Philadelphia: Lippincott, 1940.

Tarde, G. *The laws of imitation.* Elsie Clews Parsons (Trans.) (Orig. French ed. 1890). New York: Holt, 1903.

Thomas, W. I., & Znaniecki, F. *The Polish peasant in Europe and America.* Boston: R. G. Badger, 1918–1920.

Thurstone, L. L., & Chave, E. J. *The measurement of attitude.* Chicago: Univer. of Chicago Press, 1929.

Timasheff, N. S. *Sociological theory: Its nature and growth.* New York: Random House, Inc., 1955.

Tönnies, F. *Fundamental concepts of sociology.* Charles P. Loomis (Trans.) (Orig. German ed. 1887). New York: American Book Co., 1940.

Tylor, E. B. *Researches into the early history and development of mankind.* London: J. Murray, 1865.

Tylor, E. B. *Primitive culture.* London: J. Murray, 1871.

Ward, L. F. *Dynamic sociology.* New York: Appleton-Century-Crofts, Inc., 1883.

Ward, L. F. *The psychic factors of civilization.* Boston: Ginn, 1897.

Weber, M. *From Max Weber.* H. Gerth & C. W. Mills (Trans. & Ed.). New York: Oxford, 1946.

Weber, M. *The theory of social and economic organization.* A. M. Henderson & T. Parsons (Trans.). New York: Oxford, 1947.

Weber, M. *The protestant ethic and the spirit of capitalism.* T. Parsons (Trans.) (Orig. German ed. 1906). New York: Scribner, 1958.

Whyte, W. F. *Street corner society.* Chicago: Univer. of Chicago Press, 1943.

Young, K. *Introductory sociology.* New York: American Book Co., 1934.

Znaniecki, F. *The method of sociology.* New York: Farrar & Rinehart, 1934.

Znaniecki, F. The proximate future of sociology: Controversies in doctrine and method. *Amer. J. Sociol.,* 1945, 50, 514–521.

CHAPTER 25 Contemporary Theory in Sociology

GEORGE CASPAR HOMANS

Contemporary sociologists have been pre-occupied with "theory," yet have seldom tried to make clear what a theory *is*. My first task, therefore, will be to describe the essential features of a theory. I shall then consider the intellectual confusions and practical difficulties that get in the way of the construction of theories in sociology. Next, I shall examine the differences between the main types of sociological theory. Since there are few areas of sociological investigation that have not claimed to be theoretical, I shall confine myself to the theories that pretend to be "general," especially structural, functional, and psychological theories. I shall end with a few remarks about the relations between theory and research.

WHAT IS A THEORY?

We sociologists show our confusion about the nature of theory both by what we say about theory in general and by the kinds of theories we actually produce. In what follows I shall not simply accept as theory what various sociologists have called by that name, but assess the degree to which different theories meet the requirements of a classical definition. This is the definition that identifies a theory of a phenomenon with an explanation of it by means of a deductive system. See especially Braithwaite (1953) and Nagel (1961).

I cannot go further without putting an example of a theory before us, so let me take a famous one. It is Durkheim's (1951, pp. 152–170) theory of the low suicide rate in Spain:

1. In any social grouping, the suicide rate varies directly with the degree of individualism (egoism).

2. The degree of individualism varies with the incidence of Protestantism.

3. Therefore, the suicide rate varies with the incidence of Protestantism.

4. The incidence of Protestantism in Spain is low.

5. Therefore, the suicide rate in Spain is low.

I do not ask of this example, or of others I shall use, whether it is a true theory and whether its logic is absolutely watertight, but only what its general characteristics as a theory are. It consists, first, of a set of concepts or *conceptual scheme*. Some of the terms in the scheme I call *descriptive* concepts, serving to show what the theory is about: "individualism," "suicide," "Protestantism." Others I call *operative* concepts or properties of nature: "suicide *rate*," "*incidence* of Protestantism." These latter properties are variables, and the variables may be probabilities. In some cases, as in the example, the variables are treated as continuous; in others, the variables take only two values, in the sense that the property in question is either present or absent. A conceptual scheme alone is insufficient to constitute a theory.

A theory consists, second, of a set of *propositions,* each stating a relationship, such as "varies directly with," between at least two of the properties, and the propositions form a *deductive system*. That is, each proposition may be represented symbolically by signs like $x, y,$ and $=$. The set of propositions forms a calculus, and according to the rules for the manipulation of the calculus, which are here taken to be those of simple logic, proposition 3 is said to be derived or deduced from propositions 1 and 2 and proposition 5 in turn from 3 and 4. When propositions are so derived they are said to be explained. A theory is nothing if it is not an explanation.

A deductive system also provides grounds for prediction. If, for instance, one did not know what the suicide rate in Eire was, but did know that the incidence of Protestantism was low, this proposition, together with proposition 3, would allow one to predict that the suicide rate there was low, too.

Third, some of the propositions of a scientific theory must be *contingent,* in the sense that experience is relevant to their truth or falsity or to that of propositions derived from them (Braithwaite, 1953, p. 24). In my example, all the propositions are of this sort. I shall not go into the problem of testing the truth of propositions, which is of course crucial for the acceptance or rejection of theories, but which seems to me to fall within the province of methodology rather than that of theory per se.

In some deductive systems, but not the present example, noncontingent propositions like $(x + y)(x - y) = (x^2 - y^2)$ are introduced into the calculus for convenience in making deductions. They are noncontingent in that experience is irrelevant to their truth or falsity. Rather they are logically necessary, like the propositions of mathematics, as following from axioms and postulates assumed a priori. Remember that a scientific theory does not consist solely of noncontingent propositions.

The propositions in a deductive system need not always differ in generality, but they often do, and the differences in generality may be of different kinds. In the example, proposition 5 is clearly less general than proposition 1 in that it applies to only one social unit, Spain, rather than to the universe of social groupings as does proposition 1. In a different way, and less clearly, proposition 2 might be considered less general than proposition 1 if we had reason to believe (as we do) that the degree of individualism varied with other properties besides the incidence of Protestantism. In what follows the more general propositions will also be called higher-order ones and the less general, lower-order or empirical ones. A theory need not contain, as my example does, only one highest-order proposition.

The deductive system I have used as an example is, in form, a theory of the low suicide rate in Spain. Since it explains only one empirical proposition, most scholars would not consider it a theory at all. Usually we speak of a theory only when it deals with a class of phenomena, such as all variations in suicide rates. In this sense of the word a theory consists of a cluster of deductive systems, differing of course in their lower-order propositions, including the propositions to be explained, but containing one or more of the same higher-order ones. When we speak of the "power" of a theory, we refer to the fact that a wide variety of empirical propositions may be derived from a few higher-order propositions under different given conditions. This, indeed, is the justification for calling the higher-order propositions more general.

I think it idle to claim that any theory is ever complete. In the first place, the most general propositions in the theory as formulated may themselves be explainable by another, still more general set of propositions. When they are so explained, they are often said to be reduced to the more general set. I think proposition 1 in our example could be reduced to a set of psychological propositions, though Durkheim might not have agreed (Durkheim, 1927, p. 125). And even if at any given time the most general propositions are not reducible, the possibility is always open that at some future time they will be, as Newton's law of gravitation was shown to follow under specific limiting conditions from the theory of relativity.

In the second place, some of the lower-order propositions in a theory are often themselves explainable by deductive systems, though the theorist for one reason or another may not want to bother to explain them. Take, for instance, proposition 4 in our example: the incidence of Protestantism in Spain is low. This could certainly be explained, but the deductive system would be long and intricate, bringing in, in principle, nothing less than the whole history of Spain. Under these circumstances, a theorist who is concerned with suicide and not with the history of Spain, and who does not have all the time in the world, may be pardoned if he treats proposition 4 as simply given, and leaves it unexplained. In practice he is more apt to do so if he regards the incidence of Protestantism in Spain as a parameter, that is, as an independent variable, which is not itself dependent on some other variable in his system, and whose value is temporarily constant. In what follows I shall call propositions like 4 *givens* or *given conditions*. Though a theory may be treated for convenience as if it were complete or closed, it is never so in fact. Instead it is open to the universe both at the top, so to speak, and at the sides.

The example used, like those used hereafter, was obviously a very simple deductive system. Much depends on what one wants to explain or predict. If, for instance, one wants to explain, not why the suicide rate in Spain is low but why the rate in some particular year was some particular figure, one might have to introduce other "factors" besides religion, and the factors might not be independent of one another. When the higher-order propositions in a theory are many, when the relationships between the variables are intricate, when, for instance, the values of several variables cannot be taken as given but are functions of other variables in the system, then the deductive system may have to use mathematics, and a computer may be required to solve the equations for the values of the unknowns. The deductive systems of sociology are increasingly likely to have these features. My only excuse for using simple examples is that the general requirements of a theory do not change just because it is complex.

The Definition of Concepts

I have yet to deal with the most difficult problem in characterizing a theory. The calculus representing the theory must be interpreted: in ordinary language, its terms must be defined, and the problem in question arises because they may be defined in two different ways. Some are defined directly by the criteria according to which observations are classed under the concept and measured. In our example, suicide rates are defined by the ways in which deaths are classified as suicides in vital statistics and their numbers counted. Such concepts are directly, explicitly, or, if you like, operationally defined (Bridgman, 1946, p. 5). More important, the operations defining such concepts are independent of those defining others.

But concepts of another kind are also apt to appear in deductive systems, concepts that are not defined in this way but that nevertheless play an important part in the systems. The classic example is that of *force* in mechanics as it appears in the equation: $f = ma$. In the interpretation of this equation, force is not defined independently of *mass* (m) and *acceleration* (a). Yet *force* plays a useful part in the theory of mechanics, if only because a number of different force-functions, such as that of gravitation, may be substituted for f, and the deductive systems that contain these new equations can explain a wide variety of empirical propositions. Such a concept is said to be implicitly defined (see Braithwaite, 1953, p. 77). There are many other examples in physical science.

In sociology I think *individualism* in our example may be such a concept. But I am not sure, so let me take a case of which I am more sure, the concept of *value* as it occurs, for instance, in the proposition: the more valuable to a man the reward he gets from another man or the environment, the more often he will emit activity that gets him that reward. The two variables here are: (1) the frequency of emission of the activity and (2) the value of the reward. Now there are cases in which *value* can be operationally defined: the value of food to a man may be operationally defined by the length of time a man has gone without food, and this definition satisfies the proposition, for the longer a man has gone without food, the more activity that will get him food he is indeed apt to put out.

But this definition of value deals only with a single kind of reward, food, whose value is measured by the degree to which a man has been deprived of it. The problem of definition is more difficult when the theorist has to deal with the situation in which a man has to choose between two kinds of rewards, and the degree of deprivation cannot be used as a measure of value. Thus a sociologist might say: a thirsty Chinese finds tea more valuable than milk, and so, by the proposition cited above, will do more to get tea than to get milk. I

need not point out that this kind of choice among values is of great importance to sociology.

The question then arises how the relative values of tea and milk are to be measured, that is, how *value* in this situation is to be defined. If we rule out the operation of asking the Chinese which he prefers, and many sociologists do rule out this sort of operation as unreliable, what are we left with? Our only way of measuring the relative value of milk and tea to a Chinese is to observe whether he will do more work (or pay more money) to get the one than to get the other. In this case, the proposition we started with becomes, not a proposition in which each of two variables is independently defined, but a proposition like $f = ma$ in mechanics in which one of the variables is only defined implicitly.

Then we may well ask why it is worthwhile introducing the concept of value at all. Why not simply drop it out and keep the empirical proposition: Chinese will do more to get tea than to get milk? This proposition is not a tautology, since both "being Chinese" and "doing more" can be independently and explicitly defined. The trouble is that the conditions leading a man to do more to get one reward than another are infinite in kind and number. "Being Chinese" is one, but so is "being unskilled" or "being out in the rain," and so on. It is impossible to enumerate them all, and new ones are forever being discovered. Under these circumstances, it is convenient to state the high-order proposition: "The more valuable the reward, the more a man will do to get it," and leave the various conditions that create differences in value in particular circumstances to be described by lower-order propositions in the various deductive systems that have the high-order proposition at their head. This procedure secures the advantages of generality, since from the high-order proposition true empirical conclusions may be derived, whether value is defined in terms of deprivation or in terms of such things as being Chinese. This is the procedure Braithwaite has in mind when, discussing the fitting of a symbolic calculus to a deductive system, he writes:

The implicit empirical definition of the theoretical terms in a scientific deductive system consists in the fitting of the calculus to the system from the bottom upwards. This is done by first fitting derived formulae of the calculus to the empirical generalizations which are the lowest-level hypotheses in the deductive system, and then working backwards so that the formulae containing the theoretical terms are interpreted as representing those higher-level hypotheses from which the lowest-level hypotheses logically follow in the scientific deductive system (Braithwaite, 1953, pp. 78–79).

If this procedure is adopted, as Braithwaite points out, "the hypotheses of the theory will be logically deducible from the empirical generalizations which they were put forward to explain" (1953, p. 67). And how, then, can we speak of explanation? On the other hand, the procedure has the advantage of allowing the theory to be extended to take account of empirical generalizations as yet unknown, and this is an important advantage in the present case, since the conditions that may create differences in value may be innumerable. Explicit definition, Braithwaite says, does not allow such extension. His demonstration is long; I urge students to read it for themselves (1953, Ch. 3); only his final statement can be quoted here:

A theory which it is hoped may be expanded in the future to explain more generalizations than it was originally designed to explain must allow more freedom to its theoretical terms than would be given them were they to be logical constructions out of observable entities. A scientific theory which, like all good scientific theories, is capable of growth must be more than an alternative way of describing the generalizations upon which it is based, which is all it would be if its theoretical terms were limited by being explicitly defined (Braithwaite, 1953, p. 76).

The problem of implicit definition comes up again and again in the theories of social science. Thus the *cohesiveness* of a group plays a part in some theories of social psychology similar to the one *value* plays in the example I have used (see Festinger, Schachter, & Back, 1950, p. 164). The issue at stake is also, I think, that of nominal versus real definitions of concepts, which has exercised some sociologists (Bierstedt, 1959; Zetterberg, 1954, p. 30). Thus *cohesiveness* might be defined nominally by the high-order proposition: The more cohesive a group, the more often its members will take part in its activities. This is a proposition similar to the one defining *value* in the sense that there is no single measure of cohesiveness independent of the participation of the members. Instead, various lower-order propositions are brought into the theory, each stating what makes for cohesiveness under particular circumstances: the number of sociometric choices within a group, the value of the rewards obtained from the activities of the group, and the like. In terms of the distinction between nominal and real, these are the real definitions of cohesiveness.

Mathematical Models

The set of propositions that constitute a theory may be represented symbolically by a calculus, and the derivations made according to the rules for the manipulation of the calculus. When the symbols and the rules are those of mathematics, we say that the calculus is a mathematical model of the theory (see Lazarsfeld, 1954; Solomon, 1960). But remember always that a mathematical model, like a theory itself, must contain some contingent propositions (equations), even though they are stated in the language of mathematics. If it contains none, it is mathematics and not a mathematical model of a theory. The usual trouble with mathematical models in sociology is that they contain too few contingent equations to enable them, however beautiful the mathematics, to explain the empirical facts in any detail.

To set up a mathematical model, moreover, it is not enough to translate contingent propositions into mathematical symbols. The calculus must actually be used to derive new propositions. As Braithwaite says:

"No calculus without calculation;" the mere translation of tendency statements into mathematical language (as, for example, in Kurt Lewin's *Principles of Topological Psychology,* 1936) is not sufficient to make a quasi-deductive system out of them. The essence of mathematics is not its symbolism, but its methods of deduction (Braithwaite, 1953, p. 366).

A model, then, is no more than a representation of a theory. The exception to this statement occurs when to the highest-order concepts of the theory may be attributed properties irrelevant to the theory, as when models of chemical theory represented atoms as if they were hard round balls. The model may then become misleading. But I do not think this feature is characteristic of current mathematical models in sociology.

The effort to represent a theory in the form of a mathematical model has many advantages. It forces the theorist to make explicit how his variables are to be defined. It forces him to state the relationships between variables—the functions relating one to another—much more specifically than theories stated in verbal form usually do. The model enables him to avoid the fallacies in making deductions to which reasoning in ordinary language is notoriously subject. Above all, it enables him, in the case of complicated theories, to make deductions, especially new and unsuspected ones, that reasoning in ordinary language would be incapable of attaining at all. Let mathematical models flourish, then, especially those rich in the representation of contingent propositions.

In ending this description of the characteristics of theory let me make one statement as firmly as I can. As an ideal, the nature of theory, of explanation, is no different in the social sciences from what it is in the physical sciences, though some social scientists have talked as if it were. The two fields differ of course in the nature of the propositions that enter their deductive systems but not in the assumption that when they talk about theories deductive systems are what they mean.

THE DIFFICULTIES OF THEORY-CONSTRUCTION IN SOCIOLOGY

There are few theories in sociology—and perhaps no so-called general theories—that meet the definition given above of what a theory ought to be. I turn now to the practical difficulties and intellectual confusions that get in the way of theory-construction in sociology.

Many of the deductive systems in sociology, if spelled out in full, would be long and complicated. In practice, even the best of theorists, to save time and avoid boring their readers, leave out some of the steps in their arguments, take them for granted. The result is that they produce not explanations, but what Hempel (1959, p. 351) calls "explanation sketches." They write out their arguments, moreover, in ordinary discursive English, whose logic is apt to be slippery. The result is that, even when the theorist does have a deductive system latent in his mind, his readers have difficulty working it out for themselves. One remedy for this condition would be to present the theories in mathematical form. But even short of mathematics some measure of formalization would be a great help. At crucial points in his argument let the theorist state as precisely as he can what he believes to be the general propositions of his theory and draw attention to them by numbers or italics. Let him then spell out the steps in logic by which he draws empirical conclusions from the general propositions. No single procedure would do more to eliminate or resolve our interminable arguments and confusions about sociological theories. We might at least be able to decide what we were arguing about and, especially, whether we were dealing with deductive systems at all.

Some sociologists sound as if they do not know what a theory is. If, in what follows, I single out Talcott Parsons as an example of confusion, I do so only because he is the most famous of contemporary theorists, so I cannot be accused of hitting a man when he is down. In his most recent work (Parsons, Shils, Naegele & Pitts, 1961, vol. I, p. 32), he seems to be taking a more sensible view of theory, but his earlier doctrine may have led some of us astray. He wrote: "A theoretical system in the present sense is a body of logically interdependent generalized concepts of empirical reference" (Parsons et al., 1949, p. 17); and Robert Merton echoed him by saying that "the term *sociological theory* refers to logically interconnected conceptions which are limited and modest in scope, rather than all-embracing and grandiose" (Merton, 1957, p. 5). The two men differed in degree of modesty but not in their view of theory as "logically interdependent concepts."

I shall return to logic later, but what about the notion of theory as consisting of concepts? It seems to assume that a conceptual scheme is a theory. Concepts and their definitions are certainly part of a theory, but they are not sufficient by themselves to constitute a theory. Concepts are names for properties of nature, and a theory does not even begin to exist until propositions are stated about contingent relationships of the general form x varies as y between the properties. The reason is obvious: a theory is a deductive system, and no deductions can be made from concepts alone; propositions are absolutely necessary. All sociologists should know this, but it still badly needs saying.

None of this means that a conceptual scheme is useless. A scheme with clear criteria may allow investigators to identify instances of significant properties of nature, and the elaboration of such a scheme may be a useful preliminary to the construction of a theory. It may accordingly be called theoretical work; but it is not theory per se.

Much official sociological theory consists in fact of concepts and their definitions: it provides the dictionary of a language that possesses no sentences. Parsons is particularly good at practicing what he preaches. It would be going too far to say that his theories contain no propositions. He often slips at the lower or empirical levels. But at the higher ones, and since he claims to be "general" this means the very highest, his theories seem to me to consist largely of conceptual schemes. In Zetterberg's (1958) term, he is a "dimensionist." In fairness to Parsons it must be said that his schemes include most of the sorts of terms that need to enter into sociological theory. All that is lacking are contingent propositions about their relationships.

Let me now consider the claim that the concepts of a theory are "logically interdependent." What do statements like this mean? If they mean that lower-order propositions in a theory can be deduced under the rules of logic from the higher-order ones, then all is well. But if they mean that logic enters in any other way they are in trouble. The highest-order propositions in a theory are not "logically" related to one another. Though in my example proposition 3 can be logically derived from the conjuncture of propositions 1 and 2, the two latter are not themselves "logically interdependent." More important, the contingent relationships between concepts in a theory are not "logically necessary" like those of mathematics. Nature, if you like, and not logic makes them what they are.

What Parsons has in mind when he speaks of the "logical interdependence" of concepts seems to be this: concepts may be names for classes of observations, and Parsons often claims that his classifications "are exhaustive of the relevant logical possibilities" at a particular level of analysis (Parsons, 1951, p. 66). But anyone can always set up a logically exhaustive conceptual scheme in this sense. What he does is to define a class X and then say that everything else falls into the class Non-X, giving each of the classes a name, and then he has a logically exhaustive conceptual scheme. He can readily complicate the scheme, making it a fourfold or an *n*-fold one, by intersecting the first two classes with new ones like Y and Non-Y and calling the result a paradigm if he likes. But none of this work makes the conceptual scheme a theory, for it implies no contingent relationships between properties of nature. Only if, for instance, actual instances of X turned out also to be instances of Y, or instances of Non-X, instances of Non-Y would such a relationship be implied. You can make a conceptual scheme as exhaustive as you like and in any way you like, but it still remains only a conceptual scheme.

Yet Parsons claims he can make deductions or derivations from his conceptual scheme. In *Economy and Society,* for instance, he and Smelser say that their first chapter "established a presumption in favor of our thesis that economic theory is a special case of the general theory of social systems" (Parsons & Smelser, 1956, p. 296). They go on: "This presumption rested on two grounds: (1) the point-for-point correspondence of the logical structures of the two conceptual schemes, and (2) the fact that the goal of the economy is *less general* than societal goals." Now there is just one condition that must be met if one theory is to be called a special case of another: the propositions of the special theory must be derived in a deductive system from the propositions of the other. It is in this sense that the theory of the tides may be called a special case of Newtonian mechanics. Parsons and Smelser have not met this condition. Economic theory certainly possesses propositions, but Parsons and Smelser have not derived a single one of them through any deductive system. Instead they seem to feel that a special theory is derived from a general one if some "correspondence" can be found—and it is seldom hard to find—between the concepts of the general theory and those of the special one. But it is the deduction of propositions, not the translation of words, that counts. As for their second argument, it amounts to saying that a theory of the whole ought to be more general than a theory of a part. Indeed it ought to be, but the problem remains of demonstrating that it is.

Even when sociological theories do state relationships between properties of nature, they often do not state very much. To say that there is some relationship, but not to go any further, to allow the propositions to take the form that *x* is some function of *y* without further specifying the function, is to say something but not much that can take its place in a deductive system, for from the conjuncture of such propositions little can be deduced. Thus, Parsons (1951, p. 38) puts forward a "double contingency" paradigm of social behavior: when two men are interacting, the actions of each are rewards or punishments (sanctions) for the actions of the other. To say this is to say that variables characterizing the behavior of each man are functions of variables characterizing the behavior of the other. And to say this is certainly to say something: It is, I think, the statement from which our understanding of social behavior begins. But it is not to say much that can take its place in a theory. Only when the proposition is strengthened so as to say, for instance, that the more often the activity of one man rewards the activity of the other, the more often the other emits the activity—only when some beginning is made at specifying the functions relating the variables has anything been said from which conclusions can be drawn in a deductive system. When it does not consist of conceptual schemes, much sociological theory consists of statements like this one of Parsons. Again, it is theoretical work—I call it descriptive work—without being theory.

The weakest propositions properly entering a deductive system state, like the one cited above, that *x* varies directly as *y,* that *x* is some monotonically increasing function of *y.* For more precise explanation and prediction we should like, of course, to go further in specifying the function and say, for instance, that $x = y^2$ or $x = \log y$. But generally we are unable to do so. In practice we tend to assume that x is a linear function of y until the testing of conclusions drawn from the proposition shows that the assumption is untenable. Even then we are more apt to correct the deductive system by introducing new variables (factors) than by changing the form of the function.

A more serious problem with sociological propositions than that the relationship between two variables is only very roughly specified is that the propositions are suspected of holding good only under certain conditions. It is not just that the proposition holds good "other things equal," but that what the "other things" are and where they are "equal" is unknown. Braithwaite (1953, pp. 361–366) calls such propositions *tendency statements*. The use of tendency statements in a deductive system can lead to a sort of difficulty that may be illustrated from electricity. Suppose we were studying electrical circuits for the first time and had reason to believe the two separate propositions that current, I, tended to vary directly with electromotive force, E, and that E in turn tended to vary with resistance, R. We might be tempted to conclude that I varied directly with R; and we should be wrong, for the facts are summed up in the single proposition

$$I = \frac{E}{R}.$$

That is, I varies as E only under the condition that R is constant, and E with R only under the condition that I is constant.

Many sociological propositions, particularly those made by induction from observations in the field where the effects of "third variables" are uncontrolled, are tendency statements. Some people claim that tendency propositions from field research should not even be stated. They are quite wrong, for a proposition not stated is a proposition that cannot be retested, and unless it is tested and retested, the conditions in which it holds good or fails to do so cannot be discovered. Braithwaite (1953) suggests just this policy with regard to tendency statements. Construct a deductive system in which they are provisionally treated as if they were not tendency statements but fully general. Test the lowest-order propositions, the empirical conclusions of the system, against observation. Both the successes and the failures of such tests will provide information about the unknown limiting conditions. This is what sensible sociologists actually do.

GENERAL THEORIES

I turn now to the characteristics of some, but not all, actual sociological theories. Most areas of investigation in sociology have called themselves theoretical. Examples are organization theory, role theory, and reference-group theory. In accordance with this practice, there is no reason why we should not speak of demographic theory instead of demography or stratification theory instead of stratification, and we probably soon will, since "theory" is definitely an "O.K." word. The practice is justified in the sense that investigators in no area of sociology are content with "mere data collection." All try to explain empirical findings by deriving them under specified given conditions from more general propositions. Indeed some of these theories in particular areas come closer to meeting my requirements of what a theory should be than do some of the grander, all-embracing efforts.

But if I undertook to review all of these theories I should be trespassing on the substantive fields of sociology covered in other chapters of this Handbook. Accordingly I shall confine myself to "general" theories, theories whose highest-order propositions are believed to be very general indeed. I shall describe and criticize the distinguishing features of these theories, or rather, in some cases, the features I think they would have if they had ever been made fully explicit as deductive systems, which they have not.

Normative Theories

There are two classes of general theory: the normative and the nonnormative. There is no good special term in use to distinguish the latter from the former. To speak very roughly, normative theories explain how men ought to behave if they are to accomplish certain results, and nonnormative theories explain how they actually do behave. Of the normative theories there are again two classes, the one-sided and the two- or many-sided. The one-sided theories explain how one man or group ought to behave in order to accomplish certain results from other men and groups who are, so to speak, simply behaving, that is, behaving nonnormatively. Theories of applied sociology fall into this class. Their effectiveness obviously depends on the existence of good nonnormative theories. Thus the design of an effective program for reducing juvenile delinquency obviously depends on good nonnormative theories of group behavior, social stratification, urban sociology, and others. Since the applications of sociology are part of the subject-matter of the different substantive fields, I shall say no more about one-sided normative theories here.

In two- or many-sided normative theories two or more persons are assumed to be behaving normatively toward one another, that is, in accordance with some standard of rationality defined in the theory; and the theory proves a variety of propositions about what might be the outcomes of such behavior. Of these theories, the most famous is the Theory of Games as developed by Von Neumann and Morgenstern (1944) and their followers. This theory began by considering certain kinds of games between two players, games in the sense that they have rules allowing the players only a limited number of moves at each point in the game, some of the moves, perhaps, being determined by chance, as by the throw of dice. The theory also began by considering zero-sum games in the sense that what one

player wins, in terms of the values formally at stake, the other loses. From these assumptions the game-theorist is able to prove mathematically certain theorems: for instance, the Von Neumann–Morgenstern theorem that for each player there is a strategy that will minimize his maximum expected loss. This is obvious in the case of tick-tack-toe. What Von Neumann and Morgenstern did (and it was a great accomplishment) was to show that it was general for this class of games.

Great claims have been made for the contribution the Theory of Games will make to other sociological theory. There is no doubt that it has sharpened our wits, and some of the techniques by which its arguments are presented, such as the outcome-matrix, are convenient also for presenting some of the propositions of social psychology (Thibaut & Kelley, 1959).

But for the moment I think its further contribution is limited. The reason is not that its application is restricted to two persons or collectivities: it can be extended to more, as in the theory of coalitions. Nor is the reason that most social behavior can hardly be considered a zero-sum game. For the theory has also been extended to include non-zero-sum and cooperative games, in which, under the rules, both players can come out with a profit (Luce & Raiffa, 1957, chs. 5 & 6). Here the theory is largely concerned with devising proposals according to which the profits might reasonably be divided among the players.

The chief difficulties seem rather different. First, the Theory of Games as at present developed has no place for communication between players during the game itself, except insofar as the moves themselves may be considered communications. Thus, the players in a game like chess need not talk to one another but only watch the board. In the theory of some non-zero-sum games, communication is included, though only before the game itself begins, in order to allow the players to agree on some rule for dividing the profits; and the theory has nothing to say about the process by which agreement is reached through persuasion or bargaining. There is no reason why Game Theory should not be extended to games in which the moves are verbal and intended to persuade the players, but this has been little done so far. Yet a large part of actual human behavior consists of verbal communications.

The second reason is perhaps the more important. Game Theory is a theory all right but, as a normative theory, it is a noncontingent one; its general propositions about the rationality of the players and the forms of the game are assumed a priori. That is, the theory could have been developed without any observation of actual human behavior. If, of course, it could be shown that the players in actual social games did in fact behave, in some approximation, according to the assumptions of Game Theory, then the assumptions would become contingent propositions. It may be that men do so behave in some situations, precisely in those that most resemble the games of Game Theory. It may even be that, as they read more about Game Theory, they will more often act in this way in the future than thev have in the past. But for the moment we know little about the degree to which actual behavior corresponds to the normative assumptions of the theory. Game Theory is still vigorously growing; sociologists should keep their eye on it while remaining skeptical whether it will soon help them much with their own job, which is empirical research and the construction of contingent theories.

Nonnormative Theories

I turn now to nonnormative general theories of which I think there are three main kinds: structural, functional, and psychological. I shall also have something to say about historical explanations, though I do not believe they constitute a distinct type of theory. I warn the reader that I do not necessarily use these words in some of the senses in which they have been used in sociology.

Structural theories explain the existence of some element of social behavior, however "element" may be defined, by its relations to other elements and the relations of these elements to one another in some configuration, a social structure or social system. In functional theories, the highest-order propositions say that a society or other social unit will not survive, remain in equilibrium, or reach its goal unless a certain element or combination of elements of social behavior occurs in the unit. In psychological theories the highest-order propositions say that some variable in the behavior of individual men as members of a species—not the behavior of societies or groups as such—is a more or less specific function of some other variable in the behavior of individual men or of the physical environment. I do not think that any one of these types of theories often occurs in its pure form in sociological writings; it is usually mixed with other types.

Structural Theories

There is no reason in principle why structural theories, which may also be called field theories, should not be used to explain the existence of any feature of any social configuration, but in sociology they have most often been used, although in sketchy form, to explain an institution as part of a social structure or social system. An institution is a rule or set of rules for behavior, conformity to which is rewarded to some degree and nonconformity punished. Structural explanations have been least sketchy in the field of social anthropology, where the following might be an example:

1. Societies that have matrilocal or avunculocal rules of residence are organized in matrilineages.

2. Societies that have avunculocal rules vest jural authority over ego in his mother's brothers.

3. Therefore, societies that vest jural au-

thority over ego in his mother's brothers are organized in matrilineages.

4. The Trobrianders vest jural authority over ego in his mother's brothers.

5. Therefore, the Trobrianders are organized in matrilineages.

As usual, let us not worry about whether this explanation is true or about the meanings of the technical terms. Let us look only at the form of the explanation. I call it structural because its highest-order propositions (1 and 2) are general propositions about the relationships between elements in a universe of configurations (structures) of elements. In the present case, the elements are institutions and the configurations are kinship systems. This is the type of explanation social scientists have in mind when they assume, which they cannot often demonstrate, that every institution in a social system is related to all the others in the sense that if one changed the others would all change too. Then the nature of any one institution is explained by its relations with the others and by the relations of these with one another.

Now let us look at a somewhat more complex possibility. Suppose we could treat kinship systems as varying continuously along a definite number of institutional dimensions, such as "degree of matrilinearity," and that we could state a series of propositions (equations) about the relations between the variables. The propositions might well be more complicated than number 2 above, the relation between any two variables being conditioned by the values of a third, etc., so that many of the variables might enter into more than one of the equations. Then the highest-order propositions in the theory we were constructing would be relatively many in number and all (this is to say the same thing) at the same level of generality, the institutional level.

A number of concrete kinship systems, each characterized by a set of different values of the variables, would satisfy the system of propositions. If we had done our

work well, they would all do so. Then if we had reason to know of a particular kinship system, like that of the Trobrianders, what the actual values of a limited number of the variables were, if these values were given as in proposition 4 above, then we could solve the system of propositions to get the values of the other variables. In this case, any one "other" feature of the Trobriand system would be explained in the sense that it could be derived from the system of propositions together with the given values.

Many sciences besides anthropology have dreamed of this type of explanation. It is the one Cuvier, for instance, had in mind when he asserted that if he possessed, say, the jaw-bone of an extinct animal he could reconstruct the rest of the animal. No rigorous structural explanation has ever, I think, been carried out in social science, but it is the type of explanation some social scientists sound as if they were groping toward, and, accordingly, I have described here what I think they would get if they groped successfully.

Structural explanation is a perfectly valid type of explanation: its propositions may be contingent and its conclusions may follow from the other propositions in a deductive system. But even at the present stage of development in social science it may not turn out to be the most general type of explanation. In my terms, it may be open at the top.

It may be possible to show that some, though at present certainly only a few, of the structural propositions like numbers 1 and 2 above are in turn derivable from still more general propositions of the psychological sort—more general in that they stand high in deductive systems that explain other features of human behavior than the interrelations of institutions. Thus Homans and Schneider (1955) tried to show that a structural proposition about the relation between the loci of jural authority and the types of unilateral cross-cousin marriage could be psychologically explained. But it must be confessed that their explanation is not generally accepted (Needham, 1962).

Structural explanations, if we had them fully worked out, would be valid explanations but probably not the most general possible. In this sense I call them compatible with either functional or psychological explanations, to whose ideal types I now turn.

Functional Theories

The word function has been used in so many different senses in theoretical work that I must explain what I do not mean by "functional theories" before I can explain what I do mean (Nagel, 1961, pp. 398–446, 520–535). First, the fact that a theory contains propositions of the form "x is some function of y" in the mathematical sense of the word function does not make it a functional theory in my sense of the word, for the propositions of all real theories can be cast in this form. Nor is a theory functional that contains statements like "the function of institutions a, b, and c is to maintain institution x," when all the statement means is that institution x does not appear in a social system unless a, b, and c do too, that x is a function of a, b, and c, for this is what I have called a structural proposition.

Second, a functional theory is not the same as "functional analysis." Analysis is the word sociologists give to whatever it is they are doing when they do not want to be more specific but do want a fancy word. Sociologists are carrying out "functional analysis" when, in the course of their investigations, they examine the consequences of a particular item of social behavior or the results of a society's having adopted, for whatever reason, some particular institution. They then may call these consequences the "functions" of the behavior or the institution, further classifying them as "intended" or "unintended," as "manifest" or "latent," or as in some sense "good" or "bad" (functional or dysfunctional) consequences. Kingsley Davis (1959) said that functional analysis cannot be distinguished from ordinary sociological analysis, that we are all functionalists now. He is right in the sense that a sociologist would be a fool not to examine the consequences of social behavior.

But to say that an item of behavior *has* consequences and that a sociologist ought to look for them is not the same thing as saying that the item exists *because* its consequences are of a particular sort. Only when the latter kind of statement is made does functional analysis begin to become functional theory, that is, functional explanation. Until then functional analysis is a rule of method (Look for consequences!) which may result in the discovery of true propositions, but the propositions themselves have yet to be explained.

Third, to say that an item of behavior occurs or an institution exists because its consequences are "good" (functional) for individual men is not enough to make this a functional theory in my sense of the word. In my terms, as we shall see, this is a psychological theory, and not a very adequate one at that, for men will do many things that are not "good" for them, such as smoking cigarettes, so long as they find the results sufficiently rewarding (valuable). Only when the occurrence of an item of behavior or the existence of an institution is explained by arguing that it is "good" not for individuals but for a society or some smaller social group as such are we in the presence of a functional theory. Merton (1957, p. 52) lumped individual and societal functionalism together under the rubric of functional theory. I think it well to keep them separate, because the highest-order propositions in psychological theories are in fact very different from what they are in functional ones.

Having eliminated what I do not mean by functional theories, let me turn to the characteristics of the latter as now defined. A good place to begin is Radcliffe-Brown's (1952) classic definition of *function*:

The *function* of any recurrent activity, such as

the punishment of a crime, or a funeral ceremony, is the part it plays in the social life as a whole and therefore the contribution it makes to the maintenance of the structural continuity. The concept of function as here defined thus involves the notion of a *structure* consisting of a *set of relations* amongst *unit entities,* the *continuity* of the structure being maintained by a *life-process* made up of the activities of the constituent units (Radcliffe-Brown, 1952, p. 180).

Note that this definition combines at least two sorts of ideas: a notion of structure, "relations between entities"—between, for instance, the institutions of a social system—and a notion of function per se, "contribution to the maintenance of continuity"—for instance, the continuity of a society. This is characteristic of many functional theories, which are accordingly often called "structural-functional."

Radcliffe-Brown's (1952) statement is in form a definition, and, as we know, definitions are not theories. Let me therefore set up a deductive system that will display the characteristic features of functional theories. Radcliffe-Brown spoke of "the punishment of a crime," and my example will show how a functionalist might elaborate on Durkheim's (1947, p. 108) famous statement that the punishment of a crime has more important societal effects on the innocent than on the criminal himself.

1. If a society is to maintain its structural continuity, its members must conform to its norms.

2. Its members' conformity to norms is maintained by their expressing this horror collectively.

3. Their horror of nonconformity is maintained by their expressing this horror collectively.

4. The punishment of criminals, i.e., nonconformists, is the means of expressing this horror collectively.

5. Therefore, a society that maintains its structural continuity is one in which criminals are punished.

6. The Bongo are a society that maintains its structural continuity.

7. Therefore, criminals are punished among the Bongo.

The Bongo, incidentally, are a fictitious society.

Aside from the fact that proposition 1 is almost a truism, this explanation contains obvious weaknesses. It does not consider how many members "must" conform and how much. They cannot all conform or there would be no criminals to keep up the conformity of the rest. Also is the punishment of criminals the only means by which the horror of nonconformity is maintained? Functionalists try to deal with this problem through the doctrine of "functional alternatives"— different institutions that can perform the same function for a society. But I shall not dwell on these difficulties, which do not seem to me central to the problem of functionalism.

What, then, are the decisive characteristics of a theory of this sort? The *explicandum* (proposition 7) is an ordinary low-order empirical statement that a particular society possesses a particular kind of institution. It is the same sort of proposition as the one about the Trobrianders' being matrilineally organized, which I used in illustrating a structural theory. Sociological theories do not differ in what they explain but in how they explain it. Proposition 6 is also presumed to be a low-order empirical proposition: some anthropologist must have observed that a group of people who call themselves the Bongo continue to exist at least for the time being.

More interesting are the higher-order propositions, which are of two kinds. The first, represented by propositions 2, 3, and 4, are statements, in Radcliffe-Brown's (1952) terms, of relations between unit-entities, actually between types of social behavior: "horror of nonconformity" and "the punishment of criminals." I have stated these as if they were fully general, holding good of all social behavior. The deductive system might also be reconstructed so as to treat any one of them as holding good of only one type of society. In other types, the horror of nonconformity, for instance, might be maintained by other means than the punishment of criminals. In either case, these propositions could perfectly well take their place in structural theories; they are not distinctively functional. Finally, they could perhaps themselves be explained by psychological theory.

The second kind of proposition is represented by numbers 1 and 5. These are general propositions presumed to hold good of all social systems and stating one or more of the conditions under which a social system can "maintain its structural continuity" or "survive." It is the presence in deductive systems, implicitly or explicitly, of this kind of high-order proposition that makes the systems distinctively "functional." The existence of a particular institution in a particular society is explained by the function it performs in maintaining that society. A functional theory in this sense is also a "final-cause" or teleological theory in that it explains an institution by its consequences for a society rather than by its antecedents, the actual "efficient causes" that brought it into existence, which are left unexplained.

If, as I believe, functional theories provide unsatisfactory explanations in sociology, the reason must lie in their propositions like number 1 above, for these are the only propositions that are distinctively "functional." One difficulty is that of defining terms like "maintenance of the structural continuity" of a society. A society can maintain its structural continuity for many centuries in the sense that it is called by the same name, that its members reproduce themselves, and that it preserves its independence, while its institutions change by slow degrees, but in the long run markedly, from what they were in the beginning. Another way of putting the matter is: no method has been proposed for measuring the variable "degree of maintenance of structural continuity." Under these circumstances, a proposition containing this term becomes so weak that nothing definite can be derived from it.

For certain kinds of social groups it is conceivable that some precise measure could

be developed of the degree to which a group as a whole was successful in attaining its goals. Thus, the measure of success in industrial or commercial firms might be the profits of a firm as a percentage of capital. Then the highest-order proposition in a functional theory explaining particular features of the firm's organization might be a statement of the conditions that must be satisfied if the firm were to make a profit. But I do not know that such a proposition has actually been stated and used in a deductive system.

Another solution of the problem of defining "maintenance of the structural continuity" would be to state a proposition (equation) that the variables characterizing a social system would have to satisfy if the system were to be considered in equilibrium. The model would be provided by the science of mechanics, where some general equilibrium equation like D'Alembert's principle may be included if convenient as one of the system of equations to be solved for the values of the variables (Mach, 1942, pp. 421-434-. An equivalent proposition in sociology could be used as one of the propositions in a structural theory. It could be used—if we had it. In spite of the endless discussion of the "equilibrium concept" in sociology, a discussion to which I myself have contributed too much (Homans, 1950, pp. 301-308), no such equilibrium proposition (not concept) has ever been both stated and rigorously used in a sociological deductive system. Unless one is both stated and used. I consider any further discussion of equilibrium to be wasted breath.

Some sociologists have tried in effect to strengthen the highest-order propositions in a functional theory by substituting "survival." which can presumably be a matter of observation. for the undefinable term "maintenance of the structural continuity." Then the propositions take the form "certain conditions must be satisfied if a society is to survive." Thus, some sociologists talk of the "functional prerequisites for the survival of a society" (Aberle, Cohen, Davis, Levy &

Sutton, 1950). When so strengthened these propositions run into a new kind of problem —the problem of their status as contingent propositions.

Let me say at this point that a functional theory is not unsatisfactory just because it is a "final cause" theory. In biology there are plenty of "final cause" theories that meet all the conditions of being valid theories (Braithwaite, 1953, Ch. 10). Consider the following explanation why Canada geese fly south in winter.

1. If a species is to survive, its members (enough of them) must eat.

2. Canada geese nest in the Arctic in the summer, but cannot get enough to eat there in the winter.

3. Yet Canada geese are a surviving species.

4. Therefore, the geese must go south in the winter to places where they can get food.

5. Flying is their method of moving long distances.

6. Therefore Canada geese fly south in the winter.

I submit that this explanation runs more or less parallel to functional explanation in sociology. Its highest-order proposition states a condition that must be met if a collectivity is to survive and makes no reference, for instance, to the motivations of individual geese. It is also, of course, a "final cause" theory, and for that reason many ornithologists would not be satisfied with it. The geese, for instance, do not wait to fly south until their northern feeding grounds freeze over, and the ornithologists would want to look for the efficient causes: how certain stimuli actually started the gaggles of geese moving on their way. I claim, nevertheless, that the explanation is perfectly valid—it meets my requirements for being a deductive system—and that we should be wholly justified in using it to explain why geese fly south, especially until we had something better, something that would explain more of the details of the phenomenon.

How then does it differ from functional explanation in sociology? It differs in the status of the higher-order propositions. In the ornithological explanation these are clearly contingent propositions: one could carry out experiments to see whether geese survive without eating and whether they can get enough to eat in the Arctic in winter. The same sort of proposition could also be tested for human societies, and indeed from such propositions important conclusions about human society can be drawn, though they are insufficient to explain its features in any detail.

But functional theorists in sociology do not confine themselves to stating such biological conditions for the survival of a society. They also state purely "social" conditions such as the one I used in illustration (the members' conformity to the norms), and the contingent status of these propositions is much more dubious.

The criteria that define a society and accordingly those that define its survival, turn out to be far less clear than might appear at first glance. Thus, the Roman Empire, as a governmental institution, has certainly not survived, but the society of Italy has otherwise maintained its structural continuity intact up to the present time. Yet there are a few groups we should usually call societies that have certainly not survived since all their members have died out. The Tasmanian aborigines are one example. Others, like the Ona, appear to be in train to dying out. Now if we look at our information on these societies and run down one of the lists specifying the functional prerequisites for survival (Aberle, Cohen, Davis, Levy, & Sutton, 1950), we find that these societies met all the social prerequisites on the list. Thus, their members conformed to some degree to the norms of the society— perhaps that was just the trouble. How *much* did they conform? That is another question and one irrelevant to the present discussion, for functional theorists never tell us to what degree a society must possess any of the functional prerequisites on their lists. The societies in question did meet the social prerequisites in some degree and yet failed to survive. Why? They were undone by gunfire, firewater, disease, or some combination of the three. They were undone, if you like, by failure to meet the biological prerequisites, not the social ones.

One may regard functional propositions like number 1 above as not supported by evidence. Some of the conclusions that may be drawn from them are true, but some are false: e.g., that the Tasmanians are a surviving society. One may also regard them as inherently not supportable. In either case, sociologists who implicitly or explicitly use them in deductive systems are treating them as noncontingent, as if experience were irrelevant to their truth or falsity. Accordingly the deductive systems in question are not by my definition theories at all. This does not mean that contingent functional propositions in sociology could not conceivably be devised. It is conceivable that they could be, but no such propositions are at present in sight, or anywhere near it, and current functional theories are nontheories because they are noncontingent.

Psychological Theories

I turn now to the third class of nonnormative general theories, the psychological. These are theories in which the highest-order propositions are statements about the behavior of men as members of a species and not statements about the interrelations of institutions or about the conditions some group or society must meet in order to survive or remain in equilibrium. By way of illustration let me set down a psychological explanation of the institution for which I gave a functional one (see p. 964)—the punishment of criminals.

1. The more rewarding men find the results of an action, the more likely they are to take this action.

2. Men who are threatened are likely to find rewarding any action that hurts the threatener.

3. A person who violates a norm of a society, that is, a criminal, threatens the other men who are members of the society.

4. Punishment is, by definition, whatever hurts the criminal.

5. Therefore, men who are members of a society are likely to punish criminals.

How does this explanation differ from a functional one? It does not deny that the punishment of criminals may have further consequences for the behavior of men, such as an increased horror for the crime, or that the increased horror may have further favorable consequences for the society as such. But it has nothing to say about consequences of this sort. Instead it explains punishment by its antecedent, the threat the criminal poses to the members of the society (proposition 3), and by two propositions (1 and 2) about the characteristics of the behavior of men as members of a species and not just as members of a particular society. But I must remind the reader of the peculiar status (see p. 954) of the term *rewarding* (*valuable*) in proposition 1.

I call this a psychological explanation simply because propositions like these are most often formulated and tested by persons who call themselves psychologists. I shall not try to list all the essential psychological propositions here, especially as psychologists might not agree on what they are (Homans, 1961, Ch. 4). The list should certainly include propositions about how men's behavior is affected by the value of the rewards they obtain and by their degree of success in obtaining these rewards. It should also include propositions about how values themselves are acquired. It should include propositions about how men perceive the circumstances in which they act, and about the kinds of circumstances that are apt to release emotional behavior. Many of the propositions could no doubt be shown to follow as corollaries from a few more general ones. But note: to call an explanation psychological does not entail the adoption of any particular one of the many systems of psychological theory.

I claim that sociologists, even when they

are sounding most "functional," use psychological explanation all the time, though they more often use it implicitly than explicitly, because propositions like numbers 1 and 2 are so obvious that they can afford to take them for granted. Let me use an example from our sister science, history. Some of the same issues over explanation have come up in history as have come up in sociology with this difference: the historians do not worry about what kind of explanation they shall use but whether they have any explanation at all. In the course of this controversy one philosopher (Hempel, 1959) said just what I should have said, that an explanation would include general propositions or, as he called them, laws. Commenting on this view Scriven (1959) wrote: "Suppose we wish to explain why William the Conqueror never invaded Scotland. The answer, as usually given, is simple enough; he had no desire for the lands of the Scottish nobles, and he secured his northern borders by defeating Malcolm, King of Scotland, in battle and exacting homage. There seem to be no laws involved in this explanation" (Scriven, 1959, p. 444).

Scriven says that this *is* an explanation and that it does not contain any general laws. I claim that formally it is not an explanation just because it contains no general law. It is not an explanation because, with the propositions as explicitly given, no deductive system can be constructed. But if a major premise, which is now lacking, were supplied, a deductive system could be constructed, and the major premise would turn out to be a psychological proposition. I contend that the completed explanation would run something like this:

1. The more rewarding men find the results of an action, the more likely they are to take this action.

2. William the Conqueror was a man.

3. Therefore, the more rewarding William found the results of an action, the more likely he was to take this action.

4. In the given circumstances, he did not find the conquest of Scotland rewarding.

5. Therefore, he was unlikely to take action that would win him Scotland.

You see how obvious I can get if I try? The point is that the explanation as given by Scriven (1959) can be turned into a real explanation only by supplying a missing major premise (proposition 1). The major premise, moreover, is a psychological proposition. In sociology as well as in history, it is our major premises that we are most apt to leave unstated, particularly when they are psychological. We leave them unstated not only because they are obvious, but also because they are so obvious that we cannot bring ourselves to take them seriously. In the social sciences, unlike other sciences, the general laws are the ones men have always known most about, though they have not always formulated them as a psychologist would—and so they can hardly believe that they *are* general laws. Laws are things that have to be discovered; something lying around in plain sight comes too cheap to be a law.

I believe that, in view of the deficiencies in functional theory, the only type of theory in sociology that stands any chance of becoming a general one is a psychological theory, in the sense that the deductive systems by which we explain social behavior would, if completed, contain among their highest-order propositions one or more of those I call psychological. The time may come when they will lose their place at the top, when they in turn will be shown to be derivable from still more general propositions such as those of physiology. But the time has not come yet, and psychological propositions remain our most general ones.

What do I mean when I say that our deductive systems would "if completed" contain psychological propositions? Go back to my first illustration of a deductive system (p. 951). That system was perfectly valid as far as it went, but it was open at the top. Its highest-order proposition related the suicide rate to the degree of individualism. But I think that it would be possible to construct a convincing explanation why this relationship itself should exist and that the explanation would contain psychological propositions. In the same way it has been shown that propositions about the characteristics of small groups can be psychologically explained (Homans, 1961).

I said earlier that I did not think structural explanations containing, for instance, propositions about the relationships between institutions in social systems would turn out to be general explanations in sociology, though they, too, were valid as far as they went. The reason is again that some, though certainly not all, of the structural propositions can themselves be explained psychologically (Murdock, 1949, p. xvi).

An example is the study by Homans and Schneider (1955) of the two forms of unilateral cross-cousin marriage: preferred marriage with father's sister's daughter, preferred marriage with mother's brother's daughter. We did not spell out our argument in full (in this respect we sinned as much as other sociologists), but in effect it ran somewhat like this. We started with the assumption that the use of punishment as a method of control would provoke in some degree reactions of fear and avoidance in the persons controlled. This is a psychological proposition for which there is good evidence. We further argued that persons in authority over others in primitive societies would be apt to use some degree of control by punishment. Then, by a series of steps too long to be reproduced here, marriage and authority would be kept separate in the sense that ego would have some tendency to marry a cross-cousin on the opposite side of the family from where authority over him lay. We finally predicted that one form of unilateral cross-cousin marriage would occur in societies where authority over ego was vested in the father, the other where it was vested in mother's brother. This hypothesis received strong statistical support.

In the long run Schneider and Homans (1955) may turn out to be wrong. But no one so far has advanced hypotheses that

will take care of more of the cross-cultural variance in the data than ours will. And the deductive system that explained our tested hypothesis contained at least one high-order psychological proposition. We were not, of course, able to explain everything. We were not able to explain why some societies should vest authority in the father and some in the mother's brother, nor why unilateral cross-cousin marriage should exist at all. But with these things given, we were able to explain psychologically why each of the two forms of marriage was apt to occur in certain societies and not in others.

In these cases and in others, the psychological explanations seem to be the most general, in the sense that the higher-order propositions appearing in them, besides explaining, for instance, the structural propositions themselves, can also be used to explain a wide variety of other empirical propositions about social behavior including those of elementary economics as well as those of experimental psychology. It would be easy to jump to the conclusion, as I do, that all the empirical propositions characteristic of sociology could in principle be reduced to psychology. But what is "principle"? The fact is that the reduction has not often been actually carried out, and in many cases it probably never will be if only because the necessary information is lacking. Whatever it can do in principle, psychology cannot now in fact explain every social phenomenon. Under these circumstances, "principle" is a matter of faith.

Many sociologists do not feel comfortable with psychological reductionism, and so I had better discuss some of the common objections. The position taken here does not assume that men are isolated individuals. It is wholly compatible with the doctrine that human behavior is and has always been social. What it does assume is that the general propositions of psychology, the "law of effect," for instance, do not change when the source of reward for an action changes from being, say, the physical en vironment to being another human. The composition effects, the ways in which the propositions work out to produce a concrete result, are much more complicated when the actions of each of two or more men reward the actions of the others, but the propositions themselves do not change. When we say that the whole of social life is more than the sum of its parts, the actions of individuals, all we are referring to is the complexity of the composition effects.

The position taken here does not assume a "great man" theory of sociology, though some great men have made more difference than sociologists, many of whom know little history, are always ready to admit. It does not assume that to explain sociological phenomena one must account for the behavior of every single individual concerned. That would certainly be impossible, and in any event psychological theory certainly predicts that large numbers of individuals placed in similar circumstances, say members of a middle class in a period of economic expansion, are likely to behave in similar ways. The fact that many sociologists necessarily treat many of the phenomena they study as collective in this sense does not make the explanation of these phenomena any less psychological.

The position taken here does not assume that "human nature is the same the world over" if this old saw means that concrete human behavior is the same. It is obviously not the same but varies greatly over many dimensions. What the position does assume is something rather different: that a few general propositions hold good of human behavior, from which, under a great variety of different given conditions including those passed on to the men of a society from their ancestors, a great variety of different forms of concrete behavior follow. This capacity to explain the many through the few is the mark of a good theory.

Finally, though this is hardly a theoretical issue, the position taken here does not rob sociologists of their subject-matter. There is nothing in it to prevent sociologists, other than some kinds of theorists, from doing what they have always done, especially as the psychologists will not be doing it. Let them go on producing theories like the one of Durkheim's (1927) that I started with. The fact that their theories may be open at the top, that their highest-order propositions may ultimately be derivable from psychological propositions, does not make the theories invalid. Indeed I see no great reason why any sociologist should worry at all about "general" theory, except under one condition. If sociologists come along, as they do, telling me that theirs is a general theory and that it is structural-functional, I am a mere dog in the manger, though I may be correct, when I simply deny there is any general theory. To be constructive, I must put forward an alternative. The only main type of alternative general theory is psychological.

Durkheim. Though the position taken here does not rob sociology of its subject-matter, it does deny that it possesses any theory distinctively its own. That sociology does possess such a theory was one of the convictions of that great sociologist, Durkheim, and it is still dear to many of us. Speaking of what he called social facts, he wrote: "Since their essential characteristic consists in the power they possess of exerting, from outside, a pressure on individual consciousnesses, they do not derive from individual consciousnesses, and in consequence sociology is not a corollary of psychology" (Durkheim, 1927, pp. 124–125). But does this consequence follow? When I stop at a red traffic light or obey any other convention a social fact may be said to exert from outside a pressure on my consciousness. I bet we could discover the individual consciousness from whom the idea of the traffic light derived, but, leaving that argument aside, how do we explain the pressure the light exerts? We point out that, if I do not stop, there is some probability of certain unpleasant things happening to me, and it is a general psychological proposition that men are apt to act so as to avoid punishment. That is, the very facts from which Durkheim drew the conclusion that sociology was not a corollary of psychology can themselves be explained only by psychological laws. When Durkheim flew away from psychology, he flew on psychological wings.

Durkheim was prepared to advance his own apparently nonpsychological form of explanation: "The determining cause of a social fact ought to be looked for among antecedent social facts, and not among the states of the individual consciousness" (Durkheim, 1927, p. 135). The trouble with this is that Durkheim presented the two possibilities as alternatives rather than as complements. He may have had in mind his own finding (1951, Ch. 5) that *anomie* (a social fact) was a cause of high suicide rates (another social fact). I think it perfectly legitimate to call anomie a cause of suicide, but we are not interested just in causes but in explanations, and, were we to construct a deductive system explaining why anomie was a cause of suicide, I think the system would include psychological propositions.

Again, the price rise of the sixteenth century, which I take to be a social fact, was certainly a determining cause of the enclosure movement among English landlords. But were we to construct an explanation why this particular cause had this particular effect, we should have to say that the price rise presented English landlords both with great opportunities for monetary gain and great risks of monetary loss, that enclosure tended to increase the gain and avoid the loss, that the landlords found monetary gain rewarding (which is a state of individual consciousness, if you like), and, finally, that men are likely to take actions whose results they find rewarding—which, as I cannot repeat too often, is a general psychological proposition. The explanation of the price rise itself would in turn include psychological propositions and so on as far back in history as information was available. In short, the fact that social causes have social effects does not rule out psychological explanations.

Yet many able men still apparently cling to the Durkheimian (1927) position. Thus Blau writes:

If we should find that, regardless of whether or not an individual has an authoritarian disposition, he is more apt to discriminate against minorities if he lives in a community where authoritarian values prevail than if he lives in one where they do not, we would have evidence that this social value exerts external constraints upon the tendency to discriminate—structural effects that are independent of the internalized value orientations of individuals (Blau, 1960, p. 180).

A trick is being worked here, not a deliberate trick, but a trick none the less. It consists in Blau's (1960) assuming that his individual holds only one "internalized value," whereas he certainly holds many, and they are often in competition with one another. We need consider only two: antiauthoritarianism and social acceptance. The latter is just as much "internalized" as the former: both are acquired. If an individual cannot get acceptance from other members of the community except by discriminating against minorities, which is apt to be the case when the other members hold authoritarian values, the probability will increase of his foregoing the rewards of antiauthoritarianism in favor of those of social acceptance, and Blau's "structural effect" will be produced. But there are no effects here that are independent of the values of individuals, and the explanation is psychological. Psychological theory certainly does not deny that "society" exerts influence on "the individual"; it only denies that this influence must be explained through distinctively sociological propositions.

Historical theories. Psychological theories of a simple sort, like the foregoing one on punishment of criminals, appear to be adequate to explain human institutions defined so broadly as to allow great concrete variation within the class. Thus the punishment of criminals has taken many forms in different human societies and from time to time in any one society, but a single deductive system probably explains the existence of the general category of penal institutions. The problem is different when what we have to explain is the existence in a particular society of a very specific institution, very narrowly defined. Thus, a simple psychological explanation, or even a functional one, might hope to explain why the United States had some kind of institution for settling disputes, but it would never explain why the jury, in particular, was part of our legal system. The deductive systems that would explain things like juries would have to include, as simple psychological explanations do not, propositions about the past historical development of a society and about the way decisions taken long ago bent the twig in directions the trunk has followed since. Yet I do not think that these theories are distinctive just because they are historical. Though they are far from "simple," though their chains of reasoning if spelled out in full must be long and complex, they are still psychological theories, especially as the complexity lies more in the history than in the psychology.

For several reasons, of which the complexity is one, sociologists have tended to avoid historical theories. One way they have of doing so is to take propositions that would require historical explanation simply as givens in their deductive systems, that is, to leave these propositions unexplained. Thus the deductive system that I used as my first illustration (p. 951) included the proposition, "The incidence of Protestantism in Spain is low." The proposition was part of the explanation but was itself simply taken as given, left unexplained. To have explained it in turn would have required bringing in much of the history of Spain.

I appeal to what scholars would actually do were they asked to explain why a particular institution, not just some one of a general class of institutions, existed in a particular society. If they had the historical record they would never dream of using a functional explanation. Suppose, for instance, they were asked to explain why the British Parliament or the American business corporation exist as legal entities. They would show, from one point of time to another, how men and groups of men pursuing, in a context of other institutions and of traditions passed on to them by their forebears, different, often conflicting, and by no means always material values, choosing with inadequate information between alternative courses of action on the basis of the value of the results and the prospects of success in attaining them—the scholars would show how, in these conditions, men forged the prototypes of these institutions and then modified them progressively until they took the form they have today.

Indeed the history would, in principle, only end with today. A scholar explaining the existence of the modern American corporation should end by showing what persons and groups, in the light of possible alternatives, might have an interest in modifying it, what persons and groups might have an interest in maintaining it unchanged, and what prospects in a context of other institutions each would have for success in the struggle.

The explanatory chains might be very long—so long that the scholar might take the situation at a particular time as given and start from there instead of going back to the beginning of the historical record. He would also take as given the other institutions in whose structural context the particular institution he was interested in developed, and no try to explain them in turn, even though he thought it could be done. The explanations would certainly be sketchy in many places for lack of information. Nevertheless they would always include, and include at many different points in the argument, propositions of the kind I used in explaining the behavior of William the Conqueror, propositions about how men behave as members of a species. They would then bring in as lower-order propositions the fact that the men in question held particular values and acted in particular circumstances.

The circumstances in which men are placed may differ greatly, including the ways in which they perceive the circumstances. The values they hold may also differ, though they tend to hold certain earthy ones in common. But the propositions about how they behave, given the differences in circumstances and values, are the same for all men, and the same may be true of propositions about the way values are acquired. These are the propositions I call psychological.

The historical form of explanation can obviously not be used to explain the institutions of societies that possess no historical records, which include most of the so-called primitive societies. But the primitive societies make up for their lack of history by being many in number and limited in institutional variability largely to the themes of kinship and subsistence economy. For such societies it is possible to establish statistically certain general propositions, of the kind I call structural, about the relationships between institutions, and it is sometimes possible to show that these structural propositions in turn are susceptible to psychological explanation. But here, as in historical explanation, many things may have to be taken as simply given. Thus, it may be possible to explain psychologically why men in societies that vest strong jural authority in the father should tend to have especially close and warm relationships with their mother's brothers. But in the absence of historical records it may not be possible to explain in turn why the locus of jural authority should lie where it does.

Sociologists trying to account for the nature of human institutions often feel as if there were, according to the circumstances, a number of different kinds of explanation open to them, or combinations of the different kinds. They may try to explain an institution functionally, by what it does for a society. They may try to explain it structurally, by how it is related to other institutions in a social system. They may try to explain it historically, by the way it developed over time. Or they may try to explain it psychologically, by how it follows from general characteristics of the behavior of men. I have tried to show the distinctive features of each of these forms of explanation, their strengths and weaknesses, and how they are related to one another. Even if we agree in the end that the functional explanation is not contingent, the structural not fully general, and the historical really psychological, this does not mean that any of them has failed to make its contribution to the advancement of our science.

THE RELATIONS BETWEEN THEORY AND RESEARCH

I turn last and briefly to the relations between theory and research. In this field sociologists have felt especially guilty. On the one hand they feel that theory ought to guide research, and, if it does not, that they are in danger of becoming mere fact-gatherers. On the other hand, they feel that research should contribute cumulatively to the development of a body of general theory and that something is wrong if theory keeps on going with a life of its own impervious to research. It may help matters if I try to clear away some of the less justifiable sources of guilt.

Theorists are fond of saying complacently, "Nothing is more practical than a good theory." Like many old chestnuts this is a tautology, for a theory is no good unless it is practical in the only sense in which a theory can be practical. If you are aware of a theory that will explain and predict a number of the known facts, then a research strategy makes obviously good sense if it is designed to work out the further implications of the theory—what it implies under different given conditions. A mathematical model of the theory is a great advantage here, as it may enable you to grind out the further implications mechanically, as it were. In this case, theory is properly guiding research. But note: you have to have the theory first.

There are theorists who will tell you that sociology possesses such a theory and that accordingly it should guide research. Parsons writes: "Heretofore [sociology] has not enjoyed the kind of integration and directed activity which only the availability and common acceptance and employment of a well-articulated generalized theoretical system can give to a science. The main framework of such a system is, however, now available, though the fact is not as yet very generally appreciated . . ." (Parsons, 1949, p. 17). Can the system in question be Parsons' own? No doubt it is available, but is it practical in the sense given above? In the absence of evidence that it is so, I regard the claim that it ought to guide research as presumptuous. Yet according to Merton, Parsons makes such claims: "Talcott Parsons has observed that numerical data are scientifically important only when they can be fitted into analytical categories and that 'a great deal of current research is producing facts in a form which cannot be utilized by any current generalized analytical scheme'" (Merton, 1957, p. 113). The only possible comment is, "So much the worse for the scheme."

Researchers are sometimes told that they should investigate the effects of "theoretically relevant variables." But relevant to what theory? And does the researcher have any reason to feel confidence in it? I should have thought it obvious that the only variables of any importance whatever were the actually relevant variables. If the effects of some empirical variable can be predicted from a proposition about some generalized variable in a deductive system, then all is well. (See what I had to say above about the nominal and real definitions of concepts on pp. 953f.) But if they cannot, then the actual variable may not be disregarded, whatever its theoretical status.

There are few cases in sociology in which a developed deductive system has actually guided research. The reason is that there are few such deductive systems and still fewer among "general" theories. Let the sociologist feel guilty about that if he likes, but not about the lack of theoretical guidance. It makes sense to have theory guide research only if there is some reason for having confidence in the theory, and the theorist's own assertion is not sufficient reason. In the absence of such confidence, the researcher should feel free to do anything he pleases, so long as he studies men. Indeed he could do worse than indulge in "mere data collection."

In trying to allay one form of guilt, I do not want to increase another. I have argued that the researcher should feel free not to accept theoretical guidance. But even if he does allow himself to be guided by ideas that turn out to be inadequate theoretically, the fact will not necessarily hurt his research and may do it much good. I speak here of broad theoretical orientations rather than of actual deductive systems. Good theories in this sense need not lead to good researches, and bad theories certainly need not lead to bad ones. Thus I have shown the difficulties of using notions like *function* and *equilibrium* in sociological deductive systems. But if holding a functional theory implies the research maxim "Look for the consequences of institutions, near and remote, good or bad, intended or unintended" and if holding an equilibrium theory implies the maxim "Look for the way institutions work together to promote something like social stability," then these theories are apt to lead to the discovery of true propositions, even though the propositions may eventually turn out to be best explained neither through function nor through equilibrium. To use functional language, theories have other functions than theoretical ones.

Finally, some sociologists confuse the way a theory looks when it is completed—and it is never more than provisionally completed—with the way a theory is arrived at. Since a completed theory works downward, so to speak, from general propositions to less general empirical ones, they feel that the process of theory-building should work downward, too, starting from very general considerations like "the action frame of reference" and hoping eventually to reach the data. My general doctrine is that good science has been done by some of the damnedest methods, and that some of the methods scientists have said they used were not the ones they actually used. Accordingly I cannot rule out the possibility that good sociological theories will be reached by the downward-moving strategy of theory-construction.

But there is another strategy, and one that the history of science suggests is more likely to be successful in a new science like ours. This is the strategy well described by Willard Gibbs in his statement: "It is the office of theoretical work to give the form in which the results of experiment may be expressed" (Rukeyser, 1942, p. 232). Here there is no complaining that empirical research does not investigate "theoretically relevant variables." The strategy starts with the empirical findings themselves and seeks to invent the more general propositions from which these same findings, and, under different conditions, other findings may be derived. This is the strategy by which deductive systems are inductively arrived at.

This strategy has already proved its worth in sociology in the sense that our best theories, those that most nearly meet my requirements for being deductive systems, have stayed close to the empirical findings. In Merton's (1957, p. 9) terms, these are our theories of "the middle range." But I think that this strategy, which has sometimes been called *codification,* could be made more effective if it were made more explicit.

Codification begins with the assumption that the "mere empirical generalizations" of sociology are our most precious possessions and, like precious stones, least likely to change. But they exist in large numbers and great variety, and they are stated in a number of different terminologies. Collect, as far as possible, the propositions within any given field, say that of small groups. Reduce their number as far as possible by asking whether some of them do not state the same proposition under different words. This will entail examining how the named variables were actually measured and how far the methods of measurement were similar. Reduce the number of propositions at a particular level of generalization still further by asking whether some of them do not follow from the others as corollaries under specific limiting conditions. When you have reduced your set of propositions as far as you dare, ask what propositions of a higher level of generality still your set might in turn be derived from. Invent the higher-order propositions if you must; be a Newton. But I do not think that in sociology you will have to take action as drastic as that. You will find the propositions already invented for you in behavioral psychology.

Note that in arriving at deductive systems (explanations) in this way, you will have been an ex post facto explainer: you will have explained the findings after the findings are in, and there are sociologists who will be ready to tell you that ex post facto explanations are somehow illegitimate. Never fear; both Newton and Darwin were ex post facto explainers so you will be in good company. It is true that a proposition invented to explain a single empirical finding is not worth much. But it need not stop at a single finding. If it will explain at least two different findings under different given conditions, it will have done better than most theories in sociology, even if the explanation is ex post facto. Though it will do still better if it successfully predicts the truth of some proposition as yet untested, prediction is not the crucial step. All science begins with ex post facto explanations and without them could not get off the ground.

Naturally I believe that what I have said here is true. But the most important advice I can give contemporary sociologists has nothing to do with the validity of my arguments. It is this: you do not have to believe anything about theory or methodology that is told you pretentiously and sanctimoniously by other sociologists—including myself. So much guff has gotten mixed with the truth that, if you cannot tell which is which, you had better reject it all. It will only get in your way. No one will go far wrong theoretically who remains in close touch with and seeks to understand a body of concrete phenomena.

REFERENCES

Aberle, D. F., Cohen, A. K., Davis, A. K., Levy, M. J., Jr., & Sutton, F. X. The functional prerequisites of a society. *Ethics,* 1950, 60, 100–111.

Becker, H., & Boskoff, A. (Eds.) *Modern sociological theory in continuity and change.* New York: Holt, Rinehart & Winston, 1957.

Bierstedt, R. Nominal and real definitions in sociological theory. In L. Gross (Ed.), *Symposium on sociological theory.* Evanston, Ill.: Row, 1959. Pp. 121–144.

Black, M. (Ed.) *The social theories of Talcott Parsons.* Englewood Cliffs, N.J.: Prentice-Hall, Inc., 1961.

Blau, P. M. Structural effects. *Amer. sociol. Rev.,* 1960, 25, 178–193.

Borgatta, E. F., & Meyer, H. J. (Eds.) *Sociological theory.* New York: Knopf, 1956.

Braithwaite, R. B. *Scientific explanation.* Cambridge: Cambridge Univer. Press, 1953.

Bridgman, P. W. *The logic of modern physics.* New York: Macmillan, 1946.

Coser, L. A., & Rosenberg, B. (Eds.) *Sociological theory.* New York: Macmillan, 1957.

Davis, K. The myth of functional analysis as a special method in sociology and anthropology. *Amer. sociol. Rev.,* 1959, 24, 757–773.

Durkheim, E. *Les règles de la méthode sociologique.* (8th ed.) Paris: Alcan, 1927.

Durkheim, E. *The division of labor in society.* Glencoe, Ill.: Free Press, 1947.

Durkheim, E. *Suicide.* G. Simpson (Ed.). Glencoe, Ill.: Free Press, 1951.

Festinger, L., Schachter, S., & Back, K. *Social pressures in informal groups.* New York: Harper, 1950.

Gardiner, P. (Ed.) *Theories of history.* Glencoe, Ill.: Free Press, 1959.

Gross, L. (Ed.) *Symposium on sociological theory.* Evanston, Ill.: Row, 1959.

Hempel, C. G. Explanations and laws. In P. Gardiner (Ed.), *Theories of history.* Glencoe, Ill.: Free Press, 1959. Pp. 344–356.

Homans, G. C. *The human group.* New York: Harcourt, 1950.

Homans, G. C. *Social behavior: Its elementary forms.* New York: Harcourt, 1961.

Homans, G. C., & Schneider, D. M. *Marriage, authority, and final causes.* Glencoe, Ill.: Free Press, 1955.

Lazarsfeld, P. F. (Ed.) *Mathematical thinking in the social sciences.* Glencoe, Ill.: Free Press, 1954.

Levy, M. J., Jr. *The structure of society.* Princeton, N.J.: Princeton Univer. Press, 1952.

Lewin, K. *Principles of topological psychology.* New York: McGraw, 1936.

Loomis, C. P., & Loomis, Z. K. *Modern social theories.* Princeton, N.J.: Van Nostrand, 1961.

Luce, R. D., & Raiffa, H. *Games and decisions.* New York: Wiley, 1957.

Mach, E. *The science of mechanics.* LaSalle, Ill.: Open Court Publishing Co., 1942.

Martindale, D. *The nature and types of sociological theory.* Boston: Houghton, 1960.

Merton, R. K. *Social theory and social structure.* (rev. ed.) Glencoe, Ill.: Free Press, 1957.

Murdock, G. P. *Social structure.* New York: Macmillan, 1949.

Nagel, E. *The structure of science.* New York: Harcourt, 1961.

Needham, R. *Structure and sentiment.* Chicago: Univer. of Chicago Press, 1962.

Parsons, T. *Essays in sociological theory pure and applied.* Glencoe, Ill.: Free Press, 1949.

Parsons, T. *The social system.* Glencoe, Ill.: Free Press, 1951.

Parsons, T. General theory in sociology. In R. K. Merton, L. Broom, & L. S. Cottrell, Jr. (Eds.), *Sociology today.* New York: Basic Books, 1959. Pp. 3–38.

Parsons, T., Shils, E., Naegele, K. D., & Pitts, J. R. (Eds.) *Theories of society.* New York: The Free Press of Glencoe, 1961. 2 vols.

Parsons, T., & Smelser, N. J. *Economy and society.* Glencoe, Ill.: Free Press, 1956.

Radcliffe-Brown, A. R. *Structure and function in primitive society.* Glencoe, Ill.: Free Press, 1952.

Rex, J. *Key problems of sociological theory.* London: Routledge & Kegan Paul, 1961.

Rose, A. M. A systematic summary of symbolic interaction theory. In A. M. Rose (Ed.), *Human behavior and social processes.* Boston: Houghton, 1962. Pp. 3–19.

Rukeyser, M. *Willard Gibbs.* New York: Doubleday, Doran, 1942.

Scriven, M. Truisms as the grounds for historical explanations. In P. Gardiner (Ed.), *Theories of history.* Glencoe, Ill.: Free Press, 1959. Pp. 443–475.

Solomon, H. (Ed.) *Mathematical thinking in the measurement of behavior.* Glencoe, Ill.: Free Press, 1960.

Thibaut, J. W., & Kelley, H. H. *The social psychology of groups.* New York: Wiley, 1959.

Timasheff, N. S. *Sociological theory.* New York: Doubleday, 1955.

Von Neumann, J., & Morgenstern, O. *Theory of games and economic behavior.* Princeton, N.J.: Princeton Univer. Press, 1944.

Zetterberg, H. L. *On theory and verification in sociology.* New York: Tressler Press, 1954.

Zetterberg, H. L. Review of Becker and Boskoff (1957). *Amer. sociol. Rev.,* 1958, 23, 95–96.

Zetterberg, H. L. *Social theory and social practice.* New York: Bedminster Press, 1962.

CHAPTER 26 Sources and Types of Sociological Data[1]

MATILDA WHITE RILEY

Sociological data are the facts that sociologists assemble, organize, and interpret in the effort to explain human society. Sociologists deal with a wide variety of data—for example, about individuals in role conflict; about networks of influence in a community; about the economic, religious, or scientific aspects of a single complex society; or about the varied values or occupational structures of total societies. They obtain these data from many different sources. They use many different empirical methods of assembling and organizing data and various ways of interpreting them. The scientific importance of each set of data depends upon its ability to contribute to the growing body of knowledge about social behavior and man's relationships to man,

to test accepted sociological ideas and theories or to suggest new ones.

The nature of sociological data, their sources, and the methods of assembling them can best be understood within the framework of the basic research process. There are two main phases in this process, as suggested in Figure 1. In the empirical phase, the researcher is led by his sociological ideas and theories to certain facts (his research findings). In the interpretative phase, he compares these facts with his initial theories and tries to understand their larger significance. Each of these phases has its own methods, or rules of procedure. The combined methods enable the investigator to bring together for comparison specific facts from the real world of concrete social phenomena, on the one hand, and corresponding ideas and propositions from sociological theory, on the other.

Empirical Methods

Sociological investigators today employ many special empirical methods, rather than a single unified method, in seeking new facts and discovering the connections among

[1] Selected and adapted from Matilda White Riley, *Sociological Research*. New York: Harcourt, Brace & World, Inc., 1963, and prepared in association with John W. Riley, Jr., Richard Cohn, Ann Foner, Marilyn E. Johnson, Mary E. Moore, and Sarane S. Boocock. Among the many sociologists who were kind enough to read earlier versions of the manuscript and to make valuable suggestions were Robert K. Merton, Talcott Parsons, Frederick F. Stephan, and Winston White.

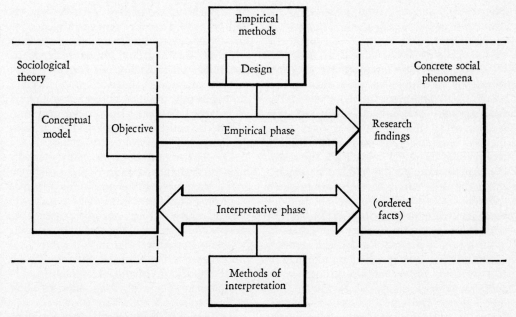

Fig. 1. Diagram of the research process.

them. Some conduct controlled experiments in the laboratory; others question cross-section samples of individuals about their opinions and attitudes; still others trace the web of interpersonal attitudes in complex organizations. Some observe and describe small group interaction; while others analyze the volume and density of human populations and the changing rates of marriages, births, and deaths. Some classify and quantify the content of mass communication; others make cross-cultural comparisons of role prescriptions and social structures. Some are concerned with using electronic computers to simulate human behavior; others with allowing for chance errors in making statistical inferences from experimental findings.

The research design. In each inquiry, the investigator selects, from the common reservoir of these and any other available methods, a particular set of methods that he will follow in obtaining his research findings. This set of selected empirical methods is referred to as the research design.

In making the broad plans for his research design and in choosing the specific technical procedures he will use to carry it out, the investigator decides how he will select certain facts (his data), how he will classify these facts, and how he will seek to uncover the order or pattern in which they actually occur. He may decide as part of his design, for example, to gather new data rather than to use available materials and to use a large rather than a small sample of cases; and he may decide to use such specific procedures as interviewing with a structured questionnaire and simple random sampling.

The Conceptual Model

But the research process does not take place entirely at the empirical level, relying exclusively upon observation or experiment. It is not merely a set of empirical procedures that yield specific findings. Whether he is aware of it or not, the researcher does not simply "look at all the facts," classifying them or finding correlations among them.

His way of selecting certain facts and his search for order among them is guided by some prior notions or theories about the nature of the social phenomena under study.

A researcher may approach the problem of success or failure in marriage, for example, with an image of marriage as the re-enactment of childhood roles; and this leads him to abstract relevant facts from the full complexity of phenomena and to report them in special ways. Both the methods that he uses and the findings he obtains might be different if his conceptions were different—if, for example, he thought of marriage as the juxtaposition of two sets of personality traits. Or another researcher, in studying the diffusion of a message through a community, may proceed on the notion that diffusion occurs mainly through interaction in which citizens talk to one another, rather than simply through mass communication to all citizens directly. Here again the researcher's conception may affect the manner in which he gathers, classifies, and analyzes the data and the character of his findings.

Since the sociologist typically wants to study certain aspects of the action and orientations of human beings in collectivities, his model generally consists of ideas, more or less clearly formulated, about (1) these human beings in collectivities (his *case*), (2) these aspects of action and orientation (the *properties*), and (3) the ways these aspects fit together and affect each other (the *rela-*

Conceptual	Empirical
Conception of the CASE	Concrete CASES
Conception of PROPERTIES	Concrete INDICANTS
Postulated RELATIONSHIPS among properties	Observed RELATIONSHIPS

Fig. 2. The translation of model into data.

tionships among properties) (see Figure 2). Thus one set of ideas in the model describes the collectivity or part of a collectivity he will use as the case or point of reference for his investigation. This may be a particular type of small group (characterized by sustained interaction), a larger society (whose members share common values although they do not all interact directly with one another), the subgroups into which the collectivity is divided, or the individuals who play roles as members of the group. The second set of ideas in the model refers to certain properties of the case, such as the integration of the group, the attitudes of group members toward one another, the norms which group members generally accept, and the like. The third set of ideas postulates certain relationships among these properties, as, for example, that increasing social interaction among the members of a group makes for a growing differentiation in their roles.

Underlying these abstract distinctions among cases, properties, and relationships among properties, the collectivity is widely viewed by sociologists as a social system. That is, the parts of the collectivity and their properties are conceived to be interdependent, so that each part influences all the others and is in turn influenced by them. In some models the roles of members are defined as the constituent parts of the small group as the higher-level system. Or a community may be viewed as a system within which families are the interdependent parts. Or a more complex model of the political structure of a state, for instance, may be defined at three levels, consisting of individual voters who make up county subsystems, while the counties in turn fit together into the higher-level system of the state. The system character of the model, and the various levels at which system and parts are defined, each present distinctive problems when the researcher comes to translate the model into empirical operations.

In short, the research process starts with a conceptual model, or an organizing image, of the phenomena to be investigated. It starts with a set of ideas—whether vague hunches or clearly formulated propositions —about the nature of these phenomena. It is this conceptual model that determines what questions are to be answered by the research and how empirical procedures are to be used as tools in finding answers to these questions.

The research objective. The researcher usually states these questions to be answered by the research in the form of a research objective: He states the purposes for which he will gather and analyze the data. The objective may be general or specific. It sometimes leads to exploration and sometimes to the testing of hypotheses. It is usually stated rather succinctly, as for example, to discover uniformities in social interaction, to explore the process of disruption of small groups, to study the conditions determining political behavior, to test the hypothesis that the spouse who talks most will be most likely to win in family arguments, or to observe quantitative fluctuations in the influence of the value systems. Each study typically states one or more major objective, and numerous minor objectives, governing specific portions of the research.

Such concisely stated objectives are only part of the larger set of underlying ideas, assumptions, and definitions in the conceptual model. Thus the objective may be regarded as a few ideas selected from the model that specify the purpose of the investigation.

The Research Findings

Guided by the conceptual model and the objective, then, the researcher applies the empirical methods he has selected in order to obtain the research findings. These findings consist of sets of facts drawn from the multitude of phenomena in the real world. Protestants are found to be more likely to commit suicide than Catholics, for example; status hierarchies are observed in corner gangs; urbanization is seen to vary concomitantly with industrialization; experi-

mentally treated delinquents show lower recidivism rates than the untreated control sample; and the like.

Thus the findings obtained by empirical methods are reports of empirical regularities —recurring processes, patterns, and structures in the data.

Methods of Interpretation

But the researcher rarely concludes the process with such specific factual findings, for he also wants to interpret them. Accordingly, having started with theory, he completes the circle in the interpretative phase by bringing the findings back into the conceptual model, setting the new facts into the context of his ideas.

Here the methods that he uses—logical reasoning, mathematics, creative imagination—are less clearly defined. Here there is often no straightforward execution of a clear-cut plan; the researcher may alternate the interpretative and empirical phases in a single study, working back and forth between theory and data. But sometimes the researcher starts with the empirical phase of his research, working from data to model by adding new ideas to the model after he has the findings in hand. As exploratory research uncovers empirical regularities, he typically looks for clues to new ideas and hypotheses that might account for these findings and uses these to amplify or specify the conceptual model. He may, for example, in order to explain the finding of a statistical correlation between religion and suicide, build a new concept into his model—the notion of the differing degrees of integration that characterize the institutional arrangements of Protestants as compared with Catholics, the differing strength of the bonds holding individuals to their fellows and to life itself. He uses this new concept to explain the observed empirical regularity in terms of a more general theoretical principle.

Or sometimes the researcher starts with the interpretative phase. Here he works from model to data, providing his interpretation as part of the model in advance of the data-gathering. In hypothesis-testing, he determines what the expected findings would be if the assumptions of the conceptual model were in accord with the facts, often using mathematical models as a precise language for formulating the interrelated ideas and implications. Then, once he has derived the implications of the conceptual model, his task is to obtain and examine the actual findings to see whether, for the particular conditions under study, they are consistent with the expected findings.

Thus, whatever procedures are used, a major step in the research process is to interpret the empirical data by incorporating them into the more general principles and theories of the conceptual model. Indeed (although particular studies often have methodological or applied objectives), the central aim of scientific research, its reason for being, is to add to or test the ideas with which the research began—to extend, revise, specify, confirm, or discard the conceptual model.

The three sections of this chapter will examine, within this basic research process, the use of sociological data to represent certain abstract properties of certain types of cases as defined in the conceptual model. The first section outlines methods for selecting concrete cases—the groups or individuals to be studied—and the second section describes methods for assembling concrete information as indicants of the properties of these cases. The third section suggests how the methods for assembling the data and the forms in which they are assembled are affected by the sociologist's special conception of societies and groups as systems.

SELECTING THE CASES

In designing and executing a study to test his conceptual model against reality, the researcher decides exactly what his data are to be—what facts he will examine for their ultimate meaning as they refer back to

this model (see Figure 2 above). Before he can study the properties of his cases, by utilizing observable acts as indicants, he must decide what kinds of concrete cases from the real world to use as specimens of the social system he has in mind.

The sociologist, in deciding what cases to study, is guided by his idea of a social system as defined in his conceptual model and by the level of that system on which his objective focuses. If his focus is on the level of the role, he may decide to study individuals in roles as his cases—actual leaders of military companies, for example, or women in a particular community who are mothers. If his focus is on the dyad (as the smallest relational unit in a social system), he may decide to study all possible pairs of members within given groups, for example, or the paired relationships between certain children and each of their parents. If his conceptual concern is with subsystems within a larger system, his research case might be the subgroup (or subcollectivity), such as wards (within hospitals) or communities (within countries). Or, at the level of the total system, he might use the total group or society as his research case—hospitals or countries, for example, or wards or communities no longer treated as subgroups. Since the focus is often on more than one level of the system the case may be the collectivity made up of subcollectivities or of roles, for example, or the role made up of dyadic relationships.

The researcher usually thinks of the empirical cases he studies as corresponding, to a greater or lesser degree, to a conceptual universe of cases to which his theory applies. Study of the entire population that matches the universe specified in the model (all communities, all primitive societies, all workers' families, for instance) is seldom practical or even possible. Hence he characteristically studies only a selected sample of cases in order to draw inferences about the total universe of interest.

The researcher must decide how to select this sample, following various possible procedures as outlined in this section. He must also decide how many cases he will select. Often (in a "case study") he works intensively with just one or just a few cases, examining in detail the structure of a single society, for example, or the patterns of relationship in just a few married couples. Often, however, he may go beyond the single case (or the few cases) to select many cases for study, so as to isolate those properties that are common to many cases from those that are peculiar only to exceptional cases. Determination of the exact size of the sample depends upon the sample design and upon the degree of accuracy required for the analysis. The conceptual model is not ordinarily limited in itself, of course, to just one or a few cases. If the sociologist uses a model of the street corner gang, for instance, he does not regard this model as applying to just one gang on one particular corner, but to all such gangs (a universe of gangs). Hence, he often wants to test his model on many gangs and to revise it when necessary so that it will fit gangs more generally.

Bases for Sample Design

There are two major bases for sample design which affect the specific procedures used in selecting the cases as well as the nature of the data obtained. First, the sample may be designed to represent the conceptual universe as closely as possible, or with a measurable degree of accuracy. Second, the sample may be designed to facilitate the analysis to be made of the data.

The importance of the representational basis is often taken for granted, since sociologists, like other scientists, typically want to generalize from the concrete cases under study to some larger universe of theoretical concern. To some degree, most sociological samples are designed as rough miniatures of a parent population.

Particular studies differ widely, however, depending upon their objectives, in the relative emphasis placed upon representa-

tiveness. At one extreme, the samples drawn by the United States Bureau of the Census, or many of the samples used in market research or public opinion polling, are designed primarily so that inferences drawn from the sample will describe the larger population with a known degree of accuracy. Other types of samples may sacrifice a degree of representativeness because the objective is purely exploratory, the conceptual universe is too general to allow representational sampling, or the requirements of the particular analysis are more compelling than the need for representativeness.

In addition to seeking representativeness, the researcher in designing his sample also considers the requirements of the analysis. Although this basis for sample design is less clearly understood and less commonly discussed in textbook treatments of sampling, the character of the sample is often markedly affected by the plans for analyzing social processes and interrelationships among variables. As one indication of the kinds of samples and data actually used in current sociological research, Anne Foner has prepared especially for this Handbook an analysis of the study designs of all the research reports published in the *American Sociological Review* and the *American Journal of Sociology* in 1962. Out of the 88 studies reported, she found that nearly half of the samples were designed primarily for purposes of the analysis. Thus a researcher may select only a few cases as his sample because he wants to examine them intensively, or a large sample of cases because he wants to make extensive cross-tabulations. Or he may choose cases that he can observe under special conditions, or cases that he can subject to experimental manipulation. Or he may design the sample so that he can control (or hold constant) certain critical variables.

Ideally, of course, the researcher emphasizes both bases in designing his sample. In a study of boys' college plans, for instance, the sample may allow analysis of the reasons behind the boys' decisions, and at the same time guarantee that the findings are a fair picture for boys in the United States today. Often, however, one basis outweighs the other in determining the sample design. Thus the researcher may concentrate either on the representativeness of the sample (from which, for example, he estimates the proportion of boys going to college) or on the sampling requirements of the analysis (from which he examines the factors in the decision).

THE REPRESENTATIONAL BASIS FOR SAMPLING

The basic procedure for drawing any representational sample rests upon a clear definition of the conceptual universe and typically consists of three phases, as outlined in Figure 3. At each of these phases, the

Phase I. Designating the Frame

In the first of these phases, the researcher seeks an empirical universe (or empirical population) of cases, for use as a sampling frame, which parallels the conceptual universe as closely as possible. Ideally he obtains a complete list (or a map) of all the empirical cases of interest, from which he will (at Phase II) draw the sample of concrete cases to be used in his research.

In practice, of course, he frequently has difficulty in securing an appropriate frame. Often he is unable to find a complete list— some of the households are not listed in the telephone directory, for example, or some of the case work records are missing from the file drawers. Whenever the list is incomplete, there is a potential danger

Research stages	Types of possible error	
Phase I: Designating (stratifying) the frame	Bias: failure to match conceptual universe	
Phase II: Drawing sample from frame	Chance error (measurable by statistical tests) Bias: failure in approximation of probability model	SAMPLING ERRORS
Phase III: Covering the entire sample	Bias: researcher's substitutions, respondents' self-selection (e.g., refusal, unavailability)	
Data-collection	Errors of observation and measurement (e.g., control effect, biased-viewpoint effect)	
Coding, punching, tabulating	Errors in data-processing	NON-SAMPLING ERRORS
Analysis and interpretation	Errors of computation, weighting, interpreting	
Inferences about conceptual universe (as drawn from the research)		TOTAL ERRORS

Fig. 3. Sampling errors and other errors in a representational sample.

researcher attempts to obtain a representative sample—a sample which is as similar as possible to the conceptual universe defined in his model—by reducing the various possibilities of sampling error.

of some systematic bias in the frame itself, that is, the unlisted cases may be consistently different from the listed ones in important respects. Inadequacies in the frame raise doubt about the correspondence between the sample and the sociological universe the researcher believes he is studying and to which he will refer his findings and his interpretations. Thus he makes every effort in Phase I to discover, and insofar as possible to eliminate or control, the potential biases in the frame.

Moreover, in many important instances of scientific research, the sociologist wants to study populations that are too general or too vaguely defined to match (at Phase I) any available empirical population (or sampling frame). If a researcher should wish, for example, to represent all preindustrial societies, or the leaders of all small groups in any place and at any time, he would be hard pressed to find a suitable sampling frame from which to draw a representative sample. Thus a major problem of representational sampling in much theoretically focused research centers in Phase I: How can a conceptual universe which is not time-bound, and perhaps not space-bound, be matched by an empirical and necessarily finite sampling frame?

Phase II. Drawing the Sample

At the second phase of the sampling procedure, the researcher selects a sample from the frame in such a way that the cases in the sample will correspond closely to the cases in the frame. He sometimes uses expert judgment in selecting representative cases. But the procedure most widely used at this phase is probability sampling, which gives each case (and each set of cases) a known chance of being selected. (Some principles of probability as applied to sampling are outlined below.)

Probability sampling has several advantages. First, a probability sample, if it is large enough, will come close to representing the sampling frame from which it is drawn. (Of course, even a carefully drawn probability sample can yield inaccurate estimates unless the research is in all other respects properly designed and executed and unless the sampling frame itself corresponds

to the conceptual universe, as in Figure 3.) Thus representativeness in a sample does not depend on the researcher's knowing the population in the frame well enough to attempt selection of "typical" cases on the basis of judgment. He need not run the risk of allowing his own special knowledge of, and interest in, the situation to bias his selection. Chance alone, if allowed to operate according to the rules of probability sampling, will take care of the problem of representativeness. Second, probability sampling allows the use of statistical tests which give the researcher some idea of how confident he can be that the findings from his sample are not distorted by chance error. Third, the researcher can govern the size and design of the sample for the level of accuracy desired.

Probability sampling is extremely useful for research situations in which an appropriate frame is available. It can produce excellent estimates of the parameters of a finite population at a given time—of the age distribution in the United States in 1960, for example, of the number of United States families owning washing machines toward the end of World War II, or of the relationship between age and conformity among American adults in a given year. (A parameter is a proportion, mean, or other number which describes the population. A statistic describes a sample; it may be used to estimate the corresponding parameter.)

But probability sampling is not always the most desirable procedure for securing representativeness, even when the frame is adequate. If the investigator knows a great deal about the cases to be sampled and if he can avoid bias in making his selections, his own judgment may, by avoiding chance error, yield the more accurate sample. To be sure, it is difficult to tell how accurate the judgment sample is, unless the findings can be checked against an outside source, because judgment sampling has no self-contained measure of sampling error. Unlike the chance error of probability sampling, which has the virtue that it can be measured, the bias or distortion of judgment sampling may be introduced by the investigator unwittingly in drawing the sample from the frame.

Judgment samples are especially recommended when the sample is very small, since chance error increases as the sample size decreases. Deming (1950, p. 23) suggests 6 or less. Thus a Malinowski (1926) probably does well to use his best judgment and all relevant information in selecting a single primitive society to represent an extreme example of "spontaneous obedience," under the theory of automatic submission to custom which he wishes to disprove. Or a Whyte (1951) does well to use his judgment in selecting just a few corner gangs in order to explore essential characteristics of their social organization.

It should be noted, too, that probability sampling sometimes requires greater expenditures of time and money than would a comparable judgment procedure (see, for example, Stouffer, 1955). But this is not invariably true—it often takes less time to draw a random sample from a list than to assemble the information needed to draw a judgment sample of the same size.

Phase III. Covering the Entire Sample

When the researcher uses probability sampling, he must meet a further procedural requirement: In Phase III, he must obtain data from all, or nearly all, the cases selected, so that the actual sample corresponds to the sample selected in Phase II. If he omits any substantial portion of the cases, some further selective principle is introduced, and the rules of probability no longer apply. An additional source of bias may thus be opened up (Phase III).

Many practical difficulties are encountered in trying to cover the entire sample, and numerous devices have been developed for dealing with such difficulties. Where interviewing is the data-gathering procedure, repeated call backs are made on respondents not easily found at home, or persuasive telegrams are sent to reduce to a minimum the tendency for certain types of respondents to "select themselves out" of the sample. The interviewer himself is not allowed to make any further selections or substitutions. A related procedure for handling the possible bias of nonresponse is to include in the sample only those respondents found at home at the first call, but to weight their answers according to their report of the proportion of days they are ordinarily at home at the time of the interview.

In studies based on mail questionnaires or other data-collection procedures in which respondents are self-selected, successive waves of follow-ups are sent out to the nonrespondents, and those answering readily are compared with those answering only after repeated prodding, or with those on the list not answering at all (see, for example, Clausen & Ford, 1947; Suchman & McCandless, 1940; Wallace, 1954). These comparisons may serve to indicate at least the existence and the general direction of the bias of nonresponse, tending to show the differentials for the lazy or the busy, though not for the stubborn and hostile.

Some Principles of Probability Sampling

Probability sampling must be understood as one application of certain general principles of probability developed by mathematicians and statisticians (used also by sociologists in mathematical models and statistical testing). If many repeated trials (or experiments) give varying results, the probability of a particular result is defined as the proportion of occurrences of that result in a very large number of trials. When the rules of probability sampling are followed, the sample obtained supports inferences about the population whose accuracy and precision can be estimated (in terms of probability).

Probability sampling rests upon the notion that very large numbers of similar samples (all the same size) are drawn successively in a specified manner from the given empirical population (frame), for which the parameter of interest is known or assumed. The results (statistics) obtained from all these samples differ from sample to sample because of chance variation (also called sampling variability, fluctuations due to chance, variability due to chance). Yet these chance variations show certain definite regularities; the regular distribution of the results of sampling from a given population is called a probability distribution for samples (or a sampling distribution). This probability distribution can be estimated either by statistical experiments in which, for instance, pennies are tossed, dice rolled, or cards drawn from a deck; or by mathematical computations which parallel such experiments.

The probability distribution serves as a statistical model against which the statistician compares and evaluates the findings of any actual single sample that he uses in estimating the true population parameter.

An example. A simple example will clarify the idea of a probability distribution and also point out how it is possible (1) to make inferences from the findings of probability samples about the parameters of interest, and (2) to make allowances for chance errors in these inferences.

Imagine that a researcher has a hypothesis that most societies (more than half) are characterized by a particular type of differentiated role structure and that he has found a list of societies (a frame) that corresponds closely to his conceptual universe. Suppose, too, that his research hypothesis is true: Three-fourths of the societies in the frame are actually differentiated, so that the population parameters are 75 per cent D (differentiated) and 25 per cent N (not differentiated). If he now proceeds to draw a probability sample consisting of just three societies, what is the chance that his sample will indicate the true situation in the population—specifically that more than half the societies in the sample will show differentiation?

The computation of probabilities for each of the possible sample outcomes is illustrated in Table 1. For any given society, the probability of D is three-fourths and the probability of N is one-fourth (taken from the known or assumed population parameters). For a sample of three societies, the probability of each possible outcome is obtained by multiplying the appropriate probabilities for the individual societies. The probability of obtaining the correct result from the sample is then found by adding together the probabilities for all those possible outcomes which contain more D's than N's: It is 54/64.

TABLE 1

	Possible Outcomes	Probability	
3 D's	DDD	27/64	
2 D's	DDN	9/64	
	DND	9/64	27/64
	NDD	9/64	
1 D	DNN	3/64	
	NDN	3/64	9/64
	NND	3/64	
0 D's	NNN	1/64	

A bar graph drawn for all these "theoretical" probabilities as in Table 1 gives the shape of the probability distribution. Experience has shown that a bar graph of the results from a large number of actual probability samples will also tend to have this same shape. Accordingly, one can say that a given sample of this size, drawn at random from this population, will have a probability of 54/64 of more D's than N's, thus representing the population correctly. True, likelihood of chance error (that is, error due to chance variation) is still considerable, but the statistical model shows how much chance error there is likely to be, indicating in what proportion of such samples the finding would not represent the population accurately. Here the probability of a misleading finding is 10/64.

This illustration of a very small sample can show the nature and use of a probability distribution because the exact probabilities can easily be computed. In the larger probability samples actually used in sociological research, various methods for estimating the distribution are employed. The researcher uses the larger estimated probability distribution in the same way as a statistical model —to locate any particular sample finding relative to the findings of all possible samples of the given size, or to determine the probability of obtaining a finding higher (or lower) than his sample finding.

Allowing for chance error. This example has demonstrated the extent to which a particular probability sample tends to resemble, or fails to resemble, the population from which it is drawn. In this example, foreknowledge of the true proportion (of D's) in the population was assumed. In practice, the researcher does not know this proportion; if he did, there would be no need of taking a sample at all. But by using probability distributions computed for various assumed population proportions, the statistician is able to calculate the margins of error attributable to chance alone.

Statisticians commonly employ, in the statistics of inference, two main types of procedures for "measuring" in this way the chance error of probability samples: the setting of confidence limits around estimated parameters, and the statistical testing of hypotheses. The United States Bureau of the Census (1961), for example, in allowing for error in estimates based on sample findings, determines a range for each possible finding. In a known proportion of all the similar samples for which such ranges are computed (in 2 samples out of every 3, for example, or in 19 out of every 20), the true proportion of the population having this characteristic will fall within this range. Here the probability distributions are used as a means of setting limits within which one can know, with a stated degree of confidence, that the true parameter lies. Statistical tests of hypotheses, at present the procedure more widely used in sociology, locate the observed sample finding in the probability distribution of all possible findings.

This is done by formulating a null hypothesis—an assumption about probabilities based on the conceptual model but usually stated in such form that the researcher hopes to disprove it—and then by determining the probability of obtaining the finding by chance if the null hypothesis is actually correct. If this probability turns out to be small enough (less than a predetermined level such as .05 or .01), the researcher decides to reject the null hypothesis.

Sample size and sampling errors. An important characteristic of probability sampling is that as the sample size increases, chance variation decreases; that is, the likelihood of drawing a misleading sample because of chance error is reduced (although in any probability sample there is always some chance error). Thus greater precision in a probability sample may be achieved by increasing the sample size. Indeed, the size is often planned to fit the level of representativeness required by the research objective.

It is important to note, however, that whether or not probability sampling is used, bias is not affected by the sample size. Large samples are no more successful than small samples in (1) overcoming distortion in the designation of the frame (at Phase I), or (2) offsetting the tendency of interviewers (if left to their own devices) to select only certain types of respondents (at Phase II), or (3) counteracting (at Phase III) the greater readiness of certain respondents to reply (if respondents are allowed to select themselves). When such selections affect variables relevant to the analysis, sample bias may produce serious error in the results, regardless of sample size. Thus, the *Literary Digest* poll of 1936 (Likert, 1948, for example), in its forecast of the presidential election, was in error by 20 percentage points (and thereby failed to predict the winner), although 10 million ballots were mailed. There would seem to have been two sources of bias in the sample design which could not be offset by the extremely large sample size: (1) The frame was constructed of *Literary Digest* and telephone subscribers, a portion of the electorate presumably having above average income; and (2) the respondents were allowed to select themselves in deciding whether to return the mail ballot and only 20 per cent did so, presumably these were the better educated, more interested members of the electorate. The problem of self-selection is similarly reflected in the Kinsey sample, which was composed entirely of volunteers. Here, too, the representativeness of the sample has been doubted, despite its large size (Cochran, Mosteller, & Tukey, 1953).

Stratified sampling. One further basic principle of probability sampling, also useful for nonprobability samples, is that stratified sampling may increase the efficiency, that is the representativeness of a probability sample of any given size. In stratified sampling, the frame is divided (in Phase I) into cells, or strata, each of which is homogeneous in respect to certain characteristics believed to be associated with the phenomenon under study. Then (Phase II) the researcher makes his sample selection, as usual, from each of the strata. This ensures that sufficient cases will be drawn from every single stratum.

As an example, imagine drawing a sample of individuals from a large business organization. It is known in advance that the top management consists of only a few individuals, that the second echelon is also relatively small in size, but that the several classes of workers are relatively populous. A sample drawn at random from the organization as a whole may happen to include nobody at all from top management, since there are so few in this stratum. Yet the researcher feels that, for proper representation, this type of individual should be included. By stratifying the individuals in advance, however, he gains assurance that each of the echelons will be represented in the sample. Stratified sampling, then, combines the advantages of probability procedures with the researcher's own knowledge of which strata are important, how these may be identified, and how the population is divided among them.

Stratified sampling is useful also in judgment samples (in improving the quota samples, for example, in which the field investigator is instructed to make his own selections of cases from designated strata), as well as in various other samples designed primarily to meet analytical requirements.

Some probability sampling procedures. In practice, a variety of probability sampling procedures are used in sociology, though they all apply the principles of probability in such a way that the selection of cases from the frame (Phase II) depends ideally upon chance alone—not upon the investigator's judgment, which may sometimes introduce bias (see, for example, Deming, 1950; Hansen, Hurwitz, & Madow, 1953; Stephan & McCarthy, 1958).

The widely useful *simple random sample* is the special procedure in which each case (and set of cases) has an equal chance of being selected. The researcher, first assigning a key number to each case in the population (frame), selects key numbers at random to designate the cases to be used in the sample. This random selection—a precise, not at all haphazard, procedure—may be made by following a table of random numbers (a list of digits generated by some mechanical mixing and drawing procedure or by computers programed for random selection). Or the selection may be made by lot. Here the researcher writes each of the key numbers on identical objects that may be mixed (for example, equal sized slips of paper, poker chips, or the like). He mixes the objects thoroughly, much more thoroughly than might be supposed necessary. Then he draws the objects one by one until the desired number of cases has been drawn.

Systematic sampling. Systematic sampling is another procedure often used when the frame consists of a list (or a card file, for example, or dwelling units arranged in sequence). Here the list must first be examined for any evidence of possible order or patterning of the characteristic under study which might allow selection at regular intervals to bias the results. The investigator determines the sampling interval (k) by dividing the total number of cases on the list by the desired size of the sample. For example, if a list contains 500 names and a sample of 125 is desired, then $k = 4$, and every fourth name on the list will be chosen. The main element of chance which is introduced into the sampling procedure here is the selection of the first case at random (the investigator may close his eyes and place his finger somewhere on the listing, or he may choose a random number within the sampling interval). After this random start, he continues selecting every kth case until the desired number of cases has been drawn.

Area sampling. Area sampling is a more complex, multi-stage procedure which was originally developed within the United States government to allow supplementation of the United States decennial census (which attempts to cover every household and every person in the country) with many interim reports (based on samples of a few thousand), which are often as accurate as the full census itself. The unique feature of this method is its ingenious device for preparing the sampling frame. Since in the United States no up-to-date lists of all citizens are either available or readily usable for the country at large, each individual is associated with the dwelling unit in which he lives and with the area in which this dwelling unit is located. Thus the initial frame consists, not of individuals, but of areas, and the sampling progresses through a series of stages, drawing on a probability basis first areas, then dwelling units, and finally the individuals themselves.

Sampling within Social Systems

Special problems frequently arise in sociological sampling of groups treated as systems made up of parts, when the sampling takes place at more than one system level. Students of voting behavior may first select a sample of all communities in the country and then select a sample of individual citizens within each community. Thus, after a researcher has drawn a sample of groups, he may still have to decide whether and how to sample within groups.

In designs where the research objective is to represent the universe (of individuals, roles, or subgroups) within each group, or to analyze selected portions of this universe, it is appropriate to sample again within each group. If, in a sample of communities (groups), the socioeconomic composition of each is to be indexed by its proportion of white-collar workers (group members), data are not required for everybody within each community—a within-group sample of the members is sufficient. Or samples of individual members within a sample of groups are used to discover whether members tend to choose certain other members as leaders.

Other designs do not sample within groups, however, but utilize all (or nearly all) the members of each group. Especially when the research objective is to uncover the relational structure of particular social systems, it often seems necessary to examine all (or nearly all) the component parts of this structure, rather than a sample of them (e.g., Coleman, 1961).

Sampling of Events

The sociologist usually talks about sampling as a selection from a universe of cases. It is convenient to think in the abstract about cases apart from their properties and, in practice, to sample by first selecting cases and then studying their properties through selected indicants at selected times.

In a more exact sense, however, because the researcher does not deal at all time periods with all the phenomena that might be used as indicants of the properties under study, sampling is a selection from this universe of phenomena. The selection of indicants and the selection of time periods, as well as the selection of cases, may affect, sometimes markedly, the representativeness of the sample findings. In a study of mathematical ability, for instance, a probability sample of individuals might yield different results depending upon which questions were selected for the test from the total population of possible questions. Or, in a study of household laundry habits, housewives interviewed on Monday (the typical washday) may respond differently from those interviewed on other days. Even though the sample of cases (households) had been chosen on a probability basis, the research findings on the phenomena under study would be biased unless the interviewing were carefully spaced over the seven days of the week in order to sample time more accurately.

The Analytical Basis for Sampling

Apart from meeting the representational aims of sampling, the sociologist frequently devotes considerable effort, time, and expense to designing a sample that will support a particular plan for analysis. The requirements of the analysis often affect the size of the sample, the stratification procedure, or the use of the sample to minimize the effects of potentially confounding extraneous variables.

Samples Designed for Experiments

One important class of analytically-based samples is designed to concentrate research attention upon the variables of immediate interest, the explanatory variables, either by holding constant or by randomizing the effects of other associated variables outside of present concern, the extraneous variables. In particular, the controlled experiment achieves much of its power in testing causal hypotheses through its use of sampling.

In the simplest experiment, two samples—an experimental sample and a control sample—are drawn in such a way that they will be as nearly alike as possible at Time 1 in regard to all factors potentially affecting the results. Then the presumed causal factor

X is introduced into the experimental sample, but withheld from the control sample, and the dependent variable Y is observed in both samples at both Time 1 and Time 2. The changes occurring in the experimental sample are compared with the changes occurring in the control sample, and any difference is attributed to the causal factor X. Although experimentation cannot afford absolute proof, it can provide a highly reasonable basis for inferring that X is (or is not) related to Y under the particular conditions studied.

Such attribution of causality is only possible through comparison of samples that were equivalent at the outset. Presumably, the experimental sample and the control sample—which might better be called the comparison sample—are exposed to all the same factors (outside events, maturation and development, indirect consequences of the research operations, characteristics associated with the cases themselves), except for the causal factor X. What comparison does is to focus attention upon the effects of X.

Procedures for equivalent sampling. In the ideal experiment, an extra phase is added to the representational sampling procedure, so that after a main sample or reservoir of cases is drawn (as in the usual sampling phases I and II in Figure 3), this main sample is then subdivided into the experimental and control samples.

Typically, a preliminary step in this subdivision is to hold constant certain extraneous variables through stratification, or through matching whereby cases are put together in similar pairs. Such matching (or stratification), though not necessary to the selection of equivalent samples in the experimental design, may greatly increase the efficiency of the design by reducing, for a sample of a given size, the error due to chance alone. The more variables are controlled, the fewer variables there are on which differences in the experimental result can occur through chance. With this reduced chance error, the matched sample design becomes more sensitive; that is, it can detect even relatively slight differences which may appear in the dependent variable as a result of the change in the independent variable.

The researcher cannot depend upon matching alone, however, to equate the experimental and control samples. He can never be sure he has recognized and been able to hold constant all the extraneous factors that may be associated with Y or with the XY relationship. Indeed, as Fisher says in his classic work on experimental design, to insist that the samples be totally alike in every respect except that to be tested is "a totally impossible requirement in . . . all . . . forms of experimentation" (Fisher, 1937, p. 21). Hence the essential step in the design of the two samples is not matching, but randomization, or the random assignment of X (the treatment), following procedures which Fisher has specified for various research situations (Fisher, pp. 20–24, *passim*). A coin may be tossed, for example, to determine which case in a given pair is assigned to the experimental sample and which to the control sample. The researcher is thereby prevented from consciously or unconsciously selecting for the experimental sample those cases apparently most likely to respond to the causal factor in the predicted direction. In addition, the effects of all those potentially confounding variables on which the researcher does not attempt to match, or on which his matching is erroneous or imperfect, are thus randomized at the outset. Since both experimental and control samples are selected at random from the same reservoir of cases, the two samples differ only by chance.

To be sure, the random assignment to experimental and control samples also results in errors—differences between the two samples which may confound the results. But these errors are not unsuspected. They are the errors due to chance variation, exactly those chance errors which the statistical tests are designed to estimate. Thus the difference between the two samples found in the dependent variable at the end of the ideal experiment is produced by just two

factors—by the independent variable X and the errors due to chance variation—for the attempt has been made to equalize, hold constant, or randomize the effects of all other factors. The statistical test, then, by estimating the probability of obtaining the observed differences on the basis of chance alone, aids the investigator in disentangling the effects of X from the effects of chance.

Elaborations of equivalent sampling. This discussion has focused on the simplest experimental design in which only two samples are used to study the effects, within the limits of random error, of a single dichotomized independent variable—X or no-X. To take care of more complex independent variables, the number of experimental and control samples may be increased. For study-

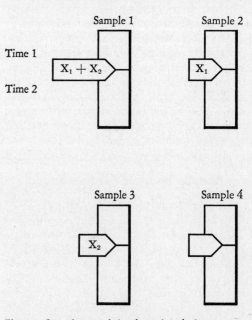

Fig. 4. Samples used in factorial design.

ing more than one explanatory variable, a factorial scheme is often employed in which a separate sample is set up for each possible combination of the factors to be examined (Fisher, 1937). Thus a sample design for two independent variables, each of which is varied in only two ways, might appear as in Figure 4. Additional samples may also be employed in experiments to handle the effects of certain extraneous factors. Solomon (1949) has worked out special designs, for example, that correct for the unsystematic control effects of pretesting. Respondents who have been pretested on the problem under study (e.g., questioned about a given set of values) may, because they thereby become sensitized to this problem, respond differently from those not pretested to the treatment X (to a mass communication, e.g., designed to change these particular values). Thus, if Boy Scouts are questioned about their adherence to Scout norms before and after being exposed to propaganda against these norms, the after-measure might show no decrease (or even an increase) in adherence (despite the propaganda) if the pretest stimulates the boys to discuss their views and reinforce one another's loyalties. In order to take care of control effects of this kind, Solomon adds to the classical design control samples which have not been exposed to the pretest (or to earlier experimentation) as a potentially confounding factor.

Modifications of Equivalent Sampling

A variety of other designs approximate such equivalent samples by holding constant certain extraneous variables, but lack the special feature of randomization of the effects of other uncontrolled variables.

For example, Chapin (1947) has described in detail the ex post facto study that, instead of manipulating the independent variable, utilizes as the presumed cause a "natural" change occurring outside of the researcher's control, such as the rehousing of slum families or the social isolation of schizophrenics. Here the experimental and control samples are selected to reflect the categories of the independent variable and are matched on a number of other associated factors. Because of the control of these factors, the sample has a sharper sensitivity to a possible relationship between the explanatory variables

than does a cross-section sample of the same size.

Although this design is a valuable means of studying causal relationships where experimentation is impossible or impractical, it cannot provide the same kind of assurance as the experiment, since it cannot detect the possible confounding effects of the uncontrolled variables. Because chance does not, indeed cannot, be allowed to operate fully in the selection of the sample, the investigator cannot rule out the possibility of systematic bias. He cannot be sure, for example, that changes in family life are produced by rehousing rather than by unsuspected differences in the economic or social stability of the two samples of families. Moreover, there are other difficulties in the design because it does not use a representative sample of all nonresidents, but only of those nonresidents who match the residents. Easily matched families may give different results from hard-to-match families, for example, or the sample may be made too small to allow investigation of additional factors through cross-tabulation (see, for example, Edwards, 1954, pp. 281–282; Strodtbeck, 1958, pp. 159–161).

Another design uses what might be called a focused sample (Matilda White Riley, 1963, I, pp. 298–300). When the objective is to discover what causal factors affect a dependent variable, the sample may be drawn from selected cells of a population already stratified on the dependent variable and on one or more extraneous variables. In one study, after an extensive analysis showed a boy's college aspirations to be correlated with his I.Q. and his father's status, subsamples were drawn for use in a further exploratory search for additional factors (Kahl, 1953). The two subsamples consisted of the two main types of boys to be compared: those expecting to go and those not expecting to go to college. Furthermore, the subsamples were alike in containing boys with enough intelligence to go to college and with lower-middle status backgrounds. This sample design thus holds constant these extraneous factors and controls, not the main causal variables as in the experimental design, but the effects or consequences of the process under study (the college plans, in this example), so as to focus on the search for causes or reasons for these plans.

Cross-section samples. Many of the samples used in cross-section studies are also designed to allow a modified form of causal analysis. The investigator, after finding that X is associated with (or seems to make a difference in) Y, typically wants to find out how much of this difference can actually be attributed to X, the independent variable in which he is interested. In order to rule out various possibly confounding factors, he makes cross-tabulations which hold these constant. In this way, he is able to study (through multivariate analysis) the XY relationship—the relationship, for example, between religious background and voting behavior—within subsamples that are homogeneous on such other variables as sex, marital status, or degree of political interest. Thus cross-tabulation for subsample comparison corresponds to the matching of samples used in experimental designs.

Plans for cross-tabulation and multivariate analysis often markedly affect both the stratification and the size of the sample employed. The sample must be stratified on each of the independent variables to be investigated, and there must be enough cases in each of the cells to allow statistical comparisons on the dependent variable. An analysis of attitudes of the American public toward civil liberties, for example, may require a sample as large as several thousand and varied enough to permit comparisons on such factors as residence, education, age, religious views, and the like (cf. Stouffer, 1955). To avoid excessive and costly increases in the overall size of a sample, small cells are often oversampled. In a sample of the United States population, for example, extra cases may be selected from the high income cell since it constitutes only a small percentage of the total; this oversampling allows separate analysis of this cell as com-pared with others, reducing the error due to chance variation. (Of course, in recombining the data for the population as a whole, appropriate weighting must be used to correct for the oversampling of the high income cases.)

Even after extensive cross-tabulation, the data from a cross-section sample can provide only limited assurance that the variable of interest, X, is indeed the true "cause" (Wold, 1956). Not only is the time order of X and Y typically problematical, but there is too often, as Stouffer has put it, "a wide-open gate through which other uncontrolled variables can march" (Stouffer, 1962, p. 294). In the ideal experimental design, it is random assignment that ensures that the X sample and the not-X sample are distributed alike (except for chance error) on all extraneous variables. In the cross-section study, however, the effects of the uncontrolled variables are merely assumed to be randomized, whereas actually, even after cross-tabulation, the X subsample and the not-X subsample may be distributed quite differently on some uncontrolled extraneous variable, W. As in the ex post facto design, it may be this uneven distribution of W, rather than X or not-X, which accounts for the differences in Y.

CONFLICTING AND COMBINED BASES

There appear to be certain situations, especially in laboratory research and experimentation, where designing a sample for purposes of the analysis may interfere with the possibility of generalizing to the universe of interest.

Suppose that an experimenter takes a main sample of individuals needing a certain treatment, holds certain variables constant through matching, then makes the random subdivision into experimental and control samples. He has doubtless thereby designed the sample properly for purposes of analyzing the relationship between the explanatory variables. Nevertheless, he may have difficulty in generalizing his results in terms of his conceptual model if the main sample was not selected by probability procedures and if the hard-to-match cases were excluded entirely. Such samples are designed to ensure what Campbell (1957) calls the internal validity of the research—"Did in fact the experimental stimulus make some significant difference in this specific instance?" rather than the external validity—"To what populations, settings, and variables can this effect be generalized?" (Campbell, 1957, p. 1).

Or suppose that a researcher is concerned with the interaction processes of small groups and defines as his conceptual universe all formal and informal student groups of certain sizes in a particular men's college. He might conceivably prepare a list of such groups and use probability procedures to obtain a fairly representative sample. But what happens to this representativeness if, alternatively, in order to facilitate laboratory observation, he depends only upon volunteers? Obviously, the kinds of groups which submit readily to such observation may be different from those which do not. Or what happens when he himself constructs the groups artificially, forming new groups to facilitate his analysis of the processes of group development? Obviously, these artificial groups may be different from the naturally established groups of interest.

In such situations, then, the two sampling bases may sometimes tend to be mutually exclusive. Out of practical considerations, moreover, the relative emphasis placed upon one or the other basis reflects the optimal allocation, for the particular objective, of the resources available for the research.

Yet the ideal design combines the two bases. Many samples designed for purposes of the analysis also attempt, where cost and inconvenience present no obstacles, to match some relevant population through representational sampling. Still other samples adhere closely to the principles of representational sampling, yet succeed in supporting elaborate analyses of social processes and the interrelationships of several variables.

ASSEMBLING THE DATA

In translating into research operations the concepts set forth in his model, the researcher must decide not only what concrete cases to select but also what kinds of concrete data he will use to index the properties of each case, so that he can then organize these data and observe their patterns and relationships. He must represent his idea of each property through selected empirical indicants or manifestations of it.

In a familiar analogue from the physical sciences, temperature is an abstract idea of a property. As a concrete indicant of the temperature of a body of water, for instance, one finds the degree of expansion of a column of mercury in an enclosed tube (a thermometer). In effect, one infers the relative amounts of the abstract quality temperature from the height of the mercury in the tube. Although the sociologist's measuring instruments may be typologies or Guttman scales rather than thermometers, he, too, must find sense data (such data as answers to questions, the talking and gesturing he observes in interaction, or the reports and documents he finds in the library) that he can use as indicants of the properties in which he is interested—the integration of the group, the group's adaptation to its environment, or the various actions, attitudes, and feelings of the individual group members.

The sociologist may either use as indicants data that are already available in one form or another that will serve his purpose, or he may gather new data. New data have the advantage that they can be gathered according to the researcher's own specifications in line with his particular objectives. Alternatively, many kinds of available materials—historical writings and documents, public records, studies completed by other researchers, to name only a few—are widely used in sociology to provide information on many otherwise inaccessible topics. First some major methods of gathering new data will be considered and then the use of available materials.

OBSERVATION VS. QUESTIONING

The researcher using new materials typically gathers them either by acting as a direct observer—watching the interaction of a group, for example; by questioning the group members themselves to learn their attitudes and perceptions; or by combining observation and questioning, as the participant observer may, for example, when he lives with certain families or certain primitive tribes. Of course, all science rests upon observation in its broadest meaning—upon data which are accessible to the researcher through his senses. But the sociologist distinguishes between the data obtained by observation in its more limited meaning of watching the group, listening to it, noting its physical characteristics and its collective products, on the one hand; and, on the other hand, the data obtained by questioning— the marks made on paper by the respondent himself or his oral reports as recorded by an interviewer.

The data from observation and from questioning differ in major focus as well as in methodological strengths and limitations. Researchers sometimes feel, mistakenly, that they can obtain a true picture of a social phenomenon only if they observe it with their own eyes. To be sure, observation and questioning often give quite different results; but this occurs not because one method is necessarily more valid than the other, but because the two focus directly on different, though interrelated, sets of social system properties.

The difference is clearly apparent when one compares two widely used forms of the two procedures—direct observation of interaction, and private questioning of the several individual group members in turn. Observation focuses on the network of overt actions and reactions among group members—the objective properties of the system. Questioning deals with the subjective network of orientations and interpersonal relationships—the underlying ideas and feelings and perceptions of the members, their hopes and fears, their dispositions to act toward others and to define and evaluate them in various ways.

Yet the data obtained by questioning and observation differ only in their direct foci. Indirectly, they are inextricably bound together, because actions and orientations, though distinguishable types of properties, are interdependent aspects of the same system. Orientations, defined as dispositions to act, are at any given moment being partially acted out (although generally a certain part of the orientations remains latent or concealed). Conversely, these orientations tend themselves to reflect this interaction, so that each actor's definitions and expectations of the other actors are constantly being tested and revised in the light of what these others actually do. Thus, orientations are indirectly reflected in data from observation, and interactions indirectly reflected in data from questioning.

The observer, then, whose chief concern is with the overt actions of a group, often goes on to make indirect inferences about orientations. He assumes that such inferences will be correct most of the time. In some instances, however, the inferences will be wrong, as individual actors successfully conceal attitudes and feelings which they do not wish to express to the group. Similarly, the questioner, concerned chiefly with orientations, may also elicit reports from respondents about their actions. Useful as such reports may often be, however, they describe the interaction as the actor himself perceives and evaluates it and thus may be quite different from the report of an outside observer of the same interaction.

In this sense, each method of data-gathering is especially valid for one set of system properties, as diagramed in Figure 5, but often misses information about the other set of properties which is directly available only through the other approach. The two methods parallel and supplement one another, and both are sometimes necessary for a full understanding. Thus Bales, for example, may supplement his observation data

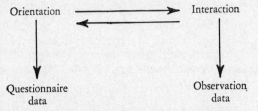

Fig. 5. Data obtained by questioning and observation.

by asking the group members to evaluate one another after the observed interaction is at an end (Bales, 1952).

DIRECT OBSERVATION OF INTERACTION

Apart from this basic difference in focus, observing and questioning as methods of data-gathering are used in many different forms, either alone or in various combinations, to compile data of varying scope, content, and accuracy. Observation, which does not depend upon any ability or willingness of the actors in the system themselves to report, often deals successfully with the whole system in the round and with its dynamic processes, revealing patterns of action and structures of roles which the participants themselves do not fully comprehend. The specific procedures of observation, as well as the nature of the data obtained, are affected by a series of design decisions about whether to use an unstructured or a structured instrument for data-gathering, whether to participate directly in the action under study, and whether and how to control this action.

Structured vs. Unstructured Observation

At one extreme, the observer may go into the field with the barest outline of the points to be covered; at the other extreme, he may employ a highly developed code (that is, a set of clearly defined categories with specifications of the ways in which the data as indicants are to be classified for purposes of measurement). The structuring of the instrument depends partly upon the conceptual model and partly upon other aspects of the research design. Unstructured observation is commonly used in exploratory research, when the conceptual model is not clearly defined in advance, and the researcher has little systematic knowledge of the properties he wants to study. Structured observation is likely to be used when the model is clearer and sufficient information is at hand to allow the advance formulation of a code which will fit the facts. Moreover, the research plans for handling single properties, studying relationships among properties, or using time as a factor in the analysis will all affect the requirements for gathering the data.

Unstructured observation. The researcher exploring an interaction process may attempt to observe as nearly as possible everything that occurs. Of course, as a sociologist, he typically focuses on social interaction, not so much on the biological or psychological processes of the multiple actors as on their social behavior and their expression to each other of underlying orientations, feelings and attitudes. He tries to record (as unobtrusively as possible) the entire sequence of interaction, describing the social situation and identifying which actor performs each of the acts. He distinguishes clearly between his observations (what he actually sees and hears) and his interpretations (the inferences he may draw about the relationships and attitudes of the actors and the patterns of their actions). He keeps an open mind toward his data, takes nothing for granted, and avoids the premature notion that he has a total grasp of the situation.

Numerous studies in the literature of cultural anthropology—each usually restricted to just one, or just a few, cases—have demonstrated the merits of the intensive, descriptive approach. In the first place, the method provides a wide range of detail. Instead of concentrating on just one specific area and selecting a few aspects for consideration, the researcher gathers such a great variety of data that he is able to see the actors in their total life situation. The reader of Malinowski's (1926) reports, for example, learns about the Trobriand native as a member of a fishing crew, as part of a complex matrilineal family, as carrying out his obligations in religious rituals and economic exchanges; the fishing excursions and other activities come to life so vividly that the reader himself feels like a participant. This wealth of detail gives an immediacy to the findings that would be difficult to duplicate by any other research method. Moreover, since the observer is actually present throughout the selected interaction under study, he can grasp the processes and patterns of behavior as a whole instead of trying to recreate them, as an interviewer might, by assembling information and assessing the consequences after they have happened. Finally, many latent patterns of behavior—patterns the actors themselves are not completely aware of and so cannot report—may become apparent through this procedure. Malinowski deals with the "hidden motives of behavior, and the hardly ever formulated spontaneous line of conduct" (Malinowski, 1926, p. 121), saying that he uncovers, though he is not always explicit about how he uncovers, a state of affairs which no native, however intelligent, can formulate.

In contrast to such potential assets of unstructured observation, an important limitation arises whenever the procedure rests on unsystematic description rather than on measurement. Because the procedure is not standardized, the researcher himself cannot always employ it consistently (although long practice in a particular descriptive procedure may lead to a degree of standardization). Because the procedure is not entirely open to inspection, the reader cannot be sure just how each piece of evidence was secured. Thus it is possible that all sorts of errors may have been introduced in the course of observing, recording, and interpreting the data. These potential errors are not fully explicated or assessed; that is, one cannot determine how reliable the evidence is.

Reliability is often considered in the methodological literature in terms of similarity of results of independent study of the same social phenomenon by two or more researchers using the same (or comparable) methods. Clearly, the unsystematic approach cannot state its procedures explicitly enough to enable others to conduct similar investigations in exactly the same way. It would therefore be difficult to compare the results obtained by different researchers using unstructured observation, even though they attempt to replicate one another's findings, for any difference in their findings might be solely a result of differences in the method. Thus, as long as observation is to remain highly flexible and to exploit every fresh opportunity, it cannot also attain the incompatible goal of maximum reliability.

To be sure, a degree of reliability may often be introduced into exploratory studies by a modified approach that supplements description with certain more systematic procedures. For example, Whyte (1951), whose approach to street corner society is largely unstructured, also introduces certain techniques that are relatively standardized and open to inspection (the mapping of the spatial positions taken by the men and the analysis of the origination of action in sets of pairs of men). Similarly, no exploratory study need remain altogether qualitative and impressionistic. Quite the contrary, the investigator making a descriptive case study in sociology remains alerted to the possibility of taking one sector of his initial observations and working out a limited but analytically informative systematic analysis.

Structured observation. In systematic observation, the researcher sets forth an organized plan for collecting and classifying the data as indicants. The basic principles may be illustrated through the widely used procedure of "interaction process analysis," developed by Bales (1950) and his colleagues at the Harvard Laboratory of Social Relations for observing, analyzing, and com-

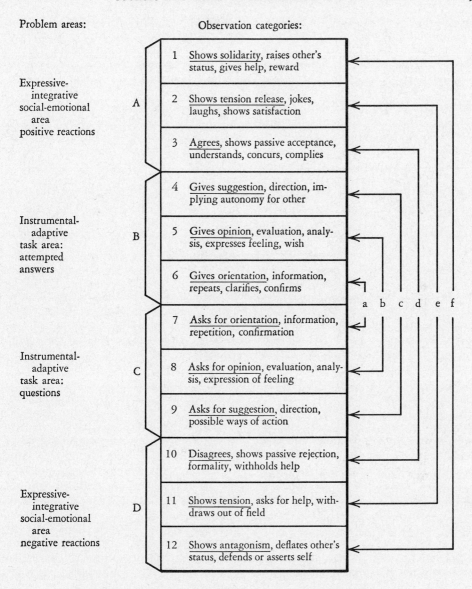

Fig. 6. Bales' categories for direct observation of the interactional process. (Reprinted with permission from Bales, 1952, p. 149.)

paring behavior in various small groups—especially groups devoted to decision-making or problem-solving.

Bales' conceptual model defines a number of properties of the interaction of any group, such as the positive or negative direction, the instrumental or expressive character, and the focus on any of six problems of communication and organization. He explicitly defines each of these rather complex properties, and within each he further defines various categories into which the property is divided. In order to measure each of these properties, Bales specifies, in his code, exactly what kinds of data are to be gathered for use as indicants, that is, which of the observed acts are to be classified in which categories as reflecting each property. The Bales categories (see Figure 6) are mutually exclusive, so that every observed act can be classified in one, and only one, category (and there is no miscellaneous or "wastebasket" category). Moreover, observers are given detailed training on how to classify each act, so that one observer's classification will accord closely with that of another observer and thus ensure a high degree of reliability.

Once such structured data have been gathered and classified, they are systematically organized for measurement and analysis and may be presented in the form of tables and graphs. One particularly useful form in which sociological data are often arranged is the who-to-whom matrix (see Figure 7). The matrix, used in mathematics and diverse fields of application, shows in the Bales (1952) analysis which members of the group interact with which other members. It provides several types of information. For example, the marginal information (that is, the totals or sums of the respective rows and columns) refers to the total roles of the group members, showing how much action each member initiates and receives. In addition, the cell information (given in the boxes or cells of the matrix) refers to the dyadic relationships between pairs of group members, showing how much action a particular member directs toward another

member, and how much he in turn receives from that other. In this manner, the data obtained from observation may be organized to yield information about several levels of the social system.

Such theoretically-based methods of structured observation achieve certain distinctive advantages. Whereas the decision to handle properties qualitatively and descriptively through unstructured observation may restrict the reliability of the findings, the alternative decision to work systematically tends to offset such restrictions. Not only does Bales explicitly demonstrate the reliability of his coding procedures (Borgatta & Bales, 1953), but he has so standardized the method that other researchers have been able to employ it. Moreover, the systematic character of the method allows widespread replications that test the conceptual model under varied conditions (the Bales method has been extended to several types of small social systems both inside and outside the laboratory), enabling the research results to become cumulative and more generally applicable (Hare, 1962).

At the same time, however, the more systematic and more precise the observation procedure, the more rigid the requirements it sets for making selections (and consequent exclusions) from the total complex of data at hand. The Bales code applied to jury deliberations, for example, does not reflect the specific content of discussions about the trial or of the arguments pro and con, but merely abstracts from these discussions those aspects that index the properties under study. The method lacks some of the flexibility of the descriptive case study, its ability to amass details, and to suggest new insights and formulations.

Consequently, sociologists often modify the highly structured procedure to provide leeway for unstructured, descriptive materials that might point to unexpected findings. Such a combined procedure is useful to the researcher who, having tentatively specified his conceptual model, is still uncertain about this specification. It may some-

Rank of person originating act	To individuals of each rank						Total to individuals	To group as a whole 0	Total initiated
	1	2	3	4	5	6			
1		1,238	961	545	445	317	3,506	5,661	9,167
2	1,748		443	310	175	102	2,778	1,211	3,989
3	1,371	415		305	125	69	2,285	742	3,027
4	952	310	282		83	49	1,676	676	2,352
5	662	224	144	83		28	1,141	443	1,584
6	470	126	114	65	44		819	373	1,192
Total received	5,203	2,313	1,944	1,308	872	565	12,205	9,106	21,311

^a Reprinted with permission from Bales, 1952, p. 154.

Fig. 7. Bales' aggregate matrix for 18 sessions of six-man groups.[a]

times prove valuable even in highly systematic, hypothesis-testing designs where the original hypotheses did not, after all, account adequately for the situation under study.

Observer Participation

Another important variable in the method of observation is the extent to which the researcher takes a direct part in the action he is observing.

Participant observation. A characteristic feature of many anthropological studies is participant observation, which is exemplified in Whyte's (1943) procedures of gathering data about the street corner gang. In trying to understand the nature of the group's interaction, Whyte found that "what people told me helped to explain what had happened and that what I observed helped to explain what people told me, so that it was helpful to observe and interview at the same time" (Whyte, 1943, p. vii). Whyte lived in Cornerville for three and a half years, boarding for a time with an Italian family and learning the Italian language so as to gain access to otherwise inaccessible material and to show his "sincere and sympathetic interest." He participated in the everyday activities of the community, joining clubs, taking part in team bowling matches, escorting local girls to dances, becoming a campaign worker for a local politician, and the like. Although the members of the group seem never to have lost their awareness of him as an "outsider" who was writing a book about their community, he did succeed in becoming a very active member of the social system he wished to study.

Participant observation of this sort may be highly effective, especially for exploratory research, in developing a remarkably full understanding of the social system as a functioning whole. Nevertheless, it is subject to two major types of errors possible in data-gathering: an unwanted and unsystematic control effect over the system under study, so that the research itself has the consequence of changing the facts; and a biased viewpoint, or failure of the researcher to perceive the facts correctly.

Control effect (like biased viewpoint) is not peculiar to participant observation, of course. (The questioner, for instance, may pretest the attitudes of an audience before exposing them to a persuasive lecture, in order to provide a basis for measuring attitude change, even though the pretest will exert an unwanted influence upon their reactions to the lecture by alerting them in advance.) But unsystematic control is a potential source of error in participant observation because the addition of a new member, like any change in a system, may affect the entire structure of interdependent parts in the group being observed. Especially in small social systems, introducing not only another person but also another role (that of observer) can affect markedly the relationships among the other members. Thus the researcher, often unintentionally and even unwittingly, controls, or changes to some extent, the action he is observing. (Similarly, the physicist, in measuring the temperature of a liquid, may change its temperature somewhat by the act of introducing into it a thermometer that may itself be initially warmer or cooler.)

The difficulty with control effect in participant observation, and in many other research designs, is that it is unsystematic, in contrast to the systematic controls which the experimenter, for example, builds into his research design when he interferes slightly with the action in order to measure the effects. The participant observer rarely attempts to measure the unsystematic control effects. Yet, as a sophisticated researcher, he recognizes the danger in advance, making every effort to minimize the changes he himself may introduce and allowing for such changes in interpreting his data.

In addition to the control effect (which changes the action under study), there may also be a biased viewpoint effect: a potential limitation affecting the observer's perception of this action. The observer, by virtue of the very fact that he plays a role in the group, tends thereby to impose certain restrictions upon his own understanding of the situation. His viewpoint may be biased in various ways. As long as he plays only one role, he perceives only those aspects of the system afforded by this role. As he forms alliances with certain members, he thus cuts himself off from the channels of information available through others. Since the leader of the gang and the lower-level followers obviously perceive the group differently, Whyte (1943), if he had taken only the leader's opinions, would not have fully understood the opinions and orientations of the other men; his conception of the corner gang would consequently have

been inaccurate and biased. (Sometimes the only feasible way to reduce the bias is to play more than one role.) Moreover, once the researcher becomes a full-fledged member of the group, familiarity may lead him to take certain phenomena for granted. He may lose his sensitivity to the possibility of latent patterns and merely adopt the attitudes and stereotypes of his informants. Or he may jump to conclusions, accepting too hastily an overly "neat" image of the action under study so that he unconsciously forecloses the possibility of further revision. To the extent that familiarity with the group dulls the researcher's sharpness of observation, his results lose their objectivity.

Even in rigorous research designs like the experiment, the investigator may lose his objectivity as he suffers from the fatigue of a long investigation, becomes increasingly immersed in the system, or allows his research hypotheses to distort his view. Error, often vital error, can arise when the experimenter, holding an expectation of an outcome, allows his judgment to be affected by what he expects to see. The results can be different, and far more accurate, when the evaluation is made through the independent judgment of some outsider who knows neither the hypothesis nor which cases are in the experimental and the control samples.

Manipulating the role of participant observer. In making participant observations, the researcher can govern to a certain extent the control effect by the way he establishes his presence in the field. He may openly let his subjects know they are being observed. Or he may enter the system incognito, assuming some plausible role that the field affords (such as taking a job). Although the incognito approach often raises ethical questions, it may reduce the control effect more than would be possible if the observer makes his presence as a researcher known. If the role he takes is already an integral part of the system, his presence in that role is less likely to affect the rest of the system. Not knowing that they are being observed, the members of the group will probably be more spontaneous in their actions.

On the other hand, the covert observer may find complete immersion in the system, and the subsequent likelihood of a biased viewpoint, more difficult to avoid. Limited to his specified role, he may be cut off from valuable channels of information, unable to solicit information not normally accessible to his role without arousing suspicion. He cannot combine questioning with direct observation as Malinowski (1926) or Whyte (1943) did. Moreover, since his project is being carried on *sub rosa,* he will not be able to stimulate interest in it, so that his subjects will be less likely to volunteer information that might be relevant to the research.

Occasionally several observers are employed, either openly identified as sociological researchers or not so identified, in order to avoid some of the difficulties. In general, however, control effect and biased viewpoint effect cannot be entirely eliminated in participant observation. Both need to be taken into consideration in planning and evaluating the results of research that utilizes this method.

Observation without participation. Another useful procedure is the direct observation of interaction in which the observer himself does not participate. The observer may watch a group of children playing in a park, for example, while the children are entirely unaware of the on-going research. The Bales method is a modification of this procedure, in which the observers behind a one-way glass cannot communicate with the actors even by exchanging glances, and the latter may soon forget that they are watched. This method minimizes any control effect over the action being studied and avoids the biased viewpoint that comes from immersion in the group; although the observer's position outside the group often limits his perceptions, restricting his view of facial expressions, for example, and his full grasp of conversation.

The Researcher's Control

Data-gathering procedures also differ in the extent to which the investigator attempts, as part of the research, to control or change the natural dynamic processes of the system he is observing. If unsystematic control occurs because of his presence in participant observation, and certain other techniques prevent his data-gathering operations from changing the observed situation in any way, there are still other procedures in which he sets out systematically to control the process, as the natural scientist often does.

The Bales procedure illustrates a special kind of systematic control. First, the researcher controls the selection of actors, bringing together aggregates of unrelated individuals who are removed from their ordinary group relations and watching how they form new social systems (instead of utilizing natural groups, such as families or corner gangs). Second, he controls the goal of the interaction by giving the group a problem to solve. Third, he controls the environment within which the interaction occurs, taking the actors from their natural settings and bringing them into the laboratory. In contrast to participant observation, the researcher now exerts this control intentionally and according to a specified plan. Bales' work demonstrates how such controls may heighten the opportunity of discovering the uniformities in the system processes.

The full potentialities of systematic controls are exploited in the experimental design, in which the researcher manipulates the independent variable (as well as the experimental conditions) in order to discover its effects. Ironically enough, though, these manipulations may themselves have indirect consequences that confound the result. The classic example of this type of control effect, the "Hawthorne effect," occurred in the studies conducted by Elton Mayo and his associates at the Western Electric Company's Hawthorne works (see, for

example, Roethlisberger & Dickson, 1940).
Here it turned out that the dependent variable (worker productivity) was governed primarily, not by the experimentally manipulated variable (the physical conditions of work), but by the informal group structure produced by the test conditions themselves.

Some Restrictions

In sum, although observation, with its direct focus upon interaction, has great value, each special observational procedure has its own special combination of advantages and disadvantages. Moreover, there are certain general restrictions shared by various observational procedures.

In the first place, strict and methodical observation seems suitable only for fairly small groups, or for selected aspects of larger groups (such as the housing in a neighborhood or the religious rituals performed in a church). To be sure, an observer (or better, several observers) can effectively record impressions of the social atmosphere of large assemblages (crowds, meetings, audiences). And sometimes he can study a strategic part which represents, in miniature, the role-structure and social processes of the larger social system which is more difficult to observe (Merton, 1959, pp. xxviff.).

In the second place, cultural taboos prevent observation of private interaction, like the intimate communications between marital partners or the deliberations of juries.

Moreover, the method is applicable to action taking place only in the present. It patently cannot be used to refer to periods prior to the inception of the research; and to extend observation into the future in order to trace a gradual development of some social system property over time may require a considerable investment of research time. Even if it were permissible to observe a married couple throughout their life together, for example, to append a sociologist-observer to the couple would be an absurdly impractical procedure.

It may be in part because of such restrictions that direct observation is comparatively little used in current sociological research; in the 88 journal reports analyzed, only 7 studies were based on data from observation and 5 of these combined the observation with questioning. The success of the Bales procedure as one example suggests the possibility, however, that observation may become more widely used as further systematic adaptations of the method are developed, and as more sociologists comprehend the possibilities of dealing directly with dynamic processes at the level of the collectivity.

QUESTIONING

Rather than observing directly the interaction of the group members, the sociologist frequently deals with the individual members removed from the interactive situation in order to question each one privately. As a sociologist, his special interest lies in the use of questioning to study, not individuals per se, but individuals as they play roles in groups, or as several individual roles may fit together to constitute a group.

Answers to questions, although they do not always report interaction as the observer might perceive it, cover a potentially wider range of content than do data from observation. They also have the peculiar merit of reflecting directly the subjective states of the actors—their feelings, attitudes, perceptions, evaluations—about the group, for example, about their own roles in it, or about the interaction as they themselves observe it. When skillfully used as a sociological tool, questioning frequently reveals dormant aspects of the system which are not displayed while the observer watches and which may even be concealed from the other group members. Thus questioning reveals the structure of orientations—the latent patterns of attitudes, feelings, mutual expectations, and interpersonal relationships among the members—that underlie the overt interaction but are not always accessible to observation.

The Nature of Questioning

The questioning of individuals as a general research procedure has been widely used in many fields, and a variety of special techniques employed in sociology were originally developed for use in personality tests, the census, public opinion polls, attitude studies, and the like. Some techniques require personal interviews, in which the questioner, following a list of topics (an interview guide) or a more structured questionnaire, interacts directly with the respondent. In other techniques, the respondent is given a form (a schedule or questionnaire) to fill out himself.

Some general principles of personal interviewing, which apply also to questioning in general, may be summarized from the accumulated experience. First, rapport is established by putting the respondent at ease and establishing a warm and friendly atmosphere; "well-liked" interviewers are found to elicit more responsive answers than interviewers who are "not liked," for example, or northern Negroes are more likely to talk freely with white interviewers than are southern Negroes. A place for the interview which provides privacy will often contribute to the feeling of rapport. Second, the legitimacy of the research must be established by a forthright statement of the purpose of the study and its sponsorship as well as by an explanation that the respondent was chosen scientifically as a member of a sample. Third, the interviewer must keep an open mind, must not stereotype the respondent from his appearance or manner, must avoid any reflection of his own ideas or hypotheses in his manner of asking the questions or recording the answers. Finally, to ensure completeness of each interview report, the interviewer must cover all the questions and must record the required answers in full.

A peculiar feature of questioning is that an interview, and to a lesser extent even the self-administration of a questionnaire, always establishes a new and temporary social system. The respondent, typically separated from the group under study, now plays a new role in relation to the questioner. The nature of this role relationship may affect not only the interviewer's perceptions of, and testimony about, the respondent's answers, but the kinds of answers the respondent gives. If the respondent thinks the interviewer expects him to make certain responses, he may adjust his answers to meet such expectations (see, for example, Merton, 1947). Both types of possible distortion—the response bias of the person being questioned and the selective perception of the questioner—combine to bias the researcher's view of the respondent's true orientations. This is akin to the biased viewpoint effect noted in the discussion of participant observation, though in the interview it is often called "interviewer bias."

Various devices have been developed for reducing such a biased viewpoint effect (see Hyman, Cobb, Feldman, Hart, & Stember, 1954, *passim*), which seek, in the main, to reduce the social interactive character of the interview relationship and to neutralize the questioner's role. The underlying principles were summed up by Winston White (see Matilda White Riley, 1963, II, p. 16) in an ingenious adaptation of Parsons' (1951, pp. 297ff.) social control paradigm in which the interviewer: (1) provides support by establishing rapport with the respondent, guaranteeing anonymity if possible, and reassuring him in various ways; (2) shows permissiveness by encouraging him to express his own views and by avoiding the communication of normative expectations as to what he ought to say; (3) denies reciprocity by refusing to allow himself to be drawn into a discussion of his own views or to be diverted from the subject matter of the interview; and (4) manipulates sanctions by pointing out inconsistent answers, probing behind obvious rationalizations, and guiding the respondent toward giving a full report.

The questioner who attempts to neutralize

his own role in some such fashion is, in one sense, similar to the observer who attempts to minimize his participation in the interaction he is studying; both are trying to avoid biased viewpoint effect. But in another sense, there is a marked difference, because ideally the questioner is not intruding upon the interaction he wants to study. In interviewing respondents about their past role relationships to their parents, for instance, the questioner himself does not enter into those relationships. Thus he does not, under the usual conditions, face the danger of control effect.

It is sometimes possible to turn into a positive advantage the interactive character of the questioner-respondent relationship, rather than trying to neutralize it. The researcher may use the new interactive system to simulate a real situation in which the interviewer acts out one of the roles. For example, the questioner may learn much about child-parent relationships by pretending to play the role of one of the child's parents. Or market researchers may make doorstep interviews that simulate the buyer-seller relationship in a store when a new product is introduced. Although it is impossible to draw any exact line between such role playing and the method of participant observation, this device has important, and largely unexplored, possibilities (cf., Stanton, Back, & Litwak, 1956).

Structured vs. Unstructured Interviewing

In questioning, as in observation, the data-gathering instrument is sometimes highly structured (consisting of set sequences of closed questions with check-list answers) and sometimes highly unstructured (consisting of open questions or of mere lists of topics to be covered).

Here again the nature of the instrument is greatly affected by the plans for coding, measurement, and analysis of the data. Procedures for complex measurement, for example, often prescribe the form in which the indicants are to be gathered. Thus Guttman (1950) scaling may impose such prescriptions on the questionnaire as that it contain several questions (some 6 to 12) to measure each property, that each question contain a check-list of mutually exclusive answers, and that the proportions of respondents who will give positive answers to the several questions range widely between 20 per cent and 80 per cent. Or a dynamic study designed to measure changes over time, like a panel study or an experiment, may require repeated questioning of the same respondents to obtain comparable sets of data.

Structured interviews. Structured interviews require that the interviewer follow the rules exactly, asking the questions stated in the questionnaire, following the specified order of questions, and avoiding explanations. The basic principle of the structured interview is that the same set of stimuli is to be administered to all respondents alike.

Unstructured interviews. Unstructured interviews, though usually more difficult to conduct since they aim at greater depth and have less standardization, serve several research purposes. A set of such interviews may themselves comprise the major data for an exploratory investigation, especially in the study of delicate topics, in which respondents are deeply involved emotionally, and of which they have little understanding. But unstructured interviews are also often used as an adjunct to other data-gathering procedures. Sometimes they serve as a pilot study to give background for defining a conceptual model and stating an objective for a larger piece of research. Sometimes they provide the basis for constructing a more highly structured questionnaire, by showing the general framework within which respondents think, the kinds of words they use, and the types of incidents and examples which have meaning for them. And sometimes unstructured interviews are conducted at a late stage of the research, to help explain an ambiguous statistical finding from an extensive study.

Whenever the research design calls for

intensive, exploratory interviews, the questioner must be able to handle lengthy conversations, often touching upon matters which are personal in nature. He must determine on the spot the arrangement and wording of the questions. He must grasp the respondent's replies quickly enough to help him express his thoughts and to probe for further information when necessary. He must deal both with respondents who have difficulty in opening up and with respondents from whom the questioning releases a flood of irrelevant material. At the same time, unless he uses a tape-recorder, he must find means of recording verbatim as much of the interview as possible, or of taking full notes so that he can reconstruct it immediately afterward.

Because such interviewing often invades personal experiences and feelings, its propriety is sometimes called into question. There is no easy answer to such ethical problems, for responsibly conducted research is the only known means of increasing scientific knowledge. Yet, if an occasional respondent turns out to be a disturbed person and seems seriously threatened by the interview, the responsible investigator usually terminates the conversation rather than forcing replies.

Questioning the Several Group Members

Well established as such techniques for questioning discrete individuals may be, the sociologist who wants to gain maximum insight into the subjective structure of the group must often find means of extending them to cover the several members of the same social system. Moreover, since questioning typically starts with the individual, he must also find means of fitting together data about individuals into collective data from which inferences may be drawn about the group, a challenging problem that will be examined further (see below). Thus the special approach open to the sociologist for studying the latent structure of orientations consists, first, of questioning many (or all) the group members individually, and, second, of combining these individual points of view (using a matrix, for example, a map, or a simple description) to refer to the larger social system.

The latent structure of orientations. In a study of marital strain, for instance, the husband and wife under investigation may have quite different goals and hopes for their marriage, and perhaps they are not fully aware of their own goals or of the absence of harmonious integration. Neither the husband nor the wife could alone provide the researcher with a clear understanding of this relationship. But by comparing and combining the two sets of answers obtained by individual questioning of both marriage partners, the researcher may well be able to uncover the discrepancies, even before they become manifest in the system at all.

Or, in a study of communications in the peer group, questioning all the members might reveal a marked status disparity in the communications reported; that is, if one member of a pair is high status and the other low, the low status person is fairly likely to name the high as somebody he talks to, whereas the high status person is unlikely to name him in return. Clearly, the mere observation of each particular pair would show only whether or not the two talk to each other. Questioning the several members, on the other hand, provides reports, partially conflicting, which indicate that the two individuals in the pair perceive and evaluate their relationship quite differently. Perhaps the relationship is important to the low-status member, whereas the high-status member has so many friends that he forgets to mention this particular friend at all.

In such ways the disparities that reflect lack of complementarity or potential strains in the system may often be uncovered through questioning. If skillful use of observation can lead to an understanding of patterns of interaction not apparent to the actors themselves, skillful use of questioning can delve still deeper to an understanding of the structures of orientations—the unrecognized disharmonies in marriage, or the lack of reciprocity in friendship—that are not yet manifested in the interactions accessible to observation. But for this purpose, the uniquely suitable approach may require the combined answers of several members of the same system (see Riley, Cohn, Toby, & Riley, 1954).

The sociometric approach. One classic approach to the structure of orientations is sociometry. Sociometry began as the more or less personal philosophy of J. L. Moreno, who drew attention to "tele"—the cathectic orientations or tendencies for members of a group to attract or repel one another. Moreno and his immediate followers worked out various useful and ingenious procedures for studying tele-relationships. Basically their procedures, which have been extended and applied to various situations, start by questioning each member of a group about each other member. Each is asked to choose those with whom he would like to interact and to indicate those with whom he would prefer not to interact. In order to make these choices as realistic as possible, the questions

are phrased in terms of some specific criterion; school children might be asked, for example, "Whom would you like to sit beside?" (Moreno, 1953).

The sociometrists have developed a number of systematic procedures useful for treating the answers to sociometric choice questions as indicants of the underlying structure of interpersonal orientations (see Lindzey & Borgatta, 1954; Proctor & Loomis, 1951). The simple answers consist merely of lists of names of persons chosen and, by themselves, do not immediately serve the research purposes of indexing the group structure. The answers must first be fitted together in some way—transformed into collective data. One procedure is the *sociogram,* or map of social space (see Figure 8). The sociogram pictures clearly and informatively the structure of a small group in respect to one or two criteria of choice, showing the positions of the various individual roles in that structure. An alternative, but conceptually similar, device is the *sociometric matrix,* which can handle data on groups as large as several hundred members. Here, as in the Bales (1952) matrix (see Figure 7 above), the group

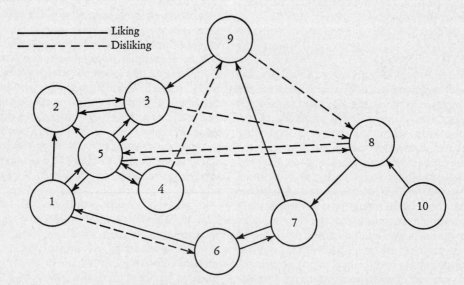

Fig. 8. A sociogram (reprinted with permission from Proctor & Loomis. p. 565).

members are listed down the side and again across the top and the choices entered in the cells. By this arrangement of data, the researcher can see how the parts of the system fit together, and he can generate several types of collective data on orientations (parallel to Bales's collective data on interactions), each referring to a different level of the system (see, e.g., Weiss & Jacobson, 1961).

Problems of questioning several group members. Although the device of questioning of many individual group members appears to hold considerable promise, as evidenced by the sociometric approach, certain special field problems are entailed. There is clearly a danger of control effect if one member, who has already been questioned, discusses the matter with another member who has not yet been questioned. The researcher may offset this effect by one of the following devices: using several interviewers in order to question all the group members simultaneously; in a two-member group, like husband and wife, conducting one interview immediately after the other without allowing any interim interaction between the group members; or administering a written questionnaire to all the members at the same time.

Another possible solution is to interview the incumbent of a representative role in the system. Le Play (1879), for example, in his early study of European families, focused upon the single role of the worker which becomes, in effect, the connecting link between the family system and the larger economic system to which it belongs. But there is no parallel solution for those frequent research situations where there is no single individual in the role of representative. The strained relationship between husband and wife cannot be fully learned from a single spouse as an "expert," nor can the interpersonal structure of attitudes in a community be revealed by a single "informant."

Interviewing the group members together, allowing them to interact during the interview, is another approach for revealing the nature of group dynamics and for gaining insight into such matters as the power structure of the group, discovering who plays instrumental and expressive roles, and the like. Since note-taking becomes difficult in such joint interviews, a tape recorder is often used to record the entire verbal interaction (the researcher can then limit his notes to nonverbal interaction). If the procedure is properly explained, and the tape recorder used unobtrusively, experience indicates that such recording usually has little effect on the interview. Joint interviewing borders closely upon direct observation of interaction, however, failing to uncover the private opinions which individuals will not express openly to the group.

The Self-Administered Questionnaire

In addition to the interview, the self-administered questionnaire is also an important tool for the sociologist, especially because it lends itself to simultaneous questioning of the members of a social system without any concomitant interaction among these members.

This method, which does not require the ministrations of an interviewer because the respondent reads the questions himself and fills out his own answers, takes various forms. Sometimes an administrator is present to guide the respondents in answering the questions, and sometimes not. Sometimes the respondents form a captive audience (such as a school class or an army unit) in which everybody is required to reply, in contrast to the self-selected set of respondents who themselves decide to reply to a mail questionnaire.

The formal requirements for the self-administered questionnaire are especially exacting because it must accomplish all the things the interviewer does in gaining entree and rapport, and preventing respondent fatigue. The auspices, statement of purpose, and guarantee of anonymity must be clearly stated. There must be some inducement for the respondent to cooperate—preferably the subject matter should be of patent interest to him. The arrangement of questions and answer spaces must be clear and consistent, and the entire form attractive and realistically paced to maintain interest and minimize boredom. Copious data are often elicited by a carefully designed format, such as a booklet, or a box in which questions appear sequentially in a window on the principle of a film-pack.

Types of questions suitable for self-administered questionnaires include those with check-list answers; those using visual devices, such as the rating scale on which the respondent can mark his answer; and even occasional open (essay) questions, which often yield interesting and suggestive answers, although different respondents answer within different frames of reference and many give no usable answers at all to such questions.

As self-administered questionnaires are increasingly used in sociological research, a new research role is being developed: that of questionnaire administrator. With captive audiences, the ratio of administrators to respondents is often pushed below 1 to 10, with excellent results. When several administrators are used in a study, they must be provided with field-tested instructions and directed not only to be sensitive to areas of respondent misunderstandings and questions, but also to give standard replies and directions.

Advantages and disadvantages. The self-administered form has a number of other advantages besides its suitability for questioning many members simultaneously. First, it is relatively inexpensive, since many cases may frequently be collected at one time without the cost of interviewing. Second, it affords a simple means of continual reporting over time, as in diary-keeping. Third, it gives the respondent a sense of privacy. Although there is, of course, always a degree of interaction between a respondent and the questioner who ultimately reads his responses, the respondent will often

report more freely because no interviewer is present. Thus the biased viewpoint effect is reduced.

Like all research procedures, the self-administered questionnaire has its disadvantages. Unless the respondents are captive, there are problems of nonresponse. Complete returns from a mail questionnaire may range as low as 10 per cent or less. Self-selection is likely to produce a bias, since persons who are especially interested in the topic, even fanatical about it in one direction or the other, are often the most likely to reply. Another disadvantage of this method is that in most cases there is no one immediately present (except possibly a busy administrator) to interpret and explain matters to the respondent, or to assess his emotional reactions. There is no possibility of probing, as there is in an interactive interview situation, although some respondents will often write long and revealing replies.

Use of Available Data

Much sociological research does not require that the investigator go into the field himself to observe interaction directly or question individuals at firsthand, but rests instead upon data that already exist in one form or another (see, for example, Riley, 1962). An impressive array of available materials lend themselves to the study of many social system problems. The researcher may make use of letters or television transcripts, historical documents or journalistic accounts, tribal artifacts or pieces of sculpture. He may analyze the records of corporations, police courts, or the United States Bureau of the Census. He may re-examine within the framework of his own conceptual model and research objective the already completed studies of other scholars. As all these and many other materials accumulate, it may well be that increasing numbers of researchers will find that the data they need have already been gathered. (Indeed, among the 88 journal reports analyzed, although 43 used new data, and 14 combined both types, there were 31 studies based primarily upon available materials.)

Forms of Available Data

Sociological data are available in diverse forms, each form requiring its own procedure of handling and interpretation. Sometimes the sociological researcher starts with data (such as letters, family case records, or works of art) which were not originally produced for research purposes. In other instances, he uses for his own objectives research data initially compiled by another researcher (such as ethnographic reports or interviews conducted by an outside polling agency). The problems entailed by these two types of materials clearly differ. The biases and limitations of data not produced for research purposes are quite different from the possible errors interjected by a researcher, whether this be an interviewer or an anthropologist describing his perceptions of a primitive society.

The sociologist may also choose between verbal and nonverbal data. Numerous techniques have been developed for analyzing verbal materials (novels, sermons, magazines, diaries, letters, documents, or case records from various fields) so as to discover underlying values or attitudes, social organization, or patterns of social behavior. Such data may be handled unsystematically and descriptively, as in Thomas and Znaniecki's (1918) use of letters in *The Polish Peasant;* or they may be arranged systematically in typologies, as in Max Weber's comparative studies of religion; or classified and quantified in various ways. One systematic procedure, "content analysis" (see Berelson, 1952), separates verbal content into small units of meaning, classifies these units, and handles them quantitatively. Somewhat less commonly used in sociology are the rich sources of nonverbal materials (art, music, clothing, dwellings, household equipment, or various artifacts), although they form a major basis for the sociology of art, music, and knowledge.

Available data may also be found at any of the several stages of research processing. At one extreme are raw data which have not yet been coded, tabulated, or analyzed. In other instances, the data may already have been partially processed. They may be coded and punched and ready to be tabulated, like the One-in-a-Thousand Population Sample issued by the United States Bureau of the Census (1963), or the polling data bank maintained at the Roper Public Opinion Research Center at Williams College. Or they may be already tabulated, but not yet fully analyzed or interpreted, like many of the statistical records of suicide used by Durkheim or the storehouse of official statistics maintained by government agencies in the United States and in many other countries throughout the world. At the opposite extreme from raw data are the findings from completed studies, which may be reanalyzed or reinterpreted through secondary analysis (see, for example, Hyman, 1959).

A Methodological Principle

Although data may be found available in such widely diversified forms and stages, one general rule applies to their use: In his analysis, the researcher must try to reconstruct the process by which the data were originally assembled by somebody else.

The researcher handling data he himself collected already knows this process. Since he selected and employed the procedures for data-gathering, he has weighed the full implications of these procedures for the research problem at hand. He is aware of the restrictions and possible biases of his materials and can evaluate their validity as indicants of the concepts which he has defined. Consequently, he can adapt his analysis and his interpretation to the nature of the new data themselves.

Such adaptation is equally important, of course, when the researcher did not gather the data. He must attempt to determine, insofar as possible, the conditions under which these data were produced, what specific methodological and technical decisions may have been made by the previous researcher, and the consequent impact on the nature of the data now to be taken over for his own use. To be sure, to make such important assessments of available data may be difficult and sometimes impossible.

Advantages

The particular data which happen to be available on given topics will range enormously, of course, in scope and in theoretical potential. In general, however, the use of available, rather than new, data tends to have certain assets. Perhaps the most obvious advantage is the greater efficiency, the possible savings of time, labor, and expense, when the researcher can go directly to the heart of his analysis, by-passing preliminary field work and sometimes also early phases of data processing. Sources of suitable available materials may be especially valuable when massive data are required beyond the scope of a single new study. The vast fund at the Bureau of the Census, for example, could not be reproduced by an individual researcher collecting his own data; yet, for study of a given problem such a fund frequently allows analysis of a wide range of potentially relevant variables and affords a high degree of refinement in the measurement of each variable. Use of data of this scope becomes increasingly feasible as materials of sociological interest are systematically accumulated and as the development of high-speed data-processing equipment facilitates storage, processing, and retrieval.

Data on past events. Probably the most important advantage of available data is that they provide the only means of studying certain kinds of problems. In particular, past events can no longer be observed directly by the researcher, nor can they be reached through questioning beyond the recollection of respondents living today. Thus the important analysis of historical situations or of long-term trends—of social change itself—

depends upon the prior existence of relevant materials. Sorokin (1937), for example, in his *Social and Cultural Dynamics,* treating the whole system of Western Europe as his macroscopic research case, dealt with social and cultural change over a period of some 2,500 years. But, it is only through his use of available materials—ranging from many thousand works of art to all the historical figures mentioned in the *Encyclopedia Britannica*—that he is able to plot the epochal alternations between Ideational and Sensate cultures, hence to postulate the governing principle of "immanent self-regulation" of broad sociocultural change.

Cross-cultural data. Similarly, study of cross-cultural phenomena from remote places may require data which would be inaccessible to new research. Consider as an example a study of family role prescriptions made by Zelditch (1955). Various previous studies by Bales (1952) and others had shown that small groups tend to develop two types of leaders: an instrumental leader, who acts principally to get the group task done, and an expressive leader, who looks after the social-emotional problems of the group. Zelditch wanted to know whether this is also true of the family—whether there is some inherent tendency within the family so that there is typically an instrumental leader (the husband) and an expressive leader (the wife). Obviously, such a universal hypothesis requires data about a wide variety of societies and cultures. The collection of new data would require not only large financing but also considerable time and an array of anthropological skills. Accordingly, the research was done from existing materials, in the following way: From lists of all societies for which ethnographers had reported relevant data on the family, the researcher drew a sample of 56. He then proceeded systematically to reanalyze the data. The method enabled him to code each society according to its predominant family structure and then to count the number of societies in which his hypothesis was supported.

Such a sweeping design was feasible in this instance and could be carried out relatively quickly and inexpensively, because Zelditch (1955) could take advantage of previously conducted research, working in a library. Thus, this example suggests how the use of available materials may contribute greatly to the sociotemporal scope of a study without commensurate increase in the costs.

Similar savings of time and expense may be possible in studies for which suitable data are already indexed in the Human Relations Area File. Started at Yale as the Cross-Cultural Survey under the leadership of Murdock (1949), duplicates of this file are housed at several universities. It covers a large number of human societies, and consists of excerpts from scholarly and scientific works, selected, classified, coded, and evaluated by specialists and available in its complete form to researchers and students. The materials are organized by societies and further divided by major categories (such as language, ideas about nature and man, socialization, kin groups) and by subtopics within categories. By consulting the index, a researcher might locate information on many subjects of possible interest—on the socialization of adolescents, for example, or on the division of labor—in all cultures for which data have been collected and processed by the File.

Public opinion studies, which are accumulating in many different countries, also lend themselves increasingly to sociological reanalysis and cross-cultural comparison (see, for example, Inkeles & Rossi, 1956; Natalie Rogoff, 1953).

Data on personal relationships. Sometimes existing materials may provide insights in depth into intimate, personal relationships. The letters used by Thomas and Znaniecki (1918) in their study of Polish peasants provide a classic illustration. These authors, studying the changing relationships within peasant primary groups as communities and families are disrupted, utilized available exchanges of letters in families from which a member had emigrated to the United States. Ideally, such a series of letters constitutes the total interaction between the Polish emigrés and their families. Through the letters the researchers catch the interaction process, just as if Bales were to record on a motion picture film and a sound track everything that goes on in his small groups.

This study shows how available data can be used as the basis for research on interaction—on the type of continuing, private interaction, indeed, which is usually inaccessible to direct observation. When the members of a group are separated, the researcher may not be able to assemble them for observation. Or when the interaction is continued over long periods of time, he may not have the resources for observation. Or, most important, the nature of the interaction may be so private that it admits of no observation at all. Nor is it likely that these difficulties could readily be overcome by the use of questioning, for the letters yield information of such complex and subtle nature that even the most skilled interviewer would have difficulty in obtaining an equivalent understanding of the constantly changing private lives of these Polish families.

Beside letters, there are other types of available data which offer comparably vivid and complete information about interaction under different conditions. Full transcriptions of court proceedings or committee meetings are often of sociological interest. Suggestive accounts (though often less accurate as factual reports) appear in newspaper stories, diplomatic memoirs, or personal diaries. Closely related, although not defined here as available data, are the life histories commissioned by the investigator for his research, like the detailed autobiography of one Polish peasant prepared for Thomas and Znaniecki (1918); such accounts, written at the instigation of the investigator, are subject to the response bias and biased viewpoint effect of self-administered questionnaires (see, for example, Abel, 1947; Stouffer, 1930). Similarly, medical, psychoanalytic, or social work case records, often obtainable in anonymous form, may serve as "expert" records of complex human relationships and processes affording insights not open to the lay investigator who himself attempts to gather such technical material.

Disadvantages

Against such impressive assets must be set certain basic restrictions on the utilization of available sources. Because the data were not originally assembled for present purposes they are often incomplete, or in a form in which they are not readily usable. Thus Zelditch (1955) had to omit many societies from his sample for lack of information about them, or Thomas and Znaniecki were obliged to make inferences from data which often lack one whole side of the family correspondence. Such incompleteness may mean that the data lack representativeness, as Zelditch feared when he was unable to determine whether his sample reflected societies in general. Another restriction may lie in the difficulty of establishing reliability; historical records, for instance, cannot be checked (unless several different accounts are available for comparison), since one can no longer observe the events reported or question the participants. Finally, the data that come to the researcher in a form he does not fully understand may not fit present definitions of the concepts under scrutiny; they may lack correspondence with the conceptual model.

Such disadvantages limit the usefulness of available materials. Indeed, the researcher may finally have to reject a given set of data because he cannot adequately assess their limitations, nor find suitable means of compensating for them. Frequently, of course, there are no data at all which are relevant to the problem under study.

Despite such limitations, the great variety of available data constitutes a highly valuable resource for the researcher. If anything, outside of such important special fields as demography (see, for example, Hauser & Duncan, 1959) or historiography (see, for example, Diamond, 1955), the sociologist has not made enough use of them and has given too little attention to the possible methods for their use. Through creative analysis of well-chosen materials from existing stores the researcher should be able to widen the scope of the problems investigated, to formulate new study objectives more clearly, and to interpret new materials within a broader framework of scientific understanding. The important caveat is to consider carefully the process by which the data were originally produced, spelling out and, insofar as possible, offsetting their limitations and biases, recasting them in a form suitable for the new problem at hand.

THE DATA AND THE SOCIAL SYSTEM MODEL

Of major importance in any classification of the types of sociological data is the level of the social system to which the data refer. The sociologist repeatedly faces the complex task of translating into research his notion of a system, in which the lower-level parts —the subgroups or the roles played by individual members—fit together to form the more inclusive, higher-level collectivity as a whole. Each level has its characteristic properties. At one level, the sociologist must find and use data that reflect the properties of the role into which the individual, with his characteristics, motivations, and orientations as a person, enters directly. At another level, he needs another type of data that index such properties of the collectivity as integration or division of labor. He may encounter some difficulty in understanding these two different types of data which, because of the systemic relationship between parts and whole, are interrelated.

Yet, in order to comprehend the full nature of social systems, the sociologist must be able to deal with properties at two or more levels of the system. Only through use of data on these levels combined is he able to investigate the interactions and interdependence of the parts and to determine func-

Type of analysis	Selective focus of model	Research case
Individual	Individual-in-role	Individuals
Contextual	Individual with reference to group context	Individuals characterized by properties of the groups to which they belong
Group	Group (collectivity)	Groups
Structural	Group with reference to internal arrangement of parts	Group segments character-ized by properties of indi-vidual members

Fig. 9. Some types of partial analysis of social systems.

tional or dysfunctional consequences for the overall system. At the same time, he must find ways of assembling and organizing these data so as to avoid treating the group either as an entity in itself that talks and thinks, or as a mere aggregate of discrete individuals whose opinions and attitudes can be simply added together to represent a "mass society."

Problems of studying the social system at various levels are particularly likely to arise when data about parts of the system are collected to refer to the system as a whole. If the sociologist questions individuals, for instance, about their satisfaction with the roles they play as parts of a group, he may then count the number of individuals who express satisfaction in order to reflect the extent of collective satisfaction for the group. Or, using income data about each of the families (constituent parts) of a country, he may take the median income of all the families to reflect the collective well-being of the country (the more inclusive system). Such collective data, although widely used, raise a number of problems of research procedure and interpretation. It is often unclear, for instance, whether a set of collective data in fact reflects a group property, as it is assumed to do, or merely the aggregation of discrete individual properties. Or, the researcher may want to go behind the collective data to identify the parts and describe the nature of their relationship to the whole. He may want to arrange his data to show which parts of the system contribute to the total group pattern.

DATA FOR PARTIAL ANALYSES

A few examples will suggest the nature of the data used at different system levels for several important types of sociological analysis—group, structural, individual, and contextual analyses (see (Figure 9)—and will point to some of the possibilities and difficulties entailed. The examples focus on the two system levels of role and collectivity, but the general principles apply as well to other levels—to dyadic relationships as parts as opposed to roles as higher-level systems, or to subgroups as opposed to more inclusive groups, or to more than just two levels of the system.

Data for Group Analysis

The data used in a group analysis deal exclusively with the higher-level system (groups), disregarding the individuals who compose each group. The value of data referring to the single level of the group is exemplified by the demographic research of Kingsley Davis and Hilda Golden (1954) which finds a negative correlation between agriculturalism and urbanization for the countries and territories of the world. Both of these group properties are indexed collectively for each country: agriculturalism by the percentage of gainfully occupied males engaged in agriculture and urbanization by the proportion of the total population living in cities.

What, then, is the nature of these collective data? The full set of facts for each country underlying the Davis-Golden (1954) analysis is suggested in Figure 10. Here each individual is first coded (in the simplest terms) as urban or rural and again as engaged in industry or in agriculture. Then these individual data are cross-tabulated for the country, so that the frequencies in the cells of Figure 10 show the within-group arrangement of individuals. The marginal totals of the table become the collective measures for the group. Thus Davis and Golden use, as their collective data for each country, the figures in the two circled marginal cells in Figure 10, taken as proportions of the total number (N) of individuals in the group.

	Variable X		Total
Variable Y	Individuals in industry	Individuals in agriculture	
Urban individuals			◯
Rural individuals			
Total	◯		N

Fig. 10. Data used in a group analysis (circles show for each country the data used in the analysis).

ginal cells in Figure 10, taken as proportions of the total number (N) of individuals in the group.

This type of analysis, then, does not make use of any individual information from the cells of such a table. Such exclusive use of marginal data distinguishes the single-level group analysis from a structural analysis, which would utilize more of the same data by also taking into account certain cell information for each group. For Davis and Golden (1954) are not immediately concerned with questions of group composition or structure. The group analysis bears directly upon their research objective, which regards the collective data as indexes of fundamental traits of the societies themselves. Such single level data are adequate for the purpose of classifying and comparing societies and explaining (in terms of agriculturalism-industrialism) why some countries and areas rather than others may be characterized by a high degree of urbanization.

Data for Structural Analysis

The data for structural analysis also focus on the group, but with some reference to the differentiated roles that interrelate to form the group's internal structure. These data may be used in different ways to support two different forms of structural analysis: segmental comparisons and within-group analysis. The study of mental disorders in urban areas by Faris and Dunham (1939) illustrates how a structural analysis may use segmental comparisons to extend and refine the results of a group analysis.

The structural analysis begins with a group analysis, which reveals in this particular study a relationship between patterns of mental illness in the various zones of the city and patterns of social disorganization. Faris and Dunham do not end their analysis at this point, however, since they want to make sure that their group-level finding cannot be ascribed solely to characteristics of the individuals themselves, but rather to social disorganization as a characteristic of the area. They want to hold constant within each area a series of extraneous individual characteristics that might account for the differing insanity rates. They see that, if schizophrenia were a function of the individual's birth place, for example, then the area differences in schizophrenia might "be explained on the basis of the varying proportions of the foreign-born in the different parts of the city." Accordingly, they make use of segmental comparisons, by comparing segments of the several areas (groups) in which individuals are alike in respect to an individual characteristic, country of birth.

One can see the nature of the data for segmental comparisons by rearranging Faris and Dunham's (1939) data, as in Figure 11. Here one imagines that the ecological investigation makes it possible, first, to classify and arrange the areas (groups) according to degree of disorganization. Next, within each area, individuals in the population are divided into native-born and foreign-born segments, and a separate insanity rate is obtained for each segment. Then, by comparing similar segments of the several areas (the circled cells in Figure 11), the researcher can control for the possible effects of the extraneous variable (the property of individuals in the segment) and make sure that the original finding holds—i.e., that there is indeed a group correlation between disorganization and rate of schizophrenia. Faris and Dunham, although they do not describe their analyses in these terms, report that they are convinced that "some factors" other than these individual characteristics "are necessary to explain these patterns [of psychosis] that are the same no

the constituent individuals are held constant.

Faris and Dunham (1939) might also have undertaken a supplementary within-group analysis. By comparing the cell percentages within each group, they could learn whether the individual's country of birth, in addition to group disorganization, might be related to insanity rates. The two forms of structural analysis combined may yield a variety of possible outcomes which help the researcher disentangle the joint effects of the independent variable as it refers, on the one hand, to the group, and, on the other hand, to the individual—or, more properly, to similar individuals as they form segments of the group.

Data for Contextual Analysis

Quite a different type of data is employed in contextual analysis, which focuses on the individual, but at the same time locates and explains the individual's role with reference

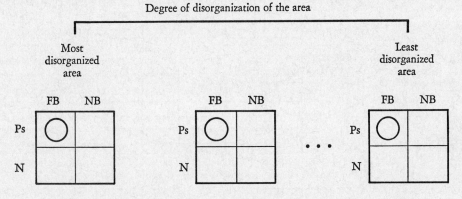

Degree of disorganization of the area

Most disorganized area

Least disorganized area

Classification of individuals in each group: FB = foreign-born, NB = native-born, Ps = psychotic, and N = normal.

Fig. 11. Data used in a structural analysis.

matter which race or nationality inhabits the area."

Segmental comparisons among groups are useful, then, in testing whether a dependent variable is associated with a group property even within similar group segments, that is, even when certain relevant characteristics of

to its group context. In a study of small discussion groups, James Davis (1961) illustrates this approach, examining the relationship between the degree of activity and the tendency to drop out of the group (see Figure 12).

Contextual analysis, like structural analy-

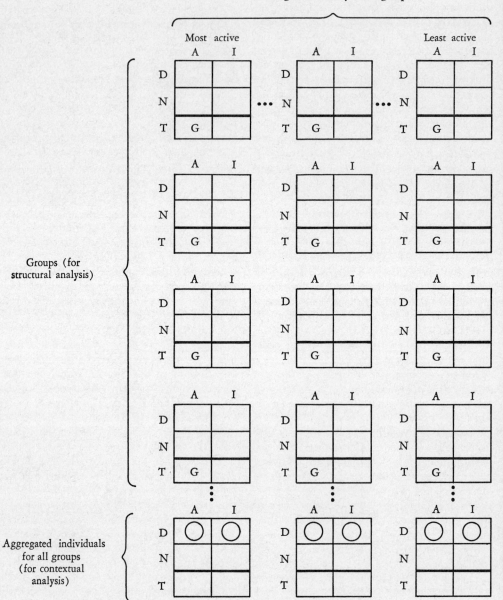

Classification of individuals: A = active (X+), I = inactive (X—), D = drops out
of group, N = does not drop out of group, and T = marginal total of individuals.
Numbers in cells are percentages.
In each group, *G* = proportion of individuals who are active.

Fig. 12. Data for a contextual analysis.

sis, aims to separate the group effects from the individual effects of an independent variable. Both forms of analysis are also alike in the data with which they start. Yet the two arrange these data quite differently and may sometimes produce very different results. In structural analysis, groups are the research case, and properties of individuals refer to homogeneous segments of individuals within each group. In contextual analysis, on the other hand, individuals aggregated from many groups are the research case, and the properties of groups are treated as contextual characteristics of discrete individuals.

In principle, just as structural analysis clarifies and specifies a group analysis, contextual analysis clarifies and specifies an individual analysis. The individual analysis itself deals exclusively with individuals in roles, disregarding the groups to which the individuals belong. Although Davis (1961) does not present an individual analysis, one might well be designed to discover why it is that some individuals rather than others drop out of study groups. Each individual is coded as active or inactive in his group and as dropping out or remaining a member of his group during the period under study. For each group these individual data are cross-tabulated and entered in the cells of a group table in the usual manner. The cell data from all the group tables are then added together to provide an aggregate individual table. This analysis (presumably) shows that individuals who are active role players are more likely than inactive individuals to stick with the study groups.

But Davis (1961), obviously not content with any such single-level analysis of individuals, wants also to take into account the composition of the group to which each individual belongs. He believes that the "role volume" of the group (the proportion of group members who are active role players) may have a further contextual effect on the individual's tendency to drop out, when the effect of the individual's own activity-inactivity is held constant.

Davis handles role volume of the group as a variable to be added to his analysis as follows. He does not change the research case: The case remains the individual, not the group. What he does is to characterize (code) each individual to show the kind of group he belongs to. A property (role-volume) of the higher-level system now becomes a contextual characteristic of the individual member (for a discussion of contextual characteristics, see Kendall & Lazarsfeld, 1950, p. 215; Lazarsfeld & Barton, 1955, p. 190). Then Davis uses this additional variable in a further cross-tabulation of individuals.

Now consider the nature of the data used in this contextual analysis. Figure 12 is an imaginary rearrangement of Davis' materials, showing a few of the group tables in which individuals are cross-tabulated according to their activity-inactivity and their readiness to drop out. The marginal totals of the independent variable provide a collective measure of the degree of activity (role volume) of the various groups. These marginal percentages of active members are keyed G in each group because Davis uses them in indexing the contextual characteristic of each individual. The group tables are also arranged in columns in Figure 12 according to the degree of group activity (G).

Davis' only direct use of these group tables is in measuring the contextual variable. His main data are obtained by adding together for each column the cell information for all the group tables in the column to give the aggregate individual tables for each column shown at the bottom of Figure 12. The circled cells in these aggregate tables contain the percentages used in the contextual analysis.

These examples begin to suggest that, in principle, structural analysis, which is aimed to study groups, and contextual analysis, which is aimed to study individuals, are quite distinct. Each aims to study a set of questions that the other cannot, and the results of the two may lead to different interpretations. The differences arise, not be-

(1) Fallacies arising because methods fail to fit model

Type of fallacy	Selective focus of model	Type of research case	Appropriate forms of partial analysis (to prevent fallacies)
Aggregative (ecological)	Individual	Group	Individual or contextual
Atomistic	Group	Individual	Group or structural

(2) Fallacies arising because methods fail to fit facts

Type of fallacy	Type of research case	Implications of the facts	Appropriate forms of partial analysis (to prevent fallacies)
Psychologistic	Individual	Interpretation of individual findings affected by group context	Contextual
Sociologistic	Group	Interpretation of group findings affected by internal structure	Structural

Fig. 13. Some possible fallacies.

cause the two sets of data are actually incompatible, but because the researcher looks at only one set and fails, in making his interpretations, to consider the possible implications of the alternative set (for a fuller discussion, see Matilda White Riley, 1963, I, pp. 700–739).

SOME POSSIBLE FALLACIES

When the researcher uses one or another of these types of data without full understanding, he is beset by a number of empirical and interpretative problems. Such difficulties potentially result in fallacious, inadequate, or misleading findings or interpretations (see Figure 13).

From Model to Method

One set of fallacies endangers the researcher who chooses his research case from a social system level that does not fit his conceptual model. If his model refers to individuals in roles, but his analysis is based on

groups (small or large collectivities or aggregates), a possible aggregative fallacy will be spoken of. Conversely, if his model refers to the group, but his analysis is based on individuals, a possible atomistic fallacy will be referred to. Strange as it may at first appear, such misuses are widespread and must be recognized if they are to be avoided.

The first of these fallacies was originally defined by Robinson (1950) in a widely quoted article. Although he called it "ecological fallacy," it is here given another name (aggregative fallacy) because the difficulty is not limited to ecological analysis, and many ecological studies (such as the one by Faris & Dunham, 1939) avoid it entirely. In Robinson's example, the research hypothesis refers to individuals. It postulates that, since educational standards are lower for the foreign-born than for the native-born, there ought to be a positive relationship between foreign birth and illiteracy. In order to test this, the researcher looks at data for groups of individuals in census areas. These data, as it turns out in this particular example, show a negative correlation (—.619) between the proportions of foreign-born inhabitants and the proportions of illiterates.

Do such group data negate the hypothesis? Do they support the contrary inference that the same individuals who are foreign-born tend necessarily to be literate? Certainly not. Indeed, if the analysis were based on individuals instead of groups, there might be no correlation at all, or even a positive correlation, between being foreign-born and being illiterate. Robinson (1950), whose article develops the mathematical relationship between group data and individual data, emphasizes this point by showing an actual rearrangement of the same census data now based on individuals, where the correlation is, after all, positive. The percentage of illiterates is in fact higher among the foreign-born than among the native-born. In these terms, then, group data are inappropriate if the hypothesis refers to the individual.

Although Robinson (who is mainly concerned with models focused on individuals) does not speak of the converse atomistic fallacy, it, too, is suggested by his data. If the researcher's hypothesis were that the foreign-born tend to predominate in those ecological groupings where illiteracy rates are low, he could scarcely draw any accurate inferences from Robinson's individual data. A conclusion about groups of individuals in census areas drawn from the individual data is subject to a possible atomistic fallacy (see the further discussion of Robinson's article in Duncan & Davis, 1953; Goodman, 1953; Menzel, 1950).

From Method to Fact

Another set of fallacies may occur, even when the research case does fit the level emphasized in the model, when the exclusive focus on a single level conceals some of the information important to an understanding of the findings. Here the method, though it fits the model, fails to discover the relevant facts. Group data alone may not be enough to prevent a sociologistic fallacy even when the focus is on the group. By the same token, individual data alone may fail to prevent a psychologistic fallacy even when the focus is on the individual.

In one example of a psychologistic fallacy, an individual analysis of older women might show that married women have more friends than do widows. But suppose that this relationship holds true, in fact, only for communities where married women are in the majority, and that, in communities with widows in the majority, the widows have more friends than do the married women. Also suppose the (imaginary) researcher does not discover this because he looks only at the facts about each discrete individual, disregarding the character of the community context. Using individual data alone, he develops an elaborate explanation of friendship patterns in terms of the marital status of the individual. This explanation would constitute a fallacy that overemphasizes the personal or psychological factors because an understanding of the individual property (having friends) also requires knowledge of a group property (the marital structure of each community).

In a different example, a group analysis for the neighborhoods in a city might show a positive correlation between transiency rates and suicide rates. Here the (imaginary) researcher explains neighborhood differences in suicide rates in terms of a social process. He postulates that transiency produces social disorganization in the area which, in turn, weakens social controls and reduces social rewards and thereby operates to encourage suicide. According to such a theory, those individuals in the neighborhood who are transients have an effect upon other individuals who are not transients themselves, but whose social ties are weakened by the general disorganization of the neighborhood.

But now suppose that, in this fictitious example, the facts are that the individual relationship between transiency and suicide is the same for all of the neighborhoods. That is, in each neighborhood the suicide rate is high among transients and low among stationary individuals, but these rates do not differ markedly from one neighborhood to another. Such facts would refute the theory that the group (or neighborhood) is in some way necessary to an understanding of the process connecting the two variables. The explanation involving interaction and between-role patterning (so that what some individuals, the transients, do and think affects what other individuals, the nontransients, do and think) would constitute a sociologistic fallacy. Indeed, the hypothetical facts in this example—that within each neighborhood the transient individuals are consistently more disposed to suicide than the nontransient individuals—would point to the need for a personal explanation of the individual correlation in psychological terms, or in terms of the cultural norms that foster tendencies toward both suicide and transiency in the same individuals. (Here the sociologist must explain why some neighborhoods have more transients than others.)

DATA FOR A FULL
SOCIAL SYSTEM ANALYSIS

Such fallacies are possible, of course, because the types of analyses discussed above (see Figure 9) are all partial analyses, based on selections from the full set of data at hand. All four types complement each other and are merely different ways of selecting from the same full set. The individual and the contextual analyses aggregate information from the cells of the group tables. The group analysis utilizes only the marginal information from these tables. And the structural analysis may either use the complete cell information for within-group comparison, or select one set of marginal data and one set of cell data for segmental comparison.

In contrast to such partial approaches, a social system analysis utilizes this full set of data. A social system analysis classifies and analyzes groups, but it also identifies the parts within each group, taking into account the internal arrangements of these parts. Thus it interrelates the group comparisons of a group analysis with the within-group and segmental comparisons of a structural analysis. Despite their potential, however, such full analyses are rarely used today except in the study of very small groups, and numerous methodological problems remain to be formulated and resolved. Yet these are highly challenging problems, because their solution will lead to the more complete utilization of sociological data, and hence to a better understanding of the internal arrangements and processes of social systems.

REFERENCES

Abel, T. The nature and use of biograms. *Amer. J. Sociol.,* 1947, 53, 111–118.

Angell, R. C. A critical review of the development of the personal document method in sociology 1920–1940. In L. Gottschalk, C. Kluckhohn, & R. C. Angell (Eds.), *The use of personal documents in history anthropology, and sociology.* Bull. No. 53. New York: Social Science Research Council, 1945. Pp. 177–232.

Angell, R. C., & Freedman, R. The use of documents, records, census materials and indices. In L. Festinger & D. Katz (Eds.), *Research methods in the behavioral sciences.* New York: Dryden, 1953. Pp. 300–326.

Bales, R. F. *Interaction process analysis: A method for the study of small groups.* Cambridge, Mass.: Addison-Wesley, 1950.

Bales, R. F. Some uniformities of behavior in small social systems. In G. E. Swanson, T. M. Newcomb, & E. L. Hartley (Eds.), *Readings in social psychology.* New York: Holt, 1952. Pp. 146–159.

Barton, A. H. *Organizational measurement.* New York: College Entrance Examination Board, 1961.

Berelson, B. Content analysis in communication research. Glencoe, Ill.: Free Press, 1952.

Berelson, B. Content analysis. In G. Lindzey (Ed.), *Handbook of social psychology.* Reading, Mass.: Addison-Wesley 1954. Pp. 488–522.

Blalock, H. M., Jr. *Social statistics.* New York: McGraw, 1960.

Blau, P. Structural effect. *Amer. sociol. Rev.,* 1960, 25, 178–193.

Bogue, D. J. Population distribution. In P. M. Hauster & O. D. Duncan (Eds.), *The study of population.* Chicago: Univer. of Chicago Press, 1959. Pp. 383–399.

Borgatta, E. F., & Bales, R. F. The consistency of subject behavior and the reliability of scoring in interaction process analysis. *Amer. sociol. Rev.,* 1953, 18, 566–569.

Campbell, D. T. Factors relevant to the validity of experiments in social settings. *Psychol. Bull.,* 1957, 54, 297–312.

Cannell C. F., & Kahn, R. L. The collection of data by interviewing. In L. Festinger & D. Katz (Eds.), *Research methods in the behavioral sciences.* New York: Dryden, 1953. Pp. 327–380.

Chapin, F. S. *Experimental designs in sociological research.* New York: Harper, 1947.

Chein I. An introduction to sampling. In Claire Selltiz, Marie Jahoda, M. Deutsch, & S. W. Cook (Eds.), *Research methods in social relations.* New York: Holt, 1959. Appendix B.

Clausen, J. A., & Ford, R. N. Controlling bias in mail questionnaires. *J. Amer. statist. Ass.,* 1947, 42, 497–511.

Cochran, W. G., Mosteller, F., & Tukey, J. W. Statistical problems of the Kinsey report. *J. Amer. statist. Ass.,* 1953, 48, 673–716.

Coleman, J. S. Relational analysis: The study of social organizations with survey methods. In A. Etzioni (Ed.), *Complex organizations.* New York: Holt, Rinehart & Winston, Inc., 1961. Pp. 441–452.

College Entrance Examination Board, Commission on Mathematics. *Introductory probability and statistical inference.* New York: Author, 1959.

Davis J. A. Compositional effects, role systems, and the survival of small discussion groups. *Publ. Opin. Quart.,* 1961, 25, 575–584.

Davis, J. A., Spaeth, J. L., & Huson, Carolyn. Analyzing effects of group composition. *Amer. sociol. Rev.,* 1961, 26, 215–225.

Davis, K., & Golden, Hilda H. Urbanization and the development of pre-industrial areas. *Econ. Devel. cult. Change,* 1954, 3, 6–24.

Dean, J. P. Participant observation and interviewing. In J. T. Doby (Ed.), *An introduction to social research.* New York: Stackpole, 1954.

Deming, W. E. *Some theory of sampling.* New York: Wiley, 1950.

Diamond, S. *The reputation of American business men.* Cambridge, Mass.: Harvard Univer. Press, 1955.

Duncan, O. D., & Davis, Beverly. An alternative to ecological correlation. *Amer. sociol. Rev.,* 1953, 18, 665–666.

Durkheim, E. *Suicide.* J. A. Spaulding & G. Simpson (Trans.). Glencoe, Ill.: Free Press, 1951.

Edwards, A. L. Experiments: Their planning and execution. In G. Lindzey (Ed.), *Handbook of social psychology.* Reading, Mass.: Addison-Wesley, 1954. Pp. 259–289.

Faris, R. E. L., & Dunham, H. W. *Mental disorders in urban areas.* Chicago: Univer. of Chicago Press, 1939.

Fisher, R. A. *The design of experiments.* Edinburgh, Scotland: Oliver and Boyd, 1937.

Furfey, P. H. *The scope and method of sociology.* New York: Harper, 1953.

Gaudet, Hazel, & Wilson, E. C. Who escapes the personal investigator? *J. appl. Psychol.,* 1940, 24, 773–777.

Gibbs, J. P., & Davis, K. Conventional versus metropolitan data in the international study of urbanization. In J. P. Gibbs (Ed.), *Urban research methods.* Princeton, N.J.: Van Nostrand, 1961. Pp. 419–436.

Goode W. J., & Hatt, P. K. *Methods in social research.* New York: McGraw, 1952.

Goodman, L. A. Ecological regressions and behavior of individuals. *Amer. sociol. Rev.,* 1953, 18, 663–664.

Guttman, L. The basis for scalogram analysis. In S. A. Stouffer, L. Guttman, E. A. Suchman, P. F. Lazarsfeld, S. A. Star, & J. A. Clausen (Eds.), *Studies in social psychology in World War II.* Vol. IV. *Measurement and prediction.* Princeton, N.J.: Princeton Univer. Press, 1950. Pp. 60–90.

Hagood, Margaret J., & Price, D. O. *Statistics for sociologists.* New York: Holt, 1952.

Hansen, M. H., Hurwitz, W. N., & Madow, W. G. *Sample survey methods and theory.* New York: Wiley, 1953.

Hare, A. P. *Handbook of small group research.* New York: The Free Press of Glencoe, 1962.

Hauser, P. M., & Duncan, O. D. The data and methods. In P. M. Hauser & O. D. Duncan (Eds.), *The study of population.* Chicago: Univer. of Chicago Press, 1959. Pp. 45–74.

Heyns, R. W., & Lippitt, R. Systematic observational techniques. In G. Lindzey (Ed.), *Handbook of social psychology*. Reading, Mass.: Addison-Wesley, 1954. Pp. 370–404.

Heyns, R. W., & Zander, A. F. Observation of group behavior. In L. Festinger & D. Katz (Eds.), *Research methods in the behavioral sciences*. New York: Dryden, 1953. Pp. 381–417.

Hughes, E. C. The place of field work in social science. Introduction to B. H. Junker, *Field work: An introduction to the social sciences*. Chicago: Univer. of Chicago Press, 1960.

Hyman, H. H., *Political socialization*. Glencoe, Ill.: Free Press, 1959.

Hyman, H. H., Cobb, W. J., Feldman, J. J., Hart, C. W., & Stember, C. H. *Interviewing in social research*. Chicago: Univer. of Chicago Press, 1954.

Inkeles, A., & Rossi, P. H. National comparisons of occupational prestige. *Amer. J. Sociol.*, 1956, 61, 329–339.

Kahl, J. A. Educational and occupational aspirations of 'common man' boys. *Harvard educ. Rev.*, 1953, 23, 186–201.

Kahn, R. L., & Cannell, C. F. *The dynamics of interviewing*. New York: Wiley, 1957.

Katz, D. Field studies. In L. Festinger & D. Katz (Eds.), *Research methods in the behavioral sciences*. New York: Dryden, 1953. Pp. 56–97.

Kendall, Patricia L., & Lazarsfeld, P. F. Problems of survey analysis. In R. K. Merton & P. F. Lazarsfeld (Eds.), *Continuities in social research: Studies in the scope and method of "the American soldier."* Glencoe, Ill.: Free Press, 1950.

Kish, Leslie. A two-stage sample of a city. *Amer. sociol. Rev.*, 1952, 17, 761–769.

Kish, Leslie. Selection of the sample. In L. Festinger & D. Katz (Eds.), *Research methods in the behavioral sciences*. New York: Dryden, 1953. Pp. 175–239.

Kornhauser, A., & Sheatsley, P. B. Questionnaire construction and interview procedure. In Claire Selltiz, Marie Jahoda, M. Deutsch, & S. W. Cook (Eds.), *Research methods in social relations*. New York: Holt, 1959. Pp. 546–587.

Lazarsfeld, P. F. The controversy over detailed interviews—An offer for negotiation. *Publ. Opin. Quart.*, 1944, 8, 38–60.

Lazarsfeld, P. F., & Barton, A. H. Some general principles of questionnaire classification. In P. F. Lazarsfeld & M. Rosenberg (Eds.), *The language of social research*. Glencoe, Ill.: Free Press, 1955. Pp. 83–92.

Lazarsfeld, P. F., & Menzel, H. On the relation between individual and collective properties. In A. Etzioni (Ed.), *Complex organizations*. New York: Holt, Rinehart & Winston, Inc., 1961. Pp. 422–440.

Lazarsfeld, P. F., & Rosenberg, M. (Eds.) *The language of social research*. Glencoe, Ill.: Free Press, 1955.

Le Play, F. *Les ouvriers Européens*. Paris: Alfred Mame et Fils, 1879.

Likert, R. Public opinion polls. *Scient. Amer.*, 1948, 179 (6), 7–11.

Lindzey, G., & Borgatta, E. F. Sociometric measurement. In G. Lindzey (Ed.), *Handbook of social psychology*. Reading, Mass.: Addison-Wesley, 1954. Pp. 405–448.

Maccoby, Eleanor E., & Maccoby, N. The interview: A tool of social science. In G. Lindzey (Ed.), *Handbook of social psychology*. Reading, Mass.: Addison-Wesley, 1954. Pp. 449–487.

McGinnis, R. Randomization and inference in sociological research. *Amer. sociol. Rev.*, 1958, 23, 408–414.

Madge, J. *The origins of scientific sociology*. New York: The Free Press of Glencoe, 1962.

Malinowski, B. *Crime and custom in savage society*. New York: Harcourt, 1926.

Menzel, H. Comment on Robinson's ecological correlations and the behavior of individuals. *Amer. sociol. Rev.*, 1950, 15, 674.

Merton, R. K. Selected properties of field work in the planned community. *Amer. sociol. Rev.*, 1947, 12, 304–312.

Merton, R. K. *Social theory and social structure*. (rev. ed.) Glencoe, Ill.: Free Press, 1957.

Merton, R. K. Notes on problem-finding in sociology. In R. K. Merton, L. Broom, & L. S. Cottrell, Jr. (Eds.), *Sociology today*. New York: Basic Books, 1959. Pp. xxviff.

Merton, R. K., Fiske, Marjorie, & Kendall, Patricia L. *The focused interview*. Glencoe, Ill.: Free Press, 1956.

Moreno, J. L. *Who shall survive?* Boston: Beacon House, 1953.

Moser, C. A. *Survey methods in social investigation*. New York: Macmillan, 1958.

Mueller, J. H., & Schuessler, K. F. *Statistical reasoning in sociology*. Boston: Houghton, 1961.

Murdock, G. P. *Social structure*. New York: Macmillan, 1949.

Parsons, T. *The social system*. Glencoe, Ill.: Free Press, 1951.

Parten, Mildred. *Surveys, polls and samples: Practical procedures*. New York: Harper, 1950.

Peak, Helen. Problems of objective observation. In L. Festinger & D. Katz (Eds.), *Research methods in the behavioral sciences*. New York: Dryden, 1953. Pp. 243–299.

Pool, I. de S. (Ed.) *Trends in content analysis*. Urbana: Univer. of Illinois Press, 1959.

Proctor, C. H., & Loomis, C. P. Analysis of sociometric data. In Marie Jahoda, M. Deutsch, & S. W. Cook (Eds.), *Research methods in social relations*. New York: Dryden, 1953. Pp. 561–586.

Riesman, D., & Glazer, N. The meaning of opinion. In D. Riesman (Ed.), *Individualism reconsidered and other essays*. Glencoe, Ill.: Free Press, 1954.

Riley, J. W., Jr. Reflections on data sources in opinion research. *Publ. Opin. Quart.*, 1962, 26, 313–322.

Riley, Matilda W. *Sociological research*. New York: Harcourt, Brace & World, 1963.

Riley, Matilda W., Cohn, R., Toby, J., & Riley, J. W., Jr. Interpersonal orientations in small groups: A consideration of the questionnaire approach. *Amer. sociol. Rev.*, 1954, 19, 715–724.

Robinson, W. S. Ecological correlations and behavior of individuals. *Amer. sociol. Rev.*, 1950, 15, 351–357.

Roethlisberger, F. J., & Dickson, W. J. *Management and the worker*. Cambridge, Mass.: Harvard Univer. Press, 1940.

Rogoff, Natalie. Social stratification in France and in the United States. *Amer. J. Sociol.*, 1953, 58, 347–357.

Selltiz, Claire, Jahoda, Marie, Deutsch, M., & Cook, S. W. *Research methods in social relations*. New York: Holt, 1959.

Sills, D. L. Three "climate of opinion" studies. *Publ. Opin. Quart.*, 1961, 25, 571–573.

Solomon, R. L. Extension of control group design. *Psychol. Bull.*, 1949, 46, 137–150.

Sorokin, P. A. *Social and cultural dynamics*. New York: American Book Company, 1937.

Stanton, H., Back, K. W., & Litwak, E. Role-playing in survey research. *Amer. J. Sociol.*, 1956, 62, 172–176.

Stephan, F. F., & McCarthy, P. J. *Sampling opinions, an analysis of survey procedures*. New York: Wiley, 1958.

Stouffer, S. A. An experimental comparison of statistical and case history methods of attitude research. Unpublished doctoral dissertation, Univer. of Chicago, 1930.

Stouffer, S. A. Sociology and sampling. In L. L. Bernard (Ed.), *Fields and methods of sociology*. New York: Long and Smith, 1934. Pp. 476–487.

Stouffer, S. A. *Communism, conformity, and civil liberties*. New York: Doubleday, 1955.

Stouffer, S. A. *Social research to test ideas*. New York: The Free Press of Glencoe, 1962.

Strodtbeck, F. L. Family interaction, values, and achievement. In D. C. McClelland, A. L. Baldwin, U. Bronfenbrenner, & F. L. Strodtbeck (Eds.), *Talent and society*. Princeton, N.J.: Van Nostrand, 1958. Pp. 135–194.

Suchman, E. A., & McCandless, B. Who answers questionnaires? *J. Appl. Psychol.*, 1940, 24, 758–769.

Sussman, Leila. F.D.R. and the White House mail. *Publ. Opin. Quart.*, 1956, 20, 5–16.

Thomas, W. I., & Znaniecki, F. *The Polish peasant in Europe and America*. Chicago: Univer. of Chicago Press, 1918.

Tippett, L. C. H. Sampling and standard error. In J. R. Newman (Ed.), *The world of mathematics*. New York: Simon & Schuster, 1956. Pp. 1459–1486.

U.S. Bureau of the Census. *U.S. census of population: 1960. Number of inhabitants, United States summary. Final report PC(1)-1A*. Washington, D.C.: Government Printing Office, 1961.

U.S. Bureau of the Census. *U.S. censuses of population and housing: 1960 1/1,000, 1/10,000, two national samples of the population of the United States, description and technical documentation*. Washington, D.C.: Government Printing Office, 1963.

Wallace, D. A case for—and against—mail questionnaires. *Publ. Opin. Quart.*, 1954, 18, 40–52.

Weber, M. *The Protestant ethic and the spirit of capitalism*. Talcott Parsons (Trans. from the German ed. of 1920). New York: Scribner, 1952.

Weiss, R. S., & Jacobson, E. A method for the analysis of the structure of complex organizations. In A. Etzioni (Ed.), *Complex organizations*. New York: Holt, Rinehart & Winston, 1961. Pp. 453–463.

Whiting, J. M. The cross-cultural method. In G. Lindzey (Ed.), *Handbook of social psychology*. Reading, Mass.: Addison-Wesley, 1954. Pp. 523–532.

Whyte, W. F. *Street corner society*. Chicago: Univer. of Chicago Press, 1943.

Whyte, W. F. Observational field-work methods. In Marie Jahoda, M. Deutsch, & S. W. Cook (Eds.), *Research methods in social relations*. New York: Dryden, 1951. Pp. 493–514.

Wold, H. Causal inference from observational data. In *J. Royal statist. Soc.*, 1956, 119, 28–50.

Young, Pauline V. *Scientific social surveys and research*. New York: Prentice-Hall, Inc., 1949.

Zelditch, M. Role differentiation in the nuclear family: A comparative study. In T. Parsons & R. F. Bales (Eds.), *Family socialization and interaction process*. Glencoe, Ill.: Free Press, 1955.

CHAPTER **27** **Mathematical Models and Computer Simulation**

JAMES S. COLEMAN

The present chapter deals with two topics that are distinct, but have many implications for each other. While there have been several surveys of mathematical models in sociology (Arrow, 1951; Berger, Cohen, Snell, & Zelditch, 1962; Coleman, 1960; Coleman, 1964a), and examinations of computer usage in the social sciences (Borko, 1962; Guetzkow, 1962), there has not been a joint examination of these two intimately related tools. The discussion in this chapter aims to show the power that each of these tools gains from the other and the problems appropriate to each.

The first section deals with mathematical models and their use in sociology. This leads directly into problems for which computers are appropriate and thus into the second section, which deals with the computer as a tool for problems in research and theory.

MATHEMATICAL MODELS AND THEIR USE IN SOCIOLOGY

Sociology is a large and diffuse discipline. Sociologists study problems all the way from friendship formation to national revolutionary movements; from attitude change to the growth of capitalism. As a consequence, different portions of sociology are at different stages in the movement toward scientific knowledge. This means that the first question that must arise in this examination is that of relevance: For what problems in sociology are mathematical models relevant?

Disciplines that are oriented to general knowledge rather than explanation of particular events engage in the development of "theory." Despite variations in the nature of theory from one area of science to another, it is concerned everywhere with relations between concepts or variables. In the formal structure of the theory, these are logical or mathematical relations; in the structure of behavior that the theory mirrors, they are causal relations.

There are several strategies that lead toward the development of such theory. One that has been frequently taken by sociologists is to identify variables or concepts that seem reasonably important in sociology, to measure them, and then to examine relations between them: for example, "social status," "group cohesiveness," "national identity," "attitude," "sentiments toward others." A great amount of empirical research consists of establishing correlations and inferring causal relations between concepts like these.

Following this strategy of building theoretical knowledge, there appear to be at least two distinct stages. The first consists of finding relationships, of establishing the overall pattern of causal connections between these concepts or variables. The results of such investigations are generally stated as propositions of the form, "as social status in a community increases, participation in activities of the community increases." The pervasiveness of such work in sociology is so great that a recent compendium of sociological facts is stated almost wholly in terms of such qualitative propositions (Berelson & Steiner, 1964).

Little use for mathematics other than statistics has been found in this stage of activity, and it appears that it has inherently little use in this stage. Precision of measurement is seldom necessary; investigators commonly report that when an attitude or behavior is measured in two different ways, the correlation with other variables tends to be strikingly the same.

The movement from this stage to one of more precise knowledge takes several paths. One path is toward refinement of these variables and relations so as to establish the form of the relation. For example, in Asch's (1951) work on the modification of judgments under group pressure, he established that the probability of an individual's succumbing to group pressure increases with the size of the group. A clear next step would be to establish the exact form of the dependence upon group size. Asch began this by showing that groups larger than four had no additional effect on the probability of succumbing; but to obtain a precise functional relation and to specify the dependent variable in a form independent of the specific situation would require a great deal of further investigation.

It is obvious that mathematics is necessary in this stage, for the result is stated as a mathematical equation embodying quantitative variables. Furthermore, the mathematics which is necessary in such work requires first of all quantitative measurement of the concepts. Consequently, it is useful here to examine the problem of quantitative measurement in some detail, a matter which has occupied a number of authors, beginning with N. R. Campbell (1928) and continuing with Hempel (1952), Koch (1951), Coombs (1950), Suppes and Winet (1955), Torgerson (1958), Von Neumann and Morgenstern (1947), Mount (1956), and others. Much has been made of the fact that sociological concepts seldom if ever conform to the constraints implied by quantitative measurement. Yet there is more to the problem than this.

Quantitative Measurement

Mathematically stated theories that employ quantitative variables use some or all of the properties of the real number system in making deductions. For example, suppose a mathematical theory states that $a(b + c) = d$, where a, b, c, and d are quantitative variables in the theory. This statement means that if one measures any three of these variables, it is possible to calculate the fourth from this equation. But note the operations that are being performed on the numbers obtained by measurement. These are addition and multiplication, the two operations that produce another real number when carried out upon real numbers.

Thus one can carry out such operations upon real numbers and expect to get a real number as a result. But will these operations, carried out upon numbers representing the concepts in questions, give a number *representing the requisite concept* as a result? The answer depends upon whether the operations of addition and multiplication, by which the numbers are manipulated, correspond to (are isomorphic with) operations that relate the concepts in question. If they do and measurement has been carried out properly, then the calculations carried out with real numbers will give a correct prediction, subject to measurement error. (The existence of measurement error, and the fact that no measurement can give an irrational number, means that there can never be exact isomorphism between the real number system and the concepts in question. This, however, causes no difficulty so long as allowance is made for measurement error.)

Thus if there are operations in the behavior in question that correspond to the operations of addition and multiplication, it is legitimate to carry out these operations upon the numbers representing these concepts. If the operations carried out in behavior imply less than this, then it is neither legitimate nor necessary to carry out these operations. A few examples will illustrate the point.

(1) Economists have a concept of utility which they use in describing behavior. The subjective utility of one set of goods for a person is higher than that of another if he chooses the first set over the other. This expression of preference implies only an order relation between utilities. Thus in all portions of economic theory which involve only such preference behavior, it is neither legitimate nor necessary to add utilities or multiply them. The concept of utility is defined only as an *ordinal* scale, obeying the property of invariant order. In that portion of economic theory, however, that deals with utility under risk (e.g., game theory), the utility of a risky outcome is conceived to be the utility of the outcome under certainty times the probability of its occurrence. In this case, therefore, it is necessary to posit a concept of utility upon which operations of addition and multiplication conforming to those in the behavior can be performed. The resulting scale of utility must be an *interval* scale, without a fixed zero point, but invariant up to a linear transformation. That is, if one scale, represented by x, gives correct predictions in the theory, then any other scale, x', must be related to it by the equation $x' = a + bx$, where a is a constant transforming the arbitrary zero point and b is a constant transforming the arbitrary scale.

(2) A similar statement may be made concerning attitudes. If, as in most propositions concerning attitudes, nothing more than order is expressed, then attitudes can only, and need only, be measured ordinally. Such propositions are usually of the form: If an individual has a stronger positive attitude toward x than toward y, he will more likely act positively toward x than y. Or: If one individual has a stronger positive attitude toward x than does another individual, he will more likely act positively toward x than will the other individual. For both such propositions to be made, the ordinal measurement of objects and individuals produced by a Guttman scale is implied. For either to be made alone, a less stringent measurement technique is implied.

But suppose the proposition is of the form: If an individual's attitudes toward x and y are together stronger than that toward z, he will more likely act in a direction favorable to x and y than one favorable to z. In this case, the proposition implies a combination operation of separate attitudes of the individual, isomorphic with addition of real numbers. For this implies that one is to measure attitudes toward x, y, and z separately, attach numbers to them, $n(x)$, $n(y)$, and $n(z)$, and then predict the individual's behavior in a situation where they are all present, based on the relative sizes of $n(x) + n(y)$, and $n(z)$.

(3) A similar example in sociological theory is the concept of authority. Suppose all the propositions in which this concept is to play a part are of the form: If role A has more authority over x than does role B, then in any conflict between A and B, the individual in role A will be able to determine x. Such propositions imply only ordinal properties for authority, and, if numbers are to be associated with the authority of A and that of B, only their ordinal prop-

erties can be legitimately used. However, suppose the theories or propositions are to contain propositions of the form: When the combined authority of A and B over x is greater than that of C, then in a conflict between A and B versus C, A and B will prevail in determining x. In this case, the nature of the proposition implies some operation by which the combined authority of A and B is applied. Only if this operation has the properties of commutativity and associativity, as does addition of real numbers, is it legitimate to attach numbers to the concept of authority and combine these numbers by addition. (Three elements a, b, c are associative under the "$+$" operation, if $a + (b + c) = (a + b) + c$, that is, the result is independent of the order in which successive operations are carried out. Two elements, a and b, are commutative under the "$+$" operation if $a + b = b + a$, that is, if the order of the elements in the operation is irrelevant to the result.)

As these examples suggest, the question of mathematical properties of concepts in sociology is not one that is relevant only to an esoteric portion of sociology, termed mathematical sociology. It is intrinsic to the very nature of these concepts and the power of the propositions that contain them. If a concept has only weak mathematical properties (such as the order relation), then it is a weak concept. The propositions in which it can play a part give only weak deductions, and the edifice of the scientific knowledge which uses it as a component will be a small edifice. A good example of this, which constructs a theoretical edifice from ordinal concepts, is Simon's formalization of Homans' (1950) and Festinger's (1950) propositions about behavior in small groups (see Simon, 1957; see also Coleman, 1960, for an extended discussion of Simon's approach).

The question arises, then, of how one can build propositions that have more power and devise concepts that will give them this power. There are two fundamental ways of doing so. The first, and classical

way, is to measure the concept through use of the proposition in which the combination operation is expressed. For example, the proposition about the combined authority of A and B would serve as the necessary proposition for measurement and for the assignment of numbers representing authority. The numbers could be assigned only after numerous comparisons of authority of different combinations of roles were carried out, and numerous ordered equivalence classes were established by use of the proposition above. The detailed procedures for such assignment of numbers can be found in Campbell (1928). In this case, the proposition serves as a definition of the concept of authority and need not be elsewhere tested. Nevertheless, it does contain empirical content and can be disconfirmed, for it implies that people so behave that the concept of authority does have the additive property of real numbers. The testing for disconfirmation comes within the process of measurement itself. Suppose one establishes by four successive measurements that the following things are true.

In conflicts of authority over an object x,

1. About half the time role A prevails over role B; about half the time, B prevails over A.

2. About half the time role A prevails over role C; about half the time, C prevails.

3. When roles A and B dictate one course of action, while D dictates another, about half the time roles A and B prevail, about half the time, D prevails.

4. When roles A and B and C dictate one course of action, and E dictates another, about half the time roles A and B and C prevail; about half the time, E prevails.

Then it is possible to tentatively think of amounts of authority, a, b, c, d, and e, associated with roles of A, B, C, D, and E respectively. If we propose "prevailing about half the time" to correspond to the mathematical relation of equality, and the combination of roles indicated above to correspond to the operation of additions on real numbers, then we can assign numbers to these amounts. The simplest assignment is to let $a = 1$. Then $b = 1$, $c = 1$, $d = 2$, and $e = 3$.

This, however, has not tested whether the proposed isomorphism holds. One important such test would be to test the deduction $e = d + c$.

The test is carried out by letting roles $D + C$ dictate one course of (1) action, and role E dictate another. If E prevails about half the time, while D and C prevail about half, then the test succeeds, and the proposed isomorphism is partially confirmed. If it does not, the test fails and real numbers cannot be assigned to the authority of A, B, C, D, and E under the operation used. This test is a partial test of both the associativity and commutativity of the operation, for these two properties imply that $a + b + c = (a + b) + c$, which is the test carried out by testing $e = d + c$.

This is the classical approach to quantitative measurement, the one used to explicate the measurement of physical concepts such as mass and length. It has the enormous advantage that its confirmation constitutes confirmation of the theory itself. The whole theory of mechanics, for example, is a logical structure that follows directly, once the concepts of mass and length have been validated as quantitative concepts through measurement. Newton's definitions and laws of motion can be construed as propositions which define mass, length, and time and are validated by the fact that the concepts as defined exhibit the additivity properties of real numbers.

When such confirmation-by-quantitative-measurement occurs, then "tests" of the theory in the usual sense are unnecessary and irrelevant. Hence the validation of a quantitative concept as having the property of additivity is a result not to be taken lightly. It implies that the concept, and the operation of combination expressed in the assignment of numbers, reflects a structure of behavior that has the properties of real numbers. It indicates that a theory of behavior may be constructed by use of this concept and proposition and that the theory will have the deductive power brought to it by the operations of addition and multiplication.

It is perhaps because such measurement would constitute a remarkable stride in the development of theories of behavior that it has been so little realized in social science. There appear to be no cases in which such measurement has been confirmed in the sense indicated above, perhaps the closest being the measurement of utility under risk and subjective probability by economists and psychologists (see Becker, De Groot, & Marschak, 1963; Edwards, 1954). The techniques of multidimensional scaling appear to be leading in the direction of quantitative measurement (see Coombs, in press; Shepard, 1962), but it is hardly to be expected that developments will come quickly or easily.

The second method of building propositions that have more power than ordinal or qualitative ones is through a somewhat different means. The assignment of numbers to a concept may be carried out in a way that appears reasonable, and then the empirical test carried out via a quantitative proposition. This method is open only when assignment of numbers may be reasonably made to two or more concepts, for a quantitative proposition inherently relates two or more quantitative concepts. For example, suppose one has a proposition: The proportion of times that a role is able to determine x, in conflicts of authority over x, is proportional to the length of time the role has had the same occupant. Confirmation of this proposition would confirm both the concepts of "length of time in a role" and "proportion of times that the role is able to determine x" as quantitative concepts, in effect confirming the assumption that each conflict of authority over x is effectively equivalent, and that each unit of time after entrance into a role is effectively equivalent. Thus a simple counting of those events gives a number that has the properties of a real number in the theory.

This mode of measurement, in which a quantitative proposition is tested, is the one that finds widespread use in mathematical sociology, and the mode that seems likely to provide the basis for mathematical sociology generally. It requires, first of all, an a priori reasonable method of assigning numbers to concepts and then a proposition which relates these concepts and thus allows their testing as quantities. Ordinarily, the only reasonable method of assigning numbers that exists in sociology (beside the intrinsically quantitative concept of time) involves counting: counting of events, of all-or-none relations, of individuals, or other entities. This approach, and the theories in which it finds a place, constitutes so radical a departure from the concept-measurement approach discussed above that it can be considered a wholly different path toward the development of theory in sociology. Rather than refinement of concepts and relations to establish a precise functional form, this approach ignores such concepts as "cohesiveness" and starts afresh.

All-or-None Observations, Counting, and Sometimes-True Theories in Social Science

Despite the difficulties that occur in measurement, as discussed above, there have arisen a number of precise, quantitative, and empirically testable mathematical models in sociology apparently unimpeded by these difficulties. These models have one attribute in common. They are based on observation of all-or-none events or elements and include only concepts based on counting of these events or elements.

A good example of such models is a stochastic process, which conceives of an entity (e.g., an individual or a group) moving among specified states. In a stochastic process, there are *states, events,* and then two sets of probabilities defined in terms of these states and events. There are *state probabilities,* the probabilities of being in given states. And there are *transition probabilities,* the probabilities of moving from one state to another at the occurrence of an event. For example, let there be two states, labelled 1 and 2, and let the probabilities of being in each state after event k be s_{1k} and s_{2k} where $s_{2k} = 1-s_{1k}$. Let the transition probabilities for moving from state 1 to 2 and 2 to 1 on event k be p_{12k} and p_{21k}. Then the process is defined by a recursive equation,

$$s_{1k} = s_{1,k-1}(1-p_{12k}) + s_{2,k-1}p_{21k}, \qquad (2)$$

and a redundant second equation,

$$s_{2k} = s_{1,k-1}p_{12k} + s_{2,k-1}(1-p_{21k}), \qquad (3)$$

with initial condition given as s_{10}, the probability of being in state 1 at the start. (In the simplest form of stochastic process, a Markov process, the transition probabilities are independent of the event k, $p_{ijk} = p_{ij,k-1}$.)

These probabilities are quantitative variables of a sort quite different from a concept like "amount of authority," but quantitative nevertheless. They are measured, or estimated, by proportions or relative frequencies. The proportions are formed by all-or-none observations of the states that individuals are in and of the shifts they make and then a counting of these observations. This counting produces two numbers for each proportion, one which serves as the denominator and one as the numerator.

What is the status of such a model as a sociological or psychological theory? It seems wholly inappropriate to conceive of such a stochastic process as ultimately, once and for all, confirmed or disconfirmed. It is far more reasonable to view this as a "model," or a sometimes-true theory, which may be confirmed in areas A, B, and C of behavior, but disconfirmed in areas D, E, and F. Thus for areas A, B, and C, the result is a quantitative, confirmed theory, having sidestepped all the problems of measurement discussed earlier.

The development of mathematical theory in sociology has progressed almost wholly through this approach of counting, based on all-or-none observations, and the application of models as sometimes-true theories. The largest class of such models consists of the direct use of all-or-none relations in those branches of mathematics, such as probability theory, graph theory, and Boolean matrices, which can use them directly. Examples of these approaches are discussed in separate sections below. These sections attempt to give an overview of the kinds of mathematical models and theories that exist in sociology at present.

Probability distributions as static models. Many probability distributions provide static models even though they were produced by a process operating through time. The simplest of these are the binomial distribution and the Poisson distribution. In both cases, the distributions are generated by a specific process or structure of events, and the models will be confirmed as theories whenever the structure of events in human behavior is isomorphic to this structure. The structure of events in the two cases is:

(1) Binomial distribution: This is generated by a sequence of n discrete and independent events, each with two possible outcomes. The outcomes in each event are governed by the same probabilities, outcome 1 occurring with probability p. The distribution produced by this structure of events is one in which the probability of k occurrences of outcome 1 in n events is given by:

$$Pr\{k|p,n\} = \binom{n}{k} p^k (1-p)^{n-k}.$$

where $Pr\{k|p,n\}$ is the probability of k occurrences, given p and n. The process equations governing these events are:

$$Pr\{1|p,1\} = p \qquad (4)$$
$$Pr\{k|p,n\} = pPr\{k-1|p,n-1\} +$$
$$(1-p)Pr\{k|p,n-1\}. \qquad (5)$$

The most common behavioral example

that mirrors this structure of events is not one of human behavior, but of physical behavior; the flipping of a coin, with heads and tails as outcomes. It is useful to reflect upon why one can say this. Is it because the distributions of coin tossing outcomes have been measured and found to conform very closely to the binomial distribution? Hardly so. It is because one sees a direct correspondence in the structure of events themselves. One knows the coin tossings are independent and that the probability of heads remains constant. Therefore one can be fairly confident that the probability of k heads in n tosses is given by the equation above.

This example illustrates a most important point. In many models of the sort under discussion, the correspondence or noncorrespondence of human behavior to the model can largely be determined by the structure of the process itself. Although seldom can correspondence be made for all aspects of the process, as in coin tossing, usually most can be, leaving only a small portion undetermined. Thus a knowledge of the process which generated a probability distribution is frequently of great aid in deciding whether there might be correspondence to a given area of human behavior.

(2) Poisson distribution: This is generated by a continuous process in which an event has a constant probability of occurrence, λdt, in a small segment of time, dt, at all points in time. The probability distribution of the number of events that has occurred in a given period of time is given by:

$$p_k = \frac{(\lambda t)^k e^{-\lambda t}}{k!} \qquad (6)$$

where p_k is the probability of k occurrences, t is the period of time, and λdt is the probability of the event's occurrence in the small segment of time, dt. The equations governing this process are:

$$\frac{dp_0}{dt} = -\lambda p_0 \qquad (7)$$

and $\quad \dfrac{dp_i}{dt} = \lambda p_{i-1} - \lambda p_i \quad$ for $i > 0 \qquad (8)$

These equations may be solved successively, beginning with p_0, by ordinary integration, or by use of the Laplace transform, to obtain the distribution above.

The Poisson distribution serves as a basic model, a baseline so to speak, for numerous situations in which there is a set of elements each constantly subject to a chance event with a given probability per unit time. Its first application was in a situation of human and animal behavior where it was used to explain the distribution of numbers of Prussian army units in which 0,1,2 . . . men had received horsekicks. Many of its applications remain in the area of human behavior. For example, if all men in a work place have the same probability per unit time of having an accident, then the distribution of men with 0,1,2 . . . accidents over a given period would be a Poisson distribution. Thus the Poisson distribution can be and is used to test whether such a conjecture is consistent with the facts. Nearly all accident data show a distribution that is more skewed than the Poisson, as if some men have higher and others lower probabilities of an accident per unit time. (Models to mirror this are discussed below.)

Apart from the standard probability distributions, such as those above, there have been other developments of static models that use numbers or proportions derived from counting. Most of these may be termed *measurement models,* for their principal use is to provide a rationally-constructed measure upon a group or individual. These may be generally classified in two areas, models of individual measurement and models of group measurement. The former consist mostly of attitude-scaling models, beginning with Guttman scales, which were generalized in two directions: beyond a single content dimension into multidimensional scaling; and away from deterministic models, toward models in which a response is only probabilistically related to the individual's position. The former have been largely developed by Coombs (1950) and his students and have been examined in detail by Torgerson (1958) and Coombs (in press). The latter has been principally developed by Lazarsfeld and his students under the label "latent structure analysis" and has been examined in some detail by Torgerson (1958) and by Lazarsfeld (1954; 1959).

This general area of work has used all-or-none (i.e., dichotomous) responses, aggregated by counting, to provide numbers that can serve in measurement of attitudes. It constitutes one of the most abundant uses of mathematical models in areas related to sociology; but since attitude measurement is more properly within psychology, since there is more theoretical relevance in process models, and since the Coombs and Torgerson reviews provide a good perspective upon the field, it is not treated in detail here.

Models of group measurement by counting events or persons are abundant. Because of the extraordinary good fortune that one can observe each individual's behavior, what is qualitative behavior at the individual level becomes quantitative for the group, merely by counting. The result is such variables as the *size* of a group, as well as *rate* of behavior determined by counting. Such simple measurement can hardly be called mathematical model-construction, but it should not be overlooked, for it provides numerous quantitative handles by which to develop quantitative models at the group level. This is illustrated by numerous models of group behavior; one of the best examples is that of the deterministic diffusion model, presented below, in which the number of persons who have adopted an innovation constitutes an important variable in the model.

Beyond such measures that derive directly from counting, mathematical models are particularly appropriate for measures having to do with group structure. Good examples are models by Katz (1953), who used a sociometric matrix of o's and 1's (see below) to give each individual in the group a status measure, and a model by Hubbell (1963), which provides more flexibility in doing a similar task. The measure is derived from manipulation of the matrix in such a way that scores are recursively determined. Each person's score is dependent on the scores of the persons who choose him, whose scores are in turn determined by the scores of the persons who choose them, and so on. Strictly speaking, these measures are individual measures, but they derive directly from the group structure.

It is possible to obtain measures upon the group itself directly from mathematical operations upon the structure matrix. For example, a measure of interdependence in making choices has been derived from the variance among persons in the number of choices received (Coleman, 1964a, Ch. 14). When most choices go to a few individuals, the statistical interdependence of choices is high; the amount of such interdependence can be measured by an explicit model.

Other models of group measurement are based on the distribution of a characteristic over a set of subgroups. For example, indices used to measure the racial segregation of a city are based on the distribution of each race in city blocks or census tracts. See Duncan and Duncan (1955) for an examination of such indices. Mathematical models based on the concomitant variation of two or more attributes over a set of subgroups have been used in conjunction with standard techniques of regression, to obtain estimates of rates of behavior (Blalock, 1964; Goodman, 1959; Harper, 1961).

There are broad possibilities for group measurement by use of explicit mathematical models. A few years ago, sociologists were content to develop indices based on more or less *ad hoc* procedures with a primary interest in well-behaved indices (fixed upper and lower bounds, preferably at 1 and 0 or 1 and −1, and similar criteria). This approach is being replaced by measures that are parameters in explicit mathematical models, and thus have explicit meaning, with dimensions that show that meaning. (Dimensions and the use of dimensional analysis in model construction cannot be treated here. Treatment may be found in Duncan [1953], Bridgman [1922], and its use in sociology is discussed in Coleman [1964a, Ch. 2].) In many cases, the models are statistical ones; in all cases, they gain their quantification from numbers derived from counting individuals' attributes.

Extensions of Bernoulli trials. The binomial and Poisson distributions discussed above were generated by dynamic processes, the binomial by a sequence of events and the Poisson by a process continuous in time. Thus, although they were treated as static models, it would be possible, by observations over time, to use them to reflect the dynamics of a process.

This leads, then, to stochastic processes, that is, processes that carry a probability distribution forward into a new distribution. Stochastic processes have begun to find applicability in social science, and it is likely that their use will expand greatly.

A very simple process of this sort, a two-state, discrete-time Markov process, is an immediate generalization of the independent events that generate a binomial distribution according to equations (4) and (5). In Bernoulli events, the outcome of the event, e.g., the state of the coin, is independent of the previous state. In a Markov process, it is dependent upon the last previous state. The defining characteristics of a simple two-state Markov process are given above, in equation (2).

The use of a Markov process, since it does have an explicit dynamic, can be to project the system forward in time by use of equations like (2) and (3). This becomes quite interesting, because one can project the expected path (as well as the probable deviation from that path) of a given individual merely by knowing the initial state and the matrix of transition probabilities that carry it forward. Furthermore, the Markov process is *ergodic,* that is, the state probabilities at equilibrium, after the process has gone on for a long time, are independent of the initial state.

One of the first applications of a simple Markov process in sociology was carried out by Anderson (1954), who fitted voting intentions (Republican, Democrat, Independent) expressed in panel survey data to a three-state Markov process. The three states were the three expressed vote intentions, and the events of the process were the panel interviews. Since each person was interviewed several times, it was possible to estimate transition probabilities from the cross-tabulation of responses on the successive waves. The two waves of interviews make possible a table like Table 1 where n_{ij} is the number of persons who expressed

TABLE 1

INTERVIEW II

		R	D	I	
Inter- view I	R	n_{11}	n_{12}	n_{13}	$n_1.$
	D	n_{21}	n_{22}	n_{23}	$n_2.$
	I	n_{31}	n_{32}	n_{33}	$n_3.$
		$n_{.1}$	$n_{.2}$	$n_{.3}$	n

intention i on interview I and j on interview II, $n_i.$ is the total number that expressed intention i at interview I, and $n._j$ the total number that expressed intention j at interview II. If p_{ij} is an element in the transition matrix, the probability of jumping from state i to state j, given that the individual is in state i, then p_{ij} may be estimated very simply as $p_{ij} = n_{ij}/n_i$. Problems of estimation and statistical tests in Markov processes were dealt with by Anderson and Goodman (1957), Goodman (1959), and elsewhere in the statistical literature. Furthermore, it is possible to test the model in several ways if there are more than two successive interviews. One test

carried out by Anderson is a test for the constancy of p_{ij} at different points in the election campaign. He found that p_{ij} was not constant, but that the frequency of change was as if the period from July to August were twice that from August to September. This illustrates an immediate use of such a process: The transition probabilities p_{ij} offer concise measures of change that can be compared.

It is easy to see that this kind of model is widely applicable to attitudinal or behavioral data from survey panels. Yet one can (and should) ask immediately, "So what?" It is no cause for excitement merely to be able to apply a mathematical model to sociological data. Mathematics in sociology must pass the same test as any other tool: Of what value is the application? When one asks that question, it becomes evident why Anderson's work was not immediately followed by widespread use of Markov chain models with panel data. For this model does little more than extrapolate an attitude or behavior forward in time, using two observations as a basis for extrapolation. It is a stochastic analog for categorical data to mere linear extrapolation of a continuous variable, and few scholars would propose that such extrapolation aids much in the understanding of behavior. To be sure, the p_{ij}'s serve as measures which may be useful for certain purposes; but it is clear that one learns more about voting behavior from relating vote intention to other characteristics of the individual than from merely relating it to itself at a prior interview.

Putting aside for a moment the application of the Markov chain to survey data, its application in other areas may be examined. It has been used for the study of epidemiology of mental illness (Marshall & Goldhamer, 1955) and for the study of short-term job mobility (Blumen, Kogan, & McCarthy, 1955)—both applications to on-going processes in society, using field data. It has been used as well to model behavior in experimental settings. Partly stemming from its intensive use in mathematical learning theory (Bush & Estes, 1959; Bush & Mosteller, 1955; Estes & Burke, 1955), the Markov chain has been applied to small-group learning situations (Hays & Bush, 1954; Suppes & Atkinson, 1960) and to the process of individual conformity in small group situations (Cohen, 1963). These uses have shown that the Markov chain could serve as a model of at least some aspects of behavior in such situations, both when applied to the group as an acting unit and to the individual. Can it be of more fundamental use, i.e., does a simple Markov chain do more than serve as a frame or a language into which the behavior data can be cast? A few further developments suggest that it will be of more fundamental use.

One of these developments has stemmed from an inability of the Markov process to fit the data. It is clear in most areas to which this model has been applied over a set of individuals that it fails to fit the data and always in the same characteristic way. When the transition matrix is estimated from points 1 and 2 and then the turnover from 1 to 3 is predicted, there is always an overprediction of turnover. (For job mobility, see Blumen, Kogan, & McCarthy [1955]; for brand choice in purchase behavior, see Kuehn [1958]; Frank [1962]; for conformity in small groups, with somewhat different data but the same difficulty, see Cohen [1963].) The reason emerges quickly: Different persons are different in their probabilities of change, yet the simple Markov chain treats them as being alike and in particular predicts the change of those people who were stable from point 1 to 2, using probabilities of change based on the total sample. It is evident that, if people are at all heterogeneous in their probabilities of change, those with high probability will have moved first and the ones remaining will be less likely to change. This glaring incompatibility of the model with behavior has led to some more interesting and more accurate models. One approach has been

to use more of the past history of the individual in predicting his future response. Two, three, or more previous responses may be used, rather than merely the last previous response. (For an example of such use in models for repetitive purchase behavior, see Kuehn [1958].) These are called second-order, third-order, and in general, n-th-order Markov chains. A second approach, that employed by Blumen, Kogan, & McCarthy (1955) and Converse (1962) is to divide the sample into two groups, the "movers" with relatively high transition probabilities, and the "stayers" who do not change at all (see Goodman [1959a; 1961], for estimation procedures and tests for n-th-order chains, and for the mover-stayer model).

Both of these approaches offer minor repairs which save the Markov chain from disconfirmation. A third approach, however, has made a more fundamental change. In previous models, the state of an individual was viewed as identical to his behavioral response: The vote intention he expresses, the brand he chooses, and so on. But in these models, there are two levels: an observed level, the response, and an unobserved level, related to but not identical with the response. (It is not strictly true that in the models considered to this point, the observed behavior was taken as his state. In particular, the models derived from learning theory treated the underlying probability of response as the basic state and applied change processes to this probability. But these models have met severe problems of estimation and found it necessary to simplify the situation. For example, Cohen's [1963] analysis runs into difficulty because he must restrict himself to four discrete underlying states.) Then the process of change can occur at the unobserved level. For example, in models of this sort which have been developed, his state at any time is viewed as his probability of giving a particular response, or, in the case of more than two possible responses, a vector of probabilities. His change, then, is only a change in the probability of his giving that response.

Those models, in application to consumer behavior involving numerous successive purchases, have been fitted to the data and have shown good ability to predict further changes. It goes without saying that further data will find this extension still to be insufficient for mirroring behavior, but it appears that this step has been a fruitful extension of Markov processes (see Wiggins [1955], Kuehn [1962], and Coleman [1964a; 1964b], for the development of these models).

It is important to see just what this step has done, particularly in view of the measurement problems discussed earlier. It began with all-or-none, dichotomous data at the individual level and turned this into numbers and proportions at the aggregate level to apply stochastic processes. But now the model allows one to de-aggregate, so to speak, and think of different individuals as characterized at any given time by different probabilities of positive response. In so doing, one now has a numerical concept at the level of the individual. This, of course, is not a sleight-of-hand trick, because the actual numerical measure of the concept for the individual is obtained only by virtue of a number of responses by the individual. But the point remains: A quantitative numerical concept, embedded in a theory, is obtained for individuals by use of the theory itself to aid in the measurement.

This sequence of models, beginning with Bernoulli independent events, moving to simple Markov chains, and then to more complex processes that better reflect behavior, shows a fruitful sequence of development of mathematics in sociology. The interplay between systematic data and formal models has made it possible to describe with far more accuracy than before the processes of change that individuals undergo in simple choice situations.

A second path of extension of the simple Markov chain can be seen best by returning to the panel survey, as exemplified by the vote intention example. Beside the fundamental defect noted above (overpredicting

subsequent change for the stable, and underpredicting it for those who have changed), there are two other defects, just as fundamental. One has to do with time of change and time of interview or observation. The first approach one might take (and that taken by Anderson [1954]) is to identify the Markov chain periods with the interview waves. Thus, if there are three interviews, there are three periods and two transitions. But it is quickly evident that this imposes an arbitrary timing upon a process that has its own timing. That is, persons change at any time, without regard for the particular spacing of interviews. As a consequence, the model is not at all structurally isomorphic with the behavioral process itself. It becomes an imposition of an arbitrary mathematical structure, one whose arbitrariness will differ depending on the particular timing of the observations. Such considerations lead to a model which is much more satisfactory for most processes which occur in nature (rather than the laboratory, where arbitrary time intervals can be imposed): a Markov process that is continuous in time. The defining equation for a two-state process is very simple:

$$\frac{dp_1}{dt} = - q_{12}p_1 + q_{21}p_2, \qquad (9)$$

where the parameters q_{12} and q_{21} are *transition rates,* analogous to the transition probabilities p_{12} and p_{21}. If these transition rates are independent of time, the process they describe is the limiting form of the simple Markov chain described earlier. That is, for $i \neq j$,

$$q_{ij} = \lim_{\Delta t \to 0} \frac{p_{ij}(\Delta t)}{\Delta t}$$

where $p_{ij}(\Delta t)$ is the transition probability for a Markov process where the time interval between jumps is Δt.

The task of estimating the q_{ij}'s becomes a little more complicated (though it requires no more data) than the simple estimation for the transition probabilities with two observations on a sample. However, this modification frees the process from the arbitrary times of data-collection and brings it closer to a process describing behavior. It also allows a second important modification of the model in the direction of mirroring behavior. For perhaps the most obvious weakness in the simple Markov chain as applied to a set of individuals is that it projects the future purely on the basis of the present state, and past change, of this single attribute, as if no other factors affected its change. But now a *partitioning* of the transition rate into components resulting from various other attributes and variables that are measured can be introduced. This partitioning, as well as estimation methods, are discussed in detail in Coleman (1964a, chs. 3–9). An example of an extension of this model to simultaneous change on two attributes is provided by McDill and Coleman (1963). For example, if there are two other attributes by which people are characterized, then the transition rate q_{12} will be as follows:

accuracy into the forward projection of the sample; the values of the components ω, β, ϵ, constitute estimates of the effects of other attributes on the one in question.

Thus this second extension of the Markov chain, into a continuous-time process, appears to lead in profitable directions, shaping it into a model that may be an appropriate abstraction of processes of change in attitudes and behavior.

Extensions of the Poisson process. Just as Bernoulli trials have been extended through Markov processes into models that are sociologically fruitful, the Poisson process has been extended. One class of models arose out of the inability of the Poisson to fit accident statistics.

Two radically different processes have been used to account for these deviations from the Poisson. One suggests that certain persons are more accident prone than others, that is, men have different parameters, λ. Under certain assumptions about the distribution of λ, this gives rise to a negative binomial distribution. The other process is a contagious process, which implies that all men begin the same, but, if a man has one

$$
\begin{aligned}
\text{(for persons with attributes } A \text{ and } B) \quad & q_{12} = \omega + \beta + \epsilon, \\
\text{(for persons with attribute } A \text{ only)} \quad & q_{12} = \omega \quad\;\; + \epsilon, \\
\text{(for persons with attribute } B \text{ only)} \quad & q_{12} = \quad\;\; \beta + \epsilon, \\
\text{(for persons with neither attribute)} \quad & q_{12} = \quad\quad\quad\; \epsilon,
\end{aligned}
$$

where ω is the effect of attribute A, β the effect of B, and ϵ is random shocks caused by other unmeasured attributes. After estimating q_{12} for each of these four types of persons, they can be used to obtain estimates of ω, β, and ϵ.

This extension of the process allows a marriage between the dynamics introduced by the Markov process and the standard procedures of data analysis which look for causal relations between attributes. For not only does this partitioning bring increased

accident, it leads to an increased chance of his having a second. The equations governing this process are only a slight modification from equations (7) and (8). If the increment to the transition rate for each accident is γ, then the transition rate after having had k accidents is $\lambda + k\gamma$, and the general differential equation for $i > 0$, is:

$$
\frac{dp_k}{dt} = -(\lambda + k\gamma)\; p_k + [\lambda + (k-1)\gamma]\; p_{k-1}. \tag{10}
$$

by the Markov process and the standard procedures of data analysis which look for causal relations between attributes. For not only does this partitioning bring increased

How is one to decide between these two explanations, one an explanation in terms of heterogeneity, and the other an explanation that says one accident leads to another?

The startling fact is that the two assumptions lead to an identical distribution, called variously the negative binomial, the Greenwood-Yule distribution, and the Polya distribution. This was first pointed out by Feller (1943). As a consequence, one cannot examine the distribution of accidents in a factory and distinguish whether it was produced merely by initial differences among the men or by a process in which one accident led to another. This is a general problem that manifests itself in numerous models; apparently the only way to break out of it is to make observations that go more deeply than the mere final distribution and intercept some of the assumed processes. In a model of within-individual contagion such as the accident model, this becomes difficult to do; in a model of between-individual contagion, such as is mentioned below, it is less difficult.

The most complete development of Poisson derivatives, and application to accident statistics, is in a little known Swedish monograph written a number of years ago (Lundberg, 1940). Applications of some of these models to other areas of behavior change may be found in Coleman (1964a, chs. 10, 11). Application to sociometric choice distributions may be found in Rapoport and Horvath (1961).

Another application of a Poisson-derivative model is in the area of "natural exposure" to cultural stimuli, such as television programs. McPhee (1963, Ch. 3) attacked the problem of explaining the characteristic pattern of differential awareness to stimuli of different strengths, by persons with different amounts of exposure, using a combination of a modified Poisson (to model the distribution of exposure) and a binomial (to reflect the probability of awareness, given exposure).

These extensions of the Poisson have largely been in the area of within-individual processes. Other extensions, perhaps of more centrality to sociology, examine between-individual processes. The most fully developed area is that of diffusion or contagion, and the principal innovations in this area have been made in the study of medical epidemics. A summary of the epidemic work up to 1957 may be found in Bailey (1957); subsequent work may be found in *Biometrika* and other British statistical journals.

These models may be illustrated by writing the equation for a simple diffusion process without removal, in which each individual is first in the have-not state, but moves into the have state. Each person has an individual transition rate toward innovation λ; but each of the k other persons who has already innovated adds to this a rate γ. The equation describing the individual who has not yet innovated when k others have innovated is

$$\frac{dp^*}{dt} = - (\lambda + k\gamma)p^*, \qquad (11)$$

where p^* is the probability that the individual has not adopted. The form of this equation shows the interaction with other individuals and the impossibility of solving for the individual's change unless one solves simultaneously for the state of the other $n - 1$ individuals. For k is a variable here, depending upon the outcome of the other $n - 1$ processes. It is, therefore, necessary in such a case to write equations for the system as a whole, since this is more than the aggregate of equations for n individuals.

The transition rate of the group out of the state of having k adopters, given that it is in the state, is $(n - k)(\lambda + k\gamma)$, that is the sum of the rates for the $n - k$ persons who have not adopted. For characterizing the group, one is interested in p_k, the probability of having k adopters, and the rate of change in p_k. This is given by the difference between the rate into state k (from $k - 1$) and the rate out of state k, or

$$\frac{dp_k}{dt} = - (n - k)(\lambda + k\gamma) p_k + (n - k + 1)[\lambda + (k - 1)\gamma]p_{k-1}. \qquad (12)$$

In order to describe the system for n persons, there are $n + 1$ equations such as the one above (with the first, $k = 0$, having only the first term on the right and the last, $k = n$, having only the second). The possibility of describing the process at either the individual or group level is a general feature of these Poisson-like processes. It can be very useful in laying out a complex process, which can often be specified more clearly first at the individual level.

This model takes one only a small step away from the Poisson; it assumes, for example, that the structure of contact among group members is complete and uniform, an assumption that is hardly true even in the smallest groups. Yet, for this model, analytical deductions, such as the distribution at any time, become exceedingly difficult.

There have, however, been a number of models for which deductions are less difficult. A contagion process in which the contagion operates in both directions does lead to a manageable model, for the equilibrium distribution may be found with little difficulty. It has been applied to voting data in groups, in which it is assumed that the vote is taken after an influence process has reached statistical equilibrium (Coleman, 1962).

Other Poisson-like models have been developed to mirror sociological processes. One area of work consists of models to account for the distribution of freely-forming groups, in which groups are continually gaining members through addition of isolates and continually losing members. With some mathematical approximations, and considering the case when the number of individuals is large and the probability of joining a group is small, the approximate distribution of group size can be derived, and it is a truncated Poisson distribution. For this and related models, the reader should see Coleman and James (1961), White (1962), and Goodman (1963a).

Altogether, the various generalizations of the Poisson process and other processes related to the Poisson (continuous-time, discrete-state models) appear extremely promising for mirroring various sociological phenomena. This is particularly the case in areas of mass behavior or loosely-structured aggregates. However, one difficulty quickly becomes apparent. Before the models are made complex enough to handle many problems, mathematical deductions become impossible. Two strategies have been used to avoid this difficulty. One lies in computer simulation, which is discussed subsequently, and the other in deterministic analogs to the stochastic processes, which are examined in the next section.

Deterministic models with variables derived from counting. Many of the same processes discussed above may be treated by deterministic models, and many have been, either as a first approximation to the stochastic process, or without regard to stochastic disturbances. (In general, such disregard is well placed when the numbers involved are large, due to the law of large numbers. But this can be misleading when there is interdependence between the elements, for great instability can occur in the face of large numbers if there is interdependence, as there is in many sociological models.) Perhaps the best example of an approximation to the stochastic process is a diffusion model, a deterministic analogue to equation (12).

$$\frac{dk}{dt} = (n - k)(a + ck) \quad (13)$$

where k is the number who have adopted, n is the total, c is the effect of each adopter on each nonadopter, and a is the individual innovation rate in the absence of others. It is assumed, of course, that n is large enough that n and k can be considered continuous for practical purposes. Dodd (1955), among other sociologists, used a variant of this model for representing sociological diffusion processes, and the British students of medical epidemics have used it and others as aproximations to the stochastic model (see

Bailey, 1957). As compared to the stochastic model, the deterministic diffusion model overestimates the rate of change, the amount of overestimation decreasing as n increases. In those models without inter-individual processes, the deterministic model is ordinarily equal to the mean value of the stochastic process, which makes the difference between stochastic and deterministic models a less important one. It is for this reason that a state probability in the Markov processes described in an earlier section can be interpreted either as the probability that a given individual will find himself in a particular state, or as the expected proportion of persons in that state.

In the case of diffusion, as well as other cases, it may be possible to make the model more realistic in other ways through making it deterministic. For example, the most grossly defective assumption implicit in the diffusion models presented above is the assumption of perfect contact between all members. In all but the smallest groups, this is wholly unrealistic. It is possible, however, to modify the above deterministic model to reduce this unreality (Coleman, 1964a, Ch. 17).

Beside deterministic models of change designed to serve as approximations to stochastic processes, there have been deterministic models still using concepts based on counting, developed without regard for stochastic disturbances. Perhaps the most interesting of these is a set of generalizations of models for growth processes. Volterra (1931) developed models for the population of two or more species in competition for the same food, for a predator-prey relation between two species, and other variations. This work has recently been extended by Davis (1960).

Of this class of models, the most widely known is a rather simple model developed by Richardson (1939), designed to illustrate the structure of an arms race that could lead to war. The resulting model is a pair of differential equations (with the variables being amounts of armament expenditure of two nations), in which the rate of increase in each variable depends on the size of the other. The result, of course, is an unstable system, leading to ever more arms and presumably to war.

Such a model as this must be regarded as even less than a "sometimes-true" theory, for one could not seriously propose such a simple model as a mirror of the processes leading to war. Instead it abstracts from the many processes one alone and shows the consequences if that process alone were operative. Models like this might be termed "what if" models, for they show what would be the case if a certain process alone were operative for an individual, a group, or a society. A more recent example of such a model is one designed to mirror addiction and other perseveration processes (McPhee, 1963, Ch. 5).

Many of the models discussed in this and preceding sections have been constructed around a mathematics of differential equations. Such models have sometimes been suspect because of the difficulties of quantification in sociology. Yet there is a wide range of possible uses, wholly from the domain of quantitative variables obtained from counting. It is clear that systems of differential equations, and the power they bring with them, can have wide use in sociology because the way to quantification can be climbed through counting. In some cases, these models will be approximations because counting provides integers rather than a continuum. But science has been built on approximations, and it is unlikely that sociology will prove to be different.

Furthermore, differential equations constitute the only intellectual device that mankind has yet invented for dealing with change that is continuous in time. Until their invention, man had no formal conceptual system for describing motion, and their invention by Newton allowed such a system to be established.

Yet for another class of problems in sociology, there have been recent mathematical developments that are particularly appropriate. These are problems of structure.

Problems of Structure and Mathematical Models of Structure

One type of social structure that has been examined mathematically by sociologists is that generated by sociometric data: choices of group members by other group members. The choices have been represented mathematically in one of two ways: (1) by matrices in which entries a_{ij} consist of 0's (representing no choice from i to j) and 1's (representing a choice from i to j); and (2) by graphs, in which group members are represented by points, and choice among them by directed lines, usually with an arrow indicating the direction of choice. As an illustration, the choice data at left below for a four person group are represented by a matrix and a graph as indicated at center and right.

this, the operations carried out are identical.

It should be made clear what the virtue is of such representation. It is not in being able to transform common sense into mathematical notation, but in the formal operations that can be carried out on the mathematical structure and their sociological interpretations. This is a point that has not always been clear in this area, particularly in the use of graph theory. The initial "applications" of graph theory were little or nothing more than giving names to points, lines, and particular configurations of points and lines (Harary & Norman, 1953). Subsequent work has begun to go beyond this, though the operations available in graph theory are rather weak ones, giving little power to the theory.

One of the more interesting areas of application of graph theory arises when relations between two individuals can be valued as positive or negative. Various social psychologists have discussed the strain that exists when there are certain configurations

Chooser	Chosen
1 =	2, 3
2 =	1, 3
3 =	1, 4
4 =	2

(Chosen)

(Chooser)	1	2	3	4
1	0	1	1	0
2	1	0	1	0
3	1	0	0	1
4	0	1	0	0

Before examining the use of these techniques one should note that the problems to which they can be applied go beyond sociometric structures. Dominance structures, in which there is at most one directed relation between each two persons, can be represented by these techniques. Communication structures, with nondirected relations, can also be represented here. Each of these types of structures implies certain conditions upon the graph or the matrix, but beyond

of positive and negative links. For example if A and B are friendly, and A and C are friendly, but B and C are hostile, there is an implicit strain, which becomes explicit whenever the three persons come together.

If one considers a graph in which the lines are not directed and are given positive and negative signs, then such a graph can represent the situation as described by social psychologists. Harary (1953) first proposed such a representation, and it has been carried further by him (1955; 1959) and others (Flament, 1963). Then, by the operation of multiplication of the signs around each cycle of the graph, the balance or imbalance of the structure can be determined, according to whether the product is positive or negative. This is equivalent to an even or odd number of negative links in the cycle respectively. The theory of graphs, weak though it be, has been then used to prove certain theorems about balanced and unbalanced graphs. For example, Harary showed that a perfectly balanced graph, whatever the size, can be divided into two sets of points (e.g., individuals) such that all the links within each set are positive, and all between the two sets are negative. Conversely, if such a partitioning can be made, the graph is perfectly balanced. This corresponds nicely to the situation that arises whenever a single issue dominates a community, for the issue divides the community into two camps, which, for the time being, are friendly within, but hostile between. Carrying this work further, Flament used the theory of graphs and the theory of lattices to determine the minimum length path through which an unbalanced graph can become balanced by successive changes of single links. An incidental area of application mentioned by Flament (1963, p. 125) is to relations within the families in primitive societies. Levi-Strauss described types of family structures consisting of the four basic members: father, son, mother, and maternal uncle. Six types of structures are observed, the most frequent being the two completely balanced and the most rare being the two which are least balanced, requiring changes of two signs to become balanced.

In this and other areas of application of graph theory, the work has proceeded little beyond common sense. Yet the pervasiveness of structural problems and the relative youth of this branch of mathematics leave room to hope that the applications will prove of real value to sociology.

With 0 — 1 matrices, the principal operation that gives some intellectual leverage on the problem is that of multiplication. Multiplication allows the study of indirect relations, at 1,2,3,4,. . . removes. The simplest example in a sociometric structure is that of multiplying the matrix by itself. In that case one has, in a four man group, chains that can be exemplified by the 1–4 example below.

$$
1 \quad \begin{array}{c} 1 \\ 2 \\ 3 \\ 4 \end{array}
$$

Thus there is one path that goes through a single other person from 1 to 4. The matrix that results from this is:

	1	2	3	4
1	2	0	1	1
2	1	1	1	1
3	0	2	1	0
4	1	0	1	0

The numbers in the cell i,j indicate the numbers of paths from i to j of length 2.

This principle of moving through the structures along extended paths has made the operation of matrix multiplication useful for numerous problems. Luce (1950), Festinger (1949), and many others have attempted to identify cliques by virtue of this operation. Use of matrix multiplication with dominance structures can show the existence of extended authority and the number of channels through which i has extended authority over j.

However, three other devices have also proved useful. The first, used by Katz (1953) and in modified form by Hubbell (1963), has been to multiply each entry by an attenuation coefficient, a, representing the attenuation of influence or information at each remove. Then numerous additional results are possible. The n-th power of the matrix can represent the amount of influence or information flowing from i to j through exactly n removes. The sum of the matrices to the $1, 2, \ldots, n$ powers represents the total influence or information from i to j at n removes or less. Furthermore, the sum of the infinite series may be either convergent or divergent for a given value of a. If it is convergent, this means that the influence flow dies out; if divergent, it means that the influence "explodes," becoming ever larger as it circulates through the structure. It may be divergent in some portions of the structure, convergent in others. As Hubbell pointed out (personal communication) this gives concreteness to the notions of expansion and contraction of influence in structural systems, as discussed by Parsons (1963) and Coleman (1963b). Hubbell's (1963) modification of Leontief input-output matrices for social structures gives an analogue to the multiplier effect in economics, which is directly relevant to the influence-expansion discussed by social theorists.

The second device is the notion of using this operation of matrix multiplication for two or more different structures or for different relations. If one has a group of n_1 boys and n_2 girls, then the structure of boy-likes-girl relation is an $n_1 \times n_2$ matrix. Multiplying this by the $n_2 \times n_1$ matrix of girl-likes-boy gives a matrix whose entries a_{ij} represent the number of girls liked by boy i, who in turn like boy j. Or in a school where students are taught by several teachers, suppose there is a group of n_1 teachers and n_2 students. In the $n_1 \times n_2$ teacher-student matrix, a 1 in cell (i, j) means that teacher i teaches student j. In the $n_2 \times n_1$, student-teacher matrix, a 1 means that student i likes teacher j. Then the $n_1 \times n_1$ product matrix has as cell entries a_{ij} the number of students, taught by teacher i, who like teacher j. The $n_2 \times n_2$ product

matrix has as a cell entry the number of teachers liked by student i who teach student j.

Finally, a third device is to let the rows and columns represent roles or statuses in an organization, and the 1 as a cell entry represent the existence of a role relation between status i and status j. In certain instances, for example in primitive tribes where marriage of a man in a given classificatory status can be only with a woman from one other status, the sum of each row is 1 and the sum of each column is 1. (Such matrices are called permutation matrices, for each such matrix is an operator which brings about a particular permutation.) If the rows represent wife's status, the matrix can be considered a husband-wife matrix which maps the husband's status into that of the wife.

Putting the last two devices together has given a useful tool for the description of classificatory marriage systems in certain primitive tribes. For in such systems, there are two necessary matrices: a marriage, or husband-wife matrix, and a descent, or father-child matrix. If these are called W and C respectively, then any relative of ego can be characterized as products of the W and C matrices (allowing the inverse matrix as well, W^{-1} and C^{-1}, which represent respectively a wife-husband matrix and a child-father relation). Then, for example, the classificatory status of ego's mother is $C^{-1}W$, and that of an uncle who is mother's sister's husband is arrived at by $C^{-1}WW^{-1}$, and an uncle who is father's sister's husband is $C^{-1}W^{-1}$.

A. Weil first proposed such correspondence, R. Bush followed the proposal (see White, 1963, appendices 1 and 2), and White (1963) has carried it out in detail and applied it to describe the relation between descent and marriage in particular primitive tribes. The allowable marriages with kin are given by the products of W and C matrices that equal W. White showed that, in some tribes, the rule is:

$W = C^{-1}WC$, that is, marriage is allowed with mother's $(C^{-1}W)$ brother's daughter (C). In others, it is $W = C^{-1}W^{-1}C$, or father's sister's daughter. Thus, the marriage system can be described by the particular products of W and C that equal W.

Beside the work noted earlier on all-or-none choice data, there is one additional body of work that uses neither the formal representative of graph theory nor $0 - 1$ matrices. This is work on "random nets," which calculates the expected structural configurations if choices were made at random among the group members. This work, which uses principally combinatorics, was carried out in the early 1950's by mathematical biophysicists and has been summarized by Coleman (1960).

It seems likely that these techniques of structural mathematics will prove increasingly valuable to sociology as their areas of application are extended. In particular, they provide a means of taking a structure that is seen only from the vantage points of the different nodes (for that is where its members are) and drawing from it its properties as a total structure.

It should be recalled in passing that certain structural problems can also be studied by stochastic processes, or more generally by systems of differential equations. For example, in modern society, where there is no fixed prescription for marriage or mobility between different statuses (i.e., occupational statuses), cell entries in a matrix would not be 0 or 1, but rather proportions, somewhere between 0 and 1. With such data, stochastic processes and systems of differential equations are appropriate. Beshers and Reiter (1963) have developed such a model for marriage and descent systems in complex societies.

Simple Processes and Complex Systems: Models and Computers

Most of the fruitful work in mathematical sociology has treated single, rather simple processes. Yet in the real world, these processes are seldom found in isolation, but are bound up in a complex system. This creates two difficulties. First, it is difficult to isolate and discover the separate processes. In survey analysis, one is sometimes able to come close to doing so, but only in a qualitative way, seldom finding the mathematical form of the process and even less often being able to estimate quantitatively the parameters. Second, even if the processes are isolated by data analysis, it is useless to synthesize them into an overall mathematical model. Such a model would hardly ever be simple enough to allow useful analytic deductions. Yet to resynthesize the components of a functioning system, in order to surmise its functioning under various conditions, is often the aim. To use an example outside sociology: Even after the laws of mechanics are known, it is not easy to calculate the functioning of a complex structure such as a bridge. Engineers must turn to either a physical model or to complex numerical calculations (which can best be carried out on a computer) to discover its behavior under various stresses. The problem is even greater when there is only partial mathematical knowledge of the behavior of the parts and the rest can be characterized only by empirically determined probabilities. In such a case, a monte carlo procedure, or simulation, can show the behavior of the system.

In sociology this is particularly true, because of the great complexity of social systems. Mathematical models and analytical deductions made from them can only mirror components of such systems. A computer becomes extremely valuable for synthesizing these into a system and carrying out numerical analysis or simulation. Thus the second part of the chapter examines computer models of social organization, as the intrinsic complement to mathematical models or mathematical theories.

COMPUTERS IN THE STUDY OF SOCIAL ORGANIZATION

This examination explicitly excludes the wide use that computers are coming to have in processing statistical data in sociology. Survey research data are now largely analyzed on computers, and techniques for statistical analysis that have seldom been possible are in current use. Some of the standard statistical techniques for which programs exist for current computers are discussed in the following paragraphs.

1. Cross-tabulation, or contingency tables.

2. Statistical tests for contingency tables, including exact tests for small cell values.

3. Correlation matrices.

4. Regression analysis, including stepwise multiple regression and attribute data as dummy variables.

5. Analysis of variance and covariance.
6. Factor analysis.
7. Item analysis.
8. Canonical analysis.
9. Linear programming.
10. Dynamic programming.

Many of these programs may be found in the program library of any large computer center. Descriptions of these and other programs may be found in *Behavioral Science,* under the heading "Computer Program Abstracts." Among the several recent books that describe current computer methods of statistical analysis is Cooley and Lohnes (1962).

There is a concurrent computer development in government and business that promises radically to increase the knowledge of society's functioning. This is the use of computers for administrative record-keeping. These records, in conjunction with statistical programs of the sort described above, should begin to provide valuable social indices for the United States and its parts, for the records cover a wide variety of behavior: television viewing, work history, family residence patterns, and many others. The time is approaching when the analytical techniques and the records can be combined to give rich information about certain aspects of society.

In addition to these techniques of statistical analysis, some work has developed with computers which is particularly appropriate for problems involving large structures. Factor analysis and regression analysis may be considered as examples of this, and certain applications have been made directly to social structural problems (Macrae, 1960). Other techniques are wholly the product of computer developments. For example, Alexander and Manheim (1963) programmed a system which takes a matrix of correlations between variables, treats the correlations as links in a graph, and then decomposes the graph into those subsets which are most empirically distinct from each other. As another example, the NASA-PERT system (1963) is a programming system for optimum scheduling of a complex sequence of activities. The sequence of activities can be represented by a set of arrows linking up each activity with its predecessors and its successors. As it stands, it has not found direct use in sociology. Yet the kind of problem it attacks, that of analyzing a complex structure of events, is at the center of much of sociology. It and several other techniques, such as linear programming and dynamic programming, have optimization rather than analysis as the end product and are thus more fitted for policy problems than analytical ones. Yet as techniques for treating complex structures, they are of interest to sociologists as the ability to gather empirical data on complex structures increases.

The Functioning of a Computer

Before examining the use of computers in studying social processes and social structure, it is useful to see the essential characteristics of a computer. Knowledge of these is not necessary in order to use a computer for straightforward purposes. It is necessary, however, if one is to innovate in use of a computer. It can be said without fear of contradiction that the greatest value of computers to sociology will be through innovations that have not yet been made.

A computer and its necessary appendages may be conceived as consisting of two parts: the *memory,* which provides large amounts of data storage, and the *operations,* which act upon data in the memory. The operations are combined into a particular sequence or *program* of operations. It is this program that provides the dynamics, for it is in fact a program or schedule of activities that the computer will carry out when it is initiated.

The program itself is stored in memory and, by virtue of that fact, can be modified by itself, as the program proceeds. It is this as much as any other single attribute of computers that makes them such powerful tools.

To give an understanding of how a computer program can operate with social structural data, a simple problem of social structure, and a very simple computer will be taken, and the computer will be used to solve the problem. Then, because nearly all programs today operate with a language one step removed from computer operations themselves, the same problem will be treated with a Fortran program.

The problem: Given one thousand persons, each of whom makes a single sociometric choice: his "best friend." (1) What is the number of persons whose friends reciprocate the choice? (2) For each person, indicate whether his friend names him in return.

Rules: Assume that the data and program are already in the computer and do not require that the results be written out from the computer. Thus input-output instructions will not be used.

The computer: The memory is composed of three thousand "words" or cells within which data can be stored. The locations or addresses of the words are 0000–2999. Each of these words is five decimal digits in length.

The instructions consist of a letter indicating the type of operation to be performed, and a four-digit address. Each instruction can be stored in a word in memory, and the program can be stored in a sequence of words.

The operations are:

B xxxx	Bring a word from location xxxx and store it in the accumulator, destroying the previous contents.
A xxxx	Add a word taken from location xxxx to the existing contents of the accumulator.
S xxxx	Subtract a word taken from location xxxx from the existing contents of the accumulator.
C xxxx	Carry the contents of the accumulator to location xxxx, replacing its existing contents.
T xxxx	Transfer computer control, taking the next operation from location xxxx rather than the next instruction in sequence.
N xxxx	Negative transfer. If accumulator is negative, transfer control to location xxxx. Otherwise continue sequence.
H 0000	Halt computer.

The computer memory is partitioned for this problem as follows:

Location
0000	(not used)
0001–1000	names of friends
1001–2000	storage space for resulting indicators in part 2 of problem
2001–2034	program
2035–2799	(not used)
2800–2804	constants used by program
2900–2901	variables used by program
2902	counter for number of mutual choices
2903–2999	(not used)

The machine-language program is given in Table 2. A Fortran program designed to do the same problem follows below. In the machine program certain instructions in the program are modified by the program itself as it proceeds. Their initial value is given in the listing, and parentheses are used to indicate that they are modified during the program's running.

Machine language program:

Address	Instruction	Description
2001	B 2800	
2002	C 2902	
2003	C 2900	
2004	B 2900	Bring previous name to accumulator
2005	A 2801	Add 1 to name, to go to next person
2006	C 2900	Carry back to storage
2007	A 2803	Add operation B 0000 to create instruction
2008	C 2013	Carry new instruction to location 2013
2009	B 2900	Bring new name to accumulator
2010	A 2804	Add C 1000 to create new instruction
2011	C 2024	Carry new instruction to location 2024
2012	C 2029	Carry new instruction to location 2029
2013	(B 0000)	Bring (0001)'s friend to accumulator
2014	A 2803	Add operation B 0000 to create instruction
2015	C 2016	Carry newly created instruction to location 2016
2016	(B 0000)	Bring friend's friend to accumulator
2017	S 2900	Subtract own name
2018	N 2028	If own name is greater, transfer
2019	C 2901	If not, carry residual to location 2901
2020	B 2800	Bring zeroes to accumulator
2021	S 2901	Subtract residual from zeroes
2022	N 2028	If own name is less, transfer
2023	B 2801	If not, prepare to carry 1 to own record
2024	(C 0000)	Carry 1 to own record
2025	A 2902	Add mutual-choice counter to 1
2026	C 2902	Carry to mutual-choice counter
2027	T 2030	Transfer to test for end
2028	B 2800	(If name is greater or less) prepare to carry 0 to own record
2029	(C 0000)	Carry 0 to own record
2030	B 2802	Bring end signal: last name
2031	S 2900	Subtract current name
2032	N 2034	If end signal surpassed, transfer to end
2033	T 2004	(If not) transfer to continue processing
2034	H 0000	Halt if end.

Storage of constants

2800	00000	zero
2801	00001	one
2802	00999	nine ninety-nine
2803	B 0000	dummy instruction
2804	C 1000	dummy instruction

Storage of variables

2900	00000	index of current chooser's name
2901	00000	temporary storage
2902	00000	mutual-choice counter

Storage of name data. In locations 0001 to 1000 are stored at the start the names (identification numbers) of friends of persons 0001 to 1000 respectively. The location of the word is the name of the chooser; the contents of the word, in the four right hand digits, is the name of the best friend.

Storage of each person's mutual-choice record. Locations 1001 to 2000 are reserved for storing the records concerning mutual choices: 0 if no mutual choice; 1 if mutual choice.

Fortran program:
```
      NUMBER = 0
      DO 10 I = 1, 1000
      J = NFRND (I)
      K = NFRND (J)
      IF (K-I) 20, 30, 20
30    NOTE (I) = 1
      NUMBER = NUMBER + 1
      GO TO 10
20    NOTE (I) = 0
10    CONTINUE
      CALL EXIT
```

Set number of mutual choices = 0
Do the loop from here to 10 1000 times, increasing I by one each time
Set J equal to name of I's friend
Set K equal to name of J's friend
If K = I go to 30
Put a 1 in I's record place
Add 1 to number of mutual choices
Go to recycle
Put a 0 in I's record place
Recycle to next person

Computers, Social Processes, and Social Structure

As the above example indicates, computers are particularly well suited to problems that involve social structure. The structure can, in a sense, be stored in the memory of the computer and then examined by the program. In this problem, a very simple structure is stored by letting persons' names be the same as their addresses or locations. Then storing the friend's name as data at ego's location gives the necessary information for the computer to go to the friend's location.

The computer program in this problem is merely a set of manipulations on the data in memory to solve the required problem. This is its task in all data-processing, in statistical analysis, and in numerical analysis methods. However, in system simulation, the program can be conceived of as a set of social and psychological processes, combined to constitute a system. The program acts through time; thus it can represent a sequence of behavior in a system. It consists of a very flexible set of logical as well as mathematical operations, so that processes difficult to put into mathematical form can nevertheless be simulated.

The problem in the example above is possible to write very simply because the structure as well as the problem is simple. It is possible to store the linkages in regular banks of memory. Fortran and languages like it will allow efficient handling of one-,

two-, and three-dimensional regular arrays, through subscripting, exemplified in the program above for a one-dimensional array by NFRND (I). However, there sometimes arises a need for more flexibility, both in storing complex structures and in modifying the links of the structure. Several computer languages have been developed to meet this need. Examples are IPL-V (Newell, 1961) and Simscript (Markowitz, 1963). These have been used particularly to represent cognitive processes (e.g., Feigenbaum & Simon, 1963), but are also appropriate for certain problems in the simulation of social processes. A language such as IPL-V restructures the memory into a series of interconnected "lists" of variable length. Each list can be thought of as a node in a structure. The information carried on the list is of two kinds: information about the node, and connections or pointers to other lists. The flexibility provided by these list structures is very great, although the flexibility is often paid for by more difficult programming.

As a general rule at present, if a problem can be programmed in a regular algebraic language like Fortran, it will be more convenient and efficient to do so. Such a rule can easily become false, of course, because of the rapid development of new languages especially designed for simulation and for problems of complex structure.

The examples of computer simulations in social organization discussed below illustrate a variety of problems that may be studied in social processes and social organization

Machine language instructions

Start

Instruction	Box
2001-2002	Set number of mutual choices = 0
2003	Set I = 0
2004-2012	Increment I by 1
2013	Find I's friend
2014-2016	Find friend of I's friend
2017-2022	Is he the same as I? — No
(Yes) 2023-2024	Set I's record = 1
2025-2026	Increment number of mutual choices by 1
2028-2029	Set I's record = 0
2030-2033	Is I > 1000? — No
(Yes) 2034	HALT

TABLE 2

FLOW CHART FOR SOCIOMETRIC PROBLEM

and a variety of approaches to these problems. They constitute not an inclusive survey of work in this field, but an examination of the various kinds of work that is being done.

Computers in Conjunction with Explicit Mathematical Models

Certain uses of computers to mirror social processes are directly tied to explicit mathematical models. These uses may be classified into three categories: parameter estimation, numerical analysis, and simulation or monte carlo techniques. An example of the first is estimating coefficients in a system of simultaneous differential equations. An example of the second is solution of such a system of equations, for the state of the system at time t. However, these procedures are possible only when an algorithm exists for carrying out such calculations. Often, the means of solution is through a recursive function which is well adapted to the computer.

Such parameter estimation and numerical analysis is not treated here, because it almost always involves algebraic or differential equations, for which there are well-developed procedures, treated in books on numerical analysis for computers.

Often, however, formulating a mathematical model of a process, analytic deductions may be impossible even with numerical analysis, and a simulation is necessary. This was mentioned earlier for the stochastic process of diffusion. In such a case, a computer program is written to mirror the structure of events described by the mathematical model. Often, this is extremely simple, although the analytic deductions may be very difficult. For example, in the case of the diffusion process described by equation (12), each individual who has not yet adopted has probability $(\lambda + k\gamma)dt$ of doing so in time dt, if k others have already done so. Thus, the simulation can be carried out by fixing a very small time unit, Δt, as the time represented by a single loop of the program, and then proceeding through this time cycle by carrying out a calculation for each individual. The calculation consists of two steps: (1) Calculate the probability of adoption in time Δt, using the fixed parameters λ and γ, together with k, the number who have already adopted, which may change after each time cycle. (2) Generate a random number, compare it with the calculated probability, and thus determine whether the individual adopts on this time cycle.

The outcome of these calculations for each of the n-k persons who have not yet adopted provides the value of k for the next time cycle, and thus the process continues.

By carrying out such calculations once over the desired number of time cycles, the behavior of a single case (i.e., group) is recorded. To obtain the expected or average behavior path, a great many such cases are necessary, thus giving the whole distribution. An example of such simulation for diffusion processes was carried out by Kendall and reproduced in Bailey (1957, p. 67).

Before turning to computer simulation designed for empirical or theoretical ends, it is useful to discuss several uses of computer models that will not be treated there.

One such use is in making population projections from census data. Several such programs are in process of development, and at least one (Tarver, 1963) has been developed and used.

A second use is in the analysis of verbal text, a problem closely related to information retrieval and automatic translation. All these areas are greatly in flux, and it is sufficient to note a few examples of such work. Analysis of verbal text is carried out by Simmons, Klein, and McClonlougue (1962), and Stone, Bales, Namenwirth, and Olgivie (1962). Translation and information retrieval work can be found in Borko (1962).

There has been a small amount of work, as yet unpublished, in the use of computers for teaching research analysis techniques. The procedure is as follows:

(1) A program is written for the computer so that the computer events simulate events in the process under study.

(2) The student may request certain data from the computer, at particular points in the process.

(3) He must infer, from the data, something about the underlying process being simulated.

One such simulation carried out by Levenson (personal communication) concerned the promotion rules in a hypothetical business organization. Students could obtain from the computer certain facts about who was in particular positions in the organization at various times. From this they had to infer what rules had been used in promotion, and what the chances were for promotion of different kinds of people. Another example of simulated social research has been developed and used by the author in teaching. In this simulated system, a diffusion process which is a slight elaboration of that described in equation (12) above is simulated in a community of one thousand. The student must then design research determining what sample size, what dates of interviews, and whether to use a panel design or separate samples. After receiving the information requested, the student then uses this to estimate the values of λ and γ. Thus to carry out the research properly, he must do both design and analysis. Furthermore, it becomes highly meaningful to use statistical inference, because there is an underlying parameter against which the student's estimate can be checked.

Though this use of computers has not yet developed far in sociology, it appears extremely promising as an aid in teaching quantitative research techniques. It provides both a kind of research laboratory to generate data and an objective criterion in terms of which the design and analysis can be evaluated.

Synthesis of Simple Propositions to Answer Systemic Questions

There are many cases in which there has not been an explicit mathematical model laid out, yet a system of behavior can be formulated as a set of quantitative processes. Two examples are given below to illustrate the use of a computer in such a case.

Interaction in a triad. This example is taken from a paper by Kirk and Coleman (1963). Georg Simmel was fascinated by triads and by the additional phenomena that can occur when there are three persons in a group, rather than two. One of the possibilities which he discussed was the tendency for a structural imbalance to occur: for a triad to degenerate into a pair and an isolate. The question then arises: What processes are necessary to explain this structural asymmetry that often arises in a group of three? It can be trivially explained by individual differences: If A and B are more compatible than either is with C, then the triad could easily become asymmetric and consist of a heavily-interacting pair and an isolate. But are such individual differences necessary? More particularly, consider a very simple process: If A and B interact, and the interaction is rewarding to each, they will have an increased tendency to interact again. This is common sense and has also been stated by a number of social psychologists. But let the same process occur for A and C, and for B and C. Then consider the fact that time is limited, so that an interaction between A and B is carried out at the expense of an interaction between A and C or B and C. Thus there are three processes, each with positive feedback, competing for a limited amount of time. Could some chance occurrence, near the beginning of the interaction, allow one process to run wild at the expense of the other two, creating a solidary pair and an isolate? Can these simple processes alone take three identical group members and create an asymmetric structure from them through the competition for limited time?

The answer is yes, that these processes can produce the isolate-dyad asymmetry. But perhaps equally important, they produce a second kind of asymmetry in which one member dominates interaction: The AB pair is strong, the AC pair is strong, but the BC pair is weak. In some cases, the structure remains balanced. In other words, these processes certainly can produce the isolate-dyad asymmetry. In some simulated sessions of one hundred interactions, over two-thirds of the interactions were between the AB pair, leaving less than one-third for BC and AC together. In contrast, the expected proportion of interactions for the strongest pair, in a total of one hundred interactions without the reward process, is only .38. In only 9 out of 50 simulated sessions was the actual proportion below .38. But the processes certainly do not always create this degeneration into isolate and

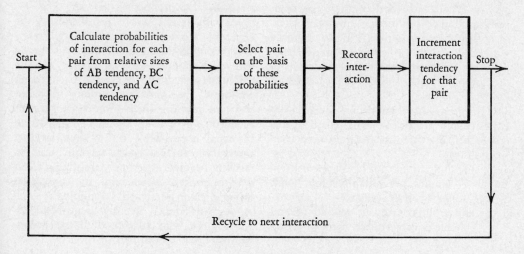

pair, and, under a wide range of initial conditions, the balanced state and the dominating-member asymmetry occur with some frequency. Thus the positive-reinforcement process can, but does not necessarily, produce the asymmetry that Simmel commented on.

It is useful, in this simple case, to show the way a computer is used in social simulation. Three words in the memory of the computer are used to keep a record of the number of interactions: one for *AB*, one for *AC*, and one for *BC*. Three more words are used to hold the current values of the interaction tendencies: one for *AB*, one for *AC*, and one for *BC*. Then the program consists of a sequence of instructions to carry out the events of one interaction, together with a device to recycle, allowing as many interactions as desired. The sequence of instructions carries out the following opera-instructions carries out the operations shown in the diagram (simplified to include only essential steps).

This example illustrates a general strategy in social simulation: to link together known microprocesses in a particular structural configuration, in order to examine consequences at the level of the system. In this case the system was a very small one, but the strategy can be used for large systems as well, as the second example will indicate.

Productive behavior in industrial work groups. There have been numerous studies of restriction of production among workers in industry, beginning with the Hawthorne studies. From these studies certain basic processes can be isolated that are relevant to the level of productivity and the level of pay:

(1) The means of monetary reward generates certain processes on the part of workers. Principally three means have been used in industry:

  (a) individual-contingent reward (examples are straight piece work and bonus systems)

  (b) group-contingent reward (example is group piece work or group bonus)

  (c) noncontingent reward (example is hourly pay).

(2) Considering only one system, straight piece work, this induces the following actions: added effort to bring added reward; a constraint on one's own work to prevent rate-cutting, if there has been a history of rate-cutting; and constraint on others whose output exceeds one's own, if there is a history of rate-cutting.

(3) The application of contraints to other workers in turn can generate negative sentiments among workers if the constraint is not obeyed. Similarly, positive sentiments may be generated by similarity of response to the work situation: similar levels of production, and similar response to constraints applied by fellow-workers.

(4) The total amount of pay per worker generates certain processes on the part of managers. The need for maintaining a relatively fixed relation to the pay of workers elsewhere in the plant will lead managers to cut piece rates if take-home pay exceeds some maximum, and increase it if it falls below a minimum

Raymond Breton (1962) synthesized a worker-management system that is governed by these processes. His interest was not merely in developing a system in which the levels of output would change as a function of the above processes, but in examining how various factors affect the structure of productive activity. For example, in initial work, he examined the effect of restrictive constraints applied by workers upon the variation in output among different members of the group. As one might expect, these constraints tended to compress the variation among different workers, making them more homogeneous in output, as if behaving in response to an informal norm. However, if their level of motivation for monetary rewards was increased beyond a certain point, the effect was opposite: Application of constraints brought about increased variability, as some workers developed negative sentiments toward those who attempted to apply constraints upon them.

This result indicates an attribute of social simulation that can be either a pitfall or extremely valuable, depending on how it is used. In this case, a surprising result occurred with the model. How is this to be taken? If directly accepted as fact, applying to industrial groups, it could be very misleading (exactly comparable to the extrapolation of results from experimental groups), for it may be incorrect, due to a defect in the simulation. However, if the result is used as a sensitizing agent, leading to a more intensive examination of the data for actual work groups, then it is extremely valuable. For one seldom expects, and thus seldom looks for, a variable to have one effect under one set of conditions and a directly opposite effect under a different set of conditions. The simulated system shows how it could be so; further research is necessary to examine whether it is so.

More than this, however, the simulation allows one to dissect and examine the mechanisms through which the result occurs (in this case, through the development of negative sentiments based on early home differences in work output). It thus suggests exactly what to look for in further empirical investigations.

These two examples have much in common. They are "simulations" of some aspect of social organizations, in which certain microprocesses are postulated (that is, processes at the level of interaction among individuals) and consequences studied at the level of the total system. Thus, they are examples of the bridge that sociological theory must constitute—a bridge between individuals, upon whom most of the sociologist's observations are made, and social systems, which are his objects of interest.

But these examples share another attribute, a complete absence of quantitative data. Their postulates are qualitative propositions, based upon common knowledge or upon results of numerous researches. But in neither case is there a close interlinking of computer model and actual data. There is developing a whole class of such models, and they should be clearly differentiated from another group that do make direct use of data.

Dynamic Surveys with Social-Psychological Processes

Simulations designed for use with data. The goal of most survey research is not that for which most statistical techniques of sampling, estimation, and hypothesis-testing are designed. It is only seldom (as in the Kinsey reports) a goal of estimating a population characteristic. It is scarcely more often that of testing a specific hypothesis. Consequently, most of the statistical techniques used in empirical research are merely bracings and buttresses, which must be deployed at appropriate points in order to reconstruct the processes from the data. For the goal is ordinarily to describe an interrelated set of processes and to project what the impact of these processes will be at the level of the system as a whole. For example, in a relatively simple use of survey research, for studying election campaigns, the goal is ordinarily to reconstruct the processes of that campaign, showing how they combined to produce the election outcome.

Thus the goal of a quantitative research project ordinarily implies some dynamics, some set of processes synthesized to mirror the system under study. Unfortunately, such work is in its infancy. There is no good example of dynamics and synthesis having been explicitly incorporated into a quantitative research project. But some examples exist that provide guideposts. There are at least two examples of research on election campaigns, and one is described below. The other was developed by McPhee, and was used in the Wisconsin primary in the 1960 presidential election in conjunction with a survey carried out by Roper Associates. A modified version of it is reported in McPhee (1963, Ch. 4). The one to be described here was also used in the 1960 election, in conjunction with a panel of eight hundred persons in Baltimore, interviewed at points throughout the campaign. It is reported in Coleman and Waldorf (1962). The data-collection and model-construction developed jointly. The model was designed to take as data a sample of persons, each with particular attitudes on issues, with a particular ranking of importance of issues, particular relations to one another, particular attention to different segments of the mass media, and particular initial attitudes toward the candidates. With these data as the initial structural conditions (both psychological and social structure), the model consisted of two simple processes to carry the system forward: development of consistency between one's vote intention and attitudes on those issues to which attention has been drawn and development of consistency between one's vote intention and the attitudes of one's associate on those issues that arise during association. Each person was carried through each time cycle (a time cycle representing one day) and subjected to the processes during that cycle. The events of the campaign, such as positions taken and issues emphasized by the candidates, constitute added inputs at particular points in time; the output of interest is the fluctuations in support for the two candidates at various points in the campaign.

About all that can be said of the results of the simulation-research is that at the aggregate level the changes at various points in the campaign corresponded well to the actual changes in the panel. These changes were sharply toward Nixon before September and then toward Kennedy after that point in the 1960 presidential election campaign.

One may well ask the question: Why not examine in detail the predictions of the model, that is, why not examine them at the individual level, to test the model more fully? The answer to this question is at first a puzzling one, reflecting more on the authors of the model than the model itself. There was little motivation to carry out a further test. But then, why not? The answer to that question indicates a peculiar defect in this work. It is not an addition to what is already done in analysis of survey data; it is a replacement of it. There was no

analysis of data, only synthesis. No analysis, for example, of the relation of religion to voting was carried out, nor an analysis to examine which issues were most important in explaining the variations in vote. Instead, at numerous points, it was necessary to arbitrarily set values for parameters. For example, the effect on vote intentions of a discussion with a friend relative to that of an exposure to television had to be arbitrarily assumed. The effects of the religious issue for those who were strong church members and for those who were nominal members were not estimated from the data, but were assumed.

Such models as these, making use of survey data, have ordinarily not integrated analysis and synthesis. The survey data are taken as parameters describing the initial state of the system; but the parameters of movement, or effects, are missing. With ordinary survey analysis, these effects are ordinarily the goal of the analysis.

It becomes evident, then, why there is little motivation to further "test" the simulation. For by choosing whatever parameters one wishes, there would be little difficulty in arriving at a reasonably good fit. Thus the test would be a weak one indeed, and there is little interest in carrying it out.

It might well be that the values of the parameters necessary to produce a good fit would themselves be valuable results. These values would be those which, operationally, led the simulated system to behave as the actual system behaved and thus would be estimates of the effects operating in the real situation. But this seems a poor means of estimating these effects, and, insofar as different combinations of values would give similar results, might be misleading.

Yet examination of the defect in this approach points the way to a better one. This is to combine analysis and synthesis, so that the empirical data are first used by the computer to estimate parameters and then these parameters used in the simulation. This proposal in essence suggests turning a panel study into a large-scale Markov process: One first calculates the probabilities of change in the dependent variables, contingent upon the independent ones. Then the system is projected forward, using these contingent probabilities.

Two kinds of results derive from such a strategy. One is the usual kind that arises from a panel study: The values of the contingent probabilities themselves show the effect of particular variables upon the ones in question. These may be thought of as the analytic results. For example, in one such study examining the interdependence between a sociometric network and a particular type of behavior of persons in it, it was found that changes in behavior depended on the person one was connected to in the network, but that changes in the network were not dependent on the behavior (Waldorf & Coleman, 1962). These are the kinds of analytic results that generally derive from survey analysis.

But when these contingent probabilities are used to project the system forward in time, a different kind of result is obtained: the impact of these processes upon the system as a whole. The projection, or simulation, resynthesizes the analytic effects and shows their aggregate or systemic effect— an effect that may not be implicit in the analytic results. For example, in the case cited above, the behavior in question was cigarette smoking by boys in high school. The systemic projections showed that the sociometric network pushed the level of smoking in the high school above what it would have otherwise been—a result that could not have been determined from the analytic effects.

An elaborate model that takes this approach is one designed to study community controversies (Abelson & Bernstein, 1963). The model is intended to use as data two or more waves of interviews with community participants, both to obtain the initial state of the system and to obtain parameters of contingent change. Then, with these data, the system would be projected forward, taking as exogenous inputs the issues raised by the principals in the controversy and the positions taken by particular leaders in the community. That is, the behavior of the leaders and the issues are taken as exogeneous, and the behavior of the community members is taken as the dependent variable of interest.

This approach eliminates the defect of the voting simulations discussed earlier, by starting with data analysis and using the results of this analysis as the basis for simulation. The approach is generally applicable and should come to constitute an important strategy in the quantitative research of the future.

Simulations involving the synthesis of hard data. Not all social simulations involving data are based on processes about which our knowledge is weak or merely qualitative. In some cases, the processes are straightforward, and the relevant probabilities can be calculated with precision. The need for simulation arises only because many factors must be taken into account. For example, the following case illustrates a problem for which a "hard" simulation is possible. A city public library wanted to obtain, by means of a survey, information that would aid it in certain policy decisions: Where to locate new branch libraries? Whether to have large branches or small ones? What kind of a collection to have in a given branch?

Data for this problem are relatively easy to obtain. They come from two sources. From a survey:

(1) reading of different types of books as related to various social characteristics: education, income, race, age;

(2) use of the library for different types of books as a function of distance from the library, estimated separately for persons with different social characteristics.

From the census:

the number of persons in a given small geographic area (e.g., a census tract), and the social characteristics of these persons.

Given these data, it becomes a relatively simple matter to design an analysis and simulation that will predict the amount of demand for books of various sorts if a branch were to be opened at a given point—and the effect on demand at other branches. As this indicates, some social simulations can give quite straightforward predictions, involving no processes about which there is great uncertainty. In general, there is a whole continuum from such precise simulations to those in which the answers are very uncertain.

Are the above examples small-scale prototypes of the approach that will prove most fruitful in the study of social organization with computers? Possibly not, for these approaches have major defects. To give a simple example: The sociometric panel example depends on data gathered at two points in time and thus obscures those processes which are very rapid, while providing no evidence on those that are very slow. It is a rigid approach, which forces all changes into the framework provided by the panel data.

A wholly different approach, more allied to that of Breton (1962) discussed earlier, has been taken in several excellent examples of socioeconomic simulation carried out by economists (Cohen, 1960; Hoggatt & Balderston, 1962). An examination of one of these will indicate the general strategy and provide clues for the future.

The Mixture of Theory and Qualitative Data: Semieconomic Simulations

Hoggatt and Balderston (1962) studied the lumber industry in the Pacific Northwest and found a structure like this: (1) lumber suppliers, who at any given time established an offering price and quantity offered at that price; (2) retailers, who made bids, requesting a particular quantity of lumber at a particular price; (3) wholesalers, whose principal activity was that of search: obtaining offer prices and quantities from suppliers, and bid prices and quantities from retailers. When a profitable transaction was possible, the wholesaler purchased from the supplier and resold to the retailer. The lumber then went directly from the supplier to the retailer. The major function of the wholesaler was indicated by his principal cost: his telephone bill.

Using this information, some of it quantitative, much of it nonquantitative, Hoggatt and Balderston constructed a simulation model that mirrored this basic structure. The decisions of the suppliers, retailers, and wholesalers were made principally on the basis of simple cost and return considerations, following roughly the behavior observed in the industry.

The most interesting results obtained with this model were in the area of social (or economic) structure. The market tended to segment, so that a given wholesaler dealt with only a small number of suppliers and retailers. Furthermore, this segmentation had continuity over time, except for certain periods at which the segmentation would collapse into a single market.

Although Hoggatt and Balderston (1962) found striking similarities in the behavior of their simulated system and the lumber industry (including the periodic collapsing of the market segmentation), they use the model principally as an analytic device: to determine the effects of particular variables, such as the cost of a unit of information, upon the functioning of the system.

What is of principal interest here, however, is the combination of elements that make up the model. There are three major kinds of elements: (1) observed information about the structure of the system and general rules of operation; (2) simple economic decision theory; (3) qualitative information about the way decisions were in fact made, which was used to modify the basic model of economic decisions.

It seems likely that much social simulation in the future will follow this general strategy. One example, based on Homans' (1961) work, has already been carried out, by Gullahorn and Gullahorn (1963). It seems probable that such future simulations will have the following characteristics:

(1) First a delineation of the principal roles in the system, and the structure of the system.

(2) A general model of purposive behavior of persons in roles, following the expanded notion of economic man set down in recent theoretical statements by Thibaut and Kelley (1959), Homans (1961), Blau (1960), Parsons (1963), and others.

(3) Detailed (though largely qualitative) observation of behavior of persons in each of the roles in the system to determine the principal costs and returns involved in each possible action by a person in the role.

(4) A synthesis of the above information into a simulated social system.

Thus if this conjecture is correct much social simulation of the future will have purposive actors in roles as its principal elements. It will combine social theory with observation of the fine structure of behavior, though these observations may often be qualitative. It will depend little if at all on systematic quantitative data such as that presently obtained in sample surveys.

It is evident, of course, that this work is still in its infancy. The work carried out to date shows the kinds of problems and difficulties that arise with particular strategies. It also shows the basis for computer techniques becoming a major tool for empirical investigation and for theory.

REFERENCES

Abelson, R. P., & Bernstein, A. A computer simulation model of community referendum controversies. *Publ. Opin. Quart.,* 1963, 27, 93–122.

Abelson, R. P., & Rosenberg, M. J. Symbolic psychologic: A model of attitudinal cognition. *Behav. Sci.,* 1958, 3, 1–13.

Alexander, C., & Manhein, M. Hidecs 2: An IBM 709/7090 program for the hierarchical decomposition of a set with an associated linear graph. *Behav. Sci.,* 1963, 8, 168–170.

Alker, H. R., Jr. An IBM 709 program for the analysis of transaction flows. *Behav. Sci.,* 1962, 7, 498–499.

Anderson, T. W. Probability models for analyzing time changes in attitudes. In P. F. Lazarsfeld (Ed.), *Mathematical thinking in the social sciences.* Glencoe, Ill.: Free Press, 1954. Ch. 1.

Anderson, T. W., & Goodman, L. A. Statistical inference about Markov chains. *Ann. math. Statist.,* 1957, 28, 89–110.

Arrow, K. J. Mathematical models in the social sciences. In D. Lerner & H. D. Lasswell (Eds.), *The policy sciences.* Stanford: Stanford Univer. Press, 1951. Pp. 129–154.

Asch, S. E. Effects of group pressure upon the modification of judgments. In H. Guetzkow (Ed.), *Groups, leadership, and men.* Pittsburgh: Carnegie Press, 1951.

Bailey, N. T. J. *The mathematical theory of epidemics.* London: Charles Griffin, 1957.

Becker, G. M., DeGroot, M. H., & Marschak, J. Stochastic models of choice behavior. *Behav. Sci.,* 1963, 8, 41–55.

Berelson, B., & Steiner, G. *Human behavior: An inventory of findings.* New York: Harcourt, 1964.

Berger, J., Cohen, B. P., Snall, J. L., & Zelditch, M. *Types of formalization in small group research.* Boston: Houghton, 1962.

Beshers, J. M., & Reiter, S. Social status and social change. *Behav. Sci.,* 1963, 8, 1–14.

Blalock, H. *Causal inferences in nonexperimental research.* Chapel Hill: Univer. of North Carolina Press, 1964.

Blau, P. M. A theory of social integration. *Amer. J. Sociol.,* 1960, 65, 545–556.

Blumen, I., Kogan, M., & McCarthy, P. J. *The industrial mobility of labor as a probability process.* Ithaca, N. Y.: Cornell Univer. Press, 1955.

Borko, H. (Ed.) *Computer applications in the behavioral sciences.* Englewood Cliffs, N.J.: Prentice-Hall, Inc., 1962.

Breton, R. Output standards and productive behavior in industrial work groups. Baltimore: Johns Hopkins Univer., 1962. (Mimeographed)

Bridgman, P. W. *Dimensional analysis.* New Haven, Conn.: Yale Univer. Press, 1922.

Bush, R. R., & Estes, W. K. (Eds.) *Studies in mathematical learning theory.* Stanford: Stanford Univer. Press, 1959.

Bush, R. R., & Mosteller, F. *Stochastic models for learning.* New York: Wiley, 1955.

Campbell, N. R. *Measurement and calculation.* London: Longmans, Green, 1928.

Cartwright, D., & Harary, F. Structural balance: A generalization of Heider's theory. *Psychol. Rev.,* 1956, 63, 277–293.

Cattell, R. B. *Factor analysis.* New York: Harper, 1952.

Cervin, V. B. Relationship of ascendant sub-missive behavior in dyadic groups of human subjects to their emotional responsiveness. *J. abnor. soc. Psychol.*, 1957, 54, 241–249.

Clarkson, G. P. S., & Simon, H. A. Simulation of group behavior. *Amer. econ. Rev.*, December, 1960, 4, 920–931.

Cohen, B. *Conflict and conformity*. Cambridge: Massachusetts Institute of Technology Press, 1963.

Cohen, K. J. *Computer models of the shoe, leather, hide sequence*. Englewood Cliffs, N.J.: Prentice-Hall, Inc., 1960.

Coleman, J. S. The mathematical study of small groups. In H. Solomon (Ed.), *Mathematical thinking in the measurement of behavior*. Glencoe, Ill.: Free Press, 1960. Part I, pp. 7–149.

Coleman, J. S. Reward structures and the allocation of effort. In Joan H. Criswell, H. Solomon, & P. Suppes (Eds.), *Mathematical methods in small group processes*. Stanford: Stanford Univer. Press, 1962. Ch. 8, pp. 119–132.

Coleman, J. S. Comment on "On the concept of influence." *Publ. Opin. Quart.*, 1963, 27, 63–82.

Coleman, J. S. *Introduction to mathematical sociology*. New York: The Free Press of Glencoe, 1964.(a)

Coleman, J. S. *Models of change and response uncertainty*. Englewood Cliffs, N.J.: Prentice-Hall, Inc., 1964.(b)

Coleman, J. S., & James, J. The equilibrium size distribution of freely-forming groups. *Sociometry*, 1961, 24, 36–45.

Coleman, J. S., & Waldorf, F. Study of a voting system with computer techniques. Baltimore: Johns Hopkins Univer., 1962. (Mimeographed)

Converse, P. E. The nature of belief systems in mass publics. Ann Arbor, Mich.: Survey Research Center, 1962. (Mimeographed)

Cooley, W. W., & Lohnes, P. R. *Multivariate procedures for the behavioral sciences*. New York: Wiley, 1962.

Coombs, C. H. Psychological scaling without a unit of measurement. *Psych. Rev.*, 1950, 57, 145.

Coombs, C. *Theory of data*. New York: Wiley, in press.

Cyert, R. M., Feigenbaum, E. A., & March, J. G. Models in a behavioral theory of the firm. *Behav. Sci.*, 1959, 4, 81–95.

Cyert, R. M., & March, J. G. Research on a behavioral theory of the firm. *Contributions to scientific research in management*, Proceedings of the scientific program following the dedication of the Western Data Processing Center, Univer. of California Graduate School of Business Administration, Los Angeles, January 29–30, 1959.

Davis, H. T. *Introduction to nonlinear differential and integral equations*. Washington: Atomic Energy Commission, 1960.

Dodd, S. C. Diffusion is predictable: Testing probability models for laws of interaction. *Amer. sociol. Rev.*, 1955, 20, 392.

Duncan, O. D., & Duncan, Beverly. A methodological analysis of segregation indexes. *Amer. sociol. Rev.*, 1955, 20, 210.

Duncan, W. J. *Physical similarity and dimensional analysis*. London: Edward Arnold, 1953.

Edwards, W. The theory of decision-making. *Psych. Bull.*, 1954, 5, 380–417.

Estes, W. K., & Burke, C. J. Application of a statistical model to simple discrimination learning in human subjects. *J. exp. Psychol.*, 1955, 50, 81–88.

Feigenbaum, E. A., & Simon, H. A. Performance of a reading task by an elementary perceiving and memorizing program. *Behav. Sci.*, 1963, 8, 72–76.

Feller, W. On a general class of contagious distributions. *Ann. math. Statist.*, 1943, 14, 389–400.

Festinger, L. The analysis of sociograms using matrix algebra. *Hum. Relat.*, 1949, 2, 153–158.

Festinger, L. Informal social communication. *Psychol. Rev.*, 1950, 57, 271–282.

Flament, C. *Applications of graph theory to group structure*. Englewood Cliffs, N.J.: Prentice-Hall, Inc., 1963.

Foster, C. C., Rapoport, A., & Orwant, C. J. A study of a large sociogram II: Elimination of free parameters. *Behav. Sci.*, 1963, 8, 56–65.

Frank, R. Brand choice as a probability process. *J. Bus.*, January, 1962, 35.

Goodman, L. A. On some statistical tests for m-th order Markov chains. *Ann. math. Statist.*, 1959, 30, 154–164.(a)

Goodman, L. A. Some alternatives to ecological correlation. *Amer. J. Sociol.,* 1959, 64, 610–625.(b)

Goodman, L. A. Statistical methods for the mover-stayer model. *J. Amer. statist. Ass.,* 1961, 56, 841–868.

Goodman, L. A. On mathematical methods for the study of systems of groups. Chicago: Univer. of Chicago, 1963. (Mimeographed) (a)

Goodman, L. A. Statistical methods for the analysis of mobility tables. Chicago: Univer. of Chicago, 1963. (Mimeographed) (b)

Guetzkow, H. (Ed.) *Simulation in social science.* Englewood Cliffs, N.J.: Prentice-Hall, Inc., 1962.

Gullahorn, J., & Gullahorn, Jean. A computer model of elementary social behavior. In E. Feigenbaum & J. Feldman (Eds.), *Computers and thought.* New York: Mc-Graw, in press.

Harary, F. On the notion of balance of a signed graph. *Mich. math. J.,* 1953, 2, 143–146.

Harary, F. On local balance and n-balance in signed graphs. *Mich. math. J.,* 1955, 3, 37–41.

Harary, F. On the measurement of structural balance. *Behav. Sci.,* 1959, 4, 316–323.

Harary, F., & Lipstein, B. The dynamics of brand loyalty: A Markovian approach. *Operat. Res.,* 1962, 10, 19–39.

Harary, F., & Norman, R. Z. Graph theory as a mathematical model in social science. Ann Arbor, Mich.: Ann Arbor Institute for Social Research, 1953.

Harary, F., & Ross, I. A procedure for clique detection using the group matrix. *Sociometry,* 1957, 20, 205–215.

Harper, D. Some new applications of dichotomous algebra to survey analysis. Unpublished doctoral dissertation, Columbia Univer., 1961.

Hays, D. G., & Bush, R. R. A study of group action. *Amer. sociol. Rev.,* 1954, 19, 693–701.

Hempel, C. G. Fundamentals of concept formation in empirical science. In *International encyclopedia of unified science.* Chicago: Univer. of Chicago Press, 1952.

Hoggatt, A. C., & Balderston, F. E. *Models for simulation of an intermediate market.* Berkeley: Univer. of California Press, 1962.

Homans, G. *The human group.* New York: Harper, 1950.

Homans, G. *Social behavior: Its elementary forms.* New York: Harcourt, 1961.

Hubbell, C. An input-output approach to clique identification. Paper presented at Amer. Sociol. Ass., Los Angeles, August, 1963.

Katz, L. A new status index derived from sociometric analysis. *Psychometrika,* 1953, 18, 39–43.

Kemeny, J. G., & Snell, J. L. *Mathematical models in the social sciences.* Boston: Ginn, 1962.

Kirk, J., & Coleman, J. S. The use of computers in the study of social structure: Interaction in a 3-person group. Baltimore: Johns Hopkins Univer., 1963. (Mimeographed)

Koch, S. The logical character of the motivation concept, I. *Psych. Rev.,* 1951, 48, 15.

Kuehn, A. A. An analysis of the dynamics of consumer behavior and its implications for marketing management. Unpublished Ph.D. dissertation, Carnegie Institute of Technology, 1958.

Lazarsfeld, P. F. A conceptual introduction to latent structure analysis. In P. F. Lazarsfeld (Ed.), *Mathematical thinking in the social sciences.* Glencoe, Ill.: Free Press, 1954. Ch. 7.

Lazarsfeld, P. F. Latent structure analysis. In S. Koch (Ed.), *Psychology: A study of a science, conceptual and systematic.* New York: McGraw, 1959. Vol. 3, pp. 476–543.

Levenson, B. Personal communication to author, 1964.

Luce, R. D. Connectivity and generalized cliques in sociometric group structure. *Psychometrika,* 1950, 15, 169–190.

Luce, R. D. *Individual choice behavior.* New York: Wiley, 1959.

Lundberg, O. *On random processes and their application to sickness and accident statistics.* Uppsala: Almqvist and Wicksells, 1940.

McDill, E. L., & Coleman, J. S. High school social status, college plans, and interest in academic achievement: A panel analysis. *Amer. sociol. Rev.,* 1963, 28, 905–918.

McPhee, W. N. *Formal theories of mass behavior.* New York: The Free Press of Glencoe, 1963.

Macrae, D., Jr. Direct factor analysis of socio-metric data. *Sociometry,* 1960, **23**, 360–372.

Markowitz, H. *Simscript: A simulation pro-gramming language.* Englewood Cliffs, N.J.: Prentice-Hall, Inc., 1963.

Marshall, A. W., & Goldhamer, H. An appli-cation of Markov processes to the study of epidemiology of mental disease. *J. Amer. statist. Ass.,* 1955, **50**, 99.

Mount, G. R. An analytic account of the prin-ciples of measurement. *Psychol. Repts,* Mon-ograph Suppl. 2, 1956.

NASA-PERT B systems manual. Washing-ton: Government Printing Office, 1963.

Newell, A. (Ed.) *Information processing lan-guage—V manual.* Englewood Cliffs, N.J.: Prentice-Hall, Inc., 1961.

Parsons, T. On the concept of influence. *Publ. Opin. Quart.,* 1963, **27**, 37–62.

Rapoport, A. Lewis F. Richardson's mathe-matical theory of war. *J. conflict Res.,* 1957, **1**, 249–299.

Rapoport, A. *Fights, games, and debates.* Ann Arbor: Univer. of Michigan Press, 1960.

Rapoport, A., & Horvath, W. J. A study of a large sociogram. *Behav. Sci.,* 1961, **6**, 279–291.

Richardson, L. F. Generalized foreign politics. *Brit. J. Psychol.,* 1939, **23**, 939. (Monograph suppl.)

Ross, I. C., & Harary, F. A description of strengthening and weakening members of a group. *Sociometry,* 1959, **22**, 139–147.

Shepard, R. N. "The analysis of proximities: Multidimensional scaling with an unknown distance function. *Psychometrika,* 1962, **27**, I, 125–140; II, 219–246.

Simmons, R. F., Klein, S., & McConlogue, K. Toward the synthesis of human language behavior. *Behav. Sci.,* 1962, **7**, 402–407.

Simon, H. *Models of man.* New York: Wiley, 1957.

Stevens, S. S., & Galanter, E. H. Ratio scales and category scales for a dozen perceptual continua. *J. exp. Psychol.,* 1957, **54**, 377–411.

Stone, P. J., Bales, R. F., Namenwirth J. Z., & Ogilvie, D. M. The general inquirer: A computer system for content analysis and retrieval based on the sentence as a unit of information. *Behav. Sci.,* 1962, **7**, 484–498.

Suppes, P., & Atkinson, R. C. *Markov learn-ing models for multiperson interactions.* Stanford Mathematical Studies in the Social Science. Stanford: Stanford Univer. Press, 1960.

Suppes, P., & Winet, Muriel. An axiomatiza-tion of utility based on the notion of utility differences. *Mangt Sci.,* 1955, **1**, 259.

Tarver, J. D. Computer programs for estimat-ing and projecting county, city, and other local subdivisional populations. *Behav. Sci.,* 1963, **8**, 165–168.

Thibaut, J., & Kelley, H. The social psychology of groups. New York: Wiley, 1959.

Torgerson, W. S. *Theory and methods of scaling.* New York: Wiley, 1958.

Volterra, V. *Leçons sur la theorie mathema-tique de la lutte pour la vie.* Paris: Gauthier-Villars, 1931.

Von Neumann, J., & Morgenstern, O. *Theory of games and economic behavior.* Princeton, N.J.: Princeton Univer. Press, 1947.

Waldorf, F., & Coleman, J. S. Analysis and simulation of reference group processes. Paper presented at the annual meeting of the Amer. Psychol. Ass., St. Louis, Septem-ber, 1962. (Mimeographed, Johns Hopkins Univer., (1962)

White, H. Chance models of systems of casual groups. *Sociometry,* 1962, **25**, 153–172.

White, H. *An anatomy of kinship.* Englewood Cliffs, N.J.: Prentice-Hall, Inc., 1963.

Wiggins, L. M. Mathematical models for the interpretation of attitude and behavior change: The analysis of multi-wave panels. Unpublished doctoral dissertation, Columbia Univer., 1955.

Wilson, A. 7090 program for analysis of vari-ance with categorical data. Berkeley: Survey Research Center, 1963. (Mimeographed)

Name and Subject Index

Rogers, Candace, 726
Rogers, E. M., 359–360
Rogers, E. S., 70, 78
Rogers, L., 813
Rogers, Martha E., 313
Rogoff, Natalie, 474, 484, 565, 569, 741, 768, 833, 901, 1013
Rokeach, M., 612
Role impingement, 513
Role relationships, 624
"Role volume" of groups, 1018–1020
Romani, J. H., 826
Roper Public Opinion Research Center, 1012
Rosberg, J., 825
Rose, A. M., 398
Rose, R. J., 324
Roseborough, Mary E., 218, 226, 228–230, 236–237, 247–248, 257, 291
Rosen, B. C., 221, 224, 243
Rosen, E., 613
Rosen, Laura, 623, 678
Rosen, S. M., 623, 678
Rosenberg, H., 211, 488
Rosenberg, M., 459, 484, 762
Rosenberg, Pearl, 592, 599
Rosow, I., 235, 240
Ross, A., 838
Ross, A. M., 633, 676
Ross, Aileen D., 725
Ross, E. A., 384, 931, 933
Ross, J. F. S., 295
Rossi, P. H., 809, 816, 1013
Rossiter, C. L., 823
Rothschild, G. H., 249, 251
Roy, D., 512
Rubenstein, A. H., 864, 868
Rudé, G., 391
Rudolph, R., 205
Ruesch, J., 226
Rukeyser, M., 975
Runkel, P. J., 233
Rural-urban patterns, 132–149; and industrialization, 137–151; and politics, 152–153; study of, 127–131
Rural and urban population: by continents, 134
Russell, J., 134, 138
Ryan, B., 546

Sabsovitch, A. M., 682–683
Sachs, L., 322
Sagi, P. C., 83–124, 242
Sahlins, M. D., 50
Salaman, R. N., 60
Salisbury, R. H., 820
Salk, J., 329
Sampling: case selection methods, 982–995; representational basis for, 984–991; probability, some principles of, 986–991; analytical basis for, 991
Sampling errors and other errors in a representational sample, 984, 992

Samuelson, P. A., 457, 484
Sanctions, various forms of, 465–466
Sanders, J. T., 144
Sanford, F. H., 244
Sanford, N., 762
Sansom, G., 781–782
Santayana, G., 775
Sarbin, T. R., 233, 235
Sarnoff, I., 192, 195
Saunders, L., 330
Sauvy, A., 276
Sayles, L. R., 652, 657, 668–669, 678
Sayre, W. S., 822, 824, 827, 871
Schacter, S., 218, 222, 224–225, 802, 955
Schaeffer, K., 319
Schattschneider, E. E., 830
Schein, E. H., 226, 501
Schellenberg, J. A., 252
Schelsky, H., 764
Schenck, H. C., 332
Schenkel, R., 530
Schermerhorn, R. A., 534, 547–548
Scheuch, E. K., 541
Schiff, H., 232
Schilling, W. R., 872
Schizophrenics, investigation of, 30
Schjelderup-Ebbe, T., 530
Schlesinger, R., 683, 685
Schmandt, H. J., 817, 820, 841
Schmidhauser, J. R., 296
Schmidt, G. P., 758
Schmitt-Eglin, P., 793–794
Schneider, D. M., 696, 709, 718, 726, 962, 969
Schneider, E. V., 623, 646, 678
Schneider, L., 770–807
Schneier, I., 226
Schnore, L. F., 72, 129–130, 136, 489
Schoenberg, Enka, 170
School integration, 588–590
Schrag, C. C., 353, 376, 566, 941–942, 946
Schramm, W., 350, 354, 357–358
Schreuder, O., 788–789
Schuessler, K., 816
Schultz, G. P., 651, 679
Schulz, J. B., 370
Schulze, R. O., 827
Schumpeter, J. A., 535, 839, 897
Schurtz, H., 278
Schutz, W. C., 230
Schwartz, M. S., 485
Schwarweller, H. K., 153
Science: nature of, 854–860, 863; as social system, 855–857; and communications system, 857–860; organization of, 863–870; national organization of, 869–870; and society, 871–874
Science, sociology of: 852–875; definitions of, 853
Scientific management in industry, 627
Scientific research: organization of, 864–869
Scientists: creativity in, 861–862
Scoble, H., 827